A GUIDE AND SUMMARY

W9-AGA-699

#36 Effects and social disadvantages of wage and price controls • *page 401*

#37 Relationship between population growth and the standard of living • *page 420*

#38 Central importance of technological change as a determinant of the rate of economic growth • *page 429*

#39 Difference between private and social costs of environmental pollution, and implications for public policy • *page 440*

#40 Role of the price system in solving shortages of resources like oil • *page 450*

#41 Effect of a price cut on the amount spent on a commodity depends on the price elasticity of demand • *page 467*

#42 Importance of distinguishing between the market demand curve for a commodity and the market demand curve of a single firm producing the commodity • *page 472*

#43 How to allocate a fixed sum of money among a variety of uses • *page 483*

#44 Shape of individual demand curves, and reasons for this shape • *page 488*

#45 The law of diminishing marginal returns • *page 505*

#46 How to minimize the cost of producing a given amount of output • *page 507*

#47 Nature and importance of the concept of marginal cost • *page 519*

#48 Relationship between a firm's average cost and its size • *page 526*

#49 Comparing the extra revenue with the extra cost of each additional unit of output to find the firm's profit-maximizing output rate • *page 539*

#50 Difference between short-run and long-run equilibrium • *page 549*

#51 Concept of marginal revenue, and determinants of a monopolist's profit-maximizing output rate • *page 565*

#52 Misallocation of resources due to monopoly • *page 571*

#53 Importance and effects of product differentiation • *page 584*

#54 Nature, effect, and instability of cartel agreements • *page 594*

#55 Purpose and effectiveness of the antitrust laws • *page 614*

#56 Ambiguity of government policies concerning competition and monopoly • *page 619*

#57 How a profit-maximizing firm determines how much labor to hire • *page 629*

#58 How unions increase wages • *page 648*

#59 The present value of a dollar received n years from now • *page 663*

#60 Role and importance of profits and losses in a capitalistic economy • *page 669*

#61 The tradeoff between equality and efficiency • *page 680*

#62 Nature and effects of government antipoverty programs • *page 690*

#63 Importance of comparative advantage in determining what a country should produce • *page 701*

#64 Effects and social disadvantages of tariffs and quotas • *page 713*

#65 Determinants of the exchange rate between two currencies • *page 727*

#66 Nature and importance of a country's balance-of-payments accounts • *page 733*

#67 The problems of the less developed countries, and the income gap between them and the developed countries • *page 757*

#68 How less developed countries should choose investment projects • *page 766*

#69 Marx's views of socialism and communism • *page 777*

#70 The basic vitality of the major capitalist economies in recent decades • *page 796*

Economics

PRINCIPLES, PROBLEMS, DECISIONS

FIFTH EDITION

Economics

PRINCIPLES, PROBLEMS, DECISIONS

EDWIN MANSFIELD

DIRECTOR, CENTER FOR ECONOMICS AND TECHNOLOGY
UNIVERSITY OF PENNSYLVANIA

FIFTH EDITION

W · W · NORTON & COMPANY · NEW YORK · LONDON

(Photograph credits and acknowledgments appear on page A50.)

To Edward Deering Mansfield (1801–1880)
and his brother-in-law Charles Davies (1798–1876)
neither of whom should be held responsible
for the views expressed here.

The text of this book is composed in Times Roman, with display type set in Times
Roman Bold. Composition by New England Typographic Service, Inc. Manufacturing by
The Murray Printing Company. Book design by Antonina Krass. Page makeup by
Ben Gamit. Cover design by Mike McIver.

Library of Congress Cataloging-in-Publication Data

Mansfield, Edwin.
  Economics : principles, problems, decisions.

  Bibliography: p.
  Includes index.
  1. Economics. I. Title.
HG171.5.M266 1986   330   85-21626

ISBN 0-393-95475-7

W. W. Norton & Company, Inc., 500 Fifth Avenue, New York, N. Y. 10110
W. W. Norton & Company Ltd., 37 Great Russell Street, London WCIB 3NU

1 2 3 4 5 6 7 8 9 0

Contents

Preface   xvii
Suggested Outlines   xxi

PART ONE   Introduction to Economics

CHAPTER 1   **Economic Problems and Analysis   1**

ECONOMIC PROBLEMS: A SAMPLER 1 • WHAT IS ECONOMICS? 5 • *Test Yourself* 8 • OPPORTUNITY COST: A FUNDAMENTAL CONCEPT 9 • THE IMPACT OF ECONOMICS ON SOCIETY 11 • *Example 1.1 How Much Does It Cost to Go to College?* 11 • *Adam Smith on the "Invisible Hand"* 13 • *Example 1.2 The Assessment of Damages* 15 • *Test Yourself* 16 • *Summary* 16 • *Concepts for Review* 17

CHAPTER 2   **Economic Models and Capitalism, American-Style   18**

THE METHODOLOGY OF ECONOMICS 19 • GRAPHS AND RELATIONSHIPS 21 • THE TASKS OF AN ECONOMIC SYSTEM 22 • *Test Yourself* 23 • THE ECONOMIC SYSTEM: A SIMPLE INTRODUCTORY MODEL 23 • *Example 2.1 Hay and Grain in Iowa* 25 • *How the Industrial Revolution Came About* 30 • CAPITALISM: AN ECONOMIC SYSTEM 31 • OUR MIXED CAPITALIST SYSTEM 34 • *Test Yourself* 35 • *Summary* 36 • *Concepts for Review* 37

PART TWO   The Private Sector and the Public Sector: An Overview

CHAPTER 3   **The Price System   39**

CONSUMERS, FIRMS, AND MARKETS 39 • THE DEMAND SIDE OF A MARKET 40 • THE SUPPLY SIDE OF A MARKET 43 • EQUILIBRIUM PRICE 44 • ACTUAL PRICE 45 • *Example 3.1 It's Not Just for Breakfast Anymore* 46 • *Test Yourself* 47 • THE EFFECTS OF SHIFTS IN THE DEMAND CURVE 48 • THE EFFECTS OF SHIFTS IN THE SUPPLY CURVE 49 • THE PRICE SYSTEM AND THE DETERMINATION OF WHAT IS PRODUCED 50 • THE PRICE SYSTEM AND THE DETERMINATION OF HOW GOODS ARE PRODUCED 51 • *Example 3.2 Tennis Anyone?* 52 • THE PRICE SYSTEM AND THE DETERMINATION OF WHO GETS WHAT 53 • THE PRICE SYSTEM AND ECONOMIC GROWTH 54 • TWO CASE STUDIES 55 • PRICE CEILINGS AND PRICE SUPPORTS 58 • THE CIRCULAR FLOWS OF MONEY AND PRODUCTS 60 • *Test Yourself* 61 • *Summary* 61 • *Concepts for Review* 62

CHAPTER 4   **The Economic Role of the Government   63**

LIMITATIONS OF THE PRICE SYSTEM 63 • WHAT FUNCTIONS SHOULD THE GOVERNMENT PERFORM? 65 • ESTABLISHING "RULES OF THE GAME" 66 • REDISTRIBUTION OF INCOME 67 • STABILIZING THE ECONOMY 67 • PROVIDING PUBLIC GOODS 68 • EXTERNALITIES 69 • SIZE AND NATURE OF GOVERNMENT ACTIVITIES 69 • *Example 4.1 The Economics of Urban Blight* 70 • CHANGES IN VIEW OF GOVERNMENT RESPONSIBILITIES 72 • *The Saga of the B-1 Bomber* 73 • WHAT THE FEDERAL, STATE, AND LOCAL GOVERNMENTS RECEIVE IN TAXES 74 • *Test Yourself* 75 • THE ROLE OF GOVERNMENT IN AMERICAN AGRICULTURE 76 • THE FARM PROBLEM 76 • GOVERNMENT AID TO AGRICULTURE 78 • PRICE SUPPORTS AND SURPLUS CONTROLS 79 • THE 1973 FARM BILL AND MORE RECENT DEVELOPMENTS 81 • EVALUATION OF GOVERNMENT FARM PROGRAMS 82 • *Test Yourself* 83 • *Summary* 84 • *Concepts for Review* 85

CHAPTER 5   **Government Expenditures, Taxation, and the Public Debt   86**

GOVERNMENT EXPENDITURES 86 • BENEFIT-COST ANALYSIS 87 • SCOPE AND EFFICIENCY OF GOVERNMENT ACTIVITIES 89 • THE THEORY OF PUBLIC CHOICE 89 • TAXATION AND GOVERNMENT REVENUES 91 • *Example 5.1 Brown-Lung Disease and Benefit-Cost Analysis* 92 • PRINCIPLES OF TAXATION 93 • THE PERSONAL INCOME TAX 94 • *More Equity and Simplicity in the Income Tax Codes* 96 • THE CORPORATE INCOME TAX 97 • *Test Yourself* 97 • THE PROPERTY TAX AND THE SALES TAX 98 • TAX INCIDENCE 98 • SUPPLY-SIDE ECONOMICS 100 • *Example 5.2 Should Income or Consumption Be Taxed?* 101 • GOVERNMENT DEBT 102 • ALTERNATIVE WAYS OF FINANCING GOVERNMENT EXPENDITURES—AND THEIR EFFECTS 104 • *The Department of the Treasury and the National Debt* 105 • *Test Yourself* 106 • *Summary* 106 • *Concepts for Review* 107

CHAPTER 6   **The Business Firm: Organization, Motivation, and Technology**   108

THE IBM CORPORATION: A CASE STUDY 108 • CHARACTERISTICS OF AMERICAN FIRMS: SOME SALIENT FACTS 110 • PROPRIETORSHIPS 111 • PARTNERSHIPS 112 • CORPORATIONS 112 • CORPORATE SECURITIES 113 • THE STOCK MARKET 115 • *Buying and Selling Common Stocks* 116 • THE GIANT CORPORATION 117 • *Test Yourself* 118 • MOTIVATION OF THE FIRM 118 • TECHNOLOGY, INPUTS, AND THE PRODUCTION FUNCTION 120 • ELEMENTS OF ACCOUNTING: THE FIRM'S BALANCE SHEET 121 • THE FIRM'S INCOME STATEMENT 122 • **Cross-Chapter Case/Part Two: Should America Adopt an Industrial Policy?** 124 • *Example 6.1 How to Depreciate a Baseball Club* 126 • ECONOMIC VERSUS ACCOUNTING PROFITS 127 • *Test Yourself* 128 • *Summary* 128 • *Concepts for Review* 129

PART THREE   **National Output, Income, and Employment**

CHAPTER 7   **National Income and Product**   131

GROSS NATIONAL PRODUCT 132 • ADJUSTING GNP FOR PRICE CHANGES 133 • USING VALUE-ADDED TO CALCULATE GNP 135 • NET NATIONAL PRODUCT 136 • THE LIMITATIONS OF GNP AND NNP 137 • *Example 7.1 Measured Economic Welfare and National Defense* 139 • *Test Yourself* 140 • TWO APPROACHES TO GNP 140 • THE EXPENDITURES APPROACH TO GNP 141 • THE INCOME APPROACH TO GNP 143 • GNP EQUALS THE TOTAL CLAIMS ON OUTPUT: A PROOF 145 • NATIONAL INCOME, PERSONAL INCOME, AND DISPOSABLE INCOME 147 • *Test Yourself* 148 • *Summary* 149 • *Concepts for Review* 150

CHAPTER 8   **Unemployment and Inflation**   151

UNEMPLOYMENT 151 • THE MEASUREMENT AND INCIDENCE OF UNEMPLOYMENT 153 • THE COSTS OF UNEMPLOYMENT 156 • THEORIES OF UNEMPLOYMENT 158 • *Example 8.1 Should We Look at Employment, not Unemployment?* 159 • *Test Yourself* 163 • INFLATION 164 • THE MEASUREMENT OF INFLATION 165 • IMPACT OF INFLATION 167 • *Example 8.2 Money Wages and Real Wages in Manufacturing* 168 • IS INDEXATION THE ANSWER TO INFLATION? 170 • THE RELATIONSHIP BETWEEN INFLATION AND UNEMPLOYMENT 171 • *Unemployment and Inflation: An International Overview* 172 • *Test Yourself* 173 • *Summary* 174 • *Concepts for Review* 174

CHAPTER 9   **Aggregate Demand, Aggregate Supply, and Business Fluctuations**   175

AGGREGATE SUPPLY AND DEMAND 175 • THE AGGREGATE DEMAND CURVE 176 • THE AGGREGATE SUPPLY CURVE 178 • NATIONAL OUTPUT AND THE PRICE LEVEL 180 • SHIFTS IN THE AGGREGATE DEMAND CURVE 180 • SHIFTS

IN THE AGGREGATE SUPPLY CURVE 184 • "SUPPLY-SIDE" GOVERNMENT POL-
ICIES 184 • *Example 9.1 A Ratchet Effect on Aggregate Supply* 185 • *Test
Yourself* 186 • BUSINESS FLUCTUATIONS 186 • BUSINESS FLUCTUATIONS DUR-
ING 1929–85: A BRIEF OVERVIEW 188 • *Test Yourself* 192 • *Summary* 193 •
Concepts for Review 194

CHAPTER 10   **The Determination of National Output**   195

THE CONSUMPTION FUNCTION 196 • THE SAVING FUNCTION 198 • THE PER-
MANENT-INCOME AND LIFE-CYCLE HYPOTHESES 200 • DETERMINANTS OF
INVESTMENT 201 • THE INVESTMENT DECISION 202 • *Test Yourself* 204 • THE
EQUILIBRIUM LEVEL OF NET NATIONAL PRODUCT 205 • AGGREGATE FLOWS
OF INCOME AND EXPENDITURE 205 • WHY NNP MUST EQUAL INTENDED
SPENDING 207 • RECONCILING AGGREGATE DEMAND AND SUPPLY CURVES
WITH INCOME-EXPENDITURE ANALYSIS 209 • LEAKAGES AND INJECTIONS:
ANOTHER APPROACH 210 • *Example 10.1 Asking "What If" Questions* 211 •
A NUMERICAL EXAMPLE 212 • LEAKAGES AND INJECTIONS: A GRAPHICAL
VIEW 213 • ACTUAL SAVING EQUALS ACTUAL INVESTMENT 214 • USEFULNESS
OF THE LEAKAGE-INJECTION APPROACH 215 • *Test Yourself* 215 • *Summary*
216 • *Concepts for Review* 217

CHAPTER 11   **Multiplier Analysis and Changes in Output**   218

THE VOLATILITY OF INVESTMENT 218 • EFFECTS OF CHANGES IN INTENDED
INVESTMENT 220 • *Example 11.1 Investment and a Great Crash* 222 • THE
MULTIPLIER • 223 • *Test Yourself* 224 • DETERMINANTS OF CONSUMPTION:
NONINCOME FACTORS 225 • SHIFTS IN THE CONSUMPTION AND SAVING
FUNCTIONS 226 • EFFECTS OF SHIFTS IN THE CONSUMPTION FUNCTION 227 •
THE ACCURACY OF POSTWAR FORECASTS: A CASE STUDY 228 • INDUCED IN-
VESTMENT 230 • THE PARADOX OF THRIFT 230 • *Example 11.2 Shifting Both
the Saving and Investment Functions* 231 • *Test Yourself* 232 • *Summary* 232
• *Concepts for Review* 233 • APPENDIX: USING BASIC ALGEBRA TO DERIVE
THE MULTIPLIER 233

CHAPTER 12   **Fiscal Policy and National Output**   236

GOVERNMENT EXPENDITURE AND NET NATIONAL PRODUCT 236 • TAXATION
AND NET NATIONAL PRODUCT 239 • HOW GOVERNMENT EXPENDITURE AND
TAXES AFFECT NNP: A TABULAR ILLUSTRATION 242 • THE BALANCED-BUD-
GET MULTIPLIER 244 • RECESSIONARY AND INFLATIONARY GAPS 244 • THE
NATURE AND OBJECTIVES OF FISCAL POLICY 245 • MAKERS OF FISCAL POL-
ICY 247 • *Example 12.1 Fiscal Policy, Deficits, and Surpluses* 247 • AUTO-
MATIC STABILIZERS 248 • *The Council of Economic Advisers* 249 • *Test Your-
self* 251 • THE TOOLS OF DISCRETIONARY FISCAL POLICY 251 • FISCAL
POLICY: THREE CASE STUDIES 253 • DEFICIT AND SURPLUS FINANCING 255 •
Martin Feldstein versus Donald Regan 258 • THE FULL-EMPLOYMENT BUD-
GET 259 • EFFECTS OF HOW A DEFICIT IS FINANCED, OR HOW A SURPLUS IS
USED 261 • *Example 12.2 Interpreting Federal Budget Deficits* 262 • RECENT
AMERICAN EXPERIENCE WITH FISCAL POLICY 262 • *Test Yourself* 264 • *Sum-*

mary 264 • *Concepts for Review* 265 • APPENDIX: THE EFFECT OF A CHANGE IN GOVERNMENT EXPENDITURE AND THE BALANCED-BUDGET MULTIPLIER (AN ALGEBRAIC TREATMENT) 266

CHAPTER 13   **Business Fluctuations and Economic Forecasting   268**

BUSINESS FLUCTUATIONS AND VARIATION IN INVESTMENT SPENDING 268 • THE ACCELERATION PRINCIPLE 269 • THE INTERACTION BETWEEN THE AC-CELERATION PRINCIPLE AND THE MULTIPLIER 271 • *Example 13.1 Invest-ment at the Howe Company* 272 • THE ROLE OF EXPECTATIONS 273 • THE EFFECT OF INNOVATIONS AND RANDOM EXTERNAL EVENTS 274 • INVEN-TORY CYCLES 275 • VARIATION IN GOVERNMENT SPENDING 276 • THE POLIT-ICAL BUSINESS CYCLE 277 • MONETARY FACTORS 278 • CAN BUSINESS FLUC-TUATIONS BE AVOIDED? 279 • *Test Yourself* 280 • CAN BUSINESS FLUCTUATIONS BE FORECASTED? 280 • LEADING INDICATORS 281 • SIMPLE AGGREGATE MODELS 283 • ECONOMETRIC MODELS 285 • ECONOMETRIC FORECASTS: THE TRACK RECORD 288 • **Cross-Chapter Case/Part Three: The Economic Forecasts of 1984** 290 • *Test Yourself* 292 • *Summary* 293 • *Concepts for Review* 293

PART FOUR   Money, Banking, and Stabilization Policy

CHAPTER 14   **Money and the Economy   295**

WHAT IS MONEY? 295 • THE MONEY SUPPLY, NARROWLY DEFINED 297 • THE MONEY SUPPLY, BROADLY DEFINED 299 • THE VALUE OF MONEY 300 • IN-FLATION AND THE QUANTITY OF MONEY 301 • UNEMPLOYMENT AND THE QUANTITY OF MONEY 302 • DETERMINANTS OF THE QUANTITY OF MONEY 302 • THE DEMAND FOR MONEY 303 • *Example 14.1 • Empirical Evidence Regarding the Demand for Money* 304 • *Test Yourself* 306 • CHANGES IN THE MONEY SUPPLY AND NATIONAL OUTPUT 306 • THE MONETARISTS 309 • THE VELOCITY OF MONEY 310 • THE EQUATION OF EXCHANGE 311 • THE CRUDE QUANTITY THEORY OF MONEY AND PRICES 312 • A MORE SOPHISTICATED VERSION OF THE QUANTITY THEORY 314 • THE IMPORTANCE OF MONEY 316 • *Test Yourself* 317 • *Summary* 317 • *Concepts for Review* 318

CHAPTER 15   **The Banking System and the Quantity of Money   319**

THE FEDERAL RESERVE SYSTEM 319 • FUNCTIONS OF THE FEDERAL RESERVE 321 • COMMERCIAL BANKS IN THE UNITED STATES 321 • HOW BANKS OPER-ATE 324 • THE BALANCE SHEET OF AN INDIVIDUAL BANK 325 • FRAC-TIONAL-RESERVE BANKING 326 • THE SAFETY OF THE BANKS 328 • *Should Deposit Insurance Be Changed?* 330 • TWO WAYS BANKS CANNOT CREATE MONEY 331 • *Test Yourself* 334 • HOW BANKS CAN CREATE MONEY 334 • THE EFFECT OF EXCESS RESERVES: A GENERAL PROPOSITION 339 • THE EFFECT OF A DECREASE IN RESERVES 340 • CURRENCY WITHDRAWALS 341 • *Example 15.1 Currency Holdings of the Public* 342 • EXCESS RESERVES 343 • *Test Yourself* 344 • *Summary* 344 • *Concepts for Review* 345

CHAPTER 16   **Monetary Policy**   346

THE AIMS OF MONETARY POLICY 346 • THE CENTRAL ROLE OF BANK RE-
SERVES 347 • MAKERS OF MONETARY POLICY 348 • THE FEDERAL RESERVE
BANKS: THEIR CONSOLIDATED BALANCE SHEET 349 • OPEN MARKET OPERA-
TIONS 350 • CHANGES IN LEGAL RESERVE REQUIREMENTS 352 • CHANGES IN
THE DISCOUNT RATE 354 • OTHER TOOLS OF MONETARY POLICY 355 • *Ex-
ample 16.1 Monetary Policy and the Aggregate Demand Curve* 356 • *Test
Yourself* 357 • WHEN IS MONETARY POLICY TIGHT OR EASY? 358 • SHOULD
THE FED PAY MORE ATTENTION TO INTEREST RATES OR THE MONEY SUP-
PLY? • 359 • DECISION MAKING AT THE FED: A CASE STUDY 360 • *Example
16.2 How Quickly Does Monetary Policy Work?* 362 • MONETARY POLICY IN
THE UNITED STATES 362 • PROBLEMS IN FORMULATING MONETARY POLICY
364 • *Is There an Independent Federal Reserve? Should There Be?* 365 • HOW
WELL HAS THE FED PERFORMED? 366 • SHOULD THE FED BE GOVERNED BY
A RULE? 368 • *Test Yourself* 369 • *Summary* 369 • *Concepts for Review* 370

CHAPTER 17   **Controversies over Stabilization Policy**   371

MONETARISTS VERSUS KEYNESIANS: THE HISTORICAL BACKGROUND 372 •
CAUSES OF BUSINESS FLUCTUATIONS: THE OPPOSING VIEWS 373 • STABILITY
OF THE ECONOMY: THE OPPOSING VIEWS 373 • EFFECTS OF THE INTEREST
RATE: THE OPPOSING VIEWS 374 • THE EFFECT OF MONETARY POLICY: THE
OPPOSING VIEWS 376 • THE EFFECT OF FISCAL POLICY: THE OPPOSING VIEWS
377 • THE CONTROVERSY OVER A MONETARY RULE 379 • *Example 17.1
What Caused the Great Depression?* 379 • *Test Yourself* 380 • THE CURRENT
STATE OF THE KEYNESIAN-MONETARIST DEBATE 381 • RATIONAL EXPECTA-
TIONS: ANOTHER ELEMENT IN THE CURRENT DEBATE 382 • SUPPLY-SIDE
ECONOMICS ENTERS THE FRAY 384 • *Test Yourself* 386 • *Summary* 386 •
Concepts for Review 387

CHAPTER 18   **Inflation and Anti-Inflationary Measures**   388

DEMAND-PULL INFLATION 388 • COST-PUSH INFLATION 389 • *Example 18.1
The Fed and Cost-Push Inflation* 390 • DIFFICULTIES IN DISTINGUISHING
COST-PUSH FROM DEMAND-PULL INFLATION 391 • THE PHILLIPS CURVE 392 •
THE INSTABILITY OF THE PHILLIPS CURVE 394 • THE LONG-RUN PHILLIPS
CURVE 395 • *Recent Developments in Economics: Rational Expectations and
Credibility in Fighting Inflation* 398 • *Test Yourself* 399 • WAGE AND PRICE
CONTROLS 400 • INCOMES POLICIES 402 • *Example 18.2 Effects of the 1971–
74 Control Program* 402 • TAX-BASED INCOMES POLICIES 405 • **Cross-Chapter
Case/Part Four: The Meeting of the Federal Open Market Committee on
November 14–15, 1983** 406 • ECONOMIC STABILIZATION: WHERE WE STAND
410 • *Test Yourself* 411 • *Summary* 411 • *Concepts for Review* 412

PART FIVE	**Economic Growth, Energy, and the Environment**	

CHAPTER 19   **Economic Growth**   413

WHAT IS ECONOMIC GROWTH? 414 • ECONOMIC GROWTH AND THE PRODUC-TION POSSIBILITIES CURVE 414 • THE AGGREGATE PRODUCTION FUNCTION 415 • THE LAW OF DIMINISHING MARGINAL RETURNS 415 • THOMAS MALTHUS AND POPULATION GROWTH 417 • *Example 19.1 "Birth Rights" and Population Control* 419 • *Test Yourself* 421 • DAVID RICARDO AND CAPI-TAL FORMATION 422 • CAPITAL FORMATION AND ECONOMIC GROWTH 424 • THE ROLE OF HUMAN CAPITAL 426 • THE ROLE OF TECHNOLOGICAL CHANGE 427 • DETERMINANTS OF TECHNOLOGICAL CHANGE 429 • ENTREPRENEUR-SHIP AND THE SOCIAL ENVIRONMENT 431 • *If the Robots Are Coming, Can Mass Unemployment Be Far Behind?* 432 • THE GAP BETWEEN ACTUAL AND POTENTIAL OUTPUT 433 • *Test Yourself* 434 • *Summary* 434 • *Concepts for Review* 435

CHAPTER 20   **Environmental and Energy Problems**   436

OUR ENVIRONMENTAL PROBLEMS 437 • THE IMPORTANT ROLE OF EXTERNAL DISECONOMIES 438 • PUBLIC POLICY TOWARD POLLUTION 439 • POLLUTION-CONTROL PROGRAMS IN THE UNITED STATES 443 • HOW CLEAN SHOULD THE ENVIRONMENT BE? 444 • *Example 20.1 How to Reduce the Costs of Cleaning Up* 445 • RECENT DIRECTIONS OF ENVIRONMENTAL POLICY 447 • *Test Your-self* 448 • OUR ENERGY PROBLEMS 448 • PUBLIC POLICY TOWARD ENERGY 450 • **Cross-Chapter Case/Part Five: Bubbles, Offsets, and Banks** 452 • *Ex-ample 20.2 Oil Price Decontrol and Imports* 454 • THE WEAKENING OF OPEC 455 • *Test Yourself* 456 • *Summary* 456 • *Concepts for Review* 457

PART SIX   **Consumer Behavior and Business Decision Making**

CHAPTER 21   **Market Demand and Price Elasticity**   459

MARKET DEMAND CURVES 459 • *Example 21.1 Speculation and the Demand Curve* 462 • THE PRICE ELASTICITY OF DEMAND 463 • DETERMINANTS OF THE PRICE ELASTICITY OF DEMAND 465 • *Why Washington's Gasoline Tax Bit the Dust* 466 • PRICE ELASTICITY AND TOTAL MONEY EXPENDITURE 467 • *Henry Ford and the Price Elasticity of Demand for Autos* 468 • *Test Yourself* 470 • THE FARM PROBLEM AND THE PRICE ELASTICITY OF DEMAND 470 • INDUSTRY AND FIRM DEMAND CURVES 472 • INCOME ELASTICITY OF DE-MAND 472 • *Example 21.2 The Demand for "Suds"* 474 • CROSS ELASTICITY OF DEMAND 475 • *Test Yourself* 475 • *Summary* 476 • *Concepts for Review* 476

CHAPTER 22   **Getting Behind the Demand Curve: Consumer Behavior** 477

CONSUMER EXPENDITURES 477 • A MODEL OF CONSUMER BEHAVIOR 479 • THE EQUILIBRIUM MARKET BASKET 482 • *Example 22.1 The Diamond-Water Paradox 484* • *Test Yourself 485* • THE CONSUMER'S DEMAND CURVE 486 • WHY DO INDIVIDUAL DEMAND CURVES GENERALLY SLOPE DOWNWARD? 488 • *Example 22.2 Meat and Consumer's Surplus 489* • *Recent Developments in Economics: The Role of Time in Consumption Decisions 490* • DERIVING THE MARKET DEMAND CURVE 491 • *Test Yourself 492* • *Summary 492* • *Concepts for Review 493* • APPENDIX: HOW INDIFFERENCE CURVES CAN BE USED TO ANALYZE CONSUMER BEHAVIOR 494

CHAPTER 23   **Optimal Input Decisions by Business Firms** 500

THE PRODUCTION FUNCTION REVISITED 501 • TYPES OF INPUTS 502 • THE SHORT RUN AND THE LONG RUN 502 • AVERAGE PRODUCT OF AN INPUT 503 • MARGINAL PRODUCT OF AN INPUT 503 • THE LAW OF DIMINISHING MARGINAL RETURNS 505 • *Example 23.1 Production Theory in the Milking Shed 506* • *Test Yourself 506* • THE OPTIMAL INPUT DECISIONS 507 • A MORE GENERAL PROOF OF THE RULE 508 • *How to Make Money in Real Estate by Logic Alone 509* • PRODUCING KANSAS CORN: A CASE STUDY 510 • *Test Yourself 511* • *Summary 511* • *Concepts for Review 512*

CHAPTER 24   **Cost Analysis** 513

WHAT ARE COSTS? 513 • SHORT-RUN COST FUNCTIONS 514 • AVERAGE COSTS IN THE SHORT RUN 516 • MARGINAL COST IN THE SHORT RUN 518 • SHORT-RUN COST FUNCTIONS OF A CRUDE-OIL PIPELINE: A CASE STUDY 521 • *Example 24.1 The Costs of a Dairy Farm 522* • *Test Yourself 523* • LONG-RUN COST FUNCTIONS 523 • RETURNS TO SCALE 525 • MEASUREMENT AND APPLICATION OF COST FUNCTIONS 526 • **Cross-Chapter Case/Part Six: How Robots Affect Firms' Cost Curves** 528 • *Test Yourself 531* • *Summary 531* • *Concepts for Review 532*

PART SEVEN   **Market Structure and Antitrust Policy**

CHAPTER 25   **Perfect Competition** 533

MARKET STRUCTURE AND ECONOMIC PERFORMANCE 533 • PERFECT COMPETITION 535 • THE OUTPUT OF THE FIRM 536 • THE MARKET SUPPLY CURVE 541 • DERIVING THE MARKET SUPPLY CURVE 542 • *Example 25.1 How Much Mercury Do We Have? 543* • *Test Yourself 544* • THE PRICE ELASTICITY OF SUPPLY 544 • PRICE AND OUTPUT: THE MARKET PERIOD 546 • PRICE AND OUTPUT: THE SHORT RUN 546 • PRICE AND OUTPUT: THE LONG RUN 547 • *Recent Developments in Economics: Laboratory Experimentation 548* • THE ALLOCATION OF RESOURCES UNDER PERFECT COMPETITION: A MORE DETAILED VIEW 550 • *Example 25.2 How Many Apples Should Be Produced?*

552 • BITUMINOUS COAL: A CASE STUDY 553 • *Test Yourself* 554 • *Summary* 555 • *Concepts for Review* 555 • APPENDIX: CONSTANT, INCREASING, AND DECREASING COST INDUSTRIES 556

CHAPTER 26 **Monopoly and Its Regulation** 558

CAUSES OF MONOPOLY 559 • DEMAND CURVE AND MARGINAL REVENUE UNDER MONOPOLY 560 • PRICE AND OUTPUT: THE SHORT RUN 562 • PRICE AND OUTPUT: THE LONG RUN 565 • PERFECT COMPETITION AND MONOPOLY: A COMPARISON 566 • *Example 26.1 Another Newspaper for Haverhill?* 568 • *Test Yourself* 569 • THE CASE AGAINST MONOPOLY 569 • PUBLIC REGULATION OF MONOPOLY 571 • DOES REGULATION AFFECT PRICES? 573 • *Example 26.2 Price Discrimination in Dentistry* 574 • INCREASE OF PRICES AND REDUCTION OF COMPETITION BY REGULATORS 575 • EFFECTS OF REGULATION ON EFFICIENCY 576 • *Test Yourself* 578 • *Summary* 578 • *Concepts for Review* 579 • APPENDIX: MARGINAL COST PRICING 580

CHAPTER 27 **Monopolistic Competition and Oligopoly** 582

MONOPOLISTIC COMPETITION AND OLIGOPOLY: THEIR MAJOR CHARACTERISTICS 582 • MONOPOLISTIC COMPETITION 583 • PRICE AND OUTPUT UNDER MONOPOLISTIC COMPETITION 584 • COMPARISONS WITH PERFECT COMPETITION AND MONOPOLY 586 • RETAILING: A CASE STUDY 587 • OLIGOPOLY 588 • MERGERS AND OLIGOPOLY 589 • OLIGOPOLY BEHAVIOR AND THE STABILITY OF PRICES 590 • *Test Yourself* 591 • COLLUSION AND CARTELS 591 • BARRIERS TO COLLUSION 593 • PRICE LEADERSHIP 594 • *Example 27.1 How Other Sources of Oil Influence OPEC's Price* 595 • COST-PLUS PRICING 596 • NONPRICE COMPETITION 597 • COMPARISON OF OLIGOPOLY WITH PERFECT COMPETITION 598 • *Recent Developments in Economics: Contestable Markets* 599 • *Test Yourself* 601 • *Summary* 601 • *Concepts for Review* 602 • APPENDIX: THE THEORY OF GAMES 602

CHAPTER 28 **Industrial Organization and Antitrust Policy** 605

THE CASE AGAINST OLIGOPOLY AND MONOPOLISTIC COMPETITION 605 • THE DEFENSE OF MONOPOLY POWER 607 • MONOPOLY POWER, BIG BUSINESS, AND TECHNOLOGICAL CHANGE 607 • HOW MUCH MONOPOLY POWER IS OPTIMAL? 608 • CONCENTRATION OF ECONOMIC POWER 609 • ASSETS OF THE 100 LARGEST FIRMS 609 • INDUSTRIAL CONCENTRATION IN THE UNITED STATES 610 • THE ANTITRUST LAWS 611 • THE ROLE OF THE COURTS 612 • THE ROLE OF THE JUSTICE DEPARTMENT 613 • POST-WORLD WAR II DEVELOPMENTS 614 • *Test Yourself* 615 • STANDARDS FOR ANTITRUST POLICY 616 • THE EFFECTIVENESS OF ANTITRUST POLICY 617 • THE *Pabst* CASE: ANTITRUST IN ACTION 617 • THE PATENT SYSTEM 618 • **Cross-Chapter Case/Part Seven:** *Berkey Photo* v. *Eastman Kodak Co.* 620 • OTHER POLICIES DESIGNED TO RESTRICT COMPETITION 622 • *Example 28.1 Resale Price Maintenance and Cosmetics* 623 • *Test Yourself* 624 • *Summary* 624 • *Concepts for Review* 625

PART EIGHT   Distribution of Income

CHAPTER 29   Determinants of Wages   627

THE LABOR FORCE AND THE PRICE OF LABOR 627 • THE EQUILIBRIUM WAGE
AND EMPLOYMENT UNDER PERFECT COMPETITION 629 • THE MARKET DE-
MAND CURVE FOR LABOR 630 • THE MARKET SUPPLY CURVE FOR LABOR 631
• EQUILIBRIUM PRICE AND QUANTITY OF LABOR 632 • WAGE DIFFERENTIALS
633 • *Example 29.1 Millionaire Geologists* 634 • THE ALL-VOLUNTEER ARMY:
A CASE STUDY 635 • *Recent Developments in Economics: Labor Market Sig-
naling* 636 • MONOPSONY 637 • *Test Yourself* 638 • LABOR UNIONS 639 • THE
AMERICAN LABOR MOVEMENT 640 • POSTWAR DEVELOPMENTS 642 • RECENT
TRENDS IN UNION MEMBERSHIP 644 • *Example 29.2 Can a Union Increase
Employment?* 645 • HOW UNIONS INCREASE WAGES 647 • COLLECTIVE BAR-
GAINING 648 • THE PROS AND CONS OF BIG UNIONS 649 • *Test Yourself* 650 •
Summary 650 • *Concepts for Review* 651

CHAPTER 30   Interest, Rent, and Profits   652

THE NATURE OF INTEREST 652 • THE DETERMINATION OF THE INTEREST
RATE 653 • FUNCTIONS OF THE INTEREST RATE 656 • CAPITAL BUDGETING
658 • CAPITAL AND ROUNDABOUT METHODS OF PRODUCTION 659 • CAPITAL-
IZATION OF ASSETS 661 • EFFECTS ON AN ASSET'S VALUE OF CHANGES IN
THE RATE OF RETURN ON OTHER INVESTMENTS 661 • THE PRESENT VALUE
OF FUTURE INCOME 661 • *What Does that Dream House Really Cost?* 662 •
Test Yourself 663 • RENT: NATURE AND SIGNIFICANCE 664 • PROFITS 666 •
Example 30.1 Exodus of Scientists and Engineers from Teaching 667 • THE
FUNCTIONS OF PROFITS 668 • THE FUNCTIONAL DISTRIBUTION OF INCOME
669 • *Test Yourself* 670 • *Summary* 671 • *Concepts for Review* 671

CHAPTER 31   Income Inequality, Poverty, and Discrimination   672

HOW MUCH INEQUALITY OF INCOME? 672 • WHY INEQUALITY? 674 • A MEAS-
URE OF INCOME INEQUALITY 674 • TRENDS IN INCOME INEQUALITY 675 •
Example 31.1 Economic Effects of Illegal Aliens 676 • EFFECTS OF THE TAX
STRUCTURE ON INCOME INEQUALITY 676 • INCOME INEQUALITY: THE PROS
AND CONS 678 • THE TRADEOFF BETWEEN EQUALITY AND EFFICIENCY 679 •
WHAT IS POVERTY? 680 • DECLINING INCIDENCE OF POVERTY 682 • CHAR-
ACTERISTICS OF THE POOR 682 • REASONS FOR POVERTY 683 • *Test Yourself*
684 • SOCIAL INSURANCE 684 • ANTIPOVERTY PROGRAMS 686 • *Example 31.2
Why Not Cure Poverty with a Check?* 689 • THE PROBLEMS OF DISCRIMINA-
TION 690 • **Cross-Chapter Case/Part Eight: How the Minimum Wage Affects
Teenage Unemployment** 692 • *Test Yourself* 695 • *Summary* 695 • *Concepts
for Review* 696

PART NINE International Economics

CHAPTER 32 International Trade 697

AMERICA'S FOREIGN TRADE 697 • SPECIALIZATION AND TRADE 698 • ABSO-LUTE ADVANTAGE 699 • COMPARATIVE ADVANTAGE 700 • A GEOMETRIC REPRESENTATION OF COMPARATIVE ADVANTAGE 701 • THE TERMS OF TRADE 702 • INCOMPLETE SPECIALIZATION 703 • INTERNATIONAL TRADE AND INDIVIDUAL MARKETS 703 • ECONOMIES OF SCALE AND LEARNING 706 • INNOVATION AND INTERNATIONAL TRADE 706 • MULTINATIONAL FIRMS 707 • *Test Yourself* 708 • TARIFFS AND QUOTAS 709 • ARGUMENTS FOR TARIFFS AND QUOTAS 711 • TARIFFS IN THE UNITED STATES 715 • *Example 32.1 The Effects of a Tariff on Shoes* 717 • *The European Economic Community* 719 • *Test Yourself* 720 • *Summary* 720 • *Concepts for Review* 721 • APPENDIX: THE EFFECTS OF FOREIGN TRADE ON NET NATIONAL PRODUCT 721

CHAPTER 33 Exchange Rates and the Balance of Payments 723

INTERNATIONAL TRANSACTIONS AND EXCHANGE RATES 723 • EXCHANGE RATES UNDER THE GOLD STANDARD 724 • THE FOREIGN EXCHANGE MAR-KET 725 • FIXED EXCHANGE RATES 728 • BALANCE-OF-PAYMENTS DEFICITS AND SURPLUSES 730 • THE BALANCE-OF-PAYMENTS ACCOUNTS 731 • *Test Yourself* 735 • EXCHANGE RATES: PRE-WORLD WAR II EXPERIENCE 736 • THE GOLD EXCHANGE STANDARD 736 • U.S. BALANCE-OF-PAYMENTS DEFICITS, 1950–72 737 • ATTEMPTS TO ELIMINATE THE DEFICITS IN THE EARLY 1970s 738 • DEMISE OF THE BRETTON WOODS SYSTEM 740 • FIXED VERSUS FLEXI-BLE EXCHANGE RATES 740 • *The International Money Game* 741 • HOW WELL HAVE FLOATING EXCHANGE RATES WORKED? 742 • THE INTERNA-TIONAL MONETARY FUND 743 • INTERNATIONAL LENDING 745 • *Example 33.1 Return to the Gold Standard?* 745 • *Test Yourself* 746 • *Summary* 747 • *Concepts for Review* 748

CHAPTER 34 The Less Developed Countries 749

LESS DEVELOPED COUNTRIES: DEFINITION AND CHARACTERISTICS 749 • BARRIERS TO DEVELOPMENT AND THE NEED FOR CAPITAL FORMATION 752 • THE POPULATION EXPLOSION 754 • TECHNOLOGY: A CRUCIAL FACTOR 756 • ENTREPRENEURSHIP AND SOCIAL INSTITUTIONS 757 • LACK OF NATURAL RESOURCES 758 • THE ROLE OF GOVERNMENT 758 • *Example 34.1 Economic Development with an Unlimited Labor Supply* 759 • *Test Yourself* 760 • BAL-ANCED GROWTH 760 • DEVELOPMENT PLANNING IN LESS DEVELOPED COUN-TRIES 762 • *Example 34.2 The Push Toward Industrialization* 763 • PLAN-NING IN ACTION: THE CASE OF INDIA 764 • CHOOSING INVESTMENT PROJECTS IN LESS DEVELOPED COUNTRIES 766 • FOREIGN AID 766 • THE WORLD BANK 769 • A NEW INTERNATIONAL ECONOMIC ORDER? 770 • *Test Yourself* 771 • *Summary* 772 • *Concepts for Review* 773

CHAPTER 35   **The Communist Countries and Marxism**   774

THE DOCTRINES OF KARL MARX 775 • THE SOVIET ECONOMY 777 • SOVIET ECONOMIC PLANNING 778 • PRIORITIES AND PERFORMANCE 780 • PRICES IN THE USSR 781 • THE DISTRIBUTION OF INCOME 783 • *Example 35.1 A Peek Behind Soviet Price Tags* 783 • SOVIET ECONOMIC GROWTH 784 • EVALUATION OF THE SOVIET ECONOMY 786 • *Test Yourself* 788 • THE CHINESE ECONOMY 788 • ECONOMIC LIFE IN CHINA 790 • DEMOCRATIC SOCIALISM 791 • RADICAL ECONOMICS 792 • **Cross-Chapter Case/Part Nine: The Mammoth Debt Problems of Argentina, Brazil, and Mexico** 793 • DOES CAPITALISM HAVE A FUTURE? 796 • *Test Yourself* 796 • *Summary* 797 • *Concepts for Review* 798

Appendices   **Digging Deeper into the Economist's Tool Box**   A1

APPENDIX A: *IS* AND *LM* CURVES AND THE KEYNESIAN-MONETARIST CONTROVERSY A1 • APPENDIX B: ISOQUANTS, ISOCOST CURVES, AND THE OPTIMAL INPUT COMBINATION A8 • APPENDIX C: LINEAR PROGRAMMING A11 • APPENDIX D: GENERAL EQUILIBRIUM ANALYSIS AND INPUT-OUTPUT MODELS A18 • APPENDIX E: OPTIMAL RESOURCE ALLOCATION AND PERFECT COMPETITION A22

Brief Answers to Odd-Numbered Test-Yourself Questions   A29

Glossary   A51

Index   A65

Preface

Any principles text must keep current with the state of economic knowledge, especially as it applies to the economic issues of the day. The fifth edition of *Economics: Principles, Problems, Decisions* does this, in ways I outline below. But the most fundamental change in this edition is not one of organization or style: it involves a new emphasis which, I believe, will lead to far greater understanding and retention of the core material of the introductory course.

To students, perhaps the biggest defect in most textbooks is their failure to sift through the many details, and present a reasonably small number of basic propositions that should be given central attention. Thus students find it difficult to separate the essential and basic from the less important, and a few years after graduation their recollection of economics is often a smudge.

Almost as formidable a barrier to learning is the tendency of textbooks to treat each topic as a separate entity, with the connections among them either unstated or mentioned in passing. Because the topics are not brought together, the student is like a chef who has the ingredients spread on the counter but lacks the recipe for blending them.

The fifth edition attempts to remedy the twin problems of excessive detail and missing linkages:

Basic Ideas. To provide direction finders through the text, the present edition focuses on 70 Basic Ideas, two highlighted per chapter, which students are encouraged to think through carefully. One can reasonably expect these 70 Basic Ideas to stick with students. If so, their time will have been well spent, because these ideas really constitute the heart of elementary economics, stripped of frills and details. Based on classroom experience, this simple pedagogical aid helps students to see (and remember) the forest, as distinct from a hodgepodge of trees. (Besides presenting each of these 70 Basic Ideas in the relevant chapters in the text, a summary of them is printed in the front and back inside covers of the book, where students can readily refer to them.)

Cross-Chapter Cases. To make connections clear—connections not only

between aspects of theory but also between theory and the uses to which it is put—this edition introduces eight Cross-Chapter Cases. Appearing near the end of each part (other than the introduction), each takes up a major issue cutting across material contained in various chapters of the part. Among the issues developed in detail are the pros and cons of America's adopting an industrial policy, the accuracy of the economic forecasts of 1984, an account of a meeting of the Federal Open Market Committee, how robots affect firms' cost curves, the antitrust case involving Berkey Photo and Eastman Kodak, the effects of the minimum wage on teenage unemployment, and the debt problems of Argentina, Brazil, and Mexico. These Cross-Chapter Cases are not mere appendages. They require students to draw on a number of tools and techniques to which they have just been exposed in the entire part.

Other New Material. While the 70 Basic Ideas and the Cross-Chapter Cases are the principal innovations in the Fifth Edition, much else has been changed. New inserts, for example, come in two varieties: some on new developments in economics (such as the role of time in economics, market signaling, contestable markets, and laboratory experimentation) while others deal with mistakes and fallacies (such as the discussion of sunk costs in Chapter 23). In addition, new materials have been introduced on such aspects of the current policy scene as tax reform, the strong dollar, the balance of trade deficit, the federal budget deficit, the B-1 bomber, and protectionism. Also, the IBM Corporation is now used to explain the operation of a giant corporation, significantly one with a strong entrepreneurial bent, in Chapter 6. Additional space is also devoted to relatively new theoretical developments such as the rational expectations hypothesis.

Glossary of Terms. Another new feature of the Fifth Edition is a Glossary of Terms, which is placed at the end of the book. I am grateful to Nariman Behravish, who supervised much of the work underlying this glossary, for permission to include it here. This new section should make it easier for students to refresh their memories concerning the definition of economic terms.

Emphasis on Doing Economics. Most textbooks do not encourage the student to get involved in the subject. They simply lay out the material, leaving the student to absorb it passively. In the previous edition, I invited students to *do* economics in order to understand it better. Scores of examples were provided, each describing a real (or realistic) situation and then calling on the student to work through the solution. Within each chapter there were two problem sets, both designated "Test Yourself." that enabled students to check their comprehension of what they had just read. The reaction of instructors and students was very favorable, and the emphasis on doing economics is maintained in this fifth edition. One new feature is that the answers for the odd-numbered Test Yourself questions are now provided at the end of the book. Many students and instructors urged me to include them in this way.

Organizational Changes. Although many new features have been included in the present edition, the book is shorter than the previous edition, due to a tough (even ruthless) editing process. A very determined effort has been made to drop extraneous material and to keep the number of words to a minimum. This has led to a reduction in the number of chapters and to shortening in such areas as consumer decision making and how banks

create money. This edition, while leaner than its predecessor, manages, I believe, to be clearer, both theoretically and empirically.

Updating. All of the empirical and policy-oriented chapters have been updated. Since a text should reflect current conditions and concerns, the government policies in all the major economic areas—fiscal, monetary, incomes, farm, energy, environmental, antitrust, and international—are reviewed in depth. The latest data available have been incorporated in the tables, diagrams, and discussions, while revisions in sections on economic forecasting, reserve requirements, Social Security, and a variety of other topics have brought them into line with current developments.

Since instructors differ considerably in their choice and ordering of topics, the fifth edition, like its predecessors, is organized for maximum flexibility. Many instructors take up microeconomics before macroeconomics. This book will work just as well for these instructors as for those who prefer to present macroeconomics first. (A suggested ordering of chapters is presented for them on p. xxi.) As an alternative to reversing the chapter sequence in the one-volume edition, some instructors may want to consider the two-volume paperbound version, *Principles of Microeconomics* and *Principles of Macroeconomics,* fifth editions.

This book can also be adapted for use in one-semester courses. Pages xxi–xxii present outlines for a one-semester course stressing microeconomics, a one-semester course stressing macroeconomics, and a one semester course covering both.

As supplements to this text, I have prepared both a book of readings and a study guide containing problems and exercises. The book of readings is in two parts, *Principles of Macroeconomics: Reading, Issues, and Cases,* fourth edition, and *Principles of Microeconomics: Readings, Issues, and Cases,* fourth edition. It provides a substantial set of supplementary articles, carefully correlated with the text for instructors who want to introduce their students to the writings of major contemporary economists. It is designed to acquaint the student with a wide range of economic analysis, spanning the spectrum from the classics to the present-day radicals. The emphasis, as in the text, is on integrating theory, measurement, and applications.

The *Study Guide,* fifth edition, contains, in addition to problems, review questions, and tests, a large number of cases that require the student to work with quantitative material in applying concepts to practical situations. In practically every chapter of the study guide, a new case study has been added. Both students and instructors have reported that such cases are important in motivating students and illuminating economic theory.

An *Instructor's Manual* has been prepared by Michael Claudon of Middlebury College to accompany the text. A *Test Item File,* prepared by Herbert Gishlick of Rider College, is available both in printed form and on computer tape. *Transparency Masters* are also available to instructors who adopt the text.

Finally, it is a pleasure to acknowledge the debts that I owe to the many teachers at various colleges and universities who have commented in detail on various parts of the manuscript. The first, second, and third editions benefited greatly from the advice I received from the following distinguished economists, none of whom is responsible, of course, for the outcome: Wallace Atherton, California State University at Long Beach; Bela Balassa, Johns Hopkins; Robert Baldwin, University of Wisconsin (Madison); Arthur Benavie, North Carolina; Lee Biggs, Montgomery College; Donald Billings, Boise State; William Branson, Princeton; Martin Bronfenbrenner, Duke; Edward Budd, Penn State; Phillip Burstein, Purdue; Wade Chio, U.S. Air Force Academy; Michael Claudon, Middlebury; Warren Coates. Federal Reserve; Richard Cooper, Yale; Alan Deardorff, Michigan; William Desvouses, Missouri (Rolla); F. Trenery Dolbear, Brandeis; Robert Dorfman, Harvard; James Duesenberry, Harvard; William Dugger, North Texas State University; Richard Easterlin, University of Southern California; Jonathan Eaton, Princeton; David Fand, Wayne State; Judith Fernandez, University of California (Berkeley); David Gay, University of Arkansas; Howard A. Gilbert, South Dakota State University; Gerald Goldstein, Northwestern; Robert Gordon, Northwestern; Edward Gramlich, Michigan; Herschel Grossman, Brown; William Gunther, Alabama; Jerry Gustafson, Beloit; Judith Herman, Queens College; Alan Heston, University of Pennsylvania; Albert Hirschman, Harvard; Ronald Jones, Rochester; John Kareken, Minnesota; Ann Krueger, World Bank; Robert Kuenne, Princeton; Simon Kuznets, Harvard; William Leonard, St. Joseph's; Richard Levin, Yale; Raymond Lubitz, Columbia and the Federal Reserve; John F. MacDonald, Illinois (Chicago Circle); Sherman Maisel, University of California (Berkeley); Leonard Martin, Cleveland State University; Thomas Mayer, University of California (Davis); William McEachern, University of Connecticut; Joseph McKinney, Baylor; Edward McNertney, Texas Christian University; Steven Morrison, University of California (Berkeley); John Murphy, Canisius; Arthur Okun, Brookings Institution; Lloyd Orr, Indiana; R. D. Peterson, Markenomics Associates (Fort Collins); E. Dwight Phaup, Union College; Roger Ransom, University of California (Berkeley); Charles Ratliff, Davidson College; Albert Rees, Princeton; Edward Renshaw, State University of New York (Albany); Anthony Romeo, University of Connecticut; Vernon Ruttan, Minnesota; Warren St. James, Nassau County Community College; Steven Sacks, University of Connecticut; Allen Sanderson, William and Mary; David Schulze, Florida; Edward Shapiro, University of Toledo; William Shugart, Arizona; Paul Sommers, Middlebury; Nicolas Spulber, Indiana; Charles Stone, Swarthmore; Richard Sutch, University of California (Berkeley); Frank Tansey, City University of New York; Michael Taussig, Rutgers; Thomas Tidrick, Clayton Junior College; Fred Westfield, Vanderbilt; Simon Whitney, Iona College; William Whitney, University of Pennsylvania; and Harold Williams, Kent State University.

Among the teachers who contributed comments and suggestions for the changes in subsequent editions are: Otis Gilley, University of Texas at Austin; Marvin E. Goodstein, University of the South; William Keeton, Yale; Walter Misiolek, University of Alabama; and Jennifer Roback, Yale.

I would like to thank Elisabeth Allison of Harvard University for contributing the inserts that appear (over her initials) in various chapters, Donald S. Lamm and Nancy K. Palmquist of W. W. Norton for their efficient handling of the publishing end of the work, and Edward D. Mansfield and Elizabeth D. Mansfield for editorial help. As always, my wife, Lucile, has contributed an enormous amount to the completion of this book.

Philadelphia, 1985.   E.M.

Outline of a One-Year Course with Macroeconomics Following Microeconomics.

1 Economic Problems and Analysis
2 Economic Models and Capitalism, American-Style
3 The Price System
4 The Economic Role of the Government
5 Government Expenditures, Taxation, and the Public Debt
6 The Business Firm: Organization, Motivation, and Technology
21 Market Demand and Price Elasticity
22 Getting Behind the Demand Curve: Consumer Behavior
23 Optimal Input Decisions by Business Firms
24 Cost Analysis
25 Perfect Competition
26 Monopoly and Its Regulation
27 Monopolistic Competition and Oligopoly
28 Industrial Organization and Antitrust Policy
29 Determinants of Wages
30 Interest, Rent, and Profits
31 Income Inequality, Poverty, and Discrimination
7 National Income and Product

8 Unemployment and Inflation
9 Aggregate Demand, Aggregate Supply, and Business Fluctuations
10 The Determination of National Output
11 Multiplier Analysis and Changes in Output
12 Fiscal Policy and National Output
13 Business Fluctuations and Economic Forecasting
14 Money and the Economy
15 The Banking System and the Quantity of Money
16 Monetary Policy
17 Controversies over Stabilization Policy
18 Inflation and Anti-Inflationary Measures
19 Economic Growth
20 Environmental and Energy Problems
32 International Trade
33 Exchange Rates and the Balance of Payments
34 The Less Developed Countries
35 The Communist Countries and Marxism

Outline of a One-Semester Course Emphasizing Microeconomics.

1 Economic Problems and Analysis
2 Economic Models and Capitalism, American-Style
3 The Price System
4 The Economic Role of the Government
6 The Business Firm: Organization, Motivation, and Technology
21 Market Demand and Price Elasticity
22 Getting Behind the Demand Curve: Consumer Behavior
23 Optimal Input Decisions by Business Firms
24 Cost Analysis
25 Perfect Competition
26 Monopoly and Its Regulation
27 Monopolistic Competition and Oligopoly

28 Industrial Organization and Antitrust Policy
31 Income Inequality, Poverty, and Discrimination [optional]
7 National Income and Product
8 Unemployment and Inflation
9 Aggregate Demand, Aggregate Supply, and Business Fluctuations
10 The Determination of National Output
11 Multiplier Analysis and Changes in Output
12 Fiscal Policy and National Output
14 Money and the Economy[1]
15 The Banking System and the Quantity of Money
16 Monetary Policy

[1] Also, assign the beginning sections of Chapter 13.

Outline of a One-Semester Course Emphasizing Macroeconomics.

1 Economic Problems and Analysis
2 Economic Models and Capitalism, American-Style
3 The Price System
4 The Economic Role of the Government
5 Government Expenditures, Taxation, and the Public Debt
6 The Business Firm: Organization, Motivation, and Technology
7 National Income and Product
8 Unemployment and Inflation
9 Aggregate Demand, Aggregate Supply, and Business Fluctuations
10 The Determination of National Output
11 Multiplier Analysis and Changes in Output
12 Fiscal Policy and National Output
13 Business Fluctuations and Economic Forecasting
14 Money and the Economy
15 The Banking System and the Quantity of Money
16 Monetary Policy
17 Controversies over Stabilization Policy
19 Economic Growth
32 International Trade
33 Exchange Rates and the Balance of Payments
34 The Less Developed Countries

Outline of a One-Semester Course Emphasizing Both Macroeconomics and Microeconomics

1 Economic Problems and Analysis
2 Economic Models and Capitalism, American-Style
3 The Price System
4 The Economic Role of the Government
5 Government Expenditures, Taxation, and the Public Debt
6 The Business Firm: Organization, Motivation, and Technology
7 National Income and Product
8 Unemployment and Inflation
9 Aggregate Demand, Aggregate Supply, and Business Fluctuations
10 The Determination of National Output
11 Multiplier Analysis and Changes in Output
12 Fiscal Policy and National Output
13 Business Fluctuations and Economic Forecasting
14 Money and the Economy
15 The Banking System and the Quantity of Money
16 Monetary Policy
17 Controversies over Stabilization Policy
18 Inflation and Anti-Inflationary Measures
21 Market Demand and Price Elasticity
22 Getting Behind the Demand Curve: Consumer Behavior
23 Optimal Input Decisions by Business Firms
24 Cost Analysis
25 Perfect Competition
26 Monopoly and Its Regulation

PART ONE

Introduction to Economics

CHAPTER 1

Economic Problems and Analysis

A recent national survey concluded that "the American public's knowledge of basic . . . economic facts of life is sadly deficient." This is a disturbing discovery, but it is not altogether surprising. Most of us grow up unaware that economics enters into nearly every activity that we engage in. To help you understand the pervasive importance of economics, we begin by looking at a sample of the major problems economists deal with. Each of these problems could have a big effect on your life.

Economic Problems: A Sampler

UNEMPLOYMENT AND INFLATION

The history of the American economy is for the most part a story of growth. Our output—the amount of goods and services we produce annually—has grown rapidly over the years, giving us a standard of living that could not have been imagined a century ago. For example, output per person in the United States was about $15,000 in 1984; in 1900, it was about $3,000. Nonetheless, the growth of output has not been steady or uninterrupted; instead, our output has tended to fluctuate—and so has unemployment. In periods when output has fallen, thousands, even millions, of people have been thrown out of work. In the Great Depression of the 1930s over 20 percent of the labor force was unemployed (see Figure 1.1). Unemployment on this scale results in enormous economic waste and social misery.

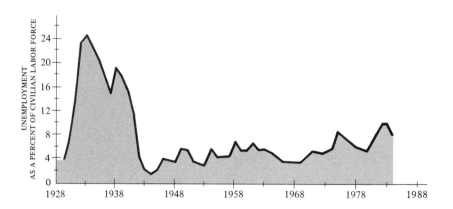

Figure 1.1
Unemployment Rates, United States, 1929–84 *The unemployment rate has varied substantially from year to year. In the Great Depression, it reached a high of over 24 percent. In 1984, it exceeded 7 percent.*

The first of our sample of economic problems is: *What determines the extent of* **unemployment** *in the American economy, and what can be done to reduce it?* This problem is complicated by a related phenomenon: The level of prices may rise when we reduce the level of unemployment. In other words, inflation may occur. Thus the problem is not only to curb unemployment, but to do this without producing an inflation so ruinous to the nation's economic health that the cure proves more dangerous than the ailment. Consequently, another major accompanying question is: *What determines the rate of* **inflation** *and how can it be reduced?* As Figure 1.2 shows, we have experienced considerable inflation since 1929; the dollar has lost over four-fifths of its purchasing power during this period. Moreover, in the 1970s and early 1980s, our economy often has been bedeviled by "stagflation": a combination of high unemployment and high inflation.

During the past 50 years, economists have learned a great deal about the factors that determine the extent of unemployment and inflation, and about the ways in which the government can promote high employment with reasonably stable prices. Any responsible citizen needs to know what economists have learned—and to be aware of the differences of opinion among leading economists on this score. To understand many of the central political issues of the day, and to vote intelligently, this knowledge is essential. Also, to understand the fallacies in many apparently simple remedies for the complex economic problems in this area, you need to know some economics.

THE PRODUCTIVITY SLOWDOWN AND THE COMPETITIVENESS OF U.S. GOODS

Labor productivity is defined as the amount of output that can be obtained per hour of labor. All nations are interested in increasing labor productivity, since it is intimately related to a nation's standard of living. Many factors, including new technologies like microelectronics and biotechnology, influence the rate of increase of labor productivity. Historically, labor productivity has increased relatively rapidly in the United States.

However, beginning in the late 1960s, U.S. labor productivity rose at a slower pace. At first, it was unclear whether this slowdown was only tempo-

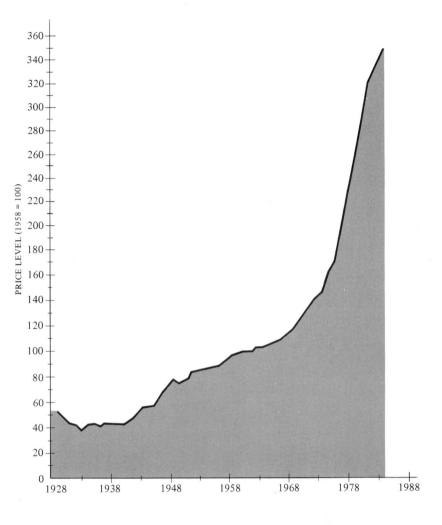

Figure 1.2
Changes in Price Level, United States, 1929-84 *The price level has increased steadily since the 1930s, and is now over eight times as high as it was in 1933.*

rary, but during the 1970s the situation got worse, not better. Between 1977 and 1980, labor productivity in the United States actually declined. (In other words, less was produced per hour of labor in 1980 than in 1977!) During the early 1980s, productivity growth picked up, but whether it would reach its old level—and stay there—was by no means obvious.

Many observers regard this productivity slowdown as being a very ominous sign for the U.S. economy. Moreover, they worry too about the fact that labor productivity in the United States has been increasing less rapidly than in many other countries like Japan and West Germany. For this and other reasons, there are questions regarding the ability of American firms to compete with their foreign rivals in industries like autos and machine tools.

Our second example of an economic problem is: *What determines the rate of increase of labor productivity? Why has this productivity slowdown occurred in the United States? What measures can and should be adopted to cope with it?* Economics provides a considerable amount of information on this score. Not only does economics tell us a good deal about the broad factors influencing national productivity levels; in addition, it provides rules and principles that are useful in increasing the productivity and efficiency of individual firms (and government agencies).

Table 1.1

MARKET SHARE OF FOUR LARGEST FIRMS, SELECTED MANUFACTURING PRODUCT MARKETS, UNITED STATES, 1977

Industry	Market share of four largest firms (percent)
Automobiles	93
Photographic equipment	72
Soap	59
Tires	70
Aircraft	59
Construction machinery	47
Blast furnaces and steel plants	45

Source: Statistical Abstract of the United States.

The 100 largest manufacturing firms control about half of all manufacturing assets in the United States (and their share of total assets seems to have increased since World War II). In certain industries, like automobiles, the 4 largest firms have accounted for over 90 percent of the market (see Table 1.1). Nonetheless, although the large corporations obviously wield considerable power in their markets, the American economic system is built on the idea that firms should compete with one another. In particular, the producers of steel, automobiles, oil, toothpicks, and other goods are expected to set their prices independently and not to collude. Certain acts of Congress, often referred to as the antitrust laws, make it illegal for firms to get together and set the price of a product.

Our third example of an economic problem is: *Why is competition of this sort socially desirable?* More specifically, why should we be in favor of the antitrust laws? What reasons are there to believe that such laws will result in a more efficient economic system? (And what do we mean by "efficient"?) To a business executive, lawyer, government official, or judge, these questions are very important, since it is likely that at one time or another these people will be concerned with an antitrust case. But these issues also matter to every citizen, because they deal with the basic rules of the game for firms in our economy. Of course, one reason why Americans have traditionally favored competition over collusion, and relatively small firms over giant ones, is that they have mistrusted the concentration of economic power, and obviously, this mistrust was based on both political and economic considerations. But beyond this, you should know when competition generally benefits society, and when it does not.

One way that society has attempted to control the economic power of corporations that dominate an entire industry is through **government regulation.** Take the case of radio and TV. The Federal Communications Commission, a government agency, monitors the activities of broadcasting stations and networks to prevent misuse of the airwaves. Other regulatory commissions supervise the activities of the power companies, the telephone companies, and other industries where it has been felt that competition cannot be relied on to produce socially desirable results.

During the late 1970s and early 1980s, there was a notable movement in the United States toward deregulation. At first, the movement was confined largely to the airlines, but then it spread to railroads, trucking, oil, and other industries. In part, this movement reflected a widespread feeling that the regulatory commissions tended to be lax or, worse still, to be captured by the industries they were supposed to regulate. In addition, it was felt that many aspects of regulation have contributed to inefficiency, both in the regulated industries themselves and in other parts of the economy. Since regulated industries produce about 10 percent of national output, we all have a big stake in understanding how they operate and whether they should be regulated and if so, how. This is another aspect of the same general problem of how industries should be organized.

THE ELIMINATION OF POVERTY

As pointed out by Philip Wicksteed, a prominent twentieth-century British economist, "A man can be neither a saint, nor a lover, nor a poet, unless he

Table 1.2

PERCENTAGE DISTRIBUTION OF PEOPLE, BY HOUSEHOLD MONTHLY CASH INCOME, UNITED STATES, 1983

Money income (dollars)	Percent of all people
Under 300	4.7
300– 599	7.8
600– 899	8.0
900–1,199	8.2
1,200–1,599	11.4
1,600–1,999	10.7
2,000–2,999	22.1
3,000–3,999	13.1
4,000 and over	14.1
Total	100ª

ª Because of rounding errors, the figures do not sum to total.

Source: U.S. Bureau of the Census. The data pertain to the third quarter of the year.

has comparatively recently had something to eat." Although relatively few people in the United States lack food desperately, about 35 million American people, approximately 15 percent of the population of the United States, live in what is officially designated as *poverty.* These people have frequently been called invisible in a nation where the average yearly income per family is over $25,000; but the poor are invisible only to those who shut their eyes, since they exist in ghettos in the wealthiest American cities like New York, Chicago, and Los Angeles, as well as near Main Street in thousands of small towns. They can also be found in areas where industry has come and gone, as in the former coal-mining towns of Pennsylvania and West Virginia, and in areas where decades of farming have depleted the soil.

Table 1.2 shows the distribution of income in the United States in 1983. Clearly, there are very substantial differences among families in income level. You as a citizen and a human being need to understand the social mechanisms underlying the distribution of income, both in the United States and in other countries, and how reasonable and just they are. Our fourth economic problem is: *Why does poverty exist in the world today, and what can be done to abolish it?* To help the poor effectively, we must understand the causes of poverty.

Since poverty is intimately bound up with our racial problems and the decay of our cities, the success or failure of measures designed to eradicate poverty may also help us determine whether we can achieve a society where equality of opportunity is more than a slogan and where people do not have to escape to the suburbs to enjoy green space and fresh air. Nor does the economist's concern with poverty stop at our shoreline. One of the biggest problems of the world today is the plight of the poor countries of Asia, Africa, and Latin America—the so-called less developed countries. The industrialized countries of the world, like the United States, Western Europe, Japan, and the Soviet Union, are really just rich little islands surrounded by seas of poverty. Over half of the world's population lives in countries where per capita income is less than $3,000 per year. These countries lack equipment, technology, and education; sometimes (but by no means always) they also suffer from overpopulation. Economists have devoted considerable attention to the problems of the less developed countries, and to developing techniques to assist them.

What Is Economics?

HUMAN WANTS AND RESOURCES

Now that we have looked at a number of specific economic problems, we must provide a definition of economics, as well as a description of the basic questions regarding any economic system that are of particular interest to economists. According to one standard definition, *economics is concerned with the way resources are allocated among alternative uses to satisfy human wants.* This definition is fine, but it does not mean much unless we define what is meant by *human wants* and by *resources.* What do these terms mean?

Human wants are the things, services, goods, and circumstances that people desire. Wants vary greatly among individuals and over time for the

Land

Labor

same individual. Some people like sports, others like books; some want to travel, others want to putter in the yard. An individual's desire for a particular good during a particular period of time is not infinite, but, in the aggregate, human wants seem to be insatiable. Besides the basic desires for food, shelter, and clothing, which must be fulfilled to some extent if the human organism is to maintain its existence, wants stem from cultural factors. For example, society, often helped along by advertising and other devices to modify tastes, promotes certain images of "the good life," which frequently entails owning an expensive car and living in a $150,000 split-level house in the suburbs.

Resources are the things or services used to produce goods which then can be used to satisfy wants. *Economic resources* are scarce, while *free resources,* such as air, are so abundant that they can be obtained without charge. The test of whether a resource is an economic resource or a free resource is price: economic resources command a nonzero price, but free resources do not. The number of free resources is actually quite limited. For instance, although the earth contains a huge amount of water, it is not a free resource to the typical urban or suburban home owner, who must pay a local water authority for providing and maintaining his or her water supply. In a world where all resources were free, there would be no economic problem, since all wants could be satisfied.

Economic resources can be classified into three categories, each of which is described below:

1. Land. A shorthand expression for natural resources, land includes minerals as well as plots of ground. Clearly, land is an important and valuable resource in both agriculture and industry. Think of the fertile soil of Iowa or Kansas, from which are obtained such abundant crops. Or consider Manhattan island, which supports the skyscrapers, shops, and theaters in the heart of New York. In addition, land is an important part of our environment, and it provides enjoyment above and beyond its contribution to agricultual and industrial output.

2. Labor. Human efforts, both physical and mental, are included in the category of labor. Thus, when you study for a final examination or make out an income tax return, this is as much labor as if you were to dig a ditch. In 1985, over 100 million people were employed (or looking for work) in the United States. This vast labor supply is, of course, an extremely important resource, without which our nation could not maintain its current output level.

3. Capital. Buildings, equipment, inventories, and other nonhuman producible resources that contribute to the production, marketing, and distribution of goods and services all fall within the economist's definition of capital. Examples are machine tools and warehouses; but not all types of capital are big or bulky: for example, a hand calculator, or a pencil for that matter, is a type of capital. American workers have an enormous amount of capital to work with. Think of the oil refineries in New Jersey and Philadelphia, the blast furnaces and open hearths in Pittsburgh and Cleveland, the aircraft plants in California and Georgia, and the host of additional types of capital we have and use in this country. Without this capital, the nation's output level would be a great deal less than it is.

TECHNOLOGY AND CHOICE

As pointed out above, economics is concerned with the way resources are allocated among alternative uses to satisfy human wants. An important determinant of the extent to which human wants can be satisfied from the amount of resources at hand is technology. *Technology* is society's pool of knowledge concerning the industrial arts. It includes the knowledge of engineers, scientists, craftsmen, managers, and others concerning how goods and services can be produced. For example, it includes the best existing knowledge regarding the ways in which an automobile plant or a synthetic rubber plant should be designed and operated. The level of technology sets limits on the amount and types of goods and services that can be derived from a given amount of resources.

To see this, suppose that engineers and craftsmen do not know how an automobile can be produced with less than 500 hours of labor being used in its manufacture. Clearly, this sets limits on the number of automobiles that can be produced with the available labor force. Or suppose that scientists and engineers do not know how to produce a ton of synthetic rubber with less than a certain amount of capital being used in its manufacture. This sets limits on the amount of synthetic rubber that can be produced with the available quantity of capital.

Given the existing technology, the fact that resources are scarce means that only a limited amount of goods and services can be produced from them. In other words, the capacity to produce goods and services is limited — *far more limited than human wants.* Thus there arises the necessity for *choice.* Somehow or other, a choice must be made as to how the available resources will be used (or if they will be used at all). And somehow or other a choice must be made as to how the output produced from these resources will be distributed among the population.

Economics is concerned with how such choices are made. Economists have spent a great deal of time, energy, and talent trying to determine how such choices *are* made in various circumstances, and how they *should* be made. Indeed, as we shall see in the next section, the basic questions that economics deals with are problems of choice of this sort. Note that these problems of choice go beyond the problems of particular individuals in choosing how to allocate their resources; they are problems of social choice.

CENTRAL QUESTIONS IN ECONOMICS

Economists are particularly concerned with four basic questions regarding the working of any economic system—ours or any other. These questions are: (1) What determines what (and how much) is produced? (2) What determines how it is produced? (3) What determines how the society's output is distributed among the members? (4) What determines the rate at which the society's per capita income will grow? These questions lie at the core of economics, because they are directed at the most fundamental characteristics of economic systems. And as stressed in the previous section, they are problems of choice.

To illustrate the nature and basic importance of these questions, sup-

Capital

Basic Idea #1: Any economic system must determine what (and how much) is produced, how it is produced, how the output is distributed among the members of society, and what provision is made for growth of per capita income. To understand how a country's economy really works, one must look carefully at how these vital decisions are made.

pose that, because of war or natural catastrophe, your town is isolated from the adjoining territory. No longer is it possible for the town's inhabitants to leave, or for people or goods to enter. (Lest you regard this as fanciful, it is perhaps worthwhile to note that Leningrad was under siege in World War II for over two years.) In this situation, you and your fellow townspeople must somehow resolve each of these questions. You must decide what goods and services will be produced, how each will be produced, who will receive what, and how much provision there will be for increased output in the future.

In a situation of this sort, your very survival will depend on how effectively you answer these questions. If a decision is made to produce too much clothing and too little food, some of the townspeople may starve. If a decision is made to produce wheat from soil that is inappropriate for wheat, but excellent for potatoes, much the same result may occur. If a decision is made to allot practically all of the town's output to friends and political cronies of the mayor, those who oppose him may have a very rough time. And if a decision is made to eat, drink, and be merry today, and not to worry about tomorrow, life may be very meager in the days ahead.

Because we are considering a relatively small and isolated population, the importance of these questions may seem more obvious than in a huge country like the United States, which is constantly communicating, trading, and interacting with the rest of the world. But the truth is that these questions are every bit as important to the United States as to the isolated town. And, for this reason, it is important that we understand how these decisions are made, and whether they are being made effectively. Just as in the hypothetical case of the isolated town, your survival depends on these decisions—but in the United States the situation isn't hypothetical!

Test Yourself

1. Explain why each of the following resources is or is not capital: (a) iron ore in Minnesota that is still in the ground; (b) a Boeing 747 airplane operated by TWA Airlines; (c) a Chrysler dealer's inventory of unsold cars; (d) a telephone used by the University of Oklahoma.

2. Alfred Marshall, the great British economist, defined economics as follows: "Economics is a study of men as they live and move and think in the ordinary business of life. But it concerns itself chiefly with those motives which affect, most powerfully and most steadily, man's conduct *in the business part of life*. . . . [The] steadiest motive to ordinary business work is the desire for the pay which is the material reward of work."* Does this definition encompass all of the examples of economic analysis and problems contained so far in this chapter?

3. C. J. Blank and E. Rosinski of Mobil Research and Development Corporation invented a new type of catalyst which enables oil refiners to save an estimated 200 million barrels of crude oil per year. Has this invention altered the technology of the oil refining industry? Has it changed the amount of goods and services that can be derived from a given amount of resources? Were resources used to obtain this invention? If so, what types of resources were used?

4. We described four basic questions that any economic system must answer. Which of these questions is involved in each of the following specific problems: (a) Should the United States use natural gas to produce ammonia? (b) Should taxes on the poor be lower? (c) Should American consumers save more? (d) Should more of our nation's industry be used to produce food?

* A. Marshall, *Principles of Economics*, London: Macmillan, 1920.

Opportunity Cost: A Fundamental Concept

In previous sections, we have emphasized that economics is concerned with the way resources are allocated among alternative uses to satisfy human wants. To help determine how resources should be allocated, economists often use the concept of *opportunity cost.* We turn now to an introductory discussion of this concept, which should help to acquaint you with how it is used.

Since a specific case is more interesting than abstract discussion, let's return to the case of the town that is isolated from the adjoining territory, because of a war or natural catastrophe. Suppose that you are a member of the town council that is organized to determine how the town's resources should be utilized. To keep things simple, suppose that only two goods—food and clothing—can be produced. (This is an innocuous assumption that allows us to strip the problem to its essentials.) You must somehow figure out how much of each good should be produced. How can you go about solving this problem?

Clearly, the first step toward a solution is to list the various resources contained within the town. Using the technology available to the townspeople, each of these resources can be used to produce either food or clothing. Some of these resources are much more effective at producing one good than the other. For example, a tailor probably is better able to produce clothing than to produce food. But nonetheless most resources can be adapted to produce either good. For example, the tailor can be put to work on a farm, even though he may not be very good at farming.

After listing the various available resources and having determined how effective each is at producing food or clothing, the next step is to see how much food the town could produce per year, if it produced nothing but food, and how much clothing it could produce per year, if it produced nothing but clothing. Also, you should determine, if various amounts of food are produced per year, the maximum amount of clothing that the town can produce per year. For example, if the town produces 100 tons of food per year, what is the maximum amount of clothing it can produce per year? If the town produces 200 tons of food per year, what is the maximum amount of clothing it can produce per year? And so on.

Having carried out this step, suppose that the results are as shown in Table 1.3. According to this table, the town can produce (at most) 200 tons of clothing per year if it produces nothing but clothing (possibility *A*). Or it can produce (at most) 400 tons of food per year if it produces nothing but food (possibility *E*). Other possible combinations (labeled *B, C,* and *D*) of food output and clothing output are specified in Table 1.3.

The data in Table 1.3 put in bold relief the basic problem of choice facing you and the other members of the town council. Because the town's resources are limited, the town can only produce limited amounts of each good. There is no way, for example, that the town can produce 200 tons of clothing per year and 200 tons of food per year. This is beyond the capacity of the town's resources. If the town wants to produce 200 tons of clothing, it can produce no food—which is hardly a pleasant prospect. And if the town wants to produce 200 tons of food, it can produce 150 (not 200) tons of clothing per year. Table 1.3 shows what combinations of food and clothing outputs are attainable.

Table 1.3

COMBINATIONS OF OUTPUT OF FOOD AND CLOTHING THAT THE TOWN CAN PRODUCE PER YEAR

Possibility	Amount of food produced per year (tons)	Amount of clothing produced per year (tons)
A	0	200
B	100	180
C	200	150
D	300	100
E	400	0

Basic Idea #2: The cost of using resources in a particular way is the value of what these resources could have produced if they had been used in the best alternative way. Thus the cost of producing a particular commodity is the value of what could have been produced instead. In other words, it is the value of what had to be given up to produce this commodity.

MORE FOOD MEANS LESS CLOTHING

A very important fact illustrated by Table 1.3 is that, whenever the town increases its production of one good, it must cut back its production of the other good. For example, if the town increases its production of food from 100 to 200 tons per year, it must cut back its production of clothing from 180 to 150 tons per year. Thus *the cost to the town of increasing its food output from 100 to 200 tons per year is that it must reduce its clothing output from 180 to 150 tons per year.*

Economists refer to this cost as **opportunity cost** (or **alternative cost**); it is one of the most fundamental concepts in economics. *The opportunity cost of using resources in a certain way is the value of what these resources could have produced if they had been used in the best alternative way.* In this case, the opportunity cost of the extra 100 tons of food per year is the 30 tons of clothing per year that must be forgone. This is what the town must give up in order to get the extra 100 tons of food.

Why is opportunity cost so important? Because for you and the other members of the town council to determine which combination of food and clothing is best, you should compare the value of increases in food output with the opportunity costs of such increases. For example, suppose that the town council is considering whether or not to increase food output from 100 to 200 tons per year. To decide this question, the council should compare the value of the extra 100 tons of food with the opportunity cost of the extra food (which is the 30 tons of clothing that must be given up). If the town council feels that the extra 100 tons of food are worth more to the town's welfare than the 30 tons of clothing that are given up, the extra food should be produced. Otherwise it should not be produced.

Parks and Opportunity Costs. As we have just seen, the concept of opportunity cost can be used to help solve the hypothetical problem of the town council described above. Used in a similar way, the concept of opportunity cost can throw significant light on many important real problems as well. For example, suppose that a bill is presented to Congress to set aside certain wilderness areas as national parks. At first glance, it may appear that such a step entails no cost to society, since the land is not being utilized and the resources required to designate the areas as national parks are trivial. But using the concept of opportunity cost, it is clear that this step may have very substantial costs to society. For instance, if these lands are made part of the national parks system, the minerals, timber, and other natural resources contained within the areas cannot be extracted nor can the lands be used as sites for factories or processing plants. As pointed out above, the opportunity cost of using resources in one way is the value of what these resources could have produced had they been used in the best alternative way. Suppose that if these lands are not turned into national parks, their most valuable alternative use is for development of copper mines which would produce benefits amounting to $25 million per year to the society. Then the actual cost to society of using these lands as parks is $25 million per year, since this is the amount that society is giving up when it uses them in this way (rather than selecting the most valuable alternative). Thus, whether these lands should be used as parks depends on whether the society believes that it is worth $25 million or more to do so.

The concept of opportunity cost is very important in analyzing personal, managerial, and judicial issues, as well as questions involving government policy. Example 1.1 shows how this concept can be applied to determine the true costs to a student of going to college. Example 1.2 indicates how this concept was used in a legal case to assess damages. Like the examples in subsequent chapters, they should be studied carefully.

The Impact of Economics on Society

In previous sections, we described some of the questions that concern economists. Now we must consider how much influence economics has had. The answer is that economics has influenced generations of statesmen, philosophers, and ordinary citizens, and has played a significant role in shaping our society today.

Example 1.1   How Much Does It Cost to Go to College?

According to the College Board, the average college student incurred the following annual costs in 1984:

	Private College (dollars)	Public College
Tuition and fees	5,016	1,126
Meals, room, books, travel, and other expenses	4,006	3,755
Total	9,022	4,881

(a) Is $9,022 the total cost to the student of a year at a private college? (*Hint:* Are there opportunity costs?) (b) John Martin is a 40-year-old executive; James Miller is an 18-year-old with no job experience. They are both full-time students. Although both must pay the same costs (given above), the true cost to Martin is more than the true cost to Miller. Why? (c) Is $1,126 the total cost to the typical public college of a student's going there for a year? (d) Is $9,022 the total cost to society of a student's going to a private college for a year?

SOLUTION

(a) No, the true cost of going to college is considerably in excess of the out-of-pocket expenses because one can obtain wages by working rather than attending classes and studying. In other words, the time spent in school has opportunity costs, since it could be devoted to a job rather than to education. For example, if the student could earn $8,000 during a school year if he or she worked rather than going to college, the true total annual cost of a college education is $9,022 + $8,000 = $17,022. (b) Martin can earn much more than Miller if, rather than going to school, he were to work. Thus the opportunity cost of his time spent in school is greater than for Miller. (c) No. Tuition and fees cover only part of the public college's costs; the rest are covered by government support, alumni contributions, and other payments. (d) No. The cost to society equals the value to society of the resources used to teach, house, feed, and maintain the student, as well as the opportunity cost to society of his or her time. Although it is not easy to pin down all of the social costs, they clearly do not equal $9,022.

ADAM SMITH, FATHER OF MODERN ECONOMICS

To illustrate the importance of economic ideas, let's consider some of the precepts of Adam Smith (1723–90), the man who is often called the father of modern economics. Much of his masterpiece *The Wealth of Nations*[1] seems trite today, because it has been absorbed so thoroughly into modern thought, but it was not trite when it was written. On the contrary, Smith's ideas were revolutionary. *He was among the first to describe how a free, competitive economy can function—without central planning or government interference—to allocate resources efficiently. He recognized the virtues of the "invisible hand" that leads the private interest of firms and individuals toward socially desirable ends, and he was properly suspicious of firms that are sheltered from competition, since he recognized the potentially undesirable effects on resource allocation.*

In addition, Smith—with the dire poverty of his times staring him in the face—was interested in the forces that determined the evolution of the economy—that is, the forces determining the rate of growth of average income per person. Although Smith did not approve of avarice, he felt that saving was good because it enabled society to invest in machinery and other forms of capital. Accumulating more and more capital would, according to Smith, allow output to grow. In addition, he emphasized the importance of increased specialization and division of labor in bringing about economic progress. By specializing, people can concentrate on the tasks they do best, with the result that society's total output is raised.

All in all, Smith's views were relatively optimistic, in keeping with the intellectual climate of his time—the era of Voltaire, Diderot, Franklin, and Jefferson, the age of the Enlightenment, when men believed so strongly in rationality. Leave markets alone, said Smith, and beware of firms with too much economic power and government meddling. If this is done, there is no reason why considerable economic progress cannot be achieved. Smith's work has been modified and extended in a variety of ways in the past 200 years. Some of his ideas have been challenged and, in some cases, discarded. But his influence on modern society has been enormous.

THE INFLUENCE OF ECONOMICS TODAY

Turning from Adam Smith's day to the present, economics continues to have an enormous influence over the shape of our society. Economics, and economists, play an extremely important part in the formulation of public policy. Skim through the articles in a daily newspaper. Chances are that you will find a report of an economist testifying before Congress, perhaps on the costs and benefits of a program to reduce unemployment among black teenagers in the Bedford-Stuyvesant area of New York City, or on the steps to be taken to make American goods more competitive with those of Japan or West Germany. Still another economist may crop up on the editorial page, discussing the pros and cons of various proposed ways to reduce the federal deficit.

Economics and economists play a key role at the highest levels of our government. The president, whether a Democrat or a Republican, relies

---

[1] Adam Smith, *The Wealth of Nations,* New York: Modern Library, 1937. Originally published in 1776.

Adam Smith (1723–90) lived during the Industrial Revolution and was one of the first scholars to understand many of the central mechanisms of a free, or unplanned, economy. Much of his life was spent as professor of moral philosophy at the University of Glasgow in Scotland. In 1759, he published *The Theory of Moral Sentiments,* which established him as one of Britain's foremost philosophers, but this was not the book for which he is famous today. His masterpiece, published in 1776 (while the American colonists were brewing rebellion), was *The Wealth of Nations,* a long encyclopedic book 12 years in the writing. It was not an instant success, but the laurels it eventually won undoubtedly compensated for its early neglect.

One of Smith's central contentions was that firms and individuals, by pursuing their own objectives, often will promote the general welfare. In a famous passage, he stated that:

"It is only for the sake of profit that any man employs [his] capital in the support of industry, and he will always, therefore, endeavor to employ it in the support of that industry of which the produce is likely to be of greatest value, or to exchange the greatest quantity either of money or of other goods. But the annual revenue of every society is always precisely equal to the exchangeable value of the whole annual produce of its industry, or rather is precisely the same thing with that exchangeable value. As every individual, therefore, endeavors as much as he can both to employ his capital in the support of domestic industry, and so to direct that industry that its produce may be of the greatest value, every individual necessarily labors to render the annual revenue of the society as great as he can: He generally, indeed, neither intends to promote the public interest, nor knows how much he is promoting it. . . . He intends only his own security; and by directing that industry in such a manner as its produce may be of the greatest value, he intends only his own gain, and *he is in this, as in many other cases, led by an invisible hand to promote an end which was no part of his intention.* Nor is it always the worse for the society that it was no part of it. *By pursuing his own interest he frequently promotes that of the society more effectually than when he really intends to promote it.* I have never known much good done by those who affected to trade for the public good. It is an affectation, indeed, not very common among merchants, and very few words need be employed in dissuading them from it. . . ."

Adam Smith, *The Wealth of Nations,* London: George Routledge, 1900, p. 345. Originally published in 1776. (Italics added.)

heavily on his economic advisers in making the decisions that help to shape the future of the country. In Congress, too, economics plays a major role. Economists are frequent witnesses before congressional committees, staff members for the committees, and advisers to individual congressmen and senators. Many congressional committees focus largely on economic matters. For example, in 1985, many congressmen spent large chunks of their time wrestling with budgetary and tax questions.

Perhaps the most dramatic evidence of the importance of economics in the formulation of public policy is provided during presidential elections, when each candidate—with his or her own cadre of economic advisers supplying ideas and reports—stakes out a position on the major economic issues of the day. This position can be of crucial importance in determining victory or defeat, and you, the citizen, must know some economics to understand whether a candidate is talking sense or nonsense (or merely evading an issue). For example, if a candidate promises to increase government expenditures, lower taxes, and reduce the federal deficit, you can be pretty certain that he is talking through his hat. This may not be obvious to you now, but it should be later on.

Also, economics and economists play an extremely important role in private decision making. Their role in the decision-making process in business firms is particularly great, since many of the nation's larger corporations hire professional economists to forecast their sales, reduce their costs, increase their efficiency, negotiate with labor and government, and carry out a host of other tasks. Judging from the fancy salaries business economists are paid, the firms seem to think they can deliver the goods; and in fact, the available evidence seems to indicate that they do provide important guidance to firms in many areas of their operations.

POSITIVE ECONOMICS VERSUS NORMATIVE ECONOMICS

Before concluding this chapter, it is essential that we recognize the distinction between positive economics and normative economics. *Positive economics contains descriptive statements, propositions, and predictions about the world.* For instance, an economic theory may predict that the price of copper will increase by $.01 a pound if income per person in the United States rises by 10 percent; this is positive economics. Positive economics tells us only what will happen under certain circumstances. It says nothing about whether the results are good or bad—or about what we should do. *Normative economics, on the other hand, makes statements about what ought to be, or about what a person, organization, or nation ought to do.* For instance, a theory might say that Chile should introduce new technology more quickly in many of its copper mines; this is normative economics.

Clearly, positive economics and normative economics must be treated differently. Positive economics is science in the ordinary sense of the word. Propositions in positive economics can be tested by an appeal to the facts. In a nonexperimental science like economics, it is sometimes difficult to get the facts you need to test particular propositions. For example, if income per person in the United States does not rise by 10 percent, it may be difficult to tell what the effect of such an increase would be on the price of copper. Moreover, even if per capita income does increase by this amount, it may be difficult to separate the effect of the increase in income per person on the price of copper from the effect of other factors. But nonetheless, we can, in principle, test propositions in positive economics by an appeal to the facts.

In normative economics, however, this is not the case. *In normative economics, the results you get depend on your values or preferences.* For example, if you believe that reducing unemployment is more important than maintaining the purchasing power of the dollar, you will get one answer to certain questions; whereas if you believe that maintaining the purchasing power of the dollar is more important than reducing unem-

---

Example 1.2   The Assessment of Damages

In a well-known legal case, the United States was sued by O'Brien Bros., Inc., the owner of a Brooklyn-bound barge that was sunk by a U.S. Navy tug that collided with the barge. O'Brien Bros. received damages stemming from the collision. The calculation of the damages was turned over to a commissioner, who found them to be as follows:

	dollars
Costs of raising the wreck	7,732.21
Repairs	43,245.22
Compensation for loss of earnings from the barge during the time it was unavailable for work	6,620.25
Miscellaneous costs	3,423.91
Total	61,021.59

(a) Why should O'Brien Bros. be compensated for the loss of earnings? It did not pay out $6,620.25 to anyone. Why should it receive this amount in damages? (b) The United States appealed the decision. Government attorneys introduced evidence that a similar barge could have been built new for $33,000. Does this mean that the damages should have been $33,000? (c) Suppose that O'Brien Bros. could have bought a similar barge for $25,000 and that its forgone earnings during the time elapsing from the sinking of the old barge to the availability of the new barge was $5,000. If the sunk barge would cause no problems either to O'Brien Bros. or anyone else, should it have been raised and repaired? (d) Suppose that O'Brien Bros. could have obtained $8,500 for the wreck (for scrap metal, salvageable parts, and so forth) if it was raised? Should it have been raised?

SOLUTION

(a) If the barge had not been sunk, O'Brien Bros. would have earned this amount. It is the opportunity cost of the barge's being sunk. (b) No. The barge that was sunk may have been worth less than $33,000, since it was not new. On the other hand, the figure of $33,000 takes no account of lost earnings in the time interval until the barge was replaced. (c) No. The cost of raising and repairing it exceeded the cost of buying a similar barge. (d) Yes, because the amount that could be obtained for the wreck would exceed the cost of raising it.*

*For further description of this case, see "O'Brien Bros., Inc. v. The Helen B. Moran et al." in R. Byrns and G. Stone, Jr., *An Economics Casebook: Applications from the Law,* Santa Monica: Goodyear, 1980.

ployment, you are likely to get a different answer to the same questions. This is not at all strange. After all, if people desire different things (which is another way of saying that they have different values), they may well make different decisions and advocate different policies. It would be strange if they did not.

This book will spend a lot of time on the principles of positive economics—the principles and propositions concerning the workings of the economic system about which practically all economists tend to agree. Normative economics will also be treated, since we must discuss questions of policy—and all policy discussions involve individual preferences, not solely hard facts. In these discussions, we shall try to indicate how the conclusions depend on one's values. Then you can let your own values be your guide. The purpose of this book is not to convert you to a particular set of values. It is to teach you how to obtain better solutions to economic problems, whatever set of values you may have.

Test Yourself

1. In a famous passage from *The Wealth of Nations,* Adam Smith said that: "It is the maxim of every prudent master of a family, never to make at home what it will cost him more to make than to buy." Suppose that Mrs. Harris spends an hour preparing a meal. She is a psychologist in private practice and can obtain $25 per hour for her services. What is the cost to the Harris family of her preparing this meal? Explain.

2. "Resources are scarce and once a decision is made to use them for one purpose, they are no longer available for another. One opportunity cost of reading [an] . . . article, for example, is not simultaneously being able to read [another article]."* Explain, and relate to the question of how a student should allocate his time among various course assignments.

3. Suppose that it costs a college student $1,000 per year more for room and board than if he or she works (and lives at home). If this assumption is correct, why is this amount, rather than the full cost of room and board, the proper amount to use in Example 1.1?

4. On the basis of positive economics alone, which of the following statements can be determined to be true or false? (a) The tax cut of 1975 reduced unemployment in the United States by 1 percent. (b) The tax cut was timed improperly. (c) The tax cut was a less equitable way of reducing unemployment than a program whereby the unemployed were hired by the government to perform important social functions.

* D. Eastburn, "Economic Man in Conflict with His Economic Self," *New York Times Magazine,* July 26, 1970.

Summary

1. According to one standard definition, economics is concerned with the way resources are allocated among alternative uses to satisfy human wants. A resource is a thing or service used to produce goods (or services) which can satisfy wants. Not all resources are scarce. Free resources, such as air, are so abundant that they can be obtained without charge.

2. Those resources that are scarce are called economic resources. The test of whether a resource is an economic resource or a free resource is price: economic resources command a nonzero price but free resources do not. Economists often classify economic resources into three categories: land, labor, and capital.

3. Since economic resources are scarce, only a limited amount of goods and services can be produced from them, and there arises the necessity for choice. For example, if an isolated town has a certain amount of resources, it must choose how much of each good it will produce from these resources. If it increases the amount produced of one good, it must reduce the amount produced of another good.

4. The opportunity cost (or alternative cost) of using a resource to increase the production of one good is the value of what the resource could have produced had it been used in the best alternative way. To illustrate the use of the concept of opportunity cost, which is one of the most important in economics, we discussed the cases of public parks and a college education.

5. Economists are particularly concerned with four basic questions regarding the working of any economic system, ours or any other. These questions are (1) What determines what (and how much) is produced? (2) What determines how it is produced? (3) What determines how the society's output is distributed among the members? (4) What determines the rate at which the society's per capita income will grow?

6. Economists often distinguish between positive economics and normative economics. Positive economics contains descriptive statements, propositions, and predictions about the world; whereas normative economics contains statements about what ought to be, or about what a person, organization, or nation ought to do.

7. In normative economics, the results you get depend on your basic values and preferences; in positive economics, the results are testable, at least in principle, by an appeal to the facts.

Concepts for Review

Unemployment	Resources	Technology
Inflation	Economic resources	Choice
Labor productivity	Free resources	Opportunity cost
Government regulation	Land	Alternative cost
Poverty	Labor	Positive economics
Economics	Capital	Normative economics
Human wants		

Economic Models and Capitalism, American-Style

The United States, like all other nations, is beset by many economic problems. As pointed out in Chapter 1, the 1970s and early 1980s were a period of bewildering inflation and excessive unemployment. We have also been confronted by serious productivity and environmental problems. Yet, despite these problems, the American economy is among the most prosperous in the world. The average American family has plenty of food, clothing, housing, appliances, and luxuries of many kinds, and the average American worker is well educated and well trained. The tremendous strength and vitality of the American economy should be recognized, as well as its shortcomings. Nothing is gained by overlooking either the successes or the faults of our system.

As a first step toward understanding why we are so well-off in some respects and so lacking in others, we need to understand how our economy works. Of course, this is a big task. Indeed, you could say that this whole book is devoted to discussing this subject. So we will not try to present a detailed picture of the operation of the American economy at this point. All we will do now is give a preliminary sketch, a basic blueprint of what an economic system must do and how our mixed capitalistic system works.

First, however, we must provide a brief description of the role of model building in economics, since this will introduce you to the methods used by economists. Without such an introduction to economic methodology, it would be difficult, if not impossible, for you to understand fully much of the material that follows in this and succeeding chapters. Only after these preliminary matters are covered will we be able to turn to a discussion of the tasks of an economic system and the way our economy functions.

The Methodology of Economics

MODEL BUILDING IN ECONOMICS

Like other types of scientific analysis, economics is based on the formulation of **models.** *A model is a theory. It is composed of a number of assumptions from which conclusions—or predictions—are deduced.* An astronomer who wants to formulate a model of the solar system might represent each planet by a point in space and assume that each would change position in accord with certain mathematical equations. Based on this model, the astronomer might predict when an eclipse would occur, or estimate the probability of a planetary collision. The economist proceeds along similar lines when he sets forth a model of economic behavior.

There are several important points to be noted concerning models:

1. To be useful, a model must simplify the real situation. The assumptions made by a model need not be exact replicas of reality. If they were, the model would be too complicated to use. The basic reason for using a model is that the real world is so complex that masses of detail often obscure underlying patterns. The economist faces the familiar problem of seeing the forest as distinct from just the trees. Other scientists must do the same; physicists work with simplified models of atoms, just as economists work with simplified models of markets. However, this does not mean that *all* models are good or useful. A model may be so oversimplified and distorted that it is utterly useless. The trick is to construct a model so that irrelevant and unimportant considerations and variables are neglected, but the major factors—those that seriously affect the phenomena the model is designed to predict—are included.

2. The purpose of a model is to make predictions about the real world; and in many respects the most important test of a model is how well it predicts. In this sense, a model that predicts the price of copper within plus or minus $.01 a pound is better than a model that predicts it within plus or minus $.02 a pound. Of course, this does not mean that a model is useless if it cannot predict very accurately. We do not always need a very accurate prediction. For example, a road map is a model that can be used to make predictions about the route a driver should take to get to a particular destination. Sometimes, a very crude map is good enough to get you where you want to go, but such a map would not, for instance, serve the hiker who needs to know the characteristics of the terrain through which he plans to walk. How detailed a map you need depends on where you are going and how you want to get there.

3. A person who wants to predict the outcome of a particular event will be forced to use the model that predicts best, even if this model does not predict very well. The choice is not between a model and no model; it is between one model and another. After all, a person who must make a forecast will use the most accurate device available—and any such device is a model of some sort. Consequently, when economists make simplifying assumptions and derive conclusions that are only approximately true, it is somewhat beside the point to complain that the assumptions are simpler than reality or that the predictions are not always accurate. This may be true, but if the predictions based on the economists' model are better than those obtained on the basis of other models, their model must, and will, be used until something better comes along. Thus, if a model can predict the price of

Figure 2.1

Relationship between Annual Clothing Expenditures and Annual Household Income *Each family is represented by a dot. The line shows the average relationship. The line does not fit all families exactly, since all the points do not fall on it. The line does, however, show average clothing expenditure for each income level.*

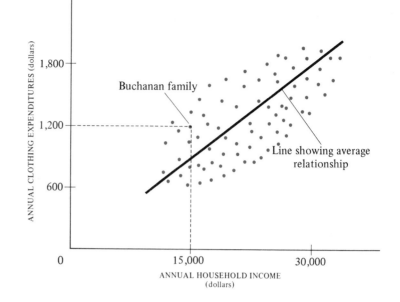

copper to within plus or minus $.01 per pound, and no other model can do better, this model will be used even if those interested in the predictions bewail the model's limitations and wish it could be improved.

ECONOMIC MEASUREMENT

To utilize and test their models, economists need facts of many sorts. For example, suppose that an economist constructs a model which predicts that a household's annual clothing expenditure tends to increase by $60 when its income increases by $1,000. To see whether this model is correct, he must gather data concerning the incomes and clothing expenditures of a large number of households and study the relationship between them. Suppose that the relationship he finds is as shown in Figure 2.1. The line represents an average relationship between household income and household consumption expenditure. Judging by Figure 2.1, his model is reasonably accurate, at least for households with incomes between $15,000 and $30,000 per year.[1]

Measurements like those in Figure 2.1 enable economists to *quantify* their models; in other words, they enable them to construct models that predict *how much* effect one variable has on another. If economists did not quantify their models, they (and their models) would be much less useful. For example, the economist in the previous paragraph might have been content with a model that predicts that higher household income results in higher household clothing expenditures; but this model would not have been interesting or useful, since you do not need an economist to tell you that. A more valuable model is one that is quantitative, that predicts how much clothing expenditure will increase if household income rises by a certain amount. This is the sort of model that economists usually try to construct.

---

[1] It is worth noting that, although it is useful to see how well a model would have fit the historical facts, this is no substitute for seeing how well it will predict the future. As a distinguished mentor of mine once observed, "It's a darned poor person who can't predict the past."

Graphs and Relationships

To conclude our brief discussion of economic methodology, we must describe the construction and interpretation of graphs, such as Figure 2.1, which economists use to present data and relationships. Such graphs are used repeatedly throughout this book, and it is essential that the following three points be understood:

1. A graph has a horizontal axis and a vertical axis, each of which has a scale of numerical values. For example, in Figure 2.1, the horizontal axis shows a household's annual income, and the vertical axis shows the annual amount spent by the household on clothing. The intersection of the two axes is called the origin and is the point where both the variable measured along the horizontal axis and the variable measured along the vertical axis are zero. In Figure 2.1, the origin is at the lower lefthand corner of the figure, labeled "0."

2. To show the relationship between two variables, one can plot the value of one variable against the value of the other variable. Thus, in Figure 2.1, each family is represented by a dot. For example, the dot for the Buchanan family is in the position shown in Figure 2.1 because its income was $15,000 and its clothing expenditure was $1,200. Clearly, the line showing the average relationship does not fit all the families exactly, since all the points do not fall on the line. This line does, however, give the average clothing expenditure for each level of income: it is an average relationship.

3. The relationship between two variables is *direct* if, as in Figure 2.1, the line of average relationship is upward sloping. In other words, if the variable measured along the vertical axis tends to increase (decrease) in response to increases (decreases) in the variable measured along the horizontal axis, the relationship is direct. On the other hand, if the line of average relationship is downward sloping, as in Figure 2.2, the relationship is *inverse*. In other words, if the variable measured along the vertical axis tends to decrease (increase) in response to increases (decreases) in the variable measured along the horizontal axis, the relationship is inverse.

To illustrate how one can graph a relationship between two variables,

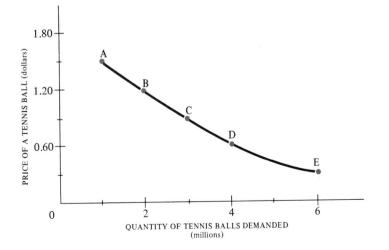

Figure 2.2

Relationship between Quantity Demanded and Price of Tennis Balls (as shown in Table 2.1)

Table 2.1

QUANTITY OF TENNIS BALLS DEMANDED
IN A PARTICULAR MARKET AT VARIOUS
PRICES

Price of a tennis ball (dollars)	Quantity of tennis balls demanded (millions)
1.50	1
1.20	2
0.90	3
0.60	4
0.30	6

consider Table 2.1, which shows the amount of tennis balls demanded in a particular market at various prices. Putting price on the vertical axis and quantity demanded on the horizontal axis, one can plot each combination of price and quantity in this table as a point on a graph; and that is precisely what has been done in Figure 2.2 (points *A* to *E*).

The Tasks of an Economic System

Having discussed the nature and quantification of economic models, we now can turn to the primary purpose of this chapter, which is to provide a preliminary sketch of what an economic system must do and how our mixed capitalistic system works. In this section, we describe what an economic system—*ours or any other*—must do. Basically, as we saw in Chapter 1, there are four tasks that any economic system must perform:

1. An economic system must determine the level and composition of society's output. That is, it must answer questions like: To what extent should society's resources be used to produce new aircraft carriers and missiles? To what extent should they be used to produce sewage plants to reduce water pollution? To what extent should they be used to produce swimming pools for the rich? To what extent should they be used to produce low-cost housing for the poor? Pause for a moment to think about how important—and how vast—this function is. Most people simply take for granted that somehow it is decided what we as a society are going to produce, and far too few people really think about the social mechanisms that determine the answers to such questions.

2. An economic system must determine how each good and service is to be produced. Given existing technology, a society's resources can be used in various ways. Should the skilled labor in Birmingham, Alabama, be used to produce cotton or steel? Should a particular machine tool be used to produce aircraft or automobiles? The way questions of this sort are answered will determine the way each good and service is produced. In other words, it will determine which resources are used to produce which goods and services. If this function is performed badly, society's resources are put to the wrong uses, resulting in less output than if this function is performed well.

3. An economic system must determine how the goods and services that are produced are to be distributed among the members of society. In other words, how much of each type of good and service should each person receive? Should there be a considerable amount of income inequality, the rich receiving much more than the poor? Or should incomes be relatively equal? Take your own case. Somehow or other, the economic system determines how much income you will receive. In our economic system, your income depends on your skills, the property you own, how hard you work, and prevailing prices, as we shall see in succeeding chapters. But in other economic systems, your income might depend on quite different factors. This function of the economic system has generated, and will continue to generate, heated controversy. Some people favor a relatively egalitarian society where the amount received by one family varies little from that received by another family of the same size. Other people favor a society where the amount a

family or person receives can vary a great deal. Few people favor a thoroughly egalitarian society, if for no other reason than that some differences in income are required to stimulate workers to do certain types of work.

4. An economic system must determine the rate of growth of per capita income. An adequate growth rate has come to be regarded as an important economic goal, particularly in the less developed countries of Africa, Asia, and Latin America. There is very strong pressure in these countries for changes in technology, the adoption of superior techniques, increases in the stock of capital resources, and better and more extensive education and training of the labor force. These are viewed as some of the major ways to promote the growth of per capita income.

Test Yourself

1. Suppose that the quantity of corn demanded annually by American consumers at each price of corn is as follows:

Price (dollars per bushel)	Quantity of corn (millions of bushels)
1	2.0
2	1.0
3	0.5
4	0.4

How much will farmers receive for their corn crop if it is 2 million bushels? If it is 1 million bushels? If you owned all of the farms producing corn, would you produce 2 million bushels? Why or why not?

2. Plot the relationship between price and quantity demanded in Question 1 in a graph. Is the relationship direct or inverse? Based on your graph, estimate how much corn is likely to be demanded if the price is (a) $1.50, (b) $2.50, and (c) $3.50.

3. Suppose that Americans begin to take up tennis in much larger numbers. Will the curve in Figure 2.2 shift? If so, will it shift to the right or to the left? Explain.

4. Suppose that you wanted to construct a model to explain and predict the breakfast food that your neighbor will choose tomorrow. What factors would you include? How well do you think you could predict?

The Economic System: A Simple Introductory Model

THE PRODUCTION POSSIBILITIES CURVE AND THE DETERMINATION OF WHAT IS PRODUCED

In a previous section, we said that economists use models to throw light on economic problems. At this point, let's try our hand at constructing a simple model to illuminate the basic functions any economic system, ours included, must perform. To keep things simple, suppose that society produces only two goods, food and tractors. This, of course, is unrealistic, but, as we stressed in a previous section, a model does not have to be realistic to be useful. Here, by assuming that there are only two goods, we eliminate a lot of unnecessary complexity and lay bare the essentials. In addition, we suppose that society has at its disposal a certain amount of resources, and that this amount is fixed for the duration of the period in question. This assumption is quite realistic. So long as the period is relatively short, the amount of a society's resources is relatively fixed (except, of course, under unusual circumstances, such as if a country annexes ad-

Table 2.2

ALTERNATIVE COMBINATIONS OF
OUTPUTS OF FOOD AND TRACTORS THAT
CAN BE PRODUCED

Possibility	Food (millions of tons)	Tractors (millions)
A	0	15
B	2	14
C	4	12
D	6	10
E	8	7
F	10	4
G	12	0

ditional land). Finally, we suppose as well that society's technology is fixed. So long as the period is relatively short, this assumption too is realistic.

Under these circumstances, it is possible to figure out the various amounts of food and tractors that society can produce. Specifically, we can proceed as in Chapter 1, where we determined the amounts of food and clothing that an isolated town could produce. Let's begin with how many tractors society can produce if all resources are devoted to tractor production. According to Table 2.2, the answer is 15 million tractors. Next, let's consider the opposite extreme, where society devotes all its resources to food production. According to Table 2.2, it can produce 12 million tons of food in this case. Next, let's consider cases where both products are being produced. Such cases are represented by possibilities B to F in the table. As emphasized in Chapter 1, the more of one good that is produced, the less of the other good that can be produced. Why? Because to produce more of one good, resources must be taken away from the production of the other good, lessening the amount of the other good produced.

Figure 2.3 shows how we can use a graph to show the various production possibilities society can attain. It is merely a different way of presenting the data in Table 2.2; the output of food is plotted on the horizontal axis and the output of tractors on the vertical axis. The curve in Figure 2.3, which shows the various combinations of output of food and tractors that society can produce, is called a *production possibilities curve.*

The production possibilities curve sheds considerable light on the economic tasks facing any society. It shows the various production possibilities open to society. In Figure 2.3, society can choose to produce 4 million tons of food and 12 million tractors (point C), or 6 million tons of food and 10 million tractors (point D), but it cannot choose to produce 6 million tons of food and 12 million tractors (point H). Point H is inaccessible with this society's resources and technology. Perhaps it will become accessible if the society's resources increase or if its technology improves, but for the present, point H is out of reach.

Figure 2.3
Production Possibilities Curve *This curve shows the various combinations of tractors and food that can be produced efficiently with given resources and technology. Point H is unattainable.*

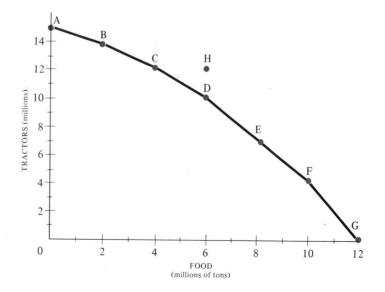

Example 2.1   Hay and Grain in Iowa

According to studies carried out at Iowa State University,* the following combinations of grain and hay could be produced in the 1940s from 100 acres of land in a particular part of Iowa:

Number of acres devoted to each use		Total production (pounds)	
Hay	Grain	Grain	Hay
0	100	224,000	0
25	75	212,920	89,600
33	67	166,194	96,400

That is, if all 100 acres were devoted to grain, 224,000 pounds of grain could be produced; if 75 of the 100 acres were devoted to grain, 212,920 pounds of grain and 89,600 pounds of hay could be produced; and so on. (a) If a 100-acre farm in this part of Iowa was producing 212,920 pounds of grain and 89,600 pounds of hay, what was the approximate cost of increasing its production of grain by 1 pound? (b) Suppose that the profit to be made from a pound of grain was five times the profit to be made from a pound of hay, and that the owner of this farm claimed that, because this was the case, he should produce no hay. Would he be correct? (c) Suppose that, if hay production was increased from zero to about 100,000 pounds, the production of grain *increased,* not *decreased* (because hay contributed elements to the soil needed in the production of grain). Under these circumstances, would the slope of the production possibilities curve be negative at all points? Would it be rational for a farmer to produce no hay? (d) Would the production possibilities curve for a farm of this sort be the same now as in the 1940s?

SOLUTION

(a) If it increased its grain output by 11,080 pounds (from 212,920 to 224,000 pounds), it had to reduce its hay output by 89,600 pounds. Thus an extra pound of grain output cost the farm about 89,600 ÷ 11,080, or 8.09 pounds of hay. (b) No. If he produced 212,920 pounds of grain and 89,600 pounds of hay, his profits would be larger than if he produced no hay, because the profit from the extra 89,600 pounds of hay was greater than the profit from the 11,080 pounds of grain forgone. (c) No. No, because by producing up to 100,000 pounds of hay, the farmer increased the output of grain too. (d) No, because of changes in technology.

* E. Heady, *Economics of Agricultural Production and Resource Use*, New York: Prentice-Hall, 1952.

If resources are fully and efficiently utilized, *the first function of any economic system—to determine the level and composition of society's output—is really a problem of determining at what point along the production possibilities curve society should be.* Should society choose point *A, B, C, D, E, F,* or *G?* In making this choice, one thing is obvious from the production possibilities curve: *you cannot get more of one good without giving up some of the other good.* In other words, you cannot escape the problem of choice. So long as resources are limited and technology is less than magic, you must reckon with the fact (emphasized in Chapter 1) that more of one thing means less of another. The old saw that you don't "get something for nothing" is hackneyed but true, so long as resources are fully and efficiently utilized.

THE LAW OF INCREASING COST

In the previous section, we stressed that an increased output of one good (say, food) means a decreased output of the other good (say, tractors). This amounts to saying (in the language of Chapter 1) that the opportunity cost of producing more food is the output of tractors that must be forgone. In this section, we go a step further; we point out that, *as more and more of a good is produced, the production of yet another unit of this good is likely to entail a larger and larger opportunity cost* and we explain why this is true.

This so-called law of increasing cost can be demonstrated in Figure 2.3. As more and more food is produced, the cost of increasing food output by 2 million tons increases. To see this, note that the *first* 2 million tons of food cost 1 million tractors (because this is the amount that tractor output must be reduced if food output increases from 0 to 2 million tons). The *second* 2 million tons of food cost 2 million tractors (because this is the amount that tractor output must be reduced if food output increases from 2 to 4 million tons). Skipping to the *sixth* 2 million tons of food, the cost of this additional food output is 4 million tractors (because this is the amount that tractor output must be reduced if food output increases from 10 to 12 million tons). Clearly, the more food that is already being produced, the greater the cost of producing an additional 2 million tons.

Why is this the case? Basically, it is because resources are not as effective in producing one good as in producing the other. When society only produces a small amount of food, it can use in food production those resources that are well suited to producing food and not so well suited to producing tractors. But as society produces more and more food, it tends to run out of such resources, and must absorb into food production those resources that are less suited to producing food and better suited to producing tractors. To increase food output by 2 million tons with the latter type of resources, a greater reduction must occur in tractor output than when the 2-million-ton increase in food output occurred with the resources that were well suited to food production (and not so well suited to producing tractors). Thus the cost of producing an additional 2 million tons of food tends to increase as more food is already being produced.

This law of increasing cost explains why a production possibilities curve has the shape shown in Figure 2.3. That is, it explains why the production possibilities curve has the "bowed out" shape (rather than the "bowed in" shape) indicated in Figure 2.4. Because the cost of increasing food output

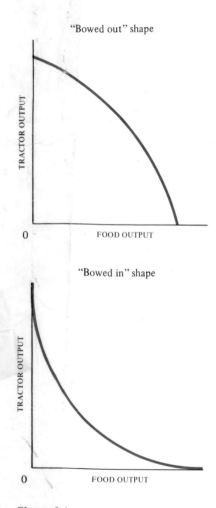

"Bowed out" shape

TRACTOR OUTPUT

0   FOOD OUTPUT

"Bowed in" shape

TRACTOR OUTPUT

0   FOOD OUTPUT

Figure 2.4

Shape of the Production Possibilities Curve So long as the law of increasing cost holds true, the production possibilities curve will have the shape at the top ("bowed out"), not the shape at the bottom ("bowed in").

by a certain amount increases as more of it is already produced, the production possibilities curve tends to fall more steeply as one moves from left to right along the horizontal axis—which explains why the production possibilities curve has the "bowed out" shape.

THE PRODUCTION POSSIBILITIES CURVE AND THE DETERMINATION OF HOW GOODS ARE PRODUCED

Let's turn now to the second basic function of any economic system: to determine how each good and service should be produced. In Table 2.2, we assumed implicitly that society's resources would be fully utilized and that the available technology would be applied in a way that would get the most out of the available resources. In other words, we assumed that the firms making food and tractors were as efficient as possible and that there was no unemployment of resources. But if there is widespread unemployment of people and machines, will society still be able to choose a point on the production possibilities curve? Clearly, the answer is no. Since society is not using all of its resources, it will not be able to produce as much as if it used them all. Thus, *if there is less than full employment of resources, society will have to settle for points inside the production possibilities curve.* For example, the best society may be able to do under these circumstances is to attain point *K* in Figure 2.5. *K* is a less desirable point than *C* or *D*—but that is the price of unemployment.

Suppose, on the other hand, that there is full employment of resources but that firms are inefficient. Perhaps they promote relatives of the boss, regardless of their ability; perhaps the managers are lazy or not much interested in efficiency; or perhaps the workers like to take long coffee breaks and are unwilling to work hard. Whatever the reason, will society still be able to choose a point on the production possibilities curve? Again, the answer is no. Since society is not getting as much as it could out of its resources, it will not be able to produce as much as it would if its resources were used efficiently. Thus, *if resources are used inefficiently, society will*

Basic Idea #3: *If there is unemployment of resources or inefficiency, society may be able to increase its output of one good (say guns) without producing less of another good (say butter). In the absence of unemployment or inefficiency, this cannot be done (so long as the quantity of resources and technology are fixed). As pointed out below, this is why the United States, but not the Soviet Union, could increase the output of guns without cutting the output of butter at the outset of World War II.*

Figure 2.5
Production Possibilities Curve *This curve, like Figure 2.3, shows the various combinations of tractors and food that can be produced efficiently with given resources and technology. Point K is less desirable than points C or D, because less output is produced at this point. But because of unemployment or inefficiency, society may wind up at point K.*

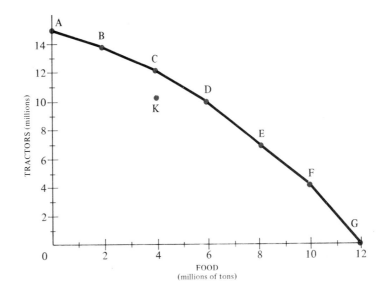

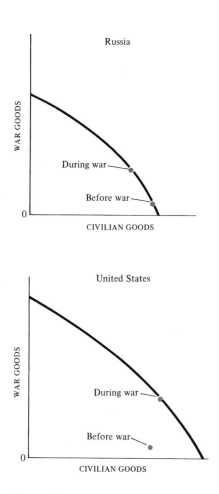

have to settle for points inside the production possibilities curve. Perhaps in these circumstances, too, the best society can do may be point *K* in Figure 2.5. This less desirable position is the price of inefficiency.

At this point, it should be obvious that our model at least partially answers the question of how each good and service should be produced. The answer is to *produce each good and service in such a way that you wind up on the production possibilities curve, not on a point inside it.* Of course, this is easier said than done, but at least our model indicates a couple of villains to watch out for: unemployment of resources and inefficiency. When these villains are present, we can be sure that society is not on the production possibilities curve. Also, the old saw is wrong, and it is possible to "get something for nothing" when society is inside the production possibilities curve. That is, society can increase the output of one good without reducing the output of another good in such a situation. Society need not give up anything—in the way of production of other goods—to increase the production of this good under these circumstances.

The U.S. and the USSR in World War II. This simple model helps illuminate the sequence of events in various countries at the beginning of World War II. In certain countries, like the Soviet Union, the war effort meant a substantial decrease in the standard of living on the home front. Resources had to be diverted from the production of civilian goods to the production of military goods, and the war struck a severe blow at the living standards of the civilian population. In other countries, like the United States, it was possible to increase the production of military goods without making such a dent in the living standards of the civilian population. This happened because the United States at the beginning of World War II was still struggling to emerge from the Great Depression, and several million people were still unemployed. The same was not true in the Soviet Union. Thus we could increase the production of both guns and butter, whereas they could not.

Suppose that we divide all goods into two classes: war goods and civilian goods. Then, as shown in Figure 2.6, *we were inside our production possibilities curve at the beginning of the war, while the Russians were not.* Consequently, for the reasons discussed above, we could increase our production of war goods without reducing our production of civilian goods, while the Russians could not. (Note that in Figure 2.6 the two goods are war goods and civilian goods, not food and tractors.)

THE PRODUCTION POSSIBILITIES CURVE, INCOME DISTRIBUTION, AND GROWTH

Let's return now to the case where our economy produces food and tractors. The third basic function of any economic system is to distribute the goods and services that are produced among the members of society. Each point on the production possibilities curve in Figure 2.5 represents society's total pie, but to deal with the third function, we must know how the pie is divided up among society's members. Since the production possibilities curve does not tell us this, it cannot shed light on this third function.

Fortunately, the production possibilities curve is of more use in analyzing the fourth basic function of any economic system: to determine the society's rate of growth of per capita income. Suppose that the society in

Figure 2.6

Effect of Increased Production of War Goods at the Beginning of World War II *Because the United States was at a point inside its production possibilities curve, we could increase our production of war goods without reducing production of civilian goods. Because the Russians were on their production possibilities curve, they could increase their output of war goods only by reducing output of civilian goods.*

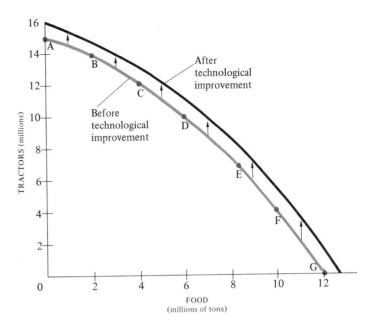

Figure 2.7

Effect of Improvement in Technology on Production Possibilities Curve *An improvement in technology results in an outward shift of the production possibilities curve.*

Figure 2.5 invests a considerable amount of its resources in developing improved processes and products. It might establish agricultural experiment stations to improve farming techniques and industrial research laboratories to improve tractor designs. As shown in Figure 2.7, the production possibilities curve will be pushed outward. This will be the result of improved technology, enabling more food and/or more tractors to be produced from the same amount of resources. Thus one way for an economy to increase its output—and its per capita income—may be to invest in research and development.

Another way is by devoting more of its resources to the production of capital goods rather than consumers' goods. **Capital goods** consist of plant and equipment that are used to make other goods; **consumers' goods** are items that consumers purchase like clothing, food, and drink. Since capital goods are themselves resources, a society that chooses to produce lots of capital goods and few consumers' goods will push out its production possibilities curve much farther than a society that chooses to produce lots of consumers' goods and few capital goods.

To illustrate this point, consider our simple society that produces food and tractors. The more tractors (and the less food) this society produces, the more tractors it will have in the next period; and the more tractors it has in the next period, the more of both goods—food and tractors—it will be able to produce then. Thus the more tractors (and the less food) this society produces, the farther out it will push its production possibilities curve—and the greater the increase in output (and per capita income) that it will achieve in the next period. If this society chooses point *F* (shown in Figures 2.7, 2.5, or 2.3), the effect will be entirely different than if it chooses point *C*. If it chooses point *F*, it produces 4 million tractors, which we assume to be the number of tractors worn out each year. Thus, if it chooses point *F*, it adds nothing to its stock of tractors: it merely replaces those that wear out. Since it has no more tractors in the next period than

One of the most remarkable developments in human history was the Industrial Revolution. Until the middle of the eighteenth century, industry (as distinct from agriculture or commerce) played a small role in the economies of Europe or America. But during the late eighteenth and early nineteenth centuries a host of important technological innovations, such as James Watt's steam engine and Richard Arkwright's spinning jenny, made possible a very rapid growth in the output of industrial goods (like textiles and pig iron). And accompanying this growth of industrial output was the advent of the factory—a social and economic institution that is taken for granted today, but which was largely unknown prior to the Industrial Revolution.

The Industrial Revolution was characterized by major improvements in technology and by large increases in the amount of capital resources available to society. Both the improvements in technology and the additional capital resulted in an outward shift in the production possibilities curve in England, where the Industrial Revolution first took hold. (See Figures 2.7 and 2.8.) Due to this shift, the standard of living in England, as measured by per capita income (total income divided by population), grew at an unprecedented rate. As the Industrial Revolution spread, this rise in living standards occurred too on the European continent and in the United States; it remained one of the lasting effects of industrialization.

As stressed above, the Industrial Revolution was characterized by considerable increases in capital. How did England (and other countries) bring about this increase in capital? By saving and investing. In other words, the English people had to set aside some of their resources, and to say in effect, "These resources will *not* be used to satisfy the current needs of our population for food, clothing, and other forms of consumption. Instead, they will be used to produce capital—factories, machines, equipment, railroads, and canals—which will increase our future productive capacity." Much more will be said about this saving process in subsequent chapters. For now, the essential point is that this saving process was one of the necessary conditions that made possible the Industrial Revolution.

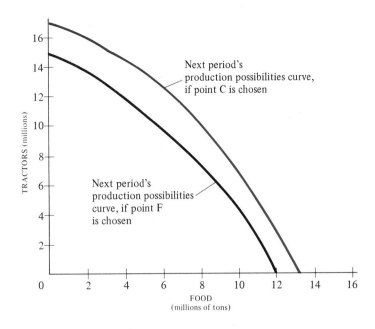

Figure 2.8
Effect of Increase in Capital Goods on Production Possibilities Curve *An increase in the amount of capital goods results in an outward shift of the production possibilities curve. The choice of point C means the production of more capital goods than the choice of point F.*

in the current period, the production possibilities curve does not shift out at all if point *F* is chosen. On the other hand, if point *C* is chosen, the society produces 12 million tractors, which means that it has 8 million additional tractors at the beginning of the next period. Thus, as shown in Figure 2.8, the production possibilities curve is pushed outward. By producing more capital goods (and less consumers' goods) our society has increased its production possibilities and its per capita income.

Capitalism: An Economic System

WHAT IS CAPITALISM?

In previous sections we have discussed the basic tasks that any economic system must perform. Now we must look at how our own economic system performs these tasks. The particular kind of economic system adopted by the United States is *capitalism*. Capitalism is one of those terms that is frequently used but seldom defined, and even less frequently understood. Its operation is complex, but its principal characteristics can be lumped into four major categories.

1. Private Ownership of Capital. Under capitalism you or I can buy the tools of production. We can own factories, equipment, inventories, and other forms of capital. In a capitalistic system, somebody owns each piece of capital—and receives the income from it. Each piece of equipment has some sort of legal instrument indicating to whom it belongs. (If it belongs to a corporation, its owners basically are the stockholders who own the corporation.) Moreover, each piece of capital has a market value. This system is in marked contrast to a Communist or socialist state where the government owns the capital. In these states, the government decides how much and what kinds of capital goods will be produced; it owns the capital goods; and it receives and distributes the income they produce. In

31

the Soviet Union or China, no one can buy or put up a new steel plant; it simply isn't allowed.

The United States is basically a capitalistic system, but there are certain areas where the government, not individuals, owns capital, and where individual property rights are limited in various ways by the government. The government owns much of the tooling used in the defense industries; it owns dams and the Tennessee Valley Authority; and it owns research laboratories in such diverse fields as atomic energy, space exploration, and health. Further, the government determines how much of a deceased person's assets can go to his or her heirs. (The rest goes to the government in the form of estate and inheritance taxes.) Also, the government can make a person sell his or her property to allow a road or other public project to be built. There are many such limitations on property rights. Ours is basically a capitalistic system, but it must be recognized that the government's role is important. More will be said about this in subsequent sections.

2. Freedom of Choice and Enterprise. Another important characteristic of capitalism is freedom of choice and freedom of enterprise. **Freedom of choice** means that consumers are free to buy what they please and reject what they please; that laborers are free to work where, when, and if they please; and that investors are free to invest in whatever property they please. By **freedom of enterprise,** we mean that firms are free to enter whatever markets they please, obtain resources in whatever ways they can, and organize their affairs as best they can. Needless to say, this does not mean that firms can run roughshod over consumers and workers. Even the strongest champions of capitalism are quick to admit that the government must set "rules of the game" to prevent firms from engaging in sharp or unfair practices. But granting such limitations, the name of the game under capitalism is economic freedom.

Freedom to do what? Under capitalism, individuals and firms are free to pursue their own self-interest. Put in today's idiom, each individual or firm can do his, her, or its own thing. However, it is important to note that this freedom is circumscribed by one's financial resources. Consumers in a capitalistic system can buy practically anything they like—if they have the money to pay for it. Similarly, workers can work wherever or whenever they please—if they don't mind the wages. And a firm can run its business as it likes—if it remains solvent. Thus an important regulator of economic activity under capitalism is the pattern of income and prices that emerges in the market place.

3. Competition. Still another important characteristic of capitalism is **competition.** Firms compete with one another for sales. Under perfect competition, there are a large number of firms producing each product; indeed, there are so many that no firm controls the product's price. Because of this competition, firms are forced to jump to the tune of the consumer. If a firm doesn't produce what consumers want—at a price at least as low as other firms are charging—it will lose sales to other firms. Eventually, unless it mends its ways, such a firm will go out of business. Of course, in real-life American markets, the number of producers is not always so large that no firm has any control over price. (Much more will be said about this below.) But in the purest form of capitalism, such imperfections do not exist. Also, lest you think that competition under capitalism is confined to producers, it must be remembered that owners of resources also compete. They are expected to offer their resources—including labor—to the buyer who gives them the best deal, and buyers of resources and products are supposed to compete openly and freely.

4. Reliance upon Markets. Finally, another very important characteristic of capitalism is its reliance upon markets. *Under pure capitalism, the market—the free market—plays a central role.* Firms and individuals buy and sell products and resources in competitive markets. Some firms and individuals make money and prosper; others lose money and fail. Each firm or individual is allowed freedom to pursue its or his or her interests in the market place, while the government guards against shady and dishonest dealings. Such is the nature of the economic system under pure capitalism.

HOW DOES CAPITALISM PERFORM THE FOUR BASIC ECONOMIC TASKS?

The **price system** lies at the heart of any capitalist economy. In a purely capitalist economy, it is used to carry out the four basic economic functions discussed above. The price system is a way to organize an economy. Under such a system, every commodity and every service, including labor, has a price. We all receive money for what we sell, including labor, and we use this money to buy the goods and services we want. If more is wanted of a certain good, the price of this good tends to rise; if less is wanted, the price of the good tends to fall. Producers base their production decisions on the prices of commodities and inputs. Thus increases in a commodity's price generally tend to increase the amount of it produced, and decreases generally tend to decrease the amount produced. In this way, firms' output decisions are brought into balance with consumers' desires.

The very important question of how the price system performs the basic economic functions we discussed above will be answered in some detail in the next chapter. All we can do here is provide a preliminary sketch of the way the price system carries out each of these four tasks.

1. How does the price system determine what society will produce? In a substantially capitalistic economy, such as ours, consumers choose the amount of each good that they want, and producers act in accord with these decisions. The importance consumers attach to a good is indicated by the price they are willing to pay for it. Of course, the principle of **consumer sovereignty**—producers dancing to the tune of consumers' tastes—should not be viewed as always and completely true, since producers do attempt to manipulate the tastes of consumers through advertising and other devices, but it is certainly a reasonable first approximation.

2. How does the price system determine how each good and service will be produced? Prices indicate the desires of workers and the relative value of various types of materials and equipment as well as the desires of consumers. For example, if plumbers are scarce relative to the demand for them, their price in the labor market—their wage—will be bid up, and they will tend to be used only in the places where they are productive enough so that their employers can afford to pay them the higher wages. The forces that push firms toward actually carrying out the proper decisions are profits and losses. Profits are the carrot and losses are the stick used to eliminate the less efficient and less alert firms and to increase the more efficient and the more alert.

3. How does the price system determine how much in the way of goods and services each member of the society is to receive? In general, an individual's income depends largely on the quantities of resources of various kinds that he or she owns and the prices he or she gets for them. For example, if a man both works and rents out farm land he owns, his income is the number of hours he works per year times his hourly wage rate plus the number of acres of land he owns times the annual rental per acre. Thus the distribution of income depends on the way resource ownership—including talent, intelligence, training, work habits, and, yes, even character—is distributed among the population. Also, to be candid, it depends on just plain luck.

4. How does the price system determine the nation's rate of growth of per capita income? A nation's rate of growth of per capita income depends on the rate of growth of its resources and the rate of increase of the efficiency with which they are used. In our economy, the rate at which labor and capital resources are increased is motivated, at least in part, through the price system. Higher wages for more skilled work are an incentive for an individual to undergo further education and training. Capital accumulation occurs in response to the expectation of profit. Increases in efficiency, due in considerable measure to the advance of technology, are also stimulated by the price system.

Our Mixed Capitalist System

Since the days of Adam Smith, economists have been fascinated by the features of a purely capitalistic economic system—an economy that relies entirely on the price system. Smith, and many generations of economists since, have gone to great pains to explain that in such an economic system, *the price system, although it is not controlled by any person or small group, results in economic order, not chaos.* The basic economic tasks any economy must perform can, as we have said, be carried out in such an economic system by the price system. It is an effective means of coordinating economic activity through decentralized decision making based on information disseminated through prices and related data.

But does this mean that the American economy is purely capitalistic? As we have noted repeatedly in previous sections, the answer is no. A purely capitalistic system is a useful model of reality, not a description of our economy as it exists now or existed in the past. It is useful because a purely capitalistic economy is, for some purposes, a reasonably close fit to our own. However, this does not mean that such a model is useful for all purposes. Many American markets are not perfectly competitive and never will be; they are dominated by a few producers or buyers who can influence price and thus distort the workings of the price system. Moreover, *the American economy is a mixed capitalistic economy, an economy where both government and private decisions are important.* The role of the government in American economic activity is very large indeed. Although it is essential

Basic Idea #4: The price system is a surprisingly effective way to organize an economy. Even though there is no small group of people directing the workings of the economy (as in the Soviet Union and other planned economies), the result is not chaos, as you might expect. Instead, prices provide the information needed for decentralized decision making.

to understand the workings of a purely capitalistic system, any model that omits the government entirely cannot purport to be adequate for the analysis of many major present-day economic issues.

To create a more balanced picture of the workings of the American economy, we must recognize that, although the price system plays an extremely important role, it is not permitted to solve all of the basic economic problems of our society. Consumer sovereignty does not extend—and cannot realistically be extended—to all areas of society. For example, certain public services cannot be left to private enterprise. The provision of fire protection, the operation of schools, and the development of weapons systems are examples of areas where we rely on political decision making, not the price system alone. Moreover, with regard to the consumption of commodities like drugs, society imposes limits on the decisions of individuals.

In addition, certain consequences of the price system are, by general agreement, unacceptable. Reliance on the price system alone does not assure a just or equitable or optimal distribution of income. It is possible, for example, that one person will have money to burn while another person will live in degrading poverty. Consequently, society empowers the government to modify the distribution of income by imposing taxes that take more from the rich than the poor, and by welfare programs that try to keep the poor from reaching the point where they lack decent food, adequate clothing, or shelter. Besides providing public services and maintaining certain minimum income standards, the government also carries out a variety of regulatory functions. Industries do not police the actions of their constituent firms, so it falls to the government to establish laws that impose limits on the economic behavior of firms. For example, these laws say that firms must not misrepresent their products, that child labor must not be employed, and that firms must not collude and form monopolies to interfere with the proper functioning of the price system. In this way, the government tries, with varying degrees of effectiveness, to establish the "rules of the game"—the limits within which the economic behavior of firms (and consumers) should lie.

Test Yourself

1. Suppose that a society's production possibilities curve is as follows:

Output (per year)

Possibility	Food (millions of tons)	Tractors (millions)
A	0	30
B	4	28
C	8	24
D	12	20
E	16	14
F	20	8
G	24	0

(a) Is it possible for the society to produce 30 million tons of food per year? (b) Can it produce 30 million tractors per year? (c) Suppose this society produces 20 million tons of food and 6 million tractors per year. Is it operating on the production possibilities curve? If not, what factors might account for this?

2. Plot the production possibilities curve in Question 1 in a graph. At what point along the horizontal axis does the curve cut the axis? At what point along the vertical axis does the curve cut the axis?

3. Suppose that, because of important technological improvements, the society in Question 1 can double its production of tractors at each level of food production. If so, is this society on its new production possibilities curve if it produces 20 million tons of food

and 16 million tractors? Plot the new production possibilities curve. At what point along the horizontal axis does the new curve cut the axis? At what point along the vertical axis does it cut the axis?

4. "[Some people] . . . fail to realize that the price system is, and ought to be, a method of coercion. . . . The very term 'rationing by the purse' illustrates the point. Economists defend such forms of rationing, but they have to do so primarily in terms of its efficiency and its fairness."* Comment.

5. "The great advantage of the [price system] . . . is that it permits wide diversity. It is, in political terms, a system of proportional representation. Each man can vote, as it were, for the color of tie he wants and get it; he does not have to see what color the majority wants and then, if he is in the minority, submit."** Comment.

* P. Samuelson, "The Economic Role of Private Activity," *A Dialogue on the Proper Economic Role of the State,* Chicago: University of Chicago Press, 1963.
** M. Friedman, *Capitalism and Freedom,* Chicago: University of Chicago Press, 1962, p. 15.

Summary

1. The methodology used by economists is much the same as that used in any other kind of scientific analysis. The basic procedure is the formulation and testing of models. A model must in general simplify and abstract from the real world. Its purpose is to make predictions, and in many respects the most important test of a model is how well it predicts. To test and quantify their models, economists gather data and utilize various statistical techniques.

2. The production possibilities curve, which shows the various production possibilities a society can attain, is useful in indicating the nature of the economic tasks any society faces. The task of determining the level and composition of society's output is really a problem of determining at what point along the production possibilities curve society should be.

3. Society has to recognize that it cannot get more of one good without giving up some of another good, if resources are fully and efficiently used. However, if they are not fully and efficiently used, society will have to settle for points inside the production possibilities curve—and it will be possible to obtain more of one good without giving up some of another good.

4. The task of determining how each good and service should be produced is, to a considerable extent, a problem of keeping society on its production possibilities curve, rather than at points inside the curve. The production possibilities curve does not tell us anything about the distribution of income, but it does indicate various ways that a society can promote growth in per capita income. By doing research and development, or by producing capital goods (rather than consumers' goods), society may push its production possibilities curve outward, thus increasing per capita income.

5. The American economy is a capitalistic economy, an economic system in which there is private ownership of capital, freedom of choice, freedom of enterprise, competition, and reliance upon markets.

6. Under pure capitalism, the price system is used to perform the four basic economic tasks. Although it is not controlled by any person or small group, the price system results in order, not chaos.

7. A purely capitalistic system is a useful model of reality, not a description of our economy as it exists now or in the past. The American economy is a mixed capitalistic economy, in which both government and private decisions are important.

8. Many public services (like defense and environmental protection) cannot be left to private enterprise, and society has said that certain consequences of the price system (like the existence of abject poverty) are unacceptable. For these reasons and others, the government carries out a long and impressive array of functions, many of which are discussed in subsequent chapters.

Concepts for Review

Model	Consumers' goods	Competition
Production possibilities curve	Capitalism	Price system
Capital goods	Freedom of choice	Consumer sovereignty
	Freedom of enterprise	

PART TWO

The Private Sector and the Public Sector: An Overview

CHAPTER 3

The Price System

Capitalist economies use the price system to perform the four basic tasks any economic system must carry out. Of course, as we pointed out in the previous chapter, the American economy is a mixed capitalist system, not a pure one. But this does not mean that the price system is unimportant. On the contrary, the price system plays a vital role in the American economy, and to obtain even a minimal grasp of the workings of our economic system, one must understand how the price system operates. This chapter takes up the nature and functions of the price system, as well as some applications of our theoretical results to real-life problems. For example, we show how the price system determines the quantity produced of a commodity like wheat, and how the pricing policies of the Broadway theater have hurt show business in a variety of ways. These applications should help illustrate the basic theory and indicate its usefulness.

Consumers, Firms, and Markets

We begin by describing and discussing consumers and firms, the basic building blocks that make up the private, or nongovernmental, sector of the economy.

Consumers. Sometimes—for example, when a person buys a beer on a warm day—the consumer is an individual. In other cases—for example, when a family buys a new car—the consumer may be an entire household. **Consumers** purchase the goods and services that are the ultimate end products of the economic system. When a man buys tickets to a ball game, he is a consumer; when he buys himself a Coke at the game, he is a consumer; and when he buys his wife a book on baseball for their twentieth wedding anniversary, he is a consumer.

Firms. There are about 16 million firms in the United States. About nine-tenths of the goods and services produced in this country are produced by firms. (The rest are provided by government and not-for-profit institutions like universities and hospitals.) A *firm* is an organization that produces a good or service for sale. In contrast to not-for-profit organizations, firms attempt to make a profit. It is obvious that our economy is centered around the activities of firms.

Markets. Consumers and firms come together in a market. The concept of a market is not quite as straightforward as it may seem, since most markets are not well defined geographically or physically. For example, the New York Stock Exchange is an atypical market because it is located principally in a particular building. For present purposes, a *market* can be defined as a group of firms and individuals that are in touch with each other in order to buy or sell some good. Of course, not every person in a market has to be in contact with every other person in the market. A person or firm is part of a market even if it is in contact with only a subset of the other persons or firms in the market.

Markets vary enormously in their size and procedures. For some goods like toothpaste, most people who have their own teeth (and are interested in keeping them) are members of the same market; while for other goods like Picasso paintings, only a few dealers, collectors, and museums in certain parts of the world may be members of the market. And for still other goods, like lemonade sold by neighborhood children for a nickel a glass at a sidewalk stand, only people who walk by the stand—and are brave enough to drink the stuff—are members of the market. Basically, however, all markets consist primarily of buyers and sellers, although third parties like brokers and agents may be present as well.

Markets also vary in the extent to which they are dominated by a few large buyers or sellers. For example, in the United States, there was for many years only one producer of aluminum. This firm, the Aluminum Corporation of America, had great power in the market for aluminum. In contrast, the number of buyers and sellers in some other markets is so large that no single buyer or seller has any power over the price of the product. This is true in various agricultural markets, for example. When a market for a product contains so many buyers and sellers that none of them can influence the price, economists call the market *perfectly competitive.* In these introductory chapters, we make the simplifying assumption that markets are perfectly competitive. We will relax that assumption later.

The Demand Side of a Market

Every market has a demand side and a supply side. The *demand* side can be represented by a *market demand curve,* which shows the amount of the commodity buyers would like to purchase at various prices. Consider Figure 3.1, which shows the demand curve for wheat in the American market during the mid-1980s.[1] The figure shows that about 2.7 billion bushels of wheat

---

[1] I am indebted to officials of the U.S. Department of Agriculture for providing me with this information. Of course, these estimates are only rough approximations, but they are good enough for present purposes.

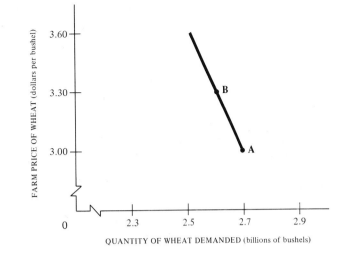

Figure 3.1

Market Demand Curve for Wheat, Mid-1980s *The curve shows the amount of wheat buyers would demand at various prices. At $3.00 per bushel, about 8 percent more wheat can be sold than at $3.60 per bushel.*

will be demanded annually if the farm price is $3.00 per bushel, about 2.6 billion bushels will be demanded annually if the farm price is $3.30 per bushel, and about 2.5 billion bushels will be demanded annually if the farm price is $3.60 per bushel. The total demand for wheat is of several types: to produce bread and other food products for domestic use, as well as for feed use, for export purposes, and for industrial uses. The demand curve in Figure 3.1 shows the total demand—including all these components—at each price. Any demand curve pertains to a particular period of time, and its shape and position depend on the length of this period.

Take a good look at the demand curve for wheat in Figure 3.1. This simple, innocent-looking curve influences a great many people's lives. After all, wheat is the principal grain used for direct human consumption in the United States. To states like Kansas, North Dakota, Oklahoma, Montana, Washington, Nebraska, Texas, Illinois, Indiana, and Ohio, wheat is a mighty important cash crop. Note that the demand curve for wheat slopes downward to the right. In other words, the quantity of wheat demanded increases as the price falls. This is true of the demand curve for most commodities: they almost always slope downward to the right. This makes sense; one would expect increases in a good's price to result in a smaller quantity demanded.

Any demand curve is based on the assumption that the tastes, incomes, and number of consumers, as well as the prices of other commodities, are held constant. Changes in any of these factors are likely to shift the position of a commodity's demand curve, as indicated below.

Consumer Tastes. If consumers show an increasing preference for a product, the demand curve will shift to the right; that is, at each price, consumers will desire to buy more than previously. On the other hand, if consumers show a decreasing preference for a product, the demand curve will shift to the left, since, at each price, consumers will desire to buy less than previously. Take wheat. If consumers become convinced that foods containing wheat prolong life and promote happiness, the demand curve may shift, as shown in Figure 3.2; and the greater the shift in preferences, the larger the shift in the demand curve.

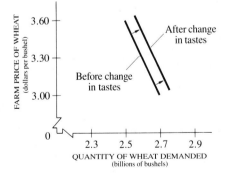

Figure 3.2

Effect of Increased Preference for Wheat on Market Demand Curve *An increased preference for wheat would shift the demand curve to the right.*

41

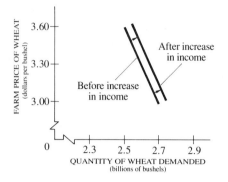

Figure 3.3

Effect of Increase in Income on Market Demand Curve for Wheat *An increase in income would shift the demand curve for wheat to the right, but only slightly.*

Income Level of Consumers. For some types of products, the demand curve shifts to the right if per capita income increases; whereas for other types of commodities, the demand curve shifts to the left if per capita income rises. Economists can explain why some goods fall into one category and other goods fall into the other, but, at present, this need not concern us. All that is important here is that changes in per capita income affect the demand curve, the size and direction of this effect varying from product to product. In the case of wheat, a 10 percent increase in per capita income would probably have a relatively small effect on the demand curve, as shown in Figure 3.3.

Number of Consumers in the Market. Compare Austria's demand for wheat with the United States'. Austria is a small country with a population of less than 8 million; the United States is a huge country with a population of over 200 million. Clearly, at a given price of wheat, the quantity demanded by American consumers will greatly exceed the quantity demanded by Austrian consumers, as shown in Figure 3.4. Even if consumer tastes, income, and other factors were held constant, this would still be true simply because the United States has so many more consumers in the relevant market.[2]

Level of Other Prices. A commodity's demand curve can be shifted by a change in the price of other commodities. Whether an increase in the price of good B will shift the demand curve for good A to the right or the left depends on the relationship between the two goods. If they are substitutes, such an increase will shift the demand curve for good A to the right. Consider the case of corn and wheat. If the price of corn goes up, more wheat will be demanded since it will be profitable to substitute wheat for corn. If the price of corn drops, less wheat will be demanded since it will be profitable to substitute corn for wheat. Thus, as shown in Figure 3.5, increases in the price of corn will shift the demand curve for wheat to the right, and decreases in the price of corn will shift it to the left.[3]

THE DISTINCTION BETWEEN CHANGES IN DEMAND AND CHANGES IN THE QUANTITY DEMANDED

It is essential to distinguish between a *shift in a commodity's demand curve* and a change in the *quantity demanded of the commodity.* A shift in a commodity's demand curve is a change in the *relationship* between price and quantity demanded. Figures 3.2, 3.3, and 3.5 show cases where such a change occurs. A change in the quantity demanded of a commodity may occur even if *no* shift occurs in the commodity's demand curve. For example, in Figure 3.1, if the price of wheat increases from $3.00 to $3.30 per bushel, the quantity demanded falls from 2.7 to 2.6 billion bushels. This change in the quantity demanded is due to a *movement along* the demand

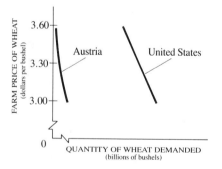

Figure 3.4

Market Demand Curve for Wheat, Austria and the United States *Since the United States has far more consumers than Austria, the demand curve in the United States is far to the right of Austria's.*

[2] Note that no figures are given along the horizontal axis in Figure 3.4. This is because we do not have reasonably precise estimates of the demand curve in Austria. Nonetheless, the hypothetical demand curves in Figure 3.4 are close enough to the mark for present purposes.

[3] If goods A and B are complements, an increase in the price of good B will shift the demand curve for good A to the left. Thus an increase in the price of gin is likely to shift the demand curve for tonic to the left. Why? Because gin and tonic tend to be used together. The increase in gin's price will reduce the quantity of gin demanded, which in turn will reduce the amount of tonic that will be demanded at each price of tonic.

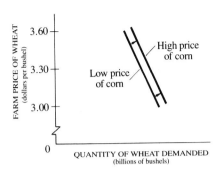

Figure 3.5

Effect of Price of Corn on Market Demand Curve for Wheat *Price increases for corn will shift the demand curve for wheat to the right.*

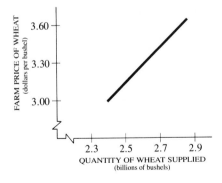

Figure 3.6

Market Supply Curve for Wheat, Mid-1980s *The curve shows the amount of wheat sellers would supply at various prices. At $3.60 per bushel, about 17 percent more wheat would be supplied than at $3.00 per bushel.*

curve (from point *A* to point *B* in Figure 3.1), not to a *shift* in the demand curve.

When economists refer to an *increase in demand,* they mean a *rightward shift* in the demand curve. Thus Figures 3.2, 3.3, and 3.5 show increases in demand for wheat. When economists refer to a *decrease in demand,* they mean a *leftward shift* in the demand curve. An increase in demand for a commodity is not the same as an increase in the quantity demanded of the commodity. In Figure 3.1, the quantity demanded of wheat *increases* if the price falls from $3.30 to $3.00 per bushel, but this is not due to an increase in demand, since there is no rightward shift of the demand curve. Similarly, a decrease in demand for a commodity is not the same as a decrease in the quantity demanded of the commodity. In Figure 3.1, the quantity demanded of wheat *decreases* if the price rises from $3.00 to $3.30 per bushel, but this is not due to a decrease in demand, since there is no leftward shift of the demand curve.

The Supply Side of a Market

So much for our first look at demand. What about the other side of the market: supply? *The* **supply** *side of a market can be represented by a* **market supply curve** *that shows the amount of the commodity sellers would offer at various prices.* Let's continue with the case of wheat. Figure 3.6 shows the supply curve for wheat in the United States in the mid-1980s, based on estimates made informally by government experts.[4] According to the figure, about 2.4 billion bushels of wheat would be supplied if the farm price were $3.00 per bushel, about 2.6 billion bushels if the farm price were $3.30 per bushel, and about 2.8 billion bushels if the farm price were $3.60 per bushel.

Look carefully at the supply curve shown in Figure 3.6. Although it looks innocuous enough, it summarizes the potential behavior of thousands of American wheat farmers—and their behavior plays an important role in determining the prosperity of many states and communities. Note that the supply curve for wheat slopes upward to the right. In other words, the quantity of wheat supplied increases as the price increases. This seems plausible, since increases in price give a greater incentive for farms to produce wheat and offer it for sale. Empirical studies indicate that the supply curves for a great many commodities share this characteristic of sloping upward to the right.

Any supply curve is based on the assumption that technology and input prices are held constant. Changes in these factors are likely to shift the position of a commodity's supply curve, as indicated below.

Technology. Recall that technology was defined in Chapter 1 as society's pool of knowledge concerning the industrial arts. As technology progresses, it becomes possible to produce commodities more cheaply, so that firms often are willing to supply a given amount at a lower price than formerly. Thus technological change often causes the supply curve to shift

---

[4] Officials of the U.S. Department of Agriculture provided me with these estimates. Although rough approximations, they are good enough for present purposes.

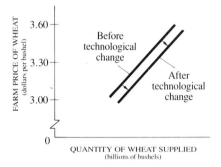

Figure 3.7

Effect of Technological Change on Market Supply Curve for Wheat *Improvements in technology often shift the supply curve to the right.*

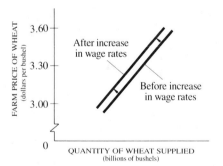

Figure 3.8

Effect of Increase in Farm Wage Rates on Market Supply Curve for Wheat *An increase in the wage rate might shift the supply curve to the left.*

to the right. This certainly has occurred in the case of wheat, as shown in Figure 3.7. There have been many important technological changes in wheat production, ranging from advances in tractors to the development of improved varieties, like semi-dwarf wheats.

Input Prices. The supply curve for a commodity is affected by the prices of the resources (labor, capital, and land) used to produce it. Decreases in the price of these inputs make it possible to produce commodities more cheaply, so that firms may be willing to supply a given amount at a lower price than they formerly would. Thus decreases in the price of inputs may cause the supply curve to shift to the right. On the other hand, increases in the price of inputs may cause it to shift to the left. For example, if the wage rates of farm labor increase, the supply curve for wheat may shift to the left, as shown in Figure 3.8.

An *increase in supply* is defined to be a *rightward shift* in the supply curve; a *decrease in supply* is defined to be a *leftward shift* in the supply curve. A change in supply should be distinguished from a change in the quantity supplied. In Figure 3.6, the quantity supplied of wheat will increase from 2.4 to 2.6 billion bushels if the price increases from $3.00 to $3.30 per bushel, but this is not due to an increase in supply, since there is no rightward shift of the supply curve in Figure 3.6.

Equilibrium Price

The two sides of a market, demand and supply, interact to determine the price of a commodity. Recall from the previous chapter that prices in a capitalistic system are important determinants of what is produced, how it is produced, who receives it, and how rapidly per capita income grows. It behooves us, therefore, to look carefully at how prices themselves are determined in a capitalist system. As a first step toward describing this process, we must define the equilibrium price of a product. At various points in this book, you will encounter the concept of an equilibrium, which is very important in economics, as in many other scientific fields.

Put briefly, an **equilibrium** is a situation where there is no tendency for change; in other words, it is a situation that can persist. Thus an **equilibrium price** is a price that can be maintained. Any price that is not an equilibrium price cannot be maintained for long, since there are basic forces at work to stimulate a change in price. The best way to understand what we mean by an equilibrium price is to take a particular case, such as the wheat market. Let's put both the demand curve for wheat (in Figure 3.1) and the supply curve for wheat (in Figure 3.6) together in the same diagram. The result, shown in Figure 3.9, will help us determine the equilibrium price of wheat.

We begin by seeing what would happen if various prices were established in the market. For example, if the price were $3.60 per bushel, the demand curve indicates that 2.5 billion bushels of wheat would be demanded, while the supply curve indicates that 2.8 billion bushels would be supplied. Thus, if the price were $3.60 a bushel, there would be a mismatch between the quantity supplied and the quantity demanded per year, since the rate at which wheat is supplied would be greater than the rate at which it is demanded. Specifically, as shown in Figure 3.9, there would be an *excess sup-*

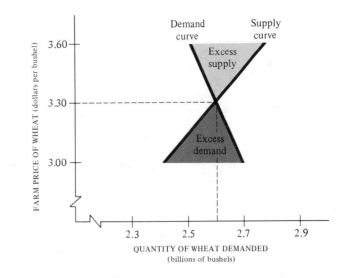

ply of 300 million bushels. Under these circumstances, some of the wheat supplied by farmers could not be sold, and, as inventories of wheat built up, suppliers would tend to cut their prices in order to get rid of unwanted inventories. Thus a price of $3.60 per bushel would not be maintained for long—and for this reason, $3.60 per bushel is not an equilibrium price.

If the price were $3.00 per bushel, on the other hand, the demand curve indicates that 2.7 billion bushels would be demanded, while the supply curve indicates that 2.4 billion bushels would be supplied. Again we find a mismatch between the quantity supplied and the quantity demanded per year, since the rate at which wheat is supplied would be less than the rate at which it is demanded. Specifically, as shown in Figure 3.9, there would be an *excess demand* of 300 million bushels. Under these circumstances, some of the consumers who want wheat at this price would have to be turned away empty-handed. There would be a shortage. And given this shortage, suppliers would find it profitable to increase the price, and competition among buyers would bid the price up. Thus a price of $3.00 per bushel could not be maintained for long—so $3.00 per bushel is not an equilibrium price.

Under these circumstances, the equilibrium price must be the price where the quantity demanded equals the quantity supplied. Obviously, this is the only price at which there is no mismatch between the quantity demanded and the quantity supplied; and consequently the only price that can be maintained for long. In Figure 3.9, the price at which the quantity supplied equals the quantity demanded is $3.30 per bushel, the price where the demand curve intersects the supply curve. Thus $3.30 per bushel is the equilibrium price of wheat under the circumstances visualized in Figure 3.9, and 2.6 billion bushels is the equilibrium quantity.

Actual Price

The price that counts in the real world, however, is the ***actual price,*** not the equilibrium price, and it is the actual price that we set out to explain. In

Example 3.1   It's Not Just for Breakfast Anymore

In recent years, many oranges grown in California and Arizona have been provided to cattle for feed or given away to juicing plants. An 11-member committee of farmers and shippers establishes the number and size of oranges that can be sold. Anyone selling oranges without the committee's permission can face civil and criminal prosecution by the Department of Justice. Although some industry spokesmen claim that the oranges held off the market are too small to be sold, it is reported that the industry's figures show that some of these oranges are as large as those sent to market.*

(a) In the absence of government intervention, suppose that the demand and supply curves for oranges would be as shown below:

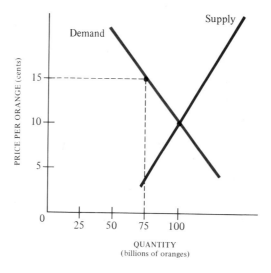

What would be the equilibrium price under these circumstances? (b) If the committee says that the quantity of oranges that can be sold must be 25 percent less than what would be sold in a free market, what will be the equilibrium price? (c) Under the committee's edict, will the growers receive more or less for their crop than under the free market? How much more or less? (d) How are consumers affected by the committee's edict?

SOLUTION

(a) 10 cents per orange. (b) In a free market, 100 billion oranges would be sold. If this quantity is reduced by 25 percent, only 75 billion oranges can be sold. Based on the demand curve, this amount can be sold for 15 cents per orange. Thus this will be the price. (c) Under the committee's edict, growers will sell 75 billion oranges at 15 cents each, so they will receive $11.25 billion. Under the free market, they will sell 100 billion oranges at 10 cents each, so they will receive $10 billion. Thus they will receive $1.25 billion more under the committee's edict than under the free market. (d) They consume fewer oranges and pay more for those they do consume.

* "Growers Bar Oranges from Market as Prices Dip," *New York Times,* February 15, 1981.

general, economists simply assume that the actual price will approximate the equilibrium price, which seems reasonable enough, since the basic forces at work tend to push the actual price toward the equilibrium price. Thus, if conditions remain fairly stable for a time, the actual price should move toward the equilibrium price.

To see that this is the case, consider the market for wheat, as described in Figure 3.9. What if the price somehow is set at $3.60 per bushel? As we saw in the previous section, there is downward pressure on the price of wheat under these conditions. Suppose the price, responding to this pressure, falls to $3.50. Comparing the quantity demanded with the quantity supplied at $3.50, we find that there is still downward pressure on price, since the quantity supplied exceeds the quantity demanded at $3.50. The price, responding to this pressure, may fall to $3.40, but comparing the quantity demanded with the quantity supplied at this price, we find that there is still a downward pressure on price, since the quantity supplied exceeds the quantity demanded at $3.40.

So long as the actual price exceeds the equilibrium price, there will be a downward pressure on price. Similarly, so long as the actual price is less than the equilibrium price, there will be an upward pressure on price. Thus there is always a tendency for the actual price to move toward the equilibrium price. But it should not be assumed that this movement is always rapid. Sometimes it takes a long time for the actual price to get close to the equilibrium price. Sometimes the actual price never gets to the equilibrium price because by the time it gets close, the equilibrium price changes (because of shifts in either the demand curve or the supply curve or both). All that safely can be said is that the actual price will move toward the equilibrium price. But of course this information is of great value, both theoretically and practically. For many purposes, all that is needed is a correct prediction of the direction in which the price will move.

Test Yourself

1. Assume that the market for electric toasters is competitive and that the quantity supplied per year depends as follows on the price of a toaster:

Price of a toaster (dollars)	Number of toasters supplied (millions)
6	4.0
8	5.0
10	5.5
12	6.0
14	6.3

Plot the supply curve for toasters. Is this a direct or inverse relationship? Are supply curves generally direct or inverse relationships?

2. Suppose that the quantity of toasters demanded per year depends as follows on the price of a toaster:

Price of a toaster (dollars)	Number of toasters demanded (millions)
6	7.0
8	6.5
10	6.2
12	6.0
14	5.8

Plot the demand curve for toasters. If the price is $8, will there be an excess demand of toasters? If the price is $14, will there be an excess demand? What is the equilibrium price of a toaster? What is the equilibrium quantity? (Use the data in Question 1.)

3. Suppose that the government imposes a price ceiling on toasters. In particular, suppose that it decrees that a toaster cannot sell for more than $8. Will the quantity supplied equal the quantity demanded? What sorts of devices may come into being to allocate the available supply of toasters to consumers? What problems will the government encounter in keeping the price at $8? What social purposes, if any, might such a price ceiling serve? (Use the data in Questions 1 and 2.)

4. Suppose that the government imposes a price floor on toasters. In particular, suppose that it decrees that a toaster cannot sell for less than $14. Will the quantity supplied equal the quantity demanded? How will the resulting supply of toasters be taken off the market? What problems will the government encounter in keeping the price at $14? What social purposes, if any, might such a price floor serve? (Use the data above.)

5. If the demand curve for butter is $Q_D = 20 - 4P$ (where Q_D is the quantity demanded and P is the price of butter) and the supply curve for butter is $Q_S = 2P$ (where Q_S is the quantity supplied), what is the equilibrium price? What is the equilibrium quantity? (Both Q_D and Q_S are measured in millions of pounds, and price is measured in dollars per pound.)

The Effects of Shifts in the Demand Curve

Heraclitus, the ancient Greek philosopher, said you cannot step in the same stream twice: everything changes, sooner or later. One need not be a disciple of Heraclitus to recognize that demand curves shift. Indeed, we have already seen that demand curves shift in response to changes in tastes, income, population, and prices of other products, and that supply curves shift in response to changes in technology and input prices. Any supply-and-demand diagram like Figure 3.9 is essentially a snapshot of the situation during a particular period of time. The results in Figure 3.9 are limited to a particular period because the demand and supply curves in the figure, like any demand and supply curves, pertain only to a certain period.

What happens to the equilibrium price of a product when its demand curve changes? This is an important question because it sheds a good deal of light on how the price system works. Suppose that consumer tastes shift in favor of foods containing wheat, causing the demand curve for wheat to shift *to the right,* as shown in Figure 3.10. It is not hard to see the effect on the equilibrium price of wheat. Before the shift, the equilibrium price is OP. But when the demand curve shifts to the right, a shortage develops at this price: that is, the quantity demanded exceeds the quantity supplied at this price.[5] Consequently, suppliers raise their prices. After some testing of market reactions and trial-and-error adjustments, the price will tend to settle at OP_1, the new equilibrium price, and quantity will tend to settle at OQ_1.

On the other hand, suppose that consumer demand for wheat products falls off, perhaps because of a great drop in the price of corn products. The demand for wheat now shifts *to the left,* as shown in Figure 3.11. What will be the effect on the equilibrium price of wheat? Clearly, the equilibrium price falls to OP_2, where the new demand curve intersects the supply curve.

In general, *a shift to the right in the demand curve results in an increase in the equilibrium price, and a shift to the left in the demand curve results in a*

[5] This shortage is equal to $OQ_1' - OQ$ in Figure 3.10.

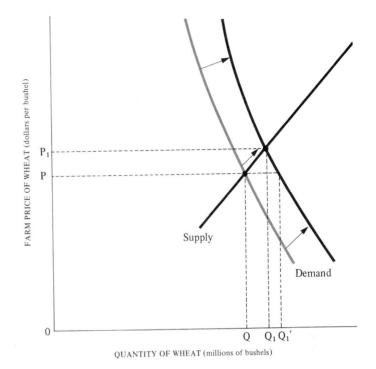

Figure 3.10
**Effect on the Equilibrium Price of a
Shift to the Right of the Market
Demand Curve** *This shift of the demand
curve to the right results in an increase
in the equilibrium price from OP to OP₁
and an increase in the equilibrium
quantity from OQ to OQ₁.*

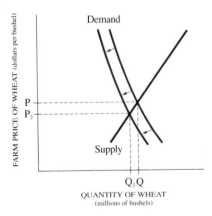

Figure 3.11
**Effect on the Equilibrium Price of a
Shift to the Left of the Market Demand
Curve** *This shift of the demand curve to
the left results in a decrease in the
equilibrium price from OP to OP₂ and a
decrease in the equilibrium quantity from
OQ to OQ₂.*

decrease in the equilibrium price. This is the lesson of Figures 3.10 and 3.11. Of course, this conclusion depends on the assumption that the supply curve slopes upward to the right, but, as we noted in a previous section, this assumption is generally true.

At this point, since all of this is theory, you may be wondering how well this theory works in practice. In 1972 and 1973, there was a vivid demonstration of the accuracy of this model in various agricultural markets, including wheat. Because of poor harvests abroad and greatly increased foreign demand for American wheat, the demand curve for wheat shifted markedly to the right. What happened to the price of wheat? In accord with our model, the price increased spectacularly, from about $1.35 a bushel in the early summer of 1972 to over $4.00 a year later. Anyone who witnessed this phenomenon could not help but be impressed by the usefulness of this model.

The Effects of Shifts in the Supply Curve

What happens to the equilibrium price of a product when its supply curve changes? For example, suppose that, because of technological advances in wheat production, wheat farmers are willing and able to supply more wheat at a given price than they used to, with the result that the supply curve shifts *to the right,* as shown in Figure 3.12. What will be the effect on the equilibrium price? Clearly, it will fall from *OP* (where the original supply curve intersects the demand curve) to *OP₃* (where the new supply curve intersects the demand curve).

On the other hand, suppose that the weather is poor, with the result that the supply curve shifts *to the left,* as shown in Figure 3.12. What will be the

49

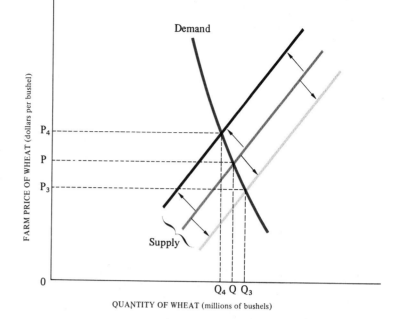

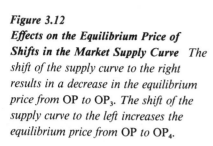

Figure 3.12
Effects on the Equilibrium Price of
Shifts in the Market Supply Curve The
shift of the supply curve to the right
results in a decrease in the equilibrium
price from OP to OP₃. The shift of the
supply curve to the left increases the
equilibrium price from OP to OP₄.

effect? The equilibrium price will increase from *OP* (where the original supply curve intersects the demand curve) to *OP₄* (where the new supply curve intersects the demand curve).

In 1984, law enforcement officers concerned with narcotics consumption in the United States were shown vividly what a shift to the right in the supply curve of a commodity will do. Because of a massive increase in the amount of coca production in South America, the supply curve for cocaine shifted dramatically to the right. The result was just what our theory would predict: a big drop in the price of cocaine. In some parts of the United States, cocaine sold in 1984 for one-half to one-third the price of a year before. According to one federal official, "At no time in the modern history of international drug control has the price of a drug dropped by half so quickly."

In general, a shift to the right in the supply curve results in a decrease in the equilibrium price, and a shift to the left in the supply curve results in an increase in the equilibrium price. Of course, this conclusion depends on the assumption that the demand curve slopes downward to the right, but, as we noted in a previous section, this assumption is generally true.

The Price System and the Determination of What Is Produced

Having described how prices are determined in free markets, we can now describe somewhat more fully how the price system goes about performing the four basic tasks that face any economic system. Let's begin by considering the determination of what society will produce: How does the price system carry out this task? Consumers indicate what goods and services they want in the market place, and producers try to meet these wants. More specifically, the demand curve for a product shows how much of that product consumers want at various prices. If consumers don't want much of it at a certain price, its demand curve will indicate that fact by being positioned close to the vertical axis at that price. In other words, the demand curve will show that, at this price for the product, the amount consumers will buy is small. On the other hand, if consumers want lots of the product at this price, its demand curve will be far from the vertical axis.

A product's demand curve is an important determinant of how much firms will produce of the product, since it indicates the amount of the product that will be demanded at each price. From the point of view of the producers, the demand curve indicates the amount they can sell at each price. In a capitalist economy, firms are in business to make money. Thus the manufacturers of any product will turn it out only if the amount of money they receive from consumers exceeds the cost of putting the product on the market. Acting in accord with the profit motive, firms are led to produce what the consumers desire. We saw in a previous section that if consumers' tastes shift in favor of foods containing wheat, the demand curve for wheat will shift to the right, which will result in an increase in the price of wheat. This increase will stimulate farmers to produce more wheat. For example, when the demand curve shifts to the right in Figure 3.10, the equilibrium quantity produced increases from OQ to OQ_1. Given the shift in the demand curve, it is profitable for firms to step up their production. Acting in their own self-interest, they are led to make production decisions geared to the wants of the consumers.

Thus the price system uses the self-interest of the producers to get them to produce what consumers want. Consumers register what they want in the market place by their purchasing decisions—shown by their demand curves. Producers can make more money by responding to consumer wants than by ignoring them. Consequently, they are led to produce what consumers want—and are willing to pay enough for to cover the producers' costs. Note that costs as well as demand determine what will be produced, and that producers are not forced by anyone to do anything. They can produce air conditioners for Eskimos if they like—and if they are prepared to absorb the losses. The price system uses prices to communicate the relevant signals to producers, and metes out the penalties and rewards in the form of losses or profits.

The Price System and the Determination of How Goods Are Produced

Next, consider how society determines how each good and service is produced. How does the price system carry out this task? The price of each resource gives producers an indication of how scarce this resource is, and how valuable it is in other uses. Clearly, firms should produce goods and services at minimum cost. Suppose that there are two ways of producing tables: Technique A and Technique B. Technique A requires 4 man-hours of labor and $10 worth of wood per table, whereas Technique B requires 5 man-hours of labor and $8 worth of wood. If the price of a man-hour of labor is $4, Technique A should be used since a table costs $26 with this

Example 3.2   Tennis Anyone?

In the early 1970s, the American public turned to tennis in droves, and many indoor tennis courts were built. In the late 1970s and early 1980s, the tennis fad began to fade. One indication: sales of tennis rackets fell by 20 percent in 1980. Also, during the late 1970s and early 1980s, the costs of operating an indoor tennis court increased markedly because of ballooning prices of electricity needed to light, heat, and air-condition the courts. For example, a 12-court facility near Philadelphia paid $8,600 a month for electricity in early 1981.*

(a) What sort of shift occurred during the late 1970s and early 1980s in the demand curve for playing time at indoor tennis courts? (b) Taken by itself, what effect did this shift in the demand curve have on the price per hour of playing time at indoor tennis courts? (c) Did the shift in the supply curve for playing time offset or reinforce this effect on price? (d) Based on the above facts, would you expect that the total amount of playing time sold by indoor tennis courts increased or decreased during the early 1980s? Why?

SOLUTION

(a) The demand curve shifted to the left because consumers demanded fewer hours of playing time at a given price. (b) Holding the supply curve constant, the leftward shift in the demand curve tended to reduce the price. (c) The supply curve shifted upward and to the left because of the increased price of electricity, a major input. Taken by itself, this shift in the supply curve tended to increase the price. Thus its effect was to offset the effect of the shift in the demand curve. (d) A leftward shift in both the demand curve and the supply curve would result in a decrease in the total amount of playing time sold (from 0Q to 0Q'), as shown below:

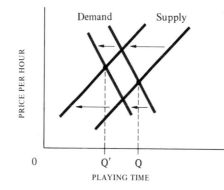

* See "As Racquet Fads Fade, Clubs Are Scrambling," *Philadelphia Inquirer,* May 4, 1981.

technique, as opposed to $28 with Technique B.[6] In other words, Technique A uses fewer resources per table.

The price system nudges producers to opt for Technique A rather than Technique B through profits and losses. If each table commands a price of $35, then by using Technique A, producers make a profit of $35 − $26 = $9 per table. If they use Technique B, they make a profit of $35 − $28 = $7 per table. Thus producers, if they maximize profit, will be led to adopt Technique A. Their desire for profit leads them to adopt the techniques that will enable society to get the most out of its resources. No one commands firms to use particular techniques. Washington officials do not order steel plants to substitute the basic oxygen process for open hearths, or petroleum refineries to substitute catalytic cracking for thermal cracking. It is all done through the impersonal market place.

You should not, however, get the idea that the price system operates with kid gloves. Suppose all firms producing tables used Technique B until this past year, when Technique A was developed: in other words, Technique A is based on a new technology. Given this technological change, the supply curve for tables will shift to the right, as we saw in a previous section, and the price of a table will fall. Suppose it drops to $27. If some firm insists on sticking with Technique B, it will lose money at the rate of $1 a table; and as these losses mount, the firm's owners will become increasingly uncomfortable. The firm will either switch to Technique A or go bankrupt. The price system leans awfully hard on producers who try to ignore its signals.

The Price System and the Determination of Who Gets What

Let's turn now to how society's output will be distributed among the people: How does the price system carry out this task? How much people receive in goods and services depends on their money income, which in turn is determined under the price system by the amount of various resources that they own and by the price of each resource. Thus, under the price system, each person's income is determined in the market place: the person comes to the market place with certain resources to sell, and his or her income depends on how much he or she can get for them.

The question of who gets what is solved at two levels by the price system. Consider an individual product—for example, the tables discussed in the previous section. For the individual product, the question of who gets what is solved by the equality of quantity demanded and quantity supplied. If the price of these tables is at its equilibrium level, the quantity demanded will equal the quantity supplied. Consumers who are willing and able to pay the equilibrium price (or more) get the tables, while those who are unwilling or unable to pay it do not get them. It is just as simple—and as impersonal—as that. It doesn't matter whether you are a nice guy or a scoundrel, or whether you are a connoisseur of tables or someone who doesn't know good workmanship from poor: all that matters is whether you are able and willing to pay the equilibrium price.

[6] To obtain these figures, note that the cost with Technique A is 4 man-hours times $4 plus $10, or $26, while the cost with Technique B is 5 man-hours times $4 plus $8, or $28.

Next, consider the question of who gets what at a somewhat more fundamental level. After all, whether a consumer is able and willing to pay the equilibrium price for a good depends on his money income. Thus the super-rich can pay the equilibrium price for an astonishing variety of things, whereas those in abject poverty can scrape up the equilibrium price for very little. As we have already seen, a consumer's money income depends on the amount of resources of various kinds that he or she owns and the price that he or she can get for them. Some people have lots of resources: they are endowed with skill and intelligence and industry, or they have lots of capital or land. Other people have little in the way of resources. Moreover, some people have resources that command a high price, while others have resources that are of little monetary value. The result is that, under the price system, some consumers get a lot more of society's output than do other consumers.

The Price System and Economic Growth

Let's turn now to the task of determining a society's rate of growth of per capita income. How does the price system do this? As pointed out in the previous chapter, a nation's rate of increase of per capita income depends on the rate of growth of its resources and the rate of increase of the efficiency with which they are used. First, consider the rate of growth of society's resources. The price system controls the amount of new capital goods produced much as it controls the amount of consumer goods produced. Similarly, the price system influences the amount society invests in educating, training, and upgrading its labor resources. To a considerable extent, the amount invested in such resource-augmenting activities is determined by the profitability of such investments, which is determined in turn by the pattern of prices.

Next, consider the rate of increase of the efficiency with which a society's resources are used. Clearly, this factor depends heavily on the rate of technological change. If technology is advancing at a rapid rate, it should be possible to get more and more out of a society's resources. But if technology is advancing rather slowly, it is likely to be difficult to get much more out of them. The price system affects the rate of technological change in a variety of ways: it influences the profitability of investing in research and development, the profitability of introducing new processes and products into commercial practice, and the profitability of accepting technological change—as well as the losses involved in spurning it.

The price system establishes strong incentives for firms to introduce new technology. Any firm that can find a cheaper way to produce an existing product, or a way to produce a better product, will have a profitable jump on its competitors. Until its competitors can do the same thing, this firm can reap higher profits than it otherwise could. Of course, these higher profits will eventually be competed away, as other firms begin to imitate this firm's innovation. But lots of money can be made in the period during which this firm has a lead over its competitors. These profits are an important incentive for the introduction of new technology.

Two Case Studies

THE PRICE SYSTEM IN ACTION BEHIND ENEMY LINES

Just as general discussions of tennis will take a neophyte only so far, after which he or she must watch and participate in a few matches, so a general discussion of the price system will take a student only so far. Then he or she should look at real-life examples of the price system at work. Our first illustration of the price system in operation is a prisoner-of-war camp in World War II. This case is not chosen because of its inherent importance, but because of its simplicity. Just as certain elementary forms of life illustrate important biological principles in a simple way, so the economic organization of a prisoner-of-war camp is an elementary form of economic system that illustrates certain important economic principles simply and well.

The prisoner-of-war camp was so elementary because no goods were produced there. All commodities were provided by the country running the camp, by the Red Cross, and by other outside donors. Each prisoner received an equal amount of food and supplies—canned milk, jam, butter, cookies, cigarettes, and so on. In addition, private parcels of clothing, cigarettes, and other supplies were received, with different prisoners, of course, receiving different quantities. Because no goods were produced in the prisoner-of-war camp, the first two tasks of an economic system (What will be produced? How will it be produced?) were not relevant; neither was the fourth task (What provision is to be made for growth?).

All that did matter in this elementary economic system was the third task: to determine who would consume the various available goods. At first blush, the answer may seem obvious: each prisoner would consume the goods he received from the detaining country, the Red Cross, and private packages. But this assumes that prisoners would not trade goods back and forth ("I'll swap you a cigarette for some milk"), which is clearly unrealistic. After all, some prisoners smoked cigarettes, others did not; some liked jam and didn't like canned beef, others liked canned beef and didn't like jam. Thus there was bound to be exchange of this sort, and the real question is in what way and on what terms such exchange took place.

How did the prisoners go about exchanging goods? According to one observer, the process developed as follows:

> Starting with simple direct barter, such as a nonsmoker giving a smoker friend his cigarette issue in exchange for a chocolate ration, more complex exchanges soon became an accepted custom. . . . Within a week or two, as the volume of trade grew, rough scales of exchange values came into existence. [Some prisoners], who had at first exchanged tinned beef for practically any other foodstuff, began to insist on jam and margarine. It was realized that a tin of jam was worth one-half pound of margarine plus something else, that a cigarette issue was worth several chocolate issues, and a tin of diced carrots was worth practically nothing. . . . By the end of the month, there was a lively trade in all commodities and their relative values were well known, and expressed not in terms of one another—one didn't quote [jam] in terms of sugar—but in terms of cigarettes. The cigarette became the standard of value.[7]

[7] R. A. Radford, "The Economic Organization of a P.O.W. Camp," reprinted in E. Mansfield, *Principles of Microeconomics: Readings, Issues, and Cases*, 4th ed., New York: Norton, 1983.

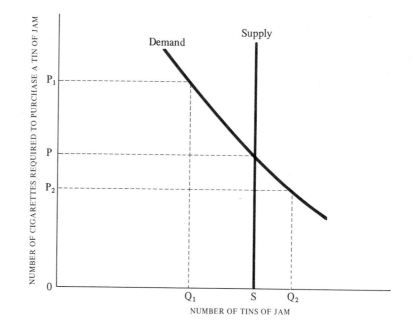

Figure 3.13
Determinants of Equilibrium Price of a Tin of Jam (in terms of cigarettes) in a P.O.W. Camp   *The market supply for jam is fixed at OS tins. Thus the equilibrium price of a tin of jam is OP cigarettes. If the price were OP_1, OQ_1 tins would be demanded; if the price were OP_2, OQ_2 tins would be demanded.*

Thus the prisoners used the price system to solve the problem of allocating the available supply of goods among consumers. A market developed for each good. This market had, of course, both a demand and a supply side. Each good had its price—but this price was quoted in cigarettes, not dollars and cents. These markets were not started in a self-conscious, deliberate way. No one said, "Let's adopt the price system to allocate available supplies," or "Let's vote on whether or not to adopt the price system." Instead, the system just evolved . . . and it worked.

To see how the supply of a particular good—jam, say—was allocated, look at Figure 3.13, which shows the market supply curve for jam. In the short run, this supply was fixed, so this supply curve is a vertical line. Figure 3.13 also provides the market demand curve for jam, which shows the amount of jam the prisoners wanted to consume at various prices of jam—expressed in terms of cigarettes. For example, the prisoners wanted OQ_1 tins of jam when a tin of jam cost OP_1 cigarettes, and OQ_2 tins of jam when a tin of jam cost OP_2 cigarettes. For the quantity demanded to equal the available supply, the price of a tin of jam had to be OP cigarettes; one tin of jam had to exchange for OP cigarettes. At this price, the available supply of jam was rationed, without resort to fights among prisoners or intervention by the prison authorities. Those prisoners who could and would pay the price had the jam—and there were just enough such consumers to exhaust the available supply. Moreover, this held true for each of the other goods (including cigarettes) as well.

THE PRICE SYSTEM IN ACTION ON THE GREAT WHITE WAY

It is a long way from a prisoner-of-war camp to the Broadway theater, but economics, like any good tool of analysis, applies to a very wide variety of problems. In this section, we discuss the theater's pricing problems—and the role of the price system in helping to solve these problems. Prices for tickets to Broadway shows are established at levels that are much the same whether the show is a success or a flop. An orchestra ticket to *Kelly* (which managed to hold out for one performance before closing) cost about as much as an orchestra ticket to such hits as *Fiddler on the Roof* or *Cats*. And once a play opens, the price of a ticket remains much the same whether the play is greeted with universal praise or with discontented critics and customers.

Because of these pricing methods, the Broadway theater has been beset for many years by serious problems. Here they are described by two veteran observers of the Broadway stage:

> For centuries the sale of theater tickets has brought on corruption and confusion. When there are more buyers than sellers, a black market results. The so-called "retail" price, the price printed on the ticket, becomes meaningless. Speculation doubles, triples, or quadruples the "real" as opposed to the "legal" asking price. A smash hit on Broadway means "ice"–the difference between the real and legal prices–a well-hidden but substantial cash flow that is divided among shadowy middlemen. Ticket scandals break out in New York as regularly as the flu. The scenario is familiar. A play opens and becomes a superhit. Tickets become difficult, then impossible, to obtain. There are letters to the newspapers.... Shocking corruption is discovered. Someone ... is convicted of overcharging and accepting illegal gratuities. Someone may even go to jail. The black market, valiantly scotched, *never stops for a single moment.*[8]

Besides enriching crooked box-office men and managers, as well as other shadowy elements of society, the black market for theater tickets has the additional undesirable effect of excluding the authors, composers, directors, and stars of the play from participation in the premium revenue. Almost all of these people receive a percentage of the play's revenues; and if the revenues at the box office are less than what customers pay for their seats (because of "ice"), these people receive less than they would if no black market existed. The amount of "ice" can be substantial. For example, Rodgers and Hammerstein estimated that, at one performance of their play, *South Pacific,* the public probably paid about $25,000 for tickets with a face value of $7,000, the amount turned in at the box office.

To focus on the problem here, let's look at the market for tickets to a particular performance of *A Chorus Line* (one of Broadway's all-time big hits) when it was at the height of its popularity. Since the supply of tickets to a given performance of this play is fixed, the market supply curve, shown in Figure 3.14, is a vertical line at the quantity of tickets corresponding to the capacity of the theater. The price set officially on a ticket was about $20. But because the show was enormously popular, the market demand curve was *D* in Figure 3.14, and the equilibrium price for a ticket was $50.[9]

Figure 3.14 makes the nature of the problem apparent: at the official price of $20, the quantity of tickets demanded is much greater than the quantity supplied. Supply and demand don't match. Obviously, there is an incentive for people to buy the tickets from the box office at $20 and sell

---

[8] S. Little and A. Cantor, *The Playmakers,* New York: Norton, 1970, p. 220.
[9] This figure is only a rough estimate, but it is good enough for present purposes.

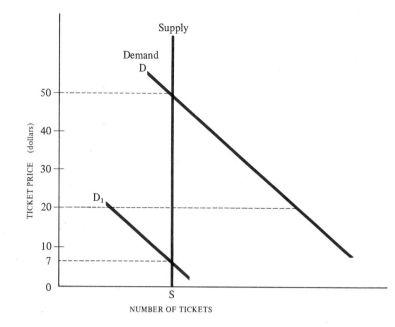

Figure 3.14
**Equilibrium Price for Tickets to A
Chorus Line** *The market supply for
tickets is fixed at* OS *per performance. If
the demand curve is* D, *the equilibrium
price of a ticket is $50. (If the demand
curve is* D_1, *the equilibrium price is $7.)
If the demand curve is* D *and the price of
a ticket is $20, the quantity of tickets
demanded will far exceed the quantity
supplied.*

them at the higher prices customers are willing to pay. There is also an
incentive for box-office men to sell them surreptitiously at higher prices
and turn in only $20. The price system cannot play the role it did in the
prisoner-of-war camp for jam and other goods. It cannot act as an effective rationing device because, to do so, the price of tickets would have to
increase to its equilibrium level, $50.

Many theater experts believe that the solution to Broadway's pricing
problems lies in allowing the price system to work more effectively by
permitting ticket prices to vary depending on a show's popularity. For
example, the official ticket price would be allowed to rise to $50 for *A
Chorus Line.* On the other hand, if *A Chorus Line* had been much less
popular and its market demand curve had been D_1 in Figure 3.14, its
official ticket price would have been allowed to fall to $7. In this way, the
black market for tickets would be eliminated, since the equilibrium
price—which equates supply and demand—would be the official price.
"Ice" would also be eliminated, since there would be no difference between the official and the actual price paid, and the people responsible for
the show would receive its full receipts, not share them with crooked
box-office men and illegal operators.[10]

Price Ceilings and Price Supports

During national emergencies, the government sometimes puts a lid on
prices, not allowing them to reach their equilibrium levels. For example,

[10] Steps have been taken toward somewhat greater price flexibility for Broadway shows.
For example, in the mid-1970s, a booth was established in Times Square where tickets to
some shows were on sale at (approximately) half of the official ticket price. In this way, a
show was enabled to cut its price, if it was unable to fill the theater at the official ticket price.
Apparently, this innovation has worked quite well, both for the producers of the shows and
the theatergoing public.

PRICE CEILINGS AND PRICE SUPPORTS

Basic Idea #6: Governments frequently establish price ceilings or price floors in an attempt to help particular parts of the population. Such intervention prevents the price system from doing the job expected of it. Price ceilings tend to result in shortages, and price floors tend to result in surpluses. Both can cause serious social waste.

during World War II, the government did not allow the prices of various foodstuffs to rise to their equilibrium levels, because it felt that this would have been inequitable (and highly unpopular). Under such circumstances, the quantity demanded of a product exceeds the quantity supplied. In other words, the situation is like that in Figure 3.14, where the quantity of tickets demanded for *A Chorus Line* exceeds the quantity supplied at a price of $20. There is a shortage.

Since the price system is not allowed to perform its rationing function, some formal system of rationing or allocating the available supply of the product may be required. Thus, in World War II, families were issued ration coupons which determined how much they could buy of various commodities. And in 1979, when the Organization of Petroleum Exporting Countries cut back oil production and reduced exports of oil to the United States, there was serious talk that gasoline and oil might be rationed in a similar way. Such rationing schemes may be justified in emergencies (of reasonably short duration), but they can result eventually in serious distortions, since prices are not allowed to do the job normally expected of them.

To illustrate the sorts of problems that can arise when price ceilings are imposed, consider the rent ceilings that exist on some apartments in New York City. Originally imposed to prevent dwelling costs from soaring during World War II, these ceilings have been defended on the ground that they help the poor, at least in the short run. Although this may be so, they have also resulted in a shortage of housing in New York City. Because they have pushed the price of housing below the equilibrium price, less housing has been supplied than has been demanded. The depressed price of housing has discouraged investors from building new housing, and has made it unprofitable for some owners of existing housing to maintain their buildings. Thus, although it would be socially desirable to channel more resources into New York housing, the rent ceilings have prevented this from occurring.

Government authorities may also impose price floors—or price supports, as they often are called. These floors are generally defended on the ground that they enable the producers of the good in question to make a better living. For example, the federal government has imposed price supports on a wide range of agricultural commodities, the purpose being to increase farm incomes. Just as in the case in Figure 3.14 where the demand curve is D_1 and where a price floor of $20 exists, the result is that the quantity supplied exceeds the quantity demanded at the support price. Thus there is a surplus of the commodity—and, in the case of agricultural commodities, the government has to buy up and store these surpluses. As in the case of a price ceiling, the result is that the price system is not allowed to do the job expected of it.

Whether price ceilings or floors are socially desirable depends on whether the loss in social efficiency resulting from them is exceeded by the gain in equity they achieve. As indicated above, their purpose is to help or protect particular parts of the population which would be treated inequitably by the unfettered price system. Since one person's view of what is equitable differ from another person's, this is an area of considerable controversy. More will be said about both price ceilings and floors in subsequent chapters, particularly Chapters 4 and 21.

The Circular Flows of Money and Products

So far we have been concerned largely with the workings of a single market—the market for wheat or tables or jam or tickets to *A Chorus Line*. But how do all of the various markets fit together? This is a very important question. Perhaps the best way to begin answering it is to distinguish between product markets and resource markets. As their names indicate, **product markets** *are markets where products are bought and sold; and* **resource markets** *are markets where resources are bought and sold.* Let's first consider product markets. As shown in Figure 3.15, firms provide products to consumers in product markets, and receive money in return. The money the firms receive is their receipts; to consumers, on the other hand, it represents their expenditures.

Next, let's consider resource markets. Figure 3.15 shows that consumers provide resources—including labor—to firms in resource markets, and they receive money in return. The money the consumers receive is their income; to firms, on the other hand, it represents their costs. Note that the flow of resources and products in Figure 3.15 is counterclockwise: that is, *consumers provide resources to firms which in turn provide goods and services to consumers.* On the other hand, the flow of money in Figure 3.15 is clockwise: that is, *firms pay money for resources to consumers who in turn use the money to buy goods and services from the firms.* Both flows—that of resources and products, and that of money—go on simultaneously and repeatedly.

So long as consumers spend all their income, the flow of money income from firms to consumers is exactly equal to the flow of expenditure from consumers to firms. Thus these circular flows, like Ole' Man River, just keep rolling along. As a first approximation, this is a perfectly good model. But as we pointed out in Chapter 1, capitalist economies have experienced periods of widespread unemployment and severe inflation that this model cannot explain. Also, note that our simple economy in Figure 3.15 has no

Figure 3.15

The Circular Flows of Money and Products *In product markets, consumers exchange money for products and firms exchange products for money. In resource markets, consumers exchange resources for money and firms exchange money for resources.*

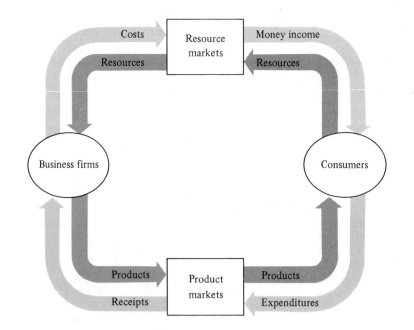

government sector. In the following chapter, we shall bring the government into the picture. Under pure capitalism, the government would play a limited role in the economic system, but in the mixed capitalistic system we have in the United States, the government plays an important role indeed.

Test Yourself

1. Will each of the following tend to shift the demand curve for toasters to the right, to the left, or not at all? (a) Consumer incomes rise by 20 percent. (b) The price of bread falls by 10 percent. (c) The price of electricity increases by 5 percent. (d) Medical reports indicate that toast prevents heart attacks. (e) The cost of producing a toaster increases by 10 percent.

2. Will each of the following tend to shift the supply curve for toasters to the right, to the left, or not at all? (a) The wage of workers producing toasters increases by 5 percent. (b) The price of the metal used to make toasters falls by 10 percent. (c) The price of bread falls by 10 percent. (d) Consumer incomes rise by 20 percent. (e) New technology makes toaster production much more efficient.

3. If both the demand and supply curve for a product shift to the right, can one predict whether the product's equilibrium price will increase or decrease? Can one predict whether its equilibrium quantity will increase or decrease?

4. In most years, New Jersey blueberry farmers can get up to 80 cents a pint. In the summer of 1984, prices were pushed to as low as 30 cents a pint. (a) Why do you think this happened? (b) New Jersey farmers complained that they couldn't make money at the 30-cent price. Should the government establish a price floor for blueberries? Explain.

5. Suppose that the American public becomes convinced that beets are more desirable than they have been, and string beans are less so. Describe the shifts that will occur in the demand and supply curves in the relevant markets, and the mechanisms that will signal and trigger a redeployment of resources.

Summary

1. There are two sides of every market: the demand side and the supply side. The demand side can be represented by the market demand curve, which almost always slopes downward to the right and whose location depends on consumer tastes, the number and income of consumers, and the prices of other commodities.

2. The supply side of the market can be represented by the market supply curve, which generally slopes upward to the right and whose location depends on technology and resource prices.

3. The equilibrium price and equilibrium quantity of the commodity are given by the intersection of the market demand and supply curves. If conditions remain reasonably stable for a time, the actual price and quantity should move close to the equilibrium price and quantity.

4. Changes in the position and shape of the demand curve—in response to changes in consumer tastes, income, population, and prices of other commodities—result in changes in the equilibrium price and equilibrium output of a product. Similarly, changes in the position and shape of the supply curve—in response to changes in technology and resource prices, among other things—also result in changes in the equilibrium price and equilibrium output of a product.

5. To determine what goods and services society will produce, the price system sets up incentives for firms to produce what consumers want. To the extent that they produce what consumers want and are willing to pay for, firms reap profits; to the extent that they don't, they experience losses.

6. The price system sets up strong incentives for firms to produce goods at minimum cost. These incentives take the form of profits for firms that minimize costs and losses for firms that operate with relatively high costs.

7. To determine who gets what, the price system results in each person's receiving an income that depends on the quantity of resources he or she owns and the prices that they command.

8. The price system establishes incentives for activities that result in increases in a society's per capita income. For example, it influences the amount of new capital goods produced, as well as the amount society spends on educating its labor force and improving its technology.

9. There are circular flows of money and products in a capitalist economy. In product markets, firms provide products to consumers and receive money in return. In resource markets, consumers provide resources to firms, and receive money in return.

Concepts for Review

Consumers	Market demand curve	Equilibrium price
Firms	Supply	Actual price
Markets	Market supply curve	Product market
Perfect competition	Equilibrium	Resource market
Demand		

CHAPTER 4

The Economic Role
of the Government

To state that the United States is a mixed capitalist system, in which both government decisions and the price system play important roles, is hardly to provoke a controversy. But going a step beyond takes us into areas where viewpoints often diverge. The proper functions of government and the desirable size and nature of government expenditures and taxes are not matters on which all agree. Indeed, the question of how big government should be, and what its proper functions are, is hotly debated by conservatives and liberals throughout the land. This is only a preliminary airing of many of these issues. As the base of economic analysis is broadened in subsequent chapters, much more will be said on these matters, and you will be in a far better position to judge them for yourself.

Limitations of the Price System

Despite its many advantages, the price system suffers from limitations. Because these limitations are both prominent and well known, no one believes that the price system, left to its own devices, can be trusted to solve all society's basic economic problems. To a considerable extent, the government's role in the economy has developed in response to the limitations of the price system, which are described below.

Distribution of Income. There is *no* reason to believe that the distribution of income generated by the price system is *fair* or, in some sense, *best*. Most people feel that the distribution of income generated by the price system should be altered to suit humanitarian needs; in particular, that help should be given to the poor. Both liberals and conservatives tend to agree on this score, although there are arguments over the extent to which the poor should be helped and the conditions under which they should be eligible for help. But the general principle that the government should step in to redistribute income in favor of the poor is generally accepted in the United States today.[1]

Public Goods. Some goods and services *cannot be provided through the price system because there is no way to exclude citizens from consuming the goods whether they pay for them or not.* For example, there is no way to prevent citizens from benefiting from national expenditures on defense, whether they pay money toward defense or not. Consequently, the price system cannot be used to provide such goods; no one will pay for them since they will receive them whether they pay or not. Further, some goods, like the quality of the environment and national defense (and others cited below), *can be enjoyed by one person without depriving others of the same enjoyment.* Such goods are called **public goods.** The government provides many public goods. Such goods are consumed collectively, or jointly, and it is inefficient to try to price them in a market. They tend to be indivisible; thus they frequently cannot be split into pieces and be bought and sold in a market.

External Economies and Diseconomies. In cases where *the production or consumption of a good by one firm or consumer has adverse or beneficial uncompensated effects on other firms or consumers, the price system will not operate effectively.* An **external economy** is said to occur when consumption or production by one person or firm results in uncompensated benefits to another person or firm. A good example of an external economy exists where fundamental research carried out by one firm is used by another firm. (To cite one such case, there were external economies from the Bell Telephone Laboratories' invention of the transistor. Many electronics firms, such as Texas Instruments and Fairchild, benefited considerably from Bell's research.) Where external economies exist, it is generally agreed that the price system will produce too little of the good in question and that the government should supplement the amount produced by private enterprise. This is the basic rationale for much of the government's huge investment in basic science. An **external diseconomy** is said to occur when consumption or production by one person or firm results in uncompensated costs to another person or firm. A good example of an external diseconomy occurs when a firm dumps pollutants into a stream and makes the water unfit for use by firms and people downstream. Where activities result in external diseconomies, it is generally agreed that the price system will tolerate too much of the activity and that the government should curb it. For example, as we shall see in Chapter 20, the government, in keeping with this doctrine, has involved itself in environmental protection and the reduction of air and water pollution.[2]

---

[1] Also, because the wealthy have more "dollar votes" than the poor, the sorts of goods and services that society produces will reflect this fact. Thus luxuries for the rich may be produced in larger amounts and necessities for the poor may be produced in smaller amounts than some critics regard as sensible and equitable. This is another frequently encountered criticism of the price system.

[2] The effects of external economies and diseconomies can also be taken care of by legal arrangements that assign liabilities for damages and compensate for benefits. However, such arrangements often are impractical or too costly to be used.

What Functions Should the Government Perform?

There are wide differences of opinion on the proper role of government in economic affairs. Although it is generally agreed that the government should redistribute income in favor of the poor, provide public goods, and offset the effects of external economies and diseconomies, there is considerable disagreement over how far the government should go in these areas, and what additional areas the government should be responsible for. Some people feel that "big government" is already a problem; that government is doing too much. Others believe that the public sector of the economy is being undernourished and that government should be allowed to do more. This is a fundamental question, and one that involves a great deal more than economics.

Conservative View. On the one hand, conservatives, such as Stanford University's Nobel laureate, Milton Friedman, believe that the government's role should be limited severely. They feel that economic and political freedom is likely to be undermined by excessive reliance on the state. Moreover, they tend to be skeptical about the government's ability to solve the social and economic problems at hand. They feel that the prevailing faith in the government's power to make a substantial dent in these problems is unreasonable, and they call for more and better information concerning the sorts of tasks government can reasonably be expected to do—and do well. They point to the slowness of the government bureaucracy, the difficulty in controlling huge government organizations, the inefficiencies political considerations can breed, and the difficulties in telling whether government programs are successful or not. On the basis of these considerations, they argue that the government's role should be carefully circumscribed.

Liberal View. To such arguments, liberals like Nobel laureate Paul Samuelson of the Massachusetts Institute of Technology respond with telling salvos of their own. Just as conservatives tend to be skeptical of the government's ability to solve important social and economic problems, so liberals tend to be skeptical about the price system's ability to solve these problems. They point to the limitations of the price system, discussed above, and they assert that the government can do a great deal to overcome these limitations, by regulating private activity and by subsidizing and providing goods and services that the private sector produces too little of. Liberals tend to be less concerned than conservatives about the effects on personal freedom of greater governmental intervention in the economy. They point out that the price system also involves coercion, since the fact that the price system awards the available goods and services to those who can pay their equilibrium price can be viewed as a form of coercion. In their view, people who are awarded only a pittance by the price system are coerced into discomfort and malnutrition.[3]

[3] See P. Samuelson, "The Economic Role of Private Activity," and G. Stigler, "The Government of the Economy," *A Dialogue on the Proper Economic Role of the State,* University of Chicago, Graduate School of Business, Selected Paper no. 7, in E. Mansfield, *Principles of Microeconomics: Readings, Issues, and Cases,* 4th ed.

Establishing "Rules of the Game"

Although there is considerable disagreement over the proper role of the government, both conservatives and liberals agree that it must do certain things. The first of these is to establish the "rules of the game"—that is, a legal, social, and competitive framework enabling the price system to function as it should. Specifically, *the government must see to it that contracts are enforced, that private ownership is protected, and that fraud is prevented.* Clearly, these matters must be tended to if the price system is to work properly. Also, *the government must maintain order (through the establishment of police and other forces), establish a monetary system (so that money can be used to facilitate trade and exchange), and provide standards for the weight and quality of products.*

As an example of this sort of government intervention, consider the Pure Food and Drug Act. This act, originally passed in 1906 and subsequently amended in various ways, protects the consumer against improper and fraudulent activities on the part of producers of foods and drugs. It prohibits the merchandising of impure or falsely labeled food or drugs, and it forces producers to specify the quantity and quality of the contents on labels. These requirements strengthen the price system. Without them, the typical consumer would be unable to tell whether food or drugs are pure or properly labeled. Unless consumers can be sure that they are getting what they pay for, the basic logic underlying the price system breaks down. Similar regulation and legislation have been instituted in fields other than food and drugs—and for similar reasons.

FDA inspectors

MAINTAINING A COMPETITIVE FRAMEWORK

Besides establishing a legal and social framework that will enable the price system to do its job, *the government must also see to it that markets remain reasonably competitive.* Only if they are will prices reflect consumer desires properly. If, on the other hand, markets are dominated by a few sellers (or a few buyers), prices may be "rigged" by these sellers (or buyers) to promote their own interests. For example, if a single firm is the sole producer of aluminum, it is a safe bet that this firm will establish a higher price than if there were many aluminum producers competing among themselves. The unfortunate thing about prices determined in noncompetitive markets—rigged prices, if you will—is that they give incorrect signals concerning what consumers want and how scarce resources and commodities are. Producers, responding to these incorrect signals, do not produce the right things in the right quantities. Consumers respond to these incorrect signals by not supplying the right resources in the right amounts, and by not consuming the proper amounts of the goods that are produced. Thus the price system is not permitted to solve the four basic economic problems properly in the absence of reasonable competition.

To try to encourage and preserve competition, the Congress has enacted a series of **antitrust laws,** such as the Sherman Antitrust Act and the Clayton Act, and it has established the Federal Trade Commission. The antitrust laws make it illegal for firms to collude or to attempt to monopolize the sale of a product. Both conservative and liberal economists, with some notable exceptions, tend to favor the intent and operation of the antitrust laws.

Redistribution of Income

We have already noted at several points the general agreement that the government should redistribute income in favor of the poor. In other words, *it is usually felt that help should be given to people who are ill, handicapped, old and infirm, disabled, and unable for other reasons to provide for themselves.* To some extent, the nation has decided that income—or at least a certain minimum income—should be divorced from productive services. Of course, this doesn't mean that people who are too lazy to work should be given a handout. It does mean that people who cannot provide for themselves should be helped. To implement this principle, various payments are made by the government to needy people—including the aged, the handicapped, the unemployed, and pensioners.

These **welfare payments** are to some extent a "depression baby," for they grew substantially during the Great Depression of the 1930s, when relief payments became a necessity. But they also represent a feeling shared by a large segment of the population that human beings should be assured that, however the wheel of fortune spins and whatever number comes up, they will not starve and their children will not be deprived of a healthy environment and basic schooling. Of course, someone has to pay for this. Welfare payments allow the poor to take more from the nation's output than they produce. In general, the more affluent members of society contribute some of their claims on output to pay for these programs, their contributions being in the form of taxes. By using its expenditures to help certain groups and by taxing other groups to pay for these programs, the government accomplishes each year, without revolt and without bayonets, a substantial redistribution of income. This is a crucial aspect of the government's role in our economy.

Stabilizing the Economy

It is also generally agreed that *the government should promote the maintenance of reasonably full employment with reasonably stable prices.* Capitalist economies have tended to alternate between booms and depressions in the past. The Great Depression of the 1930s hit the American economy—and the world economy—a particularly devastating blow, putting millions of people out of work and in desperate shape. When World War II ended, the American people vowed that they would not let a depression of this sort occur again. Congress passed the Employment Act of 1946, which stated that it was the responsibility of the federal government to maintain full employment in the United States. In particular, the federal government was not supposed to tolerate unemployment of the sort that materialized during severe depressions in the past.

Besides trying to maintain full employment, the government must also try to maintain a reasonably stable price level. No economy can function well if prices are gyrating wildly. Through its control of the money supply and its decisions regarding expenditures and taxation, the government has considerable impact on the price level, as well as on the level of employment. Unfortunately, during the 1970s in particular, the government was not very successful in maintaining price stability. According to many economists, the government's own policies (described in Chapters 12 and 16) contributed to this inflation.

Providing Public Goods

As we have indicated, the government provides many public goods. Let's consider the nature of public goods in more detail.

What Is a Public Good? One hallmark of a public good is that it can be consumed by one person without diminishing the amount that other people consume of it. Public goods tend to be relatively indivisible; they often come in such large units that they cannot be broken into pieces that can be bought or sold in ordinary markets. *Once such goods are produced, there often is no way to bar certain citizens from consuming them.* Whether or not citizens contribute toward their cost, they benefit from them. As pointed out in a previous section, this means that the price system cannot be used to handle effectively the production and distribution of such goods.

National Defense: A Public Good. National defense is a public good. The benefits of expenditure on national defense extend to the entire nation. Extension of the benefits of national defense to an additional citizen does not mean that any other citizen gets less of these benefits. Also, there is no way of preventing citizens from benefiting from them, whether they contribute to their cost or not. Thus there is no way to use the price system to provide for national defense. Since it is a public good, national defense, if it is to reach an adequate level, must be provided by the government. Similarly with flood control, environmental protection, and a host of other such services.

Decision Making Regarding Public Goods. Essentially, deciding how much to produce of a public good is a political decision. The citizens of the United States elect senators and congressmen who decide how much should be spent on national defense, and how it should be spent. These elected representatives are responsive to special-interest groups, as well as to the people as a whole. Many special-interest groups lobby hard for the production of certain public goods. For example, an alliance of military and industrial groups presses for increased defense expenditures, and other interested groups promote expenditures on other functions.

The tax system is used to pay for the production of public goods. In effect, the government says to each citizen, "Fork over a certain amount of money to pay for the expenses incurred by the government." The amount a particular citizen is assessed may depend on his or her income (as in the income tax), the value of all or specific types of his or her property (as in the property tax), the amount he or she spends on certain types of goods and services (as in the sales tax), or on still other criteria. In the 1980s, the tax system has often been the object of enormous controversy. Much more will be said about the tax system, and the controversies swirling around it, in a later section of this chapter and in the next chapter.

Externalities

It is generally agreed that *the government should encourage the production of goods and services that entail external economies and discourage the production of those that entail external diseconomies.* Take the pollution of air and water. When a firm or individual dumps wastes into the water or air, other firms or individuals often must pay all or part of the cost of putting the water or air back into a usable condition. Thus the disposal of these wastes entails external diseconomies. Unless the government prohibits certain kinds of pollution, or enforces air and water quality standards, or charges polluters in accord with the amount of waste they dump into the environment, there will be socially undesirable levels of pollution.

Effects of External Diseconomies. To see how such externalities affect the social desirability of the output of a competitive industry, consider Figure 4.1, where the industry's demand and supply curves are contained in the top panel. As shown there, the equilibrium output of the industry is OQ_0. If the industry results in no external economies or diseconomies, this is likely to be the socially optimal output. But what if the industry results in external diseconomies, such as the pollution described above? Then the industry's supply curve does not fully reflect the true social costs of producing the product. The supply curve that reflects these social costs is S_1, which, as shown in the middle panel of Figure 4.1, lies to the left of the industry's supply curve. The optimal output of the good is OQ_1, which is less than the competitive output, OQ_0.

What can the government do to correct the situation? There are a variety of ways that it can intervene to reduce the industry's output from OQ_0 to OQ_1. For example, it can impose taxes on the industry, as we shall see in Chapter 5. If these taxes are of the right type and amount, they will result in the desired reduction of output.

Effects of External Economies. What if the industry results in external economies? For example, what if the manufacture of one industrial product makes it cheaper to produce other products? Then the industry's demand curve underestimates the true social benefits of producing the product. The demand curve that reflects these social benefits correctly is D_1, which, as shown in the bottom panel of Figure 4.1, lies to the right of the industry's demand curve. The optimal output of the good is OQ_2, which is greater than the competitive output, OQ_0.

As in the case where the industry results in external diseconomies, the government can intervene in various ways to change the industry's output. But in this case, the object is to increase, not decrease, its output. To accomplish this, the government can, among other things, grant subsidies to the industry. If they are of the right type and amount, they can be used to increase the industry's output from OQ_0 to OQ_2.

Size and Nature of Government Activities

HOW BIG IS THE GOVERNMENT?

Up to this point, we have been concerned primarily with the reasons why the government must intervene in our economy—and the types of role it

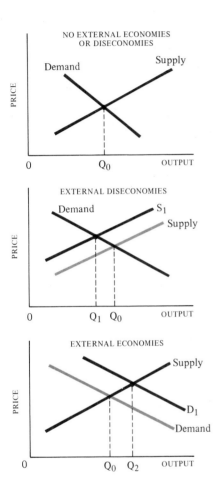

Figure 4.1
Effect of External Economies and Diseconomies on the Optimal Output of a Competitive Industry *The optimal output is* OQ_0 *if neither external economies nor diseconomies are present. If there are external diseconomies, curve* S_1 *reflects the true social costs of producing the product, and* OQ_1 *is the optimal output. If there are external economies, curve* D_1 *reflects the true social benefits of producing the product, and* OQ_2 *is the optimal output.*

Example 4.1   The Economics of Urban Blight

During the past 30 years, the federal government has promoted and encouraged the redevelopment of the inner core of our major cities. Consider two adjacent urban properties. Suppose that the two owners, Mr. Lombardi and Mr. Moore, are each trying to determine whether to invest $100,000 to redevelop their properties. If they do not invest the $100,000 in redevelopment, each can get a 10 percent return from other forms of investment. The rate of return on the $100,000 investment by each owner (which depends on whether the other owner redevelops his property as well) is shown below:

	Other Owner Redevelops	Other Owner Does Not Redevelop
	(percent)	
Redevelop	12	5
Do not redevelop	15	10

(a) If Mr. Lombardi redevelops his property, is Mr. Moore better off by redeveloping his property as well? (b) If Mr. Lombardi does not redevelop his property, is Mr. Moore better off by redeveloping his property? (c) Will either owner redevelop his property? (d) In a situation of this sort, can social gains be achieved by government intervention?

SOLUTION

(a) No, because the rate of return Mr. Moore receives if he redevelops is 12 percent, whereas the rate of return he receives if he does not redevelop is 15 percent (because his property benefits from Mr. Lombardi's investment in redevelopment even though he pays nothing). (b) No, because the rate of return Mr. Moore receives if he redevelops is only 5 percent (because little is accomplished so long as Mr. Lombardi does not redevelop too), whereas the rate of return he receives if he does not redevelop is 10 percent (which is what he can obtain from other investments). (c) No. Consider Mr. Moore. As pointed out in (a) and (b), whether or not Mr. Lombardi redevelops, Mr. Moore receives a higher return if he does not redevelop than if he does. Thus he will not redevelop. Neither will Mr. Lombardi, for the same reasons. (d) Yes. From society's point of view, or from the point of view of the two owners acting together as a unit, redevelopment may be desirable. If carried out properly, government intervention may bring this about.

should play—but we have made little or no attempt to describe its role in quantitative terms. It is time now to turn to some of the relevant facts. One useful measure of the extent of the government's role in the American economy is the size of government expenditures, both in absolute terms and as a percent of our nation's total output.

The sum total of government expenditures—federal, state, and local—was about $1.2 trillion in 1983. Since the nation's total output was about $3.3 trillion, this means that government expenditures were about one-third of our total output. The ratio of government expenditures to total output in

Figure 4.2

Government Spending as a Percent of Total Output, United States *Government expenditures—federal, state, and local—totaled about $1.2 trillion in 1983. These expenditures, which include transfer payments, have grown more rapidly than total output in this period.*

the United States has not always been this large, as Figure 4.2 shows. In 1929, the ratio was about 10 percent, as contrasted with over 30 percent in 1983. (Of course, the ratio of government spending to total output is smaller now than during World War II, but in a wartime economy, one would expect this ratio to be abnormally high.)

There are many reasons why government expenditures have grown so much faster than total output. Three of these are particularly important. First, *the United States did not maintain anything like the kind of military force in pre-World War II days that it does now.* In earlier days, when weapons were relatively simple and cheap, and when we viewed our military and political responsibilities much more narrowly than we do now, our military budget was relatively small. The cost of being a superpower in the days of nuclear weaponry is high by any standards. Second, *there has been a long-term increase in the demand for the services provided by government,* like more and better schooling, more extensive highways, more complete police and fire protection, and so forth. As incomes rise, people want more of these services. Third, **government transfer payments**—*payments in return for no products or services—have grown substantially.* For example, various types of welfare payments have increased markedly. (Another transfer payment, social security, increased from about $20 billion in 1965 to about $180 billion in 1984.) Since transfer payments do not entail any reallocation of resources from private to public goods, but a transfer of income from one private citizen or group to another, Figure 4.2 is, in some respects, an overstatement of the role of the public sector.

WHAT THE FEDERAL, STATE, AND LOCAL GOVERNMENTS SPEND MONEY ON

There are three levels of government in the United States—federal, state, and local. The state governments spend the least, while the federal government spends the most. This was not always the case. Before World War I, the local governments spent more than the federal government. In those days, the federal government did not maintain the large military establishment it does now, nor did it engage in the many programs in health, education, welfare, and other areas that it currently does. Figure 4.2 shows that federal spending is now a much larger percentage of the total than it was 40 years ago. Table 4.1 shows how the federal government spends its money. *About one-third of the federal expenditures goes for the defense and other items connected with international relations and national security. About one-half goes for social security, welfare (and other income security) programs, health, and education. The rest goes to support farm, transportation, housing, and other such programs, as well as to run Congress, the courts, and the executive branch of the federal government.*

What about the local and state governments? On what do they spend their money? Table 4.2 shows that *the biggest expenditure of the state and local governments is on schools.* After the end of World War II, these expenditures increased greatly because of the baby boom—the increase in number of school-age children. Traditionally, schools in the United States have been a responsibility of local governments—cities and towns. *State governments spend most of their money on education; welfare, old age, and unemployment benefits; and highways.* (Besides supporting education directly, they help localities to cover the costs of schooling.) In addition, the

Table 4.1

FEDERAL EXPENDITURES, FISCAL 1986

Purpose	Amount (billions of dollars)	Percent of total	Purpose	Amount (billions of dollars)	Percent of total
National defense	286	29	Transportation	26	3
International affairs	18	2	Community and		
Energy	5	1	regional		
Veterans' benefits	27	3	development	7	1
General science,			Interest	143	15
space, and			General government	5	1
technology	9	1	Income security	116	12
Agriculture	13	1	Administration of		
Education, training,			justice	5	1
employment, and			General purpose		
social services	29	3	fiscal assistance	3	b
Health	35	4	Social security		
Natural resources			and medicare	269	28
and environment	12	1	Offsetting receipts	−37	−4
Commerce and			Total[a]	974	100
housing credit	2	b			

[a] Because of rounding errors, the figures may not sum to totals.
[b] Less than ½ of 1 percent.

Source: Economic Report of the President, 1985. These are estimates made in 1985.

Table 4.2

EXPENDITURES OF STATE AND LOCAL GOVERNMENTS, UNITED STATES, 1983

Type of expenditure	Amount (billions of dollars)	Percent of total
Education	164	35
Highways	37	8
Public welfare	60	13
Other	205	44
Total	466	100

Source: Economic Report of the President, 1985.

local and state governments support hospitals, redevelopment programs, courts, and police and fire departments.

Changes in View of Government Responsibilities

We have already seen that government expenditures in the United States have grown considerably, both in absolute amount and as a percentage of our total output. This growth in government expenditures was part of a general trend in the United States toward a more extensive role of government in the economy. Two hundred years ago, there was considerable suspicion of government interference and meddling, freedom was the watchword, and governments were viewed as potential tyrants. In the nineteenth century, the United States prospered mightily under this *laissez-faire* system, but gradually—and not without considerable protest—the nation began to interpret the role of the government differently.

INCREASES IN GOVERNMENT ROLE

Responding to the dangers of noncompetitive markets, states were given the power to regulate public utilities and railroads. The Interstate Commerce Commission was established in 1887 to regulate railroads operating across state lines; and the Sherman Antitrust Act was passed in 1890 to curb monopoly and promote competition. To help control recurring business fluctuations and financial panics, banking and finance were regulated. In 1913, the Federal Reserve System was established as a central bank controlling the

About 29 percent of the federal budget goes for defense. Decisions concerning how much to spend on what kinds of weapons systems are enormously complex and involve a mixture of military, political, and economic considerations. To illustrate some of these considerations, take the case of the B-1 bomber. As early as 1954, the Air Force began to think about a replacement for the B-52 bomber, but both Presidents Kennedy and Johnson were not impressed with the need for it, since they felt that strategic missiles would be more efficient and accurate than a new manned bomber.

Nonetheless, the Air Force and its contractors did not give up on the idea of the new bomber, and even after President Carter blocked the production of such a bomber in 1977, they continued to push for it. Moreover, the Armed Services Committee of the House of Representatives approved more than $300 million for research and development on this airplane between 1977 and 1980. Within the Pentagon, a group of Air Force officers, led by General Kelly Burke, worked hard to make the bomber a reality. When the Reagan administration was elected in 1980, the political climate was much more favorable, and in January 1982 Congress voted approval of the B-1 program.

To help build political support for the B-1 program, Rockwell, the builder of the B-1, farmed out the airplane's production among thousands of subcontractors. For example, the prototype engines were built in Lynn, Massachusetts; the actuators were built in Kalamazoo, Michigan; and so on. Nearly every member of Congress had a firm in his or her district that had a stake in the B-1 program.

The B-1 program is likely to cost at least $20 billion. But the costs of weapons systems are often underestimated, since this makes it easier to sell them to Congress. For a long time, the B-1 systems program office at Wright-Patterson Air Force Base made two different cost estimates, according to one report. "One [estimate] showed what we'd said the B-1 would cost. The other showed what we really thought it would cost."*

Whether the B-1 will be an effective weapons system has been the subject of great controversy. Some argue that it will be slow, sluggish, and limited in range. Like the B-52, the B-1 would need mid-air refueling both going to and returning from the Soviet Union. According to some experts, it makes more sense to modernize the existing B-52 bombers until Stealth (a new bomber that is claimed to be more effective in avoiding enemy defenses than the B-1) comes along. In 1984, the first Stealth was tentatively scheduled to appear in 1991–92.

The amount of resources devoted to military programs of this sort is nothing less than mammoth. (In the case of the B-1, at least $20 billion will be spent for 100 airplanes!) Few people would question the need for a strong and effective national defense, but there is a widespread feeling that the weapons acquisition process is not as efficient as it might be. In August 1984, one of the first B-1 bombers crashed in the Mojave Desert, thus provoking more controversy concerning this already controversial military procurement program.

* "Is the B-1 a Plane Whose Time Has Come?" *Philadelphia Inquirer,* March 18, 1984.

member commercial banks. In 1933, the Federal Deposit Insurance Corporation was established to insure bank deposits. And in 1934, the Securities and Exchange Commission was established to watch over the financial markets.

In addition, the government's role in the fields of labor and welfare expanded considerably. For example, in the 1930s minimum-wage laws were enacted, old-age pensions and unemployment insurance were established, and the government became an important force in collective bargaining and labor relations. Furthermore, the power of government was used increasingly to ensure that citizens did not fall below a certain economic level. Food-stamp programs and programs to provide aid to dependent children were established. *In general, the broad trend in the United States in the century up to about 1975 or 1980 was for the government to be used to a greater and greater extent to achieve social objectives.*

RECENT CHANGES IN ATTITUDE

However, during the 1970s and early 1980s there was a pronounced change in the public's attitude toward the government. People seemed more inclined to question the government's capacity to solve the difficult social problems that confront our nation. In part, this seemed to be due to the apparent failure of large and expensive government programs initiated to solve a variety of social ills, such as poverty. In part, it seemed to reflect a general cynicism concerning government and politicians. One public-opinion poll after another showed that the public was irritated by the payment of what it regarded as excessively high taxes.

In 1978, California's voters supported Proposition 13 by nearly a 2-to-1 margin. Proposition 13 called for a 57 percent cut in the property tax and decreed that no local tax may increase by more than 2 percent per year. Californians were angry at the rapid increase in their property taxes during the 1970s. One Los Angeles family bought a house for $64,000 in 1968 and its property tax then was $1,800. By 1976, it had increased to $3,500, and without Proposition 13, it soon would have gone to $7,000. Californians supported Proposition 13 as a way to offset past increases and limit future increases in the property tax.

In the 1980 elections, Ronald Reagan won the presidency in part by promising to get government "off the backs" of citizens. In his first years in office, he cut back the rate of growth of federal expenditure and reduced many government programs. In 1984, he ran again on a platform that emphasized the reduction of government's role (but an increase in defense expenditure). Again he won. Certainly, the prevailing attitude was different than in the 1960s. How long this change in attitude will persist is hard to say, but while it lasts, conservatives tend to be happy and liberals tend to be concerned.

What the Federal, State, and Local Governments Receive in Taxes

To get the money to cover most of the expenditures discussed in previous sections, governments collect taxes from individuals and firms. As Table 4.3

Table 4.3

FEDERAL RECEIPTS BY TAX, FISCAL 1986

Type of tax	Amount (billions of dollars)	Percent of total
Personal income tax	359	45
Corporation income tax	74	9
Employment taxes	289	36
Excise taxes	35	4
Estate and gift taxes	5	1
Other revenues	31	4
Total[a]	794	100

[a] Because of rounding errors, the figures may not sum to totals.

Source: Economic Report of the President, 1985. These are estimates made in 1985.

Table 4.4

STATE AND LOCAL TAX REVENUES, BY
SOURCE, 1983

Source	Revenues (billions of dollars)	Percent of total
General sales tax	100	25
Property tax	89	22
Personal income tax	55	14
Corporate income tax	14	4
Other taxes	138	35
Total[a]	396	100

[a] Because of rounding errors, the figures may not sum to the totals.

Source: Economic Report of the President, 1985.

shows, *at the federal level the **personal income tax** is the biggest single money raiser.* It brings in almost one-half of the tax revenue collected by the federal government. The next most important taxes at the federal level are the Social Security, payroll, and employment taxes. Other noteworthy taxes are the corporation income tax, excise taxes (levied on the sale of tobacco, liquor, imports, and certain other items), and death and gift taxes. (Even when the Grim Reaper shows up, the Tax Man is not far behind.)

*At the local level, on the other hand, the most important form of taxation and source of revenue is the **property tax.*** This is a tax levied primarily on real estate. Other important local taxes—although dwarfed in importance by the property tax—are local sales taxes and local income taxes. Many cities—for example, New York City—levy a sales tax, equal to a certain percent—4 percent in New York City—of the value of each retail sale. The tax is simply added on to the amount charged the customer. Also, many cities—for example, Philadelphia and Pittsburgh—levy an income (or wage) tax on their residents and even on people who work in the city but live outside it. *At the state level, **sales (and excise) taxes** are the biggest money raisers,* followed by income taxes and highway-user taxes. The latter include taxes on gasoline and license fees for vehicles and drivers. Often they exceed the amount spent on roads, and the balance is used for a variety of non-highway uses. (See Table 4.4.)

Although some people claim that taxes in the United States are higher than in most other industrialized countries, this really is not true. When we compare taxes in the United States (relative to total output) with those in other countries, we learn that the governments of Sweden, France, West Germany, and the United Kingdom tax more—as a percent of total output —than we do. In part, of course, this is because of the extensive welfare programs in Sweden and the United Kingdom. It is interesting, however, that, despite our huge military programs, our government does not tax and spend more (relative to total output) than these countries.

Test Yourself

1. "I believe the government should do only that which private citizens cannot do for themselves, or which they cannot do so well for themselves." Interpret and comment. Indicate how one might determine in practice what the legitimate functions of government are, according to this proposition.

2. "The ideal public policy, from the viewpoint of the state, is one with identifiable beneficiaries, each of whom is helped appreciably, at the cost of many unidentifiable persons, none of whom is hurt much."* Interpret and comment. Indicate how this proposition might be used to help predict government behavior.

3. Explain why national defense is a public good but a rifle is not a public good.

4. "I cannot get the amount of national defense I want and you, a different amount."** Explain. Is this true of all public goods?

5. According to the 1985 *Economic Report of the President,* the federal government will spend about $8.7 billion on general science, space, and technology in fiscal 1985. Why should the government support each of these activities?

* G. Stigler, "The Government of the Economy," in E. Mansfield, *Principles of Microeconomics: Readings, Issues, and Cases.*

** M. Friedman, *Capitalism and Freedom.*

The Role of Government in American Agriculture

Thus far, we have been discussing the government's role in the American economy in rather general terms. Now we need to consider in some detail a particular example of the economic programs carried out by our government. The government's farm programs are a logical choice, because they illustrate the usefulness of the supply-and-demand analysis presented in the previous chapter. It is important to recognize at the outset that these farm programs are not being held up as a representative sample of what the government does. There are a host of other government economic programs—poverty programs, urban programs, defense programs, research programs, education programs, transportation programs, fiscal programs, monetary programs, and many more. Most of these programs will be discussed at some point in this book.

Agriculture is an enormously important sector of the American economy. Even though its size has been decreasing steadily—and this contraction has been going on for many decades—agriculture still employs about 3 million Americans. Its importance, moreover, cannot be measured entirely by its size. You need only think about how difficult it would be to get along without food to see the strategic role agriculture plays in our economic life. Also, when it comes to technological change, agriculture is one of the most progressive parts of the American economy. The efficiency of American agriculture is admired throughout the world.

The Farm Problem

Nonetheless, it is widely acknowledged that American agriculture has had serious problems. Perhaps the clearest indication of these problems is shown by a comparison of per capita income of American farmers with per capita income among the rest of the population. Until the past ten years, it is clear that farm incomes have tended to be much lower than nonfarm incomes. In 1970, per capita income on the farms was about 20 percent below that for the nonfarm population. Moreover, a large proportion of the rural population is poor. Thus the National Advisory Commission on Rural Poverty found that "rural poverty is so widespread, and so acute, as to be a national disgrace."[4] Of course, this does not mean that all farmers are poor: on the contrary, many do very well indeed. But a large percentage of the nation's farmers are poor by any standard.

This farm problem is nothing new. During the first two decades of the twentieth century, farmers enjoyed relatively high prices and relatively high incomes. But in 1920, the country experienced a sharp depression that jolted agriculture as well as the rest of the economy. Whereas the Roaring Twenties saw a recovery and boom in the nonfarm sector of the economy, agriculture did not recover as completely, and the 1930s were dreadful years; the Great Depression resulted in a sickening decline in farm prices and farm incomes. World War II brought prosperity to agriculture, but in

[4] National Advisory Committee on Rural Poverty, *The People Left Behind,* Washington, D.C., 1967.

the postwar period, farm incomes continually have been well below non-farm incomes. In 1973 to 1975, prosperity returned to the farms, but the late 1970s and 1980s saw renewed complaints by farmers about prices and incomes. All in all, agriculture has had difficulties for several decades.

CAUSES OF THE FARM PROBLEM

In Chapter 1, we claimed that relatively simple economic models are of considerable use in understanding important public and private problems. To back up this claim, we will apply the simple models of market behavior presented in the previous chapter—the models involving market demand curves and market supply curves—to explain the basic causes of the problems that have tended to besiege agriculture.

Characteristics of Demand and Supply. Let's start with the market demand curve for farm products. If you think about it for a moment, you will agree that this market demand curve must have two important characteristics. First, *its shape must reflect the fact that food is a necessity and that the quantity demanded will not vary much with the price of food.* Second, *the market demand curve for food is unlikely to shift to the right very much as per capita income rises,* because consumption of food per capita faces natural biological and other limitations.

Next, consider the market supply curve for farm products. Again, you should be aware of two important characteristics of this market supply curve. First, *the quantity of farm products supplied tends to be relatively insensitive to price,* because the farmers have only limited control over their output. (Weather, floods, insects, and other such factors are very important.) Second, because of the rapid technological change emphasized in a previous section, *the market supply curve has been shifting markedly and rapidly to the right.*

Decline in Relative Food Prices. If you understand these simple characteristics of the market demand curve and market supply curve for farm products, it is no trick at all to understand why we have had the sort of farm problem just described. Figure 4.3 shows the market demand and market supply curves for farm products at various points in time. As you would expect, the market demand curve for farm products shifts rather slowly to the right as incomes (and population) grow over time. Specifically, the market demand curve shifted from D in the first period to D_1 in the second period to D_2 in the third period. On the other hand, the market supply curve for farm products shifted rapidly to the right as technology improved over time. Specifically, it shifted from S in the first period to S_1 in the second period to S_2 in the third period.

What was the consequence of these shifts in the market demand and supply curves for food products? Clearly, *the equilibrium price of food products fell (relative to other products).* Specifically, the equilibrium price fell from OP to OP_1 to OP_2 in Figure 4.3. This price decrease was, of course, a large part of the farm problem. If we correct for changes in the general level of prices (which have tended to rise over time), there was, in general, a declining trend in farm prices. That is, agricultural prices generally fell, relative to other prices, in the last 60 years. Moreover, *given this fall in farm prices, farm incomes tended to fall, because, although lower prices were as-*

77

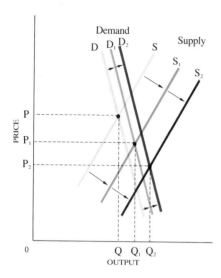

Figure 4.3

Shifts over Time in Market Demand and Supply Curves for Farm Products *The market demand curve has shifted rather slowly to the right (from D to D₁ to D₂), whereas the market supply curve has shifted rapidly to the right (from S to S₁ to S₂), with the result that the equilibrium price has declined (from OP to OP₁ to OP₂).*

sociated with greater amounts sold, the reduction was much greater than the increase in quantity sold, as shown in Figure 4.3.[5]

Thus the simple model of market behavior described in the previous chapter makes it possible to explain the fact that, in real terms, farm prices and farm incomes have tended to fall in the United States. Certainly there is nothing mysterious about these trends. Given the nature and characteristics of the market demand curve and market supply curve for farm products, our simple model shows that these trends are as much to be expected as parades on the Fourth of July.

SLOW EXIT OF RESOURCES

However, one additional fact must be noted to understand the farm problem: *people and nonhuman resources have been relatively slow to move out of agriculture in response to these trends.* Recall from the previous chapter that the price system uses such trends—lower prices and lower incomes—to signal producers that they should use their resources elsewhere. Farmers have been loath to move out of agriculture (even though they often could make more money elsewhere)—and this has been a primary cause of the farm problem that has existed over most of the past 40 years. If more people and resources had left farming, agricultural prices and incomes would have risen, and ultimately farm incomes would have come closer to nonfarm incomes. (Poor education and color were, of course, significant barriers to migration.)

Nonetheless, even though farmers have been slow to move out of agriculture, they have left the farm in the long run. In 1930 the farm population was about 30 million, or 25 percent of the total population; in 1950, it was about 23 million, or 15 percent of the total population; and in 1983, it was about 6 million, or 3 percent of the total population. Thus the price system has had its way. Resources have been moving out of agriculture in response to the signals and pressures of the price system. This movement of people and nonhuman resources unquestionably has contributed to greater efficiency and production for the nation as a whole. But during most of the past 40 years, we have continued to have a "surplus" of farmers—and this has been the root of the farm problem.

Government Aid to Agriculture

Traditionally, farmers have had a disproportionately large influence in Congress; and faced with declining economic fortunes, they appealed to the government for help. They extolled the virtues of rural life, emphasized that agriculture is a competitive industry, and claimed that it was unfair for their prices to fall relative to the prices they have had to pay. In addition, they pointed out that the movement of resources out of agriculture has entailed large human costs, since this movement, although bene-

---

[5] The amount farmers receive is the amount they sell times the price. Thus, in Figure 4.3, the amount farmers receive in income is $OP \times OQ$ in the first period, $OP_1 \times OQ_1$ in the second period, and $OP_2 \times OQ_2$ in the third period. Clearly, since the price is decreasing much more rapidly than the quantity is increasing, farm incomes are falling.

ficial to the nation as a whole, has been traumatic for the farm population. For reasons of this sort, they argued that the government should help farmers; and in particular, that the government should act to bolster farm prices and farm incomes.

THE CONCEPT OF PARITY

Their voices were heard. In the Agricultural Adjustment Act of 1933, the Congress announced the concept of parity as the major objective of American farm policy. This concept acquired great importance—and must be clearly understood. Put in its simplest terms, the concept of *parity* says that a farmer should be able to exchange a given quantity of his output for as much in the way of nonfarm goods and services as he could at some time in the past. For example, if a farmer could take a bushel of wheat to market in 1912 and get enough money to buy a pair of gloves, today he should be able to get enough money for a bushel of wheat to buy a pair of gloves.

To see what the concept of parity implies for farm prices, suppose that the price of gloves triples. Obviously, if parity is to be maintained, the price of wheat must triple too. Thus the concept of parity implies that farm prices must increase at the same rate as the prices of the goods and services farmers buy. Of course, farmers buy lots of things besides gloves, so in actual practice the parity price of wheat or other farm products is determined by the changes over time in the average price of all the goods and services farmers buy.

Two major points should be noted about parity. First, to use this concept, one must agree on some base period, such as 1912 in the example above, during which the relationship of farm to nonfarm prices is regarded as equitable. Obviously, the higher farm prices were relative to nonfarm prices in the base period, the higher farm prices will be in subsequent periods if parity is maintained. It is interesting to note that 1910–14 was used for many years as the base period. Since this was a period of relatively high farm prices and of agricultural prosperity, the farm bloc must have wielded considerable political clout on this issue. Second, note that the concept of parity is an ethical, not a scientific proposition. It states what the relative economic position of a bushel of wheat ought to be—or more precisely, it states one particular view of what the relative economic position of a bushel of wheat should be. Based on purely scientific considerations, there is no way to prove (or disprove) this proposition, since it is based on one's values and political preferences. Using the terminology of Chapter 1, it is a proposition in normative, not positive economics.

Price Supports and Surplus Controls

During the four decades up to 1973, the concept of parity was the cornerstone of a system of government price supports. In many cases, the government did not support farm prices at the full 100 percent of parity. For example, Congress may have enacted a bill saying that the secretary of agriculture could establish a price of wheat, corn, cotton, or some other

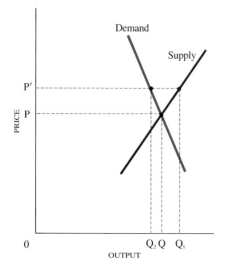

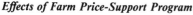

Figure 4.4

Effects of Farm Price-Support Program
The support price, OP′, *is above the
equilibrium price,* OP, *so the public buys*
OQ₂, *farmers supply* OQ₁ *units of output,
and the government buys the difference*
(OQ₁ − OQ₂).

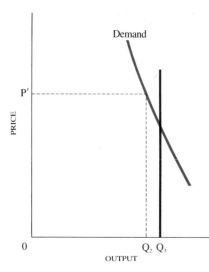

Figure 4.5

***Effects of Price Supports and Output
Restrictions*** *The government restricts
output to* OQ₃, *with the result that it
buys* (OQ₃ − OQ₂) *units of output.*

product that is between 65 and 90 percent of parity. But whatever the exact level of the price supports, the idea behind them was perfectly simple: it was to maintain farm prices above the level that would result in a free market.

Using the simple supply-and-demand model developed in the previous chapter, we can see more clearly the effects of these price supports. The situation is shown in Figure 4.4. A support price, *OP′*, was set by the government. Since this support price was above the equilibrium price, *OP*, the public bought *less* of farm products (*OQ₂* rather than *OQ*) and paid a *higher* price for them. Farmers gained from the price supports, since the amount they received for their crop under the price support was equal to *OP′* × *OQ₁*, a greater amount than what they would have received in a free market, which was *OP* × *OQ*.

Note, however, that since the support price exceeded the equilibrium price, the quantity supplied of the farm product, *OQ₁*, exceeded the quantity demanded, *OQ₂*. That is, *there was a surplus of the farm product in question,* which the government had to purchase, since no one else would. These surpluses were an embarrassment, both economically and politically. They showed that society's scarce resources were being utilized to produce products consumers simply did not want at existing prices. Moreover the cost of storing these surpluses was very large indeed: in some years, these storage costs alone hit the $1-billion mark.

POLICIES TO CUT SURPLUSES

To help reduce these surpluses, the government followed two basic strategies. First, *it tried to restrict output of farm products.* In particular, the government established an acreage allotment program, which said that farmers had to limit the number of acres they planted in order to get price supports on their crops. The Department of Agriculture estimated how much of each product would be demanded by buyers (other than the government) at the support price, and tried to cut back the total acreage planted with this crop to the point where the quantity supplied equaled the quantity demanded. These output restrictions did not eliminate the surpluses, because farmers managed to increase the yields from acreage they were allowed to plant, but undoubtedly they reduced the surpluses. With these restrictions, the situation was as shown in Figure 4.5, where *OQ₃* was the total output that could be grown on the acreage that could be planted with the crop. Because of the imposition of this output control, the surplus—which the government had to purchase—was reduced from *(OQ₁ − OQ₂)* to *(OQ₃ − OQ₂)*. Farmers continued to benefit from price supports because the amount they received for their crop—*OP′* × *OQ₃*—was still greater than they would have received in a free market, because the amount demanded of farm products was not very sensitive to their price.

Second, *the government tried to shift the demand curve for farm products to the right.* An effort was made to find new uses for various farm products. Also, various antipoverty programs, such as the food-stamp program, used our farm surpluses to help the poor. In addition, the government tried to expand the export markets for American farm products. Western Europe and Japan increased their demand for food, and the Communist countries

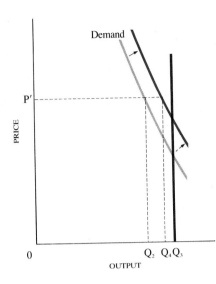

PRICE

Demand

P'

0

Q₂ Q₄Q₃

OUTPUT

Figure 4.6
Effects of Price Supports, Output Restrictions, and a Shift to the Right in the Demand Curve for Farm Products
By shifting the demand curve to the right, the government reduces the surplus from (OQ₃ − OQ₂) to (OQ₃ − OQ₄) units of output.

purchased our farm products to offset their own agricultural deficiencies. Moreover, the less developed countries were permitted by Public Law 480 to buy our farm products with their own currencies, rather than dollars. The result was a reduction in farm surpluses, as shown in Figure 4.6. Since the market demand curve for farm products shifted to the right, the surplus was reduced from $(OQ_3 - OQ_2)$ to $(OQ_3 - OQ_4)$. Because of these demand-augmenting and output-restricting measures, surpluses during the late 1960s and early 1970s were considerably smaller than they were during the late 1950s and early 1960s.

The 1973 Farm Bill and More Recent Developments

In 1973, farm prices increased markedly, due partly to very great increases in foreign demand for American agricultural products. This increase in foreign demand was due partly to poor harvests in the Soviet Union, Australia, Argentina, and elsewhere, as well as to devaluations of the dollar. (In 1972–73, the Soviet Union alone bought over $1 billion of grain—on terms that provoked considerable controversy in the United States.) As a result, farm incomes reached very high levels, farm surpluses disappeared, and for the first time in 30 years the government was trying to stimulate farm production rather than restrict it.

THE 1973 BILL

Taking advantage of this new climate, Congress passed a new farm bill which ended price supports. This bill, the Agriculture and Consumer Protection Act of 1973, aimed at reducing government involvement in agriculture and at a return to freer markets. Specifically, agricultural prices were allowed to fluctuate freely in accord with supply and demand. However, the government made cash payments to farmers if prices fell below certain "target" levels established by the law. These target levels were above the prices that generally prevailed in the past, but they were below the high levels of prices prevailing in 1973. A program of this kind was originally proposed in 1949 by Charles F. Brannan, who was secretary of agriculture under President Harry Truman. More will be said about the Brannan plan in Chapter 21.

Besides establishing these new forms of subsidies, the 1973 farm bill limited total subsidy payments to any individual farmer to $20,000 per year. This provision was meant to deal more effectively than did the prior law with the problem of very large subsidies being paid to wealthy farmers. Also, the 1973 law stated that whether or not land is taken out of production is at the discretion of the secretary of agriculture. In 1974, Secretary Earl Butz said that none should be taken out of production, and encouraged farmers to produce as much as they wanted. Nonetheless, in 1974, American crop production as a whole suffered its biggest setback in almost 40 years, due primarily to bad weather. Coupled with continued strong foreign demand for farm products, as well as domestic demand, the result was another year of high farm prices.

81

CHANGES IN GOVERNMENT INVOLVEMENT

By 1975 it appeared to many knowledgeable observers that the farm sector no longer was suffering from overcapacity, and that, in this respect at least, an equilibrium had been achieved. However, this attitude did not last long. During 1976 and 1977 U.S. farmers harvested bumper crops, with the result that prices fell considerably. The price of wheat, which had been about $3.50 per bushel in 1975, fell to about $2.30 per bushel in 1977. Farmers protested, and exerted political pressure for increased government price and income supports.

In 1977 Congress passed the Food and Agricultural Act, which contained flexible price-support levels and income supports. And in the late 1970s Secretary of Agriculture Bob Bergland said that a substantial amount of farmland had to be taken out of production. No longer was there much talk about a return to freer markets. Instead, the emphasis seemed to be on more support for farm prices and incomes.

In 1983 the Reagan administration adopted the $9 billion payment-in-kind program (PIK) in response to large grain harvests—the idea being to pay farmers for idling acreage by giving them crops stored by the government. Although this program was supposed to hold down government cash payments, expenditures soared to about $19 billion. Faced with huge government deficits, the Reagan administration announced in 1985 that it would try to persuade Congress to slash farm subsidy programs. However, many congressmen and senators (particularly from farm states) were skeptical about the chances that such a dramatic policy shift would be adopted.

Indeed, in late 1985, the trend seemed to be in the other direction. A substantial number of farmers were reported to be unable to pay their debts, and farm groups (and banks) were pressing for government help. Congress passed a bill calling for about $169 billion in spending over five years.

Evaluation of Government Farm Programs

It is obviously hard to evaluate the success of the government's farm programs. Farmers will certainly take a different view of price supports and other measures than their city cousins. Nonetheless, from the point of view of the nation as a whole, these farm programs have received considerable criticism. To understand these criticisms, we must hark back to our discussion earlier in this chapter of the proper functions of government, and ask what justification there is for the government's intervening in this way in agriculture. Perhaps the most convincing justification is that the government ought to help the rural poor. As we saw in previous sections, most people agree that the government should redistribute income in this way.

Have the Poor Been Helped? Unfortunately, however, *our farm programs have done little for the farmers most in need of help,* because the amount of money a farmer has gotten from these programs has depended on how much he produced. Thus the big farmers have gotten the lion's share of the subsidies—and they, of course, needed help least. On the other hand, the small farmers, the farmers who are mired mostly deeply in poverty, have received little from these programs. Recognizing this fact, many observers

EVALUATION OF GOV'T FARM
PROGRAMS

have pointed out that, if these programs are really aimed at helping the rural poor, it would be more sensible to channel the money to them through direct subsidies, than to finance programs where much of the benefits goes to prosperous commercial farmers.

Has the Farm Problem Been Solved? It must also be recognized that *our farm programs have not dealt with the basic causes of the farm problem.* In the past at least, we have had too many people and resources in agriculture. This, as we stressed in previous sections, is why farmers' incomes have tended to be low. Yet the government's farm programs have been directed more toward supporting farm prices and incomes (and stabilizing a sector of the economy that historically has been unstable), rather than toward promoting the needed movement of people and resources out of agriculture. Indeed, some people would say that the government's farm programs have made it more difficult for the necessary adjustments to take place.

Given these defects, many proposals have been made to alter our farm programs. In the view of many observers, agriculture should return to something more closely approximating free markets, and the price system should be allowed to work more freely. The changes that occurred in 1973 were in that direction, but it is important to note that the government is still intervening heavily in agriculture.

A BASIC MORAL

Finally, before closing this chapter, we must point out a fundamental moral of our farm programs:

The government, like the price system, can bungle the job of organizing a nation's economic activities. We began this chapter by stressing the fact that the price system breaks down under some circumstances, and that the government must intervene. It is also worth stressing that the government sometimes intervenes when it shouldn't—and that even when it should intervene, it sometimes does so in a way that wastes resources. This, of course, doesn't mean that the government should play no part in the American economy. On the contrary, the government must—and does—play an important role. What it does mean is that, just as the price system is no all-purpose cure-all, neither is the government.

Basic Idea #8: Just because the price system has well-known limitations, it does not follow that the task of organizing the nation's economic activities should be turned over to the government. As illustrated by our agricultural policies, the government has limitations of its own. Neither the price system nor the government is a panacea.

Test Yourself

1. Suppose that the demand and supply curves for paper are as shown on the right. If paper production results in serious pollution of rivers and streams, is the socially optimal output of paper less than, greater than, or equal to *OQ*? Does the supply curve reflecting the true social costs of producing paper lie to the right or to the left of the supply curve shown on the right? Why?

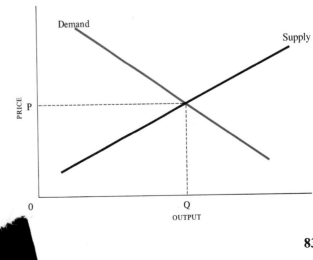

2. Suppose that paper production results in some important uncompensated benefits to other industries. If there are major external economies of this sort (and if paper production no longer results in any pollution), is the socially optimal output of paper less than, greater than, or equal to *OQ* in Question 1? Does the demand curve reflecting the true social benefits from paper output lie to the right or to the left of the demand curve shown in Question 1? Why?

3. Explain the nature of America's farm problem. To what extent have government policies solved the problem?

4. Suppose that the demand curve for corn is as follows:

Price (dollars per bushel)	Quantity demanded per year (millions of bushels)
1	70
2	65
3	60
4	55
5	50
6	45

If the government supports the price of corn at $4 per bushel, and if it restricts output to 60 million bushels per year, how much corn will the government have to buy each year? If the government stopped supporting the price of corn, what would its price be?

5. On August 8, 1982, David Stockman, director of President Reagan's Office of Management and Budget, wrote that, "There is ... [an] asymmetry between powerful and persuasive interest groups on the one hand and the general taxpayer on the other. For example, dairy subsidies are $7,000 per dairy producer but the individual taxpayer pays only about $18 a year for dairy subsidies." Explain how such an asymmetry can result in high levels of government spending.

6. "The sharp increases in the price of wheat during the mid-1970s were due primarily to shifts in the supply curve for wheat." Comment.

Summary

1. The price system, despite its many virtues, suffers from serious limitations. There is no reason to believe that the distribution of income generated by the price system is equitable or optimal. Also, there is no way for the price system to handle public goods properly, and because of external economies or diseconomies, the price system may result in too little or too much of certain goods being produced.

2. To a considerable extent, the government's role in the economy has developed in response to these limitations of the price system. There is considerable agreement that the government should redistribute income in favor of the poor, provide public goods, and offset the effects of external economies and diseconomies. Also, it is generally felt that the government should establish a proper legal, social and competitive framework for the price system, and that it should promote the maintenance of relatively full employment with reasonably stable prices.

3. Beyond this, however, there are wide differences of opinion on the proper role of government in economic affairs. Conservatives tend to be suspicious of "big government" while liberals are inclined to believe that the government should do more.

4. In the past 50 years, government spending has increased considerably, both in absolute terms and as a percent of total output. (It is now about one-third of our total output.) To a large extent, this increase has been due to our greater military responsibilities, as well as to the fact that, as their incomes have risen, our citizens have demanded more schools, highways, and other goods and services provided by government. Also, government transfer payments have grown substantially.

5. To get the money to cover most of these expenditures, governments collect taxes from individuals and firms. At the federal level, the most important form of taxation is the personal income tax; at the local level, the property tax is very important; and at the state level, sales (and excise) taxes are the biggest money raisers.

6. One example of the role of government in the American economy is the farm program. American agriculture has been plagued by relatively low incomes. In general, the demand for farm products grew slowly, while rapid technological change meant that the people and resources currently in agriculture could supply more and more farm products. Because people and resources did not move out of agriculture as rapidly as the price system dictated, farm incomes tended to be relatively low.

7. In response to political pressures from the farm blocs, the government set in motion a series of programs to aid farmers. A cornerstone of these programs was the concept of parity, which said that the prices farmers receive should increase at the same rate as the prices of the goods and services farmers buy. The government instituted price supports to keep farm prices above their equilibrium level. But since the support prices exceeded the equilibrium prices, there was a surplus of the commodities that the government had to purchase and store. To help reduce these surpluses, the government tried to restrict the output of farm products and expand the demand for them.

8. These farm programs received considerable criticism. From the point of view of income redistribution, they suffered from the fact that they did little for the farmers most in need of help. As tools of resource allocation, they suffered because they dealt more with the symptoms of the farm problem than with its basic causes. In 1973, price supports were ended, but the government pledged to make cash payments to farmers if farm prices fall below certain target levels. During the late 1970s and 1980s, the government continued to intervene heavily in agriculture.

9. The government's farm programs illustrate the fact that government intervention, like the price system, has plenty of limitations. Neither the price system nor government intervention is an all-purpose cure-all.

Concepts for Review

Public goods	**Welfare payments**	**Property tax**
External economy	**Transfer payments**	**Sales tax**
External diseconomy	**Personal income tax**	**Parity**
Antitrust laws		

CHAPTER 5

Government Expenditures, Taxation, and the Public Debt

The government plays an extremely important role in the American economy. It is obvious that it influences our economic lives and fortunes in countless ways. At this point, we must look in detail at how decisions are made concerning the level and distribution of government expenditures. Also, we must describe the theory of public choice. These topics are of central importance in understanding the public sector of our economy.

In addition, we must discuss the principles of taxation, as well as the characteristics of the major taxes used to support government activities in the United States. Further, we must describe in some detail the nature, size, and burden of the public debt, a subject that has been surrounded by as many myths as any in economics.

Government Expenditures

Determining how much the federal government should spend is a mammoth undertaking, involving literally thousands of people and hundreds of thousands of man-hours. Decisions on expenditures are part of the budgetary process. The *budget* is a statement of the government's anticipated expenditures and revenues. The federal budget is for a fiscal year, from October 1 to September 30. About 15 months before the beginning of a particular fiscal year, the various agencies of the federal government begin to prepare their program proposals for that year. Then they make detailed budget requests which the president, with his Office of Management and Budget, goes over. Since the agencies generally want more than the president w￼ spend, he usually cuts down their requests.

In January (preceding the beginning of the fiscal year), the president submits his budget to Congress, which then spends several months in intensive deliberation and negotiation. Congressional committees concerned with particular areas like defense or education recommend changes in the president's budget. The Congressional Budget Office, headed in 1985 by Rudolph Penner (formerly an economist at the American Enterprise Institute), makes various types of economic analyses to help senators and representatives evaluate alternative programs. By mid-May, Congress is supposed to pass a resolution setting tentative targets for overall spending and revenues; this resolution is based on the joint recommendations by the House and Senate Budget Committees. The targets in the resolution are to be kept in mind by the various congressional committees dealing with specific spending or tax actions. If these actions add up to bigger totals than the resolution called for, the budget committees and Congress are supposed to decide how the discrepancies are to be reconciled: by changes in expenditures, taxes, or initial targets. Before late September, Congress is supposed to adopt a second resolution, setting final ceilings for overall expenditure and a floor on revenues.

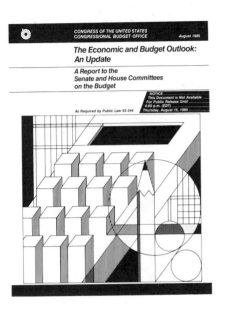

Benefit-Cost Analysis

How much should the government spend on various activities and services? Basically, the answer must be provided by the nation's political processes. For example, with regard to the provision of public goods

> voting by ballot must be resorted to in place of dollar voting. . . . Decision making by voting becomes a substitute for preference revelation through the market. The results will not please everybody, but they will approximate—more or less perfectly, depending on the efficiency of the voting process and the homogeneity of preferences—the community's preferences.[1]

Basic Idea #9: A particular government program is worthwhile if the benefits from the program exceed its costs. To see whether the program should be expanded or contracted, compare the extra benefit from the change in the program's scope to the extra cost. Although it may be difficult to obtain precise measures of benefit and cost, an analysis of this sort frequently is illuminating.

Under certain circumstances, particular types of economic analysis can prove helpful to the policy makers and citizens who must determine how much the government should spend on various programs. Let's begin by supposing that we can measure the benefits and costs of each such program. What is the optimal amount to spend on each one? The answer, clearly enough, is that *spending on the program should be pushed to the point where the extra benefit from an extra dollar spent is at least equal to the dollar of cost.* This would ensure that the amount spent on each government program yields a benefit at least as great as the value of output forgone in the private sector. This would also make sure that one government program is not being expanded at the expense of other programs that would yield greater benefits if they were expanded instead.

The principle that extra benefit should be compared with extra cost is valuable—and, as we shall see in the next section, widely applicable—but it can solve only a small part of the problem of allocating resources in the public sector. Why? Because it is impossible to measure the benefits from

[1] Richard and Peggy Musgrave, *Public Finance in Theory and Practice,* New York: McGraw-Hill, 1973, p. 8.

defense or police protection or the courts in dollars and cents. Only in certain cases can benefits be quantified at all precisely. And it is not only a question of the amount of the benefits and costs; it is also a question of who benefits and who pays. Nonetheless, it is difficult to see how rational choices can be made without paying attention to costs and benefits—even if they are measured imprecisely, and are by no means the whole story.

UPWARD BOUND: A CASE STUDY[2]

Despite the difficulties involved, in recent years more and more benefit-cost analyses have been carried out to help guide public policy. For example, consider the following study, by the Greenleigh Associates, of Upward Bound, a U.S. Office of Economic Opportunity program begun in the 1960s to select and give underprivileged young people a special college preparatory education. The study surveyed over 7,000 people who entered the Upward Bound program in 1966 to 1968. It tried to estimate the costs and benefits from the program.

On the average, the cost per person in the program was determined to be about $3,400. To estimate the benefits, each person in the program was compared with his or her older sibling with respect to earnings in the years subsequent to the program. In other words, the older siblings were viewed as a "control" group that could be used to indicate how much a person would have made if he or she had not taken part in the program. Based on such a comparison, it appeared that the benefits to society were about $7,000 per person in the program. That is, the extra earnings of such a person—used as an estimate of the value of the extra output he or she produced due to the program—was estimated to be about $7,000.

Since the benefits exceeded the costs, it appeared that the program was worthwhile. Of course, there are many difficulties in this and other such analyses, and they should be viewed with caution. Nonetheless, this study is an interesting example of a benefit-cost analysis.

OTHER EXAMPLES

Benefit-cost analyses have proved useful in many areas of government. In particular, they have been used for many years in the Department of Defense. Decisions to develop one weapons system rather than another, or to procure a certain amount of a given weapon, have been based in part on such studies. Other areas where benefit-cost analyses have been used extensively are water projects (irrigation, flood control, hydroelectric, and other projects), transportation projects, and urban renewal, recreation, and health projects. For example, in water projects, benefit-cost analysis has frequently been used by the Corps of Engineers and others to determine whether it is worthwhile to spend additional money on flood control, and if so, how much extra expenditure is justified.

A highly simplified example of a benefit-cost analysis of the construction of a dam is shown in Table 5.1. The alternative policies are to build a low dam or a high dam. Table 5.1 shows the annual costs and benefits associated with each of these policies. Clearly, the high dam should be

"Project Double Discovery" class sponsored through Upward Bound

Table 5.1

BENEFIT-COST ANALYSIS FOR CONSTRUCTING A DAM

Alternative policies	Annual cost (dollars)	Annual benefit (dollars)
Build a low dam	600,000	650,000
Build a high dam	750,000	850,000

[2] Th⋯ ⋯ction is based on E. Gramlich, *Benefit-Cost Analysis of Government Programs*, Englewo⋯ ⋯ Prentice-Hall, 1981, pp. 162–65. The figures pertain to white males.

built because the extra cost involved ($150,000 more than for the low dam) is more than outweighed by the extra benefits received ($200,000 more than for the low dam). Note, however, that this is a very simple case. In general, data on costs and benefits are not laid out so straightforwardly. Instead, there are very wide bands of uncertainty about the relevant costs and benefits.

Scope and Efficiency of Government Activities

It is not easy to decide how large government expenditures should be. As we saw in Chapter 4, opinions differ widely on the proper role of government in economic affairs, and it is often impossible to measure the costs and benefits of government programs with dependable accuracy. Thus economists differ considerably in their opinions concerning the optimal size of government expenditures. Some, like Harvard's John Kenneth Galbraith, believe that the public sector of the economy has been deprived of needed resources, whereas the private sector has catered to relatively unimportant wants. Others, like Stanford's Milton Friedman, believe that government spending is far too large, and that it should be trimmed greatly.

To a considerable extent, this argument is over the proper *scope* of government. To see what we mean, assume that we can divide all goods into publicly provided goods and privately provided goods, and that Figure 5.1 shows the society's production possibilities curve. In other words, as you recall from Chapter 2, Figure 5.1 shows the maximum amount of publicly provided goods that can be produced, given each quantity produced of privately provided goods. What Galbraith and Friedman (among others) disagree about is the point that society should choose on the production possibilities curve. Should society choose point *A* (where more publicly provided goods and less privately provided goods are produced) or point *B* (where less publicly provided goods and more privately provided goods are produced)? Galbraith would be likely to choose point *A;* Friedman would be likely to choose point *B*.

But there is another important question: How can we attain a point *on* the production possibilities curve, rather than one (like point *C*) that is *inside* it? As we know from Chapter 2, inefficiency will result in society's being on a point inside the production possibilities curve. Thus, to attain a point on the production possibilities curve, government officials (and others) must do their best to eliminate inefficiency. By doing so, society can get more from the available resources. For example, it can attain points *A* or *B* rather than point *C*. Whether society wants to use its added efficiency to attain point *A* or point *B* is then a political question. However, regardless of how this question is decided, society is better off to eliminate inefficiency.

The Theory of Public Choice

According to many economists interested in the theory of public choice, there are a variety of factors that induce the government to make decisions

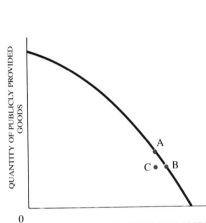

Figure 5.1
Production Possibilities Curve, Publicly Provided and Privately Provided Goods
At point B, *society produces less publicly provided goods and more privately provided goods than at point* A. *Thus a movement from point* A *to point* B *reduces government expenditures by reducing the* scope *of government services. At point* C, *society is producing inefficiently, and a movement from point* C *to point* B *or point* A *can be attained by increasing the* efficiency *of government (and/or private) operations.*

that are not efficient from an economic point of view. Thus, just as the price system suffers from the limitations cited in Chapter 4, so the government has shortcomings as a mechanism for promoting economic welfare. These factors, discussed below, often result in expanded government expenditures.

SPECIAL-INTEREST GROUPS

It is no secret that politicians try to stay in office. In some cases, they must decide whether or not to adopt a policy which benefits a small number of people each of whom will gain a great deal at the expense of a very large number of people each of whom will lose very little. The small group of gainers (the special-interest group) is likely to be well organized, well financed, and vocal. The large group of losers is likely to be unaware of its losses and indifferent to the outcome of this decision, since each member of this group has little at stake. In a case of this sort, a politician will be inclined to adopt the policy favoring the special-interest group. Why? Because the politician, if he or she does not adopt this policy, will lose the support of this group. On the other hand, by adopting this policy, the politician is unlikely to lose the support of the large group of people that are hurt by it because they are much more interested in other issues where they have more at stake.

There are many cases where politicians have adopted policies favoring special-interest groups, even though the total gains to the special-interest group are less than the total losses to other segments of society. Whereas such policies are unsound economics, they have been regarded as good politics. One example is the enactment of tariffs and quotas that reduce domestic competition and result in consumers' paying higher prices. According to many observers, another example is the farm programs described in Chapter 4. Government services that benefit special-interest groups often are expanded, to the detriment of society at large.

BUREAUCRATIC INEFFICIENCY

Many observers contend that government agencies are less efficient than private firms. As we have seen in previous chapters, the price system establishes strong incentives for firms to minimize their costs. If firms can lower their costs, they can increase their profits, at least temporarily. Government officials, on the other hand, often have less incentive to reduce costs. Indeed, it is sometimes claimed that there is an incentive to increase costs since an agency's power and influence is directly related to the size of its budget. Unfortunately, we do not have a great deal of evidence concerning whatever differences exist between the efficiency of government agencies and of private firms, due largely to the difficulties in measuring the efficiency or inefficiency of government agencies. For example, how efficient is the Environmental Protection Agency? Because it is so difficult to measure EPA's output, and because it is so difficult to find a standard against which to measure its performance, this question is exceedingly difficult to answer.

One area where there has been evidence of inefficiency has been the development and production of new weapons by the Department of Defense and its contractors. There have been spectacular overruns in development and production costs. For example, the cost of the Lockheed C5A transport plane increased from the $3.4 billion estimated in 1965 to $5.3 billion in 1968. To some extent, such cost increases reflect the fact that new weapons systems tend to push the state of the art, so that unexpected problems must be expected. But, in addition, the firms that develop and produce these weapons systems often submit unrealistically low bids to get a contract, knowing that they are likely to get approval for cost increases later on. According to some observers, like Merton J. Peck of Yale University and F. M. Scherer of Swarthmore College, these cost overruns have also been due to "inadequate attention to the efficient utilization of technical, production, and administrative manpower—areas in which major cost reductions are possible."[3]

NONSELECTIVITY

Another point made by public choice theorists is that, when citizens vote for their elected officials, they vote for a "bundle" of political programs. For example, in a particular election, the two candidates may be John Brown, who favors increased defense spending, reduced capital gains taxes, and the development of nuclear power, and Jane Smith, who opposes all of these things. If you favor increased defense spending and the development of nuclear power, but oppose reduced capital gains taxes, there is no way that you can elect a candidate that mirrors your preferences. All that you can do is vote for the candidate whose bundle of programs is closest to your preferences.

In contrast, citizens, when making choices in the market place, are better able to pick a set of goods and services that is in accord with their preferences, since they do not have to buy items that they do not want. If you want a green shirt and a purple tie (for formal occasions, of course), you can buy them without having to buy a pair of socks as well. Since citizens cannot be so selective with regard to goods and services in the public sector, public-choice theorists hold that the provision of such goods and services tends to be inefficient.

To conclude this brief section on the theory of public choice, it is important to recognize that no one is accusing government officials of being stupid, lazy, or corrupt. Some undoubtedly are, but this is true of business executives (and college professors) as well. The point is that the incentives faced by government officials and the nature of the political process result in decision making that can be suboptimal from an economic point of view. This helps to explain why the government, like the price system, can bungle the job of organizing the nation's economic activities. Neither is a panacea.

Taxation and Government Revenues

THE FEDERAL TAX LEGISLATIVE PROCESS

It is one thing for the federal government to decide how much to spend and on what; it is another to raise the money to underwrite these programs. This

[3] M. J. Peck and F. M. Scherer, *The Weapons Acquisition Process,* Cambridge, Mass.: Harvard University Press, 1962, p. 594.

section describes how the federal government decides how much to tax. Of course, this problem is not solved from scratch every year. Instead, the government takes the existing tax structure as given and changes it from time to time as seems desirable. Frequently the major initiative leading to a change in the tax laws comes from the president, who requests tax changes in his State of the Union message, his budget message, or a special tax message. (For example, in January 1985 President Reagan announced a proposal for tax simplification.) Much of the spadework underlying his proposals will have been carried out by the Treasury Department, particularly the Treasury's Office of Tax Analysis, Office of the Tax Legislative Counsel, and Internal Revenue Service.

Example 5.1   Brown-Lung Disease and Benefit-Cost Analysis

Byssinosis, commonly known as "brown-lung disease," is a major hazard for textile workers. In 1978, the Occupational Safety and Health Administration (OSHA) issued standards for levels of cotton dust in textile plants, because it felt that cotton dust was a significant cause of byssinosis and other diseases. The following table shows estimates by Robert Crandall of the Brookings Institution of the cost of avoiding an additional case of byssinosis:

Concentration of dust (milligrams per cubic foot of air)	Cost per case avoided (dollars)
0.5	31,000
0.2	572,000
0.1	1,431,000

As you can see, as the level of cotton dust decreases (from 0.5 to 0.2 to 0.1 milligrams per cubic foot), the cost per case avoided goes up.

(a) Suppose that OSHA were to say that the concentration of dust should be no higher than 0.1 milligrams per cubic foot of air. What is OSHA's estimate (explicit or implicit) of the social benefit (in dollars) of avoiding an extra case of byssinosis? (b) Is this estimate correct? (c) What are the difficulties in using benefit-cost analysis to determine how stringent OSHA's standards should be?

SOLUTION

(a) By setting this standard, OSHA is saying (implicitly) that the avoidance of an extra case is worth at least $1,431,000. If it were worth less than this, a less stringent standard should be adopted. (b) Since it is so difficult to set a dollar value on human life or health, there is no simple way to answer this question. However, it should be noted that society implicitly puts a dollar value on human life by spending no more than particular amounts to protect life. (c) As pointed out in (b), it is extremely difficult to estimate and evaluate (in dollars and cents) the social benefits from reductions of various amounts in the incidence of byssinosis. Thus it is hard to know at what point further reductions are no longer worth their cost.

The proposal of a major tax change generally brings about considerable public debate. Representatives of labor, industry, agriculture, and other economic and social groups present their opinions. Newspaper articles, radio shows, and television commentators analyze the issues. By the time the Congress begins to look seriously at the proposal, the battle lines between those who favor the change and those who oppose it are generally pretty clearly drawn. The tax bill incorporating the change is first considered by the Ways and Means Committee of the House of Representatives, a very powerful committee composed of members drawn from both political parties. After public hearings, the committee goes into executive session and reviews each proposed change with its staff and with the Treasury staff. After careful study, the committee arrives at a bill it recommends—though this bill may or may not conform to what the president asked for. Then the bill is referred to the entire House of Representatives for approval. Only rarely is a major tax bill recommended by the committee turned down by the House.

Next, the bill is sent to the Senate. There it is referred to the Finance Committee, which is organized like the House Ways and Means Committee. The Finance Committee also holds hearings, discusses the bill at length, makes changes in it, and sends its version of the bill to the entire Senate, where there frequently is considerable debate. Ultimately, it is brought to a vote. If it does not pass, that ends the process. If it does pass (and if it differs from the House version of the bill, which is generally the case), then a conference committee must be formed to iron out the differences between the House and Senate versions. Finally, when this compromise is worked out, the result must be passed by both houses and sent to the president. The president rarely vetoes a tax bill, although it has occasionally been done.[4]

Principles of Taxation

According to the English political philosopher, Edmund Burke, "To tax and to please, no more than to love and to be wise, is not given to men." What constitutes a rational tax system? Are there any generally accepted principles to guide the nation in determining who should pay how much? The answer is that there are some principles most people accept, but they are so broad and general that they leave plenty of room for argument and compromise. Specifically, two general principles of taxation command widespread agreement.

Benefit Principle. The first principle is that *people who receive more from a certain government service should pay more in taxes to support it.* Certainly few people would argue with this idea. However, it is frequently difficult, if not impossible, to apply. For example, there is no good way to measure the amount of the benefits received by a particular taxpayer from many public services, such as police protection.

Ability-to-Pay Principle. The second principle is that *people should be*

---

[4] For an excellent discussion of the federal tax legislative process, see J. Pechman, *Federal Tax Policy,* 3rd ed., Washington, D.C.: Brookings Institution, 1977, part of which is reprinted in E. Mansfield, *Principles of Macroeconomics: Readings, Issues, and Cases,* 4th ed., New York: Norton, 1983.

taxed so as to result in a socially desirable redistribution of income. In practice, this has ordinarily meant that the wealthy have been asked to pay more than the poor. This idea, too, has generally commanded widespread assent—although this, of course, has not prevented the wealthy from trying to avoid its application to them.

APPLICATIONS OF THESE PRINCIPLES

It follows from these principles that if two people are in essentially the same circumstances (their income, purchases, utilization of public services are the same), then they should pay the same taxes. This is an important rule, innocuous though it may seem. It says that equals should be treated equally—*whether one is a Republican and the other is a Democrat, or whether one is a friend of the president and the other is his enemy, or whether one has purely salary income and the other has property income, they should be treated equally.* Certainly, this is a basic characteristic of an equitable tax system.

It is easy to relate most of the taxes in our tax structure to these principles. For example, the first principle—the benefit principle—is the basic rationale behind taxes on gasoline and license fees for vehicles and drivers. Those who use the roads are asked to pay for their construction and upkeep. Also, the property tax, levied primarily on real estate, is often supported on these grounds. It is argued that property owners receive important benefits—fire and police protection, for example—and that the extent of the benefits is related to the extent of their property.

The personal income tax is based squarely on the second principle: ability to pay. A person with a large income pays a higher proportion of income in personal income taxes than does a person with a smaller income. In 1984, if a couple's income (after deductions and exemptions) were $16,000, their federal income tax would be $1,741, whereas if their income were $60,000, their federal income tax would be $15,168. Also, estate and inheritance taxes hit the rich much harder than the poor.

The principles cited above are useful and important, but they do not take us very far toward establishing a rational tax structure. They are too vague and leave too many questions unanswered. If I use about the same amount of public services as you do, but my income is twice yours, how much more should I pay in taxes? Twice as much? Three times as much? Fifty percent more? These principles throw no real light on many of the detailed questions that must be answered by a real-life tax code.

The Personal Income Tax

The federal **personal income tax** brings in over $350 billion a year. Yet many people are perhaps unaware of just how much they are contributing because it is deducted from their wages each month or each week, so that they owe little extra when April 15 rolls around. (Indeed, they may even be due a refund.) This pay-as-you-go scheme reduces the pain but, of course, it does not eliminate it; taxes are never painless.

The Tax Schedule. Obviously, how much a family has to pay in personal income taxes depends on the family's income. The tax schedule (as of 1984) is as shown in Table 5.2. The second column shows how much a couple would have to pay if their income was the amount shown in the first column. At an income of $29,900, their income tax would be $4,790; at an income of $109,400, their income tax would be $36,630. Clearly, the percentage of income owed in income tax increases as income increases, but this percentage does not increase indefinitely. The percentage of income going for personal income taxes never exceeds 50 percent, no matter how much money the couple makes.

The Marginal Tax Rate. It is instructive to look further at how the "tax bite" increases with income. In particular, let's ask ourselves what proportion of an *extra* dollar of income the couple will have to pay in personal income taxes. In other words, what is the **marginal tax rate:** the tax on an extra dollar of income? The fourth column of Table 5.2 shows that the

Table 5.2

FEDERAL PERSONAL INCOME TAX, COUPLE WITHOUT CHILDREN, 1984

Income—after deductions and personal exemptions (dollars)	Personal income tax (dollars)	Average tax rate (percent)	Marginal tax rate (percent)
5,500	231	4.2	12
16,000	1,741	10.9	18
29,900	4,790	16.0	28
60,000	15,168	25.3	42
109,400	36,630	33.5	49
1,000,000	481,400	48.1	50

marginal tax rate is 12 percent if the couple's income is $5,500, 18 percent if their income is $16,000, 42 percent if their income is $60,000, and 50 percent if their income is $1 million. Thus, the greater the couple's income, the greater the proportion of an extra dollar that goes for personal income taxes.

Effect on Income Inequality. Clearly, the personal income tax tends to reduce the inequality of after-tax income, since the rich are taxed more heavily than the poor. However, the personal income tax does not bear down as heavily on the rich as one might surmise from Table 5.2. This is because there are a variety of perfectly legal ways for people to avoid paying taxes on their incomes. Current tax laws are favorable to homeowners, who can deduct the payment of local real estate taxes and the interest on their mortgage from their income to get the adjusted level of income on which they pay income taxes. Also, money a person makes on the stock market or from some other situation where his assets go up in value, known as a **capital gain,** is subject to lower personal income tax rates than other income. Interest paid by state and local governments on their bonds is not taxable at all by the federal government. In addition, of course, there is some illegal tax evasion, such as underreporting of income, fake expenses, and imaginary dependents. But evasion is much less important than legal tax avoidance, despite Will Rogers's quip that the income tax has made more liars among the American public than golf.

MORE EQUITY AND SIMPLICITY IN THE INCOME TAX CODE?

Lawyers and accountants like to distinguish between **tax avoidance** and **tax evasion.** Tax avoidance occurs when taxpayers take legal steps to minimize their tax bill. Tax evasion occurs when taxpayers misreport their income or take other illegal steps to cut down on what they actually pay Uncle Sam.

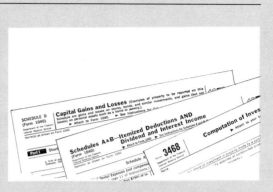

Tax avoidance is a particularly profitable pastime of the well-to-do. With the help of a good lawyer or accountant, one frequently can cut one's income taxes considerably. To illustrate, consider the actual case of a wealthy socialite who took a job as an editor. Because of this job, she may be able to deduct many expenses that she would have incurred anyhow. For example, if she takes a trip to Europe, many of her expenses may be deductible, if she can argue (convincingly) that the trip is somehow related to the development of a book. A deduction is an item that is subtracted from one's income to obtain the net income figure on which the amount of income tax is figured. If you can deduct an expense that otherwise would not be deductible, this reduces your income tax by an amount equal to your marginal income tax rate times the expense. Thus, in the case of the socialite, if she spends $5,000 on a trip to Europe, and if her marginal tax rate is 50 percent, she will save $2,500 in income taxes (that is, .50 × $5,000) if she can convince the Internal Revenue Service that the trip pertained to her business interests.

Many economists feel that the tax system would be more equitable if the tax code were simplified and if many of these ways to avoid income taxes were eliminated. In December 1984, the U.S. Treasury proposed a major revision of the tax laws which would call for only three tax rates, the highest being 35 percent. No deductions would be allowed for state and local income taxes, charitable contributions would be deductible only under certain circumstances, and deductions for interest on second-home mortgages, auto loans, and personal loans would be limited. The Treasury hailed this proposal as a major attempt to simplify the tax code and to make it more equitable.

Other proposals have been put forth as well. In 1983, Congressman Jack Kemp (NY) and Senator Robert Kasten (WIS) introduced a bill for a *"flat tax"* whereby the tax rate would be a flat 25 percent for families with incomes exceeding $3,500. Congressman Richard Gephardt (MO) and Senator William Bradley (NJ) introduced a rival bill that would simplify the tax code but keep somewhat lower tax rates for lower-income families. According to the 1985 annual report of President Reagan's Council of Economic Advisers, "Broadening the tax base would eliminate many sources of misallocation. In addition, because it also allows lower marginal tax rates for the same revenue raised, it would further reduce the inefficiencies arising from the tax system by reducing the differential between the return to taxed activities and the return to activities that are untaxed even under base-broadening."*

* Council of Economic Advisers, *Annual Report,* Washington, D.C.: Government Printing Office, 1985, p. 83.

The Corporate Income Tax

The federal government imposes a tax on the incomes of corporations as well as of people. If a corporation's profits exceed $100,000, the corporate income tax equals $25,750 plus 46 percent of the amount by which the corporation profits exceed $100,000. A corporation with annual profits of $150,000 would pay $48,750 in *corporate income tax*—$25,750 plus $23,000 (46 percent of $50,000).[5] The corporate income tax involves double taxation. The federal government taxes a corporation's earnings both through the corporate income tax (when the corporation earns the profits) and through the personal income tax (when the corporation's earnings are distributed to the stockholders as dividends).

It is generally agreed that the personal income tax is paid by the person whose income is taxed; he or she cannot shift this tax to someone else. But the incidence of the corporate income tax is not so clear. To some extent, corporations may pass along some of their income tax bill to customers in the form of higher prices or to workers in the form of lower wages. Some economists feel that a corporation shifts much of the tax burden in this way; others disagree. This is a controversial issue that has proved very difficult to resolve.

[5] If a corporation's profits are less than $100,000, the corporate income tax equals 15 percent of the first $25,000 of annual profits, 18 percent of the second $25,000 of annual profits, 30 percent of the third $25,000 of annual profits, and 40 percent of the fourth $25,000 of annual profits.

Test Yourself

1. Suppose that the government is trying to determine whether it should build a road from A to B, or whether it should build one that goes from B to C as well. The annual costs and benefits from the two alternative projects are as follows:

	Road from A to B	Road from A to B to C
Annual cost (millions of dollars)	10	15
Annual benefit (millions of dollars)	20	22

Which project, if any, should the government accept? Why?

2. Can you be sent to jail for tax avoidance? Why do people often prefer to receive capital gains rather than ordinary forms of income? If a person's marginal income tax rate is 25 percent and he receives $100 in tax-free income, how much does this equal in before-tax income?

3. Suppose that if it produces the indicated amount of private goods, the maximum amount of public goods that a society can produce is as follows:

Quantity of private goods	Quantity of public goods
0	12
1	11
5	6
8	1
10	0

If this society produces 5 units of private goods and 5 units of public goods, is it being as efficient as it could be? If not, can we tell whether the inefficiency occurs in the public or private sector? And if so, how?

4. In 1985, there was considerable discussion of the pros and cons of a "flat rate" income tax, whereby everyone would pay the same proportion of income in income taxes. Would such a tax simplify the tax code? Would it be in accord with the benefit principle? The ability-to-pay principle?

The Property Tax and the Sales Tax

The *property tax* is the fiscal bulwark of our local governments. The way it works is simple enough. Most towns and cities estimate the amount they will spend in the next year or two, and then determine a property tax based on the assessed property values in the town or city. If there is $500 million in assessed property values in the town and the town needs to raise $5 million, the tax rate will be 1 percent of assessed property value. In other words, each property owner will have to pay 1 percent of the assessed value of his property. There are well-known problems in the administration of the property tax. First, assessed values of property often depart significantly from actual market values; the former are typically much lower than the latter. And the ratio of assessed to actual value is often lower among higher-priced pieces of property; thus wealthier people tend to get off easier. Second, there is widespread evasion of taxes on *personal property*—securities, bank accounts, and so on. Many people simply do not pay up. Third, the property tax is not very flexible: assessments and rates tend to change rather slowly.

The *sales tax,* of course, is a bulwark of state taxation. It provides a high yield with relatively low collection costs. Most of the states have some form of general sales tax, the rate being usually between 3 and 6 percent. For example, New York has a 4 percent sales tax, and California has a 4¾ percent sales tax. Retailers add to the price of goods sold to consumers an amount equal to 3 to 6 percent of the consumer's bill. This extra amount is submitted to the state as the general sales tax. Some states exempt food purchases from this tax, and a few exempt medical supplies. Where they exist, these exemptions help reduce the impact of the sales tax on the poor; but in general the sales tax imposes a greater burden relative to income on the poor than on the rich, for the simple reason that the rich save a larger percentage of their income. Practically all of a poor family's income may be subject to sales taxes; a great deal of a rich family's income may not be, because it is not spent on consumer goods, but is saved.

Who really pays the property tax or the sales tax? To what extent can these taxes be shifted to other people? The answer is not as straightforward as one might expect. For the property tax, the owner of unrented residential property swallows the tax, since there is no one else to shift it to. But the owner of rented property may attempt to pass along some of the tax to the tenant. In the case of a general sales tax, it is generally concluded that the consumer pays the tax. But if the tax is imposed on only a single commodity, the extent to which it can be shifted to the consumer depends on the demand and supply curves for the taxed commodity. The following section explains in some detail why this is the case.

Tax Incidence

Suppose that a sales or excise tax is imposed on a particular good, say beer. In Figure 5.2, we show the demand and supply curves for beer before the imposition of the tax. With no tax, the equilibrium price of a case of beer is $6, and the equilibrium quantity is 100 million cases. If a

Basic Idea #10: Do not assume that a tax on a particular commodity is paid by the producers of this commodity. Taxes frequently can be shifted to other people. For example, if a price increase will not reduce appreciably the quantity demanded of the good, consumers may wind up paying most of the tax.

Figure 5.2

Effect of a $1.00 Tax on a Case of Beer
The tax shifts the supply curve upward by $1.00. Since the demand curve is unaffected, the equilibrium price of beer increases from $6.00 to $6.50 per case.

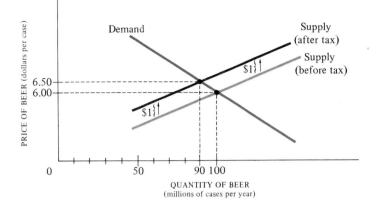

A

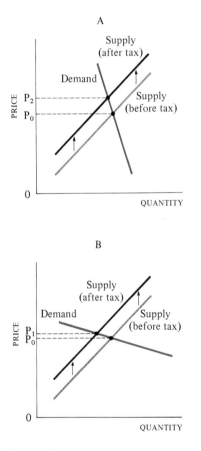

B

Figure 5.3

Effect on Tax Incidence of the Sensitivity of the Quantity Demanded to Price *The supply curve is the same in panel A as in panel B. The quantity demanded is more sensitive to price in panel B than in panel A. Before the tax the equilibrium price is OP_0 in both panels. After the tax the equilibrium price is OP_2 in panel A and OP_1 in panel B. The increase in price to the consumer is greater if the quantity demanded is less sensitive to price (panel A) than if it is more sensitive (panel B).*

tax of $1 is imposed on each case produced, what is the effect on the price of each case? Or to see it from the beer guzzler's perspective, how much of the tax is passed on to the consumer in the form of a higher price?

Since the tax is collected from the sellers, *the supply curve is shifted upward by the amount of tax,* as shown in Figure 5.2. For example, if the pretax price had to be $5 a case to induce sellers to supply 80 million cases of beer, the posttax price would have to be $1 higher—or $6 a case—to induce the same supply. Similarly, if the pretax price had to be $6 a case to induce sellers to supply 100 million cases of beer, the posttax price would have to be $1 higher—or $7 a case—to induce the same supply. The reason why the sellers require $1 more per case to supply the pretax amount is that they must pay the tax of $1 per case to the government. Thus, to wind up with the same amount as before (after paying the tax), they require the extra $1 per case.

Who Pays the Tax? Figure 5.2 shows that, after the tax is imposed, the equilibrium price of beer is $6.50, an increase of $.50 over its pretax level. Consequently, in this case, half of the tax is passed on to consumers, who pay $.50 per case more for beer. And half of the tax is swallowed by the sellers, who receive (after they pay the tax) $.50 per case less for beer. But it is not always true that sellers pass half of the tax on to consumers and absorb the rest themselves. On the contrary, in some cases, consumers may bear almost all of the tax (and sellers may bear practically none of it), while in other cases consumers may bear almost none of the tax (and sellers may bear practically all of it). The result will depend on how sensitive the quantity demanded and the quantity supplied are to the price of the good.

Sensitivity of Demand to Price. In particular, holding the supply curve constant, *the less sensitive the quantity demanded is to the price of the good, the bigger the portion of the tax that is shifted to consumers.* To illustrate this, consider Figure 5.3, which shows the effect of a $1 per case tax on beer in two markets, one (panel B) where the quantity demanded is much more sensitive to price than in the other case (panel A). As is evident, the price increase to consumers resulting from the tax is much greater in the latter case than in the former. And the amount of the tax that is absorbed by producers is much less in the latter case (panel A) than in the former (panel B).

Sensitivity of Supply to Price. It can also be shown that, holding the demand curve constant, *the less sensitive the quantity supplied is to the price of the good, the bigger the portion of the tax that is absorbed by producers.*

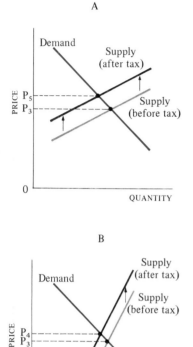

A

B

Figure 5.4

Effect on Tax Incidence of the Sensitivity of the Quantity Supplied to Price *The demand curve is the same in panel A as in panel B. The quantity supplied is more sensitive to price in panel A than in panel B. Before the tax the equilibrium price is OP$_3$ in both panels. After the tax the equilibrium price is OP$_5$ in panel A and OP$_4$ in panel B. The increase in price to the consumer is greater if the quantity supplied is more sensitive to price (panel A) than if it is less sensitive (panel B).*

To illustrate this, consider Figure 5.4, which shows the effect of a $1-per-case tax on beer in two markets, one (panel A) where the quantity supplied is much more sensitive to price than in the other (panel B). As is evident, the price increase to consumers resulting from the tax is much greater in the former case than in the latter. And the amount of the tax that is absorbed by producers is much less in the former case (panel A) than in the latter case (panel B).

Effect of Tax on Quantity. Finally, note that the tax reduces the equilibrium quantity of the good that is taxed—beer in this case. One reason why governments impose taxes on goods like cigarettes and liquor is that they are regarded (in some circles at least) as socially undesirable. Clearly, the more sensitive the quantity demanded and quantity supplied are to price, the larger the reduction in the equilibrium quantity. Thus, if the government imposes a tax of this sort to reduce the quantity consumed of the good, the effect will be greater if both the quantity demanded and the quantity supplied are relatively sensitive to price.

Supply-Side Economics

In the late 1970s and 1980s, some economists advocated tax reductions in order to stimulate national output. Their views came to be known as ***"supply-side economics,"*** and received considerable attention when some of them received high-level posts in the Reagan administration. They played an important role in formulating and helping to push through the very large tax cut passed in August 1981.

Tax Reductions on Labor Income. The supply-siders advocated cuts in taxes on labor income on the grounds that people will work longer and harder. Many economists are skeptical of this proposition. The available evidence seems to indicate that the hours worked by prime-age males would not be affected much by tax changes. But the amount of work done by married women seems more responsive to changes in tax rates. (If the marginal tax rate is high, some women feel that it is not worthwhile to take a job outside their home.)

Tax Reductions on Capital Income. Supply-siders also advocated reductions in taxes on capital income. For example, they called for cuts in taxes on dividends, interest income, and capital gains. In their view, such cuts would encourage additional saving. Although economists agree that saving and investment tend to promote the growth of an economy, there is considerable controversy over the extent to which saving is influenced by tax cuts. Early studies of consumption and saving found saving behavior to be relatively insensitive to changes in the rate of return that savers receive. (That is, if people can obtain a 15 percent annual return from their savings in banks and elsewhere, they may not save much more than if they can obtain only 10 percent.) Recent studies, particularly by Stanford's Michael Boskin, challenge this conclusion, but critics respond that the 1981 tax cut has not increased the percent of total income devoted to saving.

The Laffer Curve. According to some supply-siders, the tax burden is currently so high that further increases in the marginal tax rate would result in lower, not higher, total tax revenue. To explain why they believe this to be true, they use the **_Laffer curve,_** which relates the amount of income tax revenue collected by the government to the marginal tax rate. According to the University of Southern California's Arthur Laffer (after whom the curve was named), tax revenues will be zero if the tax rate is zero. This is indisputable. Also, he points out that tax revenues will be zero if the marginal tax rate is 100 percent. Why? Because if the government takes all the income in taxes, an individual has no incentive to earn taxable income.

According to the Laffer curve, the maximum tax revenue is reached when the tax rate is at some intermediate level between zero and 100 percent. In

---

Example 5.2   Should Income or Consumption Be Taxed?

Some economists have suggested that the income tax might be replaced by a tax on consumption expenditure. For example, a family's taxes might depend in the following way on the total amount it spends on consumption of food, clothing, and other such items:

Consumption expenditure (dollars)	Tax (dollars)
5,000	1,000
10,000	2,500
20,000	5,000
50,000	15,000
100,000	40,000

(a) Suppose that the Jones family and the Moran family both earn $20,000 a year, but that the Joneses save 10 percent of their income, whereas the Morans save nothing. Will they pay the same tax? (b) According to proponents of a consumption tax, it will encourage people to save. Do you agree? Why or why not? (c) Why should the United States be interested in increasing the amount that people save? (d) What objections can you see to the replacement of the income tax by a consumption tax? *

SOLUTION

(a) No. The Morans will pay a larger tax than the Joneses because they spend more on consumption than the Joneses. (b) It seems likely that it would encourage saving because the future consumption that can be obtained for a given sacrifice of present consumption will be greater than under an income tax. (c) As pointed out in Chapter 1, saving enables society to invest in new plant and equipment, which will promote more rapid productivity increase. In recent years, the U.S. rate of productivity increase has been relatively low. (d) There are a plethora of difficulties in making such a fundamental change in the tax system. To take but one example, consider retired people who have paid income taxes all their working lives. It would not be equitable to subject them to a consumption tax.

* For further discussion, see J. Pechman, ed., *Options for Tax Reform,* Washington, D.C.: Brookings, 1984.

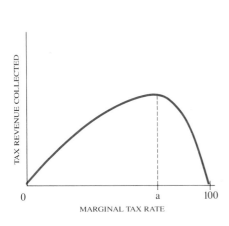

TAX REVENUE COLLECTED

0   a   100

MARGINAL TAX RATE

Figure 5.5

The Laffer Curve *Beyond point* a,
*further increases in the marginal tax rate
result in less revenue collected. According
to some economists like Arthur Laffer,
U.S. tax rates currently are at this point.
Other economists disagree. There is
considerable controversy over the shape
and usefulness of the Laffer curve.*

Figure 5.5, this level is *Oa.* According to Laffer, U.S. tax rates already have
reached or exceeded this level. Many other economists deny this. Although
they admit that a reduction in tax rates could reduce the incentive to cheat
on taxes and to find tax loopholes (as well as to encourage people to work
harder and save more), they feel that Laffer's evidence is too weak to support his conclusions.

Some supply-siders asserted that the 1981 tax cut would result in such
large increases in output and income that tax receipts would surge despite
the reduction in tax rates. Thus they felt that federal revenues would not fall
short of federal expenditures. In fact, however, federal revenues were about
$200 billion less than federal expenditures in fiscal 1985.

It seems fair to say that there is considerable uncertainty about the shape
of the Laffer curve and where the United States is located on it. Even the
existence and usefulness of such a curve is a matter of dispute.

Government Debt

THE NATIONAL DEBT: SIZE AND GROWTH

No subject in economics has more confused the public than the national
debt. When the federal government spends more than it receives in taxes, it
borrows money to cover the difference. The **national debt**—composed of
bonds, notes, and other government IOUs of various kinds—is the result of
such borrowing. These IOUs are held by individuals, firms, banks, and
public agencies. There is a large and very important market for government
securities, which are relatively riskless and highly liquid. If you look at the
New York Times or *Wall Street Journal,* for example, you can find each day
the prices at which each of a large number of issues of these bonds, notes,
and bills are quoted.

How large is the national debt? In 1984, as shown in Figure 5.6, it was
about $1.6 trillion. This certainly seems to be a large amount, but it is im-
portant to relate the size of the national debt to the size of our national
output. After all, a $1.6-trillion debt means one thing if our annual output
is $2 trillion, and another thing if our annual output is $200 billion. As a
percent of output, the national debt is smaller now than in 1939, and no
larger now than shortly after the Civil War. In 1984, the debt was about 40
percent of output; in 1939, it was about 50 percent of output; and in 1868,
it was about 40 percent of output. The debt—expressed as a percentage of
output—is shown in Figure 5.7. Surely the figures do not seem to provide
any cause for immediate alarm.[6] (However, many economists have warned
that there are problems in incurring the large deficits that were responsible
for the rapid rate of increase in the debt during the 1980s. Much more will
be said on this score in Chapter 12.)

A Burden on Future Generations? Although a discussion of many aspects
of the national debt must be postponed to later chapters, it is essential that
we look more closely at why the public has been so agitated about the debt's
size. One important reason has been that they have felt that the debt was a
burden that was being thrust on future generations. To evaluate this idea it
is important to recognize that a public debt is not like your debt or mine,

---

[6] Note too that much of the public debt is in the hands of government agencies, not held by
the public. For example, in 1984 only about $1 trillion was held by private investors.

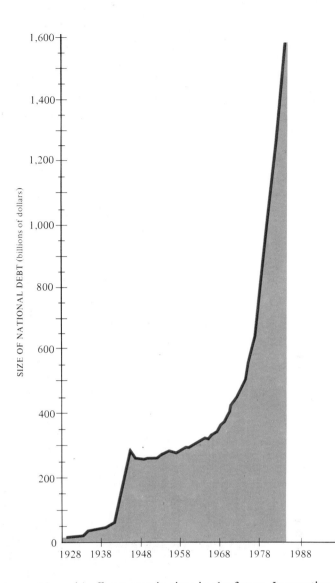

Figure 5.6

Size of the National Debt, United States, 1929–84 *The national debt, about $1.6 trillion in 1984, has been growing at a rapid rate due to huge government deficits.*

which must be paid off at a certain time in the future. In practice, new government debt is issued by the government to pay off maturing public debt. There never comes a time when we must collectively reach into our pockets

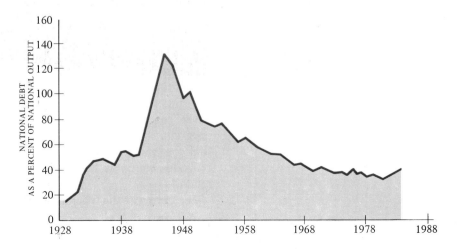

Figure 5.7

National Debt as a Percent of National Output, United States, 1929–84 *As a percent of national output, the national debt declined steadily from World War II to about 1980. During the 1980s, it increased, but not very greatly.*

to pay off the debt. And even if we did pay it off, the same generation would collect as the one that paid.

Effects of Externally Held Debt. Of course, this does not mean that the debt is of no economic consequence. On the contrary, to the extent that the debt is held by foreigners, we must send goods and services overseas to pay the interest on it. This means that less goods and services are available for our citizens. Thus, if we finance a particular government activity by borrowing from foreigners, the costs may be transferred to future generations, since they must pay the interest. But from the point of view of the world as a whole, the current generation sacrifices goods and services, since the lending country forgoes current goods and services. Also, it must be recognized that, if the debt is incurred to purchase capital goods, they may produce enough extra output to cover the interest payments.

Effects of Internally Held Debt. Even if the debt is internally held, it may have some undesirable effects. Taxes must be collected from the public at large to pay interest to the holders of government bonds, notes, and other obligations. To the extent that the bondholders receiving the interest are wealthier than the public as a whole, there is some redistribution of income from the poor to the rich. To the extent that the taxes needed to obtain the money to pay interest on the debt reduce incentives, the result also may be a smaller national output.

A final word should be added about the idea that the national debt imposes a burden on future generations. *The principal way in which one generation can impose such a burden on another is by using up some of the country's productive capacity or by failing to add a normal increment to this capacity.* This, of course, is quite different from incurring debt. For example, World War II would have imposed a burden on subsequent generations whether or not the national debt was increased. However it was financed, the war would have meant that our resources had to be used for tanks and war planes rather than for keeping up and expanding our productive capacity during 1941–45. And this imposed a burden, a real burden, on Americans living after 1945—as well, of course, as on those living during the war.

Alternative Ways of Financing Government Expenditures—and Their Effects

To complete the present discussion of public finance, it is important to recognize that there are three ways that the federal government can finance any expenditure. The first way is to *raise taxes* to cover the expenditure. The effect of this method of financing the expenditure is straightforward: purchasing power is transferred from the people paying the extra taxes to the government. Thus the costs are borne by the taxpayer. The second way is to *borrow the money* from willing lenders. In this case, too, the effect is straightforward: purchasing power is transferred from the lenders to the government. The current costs of the government programs are borne by the lenders, who receive interest subsequently in return.

The third way the federal government can finance any expenditure is to

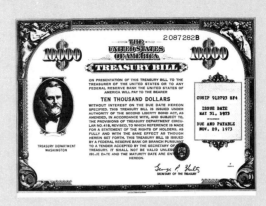

Average U.S. citizens have very little direct contact with the Department of the Treasury. If they work for the federal government, they receive a bimonthly check; if they are so fortunate as to have overpaid their income tax, they may receive a lovely green refund check. In fact, the processing of checks is (at least, to the nonrecipient economist) much less important than many other functions of the Treasury. Should the Congress or the president wish technical advice on the effect of a new tax measure, the Treasury Department will supply the analysis. In addition, it represents American interests in negotiations over international monetary arrangements with other countries; and, through the Internal Revenue Service and the Customs Service, it collects most federal taxes.*

But from an economist's point of view, one of the most interesting tasks the Treasury performs may be the management of the national debt. Imagine yourself with a debt of about $1 trillion (held by private investors), with a few billion coming due each week. Obviously, much of the Treasury's time must be spent scratching for new Peters in order to pay old Pauls. This may not sound like an easy task; and, in fact, it isn't. Over the years the Treasury has developed a bewildering array of devices—refinancing Series E bonds, U.S. savings bonds, short-term bills, long-term bonds—for coaxing new lenders to release their cash, or persuading old lenders to defer collection. One of the most important of these instruments is U.S. Treasury bills, which in 1984 amounted to over $350 billion. (Should you ever have a spare $10,000, the smallest denomination in which Treasury bills are sold, their current prices can be found in the financial pages of any major newspaper.)

Almost every month the undersecretary of the Treasury for monetary affairs must decide in what form the portion of the debt coming due should be refinanced. Are interest rates going up? If so, he might refinance by selling long-term bonds, locking up money at the present low rate. Will interest rates fall? If so, he might prefer the 90-day bill. Before an issue is floated, he gets a reading of market conditions from committees of the American Bankers Association and the Investment Bankers Association. But cost is not his only problem. He must also worry about the effect of Treasury operations on financial markets and must have developed future refunding policies. In any case, an elaborate financial network of banks, big insurance companies, pension funds, and investment houses is always waiting to respond to the Treasury's next offering.

E.A.

* Moreover, faithful television fans may realize that, through its Bureau of Customs, the Treasury is responsible for controlling the importation of narcotics.

create new money. In other words, it can print extra currency (or create new money in other ways that will be described in Chapters 14–16). If the economy is already at full employment, this procedure is likely to cause inflation. The increase in the price level will mean that households and firms will have to buy less than would otherwise have been the case. At the same time, the government will use the new money to finance the expenditure (and obtain the resources it wants). Thus purchasing power is transferred from the consumers and firms whose incomes and receipts do not keep pace with inflation to the government. One disadvantage of this means of finance is that these consumers and firms are often the weakest and least able to bear this burden.

If the economy is not at full employment, the opportunity costs of government programs may be much less than if the economy is at full employment. Recall from Chapter 1 that the opportunity cost of using resources in a particular way is the value of the output that could have been obtained if these resources had been used in some other way. Clearly, if the resources used in a particular government program would have been unemployed if this program had not been started, society is giving up very little by using these resources in this program. Why? Because they would have been idle otherwise. On the other hand, if there is full employment, these resources would not have been idle, and the opportunity costs of the program would be the value of what they could produce elsewhere.

Test Yourself

1. Suppose that the supply curve for gin is as follows:

Price of gin (dollars per quart)	Quantity supplied (millions of quarts)
4	5
5	6
6	7
7	8
8	9
9	10

Plot the supply curve on graph paper. Suppose that the government imposes a tax of $2 per quart on gin, and that the tax is collected from the sellers. Plot the posttax supply curve on graph paper.

2. Under the circumstances described in Question 1, suppose that the quantity of gin demanded is 7 million quarts, regardless of the price (so long as it is between $4 and $9 per quart). What will be the equilibrium price of gin before the tax, and after it? How much of the tax is passed on to the consumer?

3. Under the circumstances described in Question 1, suppose that the demand curve for gin is a horizontal line at $6 per quart. If this is the case, what will be the equilibrium price of gin before the tax, and after it? How much of the tax is passed on to the consumer?

4. "The national debt is of little or no economic consequence because we owe it to ourselves." Comment and evaluate.

Summary

1. The spending decisions of the federal government take place in the context of the budgetary process. The president submits his budget, which is a statement of anticipated expenditures and revenues, to Congress, which votes appropriations. The Ways and Means Committee of the House of Representatives and the

Senate Finance Committee play important roles in the federal tax legislative process.

2. Basically, the amount that the government spends on various activities and services must be decided through the nation's political processes. Voting by ballots must be substituted for dollar voting. In making such decisions, it is important to distinguish between changes in government expenditure that alter the scope of government and changes in government expenditures due to changes in efficiency.

3. Spending on each government program should be pushed to the point where the extra benefit from an extra dollar spent is at least equal to the dollar of cost. In some areas, benefit-cost analyses have proved useful in determining which of a variety of projects can accomplish a particular goal most economically, and whether any of them is worth carrying out. However, accurate measurement of the relevant benefits and costs is frequently difficult.

4. Just as the price system suffers from limitations, so does the government. Special-interest groups sometimes gain at the expense of society as a whole. Government agencies sometimes have little incentive to increase efficiency. Citizens find it difficult to be selective in their choice of goods and services in the public sector. In recent years, economists seem to have put more emphasis on these (and other) limitations of the public sector.

5. It is generally agreed that people who receive more in benefits from a certain government service should pay more in taxes to support it. It is also generally agreed that people should be taxed so that the result is a socially desirable redistribution of income, and that equals should be treated equally. But these general principles, although useful, cannot throw light on many of the detailed questions a real-life tax code must answer.

6. The personal and corporate income taxes are very important sources of federal revenues, the sales tax is an important source of state revenues, and the property tax is an important source of local revenues.

7. When the government spends more than it receives in revenues, the government borrows money to cover the difference. It could simply print money for this purpose, but it has chosen to borrow a considerable proportion of what has been needed. The resulting debt is often called the national debt.

8. Despite much public worry about the size of the national debt, as a percentage of national output it is smaller now than in 1939. There are important differences between government debt and private debt. Although the size of the debt is certainly of consequence, it is not true that it somehow may lead to bankruptcy.

Concepts for Review

Budget	Corporate income tax	Sales tax
Benefit-cost analysis		Tax incidence
Benefit principle	Tax avoidance	Supply-side economics
Ability-to-pay principle	Tax evasion	
Personal income tax	Flat tax	Laffer curve
Marginal tax rate	Property tax	National debt
Capital gain		

CHAPTER 6

The Business Firm: Organization, Motivation, and Technology

It is hard to overstate the importance of business firms in the American economy. They produce the bulk of our goods and services, hire most of the nation's workers, and issue stocks and bonds that represent a large percentage of the nation's wealth. Judged by any yardstick—even less complimentary ones like the responsibility for environmental pollution—business firms are an extremely important part of the American economy. In this chapter, we discuss the various types of business firms, such as proprietorships and corporations. Then we describe the various types of securities—common stock, bonds, and so forth—issued by firms, and discuss the workings of the stock market. Next, we take up the motivation and structure of firms, as well as their technology. Finally, we provide some essential elements of accounting. This material is a necessary introduction to the workings of the business enterprise, absolutely essential to anyone who works for, manages, or invests in a firm.

The IBM Corporation: A Case Study

To begin with, let's look in some detail at one of America's biggest firms: the IBM Corporation. A description of its history and vicissitudes should give you a better feel for what firms do and the sorts of problems they face.

ELECTRONIC COMPUTERS: COMING FROM BEHIND

The IBM Corporation operated under the strong leadership of Thomas Watson, Sr., until his death in 1956. Watson joined the Computing-Tabulating-Recording Corporation in 1914, and renamed it International Business Machines in 1924. The firm became a very successful and fast-growing office-equipment company. In the late 1940s and early 1950s, the first electronic computers were developed, but IBM did not then appreciate the commercial potential of such equipment. According to Watson's son:

> During these really earth-shaking developments in the accounting machine industry, IBM slept soundly. We had put the first electronically-operated punched card calculator on the market in 1947. We clearly knew that electronic computing even in those days was so fast that the machine waited 9/10 of every card cycle for the mechanical portions of the machine to feed the next card. In spite of this, we didn't jump to the obvious conclusion that if we could feed data more rapidly, we could increase speeds by 900 percent. Remington Rand and Univac drew this conclusion and were off to the races.
>
> Finally we awoke and began to act. We took one of our most competent operating executives with a reputation for fearlessness and competence and put him in charge of all phases of the development of an IBM large-scale electronic computer. He and we were successful.
>
> How did we come from behind? First, we had enough cash to carry loads of engineering, research, and production, which were heavy. Second, we had a sales force which enabled us to tailor our machine very closely to the market. Finally, and most important, we had good company morale. All concerned realized that this was a mutual challenge to us as an industry leader. We had to respond with all that we had to win, and we did.[1]

SNOW WHITE AND THE SEVEN DWARFS

Although IBM was a slow starter, it soon became the dominant producer of electronic computers. By 1956, it had over 80 percent of the market. According to many observers, its success was due particularly to its marketing skills. In the 1960s, it became known as Snow White, while its rivals—Burroughs, Univac, NCR, Control Data, Honeywell, GE, and RCA—were referred to as the Seven Dwarfs. In the 1970s, after GE and RCA left the computer industry, only five dwarfs remained.

On January 17, 1969, the federal government brought a massive antitrust case against IBM, accusing it of monopolistic practices. The case went on for thirteen years. According to IBM's former chairman, Frank Cary, "The suit was a tremendous cloud that was over the company. . . . It couldn't help influencing us in a whole variety of ways. Ending it lifted a huge burden from management's shoulders." In January 1982, the Justice Department dropped the case, saying that it was "without merit."

Since the settlement of the case, IBM has been selling aggressively and entering new markets. Some observers are worried that it is becoming too big and powerful; others feel that it has plenty of competition from the Japanese, among others. In 1983, its net income of $5.5 billion made IBM the

[1] T. Belden and M. Belden, *The Lengthening Shadow: The Life of Thomas J. Watson*, Boston: Little, Brown, 1962.

world's most profitable industrial corporation, although sales of $40.2 billion made it only the world's seventh largest. In 1984, its profits were over $6.5 billion.

THE IBM PERSONAL COMPUTER

One of IBM's most dramatic recent moves was its entrance into the personal computer market in 1981. The job of overseeing the development of IBM's personal computer (PC) was entrusted to a twelve-member group, which worked for about a year on the project. The group broke with tradition by making the PC's technical specifications available to other firms, thus allowing outsiders to write software and make peripheral equipment for the PC that would extend its appeal. Within a few months after its introduction, the IBM PC was setting the standard for the industry. By 1983, IBM had garnered about 28 percent of the market for personal computers.

According to some observers, IBM will eventually gain a much larger share of the personal computer market, thus cutting into the sales of Apple Computer and others. Only time will tell whether this is true. But without question IBM's very successful entrance into the personal computer market during the early 1980s has transformed the computer industry.

Characteristics of American Firms: Some Salient Facts

IBM world headquarters

IBM is an economic colossus—a huge organization with over 300,000 employees. Of course it is not typical of American business firms. If we broaden our focus to take in the entire population of business firms in the United States, the first thing we note is their tremendous number; according to government statistics, there are about 16 million. The vast majority of these firms, as one would expect, is very small. There are lots of grocery stores, gas stations, auto dealers, drugstores, clothing shops, restaurants, and so on. You see hundreds of them as you walk along practically any downtown city street. But these small firms, although numerous, do not control the bulk of the nation's productive capacity. The several hundred largest firms have great economic power, measured by their sales, assets, employment, or other such indices. The small firms tend to be weak and short-lived. Although some prosper, many small firms go out of business after only a few years of existence.

The next thing to note is that *most of the nation's business firms are engaged in agriculture, services, and retail trade.* Table 6.1 shows that about three-quarters of the firms in the United States are in these industries, an understandable figure since these industries tend to have lots and lots of small businesses. *Although manufacturing firms constitute only about 3 percent of all American firms, they account for more than one-third of all business receipts.* On the other hand, agriculture (including forestry and fisheries) includes about 25 percent of the nation's business firms, but accounts for only 3 percent of the total receipts. Clearly, this is because manufacturing firms tend to be much bigger, in terms of receipts, employment, and assets, than agricultural firms. Think, for example, of the steel plants in Pittsburgh or Cleveland, or of the aircraft plants in California or

Table 6.1

NUMBER AND RECEIPTS OF BUSINESS FIRMS, BY INDUSTRY, UNITED STATES[a]

Industry	Number of firms (millions)	Receipts of firms (billions of dollars)
Agriculture, forestry, and fisheries	4.0	170
Mining	0.1	143
Construction	1.4	318
Manufacturing	0.5	2,099
Transportation, communication[b]	0.5	456
Wholesale and retail trade	3.4	1,968
Financial	2.1	353
Services	4.5	368
Total	16.2	5,877

[a] Figures may not sum to total due to rounding.
[b] Includes electric and gas.
Source: Statistical Abstract of the United States.

Georgia. They dwarf the typical farm—and they are only parts of a manufacturing firm.

Finally, note that *most of the nation's business firms are proprietorships;* indeed, almost four-fifths fall into this category, while about 14 percent are corporations, and about 8 percent are partnerships. You often hear the terms *proprietorship, partnership, corporation.* What do these terms mean?

Proprietorships

A proprietorship is a legal form of business organization—the most common form, as we saw in the previous section, and also the simplest. Specifically, a **proprietorship** is a firm owned by a single individual. A great many of the nation's small businesses are proprietorships. For example, the corner drugstore may well be one. If so, it has a single owner. He hires the people he needs to wait on customers, deliver orders, do the bookkeeping, and so forth. He borrows, if he can, whatever money he feels he needs. He reaps the profits, or incurs the losses. All his personal assets—his house, his furniture, his car—can be taken by creditors to meet the drugstore's bills; that is, he has unlimited liability for the debts of the business.

Pros. What Lincoln said about the common man applies as well to proprietorships: God must love them, or He wouldn't have created so many of them. If proprietorships didn't have advantages over other legal forms of business organization under many sorts of circumstances, there wouldn't be so many of them. What are these advantages? First, *owners of proprietorships have complete control over their businesses.* They don't have to negotiate with partners or other co-owners. They are the boss—and the only boss. Anyone who has been in a position of complete authority knows the joy it can bring. Many proprietors treasure this feeling of independence. Second, *a proprietorship is easy and inexpensive to establish:* all you have to do is hang out your shingle and announce you are in business. This too is a great advantage.

111

Cons. But proprietorships have important disadvantages as well—and for this reason, they are seldom found in many important industries. One disadvantage is that *it is difficult for a proprietor to put together enough financial resources to enter industries like automobiles, steel, or computers.* No one in the world has enough money to establish, by himself or herself, a firm of IBM's present size. Another disadvantage is that *proprietors are liable for all of the debts of the firm.* If their business fails, their personal assets can be taken by their creditors, and they can be completely wiped out.

Partnerships

A *partnership* is somewhat more complicated than a proprietorship. As its name implies, it is a form of business organization where two or more people agree to own and conduct a business. Each partner agrees to contribute some proportion of the capital and labor used by the business, and to receive some proportion of the profits or losses. There are a variety of types of partnerships. In some cases, one or more of the partners may be "silent partners," who put up some of the money, but have little or nothing to do with the operations of the firm. The partnership is a common form of business organization in some industries and professions, like the law. But as we saw in a previous section, partnerships are found less frequently than proprietorships or corporations in the United States.

Pros. A partnership has certain advantages. Like a proprietorship, *it can be established without great expense or legal red tape.* (However, if you ever go into a partnership with someone, you would be well advised to have a good lawyer draw up a written agreement establishing such things as the salaries of each partner and how profits are to be shared.) In addition, a partnership can avoid some of the problems involved in a proprietorship. *It can usually put together more financial resources and specialized know-how than a proprietorship*—and this can be an important advantage.

Cons. But the partnership also has certain drawbacks. First, *each partner is liable without limit for the bills of the firm.* For example, even if one partner of a law firm has only a 30 percent share of the firm, he or she may be called upon to pay all the firm's debts if the other partners cannot do so. Second, *there is some red tape in keeping a partnership in existence.* Whenever a partner dies or withdraws, or whenever a new partner is admitted, a new partnership must be established. Third, like the proprietorship, *the partnership is not a very effective way to obtain the large amounts of capital required for some modern industries.* A modern automobile plant may cost $500 million, and not many partnerships could assemble that much capital. For these reasons, as well as others discussed in the next section, the corporation has become the dominant form of business organization.

Corporations

A far more complicated form of business organization than either the proprietorship or partnership, the *corporation* is a fictitious legal person, separate and distinct from its owners. A corporation is formed by having lawyers draw up the necessary papers stating (in general terms) what sorts of activities the owners of the corporation intended to engage in. The owners of the corporation are the stockholders. **Stock,** pieces of paper signifying ownership of the corporation, is issued to the owners, generally in exchange for their cash. Ordinarily, each **share** of stock gives its owner one vote. The corporation's **board of directors,** which is responsible for setting overall policy for the firm, is elected by the stockholders. The firm's owners can, if they are dissatisfied with the company's policies or think they have better opportunities elsewhere, sell their stock to someone else, assuming, of course, that they can find a buyer.

Pros. The corporation has many advantages over the partnership or proprietorship. In particular, *each of the corporation's owners has limited, not unlimited, liability.* If I decide to become one of the owners of IBM and if a share of IBM stock sells for $125 a share, I can buy ten shares of IBM stock for $1,250. And I can be sure that, if IBM falls on hard times, I cannot lose more than $1,250 I paid for the stock. There is no way that I can be assessed beyond this. Moreover, *the corporation, unlike the partnership or proprietorship, has unlimited life.* If several stockholders want to withdraw from the firm, they simply sell their stock. The corporation goes on, although the identity of the owners changes. For these reasons, *the corporation is clearly a better device for raising large sums of money than the partnership or proprietorship.* This is an enormous advantage of the corporation, particularly in industries like automobiles and steel, which could not otherwise finance their operations.

Cons. Without question, the corporation is a very important social invention. It permits people to assemble the large quantities of capital required for efficient production in many industries. Without limited liability and the other advantages of the corporation, it is doubtful that the opportunities and benefits of large-scale production could have been reaped. However, this does not mean that the corporate form will work for all firms. In many cases, a firm requires only a modest amount of capital, and there is no reason to go to the extra trouble and expense of establishing a corporation. Moreover, one disadvantage of the corporation is **double taxation of income,** since, as you will recall from Chapter 5, corporations pay income taxes—and the tax rate is often almost one-half of every extra dollar earned. Thus every dollar earned by a corporation and distributed to stockholders is taxed twice by the federal government—once when it is counted as income by the corporation, and once when the remainder is counted as income by the stockholders.

Corporate Securities

The corporation raises money by issuing various kinds of securities; of these, three kinds—common stock, preferred stock, and bonds—are particularly significant. Each of these types of securities is important to the workings of the corporation and to people's investment decisions.

Common Stock. **Common Stock** is the ordinary certificate of ownership of the corporation. Holders of common stock are owners of the firm. They share in the firm's profits—if there are any profits. At frequent intervals, the board of directors of the firm may declare a dividend of so much per share for the common stockholders. For example, the common stockholders of IBM received dividends of $4.40 per share in 1984. **Dividends** are thus the income the owners of common stock receive. (In addition, of course, common stockholders may make money by selling their stock for more than they paid for it; as noted in the previous chapter, such income is called **capital gains.**) Common stock is generally regarded as more risky than preferred stock or bonds, for reasons that will be explained.

Preferred Stock. **Preferred stock** is a special kind of certificate of ownership that pays at most a stated dividend. For example, consider the General Motors Corporation, the huge auto maker. Owners of one type of General Motors preferred stock receive $5 a share per year, as long as the firm makes enough to pay this dividend. To protect the owners of preferred stock, it is stipulated that no dividends can be paid on the common stock unless the dividends on the preferred stock are paid in full. Since the common stockholders cannot receive their dividends unless the preferred stock's dividends have been paid, common stock is obviously more risky than preferred stock. But by the same token, the amount preferred stockholders have to gain if the company prospers is less than the amount common stockholders have to gain, since however high its profits may be, the firm will pay only the stated dividend—for example, $5 per share per year in the case of General Motors—to the owners of preferred stock.

Bonds. Bonds are quite different from both common and preferred stocks. **Bonds** are debts of the firm; in other words, they are IOUs issued by the firm. In contrast to stockholders, the bondholders are not owners of a firm: they are its creditors, and receive interest, not dividends. Specifically, a bond is a certificate bearing the firm's promise to pay the interest every six months until the bond matures, at which time the firm also promises to pay the bondholders the principal (the amount they lent the firm) as well. Often bonds are sold in $1,000 denominations. For example, one type of bond issued by IBM is a 9⅜ percent bond, due in 2004. The owner of each such bond receives $93.75 per year in interest, and IBM promises to pay him or her the principal of $1,000 when the bond falls due in 2004. A firm must pay the interest on the bonds and the principal when it is due, or it can be declared bankrupt. In other words, the bondholders are legally entitled to receive what is due them before the stockholders can get anything.

Thus, from the point of view of the investor, bonds are generally considered less risky than preferred stock, and preferred stocks are considered less risky than common stock. But we have ignored another fact: inflation. The tendency for the price level in the United States to increase over time has meant that bondholders have been paid off with dollars that were worth less than those they lent. For this reason, together with the fact that owners of common stocks reaped substantial capital gains during the 1960s and early 1970s, many investors tended to favor common stocks. Indeed, during the 1960s, a "cult of equities" developed; these were the years when it appeared that stock prices were headed only one way—even higher. It became very fashionable to buy common stock. But in the middle 1970s, the public's infatuation with common stocks seemed to fade, as stock prices fell; and the 1980s have seen considerable variation in stock prices. To understand why the value of stocks can gyrate so considerably, it is necessary to look briefly at the workings of the stock market.

The Stock Market

In general, large corporations do not sell stock directly to the investor. Instead, the investor buys stock on the stock market. Two major stock exchanges in the United States are the New York Stock Exchange and the American Stock Exchange, both in New York City. On these and similar exchanges in other cities, the common stocks of thousands of corporations are bought and sold.

Price Fluctuations. The price of each common stock fluctuates from day to day, indeed from minute to minute. Basically, the factors responsible for these price fluctuations are the shifts in the demand curve and supply curve for each kind of common stock. For example, if a strike breaks out at a General Motors plant, this may cause the demand curve for General Motors stock to shift downward to the left, since the strike is liable to mean lower profits for General Motors. Because of this downward, or leftward, shift in the demand curve, the price of General Motors common stock will tend to fall, as in fact happened during a United Auto Workers strike in 1974.

The Great Crash. Occasionally, the stock market gets a case of the jitters over economic conditions, stock prices tumble, and old investors think back to the Great Crash of 1929. The 1920s witnessed a feverish interest in investing in the stock market. Along with raccoon coats, Stutz Bearcats, and the Charleston, common stocks were the rage. Both the professionals on Wall Street and the neophytes on Main Street bought common stocks and more common stocks. Naturally, as the demand curves for common stocks shifted upward to the right, their prices rose, thus whetting the appetites of investors for still more common stocks. This upward spiral continued until 1929, when the bubble burst. Suddenly the prices of common stocks fell precipitously—and continued to drop during the early 1930s. The most famous average of industrial stock prices, the Dow-Jones average, fell from 381 in 1929 to 41 in 1933. Many investors, large and small, were wiped out.

Stocks Come Back. The Great Crash made investors wary of common stocks for many years. But by the 1960s confidence in them was fully restored, and there certainly was no tendency for investors to shy away from them. In the 1970s and 1980s, although many small investors (and some large ones) lost their shirts, the stock market remained a major outlet for savings. Judging from historical experience, the public's taste for common stocks seems to be justified. Studies show that, during the course of a lifetime, the typical investor would have done better to invest in common stocks than in the best-quality bonds, because stock prices have tended to rise. This tended to apply in a great many cases, even for investors who lived through the Great Crash. And it has certainly been borne out over the past 40 or 50 years. Thus, although common stocks are riskier in some respects than bonds or preferred stocks, they seem to have performed better, on the average, at least in recent times.

MAKING MONEY ON STOCKS

During periods when the average of stock prices is going up, such as the 1920s and much of the 1950s and 1960s (as well as in more recent bull markets), it is relatively easy to be a financial wizard, whether by luck or calculation. A much more exacting test of your financial acumen is how

115

Over 30 million Americans own common stocks, which indicates that you don't have to be wealthy to be an investor. Suppose that you are interested in buying IBM stock. To determine its current price, you need only look at the financial pages of any major newspaper. For example, on April 1, 1985, the *Wall Street Journal* showed the following information concerning IBM common stock:

52-week				Sales				Net
High	Low	Stock	Div	100s	High	Low	Last	Change
138¼	99	IBM	4.40	6950	127⅛	125⅝	127	+⅜

Reading from left to right, $138.25 and $99 are the highest and lowest prices of IBM stock in the previous year, and $4.40 is the level of IBM's dividends in the previous year. The last five figures show the number of shares sold (695,000), the highest price (127.12½), the lowest price (125.62½), and the final price ($127) of a share on the previous day, as well as the change in the price from the day before (up $.37½ per share).

To determine whether IBM common stock is a good buy, you would be well advised to look at IBM's recent earnings record and to obtain as much information as you can concerning the firm's earnings prospects. This is because, as a firm's earnings (per share of common stock) go up, the price of its stock tends to go up too. Some economists and business analysts have gone so far as to publish formulas by which one can determine, on the basis of forecasts of what a firm's earnings will be, how much the stock is worth. They believe that one should buy if the current price of the stock is below this measure of the stock's intrinsic value and sell if the price is above it.

In contrast, other economists believe that the movement of stock prices has more to do with psychology than with financial valuation of this sort. As John Maynard Keynes put it, "[Most persons] are concerned, not with what an investment is really worth to a man who buys it 'for keeps,' but with what the market will value it at, under the influence of mass psychology, three months or a year hence. . . . For it is not sensible to pay 25 for an investment of which you believe the prospective yields to justify a value of 30, if you also believe that the market will value it at 20 three months hence." As Yale's Burton Malkiel observes, "This theory might . . . be called the 'greater-fool theory.' It's perfectly all right to pay three times what a stock is worth as long as later on you can find some innocent to pay five times what it's worth."*

There is no simple, foolproof way to determine whether IBM common stock is a good buy. Since even the most astute traders on Wall Street frequently do no better than one could do by buying the Dow-Jones average, you would do well to approach the stock market with caution. More than one economic savant has lost his or her shirt.

* B. Malkiel, *A Random Walk down Wall Street,* 4th ed., New York: Norton, 1985.

well you can pick which stocks will outperform the averages. If you can predict that increases will occur in a certain firm's profits, and if other people don't predict the same thing, you may be able to pass this test. However, the sobering truth is that "playing the stock market" is much more an art than a science. The stock market is affected by psychological as well as economic considerations. Moreover, when you try to spot stocks that will increase in price, you are pitting your knowledge and experience against those of skilled professionals with big research staffs and with friends and acquaintances working for the companies in question. And even these professionals can do surprisingly poorly at times.

Do economists have a nose for good investments? John Maynard Keynes was an extremely successful speculator who made millions of dollars. Other economists have been far less successful. Certainly, a knowledge of basic economics is not sufficient to enable you to make money on the stock market, but insofar as the market reflects economic realities, a knowledge of basic economics should be helpful.

The Giant Corporation

Much of the trading on the stock market centers around the relatively small number of giant corporations that control a very substantial percentage of the total assets and employment in the American economy. And well it might, for the largest 100 manufacturing corporations control about half of this country's manufacturing assets. These firms have tremendous economic and political power. They include the giant automobile manufacturers (General Motors, Ford), the big oil firms (Exxon, Standard Oil of Indiana, Mobil, Standard Oil of California, Texaco, Atlantic-Richfield), the big steel firms (U.S. Steel, Bethlehem, Armco), the big computer and office machinery producers (IBM and Xerox), the leading tobacco firms (American Brands, R. J. Reynolds, Philip Morris), the electrical equipment producers (General Electric, Westinghouse), and many others.

MANAGEMENT

Usually, the president is the chief operations officer in the firm, although sometimes the chairman of the board of directors fills this role. As for the board of directors, some members are chosen for their reputations and contacts, while others are chosen for their knowledge of the firm, the industry, or some profession or specialty.

The board generally contains at least one representative of the financial community, and a university president or former government official is often included to show that the firm is responsive to broad social issues. Members of IBM's board include Harold Brown, a former Secretary of Defense; Patricia Harris, a professor at George Washington University; and Richard Lyman, president of the Rockefeller Foundation.

The board of directors is concerned with overall policy. Since it meets only a few times a year, it seldom becomes involved in day-to-day decisions; and it usually goes along with management's policies, so long as management retains the board's confidence.

SEPARATION OF OWNERSHIP FROM CONTROL

An interesting and important feature of the large corporation is the fact that it is owned by many people, practically all of whom have little or no detailed information about the firm's operations. The owners of IBM number over 700,000, but most of them know relatively little about what is going on in the firm. Moreover, because of the wide diffusion of ownership, working control of a large corporation can often be maintained by a group with only one-fifth or less of all the voting stock. The result is a *separation of ownership from control.* In other words, the owners control the firm in only a limited and somewhat sporadic sense.

So long as a firm's management is not obviously incompetent or corrupt, it is difficult for insurgent stockholders to remove the management from office. Most stockholders do not go to the annual meetings to vote for members of the firm's board of directors. Instead, they receive *proxies,* which, if returned, permit the management to exercise their votes. Usually enough shareholders mail in their proxies to give management the votes it needs to elect a friendly board of directors. In recent years, the Securities and Exchange Commission, which oversees and regulates the financial markets, has attempted to make the giant corporations more democratic by enabling insurgent groups to gain access to mailing lists of stockholders and so forth. But there is still a noteworthy and widespread separation of ownership from control.

Test Yourself

1. In its 1979 annual report, the Exxon Corporation reported that it was building a new olefins plant (costing $500 million) in Baytown, Texas. Is this plant a firm? Why or why not? Do you think that a proprietorship would be likely to build and own such a plant? Why or why not?

2. Assume that a partnership wanted to enter the automobile industry. What problems would such a legal form of organization impose upon the potential entrants? Are any of the Big Three in the U.S automobile industry (General Motors, Ford, and Chrysler) partnerships?

3. Explain why each of the following statements is true or false. (a) The University of Texas is a firm. (b) Massachusetts General Hospital is a firm. (c) A firm must be owned by more than one person. (d) The owner of a firm must participate in its management.

4. On February 19, 1985, the common stock of Exxon Corporation closed at $47.25 per share. What effect would each of the following have on its price? (a) A marked increase in the demand for gasoline. (b) A prolonged strike at a major Exxon refinery. (c) Price ceilings on gas and oil.

5. Explain why bondholders do not vote for a corporation's board of directors and why common stockholders are not guaranteed a particular dividend rate.

Motivation of the Firm

What determines the behavior of the business firm? As a first approximation, *economists generally assume that firms attempt to maximize **profits**,* which are defined as the difference between the firm's revenue and its costs.

MOTIVATION OF THE FIRM

Basic Idea #11: Economists frequently assume that firms maximize profit. Although this is an oversimplification, models based on this assumption have proved very useful, both in explaining why firms and markets behave as they do and in indicating rules of business behavior for firms that want to try to maximize profit.

In other words, economists generally assume that firms try to make as much money as possible. This assumption certainly does not seem unreasonable; most businessmen appear to be interested in making money. Nonetheless, the assumption of profit maximization oversimplifies the situation. Although businessmen certainly want profits, they are interested in other things as well. Some firms claim that they want to promote better cultural activities or better racial relations in their community. At a less lofty level, other firms say that their aim is to increase their share of the market. Whether or not one takes these self-proclaimed goals very seriously, it is clear that firms are not interested *only* in making money—often for the same reason that Dr. Johnson gave for not becoming a philosopher: "because cheerfulness keeps breaking in."[2]

Intrafirm Politics. In a large corporation, there are some fairly obvious reasons why firms may not maximize profits. Various groups within such firms develop their own party lines, and intrafirm politics is an important part of the process determining firm behavior. Whereas in a small firm it may be fairly accurate to regard the goals of the firm as being the goals of the proprietor, in the large corporation the decision on the goals of the firm is a matter of politics, with various groups within the organization struggling for power. In addition, because of the separation of ownership from control, top management usually has a great deal of freedom as long as it seems to be performing reasonably well. Under these circumstances, the behavior of the firm may be dictated in part by the interests of the management group, resulting in higher salaries, more perquisites, and a bigger staff for their own benefit than would otherwise be the case.

Risk and Uncertainty. Also, in a world full of risk and uncertainty, it is difficult to know exactly what profit maximization means, since the firm cannot be sure that a certain level of profit will result from a certain action. Instead, the best the firm can do is to estimate that a certain probability distribution of profit levels will result from a certain action. Under these circumstances, the firm may choose less risky actions, even though they have a lower expectation of profit than other actions. In a world where ruin is ruinous, this may be perfectly rational policy.

PROFIT MAXIMIZATION IS THE STANDARD ASSUMPTION

Nonetheless, profit maximization remains the standard assumption in economics. As we agreed in our discussion of model building in Chapter 2, to be useful models need not be exact replicas of reality. Economic models based on profit maximization have been very useful indeed. For one thing, they help to show how the price system functions. For another, in the real world, they suggest how a firm should operate if it wants to make as much money as possible. Even if a firm does not want to maximize profit, these theories can be utilized. For example, they can show how much profit the firm is forgoing by taking certain courses of action. In recent years, the theory of the profit-maximizing firm has been studied more and more for the sake of determining profit-maximizing rules of business behavior.

[2] This quote is taken from R. Solow, "The New Industrial State, or Son of Affluence," *The Public Interest,* Fall 1967. Since footnotes are so often used to cite dreary material, it seems worthwhile to use them occasionally to cite humor as well.

Technology, Inputs, and the Production Function

The decisions a firm should make in order to maximize its profits are determined by the current state of technology. Technology, it will be recalled from Chapter 1, is the sum total of society's knowledge concerning the industrial arts. Just as consumers are limited by their income, firms are limited by the current state of technology. If the current state of technology is such that we do not know how to produce more than 40 bushels of corn per year from an acre of land and 2 man-years of labor, then this is as much as the firm can produce from this combination of land and labor. In making its decisions, the firm must take this into account.

INPUTS

In constructing a model of the profit-maximizing firm, economists must somehow represent the state of technology and include it in their model. As a first step toward this end, we must define an ***input.*** Perhaps the simplest definition of an input is that it is anything the firm uses in its production process. Some of the inputs of a farm producing corn might be seed, land, labor, water, fertilizer, various types of machinery, as well as the time of the people managing the farm.

PRODUCTION FUNCTION

Having defined an input, we can now describe how economists represent the state of technology. The basic concept economists use for this purpose is the production function.

For any commodity, *the **production function** is the relationship between the quantities of various inputs used per period of time and the maximum quantity of the commodity that can be produced per period of time.* More specifically, the production function is a table, a graph, or an equation showing the maximum output rate that can be achieved from any specified set of usage rates of inputs. The production function summarizes the characteristics of existing technology at a given point in time. It reflects the technological constraints the firm must reckon with.

To see more clearly what we mean by a production function, consider the Milwaukee Machine Company, a hypothetical machine shop that produces a simple metal part. Suppose that we are dealing with a period of time that is so short that the firm's basic plant and equipment cannot be altered. For simplicity, suppose that the only input whose quantity can be altered in this period is the amount of labor used by the machine shop. Suppose that the firm collects data showing the relationship between the quantity of its output and the quantity of labor it uses. This relationship, given in Table 6.2, is the firm's production function. It shows that, when 1 worker is employed, 100 parts are produced per month; when 2 workers are employed, 210 parts are produced per month; and so on. Information concerning a firm's production function is often obtained from the firm's engineers, as well as its craftsmen and technicians. Much more will be said about production functions in later chapters. All that we want to do here is to introduce the concept of the production function.

Table 6.2

PRODUCTION FUNCTION, MILWAUKEE MACHINE COMPANY

Quantity of labor used per month (number of men employed)	Output per month (number of parts)
0	0
1	100
2	210
3	315
4	415
5	500

Elements of Accounting: The Firm's Balance Sheet

Having touched on the firm's technology, we must return to the motivation of the firm. In a previous section, we stated that economists generally assume that firms attempt to maximize profits. Viewed as a first approximation, this assumption does not seem too hard to swallow, but exactly what do we mean by profit? This is an important question, of interest to businessmen and investors as well as to economists. The accounting profession provides the basic figures that are reported in the newspapers and in a firm's annual reports to its stockholders. If IBM reports that it made $5.5 billion last year, this figure is provided by IBM's accountants. How do the accountants obtain this figure? What are its limitations?

Basically, accounting concepts are built around two very important statements: the balance sheet and the income statement. A firm's **balance sheet** shows the nature of its assets, tangible and intangible, at a certain point in time.

LEFT-HAND SIDE OF THE BALANCE SHEET

Let us return to the Milwaukee Machine Company. Its balance sheet might be as shown in Table 6.3. The left-hand side of the balance sheet shows the assets of the firm as of December 31, 1985. *Current assets* are assets that will be converted into cash relatively quickly (generally within a year), whereas *fixed assets* generally will not be liquidated quickly. The firm has $20,000 in cash, $120,000 in inventory, $160,000 in equipment, and $180,000 in buildings. At first glance, these figures may seem more accurate than they are likely to be. It is very difficult to know how to value various assets. For example, should they be valued at what the firm paid for them, or at what it would cost to replace them? More will be said about these problems below.

RIGHT-HAND SIDE OF THE BALANCE SHEET

The right-hand side of the firm's balance sheet shows the claims by creditors on the firm's assets and the value of the firm's ownership. In Table 6.3,

Table 6.3

BALANCE SHEET, MILWAUKEE MACHINE COMPANY, AS OF DECEMBER 31, 1985

Assets (dollars)		Liabilities and net worth (dollars)	
Current assets		Current liabilities	
Cash	20,000	Accounts payable	20,000
Inventory	120,000	Notes payable	40,000
Fixed assets		Long-term liabilities	
Equipment	160,000	Bonds	160,000
Buildings	180,000		
		Net worth	
		Preferred stock	100,000
		Common stock	100,000
		Retained earnings	60,000
Total	480,000	Total	480,000

the Milwaukee Machine Company has total liabilities—or debts—of $220,000. There is $60,000 in *current liabilities*, which come due in less than a year; and $160,000 in *long-term liabilities*, which come due in a year or more. Specifically, there is $20,000 in *accounts payable*, which are bills owed for goods and services that the firm bought; $40,000 in *notes payable*, short-term notes owed to banks, finance companies, or other creditors; and $160,000 in *bonds payable*, or bonds outstanding.

LEFT-HAND SIDE = RIGHT-HAND SIDE

The difference between the value of a firm's assets and the value of its liabilities is its *net worth*, which is the value of the firm's owners' claims against the firm's assets. In other words, the value of the firm to its owners is the total value of its assets less the value of the debts owed by the firm. Since

total value of assets − total liabilities = net worth,

it follows that

total value of assets = total liabilities + net worth.

That is, *the sum of the items on the left-hand side of the balance sheet must equal the sum of the items on the right-hand side.* This, of course, must be true because of the way we define net worth.

In the case of the Milwaukee Machine Company, the firm's net worth—the difference between its assets and its liabilities—is $260,000. Specifically, there is $100,000 worth of preferred stock and $100,000 worth of common stock; there is also $60,000 in retained earnings. *Retained earnings* is the total amount of profit that the stockholders have reinvested in the business. In other words, the stockholders of the Milwaukee Machine Company have reinvested $60,000 of their profits in the business. Rather than withdrawing this sum as dividends, they have kept it invested in the firm.

The Firm's Income Statement

A firm's income statement shows its sales during a particular period, its costs incurred in connection with these sales, and its profits during this period. Table 6.4 shows the Milwaukee Machine Company's income statement during the period January 1, 1986 to December 31, 1986. Sales during this period were $240,000. The cost of manufacturing the items made during this period was $110,000, which includes $30,000 for materials, $40,000 for labor, $34,000 for depreciation (discussed below), and $6,000 for miscellaneous operating expenses.

However, because the firm has reduced its inventory from $120,000 to $110,000 during the period, the cost of manufacturing the items *made* during the period does not equal the cost of manufacturing the items *sold* during the period. To find the *cost of goods sold*—which is the amount that logically should be deducted from sales to get the profits made from the sale of these goods—we must add the decrease in the value of inventory to

Table 6.4

INCOME STATEMENT, MILWAUKEE MACHINE COMPANY, JANUARY 1, 1986, TO
DECEMBER 31, 1986 (DOLLARS)

Net Sales		240,000
Manufacturing cost of goods sold		120,000
Materials	30,000	
Labor	40,000	
Depreciation	34,000	
Miscellaneous operating cost	6,000	
Total	110,000	
Plus beginning inventory	120,000	
Less closing inventory	−110,000	
Adjusted total	120,000	
Selling and administrative costs		20,000
Fixed interest charges and state and local taxes		10,000
Net earnings before income taxes		90,000
Corporation income taxes		40,000
Net earnings after taxes		50,000
Dividends on preferred stock		4,000
Net profits of common stockholders		46,000
Dividends paid on common stock		20,000
Addition to retained earnings		26,000

the total manufacturing cost. (Why? Because the firm sold more items than it produced during this period. Thus the cost of the items it sold equals the cost of the items it produced during this period plus the cost of the items it sold from its inventory. Since the cost of the items it sold from its inventory equals the decrease in the value of its inventory, the cost of the items it sold equals the cost of the items it produced during this period plus the decrease in inventory.) Putting it another way, we must add the beginning inventory and subtract the closing inventory, as shown in Table 6.4. The resulting figure for cost of goods sold is $120,000.

But manufacturing costs are not the only costs the firm incurs. To estimate the firm's profits, we must also deduct from sales its selling and administrative expenses, its interest charges, and its state and local taxes, as well as its federal income taxes. Table 6.4 shows that the Milwaukee Machine Company's after tax earnings during 1986 were $50,000. This is the amount left for the owners of the business. The income statement also shows what the owners do with what is left. Table 6.4 shows that the Milwaukee Machine Company used $4,000 to pay dividends to holders of preferred stock. When this was done, the holders of common stock were free to distribute some of the profits to themselves. According to Table 6.4, they distributed $20,000 to themselves in dividends on the common stock, and plowed the rest—$26,000—back into the business as retained earnings.

DEPRECIATION

Before leaving the income statement, we should explain one element of manufacturing cost—*depreciation.* While the other elements of manufacturing cost are self-explanatory, this one is not. The idea behind depreciation is that the buildings and equipment will not last forever; eventually

Cross-Chapter Case/Part Two

SHOULD AMERICA ADOPT AN INDUSTRIAL POLICY?

In Chapters 3–6, we have been concerned primarily with the role of the price system and of firms and the government in the American economy. In the mid-1980s, one of the leading questions in this area has been: Should the United States adopt an industrial policy? It is difficult to define an "industrial policy" with precision, since economists do not all use the same definition. But all industrial policies involve some form of government action designed to stimulate and revitalize a nation's industry. In particular, according to many advocates of an industrial policy, the government should encourage new high-technology industries and help older, declining industries to adjust to lower output and employment levels.

In the United States, those favoring the adoption of an industrial policy have proposed a variety of ways in which the government's role in directing the allocation of resources might be expanded. For example, there might be a central agency to formulate the government's industrial policy. Councils including representatives of business, labor, and government might obtain data on particular industries and construct a consensus strategy. A government development bank might invest money in sectors and industries that are regarded as receiving too little capital from private financial sources. Declining industries (so-called "sunset" industries) might get protection from imports and other government help to ease the adjustment to new economic realities.

Advocates of an industrial policy argue that the United States already has an industrial policy of sorts, but that it is largely uncoordinated. For example, the U.S. government spends large amounts on research, sets import quotas, and subsidizes many kinds of firms, just as other countries do. Moreover, this is nothing new. In 1643, Massachusetts granted a fledgling firm exclusive iron-making privileges for 21 years in order to encourage the industry. More recently, the federal government provided a loan guarantee to the Chrysler Corporation to help keep the auto maker in business. Since the U.S. government is already engaged in many of the activities encompassed under the broad heading of "industrial policy," the real question, according to the proponents of an industrial policy, is whether these activities should be better coordinated. In their view, councils of business, labor, and government could do a better job than is now being done of coordinating these far-flung activities of the government, many of which conflict with one another.

Many proponents of an industrial policy also argue that a government-financed industrial development bank should provide industrial firms with money for high-risk, long-term projects. One reason why such a bank is needed, in their opinion, is that private investors tend to be averse to risk and too inclined to want quick pay-backs. Consequently, they invest too little in risky ventures extending for 5 or 10 years or more. Moreover, according to Felix Rohatyn, chairman of New York City's Municipal Assistance Corporation, such a federal bank "could make sure that the aid would be conditional on management and labor concessions needed to make the business viable." In other words, it could force firms to make tough decisions.

Many advocates of an industrial policy feel that the government should act to slow the decline in "basic" industries like steel. Besides providing loans and special tax benefits, the government would sponsor plans to spread adjustment burdens among labor, management, stockholders, creditors, and suppliers. If the industry faces competition from imports, industry commitments to restructure would be the price of protection from imports. Retraining and compensation programs would be employed to help workers whose jobs are lost.

Whereas some economists are strong advocates of an industrial policy for the United States, others feel that it would be a mistaken, and even dangerous, step to take. To begin with, they feel that councils of business, labor, and government experts would be no more effective in improving coordination of various policies of the government than the existing coordinating mechanisms. In particular, they point out that other countries with industrial policies continue to have coordination problems of this sort.

As for the creation of a government-supported industrial bank, many economists react negatively to this proposal, because they feel that political considerations would inevitably enter into the allocation of funds and that money would be wasted on "targeted growth" industries with no commercial future. According to President Reagan's Council of Economic Advisers:

> The proposal to target emerging industries suggests that government can obtain better information than the private sector. It is difficult to understand how government officials, together with private business and labor leaders, will be able to gather more accurate information and use the information more wisely than the private sector. The United States has numerous investors willing to finance new ventures through equity or bank loans. Private investment analysts spend a great deal of time and effort evaluating new technologies and advising private investors on the most promising firms. Information on emerging industries is also exchanged by job shifting among scientists and engineers who are close to the development of new technologies. Ties between industry and the academic community also contribute to the spread of new ideas. In the United States the private sector already has information at least as good as the proposed government councils and banks could expect to gather.
>
> In any event, a government agency is more likely to be short-sighted and risk averse than private investors. Since politicians face frequent elections, they often have very short time horizons. A government agency is also more likely to make decisions based on the shared expectations that are the conventional wisdom of the time; these processes tend to neglect or reject the idiosyncratic information that is the basis for decisions by the most successful private entrepreneurs.
>
> Finally, government officials will often make investments based on politics rather than economics. One country tries to develop a computer industry before it has sufficient technical workers. Other countries invest in highly visible but wasteful energy projects that private firms think are likely to fail.[1]

[1] Council of Economic Advisers, *1984 Annual Report,* Washington, D.C.: Government Printing Office, 1984.

they will have to be replaced. Clearly, it would be foolish to charge the entire cost of replacing them to the year when they are replaced. Instead, a better picture of the firm's true profitability will be drawn if the cost of replacing them is spread gradually over the life of buildings and equipment, thus recognizing that each year's output has a hand in wearing them out. One frequently used technique is so-called *straight-line depreciation,* which spreads the cost of buildings and equipment (less their scrap value) evenly over their life. Thus, if the Milwaukee Machine Company buys a piece of equipment for $20,000 and if it is expected to last ten years (its scrap value being zero), it would charge depreciation of $2,000 per year

---

Example 6.1   How to Depreciate a Baseball Club

Suppose that you decide to buy the Philadelphia Phillies for $30 million. There are some important tax advantages you should understand. According to Bill Veeck, former owner of the Chicago White Sox, "It is almost impossible not to make money on a baseball club when you are buying it new, because, unless you are inordinately successful, you pay no income tax."* In particular, half of the purchase price of the team can be regarded as the cost of the players, which are depreciable assets like machinery or breeding cattle. Suppose that you regard 5 years as being the "useful life" of the players, and that you use straight-line depreciation.

(a) How much depreciation (of the players) can you deduct from the Phillies' receipts each year to figure your profits? (b) Suppose that you pay $3 million in cash and borrow the remaining $27 million to pay for the Phillies. If you pay 15 percent interest, how much interest expense do you deduct from the Phillies' receipts each year to figure your profits? (c) Suppose that this year the Phillies' receipts equal $35 million and their operating expenses (excluding depreciation of the players and the interest on your loan) equal $28 million. Must you pay any income tax? (Assume that you have no income from sources other than the Phillies.)

SOLUTION

(a) Since the cost of the players can be regarded as one-half of the purchase price of the team, it equals one-half of $30 million, or $15 million. Since the life of the players is 5 years, annual depreciation equals $15 million divided by 5, or $3 million. (b) $27 million times 15 percent, or $4.05 million. (c) Your income from the Phillies is as follows:

Earnings (before depreciation and interest)	$7 million
Less depreciation	−3 million
Less interest	−4.05 million
	−$.05 million

Since you incurred a loss (because of the depreciation of the players), you pay no income tax.

* *Philadelphia Inquirer,* March 15, 1981.

for this machine (for ten years after its purchase). The $34,000 charge for depreciation in Table 6.4 is the sum of such charges. Clearly, this is only a rough way to estimate the true depreciation charges, but it is good enough for many purposes.

Economic versus Accounting Profits

The previous section described the nature of profit, as defined by accountants. This is the concept on which practically all published figures in business reports are based. But economists define profits somewhat differently. In particular, economists do not assume that the firm attempts to maximize the current, short-run profits measured by the accountant. Instead they assume that the firm will attempt to maximize the sum of profits over a long period of time.[3] Also, when economists speak of profit, they mean profit after taking account of the capital and labor provided by the owners. Thus, suppose that the owners of the Milwaukee Machine Company, who receive profits but no salary or wages, put in long hours for which they could receive $30,000 in 1986 if they worked for someone else. Also suppose that if they invested their capital somewhere other than in this firm, they could obtain a return of $22,000 on it in 1986. Under these circumstances, economists would say that the firm's after-tax profits in 1986 were $50,000 − $30,000 − 22,000, or −$2,000, rather than the $50,000 shown in Table 6.4. In other words, the economists' concept of profit includes only what the owners make above and beyond what their labor and capital employed in the business could have earned elsewhere. In this case, that amount is negative.

To a considerable extent, the differences between the concepts used by the accountant and the economist reflect the difference in their functions. The accountant is concerned with controlling the firm's day-to-day operations, detecting fraud or embezzlement, satisfying tax and other laws, and producing records for various interested groups. On the other hand, the economist is concerned primarily with decision making and rational choice among prospective alternatives. Although the figures published on profits almost always conform to the accountant's, not the economist's, concept, the economist's concept is the more relevant one for many kinds of decisions. (And this, of course, is recognized by sophisticated accountants.) For example, suppose the owners of the Milwaukee Machine Company are trying to decide whether they should continue in business. If they are interested in making as much money as possible, the answer depends on the firm's profits as measured by the economist, not the accountant. If the firm's economic profits are greater than (or equal to) zero, the firm should continue in existence; otherwise, it should not. Thus the Milwaukee Machine Company should not stay in existence if 1986 is a good indicator of its future profitability.

Basic Idea #12: To economists, profit is the amount that a firm's owners receive over and above what they could make from the capital and labor they provide, if this capital and labor were used outside the firm. Only if profit in this sense is non-negative should the firm stay in existence. (Note that this is closely related to Basic Idea #2 on p. 10.)

---

[3] The profits earned at various points in time should be *discounted* before being added together, but, for simplicity's sake, we neglect this point here. For some relevant discussion, see Chapter 30.

Test Yourself

1. Which of the following are inputs in the steel industry? (a) coke, (b) iron ore, (c) labor, (d) land, (e) capital, (f) water, (g) oxygen, (h) food eaten by U.S. Steel's workers.

2. The 1981 tax law allowed firms to depreciate assets more quickly. For example, they could depreciate some types of assets over 3 years, rather than 5 years. If a firm depreciates an asset more quickly, will its accounting profits in the first year after it buys the asset be increased or decreased?

3. Suppose that a firm's balance sheet is as follows:

Assets (dollars)		Liabilities and net worth (dollars)	
Current assets		Current liabilities	
Cash	200,000	Accounts payable	100,000
Inventory	300,000	Notes payable	_____
Fixed assets		Long-term liabilities	
Equipment	_____	Bonds	400,000
Buildings	800,000		
		Net worth	400,000
Total	2,000,000	Total	_____

Fill in the three blanks. What is the total amount that the firm owes? How much have the owners contributed? What is the difference between current assets and fixed assets?

4. Suppose that a firm's accounting profits for 1986 are $20,000. The firm is a proprietorship, and the owner worked 500 hours managing the business during 1986, for which she received no compensation other than the profits. If she could have gotten $10 an hour working for someone else, how much were her economic profits during 1986? Suppose that she also contributed $50,000 in capital to the firm, and that she could have obtained 6 percent interest on this capital if she had invested it elsewhere. In this case, how much were her economic profits?

Summary

1. There are three principal types of business firms: proprietorships, partnerships, and corporations. The corporation has many advantages over the other two—limited liability, unlimited life, and greater ability to raise large sums of money. Nonetheless, because the corporation also has disadvantages, many firms are not corporations.

2. The corporation raises money by issuing various kinds of securities, of which three kinds—common stock, preferred stock, and bonds—are particularly important.

3. A relatively small number of giant corporations control a very substantial proportion of the total assets and employment in the American economy. In the large corporation, ownership and control tend to be separated.

4. As a first approximation, economists generally assume that firms attempt to maximize profits. In large part, this is because it is a close enough approximation to reality for many of the most important purposes of economics. Also, economists are interested in the theory of the profit-maximizing firm because it provides rules of behavior for firms that do want to maximize profits.

5. To summarize the characteristics of existing technology at a given point in time, the economist uses the concept of the production function, which shows the maximum output rate of a given commodity that can be achieved from any specified set of usage rates of inputs.

6. Accounting concepts are built around two very important statements: the balance sheet and the income statement. The balance sheet shows the nature of the firm's assets and liabilities at a given point in time. The difference between its assets and its liabilities is its net worth, which is the value of the firm's owners' claims against its assets.

7. A firm's income statement shows its sales during a particular period, its costs incurred in connection with these sales, and its profits during the period.

8. Economists define profits somewhat differently than accountants do. In defining profit, economists deduct the amount the owners could receive from the capital and labor they provide, if this capital and labor were used outside the firm. Also, economists are interested in longer periods than those to which accounting statements apply. Although the profit figures that are published almost always conform to the accountant's concept, the economist's concept is the more relevant one for many kinds of decisions.

Concepts for Review

Proprietorship	Dividends	Balance sheet
Partnership	Preferred stock	Current assets
Corporation	Bonds	Fixed assets
Board of directors	Profits	Net worth
Double taxation of income	Input	Income statement
Common stock	Production function	Depreciation

PART THREE

National Output, Income, and Employment

CHAPTER 7

National Income and Product

America's **gross national product**—or GNP, as it is often called—was $3,663 billion in 1984, as compared with $3,305 billion in 1983. Put in the simplest terms, GNP is the value of the total amount of final goods and services produced by our economy during a particular period of time. This measure is important for its own sake, and because it helps us to understand both inflation and unemployment. The federal government and the business community watch GNP figures avidly. Government officials, from the president down, are interested because these figures indicate how prosperous we are, and because they are useful in forecasting the future health of the economy. Business executives are also extremely interested in GNP figures because the sales of their firms are related to the level of GNP, and so the figures are useful in forecasting the future health of their businesses. All in all, it is no exaggeration to say that the gross national product is one of the most closely watched numbers in existence.

In this chapter, we discuss the measurement, uses, and limitations of the gross national product, as well as a variety of other commonly-used measures of national income and output. At the outset, it is worth noting that measures of national income and national product are of comparatively recent vintage. The Department of Commerce first made such estimates in 1932, after experiments at various universities and at the National Bureau of Economic Research. A leading pioneer in this field was the late Nobel laureate Simon Kuznets, then at the University of Pennsylvania. The concepts that Kuznets and others developed are often called the **national income accounts,** and the Bureau of Economic Analysis of the U.S. Department of Commerce compiles these figures on a continuing basis. Just as the accounts of a firm are used to describe and analyze its financial health, so the national income accounts are used to describe and analyze the economic health of the nation as a whole.

131

Gross National Product

As noted above, gross national product is a measure of how much the economy produces in a particular period of time. But the American economy produces millions of types of goods and services. How can we add together everything from lemon meringue pies to helicopters, from books to houses? The only feasible answer is to use money as a common denominator and to make the price of a good or service—the amount the buyer is willing to pay—the measure of value. In other words, we add up the value in money terms of the total output of goods and services in the economy during a certain period, normally a year, and the result is the gross national product during that period.

Although the measurement of gross national product may seem straightforward ("just add up the value in money terms of the total output of the economy"), this is by no means the case. Some of the more important pitfalls that must be avoided and problems that must be confronted are the following:

Avoidance of Double Counting. Gross national product does not include the value of *all* goods and services produced: it includes only the value of *final* goods and services produced. **Final goods and services** are goods and services destined for the ultimate user. For example, flour purchased for family consumption is a final good, but flour to be used in manufacturing bread is an **intermediate good,** not a final good. We would be double counting if we counted both the bread and the flour used to make the bread as output. Thus the output of intermediate goods—goods that are not destined for the ultimate user, but are used as inputs in producing final goods and services—must not be included in gross national product.

Steel used in the production of automobiles and cotton used in the production of blue jeans must not be included. They will be counted when we count the automobiles and jeans, which are final goods. The value of the steel will be included in the price of the automobiles, and the value of the cotton will be included in the price of the jeans. To avoid double counting, we include only the value of final goods and services in gross national product.

Valuation at Cost. Some final goods and services that must be included in gross national product are not bought and sold in the market place, so they are valued at what they cost. Consider the services performed by government—police protection, fire protection, the use of the courts, defense, and so forth. Such services are not bought and sold in any market (despite the old saw about the New Jersey judge who was "the best that money could buy"). Yet they are an important part of our economy's final output. Economists and statisticians have decided to value them at what they cost the taxpayers. This is by no means ideal, but it is the best practical solution advanced to date.

Nonmarket Transactions. It is necessary for practical reasons to omit certain types of final output from gross national product. In particular, some nonmarketed goods and services, such as the services performed by housewives, are excluded from the gross national product. This is not because economists fail to appreciate these services, but because it would be extremely difficult to get reasonably reliable estimates of the money value of a housewife's services. At first glance, this may seem to be a very important weakness in our measure of total output, but so long as the value of these services does not change much (in relation to total output), the variation in gross national product will provide a reasonably accurate picture of the variation in total output—and, for many purposes, this is all that is required.

Nonproductive Transactions. Purely financial transactions are excluded from gross national product because they do not reflect current production. Such financial transactions include government transfer payments, private transfer payments, and the sale and purchase of securities. **Government transfer payments** are payments made by the government to individuals who do not contribute to production in exchange for them. Payments to welfare recipients are a good example of government transfer payments. Since these payments are not for production, it would be incorrect to include them in GNP. **Private transfer payments** are gifts or other transfers of wealth from one person or private organization to another. Again these are not payments for production, so there is no reason to include them in GNP. The sale and purchase of securities are not payments for production, as you will recall from our discussion in Chapter 6, so they too are excluded from GNP.

Secondhand Goods. Sales of secondhand goods are also excluded from gross national product. The reason for this is clear. When a good is produced, its value is included in GNP. If its value is also included when it is sold on the secondhand market, it will be counted twice, thus leading to an overstatement of the true GNP. Suppose that you buy a new bicycle and resell it a year later. The value of the new bicycle is included in GNP when the bicycle is produced. But the resale value of the bicycle is not included in GNP; to do so would be double counting.

Adjusting GNP for Price Changes

CURRENT DOLLARS VERSUS CONSTANT DOLLARS

In Chapter 1, we stressed that the general price level has changed over time. (Recall the rapid inflation of the 1970s and early 1980s.) Since gross national product values all goods and services at their current prices, it is bound to be affected by changes in the price level as well as by changes in total output. If all prices doubled tomorrow, this would produce a doubling of gross national product. Clearly, if gross national product is to be a reliable measure of changes in total output, we must correct it somehow to eliminate the effects of such changes in the price level.

To make such a correction, economists choose some **base year** and express the value of all goods and services in terms of their prices during the base year. If 1983 is taken as the base year and if the price of beef was $2 per pound in 1983, beef is valued at $2 per pound in all other years. Thus, if 100 million pounds of beef were produced in 1986, this total output is valued at $200 million even though the price of beef in 1986 was actually higher than $2 per pound. In this way, distortions caused by changes in the price level are eliminated.

Gross national product is expressed either in current dollars or in constant dollars. Figures expressed in **current dollars** are actual dollar

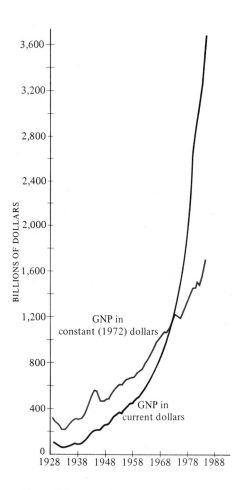

Figure 7.1 vertical axis label: BILLIONS OF DOLLARS

3,600
3,200
2,800
2,400
2,000
1,600
1,200

GNP in
constant (1972) dollars

800

400

GNP in
current dollars

0
1928 1938 1948 1958 1968 1978 1988

Figure 7.1

Gross National Product, Expressed in Current Dollars and 1972 Dollars, United States, 1929–84 *Because of inflation, GNP expressed in current dollars has increased more rapidly in recent years than GNP in constant (1972) dollars. This was particularly true in the 1970s and early 1980s, reflecting the price surge then.*

amounts, whereas those expressed in ***constant dollars*** are corrected for changes in the price level. Expressed in current dollars, gross national product is affected by changes in the price level. Expressed in constant dollars, gross national product is not affected by the price level because the prices of all goods are maintained at their base-year level. GNP, after being corrected for changes in the price level, is called ***real GNP.***

Figure 7.1 shows the behavior of both real GNP and GNP expressed in current dollars. GNP expressed in current dollars has increased more rapidly (due to inflation) than GNP in constant dollars.

PRICE INDEXES

It is often useful to have some measure of how much prices have changed over a certain period of time. One way to obtain such a measure is to divide the value of a set of goods and services expressed in current dollars by the value of the same set of goods and services expressed in constant (or base year) dollars. Suppose that a set of goods and services costs $100 when valued at 1986 prices, but $70 when valued at 1983 prices. Apparently, prices have risen an average of 43 percent for this set of goods between 1983 and 1986. How do we get 43 percent? The ratio of the cost in 1986 prices to the cost in 1983 prices is $100 \div 70 = 1.43$; thus prices must have risen on the average by 43 percent for this set of goods.

The ratio of the value of a set of goods and services in current dollars to the value of the same set of goods and services in constant (base year) dollars is a ***price index.*** Thus 1.43 is a price index in the example above. An important function of a price index is to convert values expressed in current dollars into values expressed in constant dollars. This conversion, known as ***deflating,*** can be achieved simply by dividing values expressed in current dollars by the price index. In the illustration above, values expressed in 1986 dollars can be converted into constant (i.e., 1983) dollars by dividing by 1.43. This procedure is an important one, with applications in many fields other than the measurement of gross national product. For example, firms use it to compare their output in various years. To correct for price changes, they deflate their sales by a price index for their products.

In many cases, price indexes are multiplied by 100; that is, they are expressed as percentage changes. Thus, in the case described in the previous paragraph, the price index might be expressed as 1.43×100, or 143, which would indicate that 1986 prices on the average were 143 percent of their 1983 level. In the next chapter, we shall say more about price indexes that are expressed in this way. For now, we assume that the price index is not multiplied by 100.

APPLICATIONS OF PRICE INDEXES

To illustrate how a price index can be used to deflate some figures, suppose that we want to measure how much the output of bread rose *in real terms* —that is, in constant dollars—between 1983 and 1987. Let us suppose that the value of output of bread in current dollars during each year was as shown in the first column of Table 7.1, and that the price of bread during each year was as shown in the second column. To determine the value of output of bread in 1983 dollars, we form a price index with 1983 as the base

Table 7.1

USE OF PRICE INDEX TO CONVERT FROM CURRENT TO CONSTANT DOLLARS

Year	(1) Output of bread in current dollars	(2) Price of bread (dollars)	(3) Price index (price ÷ 1983 price)	(4) Output of bread in 1983 dollars[a]
1983	1,600 million	0.50	1.00	1,600 million
1984	1,768 million	0.52	1.04	1,700 million
1985	1,980 million	0.55	1.10	1,800 million
1986	2,090 million	0.55	1.10	1,900 million
1987	2,204 million	0.58	1.16	1,900 million

[a] This column was derived by dividing column 1 by column 3.

Basic Idea #13: Output measures expressed in current dollars can be misleading because they reflect changes in prices as well as output. To correct for price changes, such an output measure should be divided by a price index, the result being an output measure expressed in constant dollars.

year, as shown in the third column. Then dividing the figures in the first column by this price index, we get the value of output of bread during each year in 1983 dollars, shown in the fourth column. Thus the fourth column shows how much the output of bread has grown in real terms. The real output of bread has risen by 19 percent—(1,900 − 1,600) ÷ 1,600—between 1983 and 1987.

Next, let's take up an actual case. The first column of Table 7.2 shows the gross national product in selected years during the 1970s. The second column shows the relevant price index for GNP for each of these years. (The base year is 1972.) What was real GNP in 1981? To answer this question, we must divide GNP in current dollars in 1981 by the price index for 1981. Thus the answer is $2,938 billion divided by 1.9358, or $1,518 billion. In other words, when expressed in constant 1972 dollars, GNP in 1981 was $1,518 billion. What was real GNP in 1978? Applying the same principles, the answer is $2,156 billion divided by 1.5005, or $1,437 billion. In other words, when expressed in constant 1972 dollars, GNP in 1978 was $1,437 billion. To test your understanding, see if you can figure out the value of real GNP in 1975. (To check your answer, consult footnote 1.)[1]

Table 7.2

CALCULATION OF REAL GROSS NATIONAL PRODUCT

Year	GNP in billions of current dollars	Price index (1972 = 1.0000)	Real GNP (billions of 1972 dollars)
1972	1,171	1.0000	1,171 (= 1,171 ÷ 1.0000)
1975	1,529	1.2718	
1978	2,156	1.5005	1,437 (= 2,156 ÷ 1.5005)
1981	2,938	1.9358	1,518 (= 2,938 ÷ 1.9358)

Using Value-Added to Calculate GNP

We have pointed out that gross national product includes the value of only the final goods and services produced. Obviously, however, the output of

[1] The real GNP in 1975 equaled $1,529 billion divided by 1.2718, or 1,202 billion of 1972 dollars.

Table 7.3

VALUE-ADDED BY VARIOUS INDUSTRIES,
UNITED STATES, 1984

Industry	Value-added (billions of dollars)
Agriculture, forestry and fisheries	91
Mining	118
Construction	148
Manufacturing	776
Transportation	130
Communication	103
Electricity, gas, and sanitation	110
Wholesale and retail trade	602
Finance, insurance, and real estate	598
Other services	529
Government[a]	422
Rest of the world	44
Gross national product	3,663[b]

[a] Equals wages and salaries of government workers.
[b] Because of rounding errors and a statistical discrepancy, figures do not sum to total.
Source: U.S. Department of Commerce.

final goods and services is not due solely to the efforts of the producers of the final goods and services. The total value of an automobile when it leaves the plant, for example, represents the work of many industries besides the automobile manufacturers. The steel, tires, glass, and many other components of the automobile were not produced by the automobile manufacturers. In reality, the automobile manufacturers only added a certain amount of value to the value of the intermediate goods—steel, tires, glass, and so forth—they purchased. This point is basic to an understanding of how the gross national product is calculated.

To measure the contribution of a firm or industry to final output, we use the concept of value-added. ***Value-added*** means just what it says: *the amount of value added by a firm or industry to the total worth of the product.* It is a measure in money terms of the extent of production taking place in a particular firm or industry. Suppose that $160 million of bread was produced in the United States in 1986. To produce it, farmers harvested $50 million of wheat, which was used as an intermediate product by flour mills, which turned out $80 million of flour. This flour was used as an intermediate product by the bakers who produced the $160 million of bread. What is the value-added at each stage of the process? For simplicity, assume that the farmers did not have to purchase any materials from other firms in order to produce the wheat. Then the value-added by the wheat farmers is $50 million; the value-added by the flour mills is $30 million ($80 million − $50 million); and the value-added by the bakers is $80 million ($160 million − $80 million). The total of the value-added at all stages of the process ($50 million + $30 million + $80 million) must equal the value of the output of final product ($160 million), because each stage's value-added is its contribution to this value.

Table 7.3 shows the value-added by various industrial groups in the United States in 1984. Since the total of the value-added by all industries must equal the value of all final goods and services, which, of course, is gross national product, it follows that 3,663 billion—the total of the figures in Table 7.3—must have been equal to gross national product in 1984. It is interesting to note that most of the value-added in the American economy in 1984 was not contributed by manufacturing, mining, construction, transportation, communication, or electricity or gas. Instead, most of it came from services—wholesale and retail trade, finance, insurance, real estate, government services, and other services. This is a sign of a basic change taking place in the American economy, which is turning more and more toward producing services, rather than goods.

Net National Product

One major drawback of GNP as a measure of national output must now be faced: it does not take into account the fact that plant and equipment wear out with use, and that a certain amount of each year's national output must be devoted to replacing the capital goods worn out in producing the year's output. Economists have therefore developed another important measure, net national product (NNP), that recognizes what every accountant knows—the relevance of depreciation. (Recall the discussion in Chapter 6.)

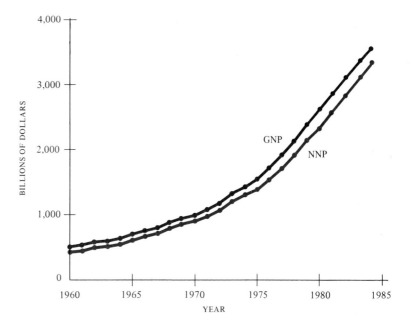

Figure 7.2

Gross National Product and Net National Product, United States, 1960–84 *It is evident that GNP and NNP move together quite closely. Thus, for many practical purposes, which one you use doesn't matter much.*

Specifically, **net national product** *equals gross national product minus depreciation.* To obtain net national product, government statisticians estimate the amount of depreciation—the amount of the nation's plant, equipment, and structures that are worn out during the period—and deduct it from gross national product. Net national product is a more accurate measure of the economy's output than gross national product because it takes depreciation into account, but estimates of net national product contain whatever errors are made in estimating depreciation (which is not easy to measure).

As we shall see in succeeding chapters, data on gross national product are more often used, even if net national product may be a somewhat better measure. Actually, since GNP and NNP move together quite closely, which one you use doesn't matter much for most practical purposes. (See Figure 7.2.)

The Limitations of GNP and NNP

It is essential that the limitations of both gross national product and net national product be understood. Although they are very useful, these figures are by no means ideal measures of economic well-being. At least five limitations of these measures must always be borne in mind.

Population. GNP and NNP are not very meaningful unless one knows the size of the population of the country in question. For example, the fact that a particular nation's GNP equals $50 billion means one thing if the nation has 10 million inhabitants, and quite another thing if it has 500 million inhabitants. To correct for the size of the population, GNP per capita—GNP divided by the population—is often used as a rough measure of output per person in a particular country.

Leisure. GNP and NNP do not take into account one of mankind's most

137

prized activities, leisure. During the past century, the average work week in the United States has decreased substantially. It has gone from almost 70 hours in 1850 to about 40 hours today. As people have become more affluent, they have chosen to substitute leisure for increased production. Yet this increase in leisure time, which surely contributes to our well-being, does not show up in GNP or NNP. Neither does the personal satisfaction (or displeasure and alienation) people get from their jobs.

Quality Changes. GNP and NNP do not take adequate account of changes in the quality of goods. An improvement in a product is not reflected accurately in GNP and NNP unless its price reflects the improvement. For example, if a new type of drug is put on the market at the same price as an old drug, and if the output and cost of the new drug are the same as the old drug, GNP will not increase, even though the new drug is twice as effective as the old one. Because GNP and NNP do not reflect such increases in product quality, it is sometimes argued that the commonly used price indices overestimate the amount of inflation, since although prices may have gone up, quality may have gone up too.

Value and Distribution. GNP and NNP say nothing about the social desirability of the composition and distribution of the nation's output. Each good and service produced is valued at its price. If the price of a Bible is $10 and the price of a pornographic novel is $10, both are valued at $10, whatever you or I may think about their respective worth. Moreover, GNP and NNP measure only the total quantity of goods and services produced. They tell us nothing about how this output is distributed among the people. If a nation's GNP is $500 billion, this is its GNP whether 90 percent of the output is consumed by a relatively few rich families or whether the output is distributed relatively equally among the citizens.

Social Costs. GNP and NNP do not reflect some of the social costs arising from the production of goods and services. In particular, they do not reflect the environmental damage resulting from the operation of our nation's factories, offices, and farms. It is common knowledge that the atmosphere and water supplies are being polluted in various ways by firms, consumers, and governments. Yet these costs are not deducted from GNP or NNP, even though the failure to do so results in an overestimate of our true economic welfare.

Economists are beginning to correct the GNP figures to eliminate some of these problems. For example, William Nordhaus and James Tobin, both of whom have served on the Council of Economic Advisers, have tried to correct the GNP figures to take proper account of the value of leisure, the value of housewives' services, and the environmental costs of production, among other things.[2] (See Example 7.1.) Unquestionably, more work along this line is needed, and will be done. However, it is also worth noting that many of these adjustments and corrections are necessarily quite rough, since there is no accurate way to measure the relevant values and costs.

[2] W. Nordhaus and J. Tobin, "Is Growth Obsolete?" *Fiftieth Anniversary Colloquium,* New York: National Bureau of Economic Research, 1972.

Example 7.1 Measured Economic Welfare and National Defense

William Nordhaus and Nobel laureate James Tobin of Yale University have attempted to adjust the net national product to obtain a better measure of economic welfare in the United States. Simplifying somewhat, they add to net national product the value of leisure and nonmarketed services, and they deduct the cost of various disamenities such as pollution. Their result, called *measured economic welfare,* is shown below:

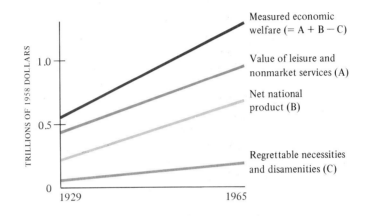

(a) Did NNP grow more or less rapidly during 1929–65 than measured economic welfare? (b) Does this mean that NNP exaggerated the percentage rate of increase of economic welfare during this period? (c) Nordhaus and Tobin include defense expenditures as "regrettable necessities," and deduct them from NNP to calculate measured economic welfare. (According to Nordhaus and Tobin, regrettable necessities are expenditures that "yield no direct satisfaction.") What do you think their reasons are for treating defense expenditures in this way? (d) What is the argument against this treatment of defense expenditures?

SOLUTION

(a) NNP increased by 206 percent (from $184 billion to $563 billion in 1958 dollars). Measured economic welfare increased by 128 percent (from $544 billion to $1,241 billion in 1958 dollars). Thus, in percentage terms, NNP grew more rapidly than measured economic welfare. (b) Yes, based on the above figures. (c) They argue that "we see no direct effect of defense expenditures on household economic welfare. No reasonable country (or household) buys 'national defense' for its own sake. If there were no war or risk of war, there would be no need for defense expenditures and no one would be the worse without them." (d) According to economists like Wilfred Beckerman, "the same sort of reasoning [used by Tobin and Nordhaus in (c)] applies to almost any component of GNP. Nobody would want hospital accident wards, or even home first aid kits, for their own sake."*

---

*See Nordhaus and Tobin, *op. cit.,* and W. Beckerman, *Two Cheers for the Affluent Society,* New York: St. Martin's Press, 1974.

Test Yourself

1. The following table shows the value of GNP in the nation of Puritania. The figures shown are in millions of 1960 dollars and current dollars. Fill in the blanks.

Year	GNP in millions of 1960 dollars	GNP in millions of current dollars	Price index $\left(\dfrac{\text{current price level}}{\text{1960 price level}}\right)$
1974	1,000	___	1.00
1976	___	1,440	1.20
1978	1,300	___	1.40
1980	1,500	___	1.60
1986	___	2,720	1.70

2. If Ronald Reagan wins $100,000 from Walter Mondale in a poker game, will this increase, decrease, or have no effect on GNP? Explain.

3. If a paper mill produces $1 million worth of paper this year, but adds considerably to the pollutants in a nearby river, are the social costs arising from this pollution reflected in the gross national product? If so, how? Should these costs be reflected in the GNP? If so, why?

4. A (small) country contains only ten firms. William Moran, the country's top statistician, calculates the country's GNP by totaling the sales of these ten firms. Do you agree with this procedure? Why, or why not?

Two Approaches to GNP

Suppose that we want to measure the market value of an automobile. One way to do this is to look at how much the consumer pays for the automobile. Although this is the most straightforward way to measure the automobile's market value, it is not the only way it can be done. Another, equally valid way is to add up all of the wage, interest, rental, and profit incomes generated in the production of the automobile. As pointed out in the circular flow model in Chapter 3 (Figure 3.15), the amount that the automobile producer receives for this car is equal to its profit (or loss) on the car plus the amount it pays the workers and other resource owners who contributed their resources to its production. Thus, if we add up all of the wage, interest, rental, and profit incomes resulting from the production of the automobile, the result is the same as if we determine how much the consumer pays for the automobile.

By the same token, there are two ways to measure the market value of the output of the economy as a whole. Or, put differently, there are two ways of looking at GNP. One is the *expenditures approach,* which regards GNP as the sum of all the expenditures on the final goods and services produced this year. The other is the *income approach,* which regards GNP as the sum of incomes derived from the production of this year's total output.

Since both of these approaches are valid, it follows that GNP can be viewed as either the total expenditure on this year's total output or as the total income stemming from the production of this year's total output. In other words,

The total expenditure on this year's total output $=$ GNP $=$ The total income stemming from the production of this year's total output.

Basic Idea #14: Gross national product, since it equals the value of all final goods and services produced, can be viewed as either the total expenditure on this year's total output or as the total income stemming from the production of this year's total output. (For the flow of output, income, and expenditure in the national economy, see Figure 7.3.)

This is an identity; the left-hand side of this equation must equal the right-hand side. (More precisely, the right-hand side should also include depreciation and indirect business taxes, as we shall see below. But this refinement can be ignored at this point.)

It is important to understand both the income and the expenditures approaches to GNP. In the following sections, we describe both approaches in more detail, and provide a more formal proof that they do in fact provide the same result.

The Expenditures Approach to GNP

To use the **expenditures approach** to determine GNP, one must add up all the spending on final goods and services. Economists distinguish among four broad categories of spending, each of which is taken up below.

PERSONAL CONSUMPTION EXPENDITURES

Personal consumption expenditures include the spending by households on durable goods, nondurable goods, and services. This category of spending includes your expenditures on items like food and drink, which are nondurable goods. It also includes your family's expenditures on a car or on an electric washer or dryer, which are durable goods. Further, it includes your payments to a dentist, who is providing a service (painful though it sometimes may be). Table 7.4 shows that in 1984 personal consumption accounted for about 64 percent of the total amount spent on final goods and services in the United States. Expenditures on consumer durable goods are clearly much less than on consumer nondurable goods, whereas expenditures on services are now larger than expenditures on either durable or nondurable goods.

GROSS PRIVATE DOMESTIC INVESTMENT

Gross private domestic investment consists of all investment spending by U.S. firms. As shown in Table 7.4, three broad types of expenditures are included in this category. First, all *final purchases of tools, equipment, and machinery* are included. Second, all *construction expenditures,* including expenditures on residential housing, are included. (One reason why houses are treated as investment goods is that they can be rented out.) Third, the *change in total inventories* is included. An increase in inventories is a positive investment; a decrease in inventories is a negative investment. The change in inventories must be included, because GNP measures the value of all final goods and services produced, *even if they are not sold this year.* Thus GNP must include the value of any increases in inventories that occur during the year. On the other hand, if a decrease occurs during the year in the value of inventories, the value of this decrease in inventories must be subtracted in calculating GNP because these goods and services were produced prior to the beginning of this year. In other words, a decline in inventories means that society has purchased more than it has produced during the year.

Table 7.4

EXPENDITURES ON FINAL GOODS AND SERVICES, UNITED STATES, 1984

Type of expenditure		Amount (billions of dollars)
Personal consumption		2,342
Durable goods	319	
Nondurable goods	857	
Services	1,166	
Gross private domestic investment		638
Expenditures on plant and equipment	426	
Residential structures	154	
Increase in inventories	58	
Net exports		−64
Exports	364	
Imports	428	
Government purchases of goods and services		747
Federal	295	
State and local	452	
Gross national product		3,663

Source: U.S. Department of Commerce.

Gross private domestic investment is "gross" in the sense that it includes all additions to the nation's stock of investment goods, whether or not they are replacements for equipment or plant that are used up in producing the current year's output. *Net private domestic investment* includes only the addition to the nation's stock of investment goods after allowing for the replacement of used-up plant and equipment. To illustrate the distinction between gross and net private domestic investment, consider the situation in 1984. In that year, the nation produced $638 billion worth of investment goods; thus gross private domestic investment equaled $638 billion. But in producing the 1984 GNP, $403 billion worth of investment goods were used up. Thus net private domestic investment equaled $638 billion minus $403 billion, or $235 billion. This was the net addition to the nation's stock of investment goods.

Net private domestic investment indicates the change in the nation's stock of capital goods. If it is positive, the nation's productive capacity, as gauged by its capital stock, is growing. If it is negative, the nation's productive capacity, as gauged by its capital stock, is declining. As pointed out in Chapter 1, the amount of goods and services that the nation can produce is influenced by the size of its stock of capital goods. (Why? Because these capital goods are one important type of resource.) Thus this year's net private domestic investment is a determinant of how much the nation can produce in the future.

GOVERNMENT PURCHASES OF GOODS AND SERVICES

This category of spending includes the expenditures of the federal, state, and local governments for the multitude of functions they perform: defense, education, police protection, and so forth. It does not include transfer payments, since they are not payments for current production. Table 7.4 shows that government spending in 1984 accounted for about 20 percent of the total amount spent on final goods and services in the United States. State and local expenditures are bigger than federal expenditures. As you recall from Chapter 4, many of the expenditures of the federal government are on items like national defense, health, and education, while at the state and local levels the biggest expenditure is for items like education and highways.

NET EXPORTS

Net exports equal the amount spent by other nations on our goods and services less the amount we spent on other nations' goods and services. This factor must be included since some of our national output is destined for foreign markets, and since we import some of the goods and services we consume. There is no reason why this component of spending cannot be negative, since imports can exceed exports. The quantity of net exports tends to be quite small. Table 7.4 shows that net exports in 1984 were equal (in absolute terms) to about 2 percent of the total amount spent on final goods and services in the United States. Because net exports are so small, we shall generally ignore them until Chapters 33 and 34, where we shall focus attention exclusively on international trade and finance.

PUTTING TOGETHER THE SPENDING COMPONENTS

Finally, because the four categories of expenditure described above include all possible types of spending on final goods and services, their sum equals the gross national product. In other words,

GNP = personal consumption expenditures +
      gross private domestic investment +
      government purchases of goods and
        services +
      net exports.

As shown in Table 7.4, the gross national product in 1984 equaled 2,342 + 638 + 747 − 64, or $3,663 billion.

The Income Approach to GNP

To use the *income approach* to determine GNP, one must add up all of the income stemming from the production of this year's output. This income is of various types: compensation of employees, rents, interest, proprietors' income, and corporate profits. In addition, for reasons described in detail in a later section, we must also include a capital consumption allowance and indirect business taxes. Each of these items is defined and discussed below.

COMPENSATION OF EMPLOYEES

This is the largest of the income categories. It includes the wages and salaries that are paid by firms and government agencies to suppliers of labor. In addition, it contains a variety of supplementary payments by employers for the benefit of their employees, such as payments into public and private pension and welfare funds. These supplementary payments are part of the employers' costs and are included in the total compensation of employees.

RENTS

In the present context, *rent* is defined as a payment to households for the supply of property resources. For example, it includes house rents received by landlords. Quite different definitions of rent are used by economists in other contexts.

INTEREST

Interest includes payments of money by private businesses to suppliers of money capital. If you buy a bond issued by General Motors, the interest payments you receive are included. Interest payments made by the government on Treasury bills, savings bonds, and other securities are excluded on the grounds that they are not payments for current goods and services. They are regarded as transfer payments.

PROPRIETORS' INCOME

What we have referred to as profits are split into two parts in the national income accounts: proprietors' income and corporate profits. ***Proprietors' income*** consists of the net income of unincorporated businesses. In other words, it consists of the net income of proprietorships and partnerships (as well as cooperatives).

CORPORATE PROFITS

Corporate profits consist of the net income of corporations. This item contains three parts: (1) dividends received by the stockholders, (2) retained earnings, and (3) the amount paid by corporations as income taxes. In other words, this item is equal to corporate profits before the payment of corporate income taxes.

DEPRECIATION

All of the items discussed above—compensation of employees, rents, interest, proprietors' income, and corporate profits—are forms of income. In addition, there are two nonincome items, depreciation and indirect business taxes, that must be added to the sum of the income items to obtain GNP. As we know from an earlier section, ***depreciation*** is the value of the nation's plant, equipment, and structures that are worn out this year. In the national income accounts, depreciation is often called a *capital consumption allowance,* because it measures the value of the capital consumed during the year. The reason why depreciation must be added to the sum of the income items to obtain GNP is given in a subsequent section.

INDIRECT BUSINESS TAXES

The government imposes certain taxes, such as general sales taxes, excise taxes, and customs duties, which firms treat as costs of production. These taxes are called ***indirect business taxes*** because they are not imposed directly on the business itself, but on its products or services instead. A good example of an indirect business tax is the tax on cigarettes; another is the general sales tax. Before a firm can pay out incomes to its workers, suppliers, or stockholders, it must pay these indirect business taxes to the government. As shown in the next section, these indirect business taxes, like depreciation, must be added to the total of the income items to get GNP.

PUTTING TOGETHER THE INCOME COMPONENTS (PLUS DEPRECIATION AND INDIRECT BUSINESS TAXES)

As we have stated repeatedly, the sum of the five types of income described above (plus depreciation and indirect business taxes) equals gross national product. In other words,

GNP = compensation of employees + rent + interest + proprietors' income + corporate profits + depreciation + indirect business taxes.

A proof that this is true is contained in the next section.

GNP Equals the Total Claims on Output: A Proof

In the previous section, we said that GNP exactly equals the total claims on output—the sum total of the wages of the workers who participated in the productive efforts, the interest paid to the investors who lent money to the firms that produced the output, the profits of the owners of the firms which produced the output, and the rents paid the owners of land or buildings used to produce the output, as well as indirect business taxes and depreciation. However, until now we have not proved that GNP equals the sum of these total claims on output.

To provide such a proof, let's start with a single firm, the General Electric Corporation, a huge producer of electrical equipment, appliances, and other products. By the simple rules of accounting discussed in Chapter 6,

$$\text{profit} = \text{sales} - \text{costs}. \tag{7.1}$$

Thus it follows that

$$\text{sales} = \text{costs} + \text{profit}. \tag{7.2}$$

Suppose we put the value of General Electric's output (i.e., its sales) on the left-hand side of Table 7.5 and its costs and profits on the right-hand side. Clearly, by Equation (7.2), the total of the right-hand side must equal the total of the left-hand side.

Now, suppose that we deduct one element of costs, "Intermediate products bought from other firms," from both sides of Table 7.5, and present the results in Table 7.6. Since the left-hand total equals the right-hand total in Table 7.5, the same must hold in Table 7.6. The total of the left-hand side of Table 7.6 equals value-added, since General Electric's value-added equals its sales minus its expenditures on intermediate goods bought from other firms. The total of the right-hand side of Table 7.6 equals the total claims against General Electric's output, which is the total income paid out (or owed) by the firm—wages, interest, rent, profits—plus

Table 7.5
SALES, COSTS, AND PROFIT, GENERAL ELECTRIC COMPANY, 1984

Sales (millions of dollars)		Costs and profit (millions of dollars)	
Sales	27,947	Employee compensation	10,939
		Interest and rent	22
		Depreciation	1,100
		Indirect business taxes	264
		Intermediate products bought from other firms	13,311
		Total costs	25,636
		Profits	2,311
Total	27,947	Total	27,947

Source: 1984 Annual Report, General Electric Company. To simplify the results, we have compressed and altered the data somewhat. Although they are adequate for present purposes, these figures are only approximate and should not be used in other contexts.

Table 7.6

VALUE-ADDED AND CLAIMS AGAINST OUTPUT, GENERAL ELECTRIC COMPANY, 1984

Value-added (millions of dollars)		Claims against output	
Sales	27,947	Employee compensation	10,939
		Interest and rent	22
Subtract: Intermediate products bought		Profits	2,311
from other firms:	13,311	Depreciation	1,100
		Indirect business taxes	264
Value-added	14,636	Total	14,636

indirect business taxes and depreciation. And, as pointed out above, the total of the left-hand side must equal the total of the right-hand side of Table 7.6.

Next, imagine constructing a table like Table 7.6 for each employer in the economy, putting sales less intermediate products bought from other firms on the left and costs plus profits less intermediate products bought from other firms on the right. For every employer, the total of the left side must equal the total of the right side. Thus, if we add up the total of the left-hand sides for all employers in the economy, the result must equal the total of the right-hand sides for all employers in the economy. But what is the total of the left-hand sides for all employers in the economy? It is the sum of value-added for all employers, which, as we saw in a previous section, equals gross national product. And the total of the right-hand sides for all employers in the economy is the total of all income paid out (or owed) in the economy—wages, interest, rent, profits—plus indirect business taxes and depreciation. Consequently, gross national product must equal the total of all income paid out (or owed) in the economy plus indirect business taxes and depreciation.

Table 7.7 shows the total amounts of various types of income paid out (or owed) in the American economy during 1984. It also shows depreciation and indirect business taxes. You can see for yourself that the total of these items equals gross national product. Besides helping to prove the point stated at the beginning of this section, this table is an interesting description of the relative importance of various types of income. For example, it shows the great importance of wages and salaries in the total income stream in the United States. In 1984, roughly 60 percent of gross national product was paid out in employee compensation.

Finally, to see how these income flows are related to the flows of output and expenditure, look carefully at Figure 7.3, which shows diagrammatically the relationships among them. Beginning at the top left-hand side of the figure, we see that the total claims on output equal GNP. Then moving to the right, we see that part of the income goes to firms, part goes to the government, and the rest goes to households. These receipts are then used by households, firms, and the government to buy the gross national product, as shown on the left-hand side of the figure. (For simplicity, this figure assumes that net exports are zero and that the government has a balanced budget.)

Table 7.7

CLAIMS ON OUTPUT, UNITED STATES, 1984

Type of claim on output	Amount of claim (billions of dollars)
Employee compensation	2,173
Rental income	62
Interest	284
Income of proprietors and professionals	154
Corporate profits	286
Indirect business taxes	304
Depreciation	403
Statistical discrepancy[a]	−3
Gross national product	3,663

[a] This also includes some minor items that need not be of concern here. See the source.
Source: U.S. Department of Commerce.

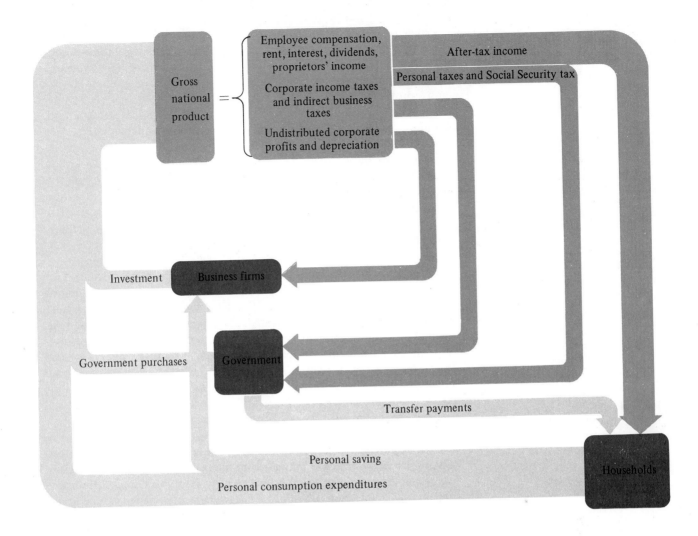

Figure 7.3

Flows of Output, Income, and Expenditures in the National Economy This diagram shows that (1) gross national product equals total income plus depreciation plus indirect business taxes; (2) part of these claims goes to households, part goes to firms, and part goes to government; and (3) households, firms, and government spend these receipts on GNP.

National Income, Personal Income, and Disposable Income

Besides gross national product and net national product, there are several other national accounting concepts that are of importance—namely, national income, personal income, and disposable income. In this section, we describe each of these concepts.

National Income. We are sometimes interested only in the total amount of income paid out (or owed) by employers, an amount called **national income.** Clearly, it is easy to derive national income if you know gross national product. All you have to do is subtract indirect business taxes and depreciation from gross national product. Or putting it another way, all you have to do is subtract indirect business taxes from net national product, since gross national product minus depreciation equals net national product.[3] Table 7.8 shows the result for 1984.

[3] Two other small items must also be taken into account. As shown in Table 7.8, we must subtract *business transfer payments*—pensions and other payments made by firms that are transfer payments—and add *subsidies less surpluses of government enterprises,* which corrects

(continued)

Table 7.8

GROSS NATIONAL PRODUCT, NET
NATIONAL PRODUCT, NATIONAL INCOME,
PERSONAL INCOME, AND DISPOSABLE
INCOME, UNITED STATES, 1984

Measure	Amount (billions of dollars)
Gross national product	3,663
Subtract: Depreciation	403
Net national product	3,260
Subtract: Indirect business taxes	304
Business transfers	17
Statistical discrepancy	−7
Add: Subsidies less surpluses of government enterprises	14
National income	2,960
Subtract: Corporate profits	286
Contributions for social insurance	306
Add: Government transfers to persons	399
Dividends	78
Business transfers	17
Other items	150
Personal income	3,012
Subtract: Personal taxes	435
Disposable income	2,577

Source: U.S. Department of Commerce.

Personal Income. For some purposes, we may need to know how much the people of a nation receive in income. This is **personal income,** and it differs from national income in two ways. First, some people who have a claim on income do not actually receive it. For example, although all a firm's profits belong to the owners, not all of its profits are paid out to them. As we saw in Chapter 6, part of the profits are plowed back into the business, and part go to the government for corporate income taxes. Also, wage earners do not actually receive the amounts they and their employers pay currently for Social Security. Second, some people receive income that is not obtained in exchange for services rendered. You will recall from an earlier section that government transfer payments are made to welfare recipients, people receiving unemployment compensation or Social Security, and so forth. Also, there are business transfer payments—pensions and other payments made by firms that are not in exchange for current productive services.

If you know national income, it is easy to derive personal income. You begin by subtracting corporate profits from national income and adding dividends to the result. This will correct for the fact that profits not distributed as dividends do not actually enter people's hands. Then you must deduct contributions for social insurance, and add government and business transfer payments. (Note once again that interest paid by governments on their debt is regarded as a transfer payment, on the grounds that it is not a payment for current goods and services.) These calculations are shown in detail in Table 7.8.

Disposable Income. It is also useful for many purposes to know how much of their personal income people get to keep after personal taxes. This is **disposable income.** If you know what personal income is, you can obtain disposable income by deducting personal taxes from personal income, as shown in Table 7.8. Disposable income plays a very important role in subsequent chapters because it has a major influence on how much consumers spend. According to Table 7.8, disposable income equaled about 70 percent of gross national product in 1984.

---

for the fact that some government agencies pay out more to income recipients than they produce in value-added. In addition, of course, there is a statistical discrepancy that must be recognized. It is purely a statistical matter.

Test Yourself

1. Given the following data (in millions of dollars) concerning the Puritanian economy in 1986, compute its gross national product and net national product.

Gross private domestic investment	400
Personal consumption expenditure	1,000
Exports	300
Imports	100
Government purchases	300
Increase in inventories	50
Depreciation	100

2. An economic historian, after careful research, makes the following estimates (in millions of dollars) concerning the Puritanian economy in 1910.

Disposable income	400
Business transfer payments	0
Statistical discrepancy	0
Subsidies less surpluses of government enterprises	0
Net national product	600
National income	550
Personal income	460

How much were personal taxes and indirect business taxes in Puritania in 1910?

3. Based on the following data (in millions of dollars), use the income approach to determine GNP.

Compensation of employees	50
Interest	10
Rents	5
Indirect business taxes	8
Corporate profits	10
Transfer payments	22
Proprietors' income	6
Depreciation	4

4. What is the difference between gross private domestic investment and net private domestic investment? Can the former be less than the latter? If the latter is negative, does this mean that the nation's capital stock is increasing or decreasing? Explain.

5. In 1977, there was an $11.6-billion increase in business inventories. Why should this be regarded as a form of investment? Explain why GNP would be calculated incorrectly if this increase in inventories were ignored.

6. Which of the following are included in calculating GNP this year? (a) Interest on a government bond; (b) Payment by the government to a person on welfare; (c) Payment by the government to a naval officer; (d) Wages paid by the University of Michigan to a professor; (e) Payment for a secondhand car by a Florida student; (f) The amount a husband would be willing to pay for his wife's housekeeping services; (g) The amount John Jones pays for 30 shares of IBM stock; (h) The allowances a father gives his 12-year-old son.

Summary

1. One of the key indicators of the health of any nation's economy is the gross national product, which measures the total value of the final goods and services the nation produces in a particular period. Since gross national product is affected by the price level, it must be deflated by a price index to correct for price-level changes. When deflated in this way, GNP is called real GNP, or GNP in constant dollars.

2. There are many pitfalls in calculating the gross national product. One must avoid counting the same output more than once. Purely financial transactions that do not reflect current production must be excluded. Also, some final goods and services that must be included in GNP are not bought and sold in the market place, so they are valued at what they cost.

3. GNP is not an ideal measure of total economic output, let alone a satisfactory measure of economic well-being. It takes no account of a nation's population, the amount of leisure time, or the distribution of income. It does not reflect many changes in the quality of goods and many social costs like pollution. Economists are beginning to correct the GNP figures to eliminate some of these problems.

4. One approach to GNP is the expenditures approach, which regards GNP as the sum of all the expenditures that are involved in taking the total output of final goods and services off the market. To determine GNP in this way, one must add up all the spending on final goods and services. Economists distinguish among four broad categories of spending: personal consumption expenditures, gross private domestic investment, government purchases, and net exports. GNP equals the sum of these four items.

5. Another approach to GNP is the income approach, which regards GNP as the sum of incomes derived from the production of this year's output (plus depreciation and indirect business taxes). To determine GNP in this way, one must add up all the income stemming from the production of this year's total output (plus depreciation and indirect business taxes). Economists identify five broad categories of income: compensation of employees, rents, interest, proprietors' income, and corporate profits. GNP equals the sum of these five items (plus depreciation and indirect business taxes).

6. Net national product is gross national product minus depreciation. It indicates the value of net output when account is taken of capital used up. National income is the total amount of income paid out (or owed) by employers; personal income is the total amount people actually receive in income; and disposable income is the total amount they get to keep after taxes.

Concepts for Review

Gross national product	Value-added	Compensation of employees
National income accounts	Net national product	Rent
Final goods and services	Expenditures approach to GNP	Interest
Intermediate good	Personal consumption expenditures	Proprietors' income
Transfer payments		Corporate profits
Base year	Gross private domestic investment	Depreciation
Current dollars		Indirect business taxes
Constant dollars	Government purchases	National income
Real gross national product	Net exports	Personal income
Price index	Income approach to GNP	Disposable income
Deflating		

CHAPTER 8

Unemployment and Inflation

Two of the most important indicators of the health of any nation's economy are its unemployment rate and its rate of inflation. In late 1985, about 7 percent of the labor force in the United States was unemployed, and the annual rate of inflation was about 3 percent. Neither the unemployment rate nor the inflation rate were as low as many government officials and private citizens desired, but, relative to some previous years, both were a marked improvement. Every government, including our own, watches these two indicators with great interest. And most societies today are committed to policies designed to keep each of them at a reasonably low level. These goals certainly seem sensible, since high rates of unemployment cause enormous economic waste and social hardship, and serious inflation causes an inequitable redistribution of income and major economic inefficiencies.

In this chapter, we begin to study unemployment and inflation. Our first objective is to discuss the nature and costs of unemployment. Then we take up the nature and costs of inflation and how the rate of inflation may be related to the rate of unemployment.

Unemployment

Almost a century ago, Pope Leo XIII said, "Among the purposes of a society should be to arrange for a continuous supply of work at all times and seasons."[1] The word **unemployment** is one of the most frightening in the English language—and for good reason. Unemployed people become de-

[1] Pope Leo XIII, "Encyclical Letter on the Conditions of Labor," May 15, 1891.

moralized, suffer loss of prestige and status, and their families tend to break apart. Sometimes they are pushed toward crime and drugs; often they feel terrible despair. Their children are innocent victims too. Indeed, perhaps the most devastating effects of unemployment are on children, whose education, health, and security may be ruined. After a few minutes' thought, most people would agree that in this or any other country, every citizen who is able and willing to work should be able to get a job.

We are not saying that all unemployment, whatever its cause or nature, should be eliminated. (For example, some unemployment may be voluntary.) According to the U.S. government, any person 16 years old or more who does not have a job and is looking for one is unemployed. Since this definition is necessarily quite broad, it is important that we distinguish among several different kinds of unemployment.

FRICTIONAL UNEMPLOYMENT

Some people quit their jobs and look for something better. They may get angry at their bosses, or they may feel that they can get more money elsewhere. Others, particularly ex-students, are looking for their first job. Still others are temporarily laid off because their work is seasonal, as in the construction industry. Unemployment of this sort is called *frictional unemployment.* Frictional unemployment is inevitable, since people find it desirable to change jobs, and such job changes often involve a period of temporary unemployment.

John Caruso may quit his job after the boss calls him a fathead. It may take him a month to find another job, perhaps because he is unaware of job opportunities or perhaps because the boss was right. During this month, he is numbered among the unemployed. We don't necessarily think that unemployment of this sort is a good thing, but it would not make much sense to try to eliminate it entirely. On the contrary, a free labor market could not function without a certain amount of frictional unemployment.

STRUCTURAL UNEMPLOYMENT

Changes continually occur in the nature of consumer demand and in technology. For example, consumers grow tired of one good and become infatuated with another. And new technologies supplant old ones. Thus some workers are thrown out of work, and because the new goods and the new technologies call for different skills than the old ones did, they cannot use their skills elsewhere. Unemployment of this sort is called *structural unemployment.* It exists when jobs are available for qualified workers, but the unemployed do not have the necessary qualifications. This sort of unemployment results from a mismatch between job requirements and the skills of the unemployed.

Consider the case of Mary Jones, a 58-year-old bookkeeper who was thrown out of work by the introduction of a new technology and who lacks the skills needed to get a job in another field. Ms. Jones is one of the structurally unemployed. To some extent, structural unemployment can be reduced by monetary and fiscal policies of the sort described in the following chapters. But in many cases, the principal way to attack it is by retraining (for jobs in other occupations, industries, or areas) workers whose skills are no longer in demand.

CYCLICAL UNEMPLOYMENT

Cyclical unemployment occurs when, because of an insufficiency of aggregate demand, there are more workers looking for work than there are jobs. Cyclical unemployment is associated with business fluctuations, or the so-called business cycle. Industrialized capitalistic economies have been subject to fluctuations, with booms often succeeding busts and vice versa. (More will be said about the nature and recent history of business fluctuations in the following chapter.) One feature of these fluctuations has been that the American economy has periodically gone through depressions, during which unemployment has been high. The Great Depression of the 1930s was particularly long and severe, and when World War II ended, the American people resolved that the gigantic social costs of the enormous unemployment of the 1930s must not be repeated in the postwar period. To avoid this, Congress passed the Employment Act of 1946, which says,

> It is the continuing policy and responsibility of the Federal Government to use all practicable means . . . [to create and maintain] conditions under which there will be afforded useful employment opportunities, including self-employment, for those able, willing, and seeking to work and to promote maximum employment, production, and purchasing power.

The Employment Act of 1946 was an extremely important piece of legislation, for it committed the federal government to combat cyclical unemployment.[2]

The Measurement and Incidence of Unemployment

Having discussed various types of unemployment, we must look next at the way in which the unemployment rate is measured in the United States and at the characteristics of the unemployed.

THE UNEMPLOYMENT RATE

Each month, the federal government conducts a scientific survey of the American people, asking a carefully selected sample of the population whether they have a job, and, if not, whether they are looking for one. According to most expert opinion, the resulting figures are quite reliable but subject to a number of qualifications. One of these is that the figures do not indicate the extent to which people are underemployed. Some

---

[2] This commitment was extended by the Humphrey-Hawkins Act of 1978, which set specific goals for the unemployment rate and the inflation rate. Although it has not been possible to meet these specific goals (for reasons discussed in subsequent chapters), the enactment of these goals was a noteworthy reaffirmation of the public commitment to fight cyclical unemployment.

people work only part-time, or at jobs well below their level of education or skill, but the government figures count them as fully employed. Also, some people have given up looking for a job and are no longer listed among the unemployed, even though they would be glad to get work if any was offered. To be counted as unemployed in the government figures, one must be actively seeking employment.

To obtain the unemployment rate, the Bureau of Labor Statistics (the government agency responsible for producing the unemployment data) divides the estimated number of people who are unemployed by the estimated number of people in the *labor force*. To be in the labor force, a person must either be employed or unemployed. Note that the unemployment rate can rise either because people who formerly were employed are thrown out of work or because people who formerly were not in the labor force decide to look for jobs. For example, an increasing number of married women who decide to enter the labor force may tend to raise the unemployment rate.

Some critics of the official unemployment statistics would use a definition of unemployment that focuses attention on "serious" cases of joblessness. They would exclude unemployed people with a working spouse, unemployed teenagers living with a parent with a job, and unemployed people who have been out of work less than a month. Also, they would have the government try harder to find out whether those who say they are unemployed are making a serious effort to find work. Officials of the Bureau of Labor Statistics reply that such a change in definition would convert the statistics into a measure of hardship rather than of unemployment.

In interpreting the unemployment statistics, do not jump to the conclusion that unemployment means starvation. For one thing, as we shall see in later chapters, unemployed workers receive unemployment compensation. In the case of some auto workers who were laid off in 1974, unemployment benefits were almost equal to what they made when they were working. But this is the exception, not the rule. In the United States, unemployment compensation typically replaces a third to a half of an unemployed worker's previous before-tax wages. But it replaces a great deal more of his or her after-tax income, because jobless benefits are exempt from taxes.

According to Martin Feldstein of Harvard University, unemployment insurance increases unemployment, since it encourages (or at least enables) the jobless to remain unemployed longer than they otherwise would. Many economists agree with Feldstein, but there is considerable argument over the extent of this effect. Stephen Marston of the Brookings Institution has estimated that unemployment insurance increases the unemployment rate by about 0.25 percentage points, while Feldstein has estimated the increase at about 1.25 percentage points.

HOW MUCH UNEMPLOYMENT IS THERE?

To get some idea of the extent of unemployment, we can consult Figure 8.1, which shows the percent of the labor force unemployed during each year from 1929 to 1984. Note the wide fluctuations in the unemployment rate, and the very high unemployment rates during the 1930s. Fortunately,

Figure 8.1

**Unemployment Rates, United States,
1929-84** *The unemployment rate has
varied substantially. Fortunately, since
World War II it has not approached the
very high levels of the Great Depression of
the 1930s. But the recession of 1981
showed that the nation is not immune to
severe bouts of unemployment.*

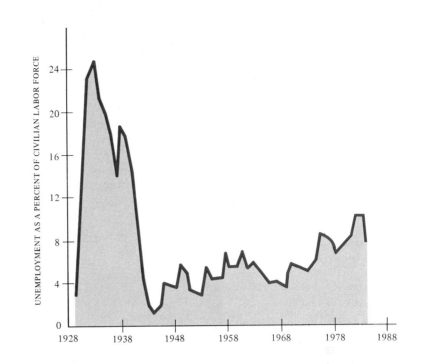

Table 8.1

UNEMPLOYMENT RATE, SELECTED
SEGMENTS OF THE POPULATION, UNITED
STATES, 1984

Population segment	Unemployment rate
Whites	
Males	
16–19 years	16.8
20 years and over	5.7
Females	
16–19 years	15.2
20 years and over	5.8
Nonwhites	
Males	
16–19 years	42.7
20 years and over	14.3
Females	
16–19 years	42.6
20 years and over	13.5
Experienced wage and salary workers	7.1
Women who maintain families	10.3
Married men, spouse present	4.6

*Source: Economic Report of the President,
1985.*

unemployment since World War II has never approached the tragically high
levels of the Great Depression of the 1930s. Between 1958 and 1964, it
averaged about 6 percent, and then declined steadily until it fell below 4
percent in 1966–69. In 1970–74, it bounced back up to 5 or 6 percent, and
then rose to 8½ percent in 1975, after which it receded to 5.8 percent in
1979. In 1981 and 1982, it rose to about 9.5 percent, after which it fell to
about 7.0 percent in 1985. Although many of these variations in the unemployment rate may seem small, they are important. With a labor force of
over 100 million in the United States, a 1 percentage point increase in the
unemployment rate means that over 1 million more people are unemployed. Any administration, Democratic or Republican, watches these figures closely and tries to avoid significant increases in unemployment.

WHO ARE THE UNEMPLOYED?

The overall unemployment rate indicates what percentage of the labor force
is out of work, but it doesn't tell us whether the unemployed are young or
old, white or nonwhite. Since it is important to know the characteristics of
the unemployed, this is the next topic to be considered.

Teenagers. The unemployment rate tends to be higher among younger
than older segments of the labor force. As shown in Table 8.1, the unemployment rate among teenagers is extremely high. In 1984, it was 17 percent
for white males, 15 percent for white females, 43 percent for nonwhite
males, and 43 percent for nonwhite females. To some extent, this is because
many teenagers are new entrants to the labor force. They must spend some
time searching for a job. Also, minimum-wage laws make it difficult for employers to hire teenagers because, in some cases, an employer would find it
worthwhile to hire teenagers only if they could be paid less than the minimum wage.

155

Nonwhites. The unemployment rate tends to be much higher among nonwhites than among whites. Among males 20 years old or more, the unemployment rate in 1984 was 14 percent among nonwhites and 6 percent among whites (Table 8.1). To a considerable extent, this difference can probably be explained by discrimination, now and in the past. Nonwhites have a more difficult time finding a job because of present discriminatory practices, such as unfair hiring practices, and previous discriminatory practices, such as inferior schooling.

The Costs of Unemployment

Basic Idea #15: Unemployment results in less goods and services being produced by society, and in obvious social and personal hardships. Government policies can help to reduce unemployment, as we will see in subsequent chapters, but these policies may have undesirable effects on inflation, at least in the short run.

As stressed at the beginning of this chapter, high levels of unemployment impose great costs on society. In this section, we describe these costs, which are both economic and noneconomic, in more detail.

ECONOMIC COSTS

The economic costs of unemployment include the goods and services that could have been produced by the unemployed. Because these people were unemployed, society had to forgo the production of the goods and services they might have produced, with the result that human wants were less effectively fulfilled than would otherwise have been the case. To determine how much society loses in this way by tolerating an unemployment rate above the minimum level resulting from frictional (and some structural) unemployment, economists estimate the ***potential GNP,*** which is the level of gross national product that could be achieved if there had been full employment. Thus, if full employment is defined as a 5 percent unemployment rate, potential GNP can be estimated by multiplying 95 percent of the labor force times the normal hours of work per year times the average output per man-hour at the relevant time.

The gap between actual and potential GNP is a measure of what society loses by tolerating less than full employment. Figure 8.2 shows the estimated size of this gap from 1952 to 1985. (Note that both actual and potential GNP are expressed in 1972 prices.) Clearly, the economic costs of unemployment have been very substantial. Consider 1975, a recession year when unemployment was about 8½ percent. As shown in Figure 8.2, society lost about $100 billion in that year alone. Although this estimate is very rough, it is accurate enough to suggest the social waste that accompanies large-scale unemployment.

One important problem in estimating this gap stems from the difficulty of defining "full employment." For many years, a common definition of ***full employment*** was a 4 percent unemployment rate, since it was felt that frictional and structural unemployment could not be reduced below this level. During the seventies, there was criticism of this definition on the grounds that an unemployment rate of about 5 percent was a more realistic measure of full employment than 4 percent because there were more young people, women, and minority workers in the labor force. All of these groups find it relatively difficult to find jobs. In 1979, the Council of Economic

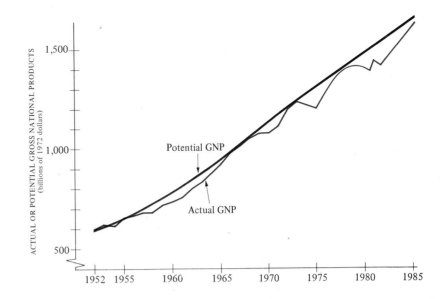

Figure 8.2
Actual and Potential GNP, United States, 1952–85 *The gap between actual and potential GNP is a measure of what society loses because there is less than full employment. In Figure 9.11, we show the size of this gap in earlier years.*

Advisers used a figure of 5.1 percent. Since this debate is unresolved, we shall not try to give a precise numerical definition of full employment.[3]

NONECONOMIC COSTS

Unemployment strikes at the social fabric of families and societies; it is not merely an economic phenomenon. Since general descriptions of the plight of the unemployed often have relatively little impact, a real-life case study may give you a better feel for what unemployment is like. Consider Joseph Torrio, a New Haven factory worker who was laid off after 18 years on the job. He describes in his own words how he spent several mornings:

> Up at seven, cup of coffee, and off to Sargent's. Like to be there when the gang comes to work, the lucky devils. Employment manager not in. Waited in his outer office.... Three others waiting, two reporting for compensation. Other one laid off two weeks ago and said he called at office every day. He inquired what I was doing and when I said "looking for work" he laughed. "You never work here? No? What chance you think you got when 400 like me who belong here out?" Employment manager showed up at 9:30. I had waited two hours. My time has no value. A pleasant fellow; told me in a kind but snappy way business was very bad. What about the future, would he take my name? Said he referred only to the present. Nothing more for me to say, so left. Two more had drifted into office. Suppose they got the same story. Must be a lot of men in New Haven that have heard it by now.
>
> [On May 21], interview with sales manager of the Real Silk Hosiery Mills. Had seen their ads for salesmen in the paper. Sales manager approached me with his hand sticking out, the first one who had offered to shake hands with

[3] Note that Figure 8.2 is based on a definition of full employment that sometimes exceeded 4 percent. For example, in 1977, it was 4.8 percent. For the definitions used, see *Economic Report of the President,* 1978, p. 84. Also see *Economic Report of the President,* 1979, 1981, and 1982.

me. I told him my name and inquired about the position. He took me into his private office, well furnished, and asked me if I had had any selling experience. I told him that I hadn't any but I thought I could do the work.... Asked me to report at 9 A.M. the next morning for further instructions.... [On May 22], I kept my appointment with the sales manager. Spent the morning learning about different kinds of stockings. Made another appointment for the afternoon which I did not keep because he wanted me to bring along $6 as security on a bag and some stock. I did not have the $6.[4]

No single case study can give you an adequate picture of the impact on people of being without a job. There are a wide variety of responses to unemployment. Some people weather it pretty well, others sink into despair; some people have substantial savings they can draw on, others are hard pressed; some people manage to shield their families from the blow, others allow their misfortunes to spread to the rest of the family. But despite these variations, being without work deals a heavy blow to a person's feeling of worth. It hits hard at a person's self-image, indicating that he or she is not needed, cannot support a family, is not really a full and valuable member of society. The impact of widespread and persistent unemployment is most clearly visible at present among the blacks and other racial minorities, where unemployment rates are much higher than among the white population. Unquestionably, the prevalence of unemployment among blacks greatly influences how the blacks view themselves, as well as the way they interact with the rest of the community.

Theories of Unemployment

THE CLASSICAL VIEW OF UNEMPLOYMENT

Until the 1930s, most economists were convinced that the price system, left to its own devices, would hold unemployment to a reasonable minimum. Thus most of the great names of economics in the nineteenth and early twentieth centuries—including John Stuart Mill, Alfred Marshall, and A. C. Pigou—felt that there was no need for government intervention to promote a high level of employment. To be sure, they recognized that unemployment was sometimes large, but they regarded these lapses from high employment as temporary aberrations that the price system would cure automatically. We begin by taking an initial, brief look at why the classical economists felt this was true. (More will be said below and in later chapters about their theories.)

The classical economists recognized the fact that the level of total spending determines the unemployment rate. They believed that total spending was unlikely to be too small to purchase the full-employment level of output, because of *Say's Law* (named after the nineteenth-century French economist, J. B. Say). According to this law, the production of a certain amount of goods and services results in the generation of an amount of income which, if spent, is precisely sufficient to buy that output. (Recall the circular flow discussed in Chapters 3 and 7.) In other words,

The ideas of John Stuart Mill (1806–73) and his arguments in support of individual freedom are particularly famous. He was one of the great philosophers of the nineteenth century. He was also a great economist; his Principles of Political Economy *(1848) is his best-known work. He advocated many social reforms, including shorter working hours and tax reform.*

[4] E. W. Bakke, *The Unemployed Worker,* Hamden, Conn.: Archon, 1969, pp. 168, 169, 174, and 175.

Example 8.1   Should We Look at Employment, not Unemployment?

Some economists believe that the rate of employment is a better measure of job availability than the rate of unemployment. The civilian rate of employment is the number of persons employed (over 16 years of age) in the civilian labor force divided by the number of persons (over 16) in the noninstitutional population (which excludes people in penal, mental, and nursing institutions and the very young). Changes over time in the rate of employment and the rate of unemployment are shown below:

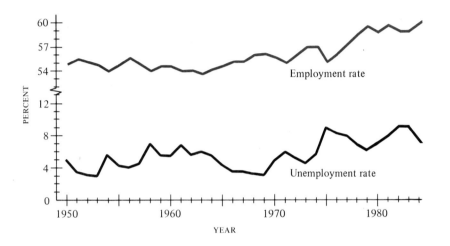

(a) What advantages are there in using the rate of employment? (b) Does it make any real difference as to which of these measures we use? (c) According to some economists, the gradual increase in the labor force participation of women has increased the rate of employment. Do you think that it has also influenced the unemployment rate? (d) Should we forget about the unemployment rate and focus attention only on the employment rate?

SOLUTION

(a) One advantage is that it does not depend on the judgment as to whether a person really is "available for work" or "actively seeking employment." Some economists feel that some people say they are looking for work, but really aren't. Other people who want work may be discouraged and give up looking for it. (b) Yes. For example, in the late 1970s, the rate of employment was high and growing, indicating that the economy was providing lots of job opportunities. At the same time, however, the unemployment rate also was high. (c) Yes. Female workers tend to move in and out of the labor force more than men. Also, men with working wives are under less pressure to stay at their present jobs or to minimize the length of time they are unemployed. (d) No. A high unemployment rate indicates that the labor market is not functioning efficiently. Both the employment rate and the unemployment rate should be considered.

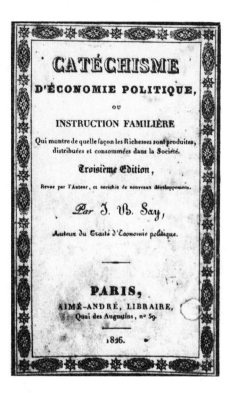

supply creates its own demand, since the total amount paid out by the producers of the goods and services to resource owners must equal the value of the goods and services. Thus, if this amount is spent, it must be sufficient to purchase all of the goods and services that are produced.

But what if resource owners do not spend all of their income, but save some of it instead? How, then, will the necessary spending arise to take all of the output off the market? The answer the classical economists offered is that each dollar saved will be invested. Therefore, investment (made largely by business firms) will restore to the spending stream what resource owners take out through the saving process. Recall that the economist's definition of investment is different from the one often used in common parlance. To the economist, investment means expenditure on plant, equipment, and other productive assets. The classical economists believed that the amount invested would automatically equal the amount saved because the interest rate—the price paid for borrowing money—would fluctuate in such a way as to maintain equality between them. In other words, there is a market for loanable funds, and the interest rate will vary so that the quantity of funds supplied equals the quantity demanded. Thus, since funds are demanded to be used—that is, invested—the amount saved will be invested.

Further, the classical economists said that the amount of goods and services firms can sell depends upon the prices they charge, as well as on total spending. For example, $1 million in spending will take 100 cars off the market if the price is $10,000 per car, and 200 cars off the market if the price is $5,000 per car. Recognizing this, the classical economists argued that firms would cut prices to sell their output. Competition among firms would prod them to reduce their prices in this way, with the result that the high-employment level of output would be taken off the market.

Looking at this process more closely, it is obvious that the prices of resources must also be reduced under such circumstances. Otherwise firms would incur losses because they would be getting less for their product, but paying no less for resources. The classical economists believed that it was realistic to expect the prices of resources to decline in such a situation. Indeed they were quite willing to assume that the wage rate—the price of labor—would be flexible in this way. They expected this flexibility because of competition among laborers. Through the processes of competition, they felt that wage rates would be bid down to the level where everyone who really wanted to work could get a job.

THE VIEWS OF KARL MARX

Quite a different view of unemployment was held by Karl Marx (1818–83), the intellectual father of communism. A man of unquestioned genius, he became an object of quasi-religious devotion to a large part of the world and a hated (and sometimes feared) revolutionary figure to another large part of the world. Because Marx the revolutionary has had such an enormous effect on modern history, it is difficult to discuss Marx the economist. But he was a very profound and influential economist. A meticulous German scholar who spent much of his life in poverty-ridden circumstances in Britain, he wrote a huge, four-volume work on economics, *Das Kapital*.[5] Eighteen years in the making, it remains one of the most influential books ever written.

To understand Marx, we need to know something about the times in which he lived. The period was characterized by revolutionary pressures against the ruling classes. In most of the countries of Europe, there was little democracy, as we know it. The masses participated little, if at all, in the world of political affairs, and very fully in the world of drudgery. For example, at one factory in Manchester, England, in 1862, people worked an average of about 80 hours per week. For these long hours of toil, the workers generally received small wages. They often could do little more than feed and clothe themselves. Given these circumstances, it is little wonder that revolutionary pressures were manifest.

1860s factory workers in Great Britain

Marx, viewing the economic system of his day, believed that capitalism was doomed to collapse. He believed that the workers were exploited by the capitalists—the owners of factories, mines, and other types of capital. And he believed that the capitalists, by introducing new labor-saving technology, would throw more and more workers into unemployment. This army of unemployed workers, by competing for jobs, would keep wages at a subsistence level. As machinery was substituted for labor, Marx felt that profits would fall. Unemployment would become more severe. Big firms would absorb small ones. Eventually the capitalistic system was bound to collapse.

To get the flavor of his reasoning and emotions, consider the following famous passage from *Das Kapital,* describing his vision of the death knell of the capitalist system:

> Along with the constantly diminishing number of the magnates of capital, who usurp and monopolize all advantages of this process of transformation, grows the mass of misery, oppression, slavery, degradation, exploitation; but with this too grows the revolt of the working-class, a class always increasing in numbers, and disciplined, united, organized by the very mechanism of the process of capitalist production itself.... Centralization of the means of production and socialization of labor at last reach a point where they become incompatible with their capitalist integument. This integument bursts asunder. The knell of capitalist private property sounds. The expropriators are expropriated.[6]

According to Marx, the inevitable successor to capitalism would be socialism, an economic system with no private property. Instead, property would be owned by society as a whole. Socialism, constituting a "dictatorship of the proletariat," would be only a transitional step to the promised land of communism. Marx did not spell out the characteristics of communism in detail. He was sure that it would be a classless society where everyone worked and no one owned capital, and he was sure that the state would "wither away," but he did not attempt to go much beyond this in his blueprint for communism. In Chapter 35, we shall discuss in detail Marx's doctrines and their limitations. The important point here is that, although the classical view (discussed in the previous section) was the dominant one, it did not go unchallenged, even in the nineteenth century.

[5] Karl Marx, *Das Kapital,* New York: Modern Library, 1906.
[6] Marx, pp. 836–837.

Crowd outside employment office, 1931

JOHN MAYNARD KEYNES AND THE GREAT DEPRESSION

Son of a British economist who was famous in his own right, John Maynard Keynes (1883–1946) was enormously successful in a variety of fields. He published a brilliant book on the theory of probability while still a relatively young man. Working for a half-hour in bed each morning, he made millions of dollars as a stock market speculator. He was a distinguished patron of the arts and a member of the Bloomsbury set, a group of London intellectuals who were the intellectual pacesetters for British society. He was a faculty member at Cambridge University, and a key figure at the British Treasury. In short, he was an extraordinarily gifted and accomplished man.

Keynes lived and worked almost a century after Marx. His world was quite different from Marx's world; and Keynes himself—polished, successful, a member of the elite—was quite different from the poverty-stricken, revolutionary Marx. But the two great economists were linked in at least one important respect. Both were preoccupied with unemployment and the future of the capitalistic system. As we saw in the previous section, Marx predicted that unemployment would get worse and worse, until at last the capitalist system would collapse. In the 1930s, when Keynes was at the height of his influence, the Great Depression seemed to many people to be proving Marx right.

In 1936, while the world was still in the throes of this economic disaster, Keynes published his *General Theory of Employment, Interest, and Money.*[7] His purpose in this book was to explain how the capitalist economic system could get stalled in the sort of depressed state of equilibrium that existed in the 1930s. He also tried to indicate how governments might help to solve the problem. Contrary to the classical economists, Keynes concluded that no automatic mechanism in a capitalistic society would generate a high level of employment—or, at least, would generate it quickly enough to be relied on in practice. Instead, the equilibrium level of national output might for a long time be below the level required to achieve high employment. His reasons for believing that this could be the case are discussed in detail in this and subsequent chapters.

To push the economy toward a higher level of employment, Keynes advocated the conscious, forceful use of the government's power to spend and tax. As we shall see in Chapter 12, many years passed before these powers became accepted tools of national economic policy, but it was Keynes who provided much of the intellectual stimulus. According to many economists, Keynes made a major contribution to saving the capitalist system.

KEYNES'S CRITICISMS OF THE CLASSICAL VIEW

There were at least two basic flaws in the classical model, as Keynes and his followers saw it. First, in their view, *there is no assurance that intended saving will equal intended investment at a level insuring high employment.* The people and firms who save are often not the same as the people and

---

[7] John Maynard Keynes, *The General Theory of Employment, Interest, and Money,* New York: Harcourt, Brace, 1936.

firms who invest, and they often have quite different motivations. In particular, a considerable amount of saving is done by families who want to put something aside for a rainy day or for a car or appliance. On the other hand, a considerable amount of investment is done by firms that are interested in increasing their profits by expanding their plants or by installing new equipment. According to Keynes, one cannot be sure that changes in the interest rate will bring about the equality of saving and investment visualized by the classical economists. In his view, intended saving may not equal intended investment at a level insuring high employment. Instead, they may be equal at a level corresponding to considerable unemployment (or to considerable inflation). Thus a purely capitalist economic system, in the absence of appropriate government policies, has no dependable rudder to keep it clear of the shoals of serious unemployment or of serious inflation.

Second, *Keynes and his followers pointed out the unreality of the classical economists' assumption that prices and wages are flexible.* Contrary to the classical economists' argument, the modern economy contains many departures from perfect competition that are barriers to downward flexibility of prices and wages. In particular, many important industries are dominated by a few producers who try hard to avoid cutting price. Even in the face of a considerable drop in demand, such industries have sometimes maintained extraordinarily stable prices. Moreover, the labor unions fight hard to avoid wage cuts. In view of these facts of life, the classical assumption of wage and price flexibility seems rather unrealistic. And to many economists, it seems unlikely that price and wage reductions can be depended on to maintain full employment.

POST-KEYNESIAN DEVELOPMENTS

Forty years have elapsed since Keynes's death, and the nature of our economic problems has changed considerably. The Great Depression of the 1930s is a distant memory, while double-digit inflation is fresh in the minds of practically everyone. The unemployment problem is still of concern to our people (particularly during 1982, when the unemployment rate reached over 9 percent), but the electorate has learned to fear inflation as well as unemployment.

The past 40 years have also witnessed considerable changes and improvements in our understanding of unemployment and its relation to inflation. While Keynes is still regarded as a very great economist (even by those who criticize the policies he espoused), the theory of unemployment has come a long way since his day, as we shall see in subsequent chapters.

John Maynard Keynes

Test Yourself

1. "Unemployed workers make about as much as when they were employed because of unemployment insurance, so the nation need not worry about the unemployed." Specify at least two fundamental errors in this statement.

2. The unemployment rate shows the percentage of the labor force out of work, but not how long they have been out of work. Does the average duration of unemployment matter too? Do you think that the average duration of unemployment is directly or inversely related to the unemployment rate? Explain.

3. Explain the differences among frictional unemployment, structural unemployment, and cyclical unemployment. Should the government attempt to reduce all types of unemployment to zero? Why or why not?

4. The data on the right came from the 1985 *Economic Report of the President.* Fill in the blanks.

	1983	1984
Percent of civilian labor force unemployed	9.6	7.5
Percent of civilian labor force employed	____	____
Civilian labor force	111.6 million	113.5 million
Total employment	____	____
Total unemployment	____	____

Inflation

It is hard to find anyone these days who does not know the meaning of inflation firsthand. Try to think of commodities you regularly purchase that cost less now than they did several years ago. Chances are that you can come up with precious few. *Inflation* is a general upward movement of prices. In other words, inflation means that goods and services that currently cost $10 may soon be priced at $11 or even $12, and wages and other input prices increase as well. It is essential to distinguish between the movements of individual prices and the movement of the entire price level. As we saw in Chapter 3, the price of an individual commodity can move up or down with the shifts in the commodity's demand or supply curve. If the price of a particular good—corn, say—goes up, this need not be inflation, since the prices of other goods may be going down at the same time, so that the overall price level—the general average level of prices—remains much the same. Inflation occurs only if most prices for goods and services in the society move upward—that is, if the average level of prices increases.

In periods of inflation, the value of money is reduced. A dollar is worth what it will buy, and what it will buy is determined by the price level. Thus a dollar was more valuable in 1940, when a Hershey chocolate bar was 5 cents, than in 1985, when it was about 40 cents. But it is important to recognize that inflations may vary in severity. *Runaway inflations* wipe out the value of money quickly and thoroughly, while *creeping inflations* erode its value gradually and slowly. There is a lot of difference between runaway inflation and a creeping inflation, as the following examples indicate.

RUNAWAY INFLATION

The case of Germany after World War I is a good example of runaway inflation. Germany was required to pay large reparations to the victorious Allies after the war. Rather than attempting to tax its people to pay these amounts, the German government merely printed additional quantities of paper money. This new money increased total spending in Germany, and the increased spending resulted in higher prices because the war-devastated economy could not increase output substantially. As more and more money was printed, prices rose higher and higher, reaching utterly fantastic levels. By 1923, it took a *trillion* marks (the unit of German currency) to buy what one mark would buy before the war.

The effect of this runaway inflation was to disrupt the economy. Prices had to be adjusted from day to day. People rushed to the stores to spend the money they received as soon as possible, since very soon it would buy much less. Speculation was rampant. This inflation was a terrible blow to Germany. The middle class was wiped out; its savings became completely worthless. It is no wonder that Germany has in recent years been more sensitive than many other countries to the evils of inflation.

CREEPING INFLATION

For the past 50 years, the price level in the United States has tended to go one way only—up. In practically all years during this period, prices have risen. Since 1955, there hasn't been a single year when the price level has fallen. Certainly, this has not been a runaway inflation, but it has resulted in a very substantial erosion in the value of the dollar. Like a beach slowly worn away by the ocean, the dollar has gradually lost a considerable portion of its value. Specifically, prices now tend to be about 6 times what they were 40 years ago. Thus the dollar now is worth about a sixth of what it was worth then. Although a creeping inflation of this sort is much less harmful than a runaway inflation, it has a number of unfortunate social consequences, which are described in detail in subsequent sections of this chapter.

The Measurement of Inflation

The most widely quoted measure of inflation in the United States is the Consumer Price Index, published monthly by the Bureau of Labor Statistics. Until 1978, the purpose of this index was to measure changes in prices of goods and services purchased by urban wage earners and clerical workers and their families. In 1978, the index was expanded to include all urban consumers (although the narrower index was not discontinued). The first step in calculating the index is to find out how much it costs in a particular month to buy a market basket of goods and services that is representative of the buying patterns of these consumers. Then this amount is expressed as a ratio of what it would have cost to buy the same market basket of goods and services in the base period (1967 at present), and this ratio is multiplied by 100. In contrast to the price indices in the previous chapter, this (like most commonly used indices) shows the *percentage,* not the proportional, change in the price level. For example, the Consumer Price Index equaled 324.5 in September 1985, which meant that it cost 224.5 percent more to buy this market basket in September 1985 than in 1967. To obtain results based on the previous chapter's definition of a price index, all we have to do is divide this index by 100.

The market basket of goods and services that is included in the Consumer Price Index is chosen with great care and is the result of an extensive survey of people's buying patterns. Among the items that are included are food, automobiles, clothing, homes, furniture, home supplies, drugs, fuel, doctors' fees, legal fees, rent, repairs, transportation fares, recreational goods, and so forth. Prices, as defined in the index, include sales and excise taxes. Also, real estate taxes, but not income or personal property taxes, are included in the index. Besides the overall index, a separate price index is computed for various types of goods or services, such as food, rent, new cars, medical services, and a variety of other items. Also, a separate index is computed for each of 28 metropolitan areas, as well as for the entire urban population.

The Consumer Price Index is widely used by industry and government. Labor agreements often stipulate that, to offset inflation, wages must increase in accord with changes in the index. Similarly, pensions, welfare payments, royalties, and even alimony payments are sometimes related to the index. However, this does not mean that it is an ideal, all-purpose measure of inflation. For one thing, it does not include the prices of industrial machinery or raw materials. For another thing, it is not confined to currently produced goods and services. For some purposes, it is less appropriate than other indices, such as the GNP deflator or the Wholesale Price Index (now the Producer Price Index).

Figure 8.3 shows the behavior of the Consumer Price Index since 1929. As pointed out in the previous section, the price level has increased considerably in the United States in the past 40 years. Substantial inflation followed World War II; the price level increased by about 34 percent between 1945 and 1948. Bursts of inflation recurred during the Korean War and then during the Vietnam War. The 1970s were a period of particularly high inflation; between 1969 and 1979 the price level doubled. The 1980s began with more double-digit inflation, but there was a reduction in the inflation rate in 1982–85. How long this respite will continue is by no means certain.

Figure 8.3

Consumer Price Index, 1929–84

Inflation has been a continual problem in the United States, particularly in the late 1970s and early 1980s. During 1979 and 1980, the Consumer Price Index rose at a double-digit annual rate.

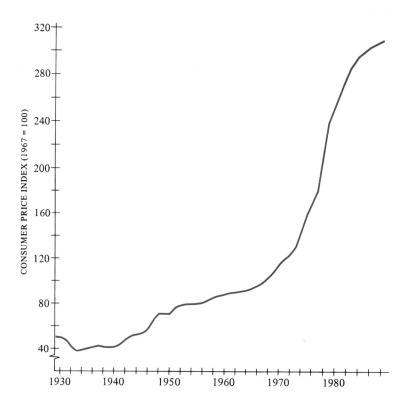

Impact of Inflation

Citizens and policy makers generally agree that inflation, like unemployment, should be minimized. Indeed, in 1981, the Council of Economic Advisers identified inflation as the chief economic problem confronting the United States. Even during 1985, when inflation had subsided substantially, there was widespread fear that it would increase again. Why is inflation so widely feared? What are its impacts? Inflation affects the distribution of income and wealth, as well as the level of output, as indicated below.

REDISTRIBUTIVE EFFECTS

Basic Idea #16: Because all incomes do not go up at the same rate as prices, inflation results in an arbitrary redistribution of income. People with relatively fixed incomes, lenders, and savers tend to be hurt by it, and major inflations tend to cripple total output as well. Government policies can help to reduce inflation, as we will see in subsequent chapters, but they may have an undesirable effect on unemployment, at least in the short run.

Perhaps the most important impact of inflation is on the distribution of income and wealth. To understand the redistributive effects of inflation, it is necessary to distinguish between *money income* and *real income.* A family's money income is its income measured in current dollars, whereas its real income is adjusted for changes in the price level. Suppose that the Murphy family earns $22,000 this year and $20,000 last year, and that the price level is 10 percent higher this year than last year. Under these circumstances, the Murphy family's money income has increased by $2,000, but its real income has not increased at all (because its money income has risen by the same percentage as the price level). The distinction between money income and real income plays an important role in understanding the effects of inflation on people with relatively fixed incomes, lenders, and savers, three groups that tend to be hit hard by inflation.

Fixed Money Incomes. Inflation may seem no more than a petty annoyance; after all, most people care about relative, not absolute, prices. For example, if the Murphy family's money income increases at the same rate as the price level, the Murphy family may be no better or worse off under inflation than if its money income remained constant and no inflation occurred. But not all people are as fortunate as the Murphys. Some people cannot increase their wages to compensate for price increases because they work under long-term contracts, among other reasons. These people take a considerable beating from inflation.

One group that tends to be particularly hard-hit by inflation is the elderly. Old people often must live on pensions and other relatively fixed forms of income. According to a study carried out by Joseph Minarik of the Brookings Institution, the effect of a 2 percent increase in the rate of inflation is to reduce the real income of elderly households (with incomes over $10,000) by about 10 percent.[8] This is a substantial, inequitable, and unwelcome impact of inflation on our older citizens.

Lenders. Inflation hurts lenders and benefits borrowers, since it results in the depreciation of money. A dollar is worth what it will buy, and what it will buy is determined by the price level. If the price level increases, a dollar is worth less than it was before. Consequently, if you lend Bill Dvorak $100 in 1985 and he pays you $100 in 1995—when a dollar will buy much less than in 1985—you are losing on the deal. In terms of what the money will buy, he is paying you less than what he borrowed. Of course, if you antici-

---

[8] J. Minarik, "Who Wins, Who Loses from Inflation," *The Brookings Bulletin,* Summer 1978.

Example 8.2 Money Wages and Real Wages in Manufacturing

In many situations, ranging from the formation of government economic policy to a particular labor negotiation between management and a union, it is important to distinguish between *money* and *real* wages. Money wages are wages expressed in current dollars, whereas real wages are adjusted for changes in the price level. The average weekly earnings in U.S. manufacturing are shown below for 1947–84, together with the Consumer Price Index for the same years.

Year	Average Weekly Earnings (current dollars)	Consumer Price Index (1967 = 100)
1947	49.13	66.9
1957	81.59	84.3
1967	114.49	100.0
1977	228.50	181.5
1984	373.22	311.1

(a) Convert the above money wages into real wages expressed in 1967 dollars. (b) In percentage terms, did real money wages in U.S. manufacturing increase as much during 1967–77 as during 1947–57? (c) John Murphy, a vegetarian who spends the bulk of his income on spinach, cauliflower, and books, received the above wages during 1947–84. Are you confident that the changes in real wages you calculated in (a) are a good indication of the changes in Mr. Murphy's standard of living during this period? (d) If the Consumer Price Index had been calculated so that 1977 = 100, would the value of this index for 1967 have been higher or lower than that shown above?

SOLUTION

(a) 1947: $49.13 \div .669 = \$73.44$
    1957: $81.59 \div .843 = \$96.79$
    1967: $114.49 \div 1.000 = \$114\ 49$
    1977: $228.50 \div 1.815 = \$125.90$
    1984: $373.22 \div 3.111 = \$119.97$

(b) During 1967–77, real wages increased by 10.0 percent (from $114.49 to $125.90). During 1947–57, they increased by 31.8 percent (from $73.44 to $96.79). Thus, percentagewise, they rose less during 1967–77 than during 1947–57. (c) No, because the prices of the goods on which he spends most of his income may have behaved quite differently from the Consumer Price Index (since the goods he buys are quite different from the market basket of goods and services bought by all urban consumers). Also, his standard of living may depend on the extent of his assets as well as the size of his earnings. (d) It would have been lower. If the 1977 price level were set equal to 100, the 1967 price level would have to be less than 100.

pate considerable inflation, you may be able to recoup by charging him a high enough interest rate to offset the depreciation of the dollar, but it is not so easy to forecast the rate of inflation and protect yourself.

Savers. Inflation can have a devastating and inequitable effect on savers. The family that works hard and saves for retirement (and a rainy day) finds that its savings are worth far less, when it finally spends them, than the amount it saved. Consider the well-meaning souls who invested $1,000 of their savings in United States savings bonds in 1939. By 1949, these bonds were worth only about 800 1939 dollars, including the interest received in the 10-year period. Thus these people had $200 taken away from them, in just as real a sense as if someone picked their pockets.[9]

EFFECTS OF ANTICIPATED AND UNANTICIPATED INFLATION

Economists are fond of pointing out that the effects of anticipated inflation tend to be less severe than those of unanticipated inflation. To see why this is the case, suppose that everyone anticipates (correctly) that the price level will be 6 percent higher next year than this year. In such a situation, everyone will build this amount of inflation into his or her decisions. Workers will realize that their money wage rates must be 6 percent higher next year just to avoid a cut in their real wage rates. The Murphy family, which earns $22,000 this year, will realize that it must earn 1.06 × $22,000, or $23,320, next year if it is to avoid a reduction in its real earnings. And people who are thinking of lending money for a year will recognize that they must charge 6 percent interest just to break even. Why? Because when the money is repaid next year, $1.06 will be worth no more in real terms than $1.00 is now.

Because people build the anticipated rate of inflation into their calculations, the effects of anticipated inflation are likely to be less pronounced than those of unanticipated inflation. However, in the real world in which we all live, this frequently is of small comfort, since it is very difficult to anticipate the rate of inflation correctly. Even the most sophisticated econometric models have not had a very distinguished record in forecasting the rate of inflation. Thus it seems foolish to believe that the typical citizen (like those who invested in United States savings bonds in 1939) can anticipate inflation well enough to protect himself or herself against its consequences.

AN ARBITRARY "TAX"

While inflation hurts some people, it benefits others. Those who are lucky enough to invest in goods, land, equipment, and other items that experience particularly rapid increases in price may make a killing. For this reason, speculation tends to be rampant during severe inflations. However, it is important to recognize that the rewards and penalties resulting from inflation are meted out with little or no regard for society's values or goals. As the late Arthur Okun, a former chairman of the Council of Economic

---

[9] However, it is important to recognize that the form of the savings matters. If one can put his or her savings in a form where its monetary value increases as rapidly as the price level, the saver is not harmed by inflation. But this isn't always easy to do.

Advisers, put it, " 'sharpies' . . . make sophisticated choices and often reap gains on inflation which do not seem to reflect any real contribution to economic growth. On the other hand, the unsophisticated saver who is merely preparing for the proverbial rainy day becomes a sucker."[10] This is one of the most undesirable features of inflation, and it helps to account for inflation's sometimes being called an arbitrary "tax."

EFFECTS ON OUTPUT

Creeping inflation, unlike unemployment, does not seem to reduce national output; in the short run, output may increase, for reasons taken up in a later section. But, although a mild upward creep of prices at the rate of a few percent per year is not likely to reduce output, a major inflation can have adverse effects on production. For one thing, it encourages speculation rather than productive use of savings. People find it more profitable to invest in gold, diamonds, real estate, and art (all of which tend to rise in monetary value during inflations) than in many kinds of productive activity. Also, businessmen tend to be discouraged from carrying out long-range projects because of the difficulty of forecasting what future prices will be. If the rate of inflation reaches the catastrophic heights that prevailed in Germany after World War I, the monetary system may break down. People may be unwilling to accept money. They may insist on trading goods or services directly for other goods and services. The result is likely to be considerable inefficiency and substantially reduced output.

Is Indexation the Answer to Inflation?

In the mid-1970s, when inflation in the United States was excessive in the eyes of practically all observers, some economists, like Milton Friedman (then at the University of Chicago), proposed a device called *indexation* to ameliorate the effects of inflation. Indexation is another word for the use of price-escalator clauses in private and public contracts. For example, in many industries, wages now rise automatically in accord with increases in the price level. And many government pensions now have similar provisions. What these economists were proposing was that such provisions be extended throughout the economy, or at least throughout much of it. For example, a person's income tax liability would be geared to the value of his or her income, after correcting for the effects of price-level changes. And interest rates would rise automatically with the rate of inflation.

Without question, indexation would help to reduce some of the harmful effects of inflation. If the U.S. Treasury were to issue bonds where the principal and interest were adjusted to compensate for rises in the price level, it would be possible for small savers to put aside some money for the future, without being victimized by inflation. To see how such bonds might work, suppose that you invested $1,000 in them, and that you cashed them in two years after you bought them. If the price level then was 20 percent higher than when you bought them, you would receive

[10] Arthur Okun, "The Costs of Inflation," in *The Battle against Unemployment*, rev. ed., New York: Norton, 1972.

$1,200 in principal. (Why $1,200? Because, since the price level was 20 percent higher, $1,200 at the time you cashed in the bonds would be the same as $1,000 at the time when you invested in them.) In addition, the interest you would receive on the bond would also be indexed.

Indexation really is not a new idea. Such great names of economics as Alfred Marshall of Cambridge and Irving Fisher of Yale were interested in the idea earlier in this century. And it has been tried on a limited scale in Canada and Israel, and to a greater extent in Brazil. But it has not received widespread support in the United States (although the 1981 tax bill introduced some indexing of people's income tax liabilities). Undoubtedly, one reason is that many people feel that indexation represents a surrender in the fight against inflation. In their view, it is better to quell inflation than to try to live with it.

Further, some observers believe that indexation of a comprehensive sort simply is not feasible. As the Council of Economic Advisers has pointed out, "A major obstacle is that many current dollar payment obligations have been incurred in past periods. Furthermore, individuals can hardly be forced to index their future contrasts if . . . they wish to make other allowances for the price movements they expect."[11] As inflation abated somewhat, talk of indexation died down. But that did not mean that the idea was abandoned. During the late 1970s and early 1980s, when the nation suffered another bout of double-digit inflation, it again received considerable attention.

The Relationship between Inflation and Unemployment

Inflation has a bad name, both among economists and with the general public. The novelist Ernest Hemingway, overstating his case more than a bit, wrote, "The first panacea for a mismanaged nation is inflation of currency: the second is war. . . . Both are the refuge of political and economic opportunists."[12] Yet according to some economists, full employment sometimes can be achieved only if a moderate amount of inflation is tolerated. In this section, we explain their reasons for believing this.

Both the unemployment rate and the inflation rate are determined by the total level of spending on the goods and services produced by the economy. Consumers, firms, and governments all spend money on the goods and services the nation produces. The level of output in our economy depends on how much money they spend. If their expenditures are very low, this means that the economy will operate in Range A in Figure 8.4, where national output is far below its maximum. Because the low level of expenditure means a low level of demand for the nation's goods and services, firms cannot sell enough goods and services to make it profitable to hire many of the workers who want to work. Thus employment is low, and the unemployment rate is high. As for the inflation rate, it is low, since there are plenty of excess capacity and unemployed resources. It is no time to raise prices.

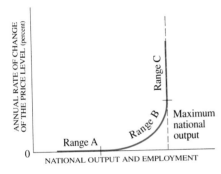

Figure 8.4

Output, Employment, and the Rate of Inflation *Chapter 2 pointed out that any economy can only produce so much, given its resources and the existing technology. The maximum output level, if all the economy's resources are fully and efficiently employed, is shown by the broken vertical line. In Range A, where national output is far below this maximum, the rate of inflation is very low but the unemployment rate is very high. In Range B, the unemployment rate is substantially less than in Range A, but the price level begins to rise. In Range C, national output is at its maximum, and increases in total spending result only in inflation.*

---

[11] Council of Economic Advisers, *Annual Report,* 1975, p. 141.
[12] Ernest Hemingway, "Notes on the Next War," *Esquire,* September 1935.

UNEMPLOYMENT AND INFLATION: AN INTERNATIONAL OVERVIEW

Economic problems, like smugglers, have no respect for international boundaries. In the 1980s, unemployment and inflation afflicted most of the industrialized world, as shown in the accompanying table.

Compared with previous experience since World War II, recent unemployment rates have been high. For example, in 1969, West Germany's unemployment rate was only 0.9 percent, as compared with 7.4 percent in 1984.

A comparison of the U.S. unemployment rate with that in other countries shows that our 1984 unemployment rate was lower

than that in Canada, France, and Great Britain, and higher than that in Germany, Italy, and Japan. To some extent, these international differences in unemployment rates are due to the fact that unemployment is defined differently in one country than in another. In some countries, to be counted as unemployed, you must register with government unemployment exchanges. Another reason for the international differences in unemployment rates is that institutional and cultural arrangements differ from country to country. In Japan many large firms commit themselves to a policy of lifetime employment for workers. This is one reason for Japan's relatively low unemployment rates.

As for the rate of inflation, the accompanying table shows that the price level increased at a rapid rate during 1978 and 1984 in most of these countries—the exceptions being Germany and Japan. U.S. performance seemed better than in a number of the other countries. While France and Italy experienced increases in consumer prices of over 7 percent per year during 1984, we managed to keep the rate of inflation down to about 4 percent per year during that period. But a 4 percent annual rate of inflation is high, relative to 25 years ago. Many economists, and citizens as well, would be glad to return to the days when the price level seldom rose at more than a couple of percentage points per year—and unemployment rarely exceeded 4 or 5 percent.

UNEMPLOYMENT AND INFLATION RATES IN THE UNITED STATES AND SIX OTHER COUNTRIES

Country	Unemployment rate[a]		Inflation rate[b]	
	1978	1984	1978	1984
United States	6.0	7.5	7.6	4.3
Canada	8.4	11.3	9.0	4.4
France	5.5	10.2	9.2	7.4
Germany	3.4	7.4	2.7	1.8
Italy	3.5	5.6	12.2	10.3
Japan	2.3	2.8	3.9	2.3
Great Britain	6.1	13.5	8.3	4.7

[a] For France and Japan, the 1984 figure pertains to the last quarter for which data are available.

[b] Estimates in *Economic Report of the President,* 1979 and 1985. The figures for 1984 are rough estimates but sufficiently reliable for present purposes. The data are not comparable with those given in other tables.

Under these circumstances, suppose that an increase occurs in the total level of spending. National output and employment will rise, and the unemployment rate will fall, but there will be little or no increase in the price level since output can be increased without bidding up the prices of labor and other inputs. When the level of expenditure increases to the point where output and employment are in Range B, the unemployment rate will be substantially lower than in Range A, but the price level will begin to rise. Why? Because bottlenecks occur in some parts of the economy, and labor pushes harder for wage increases (and firms are more willing to agree to such increases).

Finally, if the level of spending increases to the point where output and employment are in Range C, there will be no further decreases in the unemployment rate, since national output, which has reached its maximum, can grow no longer. In this range, the rate of inflation is very high, since total spending far exceeds the value of national output at initial prices. There are "too many dollars chasing too few goods."

Under the circumstances shown in Figure 8.4, the inflation rate is likely to increase as output and employment increase—which means that it is likely to increase as unemployment decreases. Thus some economists maintain that there is likely to be an inverse relationship between the unemployment rate and the inflation rate, at least in the short run. In their view, it sometimes is necessary to accept some inflation to reduce unemployment. But in recent years, this view has become increasingly controversial. More and more economists seem to have become persuaded that the reductions in unemployment due to increased inflation are only transitory and that increases in inflation bring little in the way of reduced unemployment in the long run. Much more will be said on this score in Chapter 18.

Test Yourself

1. "The Employment Act of 1946 should be amended to include the goal of stabilizing the purchasing power of the dollar as well as the goal of maintaining high-level employment." Comment and evaluate.

2. "Inflation is a necessary cost of economic progress." Comment and evaluate.

3. Suppose that a family's money income remains constant at $20,000, and that the price level increases 10 percent per year. How many years will it take for the family's real income to be cut in half?

4. If you believe that the United States is about to suffer severe inflation, would you be better off to invest money in land or in government bonds? Explain your answer.

5. According to a 1976 statement by the Research and Policy Committee of the Committee for Economic Development, "The inflation rate has receded substantially from its double-digit levels of 1974, but it still remains unacceptably high, particularly for a period in which the economy is operating far below its potential."* Why do they say this is particularly true for a period when output is far less than its potential? Explain.

* Committee for Economic Development, *Fighting Inflation and Promoting Growth,* Washington, D.C., 1976, p. 12.

Summary

1. Unemployment is of various types: frictional, structural, and cyclical. The Employment Act of 1946 committed the federal government to combat cyclical unemployment. The overall unemployment rate conceals considerable differences among types of people. The unemployment rate tends to be higher for teenagers than for older people, for nonwhites than for whites, and for females than for males. The Bureau of Labor Statistics publishes monthly data concerning unemployment rates for various segments of the population.

2. High levels of unemployment impose great costs on society. The economic costs of unemployment include the goods and services that could have been produced (but weren't) by the unemployed. The potential GNP is the level of GNP that could have been achieved if full employment had been reached. For many years, a common definition of full employment was a 4 percent unemployment rate, but many economists now believe that a figure of 5 percent or more is more realistic. The gap between actual and potential GNP is a measure of the economic costs of high unemployment.

3. Until the 1930s, most economists were convinced that the price system, left to its own devices, would ensure the maintenance of full employment. They thought it unlikely that total spending would be too small to purchase the full-employment level of output, and argued that prices would be cut if any problem of this sort developed. A notable exception was Karl Marx, who felt that the capitalistic system would suffer from worse and worse unemployment, leading to the system's eventual collapse.

4. John Maynard Keynes, in the 1930s, developed a theory to explain how the capitalist economic system remained mired in the Great Depression, with its tragically high levels of unemployment. Contrary to the classical economists, he concluded that there was no automatic mechanism in a capitalistic system to generate and maintain full employment—or, at least, to generate it quickly enough to be relied on in practice.

5. Inflation is a general upward movement of prices. Runaway inflation occurs when the price level increases very rapidly, as in Germany after World War I. Creeping inflation occurs when the price level rises a few percent per year, as in the United States during the 1950s and 1960s. The Consumer Price Index, published monthly by the Bureau of Labor Statistics, is a key measure of the rate of inflation.

6. High rates of inflation produce considerable redistribution of income and wealth. People with relatively fixed incomes, such as the elderly, tend to take a beating from inflation. Inflation hurts lenders and benefits borrowers, since it results in the depreciation of money. Inflation can also have a devastating effect on savers. The penalties (and rewards) resulting from inflation are meted out arbitrarily, with no regard for society's values or goals. Substantial rates of inflation may also reduce efficiency and total output.

Concepts for Review

Unemployment	Potential GNP	Runaway inflation
Frictional unemployment	Full employment	Creeping inflation
Structural unemployment	Say's Law	Money income
Cyclical unemployment	Inflation	Real income

CHAPTER 9

Aggregate Demand, Aggregate Supply, and Business Fluctuations

1984 was a year of rising output. Gross national product (in constant dollars) was about 7 percent higher in 1984 than in 1983. In contrast, in late 1981, the output of the American economy was not increasing. Total output, as measured by the GNP (in constant dollars), fell by over one percent in 1981's last quarter. Why the pronounced difference between these two periods? To help answer this question, as well as to understand the causes of severe unemployment and inflation, we must begin to study the nature of, and reasons for, business fluctuations.

Since aggregate demand and supply curves are useful tools in understanding why changes occur in national output and in the price level, this chapter begins by describing these demand and supply curves. Then we provide a brief introduction to business fluctuations (or "business cycles," as they are often called). Since unemployment and inflation are intimately related to business fluctuations, it is essential to have some grasp of the nature of business fluctuations in order to understand the behavior of unemployment and inflation. Only a preliminary description of business fluctuations can be presented here; much more will be said on this score in subsequent chapters.

Aggregate Supply and Demand

In Chapter 3, we described the demand and supply curves for an individual commodity like wheat. Using these demand and supply curves, we analyzed the forces determining the price and output of a commodity in a competitive market. For example, we saw that a shift to the right in the demand curve for wheat tends to increase both the price and output of wheat.

In this chapter, we will analyze the changes in the price level and output of the entire economy. That is, we are going to determine why the price level increases in some periods, but not in others, and why the gross national product soars in some periods and plummets in others. To understand the factors underlying inflation and unemployment, we must know why changes occur in the price level and in national output.

Can we use demand and supply curves for the entire economy in much the same way as we did in individual markets? Are there demand and supply curves for the whole economy that are analogous to the demand and supply curves for individual products like wheat? The answer to both questions is *yes*. And in the next few sections of this chapter, we shall indicate the nature and usefulness of these aggregate demand and supply curves.

The Aggregate Demand Curve

To begin with, consider the **aggregate demand curve**. *The aggregate demand curve shows the level of real national output that will be demanded at each price level.* (Recall from Chapter 7 that real national output is measured by real gross national product or by real net national product. Thus real national output is composed of the output of food, automobiles, machine tools, ships, and the host of other final goods and services that are produced.) As can be seen in Figure 9.1, the aggregate demand curve slopes downward and to the right. In other words, when other things are held equal, the higher the price level, the smaller the total output demanded will be; and the lower the price level, the higher the total output demanded will be. This might be expected, since the demand curve for an

Figure 9.1
Aggregate Demand Curve *The aggregate demand curve shows the level of total real output that will be demanded at each price level. If the price level is 100, a total real output of $220 billion will be demanded. If the price level is 103, a total real output of $200 billion will be demanded.*

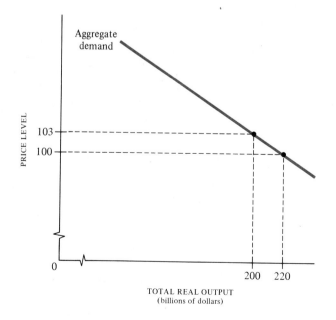

individual product also slopes downward and to the right, as we saw in Chapter 3.

There are two fundamental reasons why the demand curve for an individual commodity like wheat slopes downward and to the right. (1) As the price of the commodity falls, consumers buy more of it because it is less expensive relative to other commodities. (2) As its price falls, each consumer's money income (which is held constant) will buy a larger total amount of goods and services, so it is likely that more will be bought of this commodity.

Neither of these reasons can be used to explain the shape of the aggregate demand curve, which relates the economy's total real output to the price level. When the price level falls, the average price of *all* goods and services falls.[1] Unlike the demand curve for an individual commodity, there is not just a single price that falls, with the result that consumers find the relevant commodity relatively cheap and buy more of it. The aggregate demand curve is concerned with the effects of the price level on the economy's *total* real output, not the effects of the price of a single commodity on its output alone. Since the aggregate demand curve is concerned with the economy's price level and total real output, not the price and output of a single commodity, the reasons for the downward slope of a demand curve for an individual commodity are not applicable to the aggregate demand curve.

REASONS FOR THE AGGREGATE DEMAND CURVE'S SHAPE

Why then does the aggregate demand curve slope downward and to the right? The basic reasoning is described in the following two steps. In Chapters 14–17, we will fill in many of the details regarding the demand for money and the effects of the supply of money on interest rates and of interest rates on total spending. For present purposes, only a rough sketch is needed.

Step 1: Increases in the price level will push up interest rates. In constructing the aggregate demand curve, it is assumed that the quantity of money in the economy is fixed. An increase in the price level increases the average *money* cost of each transaction because the price of each good tends to be higher. Thus, if the price level increases considerably, people will have to hold more money in their wallets and checking accounts to pay for the items they want to buy, since prices will be so much higher. Since the quantity of money is fixed, and the demand for money increases, there will be a shortage of money. In an attempt to increase their money holdings, people will borrow or will sell government securities and other financial assets. As this happens, interest rates will be bid up.

Step 2: Increases in interest rates will reduce total output. When the interest rate goes up, firms that borrow money to invest in plant and equipment and consumers that borrow money to buy automobiles or houses tend to cut down on their spending on these items. Due to the higher interest rates, the cost of borrowing money is greater, and hence some of these investment projects and purchases no longer seem profitable

---

[1] Of course, this does not mean that the price of each good and service falls when the price level falls. Only the *average* falls.

or worthwhile. Because of the reduced spending on these items, the nation's total real output declines.[2]

The Aggregate Supply Curve

Just as the aggregate demand curve is analogous to the demand curve for an individual product, so the ***aggregate supply curve*** is analogous to the supply curve for an individual product. *The aggregate supply curve shows the level of real national output that will be supplied at each price level.* As can be seen in Figure 9.2, the aggregate supply curve slopes upward and to the right. In other words, when other things are held equal, the higher the price level, the larger the total output supplied will be; and the lower the price level, the smaller the total output supplied will be. This might be expected since the supply curve for an individual product also slopes upward and to the right, as we saw in Chapter 3.

But just as we could not derive the aggregate demand curve simply by adding up the demand curves for all the individual commodities in the economy, so we cannot derive the aggregate supply curve by adding up the supply curves for all the individual commodities. If we did this, we would commit a grave error because the factors held constant in constructing an individual supply curve are not held constant in constructing an aggregate supply curve. In particular, in constructing an individual supply curve, the price of only one commodity is allowed to vary, whereas in constructing an aggregate supply curve, the price level (and thus every price) is allowed to vary.

Figure 9.2

Aggregate Supply Curve *The aggregate supply curve shows the level of total real output that will be supplied at each price level. If the price level is 100, a total real output of $190 billion will be supplied. If the price level is 103, a total real output of $200 billion will be supplied.*

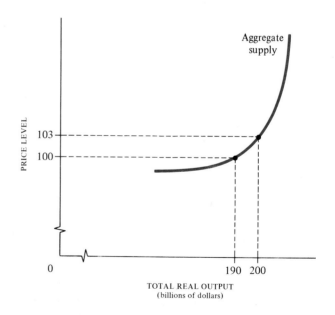

[2] There are other reasons for the shape of the aggregate demand curve. For one thing, an increase in the price level reduces the real value of the currency and government bonds held by the public. This reduction in their real wealth causes a decrease in consumption expenditure. For another thing, a rise in the U.S. price level encourages imports from abroad and discourages our exports, thus reducing the demand for American output.

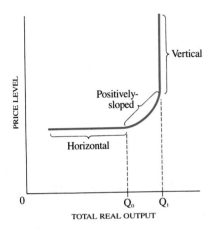

Figure 9.3

Three Ranges of the Aggregate Supply Curve *The aggregate supply curve contains three ranges: (1) a horizontal range, (2) a positively-sloped range, and (3) a vertical range.*

REASONS FOR THE AGGREGATE SUPPLY CURVE'S SHAPE

As indicated in Figure 9.3, the aggregate supply curve can be divided into three ranges: (1) a horizontal range (for output levels up to OQ_0), (2) a vertical range (when output reaches OQ_1), and (3) a positively sloped range (for output levels between OQ_0 and OQ_1). To understand the overall shape of the aggregate supply curve, we must know why each of these ranges exist.

Horizontal Range. In this range, national output can be increased without increasing the price level. This is sometimes called the *Keynesian range* because it corresponds to a situation of substantial unemployment, which is the situation (during the Great Depression) that concerned John Maynard Keynes, the great British economist (who was introduced in the previous chapter). Basically, the horizontal shape of the aggregate supply curve in this range is due to the fact that there is *no upward pressure* on prices as output increases because there are plenty of unemployed workers, equipment, and other resources. Since these resources can be used to produce additional output at about the same cost per unit of output as the existing volume of output, firms do not have to receive higher prices for their products to be willing to expand production. And since wages and the prices of other resources are relatively fixed, there is little or no downward pressure on prices as output decreases. Of course, the horizontal shape of the curve is a simplification, not an exact description of the behavior of the economy. But it seems to be a useful approximation to reality.

Vertical Range. In this range, output cannot be expanded, no matter how much the price level increases. Thus, in Figure 9.3, OQ_1 is the maximum amount that the economy can produce. This is sometimes called the *classical range* because it represents the situation that concerned the so-called classical economists (cited in Chapter 8 and discussed further in subsequent chapters). It is a situation where the economy's resources are fully employed. In contrast to the Keynesian range, there are no unemployed resources in the classical range.

Of course, this range, like the horizontal range, is a simplification. In fact, it is always possible to get a bit more output from any economic system. People can work longer hours. Equipment can be used around the clock. Children and old people can be brought into the labor force. But under normal conditions there does seem to be a point beyond which further increases in the price level result in little or no increases in output. And this is the reality that this range of the aggregate supply curve approximates.

Positively-Sloped Range. In this range, as output increases, shortages of some products begin to develop. Thus the prices of some commodities are pushed up, and the price level (which is the average of all prices of goods and services) rises. For this reason, there is a direct relationship between total real output and the price level.

This is an *intermediate* range between the horizontal range, where there is considerable unemployment of resources, and the vertical range where there is full employment. As output rises from the depressed levels in the horizontal range, some sectors of the economy reach relatively full employment before others do. Prices begin to be bid up in some markets, but not in others. As output continues to increase, more and more sectors of the economy reach their capacities, and find it increasingly difficult and

179

Figure 9.4

Equilibrium Price Level and Total Real Output *The equilibrium level of total real output and the equilibrium price level are given by the intersection of the aggregate demand and supply curves. Here the equilibrium price level is 103 and the equilibrium level of total real output is $200 billion.*

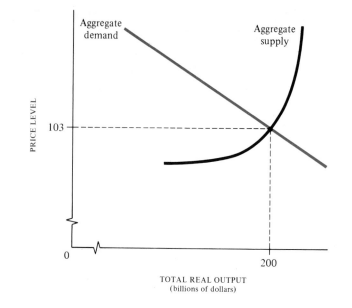

costly to increase their output further. Thus the aggregate supply curve becomes steeper as output rises—and eventually it enters the vertical range.

National Output and the Price Level

The equilibrium level of real national output and the equilibrium price level are given by the intersection of the aggregate demand curve and the aggregate supply curve. In Figure 9.4, the equilibrium level of real national output is $200 billion and the equilibrium price level is 103. The reasoning here is essentially the same as in Chapter 3, where we showed that the equilibrium price and output of a commodity are given by the intersection of the commodity's demand and supply curves. In the present case, an equilibrium can occur only at a price level and level of real national output where aggregate demand equals aggregate supply.

Shifts in the Aggregate Demand Curve

In Chapter 3, we saw that shifts in the demand curve for an individual commodity result in changes in the price and output of this commodity. We now see that shifts in the aggregate demand curve result in changes in the price level and total real output.

EFFECT OF A RIGHTWARD SHIFT

Suppose that consumers or investors decide to *increase* their spending, perhaps because of a change in their expectations. (That is, they anticipate

180

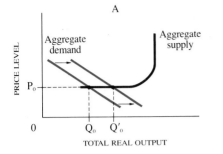

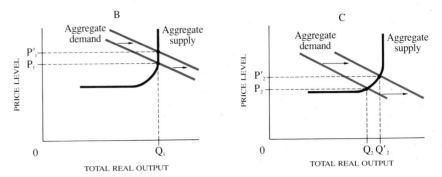

Figure 9.5

Effect of a Shift to the Right in the Aggregate Demand Curve *Panel A shows that, in the* horizontal *range of the aggregate supply curve, a rightward shift of the aggregate demand curve increases output, but not the price level. Panel B shows that, in the* vertical *range of the aggregate supply curve, a rightward shift of the aggregate demand curve increases the price level, but not output. Panel C shows that, in the* positively-sloped *range of the aggregate supply curve, a rightward shift of the aggregate demand curve increases both output and the price level.*

a marked improvement in economic conditions.) Since the level of total real output demanded at each price level increases, the aggregate demand curve shifts outward and to the right, as shown in Figure 9.5. What is the effect on the price level and on total output? The answer depends on where the aggregate demand curve intersected the aggregate supply curve before the shift in the aggregate demand curve.

Horizontal Range of the Aggregate Supply Curve. If the intersection occurred in the horizontal range of the aggregate supply curve, the rightward shift of the aggregate demand curve will increase total real output, but have no effect on the price level. (See panel A of Figure 9.5.) As pointed out above, this is because there is considerable unemployment of resources. More output does not entail increased prices.

Vertical Range of the Aggregate Supply Curve. If the intersection occurred in the vertical range of the aggregate supply curve, the rightward shift of the aggregate demand curve will increase the price level but have no impact on total real output. (See panel B of Figure 9.5.) As pointed out above, this is because there is full employment of resources. More spending bids up prices, but cannot augment total real output, which is at its maximum level.

Positively-Sloped Range of the Aggregate Supply Curve. If the intersection occurred in the positively-sloped range of the aggregate supply curve, the rightward shift of the aggregate demand curve will increase both the price level and total real output. (See panel C of Figure 9.5.) This is because increases in output can be attained in this range only if the price level increases, as we saw in a previous section.

EFFECT OF A LEFTWARD SHIFT

In contrast to the previous situation, suppose that consumers or investors decide to *reduce* their spending. Since the level of total real output demanded at each price level falls, the aggregate demand curve shifts inward and to the left, as shown in Figure 9.6. The effect of this shift depends on where the aggregate demand curve intersected the aggregate supply curve before the shift occurred.

If the intersection occurred in the horizontal range of the aggregate supply curve, the leftward shift of the aggregate demand curve will reduce total real output, but have no effect on the price level (panel A of Figure

181

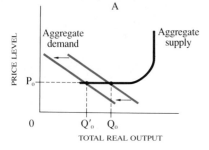

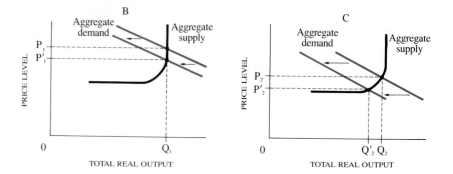

Figure 9.6

Effect of a Shift to the Left in the Aggregate Demand Curve *Panel A shows that, in the* horizontal *range of the aggregate supply curve, a leftward shift of the aggregate demand curve reduces output, but not the price level. Panel B shows that, in the* vertical *range of the aggregate supply curve, a leftward shift of the aggregate demand curve reduces the price level, but not output. Panel C shows that, in the* positively-sloped *range of the aggregate supply curve, a leftward shift of the aggregate demand curve reduces both output and the price level.*

Basic Idea #17: *To reduce unemployment, the government may shift the aggregate demand curve to the right. To do so, it must encourage and augment spending. If inflation is the principal problem, the government may shift the aggregate demand curve to the left by cutting back spending.*

9.6). If the intersection occurred in the vertical range of the aggregate supply curve, this shift will reduce the price level, but have no effect on total real output (panel B of Figure 9.6). If the intersection occurred in the positively-sloped range of the aggregate supply curve, this shift will reduce both the price level and total real output.

According to many economists, leftward shifts of the aggregate demand curve generally have much more effect on total real output than on the price level, which (as pointed out below) seldom tends to decline. If this is the case, panel A (or perhaps panel C) in Figure 9.6 is a closer approximation to reality than panel B.

GOVERNMENT STABILIZATION POLICIES

Consumers and firms are not the only actors on the economic stage that can influence the amount of spending, and thus shift the aggregate demand curve. The government can do the same thing. Through its monetary and fiscal policies, the federal government can shift the aggregate demand curve to either the right or the left. By encouraging and augmenting spending, the government can shift the aggregate demand curve to the right. By discouraging and cutting back spending, the government can shift the aggregate demand curve to the left.

Anti-Unemployment Policy. Suppose that the unemployment rate is very high, and that the nation's most important economic problem is to get its citizens back to work. This was the case in the Great Depression of the Thirties, as well as in subsequent serious recessions (which will be cited later in this chapter). Clearly, under these circumstances, the sensible strategy is for the government to shift the aggregate demand curve to the right. This situation is shown in Figure 9.7. A rightward shift of the aggregate demand curve will increase total real output and have little or no effect on the price level since the economy is in the horizontal range of the aggregate supply curve (because there is substantial unemployment). The increase in total real output will reduce unemployment because more workers and other resources will have to be employed to produce the extra output.

In fact, this is the sort of strategy that both Democratic and Republican administrations have adopted on many occasions to try to reduce unemployment. For example, in the early 1960s, President John Kennedy's (and

President Lyndon Johnson's) tax (and monetary) policies resulted in a rightward shift in the aggregate demand curve, thus reducing unemployment from about 5.7 percent in 1963 to 4.5 percent in 1965. And in the mid-1970s, President Gerald Ford's economic policies pushed the aggregate demand curve to the right, with the result that unemployment fell from 8.7 percent in March 1975 to 7.5 percent in March 1976.

Anti-Inflationary Policy. In the late 1970s and early 1980s, many American people felt that inflation, not unemployment, was the number one problem. Since the price level was increasing at over 10 percent per year during early 1980, this concern over inflation was not hard to understand. If the government anticipates that the price level is going to rise either because of a rightward shift of the aggregate demand curve or a leftward shift of the aggregate supply curve, it can reduce the prospective increase in the price level by using monetary or fiscal policy to shift the aggregate demand curve to the left. This situation is shown in Figure 9.8. If the government does not intervene, the equilibrium will be at point *A,* and the price level will be *OP,* which presumably is much higher than it is at present. To avoid reaching point *A,* the government shifts the aggregate demand curve to the left, with the result that the equilibrium will be at point *B,* and the price level will be *OP',* which is considerably lower than *OP.* Although this results in less real output (*OQ'* versus *OQ*), less inflation occurs than would otherwise be the case.

Both Democratic and Republican administrations have used this sort of anti-inflationary strategy. For example, prior to its 1975 policies to reduce unemployment (described above), the Ford administration adopted policies resulting in a leftward shift in the aggregate demand curve. By discouraging and cutting back spending, inflation was reduced in 1974. In subsequent chapters, we shall describe in detail how fiscal and monetary policies can be established to do this, and the pros and cons of such policies. All that we want to establish at present is the fact that this is the way in which governments often attempt to curb inflation.

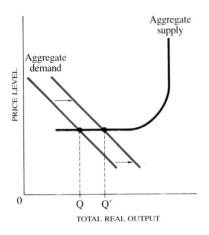

Figure 9.7
Anti-Unemployment Policy   If there is considerable unemployment, the economy is likely to be operating in the horizontal range of the aggregate supply curve. By pushing the aggregate demand curve to the right, the government can increase output and employment without pushing up the price level.

Figure 9.8
Anti-Inflation Policy   In the absence of government action, the equilibrium would be at point A, and the price level would equal OP. Since this represents an unacceptably high rate of inflation, the government pushes the aggregate demand curve to the left, so the equilibrium is at point B. The price level is lower (OP' rather than OP). Output is also somewhat lower (OQ' rather than OQ).

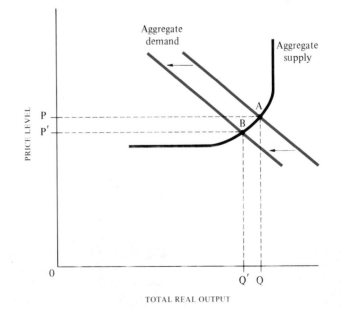

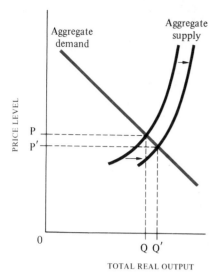

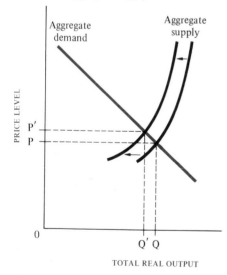

Shifts in the Aggregate Supply Curve

Shifts in the aggregate supply curve, like those in the aggregate demand curve, result in changes in the price level and total real output, as indicated below.

EFFECT OF A RIGHTWARD SHIFT

Suppose that, because of increases in productive capacity or changes in technology, firms are willing and able to supply *more* goods and services (at any given price level) than in the past. Under these circumstances, the aggregate supply curve shifts outward and to the right, as shown in Figure 9.9. What is the effect on the price level and on total output? If prior to this shift the aggregate demand curve intersected the aggregate supply curve at a point where the latter was positively sloped (or vertical), the result will be an increase in total real output and a reduction in the price level, as shown in Figure 9.9.

EFFECT OF A LEFTWARD SHIFT

On the other hand, suppose that firms are willing and able to supply *less* goods and services (at any given price level) than in the past. For example, suppose that there is a world wide shortage of important raw materials like oil or iron ore which results in increases in their prices. Given that this is the case, a given level of total real output can be produced only at a higher price level than was previously the case. That is, the aggregate supply curve shifts upward and to the left, as shown in Figure 9.10. The effect will be a reduction in total real output and an increase in the price level, as shown in Figure 9.10.

"Supply-Side" Government Policies

From the previous discussion, it is clear that rightward shifts of the aggregate supply curve are likely to result in more output and a quelling of inflationary pressures. (See Figure 9.9.) Since these are desirable goals, it is not surprising that government policies have begun to emphasize measures designed to push the aggregate supply curve outward and to the right. This emphasis on the aggregate supply curve is not new; for example, in 1776, Adam Smith recognized the importance of such shifts in the aggregate supply curve, although he did not couch his discussion in precisely these terms. But in the late 1970s and 1980s, much more talk was heard about "the supply side"—that is, shifts in the aggregate supply curve—than in previous decades.

When the Reagan administration took office, it pushed through Congress a number of measures that it felt would help to shift the aggregate supply curve to the right. In particular, the 25 percent cut in the personal income tax and the accelerated depreciation of plant and equipment (both included in the 1981 tax bill) were supposed to further this aim. According

Basic Idea #18: *A rightward shift of the aggregate supply curve is apt to result in more output and less inflationary pressure. To bring about such a shift, the government may try to encourage people and firms to work, invest, and take prudent risks. In recent years, such policies have often been dubbed "supply-side" policies.*

to the administration, the important thing was to encourage people and firms to work, invest, and take prudent risks. There has been considerable controversy inside and outside the economic profession as to the effectiveness and side-effects of some of these proposals, which have been described in Chapter 5 and which will be discussed in more detail in Chapter 17 (and elsewhere). All that we want to emphasize here is that the Reagan administration emphasized measures to shift the aggregate supply curve.

Example 9.1   A Ratchet Effect on Aggregate Supply

Suppose that prices are rigid downward; that is, they can be increased but not decreased. The aggregate supply curve (which is assumed here to have only a horizontal and a vertical range) is P_1BS, as shown below. The government adopts monetary and fiscal policies that shift the aggregate demand curve to the right (from D to D').

(a) Will the movement of the aggregate demand curve from D to D' affect the aggregate supply curve? If so, how and why? (b) If the aggregate demand curve were to return to its original position (at D), would the aggregate supply curve return to its original position? Why or why not?

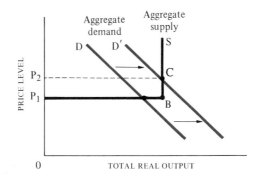

SOLUTION

(a) Yes. The movement of the aggregate demand curve from D to D' results in an increase in the price level from OP_1 to OP_2. Since the price level rises in this way, firms will be unwilling to supply the old amounts at the old prices. To supply the same amount of output as they formerly supplied when prices were OP_1, they now insist on prices of OP_2. Thus the aggregate supply curve will shift from P_1BS to P_2CS. (b) No. Because prices are rigid downward, the aggregate supply curve will remain at P_2CS (at least for a considerable period of time). Thus there is a "ratchet effect" whereby rightward shifts in the aggregate demand curve push the aggregate supply curve upward, but leftward shifts in the aggregate demand curve do not push it back to its original position.*

* A ratchet is a device that permits a wheel to turn one way but not the other.

Test Yourself

1. What sort of shifts in either the aggregate demand curve or the aggregate supply curve (or both) would result in an increase in the price level but constant real output?

2. "One of the principal reasons why the aggregate supply curve slopes upward to the right is that, as total real output increases, the quantity of money must increase as well, which means that the price level must rise, at least beyond some point." Do you agree? Why or why not?

3. Suppose that the aggregate demand curve is $P = 120 - Q$, where P is the price level and Q is real output (in billions of dollars). If the aggregate supply curve (which is a horizontal line in the relevant range) shifts upward from $P = 102$ to $P = 104$, what will happen to real output?

4. The aggregate demand curve in Country X shifts to the right, with the result that the price level rises. Do you think that this will affect Country X's aggregate supply curve? Why or why not?

5. Suppose that the Organization of Petroleum Exporting Countries raises oil prices by 50 percent in 1987. What effect will this have on the U.S. aggregate demand curve? On the U.S. aggregate supply curve?

Business Fluctuations

One of the principal reasons for presenting aggregate demand and supply curves is that they help us to understand business fluctuations—the ups and downs of the economy. Business executives, government officials, and practically everyone else is interested in business fluctuations because they influence our welfare. Business fluctuations are intimately related to the twin economic evils of unemployment and inflation, discussed in the previous chapter.

To illustrate what we mean by business fluctuations—or the business cycle—let's look at how national output has grown in the United States since World War I. Figure 9.11 shows the behavior of real GNP (in constant dollars) in the United States since 1919. It is clear that output has grown considerably during this period. Indeed, GNP is more than 5 times what it was 50 years ago. It is also clear that this growth has not been

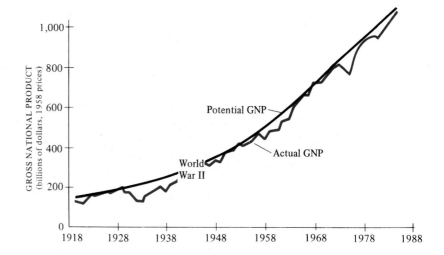

Figure 9.11

Gross National Product (in 1958 dollars), United States 1919–84, Excluding World War II *Real GNP has not grown steadily. Instead, it has tended to approach its potential level (that is, its full-employment level), then to falter and fall below this level, then to rise once more, and so on. This movement of national output is sometimes called the business cycle. (Note that GNP is expressed in 1958—not 1972—dollars here.)*

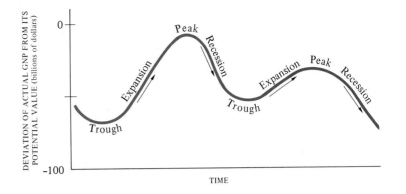

Figure 9.12

Four Phases of Business Cycle *Each cycle can be divided into four phases: trough, expansion, peak, and recession.*

steady. On the contrary, although the long-term trend has been upward, there have been periods—like 1919–21, 1929–33, 1937–38, 1944–46, 1948–49, 1953–54, 1957–58, 1969–70, 1973–75, January–July 1980, and 1981–82—when national output has declined.

Recall that the potential GNP is the total amount of goods and services that could have been produced if there had been full employment. Figure 9.11 shows that national output tends to rise and approach its potential level (that is, its full-employment level) for a while, then falter and fall below this level, then rise to approach it once more, then fall below it again, and so on. For example, output remained close to its potential level in the prosperous mid-1920s, fell far below this level in the depressed 1930s, and rose again to this level once we entered World War II. This movement of national output is sometimes called the ***business cycle,*** but it must be recognized that these cycles are far from regular or consistent. On the contrary, they are very irregular.

Each cycle can be divided into four phases, as shown in Figure 9.12. The ***trough*** is the point where national output is lowest relative to its potential level (that is, its full-employment level). ***Expansion*** is the subsequent phase during which national output rises. The ***peak*** occurs when national output is highest relative to its potential level. Finally, ***recession*** is the subsequent phase during which national output falls.[3]

Two other terms are frequently used to describe stages of the business cycle. A ***depression*** is a period when national output is well below its potential level; it is a severe recession. Depressions are, of course, periods of excessive unemployment. ***Prosperity*** is a period when national output is close to its potential level. Prosperity, if total spending is too high relative to potential output, can be a time of inflation. (Of course, in some business cycles, the peak may not be a period of prosperity because output may be below its potential level, or the trough may not be a period of depression because output may not be far below its potential level.)

Since World War II, peaks have occurred in 1948, 1953, 1957, 1960, 1969, 1973, 1980 (January), and 1981, while troughs have occurred in 1949, 1954, 1958, 1961, 1970, 1975, 1980 (July), and 1982 (November). None of these recessions has been very long or very deep (although the

---

[3] More precisely, the peak and trough are generally defined in terms of deviations from the long-term trend of national output, rather than in terms of deviations from the potential (that is, the full-employment) level of national output. But the latter definition tends to be easier for beginners to grasp.

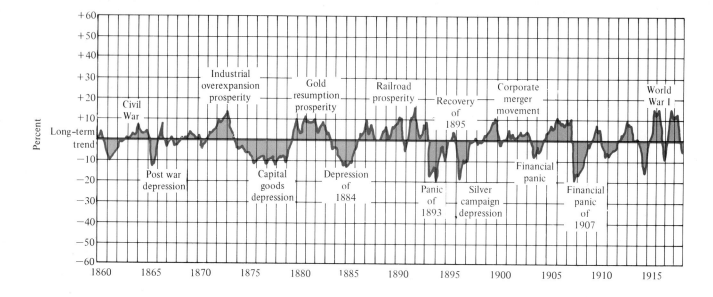

Figure 9.13

Business Fluctuations in the United States, 1860–1980 *To construct this chart, a single index of economic activity was used. After fitting a trend line to it, the deviations of this index from its trend value were plotted. The results show the fluctuations in economic activity in the U.S.*

1974–75 and 1981–82 recessions resulted in substantial unemployment). We have done better since the war at avoiding and cushioning recessions, partly because of improvements in economic knowledge of the causes and cures of business cycles.

Although business cycles have certain things in common, they are highly individualistic. (See Figure 9.13.) For certain classes of phenomena, it may be true that "if you've seen one, you've seen them all," but not for business cycles. They vary too much in length and nature. Moreover, the basic set of factors responsible for the recession and the expansion differs from cycle to cycle.[4] This means that any theory designed to explain them must be broad enough to accommodate their idiosyncrasies. In subsequent chapters, much will be said about the causes of business fluctuations.

Business Fluctuations During 1929–85: A Brief Overview

In the previous section, we described the general nature of business fluctuations. Now we turn to a description of the actual fluctuations that have occurred in the United States in recent decades. Our treatment is necessarily sketchy, since this is only a brief introductory discussion, but it should help to provide a useful background for subsequent chapters.

[4] For example, there is some evidence that every so often, a business boom, or peak, takes place at about the same time as a boom in building construction; thus such a peak is buoyed further by this favorable conjuncture—and every so often, a trough is lowered by it. These long swings in building (and other phenomena), lasting 15 to 25 years, are called Kuznets cycles after Harvard's late Nobel laureate, Simon Kuznets, who devoted considerable study to them.

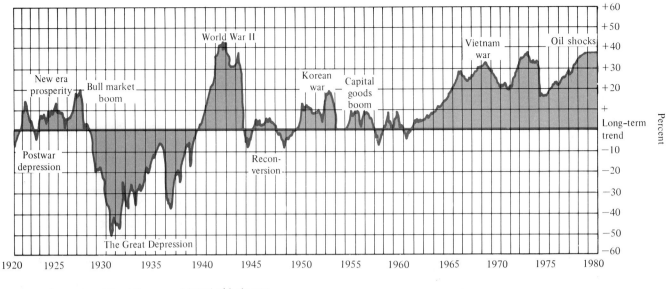

New era prosperity

Bull market boom

Postwar depression

The Great Depression

World War II

Recon- version

Korean war

Capital goods boom

Vietnam war

Oil shocks

Long-term trend

Percent

+60
+50
+40
+30
+20
+
—10
—20
—30
—40
—50
—60

1920   1925   1930   1935   1940   1945   1950   1955   1960   1965   1970   1975   1980

Source: Ameri Trust Company. Adapted with changes.

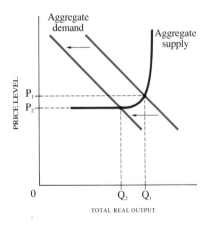

Figure 9.14

Shift of the Aggregate Demand Curve, 1929–33 *A marked shift to the left in the aggregate demand curve was the principal reason for the onset of the Great Depression. (For simplicity, we assume here that the aggregate supply curve remained fixed.) Output fell drastically (from OQ₁ to OQ₂); the price level fell too (from OP₁ to OP₂).*

THE GREAT CRASH

Let's begin with the late 1920s. During 1928 and 1929, the American economy was in the midst of a prosperity. As shown in Figure 9.11, gross national product was approximately equal to its potential value. Unemployment was low. Among the reasons for this prosperity was a relatively strong demand for machinery and equipment to produce new products (like the automobile, radio, telephone, and electric power) and to replace old machinery and equipment that had been worn out or outmoded during World War I and its aftermath.

The picture changed dramatically in 1929. After the stock market plummeted in October of that year, the economy headed down at a staggering pace. Real GNP fell by almost one-third between 1929 and 1933. Unemployment rose to an enormous 25 percent of the labor force by 1933. One important reason for this debacle was the severe contraction of gross private domestic investment. (Recall from Chapter 7 that gross private domestic investment is spending on tools, equipment, machinery, construction, and additional inventories.) Whereas gross private domestic investment was about $16 billion in 1929, it fell to about $1 billion in 1933. (The reasons for this decrease will be discussed in later chapters.) Another important factor was the decrease in the supply of money between 1929 and 1933. The money supply shrank from $26 billion in 1929 to $20 billion in 1933. This too tended to depress spending and output.

Put in terms of the aggregate demand and supply curves discussed earlier in this chapter, the situation was as shown in Figure 9.14. For the reasons given in the previous paragraph, the aggregate demand curve shifted markedly to the left; and as would be expected on the basis of Figure 9.14, total real output and the price level fell between 1929 and 1933.

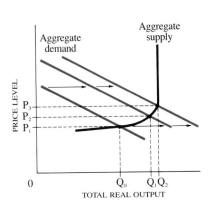

Figure 9.15

Shifts of the Aggregate Demand Curve in World War II   When we entered World War II, the aggregate demand curve shifted to the right as military expenditures mushroomed. Output increased (from OQ_0 to OQ_1 to OQ_2), and inflationary pressures mounted. (For simplicity, we assume that the aggregate supply curve remained fixed.) Much the same thing occurred during the Vietnam War.

WORLD WAR II

The United States remained mired in the Great Depression until World War II (and the mobilization period that preceded the war). To carry out the war effort, the government expanded the money supply and spent huge amounts on military personnel and equipment. One result of this increase in spending was a substantial increase in real GNP, which rose by about 75 percent between 1939 and 1945. Another result was a marked reduction in unemployment, as the armed forces expanded and as jobs opened up in defense plants (and elsewhere). Still another result was the appearance of serious inflationary pressures. As the aggregate demand curve marched to the right, there was severe upward pressure on the price level as increases in spending pushed national output to its maximum. (See Figure 9.15.) To counter this pressure, the government instituted price controls and other measures that kept a temporary lid on prices; but when these controls were lifted after the termination of the war, the price level increased dramatically. Between 1945 and 1948, the Consumer Price Index rose by about 34 percent.

THE POSTWAR YEARS

In 1948, the U.S. economy reached a peak, after which the unemployment rate increased to about 6 percent in 1949. But this recession was short-lived. The Korean conflict began in 1950, and, once again, the federal government increased its spending on armaments, resulting in substantial increases in real GNP, as well as lower unemployment and a higher rate of inflation. In 1953, another recession began, but it was relatively mild. After the trough was reached in 1954, GNP rose substantially during the next several years, only to fall back once more in the recession of 1957–58. The fifties were characterized by relatively slow growth of real GNP and by a rising unemployment rate, both of which were the cause of considerable concern.

THE PROSPEROUS SIXTIES

As previous paragraphs have shown, the American economy experienced recurring fluctuations prior to 1960. During the 1960s, this pattern seemed to change, as the United States entered a period of expansion which was uninterrupted until 1969. There were a variety of reasons for this extremely long expansion, including the tax cut of 1964, which increased after-tax income and stimulated consumer spending and investment. The increases in the money supply during this period are also given credit for this long expansion. Another important factor was the Vietnam War. Like World War II and the Korean conflict, the Vietnam War resulted in substantial increases in military spending (and a reduction in unemployment due to the draft). Due in part to Vietnam, the unemployment rate fell below 4 percent during 1966–69.

While unemployment was being squeezed to minimal levels, inflation was heating up. This is precisely what would be expected, based on our discussion of Figure 9.15. The government's spending on Vietnam was added to an already high level of expenditure on other goods and services, the result being that national output was at its maximum level in the late

1960s. Indeed, spending was so great that prices were pushed up at an increasingly alarming rate. And as prices rose, there was pressure for corresponding wage increases, which in turn pushed up firms' costs, and which were reflected in further price increases. By the end of the 1960s, inflation seemed to be the nation's foremost economic problem.

THE TURBULENT SEVENTIES

In 1969, the government adopted policies to restrict aggregate demand. Although this helped to restrain inflation, it had the undesirable effect of increasing unemployment, which rose to about 6 percent in 1971. Further, although inflation probably was reduced by these policies, it was not reduced greatly. During the first half of 1971, prices rose at an annual rate of about 4½ percent. In August 1971, the government established controls on prices, wages, and rents. This was the first time such controls had been adopted by an American government in peacetime. Although these controls seemed to hold down prices for a while, the government regarded them as increasingly unworkable, and they were phased out in 1973 and 1974.

During most of 1973, the economy was in a boom. In early 1974, the price of oil was quadrupled by the OPEC countries. This, together with a hike in farm prices, spearheaded a severe inflationary spurt. (The Consumer Price Index rose by 12 percent during 1974.) At the same time, the nation's real output fell, as the economy experienced the most serious recession since World War II. By March 1975, the unemployment rate was almost 9 percent. In mid-1975, the economy began to revive, and the unemployment rate fell gradually through 1976, 1977, and 1978. By the beginning of 1979, it was about 5.9 percent. Inflation, which had receded somewhat during 1975–77, began to reach alarming levels once again. In early 1979, the annual rate of price increase once again reached double-digit levels.

The middle and late 1970s were characterized by *stagflation,* a combination of high unemployment and high inflation. (The term stagflation was coined by putting together *stag*nation and in*flation*.) What caused this turn of events? According to many economists, it was because the aggregate supply curve shifted upward and to the left. In their view, the situation was like that in Figure 9.16. This shift in the aggregate supply curve both reduced national output and increased the price level. Since a reduction in national output means high unemployment and an increase in the price level means inflation, it is easy to see that such a shift in the aggregate supply curve might result in stagflation.

But why did the aggregate supply curve shift upward and to the left during the 1970s? The following reasons are among those frequently cited: (1) Food prices shot up, beginning in late 1972, because of bad crops around the world (and the disappearance of Peruvian anchovies, which caused a drop in the fish catch off the South American coast). (2) Many other raw material prices increased rapidly, due to worldwide shortages. (3) As pointed out above, the price of crude oil increased greatly in 1974, 1979, and other years, due to the actions of Arab and other oil-producing countries. Because of these factors, a given level of NNP could be produced only at a higher price level than was previously the case. That is, the aggregate supply curve shifted upward and to the left.

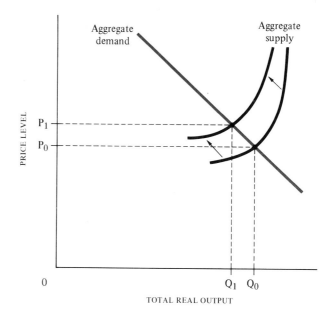

Figure 9.16

Shift of the Aggregate Supply Curve in the Seventies and Early Eighties
According to many economists, the stagflation of the late 1970s was due in considerable part to a shift of the aggregate supply curve upward and to the left due to marked shortages and price increases for oil, food, and other materials. Assuming for simplicity that the aggregate demand curve remained fixed, output fell from OQ_0 to OQ_1, and the price level rose from OP_0 to OP_1.

THE UNFOLDING EIGHTIES

In 1980, inflation continued to soar. By November 1980, the Consumer Price Index was about 13 percent above its level a year earlier. At the same time, the unemployment rate rose from about 5.8 percent in 1979 to 7.1 percent in 1980, as a very brief recession occurred early in 1980. During 1981, there seemed to be some decrease in the rate of inflation, although it was still very high by historical standards. Between December 1980 and December 1981, the price level increased by about 9 percent.

In the latter part of 1981, the economy slumped into another recession, and the unemployment rate increased considerably. By the middle of 1982, it was over 9 percent, and unemployment, not inflation, seemed to be the nation's biggest economic problem. But this did not mean that inflation was quelled. The price level continued to rise, but at a less alarming rate.

November 1982 saw the trough of the recession. During 1983, real GNP grew by about 3.4 percent. Moreover, inflation continued to fall, the increase in the Consumer Price Index during 1983 being 3.2 percent. In 1984, the economy continued to show considerable strength, with real GNP growing at about 6.8 percent and inflation being held to about 4.3 percent. Although unemployment was still about 7.0 percent, most observers seemed to regard the economy as being reasonably healthy in 1985.

Test Yourself

1. "Most depressions are caused by massive shifts to the left of the aggregate supply curve." Do you agree? Why or why not?

2. There is a seasonal cycle in many industries. For example, soft drink manufacturers have higher sales in the summer than in the winter. Is this the same as the business cycle? Why or why not?

3. In many industries, there is a long-term upward trend in

sales due to growing population and living standards. Is this the same as the business cycle? Why or why not?

4. Describe the four phases of the business cycle. In early 1985, was the U.S. economy in an expansion? A recession?

5. What policies might the United States adopt to push the aggregate supply curve to the right? If a policy has this effect, can we be sure it is desirable? Why or why not?

Summary

1. The aggregate demand curve shows the level of real national output that will be demanded at each price level. It slopes downward and to the right because (a) increases in the price level push up interest rates, and (b) increases in interest rates reduce real national output.

2. The aggregate supply curve shows the level of real national output that will be supplied at each price level. It can be divided into three ranges: (a) the horizontal or Keynesian range where there is considerable unemployment and where output can be increased without increasing the price level, (b) an intermediate range where shortages begin to develop and where increases in output require increases in the price level, and (c) a vertical or classical range where output is at its maximum and where increases in the price level have no effect on output.

3. The equilibrium level of real national output and the equilibrium price level are given by the intersection of the aggregate demand and supply curves.

4. If the equilibrium occurs in the horizontal range of the aggregate supply curve, a rightward shift of the aggregate demand curve will increase output (and thus decrease unemployment) but have no effect on the price level. This corresponds to a depression where a considerable amount of resources are unemployed. Governments frequently try to push the aggregate demand curve to the right under these circumstances.

5. If it appears likely that there will be a substantial increase in the price level, the government is likely to try to induce a leftward shift of the aggregate demand curve, thus causing the price level to be lower than it otherwise would be.

6. In recent years, there has been considerable attention given to "supply-side" economics, which focuses on shifting the aggregate supply curve to the right. If this can be done, real output will increase and inflationary forces will be quelled.

7. National output tends to rise and approach its potential (that is, its full-employment) level for a while, then falter and fall below this level, then rise to approach it once more, and so on. These ups and downs are called business fluctuations, or business cycles.

8. Each cycle can be divided into four phases: trough, expansion, peak, recession. These cycles are very irregular and highly variable in length and amplitude. Unemployment tends to be higher at the trough than at the peak; inflation tends to be higher at the peak than at the trough.

9. Our most severe recession occurred in 1929–33. Not until World War II did we really get out of the Great Depression. The war brought major inflationary pressures which subsided when it ended. Since World War II, we have had recurring recessions, and the problem of inflation has gotten worse.

10. During the late 1970s and the early 1980s, we suffered from stagflation, the combination of high unemployment and high inflation. According to many economists, this was attributable in part to a shift upward and to the left of the aggregate supply curve due to the increase in oil prices and the shortage of other raw materials. During the mid-1980s, inflation eased substantially, but the unemployment rate remained about 7 percent.

Concepts for Review

Aggregate demand curve	**Expansion**	**Depression**
Aggregate supply curve	**Peak**	**Prosperity**
Business cycle	**Recession**	**Stagflation**
Trough		

CHAPTER 10

The Determination of National Output

In the previous chapter, we presented an introductory sketch of business fluctuations and indicated how aggregate demand and supply curves can be used to analyze these fluctuations. In this chapter, we go a step further. Rather than simply taking the position of the aggregate demand curve as given, we are concerned with why the equilibrium level of national output is what it is. That is, why is the aggregate demand positioned so as to intersect the aggregate supply curve at this (rather than some other) output?

National output is defined as net national product in this chapter, since it is the best measure of how much the economy is producing when depreciation is taken into account. But since net national product and gross national product move up and down together, this theory will also enable us to explain movements in gross national product, and to help forecast them.

SIMPLIFYING ASSUMPTIONS

In this chapter, we shall make three major simplifying assumptions:

1. We assume that there are no government expenditures and that the economy is closed (no exports or imports). Thus *total spending on final output—that is, on net national product—in this simple case equals consumption expenditure plus net investment.*[1] (Why? Because the other two components of total spending—government expenditures and net exports—are zero.)

---

[1] Since personal consumption expenditure and net private domestic investment are cumbersome terms, we shall generally use consumption expenditure and net investment instead in this and subsequent chapters.

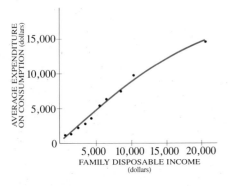

Figure 10.1

Relation between Family Expenditures on Consumption and Family Disposable Income, United States *Families with higher incomes spend more on consumption than families with lower incomes.*

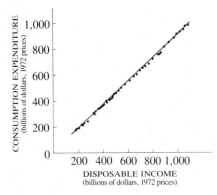

Figure 10.2

Relationship between Personal Consumption Expenditure and Disposable Income, United States, 1929–84 (excluding World War II) *There is a very close relationship between personal consumption expenditure and disposable income in the United States. In this figure a dot is given for each year. The dot's horizontal distance from the origin measures the disposable income that year, and its vertical distance from the origin measures the consumption expenditure that year. As you can see, the dots generally are very close to the line.*

2. We assume that there are no taxes, no transfer payments, and no undistributed corporate profits. Thus *NNP equals disposable income in this simple case,* because the items in Table 7.8 that are taken from, or added to, NNP to get disposable income total zero. Later chapters relax this and the first assumption.

3. We shall assume that the total amount of intended investment is *independent* of the level of net national product. This, of course, is only a rough simplification, since, as we noted in the previous chapter, the amount firms invest will be affected by the level of national output. But this simplification is very convenient and, as we shall show in the next chapter, it is relatively easy to extend the model to eliminate this assumption.

The Consumption Function

An important part of our theory of the determination of national output is the **consumption function,** *which is the relationship between consumption spending and disposable income.* It seems clear that *consumption expenditures—whether those of a single household or the total consumption expenditures in the entire economy—are influenced heavily by income.* For individual households, Figure 10.1 shows that families with higher incomes spend more on consumption than families with lower incomes. Of course, individual families vary a good deal in their behavior; some spend more than others even if their incomes are the same. But, on the average, a family's consumption expenditure is tied very closely to its income.

What is true for individual families also holds for the entire economy: total personal consumption expenditures are closely related to disposable income. This fact is shown in Figure 10.2, where personal consumption expenditure in each year (from 1929 to 1984) is plotted against disposable income in the same year (from 1929 to 1984). The points fall very near the straight line drawn in Figure 10.2, but not right on it. For most practical purposes, however, we can regard the line drawn in Figure 10.2 as representing the relationship between personal consumption expenditures and disposable income. In other words, we can regard this line as the consumption function.

The consumption function is at the heart of the modern theory of the determination of national output. It is a working tool that is used widely and often by economists to analyze and forecast the behavior of the economy. There have been many statistical studies of the consumption function. Some of these studies have been based on cross-section data—comparisons of the amount spent on consumption by families at various income levels. (Figure 10.1 is based on cross-section data.) Others have been based on time-series data—comparisons of the total amount spent on consumption in the economy with total income over various periods of time. (Figure 10.2 is based on time-series data.)

THE MARGINAL PROPENSITY TO CONSUME

Suppose that we know what the consumption function for a given society looks like at a particular period in time. For example, suppose that it is

Table 10.1
THE CONSUMPTION FUNCTION

Disposable income (billions of dollars)	Personal consumption expenditure (billions of dollars)	Marginal propensity to consume	Average propensity to consume
1,000	950		.95
		$\frac{30}{50} = .60$	
1,050	980		.93
		$\frac{30}{50} = .60$	
1,100	1,010		.92
		$\frac{30}{50} = .60$	
1,150	1,040		.90
		$\frac{30}{50} = .60$	
1,200	1,070		.89
		$\frac{30}{50} = .60$	
1,250	1,100		.88
		$\frac{30}{50} = .60$	
1,300	1,130		.87

Figure 10.3

The Marginal Propensity to Consume Equals the Slope of the Consumption Function *The slope of the consumption function between points A and B equals the vertical change (which is the change in personal consumption expenditure) divided by the horizontal change (which is the change in disposable income). Since the marginal propensity to consume equals the change in personal consumption expenditure divided by the change in disposable income, it follows that the slope equals the marginal propensity to consume.*

given by the figures for disposable income and personal consumption expenditure in the first two columns of Table 10.1. Based on our knowledge of the consumption function, we can determine the *extra* amount families will spend on consumption if they receive an *extra* dollar of disposable income. *This amount—the fraction of an extra dollar of income that is spent on consumption—is called the **marginal propensity to consume.*** For reasons discussed in the next chapter, the marginal propensity to consume, shown in column 3 of Table 10.1, plays a major role in the theory of national output determination.

To make sure that you understand exactly what the marginal propensity to consume is, consult Table 10.1. What is the marginal propensity to consume when disposable income is between $1,000 billion and $1,050 billion? The second column shows that, when income rises from $1,000 billion to $1,050 billion, consumption expenditure rises from $950 billion to $980 billion. Consequently, the fraction of the extra $50 billion of income that is consumed is $30 billion ÷ $50 billion, or 0.60. Thus the marginal propensity to consume is 0.60.[2] Based on similar calculations, the marginal propensity to consume when disposable income is between $1,050 billion and $1,100 billion is 0.60; the marginal propensity to consume when disposable income is between $1,100 billion and $1,150 billion is 0.60; and so forth.

The marginal propensity to consume can be interpreted geometrically as the slope of the consumption function. The slope of any line is, of course, the ratio of the vertical change to the horizontal change when a small movement occurs along the line. As shown in Figure 10.3, the vertical change is the change in personal consumption expenditure, and the horizontal change is the change in disposable income. Thus the ratio of the vertical change to the horizontal change must equal the marginal propensity to consume.

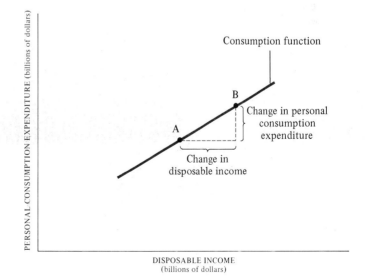

PERSONAL CONSUMPTION EXPENDITURE (billions of dollars)

Consumption function

B

A

Change in personal consumption expenditure

Change in disposable income

DISPOSABLE INCOME
(billions of dollars)

[2] Students with some knowledge of mathematics will recognize that this is an approximation since $50 billion is a substantial change in income, whereas the marginal propensity to consume pertains to a small change in income. But this is an innocuous simplification. Similar simplifications are made below.

In general, the marginal propensity to consume can differ, depending on the level of disposable income. For example, the marginal propensity to consume may be higher at lower levels than at higher levels of disposable income. Only if the consumption function is a straight line, as in Figure 10.2 and Table 10.1, will the marginal propensity to consume be the same at all levels of income. For simplicity, we assume in much of the subsequent analysis that the consumption function is a straight line, but this assumption can easily be relaxed without affecting the essential aspects of our conclusions.

THE AVERAGE PROPENSITY TO CONSUME

It is important to distinguish between the marginal propensity to consume and the *average propensity to consume.* The average propensity to consume equals the proportion of disposable income that is consumed. In other words, it equals

$$\frac{\text{personal consumption expenditure}}{\text{disposable income}}.$$

Clearly, this will not in general equal the marginal propensity to consume, which is

$$\frac{\text{change in personal consumption expenditure}}{\text{change in disposable income}}.$$

The point is that the marginal propensity to consume is the proportion of *extra* income consumed, and this proportion generally is quite different from the proportion of *total* income consumed. For example, in Table 10.1, the average propensity to consume when disposable income is $1,100 billion is 0.92; but the marginal propensity to consume when disposable income is between $1,050 billion and $1,100 billion is 0.60.

The Saving Function

If people don't devote their disposable income to personal consumption expenditure, what else can they do with it? Of course, they can save it. When families refrain from spending their income on consumption goods and services—that is, when they forgo present consumption to provide for larger consumption in the future—they save. Thus we can derive from the consumption function the total amount people will save at each level of disposable income. All we have to do is subtract the total personal consumption expenditure at each level of disposable income from disposable income. The difference is the total amount of saving at each level of disposable income. This difference is shown in the next to last column of Table 10.2. We can plot the total amount of saving against disposable income, as in Figure 10.4. The resulting relationship between total saving and disposable income is the *saving function.* Like the consumption function, it plays a major role in the theory of national output determination.

Table 10.2
THE SAVING FUNCTION

Disposable income (billions of dollars)	Personal comsumption expenditure (billions of dollars)	Saving (billions of dollars)	Marginal propensity to save
1,000	950	50	
			$\frac{20}{50} = .40$
1,050	980	70	
			$\frac{20}{50} = .40$
1,100	1,010	90	
			$\frac{20}{50} = .40$
1,150	1,040	110	
			$\frac{20}{50} = .40$
1,200	1,070	130	
			$\frac{20}{50} = .40$
1,250	1,100	150	
			$\frac{20}{50} = .40$
1,300	1,130	170	

THE MARGINAL PROPENSITY TO SAVE

If we know the saving function, we can calculate the marginal propensity to save at any level of disposable income. The *marginal propensity to save is the proportion of an extra dollar of disposable income that is saved.* To see how to calculate it, consult Table 10.2 again. The third column shows that, when income rises from $1,000 billion to $1,050 billion, saving rises from $50 billion to $70 billion. Consequently, the fraction of the extra $50 billion of income that is saved is $20 billion ÷ $50 billion, or 0.40. Thus the marginal propensity to save is 0.40. Similar calculations show that the

Figure 10.4
The Saving Function *The saving function describes the total amount of saving at each level of disposable income. The slope of the saving function equals the change in saving divided by the change in disposable income. Thus the slope of the saving function equals the marginal propensity to save.*

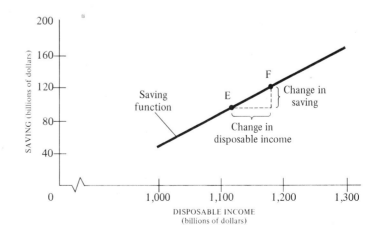

199

marginal propensity to save when disposable income is between $1,050 billion and $1,100 billion is 0.40; the marginal propensity to save when disposable income is between $1,100 billion and $1,150 billion is 0.40; and so forth.

Note that, *at any particular level of disposable income, the marginal propensity to save plus the marginal propensity to consume must equal one.* By definition, the marginal propensity to save equals the proportion of an extra dollar of disposable income that is saved, and the marginal propensity to consume equals the proportion of an extra dollar of income that is consumed. The sum of these two proportions must equal one, for, as stated above, the only things that people can do with an extra dollar of disposable income are consume it or save it. Table 10.2 shows this fact quite clearly.

Finally, it is worth noting that the marginal propensity to save equals the slope of the saving function—just as the marginal propensity to consume equals the slope of the consumption function. As pointed out above, the slope of a line equals the vertical distance between any two points on the line divided by the horizontal distance between them. Since (as shown in Figure 10.4) the vertical distance is the change in saving and the horizontal distance is the change in disposable income, the slope of the saving function must equal the marginal propensity to save.

The Permanent-Income and Life-Cycle Hypotheses

The consumption function, as described in previous sections, is a relationship between *current* consumption expenditure and *current* disposable income. In Figures 10.1 and 10.2, for example, it is presumed that current consumption expenditure in a given period, whether for a family or a nation, depends upon disposable income in that same period. Some economists, led by Milton Friedman of Stanford University, Franco Modigliani of the Massachusetts Institute of Technology, and Albert Ando of the University of Pennsylvania, have challenged this presumption. In their view, a household's current personal consumption expenditure does not depend on current disposable income; instead, it depends on the household's expected stream of disposable income over a long period of time (as well as the household's wealth). Thus two households that have the same current disposable income may spend quite different amounts on consumption goods, if their expected income streams over the long term are quite different.

To illustrate what these economists mean, consider two hypothetical families: the Rosenbergs and the Goulds. Although both Mr. Rosenberg and Ms. Gould will earn $12,000 this year, their long-run income prospects are quite different. Mr. Rosenberg is a businessman who ordinarily makes $50,000 per year, but whose income is much lower this year because of a foolish decision by one of his employees that caused a sizable one-time loss to Rosenberg's firm. Based on all available evidence, Rosenberg's annual income will return to about $50,000 in the future. Ms. Gould, on the other hand, has been unemployed for many years, and there is no prospect that she will return to work. Her $12,000 income this year was due to her having won a lottery. What Friedman, Modigliani, and Ando are saying is that one would expect each family to spend an amount on consumption goods this year that is commensurate with its long-term income, not just its income this year. Thus one would expect the Rosenbergs to spend a lot more on consumption goods than the Goulds, even though their current incomes are the same.

Although Friedman's theory (often called the permanent-income hypothesis) differs in many respects from the Modigliani-Ando theory (often called the life-cycle hypothesis), the differences need not concern us here. What is important for present purposes is that both of these theories predict that a transitory change in income may not have much impact on a household's consumption expenditure, if the household's long-run income prospects remain relatively unaffected. In contrast, the basic consumption function discussed earlier in this chapter assumes that consumption expenditure is dependent on current disposable income. To keep the analysis as simple as possible, we generally shall use the basic consumption function in subsequent chapters; but the fact that it is a simplification should be recognized. (In discussing the effects of temporary tax changes in Chapter 12, we shall put the Friedman and Modigliani-Ando theories to good use.)

Basic Idea #19: Personal consumption expenditure is closely related to disposable income. As disposable income goes up, so does personal consumption expenditure. However, personal consumption expenditure is more closely related to long-run income than to current income.

Determinants of Investment

In Chapter 7, we stressed that investment consists largely of the amount firms spend on new buildings and factories, new equipment, and increases in inventory. Investment plays a central role in the modern theory of output and employment. To understand this theory, it is essential that you understand the factors determining the level of net private domestic investment (which is gross private domestic investment less depreciation). Basically, there are two broad determinants of the level of net private domestic investment—the expected rate of return from capital, and the interest rate.

RATE OF RETURN

The *expected rate of return from capital* is the perceived rate of return that businessmen believe they can obtain if they put up new buildings or factories, add new equipment, or increase their inventories. Each of these forms of investment requires the expenditure of money. The rate of return measures the profitability of such an expenditure; it shows the annual profits to be obtained per dollar invested. Thus a rate of return of 10 percent means that, for every dollar invested, an annual profit of 10 cents is obtained. Clearly, the higher the expected rate of return from a particular investment, the more profitable the investment is expected to be.

INTEREST RATE

The *interest rate* is the cost of borrowing money. More specifically, it is the annual amount that a borrower must pay for the use of a dollar for a year. Thus, if the interest rate is 8 percent, a borrower must pay 8 cents per year for the use of a dollar. And if the interest rate is 12 percent, a borrower must pay 12 cents per year for the use of a dollar. Anyone with a savings account knows what it is to earn interest; anyone who has borrowed money from a bank knows what it is to pay interest.

The Investment Decision

To determine whether to invest in a particular project (a new building, piece of equipment, or other form of investment), a firm must compare the expected rate of return from the project with the interest rate. If the expected rate of return is less than the interest rate, the firm will lose money if it borrows money to carry out the project. For example, if the firm invests in a project with a 10 percent rate of return and borrows the money to finance the project at 12 percent interest, it will receive profits of 10 cents per dollar invested and pay out interest of 12 cents per dollar invested. So it will lose 2 cents (12 cents minus 10 cents) per dollar invested.

Even if the firm does not borrow money to finance the project, it will be unlikely to invest in a project where the expected rate of return is less than the interest rate. Why? Because, if the firm can lend money to others at the prevailing interest rate, it can obtain a greater return from its money by doing this than by investing in the project. Thus, if the interest rate is 12 percent and an investment project has an expected rate of return of 10 percent, a firm will do better, if it has a certain amount of money, to lend it out at 12 percent than to earn 10 percent from the investment project.

Since firms are likely to invest only in projects where the expected rate of return exceeds the interest rate, it is obvious that *the level of both gross and net private domestic investment depends on the total volume of investment projects where the expected rate of return exceeds the interest rate.* For example, if the interest rate is 10 percent, the level of (gross and net) investment depends on the total volume of investment projects where the expected rate of return exceeds 10 percent. The more such projects there are, the higher will be the level of (gross and net) investment. The fewer such projects there are, the lower will be the level of (gross and net) investment. In the following sections, we discuss a number of factors that influence how many such projects there are.

TECHNOLOGICAL CHANGE

The rate of technological change can have an important influence on the volume of investment projects where the rate of return exceeds the interest rate. New technology frequently opens up profitable investment opportunities. For example, Du Pont, after successfully developing nylon in 1938, found it profitable to invest millions of dollars in new plant and equipment to produce this new synthetic fiber. In other words, the invention of nylon resulted in an additional number of investment projects where the rate of return was high enough to induce firms to invest. Another case of this sort was the continuous wide strip mill, one of the most important developments in steel technology in this century. After the invention of the continuous wide strip mill by Armco in the 1920s, American steel producers invested huge sums in new rolling mills to replace the old hand mills.

In general, *a more rapid rate of technological change is likely to result in a greater dollar amount of investment projects where the rate of return exceeds the interest rate. Thus a more rapid rate of technological change is likely to increase the level of investment.*

EXISTING STOCK OF CAPITAL

Another factor that influences the volume of investment projects where the rate of return exceeds the interest rate is the size of the existing stock of capital (relative to the level of sales). As a firm's sales go up, its need for plant, equipment, and inventories clearly goes up as well. Beyond some point, increases in sales result in pressure on the capacity of existing plant and equipment, so that the firm finds it profitable to invest in additional plant and equipment. The crucial relationship is between a firm's sales and its stock of capital goods—that is, its stock of plant, equipment, and inventories. If its sales are well below the amount it can produce with its stock of capital goods, there is little pressure on the firm to invest in additional capital goods. But if its sales are at the upper limit of what can be produced with its capital goods, the firm is likely to view the purchase of additional capital goods as yielding a high rate of return.

In general, *the smaller the existing stock of capital goods—relative to present and prospective sales levels—the greater the dollar amount of investment projects where the expected rate of return exceeds the interest rate.* Conversely, *the bigger the existing stock of capital goods—relative to present and prospective sales levels—the smaller the dollar amount of investment projects where the expected rate of return exceeds the interest rate.*

BUSINESS EXPECTATIONS

Still another factor that influences the volume of investment projects where the expected rate of return exceeds the interest rate is the state of business expectations. Sometimes business executives are optimistic; sometimes they are pessimistic. If they believe that their sales are about to drop dramatically, they will be unlikely to invest much in additional capital goods. On the other hand, if they believe that their sales are about to increase greatly, they may be led to invest heavily in capital goods. Firms must make investment decisions on the basis of forecasts. There is no way any firm can tell exactly what the future will bring, and the investment decisions it makes will be influenced by how optimistic or pessimistic its forecasts are. This, in turn, will depend on existing business conditions, as well as on many other factors. Sometimes government actions and political developments have an important impact on business expectations. Sometimes unexpected changes in the fortune of one industry have a major effect on expectations in other industries.

In general, *the more optimistic business expectations are, the larger the dollar amount of investment projects where the expected rate of return exceeds the interest rate. Conversely, the more pessimistic business expectations are, the smaller the dollar amount of investment projects where the expected rate of return exceeds the interest rate.*

203

Table 10.3

EXPECTED RATES OF RETURN FROM INVESTMENT PROJECTS CONSIDERED BY A FIRM

Project	Expected rate of return (percent)
A	12
B	14
C	8
D	11
E	7
F	10

Finally, the volume of investment projects where the expected rate of return exceeds the interest rate clearly depends on the level of the interest rate. The higher the interest rate, the smaller the volume of projects that have expected rates of return exceeding the interest rate. The lower the interest rate, the larger the volume of projects that have expected rates of return exceeding the interest rate. Suppose that a firm is considering the six investment projects shown in Table 10.3. If the interest rate is 6 percent, all of them have expected rates of return exceeding the interest rate. If the interest rate is 10 percent, only three of them (projects A, B, and D) have expected rates of return exceeding the interest rate. And if the interest rate is 15 percent, none of them has an expected rate of return exceeding the interest rate.

In general, *increases in the interest rate tend to reduce investment, while decreases in the interest rate tend to increase investment.* In 1982, this fact was reiterated frequently by both President Reagan and his critics. There was a general feeling that increases in interest rates had cut back on investment which would have been helpful in getting the economy out of its recession. In 1985, reductions in interest rates were expected to increase investment.

Test Yourself

1. Suppose that only three families inhabit a nation and that (regardless of the level of its income) each family spends 90 percent of its income on consumption goods. For the nation as a whole, what is the marginal propensity to save? How much difference is there between the marginal propensity to consume and the average propensity to consume? To what extent does the nation's marginal propensity to consume depend on the distribution of income? Is this realistic?

2. Assume that the consumption function is as follows:

Disposable income (billions of dollars)	Personal consumption expenditure (billions of dollars)
900	750
1,000	800
1,100	850
1,200	900
1,300	950
1,400	1,000

(a) How much will be saved if disposable income is $1,000 billion? (b) What is the average propensity to consume if disposable income is $1,000 billion? (c) What is the marginal propensity to consume if disposable income is between $1,000 billion and $1,100 billion? (d) What is the marginal propensity to save if disposable income is between $1,000 billion and $1,100 billion?

3. Suppose that the relationship between personal consumption expenditure and disposable income in the United States were as follows:

Consumption (billions of dollars)	Disposable income (billions of dollars)
750	700
830	800
910	900
970	1,000
1,030	1,100
1,100	1,200

Draw the consumption function on a graph. On another graph, draw the saving function. Is the marginal propensity to consume constant, or does it vary with the level of disposable income? Does the average propensity to consume rise or fall as disposable income rises?

4. "Unless firms make profits, they cannot invest in plant and equipment. Profits set an upper limit on how much they can invest." Comment and evaluate.

5. What effect would each of the following have on the amount of investment? That is, would each increase it, decrease it, or have no effect on it? (a) Expectations of greater likelihood of impending recession by firms; (b) a decrease in interest rates; (c) increased rate of invention of important new synthetic materials; (d) a marked reduction in the percent of existing plant that is utilized; (e) an increase in the perceived profitability of building up inventories.

The Equilibrium Level of Net National Product

As stressed in Chapter 3, an equilibrium is a situation where there is no tendency for change; in other words, it is a situation that can persist. In Chapter 3, we studied the equilibrium value of a product's price. Here we are interested in the equilibrium value of net national product. In Chapter 3, we saw that price is at its equilibrium value when the quantity demanded equals the quantity supplied. Here we shall see that NNP is at its equilibrium value when the flow of income (generated by this value of NNP) results in a level of spending that is just sufficient (not too high, not too low) to take this level of output off the market. To understand this equilibrium condition, it is essential to keep three points in mind:

1. The production of goods and services results in a flow of income to the workers, resource owners, and managers that help to produce them. Each level of NNP results in a certain flow of income. More specifically, under the assumptions made here, NNP equals disposable income. Thus whatever the level of NNP may be, we can be sure that the level of disposable income will be equivalent to it.

2. The level of spending on final goods and services is dependent on the level of disposable income. As we saw earlier in this chapter, consumption expenditure depends on the level of disposable income. (For the moment, we assume that investment is independent of the level of output in the economy.) Thus, if we know the level of disposable income, we can predict what level of spending will be forthcoming.

3. The level of production is dependent mainly on the level of spending. If producers find that they are selling goods faster than they are producing them, their inventories will decline. If they find that they are selling goods slower than they are producing them, their inventories will rise. *If NNP is at its equilibrium value, the intended level of spending must be just equal to NNP.* Why? Because otherwise there will be an unintended increase or decrease in producers' inventories—a situation which cannot persist. Much more will be said on this score in the sections that follow.

Aggregate Flows of Income and Expenditure

OUTPUT DETERMINES INCOME

Let's look in more detail at the process whereby national output (that is, NNP) determines the level of income, which in turn determines the level of spending. Suppose that the first column of Table 10.4 shows the various possible output levels—that is, the various possible values of NNP—that the economy might produce this year. This column shows the various output levels that might be produced, *if producers expect that there will be enough spending to take this much output off the market at the existing price level.* And, as stressed above, disposable income equals NNP.

INCOME DETERMINES SPENDING

Since disposable income equals NNP (under our current assumptions), the first column of Table 10.4 also shows the level of disposable income cor-

Table 10.4

DETERMINATION OF EQUILIBRIUM LEVEL OF NET NATIONAL PRODUCT (BILLIONS OF DOLLARS)

(1) Net national product (= disposable income)	(2) Intended consumption expenditure	(3) Intended saving	(4) Intended investment	(5) Total intended spending (2) + (4)	(6) Tendency of national output
1,000	950	50	90	1,040	Upward
1,050	980	70	90	1,070	Upward
1,100	1,010	90	90	1,100	No change
1,150	1,040	110	90	1,130	Downward
1,200	1,070	130	90	1,160	Downward
1,250	1,100	150	90	1,190	Downward

responding to each possible level of NNP. From this, it should be possible to determine the level of spending corresponding to each level of NNP. Specifically, suppose that the consumption function is as shown in Table 10.1 (page 197). In this case, intended consumption expenditure at each level of NNP will be shown in column 2 of Table 10.4. For example, if NNP equals $1,000 billion, intended consumption expenditure equals $950 billion.

But consumption expenditure is not the only type of spending. What about investment? Suppose that firms want to invest $90 billion (net of depreciation) regardless of the level of NNP. Under these circumstances, total spending at each level of NNP will be as shown in column 5 of Table 10.4. (Since total intended spending equals intended consumption expenditure plus intended investment, column 5 equals column 2 plus column 4.)

OUTPUT MUST EQUAL SPENDING

Column 5 of Table 10.4 shows the level of total *intended spending* at each level of national output (and income). *If NNP is at its equilibrium value, total intended spending must equal total output.* In other words, *if NNP is at its equilibrium value, total intended spending must equal NNP.* The easiest way to show this is to show that, if intended spending is not equal to NNP, NNP is *not* at its equilibrium value. The following discussion provides such a proof. First we show that, if intended spending is greater than NNP, NNP is not at its equilibrium level. Then we show that, if intended spending is less than NNP, NNP is not at its equilibrium level.

If intended spending is *greater* than NNP, what will happen? Since the total amount that will be spent on final goods and services exceeds the total amount of final goods and services produced (the latter being, by definition, NNP), firms' inventories will be reduced. Consequently, firms will increase their output rate to avoid continued depletion of their inventories and to bring their output into balance with the rate of aggregate demand. Since an increase in the output rate means an increase in NNP, it follows that NNP will tend to increase if intended spending is greater than NNP. NNP therefore is not at its equilibrium level.

On the other hand, what will happen if intended spending is *less* than NNP? Since the total amount that will be spent on final goods and services

Basic Idea #20: For NNP to be at its
equilibrium value, total intended
spending on final goods and services
must equal NNP. If this spending
exceeds NNP, NNP will tend to rise (as
firms increase their output to avoid
continued depletion of their inventories).
If it is less than NNP, NNP will tend to
fall (as firms cut back their output in
response to increased inventories).

falls short of the total amount of final goods and services produced (the latter being, by definition, NNP), firms' inventories will increase. As inventories pile up unexpectedly, firms will cut back their output to bring it into better balance with aggregate demand. Since a reduction in output means a reduction in NNP, it follows that NNP will tend to fall if intended spending is less than NNP. Once again, NNP is not at its equilibrium level.

Since NNP is not at its equilibrium value when it exceeds or falls short of intended spending, it must be at its equilibrium value only when it equals intended spending.

Why NNP Must Equal Intended Spending: Three Cases

To get a better idea of why NNP will be at its equilibrium value only if it equals intended spending, consider three possible values of NNP—$1,050 billion, $1,100 billion, and $1,150 billion—and see what would happen in our simple economy (in Table 10.4) if these values of NNP prevailed.

CASE 1: NNP = $1,050 BILLION

What would happen if firms were to produce $1,050 billion of final goods and services? Given our assumptions, disposable income would also equal $1,050 billion (since disposable income equals NNP), so that consumers would spend $980 billion on consumption goods and services. (This follows from the nature of the consumption function: see column 2 of Table 10.4.) Since firms want to invest $90 billion, total intended spending would be $1,070 billion ($980 billion + $90 billion, as shown in column 5). But the total amount spent on final goods and services under these circumstances would exceed the total value of final goods and services produced by $20 billion ($1,070 billion − $1,050 billion), so that firms' inventories would be drawn down by $20 billion. Clearly, this situation could not persist very long. As firms become aware that their inventories are becoming depleted, they would step up their production rates, so that the value of output of final goods and services—NNP—would increase.

CASE 2: NNP = $1,150 BILLION

What would happen if firms were to produce $1,150 billion of final goods and services? Given our assumptions, disposable income would also equal $1,150 billion (since disposable income equals NNP), with the result that consumers would spend $1,040 billion on consumption goods and services. (Again, this follows from the consumption function: see column 2 of Table 10.4.) Since firms want to invest $90 billion, total spending would be $1,130 billion ($1,040 billion + $90 billion, as shown in column 5). But the total amount spent on final goods and services under these circumstances would fall short of the total value of final goods and services produced by $20 billion ($1,150 billion − $1,130 billion), so that firms' inventories would increase by $20 billion. Clearly, this situation, like the previous one, could not continue very long. When firms see that their inventories are increasing, they reduce their production rates, causing the value of output of final goods and services—NNP—to decrease.

CASE 3: NNP = $1,100 BILLION

What would happen if firms were to produce $1,100 billion of final goods and services? Disposable income would also equal $1,100 billion (since disposable income equals NNP), so that consumers would spend $1,010 billion on consumption goods and services. (Once again, this follows from the consumption function: see column 2 of Table 10.4.) Since firms want to invest $90 billion, total spending would be $1,100 billion ($1,010 billion + $90 billion, as shown in column 5). Thus the total amount spent on final goods and services under these circumstances would exactly equal the total value of final goods and services produced. Consequently, there would be no reason for firms to alter their production rates. Thus this would be an equilibrium situation—a set of circumstances where there is no tendency for NNP to change—and the equilibrium level of NNP in this situation would be $1,100 billion.

These three cases illustrate the process that pushes NNP toward its equilibrium value (and maintains it there). So long as NNP is below its equilibrium value, the situation is like that described in our first case. So long as NNP is above its equilibrium value, the situation is like that described in our second case. Whether NNP is below or above its equilibrium value, there is a tendency for production rates to be altered so that NNP moves toward its equilibrium value. Eventually, NNP will reach its equilibrium value, and the situation will be like that described in our third case. The important aspect of the third case—the equilibrium situation—is that for it to occur, intended spending must equal NNP.

USING A GRAPH TO DETERMINE EQUILIBRIUM NNP

For the sake of absolute clarity, we can represent the same argument in a diagrammatic, rather than tabular, analysis. Let's show again that the equilibrium level of NNP is at the point where intended spending equals NNP, but now using a graph. Since disposable income equals net national product in this simple case, we can plot consumption expenditure (on the vertical axis) versus net national product (on the horizontal axis), as shown in Figure 10.5. This is the consumption function. Also, we can plot the sum of consumption expenditure *(C)* and investment expenditure *(I)* against NNP, as shown in Figure 10.5. This relationship, shown by the $C + I$ line, indicates the level of total intended spending on final goods and services for various amounts of NNP. Finally, we can plot a *45-degree line,* as shown in Figure 10.5. This line contains all points where the amount on the horizontal axis equals the amount on the vertical axis. Thus, since NNP is on the horizontal axis and intended spending is on the vertical axis, it contains all points where total intended spending equals net national product.

The equilibrium level of net national product will be at the point where total intended spending equals NNP. Consequently, the *equilibrium level of NNP will be at the point on the horizontal axis where the $C + I$ line intersects the 45-degree line.* In Figure 10.5, this occurs at $1,100 billion. Under the conditions assumed here, no other level of NNP can be maintained for any considerable period of time.

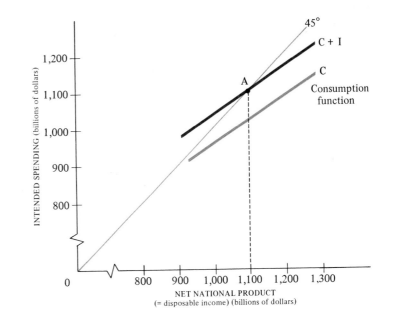

Figure 10.5
Determination of Equilibrium Value of
Net National Product *The consumption
function is C, and the sum of consumption and investment expenditure is C + I.
The equilibrium value of NNP is at the
point where the C + I line intersects the
45-degree line, here $1,100 billion.*

Why can we be sure that the point where the $C + I$ line intersects the 45-degree line is the point where intended spending equals NNP? Because a 45-degree line is, by construction, a line that includes all points where the amount on the horizontal axis equals the amount on the vertical axis. In this case, as noted above, intended spending is on the vertical axis and NNP is on the horizontal axis. Thus at point A, the point where the $C + I$ line intersects the 45-degree line, intended spending must equal NNP, because point A is on the 45-degree line.

Reconciling Aggregate Demand and Supply Curves with Income-Expenditure Analysis

At this point, we must reconcile and integrate the income-expenditure analysis presented here with the aggregate demand-aggregate supply analysis presented in Chapter 9. According to the *income-expenditure analysis,* the equilibrium level of NNP occurs at the point where the $C + I$ line intersects the 45-degree line, as shown in the top panel of Figure 10.6. This analysis assumes that firms set their output levels in accord with the level of demand at current prices. If intended spending increases, firms increase their output levels; if intended spending falls, firms cut their output levels.

The income-expenditure analysis assumes that firms will produce whatever is demanded at the going price level. In other words, it assumes that the economy is situated on the horizontal range of its aggregate supply curve. As shown in the bottom panel of Figure 10.6, the aggregate demand curve intersects the aggregate supply curve in this range. Put differently, the income-expenditure analysis assumes that the equilibrium level of output is demand determined and that supply adjusts passively to demand.

209

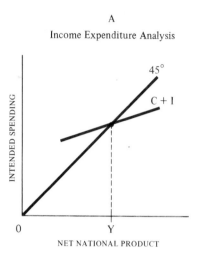

A
Income Expenditure Analysis

45°

C + I

INTENDED SPENDING

0   Y

NET NATIONAL PRODUCT

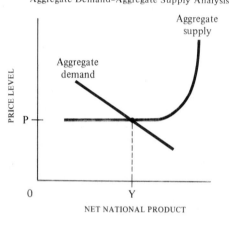

B
Aggregate Demand–Aggregate Supply Analysis

Aggregate
supply

Aggregate
demand

PRICE LEVEL

P

0   Y

NET NATIONAL PRODUCT

Figure 10.6

Relationship between Income-Expenditure Analysis and Aggregate Demand-Aggregate Supply Analysis Income-expenditure analysis uses the intersection of the C + I line and the 45-degree line to find the equilibrium level of NNP. Aggregate demand-aggregate supply analysis uses the intersection of the aggregate demand and supply curves to find the equilibrium level of NNP. Income-expenditure analysis assumes that the economy is operating on the horizontal range of the aggregate supply curve. Both types of analysis yield the same result—namely, that the equilibrium value of NNP is OY.

If the economy is experiencing considerable unemployment, and the horizontal range of the aggregate supply curve is the relevant one, the income-expenditure analysis tends to be a more revealing way of looking at the determinants of national output than the aggregate demand-aggregate supply analysis. It shows the nature of the changes in spending, which are the prime movers in the model.

But if the economy is operating at a point where the aggregate supply curve is vertical (or close to it), the aggregate demand-aggregate supply analysis is more relevant than the income-expenditure analysis because it focuses on changes in the price level, which are not included or shown in the income-expenditure analysis.

In subsequent chapters, both of these types of analysis will be used. They both are important parts of the economist's tool kit.

Leakages and Injections: Another Approach

In studying any topic, it helps to look at it from more than one angle. Another approach to income-expenditure analysis is the so-called *leakage-injection approach.* The basic idea underlying this approach is that, under our assumptions, the production of a particular level of output (that is, NNP) results in a level of disposable income that is equivalent to this level of NNP. But, as we know from our previous discussions, not all of this disposable income is spent by households; some of it is saved. This saving is a *leakage* from the spending stream, because it withdraws spending from the flow of income and expenditure. Such a leakage tends to reduce the equilibrium value of NNP because, unless it is offset, it results in total spending being too small to take the entire output (that is, NNP) off the market.

But firms do not sell their whole output to consumers. As we know from previous chapters, some of NNP (including items like blast furnaces and oil refineries) is sold to firms, this spending being called investment. Investment is an *injection* into the spending stream, because it adds spending to the flow of income and expenditure. That is, it is a supplement to consumption expenditure. Such an injection tends to increase the equilibrium value of NNP because it offsets the leakage of saving. If intended investment is less than intended saving, it is only a partial offset of this leakage. If intended investment is greater than intended saving, it more than offsets this leakage.

The equilibrium value of NNP is the one where the leakages equal the injections. Why? Because intended spending will equal NNP only if the intended amount of income not spent on output (leakages) equals the intended spending on output that is a supplement to consumer expenditure (injections). If leakages are greater than injections, NNP is above its equilibrium value, since intended spending will be too small to take the existing NNP off the market. If leakages are less than injections, NNP is below its equilibrium value, since intended spending will be more than sufficient to take the existing NNP off the market.

Example 10.1   Asking "What If" Questions

Economists find it useful to ask "what if" questions. For example, what if NNP in a particular country assumed various alternative values? What would be the results? Suppose that you know three things about the country in question. First, in this country, personal consumption expenditure = $100 million + 0.75D, where D is disposable income. Second, intended investment in this country equals $150 million. Third, this country has a primitive economy with neither a government nor foreign trade.

(a) Suppose that NNP in this country assumes the alternative values shown below. What are the corresponding values of intended consumption expenditure, intended investment, and total intended spending? Fill in the blanks below.

Net national product	Intended consumption expenditure	Intended investment	Total intended spending
	(millions of dollars)		
800	_____	_____	_____
900	_____	_____	_____
1,000	_____	_____	_____
1,100	_____	_____	_____

(b) What is the equilibrium level of net national product? (c) If NNP equals $900 million, what is the intended value of saving? (d) At what value of NNP does intended saving equal intended investment?

SOLUTION

(a) The complete table is:

Net national product	Intended consumption expenditure	Intended investment	Total intended spending
		(millions of dollars)	
800	700	150	850
900	775	150	925
1,000	850	150	1,000
1,100	925	150	1,075

(b) $1,000 million, since at this level of NNP total intended spending equals NNP. (c) $900 million minus $775 million, or $125 million. (d) When NNP equals $1,000 million, both intended saving and intended investment equal $150 million.

Table 10.5

THE LEAKAGE-INJECTION APPROACH TO THE DETERMINATION OF NET NATIONAL PRODUCT (BILLIONS OF DOLLARS)

(1) Net national product (= disposable income)	(2) Intended consumption expenditure	(3) Leakages (intended saving)	(4) Injections (intended investment)	(5) Tendency of national output
1,000	950	50	90	Upward
1,050	980	70	90	Upward
1,100	1,010	90	90	No change
1,150	1,040	110	90	Downward
1,200	1,070	130	90	Downward
1,250	1,100	150	90	Downward

A Numerical Example

To illustrate the use of the leakage-injection approach, consider Table 10.5, which is based on the same data as Table 10.4. Column 3 shows *intended saving* at each level of NNP. Saving is, as we have seen, a leakage. Thus the total leakages at each level of NNP are given in column 3. Column 4 shows *intended investment* at each level of NNP. Investment is, as we have seen, an injection. Thus the total injections at each level of NNP are given in column 4.

WHAT IF NNP IS LESS THAN $1,100 BILLION?

If NNP is *less* than $1,100, Table 10.5 indicates that the total leakages are less than the total injections. The intended amount withdrawn from the expenditure stream via saving is less than the intended amount added via investment. Thus total intended spending is greater than NNP, and, as we saw in previous sections, this will result in an increase in NNP. For example, suppose that NNP equals $1,050 billion. At this level of NNP, intended saving is $70 billion, whereas intended investment is $90 billion. Consumers withdraw $70 billion from the expenditure stream via saving, while firms want to add $90 billion to it via investment. Consequently, total intended spending exceeds NNP by $90 billion minus $70 billion, or $20 billion. Since firms' inventories are drawn down by $20 billion, there is a tendency for NNP to increase, as we saw in a previous section.

WHAT IF NNP IS GREATER THAN $1,100 BILLION?

If NNP is *greater* than $1,100 billion, Table 10.5 indicates that the total leakages are more than the total injections. The intended amount withdrawn from the expenditure stream via saving is more than the intended amount added via investment. Thus total intended spending is less than NNP, and, as we saw in previous sections, this will result in a decrease in NNP. For example, suppose that NNP equals $1,150 billion. At this level of NNP, intended saving is $110 billion, whereas intended investment is $90 billion. Consumers want to withdraw $110 billion from the expenditure stream via saving, while firms want to add $90 billion to it via investment. Consequently, total intended spending falls short of NNP by $110 billion minus $90 billion, or $20 billion. Since firms' inventories increase by $20 billion, there is a tendency for NNP to fall, as we saw in a previous section.

WHAT IF NNP EQUALS $1,100 BILLION?

Only when NNP *equals* $1,100 billion will there be no tendency for NNP to rise or fall. As shown in Table 10.5, this is the value of NNP where the total leakages equal the total injections. (Specifically, both intended saving and intended investment equal $90 billion at this level of NNP). Thus, as pointed out above, the equilibrium value of NNP is the one where the total leakages equal the total injections.

Note that the equilibrium value of NNP, as determined by the leakage-injection approach, is the same as the one determined by the approach used in previous sections. Using either approach, we get the same answer—an equilibrium NNP of $1,100 billion. This will always be true. To see why, recall that according to the approach used in previous sections, NNP is at its equilibrium value when total intended spending on output equals NNP. This condition will be met if and only if the total leakages (intended saving) equal the total injections (intended investment). Since

$$\text{total intended spending} = \text{intended consumption}$$
$$\text{expenditure} + \text{intended investment},$$

and

$$\text{disposable income} = \text{intended consumption}$$
$$\text{expenditure} + \text{intended saving},$$

it follows that, because NNP equals disposable income here, total intended spending will equal NNP if and only if intended saving equals intended investment. Thus, if we use one approach, we will get the same answer as if we use the other approach.

Leakages and Injections: A Graphical View

Graphs can be used to determine the equilibrium value of NNP when the leakage-injection approach is used. To do so, we plot the saving function and the investment function on the same graph. (The ***investment function*** is the relationship between NNP and intended investment.) The equilibrium value of NNP is the value of NNP at which these two functions intersect. Why? Because at the value of NNP at which they intersect, the total leakages (represented by the saving function) equal the total injections (represented by the investment function).

Based on the data in Table 10.5, the saving function and investment function are as shown in Figure 10.7. Thus the equilibrium value of NNP must be $1,100 billion, since this is the point where the two functions intersect. For the reasons given in the previous section, the equilibrium value of NNP, as determined by a graph of this sort, must be the same as the one determined by Figure 10.5. And in accord with this fact, both Figures 10.5 and 10.7 yield the same answer—namely, that the equilibrium value of NNP is $1,100 billion.

213

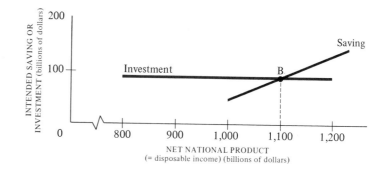

Figure 10.7

Determination of Equilibrium Value of Net National Product *The equilibrium value of NNP is at the point where the saving function intersects the investment function, which here is $1,100 billion. At this point, the total leakages equal the total injections, since the saving function represents the leakages and the investment function represents the injections.*

Actual Saving Equals Actual Investment

In the previous sections, we stressed that intended saving need not equal intended investment. This is an important fact, which must be understood. At the same time, however, it must be recognized that, whether or not intended saving equals intended investment, ***actual saving*** *must always equal* ***actual investment.*** In other words, although the amount people *set out to save* during a particular year may not equal the amount firms *set out to invest,* the *actual amount saved* will always equal the *actual amount invested.* This must be true because, as pointed out in a previous section, NNP has to equal consumption expenditure plus net investment.[3] At the same time, since it equals disposable income here, NNP must also equal consumption expenditure plus saving. Subtracting consumption expenditure from each of these expressions for NNP, saving must equal investment.

TWO ILLUSTRATIONS

Consider the case (in Table 10.4) where NNP is $1,050 billion. In this case, intended saving is $70 billion but intended investment is $90 billion. How does it turn out that actual saving equals actual investment? As pointed out in a previous section, there is an unintended ***disinvestment*** (i.e., negative investment) of −$20 billion in inventories if NNP is $1,050 billion. (Recall from Chapter 7 that a build-up of inventories is a form of investment, so a $1 billion increase in inventories equals $1 billion of investment.) Thus the actual investment is $90 billion (in intended investment) minus $20 billion (in unintended disinvestment), or $70 billion.[4] Actual saving equals intended saving, or $70 billion. Thus actual saving equals actual investment.

As a further illustration, consider the case where NNP is $1,150 billion. In this case, intended saving is $110 billion but intended investment is $90

---

[3] Recall from Chapter 7 that net national product equals consumption expenditure plus government expenditure plus net exports plus net investment. Since government expenditure and net exports are assumed to be zero, it follows that net national product equals consumption expenditure plus net investment.

[4] To make this case more concrete, suppose that the intended investment of $90 billion consists of $80 billion of expenditures on plant and equipment and a $10 billion increase in inventories. Because of the unintended disinvestment in inventories of −$20 billion, inventories will decline by $10 billion, and actual investment will equal $70 billion ($80 billion of expenditures on plant and equipment plus the −$10 billion change in inventories).

billion. How does it turn out that actual saving equals actual investment? As pointed out in a previous section, there is an unintended investment in inventories of $20 billion (because total spending falls short of NNP by this amount). Thus actual investment turns out to equal the intended investment of $90 billion plus the unintended investment of $20 billion, or $110 billion in all. Since actual saving also equals $110 billion, actual saving equals actual investment.[5]

In general, actual saving always must equal actual investment, even though intended saving does not always equal intended investment.

Usefulness of the Leakage-Injection Approach

Why bother to look at the determination of NNP in terms of the leakage-injection approach? After all, as we have stated repeatedly, we can get the same answer by comparing total intended spending on final goods and services with NNP. One important reason for looking at the determination of NNP in terms of intended saving (leakage) and intended investment (injection) is that it helps to lay bare the reasons why equilibrium NNP may be different from the level of NNP that would result in reasonably full employment at reasonably stable prices. As we pointed out in our discussion in Chapter 8 of criticisms of the classical view of unemployment, these reasons revolve about the fact that intended saving and intended investment are carried out by different parts of society and for different reasons. Households do much of the saving. They abstain from consuming now in order to provide for retirement, college educations for their children, emergencies, and other ways of consuming later. Firms, on the other hand, do most of the investing. They build plants and equipment and expand their inventories in response to profit opportunities. Because of this cleavage between the savers and the investors, *there is no assurance that intended saving will equal intended investment at a level of NNP that results in reasonably full employment at reasonably stable prices.*[6]

[5] Note that we assume here that actual saving will equal intended saving and that unintended changes in inventories will make actual investment conform to actual and intended saving. There are other ways for adjustments to take place. The important thing is that, one way or another, actual saving will equal actual investment.

[6] Note that, under the simplifying assumptions made in this chapter, there is only one leakage (saving) and one injection (investment). In subsequent chapters, we shall be concerned with models where other leakages (taxes and imports) and injections (government expenditures and exports) are involved.

Test Yourself

1. Suppose that the consumption function in a particular economy is given by the table on the right:

Disposable income (billions of dollars)	Consumption expenditure (billions of dollars)
400	300
500	360
600	410
700	440
800	470

If firms want to invest $140 billion, what is the equilibrium value of NNP? Can we be sure that this is the full-employment value of NNP? Why or why not? (The full-employment value of NNP is defined as the value of NNP that can be produced if there is full employment.)

2. Using the data in Question 1, plot the consumption function and the $C + I$ line on a graph, and derive the equilibrium value of NNP graphically. Is the consumption function a straight line? If the consumption function is not a straight line, does this affect the validity of the analysis in any way?

3. Using the data in Question 1, plot the saving function and the investment function, and show how they can be used to determine the equilibrium value of NNP. Does intended saving equal intended investment if NNP equals $800 billion? If NNP were $800 billion, show how actual saving would turn out to equal actual investment.

4. Suppose that the consumption function in a certain economy is $C = 100 + 0.8D$, where C is consumption expenditure and D is disposable income. If intended investment equals 10, what is the equilibrium value of NNP?

5. (Advanced) In a certain economy, the average propensity to consume is always equal to the marginal propensity to consume. If the equilibrium level of NNP equals $300 billion and if intended investment equals $100 billion, what is the equation for the consumption function in this economy?

Summary

1. The consumption function—the relation between personal consumption expenditure and disposable income—is at the heart of the modern theory of the determination of national output. There have been many studies of the consumption function, some based on cross-section data, some based on time-series data. From the consumption function, one can determine the marginal propensity to consume, which is the proportion of an extra dollar of income that is spent on consumption, as well as the saving function (the relationship between total saving and disposable income) and the marginal propensity to save (the proportion of an extra dollar of income that is saved).

2. Current consumption expenditure does not depend solely on disposable income in the current period. Instead, as stressed by the permanent-income and life-cycle hypotheses, it depends on the expected stream of disposable income over a long period of time.

3. The level of both gross and net private domestic investment is determined by the expected rate of return from capital and the interest rate. The expected rate of return from capital is the perceived rate of return that businesses expect to obtain if new buildings are put up, new equipment is added, or inventories are increased. The interest rate is the cost of borrowing money. The level of investment is directly related to the expected rate of return from capital, and inversely related to the interest rate.

4. The expected rate of return from capital is itself dependent upon the rate of technological change, the size of the existing stock of capital goods (relative to present and prospective sales levels), and the optimism or pessimism of business executives' expectations.

5. The equilibrium level of net national product will be at the point where intended spending on final goods and services equals NNP. If intended spending exceeds NNP, NNP will tend to increase. If intended spending falls short of NNP, NNP will tend to fall.

6. Another way to describe this equilibrium condition is to say that NNP is at its equilibrium level if intended saving equals intended investment. This is the so-called leakage-injection approach.

7. If NNP is below its equilibrium level, the total amount spent on goods and services will exceed the total amount produced, so that firms' inventories will be reduced. Firms will step up their output rates, thus increasing NNP.

8. If NNP is above its equilibrium value, the total amount spent on goods and services will fall short of the total amount produced, so that firms' inventories will rise. Firms will cut their output rates, thus reducing NNP.

9. Because of the cleavage between savers and investors, there is no assurance that intended saving will equal intended investment at a level of NNP that results in reasonably full employment at stable prices. But actual saving and actual investment always must turn out to be equal.

Concepts for Review

Consumption function	Permanent-income hypothesis	Leakage-injection approach
Marginal propensity to consume	Expected rate of return	Intended saving
Average propensity to consume	Interest rate	Intended investment
Saving function	Intended spending	Investment function
Marginal propensity to save	45-degree line	Actual saving
	Income-expenditure analysis	Actual investment
		Disinvestment

CHAPTER 11

Multiplier Analysis and Changes in Output

If you look at the business section of the morning newspaper, or if you switch on a television program dealing with the economy, there is a pretty good chance that you will find a forecast of the change in GNP or NNP in the next year or the next quarter. If so, more than one forecast may be given, for economic analysts do not always agree, particularly in detail. There is good reason why both economists and the general public are so interested in prospective changes in NNP. Besides being intrinsically important, they are related to changes in the unemployment rate and the inflation rate. In the previous chapter, we were concerned entirely with the factors determining the *level* of national output in a particular period. Now we must focus attention on the factors determining *changes* in national output.

Since changes in investment spending can result in important changes in output, we begin by describing the volatility of investment spending and the way in which changes in such spending have an amplified effect on output. Then we show that shifts in the consumption function have similar effects on national output. Finally, we discuss induced investment and the so-called paradox of thrift.

The Volatility of Investment

As shown in Figure 11.1, investment expenditure tends to be relatively unstable. That is, it varies from year to year by greater percentages than does consumption expenditure. Based on our discussion in the previous chapter, it is easy to see why this is the case.

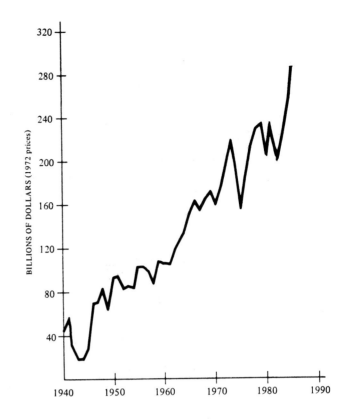

Figure 11.1
Gross Private Domestic Investment, United States, 1940–84 *Gross invest-ment varies considerably from year to year. So does net investment.*

Irregularity of Innovation Rate. Technological innovation occurs irregu-larly—that is, in fits and starts—not at a constant rate. Thus investment (which, as we have seen, is dependent on the rate of technological change) also tends to occur irregularly. Investment booms seem to have occurred in response to major innovations like the railroad and the automobile. According to some forecasts, important innovations are likely to occur during the 1980s and 1990s in microelectronics and biotechnology. If so, they may be major stimuli to investment.

Durability of Capital Goods. Because capital goods tend to be quite durable, firms frequently can postpone investment decisions. For example, they can postpone the replacement of a piece of equipment by using it even though it is not as reliable as it once was. Or they can postpone the construction of a new building by tolerating crowded conditions in their existing buildings. Since many investment decisions are postponable, the exact time when projects are accepted may depend on the state of business expectations and the level of firms' profits, both of which are highly vari-able. Also, since the optimism or pessimism of business expectations tends to be contagious, firms often tend to invest at the same time.

Capacity Utilization. There are great differences from one year to the next in the extent to which existing productive capacity is being utilized. In some years, sales are so great that firms are working their plants at full capacity. In other years, sales are so slack that firms have plenty of excess capacity. In periods when the existing stock of capital goods is more than sufficient to meet current sales, the level of investment will tend to be lower than in periods when the existing stock of capital goods is only

219

barely sufficient to meet current sales. Because of the year-to-year variation in the extent to which sales levels press against productive capacity, there is considerable variation in the level of investment.

Effects of Changes in Intended Investment

Looking at the highly simplified model we constructed in the previous chapter to explain the level of national output, what is the effect of a change in the amount of intended investment? Specifically, if firms increase their intended investment by $1 billion, what effect will this increase have on the equilibrium value of net national product?

This is a very important question, the answer to which sheds considerable light on the reasons for changes in national output. The following sections are devoted to answering this question. We assume that the change in investment is autonomous, not induced. An *autonomous* change in spending is one that *is not* due to a change in income or NNP. An *induced* change in spending is one that *is* due to a change in income or NNP. We shall discuss induced investment near the end of this chapter.

THE SPENDING CHAIN: ONE STAGE AFTER ANOTHER

If there is a $1 billion increase in intended investment, the effects can be divided into a number of stages. In the first stage, firms spend an additional $1 billion on plant, equipment, or inventories. This extra $1 billion is received by workers and suppliers as extra income, which results in a second stage of extra spending on final goods and services. How much of their extra $1 billion in income will the workers and suppliers spend? If the marginal propensity to consume is 0.6, they will spend 0.6 times $1 billion, or $.6 billion. This extra expenditure of $.6 billion is received by firms and disbursed to workers, suppliers, and owners as extra income, bringing about a third stage of extra spending on final goods and services. How much of this extra income of $.6 billion will be spent? Since the marginal propensity to consume is 0.6, they will spend 60 percent of this $.6 billion, or $.36 billion. This extra expenditure of $.36 billion is received by firms and disbursed to workers, suppliers, and owners as extra income, which results in a fourth stage of spending, then a fifth stage, a sixth stage, and so on.

TOTALING UP THE STAGES

Table 11.1 shows the total increase in expenditure on final goods and services arising from the original $1 billion increase in intended investment. The total increase in expenditures is the increase in the first stage, plus the increase in the second stage, plus the increase in the third stage, and so on. Since there is an endless chain of stages, we cannot list all the increases. But because the successive increases in spending get smaller and smaller, we can determine their sum, which in this case is $2.5 billion. Thus the $1 billion increase in intended investment results—after all stages of the spending and responding process have worked themselves out—in a

Table 11.1
THE MULTIPLIER PROCESS

Stage	Amount of extra spending (billions of dollars)
1	1.00
2	.60
3	.36
4	.22
5	.13
6	.08
7	.05
8	.03
9 and beyond	.03
Total	2.50

$2.5 billion increase in total expenditures on final goods and services. In other words, it results in a $2.5 billion increase in NNP.

WHY $2.5 BILLION?

Why does the $1 billion increase in intended investment result in a $2.5 billion increase in NNP? To see why, recall from the previous chapter that intended saving must equal intended investment, if NNP is at its equilibrium value. Thus, if intended investment increases by $1 billion, intended saving must increase by the same amount. But if intended saving must increase by $1 billion, disposable income must increase by $2.5 billion because the marginal propensity to save equals 0.4 (since it equals one minus the marginal propensity to consume, which is 0.6 in this case). In other words, *since each extra dollar of disposable income results in 40 cents of additional intended saving, and since NNP equals disposable income (under the conditions assumed here), it will take an extra $2.5 billion of NNP to result in an extra $1 billion of intended saving.*

ANOTHER WAY TO DERIVE $2.5 BILLION

An alternative way of proving that a $1 billion increase in intended investment results in a $2.5 billion increase in NNP is the following. Because 0.6 is the marginal propensity to consume, a $1 billion increase in intended investment will result in increased total spending of $(1 + .6 + .6^2 + .6^3 + \ldots)$ billions of dollars. This is evident from Table 11.1, which shows that the increased spending in the first stage is $1 billion, the increased spending in the second stage is $.6 billion, the increased spending in the third stage is $.6^2$ billion, and so on. But it can be shown that $(1 + .6 + .6^2 + .6^3 + \ldots) = \dfrac{1}{1 - .6}$. (See footnote 1.)[1] Consequently, since $1/(1-.6) = 2.5$, the total increase in NNP must be $2.5 billion.

Since the marginal propensity to save equals $(1 - .6)$, another way of stating the findings of the previous paragraph is to say that *a $1 billion increase in intended investment results in an increase in equilibrium NNP of $(1/MPS)$ billions of dollars, where MPS is the marginal propensity to save.* This is a very important conclusion. To understand more clearly what it means, let's consider a couple of numerical examples involving values of

---

[1] To see this, let's divide 1 by $(1 - m)$, where m is less than 1. Using the time-honored rules of long division, we find that

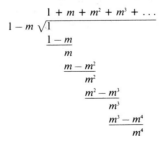

Thus letting $m = 0.6$, it follows that 1 divided by $(1 - .6)$ equals $1 + .6 + .6^2 + .6^3 + \ldots$

the marginal propensity to save other than 0.4. For instance, if the marginal propensity to save is ⅓, a $1 billion increase in intended investment will increase equilibrium NNP by 1 ÷ ⅓ billion dollars; that is, by $3 billion. Or take a case where the marginal propensity to consume equals ¾. What is the effect of a $1 billion increase in intended investment? Since the marginal propensity to save must equal 1 − ¾, or ¼, the answer must be 1 ÷ ¼ billion dollars. That is, equilibrium NNP will increase by $4 billion.

Example 11.1   Investment and a Great Crash

Between 1929 and 1933, annual investment spending in the United States fell by about $50 billion (1972 dollars). To get some idea of how a Great Crash, such as occurred then, can take place, let's consider a simple economy with no government or foreign trade. Suppose that intended investment in this economy falls from $52 billion to $2 billion. Assume that the saving function is as shown below:

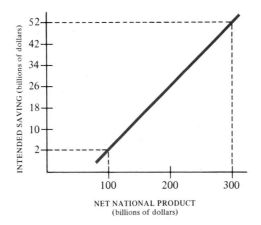

(a) What is the marginal propensity to save? (b) What is the multiplier? (c) What is the equilibrium value of NNP before the fall in investment? (c) What is the equilibrium value of NNP after the fall in investment?

SOLUTION

(a) According to the graph, intended saving equals $2 billion when NNP is $100 billion, and it equals $52 billion when NNP is $300 billion. Thus, since NNP equals disposable income under the assumed (highly simplified) conditions, the marginal propensity to save equals (52 − 2) ÷ (300 − 100) = 0.25. (b) The multiplier equals the reciprocal of the marginal propensity to save, or 1/0.25 = 4 in this highly simplified case. (c) $300 billion, since at this value of NNP intended investment ($52 billion) equals intended saving. (d) $100 billion, since at this value of NNP intended investment ($2 billion) equals intended saving.

The Multiplier

Since a dollar of extra intended investment results in (1/MPS) dollars of extra NNP, (1/MPS) is called the **multiplier.** If you want to estimate the effect of a given increase in intended investment on NNP, multiply the increase in intended investment by (1/MPS). The result will be the increase in NNP. Moreover, it is easy to show that the same multiplier holds for decreases in intended investment as well as for increases. That is, a dollar less of intended investment results in (1/MPS) dollars less of NNP. Consequently, if you want to estimate the effect of a given change in intended investment (positive or negative) on NNP, multiply the change in intended investment by (1/MPS).

It is important to note that, since MPS is less than one, *the multiplier must be greater than one.* In other words, an increase in intended investment of $1 will result in an increase in NNP of more than $1. This means that NNP is relatively sensitive to changes in intended investment. Moreover, since the multiplier is the reciprocal of the marginal propensity to save, the smaller the marginal propensity to save, the higher the multiplier—and the more sensitive is NNP to changes in intended investment. As we shall see, this result has important implications for public policy. For example, because our system of taxes and transfer payments tends to increase the marginal propensity to save out of NNP, the destabilizing effect of a sharp change in investment expenditures frequently is reduced.

USING A GRAPH TO DERIVE THE SIZE OF THE MULTIPLIER

The sort of graphical analysis we used in Figure 10.7 can be used to show the effect of an increase in intended investment on equilibrium NNP. Since such a geometric formulation provides further confirmation of our results in the previous section, it seems worthwhile presenting it at this point.

Let's begin by noting once again that, if NNP is at its equilibrium level, intended saving must equal intended investment. If the saving function in our simplified economy is as shown in Figure 11.2 and intended investment is $100 billion, what will be the effect of a $1 billion increase in intended investment on equilibrium NNP? Before the increase in intended investment, equilibrium NNP was equal to $1,000 billion. (See Figure 11.2.) The increase of $1 billion in intended investment will shift the investment function up by $1 billion, to the new position, shown in Figure 11.2. This shift in the investment function will increase the equilibrium level of NNP, but by how much?

The resulting increase in equilibrium NNP, ΔY, can be derived by the following geometrical reasoning. First, the slope of the saving function times the change in equilibrium NNP must equal the increase in intended investment, $1 billion. This follows from the definition of the slope of a line. The slope equals the vertical distance between any two points on the line divided by the horizontal difference between them. The vertical distance between points A and B in Figure 11.2 is the increase in intended investment ($1 billion), and the horizontal distance between points A and

Basic Idea #21: A $1 billion increase in intended investment results in a more than $1 billion increase in NNP. In the simple model considered here, it results in an increase in equilibrium NNP of (1/MPS) billions of dollars. Since the marginal propensity to save (MPS) is less than one, the increase in equilibrium NNP must exceed $1 billion.

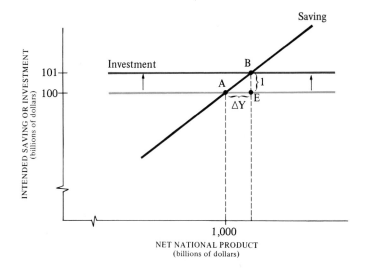

Figure 11.2
The Multiplier *If investment increases by $1 billion, the equilibrium value of NNP increases by ΔY. The slope of the saving function equals the vertical distance from A to B (which equals $1 billion) divided by the horizontal distance from A to B (which equals ΔY). Since this slope equals the marginal propensity to save (MPS), 1/ΔY = MPS. Thus ΔY = 1/MPS.*

B is the change in equilibrium NNP (Δ*Y*). Consequently, the change in equilibrium NNP must equal the increase in intended investment divided by the slope of the saving function.

Since the slope of the saving function is the marginal propensity to save—as pointed out in the previous chapter—it follows that the *change in equilibrium NNP equals the increase in intended investment divided by the marginal propensity to save. Thus a $1 billion increase in intended investment will result in an increase in equilibrium NNP of (1/MPS) billions of dollars,* which is precisely what we concluded in the previous sections.

Test Yourself

1. Suppose that the consumption function in a particular economy is given by the following table:

Disposable income (billions of dollars)	Consumption expenditure (billions of dollars)
400	300
500	360
600	410
700	440
800	470

Suppose that intended investment increases from $140 billion to $141 billion. Using a graph showing the old and new *C* + *I* line, indicate what effect this will have on the equilibrium value of NNP.

2. In question 1, plot the old and new investment functions on the same graph as the saving function. Show that you get the same answer as in question 1.

3. Suppose that the consumption function in a particular economy is *C* = 100 + 0.8*D*, where *C* is consumption expenditure and *D* is disposable income. What is the value of the multiplier?

4. Intended investment increases by $1000 in an economy where the marginal propensity to save is .2. What is the amount of extra spending in the *first* stage of the spending and responding process?

5. If the marginal propensity to consume is three times the marginal propensity to save, what is the multiplier? Why?

Determinants of Consumption: Nonincome Factors

In previous sections of this chapter, we were concerned with the effects on NNP of changes in investment spending. Now we must consider the effects of changes in consumption expenditure. It is important to recognize that many other factors besides disposable income have an effect on personal consumption expenditure. Holding disposable income constant, personal consumption expenditure is likely to vary with the amount of wealth in the hands of the public, the ease and cheapness with which consumers can borrow money, the expectations of the public, the amount of durable goods on hand, the income distribution, and the size of the population. In this section, we discuss the effects of these nonincome factors on consumption expenditure.

Amount of Wealth. Holding disposable income constant, it is clear that personal consumption expenditure will be higher if the public has a large amount of wealth—stocks, bonds, savings accounts, and so on—than if it has a small amount. Why? Because people are more willing to spend out of current income when they have large assets to tide them over if their incomes fall. Thus, if the Merriwether family has $100,000 in stocks and bonds, it is more likely to spend a large percentage of its income than if it has little or nothing in wealth.

Ease and Cheapness of Borrowing. Holding disposable income constant, it is clear that personal consumption expenditure will be higher if the public can borrow money easily and cheaply. This is particularly important for expenditures on consumer durables like automobiles and appliances. If required down payments are increased, and interest rates go up, some potential buyers will be persuaded (or forced) to postpone purchases of such items. For example, the Merriwethers may want a new car, and they may be quite willing to borrow the money to pay for it at 10 percent per year. But if the interest rate is raised to 15 percent per year, they may decide to stick with their old car until it is run into the ground.

Expectations. Holding disposable income constant, personal consumption expenditure may be higher if the public feels that price increases are in the wind or that goods will become harder to get. Why? Because the public may want to stock up on goods before their prices rise and while they are still available. (In the late 1970s, the expectation of price rises with regard to such items as autos and sugar seems to have had such an effect.) But this may not always occur. The expectation of price increases may have the opposite effect if the public is alarmed by inflation, and wants to build up its savings to cushion it against hard times ahead.

Amount of Durable Goods on Hand. Holding disposable income constant, personal consumption expenditure may be higher if the public has few durable goods on hand. For example, during World War II, very few automobiles were produced for ordinary civilian purposes. When such goods became available once again immediately after the war, there was an increase in the proportion of disposable income spent on durable goods, particularly since the public came out of the war with considerable savings and liquid assets. More will be said about this later on in this chapter.

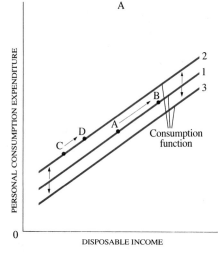

Figure 11.3A

A Shift versus a Movement in the Consumption Function *If the consumption function moves from position 1 to position 2 (or position 3), this is a* shift *in the consumption function. A movement from A to B (or from C to D) is a* movement along *a given consumption function.*

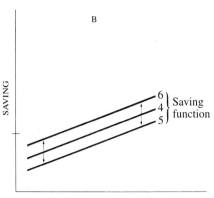

Figure 11.3B

Effects of Shifts in Consumption Function on Saving Function *An* upward *shift in the consumption function (as from position 1 to position 2 in panel A) is accompanied by a* downward *shift in the saving function (from position 4 to position 5 in panel B). A* downward *shift in the consumption function (as from position 1 to position 3 in panel A) is accompanied by an* upward *shift in the saving function (from position 4 to position 6 in panel B).*

Distribution of Income. Holding disposable income constant, personal consumption expenditure would be expected to increase as a nation's income becomes more nearly equally distributed. Why? Because one would expect that the marginal propensity to consume would be higher (and the marginal propensity to save would be lower) among poor families than among rich ones. Thus, if a dollar of income is transferred from a rich family to a poor one, the poor family would be expected to save a smaller proportion of this extra dollar than the rich family from whom it was taken. Consequently, total consumption expenditure would be expected to increase as a result of transfers of income of this sort.

Size of Population. Holding disposable income constant, personal consumption expenditure would be expected to increase as a nation's population increases. As there are more and more mouths to feed, bodies to clothe, and families to house, one would expect that more would be spent on consumption goods, and less saved.

Shifts in the Consumption and Saving Functions

Suppose that a change occurs in one of the factors discussed in the previous section. For example, suppose that there is a marked increase in the amount of wealth in the hands of the public. What effect will this have on the consumption function? Obviously, it will shift the consumption function upward, as from position 1 to position 2 in Figure 11.3A. Or suppose that it becomes more difficult and expensive for consumers to borrow money. What effect will this have on the consumption function? Obviously, it will shift the consumption function downward, as from position 1 to position 3 in Figure 11.3A.

SHIFTS IN FUNCTIONS VERSUS MOVEMENTS ALONG THEM

It is important to distinguish between a *shift* in the consumption function and a *movement along* a given consumption function. A ***shift in the consumption function*** means that the public wants to spend a different amount on consumption goods out of a given amount of disposable income than in the past. Thus, if the consumption function shifts to position 2 in Figure 11.3A, this means that the public wants to spend more on consumption goods out of a given amount of disposable income than when the consumption function was at position 1. And if the consumption function shifts to position 3 in Figure 11.3A, this means that the public wants to spend less on consumption goods out of a given amount of disposable income than when the consumption function was at position 1.

In contrast, a movement along a given consumption function is a change in personal consumption expenditure induced by a change in disposable income, with no change in the relationship between personal consumption expenditure and disposable income. For example, the movement from Point *A* to point *B* is a movement along a consumption function (in position 1). Similarly, the movement from point *C* to point *D* is a movement along a consumption function (in position 2).

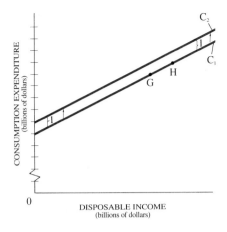

Figure 11.4
Shift in the Consumption Function *If the consumption function shifts from C_1 to C_2, this means that, at each level of disposable income, consumers intend to spend $1 billion more on consumption goods and services. Such a shift results in an increase of $\left(\dfrac{1}{MPS}\right)$ billions of dollars in equilibrium NNP, as shown in Figure 11.5.*

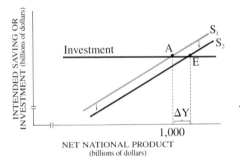

Figure 11.5
Effect of a Downward Shift of the Saving Function *A $1 billion upward shift in the consumption function results in a $1 billion downward shift in the saving function. Thus, if the consumption function shifts from C_1 to C_2 in Figure 11.4, the saving function shifts downward from S_1 to S_2, as shown here. The point where the saving function intersects the investment function shifts from A to E, and the equilibrium value of NNP increases by ΔY, which is the same amount that it increases when intended investment increases by $1 billion. (See Figure 11.2.)*

HOW SHIFTS IN THE CONSUMPTION FUNCTION ARE RELATED TO SHIFTS IN THE SAVING FUNCTION

Note that an *upward* shift in the consumption function must be accompanied by a *downward* shift in the saving function. If the public wants to spend *more* on consumption goods out of a given amount of disposable income, it must want to save *less* out of that amount of disposable income. (Why? Because personal consumption expenditure plus saving equals disposable income). Thus, if the consumption function shifts upward from position 1 to position 2 in Figure 11.3A, the saving function must shift downward from position 4 to position 5 in Figure 11.3B.

Also, a *downward* shift in the consumption function must be accompanied by an *upward* shift in the saving function. If the public wants to spend *less* on consumption goods out of a given amount of disposable income, it must want to save *more* out of that amount of disposable income. (Why? Because personal consumption expenditure plus saving equals disposable income.) Thus, if the consumption function shifts downward from position 1 to position 3 in Figure 11.3A, the saving function must shift upward from position 4 to position 6 in Figure 11.3B.

Effects of Shifts in the Consumption Function

Earlier in this chapter, we showed that changes in intended investment have an amplified effect on NNP, with the extent of the amplification measured by the multiplier. But it is important to note at this point that a shift in the consumption function will also have such an amplified effect on NNP. For example, in Figure 11.4, if the consumption function shifts from C_1 to C_2, this means that at each level of disposable income, consumers intend to spend $1 billion more on consumption goods and services than they did before. *This $1 billion upward shift in the consumption function will have precisely the same effect on equilibrium NNP as a $1 billion increase in intended investment.*

To see that this is the case, recall from the previous section that an upward shift in the consumption function results in a downward shift in the saving function. Specifically, a $1 billion upward shift in the consumption function means that the saving function shifts downward by $1 billion (because, if consumers desire to spend $1 billion *more* out of each level of disposable income than before, they must desire to save $1 billion *less* out of each level of disposable income than before). As shown in Figure 11.5, a $1 billion downward shift in the saving function results in an increase in the equilibrium value of NNP. And this increase is the same as when intended investment increases by $1 billion, the situation we observed in Figure 11.2. In either case, the increase equals $\left(\dfrac{1}{MPS}\right)$ billions of dollars.[2]

Moreover, *a $1 billion downward shift in the consumption function will have precisely the same effect on equilibrium NNP as a $1 billion decrease in*

[2] For an algebraic demonstration that this is true, see the Appendix to this chapter.

intended investment. Thus both upward and downward shifts in the consumption function—due to changes in tastes, assets, prices, population, and other things—will have a magnified effect on NNP. In other words, NNP is sensitive to shifts in the consumption function in the same way that it is sensitive to changes in intended investment. This is an important point. Finally, to prevent misunderstanding, recall from the previous sections that a *shift* in the consumption function is quite different from a *movement along* a given consumption function. (An example of the latter would be the movement from point G to point H in Figure 11.4.) We are concerned here with shifts in the consumption function, not movements along a given consumption function.

The Accuracy of Postwar Forecasts: A Case Study

Now that we have discussed some elements of the basic theory of the determination of NNP in the abstract, it is time to look at a specific application of this theory. Consider a famous incident that occurred at the end of World War II. Economists, using the best models then available, had been able to forecast the pace of the economy reasonably well during the war. When the war was coming to an end, they were charged with forecasting the level of national product in 1946, the year immediately after the war. This was an important task, since the government was worried that the economy might suffer severe postwar unemployment. The Great Depression of the 1930s was a recent—and still bitter—memory.

HOW THE GOVERNMENT FORECAST WAS MADE

Basic Idea #22: A $1 billion shift upward (or downward) in the consumption function results in the same increase (or decrease) in equilibrium NNP as a $1 billion increase (or decrease) in intended investment. In either case, the result is an increase (or decrease) in equilibrium NNP of (1/MPS) billions of dollars.

A group of economists in Washington was given the responsibility for this forecast. They made it in terms of gross national product, not net national product, but they used essentially the same theory as that discussed in previous sections. To forecast gross national product in 1946, these Washington economists began by using prewar data to estimate the consumption function. Then they estimated the amount of investment that would take place in 1946. To obtain their forecast of the change in GNP, they computed the multiplier $\left(\dfrac{1}{\text{MPS}}\right)$ and multiplied it by their estimate of the prospective change in intended investment. Then since their model—unlike ours—included government spending and taxes, other calculations, which will be discussed in Chapter 12, had to be made as well. The result was a forecast of a gross national product in 1946 of about $170 billion. This forecast received considerable attention and publicity inside and outside the government.

Before discussing the accuracy of this forecast, an important empirical question must be considered: in real-world studies like this, what is the estimated value of the multiplier? Judging from our findings in the previous sections, we would guess a figure of at least 2½, since the marginal propensity to consume should be at least 0.6. But these results are based on the assumption of no taxation. For reasons discussed in Chapter 12, the multiplier will be lower if there is taxation. Including the effects of taxation (and other factors like imports) most estimates of the multiplier seem to center around a value of 2. But these estimates can vary considerably, depending, of course, on the shape of the consumption function and other factors.

The government forecasters' estimate of a GNP of about $170 billion caused a severe chill in many parts of the government, as well as among business executives and consumers. A GNP of only about $170 billion would have meant a great deal of unemployment in 1946. Indeed, according to some predictions, about 8 million people would have been unemployed in the first quarter of 1946. Unfortunately for the forecasters—but fortunately for the nation—the GNP in 1946 turned out to be not $170 billion, but about $190 billion. And unemployment was only about a third of the forecasted amount. These are very large errors in practically anyone's book—so big that they continue to embarrass the economics profession 40 years later. Of course, our knowledge of the economy has expanded considerably over the past 40 years, and an error of this magnitude is much less likely now. Moreover, even at the end of World War II, some economists forecasted GNP in 1946 pretty well. Not everyone, by any means, agreed with the forecast of $170 billion. But it is worth bearing this notable mistake in mind when considering economic forecasts of this sort. Economics is not as exact a science as physics or chemistry—and mischief can result if one assumes otherwise.

WHY THE FORECAST WENT AWRY

What went wrong in the Washington economists' forecast? To a considerable extent, the answer lies in a topic of a previous section—a shift in the consumption function. When World War II ended, households had a great deal of liquid assets on hand. They had saved money during the war. There had been rationing of many kinds of goods, and other goods—like automobiles or refrigerators—could not be obtained at all. When the war ended and these goods flowed back on the market, consumers spent more of their income on consumption goods than in the previous years. In other words, there was a pronounced upward shift of the consumption function.

To see why this shift in the consumption function caused the forecasters to underestimate GNP in 1946, recall from the previous sections that an upward shift of $1 billion in the consumption function will result in an increase of $\left(\dfrac{1}{\text{MPS}} \right)$ billions of dollars in national product. Bearing this in mind, suppose the forecasters assumed that the consumption function remained fixed, when in fact there was an $8 billion shift upward. Then if the multiplier— $\left(\dfrac{1}{\text{MPS}} \right)$ —was 2½, national product would turn out to be $20 billion higher than the forecasters expected. (Since $\left(\dfrac{1}{\text{MPS}} \right)$ is assumed to be 2½, national product will increase $2.5 billion for every $1 billion shift in the consumption function, so an $8 billion shift in the consumption function will result in a $20 billion increase in national product.) Of course, these figures—a multiplier of 2½ and an $8 billion shift in the consumption function—are only illustrative, not precise estimates of the

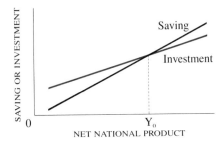

Figure 11.6

**Determination of Equilibrium Value of
Net National Product, with Induced
Investment** *If the level of investment depends on NNP, the investment function is
positively sloped, and the equilibrium
level of NNP is at the point where the investment function intersects the saving
function.*

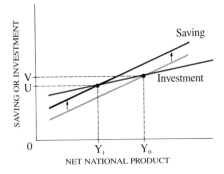

Figure 11.7

The Paradox of Thrift *If the saving
function shifts upward (as shown here),
the equilibrium value of NNP falls from
Y_0 to Y_1—and despite its attempt to save
more, the public saves less (U rather
than V).*

actual situation. For one thing, as noted above, the multiplier is wrong
because it assumes no taxation. But they indicate the sort of thing that
occurred, and they show dramatically the effects of a shift in the consumption function.

Induced Investment

In previous sections, we have assumed that intended net investment is a
certain amount, regardless of the level of NNP. This assumption has been
reflected in the fact that the investment function—for example, in Figures
11.2 and 11.5—is horizontal. Although this assumption may be a useful
first approximation, it neglects the fact that firms are much more likely to
invest in plant and equipment when NNP is high than when it is low.
After all, NNP measures output; and the greater the output of the economy, the greater the pressure on the capacity of existing plant and equipment—and the greater the pressure to expand this capacity by investing in
additional plant and equipment.

Our theory can be extended to take account of the fact that, to some extent, increases in NNP may *induce* increases in intended investment. (In
other words, not all changes in investment are autonomous.) Rather than
portraying the investment function as a horizontal line, we need only assume that it is positively sloped, as in Figure 11.6. Then, as before, the equilibrium level of NNP is at the point where the saving function intersects the
investment function—that is, at point Y_0, the point where intended saving
equals intended investment. (Much more will be said about the relationship
between investment and changes in NNP in Chapter 13.)

The Paradox of Thrift

Despite all of the praise heaped upon it by moral philosophers, thrift (as
spendthrifts have long suspected) can be a dangerous thing. If society as a
whole desires to save more, the result may well be a decrease in national
output and no increase in saving. To see why this is so, consider Figure
11.7, which shows a situation where the saving function shifts upward.
Since the investment function remains constant, the equilibrium level of
NNP falls from Y_0 to Y_1. And despite the public's attempt to save more,
saving falls from V to U, as shown in Figure 11.7.

Of course, the fact that an upward shift in the saving function is likely to
cause a decrease in the equilibrium value of NNP is really no news. As we
pointed out earlier in this chapter, an upward shift in the saving function
is accompanied by a downward shift in the consumption function. (Recall
Figure 11.3B.) And as we also saw in earlier parts of this chapter, a
downward shift in the consumption function will result in a decrease in the
equilibrium value of NNP.

The important point here is that, *although thrift may be a private virtue,
it can be a problem from the viewpoint of society as a whole.* Suppose, for
example, that a recession occurs, with the result that NNP falls and unemployment rises. Under such circumstances, the public may well be in-

clined to cut back on its spending. That is, faced with economic storm signals, the public may try to save more. But what will be the unintended result? As indicated in Figure 11.7, the equilibrium value of NNP will be reduced, thus aggravating the recession. And to add insult to injury, the public may not be able to accomplish its goal of increasing saving. Thus all that will be achieved is an undesirable reduction in national output (and employment).

Example 11.2   Shifting Both the Saving and Investment Functions

Suppose that a nation adopts economic policies to encourage both saving and investment. To get some idea of the possible effects, consider a simple economy (with zero government spending, zero taxes, and no foreign trade) which adopts such policies. Suppose that the saving and investment functions before the adoption of these policies are S and I below, and that these policies shift them to S' and I'.

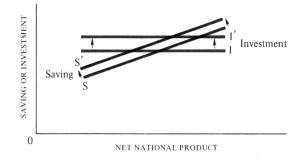

(a) Will these policies result in an increase in the equilibrium value of NNP? (b) Will these policies result in an increase in saving? (c) Will these policies result in an increase in investment? (d) How can we determine whether these policies will result in an increase in consumption expenditure? (e) Will a simultaneous upward shift in the saving and investment functions always result in an increase in the equilibrium value of NNP?

SOLUTION

(a) Yes. The intersection of the S' and I' lines lies to the right of the intersection of the S and I lines. (b) Yes. The intersection of the S' and I' lines lies above the intersection of the S and I lines. (c) The answer is the same as in (b), since saving equals investment. (d) Consider the point where the S line intersects the I line and the point where the S' line intersects the I' line. The horizontal difference between these two points equals the increase in NNP. The vertical difference between these two points equals the increase in saving. Under these highly simplified circumstances, NNP equals consumption expenditure plus saving. Thus the change in consumption expenditure equals the horizontal difference minus the vertical difference between these two points. (e) No, whether NNP will rise or fall depends on the extent of the shift of each function.

However, if a society increases *both* its saving and its investment, this may well promote a more rapid rate of growth of NNP. To see that this is the case, consult Example 11.2. Thus the effect of increased saving depends on the behavior of investment. Much more will be said on this score in Chapter 19.

Test Yourself

1. What effect would each of the following have on the position of the consumption function? That is, would each raise it, lower it, or have no effect on it? (a) An increase in interest rates; (b) expectations of greater inflation; (c) a catastrophe that wiped out half the nation's assets; (d) a marked increase in liquid assets held by people; (e) a rumor that major shortages of goods are about to occur.

2. Suppose that the consumption function in a particular economy is as follows:

Disposable income (billions of dollars)	Consumption expenditure (billions of dollars)
400	300
500	360
600	410
700	440
800	470

Suppose that consumers want to spend $50 billion more at each level of disposable income than is shown above. Using the $C + I$ line, show what effect this will have on the equilibrium value of NNP. (Assume that investment expenditure equals $140 billion.)

3. In Question 2, what effect will the indicated change in consumers' spending desires have on the saving function?

4. In Question 2, use the change in the saving function to show what change will occur in the equilibrium value of NNP.

5. If a $5 billion downward shift in the consumption function results in a $15 billion reduction in the equilibrium value of NNP, what is the marginal propensity to consume?

Summary

1. Investment expenditure tends to vary from year to year by greater percentages than does consumption expenditure. This is due in part to the irregularity of innovation, the durability of capital goods, and the differences from year to year in the extent to which existing productive capacity is utilized.

2. A $1 billion change in intended investment will result in a change in equilibrium NNP of $\left(\dfrac{1}{MPS}\right)$ billions of dollars, where MPS is the marginal propensity to save. In other words, the multiplier is $\left(\dfrac{1}{MPS}\right)$. The multiplier can be interpreted in terms of—and derived from—the successive stages of the spending process. An example of the use of the multiplier was the formulation at the end of World War II of GNP forecasts for 1946.

3. Holding disposable income constant, personal consumption expenditure is likely to depend on the amount of wealth in the hands of the public, the ease and cheapness with which consumers can borrow money, the expectations of the public, the amount of durable goods on hand, the income distribution, and the size of the population. Changes in these factors are likely to cause shifts in the consumption function.

4. A shift in the consumption function will also have an amplified effect on NNP, a \$1 billion shift in the consumption function resulting in a change of $\left(\dfrac{1}{\text{MPS}}\right)$ billions of dollars in NNP. To a considerable extent, the large error in government forecasts of GNP in 1946 was due to an unanticipated shift in the consumption function. Responding to large accumulated wartime savings and pent-up wartime demands, consumers spent more of their income on consumption goods than in previous years.

5. Our theory can be extended to take account of the fact that, to some extent, increases in NNP may induce increases in intended investment. All we need to do is assume that the investment function is positively sloped, not horizontal.

6. If society as a whole desires to save more, and if there is no shift in the investment function, the result may well be a decrease in national output and no increase in saving. This is the so-called paradox of thrift.

Concepts for Review

Multiplier
Shifts in the consumption function

Induced investment
Paradox of thrift

Appendix: Using Basic Algebra to Derive the Multiplier

Equations speak more clearly to some than words, and so for those with a taste for (elementary) algebra, we will show how some of the principal results of this chapter can be derived algebraically. We begin by recalling that the equilibrium value of NNP is attained at the point where NNP equals total intended spending on output. This condition can be expressed in the following equation:

$$NNP = C + I, \tag{11.1}$$

which says that NNP must equal intended expenditure on consumption goods *(C)* plus intended investment *(I)*. Since intended consumption expenditures plus intended investment equals total intended spending, it follows that this equation states that NNP must equal total intended spending.

Next, let's introduce a friend from this and the previous chapter, the consumption function. The consumption function in the first two columns of Table 10.4 can be represented by the following equation:

$$C = 350 + 0.6D, \tag{11.2}$$

which says that desired consumption equals \$350 billion plus 0.6 times disposable income *(D)*. Figure 11.8 shows the consumption function. As you can see, \$350 billion is the intercept on the vertical axis, while 0.6 is the slope of the consumption function. Since—as we noted in the previous chapter—the slope of the consumption function equals the marginal propensity to consume, 0.6 equals the marginal propensity to consume.

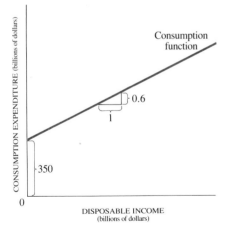

Figure 11.8

Consumption Function *The consumption function is derived from the data in Table 10.4. The marginal propensity to consume is 0.6, so the slope is 0.6.*

The next step is to substitute the right-hand side of Equation (11.2) for C in Equation (11.1). The result is:

$$NNP = 350 + 0.6D + I. \tag{11.3}$$

But recall that disposable income is equal to NNP in our simplified economy. Consequently, we can substitute NNP for D in this equation to get

$$NNP = 350 + 0.6NNP + I. \tag{11.4}$$

And going a step further, we can subtract 0.6 times NNP from both sides of Equation (11.4), which gives

$$NNP - 0.6NNP = 350 + I, \tag{11.5}$$

or, collecting terms,

$$0.4NNP = 350 + I. \tag{11.6}$$

Finally, dividing both sides by 0.4, we have

$$NNP = \frac{350}{0.4} + \frac{I}{0.4}. \tag{11.7}$$

Now we can see what happens to NNP if there is a $1 billion increase in I. In other words, suppose that I is increased from some amount, $\$X$ billion, to $\$(X + 1)$ billion. How much will this increase NNP? From Equation (11.7), it is clear that NNP will equal

$$\frac{350}{0.4} + \frac{X}{0.4}$$

if intended investment equals $\$X$ billion. It is also clear from Equation (11.7) that NNP will equal

$$\frac{350}{0.4} + \frac{(X + 1)}{0.4}$$

if intended investment is equal to $\$(X + 1)$ billion. Consequently the increase in NNP due to the $1 billion increase in intended investment is equal to

$$\left[\frac{350}{0.4} + \frac{(X + 1)}{0.4} \right] - \left[\frac{350}{0.4} + \frac{X}{0.4} \right].$$

$$= \frac{X + 1}{0.4} - \frac{X}{0.4} = \frac{X}{0.4} + \frac{1}{0.4} - \frac{X}{0.4} = \frac{1}{0.4}.$$

That is, a $1 billion increase in intended investment will result in an increase of $\frac{1}{0.4}$ billion dollars in NNP. Recalling that 0.6 is the marginal propensity to consume and that the sum of the marginal propensity to consume and the marginal propensity to save equals one—it follows that *a*

$1 billion increase in intended investment will result in an increase of $\left(\dfrac{1}{MPS}\right)$ billions of dollars in NNP, where MPS is the marginal propensity to save—0.4 in this case.

This is precisely the same conclusion we arrived at in the text of the chapter. Thus we have derived the value of the multiplier by an algebraic route rather than the other routes used before.

In addition, Equation (11.7) can be used to determine the effects of a shift in the consumption function. A $1 billion shift upward in the consumption function causes the intercept to increase from its former amount, $350 billion, to $351 billion. What is the effect of this increase in the intercept on the equilibrium value of NNP? If the intercept is $350 billion, the equilibrium value of NNP will equal

$$\frac{350}{0.4} + \frac{I}{0.4}.$$

If the intercept is $351 billion, the equilibrium value of NNP will equal

$$\frac{351}{0.4} + \frac{I}{0.4}.$$

Consequently, the increase in NNP from the $1 billion upward shift in the consumption function is

$$\left[\frac{351}{0.4} + \frac{I}{0.4}\right] - \left[\frac{350}{0.4} + \frac{I}{0.4}\right] = \frac{351}{0.4} - \frac{350}{0.4} = \frac{1}{0.4}.$$

That is, a $1 billion upward shift in the consumption function results in an increase of $\dfrac{1}{0.4}$ billions of dollars in NNP. Recalling that $0.4 = MPS$, it follows that *a $1 billion upward shift in the consumption function will result in an increase of* $\left(\dfrac{1}{MPS}\right)$ *billions of dollars in NNP.* This is precisely what we said on this score in the chapter.

CHAPTER 12

Fiscal Policy and National Output

In the period since World War II, the idea that the government's power to spend and tax should be used to stabilize the economy—that is, to reduce unemployment and fight inflation—has gained acceptance throughout the world. Most economists believe that this idea is essentially correct. However, time has also revealed that fiscal policy is far from a panacea. Witness the severe inflationary pressures and the high unemployment rates that plagued the American economy in the late 1970s and early 1980s. Both the power and the limitations of fiscal policy must be recognized.

This chapter presents a first look at fiscal policy, in the context of the simplest Keynesian model. In effect, we assume here that the money supply is fixed, and that the interest rate is not affected by changes in total intended spending (or that, if it is affected, it has little effect on total intended spending). In Chapter 17 (and in the Appendix to this book), a more sophisticated analysis of fiscal policy is presented, with money and financial assets included in the model.

Government Expenditure and Net National Product

In the previous chapters, we showed how the equilibrium level of net national product was determined in a simplified economy without government spending or taxation. We must now extend this theory to include both government spending and taxation. As we shall see, the results form the basis for some of our nation's past and present economic policy. In this section, we incorporate government spending into the theory of the determination of net national product. In so doing, we assume that government spending will not affect the consumption function or the level of intended investment. In other words, we assume that government spending does not reduce or increase private desires to spend out of each level of income. (Government includes here federal, state, and local.)

Suppose that the government purchases $50 billion worth of goods and services and that it will purchase this amount whatever the level of NNP. (As pointed out in Chapter 7, only government purchases, not transfer payments, are included here.) Clearly, adding this public expenditure to the private expenditures on consumption and investment results in a higher total level of intended spending. In an economy with government spending (but no net exports), total intended spending on output equals consumption expenditure plus intended investment expenditure plus intended government expenditure. Thus, since an increase in government expenditure (like increases in consumption or investment expenditure) results in an increase in total intended spending, and since the equilibrium value of net national product is at the point where total intended spending equals NNP, it follows that an increase in government expenditure, as well as the induced increase in private spending, brings about an increase in the equilibrium value of NNP.

To see the effects of government expenditure on the equilibrium value of NNP, we can use a simple graph similar to those introduced in Chapter 10. We begin by plotting the consumption function, which shows intended consumption expenditure at each level of NNP (since NNP equals disposable income under our assumptions): the result is line C in Figure 12.1. Then we can plot the sum of intended consumption expenditure and investment expenditure at each level of NNP. The result is line $C + I$. Next, we plot the sum of intended consumption expenditure, investment expenditure, and government expenditure at each level of NNP, to get line $C + I + G$. Since the $C + I + G$ *line* shows total intended spending, and since, as we stressed in Chapter 10, the equilibrium value of NNP is at the point where total intended spending equals NNP, it follows that the equilib-

Figure 12.1

Determination of Net National Product, Including Government Expenditure *The consumption function is* C, *the sum of consumption and investment expenditures is* C + I, *and the sum of consumption, investment, and government expenditures is* C + I + G. *The equilibrium value of NNP is at the point where the* C + I + G *line intersects the 45-degree line, which here is $1,225 billion.*

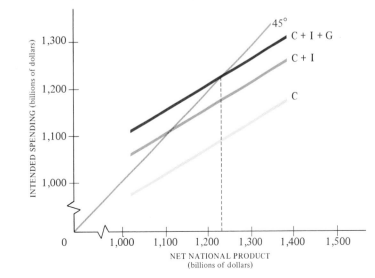

237

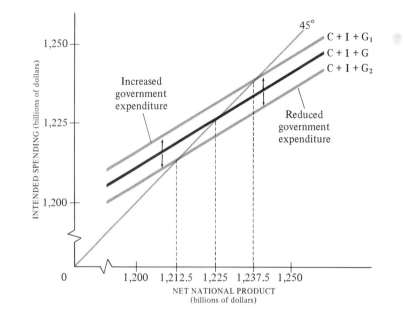

Figure 12.2
Effects on Equilibrium Net National Product of a $5 Billion Increase and Decrease in Government Expenditure *A $5 billion increase raises the equilibrium value of NNP from $1,225 billion to $1,237.5 billion. A $5 billion decrease reduces the equilibrium value of NNP from $1,225 billion to $1,212.5 billion.*

rium value of NNP is at the point where the $C + I + G$ line intersects the 45-degree line. This is at an output of $1,225 billion.

EFFECT OF INCREASED GOVERNMENT EXPENDITURE

What happens to the equilibrium level of NNP if government expenditure increases? Figure 12.2 shows the results of a $5 billion increase in government spending. The increased government expenditure (G_1) will raise the $C + I + G$ line by $5 billion, as the figure shows. Since the $C + I + G_1$ line must intersect the 45-degree line at a higher level of NNP, increases in government expenditure result in increases in the equilibrium level of NNP. In Figure 12.2, the $5 billion increase in government expenditure raises the equilibrium value of NNP from $1,225 billion to $1,237.5 billion.

EFFECT OF DECREASED GOVERNMENT EXPENDITURE

Figure 12.2 also shows what happens when government spending goes down by $5 billion (to G_2). The new $C + I + G_2$ line is $5 billion lower than the old $C + I + G$ line. Since the new $C + I + G_2$ line intersects the 45-degree line at a lower level of NNP, decreases in government expenditure result in decreases in the equilibrium level of NNP. In Figure 12.2, the $5 billion decrease in government expenditure reduces the equilibrium value of NNP from $1,225 billion to $1,212.5 billion.

WHAT IS THE MULTIPLIER EFFECT FOR GOVERNMENT EXPENDITURE?

How sensitive is the equilibrium level of NNP to changes in government spending? In the previous chapter, we found that a $1 billion change in intended investment—or a $1 billion shift in the consumption function—

results in a change in equilibrium NNP of $\left(\dfrac{1}{MPS}\right)$ billions of dollars, where MPS is the marginal propensity to save. The effect of a $1 billion change in government expenditure is exactly the same. In other words, *it will result in a change in equilibrium NNP of* $\left(\dfrac{1}{MPS}\right)$ *billion dollars.* Thus *a change in government expenditure has the same multiplier effect on NNP as a change in investment or a shift in the consumption function.* For example, if the marginal propensity to consume is 0.6, an extra $1 billion in government expenditure will increase equilibrium NNP by $2.5 billion.[1]

Taxation and Net National Product

The previous section added government expenditures to our theory, but it did not include taxes. (Here we assume taxes to be net of transfer payments.) For simplicity, it is assumed that all tax revenues stem from personal taxes. How do tax collections influence the equilibrium value of net national product? For example, if consumers pay 16⅔ percent of their income to the government in taxes, what effect does this have on NNP? Clearly, the imposition of this tax means that, for each level of NNP, people have less disposable income than they would with no taxes. In particular, disposable income now equals 83⅓ percent of NNP, whereas without taxes it equaled NNP. Thus *the relationship between consumption expenditure and NNP is altered by the imposition of the tax.* Before the tax was levied, the relationship was given by line C_0 in Figure 12.3; after the imposition of the tax, it is given by line C_1.

The relationship between consumption expenditure and national output changes in this way because consumption expenditure is determined by the level of disposable income. For instance, in the case in Figure 12.3, consumption expenditure equals $350 billion plus 60 percent of disposable income. Thus, since the tax reduces the amount of disposable income at each level of NNP, it also reduces the amount of consumption expenditure at each level of NNP. In other words, since people have less after-tax income to spend at each level of NNP, they spend less on consumption goods and services at each level of NNP. This seems eminently reasonable. It is illustrated in Figure 12.3, where, at each level of NNP, consumption expenditure after tax (given by line C_1) is less than before the tax (given by line C_0).

Because the imposition of the tax influences the relationship between consumption expenditure and NNP, it also influences the equilibrium value of NNP. As we have stressed repeatedly, the equilibrium value of NNP is at the point where intended spending on output equals NNP. Lines C_0 and C_1 in Figure 12.3 show intended consumption expenditure at each level of NNP, before and after the tax. Adding intended investment and govern-

[1] For an algebraic proof that this is true (in the context of this simple model), see the Appendix to this chapter. A more complete model is provided in Chapter 17 and in Appendix A. The conditions under which this proposition holds in this more complete model are given in footnote 1 of Appendix A.

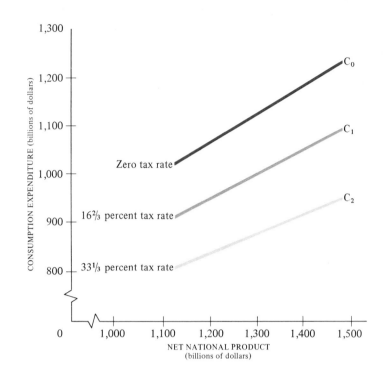

Figure 12.3
Relationship between Consumption Expenditure and Net National Product, Given Three Tax Rates *If taxes are zero, C_0 is the relationship between consumption expenditure and NNP. If consumers pay 16⅔ percent of their income in taxes, C_1 is the relationship; and if consumers pay 33⅓ percent of their income in taxes, C_2 is the relationship. Clearly, the higher the tax rate, the less consumers spend on consumption from a given NNP.*

ment expenditure to each of these lines, we get the total intended spending before and after the tax. The results are shown in Figure 12.4, under the assumption that the sum of intended investment and government spending equals $140 billion. The $C_0 + I + G$ line shows intended spending before the tax, while the $C_1 + I + G$ line shows intended spending after the tax.

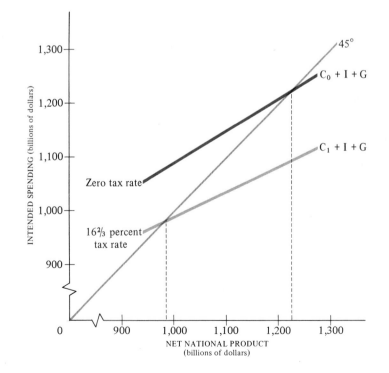

Figure 12.4
Determination of Equilibrium Value of Net National Product, with Zero and 16⅔ Percent Tax Rates *The tax rate influences the relationship between consumption expenditure and NNP. (C_0 is this relationship with a zero tax rate, while C_1 is the relationship with a 16⅔ percent tax rate. See Figure 12.3.) The $C_0 + I + G$ line shows total intended spending at each level of NNP if the tax rate is zero, and the $C_1 + I + G$ line shows total intended spending at each level of NNP if the tax rate is 16⅔ percent. Consequently, the equilibrium value of NNP is $1,225 billion if the tax rate is zero, and $980 billion if it is 16⅔ percent.*

EFFECT OF THE TAX

The equilibrium level of NNP is appreciably lower after the imposition of the tax than before. Specifically, as shown in Figure 12.4, it is $980 billion after the imposition of the tax and $1,225 billion before. The tax reduced the equilibrium level of NNP because it lowered the $C + I + G$ line from $C_0 + I + G$ to $C_1 + I + G$. It did this because, as pointed out above, it reduced the amount people wanted to spend on consumption goods at each level of NNP. People still wanted to spend the same amount *from each (after-tax) income level,* but because of the tax, their spending decisions had to be based on a *reduced (after-tax) income,* so that they spent less on consumption goods and services at each level of NNP.

EFFECT OF A TAX INCREASE

Going a step further, *the higher the tax rate, the lower the equilibrium value of NNP; and the lower the tax rate, the higher the equilibrium value of NNP.* This is a very important proposition, as we shall see in subsequent sections. To demonstrate it, let's see what will happen to the equilibrium value of NNP when the tax rate is increased from 16⅔ percent of NNP to 33⅓ percent of NNP. If the tax rate is 33⅓ percent, total intended spending at each level of NNP will be given by line $C_2 + I + G$ in Figure 12.5. Since the equilibrium value of NNP will be at the point where the $C_2 + I + G$ line intersects the 45-degree line, the equilibrium value of NNP will be $816⅔ billion, rather than $980 billion (which was the equilibrium value when the tax rate was 16⅔ percent). Thus the increase in the tax rate will reduce the equilibrium value of NNP. By reducing the amount people want to spend on consumption at each level of NNP, it will lower the $C + I + G$ line from $C_1 + I + G$ to $C_2 + I + G$.

Figure 12.5
Determination of Equilibrium Value of Net National Product, with 16⅔ Percent and 33⅓ Percent Tax Rates *The $C_1 + I + G$ line shows total intended spending at each level of NNP if the tax rate is 16⅔ percent, and the $C_2 + I + G$ line shows total intended spending at each level of NNP if the tax rate is 33⅓ percent. Consequently, the equilibrium value of NNP is $980 billion if the tax rate is 16⅔ percent and $816⅔ billion if it is 33⅓ percent.*

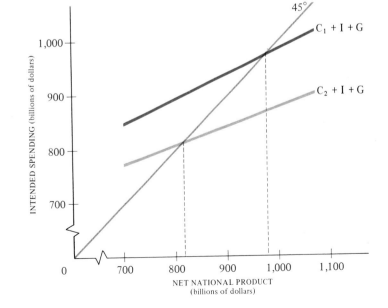

EFFECT OF A TAX CUT

On the other hand, suppose that the tax rate is lowered from 16⅔ percent of NNP to a lesser amount. What will happen to the equilibrium value of NNP? If the tax rate is less than 16⅔ percent, the intended spending on output at each level of NNP will be given by a $C + I + G$ line that lies between $C_0 + I + G$ and $C_1 + I + G$ in Figure 12.4. Since the equilibrium value of NNP will be at the point where this line intersects the 45-degree line, the equilibrium value of NNP will be greater than $980 billion. Thus the decrease in the tax rate will increase the equilibrium value of NNP. By increasing the amount people want to spend on consumption at each level of NNP, it will raise the $C + I + G$ line from $C_1 + I + G$ to a higher level.

How Government Expenditure and Taxes Affect NNP: A Tabular Illustration

To illustrate how one can determine the equilibrium level of NNP when both government expenditure and taxation are included in our model, consider the numerical example shown in Table 12.1. The numbers in this table are the same as in Table 10.4, except that we now assume that the government spends $50 billion per year on goods and services and that it receives $50 billion in taxes per year. (For simplicity, we assume in this table that the amounts of both government expenditure and taxes are independent of the level of NNP. This is in contrast to the previous section where we assumed that taxes were proportional to NNP.) Column 1 of the table shows various possible levels of NNP. To obtain the level of disposable income corresponding to each level of NNP, we must subtract taxes (in column 2) from NNP, the result being shown in column 3.

Since the consumption function is assumed to be the same as in Table 10.4 (and Table 10.1), the intended consumption expenditure at each level of disposable income is as shown in column 4. Note that disposable income no longer equals NNP, as it did in Table 10.4, because taxes have

Table 12.1

DETERMINATION OF EQUILIBRIUM LEVEL OF NET NATIONAL PRODUCT (BILLIONS OF DOLLARS)

(1) Net national product	(2) Taxes	(3) Disposable income (1) − (2)	(4) Intended consumption expenditure	(5) Intended saving (3) − (4)	(6) Intended investment	(7) Government expenditure	(8) Total intended spending (4) + (6) + (7)	(9) Tendency of national output
1,000	50	950	920	30	90	50	1,060	Upward
1,050	50	1,000	950	50	90	50	1,090	Upward
1,100	50	1,050	980	70	90	50	1,120	Upward
1,150	50	1,100	1,010	90	90	50	1,150	No change
1,200	50	1,150	1,040	110	90	50	1,180	Downward
1,250	50	1,200	1,070	130	90	50	1,210	Downward
1,300	50	1,250	1,100	150	90	50	1,240	Downward

entered the picture; this means that the relationship between intended consumption expenditure and NNP is also different. But since the consumption function is unchanged, the relationship between intended consumption expenditure and disposable income is the same as in Table 10.4.

Columns 5 to 8 of the table seem self-evident. Since intended saving equals disposable income less intended consumption expenditure, column 5 equals column 3 minus column 4. Column 6 shows intended investment, which is $90 billion. Column 7 shows government expenditure, which is $50 billion. And column 8 shows total intended spending on output at each level of NNP. Since total intended spending equals consumption expenditure plus intended investment expenditure plus intended government expenditure, column 8 equals column 4 plus column 6 plus column 7.

WHAT IS EQUILIBRIUM NNP?

As emphasized in previous discussions (in this and the previous chapters), *national output will be at its equilibrium value only if total intended spending is equal (no more, no less) to NNP.* Thus, based on the data in Table 12.1, it is clear that the equilibrium value of NNP is $1,150 billion. Why? Because a comparison of columns 1 and 8 in Table 12.1 shows that this is the only value of NNP at which total intended spending (column 8) equals NNP (column 1).

If NNP is *less* than $1,150 billion, there will be a tendency for it to increase. Total spending will exceed the value of output produced, the result being that firms' inventories will be depleted. Firms will respond by raising their production rates, thus increasing NNP. If NNP is *greater* than $1,150 billion, there will be a tendency for it to decline. Total spending will fall short of the value of output produced, the result being that firms' inventories will mount. Firms will respond by lowering their production rates, thus decreasing NNP.

USING THE LEAKAGE-INJECTION APPROACH

Finally, the leakage-injection approach described in the previous chapters is an alternative way of determining the equilibrium level of NNP. To use this approach, two points must be understood. First, *taxes are a leakage because they withdraw spending from the flow of income and expenditure.* After all, money that goes for taxes cannot be spent on output. Second, *government expenditure is an injection since it adds spending to the flow of income and expenditure.* It is a supplement to consumption expenditure and investment.

Since taxes are a leakage, the total leakages in Table 12.1 are intended saving plus taxes, or column 5 plus column 2. And since government expenditure is an injection, the total injections in Table 12.1 are intended investment plus government expenditure, or column 6 plus column 7. According to our discussion in the previous chapters, *the equilibrium value of NNP must be the value of NNP at which total leakages equal total injections*—in other words, the value of NNP at which intended saving plus taxes (column 5 plus column 2) equals intended investment plus government expenditure (column 6 plus column 7). Table 12.1 shows that this value of NNP is $1,150 billion. Of course, the answer obtained by the leakage-injection approach coincides, as it must, with that obtained by comparing the value of total intended spending (column 8) with the value of NNP (column 1).

The Balanced-Budget Multiplier

According to our previous conclusions, increases in government expenditures tend to increase NNP, while increases in tax receipts tend to reduce NNP. What will be the result when *both* government expenditures and tax receipts are increased *by the same amount?* Clearly, the increase in government expenditures will push NNP up, while the tax increase will push NNP down. But which force will prevail? According to an economic proposition called the **balanced-budget multiplier,** the result will be an *increase* in equilibrium NNP—and under the assumptions made in Table 12.1, *this increase equals the increase in both government expenditures and taxes.*

To see that this proposition is true, compare Table 10.4 with Table 12.1. The only difference between the situations represented by these two tables is that both government expenditures and taxes are $50 billion higher in Table 12.1 than in Table 10.4. (Specifically, both government expenditures and taxes equal $50 billion in Table 12.1, while both equal zero in Table 10.4.) What is the effect on NNP of this $50 billion increase in both government expenditures and taxes? In accord with the balanced-budget multiplier, the equilibrium level of NNP is $50 billion higher in Table 12.1 than in Table 10.4. (For a more general proof of the balanced-budget multiplier, see the Appendix to this chapter.)

On the other hand, suppose that both government expenditures and tax receipts are *decreased* by the same amount. What will be the effect on NNP? Clearly, the decrease in government expenditures will push NNP down, while the tax cut will push NNP up. But which force will prevail? According to the balanced-budget multiplier, the result will be a *decrease* in equilibrium NNP—and under the assumptions made in Table 12.1, *this decrease equals the decrease in both government expenditures and taxes.*

To illustrate the application of this proposition, consider a proposal made by President Ford in 1975 to cut both taxes and government expenditures by $28 billion. Assuming that both the expenditure and tax cuts went into effect at the same time, this would have reduced NNP, as we have just seen. (However, if the tax cut occurred before the expenditure cut, as some observers claimed it would, the proposal might not have had this effect at all. Recall that the balanced-budget multiplier is concerned with a *simultaneous* change in government receipts and tax revenues.)

Recessionary and Inflationary Gaps

In this and the previous chapters, we have shown how the equilibrium level of net national product is determined. But it is of central importance to recognize that *this equilibrium level of NNP may not correspond to full employment.* As pointed out in Chapter 10, a basic theme of modern economics is that there is no automatic tendency for NNP to equal its full-employment level. For example, in Table 12.1, there is no assurance that $1,150 billion is the level of NNP corresponding to full employment. It may be below the full-employment level, in which case the unemployment rate will be relatively high. Or it may be above the full-employment level, in which case there will be considerable inflation.

COPING WITH A RECESSIONARY GAP

For simplicity, suppose that, so long as total spending does not exceed the value (at initial prices) of the full-employment level of output, the price level remains constant. (As pointed out in Chapter 9, this really is not true, but it is a useful simplification to begin with.) Then if the equilibrium NNP is *below* the full-employment level, the **recessionary gap** *is the increase in intended spending required to push the equilibrium NNP up to the full-employment level.* For example, if the full-employment level of NNP is $1,400 billion in Figure 12.6, the recessionary gap is $40 billion. Why? Because this is the amount by which intended spending must be increased if NNP is to rise from its current equilibrium level, $1,300 billion, to its full-employment level of $1,400 billion. In other words, as shown in Figure 12.6, this is the amount by which the $C + I + G$ line must be raised in order to increase the equilibrium level of NNP from $1,300 billion to $1,400 billion. *To prevent excessive unemployment, such a recessionary gap should be eliminated.*

COPING WITH AN INFLATIONARY GAP

On the other hand, if the equilibrium NNP is *above* the full-employment level, the **inflationary gap** *is the reduction in intended spending required to push the equilibrium NNP down to the full-employment level.* For example, if the full-employment level of NNP is $1,400 billion in Figure 12.7, the inflationary gap is $40 billion. Why? Because this is the amount by which intended spending must be reduced if NNP is to fall from its current equilibrium level, $1,500 billion, to its full-employment level of $1,400 billion. In other words, as shown in Figure 12.7, this is the amount by which the $C + I + G$ line must fall in order to reduce the equilibrium level of NNP from $1,500 billion to $1,400 billion. Assuming that $1,400 billion is the maximum value of real NNP (in initial prices) that can be achieved, any increase of the money value of NNP above $1,400 billion is due entirely to inflation. Thus, *to curb inflationary pressures, such an inflationary gap should be eliminated.*

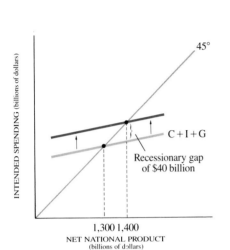

Figure 12.6
Recessionary Gap *The equilibrium level of NNP, $1,300 billion, is too low to result in full employment. The level of NNP corresponding to full employment is $1,400 billion. To raise the equilibrium level of NNP from $1,300 billion to $1,400 billion, intended spending must be increased by $40 billion. In other words, the* C + I + G *line must be raised by $40 billion. This amount—the* vertical *distance between the 45-degree line and the* C + I + G *line at the full-employment level of NNP—is called the recessionary gap.*

The Nature and Objectives of Fiscal Policy

Our discussions in previous sections make it easy to understand the basic ideas underlying modern fiscal policy. For example, suppose that the economy is suffering from an undesirably high unemployment rate. What

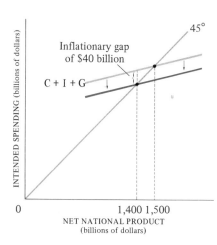

Figure 12.7
Inflationary Gap *For simplicity,
assume that $1,400 billion, the full-em-
ployment level of NNP, is the* maximum
value of real NNP (in initial prices) *that
can be achieved. Thus any increase of*
the money value of NNP above $1,400
billion *is due entirely to inflation. To
reduce the equilibrium NNP from $1,500
billion (its current level) to $1,400 billion,
intended spending must be reduced by
$40 billion. In other words, the* C + I +
G *line must be lowered by $40 billion.
This amount—the* vertical *distance
between the 45-degree line and the* C + I
+ G *line at the full employment level of
NNP—is called the inflationary gap.*

should the government do? Since there is a recessionary gap, the economy needs increased spending. In other words, as shown in Figure 12.6, the economy needs an upward lift of the $C + I + G$ line, which by increasing NNP will increase employment as well. There are three ways that the government can try to bring this about. First, *it can reduce taxes,* which, as shown in a previous section, will shift the relation between consumption expenditure and NNP—and consequently the $C + I + G$ line—upward. Second, *it can increase government expenditures,* which will also shift the $C + I + G$ line upward. Third, *the government can encourage firms to invest more,* perhaps by enacting tax credits to make investment more profitable for them. The resulting increase in intended investment will shift the $C + I + G$ line upward too.

On the other hand, perhaps we are suffering from a high rate of inflation. What should the government do? Since there is an inflationary gap, the economy needs reduced spending. In other words, what is required is a downward shift of the $C + I + G$ line, as shown in Figure 12.7. The government has three ways to try to bring this about. First, *it can increase taxes.* This, as shown in a previous section, will shift the relation between consumption expenditure and NNP—and consequently the $C + I + G$ line—downward. Second, *it can cut government expenditures,* which will also shift the $C + I + G$ curve downward. Third, *it can change the tax laws and do other things to discourage firms from investing in plant and equipment or inventories.* The resulting decrease in intended investment will shift the $C + I + G$ line downward too.

Certainly, these ideas do not seem very hard to understand. Advocates of fiscal policy maintain that, *if there is too much unemployment, the government should promote, directly or indirectly, additional public and/or private spending, which will result in additional output and jobs.* On the other hand, *if there is too much inflation, the government should reduce, directly or indirectly, spending (public and/or private). This will curb the inflationary pressure on prices.* Most economists believe that these propositions are useful—although by themselves they cannot deal as effectively as one would like with times like the 1970s and early 1980s, when excessive unemployment and inflation occurred together. (We shall discuss such situations in detail in Chapter 18.)

How can fiscal policy be included in the aggregate demand-aggregate supply analysis presented in Chapter 9? Clearly, *an anti-unemployment fiscal policy* (where government spending is increased and/or taxes are reduced) *tends to push the aggregate demand curve to the right. An anti-inflationary fiscal policy* (where government spending is reduced and/or taxes are increased) *tends to push the aggregate demand curve to the left.* The effects of each type of fiscal policy are shown in Figures 9.7 and 9.8.

Makers of Fiscal Policy

When you go to a ball game, you generally get a program telling you who on each team is playing each position. To understand the formulation and implementation of fiscal policy in the United States we need the same kind of information. Who are the people who establish our fiscal policy?

Who decides that in view of the current and prospective economic situation, tax rates or government expenditures should be changed? This is not a simple question because lots of individuals and groups play important roles. In the Congress, the House and Senate Budget Committees—as well as the Congressional Budget Office—have been charged with important responsibilities in this area. Also, the Appropriations Committees, the House Ways and Means Committee, and the Senate Finance Committee have considerable influence. In addition, another congressional committee is of importance: the Joint Economic Committee of Congress. Established by the Employment Act of 1946, this committee goes over the annual Economic

---

Example 12.1   Fiscal Policy, Deficits, and Surpluses

The following table provides some information concerning a small Latin American country:

	(billions of dollars)
Net national product (this year)	16.0
Net national product (full-employment level)	20.0
Government expenditures on goods and services	1.8

According to experts on this country's economy, the government's tax receipts are equal to 10 percent of its NNP.

(a) Is the government of this country running a deficit or a surplus? (That is, are government expenditures greater than or less than tax receipts?) (b) If the country wants to achieve full employment, should it increase government spending? Why or why not? (c) Suppose that, when NNP is at its full-employment level of $20 billion, intended saving equals $1.8 billion and intended investment equals $1.5 billion. If tax rates cannot be changed, and if government expenditures are altered to push the economy to full employment, will there be a balanced budget? (That is, will government spending equal tax receipts?) (d) If not, how large will be the deficit or surplus?

SOLUTION

(a) Government expenditures equal $1.8 billion. Tax receipts equal 10 percent of NNP, or $1.6 billion. Thus there is a deficit of $0.2 billion. (That is, spending exceeds receipts by $0.2 billion.) (b) Net national product currently is $4 billion below its full-employment level. One way to increase NNP is to increase government spending. Another way is to reduce taxes. (c) In equilibrium, taxes plus saving equal government spending plus investment. Thus, if equilibrium NNP is at its full-employment value of $20 billion, government spending must equal $2 billion + $1.8 billion − $1.5 billion, or $2.3 billion. Why? Because $2 billion is the value of taxes if NNP is at its full-employment value. (Recall that taxes equal 10 percent of NNP.) Since government spending equals taxes plus saving minus investment, it follows that government spending equals $2.3 billion. And since taxes equal $2.0 billion, the budget is not balanced. (d) Government spending ($2.3 billion) exceeds taxes ($2.0 billion) by $0.3 billion, which is the size of the deficit.

Report of the President on the state of the economy and, through its hearings, provides a major forum for review of economic issues.

In the executive branch of government, the most important person in the establishment of fiscal policy is, of course, the president. Although he must operate in the context of the tax and expenditure laws passed by Congress, he and his advisers are the country's principal analysts of the need for fiscal expansion or restraint and its leading spokesmen for legislative changes to meet these needs. Needless to say, he doesn't pore over the latest economic data and make the decisions all by himself. The Office of Management and Budget, which is part of the Executive Office of the President, is a very powerful adviser to the president on expenditure policy, as is the Treasury Department on tax policy. In addition, there is the **_Council of Economic Advisers,_** which is part of the Executive Office of the President. Established by the Employment Act of 1946, its job is to help the president carry out the objectives of that act. During the past 30 years, the Council of Economic Advisers, headed by a series of distinguished economists who left academic and other posts to contribute to public policy, has become a very important actor on the national economic policy stage.

Automatic Stabilizers

Now that we have met some of the major players, we must point out that, in their efforts to fight off serious unemployment or inflation, they get help from some **_automatic stabilizers:_** structural features of our economy that tend to stabilize national output. Although these economic stabilizers cannot do all that is required to keep the economy on an even keel, they help a lot. As soon as the economy turns down and unemployment mounts, they give the economy a helpful shot in the arm. As soon as the economy gets overheated and inflation crops up, they tend to restrain it. These stabilizers are automatic because they come into play without the need for new legislation or administrative decisions.

TAX REVENUES

Changes in income tax revenues are an important automatic stabilizer. One of the major points emphasized in Chapter 4 was that our federal system relies heavily on the income tax. The amount of income tax collected by the federal government goes up with increases in NNP and goes down with decreases in NNP. Moreover, because the income tax is progressive, the average tax rate goes up with increases in NNP, and goes down with decreases in NNP. This, of course, is just what we want to occur. When output falls off and unemployment mounts, tax collections fall off too, so disposable income falls less than NNP. This means less of a fall in consumption expenditure, which tends to brake the fall in NNP. When output rises too fast and the economy begins to suffer from serious inflation, tax collections rise too—which tends to brake the increase in NNP. Of course, corporation income taxes, as well as personal income taxes, play a significant role here.

Before World War II, there was relatively little place in the government for economists. The Treasury had a small number, the antitrust division of the Justice Department a handful, but there was no place for economists who aspired to give advice on broad policy matters. The Employment Act of 1946 changed that situation by creating a council to "gather timely and authoritative information . . . to develop and recommend to the President national economic policies . . . and to make and furnish studies . . . as the President may request."

But as demonstrated by the first chairman, Edwin Nourse, the act was really a hunting license for a chairman to peddle his good counsel. Nourse, who believed that the Council's role was to "interpret literal facts . . . without becoming involved in any way in the advocacy of particular measures," found that such services were rarely required by the president. It is hard to find any trace of the Nourse era on the economic policies of the late forties.

Beryl Sprinkel

Even the election of John F. Kennedy, who was eager to increase the U.S. rate of economic growth, did not insure the Council's future. Kennedy was inclined to fiscal conservatism and less interested in domestic than in foreign affairs. It was Walter Heller, the new chairman under Kennedy, who made the CEA an integral part of the New Frontier. The tax cut of 1964, which Heller sold to a president committed to balanced budgets, is a tribute to his success in making a body without formal powers or legislative prerogatives an integral part of the policy-making process.

The Council's influence has risen and ebbed in recent years with both the state of the economy and with other pressures on the president. In 1966, as the Vietnam War intensified, the Council urged a tax increase; Lyndon Johnson, more attuned to the political considerations, did not take action on the proposal until 1967. The Council's position in the Nixon administration further exemplified this process. Led by Paul McCracken and Herbert Stein, the Council championed restraint in fiscal and monetary policies early in Nixon's first term. But faced with mounting inflationary pressures, the Council members reluctantly joined other administration economists in setting up wage and price controls.

In the Reagan administration, the CEA's position became precarious after Martin Feldstein, its chairman until 1984 (when he returned to Harvard), clashed openly with administration officials about the dangers inherent in large federal deficits. (See p. 258.) For a time, President Reagan appointed no one to succeed Feldstein, and there was talk in early 1985 that the Council might be abolished. However, in February 1985, the president named Beryl Sprinkel, former under secretary of the treasury, as CEA chairman.

UNEMPLOYMENT COMPENSATION AND WELFARE PAYMENTS

Unemployment compensation is paid to workers who are laid off, according to a system that has evolved over the past 50 years. When an unemployed worker goes back to work, he stops receiving unemployment compensation. Thus, when NNP falls off and unemployment mounts, the tax collections to finance unemployment compensation go down (because of lower employment), while the amount paid out to unemployed workers goes up. On the other hand, when NNP rises too fast and the economy begins to suffer from serious inflation, the tax collections to finance unemployment compensation go up, while the amount paid out goes down because there is much less unemployment. Again, this is just what we want to see happen. The fall in spending is moderated when unemployment is high, and the increase in spending is curbed when there are serious inflationary pressures. Various welfare programs have the same kind of automatic stabilizing effect on the economy.

CORPORATE DIVIDENDS, FAMILY SAVING, AND FARM PROGRAMS

Since corporations tend to maintain their dividends when their sales fall off, and moderate the increase in their dividends when their sales soar, their dividend policy tends to stabilize the economy. This is very important. Also, to the extent that consumers tend to be slow to raise or lower their spending in response to increases or decreases in their income, this too tends to stabilize the economy. Finally, there are the agricultural support programs, described in Chapter 4. The government has buttressed farm prices and incomes when business was bad and unemployment was high. When output was high and inflation occurred, the government distributed the commodities in its warehouses and received dollars. In both cases, these programs acted as stabilizers.

Having painted such a glowing picture of the economy's automatic stabilizers, we are in danger of suggesting that they can stabilize the economy all by themselves. It would be nice if this were true, but it isn't. All the automatic stabilizers do is *cut down* on variations in unemployment and inflation, not *eliminate* them. Discretionary tax and spending programs are needed to supplement the effects of these automatic stabilizers. Some economists wish strongly that it were possible to set well-defined rules for government action, rather than leave things to the discretion of policy makers. Indeed, Milton Friedman, among others, forcefully argues for greater reliance on such rules, but most economists feel that it is impossible to formulate a set of rules flexible and comprehensive enough to let us do away with the discretionary powers of policy makers. Instead their concern is with sharpening the tools available to government economic decision makers.

Test Yourself

1. Suppose that the consumption function in a particular economy is given by the following table:

Disposable income (billions of dollars)	Consumption expenditure (billions of dollars)
400	350
500	425
600	500
700	575
800	650

Assuming that no taxes are imposed, what is the equilibrium value of NNP if government expenditures are $50 billion and intended investment is $50 billion?

2. Based on the data in Question 1, plot the $C + I + G$ line in a graph. Using a graph of this sort, estimate the effect on the equilibrium level of NNP of a $10 billion increase in government spending.

3. Suppose that taxes are 20 percent of NNP. Using the data in Question 1, fill in the blanks below.

NNP (billions of dollars)	Consumption expenditure (billions of dollars)
—	350
—	425
—	500
—	575
—	650

4. Using the data in Question 3, what is the equilibrium value of NNP if government expenditures are $50 billion and intended investment is $50 billion? How does this result compare with that in Question 1? Explain the difference between these two results.

5. Using the data in Question 3, is the government's budget balanced at the equilibrium level of NNP if government expenditures are $50 billion and intended investment is $50 billion? If not, how big is the surplus or deficit?

The Tools of Discretionary Fiscal Policy

Suppose that the Council of Economic Advisers, on the basis of information concerning recent economic developments, believes that national output may decline soon, causing serious unemployment, and that other agencies, like the Treasury and the Federal Reserve System, agree. What specific measures can the Council recommend that the government take under such circumstances?

1. The government can vary its expenditure for public works and other programs. If increased unemployment seems to be in the wind, it can step up outlays on roads, urban reconstruction, and other public programs. Of course, these programs must be well thought out and socially productive. There is no sense in pushing through wasteful and foolish public works programs merely to make jobs. Or if, as in 1969, the economy is plagued by inflation, it can (as President Nixon ordered) stop new federal construction programs temporarily.

2. The government can vary welfare payments and other types of transfer payments. For example, a hike in Social Security benefits may provide a very healthy shot in the arm for an economy with too much unemployment. An increase in veterans' benefits or in aid to dependent children may do the same thing. The federal government has sometimes helped the states to extend the length of time that the unemployed can receive unemployment compensation; this too will have the desired effect. On the other hand, if there is full employment and inflation is a dangerous problem, it may be worthwhile to cut back on certain kinds of transfer payments. For example, if it is agreed that some veterans' benefits should be reduced, this reduction might be timed to occur during a period when inflationary pressures are evident.

3. The government can vary tax rates. For example, if there is considerable unemployment, the government may cut tax rates, as it did in 1975. Or if inflation is the problem, the government may increase taxes, as it did in 1968 when, after considerable political maneuvering and buckpassing, the Congress was finally persuaded to put through a 10 percent tax surcharge to try to moderate the inflation caused by the Vietnam War. However, temporary tax changes may have less effect than permanent ones, since, as pointed out in Chapter 10, consumption expenditure may be influenced less by transitory changes in income than by permanent changes.

PROS AND CONS OF VARIOUS FISCAL POLICY TOOLS

Of course there are advantages and disadvantages in each of these tools of fiscal policy. *One of the big disadvantages of public works and similar spending programs is that they take so long to get started.* Plans must be made, land must be acquired, and preliminary construction studies must be carried out. By the time the expenditures are finally made and have the desired effect, the dangers of excessive unemployment may have given way to dangers of inflation, so that the spending, coming too late, does more harm than good. To some extent, this problem may be ameliorated by having a backlog of productive projects ready to go at all times. In this way, at least a portion of the lag can be eliminated.

In recent years, there has been a widespread feeling that government expenditures should be set on the basis of their long-run desirability and productivity and not on the basis of short-term stabilization considerations. The optimal level of government expenditure is at the point where the value of the extra benefits to be derived from an extra dollar of government expenditure is at least equal to the dollar of cost. This optimal level is unlikely to change much in the short run, and it would be wasteful to spend more—or less—than this amount for stabilization purposes when tax changes could be used instead. Thus many economists believe that tax cuts or tax increases should be the primary fiscal weapons to fight unemployment or inflation.

However, *one of the big problems with tax changes is that it sometimes is difficult to get Congress to take speedy action.* There is often considerable debate over a tax bill, and sometimes it becomes a political football. Another difficulty with tax changes is that it generally is much easier to reduce taxes than it is to get them back up again. To politicians, lower taxes are attractive because they are popular, and higher taxes are dangerous because they may hurt a politician's chances of re-election. In discussing fiscal policy (or most other aspects of government operations, for that matter), to ignore politics is to risk losing touch with reality.

Fiscal Policy: Three Case Studies

THE TAX CUT OF 1964

With some knowledge of the players and the plays they can call, we can look now at three examples of fiscal policy in action. When the Kennedy administration took office in 1961, it was confronted with a relatively high unemployment rate—about 7 percent in mid-1961. By 1962, although unemployment was somewhat lower (about 6 percent), the president's advisers, led by Walter W. Heller, chairman of the Council of Economic Advisers, pushed for a tax cut to reduce unemployment further. The president, after considerable discussion of the effects of such a tax cut, announced in June 1962 that he would propose such a measure to the Congress; and in January 1963, the bill was finally sent to Congress.

The proposed tax bill was a victory for Heller and the CEA. Even though it would mean a deliberately large deficit, the president had been convinced to cut taxes to push the economy closer to full employment. But the Congress was not so easily convinced. Many congressmen labeled the proposal irresponsible and reckless. Others wanted to couple tax reform with tax reduction. It was not until 1964, after President Kennedy's death, that the tax bill was enacted. It took a year from the time the bill was sent to Congress for it to be passed, and during this interval, there was a continuous debate in the executive branch and the Congress. The secretary of the Treasury, Douglas Dillon, the chairman of the Federal Reserve Board, William M. Martin, and numerous congressmen—all powerful and all initially cool to the proposal—were eventually won over. The result was a tax reduction of about $10 billion per year.

The effects of the tax cut are by no means easy to measure, in part because the rate of growth of the money supply increased at the same time, which (as we shall see in Chapter 14) should also affect GNP. But in line with the theory presented in earlier sections, consumption expenditure did increase sharply during 1964. Moreover, the additional consumption expenditure undoubtedly induced additional investment. According to some estimates, the tax cut resulted in an increase in GNP of about $24 billion in 1965 and more in subsequent years.[3] The unemployment rate, which had been about 5½ to 6 percent during 1962 and 1963, fell to 5 percent during 1964 and to 4.7 percent in the spring of 1965. It is fair to say that most economists were extremely pleased with themselves in 1965. Fiscal policy based on their theories seemed to work very well indeed! Unfortunately, however, this pleasure did not last very long, there being another, and sadder, tale to tell.

THE TAX SURCHARGE OF 1968

In late July 1965, President Lyndon Johnson announced that the United States would send 50,000 more men to Vietnam. From fiscal 1965 to fiscal 1966, defense expenditures rose from $50 billion to $62 billion—a large increase in government expenditure, and one that took place at a time of

Walter Heller

---

[3] Arthur Okun, "Measuring the Impact of the 1964 Tax Reduction," in Walter W. Heller, *Perspectives on Economic Growth,* New York: Random House, 1968, p. 33.

relatively full employment. Such an increase in government expenditure would be expected to cause inflationary pressures. The Council of Economic Advisers recognized this danger, and recommended in late 1965 that the president urge Congress to increase taxes. Johnson was reluctant. The inflationary pressures mounted during 1966, and little was done by fiscal policy makers to quell them.

Even in 1967, the Congress was unwilling to raise taxes. The case for fiscal restraint was, it felt, not clear enough. As for the president, he said, "It is not a popular thing for a President to do . . . to ask for a penny out of a dollar to pay for a war that is not popular either."[4] Finally, in mid-1968, a 10 percent surcharge on income taxes, together with some restraint in government spending, was enacted. This increase in taxes was obviously the right medicine, but it was at least two years too late, and its effects were delayed and insufficient.

THE TAX CUT OF 1975

In late 1974, the unemployment rate began to mount. Whereas it was 5.5 percent in August, it reached 7.2 percent in December. Although economists were rather slow to recognize that the economy was slumping into a severe recession, by early 1975 it was clear that some stimulus was needed. Inflation, which President Ford had labeled "Public Enemy Number One" in the fall of 1974, continued to be a problem, but most policy makers felt that unemployment rates were reaching intolerable levels. By March 1975, the unemployment rate was 8.7 percent, the highest level in over 30 years, and something clearly had to be done to lower it.

In early 1975, President Ford proposed a $16 billion tax cut. As his Council of Economic Advisers stated, its purpose was "to halt the decline in production and employment so that growth of output can resume and unemployment can be reduced."[5] In March 1975, Congress passed a $23 billion tax cut, which provided rebates (of $100 to $200) on 1974 personal income taxes as well as reductions in 1975 income taxes. Both personal and corporate income taxes were cut. Personal tax liabilities were reduced through a $30 credit for each taxpayer and each dependent, as well as through increased standard deductions and low-income allowances. Corporate tax liabilities were reduced through a liberalization of the investment tax credit, as well as changes in tax rates.

The evidence seems to indicate that the tax cut was the right kind of medicine. In accord with our theories, national output did, in fact, increase in the latter half of 1975, and unemployment eased somewhat. By the end of 1975, the recovery was well under way—due in part, according to most economists, to the tax cut. However, the tax cut had less impact than some economists predicted because consumers did not spend, but instead saved, much of the tax reduction. This behavior by consumers is what the permanent-income hypothesis (in Chapter 10) would predict. Because the tax reduction was temporary, it had less effect on consumers' permanent income —and thus less effect on consumption expenditure—than if it was permanent.

---

[4] Arthur Okun, *The Political Economy of Prosperity* New York: Norton, 1970, p. 88.
[5] Council of Economic Advisers, *1975 Annual Report,* Washington, D.C.: Government Printing Office, 1975.

IMPLICATIONS OF THE CASE STUDIES—AND THE REAGAN TAX CUT OF 1981

Based on the histories of all three of these tax changes (1964, 1968, and 1975), it is clear that, although we know a great deal more than we used to about how fiscal policy should be employed to avoid inflation or considerable unemployment, there is no guarantee that it will be used in this way. In the early 1960s and in 1974–75, policy makers seemed to make reasonably correct choices. In 1965–68, they did not. Without question, mistakes will continue to be made. All that we can do is try to learn from past mistakes.

In this connection, it is interesting to note that President Reagan, when he argued for a large tax reduction in 1981, frequently cited the beneficial effects of the tax cut of 1964. His critics pointed out that economic conditions in 1981 were different from those in 1964. Nonetheless, a huge tax cut was passed in 1981. Since much of this tax cut went into effect in 1982 and later, it was hoped in 1982 that it would help lift the economy out of the recession that afflicted the United States then. But some observers, in Wall Street and elsewhere, were worried that it might rekindle inflation, which was relatively low in early 1982.

In fact, the economy began to expand in late 1982, and 1983 was a year of vigorous cyclical recovery. (Real GNP rose by about 6 percent, and the unemployment rate fell by 2.5 percentage points in 1983.) Moreover, the expansion, which did not increase inflation substantially, continued throughout 1984—and helped to re-elect President Reagan. Although the 1981 tax cut was only one of the relevant factors, it certainly helped to bring about the desired expansion.

President Reagan signing the 1981 tax cut bill

Deficit and Surplus Financing

Now that you have studied the basic elements of fiscal policy, let's see how well you would fare with some of the problems that confront our nation's top policy makers.

CASE 1: AN IMMINENT RECESSION

Suppose that, through some inexplicable malfunctioning of the democratic process, you are elected president of the United States. Your Council of Economic Advisers reports to you that, on the basis of various forecasts, national output is likely to drop next year, and unemployment is likely to be much higher. Naturally, you are concerned; and having absorbed the ideas presented in this chapter, you ask your advisers—the Council of Economic Advisers, the Treasury, and the Office of Management and Budget —what sort of fiscal policy should be adopted to head off this undesirable turn of events. On the basis of their advice, you suggest to Congress that taxes should be cut and government expenditures should be increased.

When they receive your message, a number of key congressmen point out that if the government cuts taxes and raises expenditures it will operate in the red. In other words, government revenue will fall short of government spending—there will be a ***deficit.*** They warn that such fiscal behavior is irresponsible, since it violates the fundamental tenet of public finance that the budget should be balanced. Income should cover outgo. For further clarification on this point, you call in your advisers, who deny that the budget should be balanced each year. They point out that if a deficit is run in a particular year, the government can borrow the difference; and they claim that the national debt is in no sense dangerously large in the United States at present. Whose advice would you follow—that of your economic advisers or that of the congressmen?

CASE 2: INFLATIONARY SIGNALS

Suppose your advisers tell you that inflation is a growing problem and that you should cut back government spending and raise taxes. Since this advice seems sensible, based on the principles set forth in this chapter, you propose this course of action to Congress. Some prominent newspapers point out that by raising taxes and cutting expenditures, the government will take in more than it spends. In other words, there will be a *surplus.* They say that there is no reason for the government to take more money from the people than it needs to pay for the services it performs, and argue that taxes should not be increased because the government can cover its expenditures without such an increase. Whose advice would you follow— that of your economic advisers or that of the newspapers?

WHAT SHOULD YOU DO?

You would be wise to go along with your economic advisers in both cases. Why? Because, for reasons discussed in more detail in the next section, it is not essential or necessarily desirable for the budget to be balanced each year. Although it may well be prudent for individuals and families not to spend more than they earn, this does not carry over to the federal government. When we need to stimulate the economy and raise national output, it is perfectly legitimate and desirable for the federal government to run a deficit, provided it gets its full money's worth for what it spent. Thus, in the first case, you should not have been worried by the fact that a deficit would result. And in the second case, while it is true that the government could support its expenditures with lower taxes, this would defeat your purpose. What you want to do is to cut total spending, public and private, and raising taxes will cut private spending.

SHOULD THE BUDGET BE BALANCED ANNUALLY?

At least three policies concerning the government budget are worthy of detailed examination. The first policy says that *the government's budget should be balanced each and every year.* This is the philosophy that generally prevailed, here and abroad, until a few decades ago. Superficially, it seems reasonable. After all, won't a family or firm go bankrupt if it continues to spend more than it takes in? Why should the government be any different? However, the truth is that the government has economic capabilities, powers, and responsibilities that are entirely different from those of any family or firm, and it is misleading—sometimes even pernicious—to assume that what is sensible for a family or firm is also sensible for the government.

Budget
of the
United States
Government

Fiscal Year **1986**

EXECUTIVE OFFICE OF THE PRESIDENT
OFFICE OF MANAGEMENT AND BUDGET

If this policy of balancing the budget is accepted, the government cannot use fiscal policy as a tool to stabilize the economy. Indeed, if the government attempts to balance its budget each year, it is likely to make unemployment or inflation worse rather than better. For example, suppose that severe unemployment occurs because of a drop in national output. Since incomes drop, tax receipts drop as well. Thus, if the government attempts to balance its budget, it must cut its spending and/or increase tax rates, both of which will tend to lower, not raise, national output. On the other hand, suppose that inflation occurs because spending increases too rapidly. Since incomes increase, tax receipts increase too. Thus, for the government to balance its budget, it must increase its spending and/or decrease tax rates, both of which will tend to raise, not lower, spending.

Despite these considerations, there has been a considerable amount of political support for a constitutional amendment to mandate a balanced federal budget. In large part, this seems to be a reaction to persistent, large deficits which are widely regarded as having been inflationary. No doubt, the federal government, through inappropriate fiscal or monetary policies, has frequently been responsible for excessive inflation. Some economists go so far as to say that the real problem is how to prevent the government from creating disturbances, rather than how to use the government budget (and monetary policy) to offset disturbances arising from the private sector. But for the reasons discussed above, most economists would not go so far as to conclude that the government should balance its budget each year.

SHOULD THE BUDGET BE BALANCED OVER THE BUSINESS CYCLE?

A second budgetary philosophy says that *the government's budget should be balanced over the course of each "business cycle."* As we have seen in previous chapters, the rate of growth of national output tends to behave cyclically. It tends to increase for a while, then drop, increase, then drop. Unemployment also tends to ebb and flow in a similar cyclical fashion. According to this second budgetary policy, the government is not expected to balance its budget each year, but is expected to run a big enough surplus during periods of high employment to offset the deficit it runs during the ensuing period of excessive unemployment. This policy seems to give the government enough flexibility to run the deficits or surpluses needed to stabilize the economy, while at the same time allaying any public fear of a chronically unbalanced budget. It certainly seems to be a neat way to reconcile the government's use of fiscal policy to promote noninflationary full employment with the public's uneasiness over chronically unbalanced budgets.

Unfortunately, however, it does contain one fundamental flaw. There is no reason to believe that the size of the deficits required to eliminate excessive unemployment will equal the size of the surpluses required to moderate the subsequent inflation. Suppose that national output falls sharply, causing severe and prolonged unemployment; then regains its full-employment level only briefly; then falls again. In such a case, the deficits incurred to get the economy back to full employment are likely to exceed by far the surpluses run during the brief period of full employment. Thus there would be no way to stabilize the economy without run-

In early 1984, unemployment was receding, while sales and profits were rising substantially, and inflation remained at moderate levels. Yet President Reagan's economic advisers were engaged in a public debate that reached the front pages of the nation's newspapers and magazines. What was the fracas about? The huge and growing federal deficit.

The projected 1984 deficit was estimated to be about $200 billion; and by the Reagan administration's own projections, the cumulative deficits from 1984 through 1989 were expected to total a whopping $1 trillion. According to Martin Feldstein, chairman of President Reagan's Council of Economic Advisers, these deficits were very dangerous to the long-term health of the American economy. If they were allowed to occur, they would push up interest rates and result in a crowding out of private investment on plant and equipment. Also, U.S. exports would be hurt because high U.S. interest rates would push up the value of the dollar relative to other currencies, thus making our exports more expensive to foreign purchasers. For these and other reasons, Feldstein (and many other economists) were extremely worried about the deficit.

Martin Feldstein   **Donald Regan**

In contrast, Donald Regan, who in 1984 was secretary of the Treasury, played down the importance of the deficit. In his view, deficits do not push up interest rates and they did not result in an overvaluation of the dollar relative to other currencies. In part, his arguments seemed to be based on studies carried out by some supply-side economists, including members of the Treasury staff. But most economists did not buy these arguments. If the government increases its demands for credit because of the very large deficits, the interest rate (which is the price of borrowing money) will rise.

The contrast between the two combatants, as well as the acidity of the squabble, fascinated news commentators as well as the general public. Feldstein, the whistle blower, was a highly respected economics professor on leave from Harvard University, a winner of the John Bates Clark medal (given every two years to the most distinguished economist under 40 years of age), and a former president of the National Bureau of Economic Research. Regan, the defender of the president's program, was the former head of Merrill Lynch, the huge brokerage firm, and one of the leading lights on Wall Street. *Time Magazine* called Feldstein "a combination of gadfly, maverick, and doomsayer . . . an adviser who insists on proferring unwanted advice," and labeled Regan as "the President's chief economic cheerleader."

The clash between them was almost certainly one of the most visible and highly publicized feuds among major presidential economic advisers in the recent history of the United States. Many observers were surprised that the president allowed it to continue so openly for so long. Finally, in the summer of 1984, Feldstein resigned his post and returned to Harvard. Regan remained in the second Reagan administration and in 1985 was given the key job as White House chief of staff.

ning an unbalanced budget over the course of this business cycle. If this policy were adopted, and if the government attempted to balance the budget over the course of each business cycle, this would interfere with an effective fiscal policy designed to promote full employment with stable prices.

SHOULD WE WORRY ABOUT BALANCING THE BUDGET?

Finally, a third budgetary policy says that *the government's budget should be set so as to promote whatever attainable combination of unemployment and inflation seems socially optimal,* even if this means that the budget is unbalanced over considerable periods of time. This policy is sometimes called **functional finance.**[6] Proponents of functional finance point out that, although this policy may mean a continual growth in the public debt, the problems caused by a moderate growth in the public debt are small when compared with the social costs of unemployment and inflation.

CHANGES IN PUBLIC ATTITUDES

Certainly, the history of the past 40 years has been characterized by enormous changes in the nation's attitude toward the government budget. Forty years ago, the prevailing attitude was that the government's budget should be balanced. The emergence of the Keynesian theory of the determination of national output and employment shook this attitude, at least to the point where it became respectable to advocate a balanced budget over the business cycle, rather than in each year. In many circles, functional finance was advocated.

In the late 1970s and early 1980s, there was some movement back toward earlier views favoring balanced budgets. Conservatives emphasized the usefulness of the balanced budget as a device to limit government spending, which they regarded as excessive. The public tended to blame very high rates of inflation on large deficits. Although neither political party was prepared (even remotely) to renounce deficits, considerable lip service was paid to the desirability of a balanced budget. For example, in August 1982, the Senate approved a constitutional amendment requiring a balanced budget, while at the same time the government was running a deficit of over $100 billion!

The Full-Employment Budget

Some of the misconceptions about budget deficits and surpluses can be avoided by the use of the **full-employment budget,** which shows the difference between tax revenues and government expenditures that would result if we had full employment. For example, in 1958, the Eisenhower administration ran a deficit of over $10 billion—a reasonably large deficit by historical standards. Basically, the reason for this deficit was that, with the unemployment rate at about 7 percent, there was a substantial gap

[6] See Abba Lerner, *Economics of Control,* New York: Macmillan, 1944.

between actual and potential output. Net national product fell from 1957 to 1958, and, as a result, incomes and federal tax collections fell, and the government ran a deficit. But this $10 billion deficit was entirely due to the high level of unemployment the country was experiencing.

Had we been at full employment, there would have been a surplus of about $5 billion in 1958. NNP, incomes, and federal tax receipts would all have been higher. Government spending and the tax rates in 1958 were not such as to produce a deficit if full employment had been attained. On the contrary, the full-employment budget shows that, if full employment had prevailed, tax receipts would have increased so that federal revenues would have exceeded expenditure by about $5 billion. It is important to distinguish between the full-employment budget and the actual budget. When, as in 1958, the actual budget shows a deficit but the full-employment budget does not, most economists feel that fiscal policy is not too expansionary, since at full employment the federal government would be running a surplus.

Recognizing these considerations, recent administrations have officially adopted the full-employment budget as their measure of the stabilization impact of the budget. As you can see in Figure 12.8, President Nixon ran a full-employment surplus during his first term in office to combat inflation.

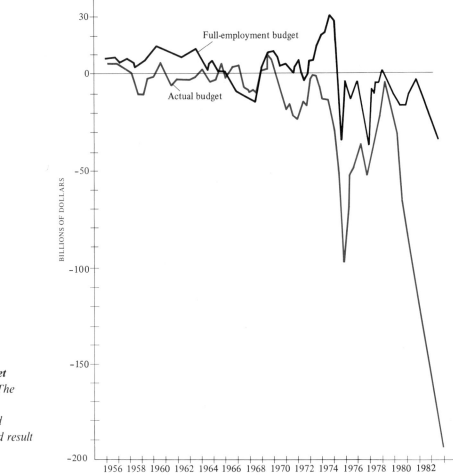

Figure 12.8

Full-Employment and Actual Budget Deficits and Surpluses, 1956–83 *The full-employment budget shows the difference between tax revenues and government expenditures that would result if there was full employment.*

In 1972, there was a full-employment deficit, but in 1973, and to a greater extent 1974, there were full-employment surpluses. This is in contrast to the actual budget, which was in deficit for most of these years. President Ford ran a large full-employment deficit in 1975 to promote recovery from the recession. In subsequent years, Presidents Carter and Reagan incurred full-employment deficits too.

As you can see in Figure 12.8, the full-employment budget can differ substantially from the actual budget. To understand whether fiscal policy is restrictive or stimulative, you must understand the difference.

Effects of How a Deficit Is Financed, or How a Surplus Is Used

Before leaving the topic of budget deficits and surpluses, it is important to note that the effect of a deficit may depend on how it is financed, as well as on its size. One way for the government to finance a deficit is *to borrow from consumers and business firms.* (Such borrowing results in increases in the national debt, discussed in Chapter 5.) When the government borrows from consumers and business firms, it takes funds from them that might otherwise be spent on consumption or investment goods. Thus some of the expansionary effect of a budget deficit may be offset by reduced private spending, if a deficit is financed by borrowing from the public.[7]

A second way for the government to finance a budget deficit is *to create new money.* For example, the government can simply print additional money to meet the deficit. (As will become clearer in Chapter 16, a similar result may be obtained if the government borrows from the central bank—the Federal Reserve in the United States.) When the government spends newly created money, it does not use funds that might otherwise be spent by the private sector. Consequently, *the expansionary effects of a deficit may be greater if it is financed by the creation of new money than if it is financed by borrowing from the public.*

Similarly, the effect of a surplus may depend on how it is used, as well as on its size. One way that the government can use a surplus is *to buy back some of its bonds from the public.* (Such purchases reduce the national debt.) When the government buys back some of its bonds, it provides the sellers of the bonds (consumers and firms) with additional spendable funds. Thus some of the anti-inflationary effects of a surplus may be offset by additional private spending.

Another way that the government can use a surplus is to *impound the funds,* that is, keep the funds idle. Since this latter use of the surplus does not provide the private sector with additional spendable funds, there is no such offset to the surplus's anti-inflationary effect. Consequently, *the anti-inflationary effects of a surplus may be greater if the surplus is impounded than if it is used to reduce the national debt.*

Basic Idea #24: If the government spends more than it receives in revenue, it will not go bankrupt. Instead, it will borrow (or create) the money to finance the deficit. If new debt is created, an intolerable burden will not be imposed on future generations (as some people claim), but this does not mean that government deficits do not have undesirable effects. For example, we must send goods and services overseas to pay interest on our foreign-held public debt, and deficit financing under the wrong circumstances can be inflationary.

[7] In Chapter 17 and in Appendix A, we shall see that a deficit financed by borrowing from the public tends to increase interest rates, which is likely to shift the investment function and possibly the consumption function downward. This will reduce the net increase in spending due to the increase in government expenditures. In other words, the increase in interest rates will reduce private spending. In the highly simplified model presented at the beginning of this chapter, we ignored this effect, which is discussed in Chapter 17 and in Appendix A.

Example 12.2   Interpreting Federal Budget Deficits

The actual deficits of the U.S. government in selected years are shown below:

Year	Billions of dollars
1954	1.2
1961	3.4
1967	8.7
1968	25.2
1975	45.2
1980	59.6

(a) Are all of these deficits the result of spendthrift government spending? (b) In 1954, 1961, 1975, and 1980, there were drops in NNP which helped to cause tax revenue to fall below government expenditure. From the above figures alone can one determine the extent to which a particular government deficit is due to high government spending or a weak economy? (c) Were the deficits in 1967 and 1968 the result of a weak economy? What information would you obtain to answer this question?

SOLUTION

(a) No. In some years, like 1954, 1961, 1975, and 1980, at least part of the reason for the deficit was a weak economy due to recession. (b) No. What one needs to know is the full-employment deficit or surplus in each year. (c) No. The unemployment rate is of use in indicating whether the economy was weak. Since the unemployment rate was less than 4 percent in 1967 and 1968, the economy certainly was not weak in these years. The full-employment deficit or surplus would help to answer this question. See Figure 12.8.

Recent American Experience with Fiscal Policy

It should be evident by now that much more is known today about the impact of fiscal policy than at the time when the economy was staggered by the Great Depression. But this does not mean that economists have all (or nearly all) the answers. Enough is known to keep the economy from careening off a bumpy road; avoiding the potholes (some of which are very large) is another matter.

THE FORD YEARS

The hard choices faced by economists in the top councils of government can be demonstrated by a close inspection of the recent attempts to give the economy a smoother side. Let's begin with the situation in the mid-1970s. In early 1974 the price of foreign oil was increased very substantially by the

OPEC countries. This price increase, as well as considerable increases in farm prices (recall Chapter 4), spearheaded a bewildering inflationary spurt. During 1974 consumer prices rose by about 12 percent! From the point of view of inflation, this was the worst year in decades. At the same time, the nation's real output fell, as the economy dropped into the most serious recession since World War II. The result was a marked increase in unemployment. By March 1975 the unemployment rate was 8.7 percent, as compared with 4.9 percent in December 1973.

Faced with a combination of excessive unemployment and excessive inflation, President Ford proposed a $16 billion tax cut, and, as we saw above, Congress passed a $23 billion tax cut in March 1975. As we have seen before, the economy began to revive in mid-1975, and unemployment fell from 8.7 percent in March 1975 to 7.5 percent in March 1976. However, stagflation (the combination of a high unemployment rate and a high rate of inflation) was by no means vanquished. On the contrary, both unemployment and inflation continued to be excessive.

THE CARTER YEARS

In 1977 the federal government ran a deficit of about $50 billion; the full-employment deficit was about $20 billion. And in January 1978 President Carter proposed personal tax reductions of $24 billion. But during 1978 the rate of inflation increased sharply, and approached double-digit levels. Since the inflation rate was higher than expected, the Carter administration scaled back its proposed tax cut to $20 billion, and Congress actually passed a $19 billion tax cut. (About $14 billion of this tax cut went to individuals, the rest to corporations.)

In the face of heightened inflation, fiscal policy did not attempt to rein in the economy very much. The deficit in 1978 was about $30 billion; the full-employment deficit was over $10 billion. There was a continuing debate within the administration over whether the inflation rate could be reduced substantially without a recession—and whether a recession was the proper medicine. In 1980, there was a very brief recession, but it did little to cool off inflation. As in previous years, the federal government ran a full-employment deficit.

THE REAGAN YEARS

When the Reagan administration took office in 1981, it was committed to cut both government expenditures and taxes. In August 1981 the administration pushed through Congress a huge tax cut for both individuals and businesses. At the same time, it reduced federal expenditures (relative to the level that former president Carter had proposed). However, the tax cuts were far in excess of the spending cuts, particularly since reductions in GNP in late 1981 also tended to reduce tax receipts. Thus the administration was faced with record deficits of over $100 billion in fiscal 1982 and about $200 billion in fiscal 1983. In early 1982 President Reagan said he would try to cut spending further in an attempt to soak up some of the red ink. But the economy was in a recession (with an unemployment rate of 9 percent) and there was little sympathy on Capitol Hill for further spending cuts. Since inflation had fallen to well under double-digits, unemployment once again seemed to be Public Enemy Number One.

In November 1982 the economy pulled out of the recession, and the expansion began. Economists of all schools, but particularly supply-side economists (recall Chapter 5), gave the 1981 tax cut considerable credit for increasing real NNP and reducing unemployment. During 1983 and 1984, both years of healthy expansion, the federal government ran huge deficits of about $200 billion. President Reagan vowed that he would not raise taxes, and proposed cuts in nonmilitary government expenditures; whereas his critics asked for tax increases and reductions in military spending. In December 1985, a bill mandating that the budget be balanced in annual steps over the next five years was passed, but there were doubts about its effectiveness and constitutionality.

Clearly, judging from our recent history, fiscal policy is no panacea. Policy makers are continually confronted with difficult choices, and the tools of fiscal policy, at least as they are currently understood and used, are not sufficient to solve or dispel many of the problems at hand. However, it is important to recognize that fiscal policy is not the only available means by which policy makers attempt to stabilize the economy. There is also monetary policy, which we shall discuss in detail in Chapter 16. A sensible fiscal policy can be formulated only in conjunction with monetary policy, and although it is convenient to discuss them separately, in real life they must be coordinated. Also, lest you become overly pessimistic, you should note that, despite the problems that remain unsolved, our improved understanding of fiscal and monetary policy has enabled us to steer a better and more stable course than in the days before World War II.

Test Yourself

1. Describe the balanced-budget multiplier. If both government expenditures and taxes rise by the same amount, what is the effect, according to the balanced-budget multiplier?

2. "An important advantage of public works as a tool of fiscal policy is that they can be started quickly. An important advantage of tax rate changes is that they almost never get embroiled in partisan politics." Comment and evaluate.

3. "The full-employment budget is just a lot of hocum to persuade the public that big deficits are smaller and less inflationary than they really are." Comment and evaluate.

4. According to Joseph Pechman of the Brookings Institution, "Among taxes, the federal individual income tax is the leading [automatic] stabilizer." Explain why, and discuss the significance of this fact. He also says that "on the expenditure side, the major built-in stabilizer is unemployment compensation." Again, explain why, and discuss the significance of this fact.

Summary

1. The equilibrium level of net national product is the level where intended consumption plus intended investment plus intended government spending equal net national product. A $1 billion change in government purchases will result in a change in equilibrium NNP of the same amount as a $1 billion change in intended investment or a $1 billion shift in the relation between consumption expenditures and NNP. In any of these cases, there is a multiplier effect.

2. An increase in the tax rate shifts the relationship between consumption expenditure and NNP downward, thus reducing the equilibrium value of NNP. A decrease in the tax rate shifts the relationship upward, thus increasing the equilibrium value of NNP.

3. The equilibrium level of NNP may not be the level corresponding to full employment. A recessionary gap is the increase in intended spending required to push the equilibrium NNP up to the full-employment level. An inflationary gap is the decrease in intended spending required to push the equilibrium NNP down to its full-employment level (at initial prices).

4. Policy makers receive a lot of help in stabilizing the economy from our automatic stabilizers—automatic changes in tax revenues, unemployment compensation and welfare payments, corporate dividends, family saving, and farm aid. However, the automatic stabilizers can only cut down on variations in unemployment and inflation, not eliminate them.

5. Discretionary programs are needed to supplement the effects of these automatic stabilizers. Such discretionary actions include changing government expenditure on public works and other programs, changing welfare payments and other such transfers, and changing tax rates. An important problem with some of these tools of fiscal policy is the lag in time before they can be brought into play.

6. At least three policies concerning the government budget have received considerable attention. First, the budget can be balanced each and every year. Second, the budget can be balanced over the course of the business cycle. Third, the budget can be set in a way that will promote full employment with stable prices whether or not this means that the budget is unbalanced over considerable periods of time.

7. The history of the past 40 years has seen enormous changes in the public's attitude toward the government budget. Forty years ago, the prevailing doctrine was that the budget should be balanced each year. Now (although a balanced budget has more support than a few years ago) the attitude seems to be that the budget should be used as a tool to reduce unemployment and inflation.

8. Some of the popular misconceptions concerning budget deficits and budget surpluses can be avoided by the use of the full-employment budget, which shows the difference between tax revenue and government expenditure that would result if we had full employment. When the actual budget shows a deficit but the full-employment budget does not, most economists feel that fiscal policy is not too expansionary.

Concepts for Review

$C + I + G$ **line**	**Council of Economic**	**Balanced budget**
Balanced-budget	**Advisers**	**Functional finance**
multiplier	**Automatic stabilizers**	**Full-employment**
Recessionary gap	**Deficit**	**budget**
Inflationary gap	**Surplus**	

Appendix: The Effect of a Change in Government Expenditure and the Balanced-Budget Multiplier (an Algebraic Treatment)

The first purpose of this Appendix is to prove that a \$1 billion change in government expenditure will result in a change in equilibrium NNP of $\left(\dfrac{1}{\text{MPS}}\right)$ billions of dollars. To prove this proposition, recall that the equilibrium value of NNP is where intended spending—$C + I + G$—equals NNP. Thus

$$NNP = C + I + G. \tag{12.1}$$

Assuming that the consumption function is as given in Table 10.1 (and Table 12.1), it follows that

$$C = 350 + 0.6 \, NNP \tag{12.2}$$

where 0.6 is the marginal propensity to consume. (Note that NNP equals disposable income. This is because there are no taxes, no transfer payments, and no undistributed corporate profits. Taxes are brought into the picture later in this appendix.) Substituting the right-hand side of Equation (12.2) for C in Equation (12.1), we have

$$NNP = 350 + 0.6 \, NNP + I + G. \tag{12.3}$$

Thus

$$(1 - 0.6) \, NNP = 350 + I + G$$
$$NNP = \frac{350}{0.4} + \frac{I}{0.4} + \frac{G}{0.4}. \tag{12.4}$$

What happens to NNP when G increases from \$$X$ billion to \$$(X + 1)$ billion? How much will this increase the equilibrium value of NNP? From Equation (12.4), it is clear that equilibrium NNP will be

$$\frac{350}{0.4} + \frac{I}{0.4} + \frac{X}{0.4}$$

if government expenditure equals \$$X$ billion. And it is equally clear from Equation (12.4) that NNP will equal

$$\frac{350}{0.4} + \frac{I}{0.4} + \frac{(X + 1)}{0.4}$$

if government expenditure is \$$(X + 1)$ billion. Consequently the increase in NNP due to the \$1 billion increase in government spending is

$$\left[\frac{350}{0.4} + \frac{I}{0.4} + \frac{(X + 1)}{0.4}\right] - \left[\frac{350}{0.4} + \frac{I}{0.4} + \frac{X}{0.4}\right],$$

which equals

$$\frac{X + 1}{0.4} - \frac{X}{0.4} = \frac{1}{0.4}.$$

That is, a \$1 billion increase in government expenditure will result in an increase of $\frac{1}{0.4}$ billion dollars of NNP—which is equal to $\left(\frac{1}{MPS}\right)$ billions of dollars of NNP, since $0.4 = MPS$. This is what we set out to prove.

The second purpose of this Appendix is to prove that, if both government expenditures and taxes are increased by \$1 billion, equilibrium NNP will be increased by \$1 billion. This is the balanced-budget multiplier. To prove this proposition, note that disposable income equals $NNP - T$, where T is the amount of taxes. Thus the consumption function is

$$C = 350 + 0.6\,(NNP - T). \tag{12.5}$$

Substituting the right-hand side of Equation (12.5) for C in Equation (12.1), we have

$$NNP = 350 + 0.6\,(NNP - T) + I + G.$$

Thus

$$(1 - 0.6)\,NNP = 350 - 0.6T + I + G$$

$$NNP = \frac{350}{0.4} - \frac{0.6T}{0.4} + \frac{I}{0.4} + \frac{G}{0.4}.$$

What happens if both G and T increase by \$1 billion? The effect of increasing T by \$1 billion is to reduce the equilibrium value of NNP by $0.6/0.4$ billions of dollars. The effect of increasing G by \$1 billion is to increase the equilibrium value of NNP by $1/0.4$ billions of dollars. Thus the effect of increasing both G and T by \$1 billion is to increase the equilibrium value of NNP by $1/0.4 - 0.6/0.4 = 0.4/0.4$, or 1 billion dollars. This is what we set out to prove.

CHAPTER 13

Business Fluctuations and Economic Forecasting

The American economy has not grown at a constant rate. Instead, as pointed out in Chapter 9, output has expanded rapidly in some periods; little, if at all, in others; and actually contracted in still others. The average citizen, as well as the government official or the business executive, needs to know why these business fluctuations occur and whether they can be avoided. This chapter investigates the causes of business fluctuations.

We also take up a related question of great practical importance. Can business fluctuations be forecasted? More and more, economic models are being used by government and industry to forecast changes in GNP and other economic variables. Economic forecasting has become a very important part of the economist's job. Although no reputable economist would claim that economic forecasting is very precise or reliable, the forecasts produced by economic models are watched closely by decision makers around the world. In the latter part of this chapter, we describe some of the more widely used forecasting techniques, and see how accurate they have proved in the past.

Business Fluctuations and Variation in Investment Spending

In Chapter 9, we described the anatomy of the business cycle. Each cycle can be divided into four phases: trough, expansion, peak, and recession. There is considerable variation in the length and severity of business fluctuations. Some recessions, like that in the early thirties, are very severe;

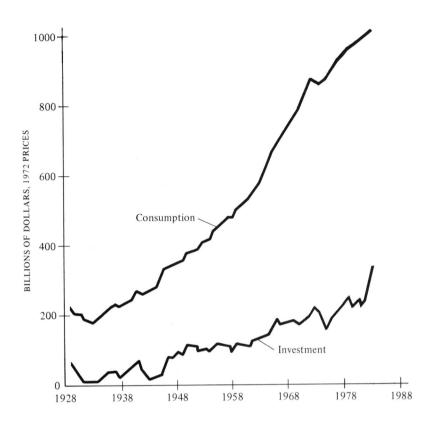

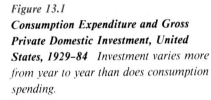

Figure 13.1

Consumption Expenditure and Gross Private Domestic Investment, United States, 1929–84 *Investment varies more from year to year than does consumption spending.*

others, like those in the fifties, are relatively mild. Some expansions, like that in the sixties, are relatively long-lived. Others, like that in the late fifties, are of relatively short duration. Moreover, the basic set of factors responsible for the recession and the expansion differs from cycle to cycle.

As we pointed out in Chapter 11, investment varies much more from year to year than does consumption expenditure. Figure 13.1 shows that investment goes up and down, while consumption climbs steadily with only slight bumps and dips.[1] *The volatility of investment is an important factor in explaining the changes in national output over time.* Why does investment in plant and equipment vary so much over the course of the business cycle? The acceleration principle throws important light on this question.

The Acceleration Principle

The acceleration principle is a theory that says that investment is related to the rate of change of output. When output is increasing beyond previous levels, investment is required to increase the capacity to produce output. When output is falling, it may be unnecessary even to replace old capital as it is scrapped, let alone to spend money on new capital.

[1] Net exports are excluded from Figure 13.1. They were almost always under $10 billion during this period. Government expenditures are considered in Figure 13.2.

Table 13.1

RELATIONSHIP BETWEEN SALES AND INVESTMENT, JOHNSON SHOE CORPORATION

Year	Sales	Needed stock of capital	Actual stock of capital	Replacement investment (millions of dollars)	Net investment	Gross investment
1977	10	20	20	1	0	1
1978	12	24	24	1	4	5
1979	14	28	28	1	4	5
1980	15	30	30	1	2	3
1981	16	32	32	1	2	3
1982	16	32	32	1	0	1
1983	15	30	31	0	−1	0
1984	15	30	30	0	−1	0
1985	15	30	30	1	0	1
1986	17	34	34	1	4	5

THE ACCELERATION PRINCIPLE IN ACTION: A NUMERICAL
EXAMPLE

Suppose that the Johnson Shoe Corporation, a maker of women's shoes, requires 1 machine to make 50,000 pairs of shoes per year. Since each machine (and related plant and facilities) costs $2 million and each pair of
shoes costs $20, it takes $2 worth of plant and equipment to produce $1
worth of output per year. In 1977, we suppose that the quantity of the
firm's plant and equipment was exactly in balance with its output. In other
words, the firm had no excess capacity; sales were $10 million and the ac-
tual stock of capital was $20 million. The firm's sales in subsequent years
are shown in Table 13.1. For example, in 1978 its sales increased to $12
million; in 1979 they increased to $14 million; and so forth.

Table 13.1 also shows the amount the firm will have to invest each year
in order to produce the amount it sells. Let's begin with 1978. To produce
$12 million worth of product, the firm must have $24 million worth of capital. This means that it must increase its stock of capital from $20 million
—the amount it has in 1977—to $24 million.[2] In other words, it must in-
crease its stock of capital by $4 million, which means that its net investment
in plant and equipment must equal $4 million. But this is not the same as
its gross investment—the amount of plant and equipment the firm must
buy—because the firm must also replace some plant and equipment that
wears out. Suppose that $1 million of plant and equipment wear out each
year. Then gross investment in 1978 must equal net investment ($4 million)
plus $1 million, or $5 million.

Next, let's look at 1979. The firm's sales in that year are $14 million. To
produce this much output, the firm must have $28 million of capital, which
means that it must increase its stock of capital by $4 million—from $24
million to $28 million. In addition, there is $1 million of replacement investment to replace plant and equipment that wear out in 1979. In all, the
firm's gross investment must be $5 million. In 1980, the firm's sales are $15

[2] Note that the firm's stock of capital is an entirely different concept than its common
stock or preferred stock. See Chapter 6.

million. To produce this output, this firm must have $30 million of capital, which means that it must increase its stock of capital by $2 million—from $28 million to $30 million. In addition, there is $1 million of replacement investment. In all, the firm's gross investment must be $3 million. Table 13.1 shows the results for subsequent years.

MAGNIFIED PERCENTAGE CHANGES IN INVESTMENT

From Table 13.1, it is clear that *changes in sales can result in magnified percentage changes in investment.* For example, between 1977 and 1978 sales went up by 20 percent, whereas gross investment went up by 400 percent. Between 1985 and 1986, sales went up by about 13 percent, whereas gross investment went up by 400 percent. The effect of a decrease in sales is even more spectacular because it tends to drive net investment to zero (or to negative values, as in 1983). Indeed, even gross investment may be driven to zero, as in 1983, if the firm wants to reduce the value of its plant and equipment. To accomplish this, the firm simply does not replace the plant and equipment that wear out.

THE IMPORTANCE OF THE RATE OF CHANGE OF SALES

Table 13.1 shows that *the amount of gross investment depends on the amount by which sales increase.* In particular, for gross investment to remain constant year after year, the annual increase of sales must also remain constant. You can see this in 1978 and 1979. In each of these years, since sales increased from the previous year by the same amount ($2 million), gross investment remained constant at $5 million per year. It is very important to note that *gross investment will fall when sales begin to increase by decreasing amounts.* The fact that sales are increasing does not insure that gross investment will increase. On the contrary, if sales are increasing by decreasing amounts, gross investment will fall. This is a very important point.

This effect of changes in sales on gross investment is often called the ***acceleration principle,*** since changes in sales result in accelerated, or magnified, changes in investment, and since an increase in investment results from an increase in the annual growth (an ***acceleration***) of sales. The acceleration principle applies to kinds of investment other than plant and equipment. For example, it is easy to show that it applies to inventories and housing as well, since firms often try to maintain a certain amount of inventory for each dollar of sales—just as they often maintain a certain amount of plant and equipment for each dollar of sales.

The Interaction between the Acceleration Principle and the Multiplier

Economists—led by Nobel laureates Paul Samuelson and Sir John Hicks—*have shown that the acceleration principle combined with the multiplier may produce business cycles like those experienced in the real world.* Suppose that national output is increasing, and the economy is moving up toward full employment. Sales are increasing at an increasing rate. Because of the acceleration principle, the increases in sales result in a high level of investment. And via the multiplier, the high level of investment promotes further increases in national output. Thus the accelerator and multiplier tend to reinforce one another, resulting in a strong upward movement of national output. The economy is in an expansion. It is a good time to be president of the United States, president of a major corporation, or an average citizen.

Example 13.1 Investment at the Howe Company

The Howe Company is a manufacturer of electrical equipment. It wants to maintain $3 worth of plant and equipment for every dollar of output per year. Each year $1 million worth of Howe Company's plant and equipment wears out. In 1983, the firm's actual value of plant and equipment is $150 million.

(a) Fill in the blanks below (all figures are in millions of dollars).

Year	Output during year	Desired value of plant and equipment	Net investment	Gross investment
1983	50	———	———	———
1984	60	———	———	———
1985	70	———	———	———
1986	80	———	———	———
1987	100	———	———	———
1988	105	———	———	———

(b) Is the rate of gross investment in plant and equipment highest in the year when output is greatest? (c) Why does gross investment drop in 1988, even though output continues to increase?

SOLUTION

(a) The complete table is:

Year	Output during year	Desired value of plant and equipment	Net investment	Gross investment
1983	50	150	0	1
1984	60	180	30	31
1985	70	210	30	31
1986	80	240	30	31
1987	100	300	60	61
1988	105	315	15	16

(b) No. (c) Because 1988 output differed from 1987 output by a smaller amount than 1987 output differed from 1986 output.

WHY A PEAK?

Eventually, however, the economy nears full employment. And since we have only a certain amount of land, labor, and capital, it simply is impossible to increase national output at the rate experienced during the recovery. Sales, which cannot increase forever at the old rate, begin to increase more slowly. But as we saw in the previous section, the reduction in the rate of increase of sales is the kiss of death for investment. Even though sales continue to increase, the drop in their rate of increase means decreasing investment. And this reduction in investment sounds the death knell for the boom, since it reduces national output directly and via the multiplier. The reduction in national output means a reduction in sales, and the reduction in sales means a drastic reduction in investment, through the acceleration principle. The drastic reduction in investment means a further reduction in national output. The economy is in a recession. Everything is moving downward, with the notable exception of unemployment. People are getting nervous—including the president of the United States, the presidents of major corporations, and many average citizens.

WHY A TROUGH?

Basic Idea #25: The level of investment is related to the rate of change of output. Gross investment is likely to fall when sales begin to increase by decreasing amounts. This is one reason for a peak. Sales cannot increase forever at a non-decreasing rate because there is only a limited amount of resources in the economy. As sales begin to increase at a decreasing rate, investment falls, thus reducing NNP (via the multiplier).

Eventually, however, firms reduce their stock of capital to the point where it is in balance with their reduced sales. In other words, they go through the sort of process shown in Table 13.1 during 1983–84, when the Johnson Shoe Corporation reduced its stock of capital by refusing to replace wornout plant and equipment. At the end of this process, the stock of capital is in balance with sales. To keep this balance, firms must now replace worn-out equipment, which means an increase in gross investment. Via the multiplier, this increase in investment results in an increase in national product, which means an increase in sales. Via the acceleration principle, this increase in sales results in an increase in investment, which in turn increases national product. The economy is once again in the midst of a recovery. It is again a good time to be president of the United States, president of a major corporation, or an average citizen. As moviegoers put it, this is where we came in.

This theory, although highly simplified, provides a great many insights into the nature of business fluctuations. One aspect of the theory in particular should be noted. Business cycles are self-starting and self-terminating. Recession, trough, recovery, peak—each phase of the business cycle leads into the next. This theory shows that one need not look outside the economic system for causes of the upper and lower turning points—that is, the points where the economy begins to turn down after a recovery or begins to turn up after a recession. These turning points can occur for the reasons we have just indicated.

The Role of Expectations

Firms' expectations concerning their future sales and profits vary a great deal from one phase to another of the business cycle. For example, in the

273

recession of 1974–75, businesses' expectations became decidedly more pessimistic. Capital spending was cut by over $15 billion and inventory investment by over $17 billion.

Firms' expectations play a significant role in amplifying business fluctuations. Decisions made at any point in time depend on expectations concerning the future. For example, when a firm builds a new warehouse, it has certain expectations concerning the extent of its sales in the future, the price it will have to pay for labor and transportation, and so on. In forming their expectations, business executives often tend to follow the leader. As more and more business executives and analysts predict a rosy future, others tend to jump on the bandwagon. This means that, as the economy advances from a trough, optimistic expectations concerning sales and profits tend to spread, slowly at first, then more and more rapidly. These expectations generate investment, which in turn increases national output. Thus the rosy expectations are self-fulfilling, at least up to a point. (In this area, even if "wishing won't make it so," expecting may turn the trick!) The result is that the expansion is fueled by self-fulfilling and self-augmenting expectations.

Eventually, however, these expectations are not fulfilled, perhaps because full-employment ceilings cause national output to grow at a slower rate, perhaps because the government cuts back its spending (as in 1953–54), perhaps for some other reason. Now the process goes into reverse. Pessimistic expectations appear; and as national output begins to decline, these expectations spread more and more rapidly. These expectations also tend to be self-fulfilling. Business executives, feeling that the outlook for sales and profits is unfavorable, cut back on their investing, which in turn reduces national output. Thus the recession is made more serious by the epidemic of gloom. In any theory of business fluctuations, it is necessary to recognize the importance of self-fulfilling expectations.

The Effect of Innovations and Random External Events

Let's turn now to a different sort of explanation of business fluctuations. The acceleration principle is only one factor influencing gross investment. Since a firm will invest in any project where the returns exceed the costs involved, many investment projects are not triggered by changes in sales. For example, a new product may be invented, and large investments may be required to produce, distribute, and market it. Consider the computer industry. It took big investments to launch the personal computers that are becoming so common in offices and homes.

TIMING OF INNOVATIONS

Major innovations do not occur every day. Neither do they occur at a constant rate. There are more in some years than in others, and sheer chance influences the number of innovations in a given year. Similarly, chance greatly influences the timing of many other types of events that bear on the level of output and investment. These include crop failures, hurricanes, and other such natural disasters, as well as man-made events,

Ragnar Frisch

like strikes in major industries and financial panics, which also affect output and investment.

Let's suppose that these events—innovations and other occurrences that have a major effect on investment—occur more or less at random. Because so many factors influence the timing of each such event, we cannot predict how many will occur in a particular year. Instead, the number is subject to chance variation, like the number thrown in a dice game or the number of spades in a poker hand. In particular, suppose that the chance that one of these events occurs in one year is about the same as in another year.

EFFECTS OF RANDOM SHOCKS

If this is the case, economists—led by Norway's Nobel laureate, Ragnar Frisch—have shown that business cycles are likely to result. The basic idea is that the economy, because of its internal structure, is like a pendulum or rocking chair. *If it is subjected to random shocks—like pushing a rocking chair every now and then—it will move up and down.* These **random shocks** are the bursts of investment that arise as a consequence of a great new invention or of the development of a major new deposit of a vital resource like oil, or for some other such reason. These bursts play the role of the forces hitting the pendulum or the rocking chair. To a considerable extent, they may be due to nonecomomic events or forces, but whatever their cause, they bang into the economy and shove it in one direction or another.

Of course, the occurrence of these shocks is not the whole story. *Business fluctuations in this model do not occur only because of the random events that affect investment. In addition, the economy must respond to—and amplify—the effects of these stimuli.* The economy must be like a rocking chair, not a sofa. (If you whack a sofa every now and then, you are likely to hurt your hand, but not to move the sofa much.) Frisch showed that the economy is likely to respond to, and amplify, these shocks. This model explains the fact, stressed in a previous section, that although cycles bear some family resemblance, no two are really alike. Thus the model has the advantage of not explaining more than it should. It does not imply that business fluctuations are more uniform and predictable than they are.

This theory provides valuable insight into the nature of business fluctuations. Like the theory of the interaction of the acceleration principle and the multiplier, it contains important elements of truth, although it obviously is highly simplified. Each of these theories focuses on factors that may be partly responsible for business fluctuations. They complement one another, in the sense that both processes—the interaction of the multiplier and the acceleration principle, and the random external stimuli to investment—may be at work. There is no need to choose between these theories. Both help to explain business fluctuations, and both are far from the whole truth.

Inventory Cycles

The "minor" or "short" business cycle, lasting about two to four years, is sometimes called an *inventory cycle* because it is often due largely to variations in inventories. This cycle proceeds as follows. Firms, having let their inventories decline during a business slowdown, find that they are short of inventories. They increase their inventories, which means that they produce more than they sell. This investment in inventories has a stimulating effect on national output. So long as the rate of increase of their sales holds up, firms continue to increase their inventories at this rate.[3] Thus inventory investment continues to stimulate the economy. But when their sales begin to increase more slowly, firms begin to cut back on their inventory investment. This reduction in inventory investment has a depressing effect on national output. As their sales decrease, firms cut back again on their inventory investment, further damping national output. Then when inventories are cut to the bone, the process starts all over again.

As an illustration, consider the recession of 1974–75. During the fourth quarter of 1974, inventories were still increasing at an annual rate of about $10 billion. Then because of a drop in sales, firms found themselves with excess inventories. They cut back their orders from suppliers, which in turn had to reduce output and employment. Inventories were reduced at an annual rate of about $20 billion during early 1975. This inventory liquidation played a major role in the recession. Production plummeted. Fortunately, the reduction in inventories all but ceased in the second half of 1975, and production and employment picked up.

Variation in Government Spending

It should not be assumed that business fluctuations are solely or necessarily due to the behavior of the private sector. Particularly during and after wars, government spending has sometimes been a major destabilizing force. Figure 13.2 shows the great bulge in government spending during World War II and the lesser bulges during the Korean War and Vietnam War. These increases in spending produced strong inflationary pressures. The price level rose over 50 percent during 1940–46 (World War II), and major inflationary spurts also occurred during the wars in Korea and Vietnam.

Government spending has been a destabilizing force after, as well as during, wars. The recession in 1953–54 was caused primarily by the reduction in government expenditures when the Korean War came to a close. When hostilities terminated, government expenditures were reduced by more than $10 billion. Government spending sometimes has also had the same destabilizing effect in other than wartime or postwar situations. The recession in 1957–58 was aggravated by a drop in defense expenditures in late 1957. Faced with this drop, the defense contractors cut their inventories and expenditures for plant and equipment.

---

[3] As noted above, the acceleration effect discussed in previous sections applies to inventories as well as to plant and equipment, since firms often try to maintain inventories equal to a certain percentage of sales. Thus the amount by which sales increase will affect the rate of investment in inventories as well as plant and equipment.

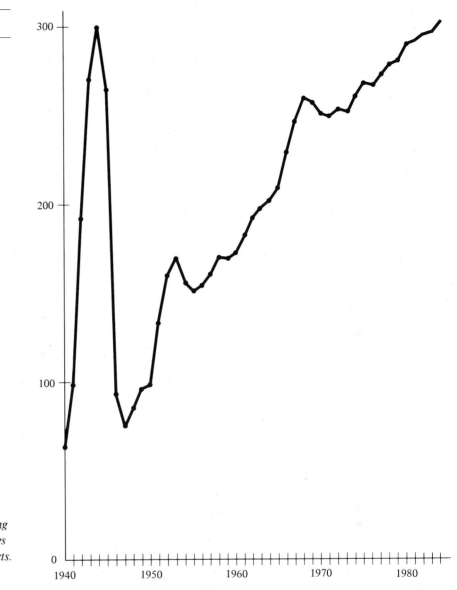

Figure 13.2
Government Purchases of Goods and Services, United States, 1940–84
Clearly, government expenditures have varied considerably from year to year. Note the big increase in spending during World War II and the smaller increases during the Korean and Vietnam conflicts.

The Political Business Cycle

Still another explanation of business fluctuations is based on the so-called political business cycle. According to a number of prominent economists, some business fluctuations, rather than being due to instability of spending by the private sector or to wartime or postwar changes in government expenditures, are caused by politicians' use of fiscal (and monetary) policy for their own political ends. As stressed in the previous chapter, economic policy in the United States is inextricably intertwined with politics, so it would not be surprising if politicians tried to use economic policy to further their own objectives.

According to economists who have studied these political business cycles, the scenario runs roughly as follows. To begin with, a year or two before the election, the incumbent president (and congressmen and senators whose eyes are fixed on the election) promotes an expansionary fiscal policy. Government expenditures are increased; taxes are cut. Also, the president may do his best to get the Federal Reserve to increase the money supply at a relatively rapid rate. Because of all this economic stimulus, the economy is in an expansion when the election comes around. The unemployment rate is relatively low—or at least, it is falling. People's money incomes are rising. The voters are put in a mood to return the incumbents to office.

After the election, the inflationary impact of the expansionary economic policy becomes evident. If the economy was reasonably close to full employment when it was stimulated in this way, much of the increase in spending is likely to result in inflation, not higher real output. But in the short run, the effect on production and employment is much greater than the effect on the price level. Thus the inflationary effects of the expansionary pre-election fiscal (and monetary) policies become evident only after the election.

Not too long after the election, the president and Congress, faced with public outcries about the accelerated rate of inflation, assume an anti-inflationary posture. They cut back on the rate of increase of government spending and, if necessary, increase taxes. Also, the Federal Reserve is likely to reduce the rate of growth of the money supply. The result is a recession—but the incumbents are likely to call it a "slowdown," a "pause," or a "readjustment." After the recession has reduced the inflationary pressures, the stage is set for the process to start all over again, since it is close to a year or two before the next presidential election.

This description of the political business cycle is clearly oversimplified. For one thing, it is not easy for the president (or anyone else) to predict the timing of the effects of an expansionary policy. Yet this simple model seems to contain a certain amount of truth, both in the United States and in other countries. During election years, the American economy has been much more likely to be expanding than slowing down. Moreover, the available evidence seems to indicate that this is true in a wide variety of other democracies around the world. It appears unlikely that this difference in economic conditions between election and nonelection years could be due to chance.

Monetary Factors

Finally, we must stress that *monetary factors are of great importance in causing business fluctuations.* By monetary factors we mean the rate at which the money supply grows, the rate of interest, and the availability of credit. As noted above, the Federal Reserve has major powers over these factors in the United States. In Chapter 16, we shall see that these factors figured significantly in slowing down the boom of the late 1960s and in reducing inflationary pressures during the mid-1970s and the early and mid-

1980s. These factors are so important that we shall devote the next several chapters entirely to them. In economics as in other aspects of life, money counts.

Can Business Fluctuations Be Avoided?

Now that we have looked at some theories designed to explain business fluctuations, we are led to ask whether these fluctuations can be avoided in the future. To some extent, a discussion of this question is premature, since we have not yet taken up monetary policy. But there is no reason to postpone answering it in general terms, waiting for subsequent chapters to provide more detailed discussions of various aspects of the answer.

On the basis of our increased knowledge of the reasons for business fluctuations and the growing acceptance of modern monetary and fiscal policy, some people have suggested that the business cycle can be licked. That is, they have felt that the government, if it makes proper use of monetary and fiscal policy, can head off a recession or a boom, and in this way offset the processes and events that destabilize the economy. This is a rather optimistic view, although the evidence does indicate that we have been able to reduce the severity and frequency of major recessions in recent years. Our record in this regard seems to have been better than in pre-World-War-II days, although the 1973–75 and 1981–82 recessions were rather severe.

Does this mean that a major depression—like that experienced in the 1930s—is impossible? The answer is no. Even though we now know how to prevent a depression, one could still occur through stupidity or some weird sequence of events. *But the probability of such a depression is very small,* given our automatic stabilizers and the fact that policy makers—and the electorate—know now that fiscal policy and monetary policy can be used to push the economy toward full employment.

There is every reason to expect, however, that the small recessions—the "dips" and "pauses"—will continue. There will be ups and downs in spending on plant and equipment, there will be fluctuations in inventories, there will be military build-ups and cutbacks, and changes in government spending and in tax rates. All these things can be destabilizing, and existing economic knowledge is not sufficiently precise to allow policy makers to iron out the resulting small deviations of national output from its long-term upward trend. *Although there has been a certain amount of optimistic talk about "fine-tuning" of the economy, the truth is that we lack the knowledge or the means to do it.*

Finally, the prospect for inflation is troublesome. The recent record of the United States has not been particularly encouraging. Serious inflationary pressures have arisen whenever the economy has gotten reasonably close to full employment. *To a considerable extent, federal policy makers have felt it necessary to engineer recessions (or "slowdowns," as they frequently are termed in Washington) to curb these pressures.* This is a very difficult problem, and an important one, which we shall discuss in much greater detail in Chapters 14, 16, 17, and 18.

Test Yourself

1. Suppose that a firm requires $3 in capital for every $1 of its sales. Suppose that none of its capital ever wears out, and that it had $450,000 in capital at the end of 1980. Its sales in subsequent years were as follows:

Year	Sales (dollars)
1981	150,000
1982	180,000
1983	210,000
1984	220,000
1985	225,000
1986	220,000

How much did the firm invest each year?

2. Describe how the multiplier and acceleration principle can interact to result in business fluctuations. Be sure to explain why the amount of investment depends on the rate of change of sales.

3. In a recent recession, the Conference Board reported the results of its latest consumer survey, which indicated that consumers' expectations concerning the economic future turned considerably more optimistic. How might this change in expectations help to pull the economy out of the recession occurring then? (*Hint:* Intentions to buy autos and appliances moved higher.)

4. "The government itself is frequently the cause of business fluctuations." Comment and evaluate.

Can Business Fluctuations Be Forecasted?

How useful are modern economic theories in forecasting NNP? This is a perfectly reasonable question. After all, when you study solid state physics, you expect to come away with certain principles that will enable you to predict physical phenomena—for example, the effects of small but controlled amounts of impurities on the properties of metal. To the extent that economics is a science, you have a right to expect the same thing, since an acid test of any science is how well it predicts.

This question is also of great practical importance. Government officials are enormously interested in what NNP is likely to be in the next year or so, since they must try to anticipate whether excessive unemployment or serious inflationary pressures are developing. Business executives are equally interested, since their firms' sales, profits, and needs for equipment depend on NNP. For these reasons, forecasting is one of the principal jobs of economists in government and industry.

FORECASTING, NO EXACT SCIENCE

The first thing that must be said is that, *in forecasting as in most other areas, economics is not an exact science.* If economists tell you they can predict exactly what NNP will be next year, you can be pretty sure that they are talking through their hats. Of course, by luck, they may be able to predict correctly, but lucky guesses do not a science make. However, although economic forecasting is not perfectly accurate, economic forecasts are still useful. Since governments, firms, and private individuals must continually make decisions that hinge on what they expect will happen, there is no way that they can avoid making forecasts, explicit or implicit. The only question is how best to make them.

There is considerable evidence that, *even though forecasts based on economic models are sometimes not very good, they are better—on the average—than those made by noneconomists.* There is no substitute for economic analysis in accurate forecasting over the long haul. This really isn't very surprising. It would be strange if economists, whose profession it is to study and predict economic phenomena, were to do worse than those without this training—even if the others are tycoons or politicians. Further, it would be strange if government and industry were to hire platoons of economists at fancy prices—which they do—if they couldn't predict any better than anyone else.

Economists have no single method for forecasting NNP or GNP. They vary in their approaches just as physicians, for example, differ in theirs. But reputable economists tend to use one of a small number of forecasting techniques, each of which is described below. Of course, many economists do not restrict themselves to one technique, but rely on a combination of several, using one to check on another.

Leading Indicators

Perhaps the simplest way to forecast business fluctuations is to use **leading indicators,** which are certain economic series that typically go down or up before national output does. The National Bureau of Economic Research, founded by Wesley C. Mitchell (1874–1948), has carried out detailed and painstaking research to examine the behavior of various economic variables over a long period of time, in some cases as long as 100 years. The Bureau has attempted to find out whether each variable goes down before, at, or after the peak of the business cycle, and whether it turns up before, at, or after the trough. Variables that go down before the peak and up before the trough are called *leading series.* Variables that go down at the peak and up at the trough are called *coincident series.* And those that go down after the peak and up after the trough are called *lagging series.*

It is worthwhile examining the kinds of variables that fall into each of these three categories, since they give us important facts concerning the anatomy of the cycle. According to the Bureau, *some important leading series are business failures, new orders for durable goods, average work week, building contracts, stock prices, certain wholesale prices, and new incorporations.* These are the variables that tend to turn down before the peak and turn up before the trough.[4] Coincident series include employment, industrial production, corporate profits, and gross national product, among many others. Some typical lagging series are retail sales, manufacturers' inventories, and personal income.

HOW LEADING INDICATORS ARE USED, AND WITH WHAT SUCCESS

Economists sometimes use leading series as forecasting devices. There are good economic reasons why these series turn down before a peak or up

---

[4] Of course, business failures turn *up* before the peak and *down* before the trough.

before a trough. In some cases, they indicate changes in spending in strategic areas of the economy, while in others they indicate changes in business executives' and investors' expectations. Both to guide the government in determining its economic policies and to guide firms in their planning, it is important to try to spot turning points—peaks and troughs—in advance. This, of course, is the toughest part of economic forecasting. Economists sometimes use these leading indicators as evidence that a turning point is about to occur. *If a large number of leading indicators turn down, this is viewed as a sign of a coming peak. If a large number turn up, this is thought to signal an impending trough.* The Department of Commerce publishes a composite index that is a weighted average of twelve leading indicators, such as those listed in the previous paragraph. The behavior of this index is shown in Figure 13.3.

Unfortunately, the leading indicators are not very reliable. It is true that the economy has seldom turned down in recent years without a warning from these indicators. This is fine. But unfortunately these indicators have turned down on a number of occasions—1952 and 1962, for example—when the economy did not turn down subsequently. Thus they sometimes provide false signals. Also, in periods of expansion, they sometimes turn down too long before the real peak. And in periods of recession, they sometimes turn up only a very short while before the trough, so that they give us little notice of the impending turning point. Nonetheless, these indicators are not worthless. They are watched closely and used to supplement other, more sophisticated forecasting techniques.

Figure 13.3

Leading Indicators and Real GNP, United States, 1950–84 *Both GNP and the composite index of leading indicators are plotted against time, the scales of the two series being constructed so that they can readily be compared. As you can see, the leading indicators often give warnings of impending troughs or peaks. But sometimes they herald troughs or peaks that never occur.*

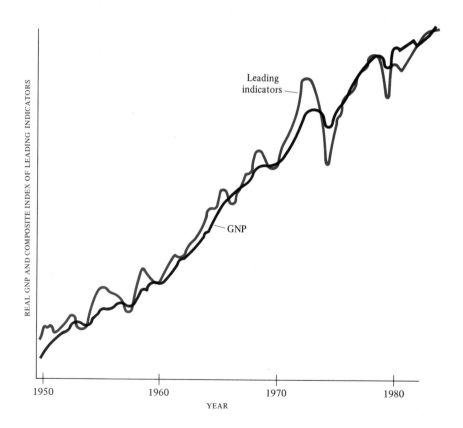

Simple Aggregate Models

Leading indicators are used primarily to spot turning points—peaks and troughs. They are of little or no use in predicting GNP (or NNP). To forecast GNP, we need a more sophisticated approach, one more firmly rooted in economic theory. (Leading indicators are largely the product of strictly empirical analysis.) To forecast GNP, it is worthwhile bringing into play the theory we described in Chapters 10–12. After all, if the theory is any good, it should help us to forecast GNP. This theory can be used in a variety of ways to help prepare such forecasts, and a first course in economics can provide no more than the most basic introduction to these methods.

A SIMPLE APPROACH

One simple way of trying to forecast GNP is to treat certain components of total spending as given and to use these components to forecast the total. This method is sometimes used by the president's Council of Economic Advisers, among others. For example, suppose that we decide to forecast investment spending and government expenditures as a first step, after which we will use these forecasts to predict GNP.[5] As we know from Chapter 7, investment spending is made up of three parts: expenditures on plant and equipment, residential construction, and changes in inventories. *To forecast expenditures on plant and equipment, the results of surveys of firms' expenditure plans for the next year are helpful.* The Department of Commerce and the Securities and Exchange Commission send out questionnaires (at the beginning of each year) to a large number of firms, asking them how much they plan to spend on plant and equipment during the year. The results, which appear in March in the *Survey of Current Business* (a Department of Commerce publication), are pretty accurate. For example, the average error in 1951–63 was only about 3 percent.

These surveys can help us forecast business expenditures on plant and equipment, but what about the other parts of investment spending—residential construction and changes in inventories? Lots of techniques are used to forecast them. *Some people use construction contracts and similar indicators as the basis for forecasts of residential construction. For inventory changes, some people watch surveys (like those that have been carried out by* Fortune *magazine and the Commerce Department) which ask companies about their inventory plans.*

Next, we need a forecast of government expenditures. At the federal level, it is possible to forecast government expenditures on the basis of the president's proposed budget or Congress's appropriations (although these forecasts can sometimes be quite wrong, as in the case of the Vietnam build-up when expenditures were higher than expected). At the state and local level, it is often possible to extrapolate spending levels reasonably well.

---

[5] We continue to ignore net exports in this part of the book because they are quite small. Chapters 32–33 will study them in some detail.

HOW CAN GNP BE FORECASTED?

Suppose that, having studied as many relevant factors as we can, we finally conclude that in our best estimate investment spending plus government expenditure will equal $600 billion next year. How do we go from this estimate to an estimate of GNP? Suppose that consumers in the past have devoted about 90 percent of their disposable income to consumption expenditure, and that disposable income has been about 70 percent of GNP. Assuming that this will also be true again next year, it follows that consumption expenditure will equal 63 percent (90 percent times 70 percent) of GNP. In other words,

$$C = .63Y, \tag{13.1}$$

where C is consumption expenditure and Y is GNP. Also, by definition,

$$Y = C + I + G,$$

where I is gross private investment and G is government expenditure. Since $I + G = 600$, it follows that

$$Y = C + 600. \tag{13.2}$$

Substituting the right-hand side of Equation (13.1) for C,

$$Y = .63Y + 600,$$

or

$$Y - .63Y = 600$$
$$.37Y = 600$$
$$Y = \frac{600}{.37}$$
$$= 1,622.$$

Thus our forecast for GNP next year is $1,622 billion.

At this point, our job may seem to be over. But it really isn't; we must check this forecast in various ways. For example, it implies that consumption expenditures next year will be $1,022 billion. (Since $C = .63Y$, according to Equation (13.1), and Y equals 1,622, C must equal 1,022.) Does this seem reasonable? For example, how does it compare with the latest results of the survey of consumer buying plans carried out at the Survey Research Center at the University of Michigan? Also, the forecasted level of GNP must be compared with the productive capacity of the economy. Do we have the physical capacity to produce this much at stable prices? To what extent will the general price level be pushed upward? Moreover, our assumptions concerning investment and government spending must be re-examined in the light of our forecast of GNP. If GNP is $1,622 billion, is it reasonable to assume that I will be the amount we initially forecasted? Or do we want to revise our forecast of investment? A great many steps must be carried out before we finally put forth a GNP forecast, if we are conscientious and professional in our approach. Moreover, even after the forecast is made, it is often updated as new information becomes available, so the process goes on more or less continuously.

Econometric Models

In recent years, more and more emphasis has been placed on econometric models. *Econometric models are systems of equations estimated from past data that are used to forecast economic variables.* Twenty years ago, econometric models were in their infancy. But now the president's Council of Economic Advisers, the Treasury, the Federal Reserve Board, and other parts of the federal government pay attention to the forecasts made by econometric models—and sometimes construct their own econometric models. Business firms too hire economists to construct econometric models for them, to forecast both GNP and their own sales.

There are many kinds of econometric models. For example, some are designed to forecast wage rates; others are designed to forecast the sales of a new product; and still others are designed to forecast a particular company's share of the market. We are concerned here only with econometric models designed to forecast GNP.

The essence of any econometric model is that it blends theory and measurement. It is not merely a general, nonquantitative theory. Useful as such a theory may be, it does not in general permit quantitative or numerical forecasts. Nor is an econometric model a purely empirical result based on little or no theoretical underpinning. Although such results may also be useful, they generally are untrustworthy once the basic structure of the economic situation changes. Most econometric models designed to forecast GNP are built, at least in part, on the theoretical foundations described in previous chapters. In other words, they contain a number of equations, one of which is designed to explain consumption expenditures, one to explain investment expenditures, and so forth.

LARGE ECONOMETRIC MODELS

Econometric models, like many of the good things in life, come in various sizes. Some are composed of lots of equations; some contain only a few. Bigger models are not necessarily to be preferred to smaller ones, or vice versa. The sort of model that is best for a particular purpose depends on which one predicts best and how costly it is to operate.

In recent years, there has been a remarkable amount of activity in the economics profession here and abroad, aimed at the construction of larger econometric models, which may be able to represent the behavior of the economy in richer and more complete detail. The leading figure in the development of such models has been Nobel Laureate Lawrence Klein of the University of Pennsylvania. The principal model that he has constructed—or helped to construct—is known as the Wharton model.

The original Wharton model, published in 1967, contained about 50 equations: 3 equations that explain various components of consumer spending (consumer nondurable goods, automobiles, and other consumer durable goods), 6 equations to explain various components of private investment (expenditure on plant and equipment, residential housing, and inventory changes), 4 explaining depreciation, 4 explaining tax receipts and transfer payments, 5 explaining the level of output in various sectors of the economy, 7 explaining price level changes in various sectors of the economy, and other equations explaining hours worked, wage rates, unemployment, interest rates, profits, and other variables. This model was used to make quarterly forecasts of GNP, unemployment, changes in the price level, and other variables a year or more ahead. It was also used to forecast the effects on the economy of alternate government policies—for example, to estimate the effects of changes in tax rates on GNP and unemployment. Its forecasts were watched closely and publicized widely in the business community and in government. In recent years, the Wharton model has been extended and refined in numerous ways. It currently contains hundreds of equations.

Other large econometric models have been built by Data Resources, Inc., Chase Econometrics, Evans Economics, the University of Michigan, UCLA, and the Bureau of Economic Analyses of the Department of Commerce, among others.

THE NUTS AND BOLTS OF A SMALL ECONOMETRIC MODEL (FOR THE MATHEMATICALLY INCLINED)

The best way to get a feel for the nature of an econometric model is to examine one. Let's consider a very simple model that might be used to forecast GNP. Although it is hypothetical and far smaller than most of the models in general use, it illustrates the nature of such models.[6] Our discussion in this section, while at an elementary level, requires familiarity with the idea of, and notation for, a set of equations. Readers who do not have this familiarity can skip this section without losing the thread of the argument.

There are four variables used in this model, and the symbol for each is as follows:

Y = gross national product
C = consumption expenditure
I = investment expenditure
G = government expenditure plus net exports.

All variables are measured in billions of dollars. Another symbol that must be explained is Δ, which means the change in a particular variable. For example, ΔY means "the change in Y," or, since Y is GNP, it means "the change in GNP." Still another symbol is the subscript $_{-1}$. Any variable with a subscript $_{-1}$ means the value of the variable in the preceding period. Thus a change with a subscript $_{-1}$ means a change occurring between the previous two periods. For example, ΔC_{-1} means the change in consumption expenditure between the last period and the period before. In this model, each period is six months.

Having disposed of the preliminaries, let's look at the model. The first equation explains ΔC, the change in consumption expenditure between this period and last period. According to this equation,

$$\Delta C = 2.18 + .37\Delta Y + .10\Delta C_{-1}. \tag{13.3}$$

---

[6] This model is not completely hypothetical. It is based in part on Irwin Friend and Paul Taubman, "A Short-Term Forecasting Model," *Review of Economics and Statistics,* August 1964. However, it is presented solely as a simple pedagogical device (for students with some mathematical background). It is not meant to be realistic.

In other words, the change in consumption expenditures equals 2.18 billion dollars plus .37 times the change in GNP between this period and last period plus .10 times the change in consumption expenditures between last period and the period before. It is reasonable to expect that the change in consumption will be directly related to the change in GNP. This follows from our discussion of the consumption function in Chapter 10. It is also reasonable to expect that the change in consumption between this period and the last will depend on the change in consumption between the last period and the one before. Basically the reason for this is that there is likely to be a lag in adjustment (due in part to the permanent-income hypothesis discussed in Chapter 10). The numbers in Equation (13.3), like those in all the equations in the model, are assumed to have been estimated from past data.

The second equation explains ΔI, the change in gross private investment expenditure between this period and the last period. According to data concerning past experience, suppose that

$$\Delta I = 1.50 + .13\ (\Delta Y - \Delta Y_{-1}). \tag{13.4}$$

In other words, the change in investment expenditure equals 1.50 billion dollars plus .13 times the change in the rate of change of GNP. From the acceleration principle, one would expect that investment expenditure would be directly related to the rate of change of GNP. Thus the change in investment expenditure would be expected to vary directly with the change in the rate of change of GNP.

Finally, the third equation merely states the obvious fact that the change in GNP must equal the change in consumption expenditures plus the change in gross private investment plus the change in government expenditures (plus net exports). In other words,

$$\Delta Y = \Delta C + \Delta I + \Delta G. \tag{13.5}$$

This must be true because $Y =$ consumption expenditure + gross private domestic investment + government expenditures (plus net exports). In other words, $Y = C + I + G$. Thus the change in Y must equal the sum of the changes in C, I, and G.

Econometric models—even small ones like this—are fairly complicated. It is easy to get so engrossed in the details of each equation that we lose sight of the basic purpose of the model—to forecast GNP, in this case. How can we use this model to forecast GNP? As a first step, let's substitute the right-hand side of Equation (13.3) for ΔC in Equation (13.5). Also, let's substitute the right-hand side of Equation (13.4) for ΔI in Equation (13.5). These substitutions give us an expression for ΔY. In particular,

$$\Delta Y = 2.18 + .37\Delta Y + .10\Delta C_{-1} + 1.50 + .13\Delta Y - .13\Delta Y_{-1} + \Delta G.$$

Collecting terms,

$$\Delta Y = 7.36 + .20\Delta C_{-1} - .26\Delta Y_{-1} + 2.00\Delta G. \tag{13.6}$$

This equation can be used to forecast the changes in gross national product between the *next* period and the *present* period. To do so, one must insert the appropriate values of ΔC_{-1}, ΔY_{-1}, and ΔG into Equation (13.6). For example, if the change in consumption between this period and the last period was \$1 billion, we would substitute 1 for ΔC_{-1} in Equation

(13.6). And if the change in gross national product between this period and the last period was \$2 billion, we would substitute 2 for ΔY_{-1}. When the value of each of the variables has been inserted in Equation (13.6), we are the proud possessor of a forecast of ΔY—the change in gross national product between the next period and the present period.

Econometric Forecasts: The Track Record

GOOD PERFORMANCE DURING THE SIXTIES

How well can econometric models forecast? Table 13.2 compares the success of the Wharton model, the Friend-Taubman model, and a model constructed at the University of Michigan's Research Seminar in Quantitative Economics in predicting GNP during 1959–67 with the forecasts of the Council of Economic Advisers and a composite forecast of GNP from about 50 economists which is tabulated each year by the Federal Reserve Bank of Philadelphia. With the exception of the Friend-Taubman model, these forecasts were made at the end of the previous year. The Friend-Taubman forecasts were made in mid-March.

In this period, the econometric models seemed to do better than the average forecast of general economists. While the general economists were off, on the average, by about \$8 billion during the period, the econometric models were off by an average of about \$5 billion. The performance of the Wharton model in this period was particularly impressive. Its average error was only about \$3 billion—or less than ½ of 1 percent. In this ball game, that is a very fancy batting average.

Basic Idea #26: Although economic forecasts should be viewed with considerable caution, they tend to be better over the long run than forecasts made by non-economists. Leading indicators, simple aggregate models, and econometric models are all useful. The important point is that economic forecasts are neither sufficiently accurate to dispel much of the fog covering the economic future, nor so inaccurate as to be completely useless.

Table 13.2

PREDICTIVE RECORD OF SOME LEADING ECONOMIC FORECASTING TECHNIQUES, 1959–67

| | | *Error (in billions of dollars)* | | | | |
Year	Actual GNP	*Average general forecast (Federal Reserve Bank of Philadelphia)*	*Council of Economic Advisers*	*Michigan model*	*Friend-Taubman model*	*Wharton model*
1959	484	−13	—	−19	—	
1960	504	4	—	−10	—	
1961	520	− 7	—	2	—	
1962	560	4	14	4	—	1
1963	591	−11	− 6	− 6	4	1
1964	632	− 7	− 4	− 4	5	1
1965	685	−10	− 6	−14	−3	−4
1966	748	− 7	−10	− 7	—	−4
1967	790	4	6	13	—	3
Average error (1963–67)		7.8	6.4	8.8	4.0	2.8

Source: Michael Evans, *Macroeconomic Activity.* New York: Harper & Row, 1969, p. 516.

MIXED RESULTS DURING THE SEVENTIES

Before you jump to the conclusion that the problem of economic forecasting is now solved, let's turn to the predictive performance of various models in more recent years. Table 13.3 shows how well five well-known models (including those of Chase Econometrics, Data Resources, Inc., General Electric, and Wharton) forecasted the annual rate of increase of GNP during the 1970s. Clearly, these forecasts were much poorer in the mid-1970s than in the early 1970s. In particular, the average one-year forecast of the percentage change in GNP (in money terms) was off by 4.1 percentage points for the year ending in the first quarter of 1975.

An important reason for this decline in performance was the difficulty in incorporating the effects of the Arab oil embargo, the drastic oil price increase, and the high inflation rate of 1973–74 into such models. The assumption underlying any econometric model is that the basic structure of the economy—the numbers in the equations of the model—will not change much. If this assumption does not hold, the model is in trouble. After all, any econometric model is powered by past data, not magic. Another reason why the models did better during 1959–67 was that this was a period of sustained prosperity. It is easier to forecast GNP during a period when it is steadily rising (or steadily falling) than at a turning point in the business cycle, such as 1970 or 1974. Unfortunately, the turning points are often of major significance to policy makers.

After 1975, economic forecasts became significantly more accurate than in 1974. As shown in Table 13.3, the average one-year forecast of the percentage change in GNP (in money terms) was off by 2.2 percentage points for the year ending in the first quarter of 1976, by 1.7 percentage points for the year ending in the first quarter of 1977, and so on. These errors are much smaller than those for the forecasts made in 1974.

In interpreting these results, note that any forecast made by an econometric model is based on assumptions concerning the future course of government policy. Indeed, one important purpose of such forecasts is to indicate what the effects of alternative policies would be. An econometric model

Table 13.3

ERROR (IN PERCENTAGE POINTS) OF AVERAGE FORECAST BY FIVE FORECASTERS OF RATE OF INCREASE OF GNP, 1971–79

Forecast pertaining to year ending in first quarter of:	Rate of increase of GNP (in money terms)	Rate of increase of GNP (in real terms)
1971	−1.0	0.5
1972	−0.5	0.6
1973	−2.3	−1.3
1974	−0.2	3.8
1975	4.1	7.0
1976	−2.2	−3.0
1977	1.7	1.0
1978	1.8	1.7
1979	−2.3	0.1

Source: Stephen McNees, "The Forecasting Record for the 1970s," *New England Economic Review,* September 1979.

Cross-Chapter Case/Part Three

THE ECONOMIC FORECASTS OF 1984

In most respects, 1983 was a good year for the American economy. In his economic report at the beginning of 1984, President Reagan stated that: "The economy's performance in 1983 was very gratifying. . . . The 3.2 percent rise in consumer prices between 1982 and 1983 was the lowest rate of inflation since 1967. The recovery produced a sharp drop in unemployment and a substantial increase in the income of American families. . . . The 6.1 percent rise in real gross national product last year means that real annual income per person in the United States rose $700."

In its annual report, the president's Council of Economic Advisers compared the composition of the expansion in real GNP during 1983 with what has generally occurred during the first year after a postwar trough of the business cycle. The results, shown in Table 1, were reported "in terms of percentage point contributions to the total change in GNP over the four quarters of 1983. For example, real personal consumption expenditures accounted for 3.6 percentage points of the total 6.1 percent growth in real GNP; by comparison, during the first four quarters of the typical postwar recovery, personal consumption accounted for 3.6 percentage points out of the total 6.8 percent increase in real GNP. The major conclusion to be drawn from Table 1 is that the magnitude and composition of the 1983 expansion was similar in most respects to the typical first four quarters of business expansion following a cyclical trough."[1]

Table 1

CONTRIBUTION OF GNP COMPONENTS TO TOTAL GNP GROWTH OVER THE FIRST YEAR OF BUSINESS CYCLE RECOVERIES

	1982 IV to 1983 IV	Typical postwar recovery
Real GNP [percentage point change]	6.1	6.8
Personal consumption expenditures	3.6	3.6
Durable goods	1.4	1.3
Nonresidential fixed investment	1.2	.5
Producers' durable equipment	1.3	.5
Structures	−.1	.0
Residential investment	1.0	1.0
Change in business inventories	2.0	1.8
Net exports of goods and services	−1.4	−.4
Exports	.3	.0
Imports (minus denotes increase)	−1.7	−.4
Government purchases of goods and services	−.4	.3
Federal	−.5	−.2
State and local	.1	.5
Final sales	4.0	5.0

[1] Council of Economic Advisers, *Annual Report,* 1984, Washington, D.C.: Government Printing Office, p. 176.

Table 2
COUNCIL OF ECONOMIC ADVISERS' FORECASTS FOR 1984

	1983	1984 forecast
Percent change (fourth quarter to fourth quarter):		
Real gross national product	6.1	4.5
Personal consumption expenditures	5.4	2.0
Nonresidential fixed investment	11.5	9.5
Residential investment	38.2	6.0
Federal purchases	−6.0	3.7
State and local purchases	.6	4.2
GNP implicit price deflator	4.1	5.0
Compensation per hour	4.6	5.5
Output per hour	3.2	2.1
Level in fourth quarter:		
Unemployment rate (percent)	8.4	7.6
Housing starts (millions of units, annual rate)	1.7	1.8

Having reviewed economic developments in 1983, the CEA proceeded to forecast what would occur in 1984. Its forecast of the economic outlook, shown in Table 2, called for the rate of growth of real GNP to fall to about 4.5 percent in 1984, for the unemployment rate to be about 7.6 percent in the fourth quarter of 1984, and for the inflation rate to rise slightly to about 5 percent.

Other private forecasts were not vastly different. Data Resources, Inc., predicted a 4.4 percent increase in real GNP, a 7.8 percent unemployment rate, and a 5 percent inflation rate. Chase Econometrics forecasted a 4 percent increase in real GNP, an 8.1 percent unemployment rate, and a 5 percent inflation rate. Wharton Econometrics came up with a 6.6 percent increase in real GNP, a 7.8 percent unemployment rate, and a 3.9 percent inflation rate.

What actually happened? In December 1984, the U.S. Department of Commerce reported that real GNP had increased by about 6.7 percent during 1984. According to the U.S. Department of Labor, the civilian unemployment rate in November 1984 was 7.2 percent, and the Consumer Price Index in November 1984 was 4 percent higher than in November 1983.

A number of magazines and newspapers ran articles criticizing economic forecasters for their performance. *Time* magazine pointed out that most forecasts had underestimated the rate of growth of real GNP and overestimated the rate of inflation. This was true for most forecasters, but not for all. Wharton's forecasts for the year as a whole seemed quite accurate.

The most important moral to be drawn from this brief case study is that it is unrealistic to expect economic forecasters to hit the target on the nose. No reputable economist would claim that he or she could do so. Moreover, to be useful, economic forecasts frequently do not have to be very accurate. For many purposes, all that is required is a rough estimate of what will occur, a partial dissipation of the fog that surrounds the economic future.

may be more accurate in forecasting the effects of such policies than in forecasting what actually occurs. Suppose that a forecast is based on the incorrect assumption that the government is going to cut taxes. Even though this incorrect assumption may result in a poor forecast, the model may forecast the effect of such a tax cut reasonably well. That is, it may be a good forecaster of the change in GNP due to the tax cut—and this may be what policy makers are most interested in.

THE EIGHTIES AND BEYOND

Economic forecasting remains a difficult and uncertain business, as illustrated by the forecasts (made at the end of 1983) of what would occur in 1984. Most economists underestimated the rate of increase of real GNP, and overestimated the inflation rate, in the first half of the year. The result was a good deal of criticism of economic forecasters in the newspapers and popular magazines. (See the cross-chapter case on pp. 290–91.)

Nonetheless, despite the rather large errors in some recent economic forecasts, neither government nor industry can swear off forecasting. For decades, economic forecasting has played an important role in the decision-making process, both in government and industry. In recent years, President Reagan has relied on economic forecasts prepared by the Council of Economic Advisers to help him formulate policies dealing with inflation, unemployment, and a host of other topics. Presidents Eisenhower, Kennedy, Johnson, Nixon, Ford, and Carter also paid close attention to economic forecasts. So do most corporate presidents. This isn't because these forecasts are always very good. It's because they are the best available. As Thomas Huxley put it, "If a little knowledge is dangerous, who is the man who has so much as to be out of danger?"

Test Yourself

1. "What goes up must come down. There is a cycle in economic activity just as in many other things, and one can use this cycle to forecast quite accurately." Comment and evaluate.

2. A leading business magazine reports that the leading indicators "are dead on center. This suggests that, although the downward trend of business has halted, there is still no clear upward thrust." Explain what this means.

3. Suppose that consumption expenditure was $100 billion in 1983 and $105 billion in 1984, and that GNP increased by $10 billion per year from 1984 to 1989. Based on Equation (13.3), what was the value of consumption expenditure from 1985 to 1989?

4. Suppose that investment spending plus government expenditure will equal $700 billion next year, and that consumption expenditure will equal 65 percent of GNP. Forecast next year's GNP.

5. In Question 4, suppose that your estimate of investment expenditure plus government expenditure is in error by $10 billion. If your other estimates are correct how big an error will occur in your forecast of GNP?

Summary

1. Changes in sales can result in magnified or accelerated changes in investment; the amount of gross investment depends on the rate of increase of sales. The fact that sales are increasing does not insure that gross investment will increase. On the contrary, if sales are increasing by decreasing amounts, gross investment is likely to fall. This effect of sales on investment is called the acceleration principle.

2. The interaction of the acceleration principle with the multiplier can cause business cycles. Thus turning points can be generated within the economic system. Investment is also determined by many events that occur more or less at random, like innovations, wars, and so on. The effects of these random shocks can also cause business fluctuations. Many short cycles are inventory cycles. The acceleration principle also applies to inventories.

3. The government's economic activities can help to cause business fluctuations. Particularly during and after wars, government spending has sometimes been a major destabilizing force. In addition, according to a number of prominent economists, some business fluctuations have been due to politicians' use of fiscal (and monetary) policy for their own political ends.

4. Although we are not in a position to erase the small dips and pauses in economic activity, it seems extremely unlikely that we will have another depression of the severity of the 1930s. The reason is that policy makers—and the electorate—know that monetary and fiscal policy can be used to push the economy back toward full employment. However, the prospect for price stability may not be so bright.

5. Although economics is by no means an exact science, economic forecasts are useful for many purposes. This does not mean that these forecasts are always very accurate. It means only that they are better than noneconomists' forecasts. Economists have a number of techniques for forecasting. One makes use of leading indicators—variables that historically have turned up or down before GNP.

6. Another technique is based on the use of simple models plus surveys and other data. Investment and government expenditures (and net exports) are sometimes estimated as a first step. Then, using the historical relationship between consumption and GNP, it is possible to forecast GNP.

7. Still another technique is based on econometric models, which are systems of equations estimated from past data. Econometric models blend theory and measurement. Econometric models may be big or small.

8. Econometric models have frequently done better than the average forecasts of general economists. However, it is important to recognize that econometric models —like any forecasting device in the social sciences—are quite fallible, as indicated by the large errors in the 1974 forecasts.

Concepts for Review

Acceleration principle	**Expectations**	**Lagging series**
Random shocks	**Leading series**	**Econometric models**
Inventory cycle	**Coincident series**	

PART FOUR

Money, Banking, and Stabilization Policy

CHAPTER 14

Money and the Economy

According to the maxim of an ancient Roman, "Money alone sets all the world in motion." Although a statement that leaves so little room for the laws of physics or astronomy may be a mite extravagant, no one would deny the importance of money in economic affairs. The quantity of money is a very significant factor in determining the health and prosperity of any economic system. Inadequate increases in the quantity of money may bring about excessive unemployment, while excessive increases in the quantity of money may result in serious inflation. To many economists, a discussion of business fluctuations and economic stabilization that ignores the money supply is like a performance of *Hamlet* that omits the prince.

In this chapter, we are concerned with the nature and value of money, as well as with the relationship between a nation's money supply and the extent of unemployment and inflation. In particular, we consider questions like: What is money? What determines its value? What factors influence the demand for money, and what factors influence its quantity? What is the relationship between the quantity of money and the price level? What is the relationship between the quantity of money and the level of net national product? To understand the workings of our economy and the nature of our government's economic policies, you must be able to answer these questions.

What Is Money?

We begin by defining money. At first blush, it may seem natural to define it by its physical characteristics. You may be inclined to say that money consists of bills of a certain size and color with certain words and symbols printed on them, as well as coins of a certain type. But this definition would be too restrictive, since money in other societies has consisted of whale teeth, wampum, and a variety of other things. Thus it seems better to define money by its functions than by its physical characteristics. Like beauty, money is as money does.

MEDIUM OF EXCHANGE

Money acts as a medium of exchange. People exchange their goods and services for something called money, and then use this money to buy the goods and services they want. To see how important money is as a medium of exchange, let's suppose that it did not exist. To exchange the goods and services they produce for the goods and services they want to consume, people would resort to *barter*, or direct exchange. If you were a wheat farmer, you would have to go to the people who produce the meat, clothes, and other goods and services you want, and swap some of your wheat for each of these goods and services. Of course this would be a very cumbersome procedure, since it would take lots of time and effort to locate and make individual bargains with each of these people. To get some idea of the extent to which money greases the process of exchange in any highly developed economy, consider all the purchases your family made last year—cheese from Wisconsin and France, automobiles from Detroit, oil from Texas and the Middle East, books from New York, and thousands of other items from all over the world. Imagine how few of these exchanges would have been feasible without money.

STANDARD OF VALUE, STORE OF VALUE

Money acts as a standard of value. It is the unit in which the prices of goods and services are measured. How do we express the price of coffee or tea or shirts or suits? In dollars and cents. Thus money prices tell us the rates at which goods and services can be exchanged. If the money price of a shirt is $30 and the money price of a tie is $10, a shirt will exchange for 3 ties. Put differently, a shirt will be "worth" 3 times as much as a tie.

Money acts as a store of value. A person can hold on to money and use it to buy things later. You often hear stories about people who hoard a lot of money under their mattresses or bury it in their back yards. These people have an overdeveloped appreciation of the role of money as a store of value. But even those of us who are less miserly use this function of money when we carry some money with us, and keep some in the bank to make future purchases.

Finally, it should be recognized that money is a social invention. It is easy to assume that money has always existed, but this is not the case. Someone had to get the idea, and people had to come to accept it. Nor has money always had the characteristics it has today. In ancient Greece and Rome, money consisted of gold and silver coins. By the end of the seventeenth century, paper money was established in England; but this paper currency, unlike today's currency, could be exchanged for a stipulated amount of gold. Only recently has the transition been made to money that is not convertible into a fixed amount of gold or silver. But regardless of its form or characteristics, anything that is a medium of exchange, a standard of value, and a store of value is money.

The Money Supply, Narrowly Defined

In practice, it is not easy to draw a hard-and-fast line between what is money and what is not money, for reasons discussed below. But everyone agrees that coins, currency, demand deposits, and other checkable deposits are money. And the sum total of coins, currency, demand deposits, and other checkable deposits is called the money supply, narrowly defined.[1]

COINS AND CURRENCY

Coins are a small proportion of the total quantity of money in the United States. This is mainly because coins come in such small denominations. It takes a small mountain of pennies, nickels, dimes, quarters, and half-dollars to make even a billion dollars. Of course, the metal in each of these coins is worth less than the face value of the coin; otherwise people would melt them down and make money by selling the metal. In the 1960s, when silver prices rose, the government stopped using silver in dimes and quarters to prevent coins from meeting this fate.

Currency—paper money like the $5 and $10 bills everyone likes to have on hand—constitutes a second and far larger share of the total money supply than coins. Together, currency and coins outstanding totaled about $159 billion in 1984, as shown in Table 14.1. The Federal Reserve System, described in the next chapter, issues practically all of our currency in the form of Federal Reserve notes. Before 1933, it was possible to exchange currency for a stipulated amount of gold, but this is no longer the case. (The price of gold on the free market varies; thus the amount of gold one can get for a dollar varies too.) All American currency (and coin) is presently "fiat" money. It is money because the government says so and because the people accept it. There is no metallic backing of the currency anymore. But this does not mean that we should be suspicious of the soundness of our currency, since gold backing is not what gives money its value. (In fact, to some extent, cause and effect work the other way. The use of gold to back currencies has in the past increased the value of gold.) Basically, the value of currency depends on its acceptability by people. And the government, to insure its acceptability, must limit its quantity.

DEMAND DEPOSITS AND OTHER CHECKABLE DEPOSITS

Demand deposits—bank deposits subject to payment on demand—are the third part of the narrowly defined money supply. They are much larger than the other two parts, as shown in Table 14.1. At first you may question whether these demand deposits—or checking accounts, as they are commonly called—are money at all. In everyday speech, they often are not considered money. But economists include demand deposits as part of the money supply, and for good reason. After all, you can pay for goods and

Table 14.1
MONEY SUPPLY, NOVEMBER 1984

	Amount (billions of dollars)
Demand deposits	248
Currency and coins[a]	159
Other checkable deposits[b]	142
Travelers checks[c]	5
Total[d]	553

[a] Only currency and coins outside bank vaults (and the Treasury and Federal Reserve) are included.
[b] Includes ATS and NOW balances at all institutions, credit union, share draft, and other minor items.
[c] See footnote 1.
[d] Because of rounding errors, figures do not sum to total.

[1] In addition, travelers checks are included in the money supply, narrowly defined, since one can pay for goods and services about as easily with travelers checks as with cash. As indicated in Table 14.1, travelers checks are only about 1 percent of the money supply, narrowly defined. Since they are so small a percentage of the money supply, we ignore them in the following discussion.

297

services just as easily by check as with cash. Indeed, the public pays for more things by check than with cash. This means that checking accounts are just as much a medium of exchange—and just as much a standard of value and a store of value—as cash. Thus, since they perform all of the functions of money, they should be included as money.

Other checkable deposits include negotiable order of withdrawal (NOW) accounts and other accounts that are very close to being demand deposits. A *NOW account* is essentially an interest-bearing checking account at banks, savings banks and other thrift institutions. First created in 1972 by a Massachusetts savings bank, such accounts became legal in more and more states, particularly in the northeast. In 1980, Congress passed a financial reform act that permitted federally chartered thrift institutions to have NOW accounts. Banking innovations like NOW accounts have blurred the distinction between checking and savings accounts. Since many savings and loan associations, mutual savings banks, and credit unions are now providing accounts against which checks can be drawn, it would make no sense to include as money only demand deposits in commercial banks. Instead, all such checkable deposits are included.

Figure 14.1 shows how the narrowly defined money supply—the sum total of coins, paper currency, demand deposits, and other checkable deposits—has behaved since World War II. You can see that the quantity of

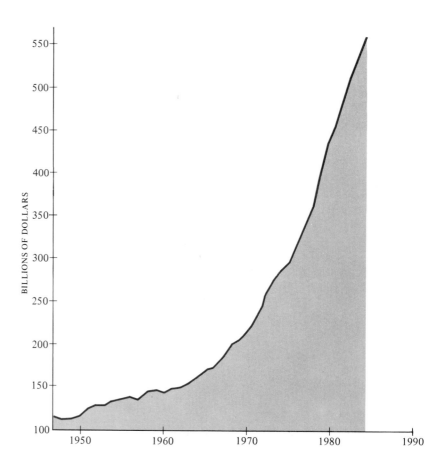

Figure 14.1

Behavior of Money Supply (Narrowly Defined), United States, 1947–84 *The money supply, about $550 billion in 1984, has generally increased from year to year, but the rate of increase has by no means been constant.*

money has generally increased from one year to the next, and that the increase has been at an average rate of about 4 or 5 percent per year. However, the rate of increase of the quantity of money has by no means been constant. In some years, like 1983, the quantity of money increased by about 9 percent; in others, like 1975, it increased by about 4 percent. A great deal will be said later about the importance and determinants of changes in the quantity of money.

The Money Supply, Broadly Defined

The narrowly defined money supply (which includes coins, currency, demand deposits, and other checkable deposits) is not the only definition of the money supply that is used by economists. There is also the money supply, broadly defined, which includes savings and small time deposits (deposits under $100,000 with a specific maturity, for example, one year) and money market mutual fund balances and money market deposit accounts, as well as coins, currency, demand deposits, and other checkable deposits. The money supply, narrowly defined, is often called M-1, while the money supply, broadly defined, is often called M-2.

The traditional reason for excluding time and saving deposits from the narrow definition of money has been that, in most instances, you could not pay for anything with them. For example, suppose that you had a savings account at a commercial bank. You could not draw a check against it, as you could with a demand deposit. And to withdraw your money from the account, you might have to give the bank a certain amount of notice (although in practice this right might be waived and the bank would ordinarily let you withdraw your money when you desired). Nonetheless, since this savings account could so readily be transformed into cash, it was almost like a checking account. Not quite, but almost.

Besides time and savings accounts, many other assets can also be transformed into cash without much difficulty—though not quite as easily as time and savings deposits. For example, it is not difficult to convert government bonds into cash. There is no way to draw a hard-and-fast dividing line between money and nonmoney, since many assets have some of the characteristics of money. Consequently, there are still other definitions of the money supply that are more inclusive than M-2. But most economists feel that, although assets like government bonds have some of the properties of money, it would be stretching things too far to include them in the money supply. (For one thing, their price varies as interest rates change.)

Economists call such assets **near-money,** and recognize that the amount of near-money in the economy has an important effect on spending habits. There is some disagreement among economists as to exactly what is and what isn't near-money, but this needn't concern us here. The major point we want to make is that any dividing line between money and nonmoney must be arbitrary.

In this book, we shall use the narrow definition, M-1, when we refer to the money supply. But it should be recognized that the choice is arbitrary.

Fortunately, our results will not depend in any very important way on this decision.

The Value of Money

Let's go back to one very important point that was mentioned briefly in a previous section. There is no gold backing for our money. In other words, there is no way that you can exchange a $10 bill for so many ounces of gold. (If you look at a $10 bill, you will see that it says nothing about what the government will give you in exchange for it.) Currency and demand (and other checkable) deposits are really just debts, or IOUs. Currency is the debt of the government, while demand deposits are the debts of the banks. Intrinsically, neither currency nor deposits have any real value. A $10 bill is merely a small piece of paper, and a deposit is merely an entry in a bank's accounts. And, as we have seen, even coins are worth far less as metal than their monetary value.

All this may make you feel a bit uncomfortable. After all, if our coins, currency, demand deposits, and other checkable deposits have little or no intrinsic value, doesn't this mean that they can easily become worthless? To answer this question, we must realize that basically, *money has value because people will accept it in payment for goods and services.* If your university will accept your check in payment for your tuition, and your grocer will accept a $20 bill in payment for your groceries, your demand deposit and your currency have value. You can exchange them for goods and services you want. And your university or your grocer accepts this money only because they have confidence that they can spend it for goods and services they want.

MONEY'S VALUE DEPENDS ON THE PRICE LEVEL

Thus money is valuable because it will buy things. But how valuable is it? For example, how valuable is $1? Clearly, *the value of a dollar is equivalent to what a dollar will buy. And what a dollar will buy depends on the price level.* If all prices doubled, the value of a dollar would be cut in half, because a dollar would be able to buy only half as many goods and services as it formerly could. On the other hand, if all prices were reduced by 50 percent, the value of a dollar would double, because a dollar would be able to buy twice as many goods and services as it formerly could. You often hear people say that today's dollar is worth only $.50. What they mean is that it will buy only half what a dollar could buy at some specified date in the past.

It is interesting and important to see how the value of the dollar, as measured by its purchasing power, has varied over time. Figure 14.2 shows how an index of the price level in the United States has changed since 1779. Over time, prices have fluctuated sharply, and the greatest fluctuations have resulted from wars. For example, the price level fell sharply after the Revolutionary War, and our next war–the War of 1812—sent prices skyrocketing, after which there was another postwar drop in prices. The period from about 1820 to about 1860 was marked by

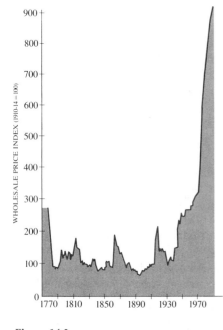

Figure 14.2

Index of Wholesale Prices, United States, 1779–1984 (1910–14 = 100) The price level has fluctuated considerably, sharp increases generally occurring during wars. Since World War II, the price level has tended to go only one way—up. In the past 20 years, the price level has more than tripled.

relative price stability, but the Civil War resulted in an upward burst followed by a postwar drop in prices. After a period of relative price stability from 1875 to 1915, there was a doubling of prices during World War I and the usual postwar drop. World War II saw an increase of about 40 percent, but there was no postwar drop in prices. Instead there has been a very sharp inflation. During the past 20 years, the price level has more than tripled.

The value of money is inversely related to the price level. In inflationary times, the value of money decreases; the opposite is true when the price level falls (an infrequent phenomenon in the past three decades). Thus the wartime periods when the price level rose greatly were periods when the value of the dollar decreased greatly. The doubling of prices during World War I meant that the value of the dollar was chopped in half. Similarly, the postwar periods when the price level fell greatly were periods when the value of the dollar increased. The 50 percent decline in prices after the Civil War meant a doubling in the value of the dollar. Given the extent of the variation of the price level shown in Figure 14.2, it is clear that the value of the dollar has varied enormously during our history.

Inflation and the Quantity of Money

As we have pointed out repeatedly, the value of money is reduced in periods of inflation. In runaway inflation, its value can be largely wiped out, as in Germany after World War I. (Recall Chapter 8.) Our own country suffered from runaway inflations during the Revolutionary War and the Civil War. You may have heard the expression that something is "not worth a continental." It comes from the fact that the inflated dollars in use during the Revolutionary War were called continentals.

Generally, such severe inflations have occurred because the government increased the money supply at an enormously rapid rate. It is not hard to see why a tremendous increase in the quantity of money will result in a runaway inflation. Other things held constant, increases in the quantity of money will result in increases in total intended spending, and once full employment is achieved, such increases in intended spending will cause more and more inflation.

Eventually, when the inflation is severe enough, households and businesses may refuse to accept money for goods and services because they fear that it will depreciate significantly before they have a chance to spend it. Instead, they may insist on being paid in merchandise or services. Thus the economy will turn to barter, with the accompanying inconveniences and inefficiency.

To prevent such an economic catastrophe, the government must manage the money supply responsibly. As we have stressed in previous sections, the value of money depends basically on the public's willingness to accept it, and the public's willingness to accept it depends on money's being reasonably stable in value. If the government increases the quantity of money at a rapid rate, thus causing a severe inflation and an accompanying precipitous fall in the value of money, public confidence in money will be shaken, and the value of money will be destroyed. The moral is *clear: the government must restrict the quantity of money, and conduct its economic policies so as to maintain a reasonably stable value of money.*

Unemployment and the Quantity of Money

In the previous section, we were concerned primarily with what happens when the quantity of money grows too rapidly. As we have seen, the result is inflation. But this is only part of the story. The quantity of money can grow too slowly as well as too rapidly; and when this happens the result is increased unemployment. If the money supply grows very slowly, or decreases, there will be a tendency for total intended spending to grow very slowly or decrease. This in turn will cause national output to grow very slowly or decrease, thus causing unemployment to increase. The result will be the social waste and human misery associated with excessive unemployment.

According to many economists, the recession of 1974–75 was due partly to an inadequate growth of the money supply. The Federal Reserve, trying to stem the inflationary tide in 1974, cut back on the rate of increase of the money supply. Looking back over past business fluctuations, it appears that an inadequate rate of increase in the quantity of money was responsible, at least in part, for many recessions. According to Harvard's James Duesenberry, "Every major depression has been accompanied by a substantial decline in the money supply, and often by a complete collapse of the banking system. Among the many causes responsible for our major depressions, money and banking difficulties have always been prominent."[2] Recall that in our discussion of business fluctuations in the previous chapter, we stressed the importance of monetary factors. In this chapter, as well as Chapters 15 to 18, we will study these factors in detail.

Determinants of the Quantity of Money

Judging from our discussion thus far, it is clear that to avoid excessive unemployment or excessive inflation, the quantity of money must not grow too slowly or too fast. But what determines the quantity of money? When the United States was on the gold standard, the amount of money in circulation was determined by the amount of monetary gold in the country. When gold flowed into the country, the money supply increased; when it flowed out, the money supply decreased. This is no longer the case, since we are no longer on the gold standard—and neither is any other major nation.

If gold doesn't determine the amount of money in circulation in the U.S., what does? The answer is that the supply of money is determined to a considerable degree by the Federal Reserve, which, as we have noted before, is our nation's central bank. Within limits, the Federal Reserve can and does control the quantity of money. But to some extent the private sector of the

[2] J. Duesenberry, *Money and Credit: Impact and Control,* Englewood Cliffs, N.J.: Prentice-Hall, 1972, p. 3.

economy also determines the quantity of money. For example, the nation's commercial banks, through their lending (and other) decisions, can influence the money supply.[3] In the remainder of this chapter, we shall make the simplifying assumption that the money supply is governed solely by the Federal Reserve. In the following chapter, we shall see how the commercial banks also play an important role in this regard.

The Demand for Money

We have discussed in general terms how changes in the quantity of money affect the tempo of economic activity. Now let's look in detail at how changes in the quantity of money affect net national product. The first step in doing this is to discuss the demand for money. Why does a family or firm want to hold money? Certainly, a family can be wealthy without holding much money, since virtually all of their wealth is tied up in factories, farms, and other nonmonetary assets. Unlike assets that yield profits or interest, money produces no direct return; so why do people and firms want to hold money, rather than other kinds of assets? Two of the most important reasons are the following.

1. Transactions Demand for Money. To carry out most transactions, money is required. Thus people and firms like to keep some money on their person and in their checking accounts to buy things. The higher a person's income—in dollars, not real terms—the more money he or she will want to hold for transaction purposes. For example, in 1985, when a doctor makes about $90,000 a year, the average physician will want to keep more money on hand for transactions purposes than in the days—many years ago—when a doctor made perhaps $10,000 a year. Because the quantity of money demanded by a household or firm increases with its income, it follows that the total quantity of money demanded for transactions purposes in the economy as a whole is directly related to net national product. That is, the higher (lower) the level of NNP, the greater (less) the quantity of money demanded for transactions purposes.

2. Precautionary Demand for Money. Besides the transactions motive, households and firms like to hold money because they are uncertain concerning the timing and size of future disbursements and receipts. Unpredictable events often require money. People get sick, and houses need repairs. Also, receipts frequently do not come in exactly when expected. To meet such contingencies, people and firms like to put a certain amount of their wealth into money and near-money. In the economy as a whole, the total quantity of money demanded for precautionary purposes (like the quantity demanded for transactions purposes) is likely to vary directly with NNP. If NNP goes up, households and firms will want to hold more money for pre-

---

[3] Of course, banks do not create money all by themselves. The public's preferences and actions, as well as bank behavior, influence the amount of demand deposits. Also, commercial banks may not be as unique in this respect as it appears at first sight. See James Tobin, "Commercial Banks as Creators of Money" in R. Teigen, ed., *Readings in Money, National Income, and Stabilization Policy,* 4th ed., Homewood, Ill.: Irwin, 1978.

cautionary purposes, because their incomes and sales will be higher than before the increase in NNP.[4]

THE INTEREST RATE AND THE DEMAND CURVE FOR MONEY

Up to this point, we have discussed why individuals and firms want to hold money. But we must recognize that there are disadvantages, as well

[4] Still another motive for holding money is the speculative motive. People like to hold some of their assets in a form in which they can be sure of its monetary value and can take advantage of future price reductions. The amount of money individuals and firms will keep on hand for speculative reasons will vary with their expectation concerning future price movements. In particular, if people feel that the prices of bonds and stocks are about to drop soon, they are likely to demand a great deal of money for speculative reasons. By holding money, they can obtain such securities at lower prices than at present.

Example 14.1   Empirical Evidence Regarding the Demand for Money

In 1973, Stephen Goldfeld of Princeton University made a study of the factors influencing the demand for money.[*] He found that a 1 percent increase in real GNP or a 1 percent increase in interest rates had the following effect on the real quantity of money demanded (that is, the quantity of money demanded divided by the price level):

	Effect of 1 percent increase in real GNP (percent)	*Effect of 1 percent increase in interest rate (percent)*
Short run	+0.19	−0.045
Long run	+0.68	−0.160

(a) The short-run effects are the effects after three months; the long-run effects are the effects after a few years. Why are the effects in the long run greater than in the short run? (b) If real GNP increases by 10 percent, what is the effect on the real quantity of money demanded in the long run? (c) If the interest rate increases from 8 percent to 10 percent, what is the effect on the real quantity of money demanded in the short run? (d) Goldfeld also found that the quantity of money demanded is proportional to the price level. Why do you think that this is the case?

SOLUTION

(a) Because it takes time for households and business firms to recognize and adapt to changing conditions. In the short run, they tend to be locked in to existing patterns of behavior, and it takes time to adjust. (b) The real quantity of money demanded will increase by about 6.8 percent. (c) Since the interest rate increases by 25 percent (from 8 to 10 percent), the real quantity of money demanded will fall by about 25 × .045, or 1.125 percent. (d) People demand money to pay for things. As the price level goes up, they require more money to pay for the same things. In other words, as the price level goes up, more money is demanded in order to have the same purchasing power as before.

[*] Stephen Goldfeld, "The Demand for Money Revisited," *Brookings Papers on Economic Activity,* 1973. For simplicity, only his results concerning the interest rate for time deposits are included. Also, see R. Dornbusch and S. Fisher, *Macroeconomics,* New York: McGraw-Hill, 1978.

---

as advantages, in holding money. One is that the real value of money will fall if inflation occurs. Another is that an important cost of holding money is the interest or profit one loses, since instead of holding money, one might have invested it in assets that would have yielded interest or profit. For example, the annual cost of holding $5,000 in money if one can obtain 6 percent on existing investments, is $300, the amount of interest or profit forgone.

With NNP constant, the amount of money demanded by individuals and firms is *inversely* related to the interest rate. *The higher the interest rate, the smaller the amount of money demanded. The lower the interest rate, the greater the amount of money demanded.* This is because the cost of holding money increases as the interest rate or yield on existing investments increases. For example, if the interest rate were 7 percent rather than 6 percent, the cost of holding $5,000 in money for one year would be $350 rather than $300. Thus, as the interest rate or profit rate increases, people try harder to minimize the amount of money they hold. So do firms. Big corporations like IBM or U.S. Steel are very conscious of the cost of holding cash balances.

Figure 14.3 summarizes two important conclusions of our discussion in this and the previous section. Panel A of Figure 14.3 shows that, *holding the interest rate constant, the quantity of money demanded is directly related to NNP.* As we explained in the previous section, the higher (lower) the level of NNP, the greater (less) the quantity of money demanded. Panel B of Figure 14.3 shows that, *with NNP constant, the quantity of money demanded is inversely related to the interest rate.*[5] This latter relationship, described in this section, is called the **demand curve for money.**

Figure 14.3

The Demand for Money   *Holding the interest rate constant, the quantity of money demanded is* directly *related to NNP, as shown in panel A. Holding NNP constant, the quantity of money demanded is* inversely *related to the interest rate, as shown in panel B. The latter relationship is known as the demand curve for money.*

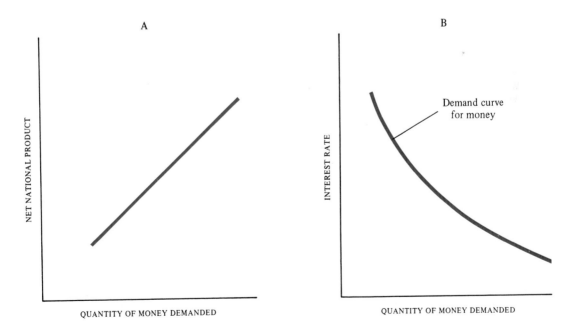

A

B

NET NATIONAL PRODUCT

INTEREST RATE

Demand curve for money

QUANTITY OF MONEY DEMANDED

QUANTITY OF MONEY DEMANDED

[5] However, this relationship between the quantity of money and the interest rate is only short-run. In the long run, increases in the money supply, if they result in increased inflation, may *raise* interest rates, because lenders will require a greater return to offset the greater rate of depreciation of the real value of the dollar. Still, however, the real rate of interest—the rate of interest adjusted for inflation—may decline.

Test Yourself

Changes in the Money Supply and National Output

EFFECTS OF AN INCREASE IN THE MONEY SUPPLY: THE KEYNESIAN MODEL

Now that we have investigated the demand for money, we are ready to show how changes in the quantity of money influence the value of NNP. Given the demand curve for money, it is a simple matter to show how the money supply can be inserted into the Keynesian model (in Chapters 10 to 12) aimed at explaining the level of NNP.

To begin with, let's trace the effects of an increase in the money supply from $200 billion to $250 billion. If the demand curve for money is as shown in panel A of Figure 14.4, the result will be a *decrease in the interest rate* from 8 percent to 6 percent. Why? Because, if the interest rate is 8 percent, people will demand only $200 billion of money, not the $250 billion that is supplied. Having more money on hand than they want, they will invest the excess in bonds, stocks, and other financial assets, with the result that the price of bonds, stocks, and other financial assets will rise.[6]

Such a rise in the price of bonds is equivalent to a fall in the rate of interest. (To see why, suppose that a very long-term bond pays interest of $300 per year. If the price of the bond is $3,000, the interest rate on the bond is 10 percent. If the price of the bond rises to $4,000, the interest rate on the bond falls to 7½ percent. Thus the increase in price amounts to a reduction in the interest rate.) When the interest rate has fallen to 6 percent, people will be willing to hold the $250 billion in money. At this interest rate, the quantity of money demanded will equal the quantity of money supplied.

The decrease in the interest rate from 8 percent to 6 percent affects the investment function.[7] Recall from Chapter 10 that the level of investment is inversely related to the interest rate. Because it is less costly to invest—and

---

[6] For simplicity, we assume that when people have excess money balances, they use the money to buy financial assets. (In the next section, we assume that when people have smaller money balances than they want, they sell financial assets to get more money.) A more complete analysis is provided in Chapter 17 and in Appendix A of this book. The results are essentially the same as those provided here.

[7] Changes in the money supply, interest rates, and credit availability affect the consumption function and government spending, as well as the investment function. For example, *increases (decreases) in interest rates shift the consumption function and the level of government spending*

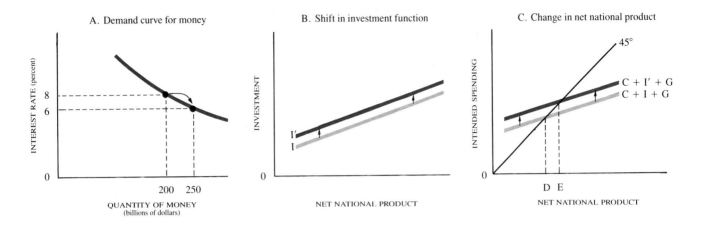

A. Demand curve for money

INTEREST RATE (percent)

8
6

0

200 250

QUANTITY OF MONEY
(billions of dollars)

B. Shift in investment function

INVESTMENT

0

I'
I

NET NATIONAL PRODUCT

C. Change in net national product

INTENDED SPENDING

45°

C + I' + G
C + I + G

0

D E

NET NATIONAL PRODUCT

Figure 14.4

Effect of an Increase in the Money Supply *If the money supply increases from $200 billion to $250 billion, the interest rate drops from 8 percent to 6 percent (panel A). Because of the decrease in the interest rate, the investment function shifts upward (panel B), and the equilibrium level of NNP increases from D to E (panel C).*

because credit is more readily available[8]—*the investment function will shift upward,* as shown in panel B of Figure 14.4. This occurs because at each level of net national product, firms will want to invest more, since investment is more profitable (because of the cut in the interest rate) and funds are more readily available.[9]

This shift in the investment function then affects the equilibrium level of net national product. As shown in panel C of Figure 14.4, *the equilibrium level of net national product will increase* from *D* to *E,* in accord with the principles discussed in Chapter 12. (Recall that the equilibrium value of NNP is at the point where the *C + I + G* line intersects the 45-degree line.) Thus *the effect of the increase in the money supply is to increase net national product.*

This, in simplified fashion, is how an increase in the money supply affects NNP, according to the Keynesian model.[10] To summarize, *the increase in the money supply results in a reduction in the interest rate, which results in an increase in investment, which results in an increase in NNP.* Obviously, this theory is of great importance in helping us to understand more completely why our economy behaves the way it does. For example, we can now understand better why vast increases in the quantity of money will result in runaway inflation. NNP (in money terms) will be pushed upward at a very rapid rate, driving the price level out of sight.

downward (upward). These factors augment the effect of monetary policy described in the text. We focus attention on the investment function in Figures 14.4 and 14.5 merely because this simplifies the exposition.

[8] Note that it is not just a matter of interest rates. Availability of credit is also important. In times when money is tight, some potential borrowers may find that they cannot get a loan, regardless of what interest rate they are prepared to pay. In times when money is easy, people who otherwise might find it difficult to get a loan may be granted one by the banks. To repeat, both availability and interest rates are important.

[9] Many firms depend to a considerable extent on retained earnings to finance their investment projects. Thus, since they do not borrow externally, the effect on their investment plans of changes in interest rates and credit availability may be reduced. However, since changes in the interest rate reflect changes in the opportunity cost of using funds to finance investment projects, they still may have an appreciable effect on the investment function.

[10] The alert reader will recognize that the increase in NNP in panel C will shift the demand curve for money in panel A of Figure 14.4. For simplicity, we ignore this feedback. It is included in the more complete model presented in Appendix A.

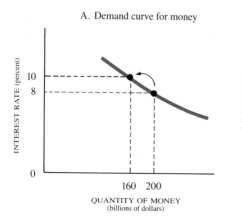

A. Demand curve for money

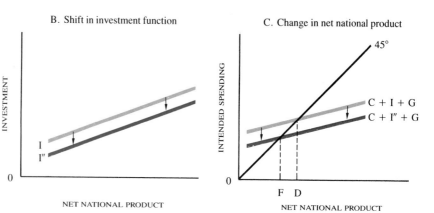

B. Shift in investment function

C. Change in net national product

Figure 14.5

Effect of a Decrease in the Money Supply *If the money supply decreases from $200 billion to $160 billion, the interest rate increases from 8 percent to 10 percent (panel A). Because of the increase in the interest rate, the investment function shifts downward (panel B) and the equilibrium level of NNP decreases from D to F (panel C).*

Basic Idea #27: Increases in the quantity of money tend to increase NNP; decreases in the quantity of money tend to decrease NNP. According to the simple Keynesian model, changes in the quantity of money influence the interest rate which in turn affects investment which in turn affects NNP.

EFFECTS OF A DECREASE IN THE MONEY SUPPLY: THE KEYNESIAN MODEL

Next, let's trace the effects of a decrease in the money supply from $200 billion to $160 billion. If the demand curve for money is as shown in panel A of Figure 14.5, the result will be an *increase in the interest rate* from 8 percent to 10 percent. Why? Because, if the interest rate is 8 percent, people will demand $200 billion in money, not the $160 billion that is supplied. Having less money on hand than they want, they will sell some of their bonds, stocks, and other financial assets to build up their money balances, with the result that the prices of bonds, stocks, and other financial assets will fall. *Such a fall in the price of bonds is equivalent to a rise in the rate of interest.* (To see why, suppose that a very long-term bond pays interest of $300 per year. If the price of the bond is $3,000, the interest rate on the bond is 10 percent. If the price of the bond falls to $2,400, the interest rate on the bond is 12½ percent. Thus the fall in price amounts to an increase in the interest rate). When the interest rate has increased to 10 percent, people will be willing to hold only the $160 billion in money. At this interest rate, the quantity of money demanded will equal the quantity of money supplied.

The increase in the interest rate from 8 percent to 10 percent affects the investment function. Because it is more costly for firms to invest—and more difficult to obtain credit—*the investment function will shift downward,* as shown in panel B of Figure 14.5. This shift occurs because, at every level of net national product, firms want to invest less. The reasons why an increase in the interest rate reduces investment were given in detail in Chapter 10.

This downward shift in the investment function has an effect in turn on the equilibrium level of net national product. As shown in panel C of Figure 14.5, *the equilibrium level of net national product will decrease from D to F* (since the equilibrium level of NNP is at the point where the C + I + G line intersects the 45-degree line). Thus *the effect of the decrease in the money supply is to decrease net national product.*

This, in simplified fashion, is how a decrease in the money supply affects NNP, according to the Keynesian model.[11] To summarize, *the decrease in the money supply results in an increase in the interest rate, which results in a decrease in investment, which results in a decrease in NNP.* This theory helps to explain, among other things, why an inadequate rate of growth of the money supply can lead to excessive unemployment. If the money supply is too small, NNP will not reach its potential level (that is, its full-employment level).[12]

The Monetarists

Some prominent economists, led by Milton Friedman of Stanford University's Hoover Institution, have expressed disagreement with the models in the previous section. They have formulated a different view of the way in which the quantity of money affects NNP. Since their criticisms of Keynesian economics have extended to many topics besides the way in which the quantity of money affects NNP, we must postpone a complete discussion of their controversies with the Keynesians to Chapter 17. All that we take up in this chapter is their view concerning the effects of the quantity of money on NNP.

These economists share a point of view called monetarism; hence they are called monetarists. It is not easy to summarize the differences between the monetarists and the Keynesians because all monetarists do not agree on all aspects of their theory, and neither do all Keynesians agree on all aspects of theirs. Consequently, not all monetarists disagree in the same way with all Keynesians. Equally important, the differences between the monetarists and the Keynesians have tended to change over time. As we shall see in Chapter 17, many of the points of disagreement during the 1950s and 1960s have become less important in the 1970s and 1980s, as one side or the other has changed its position or as economic conditions have changed. (Because of revisions in the Keynesian view, the Keynesians are often called neo-Keynesians.)

The differences between the monetarists and Keynesians lie in at least two areas. First, the monetarists couch their theory in a different set of concepts than the Keynesians. Rather than use the theory set forth in Chapters 10 and 12, they use the so-called quantity theory of money, which is described below. Although this theory employs different concepts than those used above, it is important to recognize at the outset that these concepts are not irreconcilable. One can translate a monetarist model into

Milton Friedman

---

[11] For simplicity, we ignore the fact that the decrease in NNP in panel C will shift the demand curve for money in panel A of Figure 14.5. Feedback of this sort is included in the more complete model presented in Appendix A.

[12] Harking back to Chapter 9, we are in a better position to understand now why the aggregate demand curve slopes downward and to the right. An increase in the price level increases the transactions demand for money because the average money cost of each transaction tends to go up. Thus the demand curve for money shifts to the right, with the result that the interest rate increases. As indicated in this section, the higher interest rate results in reduced spending on output. Thus there is an inverse relationship between the price level and aggregate demand.

Keynesian concepts or translate a Keynesian model into monetarist concepts. Second, the monetarists have hypothesized that certain central relationships, such as the demand curve for money, have a somewhat different shape than posited by the Keynesians. Differences of this sort are empirical matters, which can be adjudicated (at least in principle) by an appeal to facts.

Monetarists regard the rate of growth of the money supply as the principal determinant of nominal NNP. (**Nominal NNP** means NNP in money, not real terms. In other words, nominal NNP is NNP measured in current, not constant, dollars.) Some monetarists have gone so far as to say that fiscal policy, although it will alter the composition of net national product, may have little or no long-run effect on the size of nominal NNP unless it influences the money supply. This latter view, explained in more detail in Chapter 17, is not now accepted by most economists.

The monetarists have had a great impact on economic thought in the postwar period, even though theirs remains a minority view. Professor Friedman's most severe critics admit that his research in this area (which helped win him a Nobel prize) has been pathbreaking and extremely important. According to his findings,

> the rate of change of the money supply shows well-marked cycles that match closely those in economic activity in general and precede the latter by a long interval. On the average, the rate of change of the money supply has reached its peak nearly 16 months before the peak in general business and has reached its trough over 12 months before the trough in general business.[13]

Clearly, findings of this sort must be taken seriously. Moreover, research carried out at the Federal Reserve Bank of St. Louis showed a close relationship between short-run changes in the quantity of money and short-run changes in NNP. Based on this relationship, the St. Louis Bank has constructed some simple econometric models that have had some success in forecasting NNP. Although criticized on various grounds, these results have also strengthened the hand of the monetarists.

The Velocity of Money

As noted above, the monetarists have revived interest in the so-called quantity theory of money, which was developed many years ago by such titans of economics as Alfred Marshall of Cambridge and Irving Fisher at Yale. To understand this theory, it is useful to begin by defining a new term: the velocity of circulation of money. The **velocity of circulation of money** is the rate at which the money supply is used to make transactions for final goods and services. That is, it equals the average number of times per year that a dollar is used to buy the final goods and services produced

[13] Milton Friedman, testimony before the Joint Economic Committee, "The Relationship of Prices to Economic Stability and Growth," 85th Congress, 2d Session, 1958.

by the economy. In other words,

$$V = \frac{NNP}{M},$$ (14.1)

where V is velocity, NNP is the nominal net national product, and M is the money supply. For example, if our nominal net national product is $1 trillion and our money supply is $200 billion, the velocity of circulation of money is 5, which means that, on the average, each dollar of our money consummates $5 worth of purchases of net national product.

Nominal net national product can be expressed as the product of real net national product and the price level. In other words,

$$NNP = P \times Q,$$ (14.2)

where P is the price level—the average price at which final goods and services are sold—and Q is net national product in real terms. For example, suppose that national output in real terms consists of 200 tons of steel. If the price of a ton of steel is $100, then nominal NNP equals $P \times Q$, or 100×200, or $20,000.[14]

If we substitute $P \times Q$ for NNP in Equation (14.1), we have

$$V = \frac{P \times Q}{M}.$$ (14.3)

That is, velocity equals the price level *(P)* times the real NNP *(Q)* divided by the money supply *(M)*. This is another way to define the velocity of circulation of money—a way that will prove very useful.

Irving Fisher

The Equation of Exchange

Now that we have a definition of the velocity of circulation of money, our next step is to present the so-called equation of exchange. The *equation of exchange* is really nothing more than a restatement, in somewhat different form, of our definition of the velocity of circulation of money. To obtain the equation of exchange, all we have to do is multiply both sides of Equation (14.3) by M. The result is

$$MV = PQ.$$ (14.4)

To understand exactly what this equation means, let's look more closely at each side. *The right-hand side equals the amount received for final goods and services during the period,* because Q is the output of final goods and services during the period and P is their average price. Thus the product of P and Q must equal the total amount received for final goods and services during the period—or nominal NNP. For example, if national output in real terms equals 200 tons of steel, and if the price of a ton of steel is $100, then 100×200—that is, $P \times Q$—must equal the total amount received for final goods and services during the period.

---

[14] Since real NNP is measured here in physical units (tons), P is the price level. If real NNP has been measured in constant dollars, P would have been a price index. In either event, our conclusions would be basically the same.

The left-hand side of Equation (14.4) equals the total amount spent on final goods and services during the period. Why? Because the left-hand side equals the money supply—M— times the average number of times during the period that a dollar was spent on final goods and services—V. Consequently, $M \times V$ must equal the amount spent on final goods and services during the period. For example, if the money supply equals $10,000 and velocity equals 2, the total amount spent on final goods and services during the period must equal $10,000 $\times$ 2, or $20,000.

Thus, since the *amount received for* final goods and services during the period must equal the *amount spent on* final goods and services during the period, the left-hand side must equal the right-hand side.

The equation of exchange—Equation (14.4)—is what logicians call a tautology. It holds by definition. Yet it is not useless. On the contrary, economists regard the equation of exchange as very valuable, because it sets forth some of the fundamental factors that influence NNP and the price level. This equation has been used by economists for many years. It is the basis for the crude quantity theory of money used by the classical economists, as well as the recent theories put forth by the monetarists.

The Crude Quantity Theory of Money and Prices

The classical economists discussed in Chapter 8 assumed that both V and Q were constant. They believed that V was constant because it was determined by the population's stable habits of holding money, and they believed that Q would remain constant at its full employment value.[15] On the basis of these assumptions, they propounded the *crude quantity theory* of money and prices, a theory that received a great deal of attention and exerted considerable influence in its day.

If these assumptions hold, it follows from the equation of exchange—Equation (14.4)—that the price level *(P)* must be proportional to the money supply *(M)*, because V and Q have been assumed to be constant. (In the short run, the full-employment level of real net national product will not change much.) Thus we can rewrite Equation (14.4) as

$$P = \left(\frac{V}{Q}\right)M, \tag{14.5}$$

where *(V/Q)* is a constant. So P must be proportional to M if these assumptions hold.

The conclusion reached by the crude quantity theorists—namely, *that the price level will be proportional to the money supply*—is very important, if true. To see how they came to this conclusion, one must recognize that they stressed the transaction motive for holding money. Recall from an earlier section that, based on this motive, one would expect the quantity of money demanded to be directly related to the level of nominal NNP. Further, the demand for money was assumed to be stable, and little or no

---

[15] In some cases, they did not really assume continual full employment. Instead, they were concerned with the long-run changes in the economy and compared the peaks of the business cycle, where full employment frequently occurs.

attention was paid to the effect of the interest rate on the demand for money. Indeed, the crude quantity theorists went so far as to assume that the quantity of money demanded was *proportional* to the level of nominal NNP. This amounted to assuming that velocity was constant.

Suppose there is a 10 percent increase in the quantity of money. Why would the crude quantity theorists predict a 10 percent increase in the price level? To begin with, they would assert that, since the quantity of money has increased relative to the value of nominal NNP, households and firms now hold more money than they want to hold. Further, they would argue that households and firms will spend their excess money balances on commodities and services, and that the resulting increase in total intended spending will increase the nominal value, but not the real value of NNP (since full employment is assumed). In other words, the increase in aggregate demand will bid up prices. More specifically, they would argue that prices will continue to be bid up until they have increased by 10 percent, since only then will the nominal value of NNP be big enough so that households and firms will be content to hold the new quantity of money.

EVALUATION OF THE CRUDE QUANTITY THEORY

The crude quantity theory is true to its name: it is only a crude approximation to reality. One important weakness is its assumption that velocity is constant. Another is its assumption that the economy is always at full employment, which we know from previous chapters to be far from true. But despite its limitations, the crude quantity theory points to a very important truth. If the government finances its expenditures by an enormous increase in the money supply, the result will be drastic inflation. For example, if the money supply is increased tenfold, there will be a marked increase in the price level. If we take the crude quantity theory at face value, we would expect a tenfold increase in the price level; but that is a case of spurious accuracy. Perhaps the price level will go up only eightfold. Perhaps it will go up twelvefold. The important thing is that it will go up a lot.

There is a great deal of evidence to show that the crude quantity theory is a useful predictor during periods of runaway inflation, such as in Germany after World War I. The German inflation occurred because the German government printed and spent large bundles of additional money. You often hear people warn of the dangers in this country of the government's "resorting to the printing presses" and flooding the country with a vast increase in the money supply. It is a danger in any country. And one great value of the crude quantity theory is that it predicts correctly what will occur as a consequence—rapid inflation.

There is also considerable evidence that the crude quantity theory works reasonably well in predicting long-term trends in the price level. For example, during the sixteenth and seventeenth centuries, gold and silver were imported by the Spanish from the New World, resulting in a great increase in the money supply. The crude quantity theory would predict a great increase in the price level, and this is what occurred. Or consider the period during the nineteenth century, when the discovery of gold in the United States, South Africa, and Canada brought about a considerable

Basic Idea #28: If the quantity of money increases by a very large percentage, the price level is likely to increase greatly as well. According to the crude quantity theory, the price level is expected to increase by the same percentage as the quantity of money, since real NNP and velocity are assumed to be constant. Whether or not this is true, the important point is that severe inflation is likely to occur under these circumstances.

increase in the money supply. As the crude quantity theory would lead us to expect, the price level rose considerably as a consequence.

A More Sophisticated Version of the Quantity Theory

The crude quantity theory was based on two simplifying assumptions, both of which are questionable. One assumption was that real net national product *(Q)* remains fixed at its full-employment level. The other was that the velocity of circulation of money *(V)* remains constant. A more sophisticated version of the quantity theory can be derived by relaxing the first assumption. This version of the quantity theory recognizes that the economy is often at less than full employment and consequently that real net national product *(Q)* may vary a good deal for this reason.

So long as velocity remains constant, the equation of exchange—Equation (14.4)—can be used to determine the relationship between net national product in current dollars and *M,* even if *Q* is allowed to vary. On the basis of the equation of exchange, it is obvious that $P \times Q$ should be proportional to *M,* if the velocity of circulation of money *(V)* remains constant. Since $P \times Q$ is the nominal net national product, it follows that, if this assumption holds, *the nominal net national product should be proportional to the money supply.* In other words,

$$\text{NNP} = aM, \tag{14.6}$$

where NNP is the nominal net national product and *V* is assumed to equal a constant—*a.* Thus, if the money supply increases by 10 percent, the nominal value of NNP should increase by 10 percent. If the money supply increases by 20 percent, the nominal value of NNP should increase by 20 percent. And so forth.

If velocity is constant, this version of the quantity theory should enable us to predict nominal net national product if we know the money supply. Also, if velocity is constant, this version of the quantity theory should enable us to control nominal net national product by controlling the money supply. Clearly, if velocity is constant, Equation (14.6) is an extremely important economic relationship—one that will go a long way toward accomplishing the goals of Chapters 10 to 13, which were to show how net national product could be forecasted and controlled. But is velocity constant? Since Equation (14.6) is based on this assumption, we must find out.

Figure 14.6 shows hows the velocity of circulation of money has behaved since 1920.[16] Obviously velocity has not been constant. But on the other hand, it has not varied enormously. Excluding the war years, it has generally been between 2.5 and 6.5 in the United States. It has changed rather slowly, although it has varied a good deal over the business cycle. Velocity tends to decrease during depressions and increase during booms. *All in all, one must conclude from Figure 14.6 that, although velocity has not varied*

[16] The velocity figures in Figure 14.6 are based on gross national product, not net national product. But for present purposes, this makes little real difference.

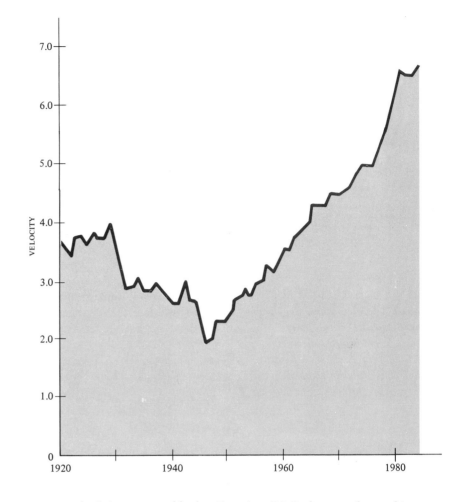

Figure 14.6
Velocity of Circulation of Money, United States, 1920–84 *The velocity of circulation of money has generally been between 2.5 and 6.5, except during World War II.*

enormously, it is not so stable that Equation (14.6) alone can be used in any precise way to forecast or control net national product.[17]

However, this does not mean that Equation (14.6) is useless, or that the more sophisticated quantity theory is without value. On the contrary, this version of the quantity theory points out a very important truth, which is that *the money supply has an important effect on net national product (in money terms). Increases in the quantity of money are likely to increase nominal NNP, while decreases in the quantity of money are likely to decrease nominal NNP.* Because velocity is not constant, the relationship between the money supply and net national product is not as neat and simple as that predicted by Equation (14.6), but there is a relationship—as shown in Figure 14.7.

Going a step further, sophisticated monetarists often relax the assumption that V is constant, and assert that it is possible to predict V as a function of other variables, like the frequency with which people are paid, the level of business confidence, and the cost of holding money (the interest rate). According to some economists, one of Friedman's major con-

[17] It is important to note that the velocity figures in Figure 14.6 are based on the narrow definition of the money supply, M-1. If M-2 is used instead, velocity is more nearly constant. For example, between 1960 and 1976, velocity based on M-2 varied within a very narrow range. See Robert Gordon, *Macroeconomics,* Boston: Little Brown, 1978.

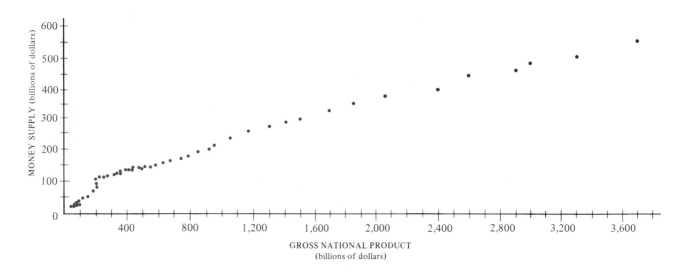

GROSS NATIONAL PRODUCT
(billions of dollars)

Figure 14.7
Relationship between Money Supply and National Product, United States, 1929–84 *There is a reasonably close relationship between the money supply and the money value of national product. As one goes up, the other tends to go up too.*

tributions was to replace the constancy of V with its predictability. Other economists feel that changes in V reflect, rather than cause, changes in NNP.

The Importance of Money

Whether one is a Keynesian using the model presented in Figures 14.4 and 14.5 or a monetarist using the more sophisticated form of quantity theory can make a considerable difference, as we shall see in Chapter 17. But it is important to underscore the fact that *the effect of the money supply on nominal NNP is qualitatively the same in both the Keynesian and monetarist models.* Whatever theory you look at, you get the same qualitative result.

Increases in the money supply would be expected to increase nominal NNP, and decreases in the money supply would be expected to decrease nominal NNP.

Furthermore, no matter which view is accepted, it would be expected that, as the economy approaches full employment, a bigger and bigger share of the increase in nominal NNP due to increases in the money supply will reflect price increases, not increases in real output. *If the economy is at considerably less than full employment, increases in the money supply would be expected to increase real NNP, while decreases in the money supply would be expected to reduce real NNP. However, once full employment is approached, increases in the money supply result more and more in increases in the price level, as distinct from increases in real NNP.*

These expectations are shared by economists of many types, which is fortunate since, as we shall see, they are important guides to the formulation of monetary policy, both here and abroad.

Test Yourself

1. If the value of NNP (in money terms) increases 10 percent and the money supply remains fixed, does velocity increase? Why or why not? What are some of the factors that might cause an increase in velocity?

2. "The history of the United States is an account of one inflation after another. The currency is being debased further and further. Soon we may experience a runaway inflation." Comment and evaluate.

3. Describe how the quantity of money influences nominal and real NNP according to (a) the Keynesian model, (b) the crude quantity theory, and (c) the more sophisticated quantity theory.

4. Suppose that a bond pays annual interest of $100 forever. What is the interest rate if its price is (a) $1,000, (b) $2,000, (c) $3,000?

Summary

1. Money performs several basic functions. It serves as a medium of exchange, a standard of value, and a store of value. The money supply, narrowly defined, is composed of coins, currency, demand deposits, and other checkable deposits. Economists include demand (and other checkable) deposits as part of the money supply because you can pay for goods and services about as easily by check as with cash.

2. Besides this narrow definition of money, broader definitions include savings and time deposits (and money market mutual fund shares). In addition, there are lots of other assets—for example, government bonds—that can be transformed without much difficulty into cash. It is not easy to draw a line between money and nonmoney, since many assets have some of the characteristics of money.

3. America's history has seen many sharp fluctuations in the price level. Generally, severe inflations have occurred because the government expanded the money supply far too rapidly. However, too small a rate of growth of the money supply can also be a mistake, resulting in excessive unemployment.

4. Most economists believe that the lower the interest rate, the greater the amount of money demanded. Thus increases in the quantity of money result in lower interest rates, which result in increased investment (and other types of spending), which results in a higher NNP. Conversely, decreases in the quantity of money result in higher interest rates, which result in decreased investment (and other types of spending), which results in a lower NNP. This is the Keynesian approach.

5. The equation of exchange is $MV = PQ$, where M is the money supply, V is velocity, P is the price level, and Q is net national product in real terms. The velocity of circulation of money is the rate at which the money supply is used to make transactions for final goods and services. Specifically, it equals NNP in money terms divided by the money supply.

6. If the velocity of circulation of money remains constant and if real net national product is fixed at its full employment level, it follows from the equation of exchange that the price level will be proportional to the money supply. This is the crude quantity theory, which is a reasonably good approximation during periods of runaway inflation, and works reasonably well in predicting long-term trends in the price level.

7. A more sophisticated version of the quantity theory recognizes that real net national product is often less than its full-employment value; consequently, Q is not fixed. Thus, if velocity remains constant, net national product in money terms should be proportional to the money supply. In fact, velocity has by no means remained stable over time. However, nominal NNP has been fairly closely related to the money supply, and the monetarists assert that velocity is predictable.

8. The monetarists, led by Milton Friedman, prefer the quantity theory over the Keynesian model. There have been many disagreements between the monetarists and the Keynesians, but both approaches agree that increases in the money supply will tend to increase nominal NNP while decreases in the money supply will tend to decrease nominal NNP.

Concepts for Review

Coins	*M*-2	**Nominal NNP**
Currency	**Near money**	**Velocity of circulation**
Demand deposits	**Time deposits**	**Equation of exchange**
Checkable deposits	**Demand curve for money**	**Crude quantity theory**
M-1		

CHAPTER 15

The Banking System and the Quantity of Money

Banking is often viewed as a colorless, dull profession whose practitioners are knee-deep in deposit slips and canceled checks. Also, when the time comes to reject a loan application, the bankers are often viewed as heartless skinflints—even if they advertise that "you have a friend at Chase Manhattan." Yet despite these notions, most people recognize the importance of the banks in our economy, perhaps because the banks deal in such an important and fascinating commodity—money.

In this chapter, we look in detail at how commercial banks operate. We begin by discussing the Federal Reserve System and the functions of commercial banks. Then we describe the nature of commercial banks' loans and investments, as well as the important concept of reserves. After looking into legal reserve requirements we go on to describe how commercial banks create money—a very important and commonly misunderstood process. Finally, we take up the effects of currency withdrawals and desired excess reserves on our results. The purpose of this chapter is to introduce you to the operations of the banking system, which is neither as colorless nor as mysterious as is sometimes assumed.

The Federal Reserve System

Any nation must exercise control over the quantity of money. In the United States, the Federal Reserve System is charged with this responsibility. The Federal Reserve System—or "Fed," as it is called by the *cognoscenti*—plays a central role in the economy as a whole. After a severe

Figure 15.1
Organization of the Federal Reserve
System *The Federal Reserve System*
contains over 5,000 commercial banks,
the 12 regional Federal Reserve Banks,
and the Board of Governors, as well as
the Federal Open Market Committee
and various advisory councils and
committees.

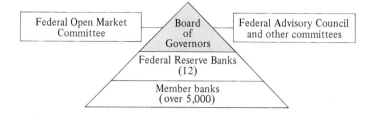

financial panic in 1907, when a great many banks failed, there was strong public pressure to do something to strengthen our banking system. At the same time, there was great fear of centralized domination of the nation's banks. The result—after six years of negotiation and discussion—was the establishment by Congress of the **Federal Reserve System** in 1913.

MEMBER BANKS

As shown in Figure 15.1, the organization of the Federal Reserve System can be viewed as a triangle. At the base are the commercial banks that belong to the system—the **member banks.** All **national banks** (so called because they receive their charters from the federal government) have to be members, and many of the larger **state banks** (chartered by the states) are members too. Member banks, which number over 5,000 out of the nation's almost 15,000 commercial banks, hold about 70 percent of the nation's demand deposits.

FEDERAL RESERVE BANKS

In the middle of the triangle in Figure 15.1 are the 12 Federal Reserve Banks, each located in a Federal Reserve district. The entire nation is divided into 12 Federal Reserve districts, with Federal Reserve Banks in New York, Chicago, Philadelphia, San Francisco, Boston, Cleveland, St. Louis, Kansas City, Atlanta, Richmond, Minneapolis, and Dallas. Each of these banks is a corporation owned by the member banks, but, despite this fact, the member banks do not in any sense act as owners of the Federal Reserve Bank in their district. Instead, each Federal Reserve Bank is a public agency. These Federal Reserve Banks act as "bankers' banks," performing much the same sorts of functions for commercial banks that commercial banks perform for the public. That is, they hold the deposits of member banks and make loans to them. In addition, as noted in previous chapters, the Federal Reserve Banks perform a function no commercial bank can perform: They issue Federal Reserve notes, which are the nation's currency.

THE BOARD OF GOVERNORS

At the top of the triangle in Figure 15.1 is the Board of Governors of the Federal Reserve System. Located in Washington, this board—generally called the Federal Reserve Board—has 7 members appointed by the president for 14-year terms. The board, which coordinates the activities of the Federal Reserve System, is supposed to be independent of partisan politics and to act to promote the nation's general economic welfare. It is responsible for supervising the operation of the money and banking system of the United States. The board is assisted in important ways by the Federal Open Market Committee, which establishes policy concerning the purchase and sale of government securities. The Federal Open Market Committee is composed of the board plus the presidents of five Federal Reserve Banks. The board is also assisted by the Federal Advisory Council, a group of 12 commercial bankers that advises the board on banking policy.

Functions of the Federal Reserve

The Federal Reserve Board, with the 12 Federal Reserve Banks, constitutes the central bank of the United States. Every major country has a central bank. England has the Bank of England, and France has the Bank of France. **Central banks** are very important organizations, whose most important function is to help control the quantity of money. One interesting feature of our central bank is that its principal allegiance is to Congress, not to the executive branch of the federal government. This came about because Congress wanted to protect the Fed from pressure by the president and the Treasury Department. Thus the Fed was supposed to be independent of the executive branch. In fact, although the Fed has sometimes locked horns with the president, it has generally cooperated with him and his administration, as we shall see in Chapter 16.

To repeat, a central bank's most important function is to control the money supply. But this is not its only function. A central bank also handles the government's own financial transactions, and coordinates and controls the country's commercial banks. Specifically, the Federal Reserve System is charged with the following responsibilities.

Member Bank Reserves. The Federal Reserve Banks hold deposits, or reserves, of the member banks. As we shall see, these reserves play an important role in the process whereby the Fed controls the quantity of money.

Check Collection. The Federal Reserve System provides facilities for check collection. In other words, it enables a bank to collect funds for checks drawn on other banks.

Currency. The Federal Reserve Banks supply the public with currency through the issuance of Federal Reserve notes.

Government Fiscal Agent. The Federal Reserve Banks act as fiscal agents for the federal government. They hold some of the checking accounts of the U.S. Treasury, and aid in the purchase and sale of government securities.

Bank Supervision. Federal Reserve Banks supervise the operation of the member commercial banks. More will be said about the nature of bank supervision and regulation later in the chapter, and much more will be said about the functions of the Federal Reserve in the next chapter.

Commercial Banks in the United States

In 1983, there were about 15,000 commercial banks in the United States. This testifies to the fact that, in contrast to countries like England, where a few banks with many branches dominate the banking scene, the United States has promoted the growth of a great many local banks. In part, this has stemmed from a traditional suspicion in this country of "big bankers." ("Eastern bankers" are a particularly suspect breed in some parts of the country.) Most of our banks are state, not national, banks. There are about 10,000 state banks, but only about 5,000 national banks.

Commercial banks have two primary functions. First, *banks hold demand deposits and permit checks to be drawn on these deposits.* This function is familiar to practically everyone. Most people have a checking account in some commercial bank, and draw checks on this account. Second, *banks lend money to industrialists, merchants, homeowners, and other individuals and firms.* At one time or another, you will probably apply for a loan to finance some project for your business or home. Indeed, it is quite possible that some of the costs of your college education are being covered by a loan to you or your parents from a commercial bank.

In addition, commercial banks perform a number of other functions, such as holding time and savings accounts. You will recall that these accounts bear interest and, although technically one must give a certain amount of notice before withdrawal, in practice they can usually be withdrawn whenever their owner likes. Commercial banks also sell money orders and traveler's checks, and handle estates and trusts. Because of their work with trusts, some banks—for example, the First Pennsylvania Bank and Trust Company, a large Philadelphia bank—include the word *trust* in their title. In addition, commercial banks rent safe-deposit boxes and provide a variety of services for customers.

Needless to say, commercial banks are not the only kind of financial institution. Mutual savings banks and savings and loan associations hold savings and time deposits and various forms of checkable deposits; "consumer finance" companies lend money to individuals; insurance companies lend money to firms and governments; "factors" provide firms with working capital; and investment bankers help firms sell their securities to the public. All these types of financial institutions play an important role in the American economy. In general, they all act as intermediaries between savers and investors; that is, they all turn over to investors money that they received from savers. As we saw in Chapter 11, this process of converting savings into investment is very important in determining net national product.[1]

THE BANK OF AMERICA: A CASE STUDY

We can learn something about banking in the United States from the history of a particular bank—the Bank of America, the nation's largest commercial bank. In 1904, Amadeo Peter Giannini, a 34-year-old son of

---

[1] The relationships among the various types of financial institutions are governed in part by law. In 1980, the Congress passed a financial reform act which changed some of these relationships. For example, federally-chartered thrift institutions were permitted to have NOW accounts, and federally chartered savings and loan associations were permitted to invest up to 20 percent of their assets in consumer loans, commercial paper, and corporate debt securities. Technological change also influences the relationships among various types of financial institutions. Many firms, such as Merrill Lynch, Sears Roebuck, and American Express, are involved in some aspects of "banking."

Amadeo Peter Giannini

an Italian immigrant, founded the Bank of Italy in the Italian district of San Francisco. Giannini was a man of enormous energy and drive. At the age of 12, he had gone to school by day, while working in his stepfather's produce firm for much of each night. At 19, he was a full-fledged member of the produce firm, and at 31 had become rich enough to retire from the produce business—and eventually to turn to banking.

Giannini showed the sort of entrepreneurial zeal in banking that would be expected from his previous track record. As an illustration, consider the following episode:

> In 1906, the city of San Francisco was rocked by earthquake and swept by fire. As the flames approached the little Bank of Italy, the young banker piled his cash and securities into a horsedrawn wagon and with a guard of two soldiers took them to his home at San Mateo, twenty miles from San Francisco, where he buried them in the garden; and then while the ruins of the city were still smoking he set up a desk in the open air down by the waterfront, put up a sign over the desk which read BANK OF ITALY, and began doing business again—the first San Francisco bank to resume.[2]

Clearly, Giannini was a banker who did not observe banker's hours.

Giannini's bank prospered and grew. By the time he was 50, it had over 25 branches. During the 1920s, he acquired more and more branches, until old-line California bankers began to realize that the Bank of Italy had become a factor to be reckoned with. They did their best to prevent its further expansion, but to no avail. A man who can turn an earthquake to his advantage is unlikely, after all, to submit to such pressures. Indeed, by 1929, Giannini had 453 banking offices in California alone, as well as a considerable number elsewhere. His was the fourth largest commercial bank in the country.

In 1930, Giannini's bank was renamed the Bank of America. The 1930s were not particularly kind to it, any more than they were to the rest of the

Table 15.1

THE TEN LARGEST COMMERCIAL BANKS IN THE UNITED STATES IN TERMS OF DEPOSITS, DECEMBER 31, 1983

Bank and location	Deposits (billions of dollars)
Bank of America, San Francisco	90
Citibank, New York	78
Chase Manhattan Bank, New York	60
Manufacturers Hanover Trust Company, New York	42
Morgan Guaranty Trust Company, New York	39
Chemical Bank, New York	33
Continental Illinois National Bank, Chicago	30
First National Bank, Chicago	28
Security Pacific National Bank, Los Angeles	28
Bankers Trust Company, New York	24

Source: Moody's.

[2] Frederick Lewis Allen, *The Lords of Creation,* New York: Harper and Bros., 1935, p. 320. Much of this section is based on Allen's account.

economy. But in the past 40 years, the Bank of America has grown and grown. In 1940, its loans (and discounts) totaled $778 million; in 1950, $3.3 billion; in 1960, $6.7 billion; and in 1970, $16 billion. Clearly, the Bank of America was on the move. By 1983, it had deposits of about $90 billion, and was the largest commercial bank in the United States. (The ten largest banks in the United States, in terms of deposits, are listed in Table 15.1.) It had come a long way since the days of the open-air desk on the waterfront.

How Banks Operate

The Bank of America, the biggest in the country, is hardly a typical commercial bank. It has had a remarkable history and a gifted founder. Many commercial banks are very small, as you would guess from the fact that there are about 15,000 of them in the United States. And there is a great deal of variation among banks in their operating procedures and styles. Some are principally for firms; they do little business with individuals. Others are heavily engaged in lending to consumers. Nonetheless, although it is difficult to generalize about the operations of commercial banks because they vary so much, certain principles and propositions generally hold.

1. Banks generally make loans to both firms and individuals, and invest in securities, particularly the bonds of state and local governments, as well as federal government bonds. The relationship between a business firm and its bank is often a close and continuing one. The firm keeps a reasonably large deposit with the bank for long periods of time, while the bank provides the firm with needed and prudent loans. The relationship between an individual and his or her bank is much more casual, but banks like consumer loans because they tend to be relatively profitable. In addition, besides lending to firms and individuals, banks buy large quantities of government bonds. For example, in the early 1970s, commercial banks held about $60 billion of state and local government bonds.

2. Banks, like other firms, are operated to make a profit. They don't do it by producing and selling a good, like automobiles or steel. Instead, they perform various services, including lending money, making investments, clearing checks, keeping records, and so on. They manage to make a profit from these activities by lending money and making investments that yield a higher rate of interest than they must pay their depositors. For example, the Bank of America may be able to get 15 percent interest on the loans it makes, while it must pay only 9 percent interest to its depositors. (Commercial banks pay interest on some, but not all, deposits. Also, they provide services at less than cost to holders of deposits.) If so, it receives the difference of 6 percent, which goes to meet its expenses—and to provide it with some profits.

3. Banks must constantly balance their desire for high returns from their loans and investments against the requirement that these loans and investments be safe and easily turned into cash. Since a bank's profits increase if it makes loans or investments that yield a high interest rate, it is clear why a bank favors high returns from its loans and investments. But those that yield a high interest rate often are relatively risky, which means that they may not be repaid in full. Because a bank lends out its depositors' money, it must be careful to limit the riskiness of the loans and investments it makes. Otherwise it may fail.

Until about 50 years ago, banks used to fail in large numbers during recessions, causing depositors to lose their money. Even during the prosperous 1920s, over 500 banks failed per year. It is no wonder that the public viewed the banks with less than complete confidence. Since the mid-1930s, bank failures have been rare, in part because of tighter standards of regulation by federal and state authorities. For example, bank examiners audit the books and practices of the banks. In addition, confidence in the banks was strengthened by the creation in 1934 of the Federal Deposit Insurance Corporation, which insures over 99 percent of all commercial bank depositors. At present, each deposit is insured up to $100,000.

The Balance Sheet of an Individual Bank

A good way to understand how a bank operates is to look at its balance sheet. Table 15.2 shows the Bank of America's balance sheet as of the end of 1983.

The Left-Hand Side. The left-hand side shows that the total assets of the Bank of America were $109.5 billion, and that these assets were made up as follows: $15.6 billion in cash, $8.4 billion in bonds and other securities, 73.0 billion in loans, and 12.5 billion in other assets. In particular, note that the loans included among the assets of the Bank of America are the loans it made to firms and individuals. As we have emphasized repeatedly, lending money is one of the major functions of a commercial bank.

The Right-Hand Side. The right-hand side of the balance sheet says that the total liabilities—or debts—of the Bank of America were $105.0 billion, and that these liabilities were made up of $89.9 billion in deposits (both demand and time), and $15.1 billion in other liabilities. Note that the deposits at the Bank of America are included among its liabilities, since the Bank of America owes the depositors the amount of money in their deposits. It will be recalled from the previous sections that maintaining these deposits is one of the major functions of a commercial bank. Returning to the balance sheet of the Bank of America, the difference between its total assets and its total liabilities—$4.5 billion—is, of course, its net worth.

Table 15.2

BALANCE SHEET, BANK OF AMERICA, DECEMBER 31, 1983 (BILLIONS OF DOLLARS)

Assets		Liabilities and net worth	
Cash	15.6	Deposits	89.9
Securities	8.4	Other liabilities	15.1
Loans	73.0	Net worth	4.5
Other assets	12.5		
Total	109.5	Total	109.5

Source: 1983 Annual Report, Bank of America.

CASH LESS THAN DEPOSITS

One noteworthy characteristic of any bank's balance sheet is the fact that *a very large percentage of its liabilities must be paid on demand.* For example, if all the depositors of the Bank of America tried to withdraw their demand deposits, a substantial proportion of its liabilities would be due on demand. Of course, the chance of everyone wanting to draw out his or her money at once is infinitesimally small. Instead, on a given day some depositors withdraw some money, while others make deposits, and most neither withdraw nor deposit money. Consequently, any bank can get along with an amount of cash to cover withdrawals that is much smaller than the total amount of its deposits. For example, the Bank of America's cash equaled about one-sixth of its total deposits. Note that "cash" here includes the bank's deposit with the Federal Reserve system and its deposits with other banks, as well as cash in its vault.

The Bank of America's practice of holding an amount of cash—including its deposits with the Federal Reserve and with other banks—much less than the amount it owes its depositors may strike you as dangerous. Indeed, if you have a deposit at the Bank of America, you may be tempted to go over and withdraw the money in your account and deposit it in some bank that does have cash equal to the amount it owes its depositors. But you won't be able to do this because *all banks hold much less cash than the amount they owe their depositors.* Moreover, this is a perfectly sound banking practice, as we shall see.

Fractional-Reserve Banking

To understand the crucial significance of *fractional-reserve banking,* as this practice is called, let's compare two situations—one where a bank must hold as reserves an amount equal to the amount it owes its depositors, another where its reserves do not have to match the amount it owes its depositors. In the first case, the bank's balance sheet might be as shown in Table 15.3, if demand deposits equal $2 million and net worth equals $500,000. The bank's loans and investments in this case are made entirely with funds put up by the owners of the bank. To see this, note that loans and investments equal $500,000, and that the bank's net worth also equals $500,000. Thus, if some of these loans are not repaid or if some of these investments lose money, the losses are borne entirely by the bank's stockholders. The depositors are protected completely because every cent of their deposits is covered by the bank's reserves.

Now let's turn to the case of fractional-reserve banking. In this case, the bank's balance sheet might be as shown in Table 15.4, if deposits equal $2 million and net worth equals $500,000. Some of the loans and investments made by the bank are not made with funds put up by the owners of the bank, but with funds deposited in the bank by depositors. Thus, though depositors deposited $2 million in the bank, the reserves are only $400,000. What happened to the remaining $1.6 million? Since the bank (in this simple case) only has two kinds of assets, loans (and investments) and reserves, the bank must have lent out (or invested) the remaining $1.6 million.

Table 15.3

BANK BALANCE SHEET: CASE WHERE RESERVES EQUAL DEMAND DEPOSITS (MILLIONS OF DOLLARS)

Assets		Liabilities and net worth	
Reserves	2.0	Demand deposits	2.0
Loans and investments	0.5	Net worth	0.5
Total	2.5	Total	2.5

Table 15.4

BANK BALANCE SHEET: FRACTIONAL RESERVES (MILLIONS OF DOLLARS)

Assets		Liabilities and net worth	
Reserves	0.4	Demand deposits	2.0
Loans and investments	2.1	Net worth	0.5
Total	2.5	Total	2.5

ORIGINS OF FRACTIONAL-RESERVE BANKING

The early history of banking is the story of an evolution from the first to the second situation. The earliest banks held reserves equal to the amounts they owed depositors, and were simply places where people stored their gold. But as time went on, banks began to practice fractional-reserve banking. It is easy to see how this evolution could take place. Suppose that you owned a bank of the first type. You would almost certainly be struck by the fact that most of the gold entrusted to you was not demanded on any given day. Sooner or later, you might be tempted to lend out some of the gold and obtain some interest. Eventually, as experience indicated that this procedure did not inconvenience your depositors, you and other bankers might make this practice common knowledge.

You might use several arguments to defend this practice. First, you would probably point out that none of the depositors had lost any money. (To the depositors, this would be a rather important argument.) Second, you could show that the interest you earned on the loans made it possible for you to charge depositors less for storing their gold. Consequently, you would argue that it was to the depositors' advantage (because of the savings that accrued to them) for you to lend out some of the gold. Third, you would probably argue that putting the money to work benefited the community and the economy. After all, in many cases, firms can make highly productive investments only if they can borrow the money, and by lending out your depositors' gold, you would enable such investments to be made.

LEGAL RESERVE REQUIREMENTS

Arguments of this sort have led society to permit fractional-reserve banking. In other words, a bank is allowed to hold less in reserves than the amount it owes its depositors. But what determines the amount of reserves banks hold? For example, the Bank of America, according to Table 15.2, held cash equal to about 17 percent of its total deposits. Probably it could get away with holding much less in reserves, so long as there is no panic among depositors and it makes sound loans and investments. One reason why the Bank of America held this much cash is very simple. *The Federal Reserve System requires every commercial bank (whether or not it is a member of the system) to hold a certain percentage of its deposits as reserves.* According to the 1980 financial reform act, the Fed can set this percentage between the limits of 8 and 14 percent for checkable deposits (that is, deposits subject to direct or indirect transfer by check).[3] Also, on the affirmative action of five of the seven members of the Fed's board of governors, it can impose an additional reserve requirement of up to 4 percent. And in extraordinary circumstances the Fed can for 180 days set the percentage at any level it deems necessary. These are *legal reserve requirements;* they also exist for time deposits (of businesses and nonprofit institutions), but are lower than for checkable deposits.

The Federal Reserve System in recent years has dictated that the average bank should hold about $1 in reserves for every $6 of demand deposits. Most of these reserves are held in the form of deposits by banks at their regional Federal Reserve Bank. Thus, for example, a great deal of the Bank of America's reserves are held in its deposit with the Federal Reserve Bank of San Francisco. In addition, some of any bank's reserves are held in cash on the bank's premises. However, its legal reserves are less than the "cash" entry on its balance sheet since its deposits with other banks do not count as legal reserves.

The most obvious reason why the Fed imposes these legal reserve re-

---

[3] For up to $25 million in checkable deposits, this percentage is 3 percent. Note too that *the 1980 law says that these reserve requirements apply to deposits in other thrift institutions (savings and loan associations, mutual savings banks, and credit unions), not just banks.*

327

quirements would seem to be to keep the banks safe, but in this case the obvious answer isn't the right one. Instead, *the most important reason for legal reserve requirements is to control the money supply.* It will take some more discussion before this becomes clear.

The Safety of the Banks

We have just argued that the reserve requirements imposed by the Federal Reserve System exceed what would be required under normal circumstances to insure the safety of the banks. To support our argument, we might cite some authorities who claim that a bank would be quite safe if it only had reserves equal to about 2 percent of its deposits. Under these circumstances it would be able to meet its depositors' everyday demands for cash. Obviously this level of reserves is much lower than the legally required level.

THE ROLE OF BANK MANAGEMENT

At the same time, one should recognize that high reserve requirements will not by themselves insure bank safety. For example, suppose that a bank lends money to every budding inventor with a scheme for producing perpetual-motion machines, and that it grants particularly large loans to those who propose to market these machines in the suburbs of Missoula, Montana. This bank is going to fail eventually, even if it holds reserves equal to 20 percent—or 50 percent, for that matter—of its demand deposits. It will fail simply because the loans it makes will not be repaid, and eventually these losses will accumulate to more than the bank's net worth. In other words, if the bank is sufficiently inept in making loans and investments, it will lose all the owners' money and some of the depositors' money besides.

The well-managed bank must make sensible loans and investments. In addition, it must protect itself against short-term withdrawals of large amounts of money. Although much-larger-than-usual withdrawals are not very likely to occur, the bank must be prepared to meet a temporary upswing in withdrawals. One way is to invest in securities that can readily be turned into cash. For example, the bank may invest in short-term government securities that can readily be sold at a price that varies only moderately from day to day. Such securities are often referred to as *secondary reserves.*

THE ROLE OF GOVERNMENT

There can be no doubt that banks are much safer today than they were 50 or 100 years ago. The reason is that the government has put its power squarely behind the banking system. It used to be that "runs" occurred on the banks. Every now and then, depositors, frightened that their banks would fail and that they would lose some of their money, would line up at the tellers' windows and withdraw as much money as they could. Faced with runs of this sort, banks were sometimes forced to close because they could not satisfy all demands for withdrawals. Needless to say, no fractional-reserve banking system can satisfy demands for total withdrawal of funds.

Runs on banks are a thing of the past, for several reasons. One is that the government—including the Federal Deposit Insurance Corporation (FDIC), the Fed, and other public agencies—has made it clear that it will not stand by and tolerate the sorts of panics that used to occur periodically in this country. The FDIC insures the accounts of depositors in practically all banks so that, even if a bank fails, the depositor will get his money back— up to $100,000. Another reason is that the banks themselves are better managed and regulated. For example, bank examiners are sent out to look over the bankers' shoulders and see whether they are solvent. It is a far cry from the situation about 80 years ago that led to the creation of the Federal Reserve System.

Nonetheless, this does not mean that bank regulation is all that it might be. In 1984, the Continental Illinois Bank, the seventh largest bank in the U.S., required a multi-billion-dollar rescue operation by federal agencies to keep it in operation. Continental Illinois bought up more than $1 billion in loans made by Penn Square Bank of Oklahoma City. When these loans went sour (and Penn Square Bank failed), Continental's depositors became worried and began to withdraw their funds. Federal agencies tried to arrange a merger between Continental and some other bank, but no partner could be found. To keep Continental going, the FDIC put up billions of dollars and established what is essentially a new Continental Illinois Bank.

THE LENDING DECISION: A CASE STUDY

To get a better feel for the workings of a bank, let's look at an actual decision faced by Robert Swift, the assistant vice-president of the Lone Star National Bank of Houston, Texas. Mr. Swift received a call from Ralph Desmond, president of the Desmond Engineering Corporation. Mr. Desmond wanted to change his bank; he was dissatisfied with the amount he could borrow from his present bank. He wanted to borrow $30,000 from the Lone Star to pay what he owed to his present bank, pay some bills coming up, and buy some material needed to fulfill a contract. Mr. Swift asked Mr. Desmond to come to his office with various financial statements regarding the Desmond Engineering Corporation and its prospects. These included recent income statements and balance sheets, as well as a variety of other data, including information indicating how rapidly the firm collected its bills and the quality of the debts owed the firm.

Mr. Swift forwarded Mr. Desmond's loan application to the credit department of the bank for further analyses. The credit department added comments on the Desmond Engineering Corporation's solvency and prospects. Besides being secured by a mortgage on some equipment owned by the Desmond Engineering Corporation, this loan was to be personally endorsed by Mr. Desmond and another principal stockholder in the firm. Consequently, Mr. Swift obtained information on the extent and nature of the personal assets of Mr. Desmond and the other stockholder. This information was used, together with all the other data on the firm, to determine whether the bank would make the loan. After a reasonable amount of time, Mr. Swift recommended the acceptance of Mr. Desmond's loan

329

In recent years, the nation's commercial banks have become deregulated in a variety of ways, and they now have considerable freedom to pay whatever interest rate they like. At the same time, they (and savings and loans and savings banks) have a unique advantage over their competitors, like the money market mutual funds and the brokerage houses, because their deposits are federally insured.

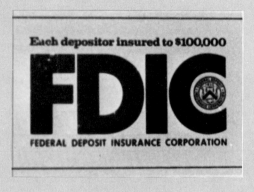

The total volume of insured deposits has grown rapidly. With the introduction by banks of new types of deposits (money market deposit accounts and Super-NOW accounts) and the elimination of ceilings on interest rates on most small time deposit accounts, investors have shifted funds out of the uninsured accounts in mutual funds and into insured deposits at the banks. Naturally, people prefer to put their money in a place where it is insured, if they can get about the same interest rate on it.

Deposit insurance dates back to the 1930s and undoubtedly has done a great deal to prevent runs on the banks. It seems very unlikely that deposit insurance will be discontinued, but there is a widespread feeling that deposit insurance has reduced the incentives for depositors to evaluate the riskiness of the banks, since their deposits are insured. Moreover, since the insurance premium charged a bank by the Federal Deposit Insurance Corporation (FDIC) is proportional to the amount of the bank's deposits (regardless of the riskiness of its assets), insured banks have an incentive to assume more risk than they otherwise would, since they do not pay higher premiums and they do obtain the higher yields that stem from riskier investments.

A number of proposals have been made to help improve matters. According to some observers, the insurance premium that the FDIC charges a particular bank should be related to the riskiness of the bank's assets. In other words, if a bank's investments are relatively risky, the FDIC should charge this bank a relatively high premium for deposit insurance. While this is an interesting suggestion, there is no simple, straightforward way to measure the riskiness of a bank's portfolio of assets.

Another proposal is that the risk exposure of large depositors should be increased. In the past, even deposits of more than $100,000 have generally been protected, because mergers have been arranged between banks that are about to fail and other healthy banks. To the FDIC, this has seemed to be the cheapest way to protect the deposits, but one consequence has been that very large depositors have little incentive to monitor the riskiness of their bank or the way it is managed. Why bother if your deposit in effect is insured, even if it does exceed $100,000?

application. In his view, Mr. Desmond had a very good chance of repaying the loan.[4]

Note two things about this decision. First, if the bank grants Mr. Desmond the loan, it will create a demand deposit for him. In other words, it will create some money. Second, the bank can do this only if it has reserves exceeding the legal reserve requirements. Both of these points are important enough to dwell on for a while.

Two Ways Banks Cannot Create Money

Genesis tells us that God created heaven and earth. Economists tell us that banks create money. To many people, the latter process is at least as mysterious as the former. Even bankers have been known to fall into serious error by claiming that they do not create money. Yet the way banks create money is a relatively simple process, which the next few sections will describe in detail. Suppose that someone receives $10,000 in newly printed currency and deposits it in his local bank. Before we see how the banks can create more than $10,000 from this deposit, we will describe two ways in which banks *cannot* create new money. Since people often jump to the conclusion that one or the other of these two processes is the correct one, it is a good idea to kill off these heresies at the outset.

CASE 1: RESERVES MUST EQUAL DEPOSITS

Suppose that ours is not a fractional-reserve banking system. In other words, assume that every bank has to maintain reserves equal to its deposits. In this case, the bank receiving the $10,000 deposit cannot create any new money. You may be inclined to think that it can be done, but it can't. To see why not, consider the changes in the bank's balance sheet, shown in Table 15.5. When the $10,000 is deposited in the bank, the bank's deposits go up $10,000. Since the bank must hold $10,000 in reserves to back up the new $10,000 deposit, it must put the $10,000 it receives from the depositor into its reserves. Thus the bank's demand deposits go up by $10,000, and its reserves go up by $10,000. Since demand deposits are on the right-hand side of the balance sheet and reserves

Table 15.5

CHANGES IN BANK BALANCE SHEET, WHERE RESERVES EQUAL DEMAND DEPOSITS (DOLLARS)

Assets		Liabilities and net worth	
Reserves	+ 10,000	Demand deposits	+ 10,000
Loans and investments	No change	Net worth	No change
Total	+ 10,000	Total	+ 10,000

[4] This case comes from Leonard Marks and Alan Coleman, *Cases in Commercial Bank Management,* New York: McGraw Hill, 1962, pp. 168–176. However, the outcome is purely conjectural.

are on the left-hand side, the balance sheet continues to balance. *No new money is created. All that happens is that the depositor gives up $10,000 in one form of money—currency—and receives $10,000 in another form of money—a demand deposit.*[5]

CASE 2: VIOLATION OF LEGAL RESERVE REQUIREMENTS

Basic Idea #29: If every bank has to maintain reserves equal to its deposits (that is, if it is not a fractional reserve system), banks cannot create new money. When a person or firm deposits a certain amount of currency in a bank, one form of money (currency) is exchanged for another form of money (demand deposit), but no new money can be created.

Next, let's turn to a second way banks cannot create money. Suppose that we have a fractional-reserve banking system and that the legal reserve requirement is 16⅔ percent. In other words, the bank must hold $1 in reserves for every $6 of demand deposits. Suppose that the bank decides to take the crisp, new $10,000 in currency that is deposited and add it to its reserves, thus increasing its reserves by $10,000. Then suppose it reasons (incorrectly) that it can increase its deposits by $50,000, since it has $10,000 in additional reserves. Why $50,000? Because the $10,000 in additional reserves will support $60,000 in demand deposits; and since the person who deposited the $10,000 has a demand deposit of $10,000, this means that it can create additional demand deposits of $60,000 minus $10,000, or $50,000.

The bank will create these additional demand deposits simply by making loans or investments. Thus when a person comes in to the bank for a loan, all the banker has to do is give her a demand deposit—a checking account—that didn't exist before. In other words, the banker can say to his staff, "Establish a checking account of $50,000 for Ms. Smith. We have just lent her this amount to buy a new piece of equipment to be used in her business." At first, this whole process looks a bit like black magic, perhaps even larceny. After all, how can checking accounts be established out of thin air? But they can, and are. In essence, this is how banks create money.

WHERE IS THE ERROR?

But we prefaced this example by saying that it contains an error. The error is the supposition that the bank can create an additional $50,000 of demand deposits on the basis of the $10,000 deposit. To see why this won't work, consider the changes in the bank's balance sheet, shown in Table 15.6. After the bank received the $10,000 deposit, its demand deposits and its reserves both increased by $10,000, as shown in the first panel of Table 15.6. Then, as we noted above, the bank made a $50,000 loan and (in the process of making the loan) created $50,000 in new deposits, as shown in the second panel. So far, so good. The bank's balance sheet continues to balance—in accord with common sense and accounting (in that order). The bank's reserves are one-sixth of its demand deposits; they satisfy the legal reserve requirements established by the Fed.

---

[5] Note that the $10,000 in currency which the depositor gives the bank is no longer counted as money once it is given to the bank. Only currency outside the vaults of all commercial banks (as well as outside the Treasury and the Federal Reserve Banks) is included in the money supply.

For simplicity, checkable deposits other than demand deposits are ignored here and below.

Table 15.6

CHANGES IN BANK BALANCE SHEET: FRACTIONAL RESERVES (DOLLARS)

		Assets		Liabilities and net worth
Bank receives deposit	Reserves	+ 10,000	Demand deposits	+ 10,000
	Loans and investments	No change	Net worth	No change
	Total	+ 10,000	Total	+ 10,000
Bank makes loan	Reserves	No change	Demand deposits	+ 50,000
	Loans and investments	+ 50,000	Net worth	No change
	Total	+ 50,000	Total	+ 50,000
Ms. Smith spends $50,000	Reserves	− 50,000	Demand deposits	− 50,000
	Loans and investments	No change	Net worth	No change
	Total	− 50,000	Total	− 50,000
Total effect	Reserves	− 40,000	Demand deposits	+ 10,000
	Loans and investments	+ 50,000	Net worth	No change
	Total	+ 10,000	Total	+ 10,000

So what is the problem? None, unless the money lent by the bank is spent. If the woman who received the loan—Ms. Smith—never used the money she borrowed, the bank could act this way and get away with it. But people who borrow money are in the habit of spending it; why pay interest on money one doesn't use? Even if Ms. Smith, the recipient of this loan, spent the money, the bank could act in accord with this example and get away with it if the people who received the money from Ms. Smith deposited it in this same bank. But the chances of this occurring are very small. The equipment Ms. Smith plans to buy is likely to be produced by a firm in some other city; and even if it is located in the same city, the firm may well have an account at another bank.

To see the problem that results when the loan is spent, suppose that Ms. Smith spends the $50,000 on a machine produced by the Acme Corporation, which has an account at the First National Bank of Boston. She sends the Acme Corporation a check for $50,000 drawn on our bank. When the Acme Corporation receives Ms. Smith's check, it deposits this check to its account at the First National Bank of Boston, which, using the facilities of the Federal Reserve System, presents the check to our bank for payment. Our bank must then fork over $50,000 of its cash—its reserves—to the First National Bank of Boston. Consequently, once the $50,000 check is paid, the effect on our bank's balance sheet is as shown in the third panel of Table 15.6. Taken as a whole, the bank's demand deposits have increased by $10,000, and its reserves have decreased by $40,000, as shown in the bottom panel of Table 15.6.

At this point, the error in this example is becoming clear. *If the bank was holding $1 in reserves for every $6 in demand deposits before the $10,000 deposit was made, these transactions must cause the bank to violate the legal reserve requirements.* This may be proved as follows. Suppose that, before the $10,000 deposit, our bank had $X in demand deposits and $\frac{X}{6}$ in

333

reserves. Then, after the transactions described above, it must have ($X + \$10,000$) in demand deposits and $\left(\$\dfrac{X}{6} - \$40,000\right)$ in reserves. Certainly, the reserves $\left(\text{which equal }\$\dfrac{X}{6} - \$40,000\right)$ are now less than one-sixth of the demand deposits (which equal $\$X + \$10,000$). This must be true whatever value X has. (Try it and see.) Thus no bank can create money in this way because, if it did, it would violate the legal reserve requirements after the newly created demand deposits were used. (As we shall see later, a monopoly bank—that is, the only bank in the country—could create money like this, but monopoly banks do not exist in the United States.)

Test Yourself

1. Suppose that John Smith deposits $50,000 in newly printed currency to his account at Bank A. What is the effect on Bank A's balance sheet?

Assets (dollars)	Liabilities and net worth (dollars)
Reserves _____	Demand deposits _____
Loans and investments _____	Net worth _____
Total _____	Total _____

2. Suppose that Bank A lends the Bugsbane Music Box Company $30,000. What is the effect on Bank A's balance sheet of both the deposit described in Question 1 and this loan? Fill in the blanks below.

Assets (dollars)	Liabilities and net worth (dollars)
Reserves _____	Demand deposits _____
Loans and investments _____	Net worth _____
Total _____	Total _____

3. After the Bugsbane Music Box Company receives the $30,000 loan, it uses the money to buy a new piece of equipment from the XYZ Tool Company. The XYZ Tool Company deposits Bugsbane's check on Bank A to its account at the Bank of America. What is the total effect on Bank A's balance sheet of the deposit described in Question 1, the loan in Question 2, and the purchase described here? Fill in the blanks below.

Assets (dollars)	Liabilities and net worth (dollars)
Reserves _____	Demand deposits _____
Loans and investments _____	Net worth _____
Total _____	Total _____

4. If Bank A had no excess reserves prior to the transactions described in Questions 1, 2, and 3, and if the legal reserve requirement is that Bank A must hold $1 in reserves for every $5 in demand deposits, does Bank A have more reserves than are legally required after these transactions? If so, how much more?

How Banks Can Create Money

Now that you have learned two ways that banks *cannot* create money, let's describe how they *can* create money. Imagine the following scenario. First, suppose once again that someone deposits $10,000 of newly printed money in our bank, which we'll call Bank A. Second, suppose that Bank A lends Ms. Smith $8,333, and that Ms. Smith uses this money to purchase some equipment from Mr. Jones, who deposits Ms. Smith's check in his account at Bank B. Third, Bank B buys a bond for $6,944 from Ms. Stone, who uses the money to pay Mr. Green for some furniture. Mr. Green deposits the check to his account at Bank C. Admittedly, this is a somewhat complicated plot with a substantial cast of characters, but life is like that.

MONEY CREATION AT BANK A

The first step in our drama occurs when someone deposits $10,000 in newly printed money in Bank A. The effect of this deposit is shown in the first panel of Table 15.7: Bank A's demand deposits and its reserves both go up by $10,000. Now Bank A is far too smart to try to make a $50,000 loan, lest it wind up with less reserves than dictated by the legal reserve requirements. Instead, it makes a loan of $8,333, since this is the amount of its **excess reserves** (those in excess of legal requirements). Because of the $10,000 increase in its deposits, its legally required reserves increase by $\frac{\$10,000}{6}$, or $1,667. (Recall that $1 in reserves must be held for every $6 in deposits.) Thus, if it had no excess reserves before, *it now has excess reserves of $10,000—$1,667, or $8,333.* When Ms. Smith asks one of the loan officers of the bank for a loan to purchase equipment, the loan officer approves a loan of $8,333, not $50,000. Ms. Smith is given a checking account of $8,333 at Bank A.

How can Bank A get away with this loan of $8,333 without winding up with less than the legally required reserves? The answer is given in the rest of Table 15.7. The second panel of this table shows what happens to Bank A's balance sheet when Bank A makes the $8,333 loan and creates a new demand deposit of $8,333. Obviously, both demand deposits and loans go up by $8,333. Next, look at the third panel of Table 15.7, which shows what happens when Ms. Smith spends the $8,333 on equipment. As pointed out above, she purchases this equipment from Mr. Jones. Mr. Jones deposits

Table 15.7
CHANGES IN BANK A'S BALANCE SHEET (DOLLARS)

	Assets		Liabilities and net worth	
Bank receives deposit	Reserves	+ 10,000	Demand deposits	+ 10,000
	Loans and investments	No change	Net worth	No change
	Total	+ 10,000	Total	+ 10,000
Bank makes loan	Reserves	No change	Demand deposits	+ 8,333
	Loans and investments	+ 8,333	Net worth	No change
	Total	+ 8,333	Total	+ 8,333
Ms. Smith spends $8,333	Reserves	− 8,333	Demand deposits	− 8,333
	Loans and investments	No change	Net worth	No change
	Total	− 8,333	Total	− 8,333
Total effect	Reserves	+ 1,667	Demand deposits	+ 10,000
	Loans and investments	+ 8,333	Net worth	No change
	Total	+ 10,000	Total	+ 10,000

Ms. Smith's check to his account in Bank B which presents the check to Bank A for payment. After Bank A pays Bank B (through the Federal Reserve System), the result—as shown in the third panel—is that Bank A's deposits go down by $8,333 since Ms. Smith no longer has the deposit. Bank A's reserves also go down by $8,333 since Bank A has to transfer these reserves to Bank B to pay the amount of the check.

As shown in the bottom panel of Table 15.7, the total effect on Bank A is to increase its deposits by the $10,000 that was deposited originally and to increase its reserves by $10,000 minus $8,333, or $1,667. In other words, reserves have increased by one-sixth as much as demand deposits. This means that Bank A will meet its legal reserve requirements. To see this, suppose that before the deposit of $10,000, Bank A had demand deposits of X and reserves of $\dfrac{X}{6}$. Then after the full effect of the transaction occurs on Bank A's balance sheet, Bank A's demand deposits will equal ($X +$ $10,000), and its reserves will equal $\left(\$\dfrac{X}{6} + \$\dfrac{10,000}{6}\right)$, since $1,667 = \dfrac{\$10,000}{6}$. Thus Bank A continues to hold $1 in reserves for every $6 in demand deposits, as required by the Fed.

It is important to recognize that *Bank A has now created $8,333 in new money.* To see this, note that Mr. Jones winds up with a demand deposit of this amount that he didn't have before; and this is a net addition to the money supply, since the person who originally deposited the $10,000 in currency still has his $10,000, although it is in the form of a demand deposit rather than currency.

MONEY CREATION AT BANK B

The effects of the $10,000 deposit at Bank A are not limited to Bank A. Instead, as we shall see, other banks can also create new money as a consequence of the original $10,000 deposit at Bank A. Let's begin with Bank B. Recall from the previous section that the $8,333 check made out by Ms. Smith to Mr. Jones is deposited by the latter in his account at Bank B. This is a new deposit of funds at Bank B. As pointed out in the previous section, Bank B gets $8,333 in reserves from Bank A when Bank A pays Bank B to get back the check. Thus the effect on Bank B's balance sheet, as shown in the first panel of Table 15.8, is to increase both demand deposits and reserves by $8,333.

Bank B is in much the same position as was Bank A when the latter received the original deposit of $10,000. Bank B can make loans or investments equal to its excess reserves, which are $6,944. (The way we derive $6,944 is explained in the footnote below.)[6] Specifically, it decides to buy a bond for $6,944 from Ms. Stone, and credits her checking account at Bank B for this amount. Thus, as shown in the second panel of Table 15.8, the effect of this transaction is to increase Bank B's investments by $6,944 and to increase its demand deposits by $6,944. Ms. Stone writes a check for

---

[6] Since Bank B's deposits increase by $8,333, its legally required reserves increase by $\dfrac{8,333}{6}$, or $1,389. Thus $1,389 of its increase in reserves is legally required, and the rest ($8,333—$1,389 = $6,944) is excess reserves.

Table 15.8

CHANGES IN BANK B'S BALANCE SHEET (DOLLARS)

	Assets		*Liabilities and net worth*	
Bank receives deposit	Reserves	+8,333	Demand deposits	+8,333
	Loans and investments	No change	Net worth	No change
	Total	+8,333	Total	+8,333
Bank buys bond	Reserves	No change	Demand deposits	+6,944
	Loans and investments	+6,944	Net worth	No change
	Total	+6,944	Total	+6,944
Mr. Green deposits money in Bank C	Reserves	−6,944	Demand deposits	−6,944
	Loans and investments	No change	Net worth	No change
	Total	−6,944	Total	−6,944
Total effect	Reserves	+1,389	Demand deposits	+8,333
	Loans and investments	+6,944	Net worth	No change
	Total	+8,333	Total	+8,333

$6,944 to Mr. Green to pay for some furniture. Mr. Green deposits the check in Bank C. Bank B's demand deposits and its reserves are decreased by $6,944 when it transfers this amount of reserves to Bank C to pay for the check. When the total effects of the transaction are summed up, Bank B, like Bank A, continues to meet its legal reserve requirements, since its increased reserves ($1,389) equal one-sixth of its increased demand deposits ($8,333).

Bank B has also created some money—$6,944 to be exact. Mr. Green has $6,944 in demand deposits that he didn't have before; and this is a net addition to the money supply since the person who originally deposited the currency in Bank A still has his $10,000, and Mr. Jones still has the $8,333 he deposited in Bank B.

THE TOTAL EFFECT OF THE ORIGINAL $8,333 IN EXCESS RESERVES

How big an increase in the money supply can the entire banking system support as a consequence of the original $8,333 of excess reserves arising from the $10,000 deposit in Bank A? Clearly, the effects of the original injection of excess reserves into the banking system spread from one bank to another, since each bank hands new reserves (and deposits) to another bank, which in turn hands them to another bank. For example, Bank C now has $6,944 more in deposits and reserves and so can create $5,787 in new money[7] by making a loan or investment of this amount. This process goes on indefinitely, and it would be impossible to describe each of the multitude of steps involved. Fortunately, it isn't necessary to do so. We can

[7] Why $5,787? Because it must hold $\frac{\$6,944}{6} = \$1,157$ as reserves to support the new demand deposit of $6,944. Thus it has excess reserves of $5,787, and it can create another new demand deposit of this amount.

Figure 15.2

Cumulative Expansion in Demand Deposits on the Basis of $8,333 of Excess Reserves and Legal Reserve Requirement of 16⅔ Percent The original deposit was $10,000, which resulted in excess reserves of $8,333. In the first stage of the expansion process, Bank A created an additional $8,333. In the second stage, Bank B created an additional $6,944.

Suppose that Bank C lent $5,787 to Mr. White, who used the money to buy a truck from Mr. Black, who deposited Mr. White's check to his account at Bank D. If so, Bank C created an additional $5,787.

Suppose that Bank D lent Ms. Cohen $4,823 which Ms. Cohen used to buy some lumber from Mr. Palucci, who deposited Ms. Cohen's check to his account at Bank E. If so, Bank D created an additional $4,823.

The process goes on until the final result is $50,000 of additional demand deposits.

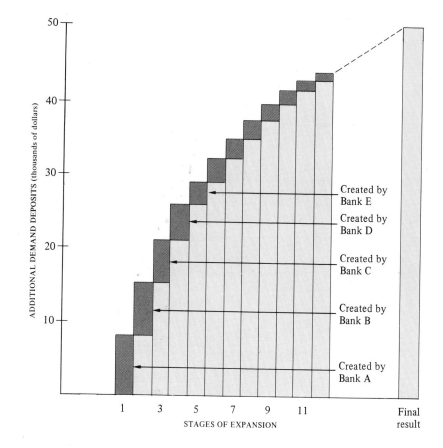

Table 15.9

INCREASE IN MONEY SUPPLY RESULTING FROM $8,333 IN EXCESS RESERVES

Source	Amount (dollars)
Created by Bank A	8,333
Created by Bank B	6,944
Created by Bank C	5,787
Created by Bank D	4,823
Created by Bank E	4,019
Created by Bank F	3,349
Created by Bank G	2,791
Created by Bank H	2,326
Created by Bank I	1,938
Created by Bank J	1,615
Created by other banks	8,075
Total	50,000

figure out the total amount of new money the entire banking system can support as a consequence of the original excess reserves at Bank A without going through all these steps.

We do this by computing how much new money each bank creates. Bank A creates $8,333, which is the amount of excess reserves provided by the $10,000 deposit. Then Bank B creates an additional $6,944, which is five-sixths of $8,333. Then Bank C creates an additional $5,787—five-sixths of $6,944 or (5/6)(5/6) $8,333, which is $(5/6)^2$ of $8,333. The amount of money created by each bank is less than that created by the previous bank, so that the total amount of new money created by the original injection of $8,333 of excess reserves—$8,333 + $6,944 + $5,787 + . . . —tends to a finite limit as the process goes on and on. Elementary algebra tells us what this sum of terms will be. *When the process works itself out, the entire banking system can support $50,000 in new money as a consequence of the original injection of $8,333 of excess reserves.*[8] For a further explanation of this fact, see Figure 15.2, which describes the cumulative expansion in demand deposits. (Table 15.9 shows the amount of new demand deposits created at each stage of this process.)

[8] The proof of this is as follows. The total amount of new money supported by the $8,333 in excess reserves is $8,333 + $6,944 + $5,787 + . . . , which equals $8,333 + 5/6 × $8,333 + $(5/6)^2$ × $8,333 + $(5/6)^3$ × $8,333 + . . . , which equals $8,333 × $(1 + 5/6 + (5/6)^2 + (5/6)^3 + . . .) = \$8{,}333 \times \dfrac{1}{1-(5/6)} = \$50{,}000$, since $1 + 5/6 + (5/6)^2 + (5/6)^3 + . . . = \dfrac{1}{1-(5/6)}$.

We must note that the banking system as a whole has accomplished what we said in a previous section that an individual bank—Bank A—could not do. It has created an additional $50,000 of demand deposits on the basis of the original $8,333 in excess reserves.[9] It seems perfectly reasonable that the banking system as a whole should be able to do this, since each $1 of reserves can back up $6 in demand deposits. But for the reasons discussed in a previous section, an individual bank cannot do it, unless, of course, it is a monopoly bank. If it is, it need have no fear of losing reserves to other banks, because there are no other banks; so it can behave this way. However, banking in the United States is not monopolized.

The Effect of Excess Reserves: A General Proposition

In general, *if a certain amount of excess reserves is made available to the banking system, the banking system as a whole can increase the money supply by an amount equal to the amount of excess reserves multiplied by the reciprocal of the required ratio of reserves to deposits.* In other words, to obtain the total increase in the money supply that can be achieved from a certain amount of excess reserves, multiply the amount of excess reserves by the reciprocal of the required ratio of reserves to deposits—or, what amounts to the same thing, *divide the amount of excess reserves by the legally required ratio of reserves to deposits.* Putting it in still another way, the banking system as a whole can increase the money supply by $(1/r)$ dollars—where r is the required ratio of reserves to deposits—for every $1 in excess reserves.[10]

Let's apply this proposition to a couple of specific cases. Suppose that the banking system gains excess reserves of $10,000 and that the required ratio of reserves to deposits is $\frac{1}{6}$. To determine how much the banking system can increase the money supply, we must divide the amount of the excess reserves—$10,000—by the required ratio of reserves to deposits—$\frac{1}{6}$—to get the answer, $60,000. Now suppose that the required ratio of reserves to deposits is $\frac{1}{5}$. By how much can the banking system increase the money supply? Dividing $10,000 by $\frac{1}{5}$, we get the answer—$50,000. Note that the higher the required ratio of reserves to deposits, the smaller the amount by which the banking system can increase the money supply on the basis of a given amount of excess reserves. More will be said about this in the next chapter.

Finally, an increase in reserves generally affects a great many banks at about the same time. For expository purposes, it is useful to trace through the effect of an increase in the reserves of a single bank—Bank A in our case. But usually this is not what happens. Instead, lots of banks experience an increase in reserves at about the same time. Thus they all have excess reserves at about the same time, and they all make loans or investments at

Basic Idea #30: If a particular amount of excess reserves is made available to the banking system, it can increase the money supply by $(1/r)$ dollars for every $1 in excess reserves, where r is the required ratio of reserves to deposits. (This is only a first approximation, since it is based on some simplifying assumptions discussed below.)

---

[9] In addition, the banking system created the original $10,000 deposit, but this was not an increase in the quantity of money since $10,000 in currency in the hands of the public was exchanged for it.

[10] The total amount of money supported by $1 of excess reserves is $1 + (1 - r) + (1 - r)^2 + (1 - r)^3 + \ldots = \dfrac{1}{1 - (1 - r)} = \dfrac{1}{r}$. We reach this conclusion by the same method we used in footnote 8.

about the same time. The result is that, when the people who borrow money spend it, each bank tends both to gain and lose reserves. Thus, on balance, each bank need not lose reserves. In real life the amount of bank money often **expands simultaneously** throughout the banking system until the legally required ratio of deposits to reserves is approached.

The Effect of a Decrease in Reserves

Up to this point, we have been talking only about the effect of an increase in reserves. What happens to the quantity of money if reserves decrease?

A NUMERICAL EXAMPLE

Suppose that you draw $10,000 out of your bank and hold it in the form of currency, perhaps by sewing it in your mattress. Let us begin with the effect on your bank. Clearly, it will experience a $10,000 decrease in deposits (because of your withdrawal) and, at the same time, a $10,000 decrease in reserves. Thus, if it was holding $1 in reserves for every $6 in deposits before you withdrew the money, it now holds less than the legally required reserves. If its deposits go down by $10,000, its reserves must legally go down by $1,667, not $10,000, if the 6:1 ratio between deposits and reserves is to be maintained. To observe the legal reserve requirements, your bank must increase its reserves by $10,000 minus $1,667, or $8,333. That is, it has a *deficiency* of reserves (negative excess reserves) of $8,333. It has several ways to get this money, one being to sell securities. It may sell a municipal bond to Mrs. Cherrytree for $8,333. To pay for the bond, she writes a check on her bank, Bank Q, for the $8,333. Thus, as shown in Table 15.10, your bank's investments decrease by $8,333, and its reserves increase by $8,333 when Bank Q transfers this amount to your bank to pay for the check.

But this is not the end of the story. Because Bank Q has lost $8,333 in deposits and $8,333 in reserves, its reserves are now less than the legal minimum. To maintain the legally required reserves, its reserves should have

Table 15.10

CHANGE IN YOUR BANK'S BALANCE SHEET (DOLLARS)

	Assets		Liabilities and net worth	
You withdraw deposit	Reserves	−10,000	Demand deposits	−10,000
	Loans and investments	No change	Net worth	No change
	Total	−10,000	Total	−10,000
Bank sells bond and gets funds from Bank Q	Reserves	+ 8,333	Demand deposits	No change
	Loans and investments	− 8,333	Net worth	No change
	Total	No change	Total	No change
Total effect	Reserves	− 1,667	Demand deposit	−10,000
	Loans and investments	− 8,333	Net worth	No change
	Total	−10,000	Total	−10,000

gone down by $\dfrac{\$8,333}{6}$, or \$1,389—not by \$8,333. Thus Bank Q must increase its reserves by \$8,333 minus \$1,389, or \$6,944. In other words, it has a deficiency of reserves of \$6,944. To make up this deficiency, it sells a bond it holds for \$6,944. But when the person who buys the bond gives Bank Q his check for \$6,944 drawn on Bank R, Bank R loses \$6,944 in deposits and \$6,944 in reserves. Thus Bank R's reserves are now below the legal requirement. To maintain the legally required reserves, its reserves should have gone down by $\dfrac{\$6,944}{6}$, or \$1,157—not by \$6,944. So Bank R must increase its reserves by \$6,944 minus \$1,157, or \$5,787. And on and on the process goes.

Let us consider the overall effect on the money supply of the \$8,333 deficiency in reserves experienced by your bank. Bank Q's demand deposits decreased by \$8,333, Bank R's demand deposits decreased by \$6,944 (that is 5/6 of \$8,333), and so on. The total decrease in the money supply—\$8,333 + \$6,944 + . . . —tends to a finite limit as the process goes on and on. This limit is \$50,000. Thus, *when the process works itself out, the entire banking system will reduce the money supply by \$50,000 as a consequence of a \$8,333 deficiency in reserves.*

A GENERAL PROPOSITION

More generally, if the banking system has a deficiency of reserves of a certain amount, the banking system as a whole will reduce demand deposits by an amount equal to the deficiency in reserves multiplied by the reciprocal of the required ratio of reserves to deposits.

In other words, to obtain the total decrease in demand deposits resulting from a deficiency in reserves, *divide the deficiency by the legally required ratio of reserves to deposits.* Putting it another way, the banking system as a whole will reduce demand deposits by $(1/r)$ dollars—where r is the required ratio of reserves to deposits—for every \$1 deficiency in reserves. Although there is often a simultaneous contraction of money on the part of many banks, just as there is often a simultaneous expansion, this doesn't affect the result.

Let's apply this proposition to a particular case. Suppose that the banking system experiences a deficiency in reserves of \$8,333 and that the required ratio of reserves to deposits is ⅙. Applying this rule, we must divide the deficiency in reserves—\$8,333—by the required ratio of reserves to deposits—⅙—to get the answer, which is a \$50,000 reduction in demand deposits. This answer checks with the result in the previous section.

Note that the effect of a \$1 deficiency in reserves is equal in absolute terms to the effect of \$1 in excess reserves. Both result in a \$(1/r) change in demand deposits. Or, more precisely, this is the case if certain assumptions, discussed in the next sections, are true. To complete our discussion of how banks create money, we turn now to these assumptions.

Currency Withdrawals

In discussing the amount of additional demand deposits that can be created by the banking system as a result of the injection of \$8,333 of excess reserves, we made the important assumption that everyone who received the new demand deposits—from Mr. Green back to the person who originally deposited his money in Bank A—wants to keep this money in the form of demand deposits rather than currency. However, this clearly may not be the case. Some people who receive new demand deposits may choose to withdraw some part of this money as currency. For example, Mr. Green may decide to withdraw some of his new demand deposit in cash.

What effect will this withdrawal of currency have on the amount of demand deposits the banking system can create? To begin with, note that this withdrawal of currency from the entire banking system reduces the reserves of the banking system. Applying the results of the previous sec-

Example 15.1   Currency Holdings of the Public

The public is free to decide how much money it wants to hold in the form of currency (and coins) and how much it wants to hold in the form of demand deposits. Suppose that the relationship between the amount it wants to hold in currency (and coins) and the amount it wants to hold in demand deposits is as follows:

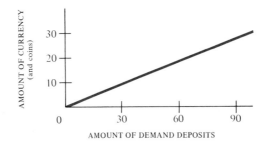

The reserve requirement is 20 percent, and commercial banks hold no excess reserves. For simplicity, assume that there are no checkable deposits other than demand deposits.

(a) If the Federal Reserve wants to reduce the quantity of money by $2 billion, how much of a decrease must occur in demand deposits? (b) To obtain this decrease in demand deposits, by how much must banks' legal reserves decline? (c) In fact, the ratio of currency (and coins) to demand deposits increased during the 1970s in the United States. Is this consistent with the above graph? (d) Some people attribute the rise in this ratio to an increase in tax evasion and the growth of the underground economy. Why?

SOLUTION

(a) The graph indicates that the public wants to hold $1 in currency (and coins) for every $3 in demand deposits. Thus, if demand deposits decrease by $1.5 billion, currency (and coin) will decrease by $0.5 billion, the total decrease in the money supply being $2.0 billion. (b) Since legal reserves equal 20 percent of demand deposits (because no excess reserves are held), legal reserves must decrease by $0.3 billion (that is, 20 percent of $1.5 billion) if demand deposits decrease by $1.5 billion. (c) No. (d) Because the underground economy tends to be based on the use of currency (which is not traceable) rather than deposits (which are traceable).

tion, this means that the banking system can create less in demand deposits than it could if the currency had not been withdrawn. Specifically, the banking system can create an amount of demand deposits equal to the amount of excess reserves *left permanently with the banking system* divided by the required ratio of reserves to demand deposits.

Similarly, in discussing how much demand deposits will be reduced as a consequence of a deficiency in reserves, we made the important assumption that everyone who buys a security from a bank pays the bank by check. But some people may pay partly or in full with currency, and this will affect how much the amount of demand deposits must be reduced by the banking system. If somebody pays in currency to one of the banks, this restores some of the reserves that the banking system lost. Thus, applying the rule set forth in the previous section, the banking system must reduce its demand deposits by less than if the bank had been paid by check.

In general, whether excess reserves are positive or negative, the change in demand deposits equals the reserves *left permanently with the banking system* divided by the required ratio of reserves to demand deposits. Thus *whether or not excess reserves have the maximum effect on demand deposits depends on how much of these reserves the public leaves in the banking system.*[11]

Excess Reserves

Another important assumption lies behind our discussion of the effects of an excess or deficiency of reserves on the amount of demand deposits. *We have assumed that no bank wants to hold excess reserves.* In other words, we have assumed that, whenever a bank has enough reserves to make a loan or investment, it will do so. Recall Bank A, which received a new deposit of $10,000. This new deposit enabled Bank A to increase its loans and investments by $8,333 without winding up with less than the legally required reserves. Thus we assumed that it would go ahead and make this much in additional loans and investments. In general, this seems to be a reasonable assumption, for the simple reason that loans and investments bring profits (in interest) into the bank while excess reserves bring none. During recent decades, banks have held relatively small amounts of excess reserves.

However, in the Great Depression of the 1930s, banks held large amounts of excess reserves. Why? Because the risks in lending and investment seemed great, and interest rates were very low. If a bank cannot find loans and investments it regards as attractive, it may decide to make no such loans or investments. After all, there isn't much profit to be made on a loan that is not repaid. Also, if interest rates are very low, the bank may feel that it isn't losing much by not lending money.

---

[11] Note too that people can convert demand deposits into time deposits, and vice versa. There are legal reserve requirements against time deposits, but they are lower than those against demand deposits. The conversion of demand deposits into time deposits will influence how much money can be supported by a certain amount of reserves. Thus the banking system can support an increase in the amount of demand deposits equal to the amount of excess reserves divided by the legally required ratio of reserves to demand deposits (no more, no less) only if there is no conversion of demand deposits into time deposits. In other words, we assume that all the demand deposits created by the banking system are converted into neither cash nor time deposits.

What difference does it make whether banks hold excess reserves? The answer is plenty. If, for example, Bank A decides to lend less than the full $8,333, this will mean that the injection of excess reserves will have a smaller effect on the amount of demand deposits than we indicated previously.[12] Similarly, if banks hold excess reserves, these reserves will offset what otherwise would be a deficiency. Thus *whether or not an injection or reduction of reserves has the maximum effect on demand deposits depends on the lending and investing policies of the bankers. If they do not lend out or invest as much as they can, the effect on demand deposits will be diminished accordingly.*

---

[12] Also, if a bank pays off some of its borrowings from the Fed, a $10,000 deposit may not increase its loans and investments by the full $8,333.

Test Yourself

1. "Banks do not create money. After all, they can only lend out money that they receive from depositors." Comment and evaluate.

2. Suppose that the legally required ratio of reserves to deposits is $1/5$. If the banking system's reserves shrink by $50 million, by how much will the money supply change? What assumptions are you making about excess reserves and currency withdrawals?

3. "Demand deposits are increased by banks when they call in loans and sell investments." Comment and evaluate.

4. Describe the way in which the banking system can create money if there is a single monopoly bank in the nation.

5. Suppose that the legally required ratio of reserves to deposits is $1/7$. If $100 million in excess reserves are made available to the banking system, by how much can the banking system increase the money supply? What is the answer if the legally required ratio of reserves to deposits is $1/6$ rather than $1/7$?

Summary

1. The Federal Reserve System is responsible for regulating and controlling the money supply. Established in 1913, the Federal Reserve System is composed of the member banks, 12 regional Federal Reserve Banks, and the Federal Reserve Board, which coordinates the activities of the system. The Federal Reserve is the central bank of the United States.

2. Commercial banks have two primary functions. First, they hold demand (and other checkable) deposits and permit checks to be drawn on them. Second, they lend money to firms and individuals. Most of our money supply is not coin and paper currency, but bank money—demand (and other checkable) deposits. This money is created by banks.

3. Whereas the earliest banks held reserves equal to deposits, modern banks practice fractional-reserve banking. That is, their reserves equal only a fraction of their deposits. The Federal Reserve System requires every commercial bank (and other thrift institution with checkable deposits) to hold a certain percentage of its deposits as reserves. The major purpose of these legal reserve requirements is to control the money supply.

4. Banks have become much safer in recent years, due in part to better management and regulation as well as to the government's stated willingness to insure and stand behind their deposits. However, bank failures still occur, and bank regulation is not as stringent as it might be.

5. A bank creates money by lending or investing its excess reserves. If banks had to keep reserves equal to their deposits, they could not create money. A bank cannot lend or invest more than its excess reserves, unless it is a monopoly bank, because it will wind up with less than the legally required reserves.

6. The banking system as a whole can increase its demand deposits by an amount equal to its excess reserves divided by the legally required ratio of reserves to deposits. Thus, if excess reserves in the banking system equal a certain amount, the banking system as a whole can increase demand deposits by the amount of the excess reserves divided by the legally required ratio of reserves to deposits.

7. If there is a deficiency in reserves in the banking system, the system as a whole must decrease demand deposits by the amount of this deficiency divided by the legally required ratio of reserves to deposits. Demand deposits are decreased by banks' selling securities or refusing to renew loans, just as demand deposits are increased by banks' making loans and investments.

8. Our argument so far has assumed that when excess reserves were made available to the banking system, there was no withdrawal of part of them in the form of currency, and that when deficiencies in reserves occur, no currency is deposited in banks. If such changes in the amount of currency take place, the change in demand deposits will equal the excess reserves left permanently with the banking system divided by the legally required ratio of reserves to deposits.

9. We have also assumed that the banks want to hold no excess reserves. Since banks make profits by lending money and making investments, this assumption is generally sensible. But when loans are risky and interest rates are low—for example, in the Great Depression of the 1930s—banks have been known to hold large excess reserves. Clearly, an injection of excess reserves or a deficiency of reserves will not have their full, or maximum, effect on demand deposits if the banks do not lend and invest as much as possible.

Concepts for Review

Federal Reserve System	State banks	Legal reserve requirements
Member banks	Central banks	Excess reserves
National banks	Fractional-reserve banking	Simultaneous expansion

CHAPTER 16

Monetary Policy

Like fiscal policy, monetary policy is no panacea, but it is a very important tool for stabilization of the economy. In recent years, monetary policy has been the subject of considerable controversy. For example, in early 1984, when the Federal Reserve loosened up on the money supply, some economists felt that improper monetary policy would rekindle very serious inflation in the United States, while others argued that a less restrictive monetary policy of this sort was needed to reduce unemployment. Without doubt, such controversies will continue in the future, since one thing is certain: Economists of all persuasions agree that monetary policy has a major impact on the economy.

In this chapter, we are concerned with a variety of basic questions about monetary policy. Who makes monetary policy? What sorts of tools can be employed by monetary policy makers? How does monetary policy affect our national output and the price level? What are some of the problems involved in formulating effective monetary policy? What has been the nature of monetary policy in the United States in recent decades?

The Aims of Monetary Policy

Monetary policy is the exercise of the central bank's control over the quantity of money and interest rates to promote the objectives of national economic policy. We described in Chapter 14 how the money supply influences net national product and the price level. If the economy is at considerably less than full employment, increases in the money supply tend to increase real NNP, and decreases in the money supply tend to decrease real NNP, with relatively little effect on the price level. As full employment is approached, increases in the money supply tend to affect the price level, as well as real output. Finally, once full employment is reached, increases in the money supply result primarily in increases in the price level, since real output cannot increase appreciably.

In formulating monetary policy, the government's objectives are to attain and maintain reasonably full employment without excessive inflation. In other words, when a recession seems imminent and business is soft, the monetary authorities are likely to increase the money supply and push down interest rates. That is, they will "ease credit" or "ease money," as the newspapers put it. This tends to push the aggregate demand curve to the right, thus increasing net national product. (Recall Figure 9.7.) On the other hand, when the economy is in danger of overheating and serious inflation threatens, the monetary authorities will probably rein in the money supply and push up interest rates. That is, in newspaper terms, they will "tighten credit" or "tighten money." This tends to push the aggregate demand curve to the left, thus curbing the upward pressure on the price level. (Recall Figure 9.8.)

At this point, you may be muttering to yourself, "But the aims of monetary policy are essentially the same as those of fiscal policy!" You are right. Monetary policy and fiscal policy are both aimed at promoting full employment without inflation. But they use different methods to attain this goal. Fiscal policy uses the spending and taxing powers of the government, whereas monetary policy uses the government's power over the money supply.

The Central Role of Bank Reserves

As you will recall from Chapter 14, there is a difference of view concerning the processes by which changes in the money supply affect NNP and the price level. On the one hand, monetarists use the quantity theory of money to link changes in the money supply directly to changes in nominal NNP. On the other hand, Keynesians believe that an increase (decrease) in the money supply decreases (increases) the interest rate, which in turn shifts the investment function upward (downward). This shift in the investment function tends to increase (decrease) national product.[1]

Regardless of which view is adopted, it is essential that we understand how the monetary authorities can promote their aims, since both Keynesians and monetarists acknowledge the importance of monetary policy. Economists of all persuasions would agree that a fundamental and key question is: How can the monetary authorities influence the money supply? And they would agree that the answer is: *by managing the reserves of the banking system.*

To see what this means in practice, suppose that the monetary authorities think that a recession is about to develop, and that, to prevent it, they want to increase the money supply more rapidly than they would other-

---

[1] Keynesians also recognize that spending by consumers and state and local governments, as well as investment, is likely to be affected by changes in the quantity of money. See Chapter 14. At this point we cannot do justice to either the Keynesian (early or modern) or monetarist views. Much of Chapter 17 and Appendix A is devoted to this subject.

wise. How can they realize this objective? By providing the banks with plenty of excess reserves. As we saw in the previous chapter, excess reserves enable the banks to increase the money supply. Indeed, we learned that if there were no desired excess reserves and no currency withdrawals, the banks could increase the money supply by $6 for every $1 of excess reserves.[2] (The ways in which the monetary authorities can increase the reserves of the banking system—and thus provide excess reserves—are discussed at length in subsequent sections.)

On the other hand, suppose that the monetary authorities smell a strong whiff of unacceptable inflation in the economic wind, and so decide to cut back on the rate of increase of the money supply. To do so, they can slow down the rate of increase of bank reserves. As we saw in the previous chapter, this will force the banks to curtail the rate of growth of their demand deposits, by easing off on the rate of growth of their loans and investments. Indeed, if the monetary authorities go so far as to reduce the reserves of the banking system, this will tend to reduce the money supply. Under the assumptions made in the previous chapter, the banks must cut back the money supply by $6 for every $1 deficiency in reserves.

Makers of Monetary Policy

Who establishes our monetary policy? Who decides that, in view of the current and prospective economic situation, the money supply should be increased (or decreased) at a certain rate? As in the case of fiscal policy, this is not a simple question to answer; many individuals and groups play an important role. Certainly, however, *the leading role is played by the* **Federal Reserve Board** *and the* **Federal Open Market Committee.** The chairman of the Federal Reserve Board is the chief spokesman for the Federal Reserve System. The recent chairmen—Paul A. Volcker, G. William Miller, Arthur F. Burns, and William McChesney Martin—undoubtedly have had considerable influence over monetary policy.

Although the Federal Reserve is responsible to Congress, Congress has established no clear guidelines for its behavior. Thus the Federal Reserve has had wide discretionary powers over monetary policy. But the Federal Reserve System is a huge organization, and it is not easy to figure out exactly who influences whom and who decides what. Formal actions can be taken by a majority of the board and of the Federal Open Market Committee (which is composed of the 7 members of the board plus 5 of the presidents of the 12 regional banks). However, this obviously tells only part of the story.

To get a more complete picture, it is essential to note too that many agencies and groups other than the Fed have an effect on monetary policy, although it is difficult to measure their respective influences. The Treasury

---

[2] This assumes that the legal reserve requirement is 16⅔ percent. If the legal reserve requirement were 10 percent, a $10 increase in the money supply could be supported by $1 of excess reserves. Also, as pointed out in the previous chapter, a much smaller increase in the money supply may result from a dollar of reserves if banks want to hold excess reserves and if currency is withdrawn.

The Federal Reserve building in Washington, DC

frequently has an important voice in the formulation of monetary policy. The Fed must take into account the problems of the Treasury, which is faced with the task of selling huge amounts of government securities each year. Also, congressional committees hold hearings and issue reports on monetary policy and the operations of the Federal Reserve. These hearings and reports cannot fail to have some effect on Fed policy. In addition, beginning in 1975, the Congress has stipulated that the Fed must publish its long-term targets for growth in the money supply, the purpose being to establish somewhat more control over monetary policy. Finally, the president may attempt to influence the Federal Reserve Board. To keep the board as free as possible from political pressure, members are appointed for long terms—14 years—and a term expires every 2 years. But since members frequently do not serve out their full terms, a president may be able to name more than two members during each of his terms in office. (President Carter was able to name 4 members in his first few years in office.)

The Federal Reserve Banks: Their Consolidated Balance Sheet

We know from a previous section that the Federal Reserve controls the money supply largely by controlling the quantity of member bank reserves. To understand how the Federal Reserve can control the quantity of member bank reserves, one must begin by examining the consolidated balance sheet of the 12 regional Federal Reserve Banks. Such a consolidated balance sheet is shown in Table 16.1. It pertains to November 30, 1984.

As shown in Table 16.1, the assets of the Federal Reserve Banks are largely of three kinds: gold certificates, securities, and loans to commercial banks. Each is explained below.

1. Gold certificates are warehouse receipts issued by the Treasury for gold bullion. For present purposes, this item is less important than securities or loans to commercial banks.

2. The *securities* listed on the Federal Reserve Banks' balance sheet are U.S. government bonds, notes, and bills. By buying and selling these securities, the Federal Reserve exercises considerable leverage on the quantity of member bank reserves (as we shall see below).

Table 16.1

CONSOLIDATED BALANCE SHEET OF THE 12 FEDERAL RESERVE BANKS, NOVEMBER 30, 1984 (BILLIONS OF DOLLARS)

Assets		Liabilities and net worth	
Gold certificates[a]	11	Reserves of member banks	25
Securities	158	Treasury deposits	2
Loans to commercial banks	5	Outstanding Federal Reserve notes	164
Other assets	31	Other liabilities and net worth	14
Total	205	Total	205

[a] Cash is included here too.

Source: Federal Reserve Bulletin.

3. The *loans to commercial banks* listed on the Federal Reserve Banks' balance sheet are loans of reserves that the Fed has made to commercial banks that are members of the Federal Reserve System. As pointed out in the previous chapter, the Fed can make such loans if it wants to. The interest rate charged for such loans—the discount rate—is discussed below.

According to the right-hand side of the balance sheet in Table 16.1, the liabilities of the Federal Reserve Banks are largely of three kinds: outstanding Federal Reserve notes, Treasury deposits, and reserves of member banks. Each is explained below.

1. The *outstanding Federal Reserve notes* are the paper currency that we use. Since these notes are debts of the Federal Reserve Banks, they are included among the Banks' liabilities.

2. *Treasury deposits* are the deposits which the U.S. Treasury maintains at the Federal Reserve banks. The Treasury draws checks on these deposits to pay its bills.

3. The *reserves of member banks* have been discussed in some detail in the previous chapter. Although these reserves are assets from the point of view of the commercial banks, they are liabilities from the point of view of the Federal Reserve Banks.

Open Market Operations

Table 16.1 shows that government securities constitute about 75 percent of the assets held by the Federal Reserve Banks. As we saw in Chapter 5, the market for government securities is huge and well developed. The Federal Reserve is part of this market. Sometimes it buys government securities, sometimes it sells them. Whether it is buying or selling—and how much—can have a heavy impact on the quantity of bank reserves. Indeed, the most important means the Federal Reserve has to control the quantity of bank reserves (and thus the quantity of excess reserves) are **open market operations,** which is the name given to the purchase and sale by the Fed of U.S. government securities in the open market.

BUYING SECURITIES

Suppose that the Federal Reserve buys $1 million worth of government securities in the open market, and that the seller of these securities is General Motors.[3] To determine the effect of this transaction on the quantity of bank reserves, let's look at the effect on the balance sheet of the Fed and on the balance sheet of the Chase Manhattan Bank, General Motors' bank.[4] In this transaction, the Fed receives $1 million in government securities and gives General Motors a check for $1 million. When General Motors deposits this check to its account at the Chase Manhattan Bank, the bank's demand deposits and reserves increase by $1 million.

Thus, as shown in Table 16.2, the left-hand side of the Fed's balance

---

[3] Large corporations often hold quantities of government securities.

[4] For simplicity, we assume that General Motors has only one bank, the Chase Manhattan Bank. Needless to say, this may not be the case, but it makes no difference to the point we are making here. We make a similar assumption regarding the investment firm of Merrill Lynch in the next section.

Table 16.2

EFFECT OF FED'S PURCHASING $1 MILLION OF GOVERNMENT SECURITIES (MILLIONS OF DOLLARS)

A. Effect on Fed's balance sheet:

Assets		Liabilities and net worth	
Government securities	+1	Member bank reserves	+1

B. Effect on balance sheet of the Chase Manhattan Bank:

Assets		Liabilities and net worth	
Reserves	+1	Demand deposits	+1

sheet shows a $1 million increase in government securities, and the right-hand side shows a $1 million increase in bank reserves. The left-hand side of the Chase Manhattan Bank's balance sheet shows a $1 million increase in reserves, and the right-hand side shows a $1 million increase in demand deposits. Clearly, *the Fed has added $1 million to the banks' reserves.* The situation is somewhat analogous to the $10,000 deposit at Bank A in the previous chapter.

SELLING SECURITIES

Suppose that the Federal Reserve sells $1 million worth of government securities in the open market. They are bought by Merrill Lynch, Pierce, Fenner, and Smith, a huge brokerage firm. What effect does this transaction have on the quantity of bank reserves? To find out, let's look at the balance sheet of the Fed and the balance sheet of Merrill Lynch's bank, which we again assume to be the Chase Manhattan. When Merrill Lynch buys the government securities from the Fed, the Fed gives Merrill Lynch the securities in exchange for Merrill Lynch's check for $1 million. When the Fed presents this check to the Chase Manhattan Bank for payment, Chase Manhattan's demand deposits and reserves decrease by $1 million.

Thus, as shown in Table 16.3, the left-hand side of the Fed's balance sheet shows a $1 million decrease in government securities, and the right-hand side shows a $1 million decrease in reserves. The left-hand side of the Chase Manhattan Bank's balance sheet shows a $1 million decrease in reserves, and the right-hand side shows a $1 million decrease in demand deposits. Clearly, *the Fed has reduced the reserves of the banks by $1 million.*

Table 16.3

EFFECT OF FED'S SELLING $1 MILLION OF GOVERNMENT SECURITIES (MILLIONS OF DOLLARS)

A. Effect on Fed's balance sheet:

Assets		Liabilities and net worth	
Government securities	−1	Member bank reserves	−1

B. Effect on balance sheet of the Chase Manhattan Bank:

Assets		Liabilities and net worth	
Reserves	−1	Demand deposits	−1

THE FEDERAL OPEN MARKET COMMITTEE

As indicated above, open market operations are the Fed's most important methods for controlling the money supply. The Federal Reserve adds to bank reserves when it buys government securities and reduces bank reserves when it sells them. Obviously, the extent to which the Federal Reserve increases or reduces bank reserves depends in an important way on the amount of government securities it buys or sells. The greater the amount, the greater the increase or decrease in bank reserves.

The power to decide on the amount of government securities the Fed should buy or sell at any given moment rests with the *Federal Open Market Committee*. This group wields an extremely powerful influence over bank reserves and the nation's money supply. Every three or four weeks, the Federal Open Market Committee meets to discuss the current situation and trends, and gives instructions to the manager of the Open Market Account at the Federal Reserve Bank of New York, who actually buys and sells the government securities.

Changes in Legal Reserve Requirements

Open market operations are not the only means the Federal Reserve has to influence the money supply. Another way is *to **change the legal reserve requirements.*** In other words, *the Federal Reserve Board can change the amount of reserves banks must hold for every dollar of demand deposits.* In 1934, Congress gave the Federal Reserve Board the power to set—within certain broad limits—the legally required ratio of reserves to deposits for both demand and time deposits. From time to time, the Fed uses this power to change legal reserve requirements. For example, in 1958 it cut the legally required ratio of reserves to deposits in big city banks from 17½ percent to 16½ percent, and the ratio remained there until 1968, when it was raised to 17 percent. Table 16.4 shows the legal reserve requirements in 1985. According to the 1980 financial reform act, the Fed can set the legally required ratio of reserves to deposits between the limits of 8 and 14 percent for checkable deposits. Also, on the affirmative action of five of the seven members of the Fed's board of governors, it can impose an additional re-

Table 16.4

LEGAL RESERVE REQUIREMENTS OF DEPOSITORY INSTITUTIONS, 1985

Type and size of deposits	Reserve requirements (percent of deposits)
Net transaction accounts	
Up to $28.9 million	3
Over $28.9 million	12
Nonpersonal time deposits, by original maturity	
Less than 1½ years	3
1½ years or more	0

Source: Federal Reserve *Bulletin.*

serve requirement of up to 4 percent. And in extraordinary conditions it can set the percentage at any level it deems necessary.

EFFECT OF AN INCREASE IN RESERVE REQUIREMENTS

The effect of an increase in the legally required ratio of reserves to deposits is that banks must hold larger reserves to support the existing amount of demand deposits. This in turn means that banks with little or no excess reserves will have to sell securities, refuse to renew loans, and reduce their demand deposits to meet the new reserve requirements. For example, suppose that a member bank has $1 million in reserves and $6 million in demand deposits. If the legal reserve requirement is 16 percent, it has excess reserves of $1 million minus $960,000 (.16 × $6 million), or $40,000. It is in good shape. If the legal reserve requirement is increased to 20 percent, this bank now needs $1.2 million (.20 × $6 million) in reserves. Since it only has $1 million in reserves, it must sell securities or refuse to renew loans.

Consider now what happens to the banking system as a whole. Clearly, an increase in the legally required ratio of reserves to deposits means that, with a given amount of reserves, the banking system can maintain less demand deposits than before. For example, if the banking system has $1 billion in total reserves, it can support $\frac{\$1 \text{ billion}}{.16}$, or $6.25 billion in demand deposits when the legal reserve requirement is 16 percent. But it can support only $\frac{\$1 \text{ billion}}{.20}$, or $5 billion in demand deposits when the legal reserve requirement is 20 percent. (See Table 16.5.)[5] Thus *increases in the legal reserve requirement tend to reduce the amount of demand deposits— bank money—the banking system can support.*

Table 16.5

CONSOLIDATED BALANCE SHEET OF ALL MEMBER BANKS, BEFORE AND AFTER AN INCREASE (FROM 16 TO 20 PERCENT) IN THE LEGAL RESERVE REQUIREMENT (BILLIONS OF DOLLARS)

A. Before the increase in the legal reserve requirement:

Assets		Liabilities	
Reserves	1.00	Demand deposits	6.25
Loans and investments	7.25	Net worth	2.00
Total	8.25		8.25

B. After the increase in the legal reserve requirement:

Assets		Liabilities	
Reserves	1.00	Demand deposits	5.00
Loans and investments	6.00	Net worth	2.00
Total	7.00		7.00

[5] We assume arbitrarily in Table 16.5 that the total net worth of the banks is $2 billion. Obviously, this assumption concerning the amount of total net worth makes no difference to the point we are making here. Also, for simplicity, we ignore checkable deposits other than demand deposits here and below.

EFFECT OF A DECREASE IN RESERVE REQUIREMENTS

What is the effect of a decrease in the legally required ratio of reserves to deposits? It means that banks must hold less reserves to support the existing amount of demand deposits, which in turn means that banks will suddenly find themselves with excess reserves. If the banking system has $1 billion in reserves and $5 billion in demand deposits, there are no excess reserves when the legal reserve requirement is 20 percent. But suppose the Federal Reserve lowers the legal reserve requirement to 16 percent. Now the amount of legally required reserves is $800 million ($5 billion × .16), so that the banks have $200 million in excess reserves—which means that they can increase the amount of their demand deposits. Thus *decreases in the legal reserve requirements tend to increase the amount of demand deposits—bank money—the banking system can support.*

Changes in legal reserve requirements are a rather drastic way to influence the money supply—they are to open market operations as a cleaver is to a scalpel, and so are made infrequently. For example, for about ten years—from April 1958 to January 1968—no change at all was made in legal reserve requirements for demand deposits in city banks. Nonetheless, the Fed can change legal reserve requirements if it wants to. And there can be no doubt about the potential impact of such changes. Large changes in reserve requirements can rapidly alter bank reserves and the money supply. When the Fed tightened credit in November 1978, it raised the reserve requirements for large certificates of deposit—and quickly cut bank reserves by several billions of dollars.

Changes in the Discount Rate

Still another way that the Federal Reserve can influence the money supply is through changes in the discount rate. As shown by the balance sheet of the Federal Reserve Banks (in Table 16.1), commercial banks that are members of the Federal Reserve System can borrow from the Federal Reserve when their reserves are low (if the Fed is willing). This is one of the functions of the Federal Reserve. The interest rate the Fed charges the banks for loans is called the ***discount rate,*** and the Fed can increase or decrease the discount rate whenever it chooses. Increases in the discount rate discourage borrowing from the Fed, while decreases in the discount rate encourage it.

The discount rate can change substantially and fairly often (Table 16.6). Take 1980. The discount rate was increased from 12 to 13 percent in early 1980, then reduced to 12 percent in May, 11 percent in June, and 10 percent in July, after which it was raised back up to 13 percent by December 1980. When the Fed increases the discount rate (relative to other interest rates), it makes it more expensive for banks to augment their reserves in this way; hence it tightens up a bit on the money supply. On the other hand, when the Fed decreases the discount rate, it is cheaper for banks to augment their reserves in this way, and hence the money supply eases up a bit.

The Fed is largely passive in these relations with the banks. It cannot

Basic Idea #31: The Federal Reserve influences the economy by managing the reserves of the banking system. By buying and selling U.S. government securities (open market operations), the Fed can increase or decrease the banks' reserves. Also, the Fed can change the legal reserve requirements and alter the discount rate. In this way, the Fed influences the money supply and interest rates.

Table 16.6

AVERAGE DISCOUNT RATE, 1960–84

Year	Discount rate (percent)
1960	3.53
1961	3.00
1962	3.00
1963	3.23
1964	3.55
1965	4.04
1966	4.50
1967	4.19
1968	5.17
1969	5.87
1970	5.95
1971	4.88
1972	4.50
1973	6.45
1974	7.83
1975	6.25
1976	5.50
1977	5.46
1978	7.46
1979	10.28
1980	11.77
1981	13.41
1982	11.02
1983	8.50
1984	8.80

Source: Economic Report of the President.

make the banks borrow. It can only set the discount rate and see how many banks show up at the "discount window" to borrow. Also, the Fed will not allow banks to borrow on a permanent or long-term basis. They are expected to use this privilege only to tide themselves over for short periods, not to borrow in order to relend at a profit. To discourage banks from excessive use of the borrowing privilege, the discount rate is kept relatively close to short-term market interest rates.

Most economists agree that changes in the discount rate have relatively little direct impact, and that the Fed's open market operations can and do offset easily the amount the banks borrow. Certainly changes in the discount rate cannot have anything like the direct effect on bank reserves of open market operations or changes in legal reserve requirements. *The principal importance of changes in the discount rate lies in their effects on people's expectations.* When the Fed increases the discount rate, this is generally interpreted as a sign that the Fed will tighten credit and the money supply. A cut in the discount rate is generally interpreted as a sign of easier money and lower interest rates.

Take the case in 1969 when the Federal Reserve announced an increase in the discount rate. What was the effect on the prices of stocks and bonds? They dropped sharply. Why? Because people interpreted this increase in the discount rate as a sure sign that the Fed was going to keep the money supply under tight reins to fight inflation.

Other Tools of Monetary Policy

In addition, the Federal Reserve has several other tools it can use, each of which is discussed below. These tools are generally less important than open market operations, changes in legal reserve requirements, and changes in the discount rate.

MORAL SUASION

This is a fancy term to describe various expressions of pleasure or displeasure by the Fed. In other words, the Fed tells the banks what it would like them to do or not do, and exhorts them to go along with its wishes. Banks may be asked not to "overexpand" credit. The Fed may appeal to the patriotism of the bankers, or it may make some statements that could be regarded as threats. Although the Fed does not have the power to force banks to comply with its wishes, the banks don't want to get into difficulties with the Fed. Thus moral suasion can have a definite impact, particularly for short periods. But banks are profit-oriented enterprises, and when the Fed's wishes conflict strongly with the profit motive, moral suasion may not work very well for very long.

INTEREST-RATE CEILINGS

The Fed has been able to vary the maximum interest rate commercial banks can pay on time deposits. Since the 1930s, the Fed has had the power, under **Regulation Q,** to establish a ceiling on the interest rates commercial banks can pay.[6] And the level at which this ceiling has been set has influenced the flow of funds into time deposits, savings and loan associa-

[6] During the 1930s, Congress forbade commercial banks from paying interest on demand deposits. Some people felt that many of the banks' problems in the 1920s and 1930s were due to too much competition. Hence this law. It is easy to see why bankers felt that their earnings would be improved if none of them was allowed to compete for deposits by paying interest, but this is hardly consistent with a competitive philosophy. In recent years, the situation has changed radically. For example, since the late 1970s (and particularly since the 1980 financial reform act), one can write checks on interest-bearing NOW accounts (discussed in Chapter 14).

Example 16.1   Monetary Policy and the Aggregate Demand Curve

Monetary policy has an important effect on the aggregate demand curve. As you will recall from Chapter 9, the aggregate demand curve is drawn on the assumption that the money supply is fixed.

(a) What effect does an increase in the money supply have on the aggregate demand curve? Does it shift it to the left or the right? Why? (b) Suppose that the economy is experiencing inflationary pressures. Specifically, assume that the price level is OP and the aggregate demand curve is AD_1, as shown below.

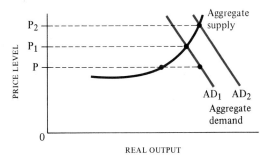

If the money supply remains fixed, in what way will these pressures work themselves out? (c) Suppose that the Fed increases the money supply to such an extent that the aggregate demand curve shifts from AD_1 to AD_2. Will the inflationary pressures subside? Will the inflation abate?

SOLUTION

(a) An increase in the money supply shifts the aggregate demand curve to the right. (A decrease in the money supply shifts the aggregate demand curve to the left.) Because an increase in the money supply lowers interest rates and increases investment, it raises aggregate demand (when the price level is held constant). (b) The price level will increase to OP_1, at which point aggregate demand and aggregate supply will be equal. (c) No. When the price level increases from OP to OP_1, there still are inflationary pressures. The price level must increase from OP_1 to OP_2, at which point aggregate demand and supply will be equal. Thus inflation does not abate after the increase in the price level to OP_1. (And so long as the Fed continues to increase the money supply at a relatively rapid rate, it will not abate.)

tions, and other financial institutions. In particular, by preventing commercial banks from paying more than a certain rate of interest on time deposits, the Fed has been able to protect the savings and loan associations, which are important sources of funds for the construction industry. In other words, the Fed could prevent the commercial banks from drawing too many deposits away from the savings and loan associations.

Because it has been aimed so directly at the construction industry, Regulation Q is often regarded as a selective credit control, not as a general tool of monetary policy. (A *selective credit control* is a control aimed at the use of credit for specific purposes.) Most economists favor the elimination of such interest ceilings on the grounds that they interfere with the functioning of free markets for funds. In 1980, the Congress passed a financial reform act phasing out Regulation Q over a six-year period.

STOCK MARKET CREDIT

Another of the Fed's tools is to vary the margin requirements for the purchase of stocks. *Margin requirements* set the maximum percentage of the price of stocks that a person can borrow. For example, in the early 1960s, you could borrow 50 percent of the cost of such securities from your broker, but in late 1972, you could borrow only 35 percent from your broker.

This is another example of a selective credit control. It may seem odd that margin requirements for the purchase of stocks were singled out for special treatment, but the severity of the stock market crash in 1929 was attributed partly to the fact that people in those days could borrow a large percentage—sometimes even 90 percent—of the value of the stock they purchased. (When stock prices slid, their small margin vanished, and unable to put up more margin, they were sold out.) Consequently, after the crash, margin requirements were imposed.

Test Yourself

1. Suppose that the Federal Reserve buys $5 million worth of government securities from U.S. Steel. Insert the effects in the blanks below.

Effects on Fed's balance sheet:

Securities _____ Member bank reserves _____

Effects on balance sheet of U.S. Steel's bank:

Reserves _____ Demand deposits _____

2. Suppose that the Federal Reserve sells $5 million worth of government securities to U.S. Steel. What is the effect on the quantity of bank reserves?

3. "When the Fed increases legal reserve requirements, it loosens credit, because the banks have more reserves." Comment and evaluate.

4. "Regulation Q interferes with the functioning of free markets, and should be abandoned. By establishing a floor under interest rates, it promotes inflation." Comment and evaluate.

5. Suppose that you have $5,000 to invest. At a restaurant you overhear someone saying that the Fed is almost certain to increase the discount rate dramatically. If this rumor is correct, do you think that you should invest now, or wait until after the increase in the discount rate? Or doesn't it matter? Be sure to explain the reasons for your preference (or lack of it) in this regard.

When Is Monetary Policy Tight or Easy?

Everyone daydreams about being powerful and important. It is a safe bet, however, that few people under the age of 21 daydream about being members of the Federal Reserve Board or the Federal Open Market Committee. Yet the truth is that the members of the board and the committee are among the most powerful people in the nation. Suppose you were appointed to the Federal Reserve Board. As a member, you would have to decide—month by month, year by year—exactly how much government securities the Fed should buy or sell, as well as whether and when changes should be made in the discount rate, legal reserve requirements, and the other instruments of Federal Reserve policy. How would you go about making your choices?

Obviously you would need lots of data. Fortunately, the Fed has a very large and able research staff to provide you with plenty of the latest information about what is going on in the economy. But what sorts of data should you look at? One thing you would want is some information on the extent to which monetary policy is inflationary or deflationary—that is, the extent to which it is *"easy"* or *"tight."* This is not simple to measure, but there is general agreement that the members of the Federal Reserve Board —and other members of the financial and academic communities—look closely at short-term interest rates and the rate of increase of the money supply.

THE LEVEL OF SHORT-TERM INTEREST RATES

As indicated in Chapter 14, Keynesians have tended to believe that changes in the quantity of money affect aggregate demand via their effects on the interest rate. High interest rates tend to reduce investment, which in turn reduces NNP. Low interest rates tend to increase investment, which in turn increases NNP. Because of their emphasis on these relationships, Keynesians tend to view monetary tightness or ease in terms of the behavior of interest rates. High interest rates are interpreted as meaning that monetary policy is tight. Low interest rates are interpreted as meaning that monetary policy is easy.

According to many economists, the *real interest rate,* not the *nominal interest rate,* is what counts in this context. The *real* interest rate is the percentage increase in *real* purchasing power that the lender receives from the borrower in return for making the loan. The *nominal* interest rate is the percentage increase in *money* that the lender receives from the borrower in return for making the loan. The crucial difference between the real rate of interest and the nominal rate of interest is that the former is *adjusted for inflation* whereas the latter is not.

Suppose that a firm borrows $1,000 for a year at 12 percent interest, and that the rate of inflation is 9 percent. When the firm repays the lender $1,120 at the end of the year, this amount of money is worth only $1,120 ÷ 1.09, or about $1,030, when corrected for inflation. Thus the real rate of interest on this loan is 3 percent, not 12 percent (the nominal rate). Why? Because the lender receives $30 in constant dollars (which is 3 percent of the amount lent) in return for making the loan. The real rate of interest is of importance in investment decisions because it measures the real cost of borrowing money.[7]

THE RATE OF INCREASE OF THE MONEY SUPPLY

As indicated in Chapter 14, monetarists have tended to link changes in the quantity of money directly to changes in NNP. Consequently, they have tended to view monetary tightness or ease in terms of the behavior of the money supply. When the money supply is growing at a relatively slow rate (much less than 4 or 5 percent per year), this is interpreted as meaning that monetary policy is tight. A relatively rapid rate of growth in the money supply (much more than 4 or 5 percent per year) is taken to mean that monetary policy is easy.

Another measure stressed by the monetarists is the **monetary base,** which by definition equals member bank reserves plus currency outside member banks. The monetary base is important because the total money supply is dependent upon—and made from—it. A relatively slow rate of growth in the monetary base (much less than 4 or 5 percent per year) is interpreted as a sign of tight money. A relatively rapid rate of growth (much more than 4 or 5 percent per year) is taken to mean that monetary policy is easy.

Should the Fed Pay More Attention to Interest Rates or the Money Supply?

We have just seen that the level of interest rates and the rate of growth of the money supply are the two principal indicators of monetary tightness or ease. Unfortunately, the Fed may not be able to control them both. To see this, suppose that the existing money supply equals $300 billion, and that the public's demand curve for money shifts upward and to the right, as shown in Figure 16.1. That is, at each level of the rate of interest, the public demands a greater amount of money than heretofore. If the interest rate remains at 12 percent, the quantity of money demanded by the public will exceed $300 billion, the existing quantity supplied. Thus the level of interest rates will rise from 12 to 14 percent, as shown in Figure 16.1. Economists who favor the use of interest rates as an indicator are likely to warn that, unless interest rates are reduced, a recession will ensue.

The Fed can push the level of interest rates back down by increasing the quantity of money. The equilibrium value of the interest rate is the one where the quantity of money demanded equals the quantity of money supplied. (Recall Chapter 14.) If the demand curve for money remains fixed at its new higher level, the Fed can push the interest rate back down to 12 percent by increasing the quantity of money to $330 billion. With this quantity of money, the equilibrium interest rate is 12 percent, as shown in Figure 16.1. However, by doing so, the Fed no longer is increas-

Basic Idea #32: To measure how tight or easy monetary policy is, economists generally look at the level of interest rates, the rate of increase of the money supply, and the rate of increase of the monetary base. Sometimes these measures point in different directions. This, together with the fact that monetary policy affects the economy with a fairly long lag, makes the Fed's job difficult.

[7] Expressed as an equation, $i_r = i_n - p$, where i_r is the real rate of interest, i_n is the nominal rate of interest, and p is the rate of inflation. In the example in the text, $i_n = 12$ percent and $p = 9$ percent; thus $i_r = 3$ percent.

Figure 16.1

**Effect of a Shift in the Demand Curve
for Money** *If the demand curve for
money shifts upward and to the right, as
shown here, the equilibrium value of the
interest rate will increase from 12 to 14
percent, if the quantity of money supplied
remains $300 billion. (Recall from
Chapter 14 that the equilibrium value of
the interest rate is the one where the
quantity of money demanded equals the
quantity supplied.) If the Fed wants to
push the equilibrium level of the interest
rate back to 12 percent, it must increase
the quantity of money supplied to $330
billion.*

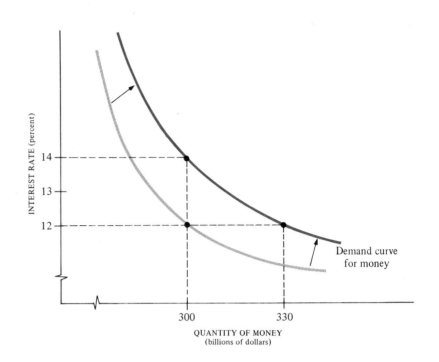

ing the money supply in accord with its previous objectives. Economists
who favor the use of the rate of growth of the money supply as an indicator are likely to warn that the Fed is increasing the money supply at too
rapid a rate.

Thus the Fed is faced with a dilemma. If it does not push interest rates
back down to their former level, some economists will claim it is promoting
recession. If it does do so, other economists will claim it is promoting inflation. Unfortunately, it is very difficult for the Fed (or anyone else) to tell
exactly how much weight should be attached to each of these indicators. In
the 1950s and 1960s, the Fed paid much more attention to interest rates
than to the rate of increase of the money supply. In the 1970s and 1980s,
due to the growing influence of the monetarists, the Fed has put more emphasis on the rate of growth of the money supply, although it continues to
pay considerable attention to interest rates.

Decision Making at the Fed: A Case Study

Let's continue to assume that you have been appointed to the Federal Reserve Board, and that the economy suddenly is confronted with what seems
to be a dangerously inflationary situation. What sort of action would you
recommend? One appropriate action might be to sell a considerable
amount of government securities, which would reduce bank reserves. You
might also recommend an increase in the discount rate or even an increase
in legal reserve requirements. To see how well you were doing, you would
watch the variables discussed in the previous section. Specifically, you
would look at the rate of increase of the money supply, as well as the rate of

increase of the monetary base, and try to reduce both. At the same time you would try to increase interest rates.

Let's compare your recommendations with what the Fed really did in a similar situation. You will recall that in 1979 the inflation rate began to hit double digits. In the second quarter of 1979 the money supply began to rise sharply. Financial managers here and abroad issued statements that inflation was reaching dangerous levels. Fiscal policy was not used to curb this inflation. Consequently, much of the responsibility for fighting inflation fell to the Federal Reserve. What actions did it take?

On Saturday, October 6, 1979, the Federal Open Market Committee held a special meeting where the members were quartered in different hotels to avoid attracting public attention. Feeling that extraordinary measures were required, the committee raised reserve requirements and increased the discount rate from 11 to 12 percent, even though it was widely believed that the economy had entered a recession. At the same time, the committee indicated that it would try to reduce the rate of growth of the money supply. Some people on Wall Street called the announcement the Saturday Night Special, since it hit the financial community hard.

In the last quarter of 1979, the rate of growth of the money supply fell to about 5 percent. Interest rates rose sharply. The prime rate, which had been about 13 percent in September 1979, hit 20 percent in April 1980. However, inflationary pressures were still great. Between December 1979 and February 1980, the Consumer Price Index rose at an annual rate of 17 percent. Financial markets were demoralized. Since there was the risk of inflation getting even worse, and of interest rates therefore going through the roof, it was difficult, if not impossible, for market participants to determine what interest rate to set on new bonds. Consequently, the long-term bond market in large part suspended operations for a while.

It was hoped that the widely anticipated recession, which finally began in January 1980, would bring down the inflation rate, as well as interest rates. When asked whether monetary tightening would result in a recession, Federal Reserve Chairman Volcker is reported to have said, "yes, and the sooner the better." Apparently, policy makers felt that the most important thing was to reduce inflation, even if a slight or moderate recession ensued. In March 1980, President Carter announced a new inflation plan. The Fed's role in the new program was to tighten monetary policy further.

Clearly, the Fed did pretty much what you would have recommended. It cut down on the rate of increase of the money supply, and pushed up interest rates. Unfortunately, such actions may reduce real output (and increase unemployment), as well as cut the inflation rate. Some liberals criticized the Fed's actions on these grounds. Others, particularly conservatives, said that the Fed moved too slowly and not vigorously enough to quell inflation. In fact, inflation, while subsiding significantly, remained at historically high levels during the early 1980s. But in early 1982, it declined substantially.[8]

[8] Much of the material in this section is taken from T. Mayer, J. Duesenberry, and R. Aliber, *Money, Banking, and the Economy,* New York: Norton, 1981; and W. Melton, *Inside the Fed,* Homewood, Illinois: Dow Jones-Irwin, 1985.

Example 16.2   How Quickly Does Monetary Policy Work?

An enormous amount of statistical and econometric research has been carried out to determine how quickly an unanticipated recession can be combated by monetary policy. According to Robert Gordon of Northwestern University, the total lag between the occurrence of such an unanticipated slowdown in economic activity and the impact of monetary policy is about 14 months. In other words, it takes about 14 months for the Federal Reserve to become aware of the slowdown, to take the appropriate actions, and to have these actions affect real GNP.

(a) On the average, how long do you think it takes for a slowdown to be reflected in the government's economic data? (b) How long do you think it takes for the Fed to pay attention to the signal and change monetary policy? (c) Once a change has been made in the rate of increase of the money supply, how long do you think it takes until real GNP is affected? (d) What problems result from the long lag between a change in economic conditions and the impact of monetary policy?

SOLUTION

(a)–(c) According to Gordon, the lags are approximately as follows:*

Lag	Months
From slowdown to reflection in economic data	2
From reflection in economic data to change in money supply	3
From change in money supply to effect on real GNP	9
Total	14

(d) By the time the effects of the expansionary monetary policy are felt, the economy may not need additional stimulus. Suppose that you were driving a car in which the wheels responded to turns of the steering wheel with a substantial lag. The problems would be analogous to those confronting the Fed.

* R. Gordon, *Macroeconomics,* Boston: Little, Brown, 1978, p. 471.

Monetary Policy in the United States

THE NIXON AND FORD YEARS

For a more complete—and more balanced—picture of monetary policy in the United States, let's look briefly at the history of monetary policy since the late 1960s. When the Nixon administration came into office in 1969, inflation was unquestionably the nation's principal economic problem. Thus practically everyone, both Republicans and Democrats, agreed that monetary policy should be tight. In accord with this view, the Federal Reserve kept a close rein on the money supply during 1969. The result, however, was to slow the growth of national output and to increase unemployment. In August 1971, President Nixon announced his new economic policy, which entailed direct controls of wages, prices, and rents, as well as an expansionary fiscal policy. In line with the more expansionary tone of his economic policies, the president announced in early 1972 that "the Federal Reserve has taken steps to create the monetary conditions necessary for rapid economic expansion." In fact, the money supply grew by about 8 percent in 1972.

After wage and price controls were largely removed in 1973, open inflation occurred with a vengeance. In the *single month* of June 1973, wholesale prices increased by 2.4 percent. President Nixon responded by slapping a 60-day freeze on most prices (but not wages) beginning in mid-June of 1973. And the Federal Reserve, whose chairman was Arthur F. Burns (who had spent much of his professional life as an economist at Columbia University and with the National Bureau of Economic Research), tightened money considerably. On June 8, 1973, the Fed raised the discount rate to 6½ percent, its highest level since 1921.

During 1973 and 1974 the Federal Reserve cut back on the rate of increase in the money supply. During 1973 the money supply grew by about 6 percent; during 1974, it grew by about 5 percent. Interest rates reached unprecedented heights in 1974. On the average, the discount rate was almost 8 percent during the year. And the prime bank rate—the interest rate that commercial banks charge their best customers—exceeded 12 percent for a time. Many critics of the Nixon and Ford administrations charged that the Federal Reserve was taking too strong a stance in its fight against inflation.

In 1974 the United States was in a recession. During the first quarter of 1975 there was little or no growth in the money supply, but in subsequent quarters the Fed permitted the money supply to grow more rapidly, with the result that the money supply increased by about 4 percent during the year as a whole. Critics of the Fed maintained that it increased the money supply much too slowly in 1975, thus impeding the recovery.

THE CARTER YEARS

In his 1976 campaign, President Carter belabored Arthur F. Burns and the Fed on these grounds, and once Carter became president, there was speculation that he and Burns might clash. During 1977 the narrowly defined money supply (*M*-1) grew by about 7 percent, and the broadly defined money supply (*M*-2) grew by about 9 percent. Interest rates increased somewhat. Velocity increased, as it had during 1976, apparently due in part to the adoption by corporations and individuals of methods to conserve on money balances. Monetary policy in 1977 was not restrictive.

In 1978 the rate of inflation once again approached double-digit levels. As many observers predicted, President Carter did not reappoint Arthur F. Burns as chairman of the Fed; instead, the job went to G. William Miller, an industrialist. In late 1978 the Fed, led by Miller, raised the discount rate to an all-time high of 9½ percent. Some reserve requirements were also increased. The narrowly defined money supply (*M*-1) grew by about 7 percent, and the broadly defined money supply (*M*-2) grew by about 4 percent in 1978.

In August 1979 Miller resigned as Fed chairman (to become secretary of the Treasury) and was succeeded by Paul Volcker, formerly president of the Federal Reserve Bank of New York. In his first months in office, Volcker was viewed as a more determined foe of inflation than his predecessor. Interest rates were pushed to record highs. Yet the rate of inflation, which was widely regarded as the nation's number one economic problem, stubbornly remained at well above 10 percent.

THE REAGAN YEARS

During 1981, the prime rate was pushed up to about 20 percent, and the general public as well as the financial community was getting the message that the Fed meant business in its fight against inflation. The widespread expectation that inflation would continue unchecked began to disappear. During 1982, the Consumer Price Index rose by about 4 percent, which was high relative to 20 years before, but low relative to the late 1970s. The money supply grew by about 8 or 9 percent in 1982 and 1983, and interest rates fell substantially. By early 1985, the prime rate was about 11 percent.

Nonetheless, the *real* interest rate (the nominal interest rate minus the rate of inflation) remained relatively high in early 1985. Since the inflation rate was about 4 percent, the real rate of interest was 11 percent (the prime rate) minus 4 percent (the inflation rate), or 7 percent. Many economists blamed the relatively high level of the real interest rate on the huge deficits run by the federal government.

In early 1985, there was considerable public sentiment that the Fed should ease money and lower interest rates to extend the recovery, which was in its third year. At the same time, some economists were warning that inflation, while reduced, was still a potential problem.

Problems in Formulating Monetary Policy

Before attempting to evaluate the Fed's record, we must recognize the three major kinds of decisions it must continually make. First, the Fed must maintain a constant watch on the economy, checking for signs that the economy is sliding into a recession, being propelled into an inflationary boom, or growing satisfactorily. As we saw in Chapter 13, there is no foolproof way to forecast the economy's short-term movements. Recognizing the fallibility of existing forecasting techniques all too well, the Fed must nonetheless use these techniques as best it can to guide its actions.

Second, having come to some tentative conclusion about the direction in which the economy is heading, the Fed must decide to what extent it should tighten or ease money. The answer depends on the Fed's estimates of when monetary changes will take effect and the magnitude of their impact, as well as on its forecasts of the economy's future direction. Also, the answer depends on the Fed's evaluation of the relative importance of full employment and price stability as national goals. If it regards full employment as much more important than price stability, it will probably want to err in the direction of easy money. On the other hand, if it thinks price stability is at least

Some say the Fed is responsible to Congress. Its enabling legislation was passed by Congress in 1913, and it could presumably be reorganized should it sufficiently rouse Congress's wrath. But Congress moves with nothing if not deliberate speed, and it seldom has sought to influence the Federal Reserve through major new legislation. The president fills vacancies on the Board of Governors, but since terms on the board run for 14 years, presidents may have to wait until their second term to appoint a majority of the board.

The Federal Open Market Committee

In fact, as knowledgeable observers often agree, there are two groups that, without appearing prominently on the organization chart, exercise considerable influence over the policies of the Fed. One is the business community—a group with a definite interest in preserving the value of a dollar. The second is the board's professional staff of senior economists. Administrations come and go, but staff economists remain, and their uniquely detailed knowledge of the workings of the Fed assure them a hearing at 20th and Constitution.

Does it matter that the Fed is a focal point for the forces in the economy who fear inflation and are willing to accept somewhat higher unemployment in the hopes prices will not rise as rapidly? It may matter less than the formal structure suggests. Virtually since its inception, the Federal Reserve has had a crop of antagonistic observers in Congress. Former Secretary of the Treasury John Connally compared one of the Fed's perennial congressional foes to a cross-eyed discus thrower. "He'll never set any records for distance but he certainly keeps the crowd on its toes."

All chairmen of the Fed—such as Paul Volcker, G. William Miller, and Arthur Burns in recent years—have been sensitive to the ultimate vulnerability of the Fed's independence, and so have been reluctant to buck administration policy too dramatically. Whether the Federal Reserve's current procedures could survive a general call for more accountability is an open question. In early 1975, Congress passed a resolution that the Federal Reserve must publish its targets for growth in the money supply. But the extent to which this really tied the Fed's hands has been by no means clear. Some critics say that the targets have been adjusted frequently to agree with the actual growth of the money supply. In 1978, the Humphrey-Hawkins Act called for annual targets for the growth in the money supply, as well as semiannual reports to Congress concerning the Fed's performance in hitting the targets. But the money supply routinely grew at rates outside the targets. In the Reagan administration, some officials have felt that the Fed's independence should be curtailed, but no such changes have been passed by Congress.

E.A.

as important as full employment, it may want to err in the direction of tight money.

Finally, once the Fed has decided what it wants to do, it must figure out how to do it. Should open market operations do the whole job? If so, how big must be the purchase or sale of government securities? Should a change be made in the discount rate, or in legal reserve requirements? How big a change? Should moral suasion be resorted to? These are the operational questions the Fed continually must answer.

In answering these questions, the Fed must reckon with two very inconvenient facts, both of which make life difficult.

1. There is often a long lag between an action by the Fed and its effect on the economy. Although the available evidence indicates that monetary policy affects some types of expenditures more rapidly than others, it is not uncommon for the bulk of the total effects to occur a year or more after the change in monetary policy.[9] Thus the Fed may act to head off an imminent recession, but find that some of the consequences of its action are not felt until later, when inflation—not recession—is the problem. Conversely, the Fed may act to curb an imminent inflation, but find that the consequences of its action are not felt until some time later, when recession, not inflation, has become the problem. In either case, the Fed can wind up doing more harm than good.

2. Experts disagree about which of the available measures—such as interest rates, the rate of increase of the money supply, or the rate of increase of the monetary base—is the best measure of how tight or easy monetary policy is. Fortunately, these measures often point in the same direction; but when they point in different directions, the Fed can be misled. During 1967–68, the Fed wanted to tighten money somewhat. Using interest rates as the primary measures of the tightness of monetary policy, it increased interest rates. However, at the same time, it permitted a substantial rate of increase in the money supply and the monetary base. By doing so, the Fed—in the eyes of many experts—really eased, not tightened money.

How Well Has the Fed Performed?

Given the difficult problems the Federal Reserve faces and the fact that its performance cannot be measured by any simple standard, it would be naïve to expect that its achievement could be graded like an arithmetic quiz. Nonetheless, just as war is too important to be left to the generals, so monetary policy is too important to be left unscrutinized to the monetary authorities. According to recent studies of Federal Reserve policy making, what have been the strengths and weaknesses of the Fed's decisions?

Forecasting. If one takes into account the limitations in existing forecasting techniques, the Fed seems to have done a reasonably good job in recent years of recognizing changes in economic conditions. As noted in previous sections, it sometimes was a bit slow to see that the economy was sinking into a recession, or that inflationary pressures were dominant. But hindsight is always much clearer than foresight (which is why Monday-

---

[9] Robert Gordon has estimated that it takes about 9 months for a change in the money supply to affect real GNP. See Example 16.2.

morning quarterbacks make so few mistakes—and get paid so little). Because the Fed did a creditable job of recognizing changes in economic conditions, the time interval between changes in economic conditions and changes in policy was rather short, particularly when compared with the corresponding time interval for fiscal policy.

Recognition of Lags. The Fed does not seem to have taken much account of the long—and seemingly quite variable—lags between changes in monetary policy and their effects on the economy. Instead, it simply reacted quickly to changes in business conditions. As pointed out in a previous section, such a policy can in reality be quite destabilizing. For example, the Fed may act to suppress inflationary pressures, but find that the consequences of its action are not felt until some time later when recession—not inflation—is the problem. Unfortunately, the truth is that, despite advances in knowledge in the past decade, economists do not have a firm understanding of these lags. Thus the Fed is only partly to blame.

Coordination. With a few notable exceptions, there generally seems to have been reasonably good coordination between the Federal Reserve and the executive branch (the Treasury and the Council of Economic Advisers, in particular). This is important because monetary policy and fiscal policy should work together, not march off in separate directions. The fact that the Fed and the executive branch have generally been aware of one another's views and probable actions does not mean that there has always been agreement between them. Nor does it mean that, even when they agreed, they could always point monetary and fiscal policy in the same direction. But at least the left hand had a pretty good idea of what the right hand was doing.

Measures. The Fed has been criticized for paying too much attention during the 1950s and 1960s to interest rates as measures of the tightness or looseness of monetary policy, and giving too little attention to the rate of growth of the money supply and the monetary base. During the 1970s and 1980s, however, the Fed has paid much more attention to the rate of growth of the money supply and the monetary base. Again, the fault is only partly the Fed's, since the experts cannot agree on the relative importance that should be attached to each measure. But wherever the fault, if any, may lie, the Fed's performance is bound to suffer if it acts on the basis of unreliable measures.

Emphasis. The Fed is often criticized for putting too much emphasis on preventing inflation and too little on preventing unemployment. According to various studies, it probably is true that the Fed has been more sensitive to the dangers of inflation than has the Congress or the administration. Liberals, emphasizing the great social costs of excessive unemployment, tend to denounce the Fed for such behavior. Without question, the costs of unemployment are high, as stressed in Chapter 8. Conservatives, on the other hand, argue that governments are tempted to resort to inflation in order to produce the short-term appearance of prosperity, even though the long-term effects may be undesirable. They say that, in the short run (when the next election is decided), unemployment is more likely than inflation to result in defeat at the polls. Whether you think that the Fed has put too much emphasis on restraining inflation will depend on the relative importance that you attach to reducing unemployment, on the one hand, and reducing inflation, on the other.

Should the Fed Be Governed by a Rule?

Many monetarists, led by Milton Friedman, go so far as to say that the Fed's attempts to "lean against the wind"—by easing money when the economy begins to dip and tightening money when the economy begins to get overheated—really do more harm than good. In their view, the Fed actually intensifies business fluctuations by changing the rate of growth of the money supply. Why? Partly because the Fed sometimes pays too much attention to measures other than the money supply. But more fundamentally, it is because the Fed tends to overreact to ephemeral changes, and because the effects of changes in the money supply on the economy occur with a long and highly variable lag. In their view, this lag is so unpredictable that the Fed—no matter how laudatory its intent—tends to intensify business fluctuations.

According to Professor Friedman and his followers, the Fed should abandon its attempts to "lean against the wind." *They propose that the Fed conform to a rule that the money supply should increase at some fixed, agreed-upon rate, such as 4 or 5 percent per year. The Fed's job would be simply to see that the money supply grows at approximately this rate.* The monetarists do not claim that a rule of this sort would prevent all business fluctuations, but they do claim that it would work better than the existing system. In particular, they feel that it would prevent the sorts of major depressions and inflations we have experienced in the past. Without major decreases in the money supply (such as occurred during the crash of 1929–33), major depressions could not occur. Without major increases in the money supply (such as occurred during World War II), major inflations could not occur. Of course, it would be nice if monetary policy could iron out minor business fluctuations as well, but in their view this simply cannot be done at present.

This proposal has received considerable attention from both economists and politicians. A number of studies have been carried out to try to estimate what would have happened if Friedman's rule had been used in the past. The results, although by no means free of criticism, seem to indicate that such a rule might have done better than discretionary action did in preventing the Great Depression of the 1930s and the inflation during World War II. But in the period since World War II, the evidence in favor of such a rule is less persuasive. Most economists seem to believe that it would be a mistake to handcuff the Fed to a simple rule of this sort. They think that a discretionary monetary policy can outperform Friedman's rule.

Nonetheless, the debate over rules versus discretionary action goes on, and the issues are still very much alive. Professor Friedman has been able to gain important converts, including the Federal Reserve Bank of St. Louis and members of the Joint Economic Committee of Congress. Indeed, after the Fed's "stop-go" policies of 1966–68 (when the Fed tightened money sharply in 1966 and loosened it rapidly in 1967–68), the Joint Economic Committee urged the Fed to adopt a rule of the sort advocated by Friedman. In 1968, the committee complained that its advice was not being followed, and special hearings were held. The Council of Economic Advisers and the secretary of the Treasury sided with the Fed against adopting such a rule. Some academic economists favor such a rule, others oppose it, and considerable economic research is being carried out to try to clarify and resolve the questions involved.

Test Yourself

1. "The Fed should keep interest rates low to promote prosperity. Unfortunately, however, it is dominated by bankers who like high interest rates because they increase bank profits." Comment and evaluate.

2. "The Fed is like a driver whose steering wheel takes about a minute to influence the car's wheels." Comment and evaluate.

3. Explain why the Federal Reserve may not be able to control both the level of interest rates and the rate of growth of the money supply. What problems does this cause?

4. According to economist Sherman Maisel, William McChesney Martin, former chairman of the Federal Reserve Board, felt "that the primary function of the Federal Reserve Board was to determine what was necessary to maintain a sound currency. . . . [To Martin] it is as immoral for a country today to allow the value of its currency to fall as it was for kings of old to clip coinage." Do you agree with Martin's views? Why or why not?

Summary

1. Monetary policy is concerned with the money supply and interest rates. Its purpose is to attain and maintain full employment without inflation. When a recession seems imminent and business is soft, the monetary authorities are likely to increase the money supply and reduce interest rates. On the other hand, when the economy is in danger of overheating and inflation threatens, the monetary authorities are likely to rein in the money supply and push up interest rates.

2. Monetary policy and fiscal policy are aimed at much the same goals, but they use different methods to promote them. One advantage of monetary policy over fiscal policy is that the lag between decision and action is relatively short. In view of the time involved in getting tax (and spending) changes enacted, this is an important point.

3. Although monetary policy is influenced by Congress, the Treasury, and other parts of the government and the public at large, the chief responsibility for the formulation of monetary policy lies with the Federal Reserve Board and the Federal Open Market Committee. To a very large extent, monetary policy operates by changing the quantity of bank reserves.

4. The most important tool of monetary policy is open market operations, which involve the buying and selling of government securities in the open market by the Federal Reserve. When the Fed buys government securities, this increases bank reserves. When the Fed sells government securities, this reduces bank reserves.

5. The Fed can also tighten or ease money by increasing or decreasing the discount rate or by increasing or decreasing legal reserve requirements. In addition, the Fed can use moral suasion.

6. As indicators of how tight or easy monetary policy is, the Fed has looked at the level of short-term interest rates, the rate of growth of the money supply, and the rate

of growth of the monetary base. During the 1950s and 1960s, the Fed paid most attention to the first indicator; in the 1970s and 1980s, the Fed increased the amount of attention paid to the last two.

7. The Federal Reserve is faced with many difficult problems in formulating and carrying out monetary policy. It must try to see where the economy is heading, and whether—and to what extent—it should tighten or ease money to stabilize the economy. This task is made very difficult by the fact that there is often a long—and highly variable—lag between an action by the Fed and its effect on the economy. There is also considerable disagreement over the best way to measure how tight or easy monetary policy is.

8. There has been criticism of various kinds regarding the performance of the Federal Reserve. Often, the Fed is criticized for paying too little attention to the long lags between its actions and their effects on the economy. Some monetarists, led by Milton Friedman, believe that monetary policy would be improved if discretionary policy were replaced by a rule that the Fed should increase the money supply at some fixed, agreed-on rate, such as 4 or 5 percent per year.

Concepts for Review

Monetary policy	Changes in legal	Selective credit control
Federal Reserve Board	reserve requirements	Margin requirements
Federal Open Market	Discount rate	Easy money
Committee	Moral suasion	Tight money
Open market operations	Regulation Q	Monetary base

CHAPTER 17

Controversies Over Stabilization Policy

During the past several decades, there has been a continuing controversy among economists over the effects of monetary and fiscal policy on output and employment, as well as over the kinds of public policies that should be adopted. This controversy has engaged the attention of many leading economists, and has had a major influence on the thinking of policy makers in both the public and private sectors of the economy. In previous chapters, we have discussed particular aspects of this controversy. Now we look at it in more detail. We begin by discussing the differences between the Keynesians and monetarists.[1] Then we describe the views of the rational expectations theorists and the "supply-side" economists.

At the outset, it is important to recognize that each of these groups is characterized by a great deal of disagreement. For example, Keynesians differ considerably among themselves, and so do monetarists. Moreover, as times have changed and evidence has accumulated, each group has changed its position. Thus the Keynesian views of the 1980s are not the same as those of the 1950s, and labels like neo-Keynesian or nonmonetarist are often used to represent the recent views of the Keynesians.

In the first part of this chapter, we describe the traditional differences between the Keynesians and monetarists. In particular, we discuss their disagreements over the causes of business fluctuations, the stability of the economy, the role of the interest rate, and the effects of monetary and fiscal policy. Then, in the second half of this chapter, we describe the current state

[1] In Appendix A, we present the Keynesian-monetarist controversy in terms of a more complete model (involving *IS* and *LM* curves) than is constructed here.

of the Keynesian—monetarist debate, as well as the views of the rational expectations and supply-side economists. The latter groups have been quite influential in the late 1970s and 1980s.

Monetarists versus Keynesians: The Historical Background

The debate between the monetarists and the Keynesians has not been limited to the classroom and scholarly gatherings. It has spilled over onto the pages of the daily newspapers and aroused considerable interest in Congress and other parts of the government. At heart, the argument has been over what determines the level of output, employment, and prices. The Keynesians have put more emphasis on the federal budget than have the monetarists; the monetarists have put more emphasis on the money supply than have the Keynesians. To understand this debate, we need to know something about the recent development of economic thought. Until the Great Depression of the 1930s, the prevailing theory was that NNP, expressed in real terms, would tend automatically to its full-employment level. (Recall from Chapter 8 the classical economists' reasons for clinging to this belief.) Moreover, the prevailing theory was that the price level could be explained by the crude quantity theory of money. In other words, the price level, P, was assumed to be proportional to the quantity of money, M, because $MV = PQ$, and both Q (real NNP) and V (the velocity of money) were thought to be essentially constant.

During the Great Depression of the 1930s, this body of theory seemed inadequate to many economists. NNP was not tending automatically toward its full-employment level. And the crude quantity theory seemed to have little value. In contrast, Keynes's ideas seemed to offer the sort of theoretical guidance and policy prescriptions that were needed. Keynesians did not neglect the use of monetary policy entirely, but they felt that it played a subsidiary role. Particularly in depressions, monetary policy seemed to be of relatively little value, since "you can't push on a string." In other words, monetary policy can make money available, but it cannot insure that it will be spent. To Keynesians, fiscal policy was of central importance.

During the 1940s, 1950s, and early 1960s, the Keynesian view was definitely predominant, here and abroad. But by the mid-1960s, it was being challenged seriously by the monetarists, led by Professor Milton Friedman and his supporters. The monetarist view harked back to the pre-Keynesian doctrine in many respects. In particular, it emphasized the importance of the equation of exchange as an analytical device and the importance of the quantity of money as a tool of economic policy. The monetarist view gained adherents in the late 1960s. Partly responsible was the long delay in passing the surtax of 1968, for the reluctance of the administration to propose and of Congress to enact the new levy vividly illustrated some of the difficulties in using fiscal policy for stabilization. Even more important was the fact that the surtax, when finally enacted, failed to have the restrictive effect on NNP (in the face of expansionary monetary policy) that some Keynesians predicted.

Causes of Business Fluctuations: The Opposing Views

Monetarists and Keynesians have tended to disagree over the basic causes of business fluctuations.

The Monetarist View. As seen by monetarists, major depressions, such as that which occurred during 1929–33, are due to decreases in the money supply. Between 1929 and 1933, for example, the money supply contracted by over one-quarter. Similarly, major inflations, in their view, are due to increases in the money supply. Looking at recent developments, they assert that the inflation of the late 1960s and the middle and late 1970s has been due to the increases that occurred in the money supply.

The Keynesian View. Keynesians, on the other hand, have tended to reject the monetarist view that money is the predominant factor accounting for business fluctuations. To the Keynesians, both monetary and nonmonetary factors cause business fluctuations. Among the important nonmonetary factors are changes (other than those predicted by changes in the money supply) in investment or shifts in the consumption function. (We have discussed many of these nonmonetary factors in Chapter 13.) Thus, in explaining the severe depression of 1929–33, Keynesians emphasize the fact that investment declined by about 90 percent during this period.

The Keynesians have not denied that there is a correlation between changes in the money supply and changes in NNP, but they have argued that the monetarists tend to mix up cause and effect. The Keynesians have suggested that increases in intended spending may bring about a greater demand for money, which in turn causes the money supply to increase. Under these circumstances, the line of causation may be the opposite of that posited by the monetarists.

Stability of the Economy: The Opposing Views

Monetarists and Keynesians also tend to differ over the extent to which our economy is stable.

The Monetarist View. The monetarists are generally more inclined to believe that, if the money supply is managed properly by the government, the free-market economy will tend automatically toward full employment with reasonably stable prices. Although the monetarists are by no means unanimous in this respect, they tend to emphasize the self-regulating characteristics of a free-enterprise economy. In their view, business fluctuations must often be laid at the door of the monetary authorities, whose well-meaning attempts to stabilize the economy frequently do more harm than good.

The Keynesian View. In contrast, the Keynesians are convinced that a free-enterprise economy has relatively weak self-regulating mechanisms. Like Keynes himself, they argue that the equilibrium level of national output may remain for a long time below the level required for full employment. (See Chapter 8 for Keynes's views.) Also, they have argued that there is nothing in the modern economy to prevent considerable inflation, even if the money supply does not increase greatly. Thus, in their view, the government has a much more positive discretionary role to play in stabilizing the economy than that visualized by the monetarists.

Effects of the Interest Rate: The Opposing Views

As pointed out above, both the Keynesian and monetarist groups contain a variety of opinions; thus it is somewhat misleading to refer to *the* Keynesian view or *the* monetarist view. Further, the consensus of opinion in each group has changed over time, as new evidence and arguments have arisen. Some of the matters that were in dispute in the past are no longer major bones of contention, as we shall see below. In the past, many of the basic disagreements between the Keynesians and the monetarists have centered about the quantitative effects of the interest rate. These disagreements have been of three kinds.

Demand for Money. The first disagreement has been over the demand for money. Recall from Chapter 14 that, because the cost of holding money is the interest forgone, the quantity of money demanded goes down as the interest rate goes up—as we saw in Figure 14.3. *According to the monetarists, the quantity of money demanded is relatively insensitive to changes in the interest rate; whereas to Keynesians, it is very sensitive to such changes.* Thus, as shown in Figure 17.1, the demand curve for money, based on monetarist views, is more nearly vertical than the demand curve for money, based on Keynesian views. The reason is that monetarists have tended to put more emphasis than Keynesians on the transactions motive for holding money (where the interest rate is less important than people's incomes in determining the demand for money). On the other hand, Keynesians have tended to put greater emphasis than monetarists on other motives for holding money where the interest rate plays a major

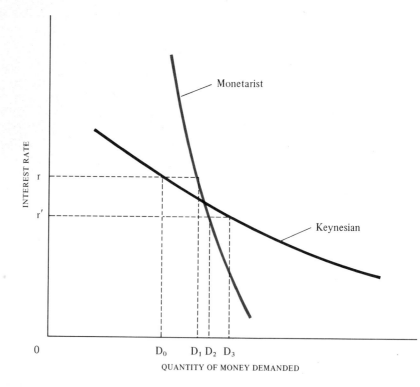

Figure 17.1

Keynesian and Monetarist Assumptions Concerning the Demand for Money
Keynesians have tended to believe that the quantity of money demanded is more sensitive to the interest rate than have monetarists. Thus, if the interest rate falls from r to r′ the quantity of money demanded increases from D_0 to D_3 under Keynesian assumptions, but only from D_1 to D_2 under monetarist assumptions.

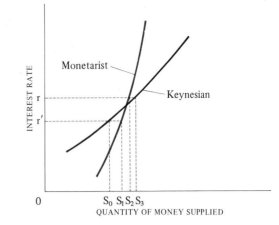

Figure 17.2

Keynesian and Monetarist Assumptions Concerning the Supply of Money *Some Keynesians have tended to believe that the supply of money is more sensitive to the interest rate than monetarists have assumed. Thus, if the interest rate falls from r to r', the supply of money drops from S_3 to S_0 under these Keynesian assumptions, but only from S_2 to S_1 under monetarist assumptions.*

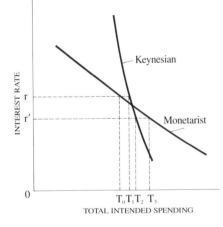

Figure 17.3

Keynesian and Monetarist Assumptions Concerning the Effect of the Interest Rate on Total Intended Spending *Some Keynesians have tended to believe that total intended spending is less sensitive to the interest rate than monetarists have assumed. Thus, if the interest rate falls from r to r', total intended spending increases from T_0 to T_3 under monetarist assumptions, but only from T_1 to T_2 under these Keynesian assumptions.*

role. Also, Keynesians have stressed that the quantity of money demanded for transactions purposes is sensitive to the interest rate.

Supply of Money. A second disagreement has been over the extent to which the supply of money is influenced by the interest rate. *Monetarists have argued that the supply of money is relatively insensitive to changes in the interest rate; whereas some Keynesians have asserted that it is quite sensitive to such changes.* In other words, monetarists have believed that the relationship between the money supply and the interest rate is nearly vertical, as shown in Figure 17.2. In their view, banks will keep few excess reserves, with the result that they are unable to vary the quantity of money in response to changes in loan demand and in interest rates. On the other hand, some Keynesians have felt that the relationship between the money supply and the interest rate is not close to vertical, as shown in Figure 17.2. Pointing to the Great Depression, they have asserted that banks may hold considerable excess reserves during depressions, and that an increase in interest rates may cause some banks to borrow more from the Fed. In their view, banks can and do increase the money supply when loan demand and interest rates are high.

Total Intended Spending. A third disagreement has been over the extent to which total intended spending is sensitive to changes in the interest rate. *According to the monetarists, total expenditure is very sensitive to changes in the interest rate; whereas to some Keynesians, it is not so sensitive to such changes.* Thus the monetarists have believed that the relationship between total intended spending and the interest rate shown in Figure 17.3 is close to horizontal, whereas some Keynesians have believed that it is closer to vertical. The reason is that the monetarists have been convinced that firms' investment decisions, as well as investment in residential housing and expenditure on consumer durable goods, depend considerably on the interest rate, whereas these Keynesians have felt that, although the interest rate has an effect, it is smaller than the monetarists assume. According to these Keynesians other factors, such as existing business conditions and business executives' expectations, have been far more important than the interest rate in determining total expenditure.

The Effect of Monetary Policy: The Opposing Views

Given the three disagreements described in the preceding section, it is easy to see why monetarists have tended to believe that monetary policy is of preeminent importance, whereas Keynesians have tended to believe that it is of lesser importance. As a first step toward understanding why this is so, it is worth emphasizing once again that *the equilibrium interest rate must be at the level where the quantity of money demanded equals the quantity of money supplied.* If the public wants to hold less money than is supplied, the interest rate will tend to decline in order to encourage people to increase the amount of money demanded. If the public wants to hold more money than is supplied, the interest rate will tend to increase in order to make people cut back on the amount of money demanded. Only if the quantity of money demanded equals the quantity of money supplied is the interest rate at its equilibrium level.

Suppose that the monetary authorities increase the money supply, with the result that the *money supply curve* (that is, the relationship between the quantity of money supplied and the interest rate in Figure 17.2) shifts to the right. Under both the Keynesian and monetarist assumptions, there will be a fall in the equilibrium interest rate, since the quantity of money supplied will exceed the quantity of money demanded at the existing interest rate. But, as shown in Figure 17.4, there will be a greater fall in the

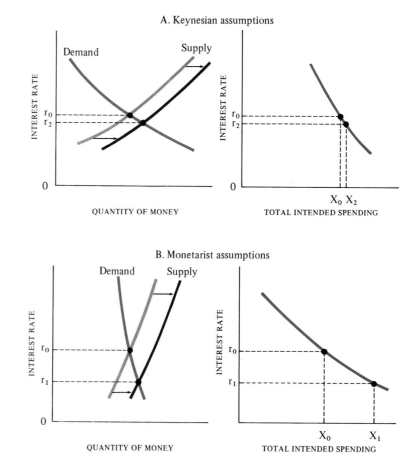

Figure 17.4

Effects of Monetary Policy under Keynesian and Monetarist Assumptions
An increase in the money supply results in a bigger drop in the interest rate, and a bigger increase in spending, under monetarist assumptions than under Keynesian assumptions.

interest rate under the monetarist assumptions (shown in panel B of Figure 17.4) than under the Keynesian assumptions (shown in panel A). Under the monetarist assumptions, the interest rate will fall to r_1, whereas under the Keynesian assumptions, it will fall to r_2.

Further, the resulting fall in the interest rate will have a greater effect on total expenditure under the monetarist assumptions than under the Keynesian assumptions. Under the monetarist assumptions, the fall in the interest rate to r_1 results in total expenditure increasing to X_1. Under the Keynesian assumptions, the fall in the interest rate to r_2 results in total expenditure increasing to X_2. Clearly, *the effect of the increase in the money supply on total expenditure is greater under the monetarist assumptions than under the Keynesian assumptions*—and it is not hard to see why monetarists have tended to emphasize the importance of monetary policy to a greater degree than Keynesians have.[2]

The Effect of Fiscal Policy: The Opposing Views

The monetarists have attacked the Keynesian view that fiscal policy works in the way described in Chapter 12.

The Monetarist View. According to the monetarists, whether the government runs a surplus or deficit has little or no long-run effect on NNP, except insofar as the government finances the surplus or deficit in a way that affects the stock of money. For example, if the government runs a deficit and finances it by borrowing from the public, the money supply will be unchanged. Thus the monetarists would argue that such a deficit has little or no long-run expansionary effect on NNP. On the other hand, if the government finances its deficit by increasing the money supply, the monetarists would expect NNP to increase, but as a result of the expansion of the money supply, not of the deficit. Thus the monetarists claim that the expansion of NNP after the tax cut of 1964 was due to considerable increases in the money supply, not to the tax cut.

Given the assumptions that they make, it is not difficult to see why the monetarists come to this conclusion. Suppose, for example, that an increase occurs in government expenditure. The result, of course, will be a shift to the right of the expenditure function in the right-hand panel of Figure 17.5B. (Note that the B panels in Figure 17.5 are the relevant ones here, since we are concerned with the monetarist assumptions.) If this function shifts from E_1 to E_2, the public will demand more money for transaction purposes, and the demand curve for money will shift to the right, as shown in the left-hand panel of Figure 17.5B. Thus the interest rate will increase to r_3. This relatively great increase in the interest rate will cut private expenditure on consumption goods and investment, and total expenditure will be X_3. (If the interest rate had not risen, total expenditure would have been X_5.) Since X_3 is not appreciably greater than X_0, the increase in government expenditure has little effect on total expenditure. Its principal effect is to substitute public for private expenditure.

---

[2] In Figure 17.4, the analysis is simplified in a number of respects, For a more complete analysis of the topics discussed in this and the following sections, see Appendix A.

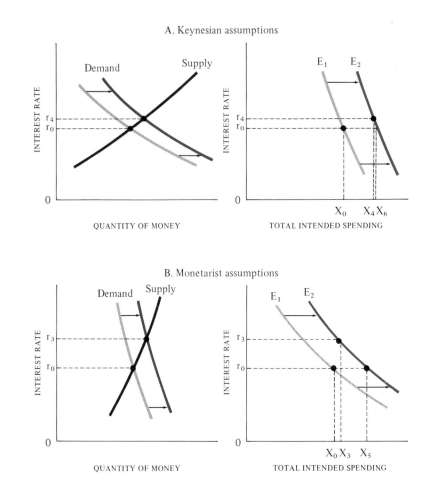

A. Keynesian assumptions

B. Monetarist assumptions

Figure 17.5
Effects of Fiscal Policy under Keynesian and Monetarist Assumptions *An increase in government expenditure results in a bigger rise in the interest rate, and a smaller increase in spending, under monetarist assumptions than under Keynesian assumptions.*

In recent years, economists have come to refer to this substitution of public for private expenditure as the ***crowding-out effect.*** More specifically, if an increase in public expenditure results in a cut in private expenditure, the public expenditure is said to crowd out the private expenditure. Under the monetarist assumptions in Figure 17.5, the rise in the interest rate caused by the increase in government expenditure reduces intended expenditure from X_5 to X_3. This reflects the crowding-out effect.

The Keynesian View. Based on their own quite different assumptions, the Keynesians conclude, of course, that fiscal policy is very effective. To see why, assume once again that an increase occurs in government expenditure, the result being a shift from E_1 to E_2 of the expenditure function in the right-hand panel of Figure 17.5A. (This time, the A panels are the relevant ones, since they contain the Keynesian assumptions.) Once again, as total expenditure rises, the public will demand more money for transactions purposes, thus increasing the interest rate. But according to the Keynesians the increase in the interest rate will be relatively small, since there will be an increase in the quantity of money supplied, and the quantity of money demanded is relatively sensitive to the interest rate. Thus the interest rate rises only to r_4, and total expenditure will be X_4. The crowding-out effect is small, since the rise in the interest rate cuts intended expenditure only from

X_6 to X_4. Since X_4 is much greater than X_0, the increase in government expenditure has a great effect on total expenditure, based on the Keynesian assumptions.

The Controversy over a Monetary Rule

The Monetarist View. Many, but not all, leading monetarists advocate the establishment of a rule to govern monetary policy. In the previous chapter, we discussed the arguments of Friedman and his supporters for such a rule.

Example 17.1   What Caused the Great Depression?

Monetarists and Keynesians have disagreed over the causes of the Great Depression of the 1930s. According to monetarists Milton Friedman and Anna Schwartz, the Great Depression was due in large measure to changes in the money supply, indicated below:

Year	*Money supply (billions of dollars)* M-1	M-2
1929	26.6	46.6
1930	25.8	45.7
1931	24.1	42.7
1932	21.1	36.0
1933	19.9	32.2
1934	21.9	34.4

(a) In response to the substantial drop in NNP after 1929, the Fed, according to Friedman and Schwartz, did not undertake large-scale open market purchases until 1932. Does this policy seem correct? (b) The Friedman-Schwartz interpretation of the Great Depression has been challenged by MIT's Peter Temin, who argues that the decline in the money supply in 1929–33 was due to a shift in the demand curve for money. What might have caused such a shift? (c) If, as Temin believes, the Great Depression was due in part to a downward shift in the consumption function, would the money supply decrease?

SOLUTION

(a) Friedman and Schwartz, among others, argue that it was an incorrect policy, and that the Fed should have adopted a more expansionary policy in the early 1930s. (b) A drop in investment or a downward shift in the consumption function might have reduced NNP. The reduction in NNP would have shifted the demand curve for money to the left. (c) As pointed out in the answer to (b), a downward shift in the consumption function would reduce NNP and shift the demand curve for money to the left. The result would be a decrease in interest rates, which could reduce the money supply. For example, banks might be induced to hold more excess reserves.*

   * For further discussion, see M. Friedman and A. Schwartz, *A Monetary History of the United States,* Princeton: Princeton University Press, 1963; and P. Temin, *Did Monetary Forces Cause the Great Depression?,* New York: Norton, 1976.

You will recall their charge that the Federal Reserve's monetary policies have often caused economic instability. Because of the difficulties in forecasting the future state of the economy and the fairly long and variable time lag in the effect of changes in the money supply, the Fed, in the eyes of many leading monetarists, frequently has caused excessive inflation or unemployment by its discretionary policies. According to the monetarists we would be better off with a rule stipulating that the money supply should grow steadily at a constant rate, say 4 or 5 percent per year.[3]

The Keynesian View. The Keynesians retort that such a rule would handcuff the monetary authorities and contribute to economic instability, since discretionary monetary policies are required to keep the economy on a reasonably even keel. The Keynesians grant that the Fed sometimes makes mistakes, but they assert that things would be worse if the Fed could not pursue the policies that a given set of circumstances seems to call for.

---

[3] When he accepted the Nobel prize in 1976, Milton Friedman jokingly said: "My monetary studies have led me to the conclusion that central banks could profitably be replaced by computers geared to provide a steady rate of growth in the quantity of money. Fortunately for me personally, and for a select group of fellow economists, the conclusion has had no practical impact . . . else there would have been no Central Bank of Sweden to have established the award I am honored to receive." (The Central Bank of Sweden donated the money for the Nobel prize in economics.)

Test Yourself

1. "Keynesians are liberal activitists who want to push our society in the direction of socialism. Their emphasis on fiscal policy is a reflection of their desire to have the government purchase more and more of the national output." Comment and evaluate.

2. "Monetarists are arch-conservatives with a strong *laissez-faire* orientation. They prefer monetary policy over fiscal policy because it involves less direct interference by government in the marketplace." Comment and evaluate.

3. "The Keynesian model can easily be translated into monetarist terms, and the monetarist model can easily be translated into Keynesian terms. Thus, there really is no basic difference between the Keynesians and the monetarists." Do you agree? Why or why not?

4. "Keynesians believe that the demand curve for money is close to vertical; consequently, they feel that monetary policy has less effect on NNP than monetarists." Comment and evaluate.

The Current State of the Keynesian-Monetarist Debate

The controversy between the Keynesians and monetarists has been going on for decades. At this point, the debate no longer focuses on some of the issues that were paramount 20 years ago. At that time, the controversy centered on the choice between monetary and fiscal policy. The more partisan monetarists claimed that fiscal policy was relatively impotent; the more partisan Keynesians claimed the same regarding monetary policy. We have discussed the arguments of each side in previous sections of this chapter. During the 1970s, as more and more evidence accumulated, this issue seemed to wane in importance. At present, most monetarists concede that fiscal policy can affect output and the price level; and most Keynesians concede the same regarding monetary policy. Although it would be incorrect to say that no differences remain on this score, there seems to be a growing recognition that the differences have narrowed considerably. Thus Milton Friedman, the leading monetarist, has been quoted as saying, "We are all Keynesians now." And Franco Modigliani, a leading Keynesian (and 1985 Nobel laureate), responded in 1976 by saying, "We are all monetarists now."

During the late 1970s and early 1980s, the focus of the debate has tended to shift. Now the clash between the monetarists and the Keynesians (who in more recent years have tended to prefer other labels like neo-Keynesian or post-Keynesian or nonmonetarist) seems to be traceable largely to the following basic disagreements which continue to exist between them.

Stability of Private Spending. The monetarists believe that, if the government's economic policies did not destabilize the economy, private spending would be quite stable. One reason for this belief is the permanent-income hypothesis, discussed in Chapter 10. Personal consumption expenditures change relatively slowly as households adjust their estimates of their long-term income prospects. Keynesians, on the other hand, believe that business and consumer spending represents a substantial source of economic instability that should be offset by monetary and fiscal policy.

Flexibility of Prices. Even if intended private spending is not entirely stable, flexible prices tend to stabilize it, according to the monetarists. The Keynesians reply that prices are relatively inflexible downward, as shown by the fact that, despite widespread unemployment, prices did not decline during the late 1930s. In their view, the length of time that would be required for the economy to get itself out of a severe recession would be intolerably long. Monetarists seem more inclined than Keynesians to believe that high unemployment will cause wages and input prices to fall, shifting the aggregate supply curve downward and increasing output in a reasonable period of time.

Rules versus Activism. Monetarists believe that, even if intended private spending is not entirely stable, and if prices are not entirely flexible, an activist monetary and fiscal policy to stabilize the economy is likely to do more damage than good. As pointed out repeatedly above, they favor a rule stipulating that the monetary supply should grow steadily at a constant rate, because of the difficulties in forecasting the future state of the economy and because of the long and variable time lag in the effect of changes in the quantity of money on output and prices. The Keynesians, while admitting that monetary and fiscal policy have sometimes been destabilizing, are much more optimistic about the efficacy of such policies in the future.

To a considerable extent, the differences between the Keynesians and the monetarists stem from divergent political beliefs. The Keynesians tend to be optimistic concerning the extent to which the government can be trusted to formulate and carry out a responsible set of monetary and fiscal policies. They recognize that some politicians are willing to win votes in the next election by destabilizing the economy, but they nonetheless believe that discretionary action by elected officials will generally be more effective than automatic rules. The monetarists, on the other hand, are skeptical of the willingness of politicians to do what is required to stabilize the economy, rather than what is politically expedient. Since this aspect of the debate is difficult to resolve (in any scientific way), a complete resolution of the Keynesian-monetarist controversy is not likely any time soon. However, many other aspects of the controversy are more amenable to scientific analysis, and these aspects almost surely will be clarified substantially in the years to come.[4]

Rational Expectations: Another Element of the Current Debate

It should not be assumed that the debate between monetarists and Keynesians is the only controversy regarding stabilization policy. In recent years, there has been considerable argument over the theory of rational expectations as well.

WHAT ARE RATIONAL EXPECTATIONS?

During the 1970s, a small band of economists, led by Robert Lucas of the University of Chicago and Thomas Sargent and Neil Wallace of the University of Minnesota, formulated a theory, based on the hypothesis of *rational expectations,* that already has had a substantial impact on economic analysis and policy. Basically, what these economists assumed was that individuals and firms do not make systematic errors in forecasting the future. In other words, forecasts, *on the average,* are assumed to be correct. Of course, this does not mean that forecasters are always right. As we saw in Chapter 13, this is far from true. Instead, these economists assumed that forecasting errors are purely random.

By assuming that people's expectations are on the average correct, they also assume in effect that these expectations are formed consistently with the relevant economic model of the economy. Thus expectations are determined as part of the model and are genuinely forward-looking, rather than being based on a mechanical extrapolation of the past (as in older economic theories). Consequently, the announcement or anticipation that a particular event will occur results in immediate effects on the economy, even before the anticipated event actually occurs.[5]

CAN STABILIZATION POLICIES WORK?

Based on these assumptions, the rational expectations theorists conclude that the *government cannot use monetary and fiscal policies in the way described in previous chapters, because the models presented in those chapters do not recognize that the expectations of firms and individuals concerning their incomes, job prospects, sales, and other relevant variables are influenced by government policies.* If firms and individuals formulate their ex-

---

[4] This section has benefited from the discussion in Robert J. Gordon, *Macroeconomics,* Boston: Little, Brown, 1978.

[5] The hypothesis of rational expectations was first developed and applied by John Muth of Indiana University.

pectations rationally, they will tend to frustrate the government's attempts to use activist stabilization policies.

To illustrate what these economists are saying, suppose that the economy is in a recession and that the government, in accord with the models in Chapters 12 and 16, increases the amount that it spends on goods and services and increases the money supply. Because prices tend to move up while wages do not, profits tend to rise and firms find it profitable to expand. But this model is based on the supposition that labor is not smart enough to foresee that prices are going to go up and that labor's real wage is going to diminish. If labor does foresee this (that is, if its expectations are rational), it will insist on an increase in its money wage, which will mean that firms will not find it profitable to expand, and the government's antirecession policy will not work as expected.

UNEMPLOYMENT AND BUSINESS FLUCTUATIONS

According to the rational expectations theorists, high rates of unemployment are not evidence of a gap between actual and potential output that can be reduced; instead, output fluctuations result from random and irreducible errors. Markets are assumed to work efficiently; and firms, acting to maximize their profits, are assumed to make the best possible decisions. According to Lucas, since unemployed workers have the option of accepting pay cuts to get jobs, excess unemployment is essentially voluntary.

Fluctuations in aggregate demand are due principally to erratic and unpredictable government policy, in his view. Changes in the quantity of money induce cyclical fluctuations in the economy. But the power of policy changes to affect real NNP is limited. People come to learn the way in which policy is made, and only unanticipated government policy changes can have a substantial impact on output or employment. Once firms and individuals learn of any systematic rule for adjusting government policy to events, the rule will have no effect.

REACTIONS PRO AND CON

These views have received considerable attention, and in the late 1970s the Federal Reserve Bank of Minneapolis stated its acceptance of them. In its annual report, the bank stated,

Robert Lucas

> The [rational expectations] view conjectures that some amount of cyclical swing in production and employment is inherent in the micro-level processes of the economy that no government macro policies can, or should attempt to, smooth out. Expected additions to money growth certainly won't smooth out cycles, if the arguments in this paper are correct. Surprise additions to money growth have the potential to make matters worse. . . . One strategy that seems consistent with the significant, though largely negative, findings of rational expectations would have monetary policy focus its attention on inflation and announce, and stick to, a policy that would bring the rate of increase in the general price level to some specified low figure.[6]

[6] The Federal Reserve Bank of Minneapolis, *Rational Expectations—Fresh Ideas That Challenge Some Established Views of Policy Making,* Minneapolis, 1977, pp. 12–13.

383

Given the fact that the rational expectations theorists have challenged the core of the theory underlying current stabilization policies, it is not surprising that many economists, particularly liberals, have challenged their conclusions. Franco Modigliani, for instance, has claimed that the rational expectations model is inconsistent "with the evidence: if it were valid, deviations of unemployment from the natural rate would be small and transitory—in which case [Keynes's] *General Theory* would not have been written."[7] Since the rational expectations theory makes excess unemployment the result of purely unexpected events, one would think that unemployment would fluctuate randomly around its equilibrium level, if this theory is true. However, as we have seen, recessions often last quite a long time.

Critics also claim that the rational expectations theory neglects the inertia in wages and prices. Contracts are written for long periods of time. Workers stick with firms for considerable periods. Consequently, wages and prices do not adjust as rapidly as is assumed by the rational expectations theorists. According to the critics, most empirical analysis does not support the rational expectations model. Contrary to the theory, price movements show only slow and adaptive changes.

Only the future will tell how successful the rational expectations theorists will be in their attack on conventional doctrines, but there can be no doubt that they have caused a remarkable stir in the economics profession.[8]

Supply-Side Economics Enters the Fray

The theory of rational expectations is not the only newcomer to the scene. In the late 1970s and 1980s, *supply-side economics* also entered the fray. To a considerable extent, as we have seen, economic policy since World War II has been dominated by measures aimed at managing aggregate demand, the two traditional tools of demand management being monetary and fiscal policy. In contrast, *supply-side economics is concerned primarily with influencing aggregate supply.*

As pointed out in Chapter 9, supply-side economics really is not new. Major economists of the eighteenth and nineteenth (as well as twentieth) centuries were concerned with the stimulation of aggregate supply. But one new twist is that some people seem to believe that the emphasis in combatting inflation should be on pushing the aggregate supply curve to the right rather than on curbing the rightward movement of the aggregate demand curve.

SUPPLY-SIDE PRESCRIPTIONS

To stimulate such a rightward shift in the aggregate supply curve, *supply-siders favor the use of various financial incentives, particularly tax cuts.* In their view, the reduction of tax rates will encourage people to work longer

[7] F. Modligliani, "The Monetarist Controversy, or, Should We Forsake Stabilization Policies," *American Economic Review,* March 1977, p. 6.

[8] For further discussion, see S. Turnovsky, "Rational Expectations and the Theory of Macroeconomic Policy," *Journal of Economic Education,* Winter 1984.

and harder, thus increasing the level of full-employment output. Also, reduced tax rates and regulations are likely to make firms willing to make risky investments in research and new plant and equipment. Further, tax reductions are likely to cut the amount of time and resources invested in finding and exploiting tax loopholes; more would be invested in productive activities.

Supply-siders argue too that tax reductions will increase saving. By cutting taxes on income from capital, the government can increase the after-tax return to capital, and encourage saving. (Recall from Chapter 5 that this is an area of controversy.) Supply-siders emphasize that saving is a very important activity which permits and encourages investment, which in turn increases the nation's productive capacity. As pointed out in Chapter 11's discussion of the paradox of thrift, Keynes took a somewhat different view of saving, emphasizing its negative effects on aggregate demand.

There is considerable uncertainty regarding the extent to which more work, risk-taking, and saving will result from tax reductions. For example, take the case of saving. In a well-known study, Stanford's Michael Boskin found that a 10-percent increase in the real after-tax rate of return will result in an increase of 2 to 4 percent in saving per year. On the other hand, other economists, such as Phillip Howrey and Saul Hymans of the University of Michigan, have criticized Boskin's findings, and have themselves come to quite different conclusions. Although the jury is still out regarding many of the relevant points, it seems fair to say that many economists are skeptical of the claims made by the more extreme supply-siders.

THE NEED FOR DEMAND MANAGEMENT

In particular, many economists seem to question the idea that supply-side policies alone can make much of a dent in our inflation problems in any reasonable time frame. For example, suppose that we accept the supply-sider's contention that their policies would increase full-employment output substantially. In a period of two or three years, it seems doubtful that these policies could increase full-employment output enough to offset the sorts of inflationary pressures experienced in the late 1970s. Even if supply-side policies could increase the annual rate of growth of full-employment output by 0.5 percentage points (a stellar performance indeed), this would be too little to make much headway against such inflationary pressures.

Thus supply-side policies should not be viewed as a replacement for demand management. This does not mean that such policies cannot be worthwhile or important. On the contrary, it is of the utmost importance that our nation devote attention to pushing its aggregate supply curve to the right. (Chapter 19 is devoted entirely to this topic.) But it is incorrect to view such policies as adequate counter-cyclical measures. The need to influence the aggregate demand curve remains.

THE TAX CUT OF 1981 AND SUPPLY-SIDE ECONOMICS

As indicated in previous chapters, supply-side economists played an important role in formulating and arguing for the huge tax cut in 1981.

Individual income taxes were cut 25 percent across the board over three years. Corporation taxes were reduced as a consequence of an increase in the pace at which depreciation can be charged against current income. Other tax reductions were enacted as well.

The first phase of the tax cut occurred in 1981 and was discounted by the administration, because it was only 5 percent and did not prevent the recession of 1981–82. Economic policy makers in the Reagan administration, therefore, counted on the larger tax cut of 10 percent in 1982 to stimulate the economy. They argued that the Reagan Economic Recovery Program could only be judged after the successive 10 percent tax cuts in 1982 and 1983 had occurred. They were banking on the success of the successive 10 percent tax cuts to show up in a strong recovery.

In fact, there was a strong recovery in 1983 and 1984; and particularly at the beginning of 1984, the supply-siders were often more accurate than other economists in forecasting how strong it would be. However, according to many observers, this substantial increase in real NNP should have been expected on the basis of the Keynesian model described in Chapter 12. To them, the strong recovery of 1983 and 1984 was testimony to the continued usefulness of the Keynesian model, highly simplified though it is.

Also, critics of supply-side economics point out that some supply-siders claimed that the 1981 tax cut would increase output so dramatically that there would be no substantial increase in the federal deficit because output would rise sufficiently to offset the cut in tax rates. Instead, as the critics stress, the deficit for fiscal 1985 may be about $200 billion. In response to such criticisms, the supply-siders blame the Fed's tight-money policies for the fact that output did not grow as much as they expected.

Test Yourself

1. "Your preferences concerning the optimal size of the government should not influence your views concerning stabilization policy." Do you agree? Why or why not?

2. Explain why an attempt by the government to stabilize interest rates may be destabilizing.

3. Do the monetarists agree with the Keynesians' interpretation of the effects of the tax cut of 1964? If not, what is their interpretation of what happened?

4. (a) "Working hours are fixed by custom at about 40 hours per week. Cutting taxes won't affect them." Do you agree? Why or why not? (b) "Business executives are working about as hard as they can to keep their heads above water. Cutting taxes won't affect how hard they work." Do you agree? Why or why not?

Summary

1. Keynesians have tended to view the private sector of the economy as inherently unstable, and they have favored the use of fiscal policy to offset this instability. They have tended to feel that fiscal policy was more important, relative to monetary policy, than have monetarists. Keynesians have based their analysis of business fluctuations on the sorts of concepts taken up in Chapter 10 and 12.

2. Monetarists have tended to view the private sector of the economy as inherently quite stable, and they have blamed much of the economy's instability on clumsy or ill-conceived policies of the government. They have emphasized the importance of monetary policy. Monetarists have based their analysis of business fluctuations on the equation of exchange, discussed in Chapter 14.

3. Many of the disagreements between the Keynesians and monetarists have centered about the effects of changes in the interest rate. (a) Monetarists have said that the quantity of money demanded is relatively insensitive to changes in the interest rate, whereas Keynesians have said that it is sensitive to such changes. (b) Monetarists have said that the supply of money is relatively insensitive to changes in the interest rate, whereas some Keynesians have said that it is quite sensitive to such changes. (c) Monetarists have said that total expenditure is very sensitive to changes in the interest rate, whereas some Keynesians have said that it is not so sensitive to such changes. These disagreements resulted in the different views of monetarists and Keynesians concerning the relative importance of fiscal and monetary policy.

4. Many leading monetarists feel that the Federal Reserve, in its attempts to stabilize the economy, does more harm than good. They favor the establishment of a rule to govern monetary policy, an idea most Keynesians oppose.

5. During the 1970s, as more evidence accumulated, the choice between monetary and fiscal policy, which had been at the center of the debate for so long, seemed to wane in importance. At present, most monetarists concede that fiscal policy can affect output and the price level, and most Keynesians concede the same regarding monetary policy.

6. At present, the debate seems to focus on the stability of private spending, the flexibility of prices, and the desirability of rules rather than discretionary government action. Monetarists tend to feel that (a) if the government's economic policies did not destabilize the economy, private spending would be quite stable; (b) even if intended private spending is not entirely stable, flexible prices tend to stabilize it; (c) an activist monetary and fiscal policy is likely to do more harm than good.

7. Keynesians tend to feel that (a) business and consumer spending represents a substantial source of economic instability that should be offset by monetary and fiscal policy; (b) price flexibility cannot be depended on to promote economic stability in a reasonable length of time; (c) an activist monetary and fiscal policy is likely to do more good than harm.

8. According to rational expectations theorists, the government cannot use monetary and fiscal policies in the way described in previous chapters because the models presented in these chapters do not recognize that the expectations of firms and individuals concerning their incomes, job prospects, sales, and other relevant variables are influenced by government policies.

9. Supply-side economics is concerned primarily with influencing aggregate supply. To stimulate rightward shifts in the aggregate supply curve, supply-siders favor the use of various financial incentives, particularly tax cuts. Supply-side policies cannot be viewed as a replacement for demand management.

Concepts for Review

Keynesians
Monetarists

Crowding-out effect
Rational expectations
Supply-side economics

CHAPTER 18

Inflation and Anti-Inflationary Measures

Whatever their attitudes toward the controversies described in the previous chapter, policy makers in the 1970s and early 1980s found it very difficult to maintain reasonably full employment with reasonably stable prices. Inflation sometimes galloped along at close to double-digit rates even when the unemployment rate was relatively high. It was a period of considerable economic discomfort for the nation—as well as a period of discomfort for economists, since they had difficulty in coming up with any solutions that were acceptable to policy makers. In 1982–85, inflation abated somewhat; in late 1985, it was about 3 percent. But no one could say how long this would last. Between 1964 and 1982, the Consumer Price Index had tripled!

In this chapter, we take up a variety of anti-inflationary measures that have been tried or proposed, often with questionable success. Among these policies are wage and price controls, incomes policies, and tax-based incomes policies. Finally, we try to indicate where we stand in our attempts to stabilize the economy and the nature of the challenges that lie ahead.

Demand-Pull Inflation

In previous chapters, we described **demand-pull inflation,** a situation in which there is too much aggregate spending. The $C + I + G$ line is too high, resulting in inflationary pressure. Or, put in terms of the equation of exchange, $M \times V$ is too high, so that P is pushed up. Too much money is chasing too few goods. This kind of inflation stems from the demand or

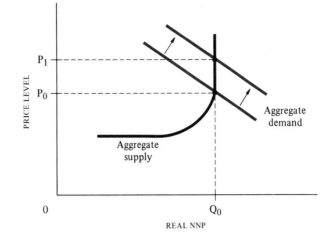

Figure 18.1

Increase in the Price Level Due to a Shift in the Aggregate Demand Curve

Major inflations during the Revolutionary and Civil Wars were due in considerable part to shifts upward and to the right in the aggregate demand curve. Such a shift results in an increase in the price level from OP_0 to OP_1. Since national output is fixed, the rise in the price level must be proportional to the increase in spending.

spending behavior of the nation's consumers, firms, and government. We have had many inflations of this kind. The major inflations during the Revolutionary War and Civil War were basically caused by demand-pull factors; and so, much more recently, was the inflation arising from the Vietnam War.

In those extreme cases in which all resources are utilized, the rise in the price level that occurs in demand-pull inflation can be viewed as a matter of arithmetic: since national output is fixed, the rise in the price level must be proportional to the increase in total spending. This is the situation shown in Figure 18.1, in which the economy is assumed to be on the vertical segment of its aggregate supply curve before the increase in aggregate demand.

Cost-Push Inflation

However, in the view of many economists, demand-pull inflation is not the only kind of inflation. There is another kind—*cost-push inflation.* The process underlying cost-push inflation is not as well understood as it should be, but, according to many economists, it works something like this. While GNP is below its potential level, costs are increased, perhaps because unions push up wages, and in an attempt to protect their profit margins, firms push up prices. These price increases affect the costs of other firms and the consumer's cost of living. As the cost of living goes up, labor feels entitled to, and obtains, higher wages to offset the higher living costs. Firms again pass on the cost increase to the consumer in the form of a price increase. This so-called *wage-price spiral* is at the heart of cost-push inflation.

One case of fairly pure cost-push inflation occurred in the late 1950s. This was a period of considerable slack in the economy. You will recall from Chapter 9 that a recession occurred in 1957–58. By 1958 6.8 percent of the labor force was unemployed. Nonetheless, wage increases took place during the late 1950s—and at a rate in excess of the rate of increase

389

of labor productivity (output per hour of labor).[1] For example, average earnings (outside agriculture) went up by 4 percent between 1957 and 1961, while labor productivity went up by 2½ percent. Moreover, prices

[1] In a later section, we shall discuss the importance of the rate of increase of output per hour of labor. For present purposes, it is sufficient to note that the greater the rate of increase of output per hour of labor, the larger the rate of increase of cost per hour of labor that can be absorbed without an increase in cost per unit of output.

Example 18.1   The Fed and Cost-Push Inflation

Suppose that labor unions suddenly demand that their wage rate (in money, not real terms) be doubled. Since firms must increase prices if they are to be willing to produce the same output as before, the aggregate supply curve will shift upward and to the left, as shown below:

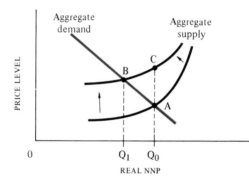

(a) If the Federal Reserve holds the money supply at its initial level, what will happen to real output and to unemployment? (b) Will real wages double? (c) Suppose that the Federal Reserve, fearing a big rise in unemployment, increases the money supply. If the increase is large enough, can a decrease in real output be avoided? (d) If a decrease in real output is avoided in this way, what will be the effect on the price level?

SOLUTION

(a) As shown in the above diagram, the economy will move from point A to point B. Thus real output will fall from OQ_0 to OQ_1 and the decrease in real output will increase unemployment. (b) No, because the price level at point B is higher than at point A. Thus, although the money wage has doubled, the real wage has less than doubled. (c) Yes. By increasing the money supply, the Fed can push the aggregate demand curve to the right. If it pushes it far enough to the right, it can make it intersect the new aggregate supply curve at point C, where real NNP is at its original level, OQ_0. (d) The price level will rise considerably. As shown in the diagram, the price level at point C is much higher than at point A. The Fed, by enabling the cost-push action of the unions to increase the price level without resulting in additional unemployment, is said to have *accommodated* the cost-push.

increased each year—by 3 percent from 1956 to 1957, and by 2 percent from 1957 to 1958.

Certainly this seemed to be a different phenomenon than the demand-pull inflation described in previous chapters. There was no evidence that too much money was chasing too few goods. Instead, this was apparently a case of cost-push inflation. Commenting on the situation in the middle and late 1950s, the Council of Economic Advisers concluded, "The movement of wages during this period reflected in part the power exercised in labor markets by strong unions and the power possessed by large companies to pass on higher wage costs in higher prices."[2]

In some cases, increases in materials prices may play a major role in cost-push inflation. When the oil-producing countries increased the price of crude oil in 1974 and in later years like 1979, this resulted in price increases in a wide variety of products that are made (directly or indirectly) from petroleum. Because these price increases were not offset by price reductions elsewhere in the economy, the overall price level increased (and at a very rapid rate) in 1974 and 1979. Of course, the price hike for crude oil (and other materials) was by no means the sole reason for this inflation. But unquestionably it did play a noteworthy role in shifting the aggregate supply curve upward and to the left, as shown in Figure 18.2. (Recall that this was pointed out in our discussion of stagflation in Chapter 9.)

Difficulties in Distinguishing Cost-Push from Demand-Pull Inflation

Generally, it is difficult, if not impossible, to sort out cost-push inflation from demand-pull inflation. For example, an increase in aggregate demand may raise firms' demand for labor, causing workers to demand higher wages, which in turn leads firms to raise their prices. In such a case,

Figure 18.2

Increase in the Price Level Due to a Shift in the Aggregate Supply Curve
According to many economists, the inflation of the middle and late 1970s was due in considerable part to shifts upward and to the left in the aggregate supply curve because of shortages and price increases in oil and other materials. Such a shift results in an increase in the price level from OP to OP'.

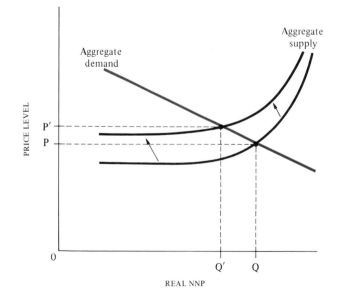

the inflation may be demand-pull in the sense that the ultimate cause was an increase in aggregate demand, but it is cost-push in the sense that the proximate cause of the increase in the price level was an increase in wages.

Also, it is important to note that a cost-push inflation of the sort shown in Figure 18.2 is unlikely to continue for a long period of time unless the Fed "accommodates" or "validates" it by following policies that shift the aggregate demand curve to the right. (See Example 18.1) If the aggregate demand curve does not shift, the inflation will die out. (Thus, in Example 18.1, once the economy moves from point *A* to point *B,* the inflation will be over. There will be no further increase in the price level.)

The Phillips Curve

As we have just seen, some economists believe that inflation can result from the power of labor to push up wages and the power of companies to pass on higher wage costs to consumers in the form of higher prices. What determines the rate at which labor can push up wages? If you think about it for a while, you will probably agree that *labor's ability to increase wages depends on the level of unemployment. The more unemployment, the more difficult it is for labor to increase wages.* Although perfect competition by no means prevails in the labor market, there is enough competition so that the presence of a pool of unemployed workers puts some damper on wage increases. In nonunion industries and occupations, workers are much less inclined to push for wage increases—and employers are much less inclined to accept them—when lots of people are looking for work. In unionized industries and occupations, unions are less likely to put their members through the hardship of a strike—and firms have less to lose from a strike—when business is bad and unemployment is high.

Because wages tend to be increased more rapidly when unemployment is low, one would expect the rate of increase of wages in any year to be inversely related to the level of unemployment. In a particular period of time in the United States, suppose that the rate of increase in wages tends to be related to the level of unemployment in the way shown in Figure 18.3. According to this figure, which is based on hypothetical, but reasonable, numbers, wages tend to rise by about 6 percent per year when 9 percent of the labor force is unemployed, by about 7½ percent per year when 7 percent of the labor force is unemployed, and by about 9 percent per year when 6 percent of the labor force is unemployed. *The relationship between the rate of increase of wages and the level of unemployment is known as the Phillips curve.* It was named after A. W. Phillips, the British economist who first called attention to it.

THE RELATIONSHIP BETWEEN INFLATION AND UNEMPLOYMENT

Given the Phillips curve in Figure 18.3, one can determine the relationship between the rate of inflation and the level of unemployment. If *C* is

---

[2] *1962 Annual Report of the Council of Economic Advisers,* Washington, D.C.: Government Printing Office, p. 175.

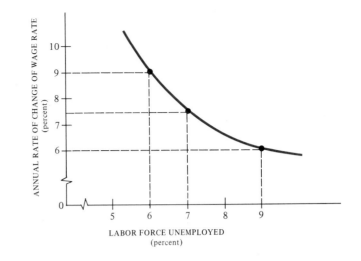

Figure 18.3
The Phillips Curve *The Phillips curve shows the relationship between the rate of increase of wages and the level of unemployment. This curve is drawn on the assumption that moderate inflation is expected.*

the total cost—wage and nonwage—per hour of labor, the total cost per unit of output equals $C \times H \div O$, where H is the total number of hours worked and O is total output. This says no more than that total cost per unit of output equals total cost per hour of labor times the number of hours of labor divided by the number of units of output. Thus total cost per unit of output equals total cost per hour of labor divided by output per hour of labor. (Output per hour of labor—that is, $O \div H$—is often called **labor productivity.**) Since the rate of increase of a ratio is the rate of increase of the numerator minus the rate of increase of the denominator, it follows that the *rate of increase of total cost per unit of output equals the rate of increase of total cost per hour of labor minus the rate of increase of output per hour of labor.*[3]

Suppose that the rate of increase of prices equals the rate of increase of total cost per unit of output, and that the rate of increase of total cost per hour of labor equals the rate of increase of wages. Then *the rate of increase of prices equals the rate of increase of wages minus the rate of increase of output per hour of labor.* Suppose too that the rate of increase of output per hour of labor (that is, labor productivity) is 2 percent per year. Then the rate of increase of prices equals the rate of increase of wages minus 2 percent.[4] Consequently, the relationship between the rate of increase in prices and the level of unemployment is as shown in Figure 18.4.

There is, of course, a simple relationship between the curve in Figure 18.3 and the curve in Figure 18.4. The curve in Figure 18.4 (which shows

[3] To see this, note that total cost per unit of output equals C (total cost per hour of labor) divided by $O \div H$ (output per hour of labor). Thus the rate of increase of total cost per unit of output equals the rate of increase of C minus the rate of increase of $O \div H$.

[4] Let p equal the rate of increase of prices, w equal the rate of increase of wages, d equal the rate of increase of output per hour of labor, a equal the rate of increase of total cost per unit of output, and b equal the rate of increase of total cost per hour of labor. The previous paragraph of the text concluded that $a = b - d$. Since we assume in this paragraph of the text that $p = a$, that $b = w$, and that $d = 2$, it follows that $p = w - 2$.

Of course, it is possible that firms will accept a lower profit rate (as a percent of sales) if they experience a decrease in demand for their products.

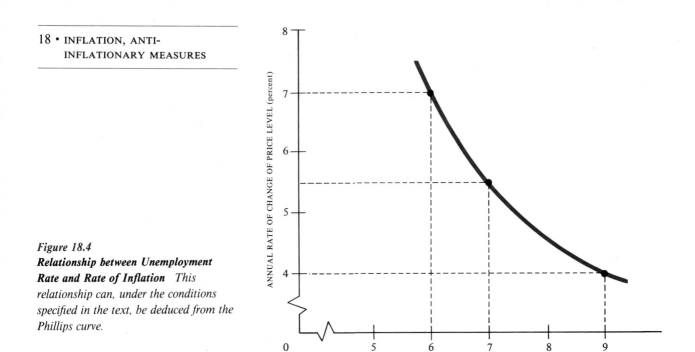

Figure 18.4
Relationship between Unemployment Rate and Rate of Inflation   *This relationship can, under the conditions specified in the text, be deduced from the Phillips curve.*

the relationship between *price* increases and unemployment) is always 2 percentage points below the curve in Figure 18.3 (which shows the relationship between *wage* increases and unemployment). Why? Because the rate of increase of prices—under the assumptions set forth above—always equals the rate of increase of wages minus 2 percent.

THE POLICY MENU

If the curve in Figure 18.4 remains fixed, the government is faced with a fundamental choice. It can reduce unemployment only if it is willing to accept a higher rate of inflation, and it can reduce the rate of inflation only if it is willing to accept a higher rate of unemployment. For example, in Figure 18.4, if the unemployment rate is 7 percent and the inflation rate is 5½ percent, the government will be anxious to reduce unemployment, but if it reduces it to 6 percent, the inflation rate will jump to 7 percent. It will also want to reduce inflation, but if it cuts it to 4 percent, the unemployment rate will jump to 9 percent. This poses a difficult problem for the government (and for society as a whole), since it would be desirable to reduce both inflation and unemployment.

The Instability of the Phillips Curve

During the 1960s, economists came to believe that the Phillips curve was a stable, predictable relationship. Panel A of Figure 18.5 shows the relationship between the inflation rate and the unemployment rate in the United States during 1955 to 1969. As you can see, there was a fairly close relationship between them in this period. Economists relied heavily on these data to buttress their belief that the Phillips curve really existed, and that it had the hypothesized shape. It is no exaggeration to say that the Phillips curve in Figure 18.5 (that is, the heavy line) had a major influence on both economic analysis and economic policy in the sixties.

But then something unforeseen (by most economists) occurred. *The inflation and unemployment rates in the seventies and eighties did not conform at all closely to the relationship that prevailed in the sixties.* As shown in panel B of Figure 18.5, the points for 1970 to 1984 lie far above and to the right of the relationship that prevailed earlier. In other words, holding constant the unemployment rate, the inflation rate tended to be much higher in the seventies than in the sixties. Or, holding the inflation rate constant, the unemployment rate tended to be much higher in the seventies than in the sixties. Whichever way you look at it, this departure from the earlier relationship between inflation and unemployment was bad news.

A REASON FOR INSTABILITY

Why did this departure from the earlier relationship occur? As stressed in a previous section, one reason was the shift to the left in the aggregate supply curve due to price hikes in oil, food, and raw materials. Because of this shift, both the inflation rate and the unemployment rate increased. And the rapid inflation of the seventies helped to bring on higher levels of unemployment. The oil price hikes acted like an excise tax levied on the consumer; they reduced the amount that consumers could spend on other things. The general inflation raised people's money incomes, thus pushing them into higher income tax brackets and increasing the amount they had to pay in taxes. (Similarly, the inflation swelled the paper profits of many firms, and increased their tax bills.) Because of the oil price increases and the effective increase in taxes, as well as other factors, like the decline in the stock market, consumers cut back on their spending. Thus the $C + I + G$ line was pushed downward, and the equilibrium value of NNP fell.

The Long-Run Phillips Curve

Many leading economists, like Milton Friedman and Edmund Phelps, deny that the Phillips curve exists as a stable "long-run" phenomenon. To them, the Phillips curve in Figure 18.3 is only a short-run relationship; in the long run, they believe that the Phillips curve is vertical. Thus they are not surprised that, holding constant the unemployment rate, the rate of inflation was higher in the seventies than in the sixties. In their view, expansionary monetary and fiscal policies that result in inflation will only reduce unemployment temporarily, with the result that the rate of inflation will tend to accelerate, for reasons given below. Thus they are often called *accelerationists.*

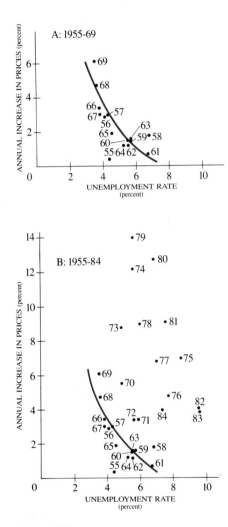

Figure 18.5

Relationship between Inflation Rate and Unemployment Rate Source: Economic Report of the President, *Washington, D.C.: Government Printing Office. 1979, 1982, and 1985.*

"NATURAL" RATE OF UNEMPLOYMENT

According to the accelerationists, there is a certain "natural" (or full-employment) rate of unemployment, which is determined by how long workers search before taking a new job. The more reluctant they are to take unattractive or low-paying jobs, the higher the "natural" rate of unemployment. Economists who stress the importance of structural unemployment argue that the "natural" rate of unemployment depends too on the rate at which changes in technology and tastes occur and the speed with which workers in declining industries can be retrained for jobs in expanding industries.

Suppose that this "natural" rate is 5½ percent, and that the government, not realizing that it is this high, uses expansionary monetary and fiscal policies to reduce unemployment to 4 percent. Because of the resulting increase in aggregate demand, the price level rises; and *if the level of money wages remains relatively constant,* firms' profits go up. Higher profits lead to expanded output and more employment. Thus the economy moves from point *C* (where it was before the government's expansionary policies) to point *D* in Figure 18.6. This movement is entirely in accord with the concept of the Phillips curve; a reduction in unemployment is gained at the expense of more inflation (6 percent rather than 4 percent).[5]

Figure 18.6

A Simplified Accelerationist Model

According to the accelerationists, expansionary monetary and fiscal policy results in a temporary reduction in the unemployment rate from 5½ to 4 percent (a movement from point C *to point* D*). But the increase in the inflation rate (from 4 to 6 percent) results in a higher expected rate of inflation, which shifts the short-run relationship from curve 1 to curve 2. If the government persists in trying to reduce the unemployment rate below the natural rate of 5½ percent, all that it will achieve is a higher and higher rate of inflation. In the long run, the unemployment rate returns to the natural rate (5½ percent in this case). Thus the long-run relationship between the unemployment rate and inflation rate is vertical.*

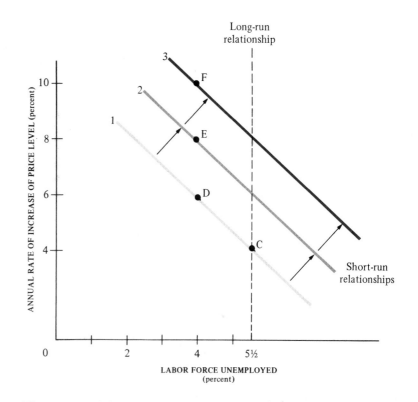

[5] To prevent confusion, note that we are not assuming that the short-run relationship between the inflation rate and the unemployment rate (curve 1 in Figure 18.6) is the same as the curve in Figure 18.4. Instead, we assume that it is below and to the left of the curve in Figure 18.4. In succeeding paragraphs, we shall show how it moves toward the position shown in Figure 18.4.

However, the accelerationists go on to argue that this movement is only temporary. To see why, it is essential to recognize that the short-run Phillips curve reflects people's expectations concerning the future rate of inflation. If people have come to expect a higher rate of inflation than in the past, this will shift the Phillips curve upward and to the right. To illustrate, let's compare two situations, one where workers and firms expect that prices will increase by 10 percent per year in the immediate future, the other where they expect no inflation at all. In the former case, unions will not be content to obtain less than a 10 percent increase in money wages, since a smaller increase would mean a cut in real wages. In the latter case, unions can afford to settle for a much more moderate increase in money wages, since none of the money wage increase is expected to be offset by inflation. Thus the rate of increase of wages is likely to be greater in the former than the latter case, if the unemployment rate is the same.

In summary, *the more inflation people expect, the further upward and out from the origin the short-run Phillips curve is likely to be. And the less inflation people expect, the further downward and close to the origin the short-run Phillips curve will be.*

According to the accelerationists, the movement from point *C* to point *D* in Figure 18.6 is only temporary because workers adjust their expectations concerning inflation. Before the government's expansionary monetary and fiscal policies were adopted, the inflation rate was 4 percent, and this was (more or less) what workers expected. The movement from point *C* to point *D* means an increase in the inflation rate to 6 percent, which the workers do not expect. Although they are fooled at first, people *adapt* their expectations; that is, the rate of inflation they expect is adjusted upward toward the new 6 percent rate. As pointed out in the previous paragraph, this increase in the expected amount of inflation will shift the short-run Phillips curve upward and out from the origin. The short-run relationship between the unemployment rate and the inflation rate will shift from curve 1 to curve 2 in Figure 18.6. Faced with this new short-run curve, the government will raise the inflation rate to 8 percent if it persists in trying to maintain the unemployment rate at 4 percent. That is, it will have to move to point *E* in Figure 18.6.

A SECOND TRY

Suppose that the government continues to try to maintain a 4 percent unemployment rate. Since the inflation rate increases to 8 percent as a consequence, people once more begin to adapt their expectations to the new inflation rate. Workers, trying to compensate for the higher inflation rate, ask for bigger wage increases, and firms are more willing to grant such increases because they recognize that the inflation rate has risen. Once again, the short-run Phillips curve shifts upward and outward from the origin. The short-run relationship between the unemployment rate and the inflation rate will shift from curve 2 to curve 3 in Figure 18.6. Thus the government will have increased the inflation rate to 10 percent if it persists in trying to keep the unemployment rate at 4 percent. That is, it will have to move to point *F* in Figure 18.6.

RECENT DEVELOPMENTS IN ECONOMICS: RATIONAL EXPECTATIONS AND CREDIBILITY IN FIGHTING INFLATION

In the previous chapter, we discussed rational expectations theories and the major impact they have had on the thinking of economists in the past decade or so. To illustrate the nature of these theories, let's consider a case where the government, rather than trying to reduce the unemployment rate (as in Figure 18.6), wants to reduce the inflation rate. Suppose that the short-run Phillips curve initially is curve 1 below, and that the government adopts a restrictive policy that moves the economy from point A to point B, with the result that the inflation rate falls from 12 percent to 10 percent. According to our argument in Figure 18.6, people will expect now that inflation will continue at 10 percent.

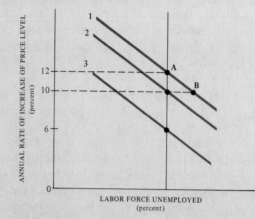

But such expectations would be irrational, if the public is convinced that the government really is serious about fighting inflation. Instead, people, if rational, will expect that inflation will fall further to perhaps 6 percent, because of the government's policies. This difference in expectations can be important. If people's expectations are rational, the short-run Phillips curve shifts downward much more rapidly than if people irrationally expect a 10 percent inflation rate. Specifically, it shifts to curve 3, whereas it would have shifted to curve 2 if people expected a 10 percent inflation rate. Thus it is much easier to tame inflation further, because of the change in expectations.

According to the rational expectations theorists, and many others as well, it is important that a government's anti-inflation policy be firm, consistent, and well understood. If firms, workers, and consumers are persuaded that the government will stick by its guns, and reduce inflation (even if it means heavy unemployment in the short run), they will relatively quickly moderate their wage and price demands, and inflation will soon be reduced. In other words, the credibility of a government's anti-inflationary policy is of the utmost importance. If such a policy is credible (and thus influences expectations), inflation will subside relatively quickly; if it is not credible, there may be great difficulties in bringing it down.

Without question, anti-inflation policy in the United States in the 1970s was not always credible. There was far more talk than action. In part, this was because government officials and their advisers were not convinced that people's expectations and behavior would change rapidly enough so that inflation could be licked without incurring considerable social costs (and political defeat at the polls).

THE LONG-RUN RELATIONSHIP

If the government persists in trying to reduce the unemployment rate below the natural rate of 5½ percent, it will continually fail to do so. All that it will achieve is a higher and higher rate of inflation. Thus, according to the accelerationists, the Phillips curve really does not exist, except in the short run, and governments that believe in its existence can cause considerable mischief. It is not possible for the economy to remain permanently at any point on the short-run curves in Figure 18.6 other than at the natural rate of unemployment (5½ percent in this case). Thus the long-run relationship between the unemployment rate and the inflation rate is a vertical line, as shown in Figure 18.6.[6]

Not all economists agree with the accelerationists' view that the long-run relationship between the unemployment rate and the inflation rate is a vertical line. Some believe that, even in the long run, this relationship is inverse. However, there seems to be little doubt that the long-run relationship is a lot steeper than the short-run relationship. Thus much, though perhaps not all, of the reduction in unemployment due to increases in inflation is likely to be illusory.

[6] The available evidence seems to indicate that the natural rate of unemployment has been higher in more recent years than in the 1960s, due in considerable part to the fact that women and teenagers have been a larger percentage of the labor force than in the 1960s. (Recall our discussion of this in Chapter 8.) This increase in the natural rate of unemployment is another factor that is partly responsible for the recent stagflation, but it is by no means the whole story.

Test Yourself

1. "The inflations arising from the Revolutionary, Civil, and Vietnam wars were largely cost-push." Comment and evaluate.

2. According to Franco Modigliani, "Acceptance of the Phillips curve ... implied ... there was no longer a unique Full Employment but rather a whole family of possible equilibrium [employment] rates, each associated with a different rate of inflation."* Explain what he means, and indicate whether you agree or not, and why.

3. Suppose that the relationship between the annual rate of change of the wage rate and the percent of the labor force unemployed is as shown below:

Rate of change of wage rate (percent per year)	Unemployment rate (percent)
5	8
6	7
7	6
8	5

Plot the Phillips curve on a graph. Would Milton Friedman accept this curve as a long-run Phillips curve? Why or why not?

4. Suppose that output per man-hour is growing at 2 percent per year. Based on the data in Question 3, plot the relationship between the annual rate of change of the price level and the unemployment rate. State the assumptions you are making.

5. During the late 1970s, Americans began to expect higher and higher rates of inflation. Explain in detail the effects of this on the short-run relationship between the unemployment rate and the rate of inflation.

* F. Modigliani, "The Monetarist Controversy or, Should We Foresake Stabilization Policies," *American Economic Review*, March 1977, p. 3.

Wage and Price Controls

Still another way that the government can try to curb inflation is by adopting *wage and price controls.* During World War II—and other wartime emergencies—the government imposed controls of this sort. In other words, the government intervened directly in the market place to see that wages and prices did not increase by more than a certain amount. The economics profession has little enthusiasm for direct controls of wages and prices, for several reasons.

1. Such controls are likely to result in a distorted allocation of resources. Recall from Chapter 3 our discussion of the functions of the price system in allocating resources. Wage and price controls do not permit prices to perform these functions, and the result is inefficiency and waste.

2. Such controls are likely to be expensive to administer. For example, during the Korean War, the Economic Stabilization Agency had 16,000 employees; even so, it was difficult to prevent violation or evasion of the controls.

3. There is widespread opposition to detailed government regulation and control of this sort, on the grounds that it impairs our economic freedom. The Council of Economic Advisers undoubtedly spoke for most of the economics profession when it said in 1968,

> The most obvious—and least desirable—way of attempting to stabilize prices is to impose mandatory controls on prices and wages. While such controls may be necessary under conditions of an all-out war, it would be folly to consider them as a solution to the inflationary pressures that accompany high employment under any other circumstance. . . . Although such controls may be unfortunately popular when they are not in effect, the appeal quickly disappears once people live under them.[7]

WAGE AND PRICE CONTROLS UNDER THE NIXON
ADMINISTRATION: A CASE STUDY

Despite the disadvantages of price controls, the Nixon administration adopted them in the summer of 1971. Wholesale prices were rising then at about 5 percent per year. The wage-price spiral was very much in evidence. Collective bargaining agreements were reached calling for wage increases far in excess of productivity increases, and there was no question but that firms would boost prices in an attempt to cover the resulting increase in costs. In August 1971, President Nixon froze wages and prices for a 3-month period. Then he appointed a 15-member Pay Board and a 7-member Price Commission, both of which were supervised by the government's Cost of Living Council.

The Pay Board was given the responsibility of administering wage controls, and the Price Commission was to administer price controls. In November 1971, these two bodies announced their initial policies. The Pay Board stated that pay increases had to be kept under 5.5 percent per year.

[7] *1968 Annual Report of the Council of Economic Advisers,* Washington, D.C.: Government Printing Office, p. 119.

A company could increase some employees' pay by more than this amount, but other employees would have to get less since total increases could not exceed this figure. The Price Commission ruled that price increases had to be kept under 2.5 percent. Both for prices and wages, exceptions could be made in some areas. Large firms were required to notify the Pay Board and Price Commission of intended wage or price increases.

From November 1971 to January 1973, this program of wage and price controls continued. Although it did not eliminate inflation, prices seemed to go up more slowly than before the freeze. (The Consumer Price Index went up by about 3 percent during 1972.) By early 1973, it appeared that controls might safely be relaxed. In January 1973, the Pay Board and the Price Commission became part of the Cost of Living Council, headed by Harvard's labor economist, John Dunlop. And controls were eliminated or relaxed for most prices and wages, with the major exceptions of the health, food, and construction industries. To a considerable extent, the Nixon administration phased out the first peacetime wage and price controls in our history.

Unfortunately, inflation occurred subsequently at a bewildering pace. During the first half of 1973, wholesale prices of farm products and processed foods and feeds rose at the unbelievable rate of 48 percent per year. At the same time, the prices of lumber, fuel, and other industrial goods rose at alarming rates. President Nixon responded by imposing a 60-day freeze on prices (but not wages), beginning in mid-June of 1973. This was only a breather, an interim measure designed to give the administration some time to deal with the serious inflationary pressures that were evident throughout the economy.

In August 1973, the administration announced that price increases could not exceed cost increases. This was the core of the new postfreeze program. But it soon became obvious that this new program was not proving effective, and that there was growing criticism and skepticism concerning price controls. In April 1974, Congress allowed the control authority to expire. This phase of the program was widely acknowledged to be a failure.

Basic Idea #36: Wage and price controls tend to result in several undesirable effects. By interfering with the functioning of the price system, they result in a distorted allocation of resources. They curtail our economic freedom, and are expensive to administer. (To a lesser extent, incomes policies may suffer from similar problems.) History indicates that wage and price controls are not a solution to the inflation problem.

It is difficult to evaluate the effects of the wage and price controls established between 1971 and 1974. According to many observers, the price level rose, once controls were relaxed, to the level that it would have attained in any event, if there had been no controls. Thus, to these observers, the effects of the controls were short-term and largely cosmetic. (See Example 18.2.) To other observers, the controls had a significant longer-term effect. According to the Council of Economic Advisers, "regardless of the overall effect of the program, whatever contribution it may have made was probably concentrated in its first 16 months, when the economy was operating well below its potential. As various industrial sectors reached capacity operations in 1973 under the stimulus of a booming domestic and world economy, the controls system began to obstruct normal supplier-purchaser relationships, and in some cases the controls became quite unworkable."[8]

---

[8] *1975 Annual Report of the Council of Economic Advisers,* Washington, D.C.: Government Printing Office, pp. 228–29.

Incomes Policies

As we have stressed repeatedly, the 1970s and early 1980s were a period of uncomfortably high inflation. For example, in 1980, the price level in the United States was increasing by more than 10 percent per year. Faced with such high rates of inflation, there has been considerable interest, both here and abroad, in using incomes policies to help curb inflation without cutting back on aggregate demand. According to one common definition, an **incomes policy** contains three elements:

1. *An incomes policy has some targets for wages (and other forms of income) and prices for the economy as a whole.* For example, the target may

---

Example 18.2   Effects of the 1971-74 Control Program

During 1971–74, the Nixon administration adopted price and wage controls. According to Northwestern's Robert Gordon, the percentage increase in the price level that would have been predicted in the absence of these controls compares as follows with the actual increase:

Period	Percent increase in price level	
	Without controls	Actual
1971 (second quarter) to 1973 (third quarter)	11.3	7.8
1973 (third quarter) to 1975 (third quarter)	11.9	15.4

(a) If these estimates are correct, did price and wage controls have a short-term effect on the price level? (b) Did they have any long-term effect on the price level? (c) Reinforcing steel bars were subject to the controls, but the steel scrap used to make the bars was not subject to them. The price of steel scrap increased much more rapidly than the price of steel bars. What do you think was the effect on the output of steel bars? (d) Steel bars are used in construction projects. What effect do you think a shortage of steel bars would have on the construction industry?*

SOLUTION

(a) Yes. During 1971–73, the price level increased less rapidly (by about 3.5 percentage points) than would have been expected without controls. (b) No. Although the price level increased less rapidly than would have been expected without controls during 1971–73, it increased more rapidly during 1973–75. In 1973–75, the positive difference in the inflation rate over what would have been expected without controls canceled the negative difference in 1971–73. In other words, when controls were lifted, the price level jumped approximately to the level it would have reached without controls. (c) Since the profits of the bar manufacturers were reduced, they cut their output of bars. (d) It interfered with the efficient operation of construction projects. In essence, the price system was not allowed to function properly.

* For further discussion, see R. Gordon, *Macroeconomics,* 2nd ed., Little Brown, 1981, pp. 317–20.

be to stabilize the price level, or to permit the Consumer Price Index to increase by less than 2 percent per year, or to allow wage increases not exceeding a certain percentage.

2. An incomes policy gives particular firms and industries some more detailed guides for decision making on wages (and other forms of income) and prices. These guides are set in such a way that the overall targets for the entire economy will be fulfilled. For example, if the aim is price stability, these guides tell firms and unions what kinds of decisions are compatible with this target. To be useful, the guides must be specific and understandable enough to be applied in particular cases. There obviously is little point in telling firms and unions to avoid "inflationary" wage and price decisions if they don't know whether a particular decision is "inflationary" or not.

3. An incomes policy contains some mechanisms to get firms and unions to follow the guides. An incomes policy differs from price and wage controls in that it seeks to induce firms and unions to follow these guides voluntarily. But if it is to have any effect, clearly the government must be prepared to use certain forms of "persuasion" beyond moral suasion. In fact, governments sometimes have publicly condemned decisions by firms and unions that were regarded as violating the guides. Government stockpiles of materials and government purchasing policies have also been used to penalize or reward particular firms and industries. Other pressures too have been brought to bear in an attempt to induce firms to follow the established guides. Thus the difference between an incomes policy and price and wage controls is one of degree and emphasis, not a clear-cut difference in kind.

An example of an incomes policy in the United States was the so-called Kennedy-Johnson guidelines. Although earlier administrations (for example, the Eisenhower and Truman administrations) had often appealed to business and labor to limit price and wage increases, the first systematic attempt at a fairly specific incomes policy in the United States occurred during the Kennedy administration, In 1961, President Kennedy's Council of Economic Advisers issued the following wage-price guidelines:

> The general guide for noninflationary wage behavior is that the rate of increase in wage rates (including fringe benefits) in each industry be equal to the trend rate of *over-all productivity advance.* General acceptance of this guide would maintain stability of labor cost per unit of output for the economy as a whole—though not of course for individual industries. The general guide for noninflationary price behavior calls for price reduction if the industry's rate of productivity increase exceeds the over-all rate—for this would mean declining unit labor costs; it calls for an appropriate increase in price if the opposite relationship prevails; and it calls for stable prices if the two rates of productivity increase are equal. [Note once again that productivity equals output per hour of labor.][9]

To see just what this means, let's consider prices and wages in the auto industry. Suppose that labor productivity in the economy as a whole was increasing at 3.2 percent per year. Then according to the guidelines, *wages in the automobile industry should increase by 3.2 percent per year.* If labor

[9] *1962 Annual Report of the Council of Economic Advisers,* Washington, D.C.: Government Printing Office, p. 189.

productivity in the auto industry increased by 4.2 percent per year, then, if the auto makers applied this guideline, the labor cost of producing a unit of output would decrease by 1 percent per year in the auto industry (since the 3.2 percent rate of increase of wages minus the 4.2 percent rate of increase of labor productivity equals −1 percent). Thus the guidelines specified that *prices in the auto industry should decrease,* perhaps by about 1 percent per year.

The Council of Economic Advisers specified several situations where these general guidelines would have to be modified. In particular, if there was a shortage of labor in a particular industry or if an industry's wages were lower than those earned elsewhere by similar labor, higher wage increases (than specified in general) would be warranted. Or if an industry's profits were insufficient to attract needed infusions of capital, or if an industry's nonwage costs rose greatly, higher price increases than specified in general would be justified. However, the Council did not attempt to set forth detailed, quantitative provisions about the extent to which higher wages or prices would be warranted under these circumstances.

THE KENNEDY-JOHNSON GUIDELINES: CRITICISM AND EXPERIENCE

Soon after the announcement of the Kennedy-Johnson guidelines, critics began to point out problems in them. The criticism was of several types.

Inefficiency. Some observers feared that the guidelines would result in inefficiency and waste. In a free-enterprise economy, we rely on price changes to direct resources into the most productive uses and to signal shortages or surpluses in various markets. If the guidelines were accepted by industry and labor, prices would not be free to perform this function. Of course, the guidelines specified that modifications of the general rules could be made in case of shortages, but critics of the guidelines felt that this escape hatch was too vague to be very useful.

Freedom. Many observers were concerned about the reduction in economic freedom. Of course, the guidelines were presented in the hope that they would be observed voluntarily. But a time was sure to come when they would be in serious contradiction with the interests of firms and unions. In such a situation, what would happen if the firms or unions decided not to follow them? To the extent that the government applied pressure on the firms or unions, there would certainly be a reduction in economic freedom; and to some observers, it seemed likely that the next step might well be direct government controls. Moreover, the nonlegislated character of the guidelines and the arbitrary choice of whom to pursue by the government raised important questions of a political nature.

Feasibility. Many people felt that the guidelines really were not workable. In other words, even if the public would go along with them, in many cases they would be impossible to use, because accurate and relevant data on changes in labor productivity in particular industries were often unobtainable, and the situations where exceptions were allowed were so vaguely specified.

Symptoms. Some economists felt that reliance on the guidelines was dangerous because it focused attention on symptoms rather than causes of inflation. In their view, inflation was largely the result of improper monetary and fiscal policies. In other words, the basic causes had to be laid at the government's own door. But by setting up guidelines, the government seemed to be saying that the fault lay with industry and labor. Thus some critics felt that the guidelines tended to cloud the real issues and so let the government escape responsibility for its actions.

During 1962–64 the government claimed that the guidelines were working well. To a considerable extent, this may have been because the economy still had considerable slack, as well as because of the noninflationary expectations of firms and individuals engendered by several years of relative price stability. By 1965, as labor markets tightened and prices rose in response to the Vietnam build-up (see Chapter 12), it became much more difficult to use the guidelines. Union leaders fought the guidelines tooth and nail, mainly because consumer prices were rising. In various important labor negotiations, unions demanded and got higher wage increases than the guidelines called for. For example, the airline machinists got a 4.9 percent increase in 1966. By 1968, the guideline were dead. No one was paying any attention to them.

What effect did the guidelines have? Some people claim that they had no real effect at all, while others claim that they reduced cost-push inflation in the early 1960s by a considerable amount. Since it is difficult to separate the effects of the guidelines from the effects of other factors, there is considerable dispute over the question. Considering the level of unemployment in the early 1960s, wages increased less rapidly then than in earlier or later periods. Prices too increased less rapidly during that period—holding unemployment constant—than earlier or later. But whether these developments were due to the guidelines, or to noninflationary expectations or some other factor, is very hard to say.

Perhaps the most important reason why the guidelines broke down was that they could not deal with the strong demand-pull inflation of the late 1960s. Even the strongest defenders of the guidelines are quick to point out that they are no substitute for proper monetary and fiscal policy. *If fiscal or monetary policy is generating strong inflationary pressures, such as existed in the late 1960s, it is foolish to think that guidelines can save the situation.* Perhaps they can cut down on the rate of inflation for a while; but in the long run, the dike is sure to burst. If the guidelines are voluntary, as in this case, firms and unions will ignore them, and the government will find it difficult, it not impossible, to do anything about it. *Even price and wage controls are no adequate antidote to strong inflationary pressures generated by an overly expansive fiscal or monetary policy. Such controls may deal temporarily with the symptoms of inflation, but over the long haul these inflationary pressures will have an effect.*

Tax-Based Incomes Policies

In the past ten years, a number of influential economists have proposed that tax-based incomes policies be adopted to slow the rate of inflation. Such incomes policies use the tax system or subsidies to induce firms to hold down prices and workers to hold down wages. Some tax-based incomes policies use a "carrot"; others use a "stick." To illustrate the nature

THE MEETING OF THE FEDERAL OPEN MARKET COMMITTEE ON NOVEMBER 14–15, 1983

On November 14–15, 1983, the Federal Open Market Committee met. To understand the factors influencing the committee's decisions, it is worthwhile describing this meeting in some detail. Information was presented by the staff of the Federal Reserve concerning economic conditions in the period since the committee's previous meeting on October 4, 1983. According to the latest information, real GNP was growing at a relatively rapid rate, although the pace of expansion seemed to have moderated from the annual growth rates of about 9¾ percent and 8 percent in the second and third quarters of 1983. The rate of increase of the Consumer Price Index, the rate of growth of industrial production, and the unemployment rate during August, September, and October were as follows:

Month	Percentage increase (from previous month) in Consumer Price Index	Percentage increase (from previous month) in industrial production	Un-employment rate
August	0.4	1.3	9.3
September	0.5	1.3	9.1
October	0.4	0.8	8.7

According to forecasts presented by the Federal Reserve staff, the rate of growth of real GNP would slow to a more moderate pace in 1984. The slowdown was expected to be due in part to less stimulus from inventory and housing investment, as well as a slower rate of growth of consumer spending. A fall in the unemployment rate was forecasted, but inflation was expected to remain generally moderate. These forecasts were based on the sorts of techniques described in Chapter 13.

At its previous meeting in October, the committee had decided that open market operations should be directed toward maintaining slightly less restraint on the economy. An annual rate of growth of the money supply (*M*-1) of around 7 percent was agreed upon. In fact, the money supply had grown at less than this rate during October. Interest rates generally fluctuated in a narrow range in the period since the October meeting. Long-term interest rates rose slightly, apparently in response to signs of continued strength in economic activity and to uncertainties about the prospective pattern of Treasury financing, as passage of legislation to increase the federal debt ceiling was delayed.

With this background in mind, the committee members discussed the economic situation and outlook. Based on the official account of this meeting, the discussion ran as follows:

> [Some] members commented that the economic expansion had remained stronger than generally anticipated. Reports from around the country suggested increasingly widespread optimism about business conditions and a high degree of consumer confidence. While all the members expected the rate of economic

growth to moderate over the year ahead, there were some differences of view with regard to the timing and likely extent of the slowdown. Some members anticipated that the slowdown might be appreciably less than projected by the staff, with unfavorable implications for inflationary pressures and the ultimate sustainability of the expansion. In support of this view, reference was made to the favorable conditions for a surge in business fixed investment created by the momentum of the expansion. In addition, it was pointed out that a highly stimulative fiscal policy remained in prospect for 1984. Thus, while the expansionary impact of housing and inventory accumulation could be expected to wane during the second year of the recovery, vigorous growth in fixed investment expenditures in conjunction with the prospective federal deficit might well sustain relatively rapid expansion in overall economic activity during the year ahead. It was also suggested that, at least for the near term, consumer spending and inventory accumulation might provide more stimulus to the economy than was generally anticipated.

Other members placed more emphasis on some elements of potential weakness in the economic outlook. It was pointed out that there was as yet no firm evidence that business fixed investment would prove to be exceptionally strong during 1984. Indeed, such investment might continue to be held down by the persistence of weak demand for the output of some traditional producers of capital equipment, and, more generally, by relatively high interest rates in the context of massive Treasury debt financings. . . .

With regard to the prospects for prices, several members questioned whether further progress could be made in containing inflationary pressures if the rate of economic expansion did not slow to a more moderate pace over the year ahead. One member observed that by late 1984, capacity utilization rates could reach levels that would tend to generate inflationary cost pressures even if unemployment were still high relative to earlier expansion periods. On the other hand, some members felt that there was little current evidence that price and wage pressures or inflationary expectations were worsening. One member also noted that the economy was still operating well below capacity and that further significant improvements in productivity, along with competitive pressures from world markets, were likely to restrain inflation during 1984.

In the Committee's discussion of policy for the period immediately ahead, all of the members found acceptable a policy directed toward maintaining the existing degree of reserve restraint. In the view of some, however, an argument could be made in favor of a small, precautionary step in the direction of firming in light of the continuing strength of the economic expansion and the associated danger of a resurgence of inflationary pressures during the year ahead. While acknowledging the risks of inflation in a rapidly expanding economy combined with large budget deficits and the relatively rapid monetary growth earlier in the year, most members saw sufficient uncertainties in the outlook to counsel against any change in reserve pressures at this time. Some members were also concerned that under the prevailing circumstances even a modest increase in restraint on reserves might have a disproportionate impact on domestic and international financial markets. The result could be an increase in domestic interest rates large enough to have damaging consequences for housing and other interest-sensitive sectors of the economy and to intensify greatly the pressures on countries with severe external debt problems.[1]

At the conclusion of the meeting, the committee decided that no change should be made in the degree of restraint on bank reserves. The committee anticipated that the money supply (M-1) would increase at an annual rate

---

[1] "Record of Policy Actions of the Federal Open Market Committee," *Federal Reserve Bulletin,* January 1984, pp. 25–26.

of about 5 or 6 percent and that the federal funds rate (the interest rate charged by financial institutions for lending reserves to one another, primarily on an over-night basis) would remain at 6 to 10 percent. Like most meetings of the Federal Open Market Committee (but unlike the Saturday Night Special described on p. 361), this one was hardly the stuff from which good drama is made. But to understand the workings of the economy, and the way in which public policy is formulated, it is essential that you know what goes on in the meetings of this committee, dramatic or not.

of those that use a "stick," suppose that a target of 6 percent were established for overall pay increases. If a firm's average pay increase was less than or equal to the 6 percent target, it would pay the basic corporate income tax of, say, 46 percent of its profits. But if its average pay increase exceeded the 6 percent target, it would be subject to a higher corporate income tax rate. For example, its income tax might be 51 percent of its profits if its pay increase was 7 percent, 56 percent of its profits if its pay increase was 8 percent, and so on. Clearly, the firm would be penalized for granting large pay increases. If it allowed pay increases far in excess of the target, its after-tax profits would be cut severely.

This is the kind of tax-based incomes policy proposed originally by Henry Wallich of the Federal Reserve Board and the late Sidney Weintraub of the University of Pennsylvania. Since their proposal, a number of other such schemes have been put forth. Lawrence Seidman of the University of Delaware has suggested that the tax system could be used both to penalize firms that grant large pay increases and to reward those that grant small pay increases. For example, if a firm were to keep pay increases to 5 percent (when the target is 6 percent), it would be rewarded with a lower income tax rate than if it did no better than the target. It might pay only 44 percent of its profits in income taxes, rather than the 46 percent that it would pay if it did no better than meet the 6 percent target.

In 1977, the late Arthur Okun of the Brookings Institution proposed a form of tax-based incomes policy that emphasized positive inducements for noninflationary behavior; that is, the "carrot" rather than the "stick." If a firm pledged to hold the average rate of wage increase of its employees below 6 percent and its average rate of price increase below 4 percent (except for the effects of increases in the costs of its materials and supplies), both the firm and its employees would receive a tax rebate. This proposal also received serious consideration from economists and policy makers.

Although tax-based incomes policies have attracted considerable interest and attention in the late 1970s and early and mid-1980s, they are not free of problems. For one thing, the administrative difficulties in implementing such policies are significant, according to Treasury officials and others. The job of the Internal Revenue Service would be complicated considerably if such policies were adopted, and firms might have difficulties in complying with them. Neither business nor labor has expressed enthusiasm for tax-based incomes policies. Labor leaders have been cool to them, because they feel that such policies seem to imply (unfairly, in their view) that inflation is due primarily to wage increases. They feel that such policies are an unwelcome interference with collective bargaining. Business leaders have been wary of them, because they feel that such policies would complicate wage negotiations and personnel management. Also, they fear that some firms (smaller or unincorporated businesses, in particular) may be exempt from the program, and that these firms, therefore, may be given a competitive edge.

Despite these problems, some form of tax-based incomes policy may eventually be tried, if for no other reason that it may seem preferable to other kinds of incomes policies. As Henry Wallich has put it, "Of course, nobody likes tax-based incomes policies *per se*. It is really a question of the alternatives."

Economic Stabilization: Where We Stand

Where do we stand in the struggle to achieve full employment without inflation? Clearly, we know much more than we did 40 years ago about how to use monetary and fiscal policies to attain this objective. Given the more advanced state of economics, it is very unlikely that a catastrophe like the Great Depression of the 1930s will occur again. But on the other hand, economists were overly optimistic in the mid-1960s when they talked about "fine-tuning" the economy. Our experience since then makes it clear that we have a long way to go before we understand the workings of the economy well enough to achieve continuous full employment without considerable inflation. Equally important, we have seen that, even if the advice of its economists were always correct, the government might still pursue destabilizing policies, as it did in the late 1960s.

The 1970s and 1980s have been characterized by both excessive inflation and excessive unemployment. Throughout the Western industrialized world, governments have been perplexed by this phenomenon of "stagflation." The standard economic remedies—monetary and fiscal policy—are not very effective in dealing with this combination of ailments. Although they can deal with either excessive unemployment or excessive inflation, they are not well designed to deal simultaneously with both of them.

To some economists, the answer (or at least a partial answer) is to rely more heavily on some form of incomes policy to fight inflation. But the evidence, here and abroad, seems to emphasize the problems in formulating an effective incomes policy. The unfortunate truth is that, although our understanding of the factors causing "stagflation" is more complete than the newspapers frequently imply, it is not complete enough to provide a workable cure that most economists can agree on. Until we obtain a better basic understanding of this phenomenon, the chances are that policy makers, both here and abroad, will continue to have problems with regard to economic stabilization—and that there will be a good deal of floundering. If the rate of inflation takes still another alarming upturn, it is likely that some form of wage and price controls will once again be applied in the United States. But it must be recognized that such controls have had limited success in restraining inflation more than temporarily, in the United States as in other countries.[10]

Finally, there has been a shift in emphasis in many public policy discussions by economists and others. During recent decades, the emphasis often was almost exclusively on the government's management of aggregate demand in an effort to maintain full employment. Now more attention is being given to the supply side of the economy. In part, this is due to the commodity shortages, sluggish productivity growth, and relatively low rates of capital investment in the United States during the 1970s. Some of the effects of these factors have been taken up in this chapter. Much more will be said concerning them in the next chapter.

[10] The Reagan administration has put less emphasis on incomes policies than did the Carter administration. As for wage and price controls, President Reagan is on record as believing that they don't "work." (See Question 4 below in "Test Yourself.") But this does not mean that such measures will not be adopted sometime in the future.

Test Yourself

1. According to Milton Friedman, "It is far better that inflation be open than that it be suppressed (by price guidelines)." Do you agree? Why or why not?

2. "The Kennedy-Johnson guidelines for noninflationary price behavior called for price reduction if an industry's rate of productivity increase exceeded the overall rate. It is unrealistic to expect price cuts of this sort." Do you agree? Why or why not?

3. "Reliance on incomes policies is dangerous because it looks at symptoms, not the basic causes of our problems." Comment and evaluate.

4. According to President Ronald Reagan, wage and price controls "didn't work when Hammurabi tried them in Babylon. They didn't work when Diocletian tried them in Rome." In this context, what does "work" mean? Why do you think they didn't "work"?

Summary

1. The Phillips curve shows the relationship between the rate of increase of wages and the level of unemployment. If the Phillips curve remains fixed, it poses an awkward dilemma for policy makers. If they reduce unemployment, inflation increases; if they reduce inflation, unemployment increases. During 1955–69, there was a fairly close relationship between the inflation rate and the unemployment rate. But then something unforeseen by most economists occurred. The inflation and unemployment rates in the seventies did not conform at all closely to the relationship that prevailed in the sixties. Both the unemployment rate and the inflation rate tended to be much higher in the seventies than in the sixties.

2. The accelerationists, led by Milton Friedman, believe that the downward-sloping Phillips curve is only a short-run relationship. In the long run, they believe that it is vertical. In their view, expansionary policies that result in inflation will only reduce unemployment temporarily, with the result that the government, if it sets out to reduce unemployment to an amount below its natural level, will have to permit higher and higher rates of inflation.

3. To reduce the inflation rate (at a given unemployment rate), governments have tried price and wage controls. Although a few economists favor such controls during peacetime, most do not agree. Such controls are likely to distort the allocation of resources, to be difficult to administer, and to run counter to our desire for economic freedom.

4. Many countries have experimented with various kinds of incomes policies. An incomes policy contains targets for prices and wages for the economy as a whole, more detailed guides for price and wage decisions in particular industries, and some mechanisms to get firms and unions to follow these guides. The Kennedy-Johnson guidelines were one form of incomes policy. Although guidelines of this sort have a short-term effect on the price level, how much effect they have in the long run is hard to say.

5. A variety of types of tax-based incomes policies has been proposed in recent years. Such policies use the tax system or subsidies to induce firms to hold down prices and workers to hold down wages. Some use a "carrot"; others use a "stick."

6. Although it is very unlikely that a catastrophe like the Great Depression will recur, our recent experience indicates that we have a long way to go before we understand the workings of the economy well enough to achieve continuous full employment without inflation. Also, even if the advice of its economists were always correct, there is no assurance that the government would always pursue policies leading toward economic stabilization.

Concepts for Review

Demand-pull inflation	Phillips curve	Wage and price controls
Cost-push inflation	Labor productivity	Incomes policies
Wage-price spiral	Accelerationist	

PART FIVE

Economic Growth, Energy, and the Environment

CHAPTER 19

Economic Growth*

Until fairly recently in human history, poverty was the rule, not the exception. As Sir Kenneth Clark puts it in his famous lectures on *Civilisation,*

> Poverty, hunger, plagues, disease: they were the background of history right up to the end of the nineteenth century, and most people regarded them as inevitable—like bad weather. Nobody thought they could be cured: St. Francis wanted to sanctify poverty, not abolish it. The old Poor Laws were not designed to abolish poverty but to prevent the poor from becoming a nuisance. All that was required was an occasional act of charity.[1]

Clearly, the human condition has changed considerably during the past century, at least in the industrialized nations of the world. Rising living standards have brought a decline in poverty, though by no means its disappearance. How has this increase in per capita output been achieved? This question has fascinated economists for a long time. Although we still are far from completely understanding the process of economic growth, our knowledge has increased considerably through the efforts of economic researchers, here and abroad. In this chapter, we discuss the process of economic growth in industrialized countries. A discussion of economic growth in less developed countries will be presented in Chapter 34.

---

*Some instructors prefer to take up this (and the following) chapter after the material on microeconomics (Chapter 21–31). This can be done, without loss of continuity. If this option is used, the section on diminishing marginal returns should be treated as a review.

[1] K. Clark, *Civilisation,* New York: Harper & Row, 1970.

What Is Economic Growth?

There are two common measures of the rate of **economic growth**. The first is the rate of growth of a nation's real gross national product (or net national product), which tells us how rapidly the economy's total real output of goods and services is increasing. The second is the rate of growth of *per capita* real gross national product (or net national product), which is a better measure of the rate of increase of a nation's standard of living. We shall use the second measure unless we state otherwise. Two aspects of the rate of growth of per capita real gross national product should be noted from the start.

1. *This measure is only a very crude approximation to the rate of increase of economic welfare.* For one thing, gross national product does not include one good that people prize most highly: leisure. For another, gross national product does not value at all accurately new products and improvements in the quality of goods and services, and does not allow properly either for noneconomic changes in the quality of life or for the costs of environmental pollution. Nor does gross national product take account of how the available output is distributed. Clearly, it makes a difference whether the bulk of the population gets a reasonable share of the output, or whether it goes largely to a favored few.

2. *Small differences in the annual rate of economic growth can make very substantial differences in living standards a few decades hence.* For example, per capita GNP in the United States was about $15,000 in 1984. If it grows at 2 percent per year, it will be about $20,600 (1984 dollars) in the year 2000, whereas if it grows at 3 percent per year, it will be about $24,100 (1984 dollars) in the year 2000. Thus an increase of 1 percentage point in growth rate means a $3,500 (or 17 percent) increase in per capita GNP in the year 2000. Even an increase of ¼ of 1 percentage point can make a considerable difference. If the growth rate increases from 1¾ percent to 2 percent per year, per capita GNP in the year 2000 will increase from $19,800 to $20,600. Of course, this is no more than arithmetic, but that doesn't make it any less important.

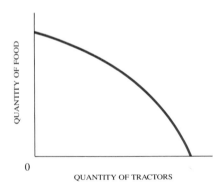

Figure 19.1
Production Possibilities Curve *The production possibilities curve shows all efficient combinations of output an economy can produce.*

Economic Growth and the Production Possibilities Curve

To represent the process of economic growth, it is convenient to use the production possibilities curve which, as you will recall from Chapter 2, shows all efficient combinations of output an economy can produce. For example, suppose that a society produces only two goods: food and tractors. If this society has at its disposal a fixed amount of resources and if technology is fixed, the production possibilities curve (like the one in Figure 19.1) shows the maximum quantity of food that can be produced, given each amount of tractors produced.

SHIFTS OF THE PRODUCTION POSSIBILITY CURVE

A nation's potential output increases when its production possibilities curve shifts outward, as from position *A* to position *B* in Figure 19.2. This happens because the society can produce (and consume) more of one good without having to produce (and consume) less of the other good. Thus its productive capacity must be greater. If the production possibilities curve shifts outward, if the economy is efficient, and if population remains constant, per capita GNP increases and economic growth occurs. Moreover, the faster the production possibilities curve shifts outward, the greater the rate of economic growth.

NO SHIFT OF THE PRODUCTION POSSIBILITY CURVE

Even if a nation's production possibilities curve does not shift outward, economic growth can occur if unemployment or inefficiency is reduced. If a nation allows some of its resources to be unemployed or underutilized because of an insufficiency of intended spending, this will cause the economy to operate at a point *inside* the production possibilities curve rather than *on* the curve. The same thing will happen if a nation allocates its resources inefficiently. Clearly, a nation can achieve some economic growth by getting closer to the production possibilities curve through a reduction in unemployment or inefficiency.

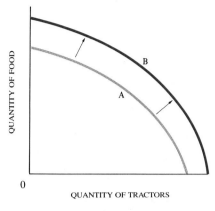

Figure 19.2
Outward Shift of Production Possibilities Curve *A nation's potential output increases when its production possibilities curve shifts outward from position* A *to position* B.

The Aggregate Production Function

A nation's potential output is directly related to the amount of resources it possesses and the extent to which they are used. These resources, or inputs, are of various kinds, including labor, capital, and land. The relationship between the amount used of each of these inputs and the resulting amount of potential output is often called the ***aggregate production function.*** It is analogous to the production function discussed in Chapter 6, which is the relationship between a firm's inputs and its output. However, the aggregate production function pertains to the entire economy, not a single firm.

Given that a nation's potential output depends on the amount of labor, capital, and land it uses, then the rate of growth of a nation's potential output must depend, in part at least, on the changes that occur in the amount of each of these inputs that is used. For example, if a nation invests heavily in additional capital, we would expect this to result in a substantial increase in potential output. Thus *a nation's rate of economic growth depends on the extent of the changes in the amounts of the various inputs used.* In addition, *a nation's rate of economic growth depends on the rate of technological change.* The aggregate production function is constructed on the assumption that technology is fixed. Changes in technology result in shifts in the production function, since more output is obtained from a given amount of resources.

The Law of Diminishing Marginal Returns

If a nation's land, labor, and capital increase, one would certainly expect its output to increase as well. But suppose the nation cannot increase the amount used of all of its resources at the same rate. Instead, suppose it can increase the quantity of one resource, say labor, while the amount of the other resources, like land, is held constant. In this situation, what will be the effect on output if the nation uses more and more of the resource that can be augmented? This is an important question, which occurs both in the present context and in the study of the production processes of the business firm.

To help answer it, economists have formulated the famous **law of diminishing marginal returns,** which states that, *if more and more of a resource is used, the quantities of other resources being held constant, the resulting increments of output will decrease after some point has been reached.*

To see what this means, suppose that we obtain data concerning the amounts of output resulting from the utilization of various amounts of one resource, holding constant the amounts of other resources. For example, suppose that data are obtained concerning the amounts of output resulting from various amounts of labor, holding constant the amounts of capital and land. Then suppose that we determine the *extra* amount of output resulting from the addition of each *extra* unit of labor. According to the law of diminishing marginal returns, this extra amount of output will eventually *decrease,* as more and more labor is utilized with the fixed amounts of capital and land. In other words, beyond some point, *an additional unit of labor will add less and less to total output.*

AN AGRICULTURAL EXAMPLE

To illustrate the workings of this law, consider Table 19.1, which shows the total output—or GNP—of a simple agricultural society under a set of alternative assumptions concerning the number of hours of labor used. For simplicity, we assume that this society produces only one product, corn, so that total output can be measured in bushels of corn. Also, we assume that the amount of land and capital that can be used is fixed in quantity. Column 1 in the table shows various alternative numbers of hours of labor that can be used with this fixed amount of land and capital. Column 2 shows the total output in each case.

Column 3 shows the additional output resulting from the addition of an

Table 19.1
THE LAW OF DIMINISHING MARGINAL RETURNS

(1) Hours of labor (millions)	(2) Bushels of corn (millions)	(3) Marginal product of labor (bushels per hour)	(4) Average product of labor (bushels per hour)
1	1.5		1.50
		2.0	
2	3.5		1.75
		2.5	
3	6.0		2.00
		3.0	
4	9.0		2.25
		2.0	
5	11.0		2.20
		2.0	
6	13.0		2.17
		1.0	
7	14.0		2.00
		0.0	
8	14.0		1.75

extra hour of labor; this is called the ***marginal product of labor.*** For example, if the quantity of labor is between 2 million hours and 3 million hours, the marginal product of labor is 2.5 bushels per hour of labor, because each extra hour of labor results in an extra 2.5 bushels of output.

In Table 19.1, the marginal product of labor increases as more and more labor is used, but only up to a point. Beyond 4 million hours of labor, the marginal product of labor goes down as more and more labor is used. Specifically, the marginal product of labor reaches a maximum of 3.0 bushels per hour when between 3 and 4 million hours of labor are used. Then it falls to 2.0 bushels per hour when between 4 and 5 million hours of labor are used, remains at 2.0 bushels per hour when between 5 and 6 million hours of labor are used, and falls once again to 1.0 bushel per hour when between 6 and 7 million hours of labor are used.

Thus, as predicted by the law of diminishing marginal returns, *the marginal product of labor eventually declines.* Moreover, as shown in column 4 of Table 19.1, the ***average product of labor,*** which is defined as total output per hour of labor, also falls beyond some point as more and more labor is used with a fixed amount of other resources. This too stems from the law of diminishing marginal returns.

REASONS FOR DIMINISHING RETURNS

It is easy to see why the law of diminishing marginal returns must be true. For example, imagine what would happen in the simple economy of Table 19.1 if more and more labor were applied to a fixed amount of land. Beyond a point, as more and more labor is used, the extra labor has to be devoted to less and less important tasks. If enough labor is used, it even becomes increasingly difficult to prevent the workers from getting in one another's way! For such reasons, one certainly would expect that, beyond some point, extra amounts of labor would result in smaller and smaller increments of output.

Finally, note two important things about this law. First, at least one resource must be fixed in quantity. The law of diminishing marginal returns does not apply to cases where there is a proportional increase in all resources. Second, technology is assumed to be fixed. The law of diminishing marginal returns does not apply to cases where technology changes.

Thomas Malthus and Population Growth

A nation's rate of economic growth depends on, among other things, how much the quantities of inputs of various kinds increase. To illuminate the nature of the growth process, we discuss the effect on the rate of economic growth of increasing each kind of input, holding the others constant. We begin by looking at the effects of changes in the quantity of labor. Economists have devoted a great deal of attention to the effects of population growth on the rate of economic growth. The classic work was done by Thomas Malthus (1776–1834), a British parson who devoted his life to academic research. The first professional economist, he taught at a college established by the East India Company to train its administrators—and was called "Pop" by his students behind his back. Whether "Pop" stood for population or not, Malthus's fame is based on his theories of population growth.

Malthus believed that the population tends to grow at a geometric rate. In his *Essay on the Principle of Population,* published in 1798, he pointed out the implications of such a constant rate of growth:

> If any person will take the trouble to make the calculation, he will see that if the necessities of life could be obtained without limit, and the number of people could be doubled every twenty-five years, the population which might have been produced from a single pair since the Christian era, would have been sufficient, not only to fill the earth quite full of people, so that four should stand in every square yard, but to fill all the planets of our solar system in the same way, and not only them but all the planets revolving around the stars which are visible to the naked eye, supposing each of them ... to have as many planets belong to it as our sun has.[2]

Thomas Malthus

In contrast to the human population, which tends to increase at a geometric rate,[3] the supply of land can increase slowly if at all. And land, particularly in Malthus's time, was the source of food. Consequently, it seemed to Malthus that the human population was in danger of outrunning its food supply: "Taking the whole earth," he wrote, "... and supposing the present population to be equal to a thousand millions, the human species would increase as the numbers 1, 2, 4, 8, 16, 32, 64, 128, 256, and subsistence as 1, 2, 3, 4, 5, 6, 7, 8, 9. In two centuries, the population would be to the means of subsistence as 256 to 9; in three centuries as 4096 to 13, and in two thousand years the difference would be incalculable."[4]

A BLEAK PROSPECT

Certainly, Malthus's view of humanity's prospects was bleak, as he himself acknowledged (in a masterpiece of British understatement) when he wrote that "the view has a melancholy hue." Gone is the optimism of Adam Smith. According to Malthus, the prospect for economic progress was very limited. Given the inexorable increase in human numbers, the standard of living will be kept at a minimum level required to keep body and soul together. If it exceeds this level, the population will increase, driving the standard of living back down. On the other hand, if the standard of living is less than this level, the population will decline because of starvation. Certainly, the long-term prospects were anything but bright. Thomas Carlyle, the famous historian and essayist, called economics "the dismal science." To a considerable extent, economics acquired this bad name through the efforts of Parson Malthus.

[2] T. Malthus, *Essay on the Principle of Population,* as quoted by R. Heilbroner, *The Worldly Philosophers,* 5th ed., New York: Simon and Schuster, 1980, p. 71. For those who would like to read more concerning the history of economic thought, Heilbroner's book is highly recommended.

[3] Of course, it does not matter to Malthus's argument whether the population doubles every 25 years or every 40 years. The important thing is that it increases at a geometric rate.

[4] T. Malthus, "The Principle of Population Growth," reprinted in E. Mansfield, *Principles of Macroeconomics: Readings, Issues, and Cases,* 4th ed. See also the full *Essay on the Principle of Population,* Philip Appleman, ed. New York: Norton, 1976, which contains critical commentary from Malthus's own time to the present.

Malthus's theory can be interpreted in terms of the law of diminishing marginal returns. Living in what was still largely an agricultural society, he emphasized the role of land and labor as resources, and assumed a relatively fixed level of technology. Since land is fixed, increases in labor—due to population growth—will eventually cause the marginal product of labor to get smaller and smaller because of the law of diminishing marginal returns. In other words, because of this law, the marginal product of labor will behave as shown in Figure 19.3, with the result that continued growth of the labor force will ultimately bring economic decline—that is, a reduction in output per worker. This happens because as the marginal product of labor falls with increases in the labor force, the

Example 19.1   "Birth Rights" and Population Control

Some observers have suggested that a nation's population might be controlled through the use of the price system. For example, the government might say that each couple should be allowed two "free births." After that, the couple would have to buy a certificate granting the right to have an additional child. The government would issue a fixed amount of certificates or "birth rights," each certificate enabling a woman to have a child. The available certificates would be sold to the highest bidders.

(a) What would the supply curve for these certificates look like? (b) Using a diagram, show how the equilibrium price of a certificate would be determined. (c) What factors would determine the location and shape of the demand curve for certificates? (d) What social, political, and religious objections can you see to such a scheme?

SOLUTION

(a) The supply curve would be a vertical line since the quantity of certificates supplied is fixed. (b) The diagram is as follows, and the equilibrium price is *OP*. (c) The demand curve

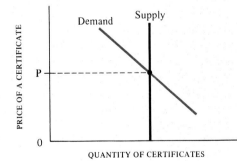

would be influenced by how much people want children, and how much they are willing to pay for the right to have them. (d) Obviously, many people would feel that such a program would be a major violation of their freedom, particularly since there are strong religious feelings and beliefs involved. People who wanted children and who were too poor to pay for a certificate would certainly object strenuously. There is no serious support for such a system in the United States.

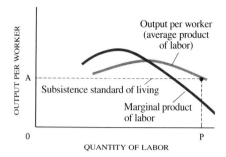

Figure 19.3

Diminishing Marginal Returns and the Effect of Population Growth According to Malthus, the labor force will tend to OP *because, if output per worker exceeds* OA, *population will increase, and if output per worker is less than* OA, *starvation will reduce the population.*

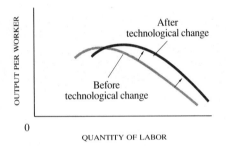

Figure 19.4

Shift over Time in the Marginal Product of Labor Technological change has shifted the marginal-product-of-labor curve to the right.

Basic Idea #37: Holding other factors constant, rapid population growth can depress living standards because of the law of diminishing marginal returns. Beyond some point, the average product of labor (and the standard of living) will fall. However, this assumes no technological change. If technology advances greatly, as it has done, rapid population growth need not result in lower standards of living.

average product of labor will eventually fall as well—and the average product of labor is another name for output per worker.

Of course, Malthus recognized that various devices could keep the population down—war, famine, birth-control measures, among others. In fact, he tried to describe and evaluate the importance of various checks on population growth. For example, suppose that population tends to grow to the point where output per worker is at a subsistence level—just sufficient to keep body and soul together. If this is the case, and if the subsistence level of output per worker is *OA*, then the labor force will tend to equal *OP* in Figure 19.3. Why? Because, as noted above, Malthus believed that if the standard of living rises appreciably above *OA*, population will increase, thus forcing it back toward *OA*. On the other hand, if the standard of living falls below *OA*, some of the population will starve, thus pushing it back toward *OA*.

EFFECTS OF POPULATION GROWTH

Was Malthus right? Among the less developed nations of the world, his analysis seems very relevant today. During the past 40 years, the population of the less developed nations has grown very rapidly, in part because of the decrease in death rates attributable to the transfer of medical advances from the industrialized countries to the less developed countries. Between 1940 and 1970, the total population of Asia, Africa, and Oceania almost doubled. There has been a tendency for growing populations to push hard against food supplies in some of the countries of Africa, Latin America, and Asia; and the Malthusian model can explain important elements of the situation.

However, Malthus's theory seems far less relevant or correct for the industrialized countries. In contrast to his model, population has not increased to the point where the standard of living has been pushed down to the subsistence level. On the contrary, the standard of living has increased dramatically in all of the industrialized nations. The most important mistake Malthus made was to underestimate the extent and importance of technological change. Instead of remaining fixed, the marginal-product-of-labor curve in Figure 19.3 moved gradually to the right, as new methods and new products increased the efficiency of agriculture. In other words, the situation was as shown in Figure 19.4. Thus, as population increased, the marginal product of labor did not go down. Instead, technological change prevented the productivity of extra agricultural workers from falling.

Among the industrialized nations, have countries with relatively high rates of growth of population had relatively low—or relatively high—rates of economic growth? In general, there seems to be little or no relationship between a nation's rate of population increase and its rate of economic growth. Figure 19.5 plots the rate of population increase against the rate of growth of output per man-year in 11 industrialized nations between 1913 and 1959. The results suggest that there is little or no relation between them; and the relationship that exists appears to be direct rather than inverse.

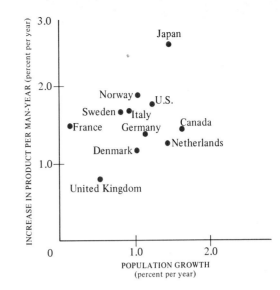

Figure 19.5

Relationship between Population Growth and Increases in National Product per Man-Year, 11 Industrialized Nations, 1913–59. *In industrialized nations, there is little or no relationship between a nation's rate of population growth and its rate of economic growth.*

Test Yourself

1. Suppose that a society produces only two goods, food and tractors, and that its production possibilities curve in 1985 and 1986 is given below:

Quantity of food (millions of tons)	Quantity of tractors (thousands of tractors)
0	9
1	8
2	7
3	5
4	3
5	0

If this society produces 4,000 tractors and 3 million tons of food in 1985 and 5,000 tractors and 3 million tons of food in 1986 (its population remaining constant), has any economic growth occurred between 1985 and 1986? If so, to what is it due?

2. Suppose that the society in Question 1 produces 6,000 tractors and 3 million tons of food in 1987 (its population remaining the same as in 1986), has any economic growth occurred between 1986 and 1987? If so, is it due entirely to a shift in the production possibilities curve? How can you tell?

3. Suppose that a society produces only one commodity, wheat, and that it has the following aggregate production function:

Hours of labor (millions)	Bushels of wheat (millions)
0	0
1	2
2	4
3	6
4	7
5	7

What is the marginal product of labor when between 1 and 2 million hours of labor are used? When between 2 and 3 million hours of labor are used? When between 4 and 5 million hours of labor are used? Do the results conform to the law of diminishing marginal returns? Why or why not?

4. Suppose that an advance in technology doubles the output that can be obtained from each amount of labor in Question 3. Under these new conditions, what is the marginal product of labor when between 1 and 2 million hours of labor are used? When between 4 and 5 million hours of labor are used? Do the results conform to the law of diminishing marginal returns? Why or why not?

5. In Question 3, suppose that the subsistence wage was 1,400 bushels of wheat. According to Malthus, what would have been the equilibrium labor force? What factors would push the labor force toward this level? What would be the effect of the technological advance in Question 4 on the equilibrium labor force?

421

David Ricardo and Capital Formation

A contemporary and good friend of Malthus's who also contributed to the theory of economic growth was David Ricardo (1772–1823). Of all the titans of economics, he is probably least known to the general public. Smith, Malthus, Marx, and Keynes are frequently encountered names. Ricardo is not, although he made many brilliant contributions to economic thought. An extremely successful stockbroker who retired at the age of 42 with a very large fortune, he devoted much of his time to highly theoretical analyses of the economic system and its workings. In contrast to Malthus, who was reviled for his pessimistic doctrines, Ricardo and his writings were widely admired in his own time. He was elected to the House of Commons and was highly respected there.

David Ricardo

RICARDO ON INCOME DISTRIBUTION

Ricardo was concerned in much of his work with the distribution of income. Unlike Adam Smith, who paid much less attention to the conflict among classes, Ricardo emphasized the struggle between the industrialists—a relatively new and rising class in his time—and the landowners—the old aristocracy that resisted the rise of the industrial class. This clash was reflected in the struggle in Britain around 1800 over the so-called Corn Laws (*corn* being a general term covering all types of grain). Because of the increase of population, the demand for grain increased in Britain, causing the price of grain to rise greatly. This meant higher profits for the landowners. But the industrialists complained bitterly about the increase in the price of food, because higher food prices meant that they had to pay higher wages. As the price of grain increased, merchants began to import cheap grain from abroad. But the landowners, who dominated Parliament, passed legislation—the Corn Laws—to keep cheap grain out of Britain. In effect the Corn Laws imposed a high tariff or duty on grain.

According to Ricardo's analysis, the landlords were bound to capture most of the benefits of economic progress, unless their control of the price of grain could be weakened. As national output increased and population expanded, poorer and poorer land had to be brought under cultivation to produce the extra food. As the cost of producing grain increased, its price would increase too—and so would the rents of the landlords. The workers and the industrialists, on the other hand, would benefit little, if at all. As the price of grain increased, the workers would have to get higher wages—but only high enough to keep them at a subsistence level (since Ricardo agreed entirely with his friend Malthus on the population issue). Thus the workers would be no better off; and neither would the industrialists, who would wind up with lower profits because of the increase in wage rates.

Ricardo felt that the Corn Laws should be repealed and that free trade in grain should be permitted. In a beautiful piece of theoretical analysis that is still reasonably fresh and convincing 170 years after its publication, he laid out the basic principles of international trade and pointed out the benefits to all countries that can be derived by specialization and free trade. For example, suppose that England is relatively more efficient at producing textiles, and France is relatively more efficient at producing wine. Then, on the basis of Ricardo's analysis, it can be shown that each country is likely to be better off by specializing in the product it is more efficient at producing—textiles in England, wine in France—and trading this product for the one the other country specializes in producing. In Chapter 32, we shall discuss this argument in considerable detail; it is a very important part of economics.

RICARDO'S VIEW OF CAPITAL FORMATION

Let's turn to the effect on economic growth of increases in physical capital, holding other inputs and technology fixed. Ricardo constructed some interesting theories concerning the effects of capital formation—i.e., investment in plant and equipment—on economic growth. Other things held constant, a nation's output depends on the amount of plant and equipment that it has and operates. Moreover, one can draw a curve showing the marginal product of capital—the extra output that would result from an extra dollar's worth of capital—under various assumptions about the total amount of capital in existence. This curve will slope downward to the right, as shown in Figure 19.6, because of the law of diminishing marginal returns. As more and more capital is accumulated, its marginal product eventually must decrease. For example, if $100 billion is the total investment in plant and equipment (or total capital), the extra output to be derived from an extra dollar of investment is worth $A; whereas if the total investment is increased to $150 billion, the economy must resort to less productive investments, and the extra output to be derived from an extra dollar of investment is only worth $B.

The curve in Figure 19.6 leads to the conclusion that investment in plant and equipment, although it will increase the growth rate up to some point, will eventually be unable to increase it further. As more and more is invested in new plant and equipment, less and less productive projects must be undertaken. Finally, when all the productive projects have been carried out, further investment in plant and equipment will be useless. At this point—$200 billion of total capital in Figure 19.6—further investment in plant and equipment will not increase output at all.

This kind of analysis led Ricardo to the pessimistic conclusion that the economy would experience decreases in the profitability of investment in

Figure 19.6

Marginal Product of Capital *This curve shows the marginal product of capital, under various assumptions concerning the total amount of capital. For example, if there is $100 billion of capital, the marginal product of capital is $A, whereas if there is $150 billion of capital, the marginal product of capital is $B.*

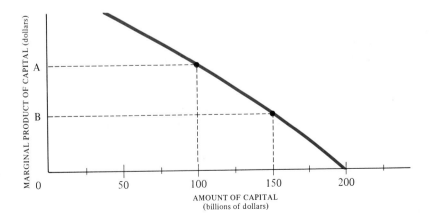

MARGINAL PRODUCT OF CAPITAL (dollars)

A

B

0   50   100   150   200

AMOUNT OF CAPITAL
(billions of dollars)

plant and equipment, and eventual termination of economic growth. Also, he expected increases in the ratio of capital to output, because he expected increases in the total amount of capital to be accompanied by decreases in the marginal product of capital.

To illustrate this, suppose that an economy's output equals $1 trillion and its total capital is $3 trillion. Suppose too that $100 billion of extra capital will result in $30 billion in extra output, another $100 billion of extra capital will result in $20 billion in extra output, and still another $100 billion in extra capital will result in $10 billion in extra output. Then the amount of capital per dollar of output will be $(3,000 + 100)/(1,000 + 30)$ if $100 billion is invested, $(3,000 + 200)/(1,000 + 50)$ if $200 billion is invested, and $(3,000 + 300)/(1,000 + 60)$ if $300 billion is invested. Since the marginal product of capital is decreasing, the amount of capital per dollar of output is increasing—from 3 to 3.01 to 3.05 to 3.11.

WAS RICARDO RIGHT?

Have we seen increases in the amount of capital per dollar of output, decreases in the profitability of investment in plant and equipment, and eventual termination of economic growth? No. Ricardo, like Malthus, was led astray by underestimating the extent and impact of future changes in technology. Suppose that, because of the development of major new products and processes, lots of new opportunities for profitable investment arise. Obviously, the effect on the curve in Figure 19.6 is to shift it to the right, because there are more investment opportunities than ever before above a certain level of productivity. But if this curve shifts to the right, as shown in Figure 19.7, we may be able to avoid Ricardo's pessimistic conclusions.

To see how this can occur, note that, if X in Figure 19.7 is the relevant curve in a particular year and if $100 billion is the total amount of capital, an extra dollar of investment in plant and equipment would have a marginal product of $C. A decade later, if Y is the relevant curve and if the total amount of capital has grown to $150 billion, the marginal product of an extra dollar of investment in plant and equipment is still $C. Thus there is no reduction in the productivity of investment opportunities despite the 50 percent increase in the total amount of capital. Because of technological change and other factors, productive and profitable new investment opportunities are opened up as fast as old ones are invested in.

The history of the United States is quite consistent with this sort of shift in investment opportunities over time. Even though we have poured an enormous amount of money into new plant and equipment, we have not exhausted or reduced the productivity or profitability of investment opportunities. The rate of return on investment in new plant and equipment has not fallen. Instead, it has fluctuated around a fairly constant level during the past 70 years. Moreover, the amount of capital per dollar of output has remained surprisingly constant. It has not increased.

Capital Formation and Economic Growth

To see more clearly the role of investment in the process of economic growth, let's extend the model we discussed in Chapters 10 and 11. Sup-

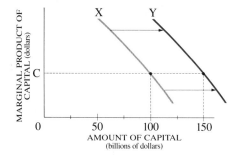

Figure 19.7
Effects of Technological Change on the Marginal Product of Capital *Technological change has shifted the marginal-product-of-capital curve to the right. (Actually, Ricardo's variable input was a combined dose of capital and labor.)*

pose we ignore the government and consider only the private sector of the economy. Suppose that the full-employment, noninflationary NNP this year is $1,000 billion, and that the consumption function is such that consumption expenditure is $900 billion if NNP is $1,000 billion. If intended investment this year is $100 billion, with the result that NNP is in fact $1,000 billion, *next year's full-employment NNP will increase because this year's investment will increase the nation's productive capacity.* In other words, this year's investment increases next year's full-employment NNP. The amount of the increase in full-employment NNP depends on the **capital-output ratio,** which is the number of dollars of investment (or extra capital goods) required to produce an extra dollar of output. For example, if the capital-output ratio is 2, $2 of investment is required to increase full-employment NNP by $1.

EFFECT OF INVESTMENT ON FULL-EMPLOYMENT NNP

Let's look more closely at the effect of investment on full-employment NNP. If the capital-output ratio is 2, full-employment NNP will increase by $50 billion as a consequence of the $100 billion of investment. Thus full-employment NNP next year is $1,050 billion. On the other hand, suppose that this year's investment is $200 billion rather than $100 billion, and that the consumption function is such that consumption expenditure is $800 billion rather than $900 billion if NNP is $1,000 billion. What will full-employment NNP be next year? If the capital-output ratio is 2, it will be $1,100 billion. Why? Because the $200 billion in investment will increase full-employment NNP by $100 billion—from $1,000 billion to $1,100 billion.

Thus the full-employment NNP will be larger if investment is $200 billion than if it is $100 billion. Similarly, the full-employment NNP will be larger if investment is $300 billion than if it is $200 billion. If the capital-output ratio is 2, the full-employment NNP will be $1,150 billion next year, if investment is $300 billion. Why? Because the $300 billion in investment will increase full-employment NNP by $150 billion—from $1,000 to $1,150 billion.

In general, the greater the percent of NNP that the society devotes to investment this year, the greater will be the increase in its full-employment NNP. Thus, *so long as the economy sustains noninflationary full employment and the capital-output ratio remains constant, the rate of growth of national output will be directly related to the percent of NNP devoted to investment.*[5]

SOME EVIDENCE CONCERNING THE EFFECTS OF INVESTMENT

Certainly, this result seems sensible enough. If a country wants to increase its growth rate, it should produce more blast furnaces, machine tools, and

---

[5] It can be shown that the rate of growth of NNP equals s/b, where s is the proportion of NNP that is saved (and invested), and b is the capital-output ratio, assuming that both s and b are constant and that full employment is maintained. For example, if b is 2 and $s = .10$, NNP will grow at 5 percent per year, since $.10/2 = .05$. This result is part of the so-called Harrod-Domar growth model developed by Sir Roy Harrod of Oxford and Evsey Domar of M.I.T. Although useful, this result must be used with caution since it is based on highly simplified assumptions.

Nation	Rate of growth of output (percent)	Percent of output invested
	Annual average	
France	2.8	18.8
Germany	3.3	18.7
Canada	2.4	19.3
Japan	5.0	26.7
United Kingdom	1.0	17.6
United States	2.6	14.5

Source: Economic Report of the President,
1982 and Table 20.10.

plows, and less cosmetics, household furniture, and sports cars. But all this is theory. What do the facts suggest? Table 19.2 shows the rate of investment and the growth rate in six major industrialized nations of the non-Communist world in the 1970s. The investment rate was highest in Japan; so was the growth rate. The investment rates were lowest in the United States and the United Kingdom, and their growth rates were among the lowest. Of course, this does not prove that there is any simple cause-and-effect relationship between the investment rate and the growth rate, but it certainly is compatible with the view that investment influences growth.

As revealed in the historical record of the United States, between 1929 and 1947 the amount of U.S. plant and equipment increased at about the same rate as the labor force. On the other hand, between 1947 and 1965, the amount of U.S. plant and equipment increased much more rapidly than the labor force. These facts would lead one to expect that the rate of economic growth would be more rapid in the latter period; and, in keeping with the theory, this turns out to be true. Again, one must be cautious about interpreting such comparisons. Lots of other things besides the investment rate were different in 1947–65 than in 1929–47, and these other things, not the investment rate, may have been responsible for the difference in growth rates. However, it seems likely that the difference in investment rates was at least partially responsible.

The Role of Human Capital

A nation's rate of economic growth is influenced by the rate at which it invests in human capital as well as physical capital. It may seem odd to speak of *human* capital, but every society builds up a certain amount of human capital through investments in formal education, on-the-job-training, and health programs. You often hear people talk about investing in their children's future by putting them through college. For the economy as a whole, the expenditure on education and public health can also be viewed—at least partly—as an investment, because consumption is sacrificed in the present in order to make possible a higher level of per capita output in the future.

The United States invests in human capital on a massive scale. In 1960 expenditures for schools at all levels of education were about $25 billion, or about 5 percent of our gross national product. Moreover, our total investment in the education of the population—the "stock" of educational capital—has grown much more rapidly than has the stock of plant and equipment. Whereas the stock of physical capital was about 4 times as big in 1956 as in 1900, the stock of educational capital was about 8 times as big. These enormous and rapidly growing investments in human capital have unquestionably increased the productivity, versatility, and adaptability of our labor force. They have certainly made a major contribution to economic growth.

Income tends to rise with a person's education. Using this relationship to measure the influence of education on a person's productivity, some economists, notably the University of Chicago's Theodore Schultz and Gary Becker, have tried to estimate the profitability, both to society and to the person, of an investment in various levels of education. Becker has tried to estimate the rate of return from a person's investment in a college education. According to his estimates, the typical urban white male in 1950 received about a 10 percent return (after taxes) on his investment in tuition, room, books, and other college expenses (including the earnings he gave up by being in college rather than at work). This was a relatively high return—much higher, for example, than if the student (or his family) simply put the equivalent amount of money in a savings bank or in government bonds.

In more recent years, however, the return from the investment in a college education seems to have fallen considerably. For example, according to Richard Freeman of Harvard University and Herbert Hollomon of M.I.T., it declined from about 11 or 12 percent in 1969 to about 7 or 8 percent in 1974.

The Role of Technological Change

A nation's rate of economic growth depends on the rate of *technological change,* as well as on the extent to which quantities of inputs of various kinds increase. Indeed, the rate of technological change is perhaps the most important single determinant of a nation's rate of economic growth. Recall from Chapter 1 that technology is knowledge concerning the industrial and agricultural arts. Thus technological change often takes the form of new methods of producing existing products; new designs that make it possible to produce goods with important new characteristics; and new techniques of organization, marketing, and management. Two examples of technological change are new ways of producing power (for example, atomic energy) and new fibers (for example, nylon or Dacron).

We have already seen that technological change can shift the curves in both Figures 19.4 and 19.7, thus warding off the law of diminishing marginal returns. But note that new knowledge by itself has little impact. *Unless knowledge is applied, it has little effect on the rate of economic growth.* A change in technology, when applied for the first time, is called an *innovation,* and the firm that first applies it is called an *innovator.* Innovation is a key stage in the process leading to the full evaluation and utilization of a new process or product. The innovator must be willing to take the risks involved in introducing a new and untried process, good, or service; and in many cases, these risks are high. Once a change in technology has been applied for the first time, the *diffusion process*—the process by which the use of the innovation spreads from firm to firm and from use to use—begins. How rapidly an innovation spreads depends heavily on its economic advantages over older methods or products. The more profitable the use of the innovation is, the more rapidly it will spread.

Joseph Schumpeter, Harvard's distinguished economist and social theorist, stressed the important role played by innovators in the process of economic growth. In Schumpeter's view, innovators are the mainspring of economic progress, the people with the foresight to see how new things can be brought into being and the courage and resourcefulness to surmount the obstacles to change. For their trouble, innovators receive profit; but this profit eventually is whittled down by competitors who imitate the innovators. The innovators push the curves in Figures 19.4 and 19.7 to the right, and once their innovations are assimilated by the economy, other innovators may shove these curves somewhat farther to the right. For example, one innovator introduces vacuum tubes, a later innovator introduces semiconductors; one innovator introduces the steam locomotive, a later innovator introduces the diesel locomotive. This process goes on and on—and is a main source of economic growth.

THE ELECTRONIC COMPUTER: A CASE STUDY

To get a better feel for the nature of technological change and the process of innovation, let's consider one of the most important technological advances of the twentieth century—the electronic computer. Many of the basic ideas underlying the computer go back to Charles Babbage, a brilliant nineteenth-century British inventor; but not until 1946 was the first electronic computer, the ENIAC, designed and constructed. John Mauchly and J. Presper Eckert, both professors at the Moore School of Electrical Engineering at the University of Pennsylvania, were responsible for the ENIAC's design and construction. The work was supported by the U.S. Army. John von Neumann, a famous mathematician at the Institute for Advanced Study at Princeton, added the important concepts of stored programming and conditional transfer.

After the war, Mauchly and Eckert established a small firm to produce electronic computers. Their firm was acquired by Remington Rand, which in 1951 marketed the Univac I, a machine used by the Census Bureau. The International Business Machines Corporation (IBM), the leading company in office machinery and data processing, which before this had been cautious about the potential market for computers (recall Chapter 6), was spurred into action by Remington Rand's success. Once it entered the field, IBM's financial resources, strong marketing organization, and engineering strength enabled it to capture a very large share of the computer market, here and abroad. In the United States, IBM's share of the market grew to about 70 percent during the 1960s.

The electronic computer has been an extremely important stimulus to economic growth. By 1966, the total number of computers installed in the Western world exceeded 50,000 at a total value of about $20 billion. These computers have had important effects on production techniques in many industries. For example, in the chemical, petroleum, and steel industries, digital computers were an important step in the evolution of control techniques. Computers helped to determine and enforce the best conditions for process operation, as well as acting as data loggers. They could also be programmed to help carry out the complex sequence of operations required to start up or shut down a plant. They have increased production, decreased waste, improved quality control, and reduced the chance of damage to equipment. In another quite different industry, banking, computers have had an important effect too. They have made it possible to eliminate conventional machines and processes for sorting checks, balancing accounts, and computing service charges. With high-speed sorters, it is possible now to process more than 1,500 checks per minute.

Obviously, the electronic computer has enabled us to produce more output from a given amount of resources. In other words, it has enabled us to push the production possibilities curve outward, thus increasing our rate of economic growth. But it must be recognized that the process by which the computer has had this effect has by no means been simple or straightforward. Many people in many countries were involved in the development of the basic ideas. Many organizations, public and private, funded the experimental work. Firms of various types were the innovators with respect to particular aspects of the modern computer. And countless individuals and organizations had to be willing to accept, work with, and invest in computers.

Determinants of Technological Change

What determines the rate of technological change and the rate at which changes in technology are applied and spread? Clearly, *the nature and extent of a nation's scientific capability, and the size and quality of its educational system are of fundamental importance.* The first thing that must be said about the influence of a nation's scientific capability on its rate of technological change is that science and technology are two quite different things that have drawn together only recently. Until the twentieth century, it was not true that technology was built on science. Even today, many technological advances rely on little in the way of science. However, in more and more areas of the economy (such as aircraft, electronics, and chemicals), the rapid application of new technology has come to depend on a strong scientific base. Merely to imitate or adapt what others have developed, a firm in these areas needs access to high-caliber scientists.

A nation's educational system also has a fundamental influence on the rate of technological change. First, and perhaps most obviously, it determines how many scientists and engineers are graduated, and how competent they are. Clearly, the rate of technological change depends on the quantity and quality of scientific and engineering talent available in the society. Second, the educational system influences the inventiveness and adaptability of the nation's work force. Despite the closer links between technology and science, workers and independent inventors remain important sources of inventions in many areas. Third, the educational system also influences the rate of technological change and innovation via the training of managers.

Industrial managers are a key agent in the innovative process. We must emphasize that the proper management of innovation is much more than establishing and maintaining a research and development laboratory that produces a great deal of good technical output. In many industries, most important innovations are not based in any significant degree on the firms' research and development (R and D). And even when the basic idea does come from a firm's own R and D, the coupling of R and D with marketing and production is crucial. Many good ideas are not applied properly because the potential users do not really understand them, and many R and D projects are technically successful but commercially irrelevant because they were not designed with sufficient comprehension of market realities. Typically, successful technological innovations seem to be stimulated by

Basic Idea #38: The rate of technological change is probably the most important single determinant of a nation's rate of economic growth. A country's rate of technological change depends on the nature and extent of its scientific capabilities and its educational system, as well as the organization of its industries and markets. For most countries, considerable technological change can be achieved by borrowing and transferring technology from the world leaders.

429

perceived production and marketing needs, not solely by technological opportunities. In other words, most of the time it takes a market-related impetus to prompt work on a successful innovation.

In addition, *the rate of technological change depends on the organization of industry and the nature of markets.* Although a certain amount of industrial concentration may promote more rapid technological change, increases in concentration beyond a moderate level probably reduce rather than increase the rate of technological change. The rate of technological change also depends on the scale and sophistication of available markets. The scale of the market determines how many units of a new product or process are likely to be sold, which in turn influences the cost per unit of developing and introducing an innovation. Our huge domestic market has often been cited as a reason for America's technological lead over many other countries. Finally, it is extremely important to note that a country that is not a technological leader can still achieve considerable technological change by borrowing and transferring technology from the leaders.

TECHNOLOGICAL CHANGE AND LABOR PRODUCTIVITY

It is difficult to measure the rate of technological change. Perhaps the most frequently used measure is the rate of growth of labor productivity: the rate of growth of output per hour of labor. Unfortunately, this measure is influenced by lots of other factors besides the rate of technological change. Nonetheless, despite its inadequacies, it is worthwhile to look briefly at how rapidly productivity has increased in the United States over the long run. Since about 1890, the nation's real output per hour of labor increased by about 2 percent per year—and these productivity gains were widely diffused, real hourly earnings growing about as rapidly, on the average, as output per hour of labor.

As indicated in Table 19.3, the rate of growth of labor productivity slowed considerably in the 1970s and early 1980s. According to some observers, this productivity slowdown has been due in part to a decline in the rate of innovation in the United States. In their opinion, the rate of introduction of new products and processes has fallen. It is true that the patent rate has been falling since about 1969, and that direct evidence of a fall in

Table 19.3

PERCENT CHANGE IN OUTPUT PER MAN-HOUR, NONFARM BUSINESS SECTOR, U.S., 1950–84

Year	Percent change[a]	Year	Percent change[a]
1984	3.1	1966	2.5
1982	0.2	1964	3.9
1980	−0.7	1962	3.6
1978	0.6	1960	0.8
1976	3.2	1958	2.4
1974	−2.5	1956	0.3
1972	3.7	1954	1.4
1970	0.3	1952	2.3
1968	3.3	1950	6.0

[a] Percent change from the previous year.
Source: Economic Report of the President, 1985.

the rate of innovation has existed in some industries, like pharmaceuticals, where one can measure the number of major innovations that are carried out per unit of time. But in other industries, such as microelectronics, the rate of innovation seems hale and hearty.

Entrepreneurship and the Social Environment

Still another set of basic factors influencing a nation's level of potential output and its rate of economic growth is the economic, social, political, and religious climate of the nation. It is difficult, if not impossible, to measure the effect of these factors, but there can be no doubt of their importance. Some societies despise material welfare and emphasize the glories of the next world. Some societies are subject to such violent political upheavals that it is risky, if not foolish, to invest in the future. Some societies are governed so corruptly that economic growth is frustrated. And some societies look down on people engaged in industry, trade, or commerce. Obviously, such societies are less likely to experience rapid economic growth than others with a more favorable climate and conditions.

The relatively rapid economic growth of the United States was undoubtedly stimulated in part by the attitude of its people toward material gain. It is commonplace to note that the United States is a materialistic society, a society that esteems business success, that bestows prestige on the rich, that accepts the Protestant ethic (which, crudely stated, is that work is good), and that encourages individual initiative. The United States has been criticized over and over again for some of these traits—often by nations frantically trying to imitate its economic success. Somewhat less obvious is the fact that, because the United States is a young country whose people came from a variety of origins, it did not inherit many feudal components in the structure of society. This too was important.

Robotics in U.S. industry

The United States has also been characterized by great economic and political freedom, by institutions that have been flexible enough to adjust to change, and by a government that has encouraged competition in the market place. This has meant fewer barriers to new ideas. Also, the United States has for a long time enjoyed internal peace, order, and general respect for property rights. There have been no violent revolutions since the Civil War, and for many years we were protected from strife in other lands by two oceans—which then seemed much broader than they do now. All these factors undoubtedly contributed to rapid economic growth.

The American economy also seems to have been able to nurture a great many entrepreneurs and a vast horde of competent business executives. During the nineteenth century, American entrepreneurs were responsible for such basic innovations as the system of interchangeable parts, pioneered by Eli Whitney and others. In many areas, the United States gained a technological lead over other nations, which was maintained for many years. Much of this lead came from superior management as well as superior technological resources. For example, the Organization for Economic Cooperation and Development concluded in 1968 that, "In the techniques of *management,* including the management of research, and of combined technological and market forecasting, the United States appears

431

Workers have long recognized and feared technological unemployment. As long ago as the mid-1700s, a mob of worried English spinners entered James Hargreave's mill and smashed the first workable multistage frames. Although the dread of technology-induced mass unemployment is not new, it was revived in the 1980s, the new scare word being *robotics*. According to some observers, robots would result in widespread unemployment.

Do increases in the rate of technological change necessarily result in increases in aggregate unemployment? To make a long story short, the answer is *no*. To see how large-scale technological unemployment can occur—and how it can be avoided—consider the figure below, which shows the $C + I + G$ line at a particular point in time. (If you are a bit hazy about the meaning and significance of this line, review Chapter 12.) Since this line intersects the 45-degree line at point A, the equilibrium level of net national product is $400 billion. If the high-employment level of net national product is also $400 billion, the economy enjoys a high level of employment. Now suppose that there is a significant amount of technological change. What will be the result? To begin with, the advance in technology will almost certainly result in an increase in productivity. In other words, it will enable the labor force to produce more than it formerly could. Thus the high-employment level of net national product will increase —say to $450 billion. Given this increase, there will be substantial unemployment if the $C + I + G$ line stays put. If output remains the same and output per man-hour increases, fewer workers will be needed and there will be unemployment.

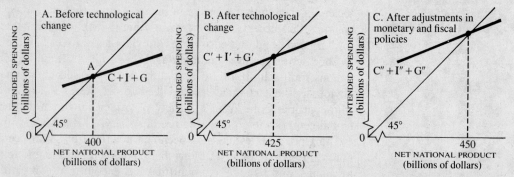

But there is no reason why the $C + I + G$ *line should remain constant.* The advance in technology itself may increase the profitability of investment, thus raising I. Moreover, the advance in technology may result in new consumer products, which prompt consumers to spend more of a given level of income, thus raising C. Suppose that, by virtue of these changes in C and I, the $C + I + G$ line shifts to $C' + I' + G'$ (shown in panel B). The new equilibrium level of net national product is $425 billion, as shown in panel B. Unfortunately, in this particular case (but not necessarily in other cases), the new equilibrium level of NNP is less than the new high-employment level of NNP. Thus, without some change in public policy, there would be some technological unemployment. But as we know, the Federal Reserve can increase I by increasing the money supply and reducing interest rates, and the government can push C upward by reducing tax rates and increase G by increasing its own expenditures. Thus there is no reason why the government cannot raise the $C + I + G$ line to the point where it intersects the 45-degree line at $450 billion. For example, the government might nudge the $C + I + G$ line up to $C'' + I'' + G''$ in panel C. And if it does this, the equilibrium level of net national product equals the high-employment level of net national product. Thus it should be possible to avoid large amounts of technological unemployment, although transitional problems obviously will remain.

to have a significant lead."[6] In the past decade, according to many observers, our technological lead has been reduced considerably. This has caused concern among American government officials and business executives.

The Gap Between Actual and Potential Output

Up to this point, our discussion of economic growth has centered on the factors that determine how rapidly a nation's potential output grows—factors like technological change, increased education, investment in plant and equipment, and increases in the labor force. Now we must examine the factors that determine how close a nation's actual output comes to its potential output. As we already know, a nation's potential output is its output under full employment. Thus, as we also know, whether or not the economy operates close to full employment is determined by the level of the $C + I + G$ line. If the $C + I + G$ line is too low, the economy will operate with considerable unemployment, and actual output will be substantially below potential output. Or, in terms of the equation of exchange, if $M \times V$ is too small, the economy will operate with considerable unemployment, and actual output will be substantially below potential output.

From previous chapters, we also know how the government can use fiscal and monetary policies to push actual output close to potential output. Cuts in tax rates, increases in government spending, incentives for private investment in plant and equipment, increases in the money supply, reductions in interest rates; all these devices can be used to push actual output closer to potential output. Such devices promote economic growth, in the sense that actual per capita output is increased. However, only so much growth can be achieved by squeezing the slack out of the economy. For example, if there is a 7 percent unemployment rate, output per capita can be increased by perhaps 6 percent simply by reducing the unemployment rate to 5 percent. *But this is a one-shot improvement.* To get any further growth, the nation must increase its potential output.

This doesn't mean that it isn't important to maintain the economy at close to full employment. On the contrary, as we stressed in Chapter 8, one of the major objectives of public policy must be full employment, and a reduction of unemployment will have a significant effect on the rate of economic growth in the short run. (Much of the economic growth in the United States in the early 1960s was caused by the transition to full employment.) But the point we are making is that, once the economy gets to full employment, no further growth can occur by this route. If a nation wants further growth, it must influence the factors responsible for the rate of growth of potential output.

---

[6] Organization for Economic Cooperation and Development, *Technology Gap: General Report,* Paris, 1968, p. 25.

433

Test Yourself

1. Suppose that a society's full-employment NNP increases between 1985 and 1986 by $100 billion. During the same period, its corporations floated $20 billion in stocks and bonds, and it invested $200 billion. What is the capital-output ratio in this society? Will the capital-output ratio in this society always be the same? Why or why not?

2. Suppose that a society's capital-output ratio is 3 and that it invests 10 percent of its NNP. If full employment is maintained, by what percentage will its NNP grow?

3. "Ricardo's pessimistic view of the prospects for economic growth stemmed from his assumptions concerning the capital-output ratio. If he had recognized that it was not fixed, he would have been closer to correct." Comment and evaluate.

4. Some studies indicate that what matters most to people is their income relative to others around them rather than the absolute level of their income. Would this fact tend to reduce the importance of growth as a means of helping the poor? Explain.

Summary

1. Economic growth is measured by the increase of per capita real gross national product, an index that does not measure accurately the growth of economic welfare, but is often used as a first approximation.

2. A nation's rate of economic growth depends on the increase in the quantity and quality of its resources (including physical and human capital) and the rate of technological change. In addition, the rate of economic growth depends on the extent to which a society maintains full employment and on the efficiency with which its resources are allocated and managed.

3. One factor that may influence a nation's rate of economic growth is the rate at which its population grows. In Malthus's view, population growth, unless checked in some way, ultimately meant economic decline, since output could not grow in proportion to the growth in population. The law of diminishing marginal returns insured that beyond some point, increases in labor, holding the quantity of land constant, would result in smaller and smaller increments of output. However, Malthus underestimated the extent and importance of technological change, which offset the law of diminishing marginal returns.

4. Another factor that determines whether per capita output grows rapidly or slowly is the rate of expenditure on new plant and equipment. Without technological change, more and more of this sort of investment would result in increases in the amount of capital per dollar of output and decreases in the profitability of investment in plant and equipment, as Ricardo pointed out. But because of technological change, none of these things has occurred. According to the available evidence, a nation's rate of economic growth seems directly related to its rate of investment in plant and equipment.

5. To a considerable extent, economic growth here and abroad has resulted from technological change. A change in technology, when applied for the first time, is called an innovation, and the firm that first applies it is called an innovator. Innovation is a key stage in the process leading to the full evaluation and utilization of a new process or product. Unless knowledge is used, it has little effect on the rate of economic growth.

6. The rate of technological change and the rate at which new technology is applied depend on a number of factors, including the nature and extent of a nation's scientific capability, the size and quality of its educational system, the quality of its managers, the attitude and structure of its firms, the organization of its industries, and the nature of its markets.

7. Another factor with an important effect on a nation's rate of economic growth is the rate at which it invests in human capital. The United States invests in human capital on a massive scale, and these enormous and rapidly growing investments have unquestionably increased the productivity, versatility, and adaptability of our labor force.

8. Still another set of basic factors influencing the rate of economic growth is the economic, social, and political climate of the nation. Some societies despise material welfare, are subject to violent political upheavals, and are governed by corrupt groups. Such societies are unlikely to have a high rate of economic growth.

9. Finally, the rate of economic growth is also affected by the extent and behavior of the gap between actual and potential GNP. However, once a nation gets to full employment, it cannot grow further by reducing this gap.

Concepts for Review

Economic growth	Marginal product of labor	Capital-output ratio
Aggregate production function	Average product of labor	Technological change
Law of diminishing marginal returns	Population growth	Innovation
	Capital formation	Innovator
		Diffusion process

435

CHAPTER 20

Environmental and Energy Problems*

Environmental pollution and energy have been two important problems in the United States, and both are related to economic growth. According to many scientists and social observers, one of the costs of economic growth is environmental pollution. For a long time, people in the United States paid relatively little attention to the environment and what they were doing to it, but this attitude changed markedly in the last twenty years. The public became genuinely concerned about environmental problems. However, in the effort to clean up the environment, choices are not always clear, nor solutions easy. In particular, the energy crisis of the 1970s brought home the fact that a cleaner environment is not costless. Many measures that would reduce pollution would increase the demand for energy.

America's energy problems have been related only partly to environmental matters. To a considerable extent, they stem from the fact that oil reserves in this country are being depleted, and that foreign sources of oil have banded together in an international cartel which raised the price of crude oil enormously in 1974 and 1979. In this chapter, we consider the economic aspects of both environmental decay and the nation's energy needs. Our purpose is to indicate the extent of these problems, the factors that are responsible for them, and the sorts of public policies that might be adopted to help deal with them.

* This chapter is written so that it can be taken up after the material on microeconomics (Chapters 21–31). Some instructors prefer to place it there.

Our Environmental Problems

WATER POLLUTION

To see what we mean by environmental pollution, let's begin with one of the most important parts of man's environment, our water supplies. As a result of human activities, large amounts of pollutants are discharged into streams, lakes, and the sea. Chemical wastes are released by industrial plants and mines, as well as by farms and homes when fertilizers, pesticides, and detergents run off into waterways. Oil is discharged into the waters by tankers, sewage systems, oil wells, and other sources. Organic compounds enter waterways from industrial plants and farms, as well as from municipal sewage plants; and animal wastes, as well as human wastes, contribute substantially to pollution.

Obviously, we cannot continue to increase the rate at which we dump wastes into our streams, rivers, and oceans. A river, like everything else, can bear only so much. The people of Cleveland know this well. In 1969, the Cuyahoga River, which flows through Cleveland, literally caught fire, so great was its concentration of industrial and other wastes. Of course, the Cuyahoga is an extreme case, but many of our rivers, including the Hudson and the Ohio, are badly polluted. Water pollution is a nuisance and perhaps a threat.[1]

AIR POLLUTION

If clean water is vital to man's survival, so too is clean air. Yet the battle being waged against air pollution in most of our major cities has not been won. Particles of various kinds are spewed into the air by factories that utilize combustion processes, grind materials, or produce dust. Motor vehicles release lead compounds from gasoline and rubber particles worn from tires, helping to create that unheavenly condition known as smog. Citizens of Los Angeles are particularly familiar with smog, but few major cities have escaped at least periodic air pollution. No precise measures have been developed to gauge the effects of air pollution on public health and enjoyment, but some rough estimates suggest that perhaps 25 percent of all deaths from respiratory disease could be avoided by a 50 percent reduction in air pollution.

One of the most important contributors to air pollution is the combustion of fossil fuels, particularly coal and oil products: by-products of combustion comprise about 85 percent of the total amount of air pollutants in the United States. Most of these pollutants result from impure fuels or inefficient burning. Among the more serious pollutants are sulphur dioxide, carbon monoxide, and various oxides of nitrogen.

At present, the automobile is the principal source of air pollution in the United States. According to some estimates, human activities pump into the air over 200 million tons of waste each year, and automobiles can be credited with the dubious honor of contributing about 40 percent of this

---

[1] See *Fortune,* February 1970; D. Rohrer, D. Montgomery, M. Montgomery, D. Eaton, and M. Arnold, *The Environment Crisis,* Skokie, Ill.: National Textbook, 1970; and Environmental Protection Agency, *The Economics of Clean Water,* 1973, Washington, D.C.: Government Printing Office, 1973.

figure. Spurred on by the public interest in pollution control, some technologists have been hard at work on substitutes for the internal combustion engine. Attempts have been—and are being—made to devise economical and convenient electric and steam-driven automobiles. To date, however, these efforts have not succeeded. Thus it seems likely that in the near future at least, we shall have to rely heavily on modifications of the internal combustion engine and its fuel to reduce air pollution.[2] (More use of nonpolluting transport like bicycles and feet would help too.)

The Important Role of External Diseconomies

The reason why our economic system has tolerated pollution of the environment lies largely in the concept of external diseconomies, which we mentioned in Chapter 4. An *external diseconomy* occurs when one person's (or firm's) use of a resource damages other people who cannot obtain proper compensation. When this occurs, a market economy is unlikely to function properly. The price system is based on the supposition that the full cost of using each resource is borne by the person or firm that uses it. If this is not the case and if the user bears only part of the full costs, then the resource is not likely to be directed by the price system into the socially optimal use.

To understand why, we might begin by reviewing briefly how resources are allocated in a market economy. As we saw in Chapter 3, resources are used in their socially most valuable way because they are allocated to the people and firms who find it worthwhile to bid most for them, assuming that prices reflect true social costs. Under these circumstances, a firm that maximizes its profits will produce the socially desirable output and use the socially desirable amounts of labor, capital, and other resources. Under these circumstances, there is no problem.

PRIVATE COST ≈ SOCIAL COST

Suppose, however, that because of the presence of external diseconomies people and firms do not pay the true social costs for resources. For example, suppose that some firms or people can use water and air for nothing, but that other firms or people incur costs as a consequence of this prior use. In this case, the *private costs* of using air and water differ from the *social costs: the price paid by the user of water and air is less than the true cost to society.* In a case like this, users of water and air are guided in their decisions by the private cost of water and air—by the prices they pay. Since they pay less than the true social costs, water and air are artificially cheap to them, so that they will use too much of these resources, from society's point of view.

Note that the divergence between private and social cost occurs if, and only if, the use of water or air by one firm or person imposes costs on other

[2] Ibid. Also, see L. Lave and E. Seskin, *Air Pollution and Human Health,* Baltimore: published for Resources for the Future by The Johns Hopkins University Press, 1977.

firms or persons. Thus, if a paper mill uses water and then treats it to restore its quality, there is no divergence between private and social cost. But when the same mill dumps harmful wastes into streams and rivers (the cheap way to get rid of its by-products), the towns downstream that use the water must incur costs to restore its quality. The same is true of air pollution. If an electric power plant uses the atmosphere as a cheap and convenient place to dispose of wastes, people living and working nearby may incur costs as a result, since the incidence of respiratory and other diseases may increase. In such cases, there may be a divergence between private and social cost.

We said above that pollution-causing activities that result in external diseconomies represent a malfunctioning of the market system. At this point, the nature of this malfunctioning should be clear. *Firms and people dump too much waste material into the water and the atmosphere. The price system does not provide the proper signals because the polluters are induced to use our streams and atmosphere in this socially undesirable way by the artificially low price of disposing of wastes in this manner. Moreover, because the polluters do not pay the true cost of waste disposal, their products are artificially cheap, so that too much is produced of them.*

Consider two examples. Electric power companies do not pay the full cost of disposing of wastes in the atmosphere. They charge an artificially low price, and the public is induced to use more electric power than is socially desirable. Similarly, since the owners of automobiles do not pay the full cost of disposing of exhaust and other wastes in the atmosphere, they pay an artificially low price for operating an automobile, and the public is induced to own and use more automobiles than is socially desirable.

Public Policy Toward Pollution

Pollution is caused by defects in our institutions, not by malicious intent, greed, or corruption. In cases where waste disposal causes significant external diseconomies, economists generally agree that government intervention may be justifiable. But how can the government intervene? Perhaps the simplest way is **direct regulation**, through the issuance of certain enforceable rules for waste disposal. For example, the government can prohibit the burning of trash in furnaces or incinerators, or the dumping of certain materials in the ocean; and make any person or firm that violates these restrictions subject to a fine, or perhaps even imprisonment. Also, the government can ban the use of chemicals like DDT, or require that all automobiles meet certain regulations for the emission of air pollutants. Further, the government can establish quality standards for air and water.

The government can also intervene by establishing effluent fees. An **effluent fee** is a fee a polluter must pay to the government for discharging waste. In other words, a price is imposed on the disposal of wastes into the environment; and the more firms or individuals pollute, the more they must pay. The idea behind the imposition of effluent fees is that they can bring the private cost of waste disposal closer to the true social costs.

Wastewater treatment plant

Basic Idea #39: A free-enterprise economy is likely to result in too much pollution because the firms and individuals who dump waste materials into the water and the atmosphere are guided by the artificially low prices they pay for disposing of wastes in this way. The true costs to society of such waste disposal are greater than the prices they pay. To remedy the situation, economists argue that polluters should be made to pay the true social costs of polluting (for example, through effluent fees).

Faced with a closer approximation to the true social costs of their activities, polluters will reduce the extent to which they pollute the environment. Needless to say, many practical difficulties are involved in carrying out this seemingly simple scheme, but many economists believe that this is the best way to deal with the pollution problem.[3]

Still another way for the government to intervene is to establish ***tax credits*** for firms that introduce pollution-control equipment. There are, of course, many types of equipment that a plant can introduce to cut down on pollution—for example, "scrubbers" for catching poisonous gases, and electrostatic precipitators for decreasing dust and smoke. But such pollution-control equipment costs money, and firms are naturally reluctant to spend money on purposes where the private rate of return is so low. To reduce the burden, the government can allow firms to reduce their tax bill by a certain percentage of the amount they spend on pollution-control equipment. Tax incentives of this sort have been discussed widely in recent years, and some have been adopted.

DIRECT REGULATION

Let's look more closely at the advantages and disadvantages of each of these major means by which the government can intervene to remedy the nation's pollution problems. At present we rely mostly on direct regulation of waste disposal (and the quality of the environment); and despite the many problems involved, it has undoubtedly done much good. As Allen Kneese, one of the country's top experts in this area, says about water pollution, "The control of water discharges through administrative orders regulating individual waste disposers has been a useful device and cannot be abandoned until we have a better substitute."[4]

However, economists agree that direct regulation suffers from some serious disadvantages:

1. Such regulations have generally taken the form of general, cross-the-board rules. For example, if two factories located on the same river dump the same amount of waste material into the river, such regulations would probably call for each factory to reduce its waste disposal by the same amount. Unfortunately, although this may appear quite sensible, it may in fact be very inefficient. Suppose that it is much less costly for one factory to reduce its waste disposal than for the other. In such a case, it would be more efficient to ask the factory that could reduce its wastes more cheaply to cut down more on its waste disposal than the other factory. For reasons of this sort, *pollution reductions are likely to be accomplished at more than minimum cost, if they are accomplished by direct regulation.*

2. To formulate such regulations in a reasonably sensible way, the responsible government agencies must have access to much more information than they are likely to obtain or assimilate. Unless the government agencies

---

[3] Another possibility is for the government to issue a certificate or license to pollute. The government might issue a limited number of certificates, to be auctioned off to the highest bidders.

[4] A. Kneese, "Public Policy toward Water Pollution." in E. Mansfield, *Microeconomics: Selected Readings,* 3d ed., New York: Norton, 1979.

have a detailed and up-to-date familiarity with the technology of hundreds of industries, they are unlikely to make sound rules. Moreover, unless the regulatory agencies have a very wide jurisdiction, their regulations will be evaded by the movement of plants and individuals from localities where regulations are stiff to localities where they are loose. In addition, the regulatory agencies must view the pollution problem as a whole, since piecemeal regulation may simply lead polluters to substitute one form of pollution for another. For example, New York and Philadelphia have attempted to reduce water pollution by more intensive sewage treatment. However, one result has been the production of a lot of biologically active sludge that is being dumped into the ocean—and perhaps causing problems there.

EFFLUENT FEES

The use of effluent fees is the approach most economists seem to prefer, for the following reasons. First, *it obviously is socially desirable to use the cheapest way to achieve any given reduction in pollution. A system of effluent fees is more likely to accomplish this objective than direct regulation, because the regulatory agency cannot have all the relevant information* (as we noted above), *whereas polluters, reacting in their own interest to effluent fees, will tend to use the cheapest means to achieve a given reduction in pollution.*

To see why this is the case, consider a particular polluter. Faced with an effluent fee—that is, a price it must pay for each unit of waste it discharges—the polluter will find it profitable to reduce its discharge of waste so long as the cost of doing so is less than the effluent fees it saves. Thus, if this firm can reduce its discharge of wastes relatively cheaply, it will be induced to make such a reduction by the prospect of increased profits. On the other hand, if it cannot reduce its discharge of wastes at all cheaply, it will not make such a reduction, since the costs will exceed the saving in effluent fees. Thus a system of effluent fees induces firms that can reduce waste disposal more cheaply to cut down more on their waste disposal than firms where such a reduction is more expensive. This means that a given reduction of pollution will occur at a relatively low cost.

Economists also favor effluent fees because this approach requires far less information in the hands of the relevant government agencies than does direct regulation. After all, when effluent fees are used, all the government has to do is meter the amount of pollution a firm or household produces (which admittedly is sometimes not easy) and charge accordingly. It is left to the firms and households to figure out the most ingenious and effective ways to cut down on their pollution and save on effluent fees. This too is a spur to inventive activities aimed at developing more effective ways to reduce pollution. Also, economists favor the use of effluent fees because financial incentives are likely to be easier to administer than direct regulation.

While economists tend to favor the use of effluent fees, they are not always against direct regulation. Some ways of disposing of certain types of waste are so dangerous that the only sensible thing to do is to ban them. For example, a ban on the disposal of mercury or arsenic in places where human beings are likely to consume them—and die—seems reasonable enough. In effect, the social cost of such pollution is so high that a very high penalty—imprisonment—is put on it. In addition, of course, economists favor direct regulation when it simply is not feasible to impose effluent fees—for example, in cases where it would be prohibitively expensive to meter the amount of pollutants emitted by various firms or households.

THE RUHR: A CASE STUDY[5]

Let's consider a well-known case of effluent fees in use: the Ruhr valley in West Germany. The Ruhr is one of the world's most industrialized areas. It includes about one-third of West Germany's industrialized capacity, and about 70 to 90 percent of West Germany's coal, coke, and iron and steel outputs. It contains about 10 million people and about 4,300 square miles. Water supplies in the Ruhr are quite limited. Five small rivers supply the area. The amazing amount of waste materials these rivers carry is indicated by the fact that the average annual natural low flow is less than the volume of effluent discharged into the rivers. Yet the local water authorities have succeeded in making this small amount of water serve the needs of the firms and households of this tremendous industrial area, and at the same the streams have been used for recreation. Moreover, all this has been achieved at a remarkably low cost. The success of water management in the Ruhr seems to be due in considerable part to institutional arrangements that allowed the German water managers to plan and operate a relatively efficient regional system. Collective water quality improvement measures are used. Water quality is controlled by waste treatment in over 100 plants, regulation of river flow by reservoir, and a number of oxidation lakes in the Ruhr itself.

Effluent fees are an integral part of the institutional arrangements governing water quality. The amount a firm has to pay depends upon how much waste—and what kind—it pumps into the rivers. A formula has been devised to indicate how much a polluter must pay to dispose of a particular type of waste. In simple terms, the formula bases the charge on the amount of clean water needed to dilute the effluent in order to avoid harm to fish. Using this formula, the local authorities can determine, after testing the effluent of any firm, the amount the firm should pay. Specifically, the amount depends on the amount of suspended materials that will settle out of the effluent, the amount of oxygen consumed by bacteria in a sample of effluent, the results of a potassium permanganate test, and the results of a fish toxicity test. You need not understand the nature or specific purposes of these measurements and tests. The important thing is that you understand their general aim—which is to measure roughly the amount of pollution caused by various kinds of wastes. Having made these measurements and tests, the local authorities use their formula to determine how much a firm must pay in effluent fees.

TAX CREDITS FOR POLLUTION-CONTROL EQUIPMENT

Many tax inducements to encourage firms and individuals to install pollution-control equipment have been proposed. A typical suggestion is that the

View of the Ruhr valley, Germany

---

[5] This section is based on A. Kneese and B. Bower, *Managing Water Quality: Economics, Technology, Institutions,* Washington, D.C.: Resources for the Future, 1968, Chapter 12.

government offer a **tax credit** equal to 20 percent of the cost of pollution-control equipment, and allow a firm to depreciate such equipment in only one to five years. In this way, the government would help defray some of the costs of the pollution-control equipment by allowing a firm that installed such equipment to pay less taxes than if no such tax inducements existed.

However, such schemes have a number of disadvantages:

1. Subsidies to promote the purchase of particular types of pollution-control equipment may result in relatively inefficient and costly reductions in pollution. After all, other methods that don't involve special pollution-control equipment—such as substituting one type of fuel for another—may sometimes be a more efficient way to reduce pollution.

2. Subsidies of this sort may not be very effective. Even if the subsidy reduces the cost to the firm of reducing pollution, it may still be cheaper for the firm to continue to pollute. In other words, subsidies of this sort make it a little less painful for polluters to reduce pollution; but unlike effluent fees, they offer no positive incentive.

3. It seems preferable on grounds of equity for the firms and individuals that do the polluting—or their customers—to pay to clean up the mess that results. Effluent fees work this way, but with tax credits for pollution-control equipment, the government picks up part of the tab by allowing the polluter to pay lower taxes. In other words, the general public, which is asked to shoulder the additional tax burden to make up for the polluters' lower taxes, pays part of the cost. But is this a fair allocation of the costs? Why should the general public be saddled with much of the bill?

Pollution-Control Programs in the United States

In recent decades, there has been considerable growth in government programs designed to control pollution. To take but one example, federal expenditures to reduce water pollution increased in the period from the mid- 1950s to 1970 from about $1 million to $300 million annually. To curb water pollution, the federal government has for years operated a system of grants-in-aid to state, municipal, or regional agencies to help construct treatment plants; and grants are made for research on new treatment methods. In addition, the 1970 Water Quality Improvement Act authorized grants to demonstrate new methods and techniques and to establish programs to train people in water control management. (The federal government has also regulated the production and use of pesticides.) The states, as well as the federal government, have played an important role in water pollution control. They have set standards for allowable pollution levels, and many state governments have provided matching grants to help municipalities construct treatment plants.

In 1969, the Congress established a new agency—the Council on Environmental Quality—to oversee and plan the nation's pollution control programs. Modeled to some extent on the Council of Economic Advisers, the Council on Environmental Quality, which has three members, is supposed to gather information on considerations and trends in the quality of the environment, review and evaluate the federal government's programs in this area, develop appropriate national policies, and conduct needed surveys and research on environmental quality. The tasks assigned to the council are obviously important ones.

In 1970, the federal government established another new agency, the Environmental Protection Agency (EPA). Working with state and local officials, this agency establishes standards for desirable air and water quality, and devises rules for attaining these goals. The 1970 Clean Air Amendments directed EPA to establish minimum ambient standards for air quality, and it set limits on the emission of carbon monoxide, hydrocarbons, and nitrous oxides from automobiles. But after a number of clashes between EPA and the auto makers, the EPA relaxed the deadlines when these limits were supposed to be met. In 1972 amendments to the Water Pollution Act authorized EPA to set up effluent standards for both privately and publicly owned plants. A stated goal of the amendments was to eliminate the discharge of pollutants into water by 1985, but, for reasons discussed in the next section, this goal was unrealistically stringent. In general, recent legislation has emphasized direct regulation, although there has been some study of the use of effluent fees. For example, the government has considered imposing a fee on the emission of sulphur oxide into the air.

Some people believe that public policy is moving too rapidly in this area: others believe that it is moving too slowly. It is not easy to determine how fast or how far we should go in attempting to reduce pollution. Those who will bear the costs of reducing pollution have an understandable tendency to emphasize (and perhaps inflate) the costs and discount the benefits of such projects. Those who are particularly interested in enjoying nature and outdoor recreation—like the Sierra Club—are understandably inclined to emphasize (and perhaps inflate) the benefits and discount the costs of such projects. Politics inevitably plays a major role in the outcome of such cases. The citizens of the United States must indicate, through the ballot box as well as the market place, how much they are willing to pay to reduce pollution. We must also decide at what level of government the relevant rules are to be made. Since many pollution problems are local, it often seems sensible to determine the appropriate level of environmental quality locally. (However, there are obvious dangers in piecemeal regulation, as pointed out above.)

How Clean Should the Environment Be?

One of the most fundamental questions about pollution control is: How clean do we want the air, water, and other parts of our environment to be? At first glance, it may seem that we should restore and maintain a pristine pure environment, but this is not a very sensible goal, since the costs of achieving it would be enormous. The Environmental Protection Agency has estimated that it would cost about $60 billion to remove 85 to 90 percent of water pollutants from industrial and municipal sources. This is hardly a trivial amount, but it is far less than the cost of achieving zero discharge of pollutants, which would be about $320 billion—a truly staggering sum.

Example 20.1   How to Reduce the Costs of Cleaning Up

According to estimates made by Allen Kneese and Charles Schultze, the cost of achieving a one-pound reduction in the amount of pollutants emitted at a petroleum refinery and a beet-sugar plant are as shown below:

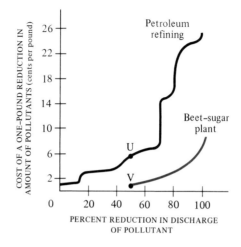

(a) Suppose that it is decided that the total amount of pollutants discharged by both plants should be reduced by 50 percent. If the government decrees that each plant should cut its discharge by 50 percent, what would be the cost of a one-pound reduction at each plant? (b) Can you suggest a way in which this total reduction in pollution can be achieved more efficiently? (c) To achieve this reduction most efficiently, which plant (the petroleum refinery or the beet-sugar plant) should reduce its discharge by the greater percentage? (d) Would an effluent fee achieve this reduction at less cost than the regulation in (a)?

SOLUTION

(a) The petroleum refinery would operate at point U, where the cost of a one-pound reduction in pollution is 6 cents. The beet-sugar plant would operate at point V, where the cost of a one-pound reduction would be 1 cent. (b) Since the beet-sugar plant can reduce pollution at less cost than the petroleum refinery (1 cent per pound rather than 6 cents per pound), it should cut its pollution more and the petroleum refinery should cut its pollution less. (c) The beet-sugar plant, for the reasons given in (b). (d) Yes. If an effluent fee were established, the cost of a one-pound reduction in pollution would tend to be the same at both plants.*

* See A. Kneese and C. Schultze, *Pollution, Prices, and Public Policy,* Washington, D.C.: The Brookings Institution, 1975; and W. Baumol and W. Oates, *Economics, Environmental Policy, and the Quality of Life,* Englewood Cliffs, N.J.: Prentice-Hall, 1979.

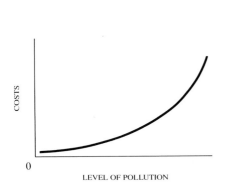

Figure 20.1

Costs to Society of Pollution *The costs to society of pollution increase with the level of pollution.*

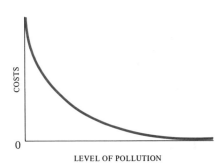

Figure 20.2
Costs to Society of Pollution Control
The more pollution is reduced, the higher are the costs to society of pollution control.

Fortunately, however, there is no reason to aim at so stringent a goal. *It seems obvious that, as pollution increases, various costs to society increase as well.* Some of these costs were described at the beginning of this chapter. For example, we pointed out that increases in air pollution result in increased deaths, and that increases in water pollution reduce the recreational value of rivers and streams. Suppose that we could get accurate data on the cost to society of various levels of pollution. Of course, it is extremely difficult to get such data, but if we could, we could determine the relationship between the amount of these costs and the level of pollution. It would look like the hypothetical curve in Figure 20.1. The greater the level of pollution, the higher these costs will be.

But these costs are not the only ones that must be considered. *We must also take into account the costs of controlling pollution.* In other words, we must look at the costs to society of maintaining a certain level of environmental quality. These costs are not trivial, as we saw at the beginning of this section. To maintain a very low level of pollution, it is necessary to invest heavily in pollution-control equipment and to make other economic sacrifices.[6] If we could get accurate data on the cost to society of controlling pollution, we could find the relationship between the amount of these costs and the level of pollution. It would look like the hypothetical curve in Figure 20.2; the lower the level of pollution, the higher these costs will be.

A GOAL OF ZERO POLLUTION?

At this point, it should be obvious why we should not try to achieve a zero level of pollution. *The sensible goal for our society is to minimize the sum of the costs of pollution and the costs of controlling pollution.* In other words, we should construct a graph, as shown in Figure 20.3, to indicate the relationship between the sum of these two types of costs and the level of pollution. Then we should choose the level of pollution at which the sum of these two types of costs is a minimum. Thus, in Figure 20.3, we should aim for a pollution level of *A*. There is no point in trying for a lower level; such a reduction would cost more than it would be worth. For example, the cost of achieving a zero pollution level would be much more than it would be worth. Only when the pollution level exceeds *A* is the extra cost to society of the additional pollution greater than the cost of preventing it. For example, the cost of allowing pollution to increase from *A* to *B* is much greater than the cost of prevention.

It is easy to draw hypothetical curves, but not so easy actually to measure these curves. Unfortunately, no one has a very clear idea of what the curves in Figure 20.3 really look like—although we can be sure that their general shapes are like those shown there. Thus no one really knows just how clean we should try to make the environment. Under these circum-

---

[6] It is important to recognize that the costs of pollution control extend far beyond the construction of more and better water treatment plants, or the more extensive control of gas emission, or other such steps. A serious pollution-control program can put firms out of business, put people out of work, and bring economic trouble to entire communities. Further, a pollution-control system can result in a redistribution of income. For example, automobiles, electric power, and other goods and services involving considerable pollution are likely to increase in price relative to other goods and services involving little pollution. To the extent that polluting goods and services play a bigger role in the budgets of the poor than of the rich, pollution controls hurt the poor and help the rich.

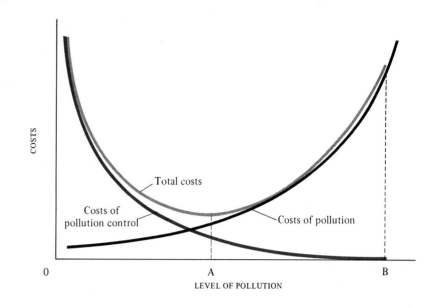

Figure 20.3
Determining Optimal Level of Pollution
The optimal level of pollution is at point
A, *since this is where the total costs are a*
minimum. Below point A, *the cost to*
society of more pollution is less than the
cost of preventing it. Above point A, *the*
cost to society of more pollution is
greater than the cost of preventing it.

stances, expert opinion differs on the nature and extent of the programs that should be carried out. Moreover, as pointed out in a previous section, political considerations and pressures enter in. But one thing is for sure: we will continue to live with some pollution—and that, for the reason just given, will be the rational thing to do.

Recent Directions of Environmental Policy

In the late seventies and early eighties, policy makers became increasingly concerned that regulatory agencies like EPA had been paying too little attention to the costs involved in reducing pollution. For example, a government study found that a relaxation of EPA's 1977 standard for water-pollution control in the steel industry *with no change in its more stringent 1983 standard* would allow savings in capital costs of $200 million. As President Carter's Council of Economic Advisers pointed out, "In making regulatory decisions on the speed of attaining standards, we should explicitly make a qualitative judgment about whether the gains from earlier attainment are worth the costs."

Going a step further, some experts, like Lester Lave and Gilbert Omenn of the Brookings Institution, have concluded from their studies that the Clean Air Act has not been very effective. In their view, "the application of pollution controls to existing plants and older cars has been limited, and costs have been excessive, largely because Congress has failed to confront [many of] the difficult issues . . ."

During the 1980s, environmentalists and others charged that the Reagan administration was dismantling, or at least emasculating, EPA. Anne Gorsuch resigned in 1983 as head of EPA, as criticism of the agency continued to build. James Watt, former Secretary of the Interior, also angered environmentalists. Administration officials retorted to such criticism by claiming that they were trying to promote and restore balance between environmental objectives and economic growth.

In 1985 a political battle raged over the superfund, the fund authorized by federal legislation to clean up sites where chemical wastes have been dumped. Environmentalists wanted a fund of $10 billion; the Reagan administration proposed $5 billion. Some observers wanted the oil and chemical firms to contribute more to the fund, while these firms bitterly opposed such a move.

Test Yourself

1. Suppose that the paper industry emits wastes into rivers and streams, and that municipalities or firms downstream must treat the water to make it usable. Do the paper industry's private costs equal the social costs of producing paper? Why or why not?

2. Suppose that each ton of paper produced results in pollution that costs municipalities and firms downstream $1.00, and that a law is passed that requires the paper industry to reimburse the municipalities and firms downstream for these costs. Prior to this law, the supply curve for paper was:

Price of paper (dollars per ton)	Quantity supplied (million tons)
1.00	10.0
2.00	15.0
2.50	17.5
3.00	20.0
4.00	25.0

After the law takes effect, what will be the quantity supplied at each price?

3. In Question 2, which output—the one prevailing before the industry has to reimburse others, or the one prevailing afterward—is socially more desirable? Why?

4. If the demand curve for paper is as shown below, what will be the equilibrium output of paper before and after the paper industry has to reimburse the municipalities and firms downstream (as indicated in Question 2)?

Price of paper (dollars per ton)	Quantity demanded (million tons)
1.00	30.0
2.00	25.0
3.00	20.0
3.50	17.5
4.00	15.0

5. Suppose that the social cost (in billions of dollars) due to pollution equals $5P$, where P is the level of pollution, and that the cost (in billions of dollars) of pollution control equals $10-2P$. What is the optimal level of pollution? Is this a typical case?

Our Energy Problems

OPEC AND THE ENERGY CRISIS

During the early 1970s, even as it began to dawn on Americans that our environment was not indestructible, other urgent concerns arose about our national resources. A nation that had taken its abundant energy supplies for granted suddenly was confronted by the prospect of shortages. In late 1973, there was the Arab oil embargo; then in 1974, there was a tremendous increase in the price of imported crude oil. In September 1973, imported crude oil cost American petroleum refiners about $4.50 per barrel; a year later, it cost them about $12.50 per barrel. This great and sudden increase in the price of imported crude oil had a very substantial effect on both the national and international economy. It helped to create inflation at home, and it transferred tens of billions of dollars from the United States to the oil-producing nations. (See Figure 20.4.) Further, this big price increase

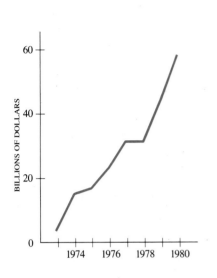

BILLIONS OF DOLLARS

60 —

40 —

20 —

0

1974   1976   1978   1980

Figure 20.4

Total U.S. Payments for Crude Oil Imports, 1973–80 *Because the price of oil skyrocketed after 1973, the amount that America paid for imported oil skyrocketed too.*

was by no means the end. For example, in 1979, after Iran began cutting its oil output, the price of oil went up about 50 percent.

Why did the price of imported crude oil increase so spectacularly? Because the Organization of Petroleum Exporting Countries (OPEC) upped the price of crude oil. OPEC is an international cartel—that is, an association of national petroleum producers that gets together and sets prices for oil.[7] Formed in the early 1960s, OPEC's charter says that "members shall study and formulate a system to ensure the stabilization of prices by, among other means, the regulation of production, with due regard to the interests of the producing and the consuming nations, and to the necessity of securing a steady income to the producing countries." In the 1960s, OPEC gained strength; in the 1970s, it lowered the boom on the oil-consuming nations.

The Arab oil embargo in late 1973 called attention to another aspect of our energy problems: the fact that the United States was coming to depend to an increasing extent on foreign sources of supply of crude oil. Oil imports supplied almost one-half of domestic petroleum demand in 1977, as compared to about one-quarter in 1965. Some people worried that our national security might be imperiled by a cutoff of foreign oil.

The argument that we should try to avoid being dependent on foreign sources of oil was by no means new. Until 1973, this argument was used to justify the adoption of oil import quotas in the united States. These import quotas set a limit on the amount of foreign oil that could be imported. Many economists were opposed to these quotas because they increased the price of petroleum and petroleum products to consumers. (See Chapter 32.) Whether self-sufficiency with regard to energy is as important a goal as some policy makers seem to believe is hard to say. But the Arab oil embargo made the potential threat much more credible.

ENERGY AND ECONOMIC GROWTH

Responding to the oil crises of the 1970s, U.S. policy makers proclaimed the importance of guaranteeing energy supplies that would meet the nation's growing energy demands. According to some observers, such as the authors of the *Limits to Growth*,[8] this could not be done. Why? Because there's only a finite supply of energy resources like oil and coal. If economic growth continues, the demand for these resources will increase exponentially. Eventually, according to these observers, we shall run out of such resources, with the result that both output and production will decline. Moreover, although this outcome is not around the corner, it is not so far off either. In their view, it will occur in the next 100 years.

Many people regard this as one of the most serious and fundamental of our energy problems. However, few economists accept the assumptions underlying these arguments. In the first place, economists charge that the authors of *Limits to Growth* underestimate very substantially the amount of the world's energy resources. Between 1944 and 1969, total world economic reserves of crude oil increased by about 12 times, due to producers'

---

[7] Although many of the oil-exporting countries are in the Middle East, OPEC also includes countries in Africa, Latin America, and other continents.

[8] D. Meadows *et al.*, *The Limits to Growth*, New York: New American Library, 1972.

efforts to find and develop new sources of supply. Since annual world consumption rose about 6 times, this meant that reserves more than kept pace with oil consumption. Yet the authors of *Limits to Growth* assumed that known economic reserves of energy resources would increase only 5 times between now and the year 2100.

More fundamentally, economists charge that the authors of *Limits to Growth* do not take proper account of the workings of the price system. When the supply of a resource becomes tight, its price rises, with the result that firms have a greater financial incentive to find more of it. Also, as the price of this resource rises, firms have an incentive to develop new technology that permits less of this resource to be used. These mechanisms have resulted in the elimination of many apparent shortages in the past, and most economists tended to believe that they would play a major role in attacking our energy problems as well.

Public Policy Toward Energy

REDUCTION OF ENERGY DEMAND

During the 1970s economists put forth a number of suggestions concerning ways to solve our energy problems. One suggestion was that we should reduce our demand for energy. Without question, there are many areas where energy could be saved with little inconvenience. One way that a reduction in energy demand could be accomplished is through the imposition of a tax on fuel. A number of economists suggested such a measure. To see how it might work, consider Figure 20.5, which shows the demand and supply curves for fuel. Without tax, the price of fuel would be OP_0, and the quantity consumed would be OQ_0.

Suppose that a tax of \$.20 per gallon[9] of fuel were imposed. If so, the supply curve would shift upward by the amount of the tax. To see why, note that, if the pretax price had to be OP_0 per gallon to induce sellers to supply OQ_0 gallons of fuel, the posttax price would have to be \$.20 higher to induce the same supply. Similarly, if the pretax price had to be OP_1 per gallon to induce sellers to supply OQ_1 gallons of fuel, the posttax price would have to be \$.20 higher to induce the same supply. The reason why the sellers require \$.20 more per gallon to supply the pretax amount is that they must pay the tax of \$.20 per gallon to the government. Thus they need the extra \$.20 to wind up with the same amount as before.

Since the tax shifts the supply curve upward by \$.20, the posttax equilibrium price and quantity are OP_2 and OQ_2, respectively. The effect of the tax on the quantity of fuel consumed is just what one would expect. It reduces fuel consumption. In Figure 20.5, the reduction is from OQ_0 to OQ_2. According to calculations by Dale Jorgensen of Harvard University and Edward Hudson of Data Resources, Inc., a tax equal to 3 percent of sales in 1985 and increasing gradually to about 15 percent in the year 2000 would result in no growth whatsoever in the quantity of energy consumed between 1985 and 2000. However, it is by no means clear that the United States

---

[9] We assume here that fuel is measured in gallons. For some fuels (like coal), this is not the case; but this simplification can easily be removed. It is used here only for convenience.

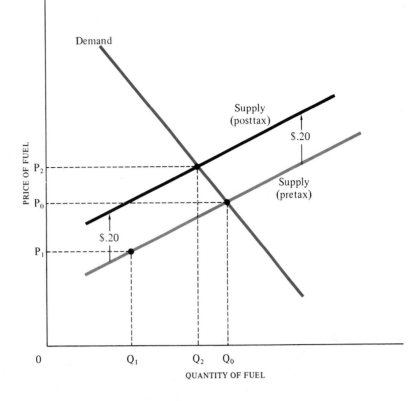

Figure 20.5
Effect of a Tax on Fuel *If a tax of $.20 per gallon is imposed on fuel, the supply curve for fuel shifts upward, as shown here. Thus the quantity of fuel consumed is cut from OQ_0 to OQ_2.*

should seek to maintain energy consumption at a constant level. For one thing, such a policy would reduce our rate of economic growth, although considerable growth would still occur.

DEVELOPMENT OF NEW ENERGY TECHNOLOGIES

Economists and others also suggested that, to avoid increased dependence on foreign oil, we might develop new technologies that can produce energy economically from our domestic resources. One important resource of this kind is shale, which is found in Colorado, Wyoming, and Utah. For many years, shale has been regarded as a promising source of synthetic oil, but so far the costs of producing oil by this route have been too high to make it economical. Also, there are many unresolved environmental problems, since it is difficult to dispose of the spent shale. In Canada, a potentially important source of synthetic oil is the tar sands located in Alberta. Here too, the costs of producing oil in this way are relatively high, but some production is occurring. In both the cases of shale and tar sands, perhaps additional investments in research and development can solve the problems that presently prevent these resources from being a more economical source of synthetic oil.

The United States has vast quantities of coal. To some extent, it might be possible to substitute our relatively plentiful coal for other fuels. However, one important problem with much of our Eastern coal is that it contains a great deal of sulphur, with the result that its combustion leads to a rise in the emission of sulphur dioxide, an important air pollutant. One way to cope with this problem is to scrub most of this chemical from power plants'

451

Cross-Chapter Case/Part Five

BUBBLES, OFFSETS, AND BANKS

Attempts to maintain an acceptable level of air quality in the United States are based on the direct regulation of individual sources of pollution. A source is defined as any installation which emits at least one pollutant; thus a single industrial plant can have several distinct sources. Each polluter is supposed to obey rules, set by the government, stipulating both the necessary amount of pollution abatement and the technology to be employed at each source. This process has proved cumbersome and time-consuming. Many studies must be made by both the regulators and the regulated. Hearings are often necessary. Moreover, for reasons discussed in this chapter, direct regulation of this sort has been inefficient. The reduction in pollution has been more costly than necessary.

In the late 1970s, the Environmental Protection Agency (EPA) began to experiment with market-like schemes for pollution control. Rather than directly controlling the behavior of each source of pollution, these schemes introduced financial incentives for firms to use their own expertise to achieve air quality levels relatively cheaply. To date, the EPA has moved very cautiously in this direction; direct regulation has not been abandoned. Only limited use of financial incentives has been approved. Three incentive schemes—bubbles, offsets, and banks—have been developed, each of which is discussed below.

The concept of a **bubble** is meant to take account of the fact that the costs of controlling pollution differ among processes within a particular plant and among plants and firms. A "bubble" is put around an entire plant or area, and it is viewed as a single source of pollution rather than several distinct sources. Regulators establish emission limits for a plant (or area) as a whole, and managers can allocate pollution abatement in any way they like as long as the overall emission target is attained. Since the managers' decisions affect their firms' profits, they have an incentive to reduce pollution in a least-cost way. The bubble concept can only be applied to existing firms, not to potential sources of pollution.

Experience with bubbles indicates that they can result in significant savings. For example, Armco Steel substituted dust-reducing actions for pollution controls in its steel-making process, the result being a saving of $20 million in capital costs and $2.5 million per year in operating costs. In Providence, Rhode Island, the New England Electric System has used different fuels at two power plants included within a bubble, and reports savings of $4 million in 2½ years. However, there are many restrictions on the use of bubbles. For example, as noted above, they can only be used by existing sources of pollution, not by new entrants.

The concept of an **offset** was developed to permit new plants to open and old ones to expand in areas that do not meet the national environmental standards, while at the same time ensuring that air quality does not get worse. Whereas bubbles apply only to existing sources of pollution, offsets apply to new sources. Offsets permit construction of new pollution sources (and enlargement of existing sources) if the resulting new emissions are *less* *than* the reduction in emissions from existing sources. The offset program allows firms that want to introduce new sources of pollution to negotiate with existing firms to purchase emission reductions from them. Also, firms can offset the increases in pollution stemming from their new sources by reducing the emissions from other sources that they own in the area.

The offset program began in 1977. According to EPA, there have been hundreds of offsets, most of which have occurred within a single firm. For example, in Brazoria County, Texas, Phillips Petroleum Company added new sources of pollution in order to enlarge the capacity of its refinery. The pollution from these new sources was offset by doing a more complete job of controlling hydrocarbon emissions from Phillips's existing storage tanks and other facilities. Through 1980, only 32 offsets involving negotiations between different firms had taken place, as shown in the table below. This seemed to be due in part to the bureaucratic difficulties in carrying out offsets.

The concept of a *bank* is an extension of an offset, the idea being to promote greater flexibility with regard to the timing of the trade of emission reductions. If a firm pushes its daily emissions below the mandated standards, it can hold these reductions in reserve at a clearinghouse, and it can trade them at some date in the future. In other words, it can "bank" these reductions. One advantage is that the basic offset program is made more efficient because firms that want to purchase emission reductions from other firms can find potential sellers of such reductions by consulting the clearinghouse inventory.

Bubbles, offsets, and banks are very partial steps toward the use of market incentives to help promote efficiency in pollution control. The United States is very far from having a system of marketable pollution rights. But as Robert Crandall of the Brookings Institution has put it, "We are surely closer to a system of economic incentives in air pollution control . . . than we were a decade ago, when a proposed sulfur tax disappeared without even serious legislative debate."[1]

Pollutant	Number of offset transactions through 1980	
	Approved	Pending, withdrawn, or uncertain
Hydrocarbons	20	8
Total suspended particulates	8	3
Sulfur dioxide	4	1
Carbon monoxide	0	1
Nitrogen oxides	2	0
Total	32	12

Source: Wes Vivian and William Hall, "An Examination of U.S. Market Trading in Air Pollution Offsets," Institute of Public Policy Studies, University of Michigan, 1981.

[1] R. Crandall, *Controlling Industrial Pollution,* Washington, D.C.: Brookings Institution, 1983, p. 98.

Example 20.2   Oil Price Decontrol and Imports

From 1971 to early 1981, the government imposed controls on the price of crude oil. Suppose that the domestic supply and demand curves for crude oil were as shown below:

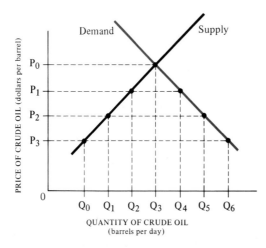

The price of imported foreign oil was OP_1 dollars per barrel. Government controls enabled buyers of crude oil to pay OP_2 dollars per barrel, but domestic suppliers received only OP_3 dollars per barrel.

(a) How much will domestic producers of crude oil supply? (b) How much will domestic buyers of crude oil demand? (c) How much crude oil will be imported? (d) If the price of crude oil were decontrolled, how much crude oil would be imported? (e) In early 1981, the price of crude oil was decontrolled. The American Petroleum Institute reported that imports of crude oil in the first six months of 1981 plunged 20 percent, to an average of 5.9 million barrels per day. Is this what would be expected, based on the above model?*

SOLUTION

(a) OQ_0 barrels per day. (b) OQ_5 barrels per day. (c) $(OQ_5 - OQ_0)$ barrels per day. (d) Under decontrol, the domestic price would have to equal the price of imported oil, OP_1. Thus the domestic producers would supply OQ_2 barrels per day, and domestic buyers would demand OQ_4 barrels per day, which means that $(OQ_4 - OQ_2)$ barrels per day would be imported. (e) Yes. The model predicts that imports will fall from $(OQ_5 - OQ_0)$ to $(OQ_4 - OQ_2)$ barrels per day under decontrol.

* See R. Leftwich and A. Sharp, *Economics of Social Issues,* Dallas: Business Publications, 1978; and "Economic Gains Tied to Ending Oil Price Curbs," *New York Times,* September 8, 1981.

flue stacks. Unfortunately, however, there does not seem to be any technology that can do this effectively and economically. Another way to cope with the problem is to convert coal to a clean gas. A number of technologies have been developed to do this, but many are still in the pilot-plant stage. Here is another area where research and development have a promising role to play.

Still another promising source of energy is the sun. Techniques for harnessing solar energy have been known for a long time. For example, flat plate collectors can be used to heat water or air, which can then be used to heat buildings. But solar energy is still very costly, and there are problems in storing it for use on cloudy days and at night. According to some experts, solar energy is potentially of great economic significance, and too little has been invested to try to develop it and reduce its cost. This is an obvious area for further research and development.

The Weakening of OPEC

During the 1980s, the power of the OPEC oil cartel was substantially reduced, for several reasons.

1. Oil consumption was reduced. Faced with the greatly increased oil prices, consumers cut back on their demand for oil. In part, this was due to the adoption of oil-saving technologies and more fuel-efficient cars. For example, a Buick Electra gets 17 miles a gallon in city driving, compared with about 10 miles that similar models got in the 1970s.

2. OPEC's share of world oil output fell. Due in part to the substantial increase in oil output by Britain, Norway, Mexico, and other non-OPEC countries, OPEC's share fell from 54 percent in 1973 to 32 percent in 1983. Countries like Britain and Norway cut oil prices, forcing OPEC producers to follow suit. In October 1984, Norway, followed by Britain, cut the price of its crude oil by $2 a barrel.

3. Some OPEC members refused to abide by the cartel agreements. In particular, Nigeria, badly needing cash, reduced its price below that set by the cartel. To help ease Nigeria's problems, other OPEC countries, such as Saudi Arabia, are reported to have allowed Nigeria to sell more oil, while cutting back their own output.

In 1983, OPEC—faced with declining demand for oil, increased competition from non-OPEC sources of oil, and price cuts within its own ranks—agreed to reduce its price from $34 to $29 a barrel. In 1984, the cartel, faced with a world oil glut and the fact that oil was trading on the world market for only about $27 a barrel, tried to muster more discipline, but without apparent success. Oil experts and analysts seemed to believe that further price declines were in the cards and that OPEC would not regain its former economic power in the foreseeable future.

However, some observers still worry about the vulnerability of the United States to oil-supply disruptions. For example, it is argued that the Soviet threat to oil-producing facilities in the Middle East is great enough to warrant the preparation of alternative energy options to supplement military contingency plans. Thus, although our energy supplies have been the subject of less worry in 1985 than in the middle and late 1970s, they continue to be the subject of some public concern.

Test Yourself

1. "A tax on fuel will reduce the quantity consumed by a greater amount if the quantity of fuel demanded is relatively insensitive to its price than if it is relatively sensitive to it." Comment and evaluate.

2. According to *Business Week,* August 19, 1985, "Falling prices have trimmed Exxon's sales, but higher profits and cash flow have fueled dividend hikes and massive share buybacks that have sent Exxon stock soaring." Interpret. Is this evidence of a crisis? If so, why?

3. During the 1970s, some economists suggested that a tax on fuel might help to solve America's energy problems. What are the disadvantages of such a tax?

4. In 1981, President Reagan decontrolled the price of oil, which had been kept below world levels by federal controls. What are the disadvantages of keeping the U.S. price of oil artificially low?

Summary

1. One of the major social issues of the 1980s is environmental pollution. To a considerable extent, environmental pollution is an economic problem. Waste disposal and other pollution-causing activities result in external diseconomies.

2. Firms and individuals that pollute the water and air (and other facets of the environment) often pay less than the true social costs of disposing of their wastes in this way. Part of the true social cost is borne by other firms and individuals, who must pay to clean up the water or air, or who must live with the consequences.

3. Because of the divergence of private from social costs, the market system does not result in an optimal allocation of resources. Firms and individuals create too much waste and dispose of it in excessively harmful ways. Because the polluters do not pay the full cost of waste disposal, their products are artificially cheap, with the result that too much is produced of them.

4. The government can intervene in several ways to help remedy the breakdown of the market system in this area. One way is to issue regulations for waste disposal and other activities influencing the environment. Another is to establish effluent fees, charges a polluter must pay to the government for discharging wastes. In recent decades, there has been considerable growth in government programs designed to control pollution.

5. It is extremely difficult to determine how clean the environment should be. Of course, the sensible goal for society is to permit the level of pollution that minimizes the sum of the costs of pollution and the costs of controlling pollution; but no one has a very clear idea of what these costs are, and to a large extent the choices must be made through the political process.

6. Another major issue has been energy. The Arab oil embargo in late 1973 and OPEC's huge price increase in early 1974 called attention to the growing dependence of the United States on foreign sources of crude oil. Billions of dollars were transferred to the oil-producing countries. A cutoff of foreign oil could disrupt our economy.

7. A variety of policy measures were proposed to help deal with our energy problems. One proposal was that we enact a tax on fuel to reduce energy demand. Another approach was to develop new energy technologies that can produce energy economically from our domestic energy resources. During the 1980s, OPEC was weakened by falling demand for oil and increased supplies. Oil prices fell, and America's energy problems seemed much less urgent.

Concepts for Review

External diseconomy	**Direct regulation**	**Bubbles**
Private costs	**Effluent fees**	**Offsets**
Social costs	**Tax credits**	**Banks**

PART SIX

Consumer Behavior and Business Decision Making

CHAPTER 21

Market Demand and Price Elasticity

What do Corfam (Du Pont's synthetic leather) and the Edsel (the new make of automobile Ford introduced in the 1950s) have in common? Both were new products that were unsuccessful because the market demand for them was too small. In a capitalist economy, market demand is a fundamental determinant of what is produced and how. The market demand curve for a commodity plays an important role in the decision-making process within each firm producing the commodity, as well as in the economy as a whole. It is no exaggeration to say that firms spend enormous time and effort trying to cater to, estimate, and influence market demand.

In this chapter, we discuss the factors influencing the market demand curve for a commodity, as well as the measurement of market demand curves and their role in decision making by private business firms and government agencies. We consider questions like: How can we measure market demand curves? What is the price elasticity of demand? What role does the price elasticity of demand play in various practical problems facing the private and public sectors of the economy? What factors underlie the market demand curve for a commodity? These are important questions, from both a theoretical and a practical point of view.

Market Demand Curves

Let's review what a market demand curve is. You will recall from Chapter 3 that a commodity's market demand curve shows how much of the commodity will be purchased during a particular period of time at various

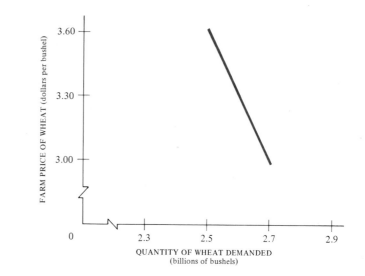

Figure 21.1

Market Demand Curve for Wheat, Mid-1980s *This curve shows how much wheat would be purchased per year at various prices.*

prices. Figure 21.1 ought to be familiar; it is the *market demand curve* for wheat in the mid-1980s, which figured prominently in our discussion of the price system in Chapter 3. Among other things, it shows that during the mid-1980s about 2.7 billion bushels of American wheat would have been purchased per year if the price was $3.00 per bushel, that about 2.6 billion bushels would have been purchased per year if the price was $3.30 per bushel, and that about 2.5 billion bushels would have been purchased if the price was $3.60 per bushel.

Since the market demand curve reflects what consumers want and are willing to pay for, when the market demand curve for wheat shifts upward to the right, this indicates that consumers want more wheat at the existing price. On the other hand, when the curve shifts downward to the left, this indicates that consumers want less wheat at the existing price. Such shifts in the market demand curve for a commodity trigger changes in the behavior of the commodity's producers. When the market demand curve shifts upward to the right, the price of wheat will tend to rise, thus inducing farmers to produce more wheat, because they will find that, given the price increase, their profits will increase if they raise their output levels. The same process occurs in other parts of the economy. Shifts in the demand curve reflecting the fact that consumers want more (less) of a commodity set in motion a sequence of events leading to more (less) production of the commodity.

MEASURING MARKET DEMAND CURVES

To be of practical use, market demand curves must be based on careful measurements. Let's look briefly at some of the techniques used to estimate the market demand curve for particular commodities. At first glance, a quick and easy way to estimate the demand curve might seem to be interviewing consumers about their buying habits and intentions. However, although more subtle variants of this approach sometimes may pay off, simply asking people how much they would buy of a certain commodity at particular prices does not usually seem very useful, since off-the-cuff answers to such questions are rarely very accurate. Thus marketing researchers and econometricians interested in measuring market demand curves have been forced to use more complex procedures.

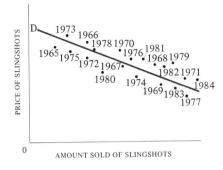

PRICE OF SLINGSHOTS

0   AMOUNT SOLD OF SLINGSHOTS

Figure 21.2
Estimated Demand Curve for Slingshots
One very crude way to estimate the market demand curve is to plot the amount sold of a commodity in each year against its price in that year, and draw a curve that seems to fit the points reasonably well. However, this technique is generally too crude to be reliable.

One such procedure is the ***direct market experiment.*** Although the designs of such experiments vary greatly and are often quite complicated, the basic idea is simple—to see the effects on the quantity demanded of actual variations in the price of the product. (Researchers attempt to hold other market factors constant or to take into account whatever changes may occur.) The Parker Pen Company conducted an experiment a number of years ago to estimate the demand curve for their ink, Quink. They increased the price from \$.15 to \$.25 in four cities, and found that the quantity demanded was quite insensitive to the price. Experiments like this are frequently made to try to estimate a product's market demand curve.

Still another technique is to use statistical methods to estimate demand curves from historical data on price and quantity purchased of the commodity. For example, one might plot the price of slingshots in various periods in the past against the quantity sold, as shown in Figure 21.2. Judging from the results, curve D in Figure 21.2 seems a reasonable approximation to the demand curve. Although this simple analysis provides some insight into how statistical methods are used to estimate demand curves from historical data, it is a vast oversimplification. For one thing, the market demand curve may have shifted over time, so that curve D is not a proper estimate. Fortunately, modern statistical techniques recognize this possibility and allow us to estimate the position and shape of this curve (at each point in time) in spite of it.

Hundreds, perhaps thousands, of studies have been made to estimate the demand curves for particular commodities. In view of the importance of the results for decision making, this is not surprising. To illustrate the role played by such studies in the formulation of public policy, let's consider the following case involving the Boston and Maine Railroad.

RAILROAD TRANSPORTATION IN METROPOLITAN
BOSTON: A CASE STUDY

In the early 1960s the Boston and Maine Railroad wanted to discontinue passenger commuter service into Boston because it felt such service was unprofitable. In 1963, the Mass Transportation Commission of Massachusetts contracted with the Boston and Maine to establish a demonstration project to estimate the effect of a lowering of fares on the quantity of commuter tickets sold. The Boston and Maine was requested not to file a petition for the discontinuance of commuter service into Boston until after the experiment. During the experiment, which lasted about a year, fares were reduced about 28 percent on the average. The result was, of course, an increase in the number of tickets sold. However, the more important thing to the railroad and the commission was the *extent* to which the fare cut would increase the number of tickets sold. *How great* would be the resulting increase in the number of tickets sold? This was the important question because to increase the railroad's profits, a fare cut had to increase the railroad's revenues more than it increased its costs. And unless the price cut increased the number of tickets sold by a greater percentage than the reduction in price, it would not increase the railroad's revenues at all.

A comparison of the Boston and Maine's commuter revenues in 1963 with those in 1962 showed that this large fare reduction resulted in only a

0.6 percent increase in the railroad's revenues. Thus the price reduction increased the railroad's revenues by little or nothing. Since the reduction in fares increased the railroad's costs—because it was more costly to handle the larger volume of traffic—and increased its revenues scarcely at all, it did not increase the railroad's profits. Thus, after the experiment, the Boston and Maine decided to continue with its petition to terminate com-

Example 21.1   Speculation and the Demand Curve

In many markets, speculators buy and sell, hoping to make money in the process. Suppose that the demand and supply curves for corn this year and next year are as shown below. Speculators, seeing that the price of corn is likely to rise (from OA to OH), decide to buy corn this year and sell it next year. Thus, including the speculators, the demand curve shifts to the right this year, and the supply curve shifts to the right next year, as shown below:

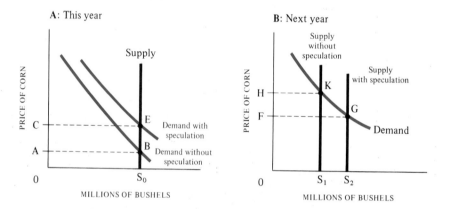

(a) In this case, do speculators even out the consumption of corn over time, thus avoiding famine-feast cycles? (b) In this case, do speculators raise the total value of the corn sold in the two periods? (c) In this case, speculators guessed correctly that the price of corn would rise. If they guess incorrectly, can they make more uneven the consumption of corn over time? (d) Once speculation is included in the analysis, does the demand curve for a product depend on its expected future price?

SOLUTION

(a) Yes. Without the speculators, much less corn would be consumed next year than this year. With them, consumption of corn is relatively constant. (b) Yes. The value (price times quantity) of the corn sold this year is increased considerably (from area $OABS_0$ to area $OCES_0$). The value of the corn sold next year does not change very much, based on the above diagram. (It is area $OHKS_1$ without speculation and area $OFGS_2$ with speculation.) Thus the total value of the corn sold in the two periods is raised. (c) Yes. (d) Yes. If there is a general feeling that the price of a product is going to increase substantially, the demand curve for this product may shift to the right.

muter service.[1] (Eventually, however, public subsidies were instituted to keep the service going.)

This is a fairly typical example of a direct market experiment designed to obtain information on relevant aspects of a market demand curve. Note the problems experiments of this sort must face. First, *the experiment can be very costly if it alienates customers or reduces the firm's profits.* Second, *it is difficult to hold other relevant variables constant.* For example, the effect of price changes was mixed up, to some extent, with the effect of increased service in the Boston and Maine case. Third, *it is hard to conduct an experiment of this sort over a long enough period to estimate long-run effects.* Thus, in the Boston and Maine case, the effect of the fare reduction on the number of tickets sold might have been much greater if the experiment had lasted longer. Nonetheless, despite these problems, experiments of this sort can produce useful evidence on the location and shape of a product's market demand curve. They are an important supplement to statistical analysis of historical data to estimate market demand curves.

The Price Elasticity of Demand

The quantity demanded of some commodities, like beef in Figure 21.3, is fairly sensitive to changes in the commodity's price. That is, changes in price result in significant changes in quantity demanded. On the other hand, the quantity demanded of other commodities, like cotton in Figure 21.3, is very insensitive to changes in the price. Large changes in price result in small changes in the quantity demanded.

To promote unambiguous discussion of this subject, we must have some measure of the sensitivity of quantity demanded to changes in price. The measure customarily used for this purpose is the ***price elasticity of demand,*** *defined as the percentage change in quantity demanded resulting from a 1 percent change in price.*[2] For example, suppose that a 1 percent reduction in the price of slingshots results in a 2 percent increase in quantity demanded. Then, using this definition, the price elasticity of demand for slingshots is 2. (Convention dictates that we give the elasticity a positive sign even though the change in price is negative and the change in quantity demanded is positive.) The price elasticity of demand is likely to vary from one point to another on the market demand curve. For example, the price elasticity of demand for slingshots may be higher when a slingshot costs $1.00 than when it costs $0.25.

Note that the price elasticity of demand is expressed in terms of *relative*—i.e., proportional or percentage—changes in price and quantity demanded, not *absolute* changes in price and quantity demanded. Thus, in

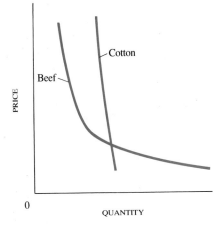

Figure 21.3

Market Demand Curves, Beef and Cotton *The quantity demanded of beef is much more sensitive to price than is the quantity demanded of cotton.*

---

[1] See *Mass Transportation in Massachusetts*, Boston: Mass Transportation Commission, 1964.

[2] What if price does not change by 1 percent? Then the price elasticity of demand is defined as the *percentage change in quantity demanded divided by the percentage change in price.* This definition will be used in the next section. Put in terms of symbols, the price elasticity of demand equals $\dfrac{-\Delta Q}{\Delta P} \times \dfrac{P}{Q}$, where P is price, ΔP is the change in price, Q is quantity demanded, and ΔQ is the change in the quantity demanded.

studying the slingshot market, we looked at the *percentage* change in quantity demanded resulting from a 1 *percent* change in price. This is because absolute changes depend on the units in which price and quantity are measured. Suppose that a reduction in the price of good Y from $100 to $99 results in an increase in the quantity demanded from 200 to 210 pounds per month. If price is measured in dollars, the quantity demanded of good Y seems quite sensitive to price changes, since a decrease in price of "1" results in an increase in quantity demanded of "10." On the other hand, if price is measured in cents, the quantity demanded of good Y seems quite insensitive to price changes, since a decrease in price of "100" results in an increase in quantity demanded of "10." By using relative changes, we do not encounter this problem. Relative changes do not depend on the units of measurement. Thus the percentage reduction in the price of good Y is 1 percent, regardless of whether price is measured in dollars or cents. And the percentage increase in the quantity demanded of good Y is 5 percent, regardless of whether it is measured in pounds or tons.

CALCULATING THE PRICE ELASTICITY OF DEMAND

The price elasticity of demand is a very important concept and one that economists use often, so it is worthwhile to spend some time explaining exactly how it is computed. Suppose that you have a table showing various points on a market demand curve. For example, Table 21.1 shows the quantity of wheat demanded at various prices, as estimated by Professor Karl Fox of Iowa State University during the early 1960s.[3] Given these data, how do you go about computing the price elasticity of demand for wheat? Since the price elasticity of demand for any product generally varies from point to point on its market demand curve, you must first determine at what point on the demand curve you want to measure the price elasticity of demand.

Let us assume that you want to estimate the price elasticity of demand for wheat when the price of wheat is between $2.00 and $2.20 per bushel. To do this, you can use the following formula:

price elasticity =

$$\frac{\text{percentage change}}{\text{in quantity demanded}} \div \frac{\text{percentage change}}{\text{in price}} =$$

$$\frac{\text{change in quantity demanded}}{\text{original quantity demanded}} \div \frac{\text{change in price}}{\text{original price}}.$$

Table 21.1 shows that the quantity demanded equals 700 million bushels when the price is $2.00, and that it equals 675 million bushels when the price is $2.20. But should we use $2.00 and 700 million bushels as the original price and quantity? Or should we use $2.20 and 675 million bushels as the original price and quantity? If we choose the former,

Table 21.1

MARKET DEMAND FOR WHEAT, EARLY 1960s

Farm price of wheat (dollars per bushel)	Quantity of wheat demanded (millions of bushels)
1.00	1,500
1.20	1,300
1.40	1,100
1.60	900
1.80	800
2.00	700
2.20	675

Source: K. Fox, V. Ruttan, and L. Witt, *Farming, Farmers, and Markets for Farm Goods.* New York: Committee for Economic Development, 1962.

[3] Note that Table 21.1 pertains to the early 1960s whereas Figure 21.1 pertains to the mid-1980s. Consequently, the demand curves are quite different, as you can see.

price elasticity =

$$-\frac{675 - 700}{700} \div \frac{2.20 - 2.00}{2.00} = .36.$$

The price elasticity of demand is estimated to be .36. (The minus sign at the beginning of this equation is due to the fact, noted above, that convention dictates that the elasticity be given a positive sign.)

But we could just as well have used $2.20 and 675 million bushels as the original price and quantity. If this had been our choice, the answer would be

price elasticity =

$$-\frac{700 - 675}{675} \div \frac{2.00 - 2.20}{2.20} = .41,$$

which is somewhat different from the answer we got in the previous paragraph.

To get around this difficulty, the generally accepted procedure is to use the average values of price and quantity as the original price and quantity. In other words, we use as an estimate of the price elasticity of demand:

price elasticity =

$$\frac{\text{change in quantity demanded}}{\text{sum of quantities}/2} \div \frac{\text{change in price}}{\text{sum of prices}/2}.$$

This is the so-called **arc elasticity of demand.** In the specific case we are considering, the arc elasticity is

price elasticity =

$$-\frac{(675 - 700)}{\dfrac{(675 + 700)}{2}} \div \frac{(2.20 - 2.00)}{\dfrac{(2.00 + 2.20)}{2}} = .38.$$

This is the answer to our problem.

Determinants of the Price Elasticity of Demand

Many studies have been made of the price elasticity of demand for particular commodities, Table 21.2 reproduces the results of some of them. Note the substantial differences among products. For example, the estimated price elasticity of demand for women's hats is about 3.00, while for cotton it is only about 0.12. Think for a few minutes about these results, and try to figure out why these differences exist. If you rack your brains for a while, chances are that you will agree that the following factors are important determinants of whether the price elasticity of demand is high or low.

Number and Closeness of Available Substitutes. If a commodity has many close substitutes, its demand is likely to be highly elastic, i.e., the price elasticity is likely to be high. If the price of the product increases, a large proportion of its buyers will turn to the close substitutes that are available.

Table 21.2

ESTIMATED PRICE ELASTICITIES OF
DEMAND FOR SELECTED COMMODITIES,
UNITED STATES

Commodity	Price elasticity
Women's hats	3.00
Gasoline	0.30
Sugar	0.31
Corn	0.49
Cotton	0.12
Hay	0.43
Potatoes	0.31
Oats	0.56
Barley	0.39
Buckwheat	0.99
Refrigerators	1.40
Airline travel	2.40
Radio and TV sets	1.20
Legal services	0.50
Pleasure boats	1.30
Canned tomatoes	2.50
Newspapers	0.10
Tires	0.60
Beef	0.92
Shoes	0.40

Source: H. Schultz, *Theory and Measurement of Demand.* Chicago: University of Chicago Press. 1938; M. Spencer and L. Siegelman, *Managerial Economics,* Homewood, Ill.: Irwin, 1959; H. Houthakker and L. Taylor, *Consumer Demand in the United States, 1929–1970.* Cambridge, Mass.: Harvard, 1966; and U.S. Department of Agriculture.

WHY WASHINGTON'S GASOLINE TAX BIT THE DUST

In August 1980, Washington, D.C. imposed a tax on gasoline, which increased the price of gasoline by 6 percent. Estimates of the price elasticity of demand for gasoline in the United States as a whole generally are about 0.3. Thus, based on such an estimate of the price elasticity of demand, one would expect that the amount of gasoline sold in Washington, D.C. would decrease by about 0.3 times 6 percent, or about 1.8 percent. In fact, there was a 33 percent drop in the amount of gasoline sold in Washington, D.C. Why was the drop so much larger than the 1.8 percent decrease forecasted above?

The answer is that the price elasticity of demand for gasoline in Washington, D.C. (when the price of gasoline outside Washington is held constant) is much higher than the price elasticity of demand for gasoline in the nation as a whole. Gasoline sold in Virginia and Maryland is a very good substitute for gasoline sold in Washington. A price increase in Washington, when no such price increase occurs in Virginia or Maryland, will induce many customers to buy their gasoline outside the nation's capital. Although this seems obvious (with hindsight), it was a surprise to Washington officials, who repealed the tax in December 1980.

One important moral of this tale is that one cannot assume that the price elasticity of demand for a good is the same, regardless of the market. Perhaps a rose is a rose is a rose; but a price elasticity can vary a lot, depending on what market you are talking about. To grab a price elasticity for a particular good off the shelf and apply it, regardless of the market to which it pertains, can be a formula for disaster.

If its price decreases, a great many buyers of substitutes will switch to this product. Naturally, the closeness of the substitutes depends on how narrowly the commodity is defined. In general, one would expect that, as the definition of the product becomes narrower and more specific, the product has more close substitutes and its price elasticity of demand is higher. Thus the demand for a particular brand of oil is more price elastic than the overall demand for oil, and the demand for oil is more price elastic than the demand for fuel as a whole. If a commodity is defined so that it has perfect substitutes, its price elasticity of demand approaches infinity. Thus, if one farmer's wheat is exactly like that grown by other farmers and if the farmer raises the price slightly (to a point above the market level), the farmer's sales will be reduced to nothing.

Importance in Consumers' Budgets. It is often asserted that the price elasticity of demand for a commodity is likely to depend on the importance of the commodity in consumers' budgets. The elasticity of demand for commodities like pepper and salt may be quite low. Typical consumers spend a very small portion of their income on pepper and salt, and the quantity they demand may not be influenced much by changes in price within a reasonable range. However, although a tendency of this sort is often hypothesized, there is no guarantee that it always exists.

Length of the Period. Every market demand curve pertains, you will recall, to a certain time interval. In general, *demand is likely to be more sensitive to price over a long period than over a short one.* The longer the period, the easier it is for consumers and business firms to substitute one good for another. If, for example, the price of oil should decline relative to other fuels, oil consumption in the month after the price decline would probably increase very little. But over a period of several years, people would have an opportunity to take account of the price decline in choosing the type of fuel to be used in new and renovated houses and businesses. In the longer period of several years, the price decline would have a greater effect on the consumption of oil than in the shorter period of one month.

Price Elasticity and Total Money Expenditure

Basic Idea #41: People commonly assume that a price reduction will lower the amount spent on a commodity, and that a price increase will raise it. The truth is that, whether the price is raised or lowered, the effect may be either an increase or decrease in the amount spent on the commodity: It all depends on the price elasticity of demand.

Many important decisions hinge on the price elasticity of demand for a commodity. One reason why this is so is that the price elasticity of demand determines whether a given change in price will increase or decrease the amount of money spent on a commodity—often a matter of basic importance to firms and government agencies. (Recall the case of the Boston and Maine Railroad.) In this section, we show how the price elasticity of demand determines the effect of a price change on the total amount spent on a commodity.

As a first step, we must define three terms—price elastic, price inelastic, and unitary elasticity. The demand for a commodity is **price elastic** if the price elasticity of demand is *greater than 1.* The demand for a commodity is **price inelastic** if the price elasticity of demand is *less than 1.* And the demand for a commodity is of **unitary elasticity** if the price elasticity of demand *equals 1.* As indicated below, the effect of a price change on the total amount spent on a commodity depends on whether the demand for

In 1905 the average automobile produced in the United States cost more than the average Datsun seventy years later. Many of the firms in the auto industry were warmed-over buggy makers who hand-crafted rich men's toys. But change was in the air. *Motor Age,* the industry's first trade magazine, prophesied that "the simple car is the car of the future—. A golden opportunity awaits some bold manufacturer of a simple car."

It remained for Henry Ford, the son of a Wisconsin farmer, to translate these words into a car—the Model T. Ford, commenting on his rural youth, declared, "It was life on the farm that drove me into devising ways and means to better transportation." Turning from the kid glove and

Henry Ford in his first automobile, 1903

checkbook set, he saw the potential market—at the right price—for car sales in the agricultural community.

The Model T was introduced in 1909. A few numbers indicate its phenomenal progress.

Year	Price (dollars)	Cars Sold
1909	900	58,022
1914	440	472,350
1916	360	730,041

However, all good things come to an end. By the twenties, Ford's unwillingness to alter the Model T in any fashion (cosmetic or mechanical), as well as increased competition from other manufacturers, and the development of trade-in and installment buying (which reduced the price elasticity of demand for automobiles) brought the Model T to an end. But the record profits of the Ford Motor Company between 1910 and 1920 vindicated Henry Ford in his belief that "it is better to sell a large number of cars at a reasonably small margin than to sell fewer cars at a larger margin of profit. Bear in mind that when you reduce the price of the car without reducing the quality you increase the possible number of purchases. There are many men who will pay $360 for a car who would not pay $440. I figure that on the $360 basis we can increase the sales to 800,000 cars for the year—less profit on each car, but more cars, more employment of labor and in the end, we get all the profit we ought to make." Needless to say, price reductions do not always result in higher profits. But in his appraisal of the auto market between 1910 and 1920, Henry Ford seemed right.*

E.A.

*Henry Ford, ed. John B. Rae, Englewood Cliffs, N.J.: Prentice-Hall, 1969, p. 112.

the commodity is price elastic, price inelastic, or of unitary elasticity. Let's consider each case.

CASE 1: DEMAND IS PRICE ELASTIC

In this case, if the price of the commodity is *reduced,* the total amount spent on the commodity will *increase.* To see why, suppose that the price elasticity of demand for hi-fi sets is 2 and that the price of the hi-fi sets is reduced by 1 percent. Because the price elasticity of demand is 2, the 1 percent reduction in price results in a 2 percent increase in quantity of hi-fi sets demanded. Since the total amount spent on hi-fi sets equals the quantity demanded times the price, the 1 percent reduction in price will be more than offset by the 2 percent increase in quantity demanded. The result of the price cut will be an increase in the total amount spent on hi-fi sets.

On the other hand, if the price of the commodity is *increased,* the total amount spent on the commodity will *fall.* For example, if the price of hi-fi sets is raised by 1 percent, this will reduce the quantity demanded by 2 percent. The 2 percent reduction in the quantity demanded will more than offset the 1 percent increase in price, the result being a decrease in the total amount spent on hi-fi sets.

CASE 2: DEMAND IS PRICE INELASTIC

In this case, if the price is *reduced,* the total amount spent on the commodity will *decrease.* To see why, suppose that the price elasticity of demand for corn is 0.5 and the price of corn is reduced by 1 percent. Because the price elasticity of demand is 0.5, the 1 percent price reduction results in a ½ percent increase in the quantity demanded of corn. Since the total amount spent on corn equals the quantity demanded times the price, the ½ percent increase in the quantity demanded will be more than offset by the 1 percent reduction in price. The result of the price cut will be a decrease in the total amount spent on corn.

On the other hand, if the price of the commodity is *increased,* the total amount spent on the commodity will *increase.* For example, if the price of corn is raised by 1 percent, this will reduce quantity demanded by ½ percent. The 1 percent price increase will more than offset the ½ percent reduction in quantity demanded, the result being an increase in the total amount spent on corn.

CASE 3: DEMAND IS OF UNITARY ELASTICITY

In this case, a price increase or decrease results in no difference in the total amount spent on the commodity. Why? Because a price decrease (increase) of a certain percentage always results in a quantity increase (decrease) of the same percentage, so that the product of the price and quantity is unaffected.

Table 21.3 summarizes the results of this section. It should help you review our findings.

Table 21.3

EFFECT OF AN INCREASE OR DECREASE
IN THE PRICE OF A COMMODITY ON THE
TOTAL EXPENDITURE ON THE
COMMODITY

Commodity's price elasticity of demand	Effect on total expenditure of:	
	Price decrease	Price increase
Price elastic (which means that elasticity is greater than 1)	Increase	Decrease
Price inelastic (which means that elasticity is less than 1)	Decrease	Increase
Unitary elasticity (which means that elasticity equals 1)	No change	No change

Test Yourself

1. Professor Kenneth Warner of the University of Michigan estimated in 1984 that a 10 percent increase in the price of cigarettes results in a 4 percent decline in the quantity of cigarettes consumed. For teenagers, he estimated that a 10 percent price increase results in a 14 percent decline in cigarette consumption. Based on his estimates, what is the price elasticity of demand for cigarettes? Among teenagers, what is the price elasticity of demand? Why is the price elasticity different among teenagers than for the public as a whole?

2. Suppose that each of the four corners of an intersection contains a gas station, and that the gasoline is essentially the same. Do you think that the price elasticity of demand for each station's gasoline is above or below 1? Why? Do you think that it is less than or greater than the price elasticity of demand for all gasoline in the U.S.?

3. The Bugsbane Music Box Company is convinced that an increase in its price will reduce the total amount of money spent on its product. Can you tell from this whether the demand for its product is price elastic or price inelastic?

4. Suppose that the relationship between the price of aluminum and the quantity of aluminum demanded is as follows:

Price (dollars)	Quantity
1	8
2	7
3	6
4	5
5	4

What is the arc elasticity of demand when price is between $1 and $2? Between $4 and $5?

The Farm Problem and the Price Elasticity of Demand

To illustrate the importance of the price elasticity of demand, let's return to the nation's farm problems. One of the most difficult problems for farmers is that, under a free market, farm incomes vary enormously between good times and bad, the variation being much greater than for nonfarm incomes. This is so because farm prices vary a great deal between good times and bad, whereas farm output is much more stable than industrial output. Why is agriculture like this?

The answer lies in considerable part with the price elasticity of demand for farm products. As we emphasized in Chapter 4, food is a necessity with few good substitutes. Thus we would expect the demand for farm products to be price inelastic. And as Table 21.2 suggests, this expectation is borne out by the facts. Given that the demand curve for farm products is price inelastic—and that the quantity supplied of farm products is also relatively insensitive to price—it follows that relatively small shifts in either the supply curve or the demand curve result in big changes in price. This is why farm prices are so unstable. Panel A of Figure 21.4 shows a market where the demand curve is much more inelastic than in panel B. As you can see, a small shift to the left in the demand curve results in a much larger drop in price in panel A than in panel B.

PRICE ELASTICITY AND THE BRANNAN PLAN

This is not the only role the price elasticity of demand plays in our farm problems. Many other questions involve it. Consider the plan proposed after World War II by Charles Brannan who served as President Truman's secretary of agriculture. The plan was later supported in somewhat modified form by Ezra Taft Benson, secretary of agriculture in the Eisenhower administration. But it drew fire from many farmers, and not until 1973,

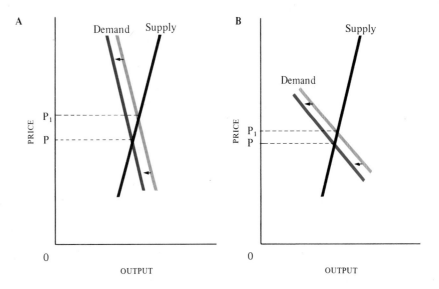

A

B

Figure 21.4
Instability of Farm Prices and Incomes
Because the demand curve in panel A is much less elastic than in panel B, a small shift in the demand curve has a much bigger impact on price in panel A than in panel B.

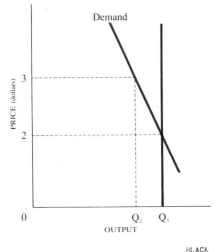

BLACK

Figure 21.5
Effect of the Brannan Plan *Under the Brannan plan, the competitive market would be let alone, so that, if output were OQ_3, the price would be $2. Then the government would pay farmers the difference between this price and the target price, $3.*

after nearly three decades of controversy, was the plan approved by Congress.

According to the **Brannan plan,** a floor is established under the price received by farmers. Suppose that the market price is below this target level. If the target level is $3 in Figure 21.5, and if the output quota is OQ_3, this plan lets the competitive market alone, so that the output of OQ_3 is sold at a price of $2. Then according to this plan, the government issues subsidy checks to farmers to cover the difference between the market price ($2) and the target price ($3).

The cost to the Treasury under the Brannan plan is $(\$3 - \$2) \times OQ_3$. Why? Because the Treasury pays a subsidy of $(\$3 - \$2)$ per bushel, and OQ_3 bushels are grown; thus the total subsidy is $(\$3 - \$2) \times OQ_3$. Before the Brannan plan was adopted, the government supported the price at $3, and bought the amount—$(OQ_3 - OQ_2)$—that private buyers would not purchase at that price. The cost to the Treasury under this system is $3 $(OQ_3 - OQ_2)$. Why? Because the Treasury buys $(OQ_3 - OQ_2)$ bushels at $3 per bushel.

An important question is: Will the cost to the U.S Treasury under the Brannan plan be greater than under the previous system? The answer can be shown to depend on the price elasticity of demand. As demonstrated in footnote 4, the cost under the Brannan plan is greater than under the previous system[4] if $\$2 \times OQ_3 < \$3 \times OQ_2$. But since $\$2 \times OQ_3$ is the total money expenditure at a price of $2 and $\$3 \times OQ_2$ is the total money expenditure at a price of $3, it follows from the previous section that $\$2 \times OQ_3$ will be less than $\$3 \times OQ_2$ if the price elasticity of demand is less than 1. (Why? Because the total amount spent on a commodity will be less at a lower price [such as $2] than at a higher price [such as $3] if demand is price inelastic.) Thus, since the elasticity of demand for farm

[4] The cost to the government under the Brannan plan is $(\$3 - \$2) \times OQ_3 = \$3 \times OQ_3 - \$2 \times OQ_3$, while the cost under the other system is $\$3 \times (OQ_3 - OQ_2) = \$3 \times OQ_3 - \$3 \times OQ_2$. Thus the difference between the former cost and the latter is $\$3 \times OQ_2 - \$2 \times OQ_3$, which means that the cost under the Brannan plan would be greater than under the other system if $\$2 \times OQ_3 < \$3 \times OQ_2$.

products is in fact less than 1, the cost to the Treasury will be greater under the Brannan plan than under a system whereby the price is supported at $3, with the government clearing the market of the farm products not purchased by the private sector at that price.[5]

Our purpose here is not to decide whether the Brannan plan is good or bad. To make such a decision, we would have to take account of many factors besides the cost to the Treasury. Instead, our point is that the price elasticity of demand is an important concept in discussing the effects of the Brannan plan, just as in discussing the instability of farm income and prices. Moreover, as we shall see in subsequent sections, the price elasticity of demand is equally as important in problems concerning the industrial sector of the economy as in problems concerning agriculture.

Industry and Firm Demand Curves

Up to this point, we have been dealing with the market demand curve for a commodity. *The market demand curve for a commodity is not the same as the market demand curve for the output of a single firm that produces the commodity, unless, of course, the industry is composed of only a single firm.* If the industry is composed of more than one firm, as is usually the case, the demand curve for the output of each firm producing the commodity will usually be quite different from the demand curve for the commodity. The demand curve for the output of Farmer Brown's wheat is quite different from the market demand curve for wheat.

In particular, the demand curve for the output of a particular firm is generally more price elastic than the market demand curve for the commodity, because the products of other firms in the industry are close substitutes for the product of this firm. As pointed out earlier, products with many close substitutes have relatively high price elasticities of demand.

If there are many, many firms selling a homogeneous product, the individual firm's demand curve becomes *horizontal,* or essentially so. To see this, suppose that 100,000 firms sell a particular commodity and that each of these firms is of equal size. If any one of these firms were to triple its output and sales, the total industry output would change by only .002 percent—too small a change to have any perceptible effect on the price of the commodity. Consequently, each firm can act as if variations in its output—within the range of its capabilities—will have no real impact on market price. In other words, the demand curve facing the individual firm is horizontal, as in Figure 21.6.

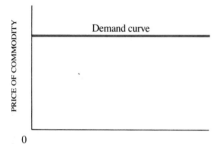

Figure 21.6

Demand Curve for Output of an Individual Firm: The Case of a Great Many Sellers of a Homogeneous Commodity *If there are many firms selling a homogeneous product, the demand curve facing an individual firm is horizontal.*

Basic Idea #42: Be careful to distinguish between the market demand curve for a commodity and the market demand curve for the output of a single firm producing the commodity. The latter is generally much more price elastic than the former. Indeed, if there are a great many firms selling a homogeneous product, the individual firm's demand curve becomes horizontal, or close to it.

Income Elasticity of Demand

So far this chapter has dealt almost exclusively with the effect of a commodity's price on the quantity demanded of it in the market. But price is not, of course, the only factor that influences the quantity demanded of

---

[5] Note that this result does not depend on our choice of $3 as the target price and of $2 as the market price. Regardless of what the target price and market price may be, this result will hold, if the price elasticity of demand is less than 1.

the commodity. Another important factor is the level of money income among the consumers in the market. The sensitivity of the quantity demanded to the total money income of all of the consumers in the market is measured by the ***income elasticity of demand,*** *which is defined as the percentage change in the quantity demanded resulting from a 1 percent increase in total money income (all prices being held constant).*

A commodity's income elasticity of demand may be positive or negative. For many commodities, increases in income result in increases in the amount demanded. Such commodities, like steak or caviar, have positive income elasticities of demand. For other commodities, increases in income result in decreases in the amount demanded. These commodities, like margarine and poor grades of vegetables, have negative income elasticities of demand. However, be careful to note that the income elasticity of demand of a commodity is likely to vary with the level of income under consideration. For example, if only families at the lowest income levels are considered, the income elasticity of demand for margarine may be positive.

Luxury items tend to have higher income elasticities of demand than necessities. Indeed, one way to define luxuries and necessities is to say that luxuries are commodities with high income elasticities of demand, and necessities are commodities with low income elasticities of demand.

EMPIRICAL STUDIES

Many studies have been made to estimate the income elasticity of demand for particular commodities, since, like the price elasticity of demand, it is of great importance to decision makers. In making long-term forecasts of industry sales, for example, firms must take the income elasticity of demand into account. Thus, if the income elasticity of demand for a product is high, and if incomes increase considerably during the next 20 years, the product's sales will tend to increase greatly during that period. On the other hand, if the income elasticity of demand for a product is close to zero, one would expect the product's sales not to increase very much on account of such increases in income.

To illustrate the findings of empirical studies in this area, consider the following results obtained by Herman Wold, a distinguished Swedish economist. According to his estimates, the income elasticity of demand is 0.37 for eggs, 0.34 for cheese, 0.42 for butter, 1.00 for liquor, −0.20 for margarine, 0.07 for milk and cream, and 1.48 for restaurant consumption of food. Certainly, these estimates seem reasonable. One would expect the income elasticity of demand to be negative for margarine, because consumers tend to view margarine as an inferior good, and as their incomes rise, they tend to switch from margarine to butter. Also, it is not surprising that the income elasticity of demand for milk and cream is close to zero, since people tend to view milk and cream as necessities, particularly for children. In addition, it is quite reasonable that the income elasticity of demand for liquor and restaurant consumption of food is higher than for the other commodities. Liquor and restaurant meals tend to be luxury items for most people.

Example 21.2   The Demand for "Suds"

According to Thomas Fogarty and Kenneth Elzinga,* the price elasticity of demand for beer in the United States is about 0.8, and the income elasticity of demand for beer is about 0.4.

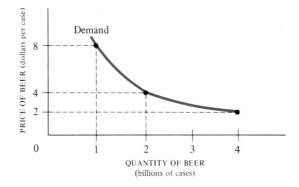

(a) Is the demand curve shown above consistent with their findings? Why or why not? (b) If the price of a case of beer increases, will this result in an increase or decrease in the amount of money spent per year on beer? (c) If consumer income increases by 15 percent, while the price of beer remains constant, what will be the effect on the amount of money spent per year on beer? (d) Holding the prices of other goods and income constant, do you think that the market demand curve for beer varies from month to month? From state to state? If so, why? (e) If Budweiser lowers the price of its beer by 1 percent, can it expect to increase the quantity it sells by 0.8 percent? Why or why not? (f) At the close of 1953, Budweiser was selling for 58 cents per case more than its rivals in the St. Louis market and had 12 percent of the market. In early 1955, Budweiser sold its beer at the same price as its rivals and had 39 percent of the market. Suppose that other brewers held their price constant at $2 per case during this period, and that the total amount of beer sold in this market was constant during this period. What was the price elasticity of demand for Budweiser beer in this market?

SOLUTION

(a) No. According to this demand curve, the price elasticity of demand for beer is 1, since the amount spent on beer is the same ($8 billion) regardless of the price. (b) Increase. (c) It will increase by about 6 percent. (d) Yes, because of differences among months and states in temperature, tastes, and other factors. (e) No. Because Budweiser is only one firm in the market, the percentage increase in the quantity it sells is likely to be greater than 0.8 percent, if other firms hold their price constant. (f) $- (.39X - .12X)/.255X \div (\$2.00 - \$2.58)/\$2.29 = 4.2.$ (X is the total amount of beer sold in this market then.)

* T. Fogarty and K. Elzinga, "The Demand for Beer," *Review of Economics and Statistics,* May 1972.

Cross Elasticity of Demand

Besides the price of the commodity and the level of total money income—the factors discussed primarily in previous sections of this chapter—the quantity demanded of a commodity also depends on the prices of other commodities. Suppose the price of butter is held constant. The amount of butter demanded will be influenced by the price of margarine. The *cross elasticity of demand, defined as the percentage change in the quantity demanded of one commodity resulting from a 1 percent change in the price of another commodity, is used to measure the sensitivity of the former commodity's quantity demanded to changes in the latter commodity's price.*

Pairs of commodities are classified as **substitutes** or **complements,** depending on the sign of the cross elasticity of demand. *If the cross elasticity of demand is positive, two commodities are substitutes.* Butter and margarine are substitutes because a decrease in the price of butter will result in a decrease in the quantity demanded of margarine—many margarine eaters really prefer the "higher-priced spread." *On the other hand, if the cross elasticity of demand is negative, two commodities are complements.* For example, gin and tonic may be complements since a decrease in the price of gin may increase the quantity demanded of tonic. The reduction in the price of gin will increase the quantity demanded of gin, thus increasing the quantity demanded of tonic since gin and tonic tend to be used together.

Many studies have been made of the cross elasticity of demand for various pairs of commodities. After all, it frequently is very important to know how a change in the price of one commodity will affect the sales of another commodity. For example, what would be the effect of a 1 percent increase in the price of pork on the quantity demanded of beef? According to Herman Wold's estimates, the effect would be a .28 percent increase in the quantity demanded of beef—since he estimates that the cross elasticity of demand for these two commodities is 0.28. What effect would a 1 percent increase in the price of butter have on the quantity demanded of margarine? According to Wold, the effect would be a .81 percent increase in the quantity demanded of margarine—since he estimates that the cross elasticity of demand for these two commodities is 0.81.

Test Yourself

1. Is each of the following statements true, partly true, or false? Explain. (a) If a good's income elasticity of demand is less than one, an increase in the price of the good will increase the amount spent on it. (b) The income elasticity of demand will have the same sign regardless of the level of income at which it is measured. (c) If Mr. Miller spends all of his income on steak (regardless of his income or the price of steak), Mr. Miller's cross elasticity of demand between steak and any other good is zero.

2. What is the sign of the cross elasticity of demand for each of the following pairs of commodities: (a) tea and coffee, (b) tennis rackets and tennis balls, (c) whiskey and gin, (d) fishing licenses and fishing poles, (e) nylon rugs and wool rugs?

3. On page 468, we saw the quantity of Model T's sold increased from about 472,000 to about 730,000 when its price was reduced from $440 in 1914 to $360 in 1916. How can this fact be reconciled with recent studies which indicate that the price elasticity of demand for automobiles is about 1.2 to 1.5?

4. According to the U.S. Department of Agriculture, the income elasticity of demand for coffee is about 0.23. If incomes rose by 1 percent, what effect would this have on the quantity demanded of coffee?

Summary

1. The market demand curve, which is the relationship between the price of a commodity and the amount of the commodity demanded in the market, is one of the most important and frequently used concepts in economics. The shape and position of a product's market demand curve depend on consumers' tastes, consumer incomes, the price of other goods, and the number of consumers in the market.

2. The market demand curve for a commodity is not the same as the demand curve for the output of a single firm that produces the commodity, unless the industry is composed of only one firm. In general, the demand curve for the output of a single firm will be more elastic than the market demand curve for the commodity. Indeed, if there are many firms selling a homogeneous commodity, the individual firm's demand curve becomes horizontal.

3. There are many techniques for measuring demand curves, such as interview studies, direct experiments, and the statistical analysis of historical data. An example of a direct experiment was the project carried out by the Boston and Maine Railroad.

4. The price elasticity of demand, defined as the percentage change in quantity demanded resulting from a 1 percent change in price, measures the sensitivity of the amount demanded to changes in price. Whether a price increase results in an increase or decrease in the total amount spent on a commodity depends on the price elasticity of demand.

5. The income elasticity of demand, defined as the percentage change in quantity demanded resulting from a 1 percent increase in total money income, measures the sensitivity of the amount demanded to changes in total income. A commodity's income elasticity of demand may be positive or negative. Luxury items are generally assumed to have higher income elasticities of demand than necessities.

6. The cross elasticity of demand, defined as the percentage change in the quantity demanded resulting from a 1 percent change in the price of another commodity, measures the sensitivity of the amount demanded to changes in the price of another commodity. If the cross elasticity of demand is positive, two commodities are substitutes; if it is negative, they are complements.

Concepts for Review

Market demand curve	Price elastic	Cross elasticity of demand
Direct market experiment	Price inelastic	
Price elasticity of demand	Unitary elasticity	Substitute
Arc elasticity of demand	Brannan plan	Complement
	Income elasticity of demand	

CHAPTER 22

Getting behind the Demand Curve: Consumer Behavior

To a considerable extent, consumers, voting with their pocketbooks, are the masters of our economic system. No wonder, then, that economists spend much of their time describing and analyzing how consumers act. In this chapter, we present the basic model economists use to analyze consumer behavior.

Consumer Expenditures

THE WALTERS OF SAN DIEGO

Since we are concerned here with consumer behavior, perhaps the best way to begin is to look at the behavior of a particular consumer. It is hard to find any consumer who is "typical." There are hundreds of millions of consumers in the United States, and they vary enormously. Nonetheless, it is instructive to look at how a particular American family—the Walters of San Diego[1]—spends its money. The Walters are in their mid-thirties, have two children (ages 8 and 6), and have Mrs. Walter's younger brother living with them. They own their own home, and both work. Mr. Walter manages a small clothing firm in San Diego, and Mrs. Walter is a designer at the same firm. Together, the Walters make about $43,000 a year.

[1] For obvious reasons, we have changed the name and residence of the family in question. Otherwise, however, the facts given in the following paragraphs are as they were stated in a national magazine. To correct for inflation, we have increased the figures in the article by the (approximate) percentage by which the price level has risen since the article appeared.

Table 22.1

MONTHLY SPENDING PATTERN OF MR. AND MRS. WALTER OF SAN DIEGO, CALIFORNIA

Item	Amount (dollars)	Percent of income
Housing	1,250	35
Food and drink	500	14
Domestic help	250	7
Private school and education	260	7
Entertainment and clothing	260	7
Medical, dental, and insurance expenses	250	7
Transportation	85	2
Taxes and savings[a]	745	21
Monthly income	3,600	100

[a]Estimated by deducting other items from monthly income.

How do the Walters spend their money? For most consumers, we cannot answer this question with any accuracy, because the people in question simply do not tell anyone what they do with their money. But because the Walters and their buying habits were scrutinized in a series of articles in a national magazine, it is possible to describe quite accurately where their money goes. As shown in Table 22.1, the Walters, who own their own home, spend about $1,250 a month—about 35 percent of their income—on housing. In addition, they spend about $500 a month—about 14 percent of their income—on food and drink. Also, they spend about $250 a month—about 7 percent of their income—on domestic help, which is needed since both parents work.

In addition, as shown in Table 22.1, the Walters spend about $260 a month—about 7 percent of their income—on private schools and other lessons for their children. Another $260 a month goes for entertainment and clothing. Because of the mild weather in San Diego (and perhaps because they can get clothing at a discount since they are in the clothing business), their expenditures on clothing are not very large. Medical, dental, and insurance expenses consume about $250 a month—again, about 7 percent of income—and $85 a month—or about 2 percent of their income—is spent on transportation. Finally, the Walters allocate about $745 a month—about 21 percent of their income—for taxes and savings.

This, in a nutshell, is how the Walters spend their money. The Walters exchange their resources—mostly labor—in the resource markets for $43,000 a year. They take this money into the product markets and spend about four-fifths of it for the goods and services described above. The remaining one-fifth of their income goes for taxes and saving. The Walters, like practically every family, keep a watchful eye on where their money goes and what they are getting in exchange for their labor and other resources. As stressed in Chapter 2, the basic purpose of our economic system is to satisfy the wants of consumers.

AGGREGATE DATA FOR THE UNITED STATES

How does the way that the Walters spend their money compare with consumer behavior in general? In Table 22.2, we provide data on how all con-

Table 22.2

ALLOCATION OF INCOME BY U.S.
HOUSEHOLDS, 1983

	Percent of total[a]
Personal taxes	15
Personal saving	4
Interest payments	2
Consumption expenditures	
Autos and parts	5
Furniture and household equipment	4
Other durable goods	2
Food and drink	15
Clothing and shoes	5
Gasoline and oil	3
Other nondurable goods	6
Housing	13
Household operations	6
Transportation	3
Other services	18
Total income	100

[a]Because of rounding errors, figures do not sum to total.

Source: Survey of Current Business, July 1984.

sumers allocated their aggregate income in 1983. These data tell us much more about the typical behavior of American consumers than our case study of the Walters. Note first of all that American households paid about 15 percent of their income in taxes. This, of course, is the price of governments services we described in Chapter 4. In addition, American households saved about 4 percent of their income. In other words, they refrained from spending 4 percent of their income on goods and services; instead, they put this amount into stocks, bonds, bank accounts, or other such channels for saving. Also, about 2 percent of their income went for interest payments to banks and other institutions from which they had borrowed money.

American consumers spent the remaining 79 percent of their income on goods and services. Table 22.2 makes it clear that they allocated much of their expenditures to housing, food and drink, and transportation. Spending on housing, household operations, and furniture and other durable household equipment accounted for about 23 percent of American consumers' total income. Spending on food and beverages accounted for about 15 percent of total income. Spending on automobiles and parts, gasoline and oil, and other transportation accounted for about 11 percent of total income. Thus taxes, savings, housing, food and drink, and transportation accounted for about 70 percent of the total income of all households in the United States.

The data in Table 22.2 make it obvious that the Walter family is not very typical of American consumers. For example, it spends a much larger percentage of its income on housing, domestic help, and education than do consumers as a whole. To some degree, this is because the Walters are more affluent than most American families, but this is only part of the reason. To a large extent, it simply reflects the fact that people want different things. Looking around you, you see considerable diversity in the way consumers spend their money. Take your own family as an example. It is a good bet that your family spends its money quite differently than the nation as a whole. If your parents like to live in a big house, your family may spend much more than the average on housing. Or if they like to go to sports events, their expenditures on such entertainment may be much higher than average.

A Model of Consumer Behavior

Why do consumers spend their money the way they do? The economist answers this question with the aid of a *model of consumer behavior,* which is useful both for analysis and for decision making. To construct this model, the economist obviously must consider the tastes of the consumer. As Henry Adams put it, "Everyone carries his own inch-rule of taste, and amuses himself by applying it, triumphantly, wherever he travels." Certainly one would expect that the amount a consumer purchases of a particular commodity is influenced by his or her tastes. Some people like beef, others like pork. Some people like the opera, others would trade a ticket to hear Luciano Pavarotti for a ticket to the Dallas Cowboys game any day of the week. Three assumptions, which seem reasonable for most purposes, underlie the economist's model of consumer preferences.

*Alfred Marshall (1842–1924) played a
major role in the construction of theories
of consumer demand, and pioneered in
many other areas of economics as well.
His* Principles of Economics *(1890),
which had eight editions, was a leading
economics text for many years.*

1. We assume that *consumers, when confronted with two alternative
market baskets, can decide whether they prefer the first to the second, the
second to the first, or whether they are indifferent between them.* For example, suppose Mrs. Walter, the San Diego designer, is confronted with a
choice between a market basket containing 3 chocolate bars and a ticket to
the movies and another market basket containing 2 chocolate bars and a
record of the Tabernacle Choir singing Chopin's Minute Waltz. Despite
the rather bizarre composition of these two market baskets, we assume
that she can somehow decide whether she prefers the first market basket to
the second, the second market basket to the first, or whether she is indifferent between them.

2. We assume that *the consumer's preferences are transitive.* The meaning of transitive in this context is simple enough. Suppose that Mrs. Walter
prefers an ounce of Chanel No. 5 perfume to an ounce of Blue Grass
perfume, and that she prefers an ounce of Blue Grass perfume to an ounce
of Sortilège perfume. Then, if her preferences are transitive, she must prefer
an ounce of Chanel No. 5 perfume to an ounce of Sortilège perfume. The
reason for this assumption is clear. If the consumer's preferences were not
transitive, the consumer would have inconsistent or contradictory preferences. Although some people may have preferences that are not transitive,
this assumption seems to be a reasonable first approximation—for the
noninstitutionalized part of the population at least.

3. We assume that *the consumer always prefers more of a commodity to
less.* For example, if one market basket contains 3 bars of soap and 2
monkey wrenches and a second contains 3 bars of soap and 3 monkey
wrenches, it is assumed that the second market basket is preferred to the
first. To a large extent, this assumption is justified by the definition of a
commodity as something the consumer desires.[2] This does not mean that
certain things are not a nuisance. If one market basket contains 3 bars of
soap and 2 rattlesnakes, we would not be at all surprised if the consumer
did *not* prefer this market basket to one containing 3 bars of soap and no
rattlesnakes. But to such a consumer, a rattlesnake would not be desired—
and thus would not be a commodity. Instead, the absence of a rattlesnake
would be desired—and would be a commodity.

TOTAL UTILITY

In Chapter 2, we pointed out that a model, to be useful, must omit many
unimportant factors, concentrate on the basic factors at work, and simplify
in order to illuminate. So that we focus on the important factors at work
here, let's assume that there are only two goods, food and clothing. This is
an innocuous assumption, since the results we shall obtain can be generalized to include cases where any number of goods exists. For simplicity,
food is measured in pounds, and clothing is measured in number of pieces
of clothing.

Consider Mrs. Walter, making choices for her family. Undoubtedly, she

---

[2] An individual's desire for a particular good during a particular period of time is not
infinite but in the aggregate human wants seem to be insatiable. Besides the basic desires for
food, shelter, and clothing, which must be fulfilled to some extent if the human organism is
to survive, wants arise from cultural factors. Advertising and the emulation of social leaders
stimulate and extend a person's wants.

regards certain market baskets—that is, certain combinations of food and clothing (the only commodities)—to be more desirable than others. She certainly regards 2 pounds of food and 1 piece of clothing to be more desirable than 1 pound of food and 1 piece of clothing. For simplicity, suppose that it is possible to measure the amount of satisfaction that she gets from each market basket by its utility. *A **utility** is a number that represents the level of satisfaction that the consumer derives from a particular market basket.* For example, the utility attached to the market basket containing 2 pounds of food and 1 piece of clothing may be 10 utils, and the utility attached to the market basket containing 1 pound of food and 1 piece of clothing may be 6 utils. (A util is the traditional unit in which utility is expressed.)

MARGINAL UTILITY

It is important to distinguish between total utility and marginal utility. The total utility of a market basket is the number described in the previous paragraph, whereas *the **marginal utility** measures the additional satisfaction derived from an additional unit of a commodity.* To see how marginal utility is obtained, let's take a close look at Table 22.3. The total utility the Walter family derives from the consumption of various amounts of food is given in the middle column of this table. (For simplicity, we assume for the moment that the Walters consume only food.) The marginal utility, shown in the right-hand column, is the extra utility derived from each amount of food over and above the utility derived from 1 less pound of food. Thus it equals the difference between the total utility of a certain amount of food and the total utility of 1 less pound of food.

For example, as shown in Table 22.3, the *total* utility of 3 pounds of food is 9 utils, which is a measure of the total amount of satisfaction that the Walters get from this much food. In contrast, the *marginal* utility of 3 pounds of food is the extra utility obtained from the third pound of food—that is, the total utility of 3 pounds of food less the total utility of 2 pounds of food. Specifically, as shown in Table 22.3, it is 2 utils. Similarly, the *total* utility of 2 pounds of food is 7 utils, which is a measure of the total amount of satisfaction that the Walters get from this much food. In contrast, the *marginal* utility of 2 pounds of food is the extra utility from the second pound of food—that is, the total utility of 2 pounds of food less the total utility of 1 pound of food. Specifically, as shown in Table 22.3, it is 4 utils.

THE LAW OF DIMINISHING MARGINAL UTILITY

Economists generally assume that, as a person consumes more and more of a particular commodity, there is, beyond some point, a decline in the extra satisfaction derived from the last unit of the commodity consumed. For example, if the Walters consume 2 pounds of food in a particular period of time, it may be just enough to meet their basic physical needs. If they consume 3 pounds of food in the same period of time, the third pound of food is likely to yield less satisfaction than the second. If they consume 4 pounds of food in the same period of time, the fourth pound of food is likely to yield less satisfaction than the third. And so on.

This assumption or hypothesis is often called the ***law of diminishing marginal utility.*** This law states that, *as a person consumes more and more*

Table 22.3

TOTAL UTILITY AND MARGINAL UTILITY DERIVED BY THE WALTERS FROM CONSUMING VARIOUS AMOUNTS OF FOOD PER DAY[a]

Pounds of food	Total utility	Marginal utility
0	0	
1	3	3 (=3–0)
2	7	4 (=7–3)
3	9	2 (=9–7)
4	10	1 (=10–9)

[a]This table assumes that no clothing is consumed. If a nonzero amount of clothing is consumed, the figures in this table will probably be altered since the marginal utility of a certain amount of food is likely to depend on the amount of clothing consumed.

of a given commodity (the consumption of other commodities being held constant), the marginal utility of the commodity eventually will tend to decline. The figures concerning the Walter family in Table 22.3 are in accord with this law, as shown in Figure 22.1, which plots the marginal utility of food against the amount consumed. Once the consumption of food exceeds about 1½ pounds, marginal utility of food declines.

The Equilibrium Market Basket

Preferences alone do not determine the consumer's actions. *Besides knowing the consumer's preferences, we must also know his or her income and the prices of commodities to predict which market basket he or she will buy.* The consumer's money income is the amount of money he or she can spend per unit of time. A consumer's choice of a market basket is constrained by the size of his or her money income. For example, although Mr. Walter may regard a Hickey Freeman as his favorite suit, he may not buy it because he may have insufficient funds (as the bankers delicately put it). Also, the market basket the consumer chooses is influenced by the prices of commodities. If the Hickey Freeman suit were offered by a discount store at $100, rather than its list price of $350, Mr. Walter might purchase it after all.

Given the consumer's tastes, economists assume that he or she attempts to maximize utility. In other words, *consumers are assumed to be rational in the sense that they choose the market basket—or more generally, the course of action—that is most to their liking.* As previously noted, consumers cannot choose whatever market basket they please. Instead, they must maximize their utility subject to the constraints imposed by the size of their money income and the nature of commodity prices.

What is the optimal market basket, the one that maximizes utility subject to these constraints? It is the one where *the consumer's income is allocated among commodities so that, for every commodity purchased, the marginal utility of the commodity is proportional to its price.* Thus, in the case of the Walter family, the optimal market basket is the one where

$$\frac{MU_F}{P_F} = \frac{MU_C}{P_C}, \qquad (22.1)$$

where MU_F is the marginal utility of food, MU_C is the marginal utility of clothing, P_F is the price of a pound of food, and P_C is the price of a piece of clothing.

WHY IS THIS RULE CORRECT?

To understand why the rule in Equation (22.1) is correct, it is convenient to begin by pointing out that $MU_F \div P_F$ is the marginal utility of the *last dollar's worth* of food and that $MU_C \div P_C$ is the marginal utility of the *last dollar's worth* of clothing. To see why this is so, take the case of food. Since MU_F is the extra utility of the *last pound* of food bought, and since P_F is the price of this *last pound,* the extra utility of the *last dollar's worth* of food must be $MU_F \div P_F$. For example, if the last pound of food results in

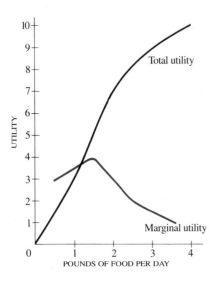

Figure 22.1
Total and Marginal Utility from Food Consumption, Walter Family *The marginal utility of the first pound of food (which, according to Table 22.3, equals 3 utils) is plotted at the midpoint between 0 and 1 pounds of food. The marginal utility of the second pound of food (which, according to Table 22.3, equals 4 utils) is plotted at the midpoint between 1 and 2 pounds of food. The marginal-utility curve connects these and other points showing the marginal utility of various amounts of food consumed.*

Beyond some point, the marginal utility curve of any commodity would be expected to fall, because of the law of diminishing marginal utility (which states that, as a person consumes more and more of a given commodity, the marginal utility of the commodity eventually will tend to decline). In the case shown here, the marginal utility curve falls when the Walter family's consumption of food exceeds about 1½ pounds per day.

an extra utility of 4 utils and this pound costs $2, then the extra utility from the last dollar's worth of food must be 4 ÷ 2, or 2 utils. In other words, the marginal utility of the last dollar's worth of food is 2 utils.

Since $MU_F \div P_F$ is the marginal utility of the last dollar's worth of food and $MU_C \div P_C$ is the marginal utility of the last dollar's worth of clothing, what Equation (22.1) really says is that *the rational consumer will choose a market basket where the marginal utility of the last dollar spent on all commodities purchased is the same.* To see why this must be so, consider the numerical example in Table 22.4, which shows the marginal utility the Walters derive from various amounts of food and clothing. Rather than measuring food and clothing in physical units, we measure them in Table 22.4 in terms of the amount of money spent on them.

Given the information in Table 22.4, how much of each commodity should Mrs. Walter buy if her money income is only $4 (a ridiculous assumption but one that will help to make our point)? Clearly, the first dollar she spends should be on food since it will yield her a marginal utility of 20. The second dollar she spends should also be on food since a second dollar's worth of food has a marginal utility of 16. (Thus the total utility derived from the $2 of expenditure is 20 + 16 = 36.)[3] The marginal utility of the third dollar is 12 if it is spent on more food—and 12 too if it is spent on clothing. Suppose that she chooses more food. (The total utility derived from the $3 of expenditure is 20 + 16 + 12 = 48.) What about the final dollar? Its marginal utility is 10 if it is spent on more food and 12 if it is spent on clothing; thus she will spend it on clothing. (The total utility derived from all $4 of expenditure is then 20 + 16 + 12 + 12 = 60.)

Thus Mrs. Walter, if she is rational, will allocate $3 of her income to food and $1 to clothing. This is the **equilibrium market basket,** the market basket that maximizes consumer satisfaction. The important thing to note is that this market basket demonstrates the principle set forth earlier in Equation (22.1). As shown in Table 22.4, the marginal utility derived from the last dollar spent on food is equal to the marginal utility derived from the last dollar spent on clothing. (Both are 12.) Thus this market basket has the characteristic described above: the marginal utility of the last dollar spent on all commodities purchased is the same. In the next section, we show that this will always be the case for market baskets that maximize the consumer's utility. If it were not true, the consumer could obtain a higher level of utility by changing the composition of his or her market basket.

FURTHER PROOF OF THE BUDGET ALLOCATION RULE

In the previous section, we stated the proposition that the consumer, to maximize utility, will choose a market basket where the marginal utility of the last dollar spent on all commodities purchased is the same. In this section, we show that, if this budget allocation rule is not followed, the consumer cannot be maximizing utility. This is offered as further proof of the proposition in the previous section. For simplicity, we assume that the consumer buys only two commodities, food and clothing.

Table 22.4

MARGINAL UTILITY DERIVED BY THE WALTERS FROM VARIOUS QUANTITIES OF FOOD AND CLOTHING

Commodity	Dollars worth				
	1	2	3	4	5
	Marginal utility (utils)				
Food	20	16	12	10	7
Clothing	12	10	7	5	3

Basic Idea #43: If any person or organization has a fixed sum of money which must be allocated among a variety of uses, the money should be allocated so that the marginal utility of the last dollar spent on each use is the same. The marginal utility of the last dollar spent on each use is the critically important factor.

---

[3] Since the marginal utility is the extra utility obtained from each dollar spent, the total utility from the total expenditure must be the sum of the marginal utilities of the individual dollars of expenditure.

Suppose that the marginal utility of the last dollar spent on food is 5 utils whereas the marginal utility of the last dollar spent on clothing is 3 utils. The consumer is not maximizing utility, because spending $1 more on food will increase total utility by 5 utils,[4] and spending $1 less on clothing will reduce total utility by 3 utils. Thus the transfer of $1 of expenditure from clothing to food will increase total utility by 2 utils—which

---

[4] We assume here that the extra utility from an *extra* dollar spent on food equals the extra utility from the *last* dollar spent on food. This is an innocuous assumption.

Example 22.1   The Diamond-Water Paradox

In 1985, a perfect blue-white diamond sold for over $10,000 per carat, while a gallon of water sold for about 2 cents per hundred gallons. For centuries, people have been fascinated by this fact. Diamonds, after all, are hardly essential to life, whereas water *is* essential. How is it, then, that people are willing to buy diamonds at a price that seems so much higher than that of water? Suppose that the typical consumer's marginal utility curves for diamonds and water are as shown below:

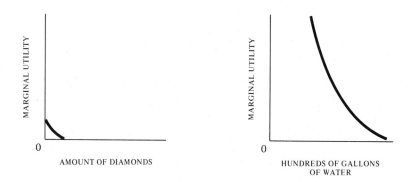

(a) If the price per carat of a diamond is 500,000 times as great as the price per hundred gallons of water, and if the consumer buys both diamonds and water, does it follow that the total utility that the consumer receives from the diamonds is 500,000 times as great as the total utility received from the water? (b) Does it follow that the marginal utility of a carat of diamonds is 500,000 times as great as the marginal utility of a hundred gallons of water? (c) If the consumer buys a great deal of water and practically no diamonds, is it possible that the marginal utility of a carat of diamonds will be 500,000 times as great as the marginal utility of a hundred gallons of water? (d) Describe in your own words why people are willing to buy diamonds at a price that seems so much higher than that of water.

SOLUTION

(a) No. If the consumer is maximizing utility, the *marginal* utility of a carat of diamonds must be 500,000 times as great as the *marginal* utility of a hundred gallons of water. But there is no reason to believe that this is true of the *total* utilities. (b) Yes. (c) Yes. (d) They buy practically no diamonds and very large quantities of water. The marginal utility of diamonds is so much higher than the marginal utility of water that the marginal utility of the last dollar spent on diamonds is equal to the marginal utility of the last dollar spent on water.

means that the consumer currently isn't maximizing utility. More generally, a transfer of expenditure from clothing to food will always increase a consumer's utility so long as the marginal utility of the last dollar spent on food exceeds the marginal utility of the last dollar spent on clothing. Thus *the consumer will not be maximizing utility if the marginal utility of the last dollar spent on food exceeds the marginal utility of the last dollar spent on clothing.*

Suppose that the situation is reversed, the marginal utility of the last dollar spent on food being 3 utils and the marginal utility of the last dollar spent on clothing being 5 utils. The consumer is not maximizing utility, because spending $1 more on clothing will increase total utility by 5 utils,[5] and spending $1 less on food will reduce total utility by 3 utils. Thus the transfer of $1 of expenditure from food to clothing will result in a net increase of utility of 2 utils—which means that the consumer currently isn't maximizing utility. More generally, a transfer of expenditure from food to clothing will always increase total utility so long as the marginal utility of the last dollar spent on clothing exceeds the marginal utility of the last dollar spent on food. Thus *the consumer will not be maximizing utility if the marginal utility of the last dollar spent on clothing exceeds the marginal utility of the last dollar spent on food.*

In the previous paragraph, we showed that the consumer will *not* be maximizing utility if the marginal utility of the last dollar spent on food *is less than* the marginal utility of the last dollar spent on clothing. In the paragraph before last, we showed that the consumer will *not* be maximizing utility if the marginal utility of the last dollar spent on food *exceeds* the marginal utility of the last dollar spent on clothing. It follows that the consumer will be maximizing utility only when the marginal utility of the last dollar spent on food *equals* the marginal utility of the last dollar spent on clothing. This is what we set out to prove.

[5] We assume here that the extra utility from an *extra* dollar spent on clothing equals the extra utility from the *last* dollar spent on clothing. This, like the assumption in footnote 4, is innocuous.

Test Yourself

1. Suppose that the total utility attached by Ms. Johnson to various quantities of hamburgers consumed (per day) is as follows:

Numbers of hamburgers	Total utility (utils)
0	0
1	5
2	12
3	15
4	17
5	18

Between 3 and 4 hamburgers, what is the marginal utility of a hamburger? Between 4 and 5 hamburgers, what is the marginal utility of a hamburger? Do these results conform to the law of diminishing marginal utility?

2. If Ms. Johnson is maximizing her satisfaction, and if the marginal utility of a hot dog is twice that of a bottle of beer, what must the price of a hot dog be if (a) the price of a bottle of beer is $.75, (b) the price of a bottle of beer is $1. (Assume that Ms. Johnson consumes both beer and hot dogs.)

3. "A good's price is related to its marginal utility, not its total utility. Thus a good like water or air may be cheap, even though its total utility is high." Comment and evaluate.

4. If the marginal utility of one good is 3 and its price is $1, while the marginal utility of another good is 6 and its price is $3, is the consumer maximizing his or her satisfaction, given that he or she is consuming both goods? Why or why not?

The Consumer's Demand Curve

In analyzing consumer behavior, economists often use the concept of an *individual demand curve.* Like the market demand curve (discussed at length in Chapter 21), the individual demand curve is the relationship between the quantity demanded of a good and the good's price. But whereas the market demand curve shows the quantity demanded in the *entire market* at various prices, the individual demand curve shows the quantity demanded by a *particular consumer* at various prices. Applying the theory of consumer behavior presented earlier in this chapter, one can derive a particular consumer's demand curve for a particular good. To see how this can be done, let's turn to Mrs. Walter and show how we can derive the relationship between the price of food and the amount of food she will buy per month.

Assuming that food and clothing are the only goods, that Mrs. Walter's monthly income is $400, and that the price of clothing is $40 per piece of clothing, we confront Mrs. Walter with a variety of prices of food. First, we confront her with a price of $1 per pound of food. How much food will she buy? Next, we confront her with a price of $2 per pound of food. How much food will she buy? The theory of consumer behavior shows how, under each of these sets of circumstances, she will allocate her income between food and clothing. (From Equation (22.1), we know that she will choose an allocation where the marginal utility of the last dollar spent on food will equal the marginal utility of the last dollar spent on clothing.) Suppose that she will buy 200 pounds of food when the price is $1 per pound, and 100 pounds of food when the price is $2 per pound. These are two points on Mrs. Walter's individual demand curve for food—those corresponding to prices of $1 and $2 per pound. Figure 22.2 shows these two points, X and Y.

It is no trick to obtain more points on her individual demand curve for food. All that we have to do is confront her with other prices of food, and see how much food she buys at each price. Plotting the amount of food she buys against the price, we obtain new points on her individual demand curve for food. Connecting up all these points, we get her complete individual demand curve for food, shown in Figure 22.2.

FACTORS INFLUENCING THE DEMAND CURVE

The location and shape of an individual demand curve depend on the tastes of the consumer. For example, if Mrs. Walter values food so much that she is determined to maintain her family's consumption of this commodity regardless of its price, her individual demand curve for food may look like demand curve *B* in Figure 22.3. But if she is less determined to maintain her family's food consumption, it may look like demand curve *A* in Figure 22.3.

Besides the consumer's tastes, other factors determining the location and shape of the consumer's individual demand curve are the income of the consumer and the prices of other goods. For example, Mrs. Walter's individual demand curve for food in Figure 22.2 is based on the assumption that her income is $400 per month and that the price of a piece of clothing is $40. If her income or the price of clothing changes, her individual demand curve

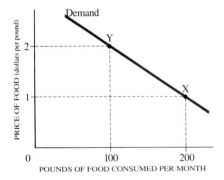

Figure 22.2
Mrs. Walter's Individual Demand Curve for Food *The consumer's individual demand curve for a commodity shows the amount of the commodity the consumer will buy at various prices. (Points* X *and* Y *on Mrs. Walter's individual demand curve for food are derived in Figure 22.13.)*

Figure 22.3

Figure 22.3

Hypothetical Individual Demand Curves *If Mrs. Walter values food so much that she is determined to buy much the same amount regardless of its price, her individual demand curve for food may look like demand curve B; but if she is less determined to maintain her family's food consumption, her individual demand curve for food may look like demand curve A.*

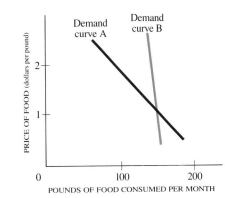

for food will change as well. Figure 22.4 shows how her individual demand curve for food may change if her income increases from $300 to $500 per month (assuming that the price of a piece of clothing remains fixed at $40). Figure 22.5 shows how her individual demand curve for food may change if the price of a piece of clothing increases from $40 to $50 (assuming that her income remains constant at $500 per month).

In Chapter 3, we pointed out the importance of distinguishing between *changes in the quantity demanded* and *changes in demand.* This is just as true for individual consumers as for the market as a whole. The shifts in Mrs. Walter's demand curve for food shown in Figure 22.4 and 22.5 are *changes in demand.* In other words, they are changes in the relationship between the quantity demanded and price. Even if there is no change in demand—that is, even if there is no shift in the demand curve—the quantity demanded may change because of a change in price. For example, in Figure 22.2, the quantity of food demanded by Mrs. Walter increases from 100 to 200 pounds per month if the price of food declines from $2 to $1 per pound. Yet Mrs. Walter's demand curve for food is unchanged in Figure 22.2, so there is no increase in demand. Instead, there has been a *movement along* Mrs. Walter's demand curve from point *Y* to point *X.* The quantity of food demanded by Mrs. Walter has changed even though her demand for food has *not* changed.

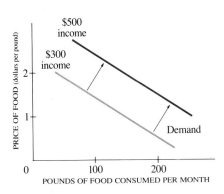

Figure 22.4

Effect of a Change in Income (from $300 to $500 per Month) on Mrs. Walter's Individual Demand Curve for Food *If Mrs. Walter's income increases from $300 to $500 per month (and if the price of a piece of clothing remains at $40), her demand curve will shift upward and to the right.*

Figure 22.5

Effect of a Change in the Price of a Piece of Clothing (from $40 to $50) on Mrs. Walter's Individual Demand Curve for Food *If the price of a piece of clothing increases from $40 to $50 (and if her income remains at $500 per month), her demand curve for food will shift upward and to the right.*

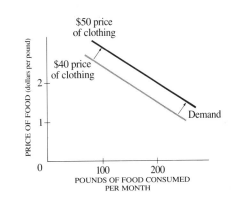

Why Do Individual Demand Curves Generally Slope Downward?[7]

Individual demand curves almost always slope downward to the right. That is, consumers almost always respond to an increase in a commodity's price by reducing the amount of it they consume. Or, put the other way around, a commodity's price almost always must be reduced to persuade the consumer to buy more of it. One way to explain this fact is by an appeal to the law of diminishing marginal utility, which (you will recall) states that, as a person consumes more and more of a particular commodity, the commodity's marginal utility declines. *Since the marginal utility—the extra utility derived from an extra unit of the commodity—declines, the price the consumer is willing to pay for an extra unit of the commodity must decline too.* This explanation relies on the assumption that marginal utility is measurable. Another way to explain the same thing makes no such assumption. According to this explanation, an increase in a commodity's price has two kinds of effects on the consumer—a substitution effect and an income effect.

SUBSTITUTION EFFECT

Basic Idea #44: Individual demand curves almost always slope downward to the right. Holding other factors (like tastes and income) constant, a commodity's price almost always must be lowered to induce the consumer to purchase more of it. This is because, as a person consumes more and more of a particular commodity, its marginal utility eventually falls.

*If the price of a commodity increases, the **substitution effect** of this price increase is the change in the quantity demanded of the commodity resulting from the commodity's becoming dearer relative to other commodities, if the consumer's level of utility is held constant.* Suppose that the price of chicken increases. Because of this price increase, the consumer may not be able to achieve as high a level of utility as he or she achieved before the price increase. Nonetheless, let's see what effect the price increase would have on the amount of chicken consumed by the consumer, *even if his or her level of utility were unchanged.* This effect is the substitution effect. *The substitution effect of a price increase always is a reduction in the quantity demanded of the commodity.* Suppose the price of chicken increases, while other prices and the consumer's level of utility are held constant. Because chicken becomes more expensive relative to other goods, the consumer will substitute other goods for chicken. Thus the substitution effect would be a *reduction* in the quantity demanded of chicken.

INCOME EFFECT

If the price of a commodity increases, the consumer's level of utility may be reduced, as pointed out above. *The **income effect** of the price increase is the change in the quantity demanded of the commodity due to this change in the consumer's utility level.* If an increase in the price of chicken cuts the consumer's level of utility by a particular amount, which in turn reduces the quantity of chicken demanded by the consumer, this reduction in the quantity demanded is the income effect. *The income effect of a price increase can be either a reduction or increase in the quantity demanded.* For

---

[7] This section is optional. Some instructors may want to skip it. The reader can go to the next section without losing the thread of the argument.

some commodities, like steak and probably chicken, a reduction in the consumer's utility level will result in the consumer's demanding *less* of them; thus the income effect of a price increase is a *reduction* in the quantity demanded of these commodities. For other commodities like margarine and poorer grades of food products, a reduction in the consumer's utility level may result in the consumer's demanding *more* of them; thus the income effect of a price increase is an *increase* in the quantity demanded of these commodities.

Example 22.2   Meat and Consumer's Surplus

It is important to recognize that consumers generally would be willing to pay more than in fact they pay for a particular good. Suppose that a consumer's demand curve for meat is as shown below, and that the price of a pound of meat is $2.

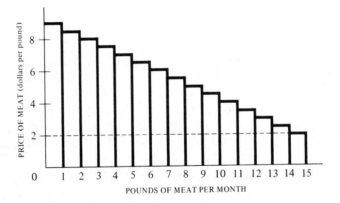

(a) What is the maximum amount that the consumer would pay for the first pound of meat per month? By how much does this exceed the actual price? (b) What is the maximum amount that the consumer would pay for the second pound of meat per month? By how much does this exceed the actual price? (c) What is the maximum amount that the consumer would pay for the 15 pounds of meat consumed per month? By how much does this exceed the actual amount paid? (d) Returning to Example 22.1, do you think that the actual amount paid for water is much less than the maximum amount that would be paid? Does this help to explain the diamond–water paradox?

SOLUTION

(a) $9. $7. (b) $8.50. $6.50. (c) $82.50. $52.50. (d) Yes. Yes, the actual amount paid for water is not a good indicator of the importance to the consumer (that is, the total utility) of water, since the actual amount paid is much less than the maximum amount that would be paid for it. *Economists use the term, **consumer's surplus,** to mean the difference between the maximum amount that the consumer would pay and what he or she actually pays.* For example, the consumer's surplus for the first pound of meat is $7.

RECENT DEVELOPMENTS IN ECONOMICS: THE ROLE OF TIME IN CONSUMPTION DECISIONS

In recent years, economists, led by Gary Becker of the University of Chicago, have begun to view a household as similar to a firm, in the sense that a household uses inputs of various kinds to produce outputs, like meals or recreation. Some of the inputs that the household uses are food, chairs, tables, and beds, but another input of great importance is *time*. The consumer has only a limited amount of time, and this time limitation, as well as his or her limited income, must be taken into account in making decisions.

To illustrate the importance of time to the consumer, take the case of a haircut. The cost to the consumer of a haircut is not only the $5 he must pay the barber; it is also the value of the time it takes for the barber to cut his hair, and, often more important, the value of the time he must wait before the barber is free to begin to cut his hair.

Gary Becker

Similarly, the cost of a vacation in Florida is not just the amount of money that must be paid for air tickets, hotels, meals, and entertainment; it is also the value placed on the reduced amount of time available to engage in non-vacation activities.

How does the economist measure the value of the time that is used up in consuming a particular item like a vacation? By the opportunity cost of the time. Thus the value of the time spent on the Florida vacation is the value of that time in its best alternative use. For example, if the consumer could have used this time to earn $100 a day, and if this would have been the best alternative use of this time to the consumer, then the value of the time spent on this vacation is $100 per day to this consumer.

Some economists have calculated the elasticity of demand for particular services with respect to the time they consume. In other words, they have estimated the percentage reduction in quantity demanded resulting from a 1 percent increase in the time taken by the service. For example, Jan Acton of the RAND Corporation studied the relationship between the number of visits to free sources of medical care by Brooklyn residents and the length of time, on the average, that such residents had to spend traveling and waiting for service. He found that a 1 percent increase in travel time was associated with slightly less than a 1 percent fall in number of visits.[1]

Of course, the value of time is not the same for all people. For example, the alternative cost of time to a teenager is generally lower than for an adult. This helps to explain the fact that teenagers frequently are more willing than adults to wait in line for tickets to various kinds of sports and musical events. Further, it has been suggested that the rise of fast-food chains has been due to an increase in the opportunity cost of time. Because of the increase in wage rates, there has been a rise in the value of time, according to this argument.

[1] Jan Acton, "Demand for Health Care among the Urban Poor," The New York City RAND Institute, April 1973.

THE TOTAL EFFECT OF A PRICE INCREASE

The *total* effect of a price increase is the *sum* of the income effect and the substitution effect. That is, the total change in the quantity demanded is the change in the quantity demanded due to the change in the consumer's utility level (the income effect) plus the change in the quantity demanded that would have occurred even if the consumer's utility level had not changed (the substitution effect). If (as is frequently the case) the income effect of a price increase is a reduction in the quantity demanded, the demand curve must slope downward. Why? Because both the income effect and the substitution effect are reductions in the quantity demanded, so the total effect of a price increase must be a reduction in the quantity demanded. Even if the income effect of a price increase is an increase in the quantity demanded, the demand curve may slope downward. Why? Because the increase in the quantity demanded due to the income effect may be more than offset by the substitution effect, which is always a reduction in the quantity demanded. Thus the demand curve will slope upward only in those *rare* cases where the income effect is an increase in the quantity demanded and where the income effect is big enough to offset the substitution effect.

Deriving the Market Demand Curve

In previous sections, we have described how each consumer's individual demand curve for a commodity can be derived, given the consumer's tastes and income, as well as the prices of other commodities. Suppose that we have obtained the individual demand curve for each of the consumers in the market. How can these individual demand curves be used to derive the market demand curve?

The answer is simple. *To derive the market demand curve, we obtain the horizontal sum of all the individual demand curves.* In other words, to find the total quantity demanded in the market at a certain price, we add up the quantities demanded by the individual consumers at that price.

Table 22.5 shows the individual demand curves for food of four families: the Walters, Joneses, Smiths, and Kleins. For simplicity, suppose that these

Table 22.5

INDIVIDUAL DEMAND CURVES AND MARKET DEMAND CURVE FOR FOOD

Price of food (dollars per pound)	Jones	Klein	Smith	Walter	Market demand
		Individual demand			
		(hundreds of pounds per month)			
1.00	50.0	45.0	5.0	2.0	102
1.20	43.0	44.0	4.2	1.8	93
1.40	36.0	43.0	3.4	1.6	84
1.60	30.0	42.0	2.6	1.4	76
1.80	25.0	41.4	2.4	1.2	70
2.00	20.0	41.0	2.0	1.0	64

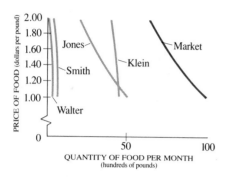

Figure 22.6
Individual Demand Curves and Market Demand Curve for Food *The market demand curve is the horizontal sum of all the individual demand curves.*

four families constitute the entire market for food. (This assumption can easily be relaxed; it just makes things simple.) Then the market demand curve for food is shown in the last column of Table 22.5. Figure 22.6 shows the families' individual demand curves for food, as well as the resulting market demand curve. To illustrate how the market demand curve is derived from the individual demand curves, suppose that the price of food is $1 per pound. Then the total quantity demanded in the market is 102 hundreds of pounds per month, since this is the sum of the quantities demanded at this price by the four families. (As shown in Table 22.5, this sum equals 50.0 + 45.0 + 5.0 + 2.0, or 102.)

Since individual demand curves for a commodity almost always slope downward to the right it follows that *market demand curves too almost always slope downward to the right.* (Why? Because, as stressed above, the market demand curve is the horizontal sum of all of the individual demand curves.) However, as emphasized in Chapter 21, the shape and location of the market demand curve vary greatly from commodity to commodity and from market to market. Market demand curves, like people, do not look alike.

Test Yourself

1. Suppose that there are five people who are the only members of a particular market. The amount that each person will buy of the product in question (at each price) is shown below. Determine five points on the market demand curve for the product.

Price (dollars)	First person	Second person	Third person	Fourth person	Fifth person
		Quantity demanded			
1	5	4	2	8	7
2	4	4	2	7	6
3	3	4	1	6	5
4	2	3	0	5	4
5	1	3	0	5	2

2. Some people judge the quality of a good by its price. If a consumer does this, how does it affect the model presented in this chapter? (*Hint:* Is utility independent of price?)

3. Bill Thompson would be willing to pay 30 cents for the first apple he consumes per day and 24 cents for the second apple he consumes per day. The current price of an apple is 24 cents. How great is Bill Thompson's consumer's surplus? What does this number mean? How might such a number be used?

4. Mrs. Moriarty (the Professor's wife) learns that the price of turkey has fallen. (a) What is the substitution effect? Do you think that it will be positive or negative? Why? (b) What is the income effect? Do you think that it will be positive or negative? Why? (c) Do you think that the Moriarty family's demand curve for turkey slopes downward to the right? Why or why not?

Summary

1. The amount of a particular commodity a consumer purchases is clearly influenced by his or her preferences. The model of consumer behavior assumes that the consumer's preferences are transitive and that commodities are defined so that more of them is preferred to less.

2. Utility is a number that represents the level of satisfaction derived by the consumer from a particular market basket. Market baskets with higher utilities are preferred over market baskets with lower utilities.

3. The model of consumer behavior recognizes that preferences alone do not determine the consumer's actions. The choices open to the consumer are dictated by the size of his or her money income and the nature of commodity prices. These factors, as well as the consumer's preferences, determine his or her choice.

4. If the consumer maximizes utility, his or her income is allocated among commodities so that, for every commodity purchased, the marginal utility of the commodity is proportional to its price. In other words, the marginal utility of the last dollar spent on each commodity is made equal for all commodities purchased.

5. The individual demand curve shows the quantity of a good demanded by a particular consumer at various prices of the good. The individual demand curve for practically all goods slopes downward and to the right. Its location depends on the consumer's income and tastes and the prices of other goods.

6. To derive the market demand curve, we obtain the horizontal sum of all the individual demand curves of the people in the market. Since individual demand curves for a commodity almost always slope downward to the right, it follows that market demand curves too almost always slope downward to the right.

Concepts for Review

Model of consumer
  behavior
Utility
Marginal utility

Law of diminishing
  marginal utility
Equilibrium market
  basket

Individual demand curve
Consumer's surplus
Substitution effect
Income effect

Appendix: How Indifference Curves Can Be Used to Analyze Consumer Behavior

In this Appendix, we show how the theory of consumer behavior can be used in cases where one is not willing to assume that marginal utility is measurable. Generally, it is exceedingly difficult to formulate meaningful measures of a person's extra satisfaction from an extra amount of a particular good. We shall show that the theory remains useful even if such measures cannot be obtained. Once again, we assume for simplicity that there are only two goods, food and clothing, since this allows us to use simple two-dimensional diagrams to illustrate the model. Since there are only these two commodities, we can represent every possible combination of goods purchased by a consumer by a point in Figure 22.7, which measures the amount of food purchased along the vertical axis and the amount of clothing purchased along the horizontal axis.

INDIFFERENCE CURVES

*An **indifference curve** contains points representing market baskets among which the consumer is indifferent.* To illustrate, consider Mrs. Walter, making choices for her family. Certain market baskets—that is, certain combinations of food and clothing (the only commodities)—will be equally desirable to her. For example, she may be indifferent between a market basket containing 100 pounds of food and 5 pieces of clothing and a market basket containing 200 pounds of food and 2 pieces of clothing. These two market baskets can be represented by two points, U and V, in Figure 22.7. In addition, other market baskets—each of which can be represented by a point in Figure 22.7—are just as desirable to Mrs. Walter as those represented by

Figure 22.7

Two of Mrs. Walter's Indifference Curves I_1 and I_2 *are two of Mrs. Walter's indifference curves. Each shows market baskets that are equally desirable to Mrs. Walter. For example, she is indifferent between 200 pounds of food and 2 pieces of clothing (point* V*) and 100 pounds of food and 5 pieces of clothing (point* U*).*

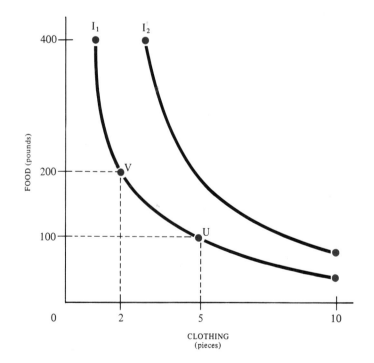

points U and V. If we connect all of these points, we get a curve that represents market baskets that are equally desirable to the consumer. In our case, Mrs. Walter is indifferent among all of the market baskets represented by points on curve I_1 in Figure 22.7. I_1 is therefore called an indifference curve.

There are three important things to note about any consumer's indifference curves:

1. Any consumer has lots of indifference curves, not just one. If Mrs. Walter is indifferent among all the market baskets represented by points on I_2 in Figure 22.7, I_2 is another of her indifference curves. Moreover, one thing is certain. She prefers any market basket on I_2 to any market basket on I_1, since I_2 includes market baskets with as much clothing and more food (or as much food and more clothing) than the market baskets on I_1. (Remember that commodities are defined so that more of them is preferred to less.) Consequently, it must always be true that market baskets on higher indifference curves like I_2 must be preferred to market baskets on lower indifference curves like I_1.

2. Every indifference curve must slope downward and to the right, to reflect the fact that commodities are defined so that more of them is preferred to less. If one market basket has more of one commodity than a second market basket, it must have less of the other commodity than the second market basket—assuming that the two market baskets are to yield equal satisfaction to the consumer. You can prove this to yourself. Suppose that you have a choice between two snacks and that you are indifferent between them. One snack consists of 1 piece of apple pie and 2 glasses of milk. The other consists of 2 pieces of apple pie and a certain number of glasses of milk. If you prefer more apple pie to less, and if you prefer more milk to less, can the number of glasses of milk in the latter snack be as large as 2? Clearly, the answer must be no.

3. Indifference curves cannot intersect. If they did, this would contradict the assumption that more of a commodity is preferred to less. For example, suppose that I_1 and I_2 in Figure 22.8 are two indifference curves and that they intersect. If this is the case, the market basket represented by point D is equivalent in the eyes of the consumer to the one represented

Figure 22.8

Intersecting Indifference Curves: A Contradiction *Indifference curves cannot intersect. If they did, the consumer would be indifferent between* D *and* E, *since both are on indifference curve* I₁; *and between* F *and* E, *since both are on indifference curve* I₂. *But this implies that he or she must be indifferent between* D *and* F, *which is impossible since* F *contains the same amount of food and 6 more pieces of clothing than* D.

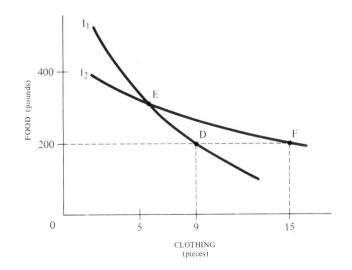

by point E, since both are on indifference curve I_1. Moreover, the market basket represented by point F is equivalent in the eyes of the consumer to the one represented by point E, since both are on indifference curve I_2. And this means that the market basket represented by point F must be equivalent in the eyes of the consumer to the one represented by point D. (Remember that consumer preferences are assumed to be transitive!) But this is impossible because market basket F contains the same amount of food and 6 more pieces of clothing than does market basket D. Since more of a commodity is preferred to less, market basket F must be preferred to market basket D.

INDIFFERENCE CURVES AND UTILITY

To continue building this new version of our model of consumer behavior, we need to return to the concept of utility. Since all market baskets on a particular indifference curve yield the same satisfaction to the consumer, they all must have the same utility. For example, all market baskets on indifference curve I_1 in Figure 22.7 must have the same utility. Moreover, market baskets on higher indifference curves must have higher utilities than market baskets on lower indifference curves. For example, all market baskets on indifference curve I_2 in Figure 22.7 must have higher utilities than market baskets on indifference curve I_1.

Given a group of indifference curves for a certain consumer, it is easy to establish an index of the utility obtained from any market basket by this consumer. *All that we have to do is attach a number to each indifference curve, this number being larger for higher indifference curves than for lower indifference curves. The utility index for any market basket is then the number attached to the indifference curve on which this market basket is located.* The resulting utility index shows at a glance which market baskets the consumer will pick over other market baskets. The rational consumer will, of course, try to pick the market basket that maximizes this index of utility.

Note that this utility index is not unique. Any set of numbers that increases as one goes from successively lower to higher indifference curves will constitute a suitable set of indices. Thus no assumption is made that we can obtain a meaningful measure of marginal utility. But it is possible to construct a utility index of this sort, so long as the three basic assumptions underlying the theory of consumer demand (described in the earlier section on "A Model of Consumer Behavior") are met.

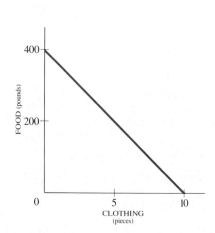

Figure 22.9

Mrs. Walter's Budget Line The consumer's budget line shows the market baskets that can be purchased, given the consumer's income and prevailing commodity prices. This budget line assumes that Mrs. Walter's income is $400 per month, that the price of a pound of food is $1, and that the price of a piece of clothing is $40.

THE BUDGET LINE

The consumer wants to maximize his or her utility, which means that he or she wants to achieve the highest possible indifference curve. But whether or not a particular indifference curve is attainable depends on the consumer's money income and on commodity prices. Exactly what constraints are imposed on the consumer by the size of his or her money income and the nature of commodity prices? To make things concrete, let's return to Mrs. Walter. Suppose that her total income is $400 per month, and that she can spend this amount only on two commodities, food and clothing. Needless to say, it is unrealistic to assume that there are only two com-

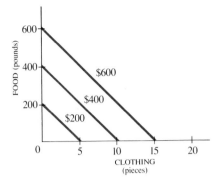

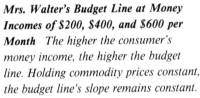

Figure 22.10

Mrs. Walter's Budget Line at Money Incomes of $200, $400, and $600 per Month *The higher the consumer's money income, the higher the budget line. Holding commodity prices constant, the budget line's slope remains constant.*

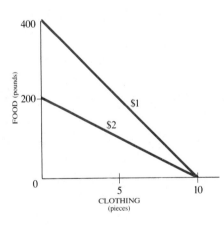

Figure 22.11

Mrs. Walter's Budget Line at Food Prices of $1 and $2 per Pound *Holding constant Mrs. Walter's money income at $400 per month and the price of a piece of clothing at $40, the budget line cuts the vertical axis farther from the origin when the price of food is $1 than when it is $2.*

modities in existence, but, to repeat what was said earlier, this makes it easier to present the model, and the results can easily be generalized to cases where more than two commodities exist.

Given these conditions, the answer to how much of each commodity Mrs. Walter can buy depends on the price of a pound of food and the price of a piece of clothing. Suppose the price of a pound of food is $1 and the price of a piece of clothing is $40. Then if she spent all of her income on food, she could buy 400 pounds of food per month. On the other hand, if she spent all of her income on clothing, she could buy 10 pieces of clothing per month. Or she could, if she wished, buy some food and some clothing. There are a large number of combinations of amounts of food and clothing that she could buy, and each such combination can be represented by a point on the line in Figure 22.9. This line is called her budget line. *A consumer's* **budget line** *shows the market baskets that he or she can purchase, given the consumer's income and prevailing market prices.*

The consumer's budget line will shift if changes occur in the consumer's money income or in commodity prices. In particular, an increase in money income means that the budget line rises, and a decrease in money income means that the budget line falls. This is illustrated in Figure 22.10, which shows Mrs. Walter's budget line at money incomes of $200, $400, and $600 per month. As you can see, her budget line moves upward as her income rises.

Commodity prices too affect the budget line. A decrease in a commodity's price causes the budget line to cut this commodity's axis at a point farther from the origin. Figure 22.11 shows Mrs. Walter's budget line when the price of a pound of food is $1 and when it is $2. You can see that the budget line cuts the vertical, or food, axis farther from the origin when the price of food is $1 per pound.

THE EQUILIBRIUM MARKET BASKET

With information on the consumer's indifference curves and budget line, we are in a position to determine the consumer's *equilibrium market basket* —the market basket that, among all those that the consumer can purchase, yields the maximum utility. The first step is to combine the indifference curves with the budget line on the same graph. Figure 22.12 brings together Mrs. Walter's indifference curves (from Figure 22.7) and her budget line (from Figure 22.9). Given the information assembled in Figure 22.12, it is a simple matter to determine her equilibrium market basket. *Her indifference curves show what she wants:* specifically, she wants to attain the highest possible indifference curve. Thus she would rather be on indifference curve I_2 than on indifference curve I_1, and on indifference curve I_3 than on indifference curve I_2. But, as we have pointed out repeatedly, she cannot choose any market basket she likes. *The budget line shows which market baskets her income and commodity prices permit her to buy.* Thus she must choose some market basket on her budget line.

Consequently, *the consumer's choice boils down to choosing that market basket on the budget line that is on the highest indifference curve. This is the equilibrium market basket.* For example, Mrs. Walter's equilibrium market basket is clearly at point *G* in Figure 22.12; it consists of 200 pounds of food and 5 pieces of clothing per month. This is her equilibrium market

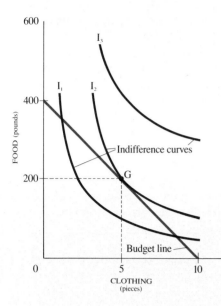

Figure 22.12

Mrs. Walter's Equilibrium Market Basket *Mrs. Walter's equilibrium market basket is at point* G, *containing 200 pounds of food and 5 pieces of clothing. This is the point on her budget line that is on the highest indifference curve,* I₂, *she can attain.*

basket because any other market basket on the budget line is on a lower indifference curve than point *G* is. But will the consumer choose this market basket? Admittedly, it may take some time and fumbling for the consumer to find out that this is the best market basket for him or her under the circumstances. Consumers, after all, do make mistakes. But they also learn, and eventually one would expect a consumer to come very close to acting in the predicted way.

DERIVING THE INDIVIDUAL DEMAND CURVE

Finally, we show how indifference curves can be used to derive the consumer's demand curve. In particular, let's return to the case of Mrs. Walter, and show how her demand curve for food can be derived.

Assuming that food and clothing are the only goods, that Mrs. Walter's monthly income is $400, and that the price of clothing is $40 per piece of clothing, Mrs. Walter's budget line is budget line 1 in Figure 22.13, when the price of food is $1 per pound. Thus, as we saw in Figure 22.2, Mrs. Walter will buy 200 pounds of food per month under these conditions.

If, however, the price of food increases to $2 per pound, her income and the price of clothing remaining constant, her budget line will be budget line 2 in Figure 22.13, and she will attain her highest indifference curve, I_1, by choosing the market basket corresponding to point *U*, a market basket containing 100 pounds of food per month. Thus, if the price of food is $2 per pound, she will buy 100 pounds of food per month.

We have derived two points on Mrs. Walter's individual demand curve for food—those corresponding to prices of $1 and $2 per pound. Figure 22.2 shows these two points, *X* and *Y.* To obtain more points on her individual demand curve for food, all we have to do is assume a particular

Figure 22.13

Effect of Change in Price of Food on Mrs. Walter's Equilibrium Market Basket *If the price of a pound of food is $1, Mrs. Walter's budget line is such that her equilibrium market basket is at point G, where she buys 200 pounds of food per month. If the price of a pound of food is $2, Mrs. Walter's budget line is such that her equilibrium market basket is at point U, where she buys 100 pounds of food per month.*

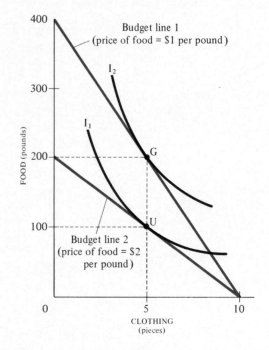

price of food, construct the budget line corresponding to this price (holding her income and the price of clothing constant), and find the market basket on this budget line that is on her highest indifference curve. Plotting the amount of food in this market basket against the assumed price of food, we obtain a new point on her individual demand curve for food. Connecting up all these points, we get her complete individual demand curve for food, shown in Figure 22.2.

CHAPTER 23

Optimal Input Decisions by Business Firms

In economies based largely on free enterprise, like our own, the managers of business firms are given considerable responsibility for deciding where, when, and how various resources are used. Thus the manager's job is a central one, from both a social and private point of view. Fortunately, the United States has been able to develop large cadres of effective managerial talent, in large part because management and business have been highly esteemed professions in the United States. As Calvin Coolidge put it, with characteristic brevity and uncharacteristic overstatement, "The business of America is business." This is quite a different sentiment from that expressed by the ancient Roman historian, Tacitus, who said that Sabinus "had talents equal to business, and aspired no higher."

In this chapter, we shall take a closer look at the decision-making process within the firm. Our discussion builds on Chapter 6, which dealt with the organization, motivation, and technology of the firm. We look in more detail at the firm's technology, and focus particular attention on the following central question: If a firm attempts to maximize profits, what production technique—that is, what combination of inputs—should it choose to produce a particular quantity of output? Two points should be noted at the outset. First, when finding the optimal input combination, we take as given the quantity of output that the firm will produce. In subsequent chapters, we shall discuss how the firm should choose this quantity. Second, just as one purpose of the previous two chapters was to show how a product's market demand curve can be derived, so an important purpose of Chapters 23 through 25 is to show how a product's market supply curve can be derived. In this chapter, we present some of the concepts and findings that are required for this purpose.

The Production Function Revisited

If the United States Steel Corporation decides to produce a certain quantity of steel, it can do so in many ways. It can use open-hearth furnaces, or basic oxygen furnaces, or electric furnaces; it can use various types of iron ore; and it can use various types of coke. Which of these many ways will maximize U.S. Steel's profits? The management of U.S. Steel—and every business firm—devotes considerable time and energy to answering this kind of question. Let's restate it in the economist's terms. Given that a firm is going to produce a certain quantity of output, what production technique—i.e., what combination of inputs—should it choose to maximize its profits?

As a first step toward answering this question, it is wise to review the concept of the production function, taken up in Chapter 6. As you will recall, *the **production function** shows the most output that existing technology permits the firm to extract from each quantity of inputs.* Consider the hypothetical case of a wheat farm with 1 acre of land. The relationship between the amount of labor used per year by this farm and the farm's output is shown in Table 23.1. This is the farm's production function. It shows that the farm can produce 30 bushels of wheat per year if 1 man-year of labor is used, 70 bushels of wheat per year if 2 man-years of labor are used, and so on.

The production function summarizes the characteristics of existing technology at a given point in time; it shows the technological constraints that a firm must reckon with. Like it or not, the most that the wheat farm in Table 23.1 can produce, if it uses 2 man-years of labor, is 70 bushels per year. This is the best that existing technology permits. Perhaps future advances in technology will permit such a farm (with 2 man-years of labor) to produce more than 70 bushels per year, but this presently cannot be done.

Table 23.1

RELATIONSHIP BETWEEN LABOR INPUT
AND OUTPUT ON 1-ACRE WHEAT FARM

Number of man-years of labor	Bushels of wheat produced per year
0	0
1	30
2	70
3	100
4	125
5	145

A CRUDE-OIL PIPELINE: A CASE STUDY

To illustrate what a production function looks like in a real case, let's consider a crude-oil pipeline that transports petroleum from oil fields and storage areas over hundreds of miles to major urban and industrial centers. We begin by noting that the output of such a pipeline is the amount of oil carried per day, and that the two principal inputs are the diameter of the pipeline and the horsepower applied to the oil carried. Both inputs are important. The bigger the diameter of the pipe, the more oil the pipeline can carry, holding constant the horsepower applied. And the greater the horsepower applied, the more oil the pipeline can carry, holding constant the diameter of the pipeline.

The production function shows the maximum output rate that can be derived from each combination of input rates. Thus, in this case, the production function shows the maximum amount of oil carried per day as a function of the pipeline's diameter and the amount of horsepower applied. On the basis of engineering estimates, one can derive the production function for crude-oil pipelines. Leslie Cookenboo of the Exxon Corporation derived such a production function, assuming that the pipeline carries Mid-Continent crude, has ¼-inch pipe throughout the lines, has lines

Table 23.2

PRODUCTION FUNCTION, CRUDE-OIL
PIPELINE[a]

Line diameter (inches)	Horsepower (thousands)				
	20	30	40	50	60
	Output rate (thousands of barrels per day)				
14	70	90	95	100	104
18	115	140	155	165	170
22	160	190	215	235	250
26	220	255	290	320	340

[a] The output rates given in this table are only approximate, since they were read from Cookenboo's graph on p. 16.

Source: Leslie Cookenboo, Crude Oil Pipe Lines and Competition in the Oil Industry, Cambridge, Mass.: Harvard University Press, 1955.

1,000 miles in length with a 5 percent terrain variation, and no net gravity flow in the line.[1] Some of his results are shown in Table 23.2. For example, the production function shows that if the diameter of the pipeline is 22 inches and the horsepower is 40,000, the pipeline can carry 215,000 barrels per day. Certainly, any firm operating a pipeline or considering the construction of one is vitally interested in such information. The production function plays a strategic role in the decision making of any firm.

Types of Inputs

As pointed out in Chapter 6, an input is anything that the firm uses in its production process. In analyzing production processes, we suppose that all inputs can be classified into two categories: fixed and variable inputs.

A **fixed input** is one whose quantity cannot change during the period of time under consideration. This period will vary. It may be six months in one case, six years in another case. Among the most important inputs often included as fixed are the firm's plant and equipment—that is, its factory and office buildings, its machinery, its tooling, and its transportation facilities. In the simple example of the wheat farm in Table 23.1, land is a fixed input since its quantity is assumed to be fixed at 1 acre.

A **variable input** is one whose quantity can be changed during the relevant period. It is generally possible to increase or decrease the number of workers engaged in a particular activity (although this is not always the case, since they may have long-term contracts). Similarly, it frequently is possible to alter the amount of raw material that is used. In the case of the wheat farm in Table 23.1, labor clearly is a variable input since its quantity can be varied from 0 to 5 man-years.

The Short Run and the Long Run

Whether an input is considered variable or fixed depends on the length of the period under consideration. The longer the period, the more inputs are variable, not fixed. Although the length of the period varies from case to case, economists have found it very useful to focus special attention on two time periods: the short run and the long run. *The **short run** is defined as the period of time in which at least one of the firm's inputs is fixed.* More specifically, since the firm's plant and equipment are among the most difficult inputs to change quickly, *the short run is generally understood to mean the length of time during which the firm's plant and equipment are fixed.* On the other hand, *the **long run** is that period of time in which all inputs are variable.* In the long run, the firm can make a complete adjustment to any change in its environment.

To illustrate the distinction between the short run and the long run, let's consider the General Motors Corporation. Any period of time during which GM's plant and equipment cannot be altered freely is the short run.

[1] L. Cookenboo, *Crude Oil Pipe Lines and Competition in the Oil Industry,* Cambridge, Mass.: Harvard University Press, 1955.

A period of one year is certainly a case of the short run, because in a year GM could not vary the quantity of its plant and equipment. It takes longer than a year to construct an automotive plant, or to alter an existing plant to produce a new kind of automobile. For example, the tooling phase of the model changeover cycle currently takes about 2 years. Also, because some of its existing contracts with suppliers and workers extend for more than a year, GM cannot vary all its inputs in a year without violating these contracts. On the other hand, any period of time during which GM can vary the quantity of all inputs is the long run. A period of 50 years is certainly a case of the long run. Whether a shorter period of time—10 years, say—is a long-run situation depends on the problem at hand. If all the relevant inputs can be varied, it is a long-run situation; if not, it is a short-run situation.

A useful way to look at the long run is to consider it a *planning horizon.* While operating in the short run, the firm must continually be planning ahead and deciding its strategy in the long run. Its decisions concerning the long run determine the sort of short-run position the firm will occupy in the future. Before a firm makes the decision to add a new type of product to its line, the firm is in a long-run situation (with regard to the new product), since it can choose among a wide variety of types and sizes of equipment to produce the new product. But once the investment is made, the firm is confronted with a short-run situation, since the type and size of equipment is, to a considerable extent, frozen.

Average Product of an Input

In order to determine which production technique—that is, which combination of inputs—a firm should use, it is necessary to define the average product and marginal product of an input. *The **average product** of an input is the firm's total output divided by the amount of input used to produce this amount of output.* The average product of an input can be calculated from the production function. Consider the wheat farm in Table 23.1. The average product of labor is 30 bushels per man-year of labor when 1 man-year of labor is used, 35 bushels per man-year of labor when 2 man-years are used, 33⅓ bushels per man-year of labor when 3 man-years are used, and so forth.

Marginal Product of an Input

As the amount of labor used on the farm increases, so does the farm's output, but the amount of extra output from the addition of an extra man-year of labor varies depending on how much labor is already being used. The extra output from the addition of the first man-year of labor is $30 - 0 = 30$ bushels per man-year of labor. The extra output due to the addition of the second man-year of labor is $70 - 30 = 40$ bushels per man-year of labor. And the extra output from the addition of the fifth

Table 23.3

AVERAGE AND MARGINAL PRODUCTS OF LABOR, 1-ACRE WHEAT FARM

Number of man-years of labor	Total output (bushels per year)	Marginal product (bushels per man-year)	Average product (bushels per man-year)
0	0		—
1	30	30	30
2	70	40	35
3	100	30	33⅓
4	125	25	31¼
5	145	20	29

man-year of labor is 145 − 125 = 20 bushels per man-year of labor. *The* **marginal product** *of an input is the addition to total output due to the addition of the last unit of input, the quantity of other inputs used being held constant.* Thus the marginal product of labor is 30 bushels when between 0 and 1 man-years of labor are used, 40 bushels when between 1 and 2 man-years of labor are used, and so on.

The concept of marginal product is analogous to that of marginal utility, which we discussed in Chapter 22. Recall that marginal utility is the extra utility resulting from an additional unit of a commodity. Substitute "output" for "utility" and "an input" for "a commodity" in the previous sentence, and you get a perfectly valid definition of marginal product. Economics is chock full of marginal "thises" and marginal "thats," and it is important that you become aware of their general family traits.

Table 23.3 shows the average and marginal products of labor at various levels of utilization of labor; Figure 23.1 shows the same thing graphically. The data in both Table 23.3 and Figure 23.1 concerning the average and marginal products of labor are derived from the production function. Given

Figure 23.1

Average and Marginal Products of Labor, 1-Acre Wheat Farm *The marginal product of the first man-year of labor (which, according to Table 23.3, equals 30 bushels per man-year) is plotted at the midpoint between 0 and 1 man-year of labor. The marginal product of the second man-year of labor is plotted at the midpoint between 1 and 2 man-years of labor. The marginal product curve connects these and other points showing the marginal product of various amounts of labor.*

The average product curve shows the average product of labor when various amounts of labor are used. As the graph shows, both the average product and the marginal product of labor rise, reach a maximum, and fall.

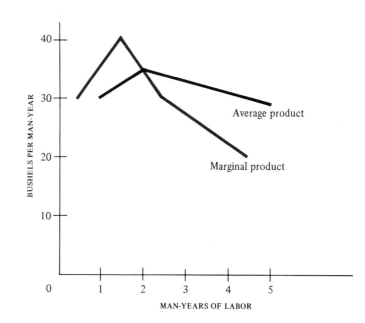

the production function, shown in Table 23.1 and reproduced in Table 23.3, the average and marginal products at each level of utilization of labor can be determined in the way we have indicated.

In Figure 23.1, as in the case of most production processes, the average product of the variable input—labor in this case—rises, reaches a maximum, and then falls. The marginal product of labor also rises, reaches a maximum, and falls. This too is typical of many production processes. Why do average and marginal product behave in this way? Because of the law of diminishing marginal returns, to which we now turn.

The Law of Diminishing Marginal Returns

Basic Idea #45: Suppose that you are the manager of a small farm. You have a fixed amount of capital and land, but you can vary the number of laborers employed. If you hire more and more laborers, there eventually will come a point where the extra output due to hiring still another laborer is less than that due to hiring the last laborer. This is an illustration of the law of diminishing marginal returns.

Perhaps the best-known—and certainly one of the least understood—laws of economics is the so-called *law of diminishing marginal returns.* Put in a single sentence, this law states that *if equal increments of an input are added, the quantities of other inputs being held constant, the resulting increments of product will decrease beyond some point;* that is, the marginal product of the input will diminish.

Suppose that a small factory that manufactures a metal automobile component has eight machine tools. If this firm hires only one or two workers, total output and output per worker will be quite low. These workers will have a number of quite different tasks to perform, and the advantages of specialization will be sacrificed. Workers will spend considerable time switching from one machine to another, and many of the eight machine tools will be idle much of the time. What happens as the firm increases its work force? As more and more workers are added, the marginal product (that is, the extra product) of each will tend to rise, as the work force grows to the point where it can man the fixed amount of equipment effectively. However, if the firm continues to increase the number of workers, the marginal product of a worker will eventually begin to decrease. Why? Because workers will have to wait in line to use the fixed number of machine tools, and because the extra workers will have to be assigned to less and less important tasks. Eventually, if enough workers are hired (and utilized within the plant), they may get in each other's way to such an extent that production may grind to a halt.

Returning to the wheat farm discussed in the previous section, Table 23.3 shows that the law of diminishing marginal returns applies in this case too. The third column of this table indicates that, beyond 2 man-years of labor, the marginal product of labor falls. Certainly, it seems entirely reasonable that, as more and more of a variable input (in this case, labor) is combined with a fixed amount of another input (in this case, land), the additional output to be derived from an additional unit of the variable input will eventually decrease. In the case of a 1-acre wheat farm, one would expect that, as more and more labor is added, the extra workers' functions eventually would become less and less important and productive.

The law of diminishing marginal returns plays a major part in determining the firm's optimal input combination and the shape of the firm's cost functions, as we shall see in this and the next chapter. To prevent misunderstanding and confusion, several points about this law should be stressed. First, *it is assumed that technology remains fixed.* If technology changes, the law of diminishing marginal returns cannot predict the effect of an additional unit of input. Second, *at least one input must be fixed in quantity,* since the law of diminishing marginal returns is not applicable to cases where there is a proportional increase in all inputs. Third, *it must be possible to vary the proportions in which the various inputs are utilized.* This is generally possible in industry and agriculture.

Example 23.1   Production Theory in the Milking Shed

According to the U.S. Department of Agriculture, the relationship between a cow's total output of milk and the amount of grain it is fed is as follows:

Amount of grain (pounds)	Amount of milk (pounds)
1,200	5,917
1,800	7,250
2,400	8,379
3,000	9,371

Forage input is assumed to be fixed at 6,500 pounds of hay.

(a) What is the average product of grain when each amount is used? (b) Should a milk producer feed a cow the amount of grain that will maximize its average product? Why or why not? (c) What is the marginal product of grain when between 1,200 and 1,800 pounds are fed; when between 1,800 and 2,400 pounds are fed; and when between 2,400 and 3,000 pounds are fed? (d) Does this production function exhibit diminishing marginal returns?

SOLUTION

(a) At 1,200 pounds, it is 4.93; at 1,800 pounds, it is 4.03; at 2,400 pounds, it is 3.49; and at 3,000 pounds, it is 3.12 pounds of milk per pound of grain. (b) No, because this generally will not maximize profit, as we shall see in subsequent discussions. (c) 2.22, 1.88, and 1.65 pounds of milk per pound of grain. (d) Yes. The marginal product of grain decreases as more of it is used.

Test Yourself

1. Suppose that a firm has the following production function:

Man-hours of labor per year (thousands)	Output per year (thousands)
0	0
1	2
2	8
3	12
4	14
5	15

Plot on a graph the marginal product of labor at various levels of utilization of labor.

2. Using the data in Question 1, plot the average product of labor at various levels of utilization of labor.

3. A tool and die shop has three types of inputs: labor, machines, and materials. It cannot obtain additional machines in less than 6 months. In the next month, do you think that labor is a fixed or variable input? Do you think that machines are a fixed or variable input? Explain.

4. The tool and die shop in Question 3 expands its use of all three types of inputs. The owner of the shop worries that by doing so the firm may encounter diminishing marginal returns. Is this a legitimate concern? Why or why not?

The Optimal Input Decision

Now we are in a position to answer the question posed at the beginning of this chapter: Given that a firm is going to produce a particular quantity of output, what production technique—i.e., what combination of inputs—should it choose to maximize profits? Note first that if the firm maximizes its profits, it must minimize the cost of producing this quantity of output. This seems obvious enough. But what combination of inputs (that will produce the required quantity of output) will minimize the firm's costs? The answer can be stated like this: *The firm will minimize cost by combining inputs in such a way that the marginal product of a dollar's worth of any one input equals the marginal product of a dollar's worth of any other input used.*

Another way to say the same thing is: *The firm will minimize cost by combining inputs in such a way that, for every input used, the marginal product of the input is proportional to its price.* Why does this say the same thing? Because the marginal product of a dollar's worth of an input equals the marginal product of the input divided by its price. If the marginal product of a man-year of labor is 40 units of output, and if the price of labor is $8,000 per man-year, the marginal product of a dollar's worth of labor is $40 \div 8,000 = .005$ units of output. Thus, if the firm is satisfying the rule for cost minimization in the previous paragraph—that is, if it is combining inputs so that the marginal product of a dollar's worth of any one input equals the marginal product of a dollar's worth of any other input used—it must at the same time be combining inputs so that, for every input used, the marginal product of the input is proportional to its price.

THE WHEAT FARM: A NUMERICAL EXAMPLE

To illustrate the application of this rule, let's take a numerical example from the wheat farm cited above. Suppose that the farm can vary the amount of labor and land it uses. Table 23.4 shows the marginal product of

Table 23.4
DETERMINATION OF OPTIMAL INPUT COMBINATION

Amount of input used		Marginal product		Marginal product ÷ price of input		Total cost
Labor (man-years)	Land (acres)	Labor	Land	Labor	Land	(dollars)
0.5	7.0	50	5	50 ÷ 8,000	5 ÷ 2,000	18,000
1.0	4.1	40	10	40 ÷ 8,000	10 ÷ 2,000	16,200
1.5	3.0	30	30	30 ÷ 8,000	30 ÷ 2,000	18,000
2.5	2.0	20	50	20 ÷ 8,000	50 ÷ 2,000	24,000

each input when various combinations of inputs (all combinations being able to produce the specified quantity of output) are used. Suppose that the price of labor is $8,000 per man-year and that the annual price of using land is $2,000 per acre. (We assume that the firm takes the prices of inputs as given and that it can buy all it wants of the inputs at these prices.) For each combination of inputs, Table 23.4 shows the marginal product of each input divided by its price. Based on our rule, the optimal input combination is 4.1 acres of land and 1 man-year of labor, since this is the only combination (capable of producing the required output) where the marginal product of labor divided by the price of labor equals the marginal product of land divided by the price of land. (See Table 23.4.)

Is this rule correct? Does it really result in a least-cost combination of inputs? Let's look at the cost of the various input combinations in Table 23.4. The first combination (0.5 man-years of labor and 7 acres of land) costs $18,000; the second combination (1.0 man-years of labor and 4.1 acres of land) costs $16,200; and so on. An examination of the total cost of each input combination shows that the input combination chosen by our rule—1.0 man-years of labor and 4.1 acres of land—is indeed the least-cost input combination, the one for the profit-maximizing firm to use.

A More General Proof of the Rule

One example really does not prove that the rule results in minimum costs; it only demonstrates that it does so in this particular case. In this section, we prove that this rule generally is valid. To do so, we show that, if this rule is violated (and the firm combines inputs so that the marginal product of a dollar's worth of one input does *not* equal the marginal product of a dollar's worth of some other input used), the firm is not minimizing its costs. Specifically, we take the case of the wheat farm, and proceed in two steps. (1) We show that if the marginal product of a dollar's worth of labor is *greater* than the marginal product of a dollar's worth of land, the firm is not minimizing costs. (2) We show that if the marginal product of a dollar's worth of labor is *less* than the marginal product of a dollar's worth of land, the firm is not minimizing costs.

Suppose that *the marginal product of a dollar's worth of labor is greater than the marginal product of a dollar's worth of land.* Since the marginal product of a dollar's worth of labor is greater than the marginal product of a dollar's worth of land, it must follow that the wheat farm can increase its output, *without increasing its costs,* if it substitutes a dollar's worth of labor for a dollar's worth of land. Suppose that the marginal product of a dollar's worth of labor is 2 bushels of wheat, whereas the marginal product of a dollar's worth of land is 1 bushel of wheat. Then, if it substitutes a dollar's worth of labor for a dollar's worth of land, the wheat farm can increase its output by 1 bushel of wheat without increasing its costs. (Why? Because the addition of an extra dollar's worth of labor increases output by 2 bushels, while the subtraction of the dollar's worth of land reduces output by 1 bushel—and the net effect is an increase in output of 1 bushel.) Thus, since the firm can increase its output without increasing its costs, it must be able to reduce its costs, if it maintains the same output. In other words, it must not be minimizing its costs.

One of the most common errors made by decision makers is that they do not ignore sunk costs. What is a sunk cost? It is a cost that has been incurred in the past and that cannot be altered or affected by any action the decision maker can take. For example, suppose that a real estate investor signs an agreement to buy a lot. The purchase price is $10,000. He makes a $2,000 down payment and will pay the remaining $8,000 in six months. Under the terms of the agreement, he will not secure title to the lot until he has paid the entire $10,000. If he fails to make the remaining payment of $8,000, the agreement states that he will lose his down payment, but he is not liable for the unpaid balance.

After buying this lot, and making the $2,000 down payment, the real estate investor travels to another city where he finds a lot which is just as desirable from his point of view as the one he has bought. Because

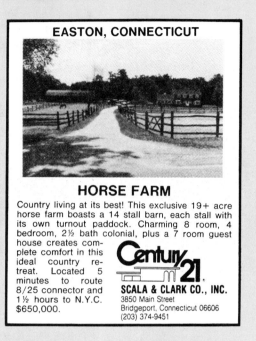

the real estate market in this city is depressed, the price of this lot is $7,000. The real estate investor wishes that he had seen this lot before purchasing the other one, but feels that there is nothing he can do. He only wants one such lot and, if he were to back out of the purchase agreement he signed, he would lose $2,000. Clearly, he doesn't want to incur such a loss!

But the real estate investor is committing a cardinal sin: he is not ignoring a sunk cost. Regardless of which lot he purchases, he loses the $2,000. Thus the $2,000 is a sunk cost. The real question is whether he will pay an *additional* $8,000 for the lot on which he has paid the down payment or whether he will pay an *additional* $7,000 for the lot he has seen more recently. Put in this way, there is no doubt about the proper course of action: he should ignore the $2,000 sunk cost, and buy the lot for $7,000. In this way, the total cost (including the sunk cost) is $9,000, which is less than the price of the lot he originally intended to purchase.

Suppose that *the marginal product of a dollar's worth of labor is less than the marginal product of a dollar's worth of land.* Since the marginal product of a dollar's worth of labor is less than the marginal product of a dollar's worth of land, it must follow that the wheat farm can increase its output, *without increasing its costs,* if it substitutes a dollar's worth of land for a dollar's worth of labor. Suppose that the marginal product of a dollar's worth of labor is 1 bushel of wheat, whereas the marginal product of a dollar's worth of land is 2 bushels of wheat. Then, if it substitutes a dollar's worth of land for a dollar's worth of labor, the wheat farm can increase its output by 1 bushel of wheat without increasing its costs. (Why? Because the addition of an extra dollar's worth of land increases output by 2 bushels, while the subtraction of a dollar's worth of labor reduces output by 1 bushel—and the net effect is an increase in output of 1 bushel.) Thus, since the firm can increase its output without increasing its costs, it must be able to reduce its costs, if it maintains the same output. In other words, it must not be minimizing its costs.

Since the firm is not minimizing the cost of producing its current output when the marginal product of a dollar's worth of labor is greater than, or less than, that of a dollar's worth of land, it must be true that *the firm is minimizing its costs only when the marginal product of a dollar's worth of labor equals that of a dollar's worth of land.* This is what we set out to prove.

Producing Kansas Corn: A Case Study

If by now you wonder about the practical payoff from this sort of analysis, consider how a distinguished agricultural economist, Earl Heady of Iowa State University, has used these methods to help farmers make better production decisions. Table 23.5 shows the various amounts of land and fertilizer that will produce 82.6 bushels of corn on Kansas Verdigras soil. As you can see, this amount of corn can be produced if 1.19 acres of land and no fertilizer are used, or if 1.11 acres of land and 20 pounds of fertilizer are used, or if .99 acres of land and 60 pounds of fertilizer are used, and so forth.

The third column of Table 23.5 shows the ratio of the marginal product of a pound of fertilizer to the marginal product of an acre of land, when each of these input combinations is used. For example, when 1.19 acres of land and no fertilizer are used, this ratio equals .0045. Based on the rule discussed in previous sections, a firm, if it minimizes costs, must set this ratio equal to the ratio of the price of a pound of fertilizer to the price of an acre of land. Why? Because the rule discussed above stipulates that the firm should choose an input combination so that

$$\frac{\text{marginal product of fertilizer}}{\text{price of fertilizer}} = \frac{\text{marginal product of land}}{\text{price of land}}.$$

So if we multiply both sides of this equation by the price of fertilizer, and divide both sides by the marginal product of land, we get

$$\frac{\text{marginal product of fertilizer}}{\text{marginal product of land}} = \frac{\text{price of fertilizer}}{\text{price of land}}.$$

Table 23.5

COMBINATIONS OF FERTILIZER AND LAND REQUIRED TO PRODUCE 82.6 BUSHELS OF CORN, AND RATIO OF MARGINAL PRODUCTS AT EACH SUCH COMBINATION

Amount of input used		Marginal product of fertilizer ÷ Marginal product of land
Fertilizer (pounds)	Land (acres)	
0	1.19	.0045
20	1.11	.0038
40	1.04	.0030
60	0.99	.0019
80	0.96	.0010
100	0.95	.0003

Source: E. Heady and L. Tweeten, *Resource Demand and Structure of the Agricultural Industry,* Ames: Iowa State University Press, 1963, p. 111.

Thus, to minimize costs, a firm should set the ratio in the third column of Table 23.5 equal to the ratio of the price of fertilizer to the price of land.

Heady and his coworkers, having obtained the results in Table 23.5, used this technique to determine the optimal input combination farmers should use to minimize their costs.[2] The optimal input combination depends on the price of land and the price of fertilizer. Suppose that a pound of fertilizer costs .003 times as much as an acre of land. Under these circumstances, the minimum-cost input combination would be 40 pounds of fertilizer and 1.04 acres of land—since, as shown in Table 23.5, this is the input combination where the ratio of the marginal product of fertilizer to the marginal product of land is .003. No matter what the ratio of the price of fertilizer to the price of land may be, the least-cost input combination can be derived this way.

Such results are of considerable practical value to farmers. Moreover, the same kind of analysis can be used by organizations in other sectors of the economy, not just agriculture. Studies of how the Defense Department could reduce its costs have utilized concepts and techniques of essentially this sort. In a more peaceful vein, this same kind of analysis has been used in various kinds of manufacturing firms. For example, steel firms have made many such studies to determine least-cost ways to produce steel, and auto firms have made similar studies to reduce their own costs.

[2] E. Heady and L. Tweeten, *Resource Demand and Structure of the Agricultural Industry,* Ames: Iowa State University Press, 1963. It is assumed that a certain amount of labor is used, this amount being proportional to the number of acres of land.

Test Yourself

1. Suppose that a cost-minimizing firm in a perfectly competitive market uses two inputs: labor and capital. If the marginal product of capital is twice the marginal product of labor, and if the price of a unit of labor is $4, what must be the price of a unit of capital?

2. In Figure 23.1, the marginal product of labor equals its average product when the latter is a maximum. Do you think that this is generally the case? Why or why not? (*Hint:* If the marginal product of an extra amount of labor exceeds the average product, will the average product increase? If it is less than the average product, will the average product decrease?)

3. A firm uses two inputs, capital and labor. The firm's chief engineer says that its output depends in the following way on the amount of labor and capital it uses:

$$Q = 3L + 4C,$$

where Q is the number of units of output produced per day, L is the number of units of labor used per day, and C is the amount of capital used per day. Does this relationship seem sensible? Why or why not?

4. In the previous problem, suppose that the price of using a unit of labor per day is $50 and the price of using a unit of capital per day is $100. What is the optimal input combination for the firm, if the relationship in the previous problem is valid? Does this seem reasonable? Why or why not?

Summary

1. Inputs can be classified into two categories: fixed and variable. A fixed input is one whose quantity cannot be changed during the period of time under consideration. A variable input is one whose quantity can be changed during the relevant period.

2. Whether an input is considered variable or fixed depends on the length of the period under consideration. The longer the period, the more inputs are variable, not fixed. The short run is defined as the period of time in which some of the firm's inputs (generally its plant and equipment) are fixed. The long run is the period of time in which all inputs are variable.

3. The average product of an input is the firm's total output divided by the amount of input used to produce this amount of output. The marginal product of an input is the addition to total output due to the addition of the last unit of input, the quantity of other inputs used being held constant.

4. The law of diminishing marginal returns states that if equal increments of an input are added (and the quantities of other inputs are held constant), the resulting increments of product will decrease beyond some point; that is, the marginal product of the input will diminish.

5. To minimize its costs, a firm must choose its input combination so that the marginal product of a dollar's worth of any one input equals the marginal product of a dollar's worth of any other input used. Put differently, the firm should combine inputs so that, for every input used, the marginal product of the input is proportional to its price. As an illustration, we showed how this sort of model can be used to determine the optimal combination of fertilizer and land in the production of Kansas corn.

Concepts for Review

Production function	**Short run**	**Marginal product**
Fixed input	**Long run**	**Law of diminishing**
Variable input	**Average product**	**marginal returns**

CHAPTER 24

Cost Analysis

The Peabody Coal Company, a huge steam-coal producer, signed many contracts with electric power companies during the 1960s, agreeing to supply coal at stipulated prices to the power companies for a number of years. By the mid-1970s, Peabody regretted these contracts because its costs had risen so much that it could not fulfill the contracts without losing money. Peabody hired McKinsey and Company, a leading management consulting firm, to figure out exactly what Peabody's costs of producing coal were in the mid-1970s. Then it went to the electric power companies and tried to renegotiate the contracts. Sometimes the power companies were willing to renegotiate; sometimes they weren't.

This example illustrates the major role played by a firm's costs in determining both its financial health and its behavior. In this chapter, we discuss the nature of costs, describe the various cost functions of the firm, and indicate some of the ways that these cost functions can be measured and used. Among the major questions taken up are: What do we mean by a firm's costs? How do various types of costs vary with the firm's output rate? Of what significance or use are the relationships between a firm's output and its various types of cost? These questions are of the utmost importance, both for the managers of a firm and for society as a whole.

What Are Costs?

The previous chapter discussed how we can determine the input combination that minimizes costs. But what do we mean by costs?

Although this question may seem foolishly simple, it is in fact tricky. *Fundamentally, the cost of a certain course of action is the value of the best*

513

alternative course of action that could have been adopted instead. The cost of producing automobiles is the value of the goods and services that could be obtained from the resources used currently in automobile production if these resources were no longer used to produce automobiles. In general, the costs of inputs to a firm are their values in their most valuable alternative uses. As we pointed out in Chapter 1, this is the so-called **opportunity cost,** or **alternative cost** doctrine. (Recall Basic Idea #2 on p. 10.)

Suppose that a firm's owner devotes 50 hours a week to the firm's business, and that, because he is the owner, he pays himself no salary. According to the usual rules of accounting, as we saw in Chapter 6, the costs of his labor are not included in the firm's income statement. But according to the economist's opportunity cost doctrine, the cost of his labor is by no means zero! Instead, this cost equals whatever amount he could obtain if he worked 50 hours a week for someone else. Both economists and sophisticated accountants agree that opportunity costs are the relevant costs for many types of problems, and that failure to use the proper concept of cost can result in serious mistakes.

Costs for the individual firm are the necessary payments to the owners of resources to get them to provide these resources to the firm. To obtain these resources as inputs, the firm must bid them away from alternative uses. The payments made to the owners of these resources may be either explicit or implicit costs. If a payment is made to a supplier, laborer, or some other resource owner besides the firm's owner, this is an explicit cost, which is paid for in an explicit way. But if a resource is owned by the firm's owner, there may be no explicit payment for it, as in the case of the labor of the owner who paid himself no salary. *The costs of such owner-supplied resources are called **implicit costs.*** As we stressed above, such implicit costs equal what these resources could bring if they were used in their most valuable alternative employments. And the firm's profits (or losses), as defined by the economist, are the difference between the firm's revenues and its total costs, both explicit and implicit.

Short-Run Cost Functions

In the previous chapter, we showed how to determine the least-cost combination of inputs to produce any quantity of output. With this information at our disposal, it is easy to determine the minimum cost of producing each quantity of output. *Knowing the (minimum) cost of producing each quantity of output, we can define and measure the firm's **cost functions,** which show how various types of costs are related to the firm's output.* A firm's cost functions will vary, depending on whether they are based on the short or long run. In the short run, the firm cannot vary the quantities of plant and equipment it uses. These are the firm's fixed inputs, and they determine the scale of its operations.

TOTAL FIXED COST

Three kinds of costs are important in the short run—total fixed cost, total variable cost, and total cost. **Total fixed cost** *is the total expenditure per period of time by the firm for fixed inputs.* Since the quantity of the fixed

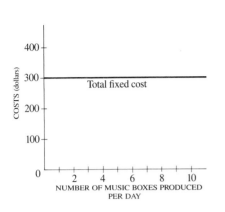

Figure 24.1

Total Fixed Cost, Bugsbane Music Box Company *The total fixed cost function is always a horizontal line, since fixed costs do not vary with output.*

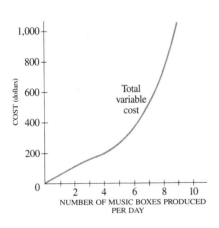

Figure 24.2

Total Variable Cost, Bugsbane Music Box Company *Total variable cost is the total expenditure per period of time on variable inputs. Due to the law of diminishing marginal returns, total variable cost increases first at a decreasing rate, then at an increasing rate.*

Table 24.1

FIXED, VARIABLE, AND TOTAL COSTS, BUGSBANE MUSIC BOX COMPANY

Number of music boxes produced per day	Total fixed cost	Total variable cost (dollars)	Total cost
0	300	0	300
1	300	60	360
2	300	110	410
3	300	160	460
4	300	200	500
5	300	260	560
6	300	360	660
7	300	510	810
8	300	710	1,010
9	300	1,060	1,360

inputs is unvarying (by definition), the total fixed cost will be the same whatever the firm's level of output. Among the firm's fixed costs in the short run are property taxes and interest on bonds issued in the past. If the firm has contracts with suppliers and workers that cannot be renegotiated (without dire consequences) in the short run, the expenses involved in meeting these contracts are also fixed costs.

To inject a whimsical note into a subject not otherwise noted for its amusement value, consider a hypothetical firm—the Bugsbane Music Box Company. This firm produces a high-priced line of music boxes that, when opened, play your favorite aria, show tune, or hymn, and emit a deadly gas that kills all insects, rodents, or pests—and, alas, occasionally a frail Chihuahua—within a 50-foot radius. Table 24.1 shows that Bugsbane's fixed costs are $300 per day; the firm's total fixed cost function is shown in Figure 24.1.

TOTAL VARIABLE COST

Total variable cost *is the firm's total expenditure on variable inputs per period of time.* Since higher output rates require greater utilization of variable inputs, they mean a higher total variable cost. Thus, if Bugsbane increases its daily production of music boxes, it must increase the amount it spends per day on metal (for the components), wood (for the outside of the boxes), labor (for the assembly of the boxes), and other variable inputs. Table 24.1 shows Bugsbane's total variable costs at various output rates; Figure 24.2 shows the firm's total variable cost function.

Up to the output rate of 4 music boxes per day, total variable cost increases at a decreasing rate; beyond that output rate, total variable cost increases at an increasing rate. It is important to understand that this characteristic of the total variable cost function results from the operation of the law of diminishing marginal returns. At small output rates, increases in the utilization of variable inputs may bring about increases in their productivity, causing total variable cost to increase with output, but at a decreasing rate. Beyond a point, however, there are diminishing marginal returns from the variable input, with the result that total variable costs increase at an increasing rate.

515

TOTAL COST

Total cost is the sum of total fixed cost and total variable cost. Thus, to obtain the Bugsbane Company's total cost at a given output, we need only add its total fixed cost and its total variable cost at that output. The result is shown in Table 24.1, and the corresponding total cost function is shown in Figure 24.3. Since the total cost function and the total variable cost function differ by only a constant amount (equal to total fixed cost), they have the same shape, as shown in Figure 24.4, which brings together all three of the total cost functions (or cost curves as they are often called).

Average Costs in the Short Run

The president of Bugsbane unquestionably cares about the average cost of a music box as well as the total cost incurred; so do economists. *Average cost tells you how much a product costs per unit of output.* There are three average cost functions, one corresponding to each of the three total cost functions.

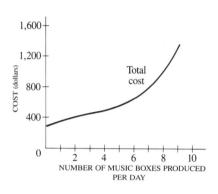

Figure 24.3
Total Cost, Bugsbane Music Box Company *Total cost is the sum of total fixed cost and total variable cost. It has the same shape as the total variable cost curve, since they differ by only a constant amount (equal to total fixed cost).*

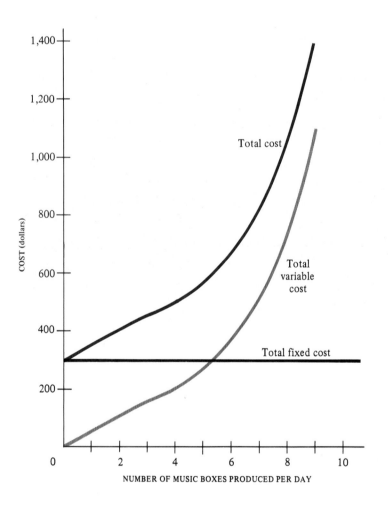

Figure 24.4
Fixed, Variable, and Total Costs, Bugsbane Music Box Company *All three cost functions, presented in Figures 24.1–24.3, are brought back for a curtain call.*

Table 24.2

AVERAGE FIXED COST, AVERAGE VARIABLE COST, AND AVERAGE TOTAL COST, BUGSBANE MUSIC BOX COMPANY

Number of music boxes produced per day	Average fixed cost	Average variable cost (dollars)	Average total cost
1	300(= 300 ÷ 1)	60(= 60 ÷ 1)	360(= 360 ÷ 1)
2	150(= 300 ÷ 2)	55(= 110 ÷ 2)	205(= 410 ÷ 2)
3	100(= 300 ÷ 3)	53(= 160 ÷ 3)	153(= 460 ÷ 3)
4	75(= 300 ÷ 4)	50(= 200 ÷ 4)	125(= 500 ÷ 4)
5	60(= 300 ÷ 5)	52(= 260 ÷ 5)	112(= 560 ÷ 5)
6	50(= 300 ÷ 6)	60(= 360 ÷ 6)	110(= 660 ÷ 6)
7	43(= 300 ÷ 7)	73(= 510 ÷ 7)	116(= 810 ÷ 7)
8	38(= 300 ÷ 8)	89(= 710 ÷ 8)	126(= 1010 ÷ 8)
9	33(= 300 ÷ 9)	118(= 1060 ÷ 9)	151(= 1360 ÷ 9)

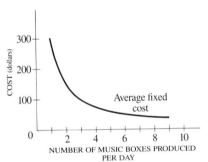

Figure 24.5

Average Fixed Cost, Bugsbane Music Box Company *Average fixed cost is total fixed cost divided by the firm's output. Since it equals a constant (total fixed cost) divided by the output rate, it must decline with increases in output.*

Figure 24.6

Average Variable Cost, Bugsbane Music Box Company *Average variable cost is total variable cost divided by the firm's output. Beyond a point (in this case, 4 music boxes per day), average variable cost rises with increases in output because of the law of diminishing marginal returns.*

AVERAGE FIXED COST

Let's begin with *average fixed cost, which is simply the total fixed cost divided by the firm's output.* Table 24.2 and Figure 24.5 show the average fixed cost function for the Bugsbane Music Box Company. Average fixed cost must decline with increases in output, since it equals a constant—total fixed cost—divided by the output rate.

AVERAGE VARIABLE COST

The next type of average cost is *average variable cost, which is total variable cost divided by output.* For Bugsbane, the average variable cost function is shown in Table 24.2 and Figure 24.6. At first, increases in the output rate result in decreases in average variable cost, but beyond a point, they result in higher average variable cost. This is because the law of diminishing marginal returns is in operation. As more and more of the variable inputs are utilized, the extra output they produce declines beyond some point, so that the amount spent on variable input per unit of output tends to increase.

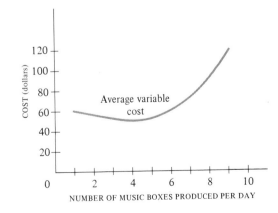

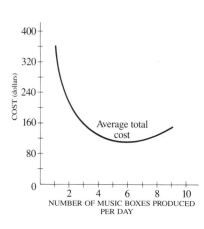

Figure 24.7
Average Total Cost, Bugsbane Music Box Company *Average total cost is total cost divided by output. It equals average fixed cost plus average variable cost. When output is 4 music boxes or less per day, both average fixed cost and average variable cost are decreasing, so average total cost must decrease too. When output is 5 or 6 music boxes per day, average total cost decreases because the fall in average fixed cost more than offsets the rise in average variable cost. When output exceeds 6 music boxes per day, the rise in average variable cost more than offsets the fall in average fixed cost, so average total cost increases.*

AVERAGE TOTAL COST

The third type of average cost is *average total cost,* *which is total cost divided by output.* For Bugsbane, the average total cost function is shown in Table 24.2 and Figure 24.7. At any level of output, *average total cost equals average fixed cost plus average variable cost.* This is easy to prove:

$$\text{average total cost} = \frac{\text{total cost}}{\text{output}} = \frac{\text{total fixed cost} + \text{total variable cost}}{\text{output}},$$

since total cost = total fixed cost + total variable cost. Moreover,

$$\frac{\text{total fixed cost} + \text{total variable cost}}{\text{output}} = \frac{\text{total fixed cost}}{\text{output}} + \frac{\text{total variable cost}}{\text{output}}$$

and the right-hand side of this equation equals average fixed cost plus average variable cost. Thus we have proved what we set out to prove.

The fact that average total cost is the sum of average fixed cost and average variable cost helps explain the shape of the average cost function. If, as the output rate goes up, both average fixed cost and average variable cost decrease, average total cost must decrease too. But beyond some point, average total cost must increase because increases in average variable cost eventually more than offset decreases in average fixed cost. However, average total cost achieves its minimum after average variable cost, because the increases in average variable cost are for a time more than offset by decreases in average fixed cost. All the average cost functions are shown below in Figure 24.9.

Marginal Cost in the Short Run

No one can really understand the operations of a business firm without understanding the concept of *marginal cost,* *the addition to total cost resulting from the addition of the last unit of output.* To see how marginal cost is calculated, look at Table 24.3, which shows the total cost function of the Bugsbane Music Box Company. When output is between 0 and 1 music

Table 24.3

CALCULATION OF MARGINAL COST, BUGSBANE MUSIC BOX COMPANY

Number of music boxes produced per day	Total cost	Marginal Cost (dollars)
0	300	60 (=360−300)
1	360	50 (=410−360)
2	410	50 (=460−410)
3	460	40 (=500−460)
4	500	60 (=560−500)
5	560	100 (=660−560)
6	660	150 (=810−660)
7	810	200 (=1,010−810)
8	1,010	350 (=1,360−1,010)
9	1,360	

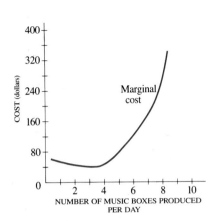

Figure 24.8

Marginal Cost, Bugsbane Music Box Company *Marginal cost is the addition to total cost arising from the addition of the last unit of output. The marginal cost of the first unit of output (which according to Table 24.3, is $60) is plotted at the midpoint between 0 and 1 units of output. The marginal cost of the second unit of output is plotted at the midpoint between 1 and 2 units of output. The marginal cost function connects these and other points showing the marginal cost of various amounts of output. Beyond a point (in this case, between 3 and 4 music boxes per day), marginal cost increases because of the law of diminishing marginal returns.*

Basic Idea #47: *Marginal cost is the addition to total cost resulting from the addition of the last unit of output. Beyond some point, a firm's marginal cost rises as more and more is produced —due to the law of diminishing marginal returns (see Basic Idea #45 on p. 505.) To comprehend how firms operate, it is extremely important that you understand the concept of marginal cost.*

box per day, the firm's marginal cost is $60, since this is the *extra cost* of producing the first music box per day. In other words, $60 equals marginal cost in this situation because it is the difference between the total cost of producing 1 music box per day ($360) and the total cost of producing 0 music boxes per day ($300).

In general, marginal cost will vary depending on the firm's output level. Thus Table 24.3 shows that at Bugsbane marginal cost is $50 when the firm produces between 1 and 2 music boxes per day, $100 when the firm produces between 5 and 6 music boxes per day, and $350 when the firm produces between 8 and 9 music boxes per day. Table 24.3—and Figure 24.8, which shows the marginal cost function graphically—indicate that marginal cost, after decreasing with increases in output at low output levels, increases with further increases in output. In other words, *beyond some point it becomes more and more costly for the firm to produce yet another unit of output.*

INCREASING MARGINAL COST AND DIMINISHING RETURNS

The reason why marginal cost increases beyond some output level is to be found in the law of diminishing marginal returns. *If (beyond some point) increases in variable inputs result in less and less extra output, it follows that a larger and larger quantity of variable inputs must be added to produce an extra unit of output. Thus the cost of producing an extra unit of output must increase.*

To illustrate how diminishing marginal returns result in increasing marginal cost, let's return for a moment to the wheat farm in Tables 23.1 and 23.3. (For convenience, the data regarding this farm are reproduced in Table 24.4.) If it is producing 70 bushels of wheat, it requires an extra 1/30 man-year of labor to produce an extra bushel—since Table 24.4 shows that the marginal product of a man-year of labor is 30 bushels. But if it is producing 100 bushels of wheat, an extra 1/25 man-year of labor is needed to produce an extra bushel, since Table 24.4 shows that the marginal product of a man-year of labor is 25 bushels. Thus more of the variable input (specifically, 1/25 man-year of labor rather than 1/30 man-year of labor) is required to produce an extra bushel of wheat. And *since more and more of the variable input is required to produce an extra unit of output, the cost of producing an extra unit of output increases as output rises.*

Table 24.4

AVERAGE AND MARGINAL PRODUCTS OF LABOR, 1-ACRE WHEAT FARM

Number of man-years of labor	Total output	Marginal product (bushels per man-year)	Average product
0	0		—
		30	
1	30		30
		40	
2	70		35
		30	
3	100		33⅓
		25	
4	125		31¼
		20	
5	145		29

RELATIONSHIP BETWEEN MARGINAL COST AND AVERAGE COST FUNCTIONS

The relationship between the marginal cost function and the average cost functions must be noted. Figure 24.9 shows the marginal cost curve together with the three average cost curves. *The marginal cost curve intersects both the average variable cost curve and the average total cost curve at their minimum points.* The reason for this is simple. If the extra cost of a unit of output is greater (less) than the average cost of the units of output already produced, the addition of the extra unit of output clearly must raise (lower) the average cost of production. Thus, if marginal cost is greater (less) than average cost, average cost must be rising (falling). And if this is so, average cost can be a minimum only when it equals marginal cost. (The same reasoning holds for both average total cost and average variable cost, and for the short and long runs.)

To make sure that you understand this point, consider the following numerical example. Suppose that the average total cost of producing 4 units of output is $10, and that the marginal cost of the fifth unit of output is less than $10. Will the average total cost be less for 5 units of output than for 4 units? It will be less, because the fifth unit's cost will pull down

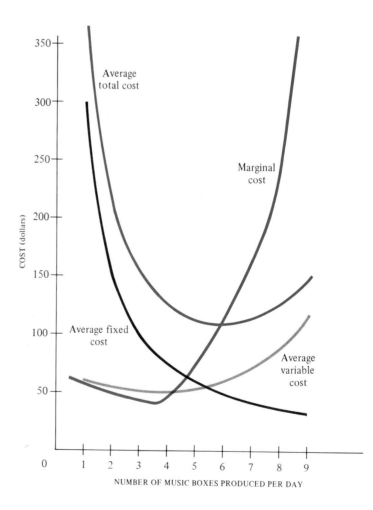

Figure 24.9

Average Fixed Cost, Average Variable Cost, Average Total Cost, and Marginal Cost, Bugsbane Music Box Company
All of the curves presented in Figures 24.5–24.8 are brought together for review. Note that the marginal cost curve intersects both the average variable cost curve and the average total cost curve at their minimum points.

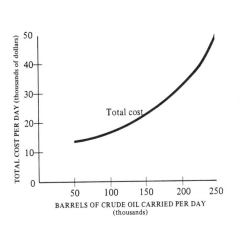

Figure 24.10

Total Cost Function, Crude-Oil Pipeline, 18-Inch Diameter *This graph shows the total cost function in an actual case. Note that it is shaped as economic theory would predict.*

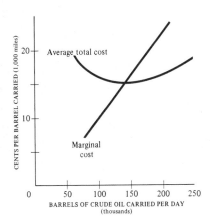

Figure 24.11

Average Total Cost Function and Marginal Cost Function, Crude-Oil Pipeline, 18-Inch Diameter *This graph shows the average cost and marginal cost functions in an actual case. Note that their shape follows economic theory.*

the average. On the other hand, if the marginal cost of the fifth unit of output had been greater than $10, the average total cost for 5 units of output would have been greater than for 4 units of output, because the fifth unit's cost would pull up the average. Thus *average total cost will fall when it is above marginal cost, and it will rise when it is below marginal cost.* Consequently, *when it is a minimum, average total cost must equal marginal cost,* as shown in Figure 24.9.

Short-Run Cost Functions of a Crude-Oil Pipeline: A Case Study

Cost functions are not academic toys, but eminently practical analytical devices that play a major role in decision making by business executives and government agencies. To illustrate the nature and use of short-run cost functions, we will take up the real-world case of crude-oil pipelines where we left off (in the previous chapter). In the short run, it is reasonable to assume that the diameter of a pipeline is fixed. Given the production function in Table 23.2, it is easy to figure out the total cost of carrying various amounts of oil per day, with a pipeline of a given diameter. In other words, we assume that the company that owns the pipeline can vary the horsepower by varying the number and type of pumping stations, but that the diameter of the pipeline is fixed.[1] Under these circumstances, if the diameter of the pipeline is 18 inches, what will the pipeline's cost functions look like?

Figures 24.10 and 24.11 answer this question. Figure 24.10 shows the *total cost function* for an 18-inch pipeline—the total daily cost of operating it, given that it carries various amounts of crude oil per day. If the pipeline carries 200,000 barrels of oil per day, the total daily cost is $33,000; if the amount of oil is increased to 250,000 barrels per day, the total daily cost rises to $48,000.

Figure 24.11 shows the *average total cost function* for an 18-inch pipeline—the total daily cost per barrel for the pipeline, given that it carries various amounts of crude oil per day. According to Figure 24.11, the total daily cost per barrel for this pipeline to carry 200,000 barrels per day is $.16½, and the total daily cost per barrel for it to carry 250,000 barrels per day is $.19⅕. Figure 24.11 also shows the *marginal cost function* for such a pipeline—the additional daily cost of carrying an extra barrel of crude oil per day. When this pipeline is carrying 200,000 barrels per day, the marginal cost runs to about $.23.

To the operators of the pipeline, a knowledge of these cost functions can mean the difference between profit and loss. For example, suppose that the operators of a particular 18-inch pipeline are thinking about increasing the amount of oil the pipeline will carry per day. Specifically, suppose that the pipeline can now carry 200,000 barrels per day and that the operators are thinking about adding enough horsepower so that it can carry 250,000 barrels per day. Suppose that, according to the best esti-

[1] Because the number and type of pumping stations must be altered, Leslie Cookenboo refers to this as the "intermediate run." See Cookenboo, *Crude Oil Pipe Lines and Competition in the Oil Industry,* Cambridge, Mass.: Harvard University Press, 1955.

mates available, the pipeline can get $5 million in additional revenue each year if it carries the additional 50,000 barrels per day. Should the operators increase in this way the amount of oil the pipeline can carry?

If they want to increase profits, they should decide against this increase in the amount of horsepower. According to the total cost function in Figure 24.10, the pipeline's daily costs would increase by $15,000 per day if horsepower were increased so that 250,000, rather than 200,000 barrels of oil could be carried per day, while the extra oil carried would increase daily revenues by $5 million ÷ 365, or about $14,000 per day. Thus the extra costs would exceed the extra revenue, which means that the pipeline's profit would be reduced by increasing the amount of horsepower. In making decisions of this sort (and they must make them repeatedly!), managers must rely heavily on information about the relevant cost functions.

Example 24.1   The Costs of a Dairy Farm

According to Leonard Weiss of the University of Wisconsin,* a typical dairy farm with 50 cows located near one of the large cities on the eastern seaboard might have the following relationship between cost and output:

Output (thousands of pounds of milk per year)	Total fixed cost (dollars per year)	Total variable cost (dollars per year)
0	24,000	0
400	24,000	9,000
440	24,000	10,650
480	24,000	13,050
520	24,000	18,000

(a) Included in the fixed cost is $5,600 in interest on the farmer's investment in the farm. If the farmer owns the farm (and does not have to pay interest to anyone else), should this item still be included? (b) Suppose that the farmer and his wife do all the work, and that the opportunity cost of their labor is the same, regardless of the farm's output. Is their labor cost a fixed or variable cost? (c) What is the marginal cost of a pound of milk when output is between 480 and 520 thousands of pounds per year? (d) At which of the above output levels is average total cost a minimum? Is this the output that the farmer should choose?

SOLUTION

(a) Yes, because if he sold this farm, he could lend out the proceeds and get $5,600 in interest. Thus this is the opportunity cost of the farmer's investment in the farm. (b) It is a fixed cost. (c) ($18,000 − $13,050) ÷ 40,000 = 12.4 cents. (d) 480 thousand pounds. In general, as we shall see in the following chapter, the farmer, if he or she wants to maximize profit, should not choose the output in the short run that minimizes average total cost.

* L. Weiss, *Case Studies in American Industry,* New York: John Wiley, 1980.

Test Yourself

1. Suppose that a firm's short-run total cost function is as follows:

Output (number of units per year)	Total cost per year (dollars)
0	20,000
1	20,100
2	20,200
3	20,300
4	20,500
5	20,800

What are the firm's total fixed costs? What are its total variable costs when it produces 4 units per year?

2. In Question 1, what is the firm's marginal cost when between 4 and 5 units are produced per year? Does marginal cost increase beyond some output level?

3. In Question 1, what is the firm's average cost when it produces 1 unit per year? 2 units per year? 3 units per year? 4 units per year? 5 units per year?

4. Fill in the blanks below:

Total output	Total fixed cost	Total variable cost	Average total cost (dollars)	Average fixed cost	Average variable cost
0	500	—			
1	—	20	—	—	—
2	—	—	300	—	—
3	—	—	—	—	133⅓
4	—	1,100	—	—	—

5. In Question 4, does marginal cost increase with increases in output? Explain.

Long-Run Cost Functions

THE LONG-RUN AVERAGE COST FUNCTION

We have held to the last one additional kind of cost function that plays a very important role in economic analysis. This is the firm's **long-run average cost function,** *which shows the minimum average cost of producing each output level when any desired type or scale of plant can be built.* Unlike the cost functions discussed in the previous sections, this cost function pertains to the long run—*to a period long enough so that all inputs are variable and none is fixed.* As pointed out in the previous chapter, a useful way to look at the long run is to consider it a *planning horizon.* The firm must continually be planning ahead and trying to decide its strategy in the long run.

Suppose a firm can build plants of three sizes—small, medium, and large. The short-run average total cost functions corresponding to these plants are AA', BB', and DD' in Figure 24.12. If the firm is still in the planning stage of plant construction, it can choose whichever plant has the lowest costs. Consequently, the firm will choose the small plant if it believes its output rate will be smaller than OQ_1, the medium plant if it believes its output rate will be above OQ_1, but below OQ_2, and the large plant if it believes that its output rate will be above OQ_2. Thus the long-run average cost curve is $AUVD'$. And if, as is generally the case, there are many possible types of plants, the long-run average cost curve looks like LL' in Figure 24.13. (Only a few of the short-run average cost curves are shown in Figure 24.13.)

The usefulness of the long-run average cost function can be illustrated by the familiar case of crude-oil pipelines. Figure 24.14 shows the long-run average cost function for these pipelines, as well as selected short-run

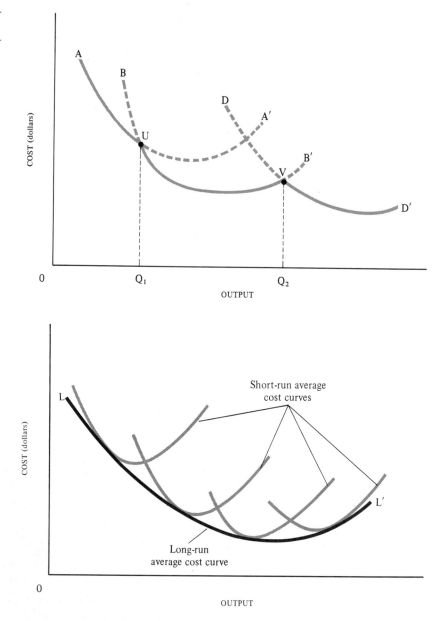

Figure 24.12
Short-Run Average Cost Curves and Long-Run Average Cost Curve *The short-run average total cost functions for three plants—small, medium, and large—are AA′, BB′, and DD′. The long-run average cost function is AUVD′, if these are the only three types of plant that can be built.*

Figure 24.13
Long-Run Average Cost Curve *If many possible types of plants can be built, the long-run average cost function is LL′.*

average cost functions (corresponding to diameters of 8, 10, 12, 14, 16, 18, 20, 24, 26, 30, and 32 inches). Note that long-run average cost—that is, cost per barrel—decreases as more and more oil is carried per day, at least up to 400,000 barrels per day. Thus it appears that costs are reduced when the greatest possible quantities of oil are transported in large-diameter pipelines.

This fact is important in evaluating the effects of various kinds of market structure in the pipeline industry. *If long-run average costs decrease with increases in output up to an output representing all, or nearly all, of the market, it is wasteful to force competition in such an industry, since costs would be greater if the industry output were divided among a number of firms than if it were produced by only one or two firms.* More will be said on this score in Chapter 26.

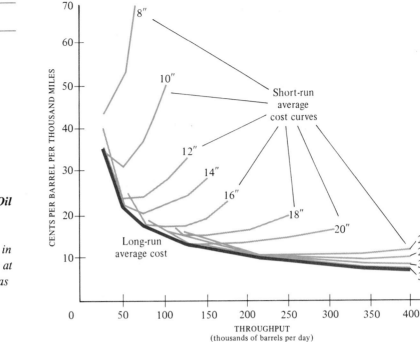

Figure 24.14
Costs per Barrel of Operating Crude-Oil Trunk Pipeline *This graph shows the long-run average cost curve (and the revelant short-run average cost curves) in an actual case. Note that in this range at least, long-run average cost decreases as output increases.*

Returns to Scale

What determines the shape of the long-run average cost function in a particular industry? Its shape must depend upon the characteristics of the production function—specifically, upon whether there are increasing, decreasing, or constant returns to scale. To understand what these terms mean, consider a long-run situation and suppose that the firm increases the amount of all inputs by the same proportion. What will happen to output? *If output increases by a larger proportion than each of the inputs, this is a case of **increasing returns to scale.** If output increases by a smaller proportion than each of the inputs, this is a case of **decreasing returns to scale.** If output increases by the same proportion as each of the inputs, this is a case of **constant returns to scale.***

At first glance it may seem that constant returns to scale must always prevail. After all, if two factories are built with the same equipment and use the same type and number of workers, it would seem obvious that they can produce twice as much output as one such factory. But things are not that simple. If a firm doubles its scale, it may be able to *use techniques that could not be used at the smaller scale.* Some inputs are not available in small units; for example, we cannot install half a numerically controlled machine tool. Because of indivisibilities of this sort, increasing returns to scale may occur. Thus, although one could double a firm's size by simply building two small factories, this may be inefficient. One large factory may be more efficient than two smaller factories of the same total capacity because it is large enough to use certain techniques and inputs that the smaller factories cannot use.

Another reason for increasing returns to scale stems from certain *geo-*

metrical relations. For example, since the volume of a box that is $3 \times 3 \times 3$ feet is 27 times as great as the volume of a box that is $1 \times 1 \times 1$ foot, the former box can carry 27 times as much as the latter box. But since the area of the six sides of the $3 \times 3 \times 3$-foot box is 54 square feet and the area of the six sides of the $1 \times 1 \times 1$-foot box is 6 square feet, the former box only requires 9 times as much wood as the latter. Greater *specialization* also can result in increasing returns to scale. As more men and machines are used, it is possible to subdivide tasks and allow various inputs to specialize.

Decreasing returns to scale can also occur; the most frequently cited reason is *the difficulty of coordinating a large enterprise.* It can be difficult even in a small firm to obtain the information required to make important decisions; in a large firm, the difficulties tend to be greater. It can be difficult even in a small firm to be certain that management's wishes are being carried out; in a larger firm these difficulties too tend to be greater. Although the advantages of a large organization seem to have captured the public fancy, there are often very great disadvantages as well.

Whether there are increasing, decreasing, or constant returns to scale in a particular situation must be settled case by case. Moreover, the answer is likely to depend on the particular range of output considered. There frequently are increasing returns to scale up to some level of output, then perhaps constant returns to scale up to a higher level of output, beyond which there may be decreasing returns to scale. This pattern is responsible for the *U*-shaped long-run average cost function in Figure 24.13. At relatively small output levels, there are increasing returns to scale, and long-run average cost decreases as output rises. At relatively high output levels, there are decreasing returns to scale, and long-run average cost increases as output rises.

As we shall see in the following section, this *U*-shaped pattern is not found in all industries. Within the range covered by the available data, there is little or no evidence in many industries that long-run average cost increases as output rises. But this may be because the data do not cover a wide enough range. Eventually, one would expect long-run average cost to rise because of problems of coordination, increased red tape, and reduced flexibility. Firms as large as General Motors or IBM are continually bedeviled by the very real difficulties of enormous size.

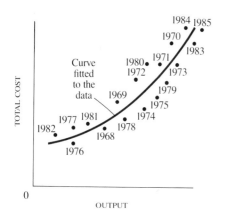

Figure 24.15

Relationship between Total Cost and Output: Time Series for a Particular Firm *One very crude way to estimate the total cost curve is to plot total cost in each year against total output in that year, and draw a curve, like the one shown in the diagram, that fits the points reasonably well. However, this technique is generally too crude to be reliable.*

Measurement and Application of Cost Functions

MEASUREMENT OF COST FUNCTIONS

Countless studies have been made to estimate cost functions in particular firms and industries. Many of these have been based on the relationship over time between cost and output. Figure 24.15 shows the total costs of a hypothetical firm in various years plotted against the firm's output in these years. Based on the data, a reasonable approximation to the firm's total cost function might be the curve that is drawn in Figure 24.15. However, there are a number of difficulties in this simple procedure. For one thing, the firm's cost function may not have remained fixed throughout this period.

For another, accounting data on costs may not be as accurate as one would like.[2] For these and other reasons, economists and statisticians have devised more sophisticated techniques to estimate cost functions.

To illustrate the sorts of results that have been obtained, Figure 24.16 shows the total cost function, average total cost function, and marginal cost function for a leather belt shop. Note that the total cost function appears linear, that is, a straight line, in the relevant range.

These results were obtained over 40 years ago by one of the pioneers in this field, Joel Dean of Columbia University.[3] Since that time, a great deal of evidence has been amassed on the shape of the cost functions of individual firms and industries. Two findings are particularly worth noting. First, *within the range of observed data, the long-run average cost curve in many industries seems to be L-shaped* (as in Figure 24.17), *not U-shaped* (as in Figure 24.13). That is, there is little or no evidence that it turns upward, rather than remains horizontal, at high output levels. As pointed out in the previous section, this may be due in part to the limited range of the data. Second, *many empirical studies indicate that marginal cost in the short run tends to be constant in the relevant output range.* However, this really does not contradict our assertions in previous sections, because the data used in these studies often do not cover periods when the firm was operating at peak capacity.

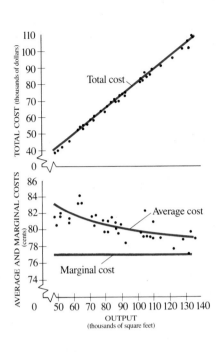

Figure 24.16

Total, Average, and Marginal Cost Functions of a Leather Belt Shop *This graph shows the short-run total, average, and marginal cost curves in an actual case. Note that marginal cost is constant in this case, but the data pertain only to a limited range of output levels.*

Figure 24.17

Apparent Shape of Many Long-Run Average Cost Curves *Within the range of observed data, there is little or no evidence in many industries that the long-run average cost curve turns upward, rather than remains horizontal, at high output levels. But the range of observed data is limited.*

BREAK-EVEN CHARTS

Estimated cost functions are used in a variety of ways by firms and government agencies. One important practical application of cost functions is to so-called **break-even charts.** To construct a break-even chart, *the firm's total revenue must be plotted on the same chart with its total cost function.* It is generally assumed that the price the firm receives for its product will not be influenced by the amount it sells, so that total revenue is proportional

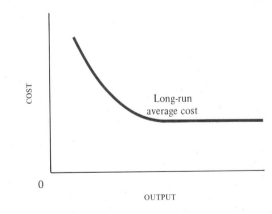

[2] Some of the difficulties are that the depreciation of an asset is often determined by the tax laws rather than economic criteria, many inputs are valued at historical, rather than opportunity cost, and accountants sometimes use arbitrary allocations of overhead and joint costs.

[3] Joel Dean, *The Relation of Cost to Output for a Leather Belt Shop,* New York: National Bureau of Economic Research, 1941.

HOW ROBOTS AFFECT FIRMS' COST CURVES

Although articles in the popular press often exaggerate the abilities and social implications of robots, it certainly is true that they will have a noteworthy effect on production costs, particularly in the metal working industries. According to the Robot Institute of America, a robot is defined as a "reprogrammable, multi-functional manipulator designed to move material parts, tools, or specialized devices through variable programmed motions for the performance of a variety of tasks."[1] The market for robots has been estimated to rise by about 30-35 percent per year over the rest of the 1980s. Many experts expect that the world stock of robots will number about 300,000 by 1990.

Robots are currently used in a variety of processes, such as forging, welding, assembly, painting, and machine tool loading. For example, at John Deere and Company, robots are handling about 80 percent of the painting on each tractor produced, resulting in a considerable saving of labor. Volvo introduced 28 robots into an automobile assembly line to make about 700 spot welds, replacing 67 workers with a handful of key staff. Often, robots are used to do difficult and dangerous jobs in foundries and welding and painting operations.

Firms generally introduce robots to reduce labor inputs. According to recent evidence from Japan, the most advanced robots currently in use sometimes displace 2 to 4 workers per shift. For example, in one Japanese factory, the operation of five die cast machines required five workers before the robot was introduced; after its introduction, only one worker was needed. However, most studies seem to indicate that the average number of workers displaced per shift by a robot is only about 1.5. Moreover, although robots reduce the amount of labor required to do some types of work, they increase the amount of labor required to do other types (such as the maintenance of the robots). Thus the reduction in labor requirements often is not as large as it may seem.

Industrial robots are a key component of flexible manufacturing systems that allow relatively low-cost production of batches of custom-tailored products. For example, John Deere's tractor plant can produce tractors in more than 5,000 configurations. This plant is often cited as a model of modern automation. In the section where transmissions are assembled, a computer identifies which of 10 different models the transmission is to be before its elements start down the assembly line. A lone worker loads the raw castings on carts, and punches a code into a computer terminal. The computer takes over from that point on.

Besides reducing labor requirements, the use of flexible manufacturing systems can reduce capital requirements. At present, machine tools are idle most of the time, because human operators have to set up, inspect, load, and unload their machines. Also, plants are closed for holidays, strikes, and other reasons; and when plants are not closed, there may not be three shifts

---

[1] "Robots: The Users and the Makers," *The OECD Observer*, July 1983, p. 12.

every day of the week. By using robots and computer control, firms can reduce considerably the amount of idle time which has been a prime factor in maintaining relatively low machine productivity. For example, a Japanese firm's flexible manufacturing system enables it to run an unmanned night shift, because the machining of parts is so completely automated.

According to engineers and business executives, the use of robots and flexible manufacturing systems is beginning to have a significant effect on the long-run average cost curve for the production of many products in the metal-working industries. Because they reduce the amount of labor and capital inputs required per unit of output, these new technologies are pushing the long-run average cost curve downward, as shown in panel A of the graph below. However, many observers report that the new long-run average cost curve is not parallel to the old one. Instead, the vertical distance between the new and old cost curves is greater at intermediate than very large output levels, as shown below, because the reduction in average cost is greater for intermediate ranges of output than for very large output levels (where mass production techniques are appropriate).

In the case of automobile production, the Organization for Economic Cooperation and Development (OECD) has reported that these technological changes have resulted in a reduction in the minimum efficient scale for an automobile assembly plant (as well as for an engine and transmission plant). Whereas such a plant formerly had to produce about 400,000 vehicles per year to have reasonably low costs, plants producing 250,000 vehicles now have low enough costs to be competitive. (The situation is shown in panel B of the graph below.) Indeed, Nissan's proposed United Kingdom plant has been planned for 200,000 units per year. Such a change in the minimum efficient scale of plant is regarded as an important development in the automobile industry.

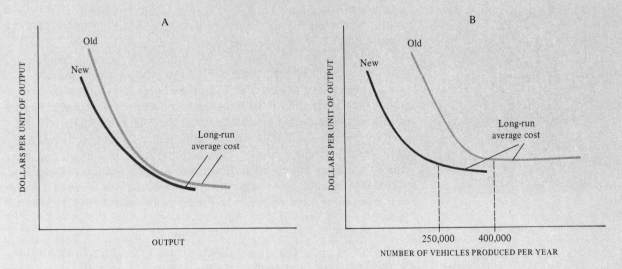

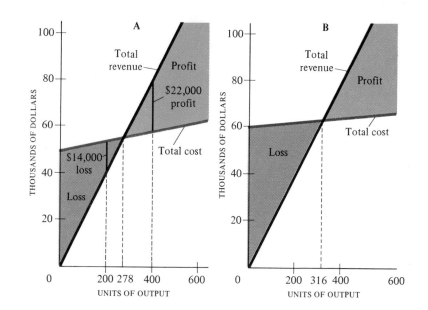

Figure 24.18

Break-Even Chart, Cable Manufacturing Firm *In panels A and B, the sales price of each unit of output is $200. In panel A, the firm's fixed costs are $50,000 per month, and its average variable cost per unit of output is $20. In panel B, the firm's fixed costs are $60,000 per month, and its average variable cost per unit of output is $10. In panel A, the firm's break-even point is 278 units of output per month, whereas in panel B it is 316 units of output per month.*

to output. Thus the total revenue curve is a straight line through the origin. Also, it is generally assumed that the firm's average variable cost and marginal cost are constant *in the relevant output range,* meaning that the firm's total cost function is also assumed to be a straight line.

Panel A of Figure 24.18 shows the break-even chart for an actual cable manufacturing firm.[4] The sales price of each unit of its output was $200. The firm's fixed costs were $50,000 per month and its average variable cost per unit of output was $20. The break-even chart shows the monthly profit or loss that will result from each sales level. Panel A (Figure 24.18) shows that the firm would have lost $14,000 per month if it had sold 200 units per month. On the other hand, it would have made a profit of $22,000 per month if it had sold 400 units per month. The chart also shows the ***break-even point,*** *the output level that must be reached if the firm is to avoid losses.* In panel A, the break-even point is 278 units of output per month.

Break-even charts are used very extensively by firms and other groups to estimate the effect of the sales rate on costs, receipts, and profits. A firm may use a break-even chart to determine the effect on profits of a projected increase in sales, or how many units of a particular product it must sell in order to break even. For instance, the cable manufacturing firm wanted to find out, among other things, how its break-even point would be affected if it installed new equipment that would increase its fixed costs to $60,000 per month and reduce its average variable cost to $10. Panel B of Figure 24.18 shows that, under these circumstances, the firm's break-even point would be 316, rather than 278, units of output per month. This information is, of course, of considerable value to the firm. It means that, if the firm installs the new equipment, it must sell at least 316 units of output per month to stay in the black.

[4] See Charles Stokes, *Managerial Economics: A Case Book,* New York: Random House, 1969. However, I have changed the numbers to make them easier to work with.

Test Yourself

1. Explain why each of the following statements is true, partly true, or false. (a) "Decreasing returns to scale occur when increased scale allows efficiencies of various sorts." (b) "The law of diminishing marginal returns is inconsistent with increasing returns to scale." (c) "John Maynard Keynes said, 'In the long run we are all dead.' He was right. What is important for the determination of the optimal number of firms in an industry is the short-run average cost function."

2. As the electronics industry has grown more mature and new technologies have been developed, the costs of many electronic products have fallen dramatically. Is this evidence that the long-run average cost curve slopes downward to the right? Explain.

3. A business analyst uses a break-even chart which assumes that her firm's total cost is a linear function of output (as in Figure 24.18). If the firm's marginal cost increases sharply as its output increases, is this break-even chart likely to be very accurate? Why or why not?

4. Suppose that you were the president of a firm that operates a crude-oil pipeline. Describe in detail the various ways in which the cost functions given in this chapter might be useful to you.

Summary

1. The cost of a certain course of action is the value of the best alternative course of action that could have been pursued instead. This is the doctrine of opportunity, or alternative, cost.

2. Three kinds of total cost functions are important in the short run—total fixed cost, total variable cost, and total cost. In addition, there are three kinds of average cost functions (corresponding to each of the total cost functions)—average fixed cost, average variable cost, and average total cost.

3. Marginal cost—the addition to total cost due to the addition of the last unit of output—is of enormous significance in the firm's decision making process. Because of the law of diminishing marginal returns, marginal cost tends to increase beyond some output level.

4. The firm's long-run average cost curve shows the minimum average cost of producing each output level when any desired type or scale of plant can be built. The shape of the long-run average cost curve is determined in part by whether there are increasing, decreasing, or constant returns to scale.

5. Suppose that a firm increases the amount of all inputs by the same percentage. If output increases by more than this percentage, this is a case of increasing returns to scale. If output increases by less than this percentage, this is a case of decreasing returns to scale. If output increases by this percentage, this is a case of constant returns to scale.

6. If long-run average costs decrease with increases in output up to an output representing all, or nearly all, of the market, it is wasteful to force competition in such an industry, since costs would be greater if the industry output were divided among a number of firms than if it were produced by only one or two firms.

7. Cost functions play a very important practical role in economics and management. There have been countless studies to estimate cost functions in particular firms and industries, based on engineering and accounting data.

8. Cost functions can be used to help solve important sorts of managerial problems, as well as problems of public policy. We have shown how estimates of cost functions have been used to construct break-even charts, commonly employed by firms to promote better decisions.

Concepts for Review

Opportunity cost	Average fixed cost	Long-run average cost function
Alternative cost	Average variable cost	
Implicit cost	Average total cost	Increasing returns to scale
Cost functions	Marginal cost	Decreasing returns to scale
Total fixed cost	Total cost function	Constant returns to scale
Total variable cost	Average total cost function	Break-even chart
Total cost		Break-even point
	Marginal cost function	

PART SEVEN

Market Structure and Antitrust Policy

CHAPTER 25

Perfect Competition

Even a country as rich as the United States cannot afford to waste resources, particularly when much of the world is hungry. One of the important determinants of how a society's resources are used is how its markets are organized. Thus, if the market for wheat contained few sellers rather than many, it would certainly use resources quite differently. Or if 20 firms, rather than one, provided local telephone service in Chicago, resources would be used differently. Economists do not have any simple formulas that will eliminate all social waste. But based on existing models and evidence, some forms of market organization tend to minimize social waste, whereas other forms seem to promote it.

In this chapter, we examine the way resources are allocated and prices are set under *perfect competition.* This type of market organization—or market structure, as it is often called—is a polar case which seldom, if ever, occurs in a pure form in the real world. But it is an extremely useful model that sheds much light on a market structure's effects on resource allocation. Anyone who wants to understand how markets work in a capitalistic economy—or why our public policies toward business are what they are—must understand perfect competition, as well as the other market structures taken up in the next two chapters.

Market Structure and Economic Performance

Many economists have come to the conclusion, based on their studies of the workings of markets, that certain kinds of market organization are better, from society's point of view, than others. This is a much stronger

Table 25.1

TYPES OF MARKET STRUCTURE

Market structure	Examples	Number of producers	Type of product	Power of firm over price	Barriers to entry	Nonprice competition
Perfect competition	Parts of agriculture are reasonably close	Many	Standardized	None	Low	None
Monopolistic competition	Retail trade	Many	Differentiated	Some	Low	Advertising and product differentiation
Oligopoly	Autos, steel, machinery	Few	Standardized or differentiated	Some	High	Advertising and product differentiation
Monopoly	Public utilities	One	Unique product	Considerable	Very high	Advertising

statement than merely saying, as we did in the previous section, that market structure influences market behavior. This statement is based on some set of values and preferences, explicit or implicit, and on certain economic models that predict that "better" behavior is more likely if markets are organized in certain ways than in other ways. Although there is considerable controversy on this score, many economists believe that, from society's point of view, market structures should be as close as possible to perfect competition (for reasons given in the next three chapters).

Economists have generally found it useful to classify markets into four broad types: ***perfect competition, monopoly, monopolistic competition,*** and ***oligopoly.*** Each of these terms describes a particular type of market structure or organization. Table 25.1 provides a capsule description of each of these types. Before looking in detail at each of them, we must go over this table to see how these market structures differ.

Number of Firms. The economist's classification of market structures is based to an important extent on the number of firms in the industry that supplies the product. In perfect competition and monopolistic competition, there are *many* sellers, each of which produces only a small part of the industry's output. In monopoly, on the other hand, the industry consists of only a *single* seller. Oligopoly is an intermediate case where there are a *few* sellers. Thus Consolidated Edison, if it is the only supplier of electricity in a particular market, is a monopoly. And since there is only a small number of computer manufacturers, the market for computers is an oligopoly.

Control over Price. Market structures differ considerably in the extent to which an individual firm has control over price. A firm under perfect competition has *no control* over price. For example, a wheat farm (which is close to being a perfectly competitive firm) has no control over the price of wheat. On the other hand, a monopolist is likely to have *considerable control* over price. Thus, in the absence of public regulation, Consolidated Edison would have considerable control over the price of electricity in New York City. A firm under monopolistic competition or oligopoly is likely to have *more* control over price than a perfectly competitive firm and *less* control over price than a monopolist.

Type of Product. These market structures also differ in the extent to which the firms in an industry produce standardized (that is, identical) products. Firms in a perfectly competitive market all produce *identical* products. Thus Farmer Brown's corn is essentially the same as Farmer Smith's. In a monopolistic competitive industry like dress manufacturing, firms produce *somewhat different* products. One firm's dresses differ in style and quality from another firm's dresses. In an oligopolistic industry, firms *sometimes,* but not always, produce identical products. And in a monopolistic industry, there can be *no difference* among firms in their products, since there is only one firm.

Barriers to Entry. The ease with which firms can enter the industry differs from one market structure to another. In perfect competition, barriers to entry are *low.* Thus only a small investment is required to enter many parts of agriculture. Similarly, there are *low* barriers to entry in monopolistic competition. But in oligopolies such as autos and steel, there tend to be *very considerable* barriers to entry because it is so expensive to build an auto or steel plant (and for many other reasons too). In monopoly, entry is blocked; once entry occurs, the monopolist is an ex-monopolist.

Nonprice Competition. These market structures also differ in the extent to which firms compete on the basis of advertising and differences in product characteristics, rather than price. In perfect competition, there is *no* nonprice competition. In monopolistic competition, there is *considerable emphasis* on nonprice competition. Thus dress manufacturers compete by trying to develop better styles and by advertising their product lines. Oligopolies also tend to rely *heavily* on nonprice competition. For example, auto firms try to increase their sales by building better and more attractive cars and by advertising. Monopolists also engage in advertising, although this advertising is not directed at reducing the sales of other firms in the industry, since no other firms exist.

Table 25.1 provides a useful summary of some of the key characteristics of each market structure. Before proceeding further, study it carefully.

Perfect Competition

When business executives speak of a highly competitive market, they often mean one in which each firm is keenly aware of its rivalry with a few others and in which advertising, styling, packaging, and other such commercial weapons are used to attract business away from them. In contrast, the basic feature of the economist's definition of **perfect competition** is its *impersonality.* Because there are so many firms in the industry, no firm views another as a competitor, any more than one small tobacco farmer views another small tobacco farmer as a competitor. A market is perfectly competitive if it satisfies the following three conditions.

Homogeneity of Product. The first condition is that *the product of any one seller must be the same as the product of any other seller.* This condition insures that buyers do not care from which seller they purchase the goods, so long as the price is the same. This condition is met in many markets. As pointed out in the previous section, Farmer Brown's corn is likely to be essentially the same as Farmer Smith's.

Many Buyers and Sellers. The second condition is that there must be a

large number of buyers and sellers. *Each participant in the market, whether buyer or seller, must be so small in relation to the entire market that he or she cannot affect the product's price.* That is, all buyers and sellers must be "price takers," not "price makers." As we know from Chapter 21, a firm under perfect competition faces a *horizontal demand curve,* since variations in its output—within the range of its capabilities—will have no effect on market price.

Mobility of Resources. The third condition is that *all resources must be able to switch readily from one use to another, and consumers, firms, and resource owners must have complete knowledge of all relevant economic and technological data.*

No industry in the real world, now or in the past, satisfies all these conditions completely; thus no industry is perfectly competitive. Some agricultural markets may be reasonably close, but even they do not meet all the requirements. But this does not mean that it is useless to study the behavior of a perfectly competitive market. The conclusions derived from the model of perfect competition have proved very helpful in explaining and predicting behavior in the real world. Indeed, as we shall see, they have permitted a reasonably accurate view of resource allocation in many important segments of our economy.

The Output of the Firm

What determines the output rate in the short run of a perfectly competitive firm? Since the firm is perfectly competitive, it cannot affect the price of its product, and it can sell any amount it wants at this price. Since we are concerned with the short run, the firm can expand or contract its output rate by increasing or decreasing its utilization of its variable, but not its fixed, inputs. The situation in the long run will be reserved for a later section.

WHAT IS THE PROFIT AT EACH OUTPUT RATE?

To see how a firm determines its output rate, suppose that your aunt dies and leaves you her business, the Allegro Piano Company. Once you take over the business, your first problem is to decide how many pianos (each of which has a price of $1,000) the firm should produce per week. Having a good deal of economic intuition, you instruct your accountants to estimate the company's *total revenue* (defined as price times output) and total costs (as well as fixed and variable costs) at various output levels. They estimate the firm's total revenue at various output rates and its total cost function (as well as its total fixed cost function and total variable cost function), with the results shown in Table 25.2. Subtracting the total cost at a given output rate from the total revenue at this output rate, you obtain the total profit at each output rate, which is shown in the last column of Table 25.2.

FINDING THE MAXIMUM-PROFIT OUTPUT RATE

As the output rate increases from 0 to 4 pianos per week, the total profit *rises.* As the output rate increases from 5 to 8 pianos per week, the total

Table 25.2

COSTS AND REVENUES, ALLEGRO PIANO COMPANY

Output per week (pianos)	Price	Total revenue (price × output)	Total fixed cost (dollars)	Total variable cost	Total cost	Total profit
0	1,000	0	1,000	0	1,000	−1,000
1	1,000	1,000	1,000	200	1,200	− 200
2	1,000	2,000	1,000	300	1,300	700
3	1,000	3,000	1,000	500	1,500	1,500
4	1,000	4,000	1,000	1,000	2,000	2,000
5	1,000	5,000	1,000	2,000	3,000	2,000
6	1,000	6,000	1,000	3,200	4,200	1,800
7	1,000	7,000	1,000	4,500	5,500	1,500
8	1,000	8,000	1,000	7,200	8,200	− 200

profit *falls*. Thus the *maximum* profit is achieved at an output rate between 4 and 5 pianos per week.[1] (Without more detailed data, one cannot tell precisely where the maximum occurs, but this is close enough for present purposes.) Since the maximum profit is obtained at an output of between 4 and 5 pianos per week, this is the output rate you choose.

Figure 25.1 gives a somewhat more vivid picture of the firm's situation by plotting the relationship between total revenue and total cost, on the one hand, and output on the other. At each output rate, the vertical distance between the total revenue curve and the total cost curve is the amount of profit the firm earns. Below an output rate of about 1 piano per week and above a rate of about 8 pianos per week, the total revenue curve lies *below* the total cost curve, indicating that profits are negative—that is, there are losses. Both Table 25.2 and Figure 25.1 show that the output rate that will maximize the firm's profits is between 4 and 5 pianos per week. At this

Figure 25.1

Costs, Revenues, and Profits, Allegro Piano Company *Profit equals the vertical distance between the total revenue curve and the total cost curve. This distance is maximized when the output rate is between 4 and 5 pianos per week. At this output rate, profit (measured by the vertical distance) is somewhat more than $2,000.*

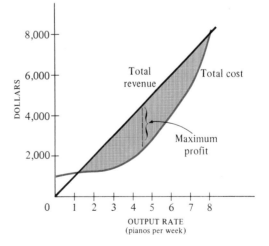

[1] This assumes that the output rate can be varied continuously and that there is a single maximum. These are innocuous assumptions.

Table 25.3

MARGINAL COST AND PRICE, ALLEGRO PIANO COMPANY

Output per week (pianos)	Marginal cost (dollars)	Price
0		1,000
	200	
1		1,000
	100	
2		1,000
	200	
3		1,000
	500	
4		1,000
	1,000	
5		1,000
	1,200	
6		1,000
	1,300	
7		1,000
	2,700	
8		1,000

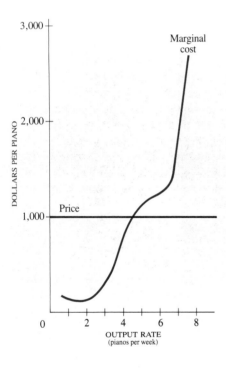

Figure 25.2
Marginal Cost and Price, Allegro Piano Company *At the profit-maximizing output rate of between 4 and 5 pianos per week, marginal cost (which is $1,000 when the output rate is between 4 and 5) equals price ($1,000). Recall from Figure 24.8 that marginal cost is plotted at the mid-point of the range of output to which it pertains.*

output rate, the firm will make a profit of over $2,000 per week, which is more than it can make at any other output rate.

There is an alternative way to analyze the firm's situation. Rather than looking at total revenue and total cost, let's look at price and marginal cost. Table 25.3 and Figure 25.2 show the product price and marginal cost of each output rate. It turns out that the maximum profit is achieved at the output rate where price equals marginal cost. In other words, both Table 25.3 and Figure 25.2 indicate that price equals marginal cost at the profit-maximizing output rate of between 4 and 5 pianos per week. This raises a question. Will price usually equal marginal cost at the profit-maximizing output rate, or is this merely a coincidence?

THE GOLDEN RULE OF OUTPUT DETERMINATION

Readers familiar with television scripts and detective stories will have recognized that the question just posed can only be answered in one way without ruining the plot. The equality of marginal cost and price at the profit-maximizing output rate is no mere coincidence. It will usually be true if the firm takes the price of its product as given. Indeed, the Golden Rule of Output Determination for a perfectly competitive firm is: *Choose the output rate at which marginal cost is equal to price.*

To prove that this rule maximizes profits, consider Figure 25.3, which shows a typical short-run marginal cost function. Suppose that the price is OP_1. At any output rate less than OQ_1, price is greater than marginal cost.[2] This means that increases in output will increase the firm's profits since they will add more to total revenues than to total costs. Why? Because an extra unit of output adds an amount equal to price to total revenue and an amount equal to marginal cost to total cost. Thus, since price exceeds marginal cost, an extra unit of output adds more to total revenue than to total cost. This is the case for the Allegro Piano Company when it is producing 3 pianos per week. As shown in Table 25.3, the extra cost of producing a fourth piano is $500, while the revenue brought in by producing and selling it is $1,000. Consequently, it pays the Allegro Piano Company to produce more than 3 pianos per week.

At any output rate above OQ_1, price is less than marginal cost. This means that decreases in output will increase the firm's profits since they will subtract more from total costs than from total revenue. This happens because one less unit of output subtracts an amount equal to price from total revenue and an amount equal to marginal cost from total cost. Thus, since price is less than marginal cost, one less unit of output subtracts more from total cost than from total revenue. Such a case occurs when the Allegro Piano Company is producing 7 pianos per week. As shown in Table 25.3, the extra cost of producing the seventh piano is $1,300, while the extra revenue it brings in is $1,000. So it pays the Allegro Piano Company to produce less than 7 pianos per week.

Since increases in output will increase profits if output is less than OQ_1, and decreases in output will increase profits if output is greater than OQ_1, it follows that profits must be maximized at OQ_1, the output rate at which

[2] Except perhaps for an irrelevant range where marginal cost decreases with increases in output.

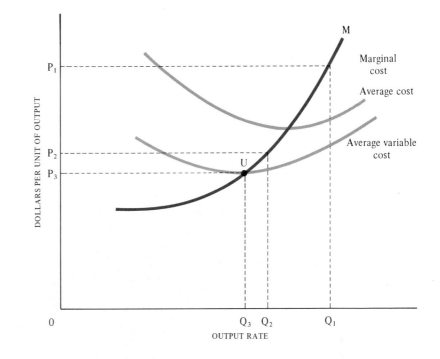

Figure 25.3

Short-Run Average and Marginal Cost Curves *If price is OP₁, the profit-maximizing output rate is OQ₁. If price is OP₂, the profit-maximizing output rate is OQ₂, even though the firm will incur a loss. If the price is below OP₃, the firm will discontinue production. (Note that, regardless of what the price is, the demand curve facing the firm is a horizontal line at this price.)*

Basic Idea #49: *To determine the profit-maximizing output rate of a firm, compare the extra revenue with the extra cost of each additional unit of output. If the extra revenue (which equals price here) is greater than the extra cost (which equals marginal cost), the extra unit should be produced; otherwise it should not be produced. (But if there is no output where price exceeds average variable cost, the firm will be better off producing nothing at all.)*

price equals marginal cost. After all, if increases in output up to this output *(OQ₁)* result in increases in profit and further increases in output result in decreases in profit, *OQ₁* must be the profit-maximizing output rate. For the Allegro Piano Company, this output rate is between 4 and 5 pianos per week, as we saw above.

DOES IT PAY TO BE A DROPOUT?

All rules—even the Golden Rule we just mentioned—have exceptions. Under some circumstances, the perfectly competitive firm will not maximize its profits if it sets marginal cost equal to price. Instead, it will maximize profits only if it becomes an economic dropout by discontinuing production. Let's demonstrate that this is indeed a fact. The first important point is that even if the firm is doing the best it can, it may not be able to earn a profit. If the price is *OP₂* in Figure 25.3, short-run average cost exceeds the price, *OP₂*, at all possible output rates. Thus the firm cannot earn a profit whatever output it produces. Since the short run is too short for the firm to alter the scale of its plant, it cannot liquidate its plant in the short run. Its only choice is to produce at a loss or discontinue production.

Under what conditions will the firm produce at a loss, and under what conditions will it discontinue production? *If there is an output rate where price exceeds average variable costs, it will pay the firm to produce, even though price does not cover average total cost. If there is no such output rate, the firm is better off to produce nothing at all.* This is true because even if the firm produces nothing, it must pay its fixed cost. Thus, if the loss resulting from production is less than the firm's fixed cost, the firm is better off producing than not producing. On the other hand, if the loss resulting from production is greater than the firm's fixed cost, the firm is better off not to produce.

539

In other words, *the firm will find it advantageous to produce if total losses are less than total fixed cost.* Since

$$\text{total losses} = \text{total cost} - \text{total revenue},$$

this will be the case if

$$\text{total cost} - \text{total revenue} < \text{total fixed cost}.$$

If we subtract total fixed cost from both sides of this inequality, and if we add total revenue to both sides, we find that the firm is better off to produce if

$$\text{total cost} - \text{total fixed cost} < \text{total revenue}.$$

Dividing each side of this inequality by output (and recognizing that total revenue = price × output), we find that the firm is better off to produce if

$$\text{average variable cost} < \text{price},$$

since average variable cost equals average total cost minus average fixed cost.

Once again, we have proved what we set out to prove—that the firm will maximize profits by producing *nothing* if there is no output rate at which price exceeds average variable cost. If such an output rate does exist, the Golden Rule applies. The firm will set its output rate at the point where marginal cost equals price.

DROPPING OUT: ILLUSTRATIVE CASES

To illustrate the conditions under which it pays a firm to drop out, suppose that the cost functions of the Allegro Piano Company are as shown in Table 25.4. In this case, there exists no output rate such that average variable cost is less than price—which, you will recall, is $1,000 per piano. Thus, according to the results of the last paragraphs, the Allegro Piano Company should discontinue production under these conditions. The wisdom of this course of action is shown by the last column of Table 25.4, which demonstrates that the profit-maximizing—or, what amounts to the same thing, the loss-minimizing—output rate is zero.

Table 25.4

COSTS AND REVENUES, ALLEGRO PIANO COMPANY

Output per week (pianos)	Price	Total revenue	Total fixed cost	Total variable cost	Average variable cost	Total cost	Total profit
				(dollars)			
0	1,000	0	1,000	0	—	1,000	−1,000
1	1,000	1,000	1,000	1,200	1,200	2,200	−1,200
2	1,000	2,000	1,000	2,600	1,300	3,600	−1,600
3	1,000	3,000	1,000	4,200	1,400	5,200	−2,200
4	1,000	4,000	1,000	6,000	1,500	7,000	−3,000
5	1,000	5,000	1,000	8,000	1,600	9,000	−4,000
6	1,000	6,000	1,000	10,200	1,700	11,200	−5,200
7	1,000	7,000	1,000	12,600	1,800	13,600	−6,600
8	1,000	8,000	1,000	15,200	1,900	16,200	−8,200

Sometimes, as in the present case, the best thing to produce is nothing. The situation is analogous to the common experience of leaving a movie after the first ten minutes indicate that it is not going to be a good one, even though the admission price is not refundable. One ignores the fixed costs (the admission price), and finding that the variable cost (the pleasure gained from activities that would be forgone by seeing the rest of the show) is going to exceed the benefits of staying, one leaves.

In 1973, many meat-processing plants discontinued production for essentially this reason. The federal government, in an attempt to control inflation, froze the price of their product, but allowed the prices of the inputs they used to go up, with the result that their average variable costs exceeded price at all possible output levels. The consequence, as our theory would predict, was that many plants closed down. In Chicago, the American Meat Institute announced that 16 plants closed down in the second quarter of 1973. As the president of Detroit's Crown Packing Company put it, "Frankly, we closed down so that we would lose less money."

The Market Supply Curve

In Chapter 3, we described some of the factors underlying a commodity's market supply curve, but we could not go into much detail. Now we can, because our Golden Rule of Output Determination underlies the market supply curve. As a first step, let's derive the *firm's supply curve,* which shows how much the firm will want to produce at each price.

THE FIRM'S SUPPLY CURVE

Since the firm takes the price of its product as given (and can sell all it wants at that price), we know from the previous sections that the firm will choose the output level at which price equals marginal cost. Or if the price is below the firm's average variable cost curve at every output level, the firm will produce nothing. These results are all we need to determine the firm's supply curve.

Suppose that the firm's short-run cost curves are as shown in Figure 25.3. The marginal cost curve must intersect the average variable cost curve at the latter's minimum point, U. If the price of the product is less than OP_3, the firm will produce nothing, because there is no output level where price exceeds average variable cost. If the price of the product exceeds OP_3, the firm will set its output rate at the point where price equals marginal cost. Thus, if the price is OP_1, the firm will produce OQ_1; if the price is OP_2, the firm will produce OQ_2; and so forth. Consequently, *the firm's supply curve is exactly the same as the firm's marginal cost curve for prices above the minimum value of average variable cost* (OP_3). For prices at or below the minimum value of average variable cost, the firm's supply curve corresponds to the price axis, the desire to supply at these prices being uniformly zero. Thus the firm's supply curve is OP_3UM.

Deriving the Market Supply Curve

Our next step is to derive the market supply curve from the supply curves of the individual firms. If one assumption holds, the **market supply curve** *can be regarded as the horizontal summation of the supply curves of all the firms producing the product.* If there were 3 firms in the industry and their supply curves were as shown in Figure 25.4, the market supply curve would be the horizontal summation of their 3 supply curves. Thus, since these 3 supply curves show that firm 1 would supply 25 units of output at a price of $2 per unit, that firm 2 would supply 40 units at this price, and that firm 3 would supply 55 units at this price, the market supply curve shows that 120 units of output will be supplied if the price is $2 per unit. Why? Because the market supply curve shows the *total* amount of the product that all of the firms together would supply at this price—and 25 + 40 + 55 = 120. If there were only 3 firms, the market would not be perfectly competitive, but we can ignore this inconsistency. Figure 25.4 is designed to illustrate the fact that the market supply curve is the horizontal summation of the firm supply curves, at least under one important assumption.

The assumption underlying this construction of the short-run market supply curve is that *increases or decreases in output by all firms simultaneously do not affect input prices.* This is a convenient simplification, but it is not always true. Although changes in the output of one firm alone often cannot affect input prices, the simultaneous expansion or contraction of output by all firms may well alter input prices, so that the individual firm's cost curves—and supply curve—will shift. For instance, an expansion of the whole industry may bid up the price of certain inputs, with the result that the cost curves of the individual firms will be pushed upward. In the aerospace industry, a sudden expansion of the industry might well increase the price of certain inputs like the services of aerospace scientists and engineers.

Figure 25.4
Horizontal Summation of Short-Run Supply Curves of Firms *If each of the three firms' supply curves is as shown here (and if each firm supplies nothing if the price is below OH), the market supply curve is the horizontal summation of the firms' supply curves, assuming that input prices are not influenced by the output of the industry. If the price is $2, firm 1 will supply 25 units, firm 2 will supply 40 units, and firm 3 will supply 55 units; thus, the total amount supplied is 120 units.*

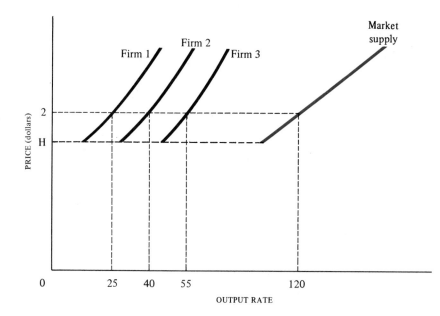

If, contrary to the assumption underlying Figure 25.4, input prices *are* increased by the expansion of the industry, one can still derive the short-run market supply curve by seeing how much the industry will supply in the short run at each price of the product. But it is incorrect to assume that the market supply curve is the horizontal summation of the firm supply curves. More will be said in the chapter Appendix about the effects of industry output on input prices.

Example 25.1   How Much Mercury Do We Have?

According to the U.S. Bureau of Mines,* the quantity of mercury reserves in the United States at selected price levels of mercury is as follows:

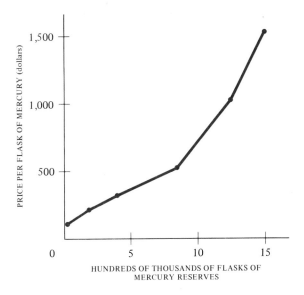

(a) Is this the supply curve for mercury? Why or why not? (b) Does this curve show how much mercury will be supplied per period of time? (c) Why is the quantity of reserves sensitive to price? (d) Does it appear that, as price increases, beyond some point increasing price begins to lose its power to elicit substantially larger supplies? Is this reasonable? Why or why not?

SOLUTION

(a) No. This curve shows how much mercury will be available (not produced) at various prices. (b) No. (c) Because, at higher mercury prices, it becomes profitable to obtain mercury from relatively high-cost sources; whereas at lower mercury prices this is not the case. (d) Yes. This is reasonable because beyond some point it becomes increasingly expensive to find and obtain an extra flask of mercury.

* U.S. Bureau of Mines, *Mercury Potential of the United States,* Washington, D.C.: Government Printing Office, 1965.

DETERMINANTS OF THE LOCATION AND SHAPE OF THE MARKET SUPPLY CURVE

Based on the preceding discussion, we now can identify the basic determinants of the location and shape of a commodity's short-run market supply curve. If increases or decreases in output by all firms do not affect input prices, the short-run market supply curve is the horizontal summation of the firm supply curves. Thus its location and shape are derived from the location and shapes of the marginal cost curves of the firms in the industry, since these marginal cost curves determine the firm supply curves. From previous chapters, we know that the location and shape of each marginal cost curve depend on *the size of the firm's plants, the level of input prices,* and *the state of technology* in particular. Thus these factors play a major role in determining the location and shape of the market supply curve. Also, its location and shape in the short run are determined by the *number of firms* in the industry. The market supply curve in Figure 25.4 would be located farther to the right if there were more firms in the industry. In addition, its location and shape are determined by *the effect of industry output on input prices.*

The short-run market supply curve generally slopes upward and to the right because marginal cost curves (in the relevant range) generally slope upward to the right. If industry output does not affect input prices, the market supply curve is the horizontal sum of the firms' marginal cost curves (in the range where they are rising). Consequently, since each of the marginal cost curves slopes upward and to the right (in this range), this is also true of their horizontal sum, the short-run market supply curve.

Test Yourself

1. Suppose that the total costs of a perfectly competitive firm are as follows:

Output rate	Total cost (dollars)
0	40
1	60
2	90
3	130
4	180
5	240

If the price of the product is $50, what output rate should the firm choose?

2. Suppose that the firm in Question 1 experienced an increase of $30 in its fixed costs. Plot its new total cost function. What effect will this increase in its fixed costs have on the output it will choose?

3. After the increase in fixed costs described in Question 2, what does the firm's marginal cost curve look like? Plot it on a graph. Does it differ from what it was before the increase in fixed costs? Why or why not?

4. After the increase in fixed costs described in Question 2, what output rate would the firm choose if the price of its product were $40? $50? $60? $70?

The Price Elasticity of Supply

Market supply curves vary in their shape. For some commodities, the quantity supplied is very sensitive to changes in the commodity's price. For others, the quantity supplied is not at all sensitive to changes in price.

To measure the sensitivity of quantity supplied to changes in price, economists use the **price elasticity of supply,** *which is defined as the percentage change in quantity supplied resulting from a 1 percent change in price.* Suppose that a 1 percent reduction in the price of slingshots results in a 1.5 percent reduction in the quantity supplied. Then the price elasticity of supply for slingshots (in the neighborhood of the existing price) is 1.5. The price elasticity of supply is likely to vary from one point to another on the market supply curve. Thus the price elasticity of supply for slingshots may be higher when the price of a slingshot is $2 than when it is $1.

The same factors that influence the location and shape of the market supply curve also determine the price elasticity of supply. But to these factors previously mentioned—the number of plants, input prices, and the nature of technology, among others—another important factor should be added—the length of the time period to which the supply curve pertains. *Market supply curves, like market demand curves, tend to be more price elastic if the time period is long rather than short.* Consider the market for watermelons. If we are dealing with a very short period—a few hours or a day—the supply of watermelons may be fixed, as shown in Figure 25.5. That is, the market supply curve may be perfectly inelastic, the price elasticity of supply being zero, because the period is too short to grow any more watermelons or transport any more watermelons into the market.

Suppose now that we lengthen the period of time to a year or so. In this period, farmers can alter the size of their watermelon crop in response to variations in price. Thus the price elasticity of supply will be higher than in the very short period of a few hours or a day. In this longer period, the price elasticity of supply has been estimated to be about .30; and the supply curve may be as shown in Figure 25.5.[3]

Finally, suppose that we lengthen the period further—to 10 years. In this period, farmers will take land out of watermelon production or put land into watermelon production. Indeed, they can make all reasonable adjustments to changes in price. So the price elasticity of supply will be higher than in a period of a year or so—and much higher than in a period of a few hours or a day. The supply curve may be as shown in Figure 25.5.

Figure 25.5

Market Supply Curves for Watermelons, Periods of Varying Length The left-hand panel shows the market supply curve in a period of a few hours or a day. The middle panel refers to a year or so. The right-hand panel refers to 10 years.

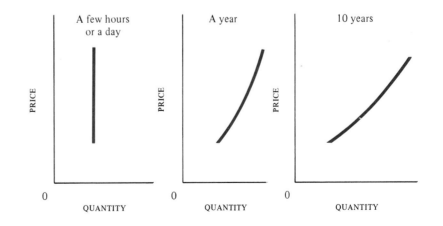

[3] D. Suits, "An Econometric Model of the Watermelon Market," *Journal of Farm Economics,* May 1955; and W. L'Esperance, "A Case Study in Prediction," *Econometrica,* 1964.

545

Price and Output: The Market Period

How much of a particular product will be produced if the market is perfectly competitive, and what will the price be? The answers depend on the length of the time period. To begin with, let's consider the relatively short period of time when the supply of the relevant good is *fixed.* This period of time is called the ***market period.*** In the market period, as in the short and long runs, the price of a good in a perfectly competitive market is determined by the market demand and market supply curves. However, in the market period, the market supply curve is a vertical line, as shown in Figure 25.6.

Thus, in the market period, output is unaffected by price. In Figure 25.6, output is *OQ*—and regardless of price, it cannot be changed. The equilibrium price depends on the position of the demand curve. Price is OP_1 if the demand curve is *A,* and OP_2 if the demand curve is *B.*

The role of the price as a rationing device is particularly obvious in the market period, where this is the major function of price. Consumers who are willing to pay a relatively high price get some of the product; others do without. The allocation of jam in the prisoner-of-war camp and the allocation of tickets to *A Chorus Line,* both taken up in Chapter 3, are among the examples you have encountered earlier of how price rations output in the market period. These cases can be regarded as taking place in the market period because the supply is fixed in each case.

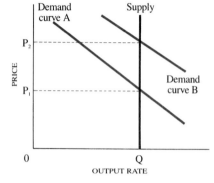

Figure 25.6

Price Determination in the Market Period *In the market period, supply is fixed at* OQ. *Equilibrium price is* OP₁ *if the demand curve is demand curve* A *and* OP₂ *if the demand curve is demand curve* B.

Price and Output: The Short Run

Let's turn now to the short run, the period during which each firm's plant and equipment are fixed. What determines the price and output of a good in a perfectly competitive market in the short run? The answer once again is the market demand and market supply curves. However, the position and shape of these curves will generally be different in the short run than in the market period. In particular, the market supply curve in the short run will not be a vertical line; it will generally slope upward to the right, as in panel B of Figure 25.7. Thus, *in the short run, price influences, as well as rations, the amount supplied.* In panel B of Figure 25.7, the equilibrium price and output in the short run are *OP* and *OQ.*

To illustrate the nature of the short-run supply curve, consider the bituminous coal industry, which in many respects comes reasonably close to perfect competition. According to Hubert Risser of the University of Kansas, the short-run supply curve for bituminous coal is very price elastic, so long as output stays within the range of existing capacity.[4] In other words, if output is less than existing capacity, small variations in price will result in large variations in output. Thus the situation in the short run is quite different from that in the market period, where output is fixed and unaffected by price. But the basic fact remains that equilibrium price and equilibrium output are determined by the intersection of the relevant demand and supply curves, in both the market period and the short run.

[4] H. Risser, *The Economics of the Coal Industry,* Lawrence: University Press of Kansas, 1958, p. 155.

Figure 25.7

Short-Run Competitive Equilibrium *In the short run, equilibrium price is* OP, *and the equilibrium output of the industry is* OQ, *since (as shown in panel* B) *the industry demand and supply curves intersect at this price and output. The demand curve facing the individual firm is a horizontal line at* OP *(as shown in panel* A). *Each firm produces* Oq *units of the product, since this is the output that maximizes its profits. The output of the industry* (OQ) *is the sum of the outputs* (Oq) *of the individual firms. In short-run equilibrium, firms may be making either profits or losses. In this particular case, the individual firm earns a profit equal to the shaded area in panel* A. *(Why? Because the profit per unit of output* equals the price [OP] minus average cost [OC], *or the vertical distance* CP. *To obtain the firm's* total *profit, this distance must be multiplied by the firm's output [Oq], the result being the shaded area.) If firms were making losses rather than profits, the demand curve confronting each firm would intersect the marginal cost curve at a point below (rather than above) the average cost curve.*

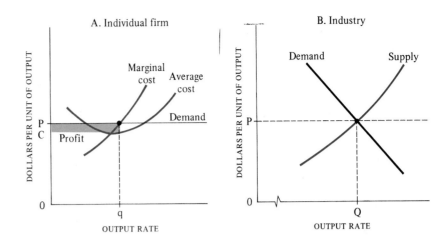

Returning to Figure 25.7, panel A shows the behavior of an individual firm in short-run equilibrium. Since *OP* is the price, the demand curve facing the firm is a horizontal line at *OP,* as shown in panel A. To maximize profit, the firm produces an output of *Oq,* because price equals marginal cost at this output. In short-run equilibrium, firms may be making either profits or losses. In the particular case described in panel A, the firm earns a profit equal to the shaded area shown there. Since the profit per unit of output equals *CP,* total profit equals *CP* multiplied by *Oq,* which is this shaded area.

Taken together, the two panels in Figure 25.7 bring out the following important point. To the *individual* firm, the price of the product is taken as given. If the price is *OP,* the firm in panel A reacts to this price by setting an output rate of *Oq* units. It cannot alter the price; it can only react to it. But *as a group* the reactions of the firms are a major determinant of the price of the product. The supply curve in panel B shows the total amount that the entire group of firms will supply at each price. It summarizes the reactions of the firms to various levels of the price. Put briefly, the equilibrium price is viewed by the individual firm as being beyond its control; yet the supply decisions of all firms taken as a group are a basic determinant of the equilibrium price.

Price and Output: The Long Run

In the long run, what determines the output and price of a good in a perfectly competitive market? In the long run, a firm can change its plant size, which means that established firms may *leave* an industry if it has below-average profits, or that new firms may *enter* an industry with above-average profits. Suppose that textile firms can earn up to (but no more than) a 15 percent rate of return by investing their resources in other industries. If they can earn only 12 percent by keeping these resources invested in the textile industry, they will leave the textile industry. On the other hand, if a rate of return of 18 percent can be earned by investing in the textile industry, firms in other industries, attracted by this relatively high return, will enter the textile industry.

In the past decade or two, economists have begun to use laboratory experiments to understand better how markets work. In an experimental market, the subjects (often college students) trade a commodity (e.g., a scrap of paper) that has no intrinsic value. Buyers make a profit by purchasing the commodity from sellers and reselling it to the experimenter. For example, the rules of the experiment may state that the experimenter will redeem the first unit of the commodity for $2.00, the second unit for $1.50, the third unit for $1.00, and so on. Sellers make a profit by buying units from the experimenter and selling them to the buyers. For example, the experimenter may provide the seller with the first unit of the commodity for $0.25, the second unit for $0.75, the third unit for $1.00, and so on.

The way in which the market is organized varies from experiment to experiment. Fre-

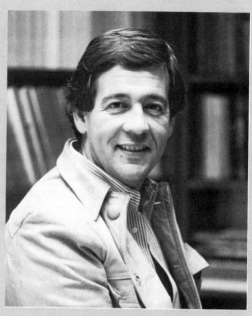

Charles Plott

quently, they are organized as double auctions, which are characterized by public bids to buy units of the commodity and public offers to sell units of it. Any participant is free to accept whatever terms he or she wants. Typically, bids are made verbally. An auctioneer, when hearing a bid or offer, writes it on the blackboard. The last bid and offer remain standing until accepted, cancelled, or replaced.

Based on the work of Caltech's Charles Plott, Arizona's Vernon Smith, and other leaders in this new field, auctions of this type tend to converge to the competitive equilibrium even with relatively few traders. In other words, if one constructs a market demand curve (based on the amount of the commodity that each buyer will purchase at a given price in order to maximize profit) and a market supply curve (based on the amount of the commodity that each seller will sell at a given price in order to maximize profit), the actual price in the experiment generally moves toward the level at which the market demand curve intersects the market supply curve.

This, of course, is an interesting test of the basic model considered in this chapter, which seems to come through with flying colors. Laboratory experiments have also been carried out to test and extend the models of monopoly, monopolistic competition, and oligopoly discussed in succeeding chapters. Without question, such experiments have been and will be useful in a variety of ways. However, as the leading experimenters are quick to point out, one must be very careful in extrapolating behavior from a very simple laboratory setting to a complex industrial environment. The real world is, of course, a lot more complicated than these simple experiments.

EQUILIBRIUM: ZERO ECONOMIC PROFIT

Equilibrium is achieved in the long run when enough firms—no more, no less—are in the industry so that *economic profits*—*defined as the excess of a firm's profits over what it could make in other industries*—are zero. This condition is necessary for long-run equilibrium because, as we have seen, new firms will enter the industry if there are economic profits, and existing firms will leave if there are economic losses. This process of entry and exit is the key to long-run equilibrium. It is discussed repeatedly in this and subsequent sections.

Note that the existence of economic profits or losses in an industry brings about a shift in the industry's short-run supply curve. If there are economic profits, new firms will enter the industry, and so shift the short-run supply curve to the right. On the other hand, if there are economic losses in the industry (i.e., if the industry's profits are less than could be obtained elsewhere), existing firms will leave the industry, causing the short-run supply curve to shift to the left. Only if economic profits are zero will the number of firms in the industry—and the industry's short-run supply curve—be stable. Putting this equilibrium condition another way, *the long-run equilibrium position of the firm is at the point at which its long-run average costs equal price.* If price exceeds average total costs, economic profits are being earned; and if price is less than average total costs, economic losses are being incurred.

EQUILIBRIUM: MAXIMUM ECONOMIC PROFIT

Going a step further, *long-run equilibrium requires that price equal the lowest value of long-run average total costs.* In other words, firms must be producing at the *minimum point* on their long-run average cost curves, because to maximize their profits they must operate where price equals long-run marginal cost,[5] and at the same time they also have to operate where price equals long-run average cost. But if both these conditions are satisfied, long-run marginal cost must equal long-run average cost—since both equal price. And we know that long-run marginal cost equals long-run average cost only at the point at which long-run average cost is a minimum.[6] Consequently, if long-run marginal cost equals long-run average cost, the firm must be producing at the minimum point on the long-run average cost curve.

This equilibrium position is illustrated in Figure 25.8. When all adjustments are made, price equals *OP*. The equilibrium output of the firm is *Oq*, and its plant corresponds to the short-run average and marginal cost curves in Figure 25.8. At this output and with this plant, long-run marginal cost equals short-run marginal cost equals price. This insures that the firm is maximizing profit. Also, long-run average cost equals short-run average cost equals price. This insures that economic profits are zero. Since the long-run marginal cost and long-run average cost must be equal, the firm is producing at the minimum point on its long-run average cost curve.

Basic Idea #50: The big difference between short-run equilibrium and long-run equilibrium is that entry and exit of firms are possible in the long run but not in the short run. For a long-run equilibrium to occur, there must be zero economic profit; otherwise, the number of firms would not be stable. In contrast, in short-run equilibrium, economic profit may be positive or negative, since the time interval is too short for firms to enter or leave the industry.

---

[5] The reasons why marginal cost must be equal to price, if profits are to be maximized, are given in earlier sections of this chapter.

[6] The previous discussion of this point on p. 520 concerned short-run cost functions, but the argument applies just as well to long-run cost functions.

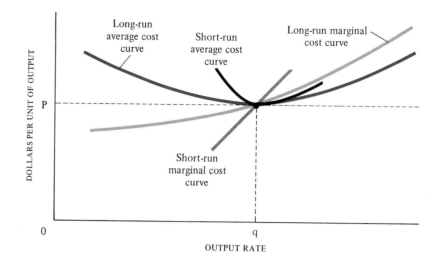

Figure 25.8

Long-Run Equilibrium of a Perfectly Competitive Firm *In long-run equilibrium, output is Oq and the firm's plant corresponds to the short-run average and marginal cost curves shown here. At Oq, long-run marginal cost equals short-run marginal cost equals price; also, long-run average cost equals short-run average cost equals price. These conditions ensure that the firm is maximizing profits and that economic profits are zero.*

To illustrate the process of entry and exit in an industry that approximates perfect competition, let's return to the bituminous coal industry. Entry into this industry is relatively easy, but exit is relatively difficult, for at least two reasons. First, it is costly to shut down a mine and reopen it later. Second, because of corrosion and water damage, it is hard to shut down a mine for longer than two years unless it is to be abandoned entirely. For these reasons, mines tend to stay open and produce even though short-term losses are incurred. In the period before World War II, the demand for coal fell substantially, but although the industry suffered substantial losses, mines were slow to close down. Nonetheless, the competitive process had its way. Slowly, but surely, the number of mines fell markedly in response to these losses.[7] Thus, despite the barriers to rapid exit, firms eventually left the industry, just as the model would predict.

The Allocation of Resources Under Perfect Competition: A More Detailed View

At this point, it is instructive to describe the process by which a perfectly competitive economy—one composed of perfectly competitive industries— would allocate resources. In Chapters 2 and 3, we stressed that the allocation of resources among alternative uses is one of the major functions of any economic system. Equipped with the concepts of this and previous chapters, we can now go much further in describing how a perfectly competitive economy shifts resources in accord with changes in tastes, technology and other factors.

CONSUMERS TURN FROM CORN TO WHEAT

To be specific, suppose that a change occurs in tastes. Consumers become more favorably disposed toward wheat and less favorably disposed toward

[7] J. B. Hendry, "The Bituminous Coal Industry," in W. Adams, *The Structure of American Industry,* New York: Macmillan, 1961.

corn than in the past.[8] In the short run, the increase in the demand for wheat increases the price of wheat, and results in some increase in the output of wheat. However, the output cannot be increased very substantially because the industry's capacity cannot be expanded in the short run. Similarly, the fall in the demand for corn reduces the price of corn, and results in some reduction in output. But the output will not be curtailed greatly because firms will continue to produce as long as they can cover variable costs.

PRICES SIGNAL RESOURCE REALLOCATION

The change in the relative prices of wheat and corn tells producers that a reallocation of resources is called for. Because of the increase in the price of wheat and the decrease in the price of corn, wheat producers are earning economic profits and corn producers are showing economic losses. This will trigger a new deployment of resources. If some variable inputs in corn production can be used as effectively in the production of wheat, they may be switched from corn production to wheat production. Even if no variable inputs are used in both wheat and corn production, adjustment can be made in various interrelated markets, with the result that wheat production gains resources and corn production loses resources. When short-run equilibrium is attained in both the wheat and corn industries, the reallocation of resources is not yet complete since there has not been enough time for producers to build new capacity or liquidate old capacity. In particular, neither industry is operating at minimum average cost. The wheat producers are operating at greater than the output level where average cost is a minimum; and the corn producers are operating at less than this level.

EFFECTS IN THE LONG RUN

What will happen in the long run? The shift in consumer demand from corn to wheat will result in greater adjustments in production and smaller adjustments in price than in the short run. In the long run, existing firms can leave corn production and new firms can enter wheat production. Because of short-run economic losses in corn production, some corn land and related equipment will be allowed to run down, and some firms engaged in corn production will be liquidated. As firms leave corn production, the supply curve shifts to the left, causing the price to rise above its short-run level. The transfer of resources out of corn production will stop when the price has increased, and costs have decreased, to the point where losses are avoided.

While corn production is losing resources, wheat production is gaining them. The prospect of positive economic profits in wheat production will cause new firms to enter the industry. The increased demand for inputs will raise input prices and cost curves in wheat production, and the price of wheat will be depressed by the movement to the right of the supply curve because of the entry of new firms. Entry ceases when economic profits are no longer being earned. At this point, when long-run equilib-

---

[8] Since we assume here that the markets for wheat and corn are perfectly competitive, it is also assumed that there is no government intervention in these markets.

Example 25.2   How Many Apples Should Be Produced?

Suppose that the demand and supply curves for apples are as shown below:

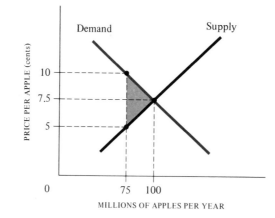

(a) If 75 million apples are produced per year, how much would an additional apple cost to produce? How much would an additional apple be worth to consumers? (b) Under these circumstances, is it socially worthwhile to increase apple production? Why or why not? (c) If 100 million apples are produced per year, how much would an additional apple cost to produce? How much would an additional apple be worth to consumers? (d) If 100 million apples are produced, is it socially worthwhile to increase apple production? Explain. (e) How great is the loss to society if 75 million, rather than 100 million, apples are produced?

SOLUTION

(a) 5 cents, since the supply curve shows marginal cost. 10 cents, because the demand curve shows the maximum amount consumers would pay for an extra apple. (b) Yes, because the extra social cost of producing an extra apple is less than the extra social benefit from doing so. Consumers would be glad to pay producers to produce extra apples. (c) 7½ cents. 7½ cents. (d) No, since the extra social cost of producing an extra apple is no less than the maximum amount that consumers would pay for an extra apple. If private benefits and costs do not differ from social benefits and costs, 100 million apples is the optimal output level. It would not be socially worthwhile to exceed or fall short of it. (e) The vertical distance from the demand curve to the supply curve is the difference between the social benefit and the social cost of an *extra* apple. (For example, if 75 million apples are produced, the social benefit of an extra apple exceeds its social cost by $10 - 5 = 5$ cents.) Thus the difference between the social benefit and social cost of the *extra 25 million apples* equals the sum of these vertical distances for all of the extra apples. This sum equals the shaded area in the above diagram, which amounts to 25 million × 2½ cents = $625,000. This is the loss to society.

rium is achieved, more resources will be used in the industry than in the short run. (Note that, if corn land and equipment can be converted to the production of wheat, some of the "entry" may occur through existing farmers' shifting of their crop mix toward wheat and away from corn.)

Finally, long-run equilibrium is established in both industries, and the reallocation of resources is complete. It is important to note that this reallocation can affect industries other than wheat and corn. If corn land and equipment can be easily adapted to the production of wheat, corn producers can simply change to wheat production. If not, the resources used in corn production are converted to some use other than wheat, and the resources that enter wheat production come from some use other than corn production.

Bituminous Coal: A Case Study

To illustrate how resources are allocated in the long run, we will look in more detail at the bituminous coal industry. Although it does not have all the characteristics of a perfectly competitive industry, it has enough of them so that the perfectly competitive model predicts many aspects of its behavior reasonably well. From the turn of the century until about 1923, the bituminous coal industry expanded rapidly. Between 1903 and 1923, the price of coal increased from $1.24 to $2.68 per ton, in considerable part because of the marked upward shift to the right of the demand curve for coal, an important fuel in this period of general industrial growth. In addition, the high prices of the period were sometimes the result of temporary shortages caused by strikes and insufficient railroad transportation. Thus temporary upward shifts to the left of the supply curve for coal, as well as shifts of the demand curve, were responsible for the increases in price.

Given the very high coal prices of 1917–23, coal mining was very profitable. Indeed, after-tax income in 1920 was about 20 percent of invested capital for all bituminous coal companies—and much higher for particular companies. These high profits signaled that more resources should be invested in the industry. And just as the perfectly competitive model would predict, more resources were invested; the number of bituminous coal firms increased by over 130 percent in nine key states between 1903 and 1923, and the industry's capacity grew by over 50 percent between 1913 and 1923.

Unfortunately, the demand for coal dropped considerably from 1923 to 1933, plunging the industry into a severe economic crisis. The downward shift to the left of the demand curve for coal during the early 1930s was due in considerable part to the fall in national output during the Great Depression. It was accompanied by a marked decrease in the price of coal. From $2.68 in 1923, the price per ton fell to $1.34 in 1933. Needless to say, this tremendous drop meant losses for bituminous coal producers. Indeed, in every year between 1925 and 1940, the bituminous coal industry as a whole showed losses.

These economic losses signaled that resources should be withdrawn from the bituminous coal industry and used elsewhere in the economy where they could be more valuably employed. And as the perfectly competitive model would predict, resources were in fact taken out of bituminous coal. Between 1923 and 1933, there was a reduction of over 40 percent in the number of coal companies operating in nine key states. And the industry's capacity fell by almost 40 percent between 1923 and 1933. Despite the difficulties in exit that we described in a previous section, the competitive process had its way. Its signals were heeded. Consequently, the industry began to move closer and closer to a position of long-run equilibrium, and although the industry remained on the nation's sick list, it began to show much smaller losses. By the onset of World War II, many of the basic adjustments had occurred.

In the postwar period, many important changes have taken place in the bituminous coal industry. Strip mining has become much more important relative to underground mining. The federal government has passed new legislation setting stricter safety requirements for coal. The energy crisis of the 1970s focused new attention on our great coal resources. But from the point of view of the present chapter, perhaps the most interesting development is the increased dominance of the industry by relatively few large firms—and the fact that many big coal companies have been purchased by the major oil firms. About half of the country's 10 biggest coal companies were bought up during the 1960s. Some observers worry that the bituminous coal industry, which tended to be relatively competitive in the past, may be less so in the future.[9]

[9] See T. Duchesneau, *Competition in the U.S. Energy Industry,* Cambridge, Mass.: Ballinger, 1975; R. Moyer, *Competition in the Midwestern Coal Market,* Cambridge, Mass.: Harvard University Press, 1964; and "Out of the Pits," *Barron's,* May 21, 1979.

Test Yourself

1. If the price elasticity of supply for corn is about 0.1 in the short run, as estimated by Marc Nerlove of the University of Pennsylvania, a 1 percent increase in the price of corn would have approximately what impact on the quantity supplied?

2. In Example 25.2, suppose that 125 million apples are produced per year. Under these circumstances, is it socially desirable to reduce apple production? Explain.

3. Suppose that the demand curve for onions is $P = 10 - 3Q$, where P is the price of a pound of onions and Q is the quantity demanded (in millions of pounds). If the supply of onions in the market period is 3⅙ million pounds, what is the equilibrium price of onions in the market period? What does the supply curve for onions look like in the market period?

4. In the short run, suppose that the demand curve for onions is as given in Question 3, and that the supply curve is $P = Q/3$. What is the equilibrium price of onions in the short run? What does the supply curve of onions look like in the short run?

5. In Chapter 3 we pointed out that, in the late 1970s and in the 1980s, consumers seemed to become less interested in playing tennis than in previous years. Describe how the price system reallocated resources in response to this change in tastes.

Summary

1. Economists generally classify markets into four types—perfect competition, monopoly, monopolistic competition, and oligopoly. Perfect competition requires that the product of any seller be the same as the product of any other seller, that no buyer or seller be able to influence the price of the product, and that resources be able to switch readily from one use to another.

2. If it maximizes profit, a perfectly competitive firm should set its output rate in the short run at the level where marginal cost equals price, so long as price exceeds average variable cost. If there is no output rate at which price exceeds average variable cost, the firm should discontinue production.

3. The firm's supply curve coincides with its marginal cost curve for prices exceeding the minimum value of average variable cost. For prices that are less than or equal to the minimum value of average variable cost, the firm's supply curve coincides with the price axis.

4. As a first approximation, the market supply curve can be viewed as the horizontal summation of the supply curves of all of the firms producing the product. This assumes that increases or decreases in output by all firms simultaneously do not affect input prices.

5. The market supply curve of a product is determined by the size of the firms' plants, the level of input prices, the nature of technology, and the other factors determining the shape of the firms' marginal cost curves, as well as by the effect of changes in the industry output on input prices and by the number of firms producing the product.

6. The sensitivity of the quantity supplied to changes in price is measured by the price elasticity of supply, defined as the percentage change in quantity supplied resulting from a 1 percent change in price. In general, the price elasticity of supply is greater if the time interval is long rather than short.

7. Price and output under perfect competition are determined by the intersection of the market supply and demand curves. In the market period, supply is fixed; thus price plays the role of the allocating device. In the short run, price influences as well as rations the amount supplied.

8. In the long run, equilibrium is achieved under perfect competition when enough firms—no more, no less—are in the industry so that economic profits are eliminated. In other words, the long-run equilibrium position of the firm is at the point where its long-run average cost equals price. But since price must also equal marginal cost (to maximize profit), it follows that the firm must be operating at the minimum point on the long-run average cost curve.

9. In a perfectly competitive economy, prices are the signals that are used to guide the reallocation of resources in response to changes in consumer tastes, technology, and other factors.

Concepts for Review

Perfect competition	**Oligopoly**	**Price elasticity of supply**
Monopoly	**Firm's supply curve**	**Market period**
Monopolistic competition	**Market supply curve**	**Economic profits**

Appendix: Constant, Increasing, and Decreasing Cost Industries

Perfectly competitive industries can be categorized into three types—constant cost industries, increasing cost industries, and decreasing cost industries.

CONSTANT COST INDUSTRIES

*In a **constant cost industry** an expansion of output does not result in a change in input prices.* Figure 25.9 shows the long-run equilibrium in a constant cost industry. Panel A shows the short- and long-run cost curves of a typical firm in the industry. Panel B shows the demand and supply curves in the market as a whole. It is assumed that the industry is in long-run equilibrium, with the result that the price line is tangent to the long-run (and short-run) average cost curve at its minimum point. The price is OP.

Let's assume that the demand curve shifts upward and to the right, as shown in panel B. In the short run, with the number of firms fixed, the price of the product will rise from OP to OP_1; each firm will expand output from Oq to Oq_1; and each firm will be making economic profits since OP_1 exceeds the short-run average costs of the firm at Oq_1. The consequence is that firms will enter the industry and shift the short-run supply curve to the right. In a constant cost industry, the entrance of the new firms does not affect the costs of the existing firms. The inputs used by this industry are used by many other industries as well, and the appearance of the new firms in this industry does not bid up the price of inputs (and consequently raise the costs of existing firms). In the long run, the price settles back to OP, the level of (minimum) long-run average cost. Thus *a constant cost industry has a horizontal long-run supply curve.* Since output can be varied by varying the number of firms producing Oq units at an average cost of OP, the long-run supply curve is horizontal at OP.

INCREASING COST INDUSTRIES

Most economists seem to regard increasing, not constant, cost industries as the most prevalent of the three types. *An **increasing cost industry** is one*

Figure 25.9

Long-Run Equilibrium: Constant Cost Industry *If the demand curve shifts upward and to the right, the price will increase in the short run from OP to OP₁. Each firm will expand output from Oq to Oq₁, and entry will occur, thus shifting the supply curve downward and to the right. The long-run supply curve in a constant cost industry is horizontal.*

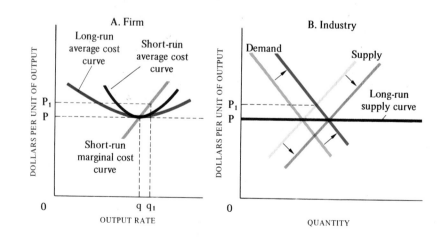

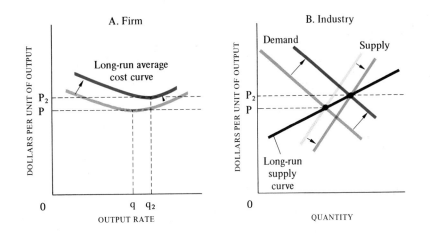

Figure 25.10

Long-Run Equilibrium: Increasing Cost Industry *If the demand curve shifts upward and to the right, the price will increase in the short run. Entry will occur, and the price of inputs will increase, thus pushing the long-run average cost curve upward. The short-run supply curve will shift downward and to the right. The long-run supply curve in an increasing cost industry slopes upward to the right.*

where the price of inputs increases with the amount the industry uses. The situation in such an industry is shown in Figure 25.10. The original conditions are the same as those in Figure 25.9, and we suppose again that the demand curve shifts upward and to the right, with the result that the price of the product increases and firms earn economic profits, thus attracting new entrants. More and more inputs are required by the industry, and in an increasing cost industry the price of inputs increases with the amount the industry uses. Consequently, the cost of inputs increases for the established firms as well as the new entrants. The long-run average cost curve of each firm is pushed up, as shown in panel A. The short-run supply curve shifts downward and to the right, as shown in panel B. Thus the new equilibrium price is OP_2 and each firm produces Oq_2 units. *An increasing cost industry has a positively sloped long-run supply curve,* as shown in Figure 25.10. That is, after long-run equilibrium is achieved, increases in output require increases in the price of the product.

DECREASING COST INDUSTRIES

Decreasing cost industries are the most unusual situation, although quite young industries may sometimes fall into this category. *In a **decreasing cost industry,** the expansion of the industry results in a decrease in the costs of the established firms.*[10] Thus *a decreasing cost industry has a negatively sloped long-run supply curve.* That is, after long-run equilibrium is reached, increases in output are accompanied by decreases in price.

Whether an industry is a constant cost industry, an increasing cost industry, or a decreasing cost industry is an empirical question that must be settled case by case. In trying to determine whether a particular industry is an increasing or constant cost industry, one important consideration is whether or not it is a relatively large user of certain inputs. Because the automobile industry uses a great deal of the nation's steel, an expansion of the automobile industry might well cause an increase in the price of steel; but an expansion of the paper-clip industry, which uses very little of the nation's steel, would be unlikely to raise the price of steel.

---

[10] Certain *external economies,* which are cost reductions that occur when an industry expands, may be responsible for the existence of decreasing cost industries. An example of such an external economy is an improvement in transportation that is due to the expansion of an industry and that reduces the costs of each firm in the industry (see Chapter 4).

CHAPTER 26

Monopoly and Its Regulation

At the opposite extreme from perfect competition is monopoly. Under a monopolistic market structure, what sorts of behavior can we expect? How much of the product will be produced, and at what level will its price be set? What are the social disadvantages of monopoly? In what ways have government commissions attempted to regulate industries whose market structures approximate monopoly? These are some of the major questions dealt with in this chapter.

To begin with, recall what is meant by *monopoly: a market where there exists one, and only one, seller.* Monopoly, like perfect competition, seldom corresponds more than approximately to conditions in real industries, but it is a very useful model. In several respects, monopoly and perfect competition stand as polar opposites. The firm in a perfectly competitive market has so many rivals that competition becomes entirely impersonal. The firm is a price taker, an inconspicuous seller in a sea of inconspicuous sellers. Under monopoly, on the other hand, the firm has no direct competitors at all; it is the sole supplier.

However, even the monopolist is affected by certain indirect and potential forms of competition. Suppose a firm managed to obtain a monopoly on wheat production. It would have to worry about competition from corn and other agricultural commodities that could be substituted for wheat. Moreover, the wheat monopolist would also have to take into account the possibility that new firms might arise to challenge its monopoly if it attempted to extract conspicuously high profits. Thus even the monopolist is subject to some restraint imposed by competitive forces.

Causes of Monopoly

There are many reasons why monopolies, or market structures that closely approximate monopoly, may arise.

Patents. A firm may acquire a monopoly over the production of a good by having patents on the product or on certain basic processes used in its production. The patent laws of the United States give an inventor the exclusive right to make a certain product or to use a certain process for 17 years. The purpose of the patent system is to encourage invention and innovation and to discourage industrial secrecy. Many firms with monopoly power achieved it in considerable part through patents. For example, the United Shoe Machinery Company became the sole supplier of certain important kinds of shoemaking equipment through control of basic patents. United Shoe was free to dominate the market until 1954, when, after prosecution under the antitrust laws, the firm was ordered to license its patents. And in 1968, when this remedy seemed insufficient, a divestiture program was agreed upon.

Control of Input. A firm may become a monopolist by obtaining control over the entire supply of a basic input required to manufacture a product. The International Nickel Company of Canada controls about nine-tenths of the proven nickel reserves in the world. Since it is hard to produce nickel without nickel, the International Nickel Company obviously has a strong monopoly position. Similarly, the Aluminum Company of America (Alcoa) kept its dominant position for a long time by controlling practically all the sources of bauxite, the ore used to make aluminum. However, as we shall see in Chapter 28, Alcoa's monopoly was broken in 1945 when the Supreme Court decided that Alcoa's control of practically all the industry's output violated the antitrust laws.

Government Action. A firm may become a monopolist because it is awarded a market franchise by a government agency. The government may give a particular firm the franchise to sell a particular product in a public facility. Or it may give a particular company the right to provide a service, such as telephone service, to people in a particular area. In exchange for this right, the firm agrees to allow the government to regulate certain aspects of its operations. The form of regulation does not matter here; the important point for now is that the monopoly is created by the government.

Declining Cost of Production. A firm may become a monopolist because the average costs of producing the product reach a minimum at an output rate that is large enough to satisfy the entire market (at a price that is profitable). In a case like this, a firm obviously has an incentive to expand until it produces all the market wants of the good. (Its costs fall as it continues to expand). Thus competition cannot be maintained in this case. If there are a number of firms in the industry, the result is likely to be economic warfare —and the survival of a single victor, the monopolist.[1]

Cases where costs behave like this are called **natural monopolies.** When an industry is a natural monopoly, the public often insists that its behavior be regulated by the government. For example, electric power is an industry where there seem to be great economies of scale—and thus de-

---

[1] Note that economies of scale are different from the external economies discussed in note 10 of the previous chapter. The individual firm has no control over external economies.

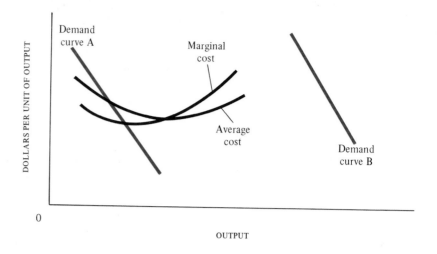

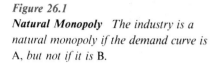
Figure 26.1
Natural Monopoly *The industry is a natural monopoly if the demand curve is* A, *but not if it is* B.

creasing average costs. Fuel consumed per kilowatt hour is lower in larger power generating units, and there are economies in combining generating units at a single site. Because of these factors, there has been little attempt to force competition in the industry, since it would be wasteful. Instead, as we describe later, the market for electric power in a particular area is a regulated monopoly.[2]

The likelihood that the long-run average cost curve will decrease up to a point that satisfies the entire market depends on the size of the market. The smaller the market, the more likely it is. In Figure 26.1, the industry is a natural monopoly if the demand curve is *A,* but not if it is *B.* In a large market like the United States, it is much less likely that an industry will be a natural monopoly than in a small market like Belgium or Denmark. One of the advantages claimed for the Common Market in Europe (which was a step toward integrating Europe into a single market) was that it would create a larger market that could support more efficient production and more competitive industries. More will be said on this score in Chapter 32. For now, the important point to recognize is that, just as stagnant marshes are the breeding ground for mosquitos, so small, insulated markets are the breeding ground for monopoly.

Demand Curve and Marginal Revenue under Monopoly

Before we can make any statements about the behavior of a monopolistic market, we must point out certain important characteristics of the demand curve facing the monopolist. Since the monopolist is the only seller of the commodity, the demand curve it faces is the market demand curve for the product. Since the market demand curve is almost always downward-sloping to the right, the monopolist's demand curve must also be downward-sloping to the right. This is quite different from perfect competition,

---

[2] However, it is worth noting that technological developments in this industry may permit more competition in the future. See L. Weiss, "Antitrust in the Electric Power Industry," in A. Phillips, *Promoting Competition in Regulated Markets,* Washington, D.C.: The Brookings Institution, 1975.

DEMAND CURVE AND MARGINAL REVENUE

Table 26.1

DEMAND AND REVENUE OF A MONOPOLIST

Quan-tity	Price	Total revenue (dollars)	Marginal revenue
1	100	100	80
2	90	180	60
3	80	240	40
4	70	280	20
5	60	300	0
6	50	300	−20
7	40	280	−40
8	30	240	

where the firm's demand curve is horizontal. To illustrate the situation faced by a monopolist, consider the hypothetical case in Table 26.1. The price at which each quantity (shown in column 1) can be sold by the monopolist is shown in column 2. The firm's ***total revenue***—its total dollar sales volume—is shown in column 3. Obviously, column 3 is the product of the first two columns. Column 4 contains the firm's ***marginal revenue,*** *defined as the addition to total revenue attributable to the addition of one unit to sales.* (Thus if $R(q)$ is total revenue when q units are sold and $R(q-1)$ is total revenue when $(q-1)$ units are sold, the marginal revenue between q units and $(q-1)$ units is $R(q) - R(q-1)$.)

Marginal revenue is very important to the monopolist. We can estimate it from the figures in the first three columns of Table 26.1. The marginal revenue between 1 and 2 units of output per day is \$180—\$100, or \$80; the marginal revenue between 2 and 3 units of output per day is \$240—\$180, or \$60; the marginal revenue between 3 and 4 units of output per day is \$280—\$240, or \$40; and so on. The results are shown in column 4 of the table (and are plotted in Figure 26.2). Note that marginal revenue is analo-

Figure 26.2

Marginal Revenue and Demand Curves
The demand curve comes from Table 26.1. Each value of marginal revenue is plotted at the midpoint of the range of output to which it pertains. Since the demand curve is downward-sloping, marginal revenue is always less than price, for reasons discussed in the text. Note that the value of marginal revenue is related to the price elasticity of demand. At outputs where demand is price elastic, marginal revenue is positive; *at outputs where it is price inelastic, marginal revenue is* negative; *and at outputs where it is of unitary elasticity, marginal revenue is zero.*

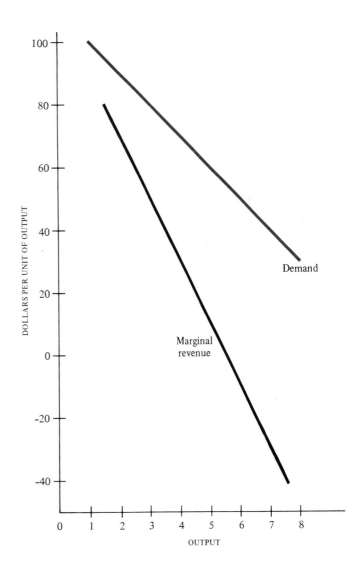

561

gous to marginal cost (and marginal utility and marginal product, for that matter). Recall that marginal cost is the extra cost resulting from an extra unit of production. Substitute "revenue" for "cost" and "sales" for "production" in the previous sentence, and what do you get? A perfectly acceptable definition of marginal revenue.

Marginal revenue will always be less than price if the firm's demand curve is downward-sloping (as it is under monopoly and other market structures that are not perfectly competitive). In Table 26.1, the extra revenue from the second unit of output is $80 whereas the price of this unit is $90. *The basic reason is that the firm must reduce the price of all units of output, not just the extra unit, in order to sell the extra unit.* Thus, in Table 26.1, the extra revenue from the second unit of output is $80 because, while the price of the second unit is $90, the price of the first unit must be reduced by $10 in order to sell the second unit. Thus the extra revenue (that is, marginal revenue) from selling the second unit of output is $90—$10, or $80, which is less than the price of the second unit.

Similarly, the marginal revenue from selling the third unit of output ($60, according to Table 26.1) is less than the price at which the third unit can be sold ($80, according to Table 26.1). Why? Because, to sell the third unit of output, the price of the first two units of output must be reduced by $10 each (that is, from $90 to $80). Thus the extra revenue (that is, marginal revenue) from selling the third unit is not $80, but $80 less the $20 reduction in the amount received for the first two units.

Price and Output: The Short Run

We are now in a position to determine how output and price behave under monopoly. If the monopolist is free to maximize its profits, it will choose the price and output rate at which the difference between total revenue and total cost is greatest. Suppose that the firm's costs are as shown in Table 26.2 and that the demand curve it faces is as shown in Table 26.1. Based on the data in these two tables, the firm can calculate the profit that it will make at each output rate. To do so, it subtracts its total cost from its total

Table 26.2
COSTS OF A MONOPOLIST

Quantity	Total variable cost	Total fixed cost (dollars)	Total cost	Marginal cost
0	0	100	100	
1	40	100	140	40
2	70	100	170	30
3	110	100	210	40
4	150	100	250	40
5	200	100	300	50
6	260	100	360	60
7	350	100	450	90
8	450	100	550	100

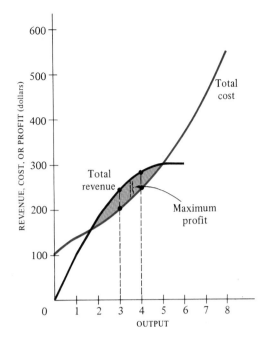

Figure 26.3

Total Revenue, Cost, and Profit of Monopolist *The output rate that will maximize the firm's profit is between 3 and 4 units per day. At this output rate, profit (which equals the vertical distance between the total revenue and total cost curves) is over $30 per day. Based on the demand curve for its product (shown in Table 26.1), the firm must set a price of between $70 and $80 to sell between 3 and 4 units per day.*

Table 26.3

PROFITS OF A MONOPOLIST

Quantity	Total revenue	Total cost	Total profit
	(dollars)		
1	100	140	−40
2	180	170	10
3	240	210	30
4	280	250	30
5	300	300	0
6	300	360	−60
7	280	450	−170
8	240	550	−310

Table 26.4

MARGINAL COST AND MARGINAL REVENUE OF A MONOPOLIST

Quantity	Total profit	Marginal cost	Marginal revenue
	(dollars)		
1	−40		
		30	80
2	10		
		40	60
3	30		
		40	40
4	30		
		50	20
5	0		
		60	0
6	−60		
		90	−20
7	−170		
		100	−40
8	−310		

revenue, as shown in Table 26.3. What output rate will maximize the firm's profit? According to Table 26.3, profit *rises* as its output rate increases from 1 to 3 units per day, and profit *falls* as its output rate increases from 4 to 8 units per day. Thus the *maximum* profit is achieved at an output rate between 3 and 4 units per day.[3] (Without more detailed data, one cannot tell precisely where the maximum occurs, but this is close enough for present purposes.) Figure 26.3 shows the same thing graphically.

What price will the monopolist charge? To maximize its profit, it must charge the price that results in its selling the profit-maximizing output, which in this case is between 3 and 4 units per day. Thus, according to Table 26.1, it must charge between $70 and $80 per unit. Why? Because if it charges $70, it will sell 4 units per day; and if it charges $80, it will sell 3 units per day. Consequently, to sell the profit-maximizing output of between 3 and 4 units per day, it must charge a price of between $70 and $80 per unit.

THE GOLDEN RULE OF OUTPUT DETERMINATION

In Chapter 25, we set forth the Golden Rule of Output Determination for a perfectly competitive firm. We can now formulate a Golden Rule of Output Determination for a monopolist: *set the output rate at the point where marginal revenue equals marginal cost.* Table 26.4 and Figure 26.4 show that this rule results in a maximum profit in this example. It is evident from Table 26.4 that marginal revenue equals marginal cost at the profit-maximizing output of between 3 and 4 units per day. Figure 26.4 shows the same thing graphically.

Why is this rule generally a necessary condition for profit maximiza-

---

[3] This assumes that the output rate can vary continuously and that there is a single maximum. These are innocuous assumptions.

tion? At any output rate at which marginal revenue *exceeds* marginal cost, profit can be increased by *increasing* output, since the extra revenue will exceed the extra cost. At any output rate at which marginal revenue is *less than* marginal cost, profit can be increased by *reducing* output, since the decrease in cost will exceed the decrease in revenue. Thus, since profit will *not* be a maximum when marginal revenue exceeds marginal cost or falls short of marginal cost, *it must be a maximum only when marginal revenue equals marginal cost.*

THE MONOPOLIST'S EQUILIBRIUM POSITION

Figure 26.5 shows the equilibrium position of a monopolist in the short run. Short-run equilibrium will occur at the output, *OQ*, where the marginal cost curve intersects the marginal revenue curve (the curve that shows the firm's marginal revenue at each output level). And if the monopolist is to sell *OQ* units per period of time, the demand curve shows that it must set a price of *OP*. Thus the equilibrium output and price are *OQ* and *OP*, respectively.

It is interesting to compare the Golden Rule of Output Determination for a monopolist (set the output rate at the point where marginal revenue equals marginal cost) with that for a perfectly competitive firm (set the output rate at the point where price equals marginal cost). The latter is really the same as the former because, *for a perfectly competitive firm, price equals marginal revenue.* Since the perfectly competitive firm can sell all it wants at the market price, each additional unit sold increases the firm's total revenue by the amount of the price. Thus, *for both the monopolist and the perfectly competitive firm, profits are maximized by setting the output rate at the point where marginal revenue equals marginal cost.*

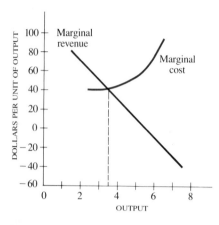

Figure 26.4

Marginal Cost and Marginal Revenue of Monopolist *At the profit-maximizing output rate of between 3 and 4 units per day, marginal cost (which is $40 between an output rate of 3 and 4 units per period) equals marginal revenue (which also is $40 between an output rate of 3 and 4 units per period). Both marginal cost and marginal revenue are plotted at the midpoints of the ranges of output to which they pertain. (See Figures 24.8 and 26.2.)*

Figure 26.5

Equilibrium Position of Monopolist
The monopolist sets its output rate at OQ, *where the marginal revenue curve intersects the marginal cost curve. At this output, price must be* OP. *And profit per unit of output equals* CP, *since average cost equals* OC.

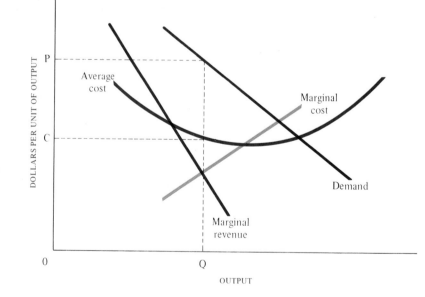

564

WHEN WILL A MONOPOLIST SHUT DOWN?

From the previous chapter, we know that perfectly competitive firms sometimes find it preferable to shut down rather than follow this rule. Is this true for monopolists as well? The answer is yes. *Just as perfectly competitive firms will discontinue production if they will lose more money by producing than by shutting down, so monopolists will do the same thing, and for the same reasons.* In other words, if there is no output such that price exceeds average variable costs, monopolists, like perfect competitors, will discontinue production. This makes sense. If by producing, monopolists incur greater losses than their fixed costs, they will "drop out," i.e., produce nothing.

TWO MISCONCEPTIONS

Finally, note two misconceptions concerning monopoly behavior. First, it is sometimes said that monopolists will charge "as high a price as they can get." This is nonsense. The monopolist in Table 26.1 could charge a higher price than $70 to $80, but to do so would be foolish since it would result in lower profits. Second, it is sometimes said that monopolists will seek to maximize their profit per unit of output. This too is nonsense, since monopolists are interested in their total profits and their return on capital, not on the profit per unit of output. Rational monopolists will not sacrifice their total profits to increase their profit per unit of output.

Price and Output: The Long Run

In contrast to the situation under perfect competition, the long-run equilibrium of a monopolistic industry may not be marked by the absence of economic profits. If a monopolist earns a short-run economic profit, it will not be confronted in the long run with competitors, unless the industry ceases to be a monopoly. The entrance of additional firms into the industry is incompatible with the existence of monopoly. Thus the long-run equilibrium of an industry under monopoly may be characterized by economic profits.

On the other hand, if the monopolist incurs a short-run economic loss, it will be forced to look for other, more profitable uses for its resources. One possibility is that the firm's existing plant is not optimal and that it can earn economic profits by appropriate alterations to its scale and characteristics. If so, the firm will make these alterations in the long run and remain in the industry. However, *if there is no scale of plant that will enable the firm to avoid economic losses, it will leave the industry in the long run.* The mere fact of having a monopoly over the production of a certain commodity does not mean that the firm must be profitable. A monopoly over the production of cut-glass spittoons would be unlikely to catapult a firm into financial glory—or even allow it to avoid losses.

To illustrate the long-run behavior of a monopolist, consider the prewar policy of the Aluminum Company of America (Alcoa). Until after World War II, Alcoa was virtually the sole producer of aluminum in the United

States. According to various observers, Alcoa recognized the dangers involved in potential competition, and adopted a policy of keeping its price low enough to ward off potential entrants. Naturally, it wanted to make money—and it did. But it was smart enough to see that, if it charged very high prices, it might encourage other firms to enter the aluminum industry. So it set a price high enough to permit it to make plenty of economic profits, but not so high that it would have to wrestle with competitors. Some other firms with monopoly power think the same way and act accordingly, but by no means all are so clever. On the contrary, some monopolists, like some newlyweds, think the *status quo* will last forever. And just as for newlyweds, sometimes it does, but sometimes it doesn't.

Perfect Competition and Monopoly: A Comparison

At the beginning of the previous chapter, we said that a market's structure would be likely to affect the behavior of the market; in other words, that a market's structure would influence how much was produced and the price that would be set. If we could perform an experiment in which an industry was first operated under conditions of perfect competition and then under conditions of monopoly (assuming that the demand for the industry's product and the industry's cost functions would be the same in either case),[4] we would find that the equilibrium price and output would differ under the two sets of conditions.

HIGHER PRICE AND LESS OUTPUT UNDER MONOPOLY

Specifically, if the product demand curve and the industry's cost functions are the same, *the output of a perfectly competitive industry tends to be greater and the price tends to be lower than under monopoly.* We see this in Figure 26.6, which shows the industry's demand and supply curves, if it is perfectly competitive. Since price and output under perfect competition are given by the intersection of the demand and supply curves, OQ_C is the industry output and OP_C is the price. But what if all of the competitive firms are bought up by a single firm, which operates as a pure monopolist? Under these conditions, what formerly was the industry's supply curve is now the monopolist's marginal cost curve.[5] And what formerly was the industry's demand curve is now the monopolist's demand curve. Since the

[4] However, the cost and demand curves need not be the same. For example, the monopolist may spend money on advertising, thus shifting the demand curve. It should be recognized that the assumption that they are the same is stronger than it appears at first glance.

[5] The monopolist will operate the various plants that would be independent under perfect competition as branches of a single firm. The marginal cost curve of a multiplant monopoly is the horizontal sum of the marginal cost curves of the individual plants. (To see why, suppose that a monopoly has two plants, A and B. The total amount that the monopoly can produce at a particular marginal cost is the sum of (1) the amount plant A can produce at this marginal cost, and (2) the amount plant B can produce at this marginal cost.) From the previous chapter, we know that this is also the supply curve of the industry if the plants are operated as separate firms under perfect competition.

Figure 26.6

Comparison of Long-Run Equilibria:
Perfect Competition and Monopoly
Under perfect competition, OQ_C is the
industry output and OP_C is the price.
Under monopoly, OQ_M is the industry
output, OP_M is the price. Clearly, output
is higher and price is lower under perfect
competition than under monopoly.

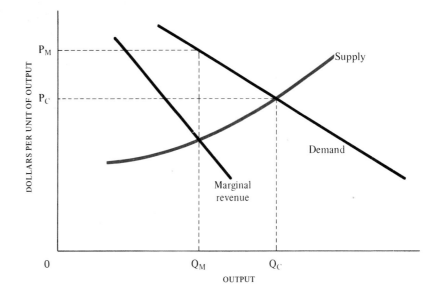

monopolist chooses the output where marginal cost equals marginal revenue, the industry output will be OQ_M and the price will be OP_M. Clearly, OQ_M is less than OQ_C, and OP_M is greater than OP_C—which is what we set out to prove.

Of course, all this is theory. But there is plenty of evidence that monopolists restrict output and charge higher prices than under competition. Take the case of tungsten carbide, which sold for $50 per pound until a monopoly was established in 1927 by General Electric. Then the price went to between $225 and $453 per pound, until the monopoly was broken by the antitrust laws in 1945. The price then dropped back to between $27 and $45 per pound.[6] This case was extreme, but by no means unique. Indeed, for centuries people have observed that when monopolies are formed, output tends to be restricted, and price tends to be driven up.

MONOPOLY AND RESOURCE ALLOCATION

Moreover, it has long been felt that the allocation of resources under perfect competition is socially more desirable than under monopoly. Society might be better off if more resources were devoted to producing the monopolized good in Figure 26.6, and if the competitive, not the monopolistic, output were produced. For example, in the *Wealth of Nations*, published about 200 years ago, Adam Smith stressed that when competitive forces are thwarted by "the great engine... of monopoly," the tendency for resources to be used "as nearly as possible in the proportion which is most agreeable to the interest of the whole society" is thwarted as well.

Why do many economists believe that the allocation of resources under perfect competition is more socially desirable than that under monopoly? This is not a simple question, and like most hard questions can be answered at various levels of sophistication. Put most simply, many econ-

---

[6] W. Adams, *The Structure of American Industry*, 5th ed., New York: Macmillan, 1977, p. 485.

omists believe that firms under perfect competition are induced to produce quantities of goods that are more in line with consumer desires, and that firms under perfect competition are induced to use the least costly methods of production. In the following section, we shall indicate in detail why they believe that these things are true. In Chapter 28 (and in Appendix E), we provide a much more complete discussion of the pros and cons of monopoly and competition.

Example 26.1   Another Newspaper for Haverhill?

In Haverhill, Massachusetts, one newspaper had been published for over a century. Then, in the 1950s, another newspaper was founded. In the Haverhill market, suppose that the market demand curve for the town's newspapers, and the demand curve facing each newspaper, were as shown below. Also, each newspaper's cost curves and marginal revenue curve are given below. (Note: In this special case, the firm's demand curve is the same as a monopolist's marginal revenue curve.)

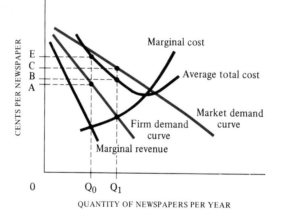

(a) If both firms stay in business, how much will each lose? (b) If only one of them stays in business, can it make a profit? How big a profit? (c) Is this a case of natural monopoly? (d) If entry by one firm may drive the other out of business, is this illegal?

SOLUTION

(a) Each firm will produce OQ_0 newspapers, since this is the output where marginal revenue equals marginal cost. To sell this output, each sets a price of OA, since this is the price on the firm's demand curve corresponding to the sale of OQ_0 newspapers. At an output of OQ_0 newspapers, each firm's average total cost equals OE. Thus it loses $(OE - OA)$ cents per newspaper sold, and since it sells OQ_0 newspapers per year, its total annual loss is $OQ_0 \times (OE - OA)$ cents. (b) The monopolist will produce OQ_1 newspapers, since this is the output where its marginal revenue equals marginal cost. (Recall that in this case the firm's demand curve is the same as the monopolist's marginal revenue curve.) To sell this output, it must charge a price equal to OC cents per newspaper. Since its average total cost is OB cents per newspaper, it makes a profit of $(OC - OB)$ cents per newspaper sold, and its total annual profit is $OQ_1 \times (OC - OB)$ cents. (c) Yes. (d) This question was taken to court by these newspapers. The decision was that it was not illegal.

Test Yourself

1. If you were the president of a firm that has a monopoly on a certain product, would you choose an output level where demand for the product was price inelastic? Explain.

2. Suppose that a monopolist's demand curve is as follows:

Quantity demanded (per year)	Price (dollars)
8	1,000
7	2,000
6	3,000
5	4,000
4	5,000
3	6,000
2	7,000
1	8,000

Plot the firm's marginal revenue curve.

3. Suppose that the monopolist in Question 2 has fixed costs of $10,000 and an average variable cost of $4,000. The average variable cost is the same for outputs of 1 to 10 units per year. What output rate will the firm choose? What price will it set?

4. Plot the marginal cost curve of the firm in Question 3. Where does this curve intersect the marginal revenue curve you drew in Question 2?

5. Suppose that the firm in Question 3 experienced a 50 percent increase in both its fixed and average variable costs. If the demand curve in Question 2 remains valid, what effect will this cost increase have on the output rate and price that the firm will choose?

The Case Against Monopoly

Many people oppose monopolies on the grounds that they "gouge" the consumers by charging a higher price than would otherwise exist—a price that can be sustained only because monopolists artificially limit the supply. In other words, these people claim that monopolists reap higher profits than would be possible under perfect competition and that these profits are at the expense of consumers, who pay higher prices than under perfect competition. Is their claim accurate? As we have just seen, a monopolist will reap higher profits than under perfect competition and consumers will pay higher prices under monopoly than under perfect competition. But is this bad?

To the extent that the monopolist is rich and the consumers are poor, we are likely to answer yes. Also, to the extent that the monopolist is less deserving than the consumers, we are likely to answer the same thing. But suppose the monopolist is a selfless philanthropist who gives to the poor. Is monopoly still socially undesirable? The answer remains yes, because *monopoly imposes a burden on society by misallocating resources. In the presence of monopoly, the price system cannot be relied on to direct the allocation of resources to their most efficient use.*

THE MISALLOCATION OF RESOURCES

To see more precisely how monopoly interferes with the proper functioning of the price system, suppose that all industries other than the shoe industry are perfectly competitive. The shoe industry, however, has been monopolized. How does this cause a misallocation of resources? Under fairly general circumstances, a good's price can be taken as a measure of the social value of an extra unit of the good. Thus, if the price of a pair of socks is $1, the value to the consumer of an extra pair of socks can be taken to be $1. Moreover, under fairly general circumstances, a good's marginal cost can be taken as a measure of the cost to society of an extra unit of the good. Thus, if the marginal cost of a pair of shoes is $30, the cost to society of producing an extra pair of shoes can be taken to be $30.

In perfectly competitive industries, price is set equal to marginal cost, as we saw in Chapter 25. Thus each of the competitive industries produces up to the point where the social value of an extra unit of the good (which equals price) is set equal to the cost to society of producing an extra unit of the good (which equals marginal cost). This is the amount each of these industries should produce—the output rate that will result in an optimal allocation of resources.

WHY IS THE COMPETITIVE OUTPUT OPTIMAL?

To see that this is the optimal output rate, consider what happens when an industry produces up to the point where the social value of an extra unit of the good is *more* than the cost to society of producing an extra unit. This isn't the socially optimal output rate because a one-unit increase in the output rate will increase the social value of output by more than the social cost of production, which means that it will increase social welfare. Thus, since a one-unit increase in the output rate will increase social welfare, the existing output rate cannot be optimal. (Recall Example 25.2.)

Next, consider what happens when an industry produces up to the point where the social value of an extra unit of the good is *less* than the cost to society of producing the extra unit. This isn't the socially optimal output rate because a one-unit decrease in the output rate will decrease the social value of output by less than the social cost of production, which means that it will increase social welfare. Thus, since a one-unit decrease in the output rate will increase social welfare, the existing output rate cannot be optimal.

Putting together the results of the previous two paragraphs, it follows that the socially optimal output rate must be at the point where the social value of an extra unit of the good *equals* the social cost of producing an extra unit of the good. Why? Because if the output rate is not optimal when the social value of an extra unit of the good exceeds or falls short of the cost to society of producing the extra unit, it must be optimal only when the two are equal.

THE MONOPOLIST PRODUCES TOO LITTLE

Now let's return to the shoe industry—the sole monopolist.[7] Is the shoe industry producing the optimal amount of shoes? The answer is no. Like any monopolist, it produces at the point where marginal revenue equals marginal cost. Thus, since marginal revenue is *less* than price (as was proved above), the monopolist produces at a point where price is *greater* than marginal cost. Consequently, *the monopolistic industry produces at a point where the social value of an extra unit of the good (which equals price) is greater than the cost to society of producing the extra unit (which equals marginal cost).* As we saw in a previous paragraph, this means that the

---

[7] Are puns really the lowest form of humor?

monopolist's output rate is too small. A one-unit increase in the output of shoes will increase the social value of output by more than the social cost of production. (The situation is similar to that in Example 25.2 when 75 million apples are produced.)

Here lies the economist's principal complaint against monopoly: it results in a misallocation of resources. Too little is produced of the monopolized good. Society is less well off—in terms of its own tastes and potentialities—than it could be. The price system, which would not lead to, or tolerate, such waste if all industries were perfectly competitive, is not allowed to perform as it should. (These inefficiencies caused by monopoly are described further and in more detail in Appendix E.)

INCOME DISTRIBUTION, EFFICIENCY, AND TECHNOLOGICAL CHANGE

Misallocation of resources is only part of the economist's brief against monopoly. As we have already pointed out, *monopoly redistributes income in favor of the monopolists.* In other words, monopolists can fatten their own purse by restricting their output and raising their price. Admittedly, there is no scientific way to prove that monopolists are less deserving than the rest of the population, but it is also pretty difficult to see why they are more deserving.

In addition, *since monopolists do not have to face direct competition, they are likely to be less diligent in controlling costs and in using resources efficiently.* As Sir John Hicks put it, "The best of all monopoly profits is a quiet life."[8] Certainly we all dream at times of being able to take life easy. It would be strange if monopolists, having succeeded in insulating themselves from direct competition, did not take advantage of the opportunity—not open to firms in perfectly competitive markets—to relax a bit and worry less about pinching pennies. For this reason, economists fear that, to use Adam Smith's pungent phrase, "Monopoly ... is a great enemy to good management."

Further, *it is often claimed that monopolists are slow to innovate and adopt new techniques and products.* This lethargy stems from the monopolist's freedom from direct competition. Innovation tends to be disruptive, while old ways, like old shoes, tend to be comfortable. The monopolist may be inclined, therefore, to stick with "time-honored" practices. Without question, competition is an important spur to innovation and to the rapid diffusion of innovations. But there are well-known arguments on the other side as well. Some economists argue that substantial monopoly power promotes innovation and technological change. Much more will be said on this score in Chapter 28.

Public Regulation of Monopoly

One way that society has attempted to reduce the harmful effects of monopoly is through *public regulation.* Suppose that the long-run cost curve in a particular industry is such that competition is not feasible. In such a case, society may permit a monopoly to be established. But a commission

[8] J. Hicks, "Annual Survey of Economic Theory: The Theory of Monopoly," *Econometrica*, 1935.

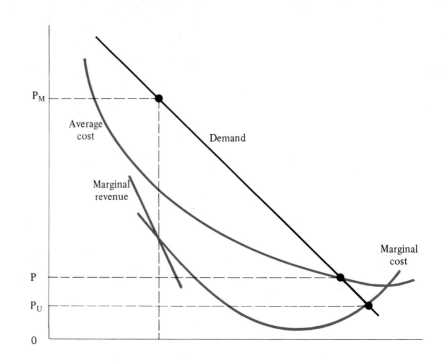

Figure 26.7

Regulation of Monopoly *The price established by a commission might be OP, where the demand curve intersects the average total cost curve. (Costs here include what the commission regards as a fair profit per unit of output.) In the absence of regulation, the monopolist would set a price of OP$_M$ (because it would set its output at the point where marginal revenue equals marginal cost). Since OP is less than OP$_M$, regulation has reduced price in this instance, but not to the point where price equals marginal cost (as in perfect competition). For price to equal marginal cost, price would have to equal OP$_u$. (For a discussion of marginal-cost pricing, see the Appendix to this chapter.)*

or some other public body is also established to regulate the monopoly's behavior. Among the many such regulatory commissions in the United States are the Federal Energy Regulatory Commission, the Federal Communications Commission, and the Interstate Commerce Commission. They regulate the behavior of firms with monopoly power in the electric power, communications, transportation, and other industries. These industries are big as well as important, taking in about 10 percent of the national output. Thus we need to know how these commissions operate and make decisions on prices and other matters.

Regulatory commissions often set the price—or the maximum price—at the level at which it equals average total cost, including a "fair" rate of return on the firm's investment. In Figure 26.7, the price would be established by the commission at *OP,* where the demand curve intersects the average total cost curve (which includes what the commission regards as a fair profit per unit of output). Needless to say, there has been considerable controversy over what constitutes a fair rate of return. Frequently, commissions have settled on 8 to 10 percent. In addition, there has been a good deal of controversy over what should be included in the company's "investment" on which the fair rate of return is to be earned. A company's assets can be valued at **historical cost** or at **reproduction cost**—at what the company paid for them or at what it would cost to replace them. If the price level does not change much, these two approaches yield much the same answer. But if prices are rising—as they have been during most of the past 40 years—replacement cost will be greater than historical cost, with the result that the company will be allowed higher profits and rates if replacement cost is used. Most commissions now use historical cost.[9]

---

[9] The use of marginal-cost pricing by regulated industries is discussed in the Appendix to this chapter.

Does Regulation Affect Prices?

The regulatory commissions and the principles they use have become extremely controversial. *Many observers feel that the commissions are lax, and that they tend to be captured by the industries they are supposed to regulate.* Regulated industries, recognizing the power of such commissions, invest considerable time and money in attempts to influence the commissions. The public, on the other hand, often has only a foggy idea of what the commissions are doing, and of whether or not it is in the public interest. According to some critics like Ralph Nader, "Nobody seriously challenges the fact that the regulatory agencies have made an accommodation with the businesses they are supposed to regulate—and they've done so at the expense of the public." For these and other reasons, some economists believe that regulation has little effect on prices.

It is difficult to isolate and measure the effects of regulation on the average level of prices. Some well-known economists have conducted studies which suggest that regulation has made little or no difference in this regard. Nobel laureate George Stigler and Claire Friedland of the University of Chicago compared the levels of rates charged for electricity by regulated and unregulated electric power companies. They found that there was no significant difference between the average rates charged by the two sets of firms.[10] Other economists challenge Stigler's and Friedland's interpretation of their factual findings, and much more research on this topic is needed. Nonetheless, it seems fair to conclude that, although the simple model of the regulatory process presented in previous sections would predict that regulated prices would be lower, on the average, than unregulated prices (of the same item), the evidence in support of this prediction is much weaker than might be supposed.

Whether or not regulation has a significant effect on the *average* level of prices, it certainly has an effect on *particular* prices charged by regulated firms. In some cases, it has reduced the price of a product. There seems to be general agreement that the Federal Energy Regulatory Commission kept the price of natural gas (in interstate commerce) below what this price would have been during the 1970s in the absence of regulation. In other cases, it has increased the price of a product. Some observers believe that prior to the deregulation of the airlines in the late 1970s, the Civil Aeronautics Board (CAB) increased the airplane fare between New York and Washington. As evidence of this, they compared at that time this fare with the fare from San Francisco to Los Angeles, which was not subject to CAB regulation since the trip was entirely within California. Although the distance from San Francisco to Los Angeles is almost twice as great as that from New York to Washington, the fare from San Francisco to Los Angeles was less than that from New York to Washington.

---

[10] G. Stigler and C. Friedland, "What Can Regulators Regulate? The Case of Electricity," *The Journal of Law and Economics,* 1962. For another point of view, see H. Trebing, "The Chicago School versus Public Utility Regulation," *Journal of Economic Issues,* March 1976.

Example 26.2　Price Discrimination in Dentistry

An isolated town of 5,000 inhabitants in the Rocky Mountains is looking for a dentist. To simplify matters, we divide the town's inhabitants into two categories: the rich and the poor. The demand curve for dental care among each type of inhabitant is shown below. Adding the two demand curves horizontally, we find that the total demand curve for dental care is DAB.

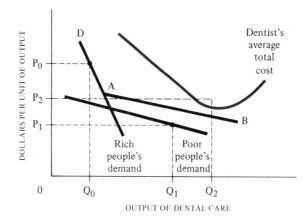

(a) If a dentist charges the same price to all inhabitants (rich or poor), can the dentist cover his or her average total costs? (b) If the dentist charges the rich a higher price than the poor, can the dentist cover his or her average total costs? (c) *Price discrimination* occurs when a producer sells the same commodity or service at more than one price. Thus the dentist in (b) is engaging in price discrimination. In fact, do physicians and dentists engage in price discrimination? (d) In some instances, is it true that a good or service cannot be produced without price discrimination? (e) Is this always the case?

SOLUTION

(a) No. The total demand curve lies below the average total cost curve. Thus, regardless of what output the dentist chooses, price would be less than average total cost. (b) Yes. If the dentist charges rich people a price of OP_0, he or she can sell OQ_0 units of dental care to them. If he or she charges poor people a price of OP_1, he or she can sell OQ_1 units of dental care to them. Thus the total output, which equals OQ_2, brings an average price of OP_2, which is greater than average total cost. (c) Yes. (d) Yes, the situation depicted in the graph is an example. Without price discrimination, this dentist could not cover his or her costs. (e) No. It is important to note that price discrimination frequently occurs in situations where the good or service could be produced without it. Price discrimination is used in these situations to increase the profits of the producer. (From the point of view of society as a whole, price discrimination frequently is objectionable because it violates the conditions for optimal resource allocation described in Appendix E.)

Increase of Prices and Reduction of Competition by Regulators

As pointed out in the previous section, regulatory commissions, far from reducing prices, sometimes actually increase them. This is because *many commissions have been concerned with the regulation of competition as much as with the regulation of monopoly.* Consider the Interstate Commerce Commission (ICC), created in 1887 to regulate the railroads, which had considerable monopoly power at that time. With the advent of the motor truck and the phenomenal growth of highways, the railroads became increasingly vulnerable to competition from trucks; and there were fears that, if the railroads continued to be regulated but the trucks were not regulated, the railroads would be hurt badly by this new competition. In 1935, the ICC and the railroads were successful in bringing most trucking under the ICC's regulation, over the objection of some truckers. Thus, despite the fact that trucking, if unregulated, would be a highly competitive industry, it was brought under the regulatory umbrella.

EFFECTS ON TRUCKING

The results, according to most accounts, were pretty dismal. In interstate trucking, firms were allowed to agree upon rates in secret, through rate-bureau negotiations. These rates were seldom challenged by the ICC except in cases of across-the-board increases. Because of this system, rates tended to be established so as to cover the costs of the less efficient firms, with the consequence that consumers paid higher prices than under a competitive market structure. In markets where only one trucking firm was certificated, this system of rate setting allowed the firm to earn excess profits by offering poorer service (at the regulated price) than if other firms were permitted to compete. In markets where two or more trucking firms were certificated, there were potential excess profits for the more efficient truckers because the rates were set to cover the costs of the less efficient truckers. But these potential excess profits tended to be eliminated by service competition; that is, the firms provided more frequent schedules or larger trucks than otherwise would be the case. This sort of nonprice competition tended to create excess capacity which had a lower value to the shipper than the extra price paid.

Many economists argued that, to help solve the problem of excess capacity in markets with more than one trucking firm and the problem of poor service in markets with only one trucking firm, the ICC should allow entry into the trucking industry and encourage price competition among trucking firms. Why would freer entry and more price competition reduce excess capacity? Because new trucking firms would enter and force rates downward if existing truckers did not reduce their rates. Why would freer entry and more price competition promote better service in markets with only one trucking firm? Because the excess profits earned by the monopolist would attract new firms that would try to take away some of the monopolist's business by offering better service. The monopolist would have to improve its service and/or lower its rates, unless it wanted to lose much of its share of the market.

In 1980, President Carter, responding in part to arguments of this sort, signed a bill to deregulate the trucking industry. The law loosens—to an extent that is open to interpretation—the ICC's regulatory controls over the industry, but does not remove them completely. By 1985, there was considerable evidence of price competition among truckers. Between 1978 and 1985, thousands of small carriers entered the market, and battled with established firms (and among themselves) for a share of the market. The number of business failures in trucking increased considerably. In January 1985 one trucking executive reported: "There's a rate war going on."

EFFECTS ON RAILROADS

The ICC was established originally to regulate railroads, not trucks. How did its policies work in the railroad industry? Unfortunately, there were serious problems here too. With the growth of the trucking industry, many low-density rail lines were used less and less, until now they are no longer economical to operate. Nonetheless, the railroads were prevented by regulatory requirements from discontinuing such services as quickly as would seem warranted. Because of the losses incurred on unprofitable lines, the overall financial position of many railroads was impaired, with the result that needed maintenance and capital investments had to be reduced.

In 1980, President Carter signed a bill to deregulate the railroads, which hoped that greater freedom to change rates would enable them to earn a profit. Opponents of deregulation feared that the railroads would raise the price of hauling coal (and other bulk commodities) very sharply. A compromise was reached which permitted a relaxation of the ICC's rate-approval authority on a prearranged schedule. The purpose was to provide the railroads with significant freedom to alter rates while trying to give the customers of the railroads some protection against abuse of this freedom.

Effects of Regulation on Efficiency

As previous chapters have stressed, competitive markets provide considerable incentives for a firm to increase its efficiency. Firms that are able to push their costs below those of their competitors reap higher profits than their competitors. As a simple illustration, suppose that firms A and B both have contracts to produce 100 airplanes, and that the price they will get for each airplane is $25,000. Firm A's management, which is diligent, imaginative, and innovative, gets the cost per airplane down to $10,000, and thus makes a healthy profit of $1,500,000. Firm B's management which is lazy, unimaginative, and dull, lets the cost per airplane rise to $30,000, and thus loses $500,000. Clearly, firm A is rewarded for its good performance, while firm B is penalized for its poor performance.

NO INCENTIVE FOR EFFICIENCY

One of the primary purposes of regulators is to prevent a monopoly from earning excessive profits. The firm is allowed only a "fair" rate of return on its investment. One problem with this arrangement is that the firm is guaranteed this rate of return, regardless of how well it performs. If the regulators decide that the Sleepy Hollow Electric and Gas Company should receive a 10 percent rate of return on its investment, this is the rate of return it will receive regardless of whether the Sleepy Hollow Electric and Gas Company is managed well or poorly. Why is this a problem? Because unlike the competitive firms discussed in the previous paragraph, there is no incentive for the firm to increase its efficiency.

The available evidence indicates that, if a firm is guaranteed a fixed amount of profit for a job (regardless of how efficiently it does this job), the firm will tend to be less efficient than if the amount of profit it receives is directly related to its efficiency. The Department of Defense has found that, when it bought goods or services on a cost-plus-fixed-fee basis, these goods and services were not produced as cheaply as when it bought them in a competitive market. This is reasonable. It takes time, energy, and lots of trouble to make a firm more efficient. Why should a firm's managers bother to induce added efficiency if the firm's profits are the same, regardless of how efficient or inefficient it is?

REGULATORY LAG AND INCENTIVE FOR EFFICIENCY

The regulatory process is characterized by long delays. In many regulated industries, a proposed rate increase or decrease may be under consideration for months before a decision is made by the commission. In cases where such a price change is strongly contested, it may take years for the required hearings to occur before the commission and for appeals to be made subsequently to the courts. Such a delay between a proposed price change and its ultimate disposition is called a *regulatory lag.* Long regulatory lags are often criticized by those who would like the regulatory process to adapt more quickly to changing conditions and to provide more timely decisions. But one advantage of regulatory lags is that they result in some rewards for efficiency and penalties for inefficiency.

To see why this is so, consider a regulated company whose price is set so that the firm can earn a rate of return of 10 percent (which is what the commission regards as a "fair" rate of return). The firm develops and introduces some improved manufacturing processes which reduce the firm's costs, thus allowing it to earn 13 percent. If it takes 18 months for the commission to review the prices it approved before and to modify them to take account of the new (lower) cost levels, the firm earns a higher rate of return (13 percent rather than 10 percent) during these 18 months than if it had not developed and introduced the improved manufacturing processes. This is a reward for efficiency.

On the other hand, suppose that this firm makes several serious blunders which result in a substantial increase in its costs, the result being that the firm earns only a rate of return of 6 percent. If once again it takes 18 months for the commission to review the prices it set before and to modify them to take account of the changes in firms' cost levels, this firm earns a lower rate of return (6 percent rather than 10 percent) during these 18 months than if it had not made these blunders. This is a penalty for inefficiency.

Although regulatory lag does restore some of the incentives for efficiency (and some of the penalties for inefficiency), it would be a mistake to believe that it results in as strong a set of incentives as does competitive markets. One of the basic problems with regulation is that, *if a regulatory commission prevents a firm from earning higher-than-average profits, there may be relatively little incentive for the firm to increase its efficiency and innovate.*

Test Yourself

1. Compare the long-run equilibrium of a perfectly competitive industry with that which would occur if all the firms were to be merged in a single monopolistic firm. Is there any reason for society to prefer one equilibrium over the other?

2. "No firm has a monopoly since every good competes to some extent with every other good. Thus there is no good that is completely sealed off from competition." Comment and evaluate.

3. "Firms with relatively high profits are bound to be monopolists. If they were competitive, the entry of new firms into the industry would drive economic profits down to zero. Thus the easiest and best way to determine whether a firm is a monopolist is to look at its profits." Comment and evaluate.

4. According to the Council of Economic Advisers, "although exit from an industry via bankruptcy is a normal characteristic of efficient competitive markets, the bankruptcy of a regulated firm tends to be viewed as a sign of regulatory failure." What problems are likely to result from this attitude?

Summary

1. A pure monopoly is a market with one, and only one, seller. Monopolies may occur because of patents, control over basic inputs, and government action, as well as decreasing average costs up to the point where the market is satisfied.

2. If average costs reach their minimum at an output rate large enough to satisfy the entire market, perfect competition cannot be maintained; and the public often insists that the industry (a natural monopoly) be regulated by the government.

3. Since the monopolist is the only seller of the product, the demand curve facing the monopolist is the market demand curve, which slopes downward (rather than being horizontal as in perfect competition).

4. The unregulated monopolist will maximize profit by choosing the output where marginal cost equals marginal revenue, marginal revenue being defined as the addition to total revenue attributable to the addition of one unit to sales. This rule for output determination also holds under perfect competition, since price equals marginal revenue under perfect competition.

5. If monopolists cannot prevent losses from exceeding fixed costs, they, like perfect competitors, will discontinue production. In contrast to the case in perfect competition, the long-run equilibrium of a monopolistic industry may not be marked by the absence of economic profits.

6. The output of a monopoly tends to be smaller and the price tends to be higher than under perfect competition. Economists tend to believe that society would be better off if more resources were devoted to the production of the good than under monopoly, the competitive output often being regarded as best.

7. One way that society has attempted to reduce the harmful effects of monopoly is through public regulation. Commissions often set price at the level at which it equals average total cost, including a "fair rate of return" on the firm's investment.

8. There has been a great deal of controversy over the practices of the regulatory commissions. Many economists have viewed them as lax or ill-conceived. In many areas, like transportation, they have been concerned as much with the regulation of competition as with the regulation of monopoly; and, according to many studies, their decisions have resulted in substantial costs and inefficiencies.

9. Regulatory commissions try to prevent a monopoly from earning excessive profits; the firm is allowed only a "fair rate of return" on its investment. One difficulty with this arrangement is that, since the firm is guaranteed this rate of return (regardless of how well or poorly it performs), there is no incentive for the firm to increase its efficiency. Although regulatory lag results in some incentives of this sort, they often are relatively weak.

10. In some industries (like airlines, trucking, and railroads), the late 1970s and early 1980s saw a strong movement toward deregulation. This has been one of the most significant recent developments in this area.

Concepts for Review

Monopoly	**Marginal revenue**	**Reproduction cost**
Natural monopoly	**Regulation**	**Regulatory lag**
Total revenue	**Historical cost**	

Appendix: Marginal Cost Pricing

In this and the previous chapter, we indicated that, under the assumptions made here, the conditions for optimal resource allocation are satisfied under perfect competition. (See Appendix E for a more detailed discussion of this point.) Economists interested in the functioning of planned, or socialist, economies have pointed out that a price system also could be used to increase social welfare in such economies. Also, it has been argued that government-owned enterprises and public utilities in capitalist economies should set price equal to marginal cost, just as perfectly competitive firms do. In this Appendix, we discuss marginal cost pricing, and how it might be used by government-owned or regulated monopolists, as well as by socialist economies.

SOCIALIST ECONOMIES

According to economists like Abba Lerner[11] of Florida State University, rational economic organization could be achieved in a socialist economy that is decentralized, as well as under perfect competition. The socialist government might solve the system of equations that is solved automatically in a perfectly competitive economy, and obtain the prices that would prevail under perfect competition. Then the government might publish this price list, together with instructions for consumers to maximize their satisfaction and for producers to maximize profit. (Of course, the wording of the instructions to consumers might be a bit less heavy-handed than "Maximize your satisfaction!")

Under a socialist system of this sort, the government does not have to become involved in the intricate and detailed business of setting production targets for each plant. It need only compute the proper set of prices. In following the rules to maximize "profits," plant managers will choose the proper production levels. Thus decentralized decision making, rather than detailed centralized direction, could be used, thus reducing administrative costs and bureaucratic disadvantages, according to Lerner.

GOVERNMENT-OWNED OR REGULATED MONOPOLIES

The prices the government would publish, like those prevailing in a perfectly competitive economy, would equal marginal cost. Many economists have recommended that government-owned enterprises in basically capitalist economies also adopt *marginal cost pricing,* i.e., that they set price equal to marginal cost. Taking the case of a bridge where the marginal cost (the extra cost involved in allowing an additional vehicle to cross) is zero, Harold Hotelling argued in a famous article that the socially optimal price for crossing the bridge is zero, and that its costs should be defrayed by general taxation. If a toll is charged, the conditions for optimal resource use are not met.[12]

Marginal cost pricing has fascinated economists during the 50 years that

---

[11] Abba Lerner, *The Economics of Control,* New York: Macmillan, 1944.
[12] Harold Hotelling, "The General Welfare in Relation to Problems of Taxation and of Railway and Utility Rates," *Econometrica,* 1938.

have elapsed since Hotelling's article,[13] but there are a number of problems in the application of this idea. One of the most important is that if the firm's average costs decrease with increases in its scale of output (as is frequently the case in public utilities), it follows from the discussion in Chapter 24 that marginal cost must be less than average cost, with the consequence that the firm will not cover its costs if price is set equal to marginal cost.[14] This means that marginal cost pricing must be accompanied by some form of subsidy if the firm is to stay in operation—and the collection of the funds required for the payment of the subsidy may also violate the conditions for optimal resource allocation. This subsidy also means that there is a change in the income distribution favoring users of the firm's output and penalizing nonusers.

THE COMMON SENSE OF MARGINAL COST PRICING

To illustrate the reasoning that underlies marginal cost pricing, consider the case of water supplies. What determines the level at which the price of water should be set?

> Suppose that at a certain moment in time [consumers are willing to pay] $30 per unit. Then, if the community as a whole can acquire and transport another unit of water for, say, $20, it would clearly be desirable to do so; in fact, any of the individual customers to whom the unit of water is worth $30 would be happy to pay the $20 cost, and none of the other members of the community would be made worse off thereby. We may say that, on efficiency grounds, additional units should be made available so long as any members of the community are willing to pay the additional or marginal costs incurred.... So the ... rule is to make the price equal to marginal cost and equal for all customers.[15]

Unfortunately, it seems that water-pricing practices do not often conform to this rule. Some types of water users are commonly charged lower prices than other types of water users, although the marginal cost of the water is the same. According to a study carried out at the RAND Corporation,

> In Los Angeles, for example, there is an exceptionally low rate for irrigation use. Domestic, commercial, and industrial services are not distinguished as such, but they are differentially affected by the promotional volume rates. More serious, because much more common, is the system of block rates, with reductions [in price] for larger quantities used.... [This system leads] to wasteful use of water by large users, since small users would value the same marginal unit of water more highly if delivered to them.... The customer paying the lower price will on the margin be utilizing water for less valuable purposes than it could serve if transferred to the customer paying the higher price.

[13] See J. Nelson, *Marginal Cost Pricing in Practice,* Englewood Cliffs, N.J.: Prentice-Hall, 1964.

[14] Recall from Chapter 24 that an increase in output results in a reduction in average cost only when marginal cost is less than average cost. Since the firm's receipts will cover its costs only if price is at least equal to average cost, it follows that, under these circumstances, the firm cannot cover its costs if it sets price equal to marginal cost.

[15] Hirshleifer, Milliman, and DeHaven, *Water Supply,* Chicago: University of Chicago Press, 1969, pp. 40–41.

CHAPTER 27

Monopolistic Competition and Oligopoly

The industries encountered in the real world are seldom perfectly competitive or monopolistic. Although perfect competition and monopoly are very useful models that shed much valuable light on the behavior of markets, they are polar cases. Economists have developed other models that portray more realistically the behavior of many modern industries. The model of monopolistic competition helps to explain market behavior in such industries as retail drug stores and barber shops, while the model of oligopoly pertains to industries like steel, oil, and automobiles.

In this chapter, we examine how resources are allocated and prices are set under monopolistic competition and oligopoly. We also compare the behavior of monopolistically competitive and oligopolistic markets with the behavior of perfectly competitive and monopolistic markets. The results are of considerable significance, both because they give us a better understanding of how many markets work, and because they provide valuable information on the social desirability of monopolistic competition and oligopoly.

Monopolistic Competition and Oligopoly:
Their Major Characteristics

To begin with, we must recall what monopolistic competition and oligopoly are. *Monopolistic competition occurs where there are many sellers (as in perfect competition) but where there is product differentiation. In other words, the firms' products are not the same.* It does not matter whether the differences among products are real or imagined. What is important is that the consumer regards the products as different.

Oligopoly occurs in markets where there are few sellers. There are two types of oligopolies, one where all sellers produce an identical product, and one where the sellers produce somewhat different products. Examples of the first type—*pure oligopoly*—are the markets for steel, cement, tin cans, and petroleum. Examples of the second type—*differentiated oligopoly*—are the markets for automobiles and machinery.

In contrast to the extremes of perfect competition and monopoly, monopolistic competition and oligopoly are intermediate cases that include an element of competition and of monopoly—an advantage from the point of view of realism.

Monopolistic Competition

The key feature of monopolistic competition is *product differentiation.* In contrast to perfect competition, where all firms sell an identical product, firms under monopolistic competition sell somewhat different products. Producers differentiate their product from that of other producers. This is the case in many American markets. In many parts of retail trade, producers try to make their product a little different, by altering the product's physical make-up, the services they offer, and other such variables. Other differences—which may be spurious—are based on brand name, image making, advertising claims, etc. In this way, the producers have some monopoly power, but it usually is small, because the products of other firms are very similar.

In perfect competition, the firms included in an industry are easy to determine because they all produce the same product. But if product differentiation exists, it is no longer easy to define an industry, since each firm produces a somewhat different product. Nevertheless, it may be useful to group together firms that produce similar products and call them a *product group.* We can formulate a product group called "toothpaste" or "toilet soap" or "chocolate bars." The process by which we combine firms into product groups is bound to be somewhat arbitrary, since there is no way to decide how close a pair of substitutes must be to belong to the same product group. But it is assumed that meaningful product groups can be established.

Besides product differentiation, other conditions must be met for an industry to qualify as a case of monopolistic competition. First, *there must be a large number of firms in the product group.* In other words, the product must be produced by perhaps 50 to 100 or more firms, with each firm's product a fairly close substitute for the products of the other firms in the product group. Second, *the number of firms in the product group must be large enough so that each firm expects its actions to go unheeded by its rivals and is unimpeded by possible retaliatory moves on their part.* If there is a large number of firms, this condition will normally be met. Third, *entry into the product group must be relatively easy, and there must be no collu-*

sion, such as price fixing or market sharing, among firms in the product group. If there is a large number of firms, collusion generally is difficult, if not impossible.

Price and Output under Monopolistic Competition

Basic Idea #53: Product differentiation is a hallmark of monopolistic competition. If there is product differentiation, each firm's product is somewhat different from that of other firms, either physically or through the image created in the minds of consumers. Thus the demand curve for each firm's output is downward-sloping, not horizontal (as it is under perfect competition).

Under monopolistic competition, what determines how much output a firm will produce, and what price it will charge? If each firm produces a somewhat different product, it follows that the demand curve facing each firm slopes downward to the right. That is, if the firm raises its price slightly it will lose some, but by no means all, of its customers to other firms. And if it lowers its price slightly, it will gain some, but by no means all, of its competitors' customers. This is in contrast to perfect competition, where the demand curve facing each firm is horizontal.

Figure 27.1 shows the short-run equilibrium of a monopolistically competitive firm. The firm in the short run will set its price at OP_0 and its output rate at OQ_0, since this combination of price and output will maximize its profits. We can be sure that this combination of price and output maximizes profit because marginal cost equals marginal revenue at this output rate. Economic profits will be earned because price, OP_0, exceeds average total costs, OC_0, at this output rate.

What will the equilibrium price and output be in the long run? One condition for long-run equilibrium is that each firm be making no economic profits or losses, since entry or exit of firms will occur otherwise—and entry and exit are incompatible with long-run equilibrium. Another condition for long-run equilibrium is that each firm be maximizing its profits. At what price and output will both these conditions be fulfilled?

Figure 27.1
Short-Run Equilibrium: Monopolistic Competition *The firm will set price at OP_0 and its output rate at OQ_0 since marginal cost equals marginal revenue at this output. It will earn a profit of C_0P_0 per unit of output.*

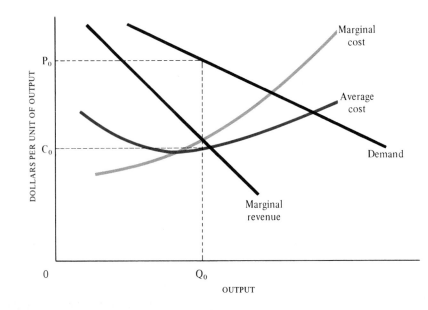

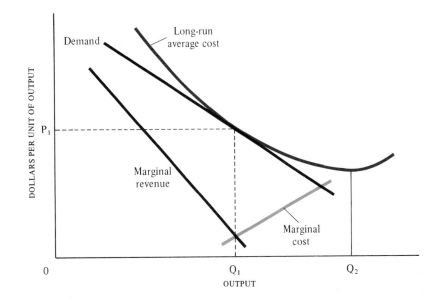

Figure 27.2
Long-Run Equilibrium: Monopolistic Competition *The long-run equilibrium is at a price of* OP$_1$ *and an output of* OQ$_1$. *There are zero profits since long-run average cost equals price. Profits are being maximized since marginal cost equals marginal revenue at this output.*

Figure 27.2 shows that the long-run equilibrium is at a price of OP_1 and an output of OQ_1. The zero-economic-profit condition is met at this combination of price and output since the firm's average cost at this output equals the price, OP_1. And the profit-maximization condition is met since the marginal revenue curve intersects the marginal cost curve at this output rate.

EXCESS CAPACITY

A famous conclusion of the theory of monopolistic competition is that *a firm under this form of market organization will tend to operate with excess capacity.* In other words, the firm will construct a plant smaller than the minimum-cost size of plant and operate it at less than the minimum-cost rate of output. Why? Because, as shown in Figure 27.2, the long-run average cost curve must be tangent in long-run equilibrium to the demand curve. Thus, since the demand curve is *downward-sloping,* the long-run average cost curve must also be *downward-sloping* at the long-run equilibrium output rate. Consequently, the firm's output must be less than OQ_2, the output rate at which long-run average costs are minimized, since the long-run average cost curve slopes downward only at output rates less than OQ_2.

This is a very important conclusion, since it suggests that monopolistically competitive industries will be overcrowded with firms. There will be too many firms (from society's point of view), each of which is smaller than required to minimize its unit costs. For this conclusion, as well as much of the entire theory of monopolistic competition, we are indebted to Edward Chamberlin of Harvard University, whose path-breaking book on the subject first appeared in 1933.[1]

---

[1] E. Chamberlin, *The Theory of Monopolistic Competition,* Cambridge, Mass.: Harvard University Press, 1933.

Edward Chamberlin

Comparisons with Perfect Competition and Monopoly

Market structure is important because it influences market behavior. We need to know how the behavior of a monopolistically competitive industry differs from that of a perfectly competitive industry or a monopoly. Suppose that there exists a magician who can transform an industry's structure by a wave of a wand. (John D. Rockefeller was a real-life magician who transformed the structure of the oil industry in the late 1800s—but he seemed to favor mergers, mixed with some ungentlemanly tactics, over wands.) Suppose that the magician makes an industry monopolistically competitive, rather than perfectly competitive or monopolistic. What difference would it make in the behavior of the industry? Or, to take a less fanciful case, what difference would it make if government action or technological change resulted in such a change in an industry's market structure? It is difficult to say how the industry's behavior would be affected, because output would be heterogeneous in one case and homogeneous in the other, and its cost curves would probably vary with its organization. But many economists seem to believe that differences of the following kind can be expected.

1. The firm under monopolistic competition is likely to produce less, and charge a higher price, than under perfect competition. The demand curve confronting the monopolistic competitor slopes downward to the right. Consequently, as we saw in the previous chapter, marginal revenue must be less than price. Thus, under monopolistic competition, marginal cost must also be less than price, since marginal revenue must equal marginal cost at the firm's profit-maximizing output rate. But if marginal cost is less than price, the firm's output rate must be smaller—and the price higher—than if marginal cost equals price, which is the case under perfect competition. On the other hand, *relative to monopoly, monopolistically competitive firms are likely to have lower profits, greater output, and lower price.* The firms in a product group might obtain positive economic profits if they were to collude and behave as a monopolist. Such an increase in profits resulting from the monopoly would benefit the producers. Consumers would be worse off because of the higher prices and smaller output of goods.

2. As noted in the previous section, *a firm under monopolistic competition may be somewhat inefficient because it tends to operate with excess capacity.* Each firm builds a smaller-than-minimum-cost plant and produces a smaller-than-minimum-cost output. More firms exist than if there were no excess capacity, resulting in some overcrowding of the industry. Inefficiencies of this sort would not be expected under perfect competition. These inefficiencies may not be very great, since the demand curve confronting the monopolistically competitive firm is likely to be highly elastic; and the more elastic it is, the less excess capacity the firm will have. But many observers seem to believe that excess capacity of this sort is a serious problem in many important industries, including textiles.

3. Firms under monopolistic competition will offer a wider variety of styles, brands, and qualities than firms under perfect competition. Moreover, they will spend much more on advertising and other selling expenses than a perfectly competitive firm would. Whether this diversity is worth its cost is hard to say. Some economists are impressed by the apparent waste in monopolistic competition. They think it results in too many firms, too many brands, too much selling effort, and too much spurious product differentiation. But if the differences among products are real and are understood by consumers, the greater variety of alternatives available under monopolistic competition may be very valuable to consumers. The proper evaluation of the social advantages and disadvantages of product differentiation is a problem economists have not solved.

Retailing: A Case Study[2]

To illustrate the case of monopolistic competition, consider retailing in the United States. Each retailer has a certain amount of monopoly power because his location, his product lines, his personality, and his salespeople are somewhat different from those of his competitors. In other words, his product is differentiated. But the extent and strength of his monopoly power is generally quite limited because he faces many competitors reasonably similar to himself in these respects. That is, lots of other firms sell products that are close substitutes for his own product. The goods carried by one drugstore, grocery store, or clothing shop are close substitutes for those carried by another drugstore, grocery store, or clothing shop. Moreover, entry into retail trade tends to be quite easy, as indicated by the fact that firms are continually entering various lines of retailing, and that the capital and skill required for entry are generally rather modest.

All in all, retailing seems to have many of the most important characteristics of monopolistic competition. Assuming that the retail industry can be approximated reasonably well by our model of monopolistic competition, we would expect that there would be some overcrowding of firms, that firms would try hard to differentiate their product through advertising and other selling expenses, and that long-run profits in the industry would tend to be low. Let us see to what extent these conditions do prevail.

There seems to be considerable evidence of overcrowding. More firms exist in retail trade than would be the case if each were operating at a point where unit costs were a minimum. But the extent of this excess capacity may not be very great, since the price elasticity of demand in retailing is normally very high—typically about 5.0, according to Leonard Weiss of the University of Wisconsin. Also, in accord with the model, firms in retail trade spend a great deal on various selling expenses, notably advertising. About one-quarter of the total expenditure on advertising in the United States is spent by retailers. Usually these ads are local and provide a valuable source of information on sales and specials in a particular neighborhood. (It is the exceptional person who does not spend some part of each week scanning the retail ads in a local newspaper.) Retail stores spend a lot on other selling expenses too—attractive décor, free parking, trading stamps, clerks to hover over the customer, and so forth.

[2] For a much more extensive discussion of retailing, see Leonard Weiss, *Case Studies in American Industry,* New York: Wiley, 1967. For further relevant discussion, see W. Shepherd, *The Economics of Industrial Organization,* Englewood Cliffs, N.J.: Prentice-Hall, 1979.

These expenses add to the prices they charge for the products they carry.

The level of profits in retail trade also accords with what theory would lead us to expect. It is low. Except for a few years right after World War II (when there was a relative scarcity of retail outlets), profits seem to have been consistently lower in retailing than in manufacturing. Moreover, this can hardly be attributed to less risk in retailing than in manufacturing, since retailing's bankruptcy rate has been exceptionally high—much higher than in other parts of the nonfarm economy. The facts seem to correspond quite well with the theory's prediction of no economic profits in the industry.[3]

Oligopoly

Oligopoly (domination by a few firms) is a common and important market structure in the United States; many industries, like steel, automobiles, oil, and electrical equipment, are oligopolistic. An example of an oligopolist is IBM, described in Chapter 6. *The key characteristic of oligopoly is interdependence, actual and perceived, among firms.* Each oligopolist formulates its policies with an eye to their effect on its rivals. Since an oligopoly contains a small number of firms, any change in one firm's price or output influences the sales and profits of its competitors. Moreover, since there are only a few firms, each must recognize that changes in its own policies are likely to result in changes in the policies of its rivals as well.

What factors are responsible for oligopoly? First, in some industries, *low production costs cannot be achieved unless a firm is producing an output equal to a substantial portion of the total available market,* with the consequence that the number of firms will tend to be rather small. Second, *there may be economies of scale in sales promotion* in certain industries, and this too may promote oligopoly. Third, entry into some industries may be blocked by *the requirement that a firm build and maintain a large, complicated, and expensive plant, or have access to patents or scarce raw materials.* Only a few firms may be in a position to obtain all these necessary prerequisites for membership in the club.

ECONOMIES OF SCALE

The automobile industry is a good example of the impact of *economies of scale in production.* According to studies made by Joe Bain of the University of California, an automobile plant of minimum efficient size can provide almost 10 percent of the total national market.[4] Thus it simply is not economical to have a great many automobile firms. It might be possible to have a dozen automobile firms rather than the four we currently have without sacrificing productive efficiency, but because of economies of scale, it would not be feasible to have 50 or 100.

The automobile industry is a good example of *economies of scale in sales promotion.* To be effective, advertising must often be carried out on a large

---

[3] Before leaving the subject of monopolistic competition, it should be recognized that Professor Chamberlin's theory has been subjected to considerable criticism. As a case in point, the definition of the product group is ambiguous. See G. Stigler, *Five Lectures on Economic Problems,* London: Longmans Green, 1949.

[4] J. Bain, *Barriers to New Competition,* Cambridge, Mass.: Harvard University Press, 1956.

scale, the result being that the advertising cost per unit of output decreases with increases in output, at least up to some point. Also, car buyers like to deal with firms with a large, dependable dealer network. Since it takes a lot of money to establish such a network, and since the better dealers are attracted by the more popular brands, the smaller automobile manufacturers are at a substantial disadvantage.

BARRIERS TO ENTRY

In addition, the automobile industry offers a good example of *barriers to entry due to large financial requirements.* An automobile plant of minimum efficient size costs about $500 million to build and put into operation. This is an enormous amount of money, beyond the reach of practically all individuals. It takes the help of major financial interests and financial institutions to break into the automobile business. Since World War II, no new firms have obtained a foothold in the American automobile industry.

The *availability of raw materials* can also be a barrier to entry. Such is the case in the steel industry, where a few big firms have most of the available iron ore, partly through foresight and partly because they were the only organizations that could afford to spend the vast sums required to obtain the ore. Also, *patents* can be a very big barrier to entry. The electric light industry is a famous example. General Electric was able to dominate the industry from 1892 to 1930 through the acquisition of the basic Edison patents and then the acquisition of patents on many of the improvements.[5]

Mergers and Oligopoly

Mergers between firms often contribute to the movement toward oligopoly in particular industries. There have been three major waves of mergers in the American economy. The first occurred between 1887 and 1904, the second between 1916 and 1929, and the third after World War II. The first wave in 1887–1904 saw the formation of such giants as U.S. Steel and John D. Rockefeller's Standard Oil. The mergers in this period tended to be *horizontal,* that is, among firms producing essentially the same product. Such was the case with U.S. Steel, formed in 1901 from a combination of about 785 plants. During the second wave of mergers in 1916–29, the emphasis was more on *vertical mergers* (mergers among firms at various stages in the production process) and *conglomerate mergers* (mergers among firms producing entirely different products). During the third wave of mergers in the 25 years following World War II, a very large number of firms was absorbed and assimilated by others. Of the 1,000 largest manufacturing firms in existence at the end of 1950, 216 had disappeared by merger by 1963.

Mergers of all types (horizontal, vertical, conglomerate) continue to occur. Sometimes they take place to reduce competition. Thomas Edison was forthright when he said in 1892 about the formation of General Elec-

[5] F. M. Scherer, *Industrial Market Structure and Economic Performance,* Skokie, Ill.: Rand McNally, 1970, pp. 391–92.

tric, "The consolidation of the companies . . . will do away with a competition which has become so sharp that the product of the factories has been worth little more than ordinary hardware."[6] Other mergers are made so that promoters can earn profits from corporate marriages. In still other cases, mergers occur because firms need the people or ideas other firms have, or because the owners want to sell out, or because there appear to be beneficial synergetic effects arising from complementary resources owned by the merging firms.

Oligopoly Behavior and the Stability of Prices

Unlike perfect competition, monopoly, and monopolistic competition, there is no single unified model of oligopoly behavior. Instead, *there are a number of models, each based on a somewhat different set of assumptions concerning the relationships among the firms that make up the oligopoly.* Basically, no single model exists because economists have not yet been able to devise one that would cover all the relevant cases adequately. Economics, like all sciences, continues to grow; perhaps someone—indeed, perhaps someone reading this book—may be able to develop such a model before too long. However, it doesn't exist now.

THE KINKED OLIGOPOLY DEMAND CURVE

Let's start with a model that sheds light on the stability of oligopolistic prices. Empirical studies of pricing in oligopolistic markets have often concluded that prices in such markets tend to be rigid. A classic example occurred in the sulphur industry. From 1926 to 1938, the price of sulphur remained at $18 a ton, despite great shifts in demand and production costs. This example is somewhat extreme, but it illustrates the basic point: Prices in oligopolistic industries commonly remain unchanged for fairly long periods. A well-known model designed to explain this price rigidity was advanced by Paul Sweezy, who asserted that, *if an oligopolist cuts its price, it can be pretty sure that its rivals will meet the reduction. On the other hand, if it increases its price, its rivals may not change theirs.*

Figure 27.3 shows the situation. The oligopolist's demand curve is represented by *DAD'* and the current price is *OP*. There is a "kink" in the demand curve because *under the postulated circumstances the demand curve for the oligopolist's product is much less elastic for price decreases than for price increases.* Why is it less elastic for price decreases than for price increases? Because price decreases will be met by the firm's rivals, which means that the firm will not be able to take any appreciable amount of sales away from its rivals by such decreases. The effect of such decreases will be to increase the quantity demanded of the firm's product, since the total quantity demanded of the entire industry's product will increase due to the price reduction. But the increase in the quantity demanded of the firm's product will be relatively modest. On the other hand, if the firm raises its price, it is assumed that its rivals do not follow suit. Thus the

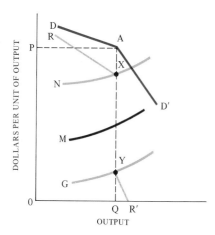

Figure 27.3

The Kinked Oligopoly Demand Curve
The oligopolist's demand curve is DAD', the current price being OP. Because of the kink in the demand curve, the marginal revenue curve consists of two segments RX and YR'. Since the marginal cost curve is M, the most profitable output is OQ. Moreover, it remains the most profitable output—and OP the most profitable price—even if the marginal cost curve shifts to N or to G or if the demand curve shifts considerably (within limits).

[6] Ibid., p. 113.

quantity demanded of the firm's product will fall considerably, if it raises its price.

PREDICTION: RIGID PRICES

Because of the kink in the demand curve, the marginal revenue curve in Figure 27.3 is not continuous. It consists of two segments, RX and YR'. Given that the firm's marginal cost curve is M, the most profitable output is OQ, where the marginal cost curve intersects the vertical line, XY. Moreover, OQ *remains the most profitable output—and* OP *the most profitable price—even if the marginal cost curve shifts considerably (even to* N *or* G) *or if the demand curve shifts (within limits).* One would expect price to be quite rigid under these circumstances, since many types of changes in cost and demand will not alter the price that maximizes profits.

This theory, although useful in explaining why price tends to remain at a certain level (*OP* in Figure 27.3), is of no use at all in explaining why this level, rather than another, currently prevails. It simply takes the current price as given. Thus this theory is an incomplete model of oligopoly pricing. Nonetheless, it seems to explain some of the relevant facts; and for this and other reasons, Sweezy's model has achieved a place in the theory of oligopoly.

Test Yourself

1. In a previous section, it was asserted that, if the demand curve confronting a monopolistically competitive firm is highly elastic, the firm is likely to have less excess capacity than if it is relatively inelastic. Explain why this is true.

2. Explain how a firm's output and price are determined under monopolistic competition in (a) the short run and (b) the long run.

3. "The kinked oligopoly demand curve is not a very effective tool of analysis because oligopolists frequently do raise their price in response to a price increase by a rival." Comment and evaluate.

4. "The Sweezy model is unrealistic because oligopolists seldom take account of how their rivals will respond to their actions. After all, there is no way to tell what their rivals will do in response to a particular action." Comment and evaluate.

Collusion and Cartels

HOW FIRMS COLLUDE

Collusion occurs when firms get together and agree on price and output. Up to this point, we have assumed that oligopolists do not collude, but conditions in oligopolistic industries tend to promote collusion, since the number of firms is small and the firms recognize their interdependence. The advantages of collusion to the firms seem obvious—increased profits, decreased uncertainty, and a better opportunity to prevent entry.

Not all collusion is disguised from the public or secret. In contrast to illicit collusion, a *cartel* is an open, formal collusive arrangement among firms. In many countries in Europe, cartels have been common and legally acceptable. In the United States, most collusive arrangements, whether secret or open cartels, were declared illegal by the Sherman Antitrust Act, which was passed in 1890.

However, this does not mean that such arrangements do not exist. Widespread collusion to fix prices occurred among American electrical equipment manufacturers during the 1950s, and when the collusion was uncovered a number of high executives were tried, convicted, and sent to jail. Moreover, collusion of this sort is not limited to a single industry—or a single country. Some cartels, like that in quinine in the early 1960s or in crude oil in the 1970s and 1980s, are international in scope.

PRICE AND OUTPUT OF A CARTEL

If a cartel is established to set a uniform price for a particular product, what price will it charge? As a first step, the cartel must estimate the marginal cost curve for the cartel as a whole. Then it must find the output where its marginal cost equals its marginal revenue, since this output maximizes the total profit of the cartel members. In Figure 27.4, this output is *OQ*. Thus, if it maximizes cartel profits, the cartel will choose a price of *OP*, which is the monopoly price. In short, *the cartel acts like a monopolist with a number of plants or divisions, each of which is a member firm.*

How will the cartel allocate sales among the member firms? If its aim is to maximize cartel profits, it will allocate sales to firms in such a way that the sum of the firms' costs is minimized. But this allocation is unlikely to occur in reality. The allocation process is a bargaining process, and firms with the most influence and the shrewdest negotiators are likely to receive the largest sales quotas, even though this decreases the total profits of the cartel. Moreover, high-cost firms are likely to receive larger sales quotas than would be the case if total cartel profits were maximized, since they would be unwilling otherwise to stay in the cartel. In practice, it appears that cartels often divide markets geographically or in accord with a firm's level of sales in the past.

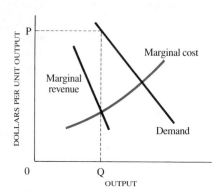

Figure 27.4
Price and Output of a Cartel *The marginal cost curve shows the marginal cost for the cartel as a whole. Based on the demand curve for the industry's product, the cartel can derive the marginal revenue curve. The output that maximizes the total profit of the cartel members is* OQ. *The corresponding price is* OP.

THE ELECTRICAL CONSPIRACY

To illustrate how firms collude, consider the electrical equipment manufacturers we mentioned above. During the 1950s, there was widespread collusion among about 30 firms selling turbine generators, switchgear, transformers, and other products with total sales of about $1.5 billion per year. Representatives of these firms got together and agreed upon prices for many products. The available evidence indicates that both prices and profits tended to be increased by the collusive agreements—or at least until the firms were prosecuted under the antitrust laws by the Department of Justice. The following statement by F. M. Scherer of Swarthmore College is a good description of some of the procedures used by these firms:

> Some of the most elaborate procedures were devised to handle switchgear pricing. As in the case of generators, book prices served as the initial departure point. Each seller agreed to quote book prices in sales to private buyers,

and meetings were held regularly to compare calculations for forthcoming job quotations. Sealed-bid competitions sponsored by government agencies posed a different set of problems, and new methods were worked out to handle them. Through protracted negotiation, each seller was assigned a specific share of all sealed-bid business, e.g., General Electric's share of the high voltage switchgear field was set at 40.3 per cent in late 1958, and Allis-Chalmers' at 8.8 per cent. Participants then coordinated their bidding so that each firm was low bidder in just enough transactions to gain its predetermined share of the market. In the power switching equipment line, this was achieved for a while by dividing the United States into four quadrants, assigning four sellers to each quadrant, and letting the sellers in a quadrant rotate their bids. A "phases of the moon" system was used to allocate low-bidding privileges in the high voltage switchgear field, with a new seller assuming low-bidding priority every two weeks. The designated bidder subtracted a specified percentage margin from the book price to capture orders during its phase, while others added various margins to the book price. The result was an ostensibly random pattern of quotations, conveying the impression of independent pricing behavior.[7]

Barriers to Collusion

The fact that oligopoly often can lead to collusion is not new. Nor is it newly understood. Back in 1776, Adam Smith warned that "people of the same trade seldom meet together even for merriment and diversion, but the conversation ends in a conspiracy against the public, or in some contrivance to raise prices." However, it must be borne in mind that collusive arrangements are often difficult to accomplish and maintain for long. In particular, there are several important barriers to collusion.

LEGAL PROBLEMS

The antitrust laws forbid outright collusion and price fixing. This does not mean that firms do not break those laws; witness the electrical equipment manufacturers just described. But the antitrust laws are an important obstacle to collusion.

TECHNICAL PROBLEMS

Collusion is often difficult to achieve and maintain because an oligopoly contains an unwieldy number of firms, or the product is quite heterogeneous, or the cost structures of the firms differ considerably. It is clear that a collusive agreement will be more difficult to achieve and maintain if there are a dozen oligopolists than if there are three or four. Moreover, if the products sold by the oligopolists differ substantially, it will probably be more difficult for them to find a common price strategy that will be acceptable to all. Similarly, if the firms' cost structures differ, it will be more difficult to get agreement, since the low-cost firms will be more inclined to cut price. For example, National Steel, after introducing low-cost continuous strip mills in the 1930s, became a price cutter in the steel industry.

---

[7] F. M. Scherer, *Industrial Market Structure and Economic Performance*, p. 160.

Basic Idea #54: Because they are few in number, firms in an oligopolistic industry may be tempted to collude to fix price and output. If this occurs, and if the firms try to maximize industry profits, the industry will act like a monopolist with a number of plants or divisions, each of which is a member firm. But there is a strong temptation for oligopolists to cheat on a collusive agreement, so agreements of this sort tend to be unstable.

CHEATING

There is a constant temptation for oligopolists to cheat on any collusive agreement. If other firms stick to the agreement, any firm that cheats—by cutting its price below that agreed to under the collusive arrangement—can take a lot of business away from the other firms and increase its profits substantially, as least in the short run. This temptation is particularly great when an industry's sales are depressed and its profits are low. Every firm is hungry for business, and it is difficult to resist. Moreover, one firm may be driven to cheating because it hears that another firm is doing so, with the eventual result that the collusive agreement is torn apart.

To illustrate the problems of maintaining a collusive agreement, let's return to the electrical equipment manufacturers. As the *Wall Street Journal* summed it up,

> One of the great ironies of the conspiracies was that no matter how hard the participants schemed, no matter how friendly their meetings and communications might be, there was an innate tendency to compete. Someone was always violating the agreements to get more business and this continually called for new illegal plans. For example, price-cutting in sales of power switching equipment to government agencies was getting out of hand in late 1958. This led to the "quadrant" system of dividing markets [described in the previous section].

As one executive of General Electric complained, "No one was living up to the agreements and we . . . were being made suckers. On every job someone would cut our throat; we lost confidence in the group." Given that these agreements were illegal, it is remarkable that such a complaint was uttered with a straight face.

Price Leadership

In order to coordinate their behavior without outright collusion, some industries contain a *price leader.* It is quite common in oligopolistic industries for one or a few firms to set the price and for the rest to follow their lead. Two types of price leadership are the dominant-firm model and the barometric-firm model. *The **dominant-firm** model applies to cases where the industry has a single large dominant firm and a number of small firms.* The dominant firm sets the price for the industry, but it lets the small firms sell all they want at that price. *The **barometric-firm** model applies to cases where one firm usually is the first to make changes in price that are generally accepted by other firms in the industry.* The barometric firm may not be the largest, or most powerful, firm. Instead, it is a reasonably accurate interpreter of changes in basic cost and demand conditions in the industry as a whole. According to some authorities, barometric price leadership often occurs as a response to a period of violent price fluctuation in an industry, during which many firms suffer and greater stability is widely sought.

In the past, the steel industry has been a good example of price leadership of the dominant-firm variety. The largest firm in the industry is U.S. Steel, which, as we know, was formed in 1901 by the merger of a number of companies. Judge Elbert Gary, the first chairman of the board of U.S.

Steel, sought the cooperation of the smaller firms in the industry. He inaugurated a series of so-called "Gary dinners," attended by all the major steel producers, which made declarations of industry policy on pricing and other matters. Since any formal pricing agreements would have been illegal, they made no such agreements. But, generally speaking, U.S. Steel set the pricing pattern and other firms followed. Moreover, this relationship continued long after Judge Gary had gone to his reward. According to Walter Adams of Michigan State University, U.S. Steel typically set the

Example 27.1   How Other Sources of Oil Influence OPEC's Price

The Organization of Petroleum Exporting Countries (OPEC) is a cartel that includes many of the world's leading oil producers, such as Saudi Arabia, Nigeria, Venezuela, Indonesia, and others. Nonetheless, OPEC does not supply all of the world's oil. Important oil producers outside OPEC include the United States, Mexico, Canada, Britain, Norway, and Australia. Suppose that the supply curve for non-OPEC oil and the world demand curve for oil are as shown below:

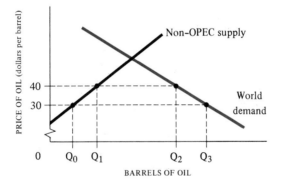

(a) If the price of oil is $30 per barrel, what is the quantity demanded of OPEC oil? (b) If the price of oil is $40 per barrel, what is the quantity demanded of OPEC oil? (c) From the above graph, how can we determine the demand curve for OPEC oil? (d) Given the demand curve for OPEC oil, how can we determine the price that would maximize OPEC's profit?

SOLUTION

(a) $(OQ_3 - OQ_0)$ barrels of oil. (b) $(OQ_2 - OQ_1)$ barrels of oil. (c) To determine the quantity of OPEC oil demanded at each price, subtract the quantity of non-OPEC oil supplied at that price from the quantity of oil demanded in the world as a whole at that price. (d) Find the marginal revenue curve corresponding to the demand curve for OPEC oil, and determine the output at which this marginal revenue curve intersects OPEC's marginal cost curve. The profit-maximizing price is the one that corresponds to this output on the demand curve for OPEC oil. That is, it is the price that results in OPEC's selling this quantity of output.

price "and the other companies follow in lockstep—both in their sales to private customers and in their secret bids on government contracts."[8]

Illustrating the attitude of other firms was the statement by the president of Bethlehem Steel to a congressional committee in 1939 that "in the main we . . . await the [price] schedules of the [U.S.] Steel Corporation." However, there was some secret price cutting, particularly during depressions. On at least one occasion, U.S. Steel responded to such price cutting by announcing publicly that it would meet any price reduction it heard of. In this way, it attempted to discourage under-the-counter price cutting. In more recent times, U.S. Steel no longer seems to be the price leader it once was. In 1962, it drew a great deal of criticism from President Kennedy for being the first steel firm to raise prices. Subsequently, smaller steel firms have often been the first. Indeed, in 1968 the world was treated to the amusing spectacle of Bethlehem announcing a price cut in order to counter some secret price cutting by the former price leader, U.S. Steel.

Cost-Plus Pricing

There is one further model of oligopoly behavior to consider. According to studies of business behavior, *cost-plus pricing* is used by many oligopolists. It occurs in two steps. First, *the firm estimates the cost per unit of output of the product.* Since this cost will generally vary with the output rate, the firm must base this computation on some assumed output rate—often two-thirds or three-quarters of the firm's capacity. Second, *the firm adds a markup to the estimated average cost.* This markup is meant to include certain costs that cannot be allocated to any specific product and to provide a return on the firm's investment. The size of the markup depends on the rate of profit the firm believes it can earn. Some firms, like General Electric and General Motors, have set a *target rate of return* figure they hope to earn, which determines the markup.

Unquestionably, many firms do compute prices on the basis of this sort of procedure. However, the cost-plus pricing model is incomplete unless it specifies more precisely what determines the size of the markup. Although firms may construct these markups to yield a certain target rate of return, the firms' income statements show that these markups do not prevail, since the firms' actual rates of return frequently vary considerably from the target rate of return. Moreover, to many economists this form of pricing seems naïve, since it takes no account, explicitly at least, of the extent or elasticity of demand or of the size of marginal, rather than average, costs.

THE CASE OF GENERAL MOTORS

Consider General Motors, which has often used cost-plus pricing. General Motors has begun by stating an objective of earning a profit of about 15 percent (after taxes) on total invested capital. Then it has assumed that it will sell enough cars in the next year to operate at about 80 percent of its capacity; and on the basis of this assumption, it has figured what its cost per car will be. Then it has added to this cost a markup big enough to pro-

[8] W. Adams, *The Structure of American Industry,* New York: Macmillan, 1961, p. 168.

duce the desired return on investment. The result is the so-called standard price. General Motors' high-echelon price policy committee has taken this standard price as a first approximation, and has made small adjustments to reflect competitive conditions, long-run goals of the firm, and other things. Typically, these adjustments have been quite small, and the actual price has turned out to be close to the standard price.

Needless to say, there is no assurance that General Motors will earn the desired 15 percent of total invested capital. If it sells fewer cars than it needs to sell in order to operate at 80 percent of capacity, its unit costs will be higher than expected and its profits—both total and per unit of output—will be less than expected. On the other hand, if it sells more cars than it needs to sell in order to operate at 80 percent of capacity, its profits will be higher than expected. In general, since World War II, General Motors has achieved sales levels that permitted it to operate at more than 80 percent of capacity, with the result that it has earned substantially more, on the average, than the target rate of 15 percent of invested capital.

But this was not true in 1974 and 1975. And in 1980, General Motors' sales dropped considerably below the 1979 level, and it lost a whopping $762 million. 1981 was not a good year either. With the increased competition from Japanese imported cars, General Motors found it more difficult to use its traditional pricing methods. However, in 1983 and 1984, due partly to quotas on auto imports, General Motors' profits increased substantially.

Nonprice Competition

Oligopolists tend to compete more aggressively through advertising and product differentiation than through direct price reductions. In other words, when we observe the behavior of major oligopolies, we find that firms try hard to get business away from their rivals by outdoing them with better advertising campaigns and with improvements in the product; but it is less common for oligopolists to slug it out, toe to toe, with price reductions. This is an important characteristic of oligopoly. In contrast to the case of perfect competition, nonprice competition plays a central role in oligopoly. It is worthwhile, therefore, to note a few salient points about the advertising and product development strategies of oligopolists.

ADVERTISING

Advertising is a very big business. In 1983 over $75 billion per year was spent on it in the United States. One important purpose of advertising is to convince the consumer that one firm's product is better than another's. In industries where there is less physical differentiation of the product, advertising expenditures often are larger than in industries where the product varies more. Thus the cigarette, liquor, and soap industries spend over 10 percent of their gross revenues (excluding excise taxes) on advertising, whereas the automobile industry spends less than 1 percent of its gross revenues on advertising.

The social desirability of much of this advertising is debatable, and much debated. While advertising can serve an important purpose by keeping the consumer better informed, some advertising is more misleading than informative. Unfortunately, it is difficult to make reliable estimates of the extent to which oligopolists may be overinvesting, from society's point of view, in advertising.[9]

PRODUCT DEVELOPMENT

The development of new and improved products is also a very big business in the United States. Currently firms spend over $40 billion per year on research and development. In many industries, R and D is a central part of oligopolistic competition. For example, a spectacular case in the drug industry was the effect of American Cyanamid's Achromycin tetracycline, introduced in 1953, on sales of Aureomycin chlortetracycline, which had been marketed since late 1948. After an almost continuous upward trend in 1950–53, Aureomycin sales dropped by nearly 40 percent during the first full year of the sale of Achromycin. Hardly a typical case, this nonetheless illustrates how one firm can take sales away from its rivals through new product development.

It is important to add, however, that much of industry's R and D is aimed at fairly minor improvements in products and processes. Moreover, a good deal of the engineering efforts of many important industries is aimed largely at style changes, not basic improvements in the product. A case in point is the automobile industry, which spends an enormous amount to produce the model changes that are familiar to car buyers throughout the land. Specifically, according to three economists—Frank Fisher, Zvi Griliches, and Carl Kaysen—such model changes in the automobile industry cost about $5 billion per year during the late 1950s.[10] From society's point of view, it is not at all clear that such huge expenditures are justifiable.

Perhaps the main reason why oligopolists would rather compete through advertising and product differentiation than through price is that a firm's rivals can easily and quickly match a price reduction, whereas they may find it difficult to match a clever advertising campaign or an attractive product improvement. Eastman Kodak had to work over six years to develop the instant camera it introduced in 1976 to compete with Polaroid's instant camera. Thus oligopolists tend to feel that they have a better chance of improving their long-run profits at the expense of their rivals in the arena of nonprice competition than by price cutting.

Comparison of Oligopoly with Perfect Competition

We have seen that economists have constructed a number of types of models of oligopoly behavior—the Sweezy model, the cartel models, price leadership models, cost-plus pricing models, and others—but there is no

---

[9] See W. Comanor and T. Wilson, *Advertising and Market Power*, Cambridge: Harvard University Press, 1975.

[10] For more recent data, see L. White, *The Automobile Industry Since 1945*, Cambridge, Mass.: Harvard University Press, 1971.

RECENT DEVELOPMENTS IN ECONOMICS: CONTESTABLE MARKETS

During the late 1970s and early 1980s, a group of economists at New York and Princeton Universities (and the Bell Laboratories), headed by William Baumol, developed a theory of contestable markets. This theory has received considerable attention. Because it is so new, it is very difficult to predict how significant it will eventually turn out to be. But it has had enough influence to warrant discussion.

What is a contestable market? According to Baumol and his colleagues, it is a market into which entry is absolutely free, *and exit is absolutely costless.* Any firm can leave the market without impediment, and can get back whatever costs it incurred in entering. The key characteristic of a contestable market is its vulnerability to hit-and-run entry. A firm can enter such a market, make a quick profit, and leave without cost, if this seems to be the most profitable course of action.

William Baumol

Just as a perfectly competitive market is only a model, so the same is true of a contestable market. Nonetheless, models of this sort can be very useful and suggestive. At least three characteristics of a contestable market are worth noting. First, it can be shown that profits are zero in equilibrium in a contestable market. If profits were positive, a firm could enter the market, undercut the price of the firm with profits, and make a profit, and leave the market if this seemed desirable. Thus profits will be eroded by such price cutting until they are zero. This is true regardless of how few firms exist in the contestable market. Because each is subject to such hit-and-run tactics, profits are eliminated.

Second, the organization of a contestable market is efficient in the sense that the average cost of production is as low as possible. Again because of the possibility of hit-and-run entry, firms in such a market must maintain their costs at the lowest possible level in the long run. If they do not do so, more efficient firms will enter, undercut their price, and force them to reduce their costs or withdraw from the market.

Third, if a contestable market contains two or more sellers, their prices, in equilibrium, must equal their marginal costs. As pointed out in Chapter 26, there are fundamental reasons why economists favor markets in which price equals marginal cost. One reason why perfect competition is favored by so many economists is that price equals marginal cost. Thus it is very interesting that this desirable feature of perfect competition exists as well in contestable markets.

In the past, it has often been presumed that these three outcomes—zero profits, minimum cost, and price equal to marginal cost—would be very unlikely to occur when there are few sellers. The theory of contestable markets implies that this is not necessarily the case.

agreement that any of these models is an adequate general representation of oligopoly behavior. For this reason, it is difficult to estimate the effects of an oligopolistic market structure on price, output, and profits. Nonetheless, if a perfectly competitive industry were turned overnight into an oligopoly, it seems likely that certain changes would occur.

1. Price would probably be higher than under perfect competition. The difference between the oligopoly price and the perfectly competitive price will depend on the number of firms in the industry and the ease of entry. The larger the number of firms and the easier it is to enter the industry, the closer the oligopoly price will be to the perfectly competitive level. Also, prices will tend to be more inflexible under oligopolistic conditions than under perfect competition.

2. If the demand curve is the same under oligopoly as under perfect competition, it also follows that *output will be less under oligopoly than under perfect competition.* However, it is not always reasonable to assume that the demand curve is the same in both cases, since the large expenditures for advertising and product differentiation incurred by some oligopolies may tend to shift the demand curve to the right. Consequently in some cases both price and output may tend to be higher under oligopoly than under perfect competition.

3. Oligopolistic industries tend to spend more on advertising, product differentiation, and style changes than perfectly competitive industries. The use of some resources for these purposes is certainly worthwhile, since advertising provides buyers with information, and product differentiation allows greater freedom of choice. Whether oligopolies spend too much for these purposes is by no means obvious. However, there is a widespread feeling among economists, based largely on empirical studies (and hunch), that in some oligopolistic industries such expenditures have been expanded beyond socially optimal levels.

4. One might expect on the basis of the models presented in this chapter that the *profits earned by oligopolists would be higher, on the average, than the profits earned by perfectly competitive firms.* This conclusion is supported by some statistical evidence. Joe Bain of the University of California has found that firms in industries in which the largest few firms had a high proportion of total sales tended to have higher rates of return than firms in industries in which the largest few firms had a small proportion of total sales. [11]

---

[11] J. Bain, "Relation of Profit Rate to Industry Concentration: American Manufacturing, 1936–1940," *Quarterly Journal of Economics,* August 1951. However, there has been much disagreement on this score. According to some recent evidence, a firm is likely to have higher-than-average profits if it has a relatively big share of the market, regardless of whether or not the industry as a whole is highly concentrated. For some relevant discussion, see L. Weiss, "The Concentration-Profits Relationship and Antitrust," in H. Goldschmid, H. M. Mann, and J. F. Weston, *Industrial Concentration, The New Learning,* Boston: Little Brown, 1974.

Test Yourself

1. Suppose that a cartel consists of four firms, each of which has a horizontal marginal cost curve. For each firm, marginal cost equals \$4. Suppose that the marginal revenue curve for the cartel is $MR = 10 - 2Q$, where MR is marginal revenue (in dollars) and Q is the cartel's output per year (in thousands of units). What output rate will the cartel choose?

2. According to the Senate Subcommittee on Antitrust and Monopoly, "Some system of marketing quotas, whether overt or carefully hidden, must underlie any price-fixing agreement." Comment and evaluate.

3. Discuss the incentives that each firm in Question 1 would have to cheat on the collusive agreement described there.

4. Suppose that a firm engages in cost-plus pricing. Assuming that it will operate next year at 80 percent of capacity, it estimates its average costs at that output rate. Then it adds a certain percentage to this average cost figure to get its price. But suppose that the demand curve shifts to the left during the next year, and that the firm can only operate at 40 percent of capacity if it maintains this price. What factors will govern whether the firm sticks with this price? What does this indicate about cost-plus pricing?

Summary

1. Monopolistic competition occurs where there are many sellers whose products are somewhat different. The demand curve facing each firm slopes downward to the right. The conditions for long-run equilibrium are that each firm is maximizing profits and that economic profits are zero. A famous conclusion of the theory of monopolistic competition is that firms under this form of market organization will tend to operate with excess capacity.

2. The firm under monopolistic competition is likely to produce less, and charge a higher price, than under perfect competition. Relative to pure monopoly, monopolistically competitive firms are likely to have lower profits, greater output, and lower prices. Firms under monopolistic competition will offer a wider variety of styles, brands, and qualities than will firms under perfect competition.

3. Oligopoly is characterized by a small number of firms and a great deal of interdependence, actual and perceived, among them. Oligopoly is a common market structure in the United States.

4. According to empirical studies, prices tend to be rigid in oligopolistic industries. A well-known theory designed to explain this phenomenon is Sweezy's model, based on the kinked demand curve. This theory is an incomplete model of oligopoly pricing, even though it may be of use in explaining the rigidity of prices.

5. Conditions in oligopolistic industries tend to promote collusion. A cartel is an open, formal, collusive arrangement. A profit-maximizing cartel will act like a monopolist with a number of plants or divisions, each of which is a member firm. In practice, it appears that the members of a cartel often divide markets geographically or in accord with each firm's level of sales in the past.

6. Price leadership is quite common in oligopolistic industries, one or a few firms apparently setting the price and the rest following their lead. Two types of price leadership are the dominant-firm model and the barometric-firm model. An example of the former kind of price leadership was the steel industry until a decade or so ago.

7. According to numerous studies of business behavior, cost-plus pricing is used by many oligopolists. However, a cost-plus model of pricing is incomplete unless it specifies more precisely the determinants of the size of the markup.

601

8. Relative to perfect competition, it seems likely that both price and profits will be higher under oligopoly. Moreover, oligopolistic industries will tend to spend more on advertising, product differentiation, and style changes than perfectly competitive industries.

Concepts for Review

Monopolistic competition	**Horizontal merger**	**Dominant firm**
Oligopoly	**Vertical merger**	**Barometric firm**
Pure oligopoly	**Conglomerate merger**	**Cost-plus pricing**
Differentiated oligopoly	**Collusion**	**Markup**
Product differentiation	**Cartel**	**Target rate of return**
Product group	**Price leader**	

Appendix: The Theory of Games

A useful model of oligopoly is one that stresses its gamelike characteristics. As in a game, in oligopoly each firm must take account of its rivals' reactions to its own actions. For this reason, an oligopolistic firm cannot tell what effect a change in its output will have on the price of its product and on its profits unless it can guess how its rivals will respond to the change. To understand game theory, you have to know what a *game* is. It is a competitive situation where two or more persons pursue their own interests and no person can dictate the outcome. Poker is a game, and so is a situation in which two firms are engaged in competitive advertising campaigns. A game is described in terms of its players, rules, payoffs, and information conditions. These elements are common to all conflict situations.

DEFINITIONS OF TERMS

More specifically, a *player,* whether a single person or an organization, is a decision-making unit. Each player has a certain amount of resources, and the *rules of the game* describe how these resources can be used. Thus the rules of poker indicate how bets can be made and which hands are better than others. A *strategy* is a complete specification of what a player will do under each contingency in the playing of the game. Thus a corporation president might tell his subordinates how she wants an advertising campaign to start, and what should be done at subsequent times in response to various actions of competing firms. The game's outcome clearly depends on each player's strategies. A player's *payoff* varies from game to game. It is win, lose, or draw in checkers, and various sums of money in poker.

For simplicity we will restrict our attention to *two-person games,* i.e., those with only two players, and to *zero-sum games,* in which the amount one player wins exactly equals the amount the other player loses. The relevant features of a two-person, zero-sum game can be shown by constructing a *payoff matrix.* To illustrate, consider the case of two big soap producers, Procter & Gamble and Lever Brothers. Suppose that these two firms are about to stage rival advertising campaigns and that each firm has a choice of strategies. Procter & Gamble can choose to concentrate on either television ads or magazine ads; Lever Brothers has the same choice. Table 27.1 shows what will happen to the profits of each firm when each combination of strategies is chosen. If both firms concentrate on TV ads, Procter & Gamble gains $3 million and Lever Brothers loses $3 million. If Procter & Gamble concentrates on TV ads and Lever Brothers concentrates on magazine ads, Procter & Gamble gains $2 million and Lever Brothers loses $2 million. And so on.

PROCTER AND GAMBLE'S VIEWPOINT

Given the payoff matrix in Table 27.1, there is a definite optimal choice for each firm. To see that this is the case, let's begin by looking at the situation from Procter & Gamble's point of view. If Procter & Gamble concentrates on magazine ads, Lever Brothers will respond by choosing to concentrate on TV ads. Why? Because Lever Brothers will lose less ($1 million) than if it too concentrates on magazine ads (in which case its loss will be $1.5 million). Thus *Procter & Gamble, if it concentrates on magazine ads, will gain $1 million.*

What if Procter & Gamble concentrates on TV ads? In this case, Lever Brothers will respond by choosing to concentrate on magazines. Why? Because Lever Brothers will lose less ($2 million) than if it too concentrates on TV ads (in which case its losses will be $3 million). Thus *Procter & Gamble, if it concentrates on TV ads, will gain $2 million.*

Consequently, if both firms know the payoff matrix, *Procter & Gamble will choose the strategy of concentrating on TV ads, since it provides Procter & Gamble with a greater gain ($2 million) than if it concentrates on magazine ads (in which case the gain is $1 million).*

LEVER BROTHERS' VIEWPOINT

Now let's look at the situation from the point of view of Lever Brothers. If Lever Brothers concentrates on TV ads, Procter & Gamble will respond by

Table 27.1
PAYOFF MATRIX

Possible strategies for Procter & Gamble	Possible strategies for Lever Brothers	
	Concentrate on TV	Concentrate on magazines
Concentrate on TV	P & G gains $3 million, and Lever loses $3 million	P & G gains $2 million, and Lever loses $2 million
Concentrate on magazines	P & G gains $1 million, and Lever loses $1 million	P & G gains $1.5 million, and Lever loses $1.5 million

also concentrating on TV ads. Why? Because Procter & Gamble will gain more ($3 million) than if it concentrates on magazine ads (in which case it will gain $1 million). Thus *Lever Brothers, if it concentrates on TV ads, will lose $3 million.*

What if Lever Brothers concentrates on magazine ads? In this case, Procter & Gamble will respond by choosing to concentrate on TV ads. Why? Because Procter & Gamble will gain more ($2 million) than if it concentrates on magazine ads (in which case it will gain $1.5 million). Thus *Lever Brothers, if it concentrates on magazine ads, will lose $2 million.*

Consequently, if both firms know the payoff matrix, *Lever Brothers will choose the strategy of concentrating on magazine ads, since it provides Lever Brothers with a smaller loss ($2 million) than if it concentrates on TV ads (in which case the loss will be $3 million).*

THE SOLUTION OF THE GAME

At this point, the solution of this game is clear. *Procter & Gamble will concentrate on TV ads, and Lever Brothers will concentrate on magazine ads.* In this way Procter & Gamble gains $2 million, Lever Brothers loses $2 million. By adopting these strategies, Procter & Gamble can guarantee itself a gain of this amount, and Lever Brothers can guarantee that its loss will not exceed this amount.

Note that each firm is assumed to maximize its payoff under the assumption that its opponent will adopt the strategy most damaging to itself. Many economists feel that this is an unnecessarily pessimistic outlook for the firm, and wonder whether such an attitude is a realistic representation of how firms actually view competitive situations. The firm that adopts this viewpoint, while his competitor does not, is likely to forgo considerable profit. Despite this and other limitations, the theory of games is a useful addition to economic theory because it provides a suggestive framework for analysis. One can structure formerly intractable problems and think about them in terms of this theory. However, in its present state, game theory cannot be used to derive specific predictions of the behavior of oligopolists; the world is much more complicated than simple examples like this one.

CHAPTER 28

Industrial Organization and Antitrust Policy

Monopoly and *monopolist* have long been dirty words—or at least slightly derogatory ones. The public has tended to view monopolists with suspicion at least since Adam Smith's famous attack on monopolies in the eighteenth century. Smith preached and generations of economists since have taught that a monopolist charges a price in excess of the price that would prevail under perfect competition. For reasons given in Chapter 26, this is likely to result in a misallocation of society's resources. One way that society has attempted to deal with problems caused by monopoly is through public regulation, discussed in Chapter 26. Another way is through antitrust policy, discussed in the present chapter.

In this chapter we begin by discussing the case against oligopoly and monopolistic competition, after which we take up the defense of monopoly power made by some economists. Then, after describing the extent of industrial concentration in the United States, we discuss the nature, history, and effectiveness of antitrust policy in the United States, together with the problems in constructing standards for antitrust policy. Finally, we describe some laws in this country that restrict, rather than promote, competition.

The Case Against Oligopoly and Monopolistic Competition

Complaints against Oligopoly. In Chapter 26, we discussed the case against monopoly. Although economists are more concerned about monopoly than about oligopoly or monopolistic competition, this does not mean

605

that they give either oligopoly or monopolistic competition a clean bill of health. Even though oligopoly has aroused less public indignation and opposition than out-and-out monopoly, an oligopoly can obviously be just as deleterious to social welfare. After all, *if oligopolists engage in collusion, open or tacit, their behavior with regard to price and output may resemble a monopolist's.* Only if there is real competition among the oligopolists can we expect price to be pushed closer to marginal cost under oligopoly than under monopoly. If oligopolists "cooperate" and "maintain orderly markets," the amount of social waste may be no less than under monopoly.

Also, *the inflexibility of prices under oligopoly tends to interfere with the effective functioning of the price system.* In a perfectly competitive industry, price will decline when the demand curve shifts to the left, thus prompting resources to move out of the industry. (We examined this process in Chapter 25, using coal and corn as examples.) But in an oligopolistic industry, price tends to remain constant when demand shifts to the left, with the result that output falls and much of the industry's plant is left idle. Although resources leave the oligopolistic industry, as they should, the resources that are stuck in the industry in the short run are not utilized adequately. And the fact that prices are not allowed to decline contributes to cost-push inflation.

Complaints against Monopolistic Competition. Monopolistic competition can also be a socially wasteful form of market organization. As we saw in Chapter 27, monopolistically competitive markets are characterized by overcrowding and excess capacity. There are more firms than would exist under perfect competition, and each firm produces less than the minimum-cost output rate. Thus the industry's output is produced inefficiently. More resources are used than are really necessary. The extent of this waste may not be very great if the demand curve facing each firm is very elastic, but there is no reason to believe that the demand curve will always be so elastic as to ensure that the waste is small.

In addition, price under monopolistic competition—as well as under monopoly and oligopoly—will exceed marginal cost, although the difference between price and marginal cost may be smaller than under monopoly or oligopoly. Thus monopolistic competition, like monopoly and oligopoly, results in a misallocation of resources. The argument leading to this conclusion is exactly like that given in Chapter 26 (and Appendix E) for monopoly. Also, monopolistic competition, as well as oligopoly, may allow waste arising from too much being spent (from society's point of view) on product differentiation, advertising, and other selling expenses. This is very difficult to prove, although many economists suspect it is so.

The Bottom Line. The moral is that many economists look with disfavor on serious departures from perfect competition, whether these departures are in the direction of monopoly, oligopoly, or monopolistic competition. Judged against the perfectly competitive model, all may lead to social waste and inefficiency. However, monopoly is generally presumed to be the greatest evil, with the result that economists usually look with most disfavor on markets dominated by one, or a very few, sellers—or buyers.[1]

---

[1] Monopsony, where a single buyer exists, is taken up in Chapter 29.

Joseph Schumpeter

The Defense of Monopoly Power

Not all economists agree that monopoly power is a bad thing. On the contrary, some respected voices in the economics profession have been raised to praise monopoly, not bury it. In discussing the social problems due to monopoly in Chapter 26, we assumed that the rate of technological change is independent of an industry's market structure. Some economists like Joseph Schumpeter and John Kenneth Galbraith challenge this assumption. *They assert that the rate of technological change is likely to be higher in an imperfectly competitive industry (i.e., monopoly, oligopoly, etc.) than in a perfectly competitive industry.* Since the rate of technological change affects productivity and living standards, in their view a perfectly competitive economy is likely to be inferior in a dynamic sense to an economy containing many imperfectly competitive industries.

Arguments by Schumpeter and Galbraith. Schumpeter and Galbraith point out that firms under perfect competition have fewer resources to devote to research and experimentation than do firms under imperfect competition. Because profits are at a relatively low level, it is difficult for firms under perfect competition to support large expenditures on research and development. Moreover, they argue that unless a firm has sufficient control over the market to reap the rewards from an innovation, the introduction of the innovation may not be worthwhile. If competitors can imitate the innovation very quickly, the innovator may be unable to make any money from it.

Rejoinders to Schumpeter and Galbraith. Defenders of perfect competition retort that there is likely to be less pressure for firms in imperfect markets to introduce new techniques and products, since such firms have fewer competitors. Moreover, firms in imperfect markets are better able to drive out entrants who, uncommitted to present techniques, are likely to be relatively quick to adopt new ones. (Entrants, unlike established producers, have no vested interest in maintaining the demand for existing products and the profitability of existing equipment.) Also, there are advantages in having a large number of independent decision-making units. There is less chance that an important technological advance will be blocked by the faulty judgment of a few men or women.

It is very difficult to obtain evidence to help settle the question, if it is posed in this way, since perfect competition is a hypothetical construct that does not exist in the real world. However, it does seem unlikely that a perfectly competitive industry (if such an industry could be constructed) would be able in many areas of the economy to carry out the research and development required to promote a high rate of technological change. Moreover, if entry is free and rapid, firms in a perfectly competitive industry will have little motivation to innovate. Although the evidence is not at all clear-cut, at least this much can be granted the critics of perfect competition.

Monopoly Power, Big Business, and Technological Change

But some economists go much further than the assertion that a certain amount of market imperfection will promote a more rapid rate of technological change. *They say that an industry composed of or dominated by a few large companies is the best market structure for promoting rapid technological change.* Galbraith has said that the "modern industry of a few large firms [is] an almost perfect instrument for inducing technical change."[2] And in some circles, it is accepted as an obvious fact that giant firms with their financial strength and well-equipped laboratories are absolutely necessary to maintain a rapid rate of technological change.

Suppose that, for a market of given size, we could replace the largest firms by a larger number of somewhat smaller firms—and thus reduce the extent to which the industry is dominated by the largest firms. Is there any evidence that this would decrease the rate of technological change, as is sometimes asserted? The evidence currently available is much more limited than one would like, but the available studies—based on detailed data concerning research expenditures, patents, important inventions and innovations, and the diffusion of innovations—do not indicate that such a decrease in industrial concentration would reduce the rate of technological change in most industries.

Specifically, the available studies do not show that total research and development expenditures in most industries would decrease if the largest firms were replaced by somewhat smaller ones. Nor do they indicate that the research and development expenditures carried out by the largest firms are generally more productive (or more ambitious or more risky) than those carried out by somewhat smaller firms. Moreover, they do not suggest that greater concentration of an industry results in a faster diffusion of innovations. However, if innovations require a large amount of capital, they do suggest that the substitution of a larger number of smaller firms for a few large ones may lead to slower commercial introduction of the innovations.[3]

Thus, *contrary to the allegations of Galbraith and others, there is little evidence that industrial giants are needed in most industries to insure rapid technological change and rapid utilization of new techniques.* This does not mean that industries composed only of small firms would necessarily be optimal for the promotion and diffusion of new techniques. On the contrary, there seem to be considerable advantages in a diversity of firm sizes. Complementarities and interdependencies exist among large and small firms. There is often a division of labor. Smaller firms may focus on areas requiring sophistication and flexibility and cater to specialized needs, while bigger firms concentrate on areas requiring large production, marketing, or technical resources. However, there is little evidence in most industries that firms considerably smaller than the biggest firms are not big enough for these purposes.

John Kenneth Galbraith

How Much Monopoly Power Is Optimal?

The discussion in previous sections makes it clear that the case against monopoly power is not open and shut. On the contrary, a certain amount

---

[2] John Kenneth Galbraith, *American Capitalism*, Boston: Houghton Mifflin, 1952, p. 91.
[3] Edwin Mansfield, *Technological Change*, New York: Norton, 1971, and the literature

of monopoly power is inevitable in practically all real-life situations, since perfect competition is a model that can only be approximated in real life. Moreover, a certain amount of monopoly power may be needed to promote desirable technological change. The difficult problem is to determine how much monopoly power is optimal under various circumstances (and how this power is to be measured). Some economists (like Galbraith) are convinced that a great deal of monopoly power is both inevitable and desirable. Others believe the opposite. And the economic arguments are not strong enough to resolve the differences of opinion.

Concentration of Economic Power

Some critics of monopoly power and big business are concerned with the centralization of power in the hands of a relatively few firms. Although this is only partly an economic matter, it is obviously relevant to public policy makers. Economic power in the United States is distributed very unevenly; a few hundred corporations control a very large share of the total assets of the nonfarm economy. Moreover, within particular industries, there is considerable concentration of ownership and production, as we shall see in the next sections. This concentration of power has been viewed with concern by observers like A. A. Berle, who asserted that the largest several hundred firms "each with its own dominating pyramid within it—represent a concentration of power over economies which makes the medieval feudal system look like a Sunday School party. In sheer economic power this has gone far beyond anything we have yet seen."[4]

It is important to note that this distrust of power leads to a distrust of giant firms, whether or not they have substantial monopoly power. Even if General Motors had little power over prices, it would still have considerable economic—and political—power because of its sheer size. Note too that a firm's size is not necessarily a good indicator of the extent of its monopoly power. A small grocery store in a remote community may be a monopolist, but a large merchandising firm with many rivals may have little monopoly power.

Assets of the 100 Largest Firms

Let's look at the 100 biggest manufacturing firms in the United States. Recognizing that bigness is not the same as monopoly power, what percentage of the nation's assets do these firms control, and is this percentage increasing or decreasing over time? According to the latest available figures, the 100 largest manufacturing firms control about half of all man-

---

cited there. Also, see E. Mansfield, J. Rapoport, A. Romeo, E. Villani, S. Wagner, and F. Husic, *The Production and Application of New Industrial Technology,* New York: Norton, 1977.

[4] A. A. Berle, *Economic Power and the Free Society,* New York: Fund for the Republic, p. 14.

ufacturing assets in the United States, and this percentage seems to have increased considerably since the end of World War II.

Willard Mueller of the University of Wisconsin has pointed out that, of the total assets of manufacturing firms, "the share held by the top one hundred companies rose from 39.3 percent to 49.3 percent [between 1947 and 1968], and the share of the top 200 rose from 47.2 percent to 60.9 percent. In other words, by 1968 the top one hundred companies held a greater share than that held by the top 200 in 1947."[5] Thus there can be no doubt about the vast economic power of the 100 largest firms—and no doubt that, after World War II, they increased their share of the nation's manufacturing assets.

Table 28.1

CONCENTRATION RATIOS IN SELECTED MANUFACTURING PRODUCT MARKETS, 1977

Industry	Market share of 4 largest firms (percent)
Automobiles	93
Photographic equipment	72
Tires	70
Aircraft	59
Blast furnaces and steel plants	45
Industrial organic chemicals	43
Petroleum refining	30
Bread and cake	33
Pharmaceuticals	24
Radio and TV equipment	20
Newspapers	19
Commercial printing	6

Source: Statistical Abstract of the United States.

Table 28.2

NUMBER OF INDUSTRIES WITH VARIOUS LEVELS OF CONCENTRATION

Concentration ratio (percent)	Number of industries	Percent of industries[a]
90–100	10	2
70–89	34	7
50–69	81	18
Less than 50	314	72
Total	439	100

[a] Because of rounding errors, figures do not sum to total.

Industrial Concentration in the United States

Economists and policy makers are interested in market structure because it influences market performance. But how can one measure an industry's market structure? How can one tell how close an industry is to being a monopoly or a perfectly competitive industry? An important measure economists have devised is the **market concentration ratio,** *which shows the percentage of total sales or production accounted for by the 4 biggest firms.* The higher the market concentration ratio, the more concentrated the industry is in a very few hands. Basing this measure on 4 firms is arbitrary. You can use 5, 6, 7, or any number of firms you like. But the figures issued by the government are generally based on 4 firms.

Table 28.1 shows the market concentration ratios for selected industries. These ratios vary widely from industry to industry. At one extreme, the automobile industry is a tight oligopoly, with the concentration ratio about as high as it can get—93 percent. At the other extreme, there is very little industrial concentration in the commercial printing industry: its concentration ratio is only 6 percent. Table 28.2 shows the number of industries that have concentration ratios of various magnitudes. Over one-quarter of the manufacturing industries in the United States have concentration ratios of 50 percent or more, and about one-tenth have concentration ratios of 70 percent or more.

Most economists who have studied trends in industrial concentration seem to agree that remarkably little change has occurred in the past 70 years in the average level of concentration in the United States. As Morris Adelman of M.I.T. puts it, "Any tendency either way, if it exists, must be at the pace of a glacial drift."[6] Also, the available evidence seems to indicate that the levels of market concentration are lower in the United States than in other major industrialized countries, with the possible exception of Great Britain and Japan.

Finally, it is important to recognize that the concentration ratio is only a

[5] W. Mueller, *A Primer on Monopoly and Competition,* New York: Random House, 1970, p. 26. Also see W. Shepherd, *The Economics of Industrial Organization,* Englewood Cliffs, N.J.: Prentice-Hall, 1979.

[6] M. Adelman, "The Measurement of Industrial Concentration," *Review of Economics and Statistics,* 1951. Also, see B. T. Allen, "Average Concentration in Manufacturing, 1947–72," *Journal of Economic Issues,* September, 1976.

rough measure of an industry's market structure. Certainly, to provide a reasonably adequate description, it must be supplemented with data on the extent and type of product differentiation in the industry, as well as on barriers to entry. Moreover, even with these supplements, it is still a crude measure. (Among other things, it takes no account of competition from foreign suppliers.) Nonetheless, the concentration ratio has proved to be a valuable tool to economists.

The Antitrust Laws

National policies are too ambiguous and rich in contradictions to be summarized neatly and concisely. Consequently, it would be misleading to say that the United States has adopted a policy of promoting competition and controlling monopoly. To a large extent, it certainly is true that "competition is our fundamental national policy," as the Supreme Court said in 1963. But it is also true that we have adopted many measures to promote monopoly and to limit competition, as we shall see in subsequent sections (and as has already been pointed out in Chapter 26). On balance, however, we probably have gone further in promoting competition than other major industrialized countries, and the principal pieces of legislation designed to further this objective are the *antitrust laws.*

THE SHERMAN ACT

In 1890, the first antitrust law, the Sherman Act, was passed by Congress. Although the common law had long outlawed monopolistic practices, it appeared to many Americans in the closing years of the nineteenth century that legislation was required to discourage monopoly and to preserve and encourage competition. The formation of "trusts"—monopolistic combines that colluded to raise prices and restrict output—brought the matter to a head. The heart of the Sherman Act lies in the following two sections:

> Sec. 1. Every contract, combination in the form of trust or otherwise, or conspiracy, in restraint of trade or commerce among the several states or with foreign nations, is hereby declared to be illegal. Every person who shall make any such contract or engage in any such combination or conspiracy, shall be deemed guilty of a misdemeanor. . . .
>
> Sec. 2. Every person who shall monopolize, or attempt to monopolize or combine or conspire with any other person or persons, to monopolize any part of the trade or commerce among the several States, or with foreign nations shall be deemed guilty of a misdemeanor.

THE CLAYTON ACT

The first 20 years of experience with the Sherman Act were not very satisfying to its supporters. The ineffectiveness of the Sherman Act led in 1914 to passage by Congress of two additional laws—the Clayton Act and the Federal Trade Commission Act. The Clayton Act tried to be more specific than the Sherman Act in identifying certain practices that were illegal because they would "substantially lessen competition or tend to create a monopoly." In particular, the Clayton Act outlawed unjustified *price discrimination,* a practice whereby one buyer is charged more than another buyer for the same product. It also outlawed the use of a *tying contract,* which makes the buyers purchase other items to get the product they want. Further, it outlawed mergers that substantially lessen competition; but since it did not prohibit one firm's purchase of a competitor's plant and equipment, it really could not stop mergers. In 1950, this loophole was closed by the Celler-Kefauver Anti-Merger Act.

THE FEDERAL TRADE COMMISSION ACT

The Federal Trade Commission Act was designed to prevent undesirable and unfair competitive practices. Specifically, it created a Federal Trade Commission to investigate unfair and predatory practices and to issue cease-and-desist orders. The act stated that "unfair methods of competition in commerce are hereby declared unlawful." However, the commission—composed of 5 commissioners, each appointed by the president for a term of 7 years—was given the unenviable task of defining exactly what was "unfair." Eventually, the courts took away much of the commission's power; but in 1938, the commission acquired the function of outlawing untrue and deceptive advertising. Also, the commission has authority to carry out economic investigations of the structure and conduct of American business.

The Role of the Courts

The antitrust laws, like any laws, are enforced in the courts. Typically, charges are brought against a firm or group of firms by the Antitrust Division of the Department of Justice, a trial is held, and a decision is reached by the judge. In key cases, appeals are made that eventually reach the Supreme Court. The real impact of the antitrust laws depends on how the courts interpret them. And the judicial interpretation of these laws has changed considerably over time.

The first major set of antitrust cases took place in 1911 when the Standard Oil Company and the American Tobacco Company were forced to give up a large share of their holdings of other companies. In these cases, the Supreme Court put forth and used the famous *rule of reason*—that only unreasonable combinations in restraint of trade, not all trusts, required conviction under the Sherman Act. In 1920, the rule of reason was used by the Supreme Court in its finding that U.S. Steel had not violated the antitrust laws even though it had tried to monopolize the industry—since the Court said it had not succeeded. Moreover, U.S. Steel's large size and its potential monopoly power were ruled beside the point since "the law does not make mere size an offense. It . . . requires overt acts."

During the 1920s and 1930s the courts, including the conservative Supreme Court, interpreted the antitrust laws in such a way that they were as toothless as a new-born babe. Although Eastman Kodak and International Harvester controlled very substantial shares of their markets, the

Court, using the rule of reason, found them innocent on the grounds that they had not built up their near-monopoly position through overt coercion or predatory practices. Moreover, the Court reiterated that mere size was not an offense, no matter how great the unexerted monopoly power might be.

In the late 1930s, this situation changed very greatly, with the prosecution of the Aluminum Corporation of America (Alcoa). This case, decided in 1945 (but begun in 1937), reversed the decisions in the *U.S. Steel* and *International Harvester* cases. Alcoa had achieved its 90 percent of the market by means that would have been considered "reasonable" in the earlier cases—keeping its price low enough to discourage entry, building capacity to take care of increases in the market, and so forth. (Recall our discussion of Alcoa in Chapter 26.) Nonetheless, the Court decided that Alcoa, because it controlled practically all the industry's output, violated the antitrust laws. Thus, to a considerable extent, *the Court used market structure rather than market conduct as a test of legality.*

The Role of the Justice Department

The impact of the antitrust laws is determined by the vigor with which the Antitrust Division of the Justice Department prosecutes cases. If the Antitrust Division does not prosecute, the laws can have little effect. Like the judicial interpretation of the laws, the extent to which the Justice Department has prosecuted cases has varied from one period to another. Needless to say, the attitude of the political party in power has been an important determinant of how vigorously antitrust cases have been prosecuted. When the Sherman Act was first passed, it was of singularly little value. For example, President Grover Cleveland's attorney general did not agree with the law and would not prosecute under it. "Trust-busting" was truly a neglected art until President Theodore Roosevelt devoted his formidable energies to it. In 1903, he established the Antitrust Division of the Justice Department. Moreover, his administration started the major cases that led to the *Standard Oil, American Tobacco,* and *U.S. Steel* decisions.

Subsequently, there was a long lull in the prosecution of antitrust cases, reflecting the Supreme Court's rule-of-reason doctrine and a strong conservative tide in the nation. The lull continued for about 25 years, until 1937, when there was a significant upsurge in activity on the antitrust front. Led by Thurman Arnold, the Antitrust Division entered one of the most vigorous periods of antitrust enforcement to date. Arnold went after the glass, cigarette, cement, and other industries, the most important case being that against Alcoa. The Antitrust Division attempted in this period to reopen cases that were hopeless under the rule-of-reason doctrine. With the change in the composition of the Supreme Court, Arnold's activism turned out to be effective.

Post-World-War-II Developments

The period since World War II generally has been a vigorous one from the viewpoint of antitrust, with at least six notable developments.

1. One of the biggest cases in the history of antitrust occurred in 1961 when, as you will recall from the previous chapter, the major electrical equipment manufacturers were convicted of collusive price agreements. Executives of General Electric, Westinghouse, and other firms in the industry admitted that they met secretly in hotels and communicated by mail in order to maintain prices, share the market, and eliminate competition. Some of the executives were sentenced to jail on criminal charges, and the firms had to pay large amounts to customers to make up for the overcharges. In particular, 1,800 triple damage suits against the firms resulted in payments estimated at between $400 and $600 million. Even the most zealous antitrusters will admit that this was no slap on the wrist!

2. Following the enactment of the Celler-Kefauver Anti-Merger Act, horizontal mergers—mergers of firms making essentially the same good—became increasingly likely to run afoul of the antitrust laws. In 1962, Chief Justice Earl Warren went so far as to say that a merger that resulted in a firm having 5 percent of the market might be undesirable. In the *Von's Grocery* case in 1965, the Court disallowed a merger between two supermarkets that together had less than 8 percent of the Los Angeles market. (In this case, the Court emphasized the trend toward increasing concentration in grocery retailing in Los Angeles.) Also, vertical mergers—mergers of firms that supply or sell to one another—have been viewed with a jaundiced eye by the courts. For example, in the *Brown Shoe* case, the Supreme Court said that the merger of Brown with R. G. Kinney would mean that other shoe manufacturers would be frozen out of a substantial part of the retail shoe market.

3. A leading problem confronting the Justice Department in the 1960s was conglomerate mergers—mergers of firms in unrelated industries. Conglomerate firms like Litton industries, International Telephone, and Ling-Temco-Vought were regarded very highly by investors during the 1960s. Inspired by their apparent success, other firms began to merge with firms in other industries in order to become conglomerates themselves. Supporters of these mergers claimed that they enabled weak companies to be revitalized by superior management, bigger research facilities, and so on. However, this merger movement was opposed by many other observers on the grounds that conglomerates were obtaining too much power in the economy. To some extent, this problem has diminished in importance since the conglomerates began to show relatively disappointing earnings in the late 1960s. But the Justice Department continues to keep a watchful eye on conglomerate mergers. In 1967 it succeeded in preventing a conglomerate merger between Procter & Gamble, the big soap manufacturer, and Clorox, a maker of liquid bleach. And in 1971 it made some attempt to force ITT to divest itself of the Hartford Fire Insurance Company, but the case was dropped.

4. In 1982, a government antitrust suit (begun in 1974) against the American Telephone and Telegraph Company (AT&T) was settled. According to the settlement, AT&T divested itself of 22 companies that provide most of

Basic Idea #55: *The antitrust laws are designed to discourage monopoly and foster competition. Their effectiveness depends greatly on the Justice Department (which has the task of prosecuting) and the courts (which must interpret them). Without question, they have had an effect on the structure of American industry, but many observers feel that they have not been as effective as they might have been.*

the nation's local telephone service, and kept its Long Lines division, Western Electric, and the Bell Laboratories. While many observers worried that one result was likely to be an increase in local telephone rates, there was also considerable feeling that, after the telephone industry was restructured in this way, AT&T would be a leaner and more dynamic firm. One immediate effect of this divestiture was a great deal of confusion among customers and costly adjustments within AT&T, but by 1985 many observers believed that it was resulting in faster introduction of new technologies and services and lower long-distance phone rates.

5. *The Antitrust Division sued IBM Corporation under Section 2 of the Sherman Act in January 1969, thus starting one of the biggest and costliest antitrust cases in history.* The government charged that IBM held a monopoly and that the firm's 360 line of computers was introduced in 1965 in a way that eliminated competition. IBM's defense was that its market position stemmed from its innovative performance and economies of scale, that its pricing was competitive, and that its profit rate really had not been high. Once the trial began in 1975, it took the government almost three years to present its case. In early 1982, on the same day that it settled the antitrust case against AT&T, the Reagan administration dropped the IBM case. It said the case was "without merit and should be dismissed."

6. *As the outcome of the IBM case indicated, antitrust policy changed in 1981 when President Reagan took office.* His Antitrust Division believed that a fair number of activities that had been deemed antitrust violations in the past not only were legal, but also were beneficial to the economy. According to this view, business decisions should be free of antitrust interference unless they are unequivocally anticompetitive. Given the huge costs (about $1 billion to IBM, according to some estimates) of the IBM case, and the feeling among some economists that economies of scale were sometimes underestimated, it is not surprising that such a change in emphasis and direction occurred. But economists who favor an aggressive antitrust policy have tended to regard this change with suspicion.

Test Yourself

1. "Perfect competition results in optimal efficiency and an optimal distribution of income. This is why the United States opts for a perfectly competitive economy." Comment and evaluate.

2. "The real impact of the antitrust laws depends on judicial interpretation." Comment and evaluate.

3. Suppose that an industry is composed of five firms. The market share of each firm is given in the table on the right:

Firm	Market share (percent)
A	10
B	10
C	20
D	25
E	35

What is the concentration ratio for this industry?

4. Suppose that firm E loses half of its sales to firm C. If the sales of the other firms remain constant, what is the effect on the concentration ratio in Question 3?

Standards for Antitrust Policy

There are at least two fairly distinct approaches to antitrust policy. *The first looks primarily and directly at **market performance**—the industry's rate of technological change, efficiency, and profits, the conduct of individual firms, and so on.* Advocates of this approach argue that, in deciding antitrust cases, one should review in detail the performance of the firms in question to see how well they have served the economy. If they have served well they should not be held in violation of the antitrust laws simply because they have a large share of the market. This test, as it is usually advocated, relies heavily on an evaluation of the technological "progressiveness" and "dynamism" of the firms in question. Although this approach seems quite sensible, it has a number of disadvantages. In particular, it is very difficult to tell at present whether a particular industry's performance is "good" or "bad." Economists simply do not have the sorts of measuring rods that would be required to obtain reasonably accurate and well-accepted readings on an industry's performance. In view of the vagueness of the criteria and the practical realities of the antitrust environment, adopting this approach would probably invite nonenforcement of the laws.

*The second approach emphasizes the importance of an industry's **market structure**—the number and size distribution of buyers and sellers in the market, the ease with which new firms can enter, and the extent of product differentiation.* According to this approach, one should look to market structure for evidence of undesirable monopolistic characteristics. The basic idea behind this approach, as George Stigler puts it, is that "an industry which does not have a competitive structure will not have competitive behavior." Two leading authorities on antitrust law, Carl Kaysen of M.I.T. and Donald Turner of Harvard (and formerly head of the Antitrust Division under President Johnson), are strong advocates of this approach. They believe that, if for 5 years or more, one firm has accounted for 50 percent or more of annual sales in a market, or if 4 or fewer firms have accounted for 80 percent of such sales, it should be presumed that "market power" exists. And they propose that such "market power" be declared illegal, unless such concentration can be defended by economies of scale or some other such justification. If it cannot be defended, divestiture and dissolution would constitute possible remedies.[7]

Although respected economists favor each of these approaches, the second is probably preferred by most experts in this field. However, this does not mean that the market structure approach does not have lots of critics. On the contrary, many economists and lawyers feel that the relationship between market structure and market performance is so weak that it is a mistake to choose, more or less arbitrarily, some level of concentration and to say that, if concentration exceeds this level, market performance is likely to be undesirable.

[7] C. Kaysen and D. Turner, *Antitrust Policy,* Cambridge, Mass.: Harvard University Press, 1959.

The Effectiveness of Antitrust Policy

How effective have the antitrust laws been? Obviously it is difficult to tell with any accuracy, since there is no way to carry out an experiment in which American history is rewritten to show what would have happened if the antitrust laws had not been on the books. Many experts seem to feel that the antitrust laws have not been as effective as they might—or should—have been, largely because they do not have sufficient public support and there is no politically powerful pressure group pushing for their enforcement.

But this does not mean that the antitrust laws have had no effect. As Edward Mason of Harvard University has pointed out, their effectiveness is due "not so much to the contribution that particular judgments have made to the restoring of competition as it is to the fact that the consideration of whether or not a particular course of action may or may not be in violation of the antitrust acts is a persistent factor affecting business judgment, at least in large firms."[8] This same idea is summed up in the old saying that the ghost of Senator Sherman sits as an *ex officio* member of every firm's board of directors.

Some indication of the effects of our antitrust laws can perhaps be obtained by looking at experience in other countries, since Britain, Germany, and many other European countries (as well as Japan) took a very tolerant view of monopoly power for a long time. After World War II, there was pressure to break up some of the powerful combines in Germany and Japan, but this pressure has been somewhat relaxed more recently—although antitrust practices seem to be gaining ground in the European Common Market. Foreign experience seems to indicate that the antitrust laws have helped prevent American firms from adopting many restrictive and predatory practices common elsewhere.

The *Pabst* Case: Antitrust in Action

Perhaps the most effective way to learn certain things about the antitrust field is to try to decide an actual antitrust case. Suppose that, over the protests of the American Bar Association, you are appointed a district court judge and that your first job is to hear a case (actually brought by the government in 1958) to prevent Pabst Brewing Company from acquiring the Blatz Brewing Company. According to the government, the effect of this merger "may be substantially to lessen competition, or to tend to create a monopoly" in the production and sale of beer in the state of Wisconsin, the three-state area of Wisconsin, Illinois, and Michigan, and the United States.

A fundamental issue in any case of this sort is the definition of market and industry boundaries. Market boundaries must be broad enough to include all relevant competitors but not so broad as to include products that are

PABST QUALITY.
IT'S A TRADITION THAT KEEPS
GROWING.

---

[8] Edward Mason, Preface to Carl Kaysen and Donald Turner, *Antitrust Policy* (and reprinted in E. Mansfield, *Monopoly Power and Economic Performance,* 4th ed. New York: Norton, 1978).

not reasonable substitutes. The delineation of market and industry boundaries—in terms of "line of commerce" and "section of the country"—is bound to involve judgment, there being no simple, mechanical rule to settle it.

In the *Pabst* case, both the government and Pabst agreed "that the line of commerce involved the production, sale, and distribution of beer and that the continental United States is a relevant geographic market." However, there was disagreement over the government's use of Wisconsin and the three-state area of Wisconsin, Illinois, and Michigan as separate geographical markets. Pabst and Blatz claimed that there was no good reason to single out these particular areas as distinct markets. The government, on the other hand, claimed that they were distinct markets because the two firms competed most intensively in these areas. Pabst was the nation's eleventh largest seller of beer; its sales were 2.67 percent of the national market and about 11 percent of the sales in Wisconsin. Blatz was the nation's thirteenth largest seller of beer, its sales being 2.04 percent of the national market and about 13 percent of the sales in Wisconsin. Thus, *if you look at the smaller geographical area (Wisconsin and the three-state area), the two firms account for a substantial proportion of the market—about 24 percent in Wisconsin. But if you look at the national market as a whole, they account for a small proportion—less than 5 percent.*

As the district judge how should you decide the case? Should you agree with the government that Wisconsin and the three-state area are relevant markets? Or should you agree with Pabst and Blatz that they are not relevant markets in themselves, but just parts of a market? Moreover, if you agree with the government concerning the market definition, should you also agree that two firms with a total of 24 percent of Wisconsin sales should not be allowed to merge? Or if you agree with Pabst and Blatz concerning the market definition, should you allow a merger between two firms that together account for about 5 percent of the national market? It is a tough problem, isn't it? To demonstrate just how tough it is, the district judge decided one way, while the Supreme Court decided the other way. The district court, agreeing with Pabst and Blatz that Wisconsin and the three-state area should not be treated as distinct relevant areas, dismissed the government's complaint. But the district court's decision was reversed by the Supreme Court, which agreed with the government's position that the smaller areas should be treated as relevant, distinct markets.

The antitrust field is characterized by many complexities and uncertainties, as well as by legal and economic vagueness and ambiguity. This case illustrates how difficult it is even to decide what the relevant market is!

The Patent System

In a previous section, we pointed out that our national economic policies are by no means free of contradiction. In particular, although many of our policies are designed to promote competition and limit monopoly, one should not assume that all of them are meant to promote these objectives. On the contrary, quixotic as it may seem, some are designed to do just the opposite—to restrict competition. Among the most important of these pol-

icies are our laws concerning patents, which grant inventors exclusive control over the use of their inventions for 17 years. That is, inventors are given a temporary monopoly over the use of their inventions.

THE PROS

Since Congress passed the original patent act in 1790, the arguments used to justify the existence of the patent laws have not changed very much. First, *these laws are regarded as an important incentive to induce the inventor to put in the work required to produce an invention.* Particularly in the case of the individual inventor, it is claimed that patent protection is a strong incentive. Second, *patents are regarded as a necessary incentive to induce firms to carry out the further work and make the necessary investment in pilot plants and other items that are required to bring the invention to commercial use.* If an invention became public property when made, why should a firm incur the costs and risks involved in attempting to develop, debug, and perfect it? Another firm could watch, take no risks, and duplicate the process or product if it were successful. Third, it is argued that because of the patent laws, *inventions are disclosed earlier than otherwise, the consequence being that other inventions are facilitated by the earlier dissemination of the information.* The resulting situation is often contrasted with the intense secrecy about processes that characterized the medieval guilds and which undoubtedly retarded technological progress and economic growth.

THE CONS

Not all economists agree that the patent system is beneficial. A patent represents a monopoly right, although as many inventors can testify, it may be a very weak one. Critics of the patent system stress the social costs arising from the monopoly. After a new process or product has been discovered, it may cost very little for other persons who could make use of this knowledge to acquire it. The patent gives the inventor the right to charge a price for the use of the information, with the result that the knowledge is used less widely than is socially optimal. Critics also point out that patents have been used to create monopoly positions, which were sustained by other means after the original patents had expired. They cite as examples the aluminum, shoe machinery, and plate-glass industries. In addition, the cross-licensing of patents often has been used by firms as a vehicle for joint monopolistic exploitation of their market.

Critics also question the extent of the social gains arising from the system. They point out that the patent system was designed for the individual inventor, but that over the years most research and development has been institutionalized. They assert that patents are not really important as incentives to the large corporation, since it cannot afford to fall behind in the technological race, whether or not it receives a patent. Also, they say that because of long lead times, most of the innovative profits from many innovations can be captured before imitators have a chance to enter the market, whether or not the innovator is granted a patent. Finally, they claim that firms keep secret what inventions they can, and patent those they cannot.

These questions concerning the effects and desirability of the patent

Basic Idea #56: Although it is sometimes claimed that government policy supports competition and discourages monopoly, many of our laws are designed to do just the opposite. For example, the patent laws grant a temporary monopoly to inventors.

619

BERKEY PHOTO INC. V. EASTMAN KODAK CO.

One of the most celebrated antitrust cases of recent years involved Eastman Kodak and Berkey Photo. Eastman Kodak has long been a dominant producer of cameras and film. Berkey Photo competes with Kodak as a photofinisher, and less successfully (until 1978) as a camera manufacturer. Berkey buys much of its film and photofinishing equipment and supplies from Kodak. In 1973, Berkey filed suit, saying that Kodak had violated the antitrust laws when in 1972 it introduced its new 110 "Pocket Instamatic" camera. Because the camera was introduced with no advance notice to Kodak's competitors, Berkey could not introduce its own version of the new camera until late 1973, and did not reach a substantial sales volume until 1974. Berkey claimed that Kodak's failure to disclose the innovation to its competitors before introducing it violated section 2 of the Sherman Act.

The jury was instructed that if it found monopoly power in the relevant markets (cameras or film), it could then consider "whether in the light of other conduct [it] determine[d] to be anticompetitive, Kodak's failure to predisclose was on balance an exclusionary course of conduct,"[1] and thus in violation of section 2. The jury found that Berkey should be awarded damages, after trebling, of $45,750,000 for lost profits on the 110 camera and $167,100 for lost profits on photofinishing services. The court also instructed Kodak to disclose (before introduction) to competitors all camera and film innovations that it provides its own photofinishing division.

Eastman Kodak appealed the decision, and the Second Circuit Court reversed the damage awards. The court pointed out that "withholding from others advance knowledge of one's new products . . . ordinarily constitutes valid competitive conduct."[2] To insist on such disclosure would reduce the incentives to innovate. Regardless of whether Kodak had monopoly power in cameras or in film, Kodak did not have a duty to predisclose information about the 110 camera to its competition. "Because, as we have already indicated, a monopolist is permitted, and indeed encouraged . . . to compete aggressively on the merits, any success that it may achieve through the process of invention and innovation is clearly tolerated by the antitrust laws."[3]

In addition, Berkey claimed that Kodak engaged in two separate conspiracies, with General Electric and with Sylvania, to restrain trade in the use of new flash devices with amateur cameras. In 1963, Sylvania approached Kodak with a prototype of a new battery-powered light device: the flashcube. Berkey said that Kodak, although it did not make any real technical contributions to the flashcube, required Sylvania not to provide information concerning this invention to other camera producers. Thus Kodak was for some time the only firm able to sell cameras using this device. Similarly, Kodak insisted that Sylvania not disclose its magicube invention and that General Electric not disclose its flipflash invention. Consequently, Kodak's cameras were for a time the only ones that used these new devices.

[1] *Berkey Photo, Inc.* v *Eastman Kodak Co.*, 603 F. 2d 263 (1979), p. 281.
[2] Ibid.
[3] Ibid.

While the circuit court did not conclude that joint development projects between monopolists and manufacturers of complementary products are per se violations of section 1 of the Sherman Act, it did find that the secrecy agreements in this case were unreasonable restraints of trade. In the words of the circuit court judge, "Kodak and GE, of course, are not direct competitors, and Kodak and Sylvania were at best potential competitors when the magicube was being developed. Nevertheless, because of Kodak's market power over cameras, the exclusionary potential of horizontal research pools was present. In the case of the flipflash, for example, GE indicated early in 1971 that it could be at maximum production in two years. Kodak, however, counselled delay, at one point urging GE project officials to make a show of progress, "even if all you do is 'paint the red base black,'" so that "we'll feel free to work with you." Otherwise, Kodak said, GE could not be assured of being part of Kodak's future flash plans, for "we would then have to ask all [lamp] manufacturers" to submit ideas. A few months later, the two firms executed the formal agreement binding them to join development of flipflash and nondisclosure to rival lamp and camera manufacturers. From this and other evidence, the jury could have found in the verdict it returned that, without any technological justification, GE kept a desirable innovation off the market for two years solely to suit Kodak's convenience. There is a hollow ring to a claim of justification by appeal to the need to promote innovation, where the result of the conduct was such a clear loss to consumers."

system have proven extremely difficult to settle. But most observers seem to agree that, despite its faults, it is difficult to find a realistic substitute for the patent system. However, over the past 30 years, there has been a discernible trend for the courts and Congress to resolve conflicts between the patent system and antitrust policy in favor of the latter. The courts have found more and more patents invalid; Congress has set higher standards of patentability; and the courts have curtailed the extension of the effects of the patent beyond the invention described in the patent claim.

Other Policies Designed to Restrict Competition

The reasons why laws are enacted to restrict, rather than promote, competition are not difficult to understand. People want competition for the other guy, but not for themselves. Moreover, certain sectors of the economy seem to need help, and have the political muscle to get it—partly in the form of laws designed to take some of the competitive heat off them.

ROBINSON-PATMAN ACT

A case of this sort is retail trade, where the small independent retailers felt threatened by the advent of the chain store. The chain stores were able to reduce the costs of distribution below those of the smaller retailers, with the result that the total number of grocery stores and drug stores fell considerably in the 1920s and 1930s. The small retailers charged that their smaller numbers were due to the predatory tactics of the chain stores. They took their charges to Congress and succeeded in getting the Robinson-Patman Act enacted in 1936.

The Robinson-Patman Act says that sellers must not discriminate in price among purchasers of similar grade and quality where the effect might be to drive competitors out of business. The act was aimed at preventing price discrimination in favor of chain stores that buy goods in large quantities. Most economists do not regard the Robinson-Patman Act with enthusiasm because it attempts to keep competitors in existence even if they are inefficient. (The social virtues of the competitive system do not lie in maintaining a lot of inefficient small businessmen in operation.) Moreover, most observers seem to believe that the act has had the effect of reducing the vigor of price competition in retail trade.

MILLER-TYDINGS ACT

Another law designed to limit competition in U.S. retail trade was the Miller-Tydings Act of 1937, which exempted from the antitrust laws the use of resale price maintenance agreements in states permitting such agreements. *Resale price maintenance agreements* permitted manufacturers of a trademarked or branded item to establish the retail price of the item by contracts with retailers. Moreover, the Miller-Tydings Act permitted the manufacturer to bind *all* retailers in a state to a contract simply by signing such a contract with *any one* of the retailers in the state. The result was to reduce the amount of price competition in retail trade. In 1975, Congress passed a bill nullifying such agreements.

OTHER POLICIES LIMITING COMPETITION

Finally, you should recognize that policies designed to limit competition are found in many other areas besides retail trade. In Chapter 4, we saw that our national farm policies have been aimed at keeping the prices of agricultural products at a level exceeding what they would be under competition. In Chapter 29, we shall see that the government has promoted the growth of strong labor unions, which try to raise wages above competitive levels. In

---

Example 28.1   Resale Price Maintenance and Cosmetics

Until 1975, resale price maintenance agreements allowed manufacturers of a trademarked item to establish a floor under the retail price of the item. Suppose that the manufacturer of a cosmetic established OP as its minimum retail price, and that D_0 is the demand curve for this cosmetic at a particular drugstore. The drugstore's average costs are also shown in the diagram.

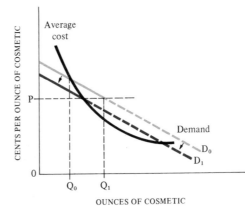

(a) Only the solid portion of demand curve D_0 is relevant to the drugstore. Why? (b) Can the drugstore make a profit on the sale of the cosmetic? (c) Will there be a change in the number of drugstores selling the cosmetic? What sort of a change? Why? (d) As changes occur in the number of drugstores selling the cosmetic, the demand curve eventually moves to D_1. Why? At this point, can a drugstore make a profit on the sale of the cosmetic?

SOLUTION

(a) Because the drugstore cannot sell the cosmetic at a price less than OP without running afoul of the resale price maintenance agreements. (b) Yes. If it sells between OQ_0 and OQ_1 ounces of the cosmetic, the price it receives will exceed its average cost. (c) Yes. Because profits are made on this cosmetic, other stores will begin to sell it, the result being that the number of stores selling it will increase. (d) Because more and more stores sell the cosmetic, the total volume is spread more thinly among the stores. In other words, the demand curve facing a particular drugstore shifts to the left. When the demand curve reaches D_1, a drugstore can no longer make a profit from the sale of the cosmetic. Thus entry ceases.*

   * For further discussion, see L. Weiss, *Case Studies in American Industry,* New York: Wiley, 1980.

the field of international trade, the Webb-Pomerene Act of 1918 allowed American exporters to get together to form export trade associations, which, according to some observers, may have tended to reduce competition. Even in the bituminous coal industry, which we looked at in some detail in Chapter 25, Congress passed the Bituminous Coal Act of 1937 to establish minimum prices and reduce "cutthroat" competition, though in 1943 the act was not renewed.

Thus it is erroneous to think that the United States has opted decisively for competition. On the contrary, although the antitrust laws are clearly designed to promote competition and limit monopoly, a number of other laws are designed to do just the opposite. In many of the industries where laws designed to restrict competition have been enacted—for example, agriculture, retail trade, and bituminous coal—the basic problem has been that too many people and too much capital were tied up in the industry. Economists generally believe that it would be wiser to encourage people and capital to leave these industries than to attempt to limit competition. (Recall our discussion in Chapter 4 of American farm policies.)

Test Yourself

1. According to John Kenneth Galbraith, "The antitrust laws effectively protect the large business from social pressure or regulation by maintaining the myth that the market does the regulating instead." Do you agree? Why or why not?

2. On November 4, 1985, *Business Week* reported that, "In the Antitrust Division, with enforcement in the doldrums, many senior lawyers want to leave but can't find jobs at private firms because the lack of enforcement activity has reduced private practice, as well." Is this necessarily bad? Why or why not?

3. Chief Justice Hughes observed, "Good intentions will not save a plan otherwise objectionable, but knowledge of actual intent is an aid in the interpretation of facts and prediction of consequence." Relate this to the construction of standards for antitrust policy.

4. What are the arguments in favor of the patent system? What are the arguments against it? Is there currently considerable political support for the abolition of the patent system?

Summary

1. A monopolistic industry produces too little of the monopolized good. Society is less well off than it could be. Oligopoly can be as bad as monopoly if oligopolists engage in collusion; and even if they don't collude, inefficiencies are likely to result. Monopolistic competition can also be a socially wasteful form of market organization.

2. In defense of monopoly power, some economists, such as Galbraith, have asserted that the rate of technological change is likely to be greater in an imperfectly competitive industry than under perfect competition. It does seem unlikely that a perfectly competitive industry would be able—and have the incentive—to carry out the research and development required to promote a rapid rate of technological change in many sectors of the economy.

3. Contrary to the allegations of Galbraith and others, there is little evidence that giant firms are needed to insure rapid technological change in a great many sectors of the economy. The situation is much more complex than such statements

indicate, and the contributions of smaller firms are much greater than is commonly recognized.

4. Economic power in the United States is distributed very unevenly; 100 corporations control about half the total manufacturing assets of the economy. Moreover, many individual industries are dominated by a few firms. This concentration of power is viewed with concern by some economists and lawyers.

5. In 1890, the Sherman Act was passed. It outlawed any contract, combination, or conspiracy in restraint of trade and made it illegal to monopolize or attempt to monopolize. In 1914, Congress passed the Clayton Act, and the Federal Trade Commission was created. A more recent antitrust development was the Celler-Kefauver Anti-Merger Act of 1950.

6. The real impact of the antitrust laws depends on the interpretation placed on these laws by the courts. In its early cases, the Supreme Court put forth and used the famous rule of reason—that only unreasonable combinations in restraint of trade, not all trusts, required conviction under the Sherman Act. The situation changed greatly in the 1940s when the Court decided that Alcoa, because it controlled practically all of the nation's aluminum output, was in violation of the antitrust laws.

7. There are at least two fairly distinct approaches to antitrust policy. One looks primarily and directly at market performance; the other emphasizes market structure. Although there are respected economists in favor of each of these approaches, the second is probably preferred by most experts in this field.

8. Many observers seem to feel that the antitrust laws have not been as effective as they might—or should—have been, largely because they do not have sufficient public support. At the same time, many feel that the evidence, although incomplete and unclear, suggests that they have had a nonnegligible effect on business behavior and markets.

9. Not all our laws are designed to promote competition and restrict monopoly. On the contrary, some laws are designed to do just the opposite. The patent system confers a temporary monopoly on inventors. And the Robinson-Patman Act and many other laws have been designed to restrict competition. The truth is that, despite some protests to the contrary, our nation is by no means fully committed to promoting competition and preventing monopoly.

Concepts for Review

Market concentration ratio	**Tying contract**	**Patent system**
Antitrust laws	**Rule of reason**	**Resale price maintenance**
Price discrimination	**Market performance**	
	Market structure	

PART EIGHT

Distribution of Income

CHAPTER 29

Determinants of Wages

Everyone has a healthy—indeed, sometimes an unhealthy—interest in income. Organizations as holy as the church and as unholy as the Mob exhibit an interest in this subject. Surely we all need to look carefully at the social mechanisms underlying the distribution of income in our society. Most income is in the form of wages and salaries; that is, it is labor income. What determines the price paid for a particular kind of labor? Why is the wage rate for surgeons frequently in the neighborhood of $100 an hour, while the wage rate for relatively unskilled labor is frequently in the neighborhood of $4 or $5 an hour? Or why is the wage rate for a secretary higher in 1986 than in 1960?

Economists frequently classify inputs into three categories—labor, capital, and land. The disadvantage of this simple classification is that each category contains an enormous variety of inputs. Consider the services of labor, which include the work of a football star like Eric Dickerson, a salesman like Willy Loman, and a knight like Don Quixote. But it does have the important advantage of distinguishing between different classes of inputs. In this chapter, we are concerned with the determinants of the price of labor. The next chapter will deal with the determinants of the prices of capital and land, as well as profits.

The Labor Force and the Price of Labor

At the outset it is important to note that, to the economist, labor includes a great deal more than the organized labor that belongs to trade unions. The secretary who works at IBM, the young account executive at Merrill Lynch, the auto mechanic at your local garage, the professor who teaches molecular

Table 29.1

OCCUPATIONAL COMPOSITION OF THE EMPLOYED LABOR FORCE,
UNITED STATES, AUGUST 1984[a]

		Percent of employed labor force
Managerial and professional workers		22.9
Executive	11.0	
Professional	11.9	
Technical, sales, and administrative support workers		30.9
Technicians	3.0	
Sales	12.1	
Administrative support	15.8	
Service workers		13.4
Private household	0.9	
Protective service	1.6	
Other service	10.8	
Precision production, craft, repair workers		12.8
Operators, fabricators, and laborers		16.1
Machine operators	7.6	
Transportation and material moving	4.2	
Handlers and laborers	4.3	
Farming, forestry, and fishing		3.9
Total		100.0

[a] Because of rounding errors, figures may not sum to total.
Source: Bureau of Labor Statistics.

biology, all put forth labor. Table 29.1 shows the occupational distribution of the labor force in the United States. You can see that almost two-thirds of the people employed are white collar workers (such as salesmen, doctors, secretaries, or managers) and service workers (such as waiters, bartenders, or cooks), while only about one-third are blue-collar workers (such as carpenters, mine workers, or foremen) and farm workers.

It is also worthwhile to preface our discussion with some data concerning how much people actually get paid. As shown in Table 29.2, average weekly earnings vary considerably from one industry to another. For example, in 1984, workers in manufacturing averaged about $373 a week, while construction workers averaged $455 a week, and workers in retail trade averaged $177 a week. Also, average weekly earnings vary considerably from one period to another. Table 29.2 shows that average weekly earnings in manufacturing in 1965 were only $108, as contrasted with $373 in 1984. In subsequent sections, we shall investigate the reasons for these differences in wages, both among industries and among periods of time.

More broadly, we shall be concerned in subsequent sections with the price of labor, which includes a great many forms of renumeration other than what are commonly regarded as wages. As noted above, economists include as labor the services performed by professional people (such as lawyers, doctors, and professors) and self-employed businessmen (such as

Table 29.2

AVERAGE WEEKLY EARNINGS, SELECTED INDUSTRIES, 1955–84 (DOLLARS)

Year	Manufact-uring	Construction	Retail trade
1955	76	91	49
1960	90	113	58
1965	108	138	67
1970	134	195	82
1975	190	265	108
1980	289	368	147
1984	373	455	177

electricians, mechanics, and barbers). Thus the amount such people receive per unit of time is included here as a particular sort of price of labor, even though these amounts are often called fees or salaries rather than wages.

Finally, it is important to distinguish between *money* wages and *real* wages. Whereas the money wage is the amount of money received per unit of time, the real wage is the amount of real goods and services that can be bought with the money wage. The real wage depends on the price level for goods and services as well as on the magnitude of the money wage. In recent years (particularly during the late 1970s and early 1980s), the inflation we have experienced has meant that real wages have increased less than money wages; thus the increases in earnings in Table 29.2 exaggerate the increase in real wages. In subsequent sections, since we shall assume that product prices are held constant, our discussion will be in terms of real wages.

The Equilibrium Wage and Employment Under Perfect Competition

THE FIRM'S DEMAND CURVE FOR LABOR

Let's begin by discussing the determinants of the price of labor under perfect competition. That is, we assume that firms take the prices of their products, as well as the prices of all inputs as given; and we assume that owners of inputs take input prices as given. Under these circumstances, what determines how much labor an individual firm will hire (at a specified wage rate)? Once we answer this question, we can derive a firm's demand curve for labor. A *firm's demand curve for labor* is the relationship between the price of labor and the amount of labor utilized by the firm. That is, it shows, for each price, the amount of labor that the firm will use.

Table 29.3

THE FIRM'S DEMAND FOR LABOR UNDER PERFECT COMPETITION

Number of workers per day	Total output per day	Marginal product of labor	Value of marginal product (dollars)
0	0		
		7	70
1	7		
		6	60
2	13		
		5	50
3	18		
		4	40
4	22		
		3	30
5	25		

THE PROFIT-MAXIMIZING QUANTITY OF LABOR

Let us assume that we know the firm's production function, and that labor is the only variable input. Given the production function, we can determine the marginal product of labor when various quantities are used. The results of such a calculation are as shown in Table 29.3. If the price of the firm's product is $10, let's determine the value to the firm of each additional worker it hires per day.[1] According to Table 29.3, the firm achieves a daily output of 7 units when it hires the first worker; and since each unit is worth $10, this brings the firm's daily revenues up to $70. By hiring the second worker, the firm increases its daily output by 6 units; and since each unit is worth $10, the resulting increase in the firm's daily revenues is $60. Similarly, the increase in the firm's daily revenues from hiring the third worker is $50, the increase from hiring the fourth worker is $40, and so on.

How many workers should the firm hire per day if it wants to maximize profit? It should hire more workers as long as the extra workers result in at least as great an addition to revenues as they do to costs. If the price of a

Basic Idea #57: How much labor a firm finds it profitable to hire depends on labor's productivity and price. If the value of the marginal product of labor is greater than labor's price, a firm can increase its profit by hiring more labor; otherwise, it is not profitable to do so.

[1] For simplicity, we assume that the number of workers that the firm hires per day must be an integer, not a fraction. This assumption is innocuous, and can easily be relaxed.

worker is $50 per day, it is profitable for the firm to hire the first worker since this adds $70 to the firm's daily revenues but only $50 to its daily costs. Also, it is profitable to hire the second worker, since this adds $60 to the firm's daily revenues but only $50 to its daily costs. The addition of the third worker does not reduce the firm's profits. But beyond 3 workers per day, it does not pay the firm to hire more labor. (The addition of a fourth worker adds $50 to the firm's daily costs but only $40 to its daily revenues.)

THE VALUE OF THE MARGINAL PRODUCT OF LABOR

Thus the optimal number of workers per day for this firm is 3. Table 29.3 shows that this is the number of workers at which the value of the marginal product of labor is equal to the price of labor. What is the *value of the marginal product of labor?* It is the marginal product of labor multiplied by the product's price. In Table 29.3, the value of the marginal product of labor is $70 when between 0 and 1 workers are used per day. Why? Because the marginal product of labor is 7 units of output, and the price of a unit of output is $10. Thus this product—7 times $10—equals $70.

To maximize profit, the value of the marginal product of labor must be set equal to the price of labor, because if the value of the marginal product is greater than labor's price, the firm can increase its profit by increasing the quantity used of labor; while if the value of the marginal product is less than labor's price, the firm can increase its profit by reducing the quantity used of labor. Thus *profits must be at a maximum when the value of the marginal product is equal to the price of labor.*

Given the results of this section, it is a simple matter to derive the firm's demand curve for labor. Specifically, its demand curve must be the value-of-marginal-product schedule in the last column of Table 29.3. If the daily wage of a worker is between $51 and $60, the firm will demand 2 workers per day; if the daily wage of a worker is between $41 and $50, the firm will demand 3 workers per day; and so forth. Thus *the firm's demand curve for labor is its value-of-marginal-product curve,* which shows the value of labor's marginal product at each quantity of labor used. This curve is shown in Figure 29.1.[2]

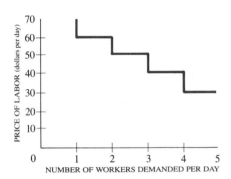

Figure 29.1

The Firm's Demand Curve for Labor under Perfect Competition *The firm's demand curve for labor is the firm's value-of-marginal-product curve, which shows the value of labor's marginal product at each quantity of labor used. The data for this figure come from Table 29.3.*

The Market Demand Curve for Labor

In previous sections, we were concerned with the demand curve of a single firm for labor. But many firms, not just one, are part of the labor market, and the price of labor depends on the demands of all of these firms. The situation is analogous to the price of a product, which depends on the demands of all consumers. *The **market demand curve for labor** shows the relationship between the price of labor and the total amount of labor demanded in the market. That is, it shows, for each price, the amount of labor*

---

[2] Strictly speaking, the firm's demand curve is the same as the curve showing the value of the input's marginal product only if this input is the only variable input. For a discussion of the more general case, see my *Microeconomics: Theory and Applications,* 5th ed., New York: Norton, 1985, Chapter 12.

that will be demanded in the entire market. The market demand curve for labor, like any other input, is quite analogous to the market demand curve for a consumer good, which we discussed in detail in Chapter 21.

But there is at least one important difference. *The demand for labor and other inputs is a **derived demand,** since inputs are demanded to produce other things, not as an end in themselves.* This fact helps to explain why the price elasticity of demand is higher for some inputs than for others. In particular, the larger the price elasticity of demand for the product the input helps produce, the larger the price elasticity of demand for the input. (In addition, the price elasticity of demand for an input is likely to be greater in the long run than in the short run, and greater if other inputs can readily be substituted for the input in question.)

The Market Supply Curve for Labor

We have already seen that a product's price depends on its market supply curve as well as its market demand curve. This is equally true for labor. Its **market supply curve** is *the relationship between the price of labor and the total amount of labor supplied in the market.* When individuals supply labor, they are supplying something they themselves can use, since the time that they do not work can be used for leisure activities. (As Charles Lamb, the English essayist, put it, "Who first invented work, and bound the free and holiday-rejoicing spirit down ... to that dry drudgery at the desk's dead wood?"[3]) Because of this fact, the market supply curve for labor, unlike the supply curve for inputs supplied by business firms, may be **backward bending,** particularly for the economy as a whole. That is, *beyond some point, increases in price may result in smaller amounts of labor being supplied.*

An example of a backward-bending supply curve is provided in Figure 29.2. What factors account for a curve like this? Basically, the reason is that as the price of labor is increased, individuals supplying the labor become richer. And when they become richer, they want to increase their amount of leisure time, which means that they want to work less. Even though the amount of money per hour they give up by not working is greater than when the price of labor was lower, they nonetheless choose to increase their leisure time. This sort of tendency has shown up quite clearly in the last century. As wage rates have increased and living standards have risen, the average work week has tended to decline.

Note that there is no contradiction between the assumption that the supply curve of labor or other inputs *to an individual firm* is horizontal under perfect competition and the fact that the *market* supply curve for the input may not be horizontal. For example, unskilled labor may be available to any firm in a particular area at a given wage rate in as great an amount as it could possibly use. But the total amount of unskilled labor supplied in this area may increase relatively little with increases in the wage rate. The situation is similar to the sale of products. As we saw in Chapter 21, any firm under perfect competition believes that it can sell all

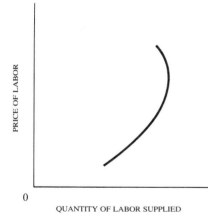

PRICE OF LABOR

0

QUANTITY OF LABOR SUPPLIED

Figure 29.2

Backward-bending Supply Curve for Labor *Beyond some point, increases in the price of labor may result in smaller amounts of labor being supplied. The reason for a supply curve of this sort is that, as the price of labor increases, the individual supplying the labor becomes richer and wants to increase his amount of leisure time.*

---

[3] The answer to Lamb's question is perhaps to be found in Genesis 3:19.

it wants at the existing price. Yet the total amount of the product sold in the entire market can ordinarily be increased only by lowering the price.

Equilibrium Price and Quantity of Labor

Labor's price (or wage rate) is determined under perfect competition in essentially the same way that a product's price is determined—by supply and demand.

The price of labor will tend toward equilibrium at the level where the quantity of labor demanded equals the quantity of labor supplied. Thus, in Figure 29.3, the equilibrium price of labor is *OP.* If the price were higher than *OP,* the quantity supplied would exceed the quantity demanded and there would be downward pressure on the price. If the price were lower than *OP,* the quantity supplied would fall short of the quantity demanded and there would be upward pressure on the price. By the same token, *the equilibrium amount of labor utilized is also given by the intersection of the market supply and demand curves.* In Figure 29.3, *OQ* units of labor will be utilized in equilibrium in the entire market.

Graphs such as Figure 29.3 are useful, but it is important to look behind the geometry, and to recognize the factors that lie behind the demand and supply curves for labor. Consider the market for surgeons and that for unskilled labor. As shown in Figure 29.4, the demand curve for the services of surgeons is to the right of the demand curve for unskilled labor (particularly at high wage rates). Why is this so? Because an hour of a surgeon's services is worth more to people than an hour of an unskilled laborer's services. In this sense, surgeons are more productive than unskilled laborers. Also, as shown in Figure 29.4, the supply curve for the services of surgeons is far to the left of the supply curve for unskilled labor. Why is this so? Because very few people are licensed surgeons, whereas practically everyone can do un-

Figure 29.3

Equilibrium Price and Quantity of Labor *The equilibrium price of labor is* OP, *and the equilibrium quantity of labor used is* OQ.

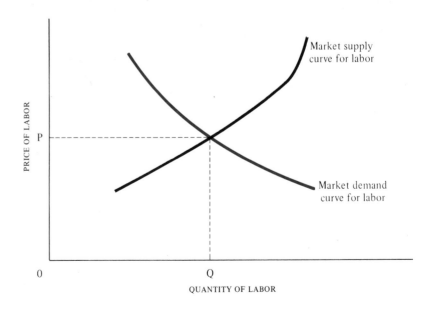

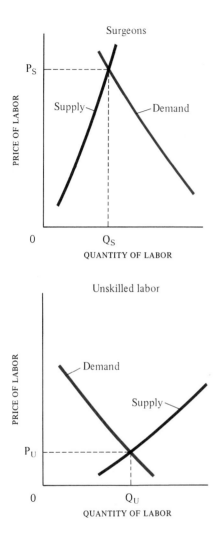

Figure 29.4
The Labor Market for Surgeons and Unskilled Labor *The wage for surgeons is higher than for unskilled labor because the demand curve for surgeons is farther to the right and the supply curve for surgeons is farther to the left than the corresponding curves for unskilled labor.*

skilled labor. In other words, surgeons are much more scarce than unskilled laborers.

For these reasons, surgeons receive a much higher wage rate than do unskilled laborers. As shown in Figure 29.4, the equilibrium price of labor for surgeons is much higher than for unskilled labor. If unskilled laborers could quickly and easily turn themselves into competent surgeons, this difference in wage rates would be eliminated by competition, since unskilled workers would find it profitable to become surgeons. But unskilled workers lack the training and often the ability to become surgeons. Thus surgeons and unskilled labor are examples of **noncompeting groups.** Wage differentials can be expected to persist among noncompeting groups because people cannot move from the low-paid to the high-paid jobs. But this is not the only reason for wage differentials, as we shall see in the next section.

Wage Differentials

Everyone realizes that, even in the same occupation, some people get paid more than others. Why is this true?

Differences in Ability or Skill. One reason for such wage differentials is that people differ in productive capacity; thus each worker differs from the next in the value of his or her output. Under these circumstances, the difference in wages paid to workers equals the difference in their marginal products' value. Consider the case of two lathe operators—Roberta and Leo. Roberta works for firm X and Leo works for firm Y. Roberta (together with the appropriate tools and materials) can produce output worth $2,000 per month and Leo (with the same tools and materials) can produce output worth $1,900 per month. In equilibrium, Roberta will earn $100 more per month than Leo. If the difference in wages were less than $100, Leo's employer would find it profitable to replace Leo with Roberta, since this would increase the value of output by $100 and cost less than $100. If the difference were more than $100, Roberta's employer would find it profitable to replace Roberta with Leo; although this would reduce the value of output by $100, it would reduce costs by more than $100.

Differences in Training. Besides differences in productive capacity and ability, there are many other reasons for wage differentials. Even if all workers were of equal ability, these differentials would still exist to offset differences in the characteristics of various occupations and areas. Some occupations require large investments in training, while other occupations require a much smaller investment in training. Chemists must spend about eight years in undergraduate and graduate training. During each year of training, they incur direct expenses for books, tuition, and the like, and they lose the income they could make if they were to work rather than go to school. Clearly, if their net remuneration is to be as high in chemistry as in other jobs they might take, they must make a greater wage when they get through than persons of comparable age, intelligence, and motivation whose job requires no training beyond high school. The difference in wages must be at least sufficient to compensate for their investment in extra training.

Other Differences. Similarly, members of some occupations must bear larger occupational expenses than others. A psychologist may have to buy testing materials and subscribe to expensive journals. For net compensation to be equalized, such workers must be paid more than others. Also, some jobs are more unstable than others. Some types of construction workers are subject to frequent layoffs and have little job security, whereas many government employees (but not the top ones) are assured stable and secure employment. If the former jobs are to be as attractive as the latter, they must pay more. In addition, other differences among jobs must be offset by

Example 29.1   Millionaire Geologists

On April 16, 1981, the *Wall Street Journal* reported that "many geologists earn more than many chief executive officers. Salaries of $1 million a year are routine for the experienced geologists who are in greatest demand. An independent [oil] company recently offered a senior exploration man at another company $1.5 million; he turned down the offer."

(a) What factors were responsible for the sharp rise in the wage rate for geologists? (b) During the late 1950s and 1960s, when the U.S. began to rely more heavily on foreign crude oil, domestic exploration fell. What do you think was the effect on the number of people entering petroleum engineering? Why? (c) In 1976, the University of Pittsburgh reinstated its petroleum program as part of chemical engineering, but had trouble obtaining faculty for it. Why do you think this trouble developed?

SOLUTION

(a) Because of the hefty increase in the price of crude oil, there was in 1981 a boom in oil drilling, which pushed the demand curve for geologists far to the right (from D_1 to D_2), as shown below. The result is that the wage of a geologist increased from OP_1 to OP_2. (b) Since there was a reduction in the demand for petroleum engineers, less jobs were available, and people turned to other fields. (c) Because potential faculty members were reluctant to leave lucrative jobs in industry to take teaching jobs.*

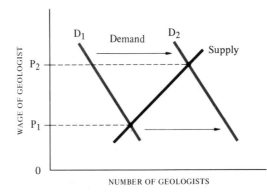

* For further discussion, see "Heated Energy Search Creates Class of Millionaire Oil-Firm Geologists," *Wall Street Journal*, April 16, 1981.

wage differentials if the net remuneration is to be equalized. For instance, there are differences among regions and communities in the cost of living. (Living costs are generally lower in small towns than in big cities.)

The All-Volunteer Army: A Case Study

In recent years there has been considerable controversy concerning the advantages and disadvantages of an all-volunteer army, the system used in this country since the early 1970s. Many economists have argued that recruiting an all-volunteer army is more efficient and equitable than relying on the draft, which through a complicated system of deferments and exemptions, as well as a lottery system, selected a certain number of young men for military service. Proponents of an all-volunteer army point out that it is more compatible with freedom of choice than the draft. In addition, they say that military personnel are used more effectively because the price of such personnel is a more realistic indicator of its value in alternative uses. Further, they point out that the cost of military manpower is distributed more equitably among the members of society. Under the draft a small group of draftees bore a large share of the cost, because they received less in wages than would have been required to induce them to volunteer.

Other economists and social observers oppose an all-volunteer army. They point out that the present system can hardly be expected to produce the necessary military manpower in a full-scale war. They also contend that an army of "paid mercenaries" might constitute a political danger by attempting to gain improper power. Some claim too that an all-volunteer army relies disproportionately on the black population, since young blacks constitute a much larger percentage of those without civilian jobs than their white counterparts.

How did the all-volunteer army come into being? In 1964, President Johnson asked that a study be made to determine whether it would be possible to shift from reliance on the draft to a system in which defense manpower needs would be met entirely by volunteers. A team of economists attempted to learn what it would cost.[4] Essentially they applied the kind of analysis described in this chapter. The basic approach was to estimate the supply curve for labor to the Department of Defense.

Figure 29.5 shows the relationship between the proportion of the male population that enlists and the level of military pay (as a percent of civilian pay), the unemployment rate being held constant at two alternative levels. As would be expected, the number of enlistments increases with the level of military pay and the unemployment rate. Using this supply curve, which was estimated by the economists, one could determine (for given values of the unemployment rate) the level of military pay that was required to bring forth the number of extra enlistments needed to eliminate the draft.

According to the economists, a 60 to 90 percent increase in enlistments

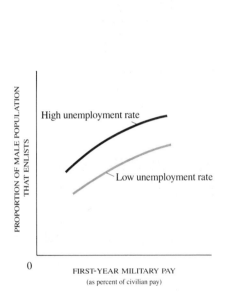

Figure 29.5

Relationship between Military Pay and Number of Enlistments *Holding the unemployment rate constant, the proportion of the male population that enlists is directly related to the level of military pay (as a percent of civilian pay). Using this supply curve, economists determined the level of military pay required to bring forth the extra enlistments needed to eliminate the draft.*

---

[4] See S. Altman and A. Fechter, "The Supply of Military Personnel in the Absence of a Draft," *American Economic Review,* May 1967; and literature cited there.

An interesting development in recent years, due to Harvard's Michael Spence, is the theory of market signaling. In 1981, Spence received the John Bates Clark medal (given every two years by the American Economic Association to the most distinguished economist under 40 years of age), in part for his seminal work on this topic. To illustrate what signaling is, suppose for simplicity that there are two distinctly different types of workers (high ability and low ability) that an employer can hire. The marginal product of high-ability workers is greater than that of low-ability workers. However, the employer cannot be sure whether a particular worker is high-ability or low-ability until after the worker has been hired. This is because it takes time on the job for the employer to determine the capabilities and productivity of the worker.

Michael Spence

If the employer regards the educational level of a job applicant as a signal, or indicator, of the worker's ability, it may pay workers to invest in their education in order to signal the employer that they in fact are able. Of course, Mary Stuart, in getting an education, may not think of herself as signaling. She will invest in education if there is sufficient return, which will depend on how much more the employer is willing to pay for highly educated than for poorly educated workers.

Assuming that the difficulty (and thus the cost) of attaining a higher educational level is less for high-ability than for low-ability people, it is clear that high-ability people will have more incentive than low-ability people to get high levels of education. Thus the employer's belief that educational level is an effective indicator, or signal, of ability and productivity will be reinforced by experience. Consequently, the employer will continue to find it profitable to offer a higher wage to job applicants with relatively high levels of education, since such applicants are more likely to be high-ability people. Thus high-ability individuals will continue to find it economically worthwhile to invest relatively heavily in their educations.

An important thing to note is that, to the individual, it appears that higher education is a prerequisite to a high-paying job. After all, under these circumstances, the employer pays more for people with more education. Also, to an outside observer, it appears that education enhances the productivity of the worker. This seems to be true because the better-educated people have higher productivity and earn bigger wages than the less-educated people. In fact, however, even if education has no effect on productivity and is only a signal of a person's ability, there will be a direct relationship between a person's education, on the one hand, and his or her productivity and wages, on the other.

was needed to eliminate the draft. To bring forth these extra enlistments, they estimated on the basis of the supply curve that first-term military pay for enlisted men had to be increased by about 110 percent (if the unemployment rate were 5.5 percent). Using 1964 military earnings as a base, increases in first-term pay for enlisted men had to be about $3,000 to attract enough volunteers to maintain a 2.65-million-man defense force. Multiplying 2.65 million men by the average increase in pay, the economists estimated that the increased cost to the Defense Department would be about $5 billion per year.[5] This estimate was very crude, as the economists stressed, since many noneconomic factors influenced the enlistment rate and the data and underlying assumptions were rough.

By 1973, the draft was no longer being used to obtain military manpower. Whether it will be reactivated in the near future is hard to say. For present purposes, the important point is that economic analysis, based on the fundamental concepts in this chapter, played a very significant role in the discussion and resolution of this major issue. And if conditions or attitudes change so that this issue must be reconsidered, you can be sure that economists will continue to play a significant role in its resolution.

Monopsony

In previous sections, we have assumed that perfect competition exists in the labor market. In some cases, however, *monopsony* exists instead. *A monopsony is a market structure where there is a single buyer.* Thus a single firm may hire all the labor in an isolated "company town," such as exists in the coal-mining regions of West Virginia and Kentucky. What determines the price of labor under monopsony? Suppose the firm's demand curve for labor and the supply curve of labor are as shown in Figure 29.6. Because the firm is the sole buyer of labor, it takes into account the fact that to acquire more labor it must pay a higher wage to *all* workers, not just the extra workers. For example, if the firm wants to increase the number of workers it employs from 5 to 6, it may have to pay the sixth an hourly wage of $5. If the supply curve of labor slopes upward to the right, this wage is more than was required to obtain the first 5 workers. Since the firm must pay all workers the same wage to avoid labor unrest, it must raise the wages of the first 5 workers to the level of the sixth, if it hires the sixth worker. Thus *the cost of hiring the sixth worker exceeds the wage that must be paid this worker.*

The supply curve for labor in Figure 29.6 shows the cost of hiring an additional worker, if workers already employed do *not* have to be paid a higher wage when the additional worker is hired. Thus this supply curve does *not* show the true additional cost to the monopsonist of hiring an additional worker, for the reasons given in the previous paragraph. Instead, curve *A,* which includes the extra wages that must be paid to the workers already employed, shows the true additional cost. For the reasons given above, curve *A* lies above the supply curve.

[5] Note that the average increase in pay is less than the average increase in first-term pay. The way Altman and Fechter proceed from the latter to the former is described in their work. Also, note that the costs to the Defense Department, which are estimated here, may be quite different from the social costs of switching to an all-volunteer army.

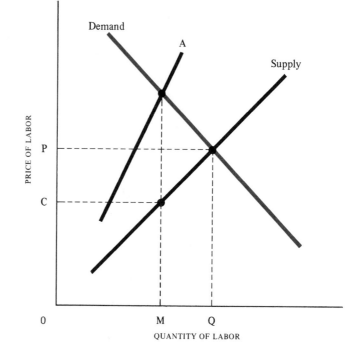

Figure 29.6
Equilibrium Wage and Quantity of Labor under Monopsony *The monopsonistic firm, if it maximizes profit, will hire laborers up to the point where the extra cost of adding an extra laborer, shown by curve* A, *equals the extra revenue from adding the extra laborer, shown by the demand curve for labor.*

If profit is maximized, the monopsonistic firm will hire labor up to the point at which the extra cost of adding an additional laborer (shown by curve *A*) equals the extra revenue from adding the additional laborer (shown by the demand curve). Thus the quantity of labor purchased will be *OM* and the price of labor will be *OC* in Figure 29.6. In contrast, under perfectly competitive conditions the equilibrium quantity and price would be at the intersection of the demand and supply curves. That is, the quantity of labor purchased would be *OQ* and the price of labor would be *OP*.

What is the effect of monopsony on the wage rate and the amount of labor hired? In general, *the wage rate, as well as the quantity hired, is lower under monopsony than under perfect competition.* This is the case in Figure 29.6, and it will generally hold true. This makes sense. One would expect a monopsonist, free from the pressures of competition, to pay workers less than would be required under perfect competition.

Test Yourself

1. Suppose that a perfectly competitive firm's production function is as follows:

Quantity of labor (man-years)	Ouput per year (thousands of units)
0	0
1	3.0
2	5.0
3	6.8
4	8.0
5	9.0

The firm is a profit maximizer, and the labor market is competitive. Labor must be hired in integer numbers and for a year (no more, no less). If the firm hires 4 man-years of labor, and if the price of a unit of the firm's product is $3, one can establish a range for what the annual wage prevailing in the labor market must be. What is the maximum amount it can be? What is the minimum amount? Why? Do these numbers seem realistic? Why or why not?

2. Based on the data in Question 1, plot the marginal product of labor at various utilization rates of labor. Also, plot the value of labor's marginal product at each quantity of labor used.

3. Suppose that the firm in Question 1 were a monopsonist. Do you think that it would pay a lower, higher, or the same wage rate as under the conditions described in Question 1? Why?

4. Suppose that the marginal product of skilled labor to a perfectly competitive firm is 2 units and the price of skilled labor is $4 an hour, while the marginal product of unskilled labor is 1 unit and the price of unskilled labor is $2.50 an hour. Is the firm minimizing its costs? Explain. (*Hint:* Regard skilled labor and unskilled labor as two separate inputs, and apply the cost-minimization rule in Chapter 23.)

Labor Unions

About 1 in 6 nonfarm workers in the United States belongs to a union, and the perfectly competitive model does not apply to these workers any more than it does to monopsonistic labor markets. There are about 200 national unions in the United States; the biggest are the Teamsters, the National Education Association, and the Food and Commercial Workers, each with 1.3 million members or more. Next come the United Auto Workers, the United Steel Workers, the Electrical Workers, the Machinists, the Carpenters, the State, County, and Municipal Employees, and the Service Employees, each with over 800,000 members.

The *national unions*[6] are of great importance in the American labor movement. The supreme governing body of the national union is the convention, which is held every year or two. The delegates to the convention have the authority to set policy for the union. However, considerable power is exercised by the national union's officers. Union presidents—men like Owen Bieber of the Auto Workers and Jackie Presser of the Teamsters—exercise great power.

A national union is composed of *local unions,* each in a given area or plant. Some local unions have only a few members, but others have thousands. The local union, with its own president and officers, often plays an important role in collective bargaining. The extent to which the local unions maintain their autonomy varies from one national union to another. In industries where markets are localized (like construction and printing), the locals are more autonomous than in industries where markets are national (like steel, automobiles, and coal).

Finally, there is the AFL-CIO, a federation of national unions created by the merger of the American Federation of Labor and the Congress of Industrial Organizations in 1955. The AFL-CIO does not include all national unions. The United Mine Workers refused to join the AFL-CIO, the Auto Workers left it in 1968, and the Teamsters were kicked out (because of corruption). The AFL-CIO is a very important spokesman for the American labor movement; but because the national unions in the AFL-CIO have given up relatively little of their power to the federation, its authority is limited.

---

[6] Sometimes they are called international unions because some locals are outside the United States—for example, in Canada.

The American Labor Movement

EARLY HISTORY OF AMERICAN LABOR UNIONS

To understand the nature and behavior of labor unions, it is necessary to look briefly at the history of the American labor movement. Unions arose because workers recognized that acting together gave them more bargaining power than acting separately. They frequently felt that they were at the mercy of their employers, and they formed fraternal societies and unions to promote economic and social benefits for the members. The first recorded case of collective bargaining in the United States took place in 1799, when Philadelphia shoemakers negotiated collectively with their employers.

However, until the 1930s unions in the United States were not very strong, partly because of employers' efforts to break up unions, and partly because the courts held that the unions' attempts to increase wages and influence working conditions were conspiracies in restraint of trade. It is not difficult to understand the antiunion feelings of management, but it is difficult to exonerate the ruthlessness with which some managements attempted to stamp out unionism. Not only were prounion workers fired and blacklisted; they were sometimes beaten up or locked out of the plant. And when strikes occurred, strike breakers were sometimes hired to teach the striking workers a lesson.

The courts were also hostile to unions. The prevailing doctrine in much of the nineteenth century was that unions were criminal conspiracies, and even when this doctrine was abandoned, the courts frequently regarded strikes, picketing, and other such union tactics as illegal. In addition, they sometimes used the Sherman Act of 1890 to stop unions, on the grounds that unions were conspiracies to restrain trade. Moreover, the courts often issued *injunctions,* which are cease-and-desist orders, to prevent unions from striking, boycotting, picketing, or carrying out other activities against the interests of their employers. In this way, the courts prevented unions from utilizing their potential power effectively.

THE AMERICAN FEDERATION OF LABOR

In 1886, the *American Federation of Labor* came into existence. In contrast to many early unions, which were aimed at political goals, the AFL, led by Samuel Gompers, concentrated on economic issues. Basically, the AFL was an association of national *craft unions,* each of which was autonomous; but although it had limited power over the national unions, Gompers was a very important spokesman for the American labor movement.

The AFL came to be the dominant federation in American labor history, and its philosophy exerted great influence on the development of trade unionism in the United States. This philosophy was built on several tenets. First, *Gompers and his associates felt that it would be a mistake to promote the development of a labor party in the United States.* The AFL would try to elect its friends and defeat its enemies, but it would not form a third party and it would not align itself with either of the two major political parties. Second, *the AFL would concentrate its efforts on bread-*

and-butter economic issues, not on attempts to alter the basic form of society. Higher wages and better working conditions, not social revolution or elimination of private property, were its aims. Third, *the AFL was suspicious of government regulation.* It felt that the interests of labor would be served best if the government interfered as little as possible in collective bargaining.

The AFL was relatively successful in increasing union membership; total union membership was about 2 million in 1904 and about 5 million in 1920. In part, this increase resulted from tight labor markets and the government's support of collective bargaining during World War I in return for labor's help in the war effort. After the war, union membership dropped from more than 5 million to about 2.6 million in 1933 (due in part to the onset of the Great Depression). The period after World War I was marked by strong antiunion sentiments. Employers resisted unions strenuously—and successfully. For example, in 1919 the U.S. Steel Corporation—led by our old friend from Chapter 27, Elbert Gary—crushed a strike resulting from an attempt to organize its plants. Firms pushed hard for an "American Plan" under which union members would not be hired. Certainly the 1920s were a difficult period for American labor unions.

THE NEW DEAL AND WORLD WAR II

During the early 1930s, the tide began to turn. To a great extent, this was because of government encouragement of unions, in which the first important step was the *Norris-La Guardia Act* of 1932. This act made it much more difficult for courts to issue injunctions against unions, and it made *yellow-dog contracts*—agreements in which workers promised their employers not to join a union—unenforceable in federal courts. The next important step occurred in 1935, when Congress passed the *Wagner Act,* which made it an unfair labor practice for employers to refuse to bargain collectively with unions representing a majority of their workers, or to interfere with their workers' right to organize. In addition, this act established the *National Labor Relations Board* to investigate unfair labor practices, to issue orders enforceable in federal courts, and to hold elections to determine which, if any, union would represent various groups of employees. The Wagner Act was a very important factor in encouraging the growth of labor unions in the United States—so important that it has often been called American labor's Magna Carta.

Another important factor in the growth of unions during the 1930s was the emergence of *industrial unions.* The more favorable atmosphere for union organization and growth led to the creation in 1935 of a new federation, the *Congress of Industrial Organizations.* The unions that created and formed the CIO rebelled against the AFL's apparent inability to take advantage of the opportunity to organize the mass-production industries like autos and steel. The AFL was composed primarily of unions organized along craft lines. The carpenters had one union, the machinists had another union, and so on for other crafts. This is in contrast to industrial unions, which include all workers in a particular plant or industry.

The young CIO, led by the United Mine Workers' president John L. Lewis, set out to establish industrial unions in the mass-production indus-

tries.[7] The CIO was very successful in its organization drives during the late 1930s. In 1937 U.S. Steel, formerly a bulwark of antiunionism, recognized the Steelworkers as bargaining agent for its more than 200,000 workers. Using the sit-down strike—in which strikers occupy the plant—as a weapon, workers in the automobile and rubber industries organized CIO unions too. In addition, the CIO organized unions in electrical machinery, petroleum refining, textiles, meat packing, longshoring, and other industries.[8]

The 1930s were a period of spectacular union growth. Aided by the prounion attitude of the Roosevelt administration, the new legislation, and the energy of its leaders, total union membership rose from less than 3 million in 1933 to more than 10 million in 1941. World War II witnessed a further growth in total union membership. Stimulated by the increase in total employment and the government's favorable attitude toward their growth, unions increased their membership from over 10 million in 1941 to almost 15 million—or about 36 percent of all nonfarm workers—in 1945. As in World War I, the government helped unions gain recognition in exchange for union cooperation in promoting war production. By the end of World War II, labor unions were conspicuous and powerful features of the economic landscape.

Postwar Developments

CREATION AND STRUCTURE OF THE AFL-CIO

In 1955, a merger occurred between the AFL and the CIO. Given the acrimony marking the relationship between these two organizations in the 1930s, the merger may seem surprising. But the differences in their attitudes toward the question of organization along industrial versus craft lines had diminished in importance over the years. And the old leaders, including those like Lewis of the Mine Workers and Hutcheson of the Carpenters who had traded blows in earlier days, had died—or, as in Lewis's case, were no longer in either federation.[9]

Moreover, the merger had advantages. The labor movement, despite large-scale organization drives in the south after the war, was unable to increase union membership appreciably during the 1950s. Many unions attributed this fact to the rivalry between the AFL and the CIO and argued that a united front would result in increased membership. Also, and perhaps most important, Congress passed several pieces of legislation, including the Taft-Hartley Act of 1947, that were heartily disliked by the

[7] Before leaving the AFL, Lewis emphasized the strength of his convictions by knocking down and bloodying up his principal opponent, William Hutcheson, president of the Carpenters' Union, on the floor of the 1935 AFL convention.

[8] Confronted with the CIO's successes, the AFL also organized new industrial unions, although craft unions remained by far the most important part of the federation.

[9] Lewis resigned from the presidency of the CIO because workers would not follow his lead and vote for Wendell Willkie for president of the United States in 1940. Later he took his union back into the AFL, but withdrew from the AFL in 1947 because the AFL did not boycott the National Labor Relations Board in an effort to defeat the Taft-Hartley Act.

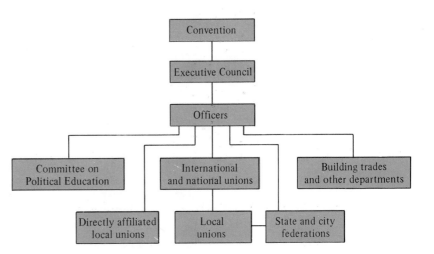

Figure 29.7
Structure of AFL-CIO *The AFL-CIO, which resulted from a merger of the AFL and CIO in 1955, is organized with the governing power in the hands of a biennial convention.*

unions, and it was felt that the merger would increase labor's political clout.

The AFL-CIO is organized along the lines indicated in Figure 29.7. The organization closely resembles that of the AFL (the larger of the merging federations). The constitution of the AFL-CIO puts supreme governing power in the hands of a biennial convention. The national unions are represented at these conventions on the basis of their dues-paying membership. Between conventions, the AFL-CIO's business is directed by its president (Lane Kirkland in 1985) and secretary-treasurer, as well as by various committees and councils composed of representatives of various national unions or people elected at the convention. The AFL-CIO contains seven trade and industrial departments, such as building trades, food and beverage trades, maritime trades, and so forth. Also, as indicated by Figure 29.7, a few local unions are not affiliated with a national union, but are directly affiliated with the AFL-CIO.

INTERNAL PROBLEMS IN LABOR UNIONS

As unions have grown older and more secure and powerful, there has been more and more concern about the nature of their internal practices and leadership. After all, they are no longer the underdogs that they were 50 years ago. They are huge organizations with immense power. Both in this country and in Europe, observers have charged that unions are often far from democratic. Members are frequently apathetic, for there is less interest in union affairs now than in the early days when unions were fighting for survival; and the leadership of some unions has become entrenched and bureaucratic. Moreover, there are frequent charges that unions engage in racial and other forms of discrimination.

Another problem is *corruption within labor unions*. In the 1950s, a Senate committee—the so-called McClellan Committee—conducted lengthy and revealing investigations which showed that the leaders of the Teamsters Union had misused union funds, had questionable relations with the underworld, and had "shamefully betrayed their own members." Other unions were also accused of corrupt practices. It is important, however, to avoid smearing the entire labor movement. Although racketeering and fraud unquestionably are problems, they tend to be localized in relatively few industries—particularly the building trades, trucking, longshoring, laundries, and hotels. Many responsible and honest leaders of the labor movement have tried hard to rid the labor movement of these unsavory practices.

POSTWAR LABOR LEGISLATION

After World War II, public sentiment turned somewhat against unions. Strikes and higher prices got under the skin of the consumer as well as the employer, and there began to be a lot of talk in Congress and elsewhere about the prewar Wagner Act having been too one-sided, giving the advantages to labor and the penalties to the employer. In 1947, despite bitter labor opposition, the *Taft-Hartley Act* was passed, with the purpose of redressing the balance between labor and employers. The act established standards of conduct for unions as well as employers, defined unfair union practices, and stated that unions can be sued for acts of their agents. Also, the act outlawed the closed shop, which requires that firms hire only workers who are already union members, and stipulated that, unless the workers agree in writing, the ***checkoff*** is illegal. (The checkoff is a system in which the employer deducts union dues from each worker's pay and hands them over to the union.)

In addition, the act tried to increase protection against strikes in which the public's safety and health are involved. If the president decides that an actual or impending strike imperils the national health or safety, he can appoint a fact-finding committee to investigate the situation. After receiving the committee's report, he can tell the attorney general to obtain an injunction forbidding a strike for 80 days, during which the parties can continue to negotiate. A Federal Mediation Service was established to help the parties settle such negotiations. The act does not forbid a strike at the end of the 80 days, if no agreement has been reached.

In response to the evidence of union corruption presented by the McClellan Committee, Congress passed the *Landrum-Griffin Act* in 1959. This act attempts to protect the rights of individual union members from abuse by union leaders. It contains a "bill of rights" for labor, guaranteeing that each member can participate in union elections, that elections be held by secret ballot, and that other steps be taken to protect the rights of the members. It also requires unions to file financial reports, forbids payments (beyond wages) by employers to union representatives, and prohibits loans exceeding $2,000 by unions to union officials.

Recent Trends in Union Membership

In recent years, union membership has increased rather modestly; indeed, during the late 1950s and early 1960s, it didn't increase at all. To some extent, this has been due to dissension within the labor movement and to a diminution of the zeal that characterized the movement in earlier years. Also, rightly or wrongly, unions have lost a certain amount of public sympathy and respect because of racial discrimination, unpopular strikes, evidence of corruption, and the belief that they are responsible in considerable part for cost-push inflation. But these factors only partly explain this lack of growth. In addition, important changes in the labor force have tended to reduce union membership.

Specifically, the increasing proportion of *white-collar workers* seems to have raised important problems for unions. To date, unions have made relatively little progress in organizing white-collar workers. In the early 1960s, only about 3 percent of engineers, and about 9 percent of office workers were union members. One reason for this lack of progress is that white-collar employees tend to identify with management. Also, the increasing proportion of *women* in the labor force seems to raise important problems for unions. It is sometimes claimed that female workers are harder to organize because they do not stay in the labor force very long

Example 29.2   Can a Union Increase Employment?

In many isolated areas, a single firm is the only employer of a certain kind of labor. Suppose that a textile firm is in this position, and that its demand curve for labor, as well as the supply curve for labor, are shown below. Curve A shows the extra cost to the firm of adding an extra laborer.

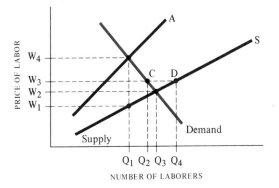

(a) How many laborers will the firm hire, and how much will each be paid? (b) Suppose that a union enters the market and that it sets a wage of OW_3. What now is the supply curve for labor? (c) How many laborers will the firm hire now? Is employment higher than before the union entered? (d) Will there be involuntary unemployment now?

SOLUTION

(a) The firm will hire OQ_1 laborers and pay a wage of OW_1, in accord with our discussion of monopsony. (b) It is W_3DS, because the firm cannot pay a wage below OW_3 under the assumed circumstances. (c) The firm will hire OQ_2 workers, since the extra cost of hiring an extra worker equals OW_3 so long as less than OQ_4 workers are hired. Employment is higher than before the union entered (when it was OQ_1). (d) Yes. At a wage of OW_3, OQ_4 workers will seek employment but only OQ_2 workers will be hired. Thus $(OQ_4 - OQ_2)$ workers will be involuntarily unemployed.

and because they are concentrated in jobs—clerical and sales positions—that are difficult to organize. Nonetheless, almost 1 in 5 union members in 1962 were women; and the majority of the Retail Clerks, the Clothing Workers, and the International Ladies' Garment Workers were women.

However, even though union membership has not been growing in recent years, it would be a mistake to jump to the conclusion that the American labor movement is stagnant or that unions are declining in importance. For one thing, membership is not a very good measure of power. A small union can sometimes bring an enormous amount of pressure to bear if it is located strategically in the economy. Also, union membership has been growing rapidly in some areas, notably *public employment.* Between 1956 and 1968, union membership among public employees grew from 915,000 to 2,155,000, with the bulk of the membership in six unions, three of federal employees and three of state and local employees.[10] For many years, there was a tradition, as well as legal prohibitions, against strikes by public employees. But during the 1960s, when these workers seemed to be left behind economically, various executive orders and legislative enactments encouraged unionism among public employees.

STRIKES BY PUBLIC EMPLOYEES

A nettlesome problem regarding the unionization of public employees is related to strikes. Since such employees man vital public services, a strike can bring a community or state to its knees. In four states—Pennsylvania, Hawaii, Oregon, and Vermont—strikes of this sort are legal. But the fact that they are forbidden by law in other states, such as New York, does not prevent walkouts by teachers, sanitation workers, or other state and local employees from being a fairly common occurrence. The public, naturally, becomes indignant when strikes of this sort occur, and the question of whether or not public employees should be able to walk off the job provokes heated debate.

In 1981, there was a well-publicized confrontation between a public-employee union and the government. When the Professional Air Traffic Controllers Organization (PATCO) went on strike, President Reagan responded by saying that the strike was illegal, and he ultimately fired the striking controllers. The nation managed to get along with only 10,000 controllers—supervisors, nonstrikers, military personnel, and new trainees. In October 1981, the Federal Labor Relations Authority stripped the union of its right to represent controllers. This was a stern message to unionized public employees, and one that has not been forgotten. In the immediate future, it seems likely that they will be less likely to call strikes of this sort.

---

[10] The three unions of federal employees are the American Federation of Government Employees, the National Association of Letter Carriers, and the United Federation of Postal Clerks. The three unions of state and local employees are the American Federation of State, County, and Municipal Employees; the American Federation of Teachers; and the International Association of Firefighters.

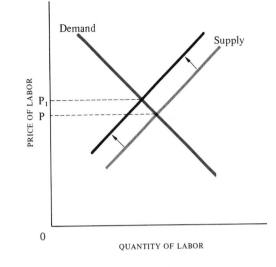

Figure 29.8

Shift of Supply Curve for Labor *A union may shift the supply curve to the left by getting employers to hire only union members and then restricting union membership, or by other techniques.*

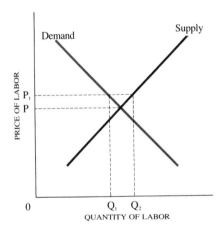

Figure 29.9

Direct Increase in Price of Labor *A union may get the employer to raise the wage from OP to OP₁, and let the higher wage reduce the opportunity for work. This is commonly done by strong industrial unions.*

How Unions Increase Wages

Unions wield considerable power, and economists must include them in their analysis if they want their models of the labor market to reflect conditions in the real world. We shall now see how this is done. Let us begin by supposing that a union wants to increase the wage rate paid its members. How can it accomplish this objective? In other words, how can it alter the market supply curve for labor, or the market demand curve for labor, so that the price of labor—its wage—will increase?

1. The union may try to shift the supply curve of labor to the left. It may shift the supply curve, as shown in Figure 29.8, with the result that the price of labor will increase from OP to OP_1. How can the union cause this shift in the supply curve? Craft unions have frequently forced employers to hire only union members, and then restricted union membership by high initiation fees, reduction in new membership, and other devices. In addition, unions have favored legislation to reduce immigration, shorten working hours, and limit the labor supply in other ways.

2. The union may try to get the employers to pay a higher wage, while allowing some of the supply of labor forthcoming at this higher wage to find no opportunity for work. In Figure 29.9, the union may exert pressure on the employers to raise the price of labor from OP to OP_1. At OP_1, not all of the available supply of labor can find jobs. The quantity of labor supplied is OQ_2, while the amount of labor demanded is OQ_1. The effect is the same as in Figure 29.8, but in this case the union does not limit the supply directly. It lets the higher wage reduce the opportunity for work. Strong industrial unions often behave in this fashion. Having organized practically all the relevant workers and controlling the labor supply, the union raises the wage to OP_1. This is a common and important case.

3. The union may try to shift the demand curve for labor upward and to the right. If it can bring about the shift described in Figure 29.10, the price of labor will increase from OP to OP_2. To cause this shift in the demand for labor, the union may resort to **featherbedding.** That is, it may try to restrict

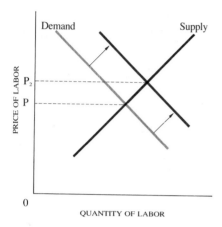

Figure 29.10
Shift in Demand Curve for Labor *A
union may shift the demand curve for
labor to the right by featherbedding or
other devices, thus increasing the wage
from OP to OP₂.*

Basic Idea #58: *Unions were organized
because workers recognized that acting
together gave them more bargaining
power than acting separately. To
increase wages, unions frequently have
shifted the supply curve for labor to the
left, and shifted the demand curve for
labor to the right. Besides higher wages,
unions have tried to promote job
security and other benefits for their
members.*

output per worker in order to increase the amount of labor required to do a
certain job. (To cite but one case, the railroad unions have insisted on much
unnecessary labor.) Unions also try to shift the demand curve by helping
the employers compete against other industries, or by helping to make
Congress pass legislation that protects the employers from foreign competition.

Collective Bargaining

Collective bargaining is the process of negotiation between the union and
management over wages and working conditions. Representatives of the
union and management meet periodically to work out an agreement or
contract; this process generally begins a few months before the old labor
contract runs out. Typically, each side asks at first for more than it expects
to get, and compromises must be made to reach an agreement. The union
representatives take the agreement to their members, who must vote to
accept or reject it. If they reject it, they may vote to strike or to continue to
negotiate.

Collective bargaining agreements vary greatly. Some pertain to only a
single plant while others apply to an entire industry. However, an agreement generally contains the following elements. It specifies the extent and
kind of recognition that management gives the union, the level of wage
rates for particular jobs, the length of the work week, the rate of overtime
pay, the extent to which seniority will determine which workers will be
first to be laid off, the nature and extent of management's prerogatives,
and how grievances between workers and the employer will be handled.

Historically, industries and firms have extended recognition to unions
by accepting one of three arrangements—the closed shop, the union shop,
or the open shop. In a *closed shop,* workers must be union members before
they can be hired. This gives the union more power than if there is a *union
shop,* in which the employer can hire nonunion workers who must then
become union members in a certain length of time after being hired. In an
open shop, the employer can hire union or nonunion labor, and nonunion
workers need not, once employed, join the union. As we have seen, the
closed shop was banned by the Taft-Hartley Act. The Taft-Hartley Act
also says that the union shop is legal unless outlawed by state laws; and in
about 20 states there are "right to work" laws that make the union shop
illegal. Needless to say, these right-to-work laws are hated by organized
labor, which regards them as a threat to its security and effectiveness.

BASIC FORCES AT WORK

Collective bargaining is a power struggle. At each point in their negotiations, both the union and the employer must compare the costs (or benefits) of agreeing with the other party with the costs (or benefits) of continuing to disagree. The costs of disagreement are the costs of a strike,
while the costs of agreement are the costs of settling on terms other than
one's own. These costs are determined by basic market forces. For example, during periods when demand is great, employers are more likely to

grant large wage increases because the costs of disagreement seem higher (a strike will prove more costly) than those of settlement. The outcome of the negotiations will depend on the relative strength of the parties. The strength of the employers depends on their ability to withstand a strike. The strength of the unions depends on their ability to keep out nonunion workers and to enlist the support of other unions, as well as on the size of their financial reserves.

In the early 1980s, many important unions cut back on their wage requests. In the automobile industry, American firms were finding it difficult to compete with their Japanese rivals, and many experts attributed this partly to the very high wages in the U.S. auto industry. In the trucking industry, unionized firms were finding it increasingly difficult to compete with nonunion firms. More and more union members in industries like autos, trucking, steel, rubber, and the airlines began to worry about the effects of hefty wage increases on whether or not they would have jobs. The climate for collective bargaining was quite different than in earlier years.

To illustrate, consider the labor negotiations in the auto industry in 1984. In September 1984, after two months of bargaining, the United Auto Workers struck 13 General Motors plants. About a week later, a settlement was reached, which called for wage increases of only about 2 percent per year. However, General Motors agreed to put $1 billion into a pool to pay workers whose jobs have been eliminated due to automation or the movement of production to overseas plants.

The Pros and Cons of Big Unions

Finally, we should discuss briefly some of the criticisms that are made of the big unions. These criticisms are based largely on their monopoly power. Critics charge that by exerting such power, unions push up the price of labor and reduce the level of employment in various industries. This results in badly allocated resources, since wage rates no longer signal accurately the relative scarcity of labor of various types. Moreover, it is argued that the resulting upward pressure on wages is an important element in cost-push inflation. Opponents of big unions have proposed at least four policies designed to reduce their power—first, that the antitrust laws be applied to unions as well as firms; second, that industry-wide bargaining, which allows a union to shut down an entire industry, be banned; third, that the union shop be banned; and fourth, that big unions be broken up into a number of smaller ones.

On the other hand, many economists feel that labor unions are an important positive force in the American economy. They argue that it is foolish to believe that without unions labor markets would be perfectly competitive—and that the price of labor would be the proper one from the point of view of resource allocation. They point out that unions tend to be an antidote to the monopsonistic power held by some employers in the labor market. And they argue that unions are not really the prime movers in cost-push inflation, but rather that unions often respond to prior price increases by firms. Thus economists are divided in their attitudes toward the growth and power of big unions.

649

Test Yourself

1. "The unions should not be exempt from the antitrust laws." Comment and evaluate.

2. State the principal provisions of (a) the Wagner Act, (b) the Taft-Hartley Act, (c) the Landrum-Griffin Act, and (d) the Norris-La Guardia Act.

3. Suppose that you were the president of a small firm that hired nonunion labor. How would you go about estimating the marginal product of a certain worker, or of certain types of workers? Would it be easy? If not, does this mean that the theory of wage determination is incorrect or useless?

4. Describe the various ways that labor unions can influence the wage rate. Do you think that they attempt to maximize the wage rate? If not, what do you think their objectives are?

Summary

1. Assuming perfect competition, a firm will employ each type of labor in an amount such that its marginal product times the product's price equals its wage. In other words, the firm will employ enough labor so that the value of the marginal product of labor equals labor's price.

2. The firm's demand curve for labor—which shows, for each price of labor, the amount of labor the firm will use—is the firm's value-of-marginal-product curve (if labor is the only variable input). The market demand curve for labor shows the relationship between its price and the total amount of labor demanded in the market.

3. Labor's price depends on its market supply curve as well as on its market demand curve. Labor's market supply curve is the relationship between the price of labor and the total amount of labor supplied in the market. (Labor's market supply curve may be backward bending.)

4. An input's price is determined under perfect competition in essentially the same way that a product's price is determined—by supply and demand. The price of labor will tend in equilibrium to the level at which the quantity of labor demanded equals the quantity of labor supplied. By the same token, the equilibrium amount of labor utilized is also given by the intersection of the market supply and demand curves.

5. If there are qualitative differences among workers, the differential in their wages will reflect the differential in their marginal products. Also, even if all workers were of equal ability, there would still be differences in wage rates to offset differences among occupations in the cost of training and stability of earnings, and geographical differences in the cost of living.

6. There are about 200 national unions in the United States, the biggest being the Teamsters. Each national union is composed of local unions, which operate within the context of the constitution of the national union.

7. The AFL-CIO is a federation of national unions created by the merger in 1955 of the American Federation of Labor and the Congress of Industrial Organizations. The AFL-CIO is a very important spokesman for the American labor

movement, but because the national unions in the AFL-CIO have given up relatively little of their power to the federation, its authority is limited.

8. There are several ways that unions can increase wages—by shifting the supply curve of labor to the left, by shifting the demand curve for labor to the right, and by influencing the wage directly. Collective bargaining is the process of negotiation between union and management over wages and working conditions. An agreement generally specifies the extent and kind of recognition that management gives the union—such as the union shop or open shop. In addition, it specifies the level of wage rates for particular jobs, the length of the work week, the rate of overtime pay, the extent to which seniority will determine which workers will be first to be laid off, the nature and extent of management's prerogatives, and how grievances between workers and the employer will be handled. The union's power is based to a considerable extent on its right to strike.

9. Critics of big unions charge that they possess considerable monopoly power, and that, by pushing up the price of labor and reducing the level of employment, they cause a misallocation of resources and contribute to cost-push inflation. Opponents of big unions often suggest that the antitrust laws be applied to them and that other measures be adopted to curb their power. Supporters of big unions reply that it is foolish to believe that the price of labor would be the proper one from the point of view of resource allocation if there were no big unions. Moreover, they argue that unions are needed to offset the monopsonistic power of employers, and they deny that unions are the prime movers in cost-push inflation.

Concepts for Review

Firm's demand curve for labor	**Noncompeting groups**	**Congress of Industrial Organizations**
Value of the marginal product of labor	**Monopsony**	**Checkoff**
	National union	
Market demand curve for labor	**Local union**	**Featherbedding**
	Injunction	**Collective bargaining**
Derived demand	**American Federation of Labor**	**Closed shop**
Market supply curve for labor	**Craft union**	**Union shop**
		Open shop
Backward-bending supply curve	**Yellow-dog contract**	**Strike**
	Industrial union	

CHAPTER 30

Interest, Rent, and Profits

Not all income is received in the form of wages. The school teacher who has a savings account at the Bank of America receives income in the form of *interest*. The widow who rents out 100 acres of rich Iowa land to a farmer receives income in the form of *rent*. And the engineer who founds and owns a firm that develops a new type of electronic calculator receives income in the form of *profit*. All of these types of income—interest, rent, and profit—are forms of property income. That is, they are incomes received by owners of property. In this chapter, we are concerned with the determinants of interest, rent, and profit. Also, we try to explain the social functions of each of these types of property income.

The Nature of Interest

Charles Lamb, the English essayist, said, "The human species, according to the best theory I can form of it, is composed of two distinct races, the men who borrow and the men who lend." Whether or not such a cleavage exists, most of the human species, at one time or another, are borrowers or lenders of money. Thus practically everyone is familiar with **interest,** which is a payment for the use of money. More specifically, *the **rate of** **interest** is the amount of money one must pay for the use of a dollar for a year.* Thus, if the interest rate is 8 percent, you must pay 8 cents for the use of a dollar for a year.

Everyone who borrows money pays interest. Consumers pay interest on personal loans taken out to buy appliances, mortgages taken out to buy houses, and many other types of loans. Firms pay interest on bonds issued to purchase equipment and on short-term bank loans taken out to finance inventories. And governments pay interest on bonds issued to finance schools, highways, and other public projects.

Interest rates vary, depending on the nature of the borrower and the type of loan. One of the most important determinants of the rate of interest charged borrowers is the *riskiness* of the loan. If lenders have doubts about their chances of getting their money back, they will charge a higher interest rate than if they are sure of being repaid. Thus small, financially rickety firms have to pay higher interest rates than large blue-chip firms; and the large, well-known firms have to pay higher interest rates than the federal government. Another factor that influences the interest rate is the *cost of bookkeeping and collection.* If a firm makes many small loans and must hound the borrowers to pay up, these costs are a great deal larger than if it makes one large loan. Consequently the interest rate that must be charged for such small loans is often considerably higher than for bigger loans.

Despite the diversity of interest rates encountered at any point in time in the real world, it is analytically useful to speak of the **pure rate of interest,** which is the interest rate on a riskless loan. The rate of interest on U.S. government bonds—which are about as safe as one can get in this world—comes close to being a pure rate of interest. Actual interest rates will vary from the pure rate, depending on the riskiness of the loan together with other factors, but the configuration of actual interest rates will tend to move up and down with the pure interest rate.

The Determination of the Interest Rate

THE DEMAND FOR LOANABLE FUNDS

Since the interest rate is the price paid for the use of loanable funds, it—like any price—is determined by demand and supply. The **demand curve for loanable funds** shows the quantity of loanable funds demanded at each interest rate. The demand for loanable funds is a demand for what these funds will buy. Money is not wanted for its own sake, since it cannot build factories or equipment. Instead, it can provide command over resources— men and equipment and materials—to do things like build factories or equipment.

As shown in Figure 30.1, the demand curve slopes downward to the right, indicating that more loanable funds are demanded at a lower rate of interest than at a higher rate of interest. A very large demand for loanable funds stems from firms who want to borrow money to invest in capital goods like machine tools, buildings, and so forth. At a particular point in time a firm has available a variety of possible investments, each with a certain rate of return, which indicates its profitability or net productivity. At higher interest rates, a firm will find it profitable to borrow money for fewer of these projects than if interest rates are lower.

To be more specific, *an asset's* **rate of return** *is the interest rate earned on the investment in the asset.* Suppose that a piece of equipment costs $10,000 and yields a permanent return to its owner of $1,500 per year.[1] (This

---

[1] It is unrealistic to assume that the yield continues indefinitely, but it makes it easier to understand the principle involved.

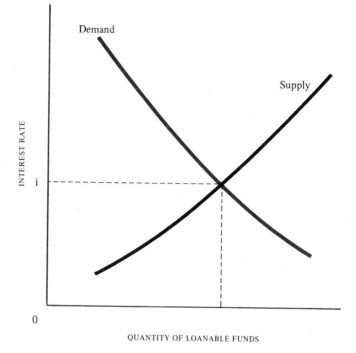

INTEREST RATE

i

0

QUANTITY OF LOANABLE FUNDS

Demand

Supply

Figure 30.1

Determination of Equilibrium Rate of Interest *The interest rate is determined by the demand and supply of loanable funds, the equilibrium level of the interest rate being* Oi.

return allows for the costs of maintaining the machine.) The rate of return on this piece of capital is 15 percent. Why? Because if an investment of $10,000 yields an indefinite annual return of $1,500, the interest rate earned on this investment is 15 percent.

If a firm maximizes profit, it will borrow to carry out investments where the rate of return, adjusted for risk, exceeds the interest rate. For example, it is profitable for a firm to pay 10 percent interest to carry out a project with a 12 percent rate of return, but it is not profitable to pay 15 percent interest for this purpose. (More will be said on this score in a subsequent section.) Consequently, the higher the interest rate, the smaller the amount that firms will be willing to borrow.

Large demands for loanable funds are also made by consumers and the government. Consumers borrow money to buy houses, cars, and many other items. The government borrows money to finance the building of schools, highways, housing, and many other types of public projects. As in the case of firms, the higher the interest rate, the smaller the amount that consumers and governments will be willing to borrow. Adding the demands of firms, consumers, and government together, we find the aggregate relationship at a given point in time between the pure interest rate and the amount of funds demanded—which is the demand curve for loanable funds. For the reasons given above, this demand curve looks the way a demand curve should. It is downward-sloping to the right.

THE SUPPLY OF LOANABLE FUNDS

The ***supply curve for loanable funds*** is the relationship between the quantity of loanable funds supplied and the pure interest rate. The supply of loanable funds comes from households and firms that find the available rate of

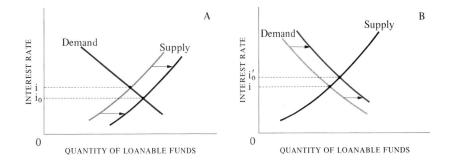

Figure 30.2

Effects on the Equilibrium Interest Rate of Shifts in the Demand or Supply Curves for Loanable Funds *If people become more willing to postpone consumption to future time periods, the supply curve will shift to the right, and the equilibrium interest rate will fall from i to i$_o$.*

If very profitable new investment opportunities are opened up, the demand curve will shift to the right, and the equilibrium interest rate will rise from i to i'$_o$.

interest sufficiently attractive to get them to save. In addition, the banks play an extremely important role in influencing the supply of loanable funds. Indeed, banks can actually create or destroy loanable funds (but only within limits set by the Federal Reserve System, our central bank).

The equilibrium value of the pure interest rate is given by the intersection of the demand and supply curves. In Figure 30.1 the equilibrium rate of interest is *Oi*. Factors that shift the demand curve or supply curve for loanable funds tend to alter the interest rate. If people become more willing to postpone consumption to future time periods, the supply curve for loanable funds will shift to the right, and the interest rate will decline. Or if inventions result in very profitable new investment possibilities, the demand curve will shift to the right and the interest rate will increase. (See Figure 30.2.)

However, this is only part of the story. Because of the government's influence on both the demand and supply sides of the market for loanable

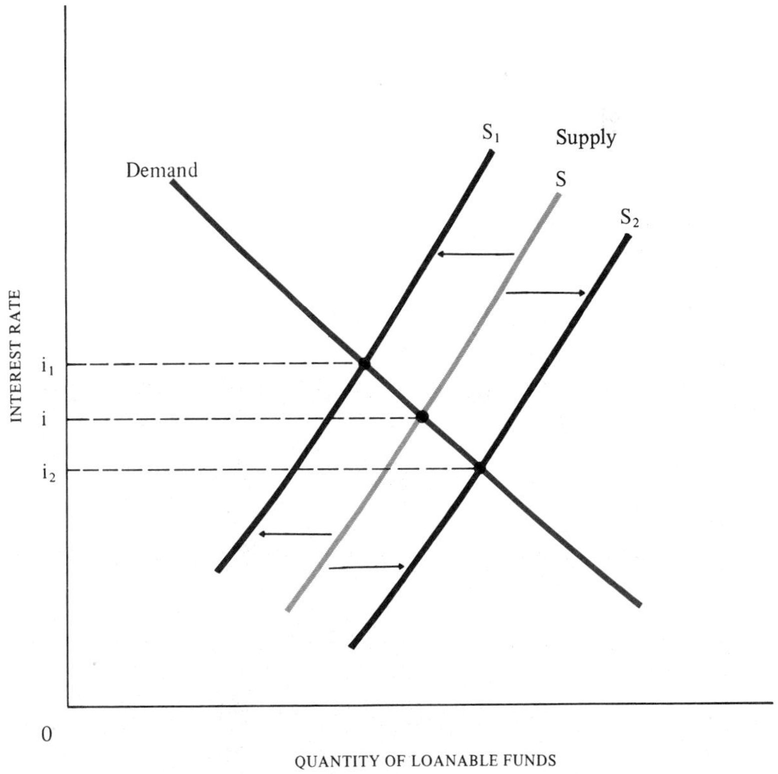

Figure 30.3

Effects on the Equilibrium Interest Rate of Federal Reserve Policies Influencing the Supply Curve for Loanable Funds *When the Federal Reserve pushes the supply curve to the right (from S to S$_2$), the equilibrium interest rate falls from i to i$_2$. When the Federal Reserve pushes the supply curve to the left (S to S$_1$), the equilibrium interest rate increases from i to i$_1$.*

funds, the interest rate at any point in time is to a considerable extent a matter of public policy. A nation's monetary policy can have a significant effect on the level of the interest rate. More specifically, when the Federal Reserve pursues a policy of easy money, this generally means that interest rates tend to fall in the short run because the Fed is pushing the supply curve for loanable funds to the right. On the other hand, when the Federal Reserve pursues a policy of tight money, interest rates generally tend to rise in the short run because the Fed is pushing the supply curve for loanable funds to the left. (See Figure 30.3.)

The government is also an important factor on the demand side of the market for loanable funds, because it is a big borrower, particularly during wartime. (Between 1941 and 1945, it borrowed almost $200 billion to help finance World War II.) During the early 1980s, it borrowed huge amounts to finance the mammoth federal deficits. At the present time, total federal debt (excluding the debt of state and local governments) held by the public is over $1 trillion.

Finally, note that the equilibrium level of the pure interest rate can be determined by John Maynard Keynes's *liquidity preference theory,* as well as by the loanable funds theory described in this section. The liquidity preference theory focuses attention on all money, not just loanable funds, and says that the interest rate is determined by the demand and supply of all money in the economy. The two approaches are not contradictory; rather, they complement one another.

Functions of the Interest Rate

Interest has often been a relatively unpopular and somewhat suspect form of income. Even Aristotle, who was hardly noted for muddle-headedness, felt that money was "barren" and that it was improper to charge interest. And in the Middle Ages, church law outlawed usury, even though interest continued to be charged. In real life and in fiction, the money lender is often the villain, almost never the hero. Yet it is perfectly clear that *interest rates serve a very important function. They allocate the supply of loanable funds.*

At a given point in time, funds that can be used to construct new capital goods are scarce, and society faces the problem of allocating these scarce funds among alternative possible uses. One way to allocate the loanable funds is through freely fluctuating interest rates. When such funds are relatively scarce, the interest rate will rise, with the result that only projects with relatively high rates of return will be carried out since the others will not be profitable. On the other hand, when such funds are relatively plentiful, the interest rate will fall, and less productive projects will be carried out because they now become profitable.

CHOOSING THE MOST PRODUCTIVE PROJECTS

The advantage of using the interest rate to allocate funds is that only the most productive projects are funded. To see why, assume that all investments are riskless. *If firms can borrow all the money they want (at the prevailing interest rate), and if they maximize their profits, they will buy all capital goods and accept all investment opportunities where the rate of return on these capital goods or investment opportunities exceeds the interest rate at which they can borrow.*[2] The reason for this is clear enough. If one can borrow money at an interest cost that is less than the rate of return on the borrowed money, clearly one can make money. Thus, if you borrow $1,000 at 3 percent per year interest and buy a $1,000 machine that has a rate of return of 4 percent per year, you receive a return of $40 per year and incur a cost of $30 per year. Since you make a profit of $10 per year, it obviously pays to buy this machine.

At a particular point in time, there is a variety of possible capital goods that can be produced and investment projects that can be carried out. Their rates of return vary a great deal; some goods or projects have much higher rates of return than others. Suppose that we rank the capital goods or projects according to their rates of return, from highest to lowest. If only a few of the goods or projects can be accepted, only those at the top of the list will be chosen. But as more and more can be accepted, society and private investors must go further and further down the list, with the consequence that projects with lower and lower rates of return will be chosen. How many of these capital goods and investment projects will be carried out? As noted above, firms will continue to invest as long as the rate of return on these goods or projects exceeds the interest rate at which they can borrow. Thus it follows that *the most productive projects—all those with rates of return exceeding the interest rate—will be carried out.*

SOCIALISM AND THE INTEREST RATE

Although interest is sometimes represented as a product of greedy capitalists, even socialist and Communist economies must use something like an interest rate to help allocate funds. After all, the socialists and Communists face the same sort of allocation problem that capitalists do. And when they try to screen out the less productive projects and to accept only the more productive ones, they must use the equivalent of an interest rate in their calculations, whether they call it that or not. (However, they do not pay interest income.) In the Soviet Union there have been published acknowledgments that a misallocation of resources resulted from decisions made in earlier years when interest rates—or their equivalent—were ignored. At present, Soviet decision makers use what amounts to interest rates in their calculations to determine which capital investments should be made and which should not.

Finally, besides its role in allocating the supply of loanable funds, the interest rate plays another important part in our economy: *It influences the level of investment, and thus the level of net national product.* Increases in the interest rate tend to reduce aggregate investment, thereby reducing total spending, whereas decreases in the interest rate tend to increase aggregate investment, thereby increasing total spending. Through its monetary policies, the government attempts to influence the interest rate

---

[2] We assume here that the investment opportunities are independent in the sense that the rate of return from each opportunity is not influenced by whether some other opportunity is accepted.

(and the quantity of money) so that total spending pushes net national product toward its full-employment level with reasonably stable prices.

Capital Budgeting

The principles discussed in the previous section can be applied to individual firms as well as entire societies. In particular, they help to indicate how a firm should make decisions on the choice of investment projects. Suppose that the Bugsbane Music Box Company believes that it will have $10 million from internal sources—primarily retained earnings and depreciation allowances—to invest next year. *To decide which investment projects to accept, it should estimate the rate of return from each one.* Suppose that it finds that it can invest $2 million in projects with rates of return of 30 percent, that it can invest $4 million in projects with rates of return of 25 percent, and so on, as shown in Table 30.1. Applying the principles just discussed, Bugsbane can maximize its profits by allocating the $10 million available from internal sources as follows. All projects yielding rates of return of 20 percent or more should be accepted; and all projects yielding less than 20 percent should not be undertaken. In other words, the projects with the highest rates of return—and with a total cost of $10 million—should be chosen.

This is a very useful step toward solving the firm's problem, but it assumes that the firm is unable or unwilling to borrow. If this is true, then nothing more needs to be said. But, as shown in Table 30.1, the firm has investment opportunities yielding 15 percent per year that it is not undertaking. It would pay the firm to undertake these projects even if it had to pay 10 or 12 percent interest—or anything less than 15 percent, for that matter. If the firm can borrow all the money it wants (within reason), but must pay 12 percent interest, what investment opportunities should it accept? All whose rate of return exceeds 12 percent. Thus, looking at Table 30.1, we see that the firm should invest its $10 million from internal sources and borrow an additional $6 million in order to undertake projects totaling $16 million.

This is an extremely simple case, but it illustrates how the interest rate and the concept of an asset's rate of return are used in practical business situations. *Capital budgeting*—the term applied to this area—has become an extremely important part of a firm's operations, as managers have relied more and more on economic concepts in allocating their firms' resources. Unaided hunch and intuition will no longer do in most major firms. Instead, most big firms insist that the prospective rate of return be estimated for each proposed investment, and that, making allowances for differences in risk, funds be allocated to the projects with the highest rates of return.[3] It is often difficult to make such estimates, but if funds are to be allocated rationally, it is essential that an analysis of this sort be carried out, formally or on the back of an envelope.

Table 30.1

INVESTMENT OPPORTUNITIES FOR BUGSBANE MUSIC BOX COMPANY

Rate of return (percent)	Amount of money the firm can invest at given rate of return (dollars)
30	2 million
25	4 million
20	4 million
15	6 million
10	7 million

[3] In practice, firms often base their decisions on discounted cash flow rather than rates of return. The present discussion is necessarily simplified. For a more complete treatment, see any managerial economics text.

Capital and Roundabout Methods of Production

Labor and land are often called the **primary inputs** because they are produced outside the economic system. Labor is created by familiar biological processes (which usually are not economically oriented, one would hope), and land is supplied by nature. *Capital,* on the other hand, *consists of goods that are created for the purpose of producing other goods.* Factory buildings, equipment, raw materials, inventories—all are various types of capital. In contrast to labor and land, capital is an input produced by the economic system itself.[4] A machine tool is capital; so is a boxcar or an electric power plant. These inputs are produced by firms, and they are purchased and used by firms. But they are not final consumption goods; instead, they are used to produce the final goods and services consumed by the public.

Our economy devotes a considerable amount of its productive capacity to the production of capital. The giant electrical equipment industry produces generators used by the electric power industry. The machine tool industry produces the numerically controlled tools used by the automobile, aircraft, and hundreds of other industries. The result in many sectors of the economy is a *roundabout method of production.* Consider the stages that lead to the manufacture of an automobile. Workers dig iron ore to be used to make pig iron to be used to make steel to be used to make machine tools to be used to make cylinders to be used to make a motor to be used to make the automobile.

Why Capital?

Why does the economy bother to product capital? After all, it may seem unnecessarily circuitous to construct capital to produce the goods and services consumers really want. Why not produce the desired goods and services—and *only* the desired goods and services—directly? Why produce plows to help produce agricultural crops? Why not forget about the plows and just produce the crops the consumers want? The answer is that the other inputs—labor and land—can produce more of the desired consumer goods and services when they are used in combination with capital than when they are used alone. A given amount of labor and land can produce more crops when used in combination with plows than when used alone.

The production and use of lots of capital make the other inputs—labor and land—more productive. But this does not mean that any society would be wise to increase without limit its production and use of capital. After all, the only way a society can produce more capital is to produce less goods and services of direct use to consumers. (For society as a whole, there are no free lunches, if resources are used fully and efficiently.) As the production of capital increases, consumers must cut further and further into their level of consumption at the present time in order to increase their capacity to produce in the future. Beyond a point, the advantage of

---

[4] Obviously, this distinction requires qualification. After all, land can be improved, and the quality of labor can be enhanced (by training and other means). Thus land and labor have some of the characteristics of capital since to some extent they can be "produced"—or at least enhanced—by the economic system.

having more in the future is overbalanced by the disadvantage of having less now. At this point, a society should stop increasing its production of capital goods.

The process by which people give up a claim on present consumption goods in order to receive consumption goods in the future is called *saving*. Just as a child may (infrequently) give up a lollipop today in order to get a lollipop and a candy cane next week, so an entire society may give up the present consumption of automobiles, food, tobacco, clothing, and so forth in order to obtain more of such goods and services later on.[5]

Capitalization of Assets

In a capitalist economy, each capital good has a market value. How can we determine what this value is? How much money is a capital good worth? To keep things reasonably simple, suppose that you can get 5 percent on various investments open to you; specifically, you can get 5 percent by investing your money in the stock of a local firm. That is, for every $1,000 you invest, you will receive a permanent return of $50 a year—and this is the highest return available. Now suppose that you have an opportunity to buy a piece of equipment that will yield you a permanent return of $1,000 per year. This piece of equipment is worth $1,000 ÷ .05 = $20,000 to you. Why? Because this is the amount you would have to pay for any other investment open to you that yields an equivalent amount—$1,000—per year. (If you must invest $1,000 for every $50 of annual yield, $20,000 must be invested to obtain an annual yield of $1,000.)

In general, if a particular asset yields a permanent amount—X dollars—each year, how much is this asset worth? In other words, how much should you be willing to pay for it? If you can get a return of $100 \times r$ percent per year from alternative investments, you would have to invest $X \div r$ dollars in order to get the same return as this particular asset yields. Consequently, this asset is worth

$$\frac{\$X}{r}.$$

This process of computing an asset's worth is called *capitalization.*

Thus, if the rate of return on alternative investments had been 3 percent rather than 5 percent in the example above, the worth of the piece of equipment would have been $1,000 ÷ .03 = $33,333 (since $X = \$1,000$ and $r = .03$). This is the amount you would have to pay for any other investment open to you that yields an equivalent amount—$1,000—per year. To see this, note that, if you must invest $1,000 for every $30 (not $50, as before) of annual yield, $33,333 (not $20,000, as before) must be invested to obtain an annual yield of $1,000.

[5] In a more poetic vein, this process of saving has been described as follows by William M. Thackeray:

Though small was your allowance,
    You saved a little store;
And those who save a little
    Shall get a plenty more.

If it does nothing else, the foregoing helps explain why Thackeray is better known as a novelist than a poet.

Effects on an Asset's Value of Changes in the Rate of Return on Other Investments

Note one important point about an asset's capitalized value. Holding constant an asset's annual returns, the asset's worth is higher the lower the rate of return available on other investments. Thus the piece of equipment discussed above was worth $33,333 when you could get a 3 percent return on alternative investments, but only $20,000 when you could get a 5 percent return on alternative investments. This makes sense. After all, the lower the rate of return on alternative investments, the more you must invest in them in order to obtain annual earnings equivalent to those of the asset in question. Thus the more valuable is the asset in question.

This principle helps to explain why in securities markets bond prices fall when interest rates rise, and rise when interest rates fall. As we pointed out in Chapter 6, a bond is a piece of paper that states that the borrower will pay the lender a fixed amount of interest each year (and the principal when the bond comes due). Suppose that this annual interest is $100, and that the interest rate equals $100 \times r$ percent per year. Then, applying the results of the previous paragraphs, this bond will be worth $100 \div r$ dollars, if the bond is due a great many years hence. Suppose the interest rate is 5 percent. Then it is worth $2,000. But if the interest rate rises to 10 percent, it will be worth only $1,000; and if the interest rate falls to 4 percent, it will be worth $2,500. Securities dealers make these sorts of calculations all the time, for they recognize that the value of the bond will fall when interest rates rise, and rise when interest rates fall.

The Present Value of Future Income

In the previous section, we determined the value of an asset that yields a perpetual stream of earnings. Now let's consider a case where an asset will provide you with a single lump sum at a certain time in the future. Suppose that you are the heir to an estate of $100,000, which you will receive in two years. How much is that estate worth now?

To answer this question, we must recognize the basic fact that *a dollar now is worth more than a dollar later.* Why? Because one can always invest money that is available now and obtain interest on it. If the interest rate is 6 percent, a dollar received now is equivalent to $1.06 received a year hence. Why? Because if you invest the dollar now, you'll get $1.06 in a year. Similarly, *a dollar received now is equivalent to $(1.06)^2$ dollars two years hence.* Why? Because if you invest the dollar now, you'll get 1.06 dollars in a year; and if you reinvest this amount for another year at 6 percent, you'll get $(1.06)^2$ dollars.

Consequently, if the interest rate is 6 percent, the estate is worth $100,000 \div (1.06)^2$ dollars now. Since $(1.06)^2 = 1.1236$, it is worth

$$\frac{\$100,000}{1.1236} = \$88,100.$$

In general, *if the interest rate is $100 \times r$ percent per year, a dollar received now is worth $1 \div (1 + r)^2$ dollars two years from now.* Thus, whatever the

WHAT DOES THAT DREAM HOUSE REALLY COST?

The biggest investment you'll probably ever make is in a house. The ordinary procedure is for a house buyer to take out a mortgage, often from a savings and loan association or a bank. A mortgage is a loan; the house it-self becomes security (or collateral) for the loan. If you fail to meet the mortgage payments, the lender can foreclose the mortgage, which means that the lender is entitled to take possession of the house.

To figure out how much your payments must be each month, the lender determines how much you must pay so that, when the mortgage terminates, you will have repaid the amount you borrowed and paid the stipulated interest on your debt. The size of the monthly mortgage payment depends on three things—(1) the amount you borrow, (2) how long the mortgage extends, and (3) the interest rate. The more that you borrow, the higher your monthly payment, holding all other things equal. And the higher the interest rate and the shorter the period of the mortgage, the higher your monthly payment.

To be more specific, look at the accompanying table, which shows the monthly payment per $1,000 borrowed. As you can see, the monthly payment is $9.66 per $1,000 borrowed, if the mortgage extends for 20 years and the interest rate is 10 percent. Thus, if you take out a $60,000 mortgage (at 10 percent for 20 years), the monthly payment is 60 times $9.66, or $579.60.

MONTHLY MORTGAGE PAYMENTS (PER $1,000 BORROWED)

Interest rate	Length of mortgage (years)			
	15	20	25	30
(percent)		(dollars)		
7	8.99	7.76	7.07	6.66
7½	9.28	8.06	7.39	7.00
8	9.56	8.37	7.72	7.34
8½	9.85	8.68	8.06	7.69
9	10.15	9.00	8.40	8.05
9½	10.45	9.33	8.74	8.41
10	10.75	9.66	9.09	8.78

As noted above, much of the monthly payment is used to repay part of the principal of the loan. The rest goes for interest on the portion of the loan that is not yet repaid. Over the lifetime of a mortgage, a very substantial amount is paid by the borrower for interest. If you take out a 20-year, $60,000 mortgage at an interest rate of 10 percent, you will pay $79,104 in interest over the life of the mortgage. And the higher the interest rate, the bigger the amount that you will pay in interest. Thus, if the interest rate is 9½ percent (rather than 10 percent), you will pay $74,352 (rather than $79,104) in interest over the life of a 20-year, $60,000 mortgage. As you can see, *a difference of ½ percentage point in the interest rate increases the total interest payments by about $5,000!*

value of the interest rate may be, the estate is worth

$$\frac{\$100,000}{(1 + r)^2}.$$

The principle that a dollar now is worth more than a dollar later is of fundamental importance. If you don't understand it, you don't understand a basic precept of the world of finance. Although the example considered in previous paragraphs pertains only to a two-year period, this principle remains valid no matter how long the period of time we consider. Table 30.2 shows the present value of a dollar received at various points of time in the future. As you can see, its present value declines with the length of time before the dollar is received (so long as the interest rate remains constant).

Table 30.2
PRESENT VALUE OF A FUTURE DOLLAR

Number of years hence (that dollar is received)	Interest rate (percent)			
	4	6	8	10
	(cents)			
1	96.2	94.3	92.6	90.9
2	92.5	89.0	85.7	82.6
3	89.0	83.9	79.4	75.1
4	85.5	79.2	73.5	68.3
5	82.3	74.7	68.1	62.0
10	67.6	55.8	46.3	38.5
15	55.5	41.7	31.5	23.9
20	45.6	31.1	21.5	14.8

Test Yourself

1. Suppose that the demand curve for loanable funds is as follows:

Quantity demanded (billions of dollars)	Interest rate (percent)
50	4
40	6
30	8
20	10

Plot the demand curve on a graph. Describe the various kinds of borrowers that are on the demand side of the market for loanable funds.

Suppose that the supply curve for loanable funds is as follows:

Quantity supplied (billions of dollars)	Interest rate (percent)
20	4
25	6
30	8
35	10

Plot the supply curve on the same graph you used to plot the demand curve. What is the equilibrium rate of interest? If usury laws do not permit interest rates to exceed 6 percent, what do you think will happen in this market?

2. Describe the social functions of the interest rate. Do you agree with Aristotle that it is improper to charge interest?

3. Suppose that you can get 10 percent per year from alternative investments and that, if you invest in a particular business, you will get $1,000 per year indefinitely. How much is this investment worth to you?

4. If a firm can borrow money at 10 percent per year and will accept only (riskless) investments that yield 12 percent per year or more, is the firm maximizing profit? Explain.

Rent: Nature and Significance

Besides interest, another type of property income is rent. To understand rent, one must understand what economists mean by land. ***Land*** is defined by economists as *any input that is fixed in supply, its limits established by nature.* Thus, since certain types of minerals and natural resources are in relatively fixed supply, they are included in the economist's definition of land. Suppose that the supply of an input is completely fixed. Increases in its price will not increase its supply and decreases in its price will not decrease its supply. Following the terminology of the classical economists of the nineteenth century, *the price of such an input is **rent**.* Note that rent means something quite different to an economist than to the man in the street, who considers rent the price of using an apartment or a car or some other object owned by someone else.

If the supply of an input is fixed, its supply curve is a vertical line, as shown in Figure 30.4. Thus the price of this input, its rent, is determined entirely by the demand curve for the input. If the demand curve is D_0, the rent is OP_0; if the demand curve is D_1, the rent is OP_1. Since the supply of the input is fixed, the price of the input can be lowered without influencing the amount supplied. Thus *a rent is a payment above the minimum necessary to attract this amount of the input.*[6]

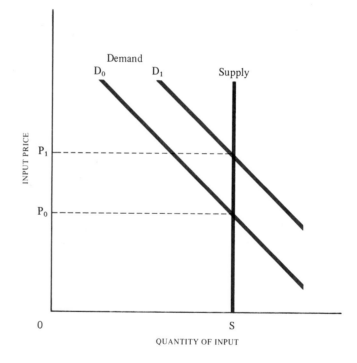

Figure 30.4

Rent *Rent is the price of an input in fixed supply. Since its supply curve is vertical, the price of such an input is determined entirely by the demand curve for the input. If the demand curve is D_0, the rent is OP_0; if the demand curve is D_1, the rent is OP_1.*

[6] In recent years, there has been a tendency among economists to extend the use of the word *rent* to encompass all payments to inputs above the minimum required to make these inputs available to the industry or to the economy. (See Example 30.1.) To a great extent these payments are costs to individual firms; the firms must make such payments to attract and keep these inputs, which are useful to other firms in the industry. But if the inputs have no use in other industries, these payments are not costs to the industry as a whole (or to the economy as a whole) because the inputs would be available to the industry whether or not these payments are made.

Why is it important to know whether a certain payment for inputs is a rent? Because a reduction of the payment will not influence the availability and use of the inputs if the payment is a rent; whereas if it is not a rent, a reduction of the payment is likely to change the allocation of resources. If the government imposes a tax on rents, there will be no effect on the supply of resources to the economy.

THE VIEWS OF HENRY GEORGE

Henry George

In 1879, Henry George (1839–97) published a book, *Progress and Poverty,* in which he argued that rents should be taxed away by the government. In his view, owners of land were receiving substantial rents simply because their land happened to be well situated, not because they were doing anything productive. Since this rent was unearned income and since the supply of land would not be influenced by such a tax, George felt that it was justifiable to tax away such rent. Indeed, he argued that a tax of this sort should be the only tax imposed by the government.

Critics of George's views pointed out that land can be improved, with the result that the supply is not completely price-inelastic. Moreover, they argued that if land rents are unearned so are many other kinds of income. In addition, they pointed out that it was unrealistic to expect such a tax to raise the needed revenue. George's single-tax movement gained a number of adherents in the last decades of the nineteenth century, and he even made an unsuccessful bid to become mayor of New York. Arguments in favor of a single tax continue to surface from time to time.

RENT: AN EXAMPLE

To make the concept of rent more concrete, consider the following example. There is a lot at the corner of Third Avenue and Winchester Street in a California suburb; this property is on the edge of the town. What will be the rent for this lot? It has various possible uses. It could be the location of a store or restaurant, a small farm, a site for an apartment building, or used for some other purpose. In each possible use, this lot has a certain value as an input.

In a competitive market, this lot will tend to rent for an amount equal to its value in its most productive use. That is, if the value of its marginal product is highest when it is used as the location for a store, a store will be built on it, and the lot will command a rent equal to the value of its marginal product. In this way, the lot will be drawn into the use that seems to yield the highest returns to the renter. From society's point of view, this has much to recommend it, since the use that yields the highest returns is likely to be the one consumers value most highly.

Classical economists viewed rent as a differential that had to be paid for the utilization of better rather than poorer land. They argued as follows. If land becomes scarce, the better lands will receive a nonzero price before the poorer lands. The rent on any acre will rise to the point where it is equal to the difference in productivity between this acre and an acre of no-rent land. Why? Because, as we saw in Chapter 29, the price differential between two inputs will equal the differential in their marginal products.

665

Profits

Besides interest and rent, another important type of property income is profit. Profit is not new to us. In Chapter 6, we discussed at some length the economist's concept of profit and how it varies from the accountant's concept. According to accountants, profit is the amount of money the owner of a firm has left after paying wages, interest, and rent—and after providing proper allowance for the depreciation of buildings and equipment. Economists dissent from this view; their position is that the opportunity costs of the labor, capital, and land contributed by the owner should also be deducted.

PROFIT STATISTICS

Available statistics concerning profits are based on the accountant's concept, not the economist's. Before taxes, corporation profits average about 10 percent of gross national product. Profits—expressed as a percent of either net worth or sales—vary considerably from industry to industry and from firm to firm. (For example, the drug industry's profits in the postwar period have frequently been about 15–20 percent of net worth—considerably higher than in most other manufacturing industries.) Also, profits vary greatly from year to year, and are much more erratic than wages. They fall more heavily in recessions and rise more rapidly in recoveries than wages do. Table 30.3 shows profit as a percent of stockholders' equity in manufacturing in the United States in 1980–84.

To some extent, the measured differences in profits among firms come about because the profit figures are not corrected for the value of the inputs contributed by the owners. Because they are smarter and more resourceful, some owners provide managerial labor of a much higher quality than other owners do. Profits arising from this fact are, at least in part, wages for superior management. Similarly, some owners put up a lot of the capital and work long hours. Profits arising from these sources are, at least in part, interest on capital and wages for time spent working in the firm.

INNOVATION, UNCERTAINTY, AND MONOPOLY POWER

Why do profits—as economists define them—exist? Three important factors are innovation, uncertainty, and monopoly power. Suppose that an economy was composed of perfectly competitive industries, that entry was completely free, and that no changes in technology—no new processes, no new products, or other innovations—were permitted. Moreover, suppose that everyone could predict the future with perfect accuracy. Under these conditions, there would be no profits, because people would enter industries where profits exist, thus reducing these profits eventually to zero, and leave industries where losses exist, thus reducing these negative profits eventually to zero. This sort of no-profit equilibrium has already been discussed in Chapter 25.

But in the real world, innovations of various kinds are made. For example, Du Pont introduces a new product like nylon, or Henry Ford introduces the assembly line, or Marconi introduces the radio. The people who carry out these bold schemes are the ***innovators,*** those with vision and

Table 30.3

ANNUAL PROFIT (AFTER TAXES) AS A PERCENTAGE OF STOCKHOLDERS' EQUITY, UNITED STATES, 1980–84

Year	All manu-facturing corpor-ations	Durable goods industries	Non-durable goods industries
	(percent)		
1980	13.9	11.2	16.3
1981	13.6	11.9	15.2
1982	9.2	6.1	11.9
1983	10.6	8.1	12.7
1984	11.9	11.3	12.4

Source: Economic Report of the President, 1985. The 1984 figures pertain to the third quarter.

the daring to back it up. The innovators are not necessarily the inventors of new techniques or products, although in some cases the innovator and the inventor are the same. Often the innovator takes another's invention, adapts it, and introduces it to the market. According to economists like the late Joseph Schumpeter of Harvard, profits are the rewards earned by innovators. The profits derived from any single innovation eventually erode with competition and imitation, but other innovations replace them, with the result that profits from innovation continue to be made.

Example 30.1   Exodus of Scientists and Engineers from Teaching

D. Allan Bromley, president of the American Association for the Advancement of Science, has pointed out that, in mathematics, physics, and engineering, many college teachers have been leaving their jobs to work in industry.

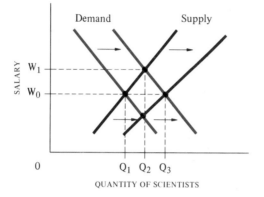

(a) Why do you think that this has been occurring? (b) What might be the effect of such a trend on the size and quality of *future* supplies of scientists and engineers? (c) If society feels that more scientists of a particular type are needed, one way of achieving an increase in supply is to shift the supply curve for this type of scientist to the right, as shown in the graph above. How can the government effect such a shift? (d) Suppose that the supply curve does not shift to the right. If the demand curve for this type of scientist shifts to the right, as shown in the graph above, does this result in some scientists of this sort receiving a higher salary than they would be willing to work for? If so, is this a rent?

SOLUTION

(a) Because new Ph.D.'s have been offered higher salaries by industry than by universities. (b) If the quality and number of college teachers were reduced, there might well be an adverse effect on the size and quality of future supplies of scientists and engineers. (c) By scholarship and other programs subsidizing the training of such scientists. (d) If the supply curve does not shift to the right, the equilibrium salary increases from OW_0 to OW_1, and those scientists that were willing to work for a salary of OW_0 receive a windfall of $(OW_1 - OW_0)$. Thus it is a rent in the sense that it is a payment above the minimum necessary to attract this amount of this input. But it is not a rent in the sense that the supply curve is vertical. (See footnote 6.)*

* For further discussion, see D. Allan Bromley, "The Fate of the Seed Corn," *Science,* July 10, 1981.

Frank Knight

In the real world, uncertainty also exists. Indeed, one of the real hazards in attempting to be an innovator is the **risk** involved. According to a theory set forth several decades ago by Frank Knight of the University of Chicago, all economic profit is due to uncertainty. Profit is the reward for risk bearing. Assuming that people would like to avoid risk, they will prefer relatively stable, sure earnings to relatively unstable, uncertain earnings—*if the average level of earnings is the same.* Consequently, to induce people to take the risks involved in owning businesses in various industries, a profit—a premium for risk—must be paid to them. This is similar to the higher wages that, according to the previous chapter, must be paid for jobs where earnings are unstable or uncertain.

Still another reason for the existence of profits is the fact that markets are not perfectly competitive. Under perfect competition, there will be a tendency in the long run for profits to disappear. But, as we have seen, this will not be the case if an industry is a monopoly or oligopoly. Instead, profits may well exist in the long run in such imperfectly competitive industries. And, as we know from Chapter 28, much of our entire economy is composed of imperfectly competitive industries. Monopoly profits are fundamentally the result of "contrived scarcities." Since a firm's demand curve is downward-sloping if competition is imperfect, it pays the firm to take account of the fact that the more it produces, the smaller the price it will receive. In other words, the firm realizes that it will spoil the market if it produces too much. Thus it pays firms to limit their output, and this contrived scarcity is responsible for the existence of the profits they make as a consequence.

The Functions of Profits

To many people, profit seems to be "something for nothing." They do not recognize the innovative or risk-bearing functions of the owners of the firm, and consequently see no reason for the existence of profits. Other people, aware that profits arise because of imperfect competition, ignore the other functions of profit and regard it as entirely the ill-gotten gain of fat monopolists, often smoking big cigars and properly equipped with a rapacious leer. But no group is more hostile to profits than the followers and disciples of Karl Marx. According to Marx, laborers in a capitalist system receive a wage that is barely enough to cover the minimum amount of housing, food, clothing, and other commodities needed for survival. The difference between the amount the employers receive for their products and the amount they pay the laborers that produce them is "surplus value." And, according to Marx, this "surplus value," which includes what we would call profit, is a measure of, and consequence of, exploitation of labor by owners of firms.

Marx's views and those of others who look on profits with suspicion and even distaste are rejected by most economists, who feel that profits play a legitimate and very important role in a capitalistic system. In such a system, consumers, suppliers of inputs, and firms, try to advance their own interests. Workers try to maximize their earnings, capitalists look for the highest interest returns, landlords try to get the highest rents, and firm

Basic Idea #60: Although some people regard profits with suspicion, the truth is that profits (and losses) are at the heart of a capitalistic economy. They indicate where resources are needed and where they are too abundant. They are incentives for risk-bearing and innovation, and they are a reward for efficiency.

owners seek to maximize their profits. At first glance, this looks like a chaotic, dog-eat-dog situation; but, as we have seen, it actually turns out to be an orderly and efficient system—if competition is present.

PROFITS AND LOSSES: MAINSPRINGS OF A CAPITALISTIC SYSTEM

Profits and losses are mainsprings of this system for several reasons.

1. They are signals that indicate where resources are needed and where they are too abundant. When there are economic profits in an industry, this is the signal for resources to flow into it; when economic losses exist in an industry, this is the signal for resources to leave it.

2. Profits are very important incentives for innovation and for betting on the future. For an entrepreneur like Joseph Wilson of Xerox, profits are the bait society dangles before him to get him to take the risks involved in marketing a new product, like xerography. If his judgment turns out to be faulty, losses—negative profits—are the penalties society imposes on him.

3. Profits are society's reward for efficiency. Firms that use inefficient techniques or produce an inappropriate amount or type of product are penalized by losses. Firms that are particularly alert, efficient, and adaptive receive profits. Further, profits enable firms to embark on new projects. Thus the profits that Xerox earned on xerography are currently being used to support its new ventures into other types of business machines.

The importance of profits in a free-enterprise economy is clear enough. However, this does not mean that all profits are socially justified or that the system as a whole cannot be improved. Monopoly profits may not be socially justified, and a competitive system, despite its advantages, may produce many socially undesirable effects—for example, an undesirable income distribution. Much more will be said on this score in the next chapter.

The Functional Distribution of Income

In this and the previous chapter, we have been concerned with wages, interest, rent, and profit. How is the total income of the nation as a whole divided among these categories? In other words, what proportion of all income goes to employees? What proportion goes for interest? For rent? For profits? In this section, we take up these questions.

Table 30.4 shows the proportion of national income going for (1) wages and salaries, (2) proprietors' income, (3) corporate profits, (4) interest, and (5) rent.[7] It is clear that wages and salaries are by far the largest of these five income categories. In 1984, about three-fourths of national income went for wages and salaries (including employer contributions to Social Security and pensions). Moreover, this is an understatement of the share of employee compensation in national income, because part of proprietors' income is really wages. As we pointed out in an earlier section, a portion of what the proprietor of the corner drugstore or the local shoestore makes is compensation for the proprietor's labor, not profit as defined by the economist.

---

[7] The concept of rent on which these figures are based is different from the one presented in this chapter, but this does not affect the conclusions presented below.

Table 30.4
PERCENTAGE SHARES OF NATIONAL INCOME, 1900–84

Period	Wages and salaries	Proprietors' Income	Corporate profits (percent)	Interest	Rent	Total
1900–09	55	24	7	5	9	100
1910–19	54	24	9	5	8	100
1920–29	60	18	8	6	8	100
1930–39	67	15	4	9	5	100
1939–48	65	17	12	3	3	100
1949–58	67	14	13	3	3	100
1963–70	70	12	11	4	3	100
1984	73	5	10	10	2	100

Source: I. Kravis, "Income Distribution: Functional Share," *International Encyclopedia of the Social Sciences,* New York: Macmillan, 1968, and *Annual Reports of the Council of Economic Advisers.* These figures may not be entirely comparable over time, but they are sufficiently accurate for present purposes.

The figures in Table 30.4 indicate a marked reduction over time in the proportion of national income going to proprietors, and a marked increase over time in the proportion going for wages and salaries. Part of this shift is due to the fact that the corporation has become a more dominant organizational form, with the result that many people who would have been individual proprietors owning their own small businesses 50 years ago now work as employed managers for corporations. Another fact that may help to explain this shift is the long-term shift from agriculture (where labor's share of income is low) to manufacturing and services (where labor's share is higher).

Some economists are impressed by the constancy of the share of national income going to labor. Using definitions that are somewhat different than those underlying Table 30.4, they come up with numbers indicating that labor's share has not varied much over time. Other economists, using somewhat different definitions, conclude that labor's share has varied considerably. But one thing is for sure. There is no evidence that a bigger share of the economic pie is going to capitalists in the form of interest, rent, or profits. Perhaps the figures in Table 30.4 exaggerate the extent to which labor's share has increased, but there is certainly no evidence that it has decreased.

Test Yourself

1. Assume that you inherit $1,000, which will be paid to you in two years. If the interest rate is 8 percent, how much is this inheritance worth now? Why?

2. "The supply curve for iron ore is horizontal, so its price is a rent." Comment.

3. "Based on the available data concerning changes over time in labor's share of total income in the United States, it is evident that labor is getting so powerful that it is receiving more and more of the total. This is an important reason for the shortage of capital in the United States." Comment and evaluate.

4. Suppose that a candidate for president proposes that all profits be taxed away. Would you support this proposal? Why or why not?

Summary

1. Interest is a payment for the use of money. Interest rates vary a great deal, depending on the nature of the borrower and the type and riskiness of the loan. One very important function of interest rates is to allocate the supply of loanable funds.

2. The pure interest rate—the interest rate on riskless loans—is, like any price, determined by the interaction of supply and demand. However, because of the influence of the government on both the demand and supply sides of the market, it is clear that the pure interest rate is to a considerable extent a matter of public policy.

3. Capital is composed of inputs produced by the economic system itself. Our economy uses very roundabout methods of production and devotes a considerable amount of its productive capacity to the production of capital.

4. If more and more capital is produced during a particular period, consumers must cut further and further into their consumption during that period. This process is called saving.

5. In a capitalist system, each capital good has a market value that can be determined by capitalizing its earnings. Holding constant an asset's annual return, the asset's worth is higher, the lower the rate of return available on other investments.

6. Any piece of capital has a rate of return, which indicates its net productivity. An asset's rate of return is the interest rate earned on the investment in the asset. If firms maximize profits, they must carry out all projects where the rate of return exceeds the interest rate at which they can borrow.

7. Rent is the return derived by inputs that are fixed in supply. Since the supply of the input is fixed, its price can be lowered without influencing the amount supplied. Thus, if the government imposes taxes on rents, there will be no effect on the supply of resources to the economy.

8. Another important type of property income is profits. Available statistics on profits are based on the accountant's concept, not the economist's, with the result that they include the opportunity costs of the labor, capital, and land contributed by the owners of the firm. Profits play a very important and legitimate role in a free enterprise system.

9. Two of the important factors responsible for the existence of profits are innovation and uncertainty. Profits are the rewards earned by innovators and a payment for risk-bearing. Still another reason for the existence of profits is monopoly power; due to contrived scarcity, profits are made by firms in imperfectly competitive markets.

Concepts for Review

Interest	Supply curve for	Saving
Rate of interest	loanable funds	Capitalization
Pure rate of interest	Liquidity preference theory	Land
Demand curve for	Capital budgeting	Rent
loanable funds	Primary inputs	Innovator
Rate of return	Capital	Risk

671

CHAPTER 31

Income Inequality, Poverty, and Discrimination

Although the United States is one of the richest countries on earth, it is not a land of milk and honey to all its inhabitants. Some Americans are poor—so poor that they suffer from malnutrition—and while poverty may not be a sin, it is no less an inconvenience to the poor. Given the affluence of American society, one is led to ask why poverty exists and whether it cannot be abolished by proper public policies. One purpose of this chapter is to examine these questions.

Poverty does not exist in a social vacuum; for one thing, it is intimately bound up with the problems of discrimination that have played an important role in American life for many years. Unquestionably, discriminatory barriers have tended to depress the incomes of females, nonwhites, and other minority groups. Besides looking at poverty in the United States, this chapter also discusses some relevant aspects of discrimination.

How Much Inequality of Income?

We don't have to be very perceptive social observers to recognize that there are great differences in income levels in the United States. But our idea of what the distribution of income looks like depends on the sort of family and community we come from. A child brought up in Lake Forest, a wealthy suburb of Chicago, is unlikely to be as aware of the incidence of poverty as a child brought up on Chicago's poor South Side. For a preliminary glimpse of the extent of *income inequality* in the United States, scan Table 31.1,

Table 31.1

PERCENTAGE DISTRIBUTION OF FAMILIES, BY INCOME, 1983

Money income (dollars)	Percent of all families	Percent of total income received	Percent of families with this and lower incomes	Percent of income received by families with this and lower incomes
Under 11,629	20	5	20	5
11,629–20,059	20	11	40	16
20,060–29,203	20	17	60	33
29,204–41,823	20	24	80	57
41,824–67,325	15	27	95	84
67,326 and over	5	16	100	100
Total	100	100		

Source: Department of Commerce.

which shows the percentage of all families in the United States that were situated in various income classes in 1983. According to the table, the bottom fifth of the nation's families received an income of less than $11,629 in 1983. On the other hand, the top fifth of the nation's families received an income of $41,824 or more in 1983.

It may come as a surprise to some that so large a percentage of the nation's families made less than $11,629. The image of the affluent society projected in the Sunday supplements and on some television programs is strangely out of tune with these facts. Yet, to put these figures in world perspective, it should be recognized that Americans are very rich relative to other peoples. This fact is shown clearly by Table 31.2, which gives for various countries the 1983 level of income per person, which is the total in-

Table 31.2

SELECTED COUNTRIES GROUPED BY APPROXIMATE LEVEL OF INCOME PER CAPITA, 1983[a]

I. Countries with income per capita exceeding $6,000		
United States	Denmark	Sweden
Australia	France	Japan
Canada	Germany	Switzerland

II. Countries with income per capita between $2,500 and $6,000		
Argentina	Greece	Yugoslavia
Ireland	Hong Kong	Italy
Soviet Union	United Kingdom	Venezuela

III. Countries and regions with income per capita between $1,000 and $2,500		
Algeria	Congo	Guatemala
Brazil	Malaysia	Turkey

IV. Countries and regions with income per capita less than $1,000		
India	El Salvador	Most of Africa
Indonesia	Haiti	Much of Asia

[a] Where 1983 figures are not yet published, the most recent available data are used. Note that all figures are expressed in 1975 dollars.

come of each nation divided by its population. The United States is among the leaders in this table.

Why Inequality?

Nonetheless, recognizing that our poor are better off than the bulk of the population in many other countries, the fact remains that there is substantial inequality of income in this country. Why is this the case? Based on our discussion of labor and property incomes in previous chapters, this question is not hard to answer. One reason is that some people possess greater abilities than others. Since Ozzie Smith and Dave Winfield have extraordinary skill as baseball players, it is easy to understand why they make a lot of money. Another reason is differences in the amount of education and training people receive. Thus physicians or lawyers must receive a higher income than people in occupations requiring little or no training. (Otherwise it would not pay people to undergo medical or legal training.) Still another reason is that some people own large amounts of property. Thus, because of a shrewd choice of ancestry, the Fords, Rockefellers, and Mellons get high incomes from inherited wealth. Still other reasons are that some people have managed to obtain monopoly power, and others have had an extraordinary string of good luck.

A Measure of Income Inequality

To what extent has income inequality in the United States decreased? Some people say that because of the advent of the "welfare state" the nation has moved rapidly toward greater equality of income. Others say that the rich are getting richer and the poor are getting poorer. Who is right? To answer this question, we need some way to measure the degree of income inequality. The most commonly used technique is the **Lorenz curve,** which plots the percentage of people, going from the poorest up, on the horizontal axis, and the percentage of total income they get on the vertical axis.

The Lorenz curve based on the figures in Table 31.1 is shown in Figure 31.1. To see how this diagram was constructed, note that in Table 31.1 families with incomes under $11,629 accounted for 20 percent of all families, but only 5 percent of all income. Thus, plotting 20 percent on the horizontal axis against 5 percent on the vertical axis, we get point A. The table also indicated that families with incomes under $20,060 accounted for 40 percent of all families, but only 16 percent of all income. Plotting these figures in the same way, we get point B. Connecting up all points like A and B, we obtain the Lorenz curve in Figure 31.1.

Case 1: No Inequality. Two extreme cases must be understood to see how the Lorenz curve is used. First, suppose that *incomes were the same for all families* (or whatever kinds of recipients are under consideration). Then the Lorenz curve would be a straight line connecting the origin of the diagram with its upper right-hand corner. That is, it would be *OP* in Figure 31.1. To see this, note that, if incomes are distributed equally, the lowest 10 percent of the families receive 10 percent of the total income, the lowest 20 percent

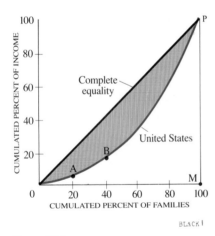

Figure 31.1

Lorenz Curve for Family Income, United States, 1983 *OP is the Lorenz curve if income were distributed equally. The shaded area between this hypothetical Lorenz curve and the actual Lorenz curve is a measure of income inequality.*

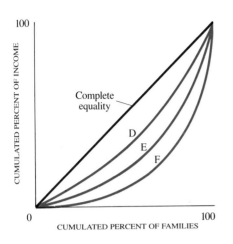

Figure 31.2
Lorenz Curves for Countries D, E, and
F *Income inequality is greater in*
country F than in country E, and greater
in country E than in country D.

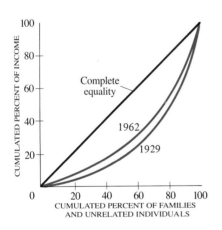

Figure 31.3
Changes over Time in Lorenz Curves for
Family Income in the United States
Income inequality in the United States
has decreased over time, as indicated by
the Lorenz curves for 1929 and 1962.

of the families receive 20 percent of the total income, and so forth. Plotting 10 percent on the horizontal axis against 10 percent on the vertical axis, 20 percent on the horizontal axis against 20 percent on the vertical axis, and so forth, one gets a Lorenz curve of *OP*.

Case 2: Complete Inequality. Suppose that *incomes were distributed completely unequally*—that is, one person has all of the income and the rest have none. In this case, the Lorenz curve would lie along the horizontal axis from *O* to *M* and along the vertical line from *M* to *P*. It would be *OMP* in Figure 31.1. Why? Because the lowest 10 percent of the families have zero percent of the total income, the lowest 20 percent of the families have zero percent of the total income, and so, in fact, do the lowest 99 percent of the families. Plotting 10 percent on the horizontal axis against zero percent on the vertical axis, 20 percent on the horizontal axis against zero percent on the vertical axis, and so on, one gets a Lorenz curve that lies along the horizontal axis from *O* to *M*. But since 100 percent of the families must receive 100 percent of the income, the Lorenz curve must then jump up from *M* to *P*.

The Importance of the Shaded Area. These two cases make it clear that *the shaded area in Figure 31.1*—the deviation of the actual Lorenz curve from the Lorenz curve corresponding to complete equality of income—*is a measure of income inequality.* The larger this shaded area, the greater the extent of income inequality. Figure 31.2 shows the Lorenz curve for the income distributions in three countries—*D, E,* and *F.* As reflected in the Lorenz curves, income inequality is greater in *F* than in *E,* and greater in *E* than in *D.* Why? Because the area between the actual Lorenz curve and the Lorenz curve corresponding to complete equality is greater in *F* than in *E,* and greater in *E* than in *D.*

Trends in Income Inequality

Let us now return to the question posed at the beginning of the previous section: To what extent has income inequality in the United States decreased? Figure 31.3 shows the Lorenz curves for the income distributions in 1929 and 1962. These curves make it clear that there was a considerable reduction in income inequality. The share of income going to the top 20 percent declined by one-fifth between 1929 and 1962. This change, described by some writers as an "income revolution," did not occur gradually throughout the period. Instead, essentially all the reduction in income inequality occurred before the end of World War II. Since then, there has been little change in the degree of income inequality.

One of the reasons for the reduction in income inequality between 1929 and the end of World War II was the increased importance of wages and salaries relative to other sources of income. Wages and salaries are more equally distributed than income from self-employment and property. Also, many public programs were established to provide income for the poor. (The details of these programs are described below.) In addition, the shift from substantial prewar unemployment to the full employment of World War II narrowed wage differentials among various types of workers. Further, the inequality in the distribution of wealth was reduced during this period.

675

Example 31.1   Economic Effects of Illegal Aliens

In recent years, the number of illegal aliens in the United States has been estimated to be between 2 and 12 million. Most of the apprehended aliens have been Mexican nationals. Suppose that the value-of-marginal-product curve for labor in the U.S. market is as follows:

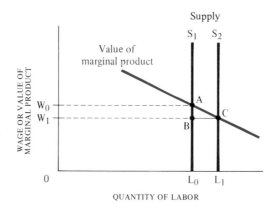

(a) If S_1 is the supply curve for labor *without* immigration of illegal aliens, what would be total labor income under these circumstances? (b) If S_2 is the supply curve for labor *with* immigration of illegal aliens, what would be the total labor income of the native U.S. population under these circumstances? (c) Will the owners of U.S. capital and land benefit from this immigration? Why or why not? (d) Why does La Raza Unidad, a farm labor union representing many Spanish-speaking American citizens, oppose such immigration?

SOLUTION

(a) Total labor income will equal the area of rectangle OW_0AL_0, since it will equal the wage (OW_0) times the quantity of labor employed (OL_0). (b) Since the total supply of native U.S. labor is OL_0, total labor income will equal the area of rectangle OW_1BL_0, since it will equal the wage (OW_1) times OL_0. (c) Yes. The value of the marginal product of the extra ($OL_1 - OL_0$) workers exceeds their wage, OW_1, as can be seen in the above graph. Also, the owners of U.S. capital and land benefit from the fact that they can pay native U.S. labor a lower wage. (d) One reason may be that such immigration lowers the wage received by American citizens engaged in farm labor.*

* For further discussion, see B. Chiswick, "Immigrants and Immigration Policy," in W. Fellner, ed., *Contemporary Economic Problems, 1978,* Washington, D.C.: American Enterprise Institute, 1978.

Effects of the Tax Structure on Income Inequality

So far we have looked at the distribution of before-tax income. But we must also consider the effect of the tax system on income inequality.

A tax is **progressive** if the rich pay a higher proportion of their income for the tax than do the poor. A tax is **regressive** if the rich pay a smaller proportion of their income for the tax than do the poor.

Needless to say, people who feel that the tax system should promote a redistribution of income from rich to poor favor progressive, not regressive taxes. Obviously, the personal income tax is progressive, since the tax rate is greater for high-income people than for low-income people. Other progressive taxes are inheritance or estate taxes. (The federal government levies a gift tax to prevent wealthy people from circumventing the estate tax by giving their money away before death.) This is applauded by reformers who oppose accumulation and preservation of inherited wealth. But, as in the case of the personal income tax, the portion of an estate subject to taxes can be reduced through clever use of various loopholes, all quite legal. Thus the estate tax is not as progressive as it looks.

Not all taxes are progressive; examples of regressive taxes are not hard to find. General sales taxes of the sort used by most states and some cities are regressive, since high-income people pay a smaller percentage of their income in sales taxes than do low-income people. The Social Security tax is also regressive. It is difficult to tell whether the corporation income tax is progressive or regressive. At first glance, it seems progressive because the owners of corporations—the stockholders—tend to be wealthy people; and to the extent that the corporate income tax is paid from earnings that might otherwise be paid to the stockholders, one might conclude that it is progressive. But this ignores the possibility that the corporation may pass the tax on to the consumer by charging a higher price; in this case the tax may not be progressive.

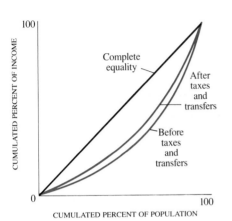

Figure 31.4

Effect of Federal Income Tax and Transfer Payments on Lorenz Curve, United States, 1980 *In the United States, inequality of income after taxes and transfers is less than inequality of income before taxes and transfers.*

WHO PAYS THE TAXES AND RECEIVES THE TRANSFER PAYMENTS?

To get a better picture of the extent to which the government—in terms of both the money it spends and the taxes it levies—takes from the rich and gives to the poor, studies have been carried out to determine how much people in various income brackets pay in taxes and receive in transfer payments (social security, welfare payments, food stamps, medicare, and medicaid). The results of one important study of this sort are shown in Figure 31.4. As you can see, the effect of taxes (federal, state, and local) and transfers is to reduce income inequality. However, this is due largely to the fact that transfer payments go mainly to the poor. Taken by itself, the tax system is only mildly progressive or slightly regressive, depending on the study's assumptions. Moreover, there is evidence that the tax system is less progressive (or more regressive) in 1985 than in 1966.[1]

Estimates of this sort are interesting, but it is difficult to predict the ***incidence*** of some taxes—that is, it is difficult to know who *really* pays them. The incidence of certain taxes is relatively easy to determine, as we saw in Chapter 5. It is generally accepted that the personal income tax is paid by the person whose income is taxed. But there are other cases—such as the corporation income taxes we just mentioned—where it is difficult to tell how much of the tax burden the firm shifts to the consumer.[2] For these and

[1] J. Pechman, *Who Paid the Taxes, 1966–85?*, Washington, D.C.: Brookings Institution, 1985. Based on different assumptions about tax incidence, E. Browning and W. Johnson have concluded that the tax system is more progressive than Pechman concludes.

[2] To see how the burden of a tax can be shifted, recall our discussion in Chapter 5 of the effects of an *excise* tax—a tax imposed on each unit sold of a particular product. The federal government imposes excise taxes on liquor and tobacco, among many other products. The im-

(continued)

other reasons, there is considerable controversy over the extent to which the spending and taxing activities of the government really are progressive or regressive.

Income Inequality: The Pros and Cons

THE CASE AGAINST INCOME INEQUALITY

Many distinguished social philosophers have debated the merits and demerits of making the income distribution more equal. We cannot consider all the subtler points, but those who favor greater equality make four main arguments.

1. They say that inequality of income lessens total consumer satisfaction because an extra dollar given to a poor man provides him with more extra satisfaction than the loss of a dollar takes away from a rich man. According to A. C. Pigou, "It is evident that any transference of income from a relatively rich man to a relatively poor man of similar temperament, since it enables more intense wants to be satisfied at the expense of less intense wants, must increase the aggregate sum of satisfactions."[3]

A problem in this very appealing argument is its assumption that the rich man and the poor man have the same capacities to gain enjoyment from income. Most economists believe that there is no scientific way to make such comparisons (as emphasized in Appendix E). They deny that the satisfaction one person derives from an extra dollar of income can be measured against the satisfaction another person derives from an extra dollar. Although such comparisons may be drawn, they rest on ethical, not scientific, grounds.

2. It is argued that income inequality is likely to result in unequal opportunities for young people to gain advanced education and training. The children of the rich can get an education, while the children of the poor often cannot. The result is that some able and productive people may be denied an education simply because their parents are poor. This is a waste of resources.

3. It is argued that income inequality is likely to lead to political inequality. The rich may well influence legislation and political decisions more heavily than the poor, and there is likely to be one kind of justice for the rich and another kind for the poor.

4. In the past few years, the arguments for income equality have been carried a step forward by John Rawls, the Harvard philosopher. He says

---

mediate effect of these taxes is to raise the price of the commodity since the supply curve will be shifted upward and to the left. If demand is price inelastic, most of the burden of the tax is shifted to the consumer. Under these circumstances, firms sell almost as many units of the product as before the tax was imposed, despite the higher price induced by the tax. On the other hand, if supply is relatively inelastic, the burden is borne mainly by the producer. Usually, the aim of excise taxes is to put the burden on consumers. In the case of liquor and tobacco there clearly is a feeling that drinking and smoking smack of sin, and sinners should pay, in this world and the next. For a discussion of excise taxes, see J. Pechman, *Federal Tax Policy,* 3d ed., Washington, D.C.: The Brookings Institution, 1977.

[3] A. C. Pigou, *Economics of Welfare,* 4th ed., London: Macmillan, 1948, p. 89.

that, *if people were framing a constitution for society without knowing what their class position would be, they would opt for equality.* And he argues that "all social values . . . are to be distributed equally unless an unequal distribution . . . is to everyone's advantage"—that is, unless an unequal distribution is to the advantage of society's least privileged group. Although Rawls's book, *A Theory of Justice,* has had considerable impact, many economists have pointed out that his prescription for society might not appeal to people who were willing to take risks. Suppose that you were framing a social constitution and that you could establish a society that guaranteed every family $15,000 a year (no more, no less) or one where 99 percent of all families would receive $20,000 and 1 percent would receive $12,000. You might choose the latter kind of society because, although there is a small chance that you would do worse than in the egalitarian case, the chance of doing better seems worth this risk.

THE CASE FOR INCOME INEQUALITY

In general, people who favor income inequality also make four arguments.

1. They argue that income inequality is needed to give people an incentive to work and create. After all, if everyone receives the same income, why bother to increase your production, or to try to invent a new process, or to work overtime? Whatever you do, your income will be the same. This is an important point, though it overlooks the fact that nonmonetary incentives like pride in a job well done can be as important as monetary incentives.

2. Advocates of income inequality claim that it permits greater savings, and thus greater capital formation. Although this seems reasonable, it is not hard to cite cases where countries with greater inequality of income invest less, not more, than countries with less inequality of income. Thus some Middle Eastern countries with great income inequality have not had relatively high investment rates.

3. Advocates of income inequality say that the rich have been important patrons of new and high-quality products that benefit the entire society. They argue that there are social advantages in the existence of certain people with the wherewithal to pioneer in consumption and to support art and culture. In their view, a completely egalitarian society would be a rather dull affair.

4. Advocates of income inequality point out that even if everyone received the same income, the poor would not be helped a great deal, because the wealthy are relatively few. If the riches of the rich were transferred to the poor, each poor person would get only a little, because there are so many poor and so few rich.

The Tradeoff between Equality and Efficiency

In trying to decide how much income inequality you favor, it is important to recognize that measures taken to reduce inequality are likely to decrease economic efficiency. In other words, *if we reduce inequality, we may well cut society's total output.* Why? Because, as pointed out in the previous section, people are likely to have less incentive to produce if their incomes are much the same regardless of how much they produce. This does not mean that all measures designed to reduce income inequality are bad. What it does mean is that, if you want to reduce income inequality, you should be sensitive to the effects on output. In particular, you should try to find policies that will attain a given reduction in inequality at a minimum cost in terms of reduced output.

In view of the strong feelings of many advocates and opponents of reduced income inequality, it is not surprising that they sometimes make extreme statements about the nature of the tradeoff between equality and efficiency. Some egalitarians deny that there is any tradeoff at all. They claim that inequality can be reduced without any cut in output. Some opponents of reductions in income inequality assert that there will be a catastrophic fall in output if the existing income distribution is tampered with. Although far too little is known about the quantitative character of this tradeoff, there seems to be general agreement among economists that the truth lies somewhere between these two extremes.

People vary considerably in their evaluation of how much society should pay (in terms of decreased total output) for a particular reduction in income inequality. The late Arthur Okun of the Brookings Institution suggested that, to characterize your own feelings on this score, it is useful to view money as a liquid and to visualize a bucket which carries money from the rich to the poor.[4] The bucket is leaky, so only part of what is taken from the rich can be given to the poor. If the leak is very small, a dollar taken from the rich may result in 99 cents going to the poor. Many people would accept a loss of this magnitude. If the leak is very large, a dollar taken from the rich may result in only 5 cents going to the poor. Few people would accept this big a loss. How big a loss would you accept? The larger the leak that you would find acceptable, the more willing you are to accept output losses in order to attain decreases in income inequality.

The argument between the advocates and opponents of reduced income inequality involves much more than economics. Whether you favor greater or less income inequality depends on your ethical and political beliefs. It is not a matter economics alone can settle. What economists can do is assess the degree of income inequality in a country and suggest ways to alter the gap between the haves and have-nots in accord with the dictates of the people or their leaders. In recent years, economists in and out of government have devoted much effort to designing programs aimed at reducing poverty. To understand these programs, we must discuss what poverty is, and who the poor are.

Basic Idea #61: Attempts to promote economic equality may well result in a reduction in national output, since such attempts are likely to weaken incentives to work hard, save, and invest productively. Conversely, attempts to increase national output via the strengthening of such incentives may result in more inequality.

What Is Poverty?

Some people are fond of saying that everything is relative. Certainly this is true of poverty. Relative to the Mellons or Rockefellers, practically all of us are poor; but relative to the homeless who sleep in railroad and bus termi-

---

[4] Arthur Okun, *Equality and Efficiency,* Washington, D.C.: Brookings Institution, 1975. For an excerpt from this book, see E. Mansfield, *Principles of Microeconomics: Readings, Issues, Cases,* 4th ed., New York: Norton, 1983.

nals, practically all of us are rich. Moreover, poverty is certainly subjective. Consider the average young executive making $50,000 a year. After a bad day at the office or a particularly expensive family shopping spree, he is likely to tell anyone who will listen that he is as poor as a church mouse.

There is no well-defined income level that can be used in all times and places as a touchstone to define poverty. Poverty is partly a matter of how one person's income stacks up against that of others. What most people in America today regard as stark poverty would have seemed like luxury to many Americans of 200 years ago—and would seem like luxury in parts of Asia and Africa today. Consequently, one must be careful not to define poverty in such a way that it cannot be eliminated—and then try to eliminate it. If poverty is defined as being in the bottom 10 percent of the income distribution, how can a war against poverty ever be won? Regardless of what measures are taken, there will always be a bottom 10 percent of the income distribution, unless all income inequality is eliminated (which is highly unlikely).

Perhaps the most widely accepted definition of *poverty* in the United States today is the one developed by the Social Security Administration, which began by determining the cost of a *minimal* nutritionally sound food plan (given by the Department of Agriculture). Then, since low-income families spend about one-third of their incomes on food, this food cost was multiplied by 3 to obtain an income level that was used as a criterion for poverty. Families with less income were regarded as "living below the poverty level."

Based on such computations, an urban family of four needed an income of about $10,178 to make it barely over the Social Security Administration's poverty line in 1983. (Since farm families typically have lower food costs, the estimates for them are somewhat lower.) Although one could quarrel with this figure on various counts, most people probably would agree that families with income below this level are poor.[5]

TWO CASE STUDIES

Particular cases of poverty are generally more illuminating and impressive than discussions in the abstract. Consider the following two actual cases in New York City (the names are fictitious).

The Smith Family. The Smiths—Christopher, 47, and Irene, 35—opened a small restaurant after years of saving. Within a month, Christopher had a severe heart attack and was laid up in the hospital. The Smiths lost the restaurant, and Irene went to work as a nurse's aide to supplement her husband's small disability benefits. After about a year of working and trying to take care of her husband and two children—John, 13, and Deborah, 12—Irene collapsed from the strain and had to enter a mental hospital. While she was away, a relative took care of Christopher and the children. After getting out of the hospital, Irene learned that her husband

[5] The basic figures come from the Department of Commerce's *Current Population Reports,* which explain in detail the way in which these figures are derived. The method described in the text is crude, but it provides results that are quite close to those of more complicated methods. Since 1969, the poverty line has been calculated on the basis of the Consumer Price Index, not the price of food.

had cancer and required expensive surgery. She became so upset that the doctor called in one of the city's charity agencies, which tried to help this troubled and impoverished family as best it could.

The Jones Family. Jean Jones, 35, is trying to raise seven children. Her husband, an unskilled laborer, never made much money. He drank a lot, terrified Mrs. Jones and the children with his abuse, and was an unfaithful husband. Four years ago, Mrs. Jones separated from him. She gets along as best she can on public assistance, but is having a difficult time. Two of the children have been arrested for theft; two others are in trouble in school; and one daughter is pregnant out of wedlock. Mrs. Jones feels beaten. In recent months, through the help of neighbors, she has consulted a community service bureau where the social workers have given her help and encouragement. But she obviously needs a great deal of aid if she and her family are to get their heads above water.

Neither of these cases is typical. Since they were cited by the *New York Times* as being among New York's 100 neediest cases, it is fair to say that their plight is probably worse than that of the great bulk of America's poor. But they provide some idea of just how bad things can get; and one has to be hardhearted indeed not to feel compassion for people like the Smiths and Mrs. Jones.

Declining Incidence of Poverty

Because college students tend to come from relatively well-off families, they often are unaware of the number of families in the United States whose incomes fall below the Social Security Administration's poverty line. According to estimates made by the federal government in 1984, about 15 percent of the population in the United States was below this line. In absolute terms, this means that over 35 million people were poor—usually not as poor as the Smiths or Mrs. Jones, but poor enough to fall below the criterion described above.

Fortunately, the incidence of poverty (measured by this criterion) generally has been declining in the United States. In 1947, about 30 percent; in 1960, about 20 percent; and in 1977, about 12 percent of the people were poor by this definition. This is what we would expect. As the average level of income rises, the proportion of the population falling below the poverty line (which is defined by a relatively fixed dollar amount of income) will tend to decrease. Nonetheless, the fact that poverty is being eliminated in the United States does not mean that this process is going on as fast as it should. Many observers feel, as we shall see in subsequent sections, that poverty could and should be eradicated more rapidly.

Characteristics of the Poor

Naturally, the poor are not confined to any particular demographic group, but some types of families are much more likely than others to be below the poverty line. In particular, *nonwhites are much more likely to be poor than whites.* In 1983, 36 percent of nonwhites were poor, whereas 12 percent of whites were poor. Also, *families headed by females are much more likely to be poor than families headed by males.* In addition, very large families—7 persons and over—are much more likely than others to be poor.

Poverty strikes a particularly hard blow at children. Even the most hardhearted citizens are prone to agree that the young should be shielded from the crippling impact of dire poverty. According to a government survey carried out in 1975, *over 8 million children under 16 in the United States were being raised in families below the poverty line.* This is a very striking fact indeed.

Reasons for Poverty

To a considerable extent, the reasons why families are poor lie beyond the control of the families themselves. About one-third of the poor adults have suffered a disability of some sort, or the premature death of the family breadwinner, or family dissolution. Some have had to face a smaller demand for their occupation (because of technological or other change) or the decline of their industry or geographical area. Some have simply lived "too long"—their savings have given out before their minds and bodies did. Another instrumental factor in making some families poor is discrimination of various kinds. The most obvious type is racial, but others exist as well—discrimination based on sex, religion, age, residence, education, and seniority. In addition, some people are poor because they have very limited ability or little or no motivation. These factors should not be overlooked.

There are important barriers which tend to separate the poor from the rest of society. As the University of Wisconsin's Robert Lampman points out,

> Barriers, once established, tend to be reinforced from the poverty side by the alienated themselves. The poor tend to be cut off from not only opportunity but even from information about opportunity. A poverty subculture develops which sustains attitudes and values that are hostile to escape from poverty. These barriers combine to make events nonrandom; e.g., unemployment is slanted away from those inside the feudalistic walls of collective bargaining, disability more commonly occurs in jobs reserved for those outside the barriers, the subculture of poverty invites or is prone to self-realizing forecasts of disaster.[6]

Judging from the available evidence, poverty tends to be self-perpetuating. Families tend to be poor year after year, and their children tend to be poor. Because the families are poor, the children are poorly educated, poorly fed, and poorly cared for, and poverty is transmitted from one generation to the next. It is a vicious cycle.

[6] Robert Lampman, "Approaches to the Reduction of Poverty," *American Economic Review,* May 1965.

Test Yourself

1. Suppose that the following data pertain to the income distribution in the nation of Upper Usher in 1984:

Income (dollars)	Percent of families with indicated income
2,000	40
4,000	30
6,000	20
10,000	10

Plot the Lorenz curve for this nation in 1984.

2. In 1985, suppose that the income distribution in Upper Usher is as follows:

Income (dollars)	Percent of families with indicated income
2,000	20
4,000	40
6,000	35
10,000	5

Plot the 1985 Lorenz curve, and compare it with the 1984 curve. Did income inequality in this nation increase or decrease between 1984 and 1985?

3. People are classified as poor on the basis of their current money income. Should the following items also be taken into account? (a) The assets of the person or family; (b) the existence of rich relatives of the person or family; (c) the person's or family's income over a period of years, not a single year.

Social Insurance

OLD-AGE INSURANCE

Until about 50 years ago, the federal government played little or no role in helping the poor. Private charity was available in limited amounts, and the state and local governments provided some help, but the general attitude was "sink or swim." Self-reliance and self-support were the watchwords. The Great Depression of the 1930s, which changed so many attitudes, also made a marked change in this area. In 1935, with the passage of the Social Security Act, the federal government established a social insurance system providing compulsory old-age insurance for both workers and self-employed people, as well as unemployment insurance. By 1984, about 36 million Americans were receiving well over $100 billion in benefits from the resulting system of old-age and survivors' insurance.

Every wage earner covered under the Social Security Act pays a tax, which in 1984 amounted to 7 percent of the first $37,800 of his or her annual earnings. The employer also pays a tax, which is equal to that paid by the employee. The amount that one can expect to receive each month in *old-age insurance* benefits depends on one's average monthly earnings. Also, the size of the benefits depends on the number of years one has worked. Table 31.3 shows the maximum monthly benefits in 1984. The benefits in the table are a retirement annuity. In other words, they are paid to the wage earner from the date of retirement to the time he or she dies. In addition, when a wage earner dies, *Social Security* provides payments to his or her spouse, to dependent parents, and to children until they are about 18 years of age. Further, payments are made to a wage earner (and dependents), if he or she is totally disabled and unable to work.

Table 31.3

MAXIMUM INITIAL SOCIAL SECURITY BENEFITS, 1984

	Monthly payment
Retired worker alone	
65 years old	$703
62 years old	559
Retired worker with spouse	
65 years old	908
62 years old	821

Source: World Almanac.

CONTROVERSIES OVER SOCIAL SECURITY

There are a number of controversial aspects of the Social Security program.

1. *If you work past the retirement age of 65, you can be penalized considerably.* For every dollar in wages that you earn above and beyond $6,960 in 1984, you lose 50 cents in Social Security benefits. Thus, since you must pay taxes on your earnings, you get to keep well under one-half of every extra dollar that you earn in wages (over $6,960 per year). But you can earn any amount of interest or dividends or pensions without your Social Security benefits being reduced. To some observers, this is unfair discrimination against older people who want to hold down jobs.

2. *The Social Security tax is regressive,* since those with annual earnings above $37,800 pay a smaller proportion of their income in Social Security taxes than do those with annual earnings below $37,800. For this and other reasons, many observers believe that the system is not as generous to the poor as it should be.

3. *Some people are disturbed that the Social Security system is not really an ordinary insurance system at all.* An ordinary insurance program must have assets that are sufficient to finance all of the benefits promised to the people in the program. This is not the case for Social Security. But this does not mean that you won't receive your Social Security benefits. What it does mean is that the Social Security system is a means of transferring income each year from the working young and middle-aged to the retired old people. It will be up to future Congresses to determine what these benefits will be. (In 1983, Congress made a number of important changes: for example, up to half of the Social Security benefits of the well-to-do will be taxable under the personal income tax.) Perhaps you will receive much more than the amounts in Table 31.3—but then again, perhaps you won't. Only time will tell.

4. *Some people are disturbed that Social Security is mandatory.* Milton Friedman is concerned that the government interferes with an individual's freedom to plan for the future by forcing him or her to be a member of the Social Security system. (Workers might be able to obtain larger pensions by investing the money that they contribute to Social Security in investments of their own choosing.) Other observers retort that without a mandatory system, some workers would make inadequate provision for their old age and might become public charges.

5. *Some people are concerned that Social Security is an impediment to saving and capital formation.* Martin Feldstein, former chairman of President Reagan's Council of Economic Advisers, feels that Americans save relatively little because they depend on Social Security to take care of their old age. This, he believes, tends to depress capital formation in the United States, since savings can be used to build factories, expand old plants ,and add in various ways to the nation's stock of capital. He favors a slowdown in the rate of growth of Social Security, and more reliance on private pensions and personal savings.

MEDICARE, UNEMPLOYMENT INSURANCE, OTHER PROGRAMS

In 1965, the Congress extended the Social Security program to include **Medicare,** a compulsory hospitalization insurance plan plus a voluntary insurance plan covering doctors' fees for people over 65. The hospitalization insurance pays for practically all the hospital costs of the first 90 days of each spell of illness, as well as some additional costs. The voluntary plan covers about 80 percent of doctors' fees after the first $60. The cost of the compulsory insurance is included in the taxes described above.

Besides instituting old-age, survivors, and medical insurance, the Social Security Act also encouraged the states to set up systems of *unemployment insurance.* Such systems now exist in all states, financed by taxes on employers. Once an insured worker is unemployed, he can obtain benefits after a short waiting period, generally a week. The average weekly benefits differ from state to state; in 1982 they ranged from about $150 in Michigan to about $80 in Mississippi. (Since these benefits are not subject to income taxes, these figures understate the value of the benefit to the recipient.) In most states, there is a 26-week ceiling on the duration of benefits, but in 1975, there was a temporary extension of benefits to a maximum duration of 65 weeks. Clearly, unemployment insurance is another important device to keep people from falling below the poverty line.

Finally, in 1974, a new program was created to replace federal grants to the states to help the aged, the blind, and the disabled. This program, called the *Supplemental Security Income* program, establishes a uniform national minimum income for people in these categories who are unable to work. (Also, many states supplement these federal payments.) In 1984, about 4 million people received income from this program.

Antipoverty Programs

According to the English poet and essayist Samuel Johnson, "A decent provision for the poor is the true test of civilization." There is general agreement that our social insurance programs, although useful in preventing and alleviating poverty, are not an adequate or complete antipoverty program. For one thing, they focus largely on the elderly, which means that they do not aid many poor people. They do not help the working poor; and even for the unemployed, they provide only limited help for a limited period of time.

Consequently, the government has started a number of additional programs specifically designed to help the poor, although many of them are aimed more at the symptoms of poverty than at its basic causes. There are programs that provide goods and services to the poor. Perhaps the most important of these are the *food programs,* which distribute food to needy families. (Before 1973, this food generally came from surpluses due to the farm programs described in Chapter 4.) The federal government gives *stamps* that can be used to buy food to local agencies, which sell them (at less than the equivalent of market prices) or give them to low-income families. In 1983, the cost of this program to the federal government exceeded $11 billion. On the whole, this program has reached people who were truly needy, but critics have pointed out that some recipients, like college students from well-off families, qualified for the program and received this subsidy.

More important in quantitative terms than programs that give particular commodities to the poor are programs that provide them with cash. These are what people generally have in mind when they refer to *welfare.* There are advantages to cash payments. They allow a family to adapt its purchases

to its own needs and circumstances. There are obvious disadvantages too, since the money may be spent on liquor and marijuana rather than on food and milk. The most important single program of cash payments gives **aid to families with dependent children.** In 1984, this program alone paid out over $13 billion.

To qualify for this program, a family must contain dependent children who are without the support of a parent (usually the father) through death, disability, or absence (and in some states, through unemployment as well). The amount paid to a family under this program varies from state to state, since each state administers its own program and sets its own schedule of payments—as well as contributes part of the cost of the program, with the federal government providing the balance. In 1980, the average payment was about $3,400, but it was higher in states like New York and Massachusetts and lower in states like Mississippi and Alabama. To determine eligibility, the family's affairs are examined; and while receiving aid the family may be under the surveillance of a social worker who supervises its housekeeping and child care.

In 1981, President Reagan cut back the food stamp program, aid to families with dependent children, and other such programs. With regard to aid for families with dependent children, the changes reduced or eliminated the benefits for some low-income people who work. With regard to food stamps, the changes stiffened income eligibility requirements. Liberals tended to be angry at these cuts; many conservatives tended to view them as overdue.

THE NEGATIVE INCOME TAX

There is widespread dissatisfaction with current antipoverty—or welfare—programs. The cost of these programs has risen alarmingly; the programs themselves are judged by many experts to be inefficient; and, in some people's view, the welfare recipients are subjected to unnecessary meddling and spying. Moreover, there is little incentive for many people to get off welfare. Both Republicans and Democrats seem to agree that current welfare programs need improvement. What changes might be made? One suggestion that has received serious consideration is the negative income tax, an idea proposed by Stanford University's Milton Friedman (an adviser to presidential candidate Barry Goldwater in 1964 and to President Nixon) and Yale's James Tobin (an adviser to President Kennedy).

A **negative income tax** would work as follows: Just as families with reasonably high incomes *pay* taxes, families with low incomes would *receive* a payment. In other words, the poor would pay a *negative* income tax. Figure 31.5 illustrates how a negative income tax might work; it shows the amount a family of four would pay—or receive—in taxes for incomes at various levels. According to Figure 31.5, $4,000 is the **break-even income**—the income at which a family of four neither pays nor receives income taxes. Above $4,000, a family pays taxes. Thus a family with an income of $6,000 pays $500 in taxes. Below $4,000 a family receives a payment. Thus a family with an income of $1,000 is paid $1,500.

There are several advantages of a negative income tax.

1. It would give people on welfare more incentive to work. As indicated in Figure 31.5, for every extra dollar it earns, the family receives only 50

Figure 31.5

Example of Negative Income Tax *A family with more than $4,000 in income pays taxes. Thus a family with an income of $6,000 pays $500 in taxes. A family with an income less than $4,000 receives a payment. Thus a family with an income of $1,000 is paid $1,500.*

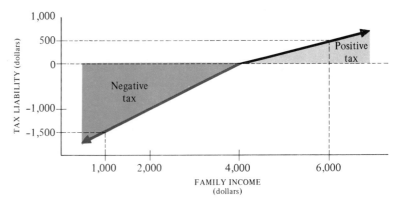

[Fig. 32.6]

cents less from the government under this kind of negative income tax. Thus the family gets to keep half of every extra dollar (up to $4,000) it earns, which is a larger portion of this extra dollar than under the present system.

2. There would be no intrusion into the internal affairs of families on welfare and no regulations that cut off welfare payments if the husband remains with his family. In the past, the welfare system has given families an incentive to break up, and encroached on the dignity of poor people.

3. It might cost less to administer the negative income tax than the present system, and differences among states in benefits might be reduced.

Despite these advantages, many citizens remain skeptical about the negative income tax. For one thing, they are antagonistic to the idea of giving people an income without requiring any work in return. They also are unwilling to transfer large amounts from rich to poor. This amount would depend on how high the break-even income was set and on the negative tax rates. In the late 1960s, it was estimated that a negative income tax based on the sort of plan described in Figure 31.5 would have meant that those above the break-even income level would transfer about $25 billion to those below the break-even level. Despite the attractive features of a negative income tax, a transfer of this magnitude has proved unacceptable in many quarters.

Also, some economists regard the results of the experiments with a negative income tax in Seattle and Denver to have been disappointing. These experiments, carried out with a sample of households, seem to indicate that under a negative income tax people work less, apparently because they are more willing to quit work, and less willing to search hard for a new job.

HAS THE WAR ON POVERTY BEEN WON?

The official government statistics concerning the incidence of poverty do not recognize the fact that many people below the official poverty line receive noncash benefits from the government, such as food stamps, subsidized school lunches, public housing, Medicaid, and Medicare. These benefits accounted in 1980 for more than two out of every three dollars of government assistance. According to a report published by the U.S. Bureau of the Census in 1984, the percentage of the U.S. population below the poverty line is much smaller than the official statistics indicate, when these government noncash benefits are taken into account. Specifically, the figure according to official statistics is about 10 percent. When underreporting of incomes is taken into consideration, some economists conclude that only about 4 percent of the population have fallen below the poverty line in recent years. Based on these statistics, some observers claim that the war on poverty in the United States has been won. But it is important to recognize that, even if only 4 percent fall below the poverty line, this means that about 9 million people remain poor. And among blacks, the percentage of poor people is much higher than 4 percent. Also, the statistics themselves are subject to a great many limitations, and should be viewed with caution.

Example 31.2   Why Not Cure Poverty with a Check?

If the United States government were to mail checks to all poor families to raise their incomes to the poverty level, these checks would amount to less than 1 percent of our gross national product. Suppose that the government decides to solve the poverty problem in this way.

(a) If the poverty level is $5,000 per year, what is the relationship between a family's income before subsidy and its income after subsidy? (b) Up to $5,000, does a family's earnings influence its income after subsidy? (c) For people whose pre-subsidy earnings are below the poverty level, what would be the effect of this program on the incentive to work? (d) For people whose pre-subsidy earnings are slightly above the poverty level, what would be the effect of this program on the incentive to work? (e) Would the cost of this program be greater than the amount of the checks mailed to the poor?

SOLUTION

(a) This relationship is shown below:

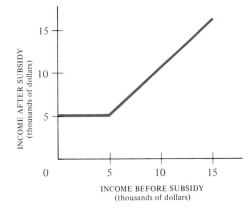

(b) No. (c) Because they can get $5,000 without working, some would be likely to quit working, or to work less hard. (d) Because they can get almost as much as their current income without working, some would be likely to quit working, or to work less hard. (e) Yes. There would be the additional costs due to the diminished incentives to work. For reasons discussed above, people would work less, and fewer goods and services would be produced.

Although they suggest that considerable progress against poverty has been made, these statistics do not indicate that poverty is no longer of concern to the American people.

The Problems of Discrimination

RACIAL DISCRIMINATION

Poverty, discrimination, and race are closely intertwined. Despite recent improvements, the sad fact is that racial discrimination occurs in many walks of life in many areas of the United States. Table 31.4 shows certain aspects of the relative position of the white and nonwhite populations in the United States. The average income of nonwhites is less than two-thirds that of whites. About one-third of the nonwhite population is below the poverty line, compared to only about one-eighth of the white population. On the average, whites complete more years of schooling than nonwhites, and a larger percentage of whites than of nonwhites are college graduates.

There is considerable agreement that at least part of these economic differences is the result of discrimination. Nonwhites are often prevented from reaching certain occupational or managerial levels. It is rare to find a black in the higher reaches of management in a major corporation. To a considerable extent they are cut off from job opportunities at this level by lack of education. But even at much lower levels, they are kept out of certain occupations by union policy (the building trades are a good example); and even when nonwhites do essentially the same kind of work as whites, there is sometimes a tendency to pay nonwhites less.

EFFECTS OF DISCRIMINATION

Some important effects of racial discrimination can be demonstrated by using the theory of wages discussed in Chapter 29. (The general point of this discussion holds true whether discrimination is on racial or other grounds.) The important thing to recognize at the outset is that nonwhite labor is not allowed to compete with white labor. This results in two different labor markets, one for whites and one for nonwhites. As shown in Figure 31.6, the demand curve for nonwhite labor is quite different from the demand curve for white labor, reflecting the fact that nonwhites are not allowed to enter many of the more productive occupations. Because of the difference in the demand (and supply) curves, the equilibrium wage for nonwhites, P_B, is lower than for whites, P_W.

How does this equilibrium differ from a situation of no discrimination? If nonwhites and whites competed in the same labor market, the total demand for labor—regardless of color—and the total supply of labor—regardless of color—would be as shown in panel B of Figure 31.6, and the wage for all labor—regardless of color—would be P_T. A comparison of P_T with P_B shows that the wage rate of nonwhites would be increased considerably. A comparison of P_T with P_W shows that the wage rates of whites would be decreased slightly. The slight cut in white wages would be much smaller than the considerable increase in nonwhite wages, since the nation's total production

Table 31.4

ECONOMIC CHARACTERISTICS OF WHITES AND NONWHITES, UNITED STATES, 1983

	White	Non-white
Median family income (dollars)	25,757	14,506
Percent of persons in poverty	12.1	35.7
Percent unemployed (males)	6.4	16.4
Percent unemployed (females)	6.5	15.4
Percent unemployed (male teenagers)	16.8	42.7
Percent of people (25 years and over) with 4 years or more of college	19.5	9.5

Source: Economic Report of the President, 1985, and World Almanac. Unemployment rates pertain to 1984.

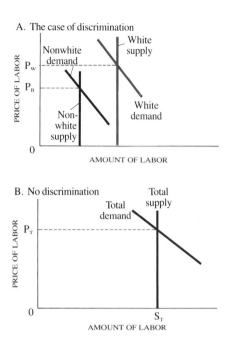

A. The case of discrimination

B. No discrimination

Figure 31.6

Racial Discrimination *Under discrimination, the demand curve for white labor is quite different from that for nonwhite labor, and the supply curve of white labor is quite different from that of nonwhite labor, so that the equilibrium wage for nonwhites, P_B, is lower than for whites, P_W. If there were no discrimination, the wage for all labor, nonwhite or white, would be P_T.*

(and income) would increase because nonwhites could be put to more productive use.

Thus the effect of discrimination is to exploit nonwhites—by reducing their wages relative to whites—and to lower the nation's total output. Fortunately, there is evidence that racial discrimination is lessening. In part because of changing attitudes among whites, the growing restiveness of the nonwhites, and the coming of age of new leadership, the old patterns of segregation and discrimination are breaking down. Blacks are now being recruited actively by many prestigious colleges, and they are being hired and promoted to responsible positions in firms where formerly they remained at a relatively menial level. Progress is slow, but it unquestionably exists.

DISCRIMINATION AGAINST WOMEN

Needless to say, discrimination is not limited to nonwhites. There is also some discrimination against older workers. Even more widespread is discrimination against women. Holding age and education constant, women earn much less than men. To some extent, this difference in earnings arises because women work shorter hours and often have less experience in their jobs than men. But even after adjusting for factors such as education, work experience during the year, and lifetime work experience, there remains a differential of about 20 percent between the earnings of men and women. To a considerable extent, this differential is probably the result of discrimination, the nature of which has been described in the following terms by the Council of Economic Advisers:

There is clearly prejudice against women engaging in particular activities. Some patients reject women doctors, some clients reject women lawyers, some customers reject automobile saleswomen, and some workers reject women bosses. Employers also may have formulated discriminatory attitudes about women, exaggerating the risk of job instability or client acceptance and therefore excluding women from on-the-job training which would advance their careers. In fact, even if employers do estimate correctly the average job turnover of women, women who are strongly committed to their jobs may suffer from "statistical discrimination" by being treated as though their own behavior resembled the average. The extent to which this type of discrimination occurs depends on how costly it is for employers to distinguish women who will have a strong job commitment from those who will not. Finally, because some occupations restrict the number of newcomers they take in and because women move in and out of the labor force more often, more women than men tend to fall into the newcomer category and to be thus excluded. For example, restrictive entry policies may have kept women out of the skilled crafts.

On the other hand, some component of the earnings differential and of the occupation differential stems from differences in role orientation which start with differences in education and continue through marriage, where women generally are expected to assume primary responsibility for the home and subordinate their own outside work to their household responsibilities. It is not now possible to distinguish in a quantitative way between the discrimination which bars women from jobs solely because of their sex, and the role differentiation whereby women, either through choice or necessity, restrict their careers because of the demands of their homes. Some may label the

691

Cross-Chapter Case/Part Eight

HOW THE MINIMUM WAGE AFFECTS TEENAGE UNEMPLOYMENT

The minimum wage goes back almost half a century in the United States. In 1938, the Congress passed the Fair Labor Standards Act, which established a minimum wage of 25 cents per hour. With inflation and changes in social attitudes and values, the minimum wage has been increased. Between 1938 and 1981 it was increased 15 times. Moreover, it has been extended to more and more workers. By 1984, it reached $3.35 an hour, and was applicable to more than 80 percent of all jobs.

At first glance, the minimum wage seems to be a sensible way to help the poor. After all, it seems reasonable to believe that people in very low-paying jobs tend to be poor, and a minimum wage would seem to increase their income. But a superficial analysis of this sort can be very misleading. As a matter of fact, many economists are convinced that the minimum wage has harmed many of the nation's poor. Few economists, if any, would argue that the minimum wage is the optimal way to fight poverty.

The difficulties with a minimum wage are demonstrated in the following figure, which shows the demand and supply curves for unskilled labor in a competitive labor market. Without the minimum wage, the equilibrium wage rate is $3.00 per hour, and OL_2 hours of labor are hired. If a minimum wage of $4.00 per hour is put into effect, employers will cut back on the amount of labor that they hire. Rather than employing OL_2 hours of labor, they will employ only OL_1 hours of labor. Unemployment will be created. Whereas workers would like to work OL_3 hours, they will only be able to work OL_1 hours. Not all of this unemployment will be reflected in

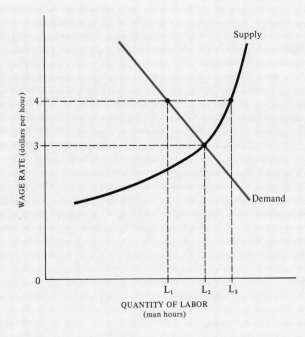

the government's unemployment statistics, since some people who are unable to find jobs may give up looking for work (and thus not be counted in the government's figures).

Clearly, the unskilled workers who keep their jobs are better off because of the minimum wage; they get $4 an hour rather than $3 an hour. But those who lose their jobs or are unable to find jobs are worse off. In general, one would expect that the least skilled and most disadvantaged would be the ones that would be hardest hit by the minimum wage. Specifically, one would expect the unemployment rate among teenagers, particularly black teenagers, to be increased by the minimum wage—and by increases in the minimum wage.

To illustrate how increases in the minimum wage can affect teenage employment, consider the fast-food industry (including firms like McDonald's), a leading employer of teenagers. When the minimum wage increased from $2.30 to $2.65 per hour in the late 1970s, the fast-food chains reduced their employees' average hours (by closing earlier and opening later), and introduced new equipment (like computerized cash registers) to save labor. Also, they sometimes substituted adults for teenagers. The overall result of the increase in the minimum wage was a decrease in the employment of teenagers.

Statistical studies have been carried out by economists to estimate the extent to which increases in the minimum wage affect the employment of teenagers. Dozens of such studies have been done. Although the results vary from study to study, most such investigations have found that a 10 percent increase in the minimum wage causes about a 1 to 3 percent reduction in teenage employment.[1]

Many observers, including President Reagan, favor a lower minimum wage for teenagers than for other workers. According to Daniel Hamermesh of Michigan State University, if the minimum wage for teenagers were reduced to $2.50 an hour, the unemployment rate for teenagers could be reduced considerably. Indeed, among black teenagers, the unemployment rate might be cut in half.[2]

In 1977, the House of Representatives established a Minimum Wage Study Commission, which was asked to investigate the effects of increasing the minimum wage on inflation, employment, and unemployment; and the ability of the minimum wage to combat poverty. In May 1981, the Commission issued a 250-page report summarizing its findings. Two principal recommendations were that the minimum wage should be indexed to adjust for inflation, and that there should not be a lower minimum wage for young workers than for older workers. Some observers, particularly conservatives, were critical of the Commission for its generally favorable attitude toward the minimum wage.[3]

As indicated above, many economists feel that the minimum wage is a poor way to fight poverty. One reason is that it creates unemployment. Another reason is that relatively few families seem to be poor because their

[1] C. Brown, C. Gilroy, and A. Kohen, "The Effect of the Minimum Wage on Employment and Unemployment," *Journal of Economic Literature*, June 1982.

[2] J. Shaw, "The Case for Paying Teenagers A Lower Minimum Wage," *Business Week*, April 2, 1984.

[3] M. Eccles and R. Freeman, "What! Another Minimum Wage Study?," *American Economic Review*, May 1982.

members earn low wages. (Instead, most do not have jobs or work only part-time.) Thus the minimum wage can have only a limited positive effect on the incomes of the poor. Nonetheless, some powerful groups, including organized labor, are strong believers in the minimum wage, and there is little prospect of fundamental changes in the minimum wage laws in the immediate future.

latter as a pervasive social discrimination which starts in the cradle; nonetheless, it is useful to draw the distinction.[7]

In various ways, the government has set out to discourage discrimination against women. The Equal Pay Act of 1963 requires employers to pay men and women equally for the same work, and Title VII of the Civil Rights Act of 1964 bars discrimination in hiring, firing, and other aspects of employment. In addition, a number of women have been appointed to high-ranking government jobs, including economists Juanita Kreps (who has been secretary of commerce), Marina Whitman (who has served as member of the President's Council of Economic Advisers), Alice Rivlin (who has headed the Congressional Budget Office), and Nancy Teeters (who has been a member of the Federal Reserve Board). All these measures undoubtedly will have a beneficial effect, but it must be recognized that eliminating discrimination of this kind will require basic changes in the attitudes of both males and females. The problem of discrimination against women is likely to be with us for a long time.

[7] *The Economic Report of the President*, 1973, pp. 106–7.

Test Yourself

1. "Since there cannot be two different prices for a homogeneous input, the existence of discrimination can be expected to disappear over time due to market forces." Comment and evaluate.

2. "The Social Security system is actuarially unsound. The amounts currently collected in Social Security taxes do not equal the amounts currently paid out in benefits. We cannot keep this up!" Comment and evaluate.

3. According to some economists, Social Security should be voluntary, not mandatory. Present the arguments on each side of this issue in as much detail as you can.

4. Do the official government statistics concerning poverty recognize that many people below the poverty line receive non-cash benefits from the government? If not, does this mean that these statistics are useless? Explain.

Summary

1. Lorenz curves are used to measure the extent of income inequality. They make it clear that there has been a considerable reduction in income inequality in the United States since the late 1920s. Practically all this reduction occurred before the end of World War II.

2. Many factors are responsible for existing income differentials. Some people are abler, better educated, or luckier than others. Some people have more property, or more monopoly power, than others.

3. Critics of income inequality argue that it lessens total consumer satisfaction because an extra dollar given to the poor provides them with more extra satisfaction than the loss of a dollar taken away from the rich. Also, they argue that income inequality leads to social and political inequality.

4. Defenders of income inequality point out that it is scientifically impossible to make interpersonal comparisons of utility, and argue that income inequality is needed to provide incentives for people to work and create, and that it permits greater capital formation.

5. There is no well-defined income level that can be used in all times and all places to determine poverty. Perhaps the most widely accepted definition of poverty in the United States today is the one developed by the Social Security Administration, according to which about 15 percent of the population in the United States—over 35 million people—fall below the poverty line. In recent decades, the incidence of poverty has been declining in the United States.

6. Nonwhite families, families headed by a female, and very large families are more likely than others to be poor. To a considerable extent, the reasons for their poverty lie beyond the control of the poor people. About one-third of poor adults have suffered a disability of some sort, or the premature death of the family breadwinner, or family dissolution. Most heads of poor families do not have jobs.

7. Because private charity is judged to be inadequate, the nation has authorized its government to carry out various public programs to aid the poor. There are programs to provide them with goods and services—food-stamp programs, for instance. Other programs, like aid to families with dependent children, give them cash. When these programs are taken into account, the percentage of the population falling below the poverty line is reduced considerably.

8. There is widespread dissatisfaction with existing antipoverty—or welfare—programs. They are judged to be inefficient; their costs have been increasing at an alarming rate; and they provide little incentive for people to get off welfare. One suggestion to remedy these problems is a negative income tax. In most of the forms put forth it involves a transfer of income that may be beyond the realm of political feasibility.

9. Despite recent improvements, the sad fact is that racial discrimination occurs in many walks of life in many areas of the United States. Nonwhites often are cut off from educational and job opportunities; and even when nonwhites do essentially the same kind of work as whites, there is sometimes a tendency to pay them less. The effects of discrimination are to reduce the wages of nonwhites relative to whites and to lower the nation's total output.

10. There is also much discrimination against women, making them less likely than men to enter the better-paying occupations. Even after adjusting for factors such as education and work experience, women earn about 20 percent less than men.

Concepts for Review

Income inequality	**Old-age insurance**	**Welfare**
Lorenz curve	**Social Security**	**Aid to families with**
Progressive tax	**Medicare**	**dependent**
Regressive tax	**Unemployment insurance**	**children**
Tax incidence	**Supplemental Security**	**Negative income tax**
Poverty	**Income Program**	**Break-even income**
	Food programs	**Discrimination**

PART NINE

International Economics

CHAPTER 32

International Trade

Practically all human beings realize that they are not islands unto themselves, and that they benefit from living with, working with, and trading with other people. Exactly the same is true of nations. They too must interact with one another, and they too benefit from trade with one another. No nation can be an island unto itself—not even the United States. To understand how the world economy functions, you must grasp the basic economic principles of international trade.

This chapter discusses many of the fundamental questions about international trade. What is the nature of American foreign trade? What are the effects of international trade? What determines the sorts of goods a nation will import or export? What are the advantages of free trade and the arguments against it? What are the social costs of tariffs and quotas, and what has been their history in the United States? What are some of the major issues regarding protectionism in the United States today? Some of these questions have occupied the attention of economists for hundreds of years; some are as current as today's newspaper.

America's Foreign Trade

America's foreign trade, although small relative to our national product, plays a very important role in our economic life. Many of our industries depend on other countries for markets or for raw materials (like coffee, tea, or tin). Our *exports*—the things we sell to other countries—amount to about 10 percent of our gross national product, which seems small relative to other countries like Germany, France, Italy, and the United Kingdom,

Table 32.1

U.S. MERCHANDISE EXPORTS, 1984

Product	Amount (billions of dollars)
Food, feed, and beverages	32
Industrial supplies and materials	63
Machinery	62
Automotive vehicles and parts	22
Aircraft	10
Other	31
Total	220

Source: Survey of Current Busness, March 1985.

Table 32.2

PERCENT OF U.S. EXPORTS, BY AREA, 1984

Country	Percent
Japan	10
Western Europe	26
Latin America	14
Canada	24
Eastern Europe	2
Other	24
Total	100

Source: See Table 32.1.

Table 32.3

U.S. MERCHANDISE IMPORTS, 1984

Product	Amount (billions of dollars)
Food, feed, and beverages	21
Petroleum and oil products	57
Other industrial supplies and materials	67
Capital goods	60
Automotive vehicles and parts	55
Consumer goods (excluding autos)	60
Other	8
Total	328

Source: See Table 32.1.

where exports are about 15 to 20 percent of gross national product. But this is because our domestic market is so large. In absolute terms, our exports (and imports) are bigger than those of any other nation. Without question, our way of life would have to change considerably if we could not trade with other countries.

When we were a young country, we exported raw materials primarily. During the 1850s about 70 percent of our exports were raw materials and foodstuffs. But the composition of our exports has changed with time. More are now finished manufactured goods and less are raw materials. In the 1960s, about 60 percent of our exports were finished manufactured goods, and only about 20 percent were raw materials and foodstuffs. Table 32.1 shows the importance of machinery and industrial supplies in our merchandise exports. Table 32.2 indicates to whom we sell. Western Europe and Canada take about one-half of our exports, and Latin America takes over 10 percent.

What sorts of goods do we buy from abroad? About 10 percent of our *imports* are agricultural commodities like coffee, sugar, bananas, and cocoa. Almost 20 percent are petroleum and its products. But a considerable proportion is neither raw materials nor foodstuffs. Over one-half of our imports, as shown in Table 32.3, are manufactured goods like bicycles from England or color TVs from Japan. Just as we sell more to Canada and Western Europe than any other area, so we buy more from these countries too (see Table 32.4). But the pattern varies from product to product. Thus Canada is our leading foreign source for wood pulp and nonferrous metals, while Latin America is our leading source of imported coffee and sugar.

Specialization and Trade

We have discussed the extent and nature of our trade with other countries, but not *why* we trade with other countries. Do we—and our trading partners—benefit from this trade? And if so, what determines the sorts of goods we should export and import? These are very important questions, among the most fundamental in economics. The answers are by no means new. They have been well understood for considerably more than a century, due to the work of such great economists as David Hume, David Ricardo, Adam Smith, and John Stuart Mill.

WHY DO INDIVIDUALS TRADE?

As a first step, it is useful to recognize that the benefits *nations* receive through trade are essentially the same as those *individuals* receive through trade. Consider the hypothetical case of John Barrister, a lawyer, with a wife and two children. The Barrister family, like practically all families, trades continually with other families and with business firms. Since Mr. Barrister is a lawyer, he trades his legal services for money which he and his wife use to buy the food, clothing, housing, and other goods and services his family wants. Why does the Barrister family do this? What advantages does it receive through trade? Why doesn't it attempt to be self-sufficient?

ABSOLUTE ADVANTAGE

Table 32.4

PERCENT OF U.S. IMPORTS, BY AREA, 1984

Country	Percent
Japan	17
Western Europe	22
Latin America	15
Canada	21
Eastern Europe	1
Other	25
Total[a]	100

Source: See Table 32.1.

[a] Because of rounding errors, figures do not sum to total.

To see why the Barrister family is sensible indeed to opt for trade rather than self-sufficiency, let's compare the current situation—where Mr. Barrister specializes in the production of legal services and trades the money he receives for other goods and services—with the situation if the Barrister family attempted to be self-sufficient. In the latter case, the Barristers would have to provide their own transportation, telephone service, foodstuffs, clothing, and a host of other things. Mr. Barrister is a lawyer—a well-trained, valuable, productive member of the community. But if he were to try his hand at making automobiles—or even bicycles—he might be a total loss. Thus, if the Barrister family attempted to be self-sufficient, it might be unable to provide many of the goods it now enjoys.

WHY DO NATIONS TRADE?

Trade permits specialization, and specialization increases output. This is the advantage of trade, both for individuals and for nations. In our hypothetical case, it is obvious that, because he can trade with other families and with firms, Mr. Barrister can specialize in doing what he is good at—law. Consequently, he can be more productive than if he were forced to be a Jack-of-all-trades, as he would have to be if he could not trade with others. The same principle holds for nations. Because the United States can trade with other nations, it can specialize in the goods and services it produces particularly well. Then it can trade them for goods that other countries are especially good at producing. Thus both we and our trading partners benefit.

Some countries have more and better resources of certain types than others. Saudi Arabia has oil, Canada has timber, Japan has a skilled labor force, and so on. *International differences in resource endowments, and in the relative quantity of various types of human and nonhuman resources, are important bases for specialization.* Consider countries with lots of fertile soil, little capital, and much unskilled labor. They are likely to find it advantageous to produce agricultural goods, while countries with poor soil, much capital, and highly skilled labor will probably do better to produce capital-intensive, high-technology goods. We must recognize, however, that the bases for specialization do not remain fixed over time. Instead, as technology and the resource endowments of various countries change, the pattern of international specialization changes as well. As we saw in the previous section, the United States specialized more in raw materials and foodstuffs about a century ago than it does now.

Absolute Advantage

To clarify the benefits of trade, consider the following example. Suppose that the United States can produce 2 electronic computers or 5,000 cases of wine with 1 unit of resources. Suppose that France can produce 1 electronic computer or 10,000 cases of wine with 1 unit of resources. Given the production possibilities in each country, are there any advantages in trade between the countries? And if so, what commodity should each country export, and what commodity should each country import? Should

699

France export wine and import computers, or should it import wine and export computers?

To answer these questions, assume that the United States is producing a certain amount of computers and a certain amount of wine—and that France is producing a certain amount of computers and a certain amount of wine. If the United States shifts 1 unit of its resources from producing wine to producing computers, it will increase its production of computers by 2 computers and reduce its production of wine by 5,000 cases of wine. If France shifts 1 unit of resources from the production of computers to the production of wine, it will increase its production of wine by 10,000 cases and reduce its production of computers by 1 computer.

Table 32.5 shows the *net* effect of this shift in the utilization of resources on *world* output of computers and of wine. World output of computers increases (by 1 computer) and world output of wine increases (by 5,000 cases) as a result of the redeployment of resources in each country. Thus *specialization increases world output.*

Moreover, if world output of each commodity is increased by shifting 1 unit of American resources from wine to computers and shifting 1 unit of French resources from computers to wine, it follows that world output of each commodity will be increased further if each country shifts *more* of its resources in the same direction. This is because the amount of resources required to produce each good is assumed to be constant, regardless of how much is produced.

Thus, in this situation, one country—the United States—should specialize in producing computers, and the other country—France—should specialize in producing wine. This will maximize world output of both wine and computers, permitting a rise in both countries' standards of living. Complete specialization of this sort is somewhat unrealistic, since countries often produce some of both commodities, but this simple example illustrates the basic principles involved.

Table 32.5
CASE OF ABSOLUTE ADVANTAGE

| | Increase or decrease in output of: | |
	Computers	Wine (thousands of cases)
Effect of U.S.'s shifting 1 unit of resources from wine to computers	+2	− 5
Effect of France's shifting 1 unit of resources from computers to wine	−1	+ 10
Net effect	+1	+ 5

Comparative Advantage

The case just described is a very special one, since one country (France) has an absolute advantage over another (the United States) in the production of one good (wine), whereas the second country (the United States) has an absolute advantage over the first (France) in the production of another good (computers). What do we mean by the term *absolute advantage?* Country A has an **absolute advantage** over Country B in the production of a good when Country A can produce a unit of the good with less resources than can Country B. Since the United States can produce a computer with fewer units of resources than France, it has an absolute advantage over France in the production of computers. Since France requires fewer resources than the United States to produce a given amount of wine, France has an absolute advantage over the United States in the production of wine.

But what if one country is more efficient in producing both goods? If the United States is more efficient in producing both computers and wine, is there still any benefit to be derived from specialization and trade? At first glance, you are probably inclined to answer no. But if this is your inclination, you should reconsider—because you are wrong.

COMPARATIVE ADVANTAGE GEOMETRICALLY

Table 32.6

CASE OF COMPARATIVE ADVANTAGE

| | Increase or decrease in output of: | |
	Computers	Wine (thousands of cases)
Effect of U.S.'s shifting 2 units of resources from wine to computers	+4	−10
Effect of France's shifting 3 units of resources from computers to wine	−3	+12
Net effect	+1	+2

Basic Idea #63: Trade between two countries can be mutually beneficial even if one country is more efficient at producing everything than the other country. Each country can specialize in products where it has a comparative advantage and import those where the other country has a comparative advantage. What is important in determining what a country should produce is comparative, not absolute, advantage.

A NUMERICAL EXAMPLE

To see why specialization and trade have advantages even when one country is more efficient than another at producing both goods, consider the following example. Suppose the United States can produce 2 electronic computers or 5,000 cases of wine with 1 unit of resources, and France can produce 1 electronic computer or 4,000 cases of wine with 1 unit of resources. In this case, the ·United States is a more efficient producer of both computers and wine. Nonetheless, as we shall see, world output of both goods will increase if the United States specializes in the production of computers and France specializes in the production of wine.

Table 32.6 demonstrates this conclusion. If 2 units of American resources are shifted from wine to computer production, 4 additional computers and 10,000 fewer cases of wine are produced. If 3 units of French resources are shifted from computer to wine production, 3 fewer computers and 12,000 additional cases of wine are produced. Thus the combined effect of this redeployment of resources in both countries is to increase world output of computers by 1 computer and to increase world output of wine by 2,000 cases. Even though the United States is more efficient than France in the production of both computers and wine, world output of both goods will be maximized if the United States specializes in computers and France specializes in wine.

Basically, this is so because, although the United States is more efficient than France in the production of both goods, it has a greater advantage in computers than in wine. It is twice as efficient as France in producing computers, but only 25 percent more efficient than France in producing wine. To derive these numbers, recall that 1 unit of resources will produce 2 computers in the United States, but only 1 computer in France. Thus the United States is twice as efficient in computers. On the other hand, 1 unit of resources will produce 5,000 cases of wine in the United States, but only 4,000 cases in France. Thus the United States is 25 percent more efficient in wine.

TRADE DEPENDS ON COMPARATIVE ADVANTAGE

A nation has a ***comparative advantage*** in those products where its efficiency relative to other nations is highest. Thus, in this case, the United States has a comparative advantage in the production of computers and a comparative disadvantage in the production of wine. So long as a country has a comparative advantage in the production of some commodities and a comparative disadvantage in the production of others, it can benefit from specialization and trade. A country will specialize in products where it has a comparative advantage, and import those where it has a comparative disadvantage. The point is that *specialization and trade depend on comparative, not absolute advantage.* One of the first economists to understand the full significance of this fact was David Ricardo, the English economist of the early nineteenth century.

A Geometric Representation of Comparative Advantage

The principle of comparative advantage, like so many important economic concepts, can be displayed diagrammatically. Again, we suppose that in the United States 1 unit of resources will produce 2 electronic computers or 5,000 cases of wine. Consequently, the **production possibilities curve** in the United States—the curve that shows the maximum number of computers that can be produced, given various outputs of wine—is the one in panel A of Figure 32.1. The United States must give up 1 computer for every additional 2,500 cases of wine that it produces; thus the slope of the American production possibilities curve is $-\dfrac{1}{2,500}$.[1]

Also, as in the previous section, we suppose that in France 1 unit of resources will produce 1 electronic computer or 4,000 cases of wine. Thus the production possibilities curve in France is as shown in panel B of Figure 32.1. France must give up 1 computer for every additional 4,000 cases of wine it produces; thus the slope of France's production possibilities curve is $-\dfrac{1}{4,000}$.

Now suppose that the United States uses all its resources to produce computers and that France uses all its resources to produce wine. In other words, the United States operates at point A on its production possibilities curve and France operates at point B on its production possibilities curve. Then suppose that the United States trades its computers for France's wine. AC in panel A of Figure 32.1 shows the various amounts of computers and wine the United States can end up with if it specializes in computers and trades them for French wine. AC is called the **trading possibilities curve** of the United States. The slope of AC is minus 1 times the ratio of the price of a case of wine to the price of a computer, since this ratio equals the number of computers the United States must give up to get a case of French wine. Similarly, the line BD in panel B of Figure 32.1 shows France's trading possibilities curve. That is, BD represents the various amounts of computers and wine France can wind up with if it specializes in wine and trades it for U.S. computers.

The thing to note about both panels of Figure 32.1 is that each country's trading possibilities curve—AC in panel A, BD in panel B—lies above its production possibilities curve. This means that *both countries can have more of both commodities by specializing and trading than by trying to be self-sufficient*—even though the United States is more efficient than France at producing both commodities. Thus Figure 32.1 shows what we said in the previous section: If countries specialize in products where they have a comparative advantage and trade with one another, each country can improve its standard of living.

The Terms of Trade

The **terms of trade** are defined as the quantity of imported goods that a country can obtain in exchange for a unit of domestic goods. Thus, in Figure 32.1, the terms of trade are measured by the ratio of the price of a

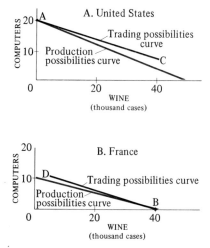

Figure 32.1

Benefits of Specialization and Trade
AC *represents the various amounts of computers and wine that the United States can end up with, if it specializes in computers and trades them for French wine. The slope of* AC *equals* −1 *times the ratio of the price of a case of wine to the price of a computer, assumed to be* $\dfrac{1}{3,333}$. BD *represents the various amounts of computers and wine that France can wind up with, if it specializes in wine and trades for U.S. computers.* AC *lies above America's production possibilities curve and* BD *lies above France's production possibilities curve. Thus both countries can have more of both commodities by specializing and trading than by attempting to be self-sufficient.*

[1] As we know from Chapter 2, the production possibilities curve shows the maximum amount of one commodity that can be produced, given various outputs of the other commodity. Since the United States must give up 1/2,500 computer for each additional case of wine that it produces, the slope must be − 1/2,500.

computer to the price of a case of wine—since this ratio shows how many cases of French wine the United States can get in exchange for an American computer. In Figure 32.1, we asume that this ratio equals 3,333:1. It is important to note that this ratio must be somewhere between 2,500:1 and 4,000:1. By diverting its own resources from computer production to wine production, the United States can exchange a computer for 2,500 cases of wine. Since this is possible, it will not pay the United States to trade a computer for less than 2,500 cases of wine. Similarly, since France can exchange a case of wine for 1/4,000 of a computer by diverting its own resources from wine to computers, it clearly will not be willing to trade a case of wine for less than 1/4,000 of a computer.

But where will the price ratio lie between 2,500:1 and 4,000:1? The answer depends on *world supply and demand for the two products*. The stronger the demand for computers (relative to their supply) and the weaker the demand for wine (relative to its supply), the higher the price ratio. On the other hand, the weaker the demand for computers (relative to their supply) and the stronger the demand for wine (relative to its supply), the lower the price ratio.

Incomplete Specialization

Figure 32.1 shows that the United States should specialize completely in computers, and that France should specialize completely in wine. This result stems from the assumption that the cost of producing a computer or a case of wine is constant. If, on the other hand, the cost of producing each good increases with the amount produced, the result is likely to be incomplete specialization. In other words, although the United States will continue to specialize in computers and France will continue to specialize in wine, each country will also produce some of the other good as well. This is a more likely outcome, since specialization generally tends to be less than complete.

International Trade and Individual Markets

We have emphasized that nations can benefit by specializing in the production of goods for which they have a comparative advantage and trading these goods for others where they have a comparative disadvantage.[2]

---

[2] The principle of comparative advantage is useful in explaining and predicting the pattern of world trade, as well as in showing the benefits of trade. For example, consider the exports of Great Britain and the United States. Robert Stern of the University of Michigan compared British and American exports of 39 industries. In 21 of the 24 industries where our labor productivity was more than three times that of the British, our exports exceeded British exports. In 11 of the 15 industries where our labor productivity was less than three times that of the British, our exports were less than British exports. Thus, in 32 out of 39 industries, the principle of comparative advantage, as interpreted by Stern, predicted correctly which country would export more. This is a high batting average, since labor is not the only input and labor productivity is an imperfect measure of true efficiency. Moreover, as we shall see in subsequent sections, countries raise barriers to foreign trade, preventing trade from taking place in accord with the principle of comparative advantage.

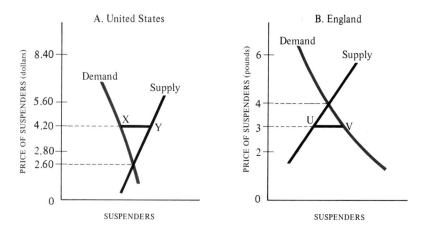

Figure 32.2

Determination of Quantity Imported and Exported under Free Trade *Under free trade, price will equal $4.20 or £3. The United States will export* XY *units, the English will import* UV *units, and* XY = UV.

But how do a nation's producers know whether they have a comparative advantage or disadvantage in the production of a given commodity? They do not call up the local university and ask the leading professor of economics (although that might not always be such a bad idea). Instead, as we shall see in this section, the market for the good provides the required signals.

To see how this works, let's consider a new (and rather whimsical) product—bulletproof suspenders. Suppose that the Mob, having run a scientific survey of gunmen and policemen, finds that most of them wear their suspenders over their bulletproof vests. As a consequence, the Mob's gunmen are instructed to render a victim immobile by shooting holes in his suspenders (thus making his trousers fall down and trip him). Naturally, the producers of suspenders will soon find it profitable to produce a new bulletproof variety, an innovation which, it is hoped, will make a solid contribution to law and order. The new suspenders are demanded only in the United States and England, since the rest of the world wear belts. The demand curve in the United States is as shown in panel A of Figure 32.2, and the demand curve in England is as shown in panel B. Suppose further that this product can be manufactured in both the United States and England. The supply curve in the United States is as shown in panel A, and the supply curve in England is as shown in panel B.

Take a closer look at Figure 32.2. Note that prices in England are expressed in pounds (£) and prices in the United States are expressed in dollars ($). This is quite realistic. Each country has its own currency, in which prices in that country are expressed. As of 1985, £1 was equal to about $1.40. In other words, you could exchange a pound note for $1.40—or $1.40 for a £1 note. For this reason, the two panels of Figure 32.2 are lined up so that a price of $2.80 is at the same level as a price of £2, $4.20 is at the same level as £3, and so on.

NO FOREIGN TRADE

To begin with, suppose that bulletproof suspenders cannot be exported or imported, perhaps because of a very high tariff (tax on imports) imposed on them in both the United States and England. (One can readily imagine members of both Congress and Parliament defending such a tariff on the grounds that a capacity to produce plenty of bulletproof suspenders is important for national defense.) If this happens, the price of bulletproof suspenders will be $2.60 in the United States and £4 in England. Why? Because, as shown in Figure 32.2, these are the prices at which each country's demand curve intersects its supply curve.

FOREIGN TRADE PERMITTED

Next, suppose that international trade in this product is permitted, perhaps because both countries eliminate the tariff. Now what will happen? Since the price is lower in the United States than in England, people can make money by sending this product from the United States to England. After all, they can buy it for $2.60 in this country and sell it for £4 (= $5.60) in England. But they will not be able to do so indefinitely. As more and more suspenders are supplied by the United States for the English market, the price in the United States must go up (to induce producers to produce the additional output) and the price in England must go down (to induce consumers to buy the additional quantity).

When an equilibrium is reached, *the price in the United States must equal the price in England.* If this did not happen, there would be an advantage in increasing American exports (if the price in England were higher) or in decreasing American exports (if the price in the United States were higher). Thus only if the prices are equal can an equilibrium exist.

At what level will this price—which is common to both countries—tend to settle? Obviously, *the price must end up at the level where the amount of the good one country wants to export equals the amount the other country wants to import.* In other words, it must settle at $4.20 or £3. Otherwise, the total amount demanded in both countries would not equal the total amount supplied in both countries. And any reader who has mastered the material in Chapter 3 knows that such a situation cannot be an equilibrium.

THE SIGNAL OF MARKET FORCES

At this point, we can see how market forces indicate whether a country has a comparative advantage or a comparative disadvantage in the production of a certain commodity. *If a country has a comparative advantage, it turns out—after the price of the good in various countries is equalized and total world output of the good equals total world demand for it—that the country exports the good under free trade and competition.* In Figure 32.2, it turns out—as we've just seen—that the United States is an exporter of bulletproof suspenders under free trade, because the demand and supply curves in the United States and England take the positions. they do. The basic reason why the curves take these positions is that the United States has a comparative advantage in the production of this good. Thus, to put things in a nutshell, a nation's producers can tell (under free trade) whether they have a comparative advantage in the production of a certain commodity by seeing whether it is profitable for them to export it. If they can make a profit, they have a comparative advantage.[3]

---

[3] In reality things are not quite so simple. For one thing, high transport costs are often involved in moving goods from one country to another. These costs can impede trade in certain commodities. Also, tariffs or quotas can be enacted by governments to interfere with free trade. Much more will be said on this score in later sections.

Economies of Scale and Learning

Specialization and trade may be advantageous even if there is no difference among countries in the efficiency with which they can produce goods and services. In a case like this, although no nation has a technological advantage over any other, specialization and trade may still be of benefit, because there may be economies of scale in producing some commodities. Thus, if one country specializes in one good and another country specializes in another good, firms can serve the *combined* markets of both countries, which will make their costs *lower* than if they could only reach their domestic markets. This is a major argument for forming an international economic association like the European Common Market, discussed later in this chapter.

Another reason for specialization is that it may result in learning. It is well known that the cost of producing many articles goes down as more and more of the articles are produced. In the aircraft and machine tool industries, producers are well aware of the reduction in costs from learning. The unit costs of a new machine tool tend to be reduced by 20 percent for each doubling of cumulated output, due to improved efficiency through individual and organizational learning. If such learning is an important factor in an industry, there are advantages in having one nation's producers specialize in a certain good. Specialization can reduce costs to a lower level than if each nation tries to be self-sufficient. Longer production runs cut costs since *the more a producer makes, the lower the unit costs.*

Innovation and International Trade

International trade also arises because of technological change. Suppose that a new product is invented in the United States and an American firm begins producing and selling it in the American market. It catches on, and the American innovator decides to export the new product to Europe and other foreign markets. If the new product meets European needs and tastes, the Europeans will import it from the United States; and later, when the market in Europe gets big enough, the American firm may establish a branch plant in Europe. For a time at least, European firms do not have the technological know-how to produce the new product, which is often protected to some extent by patents.

Trade of this sort is based on a *technology gap* between countries. Consider the plastics industry. After the development of a new plastic, there generally has been a period of 15 to 25 years when the innovating country has had a decisive advantage and has been likely to lead in per capita production and exports. It has had a head start, as well as the benefits of patents and commercial secrecy. Production has been licensed to other countries, but often on a limited scale and only after a number of years. Soon after the patents expire, a different phase begins. Imitation is easier, technical know-how spreads more readily, direct technical factors lose importance, and such other factors as materials costs become much more important. Industry from other countries may challenge the innovator in export markets, and sometimes in the innovator's home market as well, although the innovating firm still benefits to some extent from its accumulated knowledge and experience and its ongoing research and development.

The United States tends to export products with a high technological component—relatively new products based on considerable research and development. If the 5 U.S. industries with the largest research programs are compared with the 14 other major industries, it turns out that the high-research industries export 4 times as much per dollar of sales as the others.[4] During the 1960s, Europeans expressed considerable concern over the technological gap between the United States and Europe. They asserted that superior know-how stemming from scientific and technical development in the United States had allowed American companies to obtain large shares of European markets in areas like aircraft, space equipment, computers, and other electronic products. More recently, our technological lead has narrowed considerably in many industries, as the Japanese, Germans, and others have upgraded their technology. Indeed, in some areas, their technology now surpasses our own. According to many observers, some American exports will be, and are being, hurt as a consequence.[5]

Multinational Firms

One of the most remarkable economic phenomena of the last 30 years has been the growth of *multinational firms*—firms that make direct investments in other countries and produce and market their products abroad. For example, Coca-Cola is produced and bottled all over the world. Most multinational firms are American, but companies like Shell in petroleum and Hoffman-La Roche in drugs are examples of foreign-based multinational firms. The available data indicate that the multinational firms have grown by leaps and bounds, and that their shipments have become a bigger proportion of international trade.

The reasons why firms have become multinational are varied. In some cases, firms have established overseas branches to control foreign sources of raw materials. In other cases, they have invested overseas in an effort to defend their competitive position. Very frequently, firms have established foreign branches to exploit a technological lead. After exporting a new product (or a cheaper version of an existing product) to foreign markets, firms have decided to establish plants overseas to supply these markets. Once a foreign market is big enough to accommodate a plant of minimum efficient size, this decision does not conflict with economies of scale. Moreover, transport costs often hasten such a decision. Also, in some

---

[4] Charles Kindleberger, *International Economics,* Homewood, Ill.: Irwin, 1968, p. 67. Also, see R. Vernon, "International Investment and International Trade in the Product Cycle," *Quarterly Journal of Economics,* May 1966; and R. Caves and R. Jones, *World Trade and Payments,* 2d ed., Boston: Little, Brown, 1977.

[5] Besides differences in technology, another reason for trade is a difference in national tastes. If Country A likes beef and Country B likes pork, it may pay both countries to produce beef and pork, and Country A may find it advantageous to import beef from Country B and Country B may find it advantageous to import pork from Country A.

cases, the only way a firm can introduce its innovation into a foreign market is through the establishment of overseas production facilities.

EFFECTS OF MULTINATIONAL FIRMS

By carrying its technology overseas, the multinational firm plays a very important role in the international diffusion of innovations. A firm with a technological edge over its competitors often prefers to exploit its technology in foreign markets through wholly owned subsidiaries rather than through licensing or other means. To some extent, this is because of difficulties in using ordinary market mechanisms to buy and sell information. The difficulties of transferring technology across organizational, as well as national, boundaries also contribute to the decision. For these and other reasons, the innovating firm may find it advantageous to transfer its technology to other countries by establishing subsidiaries abroad.

One of the most important effects of the multinational firm has been to integrate the economies of the world more closely into a worldwide system. In other words, multinational firms have tended to break down some of the barriers between nations. Besides speeding the diffusion of new technology, they have linked the capital markets of many countries and promoted the international transfer of important managerial labor.

Particularly in the less developed countries, there has been an impassioned debate over the pros and cons of the multinational firm, which sometimes is viewed with suspicion by the nation-states in which it operates. These nation-states feel that their sovereignty is threatened by the great power of the multinational firm over their national economies. And the tragedy at Bhopal, India, where thousands of people were killed in 1984 by an accident at a plant owned by a major multinational firm—Union Carbide Corporation—has caused further conflict of this sort. Also, some observers are wary of multinational firms because of the possibility that they will attain undesirable monopoly power. In addition, as we shall see in subsequent chapters, they may put undesirable stress on the international financial system.

Test Yourself

1. Suppose that the United States can produce 3 electronic computers or 3,000 cases of wine with 1 unit of resources, while France can produce 1 electronic computer or 2,000 cases of wine with 1 unit of resources. Will specialization increase world output?

2. Suppose that the United States has 100 units of resources while France has 50 units. Based on the data in Question 1, draw the production possibilities curve in each country. Without international trade, what will be the ratio of the price of an electronic computer to the price of a case of wine in each country?

3. Given the information in Questions 1 and 2, how will firms in France and the United States know whether they should produce wine or electronic computers? Must the government instruct them on this score? Why or why not?

4. Under the circumstances described in Questions 1 and 2, will each country specialize completely in the production of one or the other good? Why or why not? What factors result in incomplete specialization in the real world?

Tariffs and Quotas

WHAT IS A TARIFF?

Despite its advantages, not everyone benefits from free trade. On the contrary, the well-being of some firms and workers may be threatened by foreign competition; and they may press for a *tariff*, a tax the government imposes on imports. The purpose of a tariff is to cut down on imports in order to protect domestic industry and workers from foreign competition. A secondary reason for tariffs is to produce revenue for the government.

To see how a tariff works, consider the market for wristwatches. Suppose that the demand and supply curves for wristwatches in the United States are as shown in panel A of Figure 32.3, and that the demand and supply curves for wristwatches in Switzerland are as shown in panel B. Clearly, Switzerland has a comparative advantage in the production of wristwatches, and under free trade the price of a wristwatch would tend toward $10 in the United States and toward 25 Swiss francs in Switzerland. (Note that 1 Swiss franc is assumed to equal 40 cents.) Under free trade, the United States would import 10 million wristwatches from Switzerland.

Now if the United States imposes a tariff of $10 on each wristwatch imported from Switzerland, the imports will completely cease. Any importers who buy watches in Switzerland at the price (when there is no foreign trade) of 15 Swiss francs—which equals $6—must pay a tariff of $10; this makes their total cost $16 per watch. But this is more than the price of a watch in the United States when there is no foreign trade (which is $15). Consequently, there is no money to be made by importing watches—unless Americans can be persuaded to pay more for a Swiss watch than for an identical American watch.

THE SOCIAL COSTS OF TARIFFS

What is the effect of the tariff? The domestic watch industry receives a higher price—$15 rather than $10—than it would without a tariff. And the workers in the domestic watch industry may have more jobs and higher

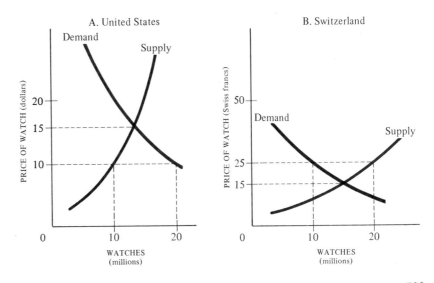

Figure 32.3

Effect of a Tariff on Swiss Watches

Under free trade, price would equal $10, or 25 Swiss francs. If a tariff of $10 is imposed on each watch imported from Switzerland, there will be a complete cessation of imports. Price in the United States will increase to $15, and price in Switzerland will fall to 15 Swiss francs.

wages than without the tariff. The victim of the tariff is the American consumer, who pays a higher price for wristwatches. Thus the domestic watch industry benefits at the expense of the rest of the nation. But does the general public lose more than the watch industry gains? In general, the answer is yes. The tariff reduces the welfare of the nation as a whole.

The tariff in Figure 32.3 is a **prohibitive tariff**—a tariff so high that it stops all imports of the good in question. Not all tariffs are prohibitive. (If they were, the government would receive no revenue at all from tariffs.) In many cases, the tariff is high enough to stop some, but not all, imports; and, as you would expect, the detrimental effect of a nonprohibitive tariff on living standards is less than that of a prohibitive tariff. But this does not mean that nonprohibitive tariffs are harmless. On the contrary, they can do lots of harm to domestic consumption and living standards.

The detrimental effects of tariffs have long been recognized, even in detective stories. Thus, in the course of solving the mystery concerning the Hound of the Baskervilles, Sherlock Holmes expressed his enthusiastic approval of a newspaper editorial that read as follows:

> You may be cajoled into imagining that your own special trade or your own industry will be encouraged by a protective tariff, but it stands to reason that such legislation must in the long run . . . lower the general conditions of life on this island.

Of course, Holmes considered this point elementary (my dear Watson) but worth hammering home.

WHAT IS A QUOTA?

Besides tariffs, other barriers to free trade are **quotas,** which many countries impose on the amount of certain commodities that can be imported annually. The United States sets import quotas on sugar and exerts pressure on foreigners to get them to limit the quantity of steel and textiles that they will export to us. To see how a quota affects trade, production, and prices, let's return to the market for wristwatches. Suppose the United States places a quota on the import of wristwatches: no more than 6 million wristwatches can be imported per year. Figure 32.4 shows the effect of the quota. Before it was imposed, the price of wristwatches was $10 (or 25 Swiss francs), and the United States imported 10 million wristwatches from Switzerland. The quota forces the United States to reduce its imports to 6 million.

What will be the effect on the U.S. price? The demand curve shows that, if the price is $12, American demand will exceed American supply by 6 million watches; in other words, we will import 6 million watches. Thus, once the quota is imposed, the price will rise to $12, since *this is the price that will reduce our imports to the amount of the quota.* A quota—like a tariff—increases the price of the good. (Note too that the price in Switzerland will fall to 20 francs. Thus the quota will reduce the price in Switzerland.)

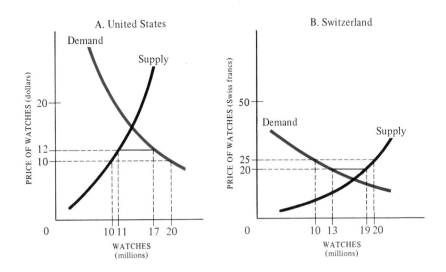

Figure 32.4

Effect of a Quota on Swiss Watches
*Before the quota is imposed, the price is
$10, or 25 Swiss francs. After a quota of 6
million watches is imposed, the price in
the United States rises to $12, and the
price in Switzerland falls to 20 Swiss
francs.*

THE SOCIAL COSTS OF QUOTAS

Both a quota and a tariff reduce trade, raise prices, protect domestic industry from foreign competition, and reduce the standard of living of the
nation as a whole. But most economists tend to regard quotas with even
less enthusiasm than they do tariffs. Under many circumstances, a quota
insulates local industry from foreign competition even more effectively
than a tariff does. Foreigners, if their costs are low enough, can surmount
a tariff barrier; but if a quota exists, there is no way they can exceed the
quota. Moreover, a (nonprohibitive) tariff provides the government with
some revenue, while quotas do not even do that. The windfall price increase from a quota accrues to the importer who is lucky enough or influential enough—or sufficiently generous with favors and bribes—to get an
import license. (However, if the government auctions off the import licenses, it can obtain revenue from a quota.)

EXPORT SUBSIDIES AND OTHER NONTARIFF BARRIERS TO FREE
TRADE

Finally, ***export subsidies,*** another means by which governments try to give
their domestic industry an advantage in international competition, are
also a major impediment to free trade. Such subsidies may take the form
of outright cash disbursements, tax exemptions, preferential financing or
insurance arrangements, or other preferential treatment for exports. Export subsidies, and other such measures, frequently lead to countermea-
sures. Thus, to counter foreign export subsidies, the U.S. government has
imposed duties against such subsidies on goods sold here.

Other nontariff barriers to free trade include licensing requirements and
unreasonable product quality standards. By granting few licenses (which
are required in some countries to import goods) and by imposing unrealistically stringent product quality standards, governments discourage imports.

Arguments for Tariffs and Quotas

Given the disadvantages to society at large of tariffs and other barriers to free trade, why do governments continue to impose them? There are many reasons, some sensible, some irrational.

THE NATIONAL DEFENSE ARGUMENT

One of the most convincing arguments is the desirability of maintaining a domestic industry for purposes of *national defense.* Thus, even if the Swedes had a comparative advantage in producing airplanes, we would not allow free trade to put our domestic producers of aircraft out of business if we felt that a domestic aircraft industry was necessary for national defense. Although the Swedes are by no means unfriendly, we would not want to import our entire supply of such a critical commodity from a foreign country, where the supply might be shut off for reasons of international politics. (Recall the Arab oil embargo of 1973.)

This is a perfectly valid reason for protecting certain domestic industries, and many protective measures are defended on these grounds. To the extent that protective measures are in fact required for national defense, economists go along with them. The restrictions entail social costs (some of which were described in previous sections), but these costs may well be worth paying for enhanced national security. The trouble is that many barriers to free trade are justified on these grounds when in fact they protect domestic industries only tenuously connected with national defense. Moreover, even if there is a legitimate case on defense grounds for protecting a domestic industry, subsidies are likely to be a more straightforward and efficient way to do so than tariffs or quotas.

Besides national defense, there are other noneconomic reasons for protecting particular domestic industries. Some countries—Canada, for one—use a tariff to protect certain industries that they feel help them to be more independent of foreign domination and influence. Many Canadians, for understandable reasons, are intent on maintaining their traditions and values, and on resisting the penetration of American ways. Such noneconomic reasons for protection are perfectly reasonable if the nation as a whole understands the economic cost and agrees that the game is worth the candle (and if the reasons are sufficiently understood by foreigners that the measures do not provoke retaliation).

OTHER ARGUMENTS FOR TARIFFS

Besides national defense, several other arguments for tariffs or quotas can make sense.

1. Tariffs or other forms of protection can be justified to foster the growth or development of young industries. Suppose that Japan has a comparative advantage in the production of a certain semiconductor, but Japan does not presently produce this item. It may take Japanese firms several years to become proficient in the relevant technology, to engage in the learning described in a previous section and to take advantage of the relevant economies of scale. While this industry is "growing up," Japan may impose a tariff on such semiconductors, thus shielding its young industry from competition it cannot yet handle. This "infant industry" argument for tariffs has a long history; Alexander Hamilton was one of its early exponents. Needless to say, it is *not* an argument for *permanent* tariffs, since infant industries are supposed to grow up—and the sooner the better. (Moreover, a subsidy for the industry would probably be better and easier to remove than a temporary tariff, according to many economists.)

2. Tariffs sometimes may be imposed to protect domestic jobs and to reduce unemployment at home. In the short run the policy may succeed, but we must recognize that other nations are likely to retaliate by enacting or increasing their own tariffs, so that such a policy may not work very well in the long run. A more sensible way to reduce domestic unemployment is to use the tools of fiscal and monetary policy described in Chapters 12 and 16 rather than tariffs. If workers are laid off by industries that cannot compete with foreign producers, proper monetary and fiscal policy, together with retraining programs, should enable these workers to switch to other industries that can compete.

3. Tariffs sometimes may be imposed to prevent a country from being too dependent on only a few industries. Consider a Latin American country that is a major producer of bananas. Under free trade, this country might produce bananas and little else, putting its entire economy at the mercy of the banana market. If the price of bananas fell, the country's national income would decrease drastically. To promote industrial diversification, this country may establish tariffs to protect other industries—for example, certain types of light manufacturing. In a case like this, the tariff protects the country from having too many eggs—or bananas (if you want to avoid mixing a metaphor)—in a single basket.

4. Tariffs may sometimes improve a country's terms of trade—that is, the ratio of its export prices to its import prices. The United States is a major importer of bananas. If we impose a tariff on bananas, thus cutting down on the domestic demand for them (because the tariff will increase their price), the reduction in our demand is likely to reduce the price of bananas abroad. Consequently, foreign producers of bananas will really pay part of the tariff. However, other countries may retaliate; and if all countries pursue such policies, few, if any, are likely to find themselves better off.

FREQUENTLY ENCOUNTERED FALLACIES

Although, as we have just seen, tariffs can be defended under certain circumstances, many of the arguments for them frequently encountered in political oratory and popular discussions are misleading. Although no field of economics is free of popular misconceptions and fallacies, this one is particularly rich in pious inanities and thunderous *non sequiturs*.

Fallacy 1. One frequently encountered fallacy is that, if foreigners want to trade with us, they must be benefiting from the trade. Consequently, according to this argument, we must be giving them more than we get—and it must be in our interest to reduce trade. This argument is entirely erroneous in its assumption that trade cannot be beneficial to *both* trading partners. On the contrary, as we have seen, the heart of the argument for trade is that it can be mutually beneficial.

Basic Idea #64: Tariffs and quotas reduce trade, raise prices, protect domestic industry from foreign competition, and reduce the standard of living of the nation as a whole. The industries (and workers) that are protected by tariffs and quotas gain at the expense of the general public. However, national defense and "infant industry" arguments (and others) are often advanced to support tariffs and quotas.

713

Fallacy 2. Another fallacy one often encounters in polite conversation—and not-so-polite political debate—is that a tariff is required to protect our workers from low-wage labor in other countries. According to this argument, since American labor (at $8 an hour) clearly cannot compete with foreign labor (which works at "coolie" wage levels), we have no choice but to impose tariffs. If we do not, cheap foreign goods will throw our high-priced laborers out of work. This argument is wrong on two counts. First, *high wages do not necessarily mean high unit costs of production.* Because the productivity of American workers is high, unit labor costs in the United States are roughly in line with those in other countries. (Recall from Chapter 18 that unit labor cost equals the wage rate divided by labor productivity. Thus unit labor cost may be no higher here than abroad, even though the wage rate here is much higher, if labor productivity here is also much higher than abroad.) Second, *if our costs were out of line with those of other countries, there should be a change in exchange rates, which would tend to bring them back into line.* As we shall see in Chapter 33, exchange rates should move to bring our exports and imports into balance.

Fallacy 3. Still another fallacy that makes the rounds is that it is better to "buy American" because then we have both the goods that are bought and the money, whereas if we buy from foreigners we have the goods but they have the money. Like some jokes, this fallacy has an ancient lineage—and one that borders on respectability, since Abraham Lincoln is supposed to have subscribed to it. Basically, the flaw is the implicit assumption that money is somehow valued for its own sake. In reality, all foreigners can do with the money is buy some of our goods, so that really we are just swapping some of our goods for some of theirs. If such a trade is mutually advantageous, fine.

WHY SO MUCH NONSENSE?

Why do politicians (both Democrats and Republicans) sometimes utter these fallacies? No doubt an important reason is simply ignorance. There is no law that prevents people with little understanding of economics from holding public office. But this may not be the only reason. Special-interest groups—particular industries, unions, and regions—have a lot to gain by getting the government to enact protective tariffs and quotas. And Congress and the executive branch of the government are often sensitive to the pressures of these groups, which wield considerable political power.

Faced with a choice between helping a few powerful, well-organized groups and helping the general public—which is poorly organized and often ignorant of its own interests—politicians frequently tend to favor the special-interest groups. After all, these groups have a lot to gain and will remember their friends, while the general public—each member of which loses only a relatively small amount—will be largely unaware of its losses anyhow. Having decided to help these groups, representatives or senators may not exert themselves unduly to search out or expose the weakness in some of the arguments used to bolster their position. Thus there is the story of a well-known senator who, about to deliver a certain oration, wrote in the margin of one section of his speech: "Weak point here. Holler like hell."

Finally, it is important to recognize once again that, although the majority of citizens benefit from free trade, some are likely to be hurt by it. A reduction in the tariff on shoes is likely to hurt people who own and work in American shoe factories. If our domestic shoe industry cannot compete with foreign producers, workers will be laid off and plants will close. The result will be a considerable loss to domestic shoe producers and workers. Most people believe that society as a whole, which benefits from free trade, should help the minority that is victimized by it. To promote this objective, the United States has established "adjustment assistance" for firms or workers who, because of government agreement to reduce barriers to free trade, have suffered idleness or unemployment due to an increase in imports. Workers can enter retraining programs and can obtain allowances to help pay for moving to other jobs.

Tariffs in the United States

How high are American tariffs, now and in the past? In our early years, we were a very protectionist nation. The argument for protecting our young industry from the competition of European manufacturers was the "infant industry" argument, which, as we saw above, can be perfectly sensible. However, our own industries understandably found it advantageous to prolong their childhood for as long as possible—and to press for continuation of high tariffs. During the nineteenth century and well into the twentieth, the industrial Northeast was particularly strong in its support of tariffs. Furthermore, the Republican party, which generally held sway in American politics between the Civil War and the New Deal, favored a high tariff. Thus, as shown in Figure 32.5, the tariff remained relatively high from about 1870 until the early 1930s. With the exception of the period around World War I, average tariff rates were about 40 to 50 percent. With the enactment of the Smoot-Hawley Tariff of 1930, the tariff reached its peak—about 60 percent. Moreover, these tariff rates understate the extent to which the tariff restricted trade: Some goods were completely shut out of the country by the tariff, and do not show up in the figures.

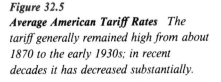

Figure 32.5
Average American Tariff Rates The tariff generally remained high from about 1870 to the early 1930s; in recent decades it has decreased substantially.

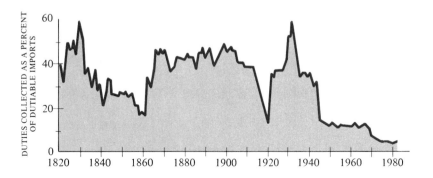

With the Democratic victory in 1932, a movement began toward freer trade. The Trade Agreements Act of 1934 allowed the president to bargain with other countries to reduce barriers to trade. He was given the power to lower U.S. tariffs by as much as 50 percent. In 1945, he was given the power to make further tariff reductions. Between 1934 and 1948, tariff rates fell substantially, as shown in Figure 32.5. By 1948, the United States was no longer a high-tariff country; the average tariff rate was only about 10 percent.[6]

THE KENNEDY ROUND

During the 1950s, there were no further decreases in the tariff—but there were no substantial increases either. The movement toward freer trade was continued by President Kennedy in 1962, and during the 1960s, the "Kennedy Round" negotiations took place among about 40 nations in an attempt to reduce tariffs. In 1967, the United States agreed to cut tariffs by about one-third on a great many items.

The negotiations during the 1960s were prompted by the establishment of the **European Economic Community**—or **"Common Market."** The EEC was composed originally of Belgium, France, West Germany, Holland, Italy, and Luxembourg; and in the late 1970s, Britain, Denmark, and Ireland joined. When the EEC was formed, the member countries agreed to reduce the tariff barriers against one another's goods—but not against the goods of other nations, including the United States.

The formation and success of the Common Market—and the likelihood that other European countries would join—posed a problem for the United States. The Common Market is a large and rich market, with over 200 million people and a combined gross national product in the trillions of dollars. With the reduction of tariff barriers *within* the Common Market, trade *among* the members of the Common Market increased rapidly, and prices of many items were cut. But American exporters were less than ecstatic about all of this, because the members of the Common Market still maintained their tariff barriers against American goods. While the "Kennedy Round" negotiations succeeded in reducing some of the tariff barriers between the United States and the Common Market, important tariff barriers remained, particularly for agricultural products.

THE TRADE REFORM ACT AND THE TOKYO ROUND

In 1974, the Congress passed the Trade Reform Act of 1974, which enabled the president, after international negotiations, to reduce any tariff presently above 5 percent by three-fifths and to abolish any tariff presently equal to 5 percent or less. Also, the act allowed workers, firms, and communities that are hurt by import competition to obtain payments and other forms of assistance. As pointed out in a previous section, such as-

---

[6] In 1947, the United States and 22 other nations signed the *General Agreement on Tariffs and Trade* (GATT), which calls for all participating countries to meet periodically to negotiate bilaterally on tariff cuts. Any tariff cut negotiated in this way will be extended to all participating nations.

Example 32.1 The Effects of a Tariff on Shoes

The quantity of shoes demanded in the United States at each price of a pair of shoes is shown below. In addition, the quantities of shoes supplied by American producers and by foreign producers at each price are shown too.

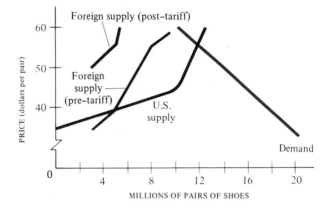

(a) Assuming that the market for shoes is competitive, what is the equilibrium price of a pair of shoes in the United States? (b) What proportion of the U.S. market goes to foreign producers of shoes? (c) Suppose that the United States imposes a tariff of $15 per pair of shoes. How many pairs of shoes will foreign producers now supply if the price is (1) $50, (2) $55, (3) $60. (Note that a $50 price together with a $15 tariff means that the price to the foreign producer is $50 − $15, or $35.) (d) After the imposition of the tariff, what is the equilibrium price? (e) After the imposition of the tariff, what proportion of the U.S. market goes to foreign producers of shoes? (f) How much revenue does the U.S. government get from this tariff?

SOLUTION

(a) $45, since at this price U.S. supply (10 million pairs) plus foreign supply (6 million pairs) equals the quantity demanded (16 million pairs). (b) 6/16. (c) 3 million pairs (since this is what would have been supplied at a price of $35 without the tariff), 5 million pairs (since this is what would have been supplied at a price of $40 without the tariff), 6 million pairs (since this is what would have been supplied at a price of $45 without the tariff). (d) $50, since at this price U.S. supply (11 million pairs) plus foreign supply (3 million pairs) equals the quantity demanded (14 million pairs). (e) 3/14. (f) 3 million × $15, or $45 million.

sistance is a way of helping the minority of workers and firms that may be victimized by freer trade.

In 1973, over 100 nations met in Tokyo to plan a new round of trade negotiations. The aim was to make progress toward the reduction of both tariffs and nontariff barriers to trade. (In recent years, tariffs have been replaced to some extent by nontariff barriers to trade.) After over 5 years of difficult negotiations, an agreement was approved in April 1979. This agreement called for the industrial nations to reduce tariffs on thousands of goods by an average of about 33 percent during an 8-year period. It also tried to reduce export subsidies, phony technical standards for imports (used to keep out foreign goods), and barriers to international bidding for government contracts.

INCREASED PROTECTIONISM

Recent years have seen a marked increase in protectionist feelings in the United States. As Western Europe and Japan have become more formidable competitors abroad and at home, many industries have begun to press for quotas and higher tariffs. The automobile, steel, and textile industries have been among the most frequent petitioners for protection. In 1981, the Japanese agreed to limit import of Japanese autos into the U.S. to 1.68 million per year; in 1984, the ceiling was raised to 1.85 million per year, and the agreement called for the industrial nations to reduce tariffs on thousands of goods by an average of about 33 percent during an 8-year period. It also tried to reduce export subsidies, phony technical standards for imports (used to keep out foreign goods), and barriers to international bidding for government contracts.

In the mid-1980s, hundreds of petitions have been filed by industry and labor, asking the federal government to protect them from imports. In considerable part, this was due to the very strong dollar. As we shall see in the following chapter, the dollar's value relative to other currencies rose markedly from 1980 to 1983, the result being that foreign goods became much cheaper to American buyers. Also, in some industries like semiconductors, the quality of foreign goods sometimes exceeded that of American suppliers. Faced with very stiff competition from imports, American firms asked the government for protection.

As indicated in earlier sections of this chapter, the American consumer is the loser. Robert Crandall of the Brookings Institution has estimated that in 1983 the auto import quotas resulted in about a $400 per car increase in the price of U.S. cars and a $1,000 per car increase in the price of Japanese imports, the total cost to American consumers being over $4 billion in 1983 alone. According to Crandall, "The cost per job saved, therefore, was nearly $160,000 per year. Employment creation at this cost is surely not worth the candle."[7]

Most economists feel that the upsurge in protectionism in the mid-1980s

---

[7] R. Crandall, "Import Quotas and the Automobile Industry," *The Brookings Review,* Summer 1984, p. 16.

The EEC, born in the embers of World War II, was fathered by a desire to bind Germany to the rest of Europe. The success of the European Steel and Coal Community and the Benelux union encouraged the "Europeanists," and in 1957 the Treaty of Rome formally proclaimed the birth of a six-country free-trade area in which labor, capital, and goods were to move freely. None of this was to happen instantaneously, but the six countries—France, Germany, Italy, Belgium, the Netherlands, and Luxembourg—did agree on a timetable for the removal of centuries-old barriers and on a commission and council to manage the details of the process.

Headquarters of the European Economic Community, Brussels

There are ample statistics to tell what happened after the EEC was formed—relatively high growth rates, increased competitiveness by European firms, increases in per capita incomes, and increased membership (including Great Britain). But the flavor of this customs union comes through best by seeing what it has meant to three prototype economic people.

Nino T. was born in southern Italy, where reported unemployment has been 14 percent. If disguised unemployment were included, the rate might run as high as double that. Wages, for those with jobs, averaged about $20 per week. In 1965, he migrated to Germany to work in an automobile plant in Frankfort, where he could make $75 a week, and send back $40 to his family. He planned to stay for another two years—perhaps until he had saved enough to buy a small business.

Elizabeth C. works for a leather-goods firm in London. When Britain joined the Common Market, her chief worry was that it would mean higher food prices. Why? Because the technologically inefficient but politically powerful French farmer demanded protection from cheap American and Canadian food. Thus, while French wheat would flow freely into Great Britain, the high external tariff would now keep out North American wheat.

Richard B., an American businessman, now lives in Paris, managing the French subsidiary of a large New York-based corporation. He was moved to Paris about 20 years ago, when company officials decided that the removal of internal barriers by the EEC would allow U.S. companies to operate on the scale to which they were accustomed. To stay competitive in the European market, they decided to build production facilities inside the EEC, rather than producing in the U.S. and shipping abroad. Richard now finds himself very much at home in France, and seriously considers living out his days in Paris.

E.A.

is an unfortunate development. Although they understand that it will be difficult to beat back the protectionist tide, they hope that this upsurge of protectionist spirit will be short-lived, and that developments here and abroad will enable us and our trading partners to move closer to the realization of the benefits of free trade.

Test Yourself

1. According to Hendrik Houthakker, "Our workers get high real income not because they are protected from foreign competition, but because they are highly productive, at least in certain industries." Do you agree? Why or why not?

2. According to Richard Cooper, "Technological innovation can undoubtedly strengthen the competitive position of a country in which the innovation takes place, whether it be one which enlarges exports or displaces imports." Give examples of this phenomenon, and discuss various ways that one might measure the effects of technological innovation on a country's competitive position.

3. "The principle of comparative advantage doesn't work. The U.S. exports electronic computers to Japan and imports electronic consumer goods like TV sets from Japan." Comment and evaluate.

4. Would you favor a high tariff on imported steel if you were (a) an automobile worker, (b) a steel worker, (c) an automobile buyer, (d) a plastics worker? Explain your reasoning in each case.

Summary

1. International trade permits specialization, and specialization increases output. This is the advantage of trade, both for individuals and for nations.

2. Country A has an absolute advantage over Country B in the production of a good when Country A can produce a unit of the good with less resources than can Country B. Trade can be mutually beneficial even if one country has an absolute advantage in the production of all goods.

3. Specialization and trade depend on comparative, not absolute, advantage. A nation is said to have a comparative advantage in those products where its efficiency relative to other nations is highest. Trade can be mutually beneficial if a country specializes in the products where it has a comparative advantage and imports the products where it has a comparative disadvantage.

4. If markets are relatively free and competitive, producers will automatically be led to produce in accord with comparative advantage. If a country has a comparative advantage in the production of a certain good, it will turn out—after the price of the good in various countries is equalized and total world output of the good equals total world demand—that this country is an exporter of the good under free trade.

5. Specialization may occur because of economies of scale and learning. Also, some countries develop new products and processes, which they export to other countries until the technology becomes widely available.

6. A tariff is a tax imposed by the government on imports, the purpose being to cut down on imports in order to protect domestic industry and workers from foreign competition. Tariffs benefit the protected industry at the expense of the general public, and, in general, a tariff costs the general public more than the protected industry (and its workers and suppliers) gains.

7. Quotas are another barrier to free trade. They too reduce trade, raise prices, protect domestic industry from foreign competition, and reduce the standard of living of the nation as a whole.

8. Tariffs, quotas, and other barriers to free trade can sometimes be justified on the basis of national security and other noneconomic considerations. Moreover, tariffs and other forms of protection can sometimes be justified to protect infant industries, to prevent a country from being too dependent on only a few industries, and to carry out other national objectives. But many arguments for tariffs are fallacious.

9. In our early years, we were a very protectionist country. Our tariffs remained relatively high until the 1930s, when a movement began toward free trade. Between 1934 and 1948, our tariff rates dropped substantially. Again during the 1960s, there was a significant reduction in our tariffs. But more recently, as some of our industries (like steel) have been hit hard by imports, there has been a tendency to push for more protectionist measures. During the 1980s, the protectionist tide was very strong.

10. Although it has equaled only about 10 percent of our gross national product, foreign trade is of very considerable importance to the American economy. Many of our industries rely on foreign countries for raw materials or for markets, and our consumers buy many kinds of imported goods. In absolute terms, our exports and imports are larger than those of any other nation.

Concepts for Review

Exports	**Trading possibilities**	**Quota**
Imports	**curve**	**Export subsidy**
Absolute advantage	**Terms of trade**	**European Economic**
Comparative advantage	**Multinational firm**	**Community**
Production possibilities	**Tariff**	**(Common Market)**
curve	**Prohibitive tariff**	

Appendix: The Effects of Foreign Trade on NNP

In Chapters 10–12, we discussed how the level of net national product is determined. As a first approximation, it seemed adequate to ignore exports and imports in our discussion there. Now we must take account of exports and imports and see how they affect NNP. Recall from Chapter 7

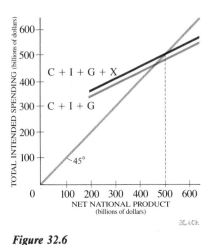

Figure 32.6

Effects of Foreign Trade on Net National Product *The equilibrium level of NNP is at the point where the* C + I + G + X *line intersects the 45-degree line; in this case, $500 billion.*

that net national product = consumption expenditure + investment + government spending + net exports, where net exports equal exports minus imports. In other words,

$$Y = C + I + G + X, \qquad (32.1)$$

where Y is NNP, C is consumption expenditure, I is investment, G is government spending, and X is net exports. Recall too that *the equilibrium level of NNP will be at the point where intended spending on NNP*—which equals intended consumption expenditure + intended investment + government spending + intended net exports—*equals NNP.*

Thus, in Figure 32.6, the equilibrium level of NNP must be $500 billion, since this is the level at which the $C + I + G + X$ line intersects the 45-degree line. To see this, note that we are merely carrying out a straightforward extension of the analysis in Chapter 12, where we assumed that net exports were zero. Once this assumption is relaxed, intended net exports must be added to the $C + I + G$ line to get total intended spending, and the equilibrium level of NNP is at the point where the resulting total-intended-spending line—$C + I + G + X$—intersects the 45-degree line.

We can also use the leakage-injection approach (described in Chapters 10 to 12) to show the effects of foreign trade on the equilibrium value of NNP. Clearly, *exports are an injection* since they add spending to the domestic flow of income and expenditure. In other words, foreign spending on American products and services results in additional output and jobs in the United States. On the other hand, *imports are a leakage* because they withdraw spending from the domestic flow of income and expenditure. In other words, they constitute a use for income other than spending on U.S. goods and services.

Once this is understood, it is clear why governments during the 1930s wanted to increase their exports and decrease their imports. Spending on net exports results in increases in NNP. If intended spending on net exports increases from X to X', as shown in Figure 32.7, the equilibrium level of NNP increases from $500 billion to $550 billion. Moreover, *increases in spending on net exports have a multiplier effect,* which is like the multiplier effect for investment or government spending. Thus a $1 increase in intended spending on net exports results in more than a $1 increase in NNP.[8] Since governments during the 1930s wanted desperately to increase their NNP to reduce unemployment, it is clear why they tried to increase their net exports. However, all that resulted was a reduction in international trade, because of retaliatory measures.

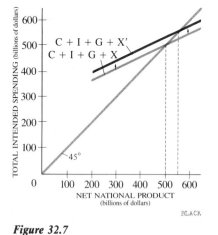

Figure 32.7

Effect of Increase in Net Exports on Net National Product *If net exports increase from* X *to* X', *the equilibrium level of* NNP *increases from $500 billion to $550 billion.*

[8] If we assume that exports, government expenditures, and tax receipts are the same at all levels of NNP, then a $1 increase in intended spending on net exports will result in an increase in equilibrium NNP of $\dfrac{1}{MPS + MPI}$ dollars, where *MPS* is the marginal propensity to save and *MPI* is the marginal propensity to import. (The *marginal propensity to import* is the proportion of an extra dollar of income that is spent on imports.) Note that the multiplier is smaller now than in the case of a closed economy (where *MPI* equals zero).

CHAPTER 33

Exchange Rates and the Balance of Payments

In late 1984, the financial pages of newspapers around the world trumpeted that the value of the dollar had reached its highest level in over a decade. (*Business Week,* for example, published a cover story on the "superdollar.") American tourists visiting other countries and U.S. importers were happy because a dollar was worth more German marks, Japanese yen, and Swiss francs. The situation was quite different from 1978, when the value of the dollar plunged, also resulting in headline news.

To understand these developments, we must consider several questions. What are exchange rates and how are they determined? How are international business transactions carried out? Should there be fixed or flexible exchange rates? What is a balance-of-payments deficit, and what is its significance? What problems have afflicted the international monetary system in recent years? These questions, which are both fundamental and timely, are taken up in this chapter.

International Transactions and Exchange Rates

Suppose you want to buy a book from a German publisher, and that book costs 20 marks. (The German currency consists of marks, not dollars.) To buy the book, you must somehow get marks to pay the publisher, since this is the currency in which the publisher deals. Or, if the publisher agrees, you might pay in dollars; but the publisher would then have to exchange the dollars for marks, since its bills must be paid in marks. Whatever happens, either you or the publisher must somehow exchange dollars for marks, since international business transactions, unlike transactions within a country, involve two different currencies.

If you decide to exchange dollars for marks to pay the German publisher, how can you make the exchange? The answer is simple. You can buy German marks at a bank, just as you might buy lamb chops at a butcher shop. Just as the lamb chops have a price (expressed in dollars), so the German marks have a price (expressed in dollars). The bank may tell you that each mark you buy will cost you $.40. This makes the **exchange rate** between dollars and marks .4 to 1, since it takes .4 dollars to purchase 1 mark (or 2½ marks to purchase 1 dollar).

In general, *the exchange rate is simply the number of units of one currency that exchanges for a unit of another currency.* The obvious question is: What determines the exchange rate? Why is the exchange rate between German marks and American dollars what it is? Why doesn't a dollar exchange for 10 marks, rather than 2½ marks? This basic question will occupy us in the next several sections.

Exchange rate board showing international currencies

Exchange Rates under the Gold Standard

As a starter, let's see how exchange rates were determined under the **gold standard,** which prevailed before the 1930s. *If a country was on the gold standard, a unit of its currency was convertible into a certain amount of gold.* Before World War I the dollar was convertible into one-twentieth of an ounce of gold, and the British pound was convertible into one-quarter of an ounce of gold. Thus, since the pound exchanged for 5 times as much gold as the dollar, the pound exchanged for $5. The currency of any other country on the gold standard was convertible into a certain amount of gold in the same way; and *to see how much its currency was worth in dollars, you divided the amount of gold a unit of its currency was worth by the amount of gold (one-twentieth of an ounce) a dollar was worth.*

Why did the exchange rate always equal the ratio between the amount of gold a foreign currency was worth and the amount of gold a dollar was worth? Why did the price of a British pound stay at $5 before World War I? To see why, suppose that the price (in dollars) of a pound rose above this ratio—above $5. Instead of exchanging their dollars directly for pounds, Americans would have done better to exchange them for gold and then exchange the gold for pounds. By this indirect process, Americans could have exchanged $5 for a pound, so they would have refused to buy pounds at a price above $5 per pound.

Similarly, if the price of a pound fell below $5, the British would have refused to sell pounds, since they could have obtained $5 by converting the pound into gold and the gold into dollars. Thus, *because Americans would refuse to pay more than $5, and the British would refuse to accept less, for a pound, the price of a pound had to remain at about $5.* (In practice, the pound could be a few cents above or below $5, because it costs money to transport gold in order to carry out the conversion.)

BALANCE BETWEEN EXPORTS AND IMPORTS

But what ensured that this exchange rate, dictated by the gold content of currencies, would result in a rough equality of trade between countries? If one pound exchanged for $5, perhaps the British might find our goods so cheap that they would import a great deal from us, while we might find their goods so expensive that we would import little from them. Under these circumstances, the British would have to ship gold to us to pay for the excess of their imports from us over their exports to us, and eventually they could run out of gold. Could this happen? If not, why not? These questions occupied the attention of many early economists. The classic answers were given by David Hume, the Scottish philosopher, in the eighteenth century.

Hume pointed out that under the gold standard a mechanism ensured that trade would be brought into balance and that neither country would run out of gold. This mechanism was as follows. If, as we assumed, the British bought more from us than we bought from them, they would have to send us gold to pay for the excess of their imports over their exports. As their gold stock declined, their price level would fall. (Recall the quantity theory of money.) As our gold stock increased, our price level would rise. Thus, because of our rising prices, the British would tend to import less from us; and because of their falling prices, we would tend to import more from them. Consequently, the trade between the two countries would tend toward a better balance. Eventually when enough gold had left Britain and entered the United States, prices here would have increased enough, and prices in Britain would have fallen enough, to put imports and exports in balance.

The Foreign Exchange Market

The gold standard is long gone; and after many decades of fixed exchange rates (discussed in a later section), the major trading nations of the world began to experiment with flexible exchange rates in early 1973. Let's consider a situation where exchange rates are allowed to fluctuate freely, like the price of any commodity in a competitive market. In a case of this sort, exchange rates—like any price—are determined by supply and demand. There is a market for various types of foreign currency—German marks, British pounds, French francs, and so on—just as there are markets for various types of meat.

In the case of the German mark, the demand and supply curves may look like those shown in Figure 33.1. The demand curve shows the amount of German marks that people with dollars will demand at various prices of a mark. The supply curve shows the amount of German marks that people with marks will supply at various prices of a mark. Since the amount of German currency supplied must equal the amount demanded in equilibrium, *the equilibrium price (in dollars) of a German mark is given by the intersection of the demand and supply curves.* In Figure 33.1, this intersection is at $.40.

THE DEMAND AND SUPPLY SIDES OF THE MARKET

Let's look in more detail at the demand and supply sides of this market. On the *demand* side are people who want to import German goods (like the book you want to buy) into the United States, people who want to

725

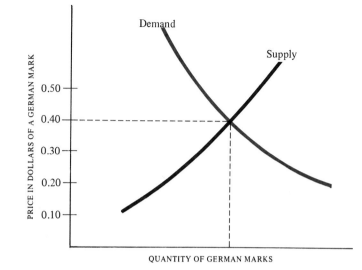

Figure 33.1

Determination of the Exchange Rate between Dollars and German Marks under Freely Fluctuating Exchange Rates *Under freely fluctuating exchange rates, the equilibrium price of a German mark would be $.40 if the demand and supply curves for marks are as shown here.*

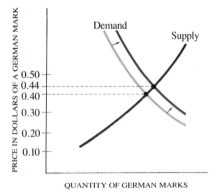

Figure 33.2

Effect of Shift in Demand Curve for German Marks *Because of the demand curve's shift to the right, the equilibrium price of a German mark increases from $.40 to $.44.*

travel in Germany (where they'll need German money), people who want to build factories in Germany, and others with dollars who want German currency. The people on the *supply* side are those who want to import American goods into Germany, Germans who want to travel in the United States (where they'll need American money), people with marks who want to build factories in the United States, and others with marks who want American currency.

When Americans demand more German cameras or Rhine wine (causing the demand curve to shift upward and to the right), the price (in dollars) of the German mark will tend to increase. Thus, if the demand curve for marks shifts as shown in Figure 33.2, the result will be an increase in the equilibrium price (in dollars) of a mark from $.40 to $.44. Conversely, *when the Germans demand more American cars or computers (resulting in a shift of the supply curve downward and to the right), the price (in dollars) of the German mark will tend to decrease.*

To see why an increase in German demand for American cars or computers shifts the supply curve downward and to the right, recall that the supply curve shows the amount of marks that will be supplied at each price of a mark. Thus a shift downward and to the right in the supply curve means that more marks will be supplied at a given price (in dollars) of the mark. Given the posited increase in German demand for American goods, such a shift in the supply curve would be expected.

APPRECIATION AND DEPRECIATION OF A CURRENCY

Two terms frequently encountered in discussions of the foreign exchange market are **appreciation** and **depreciation.** When Country A's currency becomes more valuable relative to Country B's currency, Country A's currency is said to appreciate relative to that of Country B, and Country B's currency is said to depreciate relative to that of Country A. In Figure 33.2, the mark appreciated relative to the dollar and the dollar depreciated relative to the mark. This use of terms makes sense. Since the number of dollars commanded by a mark increased, the mark became more valuable relative to the dollar and the dollar became less valuable relative to the mark.

Note that such a change in exchange rates would not have been possible under the gold standard. Unless a country changed the amount of gold that could be exchanged for a unit of its currency, exchange rates were fixed under the gold standard. Sometimes governments did change the amount of gold that could be exchanged for their currencies. For example, in 1933 the United States increased the price of gold from $21 an ounce to $35 an ounce. When a country increased the price of gold, this was called a ***devaluation*** of its currency.

DETERMINANTS OF EXCHANGE RATES

In a previous section, we have seen that flexible exchange rates are determined by supply and demand. But what are some of the major factors determining the position of these supply and demand curves?

Relative Price Levels. In the long run, the exchange rate between any two currencies may be expected to reflect differences in the price levels in the two countries. (This is the so-called purchasing-power parity theory of exchange rate determination.) To see why, suppose that Germany and the United States are the only exporters or importers of automobiles, and that automobiles are the only product they export or import. If an automobile costs $4,000 in the United States and 10,000 marks in Germany, what must be the exchange rate between the dollar and the mark? Clearly, a mark must be worth .40 dollars, because otherwise the two countries' automobiles would not be competitive in the world market. If a mark were set equal to 0.60 dollars, this would mean that a German automobile would cost $6,000 (that is 10,000 times $0.60), which is far more than what an American automobile would cost. Thus foreign buyers would obtain their automobiles in the United States.

Based on this theory, one would expect that, *if the rate of inflation in Country A is higher than in Country B, Country A's currency is likely to depreciate relative to Country B's.* Suppose that costs double in the United States but increase by only 25 percent in Germany. After this burst of inflation, an automobile costs $8,000 (that is, 2 times $4,000) in the United States and 12,500 marks (that is, 1.25 times 10,000 marks) in Germany. Thus, based on the purchasing-power parity theory, the new value of the mark must be 0.64 dollars, rather than the old value of 0.40 dollars. (Why 0.64 dollars? Because this is the exchange rate that makes the new cost of an automobile in the United States, $8,000, equivalent to the new cost of an automobile in Germany, 12,500 marks.) Because the rate of inflation is higher in the United States than in Germany, the dollar depreciates relative to the mark.

Relative Rates of Growth. Although relative price levels may play an important role in the long run, other factors tend to exert more influence on exchange rates in the short run. In particular, *if one country's rate of economic growth is higher than the rest of the world, its currency is likely to depreciate.* If a country's economy is booming, this tends to increase its imports. If there is a boom in the United States, Americans will tend to import a great deal from other countries. If a country's imports tend to

Basic Idea #65: Under flexible exchange rates, the exchange rate between any two currencies will reflect differences in the price levels in the two countries. If the rate of inflation in Country A is higher than in Country B, Country A's currency is likely to depreciate relative to Country B's. Also, if one country's rate of economic growth is higher than that of the rest of the world, or if its interest rates decline, its currency is likely to depreciate.

727

grow faster than its exports, its demand for foreign currency will tend to grow more rapidly than the amount of foreign currency that is supplied to it. Consequently, its currency is likely to depreciate.

Relative Interest-Rate Levels. If the rate of interest in Germany is higher than in the United States, banks, multinational corporations, and other investors in the United States will sell dollars and buy marks in order to invest in the high-yielding Germany securities. Also, German investors (and others) will be less likely to find American securities attractive. Thus the mark will tend to appreciate relative to the dollar, since the demand curve for marks will shift to the right and the supply curve for marks will shift to the left. In general, *an increase in a country's interest rates leads to an appreciation of its currency, and a decrease in its interest rates leads to a depreciation of its currency.* In the short run, interest-rate differentials can have a major impact on exchange rates, since there is estimated to be over $100 billion in funds that are moved from country to country in response to differentials in interest rates.

THE ADJUSTMENT MECHANISM UNDER FLEXIBLE EXCHANGE RATES

Under flexible exchange rates, what insures a balance in the exports and imports between countries? The situation differs from that described by David Hume, since Hume assumed the existence of the gold standard. Under flexible exchange rates, the balance is achieved through changes in exchange rates. Suppose that for some reason Britain is importing far more from us than we are from Britain. This will mean that the British, needing dollars to buy our goods, will be willing to supply pounds more cheaply. In other words, the supply curve for British pounds will shift downward and to the right, as shown in Figure 33.3. This will cause the price of a pound to decline from P_1 dollars to P_2 dollars. Or, from Britain's point of view, the price (in pounds) of a dollar will have been bid up by the swollen demand for imports from America.

Because of the increase in the price (in pounds) of a dollar, our goods will become more expensive in Britain. Thus the British will tend to reduce their imports of our goods. At the same time, since the price (in dollars) of a pound has decreased, British goods will become cheaper in the United States, and this will stimulate us to import more from Britain. Consequently, as our currency appreciates in terms of theirs—or, to put it another way, as theirs depreciates in terms of ours—the British are induced to import less and export more. Thus there is an automatic mechanism (just as there was under the gold standard) to bring trade between countries into balance.

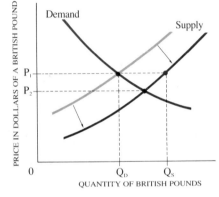

Figure 33.3
Adjustment Mechanism *If Britain imports more from us than we do from Britain, the supply curve for British pounds will shift downward and to the right, resulting in a decline of the price of the pound from* P_1 *to* P_2 *dollars. If Britain tries to maintain the price at* P_1 *dollars, the British government will have to exchange dollars for* $(Q_S - Q_D)$ *pounds.*

Fixed Exchange Rates

Although many economists believed that exchange rates should be allowed to fluctuate, very few exchange rates really did so in the period from the end of World War II up to 1973. Instead, *most exchange rates were fixed by government action and international agreement.* Although they may have varied slightly about the fixed level, the extent to which they were allowed to vary was small. Every now and then, governments changed the exchange rates, for reasons discussed below; but for long periods of time, they remained fixed.

If exchange rates remain fixed, the amount demanded of a foreign currency may not equal the amount supplied. Consider the situation in Figure 33.4. If A is the demand curve for German marks, the equilibrium price of a mark is $.40. But suppose the fixed exchange rate between dollars and marks is .35 to 1—that is, each mark exchanges for $.35. Unless the government intervenes, more German marks will be demanded at a price of $.35 per mark than will be offered. Specifically, the difference between the quantity demanded and the quantity supplied will be $Q_D - Q_S$. Unless the government steps in, a black market for German marks may develop, and the real price may increase toward $.40 per mark.

TYPES OF GOVERNMENT INTERVENTION

To maintain exchange rates at their fixed levels, governments can intervene in a variety of ways. For example, they may reduce the demand for foreign currencies by reducing defense expenditures abroad, by limiting the amount that their citizens can travel abroad, and by curbing imports from other countries. Thus, in the case depicted in Figure 33.4, the American government might adopt some or all of these measures to shift the demand curve for German marks downward and to the left. If the demand curve can be pushed from A to B, the equilibrium price of a German mark can be reduced to $.35, the fixed exchange rate. For the time being, there will no longer be any mismatch between the quantity of marks demanded and the quantity supplied.

When exchange rates are fixed, mismatches of this sort cannot be eliminated entirely and permanently. To deal with such temporary mismatches, governments enter the market and buy and sell their currencies in order to maintain fixed exchange rates. Take the case of post-World-War-II Britain. At times the amount of British pounds supplied exceeded the amount demanded. Then the British government bought up the excess at the fixed exchange rate. At other times, when the quantity demanded exceeded the amount supplied, the British government supplied the pounds desired at the fixed exchange rate. As long as the equilibrium exchange rate was close to (sometimes above and sometimes below) the fixed exchange rate, the amount of its currency the government sold at one time equaled, more or less, the amount it bought at another time.

But in some cases governments have tried to maintain a fixed exchange rate far from the equilibrium exchange rate. The British government tried during the 1960s to maintain the price (in dollars) of the pound at $2.80, even though the equilibrium price was about $2.40. The situation was as shown in Figure 33.5. Since the quantity of British pounds supplied exceeded the quantity demanded at the price of $2.80, the British government had to buy the difference. That is, it had to buy $(Q_S - Q_D)$ pounds with dollars. Moreover, it had to keep on exchanging dollars for pounds in these quantities for as long as the demand and supply curves remained in these positions. Such a situation could not go on indefinitely, since the British government eventually had to run out of dollars. How long it could

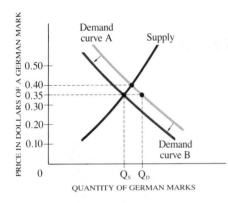

Figure 33.4

Fixed Exchange Rate *The equilibrium price of a German mark is $.40, if A is the demand curve. If $.35 is the fixed exchange rate, the U.S. government may try to shift the demand curve for marks from A to B, thus bringing the equilibrium exchange rate into equality with the fixed exchange rate.*

go on depended on how big Britain's reserves of gold and foreign currency were.

Balance-of-Payments Deficits and Surpluses

Under a system of fixed exchange rates, economists and financial analysts look at whether a country has a balance-of-payments deficit or surplus to see whether its currency is above or below its equilibrium value. What is a **balance-of-payments deficit?** What is a **balance-of-payments surplus?** It is important that both of these terms be understood.

BALANCE-OF-PAYMENTS DEFICIT

If a country's currency is *overvalued* (that is, if its price exceeds the equilibrium price), the quantity supplied of its currency will exceed the quantity demanded. Let's return to the case where the price of the British pound was set at $2.80. Under these circumstances, the quantity supplied of pounds exceeds the quantity demanded by $(Q_S - Q_D)$ pounds, as shown in Figure 33.5. This amount—$(Q_S - Q_D)$ pounds—is Britain's balance-of-payments deficit. (See Figure 33.5.) As pointed out in the previous section, it is the number of pounds that Britain's central bank, the Bank of England, must purchase. To pay for these pounds, the Bank of England must give up some of its *reserves* of foreign currencies or gold.

In a situation of this sort, there may be a "run" on the overvalued currency. Suppose that speculators become convinced that the country with the balance-of-payments deficit cannot maintain the artificially high price of its currency much longer because its reserves are running low. Because they will suffer losses if they hold on to a currency that is devalued, the speculators are likely to sell the overvalued currency (in Figure 33.5, the British pound) in very large amounts, thus causing an even bigger balance-of-payments deficit for the country with the overvalued currency. Faced with the exhaustion of its reserves, the country is likely to be forced to allow the price of its currency to fall.

BALANCE-OF-PAYMENTS SURPLUS

If a country's currency is *undervalued* (that is, if its price is less than the equilibrium price), the quantity demanded of its currency will exceed the quantity supplied. During the early 1970s, the price of the German mark was set at $0.35, even though its equilibrium price was about $0.40. As shown in Figure 33.6, the quantity of marks demanded exceeds the quantity supplied by $(Q'_D - Q'_S)$ marks under these circumstances. This amount—$(Q'_D - Q'_S)$ marks—is Germany's balance-of-payments surplus. (See Figure 33.6.) Germany can keep the price of the mark at $0.35 only if it provides these $(Q'_D - Q'_S)$ marks in exchange for foreign currencies and gold. By doing so, it increases its reserves.

Whereas a country with an overvalued currency is likely to be forced by the reduction in its reserves to reduce the price of its currency, a country with an undervalued currency is unlikely to be forced by the increase in its reserves to increase the price of its currency. And a country with an un-

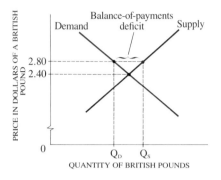

Figure 33.5

Balance-of-Payments Deficit *Because the British pound is overvalued at $2.80, the quantity of pounds demanded (Q_D) is less than the quantity supplied (Q_S). The shortfall—that is, $(Q_S - Q_D)$ pounds—is the balance-of-payments deficit.*

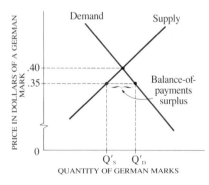

Figure 33.6

Balance-of-Payments Surplus *Because the German mark is undervalued at $.35, the quantity of marks demanded (Q'_D) is greater than the quantity supplied (Q'_S). The surplus—that is, $(Q'_D - Q'_S)$ marks—is the balance-of-payments surplus.*

dervalued currency often is reluctant to increase the price of its currency because of political pressures by its exporters (and their workers) who point out that such a revaluation would make the country's goods more expensive in foreign markets and thus would reduce its exports. Consequently, when exchange rates were fixed, countries with undervalued currencies were less likely to adjust their exchange rates than countries with overvalued currencies.

MEASURING DEFICITS AND SURPLUSES

If we are given the demand and supply curves for a country's currency, it is a simple matter to determine the deficit or surplus in its balance of payments. All that we have to do is subtract the quantity demanded of the currency from the quantity supplied. However, since we do not observe these demand and supply curves in the real world, this method of determining the deficit or surplus, while fine in principle, is not practical. The available data show only the total amount of the country's currency bought and the total amount of the country's currency sold. Since each unit of the country's currency that is bought must also be sold, it is evident that the total amount bought must equal the total amount sold. Given that this is the case, how can one identify and measure a balance-of-payments deficit or surplus?

The answer lies in the transactions of the country's central bank. If the central bank's purchases or sales of currency make up for the difference between the quantity demanded and the quantity supplied, it will purchase currency if there is a balance-of-payments deficit and sell currency if there is a balance-of-payments surplus. The amount it purchases or sells measures the size of the deficit or surplus. In other words, the official transactions of this country's government with other governments are used to measure the deficit or surplus. Roughly speaking, this is how a balance-of-payments deficit or surplus has been measured. However, beginning in May 1976, the U.S. government stopped publishing figures on the deficit or surplus in our balance of payments. Under the current regime of flexible exchange rates, changes in demand and supply for foreign exchange generally show up as changes in exchange rates, rather than in the transactions of the central bank. Thus figures regarding the deficit or surplus in our balance of payments have lost much of their previous meaning.

The Balance-of-Payments Accounts

Although the U.S. government no longer calculates the deficit or surplus in our balance of payments, it does publish our **balance-of-payments accounts,** which are an important record of *the flow of payments between the United States and other countries.* There are two types of items in the balance-of-payments accounts: debit items and credit items. **Debit items** are items for which we must pay foreigners—items that use up our foreign currency. **Credit items** are items for which we are paid by foreigners—items that provide us with a stock of foreign currency. If a French importer buys an American car to sell in France, this is a credit item in the U.S. balance-of-payments accounts because a foreigner—the French importer—

Table 33.1

UNITED STATES BALANCE-OF-PAYMENTS ACCOUNTS, 1983

	Credit	Debit
	(billions of dollars)	
Current Account		
Merchandise exports	200	
Merchandise imports		261
Net travel and transportation receipts		5
Investment income (and other services)	32	
Net military transactions	1	
Unilateral transfers		9
Capital account		
Change in U.S. assets abroad		48
Change in foreign assets in U.S.	76	
Change in U.S. reserve assets		1
Change in foreign official assets in the U.S.	5	
Statistical discrepancy	9	
Total[a]	324	324
Balance on goods and services = $233 billion − $266 billion = −$33 billion		
Balance on current account = $233 billion − $275 billion = −$42 billion		

[a] Because of rounding, numbers may not sum to total.

must pay us for the car. On the other hand, if an American importer buys some French wine to sell in the United States, this is a debit item in the U.S. balance-of-payments accounts. We must pay the foreigner—the French winemaker—for the wine.

It is essential to understand at the outset that *the balance-of-payments accounts always balance*. The total of credit items must always equal the total of debit items, because the sum of the debit items is the total value of goods, services, and assets we received from foreigners. These goods, services, and assets must be paid for with credit items, since credit items provide the foreign currency required by foreigners. Since the debit items must be paid for by the credit items, *the sum of the credit items must equal the sum of the debit items.*

Let's consider the U.S. balance-of-payments accounts in 1983, shown in Table 33.1. Debit items are negative; credit items are positive. The entire balance-of-payments accounts are divided into two parts, the current account and the capital account, each of which is described below.

THE CURRENT ACCOUNT

The current account in Table 33.1 summarizes America's international trade in currently produced goods and services. It contains entries pertaining to six types of international transactions.

Merchandise Exports. During 1983, the United States exported about $200 billion worth of merchandise. This is a credit item since it represents payments to us by foreign purchasers of American goods.

Merchandise Imports. During 1983, the United States imported about $261 billion worth of merchandise. This is a debit item since it requires payments to manufacturers abroad.

Net Travel and Transportation Receipts. Travel and transportation services must be accounted for in the balance-of-payments accounts, since they entail payments by one country to another. When a British vessel carries our merchandise, we must pay for this service. Or when an American tourist stays at the George V Hotel in Paris, we must pay for this service—and judging from the George V's rates, pay dearly at that. You will recall from the previous section that credit items supply us with foreign currency while debit items use up our foreign currency. Thus it is clear that when foreign carriers transport our goods or people, this is a debit item, but when we carry other countries' goods or people, this is a credit item in our balance of payments. Similarly, expenditures by American tourists traveling abroad are debit items, but money spent here by foreign tourists is a credit item. Table 33.1 shows that, during 1983, the United States had a debit balance of about $5 billion with regard to travel and transportation.

Investment Income and Other Services. This item includes, among other things, the flow of profits from U.S. firms in foreign countries to their headquarters in the United States, minus the flow of profits from foreign firms in the United States to their headquarters abroad. When the Ford Motor Company's British subsidiary sends its profits home, this provides us with foreign currency, and thus is a credit item. When Ciba-Geigy's American subsidiary sends its profits to the firm's headquarters in Switzerland, this uses up our foreign currency and thus is a debit item. In addition, this item includes interest we pay foreigners for money lent to us, and interest paid to us for money we lent foreigners. Interest we pay foreigners is a debit item, since it uses up our foreign currency, while interest paid to us by foreigners is a credit item. Table 33.1 shows that, during 1983, the United States had a credit balance of about $32 billion with regard to investment income and other services.

Net Military Transactions. Besides the transactions made by private citizens, the government's transactions must be included too in our balance-of-payments accounts. The United States government supports a vast network of military bases around the world. We also engage in a host of other government activities abroad (like the Peace Corps), and all these programs affect our balance of payments. Frequently, they result in debit items since they involve payments abroad. Money spent by U.S. military authorities stationed in Wiesbaden, Germany, to buy supplies from local German companies is a debit item. However, we also earn a large amount of foreign currency by selling armaments to foreign nations; these transactions result in credit items. Table 33.1 shows that, during 1983, the United States had a credit balance of about $1 billion with regard to military transactions.

If we add up the foregoing five entries (merchandise exports, merchandise imports, net travel and transportation receipts, investment income and other services, and net military transactions), we get the so-called *balance on goods and services.* This balance, shown in Table 33.1, equaled about −$33 billion, which means that foreigners spent about $33 billion less on our goods and services than we spent on foreign goods and services.

Unilateral Transfers. This final item in the current account includes the amount that residents of the United States send abroad minus the amount that Americans residing abroad send home. If an American working in St. Louis sends part of her pay to her relatives in Italy, this is a debit item since it uses up our foreign currency. In addition, the amount that the government sends abroad for foreign aid is also counted as a unilateral transfer.

Table 33.1 shows that, during 1983, the United States had a debit balance of about $9 billion with regard to unilateral transfers.

If all six entries in the current account are totaled, we get the so-called *balance on current account*. This balance, shown in Table 33.1, equaled about −$42 billion, which means that we had a deficit of about $42 billion on current account. Any deficit of this sort must be offset by a surplus in the rest of the balance-of-payments accounts (that is, in the capital account) because, as stressed in a previous section, the total of the debit items must equal the total of the credit items.

THE CAPITAL ACCOUNT

The capital account in Table 33.1 summarizes America's international transactions associated with capital investments (but not the income from these investments, since it is included in the current account). It contains entries pertaining to four types of international transactions.

Change in U.S. Assets Abroad. When Americans buy plants in foreign countries, or purchase the securities of foreign firms, or make deposits in foreign banks, such transactions require that we use foreign currency, since we will be buying foreign assets. Thus these transactions result in debit items. During 1983, increases in U.S. *private* assets abroad resulted in a debit balance of about $43 billion, and increases in U.S. *government* assets abroad resulted in a debit balance of about $5 billion. Thus, as shown in Table 33.1, the total debit balance due to the increase in both U.S. private and government assets abroad was about $48 billion.

Change in Foreign Assets in the U.S. When Saudi Arabians buy American firms or farmland, or purchase U.S. Treasury securities, or make deposits in the Bank of America, such transactions provide us with foreign currency, since foreigners use their currency to purchase our assets. Thus these transactions result in credit items. Table 33.1 shows that, during 1983, increases in foreign assets in the U.S. resulted in a credit balance of about $76 billion.

Change in U.S. Reserve Assets. The U.S. government holds reserve assets, such as gold and foreign currencies. When we transfer some of these reserves to a foreign government, we can exchange them for dollars or foreign currencies. Thus a decrease in our reserves is a credit item. Prior to 1971, the U.S. government offset many of the debit items in its balance-of-payments accounts by transferring gold to other governments. That is, it helped to finance the deficits in its balance of payments in this way. Since 1971, the U.S. government no longer has been willing to transfer gold to foreign governments, but it has used other reserve assets such as foreign currencies. As shown in Table 33.1, there was a $1 billion increase in U.S. reserves in 1983.

Change in Foreign Official Assets in the U.S. Increases in foreign official assets in the United States are increases in dollars held by foreign governments, generally in the form of U.S. Treasury bills. Since such increases provide us in effect with foreign currency, they are credit items. For many years, they have helped in a major way to finance deficits in the U.S. balance of payments. During 1983, increases in foreign official assets in the United States resulted in a credit balance of about $5 billion.

All of the entries in both the current and capital account are subject to error. To some extent, this may be due to faulty and incomplete data collection, but a more important reason for the errors and omissions in the balance-of-payments accounts is that the United States finds it difficult to keep track of all the movements of goods, services, and money to and from other countries. Table 33.1 shows that, because of this *statistical discrepancy,* the government underestimated the credit items during 1983 by about $9 billion.

Finally, when we get down to the bottom of the balance-of-payments accounts, we find that the total of the credit items equals the total of the debit items. (Both are $324 billion.) As pointed out in a previous section, logic assures us that this equality will always prevail, since we must pay in cash or IOUs for what we get from other nations.

THE BALANCE OF TRADE

The newspapers often mention the balance of trade. The **balance of merchandise trade** refers only to a part of the balance-of-payments accounts. A nation is said to have a *favorable* balance of merchandise trade if its exports of merchandise are more than its imports of merchandise, and an *unfavorable* balance of merchandise trade if its exports of merchandise are less than its imports of merchandise. As Table 33.1 shows, the United States had an unfavorable balance of merchandise trade of about $61 billion in 1983. Until 1970, the United States generally had a favorable balance of trade, but in recent years this seldom has been the case.

Indeed, the 1983 trade deficit was a record, and it prompted considerable concern. To some extent, it was due to the strength of the dollar. Because the dollar appreciated considerably relative to other currencies in the early 1980s, American exports were expensive to foreigners and foreign imports were cheap to Americans. Also, the American economy was growing more rapidly than Europe and Japan, thus stimulating our imports.

Although the balance of merchandise trade is of interest, it tells us only part of what we want to know about a country's transactions with other countries. As shown in Table 33.1, there is much more to the balance of payments than a comparison of merchandise exports with merchandise imports. Moreover, a "favorable" balance of trade is not necessarily a good thing, since imports, not exports, contribute to a nation's standard of living.

Test Yourself

1. Suppose that the demand curve for German marks is as follows:

Quantity demanded (billions of marks)	Price (in dollars) of a mark
20	0.20
15	.30
10	.40
5	.50

Plot this demand curve on a graph. What sorts of groups, organizations, and individuals are part of the demand side of this market?

2. Suppose that the supply curve for German marks is as follows:

Quantity supplied (billions of marks)	Price (in dollars) of a mark
8	0.20
9	.30
10	.40
11	.50

Plot this supply curve on the same graph as the demand curve in Question 1. What sorts of groups, organizations, and individuals are part of the supply side of this market?

3. Based on the information in Questions 1 and 2, what is the equilibrium value of the exchange rate, if it is completely flexible? Why? Is the exchange rate between the U.S. dollar and the German mark completely flexible at present?

4. Suppose that the exchange rate is fixed, and that the price (in dollars) of a mark is set at $0.30. Based on the data in Questions 1 and 2, will the quantity of marks demanded equal the quantity supplied? What sorts of government actions will have to be taken?

Exchange Rates: Pre-World War II Experience

Now that we are familiar with a balance-of-payments deficit and surplus (and the balance-of-payments accounts), we can begin to see how various types of exchange rates have worked out. What has been our experience with the gold standard? With fixed exchange rates? With flexible exchange rates?

During the latter part of the nineteenth century, the gold standard seemed to work very well, but serious trouble developed after World War I. During the war, practically all of the warring nations went off the gold standard to keep people from hoarding gold or from sending it to neutral countries. After the war, some countries tried to re-establish the old rates of exchange. Because the wartime and postwar rates of inflation were greater in some countries than in others, under the old exchange rates the goods of some countries were underpriced and those of other countries were overpriced. According to the doctrines of David Hume, this imbalance should have been remedied by increases in the general price level in countries where goods were underpriced and by reductions in the general price level in countries where goods were overpriced. But wages and prices proved to be inflexible, and, as one would expect, it proved especially difficult to adjust them downward. When the adjustment mechanism failed to work quickly enough, the gold standard was abandoned.

During the 1930s, governments tried various schemes. This was the time of the Great Depression, and governments were trying frantically to reduce unemployment. Sometimes a government allowed the exchange rate to be flexible for a while, and when it found what seemed to be an equilibrium level, fixed the exchange rate there. Sometimes a government depreciated the value of its own currency relative to those of other countries in an attempt to increase employment by making its goods cheap to other countries. When one country adopted such policies, others retaliated, causing a reduction in international trade and lending, but little or no benefit for the country that started the fracas.

The Gold Exchange Standard

In 1944, the Allied governments sent representatives to Bretton Woods, New Hampshire, to work out a more effective system for the postwar era. It was generally agreed that competitive devaluations, such as occurred in the 1930s, should be avoided. Out of the Bretton Woods conference came the *International Monetary Fund* (IMF), which was set up to maintain a stable system of fixed exchange rates and to insure that when exchange rates had to be changed because of significant trade imbalances, disruption was minimized.

The system developed during the postwar period was generally labeled the **gold-exchange standard,** as opposed to the gold standard. Under this system, the dollar—which had by this time taken the place of the British pound as the world's key currency—was convertible (for official monetary purposes) into gold at a fixed price. And since other currencies could be converted into dollars at fixed exchange rates, other currencies were convertible indirectly into gold at a fixed price.

U.S. Balance-of-Payments Deficits, 1950–72

During the early postwar period, the gold-exchange standard worked reasonably well. However, it was not too long before problems began to develop. As noted in a previous section, when exchange rates are fixed, a U.S. balance-of-payments deficit is evidence of pressure on the dollar in foreign exchange markets. Figure 33.7 shows that, *during the period from 1950 to 1972 (the last full year when exchange rates were fixed), the United States showed a chronic deficit in its balance of payments.* This chronic deficit caused considerable uneasiness and concern, both here and abroad. Several factors were responsible for it.

Postwar Recovery of Western Europe and Japan. As the Western European and Japanese economies recovered from the devastation of World War II, they adopted new technology, and became tough competitors. To cite but one example, the Japanese were particularly adept at absorbing modern electronic technology and at producing electronic goods for civilian markets. In many areas of technology, the United States continued to enjoy a lead, but the gap seemed to be narrowing. As productivity in Western Europe and Japan rose more rapidly than ours, their costs fell relative to ours, and they were able to undersell us much more in their own markets, third markets, and sometimes even our own market.

Military and Foreign Aid. We spent enormous amounts abroad for military purposes and for foreign aid. Our military expenditures abroad were particularly high during the Vietnam War. They were about $4.5 billion in 1968 alone. Not only did this war take a heavy toll in lives and in social disruption; it also helped keep our balance of payments in deficit. Note, however, that some of our government spending abroad has involved the use of "tied" funds, which can be used only to buy American goods. Since these programs result in exports that would not otherwise be made, the elimination of some of these programs would not reduce the deficit. If the government spending were cut, the exports it financed would be cut as well.

Private Investment Abroad. American firms invested enormous amounts of money abroad. U.S. investors acquired oil refineries, assembly lines, and hundreds of other types of plants. The rate of private investment abroad increased spectacularly during the 1950s and 1960s. In the early 1950s, new American private investment abroad was about $2 billion per year; in the late 1950s over $3 billion per year; in the early 1960s, over $4 billion per year; and in the late 1960s, over $8 billion per year. The reason

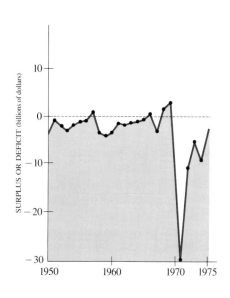

Figure 33.7
**Deficit or Surplus in U.S. Balance of
Payments 1950–75**

for this growth is fairly obvious. The markets of Western Europe (and other parts of the world) were growing rapidly and the construction of plants abroad was a profitable move. To help reduce our balance-of-payments deficit, the government introduced a voluntary program to limit such investment abroad in 1965, and made the program compulsory in 1968. (It lapsed in the 1970s.)

Inflation and Discrimination. A number of other factors, including inflation in the United States and discrimination abroad against U.S. products, also contributed to our balance-of-payments deficits. Clearly, inflation in the United States made our exports more expensive abroad. It is true that inflation in the United States was not as great as in many other countries, but in many industries, like steel, our prices rose relative to those abroad. Also, foreigners maintained various quotas, tariffs, and other devices to keep out American exports. Many of these discriminatory regulations were enacted during earlier days when such policies were more understandable than during the period under consideration.

Attempts to Eliminate the Deficits in the Early 1970s

Under a regime of fixed exchange rates, what can a country do to eliminate a balance-of-payments deficit? In general there are three routes it can take. (1) It can adjust its exchange rate. (2) It can change its price level. (3) It can adopt various kinds of controls to interfere with market forces. To illustrate each of these ways to eliminate deficits, consider the situation facing the United States in 1970. The dollar at that time was overvalued relative to other currencies, like the German mark. The situation was as shown in Figure 33.8, which contains the demand and supply curves for marks. In a free market for foreign exchange, the price (in dollars) of a German mark would have risen from the fixed exchange rate, P_F, to P_E. This would have discouraged American imports, encouraged American exports, and eliminated the U.S. balance-of-payments deficit.

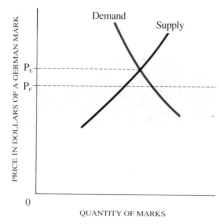

Figure 33.8
"Overvaluation" of the Dollar   Whereas the fixed exchange rate was only P_F dollars for a German mark, the equilibrium price was P_E dollars. Note the similarity between this diagram and Figure 33.6.

DEPRECIATE THE DOLLAR?

Thus one step the United States might have taken in 1970 to eliminate the deficit was to *depreciate the dollar.* But the United States was reluctant to depreciate its currency relative to others. Depreciation of our currency would hurt friendly nations who had been willing to hold large dollar balances. The United States wanted to discourage speculation against the dollar. And there was a chance that depreciation of the world's leading currency would seriously disrupt the entire world monetary system. Also, it must be noted that depreciation would have required the cooperation of other countries. Unless the Germans were prepared to let the mark rise in value relative to the dollar, they could stop it by also depreciating the mark.

CHANGE THE PRICE LEVEL?

A second way to eliminate the deficit was to *change the price level.* This was the sort of mechanism the gold standard used to eliminate a deficit. In a country with a chronic deficit, like the United States, the remedy would be a lowering of its general price level relative to that of other countries. This would reduce our imports and promote our exports. In contrast to the previous alternative, it would not have meant any alteration in exchange rates. However, it might well have led to a depression in the United States. Because wages and prices are very difficult to push downward, any serious attempt to reduce aggregate spending in an effort to reduce the price level would probably cut output and increase unemployment. For this reason, economists were not enthusiastic about this route to equilibrium. However, they did counsel the president to keep inflation to a minimum—for balance-of-payments reasons as well as others discussed in previous chapters. In an inflationary world, all that the United States really had to do was have a lower inflation rate than other countries, not reduce its price level.

ADOPT CONTROLS?

A third way to eliminate the deficit was to *adopt various types of controls.* For one thing, a country might impose controls over the exchange market. Thus the United States government might have required all foreign exchange received by exporters (or others) to be sold to the government, and the government might have rationed this foreign exchange among importers and others who wanted it. By so doing, the government would see that the deficit in the balance of payments was eliminated. However, this kind of scheme has many disadvantages, such as it limits freedom of choice and is difficult for the government to enforce.

Another type of government control is aimed at trade rather than the exchange markets. In this case, the government tries to influence imports and exports through quotas, tariffs, subsidies, and other such controls. The United States might have raised tariffs and imposed quotas to cut its imports, and subsidized some of its exports to increase their volume. It might also have imposed limits on the amount American tourists could spend abroad. An important difficulty with such interference with free trade is that it reduces world efficiency, as we saw in Chapter 32.

In addition, the government might have discouraged American investment abroad—and in fact it did so in various ways, including the imposition in 1963 of an "interest equalization tax" of 15 percent (later reduced to 11½ percent) on any purchase of a foreign stock or bond by an American from a foreigner. Also, in the special circumstances facing the United States, one way to eliminate the deficit in our balance of payments might have been to convince other countries to increase their share of the responsibilities for defense and foreign aid. Western Europe might have paid a larger share of the costs of maintaining a defensive shield that protects us all. The United States pressed for this for many years, with some success. Also, the United States might have tried to persuade other countries to remove discriminatory barriers to our goods. And finally, the United States might have tried to step up its rate of productivity increase and product innovation. This would have made our exports more competitive.

WHAT WAS DONE?

In fact, what did the United States do in the early 1970s to eliminate the deficit in its balance of payments? As you might expect, we adopted many of the measures described above. In 1971, we depreciated the dollar relative to all major foreign currencies. On the average, the dollar was depreciated by about 10 to 15 percent. Moreover, throughout the early 1970s a serious effort was made to contain inflation at home, and, for better or worse, some protectionist controls were established or continued. Also, the president's special assistant on international economic policy, Peter Peterson (later secretary of commerce), beat the drum for subsidies or encouragement for added research and development by American industry to make our exports more competitive in world markets.

Demise of the Bretton Woods System

As pointed out in the previous section, the dollar was depreciated relative to all major foreign currencies in 1971. And a new system of fixed exchange rates was approved by representatives of the major trading nations at a meeting at the Smithsonian Institution. Although President Nixon hailed the Smithsonian agreement as "the greatest international monetary agreement in the history of the world," events were to prove it unequal to the tasks it faced. In February 1973, scarcely more than a year after the agreement, the United States felt obliged to devalue the dollar again, as the outflow of dollars to other countries continued. Then, in March 1973, representatives of the major trading nations met in Paris to establish a system of fluctuating exchange rates, thus abandoning the Bretton Woods system of fixed exchange rates. This was a major break with the past, and one that was greeted with considerable apprehension as well as hope.

However, the major trading nations did not go so far as to establish completely flexible exchange rates. Instead, the float was to be managed. Central banks would step in to buy and sell their currency. Thus the United States agreed that "when necessary and desirable" it would support the value of the dollar. Also, some European countries decided to maintain fixed exchange rates among their own currencies, but to float jointly against other currencies.

Fixed versus Flexible Exchange Rates

Why, until 1973, did most countries fix their exchange rates, rather than allow them to fluctuate? One important reason was the feeling that flexible exchange rates might vary so erratically that it might be difficult to carry out normal trade. Thus American exporters of machine tools to Britain might not know what British pounds would be worth six months from now, when they would collect a debt in pounds. According to the proponents of fixed exchange rates, fluctuating rates would increase uncertainties for people and firms engaged in international trade and thus reduce the volume of such trade. Moreover, they argued that the harmful

THE INTERNATIONAL MONEY GAME

Q: During the early 1970s, what contributed to, or aggravated, an international monetary crisis?

A: It's not a what, but a who. In periods of international financial stress, speculators moved vast sums of money out of weak currencies into strong currencies, and forced the central banks to intervene in order to maintain orderly foreign exchange markets.

Q: Why did speculators do a thing like that?

A: Because it was very profitable.

Q: Who were the speculators?

A: Right after the war (World War II, that is), the "in" speculator was a small Swiss banker (sometimes referred to as a Gnome of Zurich). More recently, much of the speculation business was rumored to be centered in OPEC (Organization of Petroleum Exporting Countries). As long as the U.S. kept exchanging billions of U.S. dollars for oil, the shieks had plenty to speculate with.

International money desk at a Swiss bank, Zurich

Q: Were there other speculators?

A: Sure. Multinational corporations.

Q: I thought companies dealt in foreign exchange only to cover costs of their imports. Aren't they the honest merchants?

A: Some do. Most small companies deal in foreign exchange only when converting receipts from an overseas customer into dollars. But a select group of multinationals have come to be major powers in foreign exchange markets. The biggest 200 American-based MNFs (multinational firms) own huge amounts of cash, and even larger amounts of inventories and receivables. Their holdings are large even when compared with the reserves of individual nations. During the currency crises of the sixties, these MNFs learned that it was not wise to be caught in pounds sterling or dollars, and so began to move money on a large scale.

Q: By ship?

A: No, by prepayment and borrowings. For example, branches of a multinational firm continuously buy and sell from each other. If a treasurer saw an appreciation of the mark coming on, he urged the German subsidiaries to pay its sister subsidiaries as slowly as possible.

Q: It sounds unpatriotic.

A: Depends on whom you ask. The treasurer would claim enlightened profit-maximizing. Isn't that what you want a firm to do?

E.A.

effects of speculation over exchange rates would increase if exchange rates were flexible, because speculators could push a currency's exchange rate up or down, and destabilize the exchange market. Further, they argued that flexible exchange rates might promote more rapid inflation, because countries would be less affected by balance-of-payments discipline.

Many economists disagreed, feeling that flexible exchange rates would work better. They asked why flexible prices are used and trusted in other areas of the economy, but not in connection with foreign exchange. They pointed out that a country would have more autonomy in formulating its fiscal and monetary policy if exchange rates were flexible, and they claimed that speculation regarding exchange rates would not be destabilizing. But until 1973, the advocates of flexible exchange rates persuaded few of the world's central bankers and policy makers.

How Well Have Floating Exchange Rates Worked?

From 1973 to date, exchange rates have been flexible, not fixed. As noted above, there has been some intervention by central banks to keep the movement of exchange rates between broad bounds, but this intervention generally has not been very great. The result has been considerable volatility in exchange rates. The exchange rate between the dollar and the German mark has sometimes varied by 2 percent or more from one day to the next, and by 15 percent or more over a period of several months.

Unquestionably, the variations in exchange rates, some of which are erratic and without fundamental economic significance, have made international transactions more difficult. Thus Renault, the French auto manufacturer, is reported to have hesitated to launch an export drive into the U.S. market because of the erratic behavior of the dollar-franc exchange rate. However, businesses seem to have coped rather successfully with such exchange rate variation, as reflected in the following statement in late 1975 by the National Foreign Trade Council: "[Floating exchange rates have] . . . responded well to the shocks of the fast-moving developments of recent years, . . . [although] at times business has been unfavorably affected by sharp fluctuations of key currencies."

One of the greatest "shocks" of recent years was the increase in oil prices at the beginning of 1974. This sharp price increase meant that oil-importing countries suddenly had to pay unprecedented bills to the oil-producing countries, with the result that massive strain was put on the international financial system. Although the difficulties were not surmounted easily, the new system of floating exchange rates seemed to show the required resilience to overcome this crisis.

A crisis of another sort occurred in 1977 and 1978, when the value of the dollar dropped dramatically. Between September 1977 and March 1978, and again between June and October 1978, the value of the dollar fell by about 10 percent, due in part to our unfavorable balance of trade (because we pursued a more expansionary policy than our major trading partners) and to interest rates being higher abroad than here.

During the early 1980s, the dollar staged a very impressive rebound. Between 1980 and 1983, its value rose by about 50 percent. In large part, this was due to the fact that inflation in the U.S. seemed to have moderated, real interest rates here were higher than in other countries (partly the result of huge government borrowing to finance its deficits), and the rates of return from investments here seemed relatively high. This marked appreciation of the dollar hurt American exporters, since their goods became very expensive to foreigners, but it helped to keep a lid on inflation, since imported goods were relatively cheap, and many American firms could not raise their own prices very much without losing business to imported goods.

Although there is no indication that flexible exchange rates will be forsaken (and fixed exchange rates restored), some observers feel that central banks should intervene to a greater extent to influence exchange rates. In September 1985, the U.S., Britain, France, Germany, and Japan agreed to intervene to help bring down the value of the dollar.

The International Monetary Fund

Having described our experience with the gold standard, fixed exchange rates, and flexible exchange rates, we must look more closely at the role of the International Monetary Fund. As pointed out above, representatives of 16 countries met in 1944 in Bretton Woods, New Hampshire, to try to establish a new international monetary system. Out of these historic conferences came a system that survived—with some crises and changes—for almost 30 years. A cornerstone of this system was the International Monetary Fund (IMF), established by 40 nations to insure reasonable stability of exchange rates. The Fund was composed initially of about $30 billion of gold and currency, contributed by the member countries. It has been enlarged greatly since then, and membership has grown to over 100 countries.

Bretton Woods, New Hampshire

THE IMF UNDER FIXED EXCHANGE RATES

The IMF had three purposes. First, it provided a permanent mechanism for consultation by various countries on international financial problems. Second, it tried to promote the stability of exchange rates and to avoid competitive depreciation of currencies. Third, it was empowered to make temporary loans to member countries to give them time to correct disequilibria in their balances of payments, thus promoting smoother international financial adjustments.

Note that the Fund was built on a philosophy of *fixed* exchange rates. The men who met at Bretton Woods were impressed with the problems of flexible exchange rates, at least as they were used in the 1930s, and agreed that exchange rates should be reasonably stable. Of course, they recognized that from time to time changes in certain exchange rates would be required. (Among the people at Bretton Woods was John Maynard Keynes, which suggests that the conferees were hardly financial babes in the woods.) But changes in exchange rates should, they felt, be made only in response to persistent disequilibria. In this respect, the spirit behind the IMF differed substantially from the old gold standard. Whereas the IMF recognized that exchange rates should sometimes change, the gold standard emphasized exchange stability under all circumstances.

743

THE IMF UNDER FLEXIBLE EXCHANGE RATES

The role of the IMF in the international monetary system had to be altered considerably when flexible exchange rates were adopted. In 1976, the IMF Board of Governors adopted an amendment to the IMF Articles of Agreement. This amendment formalized a number of major changes in the functioning of the IMF. To a considerable extent, it ratified the changes that already had occurred.

Specifically, this amendment permitted each country belonging to the IMF to choose its own preferred exchange-rate arrangement. A country could allow the value of its currency to be determined entirely by supply and demand. Or it could fix the exchange rate between its currency and that of some other country. Or it could adopt some other arrangement. All that the country had to undertake to do was to foster orderly economic and financial conditions and to avoid preventing the effective adjustment of balance-of-payments problems. Although the reintroduction of a system of "stable but adjustable" exchange rates was mentioned as a possibility in the amendment, such a change would require a "high majority" of the voting power and could be vetoed by the United States (which has 20 percent of the votes).

SDRs AND GOLD

The leading Western economic powers agreed in 1968 to allow the International Monetary Fund to establish *special drawing rights (SDRs)*. These SDRs were a new kind of reserve asset, which could be used by member countries much as they used gold in the past. New SDRs can be created by a vote of 85 percent of the IMF's membership. Unlike garden-variety IMF loans, SDRs do not have to be repaid to the IMF, but their allocation among countries must be in accord with IMF quotas. SDRs are sometimes called "paper gold."

"Paper gold" is backed by nothing other than the member countries' pledge to accept it in exchange for currencies. It is much like our domestic money—which, as we know from Chapter 14, is not convertible into gold or silver. In 1970, over $3 billion worth of "paper gold" was created by the IMF. The United States received about $900 million, the United Kingdom received about $400 million, and France and Germany about $200 million each. More SDRs were issued in later years. For example, by early 1976 about $7.7 billion of SDRs had been created, of which the United States got about $2.8 billion.

The trend during the 1970s was toward a declining role for gold in the international monetary system. In 1976, it was agreed that gold would no longer be a medium of settlement in International Monetary Fund transactions. But it is still possible for countries to trade in gold. There is now a free market where anyone can buy or sell gold. The price of gold varies substantially from month to month. Since gold is viewed by many as a hedge against inflation, its price tends to rise as fears of inflation mount. While many economists favor the expanded reliance on SDRs, many of the world's bankers are suspicious of "paper gold."

International Lending

Before concluding this chapter, we must discuss international capital movements in somewhat more detail. The factors underlying international transactions with regard to goods and services are clear enough. We saw in

---

Example 33.1   Return to the Gold Standard?

Confronted by very high rates of inflation, the United States in the late 1970s and early 1980s looked hard for a remedy. To some, the answer seemed to be a return to the gold standard. In 1981, President Reagan appointed an official commission to examine the potential role of gold in the domestic and international monetary system. The commission included congressmen, senators, businessmen, and government officials, including Secretary of the Treasury Donald Regan. Many groups, including President Reagan's Council of Economic Advisers, were skeptical about the advantages of a return to the gold standard.

(a) Did the gold standard result in price stability in the United States? (b) What if we returned to the gold standard and set a price for gold that was too low? (c) What if we returned to the gold standard and set a price that was too high? (d) How could the public be reasonably sure that the gold standard, if adopted, would not be abandoned again? (e) If they couldn't be sure, does this matter?

SOLUTION

(a) No. According to the available historical evidence, the Wholesale Price Index varied as follows during 1814 to 1920:

Year	Price Level (1910–14 = 100)
1814	182
1843	75
1865	185
1889	81
1920	225

(b) As pointed out by Henry Wallich, a member of the commission, the United States would lose gold, our money supply would contract, and (if the contraction were too great), there might be very large unemployment. (c) We would have to buy large quantities of gold, our money supply would increase, and serious inflation might result. The Soviet Union and South Africa, two principal gold producers, would benefit. (d) It is hard to see how they could be sure of this. A Congress that implements a gold standard one year can terminate it the next. Even if the gold standard were put in the constitution, it could be changed. (e) Yes. For example, if the government's gold stock fell, the public might view this as meaning that the gold standard would be abandoned or that the price of gold would be increased. Thus speculators might demand gold, causing the government's gold stock to fall further, a serious recession might ensue, and there might be pressure to abandon the gold standard.*

* For further discussion, see E. Bernstein, "Back to the Gold Standard?," *Brookings Bulletin,* Fall 1980; L. Lehrman and H. Wallich, "Should We (and Could We) Return to the Gold Standard?," *New York Times,* September 6, 1981; and R. Penner, "In the Wings, the Gold Standard," *New York Times,* September 13, 1981.

the previous chapter why countries find it profitable to import and export goods and services. But we need to know more about the reasons why nations lend to one another. What factors are responsible for the fact (shown vividly in the balance-of-payments accounts in Table 33.1) that one nation invests in another?

If the world were free of political problems and nationalist fervor, the answer would be easy. Because different parts of the world are endowed with different amounts and qualities of land and other resources, and have different population densities and amounts of capital, the rate of return to be derived from investments will vary from place to place. Consequently, nations where savings rates are high and investment opportunities are relatively poor will invest their capital in nations where the investment opportunities are better.

Such international lending helps both the lender and the borrower. The lender receives a higher rate of return than it would otherwise, and the borrower gains by having more capital to work with, so that the borrower's output and wages are higher than they would be otherwise. So long as the lender receives a relatively high return from the borrowing country, there is no reason why it should ask for repayment. It may continue to lend money to the borrowing country for years and years. England, for instance, was a net lender to the United States for about a century. To pay interest to the lender, the borrowing country must sell the lender more goods than it buys, thus building up a credit in its balance of payments that it can use to finance the interest, which is a debit item.

But the world is not free of political problems and nationalist fervor. Wars occur, governments topple, devastating inflations take place, property is confiscated. Only a fool contemplates investment in another country without taking some account of these and other risks; and because these risks are present, international lending that would otherwise be profitable and beneficial—and would take place if only economic considerations were involved—is sometimes stymied. Suppose that you had $1 million to invest, and that you could invest it at 15 percent interest in a country with an unstable government, where the chances were substantial that your investment would be confiscated and that you would get back only a fraction of the $1 million. Would you make the loan? Maybe; maybe not. Unfortunately, such risks discourage many international loans that would otherwise be advantageous to both lender and borrower.

Test Yourself

1. During the 1950s and 1960s, the British government reacted to deficits in its balance of payments by adopting deflationary monetary and fiscal policies (temporarily at least). Was this sensible? Why or why not?

2. Under what circumstances would you be willing to invest $10,000 (if you had $10,000) in (a) El Salvador, (b) Poland, (c) Japan, (d) India? What interest rate would you expect? What guarantees would you expect? Why?

3. "Under floating exchange rates, reserves play a much less important role than under fixed exchange rates." What does this mean? Do you agree? Why or why not?

4. Country X has been confronted with a balance-of-payments deficit. Explain how it can eliminate this deficit by: (a) changing its exchange rate, (b) changing its price level, (c) adopting controls.

Summary

1. An important difference between international business transactions and business transactions within a country is that international business transactions involve more than one currency. The exchange rate is the number of units of one currency that exchanges for a unit of another currency.

2. Before the 1930s, many major countries were on the gold standard, which meant that their currency was convertible into a certain amount of gold, and that the relative gold content of currencies determined exchange rates.

3. From 1945 to 1973, when exchange rates became more flexible, most exchange rates were fixed by government action and international agreement. They were allowed to vary slightly, but only slightly, about the official rate.

4. If exchange rates are fixed, the amount of a foreign currency demanded may not equal the amount supplied. To maintain exchange rates at the official levels, governments enter the market and buy and sell their currencies as needed. They also intervene by curbing imports, limiting foreign travel, and other measures.

5. Under a system of fixed exchange rates, a country will have a balance-of-payments deficit if its currency is overvalued and a balance-of-payments surplus if its currency is undervalued. A balance-of-payments deficit is the difference between the quantity supplied and quantity demanded of the currency. A balance-of-payments surplus is the difference between the quantity demanded and quantity supplied of the currency.

6. The United States experienced a chronic balance-of-payments deficit during the 1950s, 1960s, and 1970s. This deficit—the result of the growing productivity of other economies, our large investments abroad, and our military and foreign aid expenditures abroad—was financed by reductions in our gold stock and by foreigners' acceptance of our short-term debt. In 1973, the system of fixed exchange rates was abandoned.

7. Under a system of flexible exchange rates, the market for foreign exchange functions like any other free market, the exchange rate being determined by supply and demand. Under such a system, exchange rates tend to move in a way that removes imbalances among countries in exports and imports. The price of a country's currency tends to fall (rise) if its inflation rate and growth rate are relatively high (low) or if its interest rate is relatively low (high).

8. A country's balance-of-payments accounts measure the flow of payments between it and other countries. Debit items result in a demand for foreign currency, whereas credit items supply foreign currency. The total of the debit items must equal the total of the credit items because the total of the debit items is the total amount of goods, services, and assets we received from foreigners, and these goods, services, and assets must be paid for with credit items.

9. The balance of merchandise trade refers only to part of the balance of payments. A nation is said to have a favorable (unfavorable) balance of merchandise trade if its exports of merchandise exceed (are less than) its imports of merchandise. During the early 1980s, the United States had a very unfavorable balance of merchandise trade.

Concepts for Review

Exchange rate
Gold standard
Appreciation
Depreciation
Devaluation of currency
Balance-of-payments
  deficit

Balance-of-payments
  surplus
Balance-of-payments
  accounts
Debit items
Credit items
Balance of
  merchandise trade

International
  Monetary Fund
Gold exchange
  standard
Special drawing
  rights (SDRs)

CHAPTER 34

The Less Developed Countries

Fresh from a raid on the well-stocked family refrigerator or comfortably placed in front of a television set, the average American finds it difficult to believe that hunger is a major problem in the world. Yet it is. The industrialized countries—like the United States, Western Europe, Japan, and the USSR—are really just rich little islands surrounded by seas of poverty in Asia, Africa, and much of Latin America. This chapter deals with the problems of these so-called "less developed countries" (LDCs): the poor countries of the world. We take up several questions. Which countries are poor and why? How badly do they need additional capital? How great is the danger of overpopulation? To what extent do they lack modern technology? How can they stimulate their rate of economic growth? What can the United States do to help them? These questions are crucial, both to the people in the less developed countries and to us.

Less Developed Countries: Definition and Characteristics

WHAT IS A LESS DEVELOPED COUNTRY?

Economics abounds with clumsy terms. A profession responsible for cross elasticity of demand and average propensity to consume cannot claim a prize for elegant language. The term *less developed country* is not a model of clarity. For a country to be less developed it must be poor, but *how* poor? Any answer has to be arbitrary. We shall define any country with a per capita income of under $3,000 (1975 dollars) as less developed. Although the

749

Table 34.1

COUNTRIES CLASSIFIED BY LEVEL OF PER CAPITA INCOME, 1983[A]

A. *Countries with per capita income of $3,000 or more*

Australia	Finland	Luxembourg	Sweden
Austria	France	Netherlands	Switzerland
Belgium	Germany	New Zealand	United Kingdom
Canada	Iceland	Norway	United States
Denmark	Japan	Soviet Union	

B. *Countries with per capita income of $1,000 to $2,999*

Algeria	Congo	Mexico	Paraguay
Bolivia	Jamaica	Morocco	Peru
Brazil	Korea	Nicaragua	Syria
China	Malaysia	Panama	Turkey

C. *Countries with per capita income of less than $1,000*

Afghanistan	Ethiopia	Kenya	Sudan
Bangladesh	Ghana	Madagascar	Tanzania
Burma	Haiti	Nepal	Uganda
Chad	India	Pakistan	Zaire
El Salvador	Indonesia	Sri Lanka	Zambia

[a] Where 1983 figures are not yet published, the most recent available data are used. Note that all figures are expressed in 1975 dollars.

Source: Calculations by Irving Kravis, Alan Heston, and Robert Summers, University of Pennsylvania.

$3,000 cutoff point is arbitrary, it certainly is low enough so that any country unfortunate enough to qualify is most certainly poor.[1]

Table 34.1 shows that many countries have a per capita income of under $3,000. Thus much of the world is, by this definition, less developed. Indeed, the staggering fact is that well over half of the world's population lives in the less developed countries. Indeed, hundreds of millions of people live in countries where per capita income is less than $1,000.

Imagine what life might be like if you grew up in a country with per capita income of less than $1,000 per year. Chances are that you would be illiterate. You would probably work on a farm with meager tools and little technology. You would have few possessions (and sometimes only enough food to keep body and soul together) and be likely to die young.

The unpleasant fact is that this harsh existence is the lot of a great many earth dwellers. This does not mean that the less developed countries do not have rich citizens. Indeed they do. But the rich are a tiny minority surrounded by masses of poor people. Nor does it mean that many of these people do not live in cities. Bombay is a city that is the home of over 4 million, most of them poor.

NATIONALISM, RISING EXPECTATIONS, AND A PERSISTENT GAP

It must also be recognized that many of the less developed countries have gained their political independence in recent years. Before World War II,

[1] The figures in Table 34.1 are based on the calculations of Irving Kravis, Alan Heston, and Robert Summers of the University of Pennsylvania. These figures are not comparable with many of the other per capita income figures in this book, but the differences in concept need not concern us here. The important point is that these figures are designed to be comparable from one country to another in Table 34.1.

Table 34.2

ANNUAL RATE OF GROWTH OF
INDUSTRIAL PRODUCTION, 1976–83

Less developed country	Annual growth rate
Brazil	− 0.6
Chile	2.7
India	4.4
Malaysia	5.8
Mexico	4.5
Pakistan	10.7
Philippines	5.5
South Korea	11.4
Tunisia	7.2
Zimbabwe	1.9
Average	5.3

Source: United Nations. For
Pakistan and Philippines, the data
pertain to 1976–82.

the major European powers had substantial empires. The British had colonies all over the globe. In the postwar period, many countries have achieved independence. These new countries are often fiercely nationalistic. They resent what they regard as exploitation at the hands of the former European colonists and demand power and status. Although weak individually, together they represent a force that must be reckoned with.

Moreover, because of better communications and altered religious and cultural beliefs, the expectations and demands of people in less developed countries have changed enormously. Years ago, they were more likely to accept a life of privation and want, since their eye was on the next world. Now the emphasis has shifted to this world, and to material comforts—and getting them quickly. People in less developed countries have become aware of the high standards of living in the industrialized societies, and they want to catch up as fast as they can.

Although the available data on the less developed countries are not as accurate as one would like, these countries seem to have increased their per capita output in recent years. As Table 34.2 shows, the average rate of growth of industrial production in 10 major less developed countries was about 5 percent per year during 1976–83. *But the gap between income per capita in the less developed countries and in the developed countries has not been decreasing appreciably in recent decades.* This is a disturbing fact. Apparently, the gap between rich and poor will not decrease, unless recent trends are altered.

A CLOSER LOOK AT THE LESS DEVELOPED COUNTRIES

The less developed countries vary enormously. Some, like China, are huge; others, like Paraguay, are small. Some, like Taiwan, have lots of people jammed into every square mile of land; others, like Brazil, have relatively few people spread over lots of land. Some, like Iraq, have important natural resources (notably oil); others have few resources. Some, like India, have had great civilizations many, many centuries old; others have had ruder histories. Nonetheless, although it is not easy to generalize about the less developed countries, many of them, besides suffering from relatively low productivity, have the following characteristics.

Stress on Agriculture. The less developed countries generally devote most of their resources to food production. Agriculture is by far their largest industry. This contrasts markedly with industrialized countries like the United States, where only a small percentage of output is food. Moreover, food makes up most of the goods consumed in less developed countries. They are so poor that the typical family has very little besides food, a crude dwelling, some simple clothing, and other such necessities.

Dual Economy. Many less developed countries have two economies, existing side by side. One of these is a ***market-oriented economy*** much like that in developed countries. This economy is generally found in the big cities, where there may be some modern manufacturing plants, as well as government agencies, wholesale and retail outlets, and services for the small number of rich people in the country. Coexisting with this relatively modern economy is a ***subsistence economy*** based largely on barter, innocent of all but the crudest technology and capable of producing little more—and sometimes less—than a subsistence wage for the inhabitants.

This subsistence economy often includes most of the rural areas. It has little or no capital, few decent roads, only the most rudimentary communications. Unfortunately, this is the economy in which the bulk of the population exists.

Political Problems. Some of the less developed countries have relatively weak, unstable governments. Thus the climate for long-term investment and planning is relatively poor in such countries. Moreover, some governments are controlled by a small group of wealthy citizens or by other groups with a vested interest in resisting social change. Corruption among government officials is encountered too often, and honest officials are sometimes not very well trained or experienced in their duties. To some extent these problems stem from the relative youth of many of these countries. But whatever the reasons, they hamper the effect of government on economic development.

Income Inequality. Most of the less developed countries have a relatively high degree of income inequality. Indeed, there is much more income inequality than in the industrialized countries. Typically, a few landowners or industrialists in a less developed country are rich, sometimes enormously rich. But all outside this tiny group are likely to be very poor. The middle class, so important in the industrialized countries, is very small in most less developed countries.

Barriers to Development and the Need for Capital Formation

Why are the less developed economies so poor, and what can they do to raise their income levels? These are very difficult questions, both because the answers vary from country to country and because the answers for any single country are hard to determine. A variety of factors generally is responsible for a country's poverty, and these factors are so intermeshed that it is difficult to tell which are most important. Nonetheless, certain factors stand out; among these is the lack of capital in less developed countries.

Without exception, the people in the less developed countries have had relatively little capital to work with. There have been few factories, machine tools, roads, tractors, power plants, miles of railroad, and so on. If you visited one of these countries, you would be struck by the absence of mechanical aids to production. Workers use their hands, legs, and simple tools, often as their ancestors did long ago.

There are several reasons why the less developed countries have not accumulated much capital. First, a country must usually reduce consumption to accumulate capital, but for the less developed countries, with their very low income levels, a reduction in consumption can be painful. Equally important, much of the saving that does go on in less developed countries is not utilized very effectively. Second, there are important barriers to domestic investment, such as the smallness of local markets, the lack of skilled labor, and the lack of qualified entrepreneurs (faced with the right incentives) who are willing and able to take the risks involved in carrying out investment projects. Third, fear that property will be confis-

Tobacco farming in Paraguay

Table 34.3

PERCENTAGE INCREASE OF THE
DOMESTIC PRICE LEVEL, 1970–83

Country	Percent increase
Brazil	11,442
Colombia	1,205
Egypt[a]	210
Ghana	17,307
India	189
Malaysia	20
Mexico[a]	1,617
Pakistan	61
Peru	8,480
Philippines	91
South Korea	506
Sri Lanka	243
Thailand	208
Turkey	3,525
Average	3,222

[a] The data pertain to 1970-82, not 1970-83.
Source: See Table 34.2. Note that these figures show the percentage increase over the entire period, not the average annual increase.

cated deters industrialized countries from investing in the less developed countries. As we pointed out above, many of the less developed countries are relatively young nations, filled with nationalistic fervor and fearful of becoming economically dependent. They are suspicious of foreign investment in their countries—and in some cases are quite capable of confiscating foreign-owned property. Needless to say, this does not make foreigners particularly anxious to invest in some of them.

METHODS TO INCREASE INVESTMENT

Recognizing their need for additional capital, the less developed countries have used three principal methods to increase investment. First, they have *taxed away part of the nation's resources and used them for investment purposes or made them available to private investors.* Second, they have tried to *mobilize "surplus labor" from agriculture to carry out investment projects.* Third, they have *increased government spending on investment projects without increasing taxes, thus producing inflation.* Although effective within limits, each of these methods has important limitations. Taxes may dull incentives and in any event are often evaded; "surplus labor" is difficult to transfer and utilize; and a little inflation may soon develop into a big inflation. (As shown in Table 34.3, the rate of inflation in some less developed countries has been impressive indeed.) Besides these three methods, a country can *use **foreign aid** to increase investment.* It too has its problems and limitations, but it is hard to see how many less developed countries can scrape up the capital they need without it.

Methods of this sort have enabled many less developed countries to increase the proportion of their national output devoted to capital formation. For example, Table 34.4 shows that in major LDCs the average proportion of national output devoted to capital formation was about 21 percent in

Table 34.4

GROSS FIXED CAPITAL FORMATION AS A PERCENTAGE OF NATIONAL PRODUCT, 1982[a]

Less developed countries		Developed countries	
Country	Percentage	Country	Percentage
Brazil	19	France	21
Colombia	18	Germany	21
Egypt	27	Italy	19
Ghana	3	Japan	30
India	20	United Kingdom	15
Malaysia	36	United States	15
Mexico	22	Average	20
Pakistan	15		
Peru	18		
Philippines	26		
Sri Lanka	29		
Thailand	21		
Turkey	19		
Average	21		

[a] Where 1982 figures are unavailable, these data pertain to 1981, or whatever is the latest year for which data are given.
Source: United Nations.

1982 (whereas it was less than 10 percent in 1950). This proportion is about the same as in the developed countries, where it averaged about 20 percent in 1982. Needless to say, these figures are very rough, and not too much reliance should be placed on them. But they do indicate that the less developed countries are progressing in their attempts to increase their rate of capital formation.

The Population Explosion

Another very important reason why per capita income is so low in some (but by no means all) less developed countries is that they suffer from overpopulation. Many less developed countries have sizably increased their total output. In Latin America, Africa, and Southeast Asia, it may have grown at about 5 percent per year in some recent years. If population in these areas had remained approximately constant, output per capita would also have increased at about 5 percent per year. But population has not remained constant. It has grown at almost 3 percent per year, so that output per capita has increased at only about 2 percent per year.

Table 34.5 shows the rate of population growth in a variety of less developed countries, as well as some major developed countries. The rate has been higher, without exception, in the less developed countries than in the developed ones. The most important reason is that modern methods of preventing and curing diseases have been introduced into the LDCs, thus reducing the death rate, particularly among children. It used to be that,

Table 34.5

ANNUAL RATES OF GROWTH OF POPULATION, LESS DEVELOPED AND DEVELOPED COUNTRIES, 1950–67 AND 1970–80 (PERCENTAGES)

Less developed countries			Developed countries		
Country	1950–67	1970–80	Country	1950–67	1970–80
Brazil	3.1	2.9	France	1.1	0.6
Colombia	3.2	2.8	Germany	1.2	0.1
Egypt	2.5	2.3	Italy	0.7	0.6
Ghana	2.7	2.9	Japan	1.1	1.2
India	2.2	2.1	United Kingdom	0.5	0.1
Malaysia	3.0	2.6	United States	1.6	1.1
Mexico	3.3	3.6	Average	1.0	0.6
Pakistan	2.4	3.1			
Peru	2.6	2.8			
Philippines	3.2	2.7			
South Korea	2.8	1.7			
Sri Lanka	2.5	1.7			
Taiwan	3.1	n.a.			
Thailand	3.0	2.7			
Turkey	2.7	2.4			
Average	2.8	2.6			

Source: A. Madison, *Economic Progress and Policy in Developing Countries,* New York: Norton, 1970; and United Nations.

although the birth rate in the less developed countries was higher than in the developed countries, the death rate was also higher, so that the rate of population growth was about the same in the less developed countries as in the developed ones. But in recent years, the death rate in the LDCs has been reduced by better control of malaria and other diseases, whereas the birth rate has remained high. The result has been a ***population explosion.*** Thus in parts of Latin America the population is doubling every 20 years.

This growth of sheer numbers, which recalls the work of Thomas Malthus (Chapter 19), is only part of the problem. The populations of the less developed countries also tend to be illiterate and ill-nourished. Thus they do not have the skills required to absorb much modern technology. In addition, many workers have little or nothing to do. They live with their relatives and occasionally hold a job. Although they may not be included in the official unemployment figures, they represent a case of *disguised unemployment.* In sum, the population of many less developed countries is large (relative to the available capital and natural resources), fast-growing, of relatively poor economic quality, and poorly utilized.

POLICY RESPONSES TO POPULATION PROBLEMS

The less developed countries have responded to the population explosion in at least two ways. Where birth control is opposed on religious or cultural grounds, the LDCs often concentrate on the widespread unemployment that results from population increase. The rapidly expanding labor force cannot be employed productively in agriculture, since there is already a surplus of farm labor in many LDCs, and the capital stock is not increasing rapidly enough to employ the growing numbers in industry. Governments faced with serious unemployment of this sort often are induced to *create public works programs and other projects to make jobs, even if these projects do not really promote economic growth.*

The LDCs have also responded to the population explosion by *attempting to lower the birth rate through the diffusion of contraceptive devices and other birth control techniques.* In many of the less developed countries, there is no religious barrier to the adoption of such techniques. Consider Hinduism, which does not frown on birth control. However, their adoption has been slow. One reason is the medical drawbacks of existing contraceptive devices. Also, there are obvious problems in communicating the necessary information to huge numbers of illiterate and often superstitious people. India has made considerable efforts to disseminate birth control information, but the problems have been enormous. Nonetheless, in some LDCs like South Korea, birth control programs seem to have had a noteworthy effect.

Besides trying to cope with or influence the growth rate of their populations, the LDCs have also tried to increase the economic quality of their human resources. In other words, *they have been investing in human capital.* Such an investment seems warranted; educational and skill levels in many less developed countries have been quite low. Table 34.6 shows that in 14 major less developed countries, the average percentage of public expenditure devoted to education is now about as high as in the United States. In many LDCs, the proportion of children in school is substantially higher

Table 34.6

PERCENTAGE OF TOTAL PUBLIC EXPENDITURE DEVOTED TO EDUCATION

Country	Percentage
Brazil	21
Colombia	21
Egypt	n.a.
Ghana	20
India	26
Malaysia	n.a.
Mexico	13
Pakistan	5
Peru	22
Philippines	9
South Korea	23
Sri Lanka	10
Thailand	21
Turkey	21
Average	18
United States	18

Source: See Table 34.2.

than it used to be. This is certainly a step in the right direction, although enrollment in school is only a crude measure of the quality of the labor force. In order to absorb and utilize, and eventually develop, modern technology, the LDCs must continue to invest in a more productive labor force.

Technology: A Crucial Factor

Still another very important reason why per capita income is so low in the less developed countries is that these countries use rudimentary and often backward technology. In previous chapters, we have seen that to a considerable extent the increase in per capita income in the developed countries has resulted from the development and application of new technology. Too often, the less developed countries still use the technology of their forefathers—the agricultural and manufacturing methods of long, long ago. Why is this the case? Why don't the less developed countries copy the advanced technology of the industrialized countries, following the examples of the Japanese and Russians, among others, who promoted their economic development during the twentieth century by copying Western technology?

PROBLEMS IN ADOPTING MODERN TECHNOLOGY

One barrier to the use of modern technology is lack of capital. Modern petroleum refining technology, to choose one, cannot be used without lots of capital, which the less developed countries find difficult to scrape up. But many technological improvements do not require substantial capital. Indeed, some technological improvements are capital-saving. That is, they reduce the amount of capital needed to produce a given amount of output.

A second reason why the less developed countries find it difficult to copy and use modern technology is that they lack both a skilled labor force and entrepreneurs. Imagine the difficulties in transplanting a complicated technology—for example, that involved in steel production—from the United States to a less developed country where there are few competent engineers, fewer experienced and resourceful managers, and practically no laborers with experience in the demanding work required to operate a modern steel plant.

Even more fundamental is the fact that much of our advanced Western technology is really not very well suited to circumstances in the less developed countries. Because the industrialized countries have relatively great amounts of capital and relatively little labor, they tend to develop and adopt technology that substitutes capital for labor. But this technology may not be appropriate for less developed countries where there is little capital and lots of labor. Thus *it is very important that the less developed countries pick and choose among the technologies available in the industrialized countries, and that they adapt these technologies to their own conditions.* Mindless attempts to ape the technologies used in the industrialized countries can result in waste and failure.

TECHNOLOGICAL CHANGE IN THE LDC'S

In agriculture, important technological advances have taken place in the less developed countries in recent years. In particular, new types of seeds have been developed, increasing the yields of wheat, rice, and other crops. Some of this research was supported by the Rockefeller and Ford Foundations. The resulting increase in agricultural productivity has been so impressive that many observers call it a *"green revolution."* There is no question that wheat and rice production has increased greatly in countries like Mexico, the Philippines, Iran, Sri Lanka, India, and Pakistan. Plenty of opportunity remains for improvements in livestock yields as well, but religious beliefs and traditional prejudices are sometimes an important barrier to change.

In industry, most of the new technology adopted by the less developed countries is taken from the developed countries. Very little attempt is being made to devise new technologies more appropriate to conditions in the less developed countries, both because the less developed countries do not have the engineering and scientific resources to develop them, and because such attempts have not been very successful in the past. In countries where the private sector finds it unprofitable to carry out research and development, government research institutes sometimes try to fill the void, but these institutes frequently devote too much of their limited resources to projects not closely related to economic development. In addition, productivity centers have been created in some countries to teach managers and supervisory personnel how to make better use of a new technology. Such centers have helped promote the diffusion of new technology in Mexico and Taiwan, among other countries.

Entrepreneurship and Social Institutions

Basic Idea #67: The majority of the world's population lives in countries with per capita income below $3,000. The gap between income per capita in the less developed countries and in the developed countries has not been decreasing appreciably in recent years. The LDCs need technology, capital, and a more effective allocation of resources. Some suffer from overpopulation.

Yet another important reason why per capita income is so low in the less developed countries is that they lack entrepreneurs and favorable social institutions. This point was noted in a previous section but needs more discussion. In some LDCs there is a rigid social structure. One "knows one's place" and stays in it, people distrust and resist change, and things are done in the time-honored way they have always been done (as far as anyone can remember). No wonder these countries lack entrepreneurs! The basic social and political institutions discourage entrepreneurship. Moreover, these institutions also are at least partially responsible for the ineffective utilization of savings, relatively high birth rates, and difficulties in transferring technology noted above.

The governments of many less developed countries are relatively weak and unstable. It is difficult enough for any government to give these countries an effective tax system and a rational program of public expenditures, including proper provision for the highways, public utilities, communications, and other "social overhead capital" they need. But the problems are made even more difficult when the government is weak, unstable, and perhaps somewhat corrupt. Further, the population's value systems and attitudes sometimes do little to promote economic development. Willingness to work hard, punctually, and regularly, and an awareness of the future benefits of present sacrifice are sometimes absent.

757

Lack of Natural Resources

Finally, it should also be pointed out that some of the LDCs have little in the way of natural resources. Moreover, technological change has made some of their resources less valuable, as in the case of synthetic rubber, which affected the market for natural rubber, an important natural resource of Malaya. But this is not true of all the less developed countries. Iraq and Indonesia, among others, are endowed with oil, which (as members of the OPEC cartel) they are using to try to promote their affluence. In any event, the skimpiness of natural resources in some less developed countries does not mean that they are condemned to poverty. Neither Denmark nor Switzerland is endowed with great natural resources, but both are prosperous.

The important thing is how a country uses what it has. International trade allows a country to compensate, at least in part, for its deficiencies in natural resources. Thus, although some of the less developed countries have been dealt a poor hand by Mother Nature, this lack alone does not explain their poverty. They might have been more prosperous with more natural resources; but even with what they have, they might have done much better.

There are several ways for them to use their resources more effectively. In many of the less developed countries, a peasant may farm several strips of land that are very small and distant from one another, working a small patch here and a small patch there. Obviously, this procedure is very inefficient. If these small plots could be put together into larger farms, output and productivity could be increased. In other LDCs, huge farms are owned by landlords and worked by tenant farmers. This system too tends to be inefficient, because the tenant farmers have little incentive to increase productivity (since the extra output will accrue to the landlord) and the landlords have little incentive to invest in new technology (since they often fear that the tenant farmers will not know how to use the new equipment).

Land reform is a very lively—indeed an explosive—issue in many less developed countries, and one of the issues the Communists try to exploit. Recall that agriculture is a very important part of the economy of most of the less developed countries. Thus the land is the major form of productive wealth. No wonder there is a bitter struggle in some countries over who is to own and work it.

The Role of Government

There are several opinions on the role the governments of the less developed countries should play in promoting economic growth. Some people go so far as to say that these countries would fare best if they allowed market forces to work with a minimum of government interference. But the less developed countries themselves generally seem to believe that such a free enterprise system would produce results too slowly, if at all. Thus the prevailing view in the less developed countries is that the government must intervene—and on a large scale.

Example 34.1   Economic Development with an Unlimited Labor Supply

According to a famous theory put forth by Nobel Laureate W. Arthur Lewis of Princeton University, the supply curve of unskilled labor in some less developed countries is a horizontal line, as shown below. In other words, unlimited supplies of unskilled labor are available in this country at the existing wage rate, OW. Suppose that the value of the marginal product of each amount of unskilled labor in this country is as shown below. For example, the value of the marginal product (which equals the price of the product times labor's marginal product) is L_1B when OL_1 workers are employed.

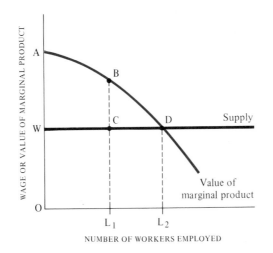

(a) How many unskilled workers will be employed in the country? (b) How much profit will be realized by hiring the $OL_1{}^{th}$ worker? (c) If firms invest their profit (from hiring the first, second, ..., $OL_2{}^{th}$ workers) in plant and equipment, what effect will this have on the value-of-marginal-product curve? (d) If the value-of-marginal-product curve shifts, will this affect the equilibrium wage rate?

SOLUTION

(a) OL_2 workers, since this is the point where the supply curve intersects the value-of-marginal-product curve. So long as the value of the marginal product of an extra worker exceeds his or her wage, it pays firms to hire the extra worker. Thus extra workers will be hired up to the point where employment equals OL_2. (b) The profit earned from the hiring of each extra worker equals the difference between the value of this worker's marginal product and this worker's wage. Thus the profit realized by hiring the $OL_1{}^{th}$ worker equals L_1B minus OW, or CB. (c) The value-of-marginal product curve will shift to the right. With more plant and equipment, the marginal product of a particular amount of labor will increase. (d) No, because the value-of-marginal-product curve will still intersect the supply curve at a wage of OW.*

＊For further discussion, see W. Arthur Lewis, "Economic Development with Unlimited Supplies of Labour," *The Manchester School of Economic and Social Studies,* May 1954.

In some less developed countries—China, for example—the government exercises almost complete control over the economy. As we shall see in Chapter 35, China's economy is planned. The government makes the basic decisions on what is produced, how it is produced, and who gets it. But even in the non-Communist LDCs, such as India, the government makes many decisions on what sorts of investment projects will be undertaken, and it controls foreign exchange. And, needless to say, the government has the responsibility for providing the important social overhead capital—roads, public utilities, schools, and so on—that is so badly needed.

Further, the government may also foster social and political change. As Nobel laureate Simon Kuznets has put it, "The problem of strategy is essentially the problem of how fast you can change an inadequate set of social and political institutions, without provoking a revolution internally, or losing allies and partners externally. The question is to know what institutions you want to change, and how."

Most economists would agree that the government has a very important role to play in promoting economic development. But there is a tendency to put less weight on the government's role than in the past. Experience has made it clear that some of the less developed countries are plagued by incompetent and corrupt government officials and by a plethora of bureaucratic red tape. Moreover, many governments have gone on spending sprees that have resulted in serious inflation. Even those who are very mistrustful of free markets find it difficult to put their complete faith in such governments, well-intentioned though they may be. Recent years have seen more and more emphasis on self-interest and individual action as contributors to growth. (If Adam Smith is peering down from the Great Beyond, he probably is smiling in agreement.) But this in no way denies the fact that governments have a key role to play.

Test Yourself

1. Between 1950 and 1967, the annual rate of growth of per capita national product was 5.3 percent in Taiwan, and 1.6 percent in India. Suggest as many hypotheses as you can to explain this difference.

2. In 1950, gross nonresidential investment was 9.8 percent of national product in Taiwan, and 7.4 percent of national product in India. In 1966, it was 16.7 percent of national product in Taiwan, and 13.8 percent of national product in India. Does this help to explain the difference in Question 1? Why or why not?

3. Between 1950 and 1967, the annual rate of growth of population was 3.1 percent in Taiwan and 2.2 percent in India. Does this help to explain the difference in Question 1? Why or why not?

4. Explain why the less developed countries have not adopted the advanced technology used in industrialized countries.

Balanced Growth

An important issue facing the governments of most less developed countries is the extent to which they want to maintain a balance between the agricultural and industrial sectors of the economy. That is, how much more rapidly should they expand industry than agriculture? According to some economists, less developed countries should invest heavily in industry, since the long-term trend of industrial prices is upward, relative to agricultural prices. In addition, advocates of unbalanced growth argue that the development of certain sectors of the economy will result in pressures for development elsewhere in the economy. Advocates of this approach point to the Soviet Union, which stressed industrialization in its growth strategy.

Other economists argue that industry and agriculture should be expanded at a more nearly equal rate. Successful industrial expansion requires agricultural expansion as well, because industry uses raw materials as inputs and because, as economic growth takes place, the people will demand more food. Balanced growth has other advantages. Various sectors of the economy are closely linked and an attempt to expand one sector in isolation is unlikely to succeed. Proponents of balanced growth deny that the long-term trend of industrial prices is upward, relative to agricultural prices. And to illustrate the wisdom of their approach, they cite as examples the United States and Britain, where industry and agriculture both expanded in the course of the development process.

INCREASES IN INDUSTRIALIZATION

In practically all of the 13 LDCs included in Table 34.7, industrial employment increased more rapidly than agricultural employment during the 1970s. Without question, the less developed countries expanded industry relative to agriculture. In some cases, such as India and Pakistan, it is generally agreed that more balance—more emphasis on agriculture—would have been preferable. Moreover, in many cases, the allocation of resources within industry could certainly have been improved. Countries sometimes put too

Table 34.7
AVERAGE ANNUAL RATE OF GROWTH OF PRODUCT, BY SECTOR, 1970–76

Country	Industry	Agriculture (percentage)	Wholesale and retail trade
Brazil[c]	13.8	6.2	12.3
Colombia[a]	6.3	5.4	6.1
Egypt[d]	2.8	4.0	6.6
Ghana[b]	3.0	3.6	3.2
India[b]	3.2	−0.7	2.2
Mexico	6.3	1.1	5.0
Pakistan	2.7	2.1	4.6
Peru	5.9	−0.4	6.8
Philippines	6.8	4.6	4.7
South Korea	19.3	4.9	10.7
Sri Lanka	9.1	1.7	4.5
Thailand	10.6	4.4	5.9
Turkey[a]	9.7	2.5	11.4
Average	7.7	3.0	6.5

[a] 1970–75. [b] 1970–74. [c] 1970–73. [d] 1970–71.
Source: United Nations.

much emphasis on substituting their own production—even when it is not efficient—for imports. Thus Chile prohibited the import of fully assembled cars to promote domestic production, but Chile's automobile plants have been uneconomic.

One reason why the less developed countries tend to push industrialization is that they see heavy industrialization in the wealthier countries. The United States, Western Europe, Japan, the USSR, all have lots of steel plants, oil refineries, chemical plants, and other kinds of heavy industry. It is easy for the less developed countries to jump to the conclusion that, if they want to become richer, they must become heavily industrialized too. It certainly seems sensible enough—until you think about the theory of comparative advantage. After all, if the less developed countries have a comparative advantage in areas other than heavy industry, they may do better to put more of their resources where their comparative advantage lies.

Another reason why the leaders of some less developed countries are fascinated by steel plants, airlines, and other modern industries, is that they think such industries confer prestige on their countries and themselves. Such prestige may be costly. Given their current situation, many of these countries might be well advised to invest much of their scarce resources in promoting higher productivity in agriculture, where they have a comparative advantage. We are not saying that many of these countries should not attempt to industrialize. We *are* saying that some of them have pushed industrialization too far—and that many have pushed it in uneconomic directions.

Development Planning in Less Developed Countries

The governments of many LDCs have established *development plans* to specify targets or goals for the economy. In some countries, these goals are set forth in very specific, detailed form; in others, they are more generally formulated. An important purpose of these plans is to allocate scarce resources, such as capital, in order to achieve rapid economic growth (or whatever the country's social objectives may be). Thus, in India, estimates have been made of the amount of capital that would be generated internally, as well as the capital that could be imported from abroad. Then the plan attempted to set a system of priorities for the use of this capital.

Some plans are merely window dressing, full of bold words and little else. But others are the result of careful investigation and hard work. To be useful, a plan must set realistic goals, which take proper account of the country's resources, available capital, and institutions. An unrealistically ambitious plan, if actually put in effect, is likely to lead to inflation, while a plan that is too easily satisfied is likely to mean a less than optimal rate of economic growth.

A useful plan should specify the policies to be used to reach the plan's goals, as well as the goals themselves. It should also forecast carefully how the various components of gross national product will change over time, the extent to which inflationary pressures will develop, the adequacy of the supply of foreign exchange, and the effects of the development program on various regions and parts of the population.

Planning techniques have benefited from the application of many tools of modern economic analysis, among them linear programming and input-output analysis. Linear programming can be used to determine how resources should be allocated to maximize output, and input-output analysis can determine how much capacity there must be in various industries to satisfy certain consumption targets (see Appendices C and D to this

Example 34.2   The Push Toward Industrialization

Governments of less developed countries sometimes force industrialization, even though many of their people would prefer a different strategy. Suppose that a particular country's production possibilities curve is as shown below:

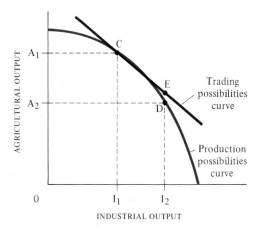

This country's government wants to increase its industrial output from $0I_1$ to $0I_2$.

(a) If its industrial output is increased in this way (and if the society remains on this production possibilities curve), what will be the cost to consumers? (b) How can the government push the society from point C to point D on the production possibilities curve? (c) Suppose that this country can trade its agricultural output for industrial goods in world markets, and that its trading possibilities curve (recall Chapter 32) is as shown above. Is there a way to reduce the cost of obtaining the extra $(0I_2 - 0I_1)$ of industrial goods? If so, what is it? (d) If the price of agricultural goods rises relative to the price of industrial goods in world markets, how will this affect the trading possibilities curve? Will it affect the cost of obtaining the extra $(0I_2 - 0I_1)$ of industrial goods? If so, how?

SOLUTION

(a) Agricultural output will have to be reduced from $0A_1$ to $0A_2$. (b) It can subsidize production of industrial goods and tax consumption of agricultural goods. Or it can intervene directly to increase industrial output and reduce agricultural output. (c) The country can move from point C to point E by trading its agricultural goods for industrial goods in world markets. Since point E lies above point D, the cost (that is, the reduction in agricultural goods) of the extra industrial goods is less than at point D. (d) It will reduce the slope of the trading possibilities curve, which will be closer to horizontal. The cost of obtaining the extra industrial goods will fall, since point E will be raised.

book). These modern tools have undoubtedly helped in formulating development plans, but their importance should not be exaggerated. It would be a great mistake to think that making a good plan is merely a job for an electronic computer.

If the plan is realistic, it can be a useful tool, but unless it is implemented properly, it will achieve very little for the economy. How well it is implemented will depend on the government's ability to marshal resources through taxation and foreign aid, to work effectively with the private sector, and to pick productive public investment projects. In some countries, like India, "the plan" has sometimes become a political symbol, but in many others, like Mexico, planning has been politically less visible. Countries where economic growth has been most rapid seem to have viewed "the plan" less as holy writ, and planning has tended to be more modest and low-keyed.

Planning in Action: The Case of India

Perhaps the best way to understand the operation of development plans is to look at the nature of a particular country's plans and how they have been fulfilled. Consider the interesting case of India, which has had a series of five-year plans.[2]

First Five-Year Plan. The First Five-Year Plan was for 1951–56. Its targets were to increase net investment in India from 5 to 6.75 percent of national income, to reduce income inequality, to cut the rate of population increase to 1 percent per year, and to lay the groundwork for a doubling of per capita output in a generation. To achieve these targets, the government relied heavily on capital formation. In particular, it sought to carry out many of the investment projects that had been discussed and planned under the British for 50 years or more. The First Five-Year Plan was accompanied by moderate growth. Per capita output grew by about 1.7 percent per year, and net investment rose from 5 to 8 percent of national income.

Second Five-Year Plan. At the beginning of 1956, the Indian Planning Commission published its Second Five-Year Plan, which called for much heavier investments—and more emphasis on investment in industry and mining, rather than agriculture and power—than the First Plan. Moreover, the Second Plan relied more heavily on deficit financing than did the First Plan, and devoted much more attention to the expansion of employment opportunities, since unemployment was a considerable problem. Unfortunately, the Second Plan ran into severe difficulties. One big problem was the loss of foreign exchange, as imports grew much more rapidly—and exports less rapidly—than expected. But perhaps more important was the fact that output did not grow as rapidly as the plan called for. By the end of the Second Five-Year Plan, all sectors of the economy, other than the service sector, were producing less than the planned targets. Nonetheless, per capita output grew about 1.8 percent per year.

Bokaro power station on the Konar river, India

[2] It is worthwhile emphasizing that the development strategies of *small* LDCs, because of their necessarily greater reliance on foreign trade, must be quite different from that of *large* LDCs, like India.

Inspecting maize field production during India's "green revolution"

Third Five-Year Plan. India's Third Five-Year Plan—for 1961–66—involved bigger investments and somewhat more emphasis on agriculture than the Second Plan. Responding to the fact that agricultural imports had been much higher than expected under the Second Plan, the Third Plan called for more investment in agriculture. Unfortunately, however, agricultural production during the Third Plan did not come up to expectations. Indeed, India might have experienced a serious famine in 1966 if it had not received substantial food imports from the United States. During the course of the Third Plan, India did increase the percentage of national income devoted to investment from 11 to 14 percent, but a substantial proportion of her investment was financed by foreign aid. Unfortunately, India's output grew by one-sixth, instead of the planned one-third, during the Third Plan, and there was little or no increase in per capita output.

Fourth Five-Year Plan. Although the failure of the Third Plan was due in considerable measure to India's involvement in two wars and two bad harvests, it nonetheless shook many Indians' confidence in the planning process. There was a three-year delay before the Fourth Five-Year Plan was unveiled, and its political significance was played down. The Fourth Plan shifted the emphasis to agricultural development, including irrigation and fertilizers; it stressed a large birth control program; and it called for a 5½ percent increase per year in national output, as well as further increases in investment. The Fourth Plan put somewhat more emphasis on the price system and somewhat less on detailed planning. In practice, however, the latter changes seemed to have been slow to occur.

The Late 1970s and 1980s. In 1975, when the late Prime Minister Indira Gandhi declared a national emergency, she claimed that many of the stern measures taken at that time were designed to help improve India's economic condition. She put forth a 20-Point Economic Program which emphasized the reduction of inflation, the encouragement of agriculture, and the reduction of the birth rate. Mrs. Gandhi's program of sterilization (sometimes forced) caused considerable resentment, and was one factor in her defeat at the polls in 1977. India's Janata party, which won the election over Mrs. Gandhi, promised to limit the role of centralized economic planning, and to emphasize agriculture and labor-intensive manufacturing in rural areas. In line with this objective, the Sixth Five-Year Plan, put forth in 1978, allocated 20 to 25 percent of the total investment outlay to labor-intensive industrial projects. However, many observers questioned whether the plan's targets were entirely realistic.

During the early 1980s, the Indian economy continued to experience problems. Many industrial goals were not met. India's oil import bill ate up 80 percent of its export earnings. The Indians went to the International Monetary Fund and the World Bank for massive loans. The Seventh Five-Year Plan, put forth in 1984, called for total investment of $320 billion (including $180 billion of public investment) and an annual rate of economic growth of about 5 percent. Only time will tell how much this plan will contribute to the achievement of India's economic goals.

Choosing Investment Projects in Less Developed Countries

Clearly, one of the crucial problems any less developed country must face is how the available capital should be invested. Countless investment projects could be undertaken—roads, irrigation projects, power plants, improvements in agricultural equipment, and so on. Faced with this menu of alternatives, how should a country choose?

One procedure often used is to accept projects resulting in high output per unit of capital invested. That is, projects are ranked by the ratio of the value of the output they produce to the capital they require. If a project yields $2 million worth of output per year and requires $1 million of capital, its ratio would be 2. Projects with high values of this ratio are accepted. This procedure, which is crude but sensible, is based on the correct idea that capital is the really scarce resource in many of the less developed countries. It is aimed at maximizing the output to be derived from a certain amount of capital.

However, a better technique for choosing projects is the concept of rate of return, which is used by profit-maximizing firms to choose among alternative investment opportunities. A less developed country, like a firm, can compute the rate of return from each investment opportunity. That is, it can estimate the rate of interest that will be obtained from each investment. Then it, like a firm, should choose the *projects with the highest rates of return.*[3]

In computing the rate of return from each investment project, it is necessary to attach values to the resources it uses and to the returns it produces. At first glance, it may seem adequate to use market prices of inputs and outputs as these values. Thus, if unskilled labor's market price is $.10 an hour, this would be the value attached to unskilled labor. Unfortunately, there are some important pitfalls in using market prices in this way. In particular, *market prices of inputs in the less developed countries often do not indicate social costs properly.* Although the market price of unskilled labor may be $.10 an hour, there may be lots of unskilled labor doing essentially nothing in the countryside, with the result that the social cost—the true opportunity cost—of using such labor is zero, not $.10 an hour. Moreover, *the market prices of some outputs may not indicate their social worth.* Because of tariffs and quotas, domestic prices may differ significantly from world prices, which may be closer to the appropriate price for some analyses of this sort.

Thus, when computing each project's rate of return, it is important to make proper adjustments so that inputs are valued at their social cost and outputs are valued at their social worth. This is easier said than done, but even crude adjustments in the right direction can be worthwhile.

Basic Idea #68: To allocate resources, an LDC, like a firm, can compute the rate of return from each investment opportunity and choose projects with relatively high rates of return. However, since market prices may be misleading, an attempt should be made to value inputs at their social cost and outputs at their social worth.

Foreign Aid

The plight of the less developed countries is of concern to Americans, both because it is good morality and good policy to help them. From the point

---

[3] More sophisticated criteria are presented in more advanced texts. Even for a firm, the above criterion is over-simplified, although, for important classes of problems, it generally gives the correct answer.

of view of humanitarianism, the United States and the other rich nations have a moral responsibility to help the poor nations. From the point of view of our self-interest, the promotion of growth in the less developed countries should help to preserve and encourage political and international stability and to make them more effective trading partners.

How can the United States be of help? With regard to many of their problems, we can do relatively little. But one thing that we can do is to provide badly needed capital. Responding to that need, we have given and lent a substantial amount of capital to the less developed countries in the past 25 years.

U.S. AID PROGRAMS

American financial assistance took several forms in the period after World War II. In the immediate postwar period, the primary objective was to help the populations of the war-ravaged countries and to get the European economies back on their feet. The United Nations Relief and Rehabilitation Administration (UNRRA) provided $4 billion of food, clothing, and medical services, about three-quarters of which was financed by the United States. In addition, other forms of relief, aid, and loans were extended. In all, the United States provided about $17 billion in aid between the war's end and 1948, about half in loans and about half in grants.

By the early 1950s, Europe's economy was in pretty good shape, but this did not spell the end of our foreign aid programs. On the contrary, much of our aid shifted toward the less developed nations. Table 34.8 shows the total

Table 34.8

U.S. FOREIGN ECONOMIC AND MILITARY AID PROGRAM, 1946–83

| Year | Economic | | Military | | Total |
| | Loans | Grants | Loans | Grants | |
		(billions of dollars)			
1946–52	8.5	22.7	–	3.8	35.0
1953–61	5.9	18.2	0.2	24.1	48.3
1962–65	8.3	8.7	0.4	8.1	25.6
1966–69	7.1	9.3	1.2	9.6	27.1
1970	1.4	2.3	0.1	3.0	6.8
1971	1.3	2.1	0.7	3.9	8.1
1972	1.6	2.3	0.6	4.8	9.2
1973	1.4	2.7	0.6	5.2	9.9
1974	1.2	2.8	1.4	3.7	9.0
1975	1.7	3.2	0.8	1.6	7.2
1976	1.8	2.1	1.4	1.3	6.6
1976TQ[a]	0.8	1.1	0.5	0.2	2.6
1977	2.1	3.5	1.4	0.8	7.8
1978	2.5	4.1	1.6	0.8	9.0
1979	1.9	5.2	5.2	1.6	13.8
1980	2.0	5.6	1.4	0.7	9.7
1981	1.5	5.8	2.5	0.7	10.6
1982	1.4	6.7	3.1	1.1	12.3
1983	1.6	7.0	3.9	1.7	14.2

[a] Transition quarter, July-September 1976. In the earlier data, the year ends June 30; in the later data, it ends September 30.

Source: Statistical Abstract of the United States.

amount the United States spent on foreign aid between 1946 and 1983. During this period, we spent about $270 billion—a huge sum by any standard. About 40 percent of these expenditures have been for military purposes, about 60 percent have been for economic purposes. No nation has ever contributed as much to the economic development of poorer countries as we have.

Much of this aid has been in the form of loans or grants that must be spent on American goods and services. Also, much of it consisted of our giving away part of what were then surplus stocks of food. (Recall the agricultural programs discussed in Chapter 4.)

In addition, the United States has established various kinds of technical assistance programs designed to help the less developed countries borrow some of our technology, administrative techniques, medical knowledge, educational methods, and so on. The emphasis frequently is on training people from the less developed countries to the point where they can teach their fellow countrymen. Often the costs of these programs are shared by United States and by the recipient of the aid. Most observers seem to believe that these technical assistance programs have been worthwhile and successful.

OTHER U.S. ASSISTANCE TO LDC'S

Some other aspects of American policy are also important, although they are not aid programs. For one thing, the United States and other developed countries can help the LDCs by reducing trade barriers, thus allowing them to increase their national incomes through trade. However, it seems unlikely that trade alone can substitute for aid, and the situation is clouded by the trade barriers the LDCs themselves have been erecting to protect their own industry. Another way that the United States can help is through private investment. American corporations have invested many billions of dollars in the less developed countries. To the less developed countries, this is a significant source of capital.

Besides providing capital, the multinational corporations have also been a source of needed technology. However, these firms have faced much more difficult problems in transmitting technology to less developed countries than to industrialized countries. Many of the techniques of the multinational firms are not very well suited to the less developed countries, with their plentiful unskilled labor, few skills, and little capital. Moreover, there is sometimes little incentive for multinational firms to adapt their products, production techniques, and marketing methods to the conditions present in developing countries. And when they do manage to make a technological transplant, its effects are often restricted to narrow segments of the economy. Still further, it should be noted that the multinational firms are often viewed with some suspicion and fear by the host governments.

CONTROVERSIES OVER FOREIGN AID

For many years, foreign aid has been a controversial subject in the United States. Many critics argue that the money could better be spent at home to alleviate domestic poverty. They claim that other industrialized countries—like Germany and Japan—should contribute a bigger share of the aid to the less developed countries. And they assert that our aid programs have not had much impact on the less developed countries so far. Liberals object to our giving aid to governments charged with serious violation of human rights. Conservatives are disturbed that some aid channeled through international organizations may go to Marxist governments.

Many suggestions have been made for ways to improve the effectiveness of our foreign aid. One prominent suggestion is that we go further in concentrating the bulk of our aid on a relatively few countries—those that really want to do what is necessary to develop, that can use the money well, and that are important from the point of view of size and international politics. Obviously adopting this suggestion means reducing aid to some other countries. Another suggestion is that, rather than impose political conditions on aid, we should give money with no strings attached. This suggestion entails a great deal more than economics. To evaluate it, one must decide what the goals of foreign aid should be. To what extent should it be aimed at raising the standard of living of the world's population, whatever the effect on the United States? To what extent should it be aimed at furthering American goals and American foreign policies? In practice, foreign aid has been bound up closely with our foreign policy. Given the political facts of life, it is difficult to see how it could be otherwise.

OTHER COUNTRIES' AID PROGRAMS

The United States has provided a large percentage of the aid that has flowed from the industrialized countries to the less developed countries, but it has by no means been the sole contributor. Other industrialized nations also have aid programs. For example, France has contributed over $2 billion per year in official development assistance and Japan and Germany have contributed over $1 billion. Moreover, the Soviet Union has formulated a significant aid program. Indeed, it is often claimed that the Russian programs have had more political effect than our own because they allow the recipient countries more freedom to build "prestige" projects like steel mills and because they make their aid look somewhat less like charity.

The World Bank

Another source of capital is the *World Bank.* In 1944, late in World War II, the major economic powers agreed to establish the International Bank for Reconstruction and Development, also known as the World Bank. Although its first loans were for postwar reconstruction, the bank's principal function now is to make long-term loans to the less developed countries—in Latin America, Asia, and elsewhere. They desperately need capital, while the rich, economically advanced countries have capital to lend. The World Bank's purpose was to channel funds from rich nations to poor, thus supplementing private investment, which was often scared off

World Bank "Equal Access" program in the Upper Volta

by the apparent risks. More specifically, the major economic powers contributed a certain amount of money to form the bank, with each country's share determined by its economic size. About one-third of the total was put up by the United States. The Soviet Union helped organize the World Bank, but later declined to join.

Now about 40 years old, the World Bank still makes loans to people or governments with sound investment projects who have been unable to get private financing. Moreover, by floating its own bond issues it can lend money above and beyond what was originally put up by the major powers. In other words, the World Bank sells its own IOUs, which are considered safe by investors because they are guaranteed by member countries. In addition, it helps less developed countries get loans from private lenders by insuring the loans. That is, the World Bank can tell the lender that if the loan goes sour it will see that the lender is paid back.

This movement of capital from the capital-rich nations to the capital-poor nations should prove beneficial for both rich and poor. The poor countries are enabled to carry out projects that will result in economic returns high enough to pay off the lender with interest and have some net benefits left over. The rich countries are enabled to invest their capital at a higher rate of return than they could obtain at home. Thus both parties benefit, as long as the loans are economically sound.

The World Bank has established the *International Development Agency* to make "soft" loans, as well as the *International Finance Corporation,* which lends to foreign development banks. An increased percentage of the bank's financing has been channeled through these two agencies.

The bank's activities have grown substantially: in 1965, its loan authorizations were about $1 billion; in 1974, they were about $4 billion; and in 1979, its loans exceeded $10 billion. Nonetheless, despite its achievements, many economists believe that in the past the World Bank has sometimes been too conservative and that it should have been willing to take bigger risks. Since the late 1960s, when Robert McNamara (now succeeded by A. W. Clausen, former president of the Bank of America) became its head, the bank has become less conservative in this respect. By 1984, a substantial proportion of its loans were aimed at helping the LDCs with their balance-of-payments problems; and there were reports of a clash between Clausen and the Reagan administration over whether such loans should be restricted. In the administration's view, the bank should concentrate on the provision of financing for development projects.

A New International Economic Order?

Since the early 1970s, the less developed countries have been voicing their extreme displeasure with the state of the world economic system as it affects them. A special session of the UN General Assembly was called in 1975 to deal with their demands for a "new international economic order." Subsequently, many other meetings have been devoted to this topic. What the LDCs want is (1) greater control by the LDCs over their own economic destiny, (2) acceleration of their growth rate (and a narrowing of the gap in per capita income between the developed and less developed countries), and (3) a major increase in the share of the world's industrial production carried out in the LDCs. To attain these objectives, they have pressed for tariff preferences for their manufactured exports, agreements to stabilize and support their commodity prices, and the accelerated transfer of resources to them from the industrialized countries.

Tariff Preferences. To gain freer access to industrial nations' markets, the LDCs want tariff preferences for their manufactured exports; specifically, they want to be charged no tariff. This idea of preferential tariffs seems to be accepted in many industrialized countries. Consider the Trade Reform Act of 1974, which authorized the United States to join with other industrial countries in reducing tariffs to zero for many products from LDCs. But there was a catch. Items like textiles and shoes cannot be granted zero duties if they are found to be "import sensitive." In practice, how much the LDCs will get in the way of tariff preferences is hard to say.

Stabilization and Support of Commodity Prices. Most LDCs derive 80 percent or more of their foreign exchange from the sale of commodities like coffee, cocoa, and sugar. Since the price of such commodities tends to fluctuate considerably, the LDCs would like the developed countries to cooperate in the stabilization of individual commodity prices. They would like to establish commodity agreements among the countries producing a commodity, binding them not to sell at less than the agreed price. In effect, these are international cartels, like OPEC. (See p. 449.) Since such cartels generally want to raise, as well as stabilize, the price of commodities, there are obvious disadvantages to the developed countries in the establishment of such agreements.

Transfer of Resources. The LDCs would like economic aid to be increased to about 1 percent of the GNP of the donor countries. Also, they would like the developed countries to forgive at least part of the large debts they have run up in recent years. If the LDCs refuse to pay these debts, their credit standing would be undermined, and their ability to secure future loans would be impaired. Nonetheless, there is considerable worry about the possibility that some of these countries may default, and impose large losses on the commercial banks and others that have lent them money.

As one would expect, these demands for a "new international economic order" have provoked a considerable amount of controversy. Some observers have pointed out that these demands ignore the fact that, to a large extent, economic development is something that the LDCs must do for themselves, by creating the necessary political stability, social mobility, and economic incentives. Other observers are suspicious of the commodity agreements the LDCs favor, since they feel that such cartel arrangements would be relatively inefficient ways to accomplish the aims of the LDCs. Only time will tell how far the developed countries will go in trying to meet these demands of the LDCs.

Test Yourself

1. "It is always a good idea for less developed countries to substitute their own production for imports. This is the only way they can become economically independent." Comment and evaluate.

2. According to Simon Kuznets, "A substantial economic advance in the less developed countries may require modification in the available stock of material technology, and probably even greater innovations in political and social structure." What does he mean? If he is correct, what are the implications for the less developed countries? For the developed countries?

3. According to Hans Morgenthau, "Foreign aid for economic development has a chance to be successful only within relatively narrow limits which are raised by cultural and political conditions impervious to direct outside influence." Do you agree? If he is correct, what are the implications for the less developed countries? For the developed countries?

4. Why don't some market prices of inputs correspond closely to social costs in less developed countries? Give examples. What implications does this have for the economic analysis of investment projects in LDCs?

Summary

1. A country is defined here as a less developed country if its per capita income is less than $3,000. Well over half of the world's population live in the less developed countries, which include many of the countries in Asia, Africa, and Latin America. In recent years, there has been a great increase in the expectations and material demands of the people in these countries.

2. The less developed countries vary greatly, but they generally devote most of their resources to the production of food, are composed of two economies (one market-oriented, the other subsistence), and often have relatively weak, unstable governments and a relatively high degree of income inequality.

3. One obvious reason why income per capita is so low is that the people in the less developed countries have so little capital to work with. The less developed countries, with their low incomes, do not save much, they lack entrepreneurs, and the climate for investment (domestic or foreign) often is not good.

4. Some less developed countries suffer from overpopulation; and as total output has increased, these gains have been offset by population increases. Modern medical techniques have reduced the death rate, while the birth rate has remained high. The result is a population explosion.

5. Another very important reason why per capita income is so low in these countries is that they often use backward technology. The transfer of technology from one country to another is not as easy as it sounds, particularly when the recipient country has an uneducated population and little capital. Also, these countries lack favorable social institutions and sometimes have few natural resources.

6. An important issue facing the governments of most less developed countries is the extent to which they want to promote a balance between the agricultural and industrial sectors of the economy. Without question, the LDCs are expanding industry relative to agriculture. In some cases, such as India and Pakistan, more balance—less emphasis on industry, more on agriculture—would have been preferable. Moreover, some countries have put too much emphasis on substituting their own production for imports, even when their own production is uneconomic.

7. Many of the less developed countries have established development plans that specify targets or goals for the economy and policies designed to attain them. One criterion often used to determine whether a given investment project should be accepted or rejected is the ratio of the value of the output produced to the capital used. Only projects with high values of this ratio are accepted.

8. A more sophisticated criterion is the rate of return from the project, the method used by firms in capital budgeting. When computing each project's rate of return, it is important that inputs be valued at their social cost and that outputs be valued at their social worth.

9. The United States has been involved in a number of major aid programs to help the less developed countries. In recent years, these aid programs have come under increasing attack, because of a feeling in Congress and elsewhere that they have not been working well.

10. Besides the United States, other countries—including the Soviet Union—have carried out significant aid programs. And the World Bank has channeled major amounts of capital into the less developed countries.

Concepts for Review

Less developed country	**Foreign aid**	**Balanced growth**
Market-oriented economy	**Population explosion**	**Development plan**
Subsistence economy	**Green revolution**	**World Bank**

CHAPTER 35

The Communist Countries and Marxism

Everybody talks and reads about *communism.* You hear the word frequently on television and see it frequently in the newspapers, but if you really know what it means, you are in the minority. It is a safe bet that most people have only a vague and distorted idea of what communism is, partly because the relationship in recent years between the Communist and non-Communist countries has been marked by suspicion, dissension, and sometimes war. Yet about a third of the world's population lives under Communist rule. The Soviet Union, China, Yugoslavia, Cuba, and many other countries are Communist. You should know something about the nature of communism to understand what is going on in a large part of the world.

In this chapter we describe and analyze the nature and workings of the economic system in various Communist countries, with our major emphasis on the Soviet Union. After a brief discussion of the doctrines of Karl Marx, the intellectual father of communism, we describe how the Soviet economy works. Since economic planning plays a major role in its functioning, the USSR's planning system is described in some detail. Next, we turn to the economy of China, and to some of the major differences between communism and democratic socialism. Finally, we describe briefly the nature of radical economics, a recent, and still very small, movement in the United States that draws heavily on Marx's views.

Karl Marx

The Doctrines of Karl Marx

THE CLASS STRUGGLE

The name Karl Marx probably makes you think of revolutionaries meeting by candlelight in damp cellars to plot the overthrow of nineteenth-century European governments. If this is the picture you associate with the name, you are quite right! Karl Marx was a revolutionary who wanted the masses to revolt against the existing social order. In 1848, he and Friedrich Engels published the famous *Communist Manifesto,* the spirit of which is given by its closing lines:

> Communists ... openly declare that their ends can be attained only by the forcible overthrow of all existing social conditions. Let the ruling classes tremble at a Communist revolution. The proletarians have nothing to lose but their chains. They have a world to win. Workers of the world, unite!

This is stirring language, no doubt about it. But why did Marx preach revolution, and what goals do the communists want to achieve?

To understand their aims, it is helpful to look at Marx's famous treatise, *Capital* (the first part of which was published in 1867), which states much of his economic and political thought. According to Marx, the fundamental causes of political and social change are socioeconomic factors. Changes in the ways goods and services are produced and distributed—and in the ways in which people enter into "productive relations" with one another (the feudal lord with the serf under feudalism, or the capitalist with the worker under capitalism)—are responsible for the great political and social movements of history. History can be viewed as a series of class struggles. In ancient times, the struggle was between masters and slaves. In feudal times, it was between lords and serfs. And in modern times, it is between the *capitalists,* who own the means of production, and the workers, or *proletariat.*

According to Marx, every economic system—ancient, feudal, or modern—develops certain defects or internal contradictions, which eventually cause it to give way to a new system. As the old system begins to weaken, the new system gains strength. Thus the feudal system grew out of the ancient system, and the modern system grew out of the feudal system. In Marx's view, *the struggle between the capitalists and the proletariat will eventually result in the defeat of the capitalists. This will set the stage for a new economic system—socialism, a transitional phase toward communism.* Communism, according to Marx, is the ultimate, perfect form of economic system.

THE THEORY OF VALUE AND WAGES

The reasons for Marx's belief that in modern times there must be a struggle between capitalists and workers lie in his theory of value and wages. *According to Marx, the value of any commodity—that is, its price relative to other commodities—is determined by the amount of labor time used in its manufacture.* In other words, if a shirt requires twice as much labor time to produce as a tie, its price is twice that of a tie. By labor time, Marx meant both the amount of labor used in making a commodity and the amount of labor time "congealed" in the machinery used to make the commodity. According to Marx, wages tend to equal the lowest level consistent with the subsistence of the workers, because capitalists, driven by the profit motive, pay the lowest wage they can.

Combining his theory of value and his theory of wages, Marx concluded that workers produce a ***surplus value***—a value above and beyond the subsistence wage they receive—which is taken by the capitalists. This surplus value arises because the capitalists make the workers labor for longer hours than are required to produce an amount of output equal to their wage. Consider the worker who may be made to work 10 hours a day, even though her output in 6 hours equals the value of her wage. The output produced in the remaining 4 hours is surplus value.

According to Marx, surplus value is what makes the capitalist world tick. Indeed, the reason why capitalists engage in production is to make this surplus value, which they steal from the workers. Capitalists also use some of it to purchase new capital. Thus capital formation, in Marx's view, comes about as a consequence of surplus value. If the capitalist class is exploiting the workers in the way Marx visualized, it is not difficult to see why he felt that a class struggle between capitalists and workers was inevitable, and even easier to see why he was on the workers' side.

MARX'S VISION OF THE FUTURE

In Marx's view, capitalism would eventually reveal certain fundamental weaknesses that would hasten its demise. As more and more capital is accumulated, Marx felt that the profit rate would be driven down, that unemployment would increase (because of a rise in technological unemployment), that business cycles would become more severe (depressions becoming more devastating), and that monopoly would grow more widespread. As these developments imposed greater and greater hardships on the working class, the chance of revolution would increase. Eventually the workers, recognizing that they "have nothing to lose but their chains," would throw off the yoke of capitalism.

However, Marx did not visualize an immediate progression to communism. Instead, he saw socialism as a way station on the road to communism. *Socialism would be a "dictatorship of the proletariat."* The workers would rule. Specifically, they would control the government, which, according to Marx, is merely a tool of the propertied class under capitalism. Moreover, the socialist government would own the means of production— the factories, mines, and equipment. Under socialism each person would receive an amount of income related to the amount he or she produced.

Finally, after an unspecified length of time, Marx felt that socialism would give way to communism, his ideal system. Communism would be a classless society, everyone working, and no one owning capital or exploiting the other person. Under communism, the state would become obsolete and wither away. The principle of income distribution would be, "From each according to his ability, to each according to his needs." Marx was a visionary and a social prophet, and communism was his promised land, the ultimate goal for which he prodded the workers to revolt—and the land into which the forces of history would ultimately propel them.

CRITICISMS OF MARX

Since Marx's doctrines have captured the imagination of huge numbers of people, and hundreds of millions now march under his banners, it is clear that Marx was a remarkable success as a social philosopher and political activist. But what about Marx the economist? Most economists feel that his economic theories have basic flaws, and that many of his economic predictions have gone badly astray. Although there is almost universal admiration for the power and originality of his mind, few economists in the non-Communist world buy his economic doctrines.

Specifically, there are the following problems with his theories:

1. His labor theory of value simply will not hold water. As we have seen in previous chapters, the price of a commodity depends on nonlabor costs as well as labor costs. In particular, capital, land, and entrepreneurship contribute to production. Moreover, the price of a commodity depends on the demand for it as well as on its costs. (You will recall that price is determined by the intersection of the demand curve and the supply curve.)

2. Marx's subsistence theory of wages has long been discredited. It simply isn't true that wages are set at the subsistence level. Far from being barely sufficient to keep the worker alive, wages in the United States are high enough to provide the typical worker with a car, television, travel, and a variety of other conveniences. Further, Marx's prediction that the working class would experience greater and greater misery has not been fulfilled. On the contrary, the standard of living of workers in the West has increased at a remarkable rate in the century since Marx wrote *Capital.*

3. His prediction that the rate of profit would fall has been wrong. Instead, the rate of profit has moved up and down, with no clear trend in either direction. And his prediction of greater warfare between capitalists and workers has not materialized either. On the contrary, workers have tended to buy shares in corporations, thus joining the capitalist class. And the lines of demarcation between the working class and the capitalist class have been blurred, not accentuated, by time.

Nonetheless, despite these and other flaws in his theories, Marx was a very important figure in economics. He recognized some of the most important problems of capitalism—in particular the problems of unemployment, income inequality, and monopoly power—and analyzed these problems forcefully and originally. One need not agree with his ideas, or sympathize with some of his followers, to recognize his remarkable talents.

The Soviet Economy

COMMUNISM IN THE USSR

The economy of the Soviet Union provides an important example of the application of Marxian theories. By the beginning of the twentieth century, **Marxism** was an international political force of some significance. In 1917,

---

Basic Idea #69: *According to Marx, socialism would be characterized by government ownership of the means of production. The workers would rule, and each person would receive an income related to the amount he or she produced. Eventually, in Marx's view, socialism would lead to communism, in which everyone would work, no one would own capital, the state would wither away, and income would be distributed according to need.*

May Day in Moscow

a Marxist-oriented party established itself in Russia. This was the first time any major country went communist. With V. I. Lenin at its helm, the Communist party overthrew the Russian government in November 1917, and set up the Union of Soviet Socialist Republics several years later. The stated goal of the party was to establish Marxian socialism—and eventually communism—in the USSR. When Lenin died in 1924, his place was taken by Josef Stalin, who ruled until his death in 1953. Since the USSR is now by far the most economically advanced and militarily strongest Communist country, we need to understand how its economy works.

Two characteristics of the Soviet economy should be stressed at the outset:

1. Although Marx seemed to want the state eventually to wither away, the Soviet government is a remarkably hardy perennial. The Kremlin's influence over Russian life is well known. Power is centralized in the hands of a relatively few Communist officials who make the big decisions about what is to be produced, how it is to be produced, and who is to receive how much. This contrasts with capitalist economies like ours, where these decisions are made largely in the market place.

2. In accord with Marx's views, most productive resources in the Soviet Union are publicly owned. The government owns the factories, mines, equipment, and so on. This too is quite different from the situation in the United States, where most productive resources are privately owned. Specifically, the Soviet government owns practically all industry, most retail and wholesale stores, and most urban housing. Some farms are government-owned, but most are collective farms. The principal case of private ownership in the Soviet Union is the small strip of land each family on a collective farm is allowed to work for itself. In addition, people are allowed to own furniture, clothing, utensils, and sometimes houses.

Soviet Economic Planning

The Soviet Union's central planners decide what the country will produce. How do they go about making these decisions, what steps do they follow, and who is involved in this process? Before trying to answer these questions, it is important to recognize that the procedures followed by the central planners change from time to time as they recognize their mistakes and try to rectify them. Planning and controlling a vast economy like the Soviet Union's is enormously complicated. In the period immediately after the Russian Revolution of 1917, the Communists made some whopping mistakes, but as time went on, the planners became better able to carry out their jobs.

This is the general procedure that evolved. First, the principal officials of the Communist party made the fundamental decisions as to how much output would be allocated for consumption and how much for investment, which industries would be expanded and which would be cut back. Once these decisions were made, people at a lower level decided the details concerning how various plants should be operated. Then these decisions were transmitted to and carried out by managers, engineers, and workers. This decision-making process is clearly very centralized. During the 1960s.

Table 35.1

THE ELEVENTH FIVE-YEAR PLAN FOR THE SOVIET UNION, 1981–85

Item	Actual output in 1980	Planned output for 1985
Electric power (billions of kilowatt hours)	1,295	1,550–1,600
Oil (million tons)	603	620–645
Natural gas (billion M³)	435	600–640
Coal (million tons)	716	770–800
Steel (million tons)	148	n.a.
Grain (million tons)	205	238–243
Meat (million tons)	14.9	17–17.5
Cement (million tons)	125	140–142

Source: D. Bond and H. Levine, "The Eleventh Five-Year Plan, 1981–85," 1981.

the Russians began to experiment with greater decentralization, delegating more of the planning to the individual plants and industries, and doing less of it centrally. But these reforms met with resistance, as we shall see below.

Several groups are involved in planning. The top officials of the Communist party establish the overall goals for the economy. These goals are generally enunciated in a *five-year plan*, which shows where the economy should be in five years. Table 35.1 shows part of the Soviet Union's Eleventh Five-Year Plan, for 1981–85. One goal was to increase electric power production by about 22 percent (about 4 percent per year). When the broad goals are decided, the detailed production plans are drawn up by *Gosplan*, the State Planning Commission. Gosplan obtains enormous amounts of data from the ministries responsible for the performance of particular industries. These data describe production capacities of various productive units and available productive resources. On this basis, Gosplan formulates a tentative production plan.

Once Gosplan's tentative plan is formulated, a host of other groups enters the picture. A number of ministries, each concerned with a particular industry, reports to Gosplan in the Soviet administrative hierarchy. These ministries review Gosplan's tentative plan, as do individual plant managers. The purpose of this evaluation is to make sure that the plan is realistic and feasible. Some plant managers will argue that the amount they are asked to produce is too high or that the amount of labor and materials they are allocated is too low. Negotiations take place, and suggestions for revision are sent back to Gosplan. Eventually Gosplan produces the final five-year plan.

ECONOMIC PLANNING: A SIMPLE ILLUSTRATION

The job faced by the Soviet planners is difficult and complex. Unless you have some appreciation of how tough it is, you cannot understand the difficulties any planned economy must face. Suppose you are handed the job of planning the performance of a small economy consisting of a chemical industry, a coal industry, and an electric power industry. To produce electric power, one needs coal, chemicals, electric power, and

Table 35.2
AMOUNT OF EACH INPUT USED PER
DOLLAR OF OUTPUT

Type of input	Type of output		
	Electric power	Coal	Chemicals
	(dollars)		
Electric	0.1	0.3	0.0
Coal	0.5	0.1	0.0
Chemicals	0.2	0.0	0.9
Labor	0.2	0.6	0.1
Total	1.0	1.0	1.0

labor as inputs. To produce coal, one needs electric power, coal, and labor as inputs. To produce chemicals, one needs chemicals and labor as inputs. Suppose that the country's political rulers have said that in five years they want the country to consume $100 million of electric power, $50 million of coal, and $50 million of chemicals.

It is not easy to decide what production targets to establish for each industry. For one thing, the output set for one industry must depend on the output set for another industry because each industry uses another's output. Thus, if you are not careful, one industry will be unable to achieve its target because another industry has produced too little. Suppose that each industry uses the products of the other industries in the proportions shown in Table 35.2. (The second column of figures, for example, states that every dollar's worth of coal requires $.30 worth of electric power, $.10 worth of coal, and $.60 worth of labor.) Under these circumstances, what should the production targets be? The answer isn't obvious. Try it and see. (It can be shown that the production targets must be as follows. In five years, $144 million of coal, $159 million of electric power, and $818 million of chemicals must be produced. For a proof, see pp. A20–A21.)

This illustration gives you some inkling of the problems faced by the Soviet planners—but only an inkling. Our illustration has only three industries, while in fact the Russians have to deal with thousands. In the illustration, the input-output coefficients (in Table 35.2) were assumed known. In fact, these coefficients change over time and are not very accurately known. In this simple illustration, we can work out the production target for each industry, using straightforward mathematical techniques. The Soviet planning problem is so much bigger and more complicated that it is impossible, even with the most sophisticated mathematical techniques and the biggest computers, to solve their planning problem the way we could solve it for the three-industry economy.

Priorities and Performance

To make the planning problem more tractable, the Soviets set higher priorities for certain production goals than for others. Thus they may set a goal for the production of houses and a goal for the production of missiles, but the production of missiles may be given higher priority. If trouble arises in meeting this production goal, the planners may take resources away from the housing industry to make sure the higher-priority goal is achieved. This makes the planner's job a little easier, but does not guarantee that the economy will be very efficient.

The best-laid plans can go awry. To make sure theirs do not, the Russians have a number of important organizations to check on the performances of plants and managers. First, there is the **Gosbank,** the state-run banking system. When the plan is published, the Gosbank gives the managers of each plant enough money to buy the resources—labor, materials, and so on—allocated to their plant. If the managers run out of money, they are using more resources than the plan called for. Also, when the managers sell the plant's output, the receipts must be deposited in the Gosbank If the deposit is less than the value of output specified in the plan, it is clear that the plant has produced less than the plan called for. In this way, the Gosbank keeps close tabs on the performance of various plants. Second, the *State Control Commission* has inspectors who visit plants and go over the records of the Gosbank. Third, officials of the Communist party are expected to report poor performance to the party bosses.

SOVIET MANAGERS AND WORKERS

The Soviet economy is a **command economy**—people are told what to do. The managers of an industrial plant are told that to fulfill the plan, they must produce a certain amount, their **quota.** Moreover, they are authorized to spend a specific amount on wages (they are free to hire labor in the labor market), and to purchase a specified amount of raw materials and equipment. Their job is to carry out these orders, but they are not told *how* to run their plant. That is up to them. The Soviets have introduced managerial incentives not too different from those in the West. If managers are resourceful and diligent, they may be able to exceed their quota. In this case the Soviets—like good capitalists—reward them with extra pay, honors, and perhaps a promotion. If they are lazy, foolish, or unlucky, they may fall short of their quota, which may lead to a pay cut or disgrace.

However, because managers have generally been judged on whether they have met their quotas, certain problems have arisen. Managers have tried to underestimate what their plants could produce in order to get easy quotas. They have tried to hoard and conceal materials and labor so that they would appear to use less resources than they did. And they have sometimes allowed the quality of their product to decline in order to meet their quota. Moreover, managers have been loath to introduce new methods or other innovations because of the risks involved. If a new method did not pan out, it could mean Siberia for the manager. Better play it safe, even though this hurts productivity over the long run.

Soviet workers have considerable freedom to determine where they work. However, farm workers are not allowed to leave the farms, and personnel are not allowed to leave certain projects of great importance to the government. To get work of the right kind done to fulfill the plan, the planners set up wage differentials to induce people to do the needed work. This is quite similar to the sorts of incentives that prevail under capitalism. In addition, however, other pressures are used to get people to work hard and in accord with the plan. The government provides medals and awards to workers who do very well. The labor unions, which are really part of the state, push for higher productivity. And people who perform poorly may be fined or penalized in other ways. Nonetheless, labor problems of various kinds exist. There are many complaints that Soviet workers are unnecessarily late and absent from their jobs, and that labor turnover is far higher than it should be.

Prices in the USSR

As we have seen in earlier chapters, prices in a market economy allocate resources in a way that promotes the goals and satisfactions of the con-

State Department Store, Moscow

sumers. Obviously, prices in the Soviet Union do not function like this. On the contrary, they are set by the government to promote the goals of the state. Note that there are two fundamental differences here between the United States and the Soviet Union. Prices are set largely by the market in the United States; they are set by the government in the USSR. And prices should promote the goals of consumers in the United States, but promote the goals of the government in the USSR.

PRICES TO PRODUCERS

More specifically, how are prices set—and how are they used—in the Soviet Union? The answer varies depending on whether one adopts the point of view of a producer or a consumer. First, consider a producer—a plant producing shoes, say. The government sets the price of the shoes, as well as the prices of the labor, materials, and other inputs the producer uses. The government tries to set these prices so that a firm of average efficiency will run neither a profit nor a loss. Thus the system of prices is used to determine whether a producer is relatively efficient or relatively inefficient. If a plant makes a profit, this is evidence that it is efficient; a loss is evidence that it is inefficient.

This is no different from capitalism. But in the USSR, prices of inputs do not reflect the relative scarcity of inputs, as they do in capitalistic economies. Moreover, the price system in the USSR does not determine the output of each commodity, as it does under capitalism. Instead, as we saw in the previous section, government planning determines target output levels.

PRICES TO CONSUMERS

Next, let's consider the prices consumers must pay for goods and services. The function performed by these prices is quite different from that performed by the prices that producers must pay. While the prices facing producers are used to gauge the producers' efficiency (and how well they perform according to the plan), the prices facing consumers are used to ration the consumer goods that are produced. Thus the price of a commodity to the producer is likely to be quite different from its price to the consumer. For example, the price of a pair of shoes may be 10 rubles to the producer and 20 rubles to the consumer. Why 20 rubles to the consumer? Because 20 rubles is the price the government feels will equate the amount demanded with the amount being produced.

Consumer prices are set with an eye toward raising the planned revenue needed for investment. The gap between the price to the consumer and the price to the producer is the **turnover tax.** The turnover tax rate—100 percent in the case of the shoes, since the difference between the two prices, 10 rubles, is the same as the price to the producer—varies considerably from commodity to commodity. It provides a good deal of the Soviet government's revenue, and is a way to reduce inflationary pressures and make consumer spending fit in with the government's economic plan.

The Distribution of Income

At this point, recall that one of the fundamental tasks of any economic system is to distribute the society's output among the people. Do citizens in the Soviet Union receive income in accord with their needs, as Marx envisioned? The answer clearly is no. The Soviet planners set incomes in accord with the type of work people do, how hard they work, and how productive they are. The result is a great deal of income inequality in the Soviet Union. If we look only at income from labor, the extent of income inequality is about as great there as in the United States. However, for all types of income (including interest, dividends, and capital gains, none of which exist in the Soviet Union), there is more income inequality in the United States.

Example 35.1   A Peek Behind Soviet Price Tags

Consider two goods, X and Y, produced and sold in the Soviet Union. The average production cost, factory profit margin, turnover tax, wholesalers' margin and retail margin of each good is shown below (in rubles):

	Good X	Good Y
Average cost of production	100	100
Factory's profit margin	5	5
Factory wholesale price	105	105
Turnover tax	50	15
Wholesalers' margin	5	5
Retail margin	10	10
Retail price	170	135

(a) Do consumers value an extra unit of good X more or less than an extra unit of good Y? (b) Is the cost of producing a unit of good X more or less than that of producing a unit of good Y? (c) Given that the ratio of retail price to cost of production is so much higher for good X than for good Y, will the planners increase the output of good X relative to that of good Y? (d) Why is the turnover tax higher for good X than for good Y?

SOLUTION

(a) They value an extra unit of good X more than an extra unit of good Y, since they are willing to pay 170 rubles for an extra unit of good X but only 135 rubles for an extra unit of good Y. (b) The cost is 100 rubles for both a unit of good X and a unit of good Y. (c) Not if this is counter to their objectives. Output levels are determined to promote the goals of the state. (d) Because the government feels that it must be higher for good X in order to equate the amount demanded with the amount being produced.*

* For further discussion, see Alec Nove, *The Soviet Economy*. New York: Praeger, 1968.

It is important to recognize that about three-fourths of all Soviet industrial workers are paid according to *piece rates.* The amount these workers receive is determined by how much output they turn out. Thus, to a much greater extent than in the United States, income is tied directly to a person's production. This is an important reason for the considerable income inequality in the USSR. Moreover, the Soviet labor unions do not play the same role American unions do. Whereas wage differentials in the United States have often been narrowed by union pressures, such pressures have not been exerted by unions in the USSR. It is very interesting, and understandable, that the Communists have emphasized monetary incentives to coax people to produce more.

INCOME DIFFERENTIALS

In the Soviet Union, as in the United States, occupations differ greatly in pay and status. Distinguished Soviet scientists and professors, leading ballet and opera stars, and important government officials and industrial managers are at the top of the heap. Their incomes are perhaps 20 times as high as that of an unskilled laborer, and they have the good housing, the plush vacations, the cars, and other luxuries that are scarce in the Soviet Union. The unskilled and semiskilled workers get the lowest incomes in the Soviet Union, as they do elsewhere. This doesn't mean, however, that various occupations cannot change their position in the salary scale. On the contrary, the Soviet planners push wages for various types of work up or down in order to get the labor required to help fulfill the plan.

To put a floor under the living standards of the poor, the Soviet government provides many free services, including education and health care. Also, the government provides other services at a very low price. For example, very low-rent housing—most of which is government-owned—is available. These programs help reduce income inequality by supplementing the incomes of the poor. The turnover tax, discussed above, is used to finance these programs.

Soviet Economic Growth

A nation's rate of economic growth is often used as an indicator of its performance. Has the Soviet economy been growing more rapidly than the economies of the United States and other non-Communist countries? Before trying to answer this question, it is essential to recognize that the United States is far in front of the Soviet Union economically. *Our gross national product (in real terms) is about double that of the Soviet Union. Consequently, since our population is smaller than theirs, per capita gross national product in the United States is more than twice that in the Soviet Union.* When comparing the growth rates of the two countries, keep these facts in mind.

The Fifties. In the 1950s, the Soviet Union achieved a very rapid rate of economic growth. American observers watched with some uneasiness as the

Soviet industry in the 1980s

Soviet gross national product increased at about 7 percent per year, while our own increased much more slowly. This remarkable Soviet performance was partly responsible for President Kennedy's decision in the early 1960s to attempt to increase our own growth rate. One important reason for the rapid Soviet growth was the heavy investment by the Russians in plant and equipment. Investment constituted about 30 percent of gross national product, in contrast to about 15 percent in the United States. Soviet planners kept a tight lid on consumption. Indeed, consumption per capita grew little, if at all, from the late 1920s to the late 1950s. Soviet consumers were not allowed to increase their standard of living. The increases in production went primarily to build factories and equipment and to build military power. Other reasons for the high Soviet growth rate were the fact that the Soviets could—and did—borrow Western technology, and that the Soviet system does not tolerate unemployment.

The Sixties and Seventies. In the 1960s and 1970s, the Soviet growth rate seemed to slump. This, together with the fact that many people began to place somewhat less emphasis on the growth rate as a measure of economic performance, resulted in less concern in the United States over the Soviet growth rate, less pressure for government measures to increase our growth rate, and less talk about "growthmanship." According to leading Kremlin watchers, an important reason for the decline in the Soviet growth rate was the greater emphasis on consumption in the post-Stalin Soviet Union. The Communist leaders began to allocate more to the consumer, and this increase in consumption goods meant a decrease in the production of investment goods, which in turn lowered the growth rate.

The Eighties and Beyond. According to the best available estimates, the Soviet growth rate has remained relatively low during the 1980s, a fact which has caused considerable concern among Soviet leaders. At this point, it should be clear that the social mechanisms determining the rate of economic growth in the Soviet Union are entirely different from those that determine the rate of economic growth in the United States. In the Soviet Union, the central planners attempt to determine the growth rate by their decisions on the rate of investment in various industries, the amount spent on research and development, and the rate of expansion of the educational system. In the United States, on the other hand, decision making is decentralized. The American growth rate is determined largely by countless decisions by consumers and producers attempting to reach their own goals.

Since per capita gross national product is so much lower in the Soviet Union than in the United States, it seems extremely doubtful that the Soviet Union will catch up with us for a long time. Even if the Soviet growth rate were to exceed ours by a full percentage point, it would be sometime in the twenty-first century before their GNP catches up with ours, and since their population exceeds ours, it would be even further in the future before their per capita GNP equals ours. In addition, an even more fundamental question is whether any real tragedy would ensue if the Russians did narrow the income gap considerably. Since gross national product is a poor measure of military power, an increase in Soviet GNP by itself certainly would not imperil American security.

Evaluation of the Soviet Economy

SOVIET ECONOMIC PERFORMANCE

In previous sections, we've described the salient features of the Soviet economy. Now let's try to evaluate its performance. Needless to say, any such evaluation must be incomplete. And since we look at the Soviet economy through American eyes, it is sure to be biased—at least in the eyes of the Soviets and other Communists. But we cannot avoid trying to make such an evaluation, despite the many formidable problems involved.

Freedom. One's evaluation of the Soviet economy must depend fundamentally on the value one places on freedom. The USSR is a command economy; to us, its economy is not free. The planners decide what is produced, how it is produced, and who is to get what. A centrally planned economy of this sort may be able to push industrialization and economic growth at a rapid rate, but at a great cost in economic freedom and in living standards. The Soviet planners have decided to build tractors, not cars; dams, not housing; and blast furnaces, not refrigerators. This emphasis on investment has increased future living standards, but that may be small comfort to those called on to make these sacrifices—people who, it should be recalled, have had a much lower standard of living than their counterparts in the industrialized Western countries.

Equity. It is difficult to say much about the equity of the income distribution, since there is no scientifically valid way to say that one income distribution is better than another. This is an ethical question, which people must answer for themselves. Perhaps the most interesting aspect of the income distribution in the Soviet Union is that it contains so much inequality. There is less difference between the Soviet Union and the Western industrialized countries in the extent of income inequality than one might expect. Thus those who favor more income equality may find less to say for the Soviet economy than might be expected.

Efficiency. It is clear that the Russian economy works—and that in many respects it works very well indeed. However, it is also plagued by problems. First, as noted above, incentives for innovation have been weak. Managers, fearful of not meeting their quotas, often resist new techniques. Second, since the planners, not the market, dictate what will be produced, goods consumers do not want are sometimes produced. The link between consumers and producers is not as firm as in the Western economies. Third, the use of production quotas and targets has led to inefficiency. Thus, if the quota for a pencil factory is expressed in terms of number of pencils, the manager of the factory may reduce the quality or size of the pencils in order to meet the quota. Fourth, since input prices do not reflect relative scarcities, they may give improper signals to producers. Fifth, the Soviet Union has had many setbacks in agriculture. Its farms produced about 6 percent less in 1975 than in 1974, and about 4 percent less in 1974 than in 1973. In 1979, its wheat crop was about 25 percent less than expected, due largely to bad weather. In 1980 and 1981, its grain production was considerably less than its grain consumption. To some extent, the poor performance of Soviet agriculture seems due to the fact that many farms are too big, and that there are too few incentives for efficiency.[1]

---

[1] Responding to this situation, the United States, as well as Canada, Australia, and other countries, has sold many billions of dollars of grain to the Soviets.

EVALUATION OF THE SOVIET ECONOMY

The Soviet economy experienced a substantial decrease in its growth rate in the early 1960s. This led to a considerable amount of self-criticism by Soviet economists. Many of the problems just cited—resistance to innovation, mismatches between what is produced and what consumers want, inefficiency due to the stress on production quotas—were admitted by some Soviet economists, and there was much discussion of possible solutions. Among the most influential economists arguing for economic reforms was Professor Y. Liberman of Kharkov University, who proposed several kinds of changes. First, he favored more decentralized decision making. Plant managers should be allowed to decide on their work force, the wages they want to pay, the supplies they want to use, and the improvements they want to make in their equipment. Second, a plant's efficiency should be gauged by the ratio of its profit to its capital investment—a dangerously capitalistic concept. To prod managers and workers to increase efficiency, the bonuses received by managers and the benefits received by workers should vary with the plant's profits. Third, to promote a better match between the goods produced and what consumers want, the profits of a plant should be linked to the amount of goods sold rather than the amount of goods produced. Fourth, interest—long banished from the Communist world—should be resurrected. Recognizing that the interest rate is a device to ration scarce capital, Liberman proposed that interest charges, imposed as a tax, be made for the use of capital by plants.

During the early 1960s, the Communists began to experiment with changes of this sort. As favorable results were achieved by the decentralized decision making and emphasis on "profits" that Liberman proposed, these innovations spread throughout the economy. By 1968, perhaps one-fourth of the Soviet economy was characterized by this "new look"—a remarkable shift toward decentralization and Western economic concepts. But the Soviets have had difficulties in operating an economy that is part planned and part market-oriented, and many of the Soviet central planners distrust the "new look." When the Soviet economy fell short of its production goals in the late 1960s, there was a shift back toward centralization.

In 1983, the late Yuri Andropov, who briefly was head of the Soviet government, made some sweeping criticisms of the inefficiencies in the Soviet economic system. He called for greater authority for local plant managers and increased labor discipline (e.g., less absenteeism and drunkenness). In 1985, Mikhail Gorbachev, a protégé of Andropov, became leader of the Soviet government, after the death of Konstantin Chernenko. In his acceptance speech, he called for "restructuring the material and technical base of production." But the extent of the changes he will bring about, and the future direction of the Soviet economy, remains uncertain. It may move further toward greater decentralization and Western economic concepts, or it may revert to its older style of operation. In his first months in office, Gorbachev seemed to encourage manager autonomy, pay incentives, and the full-scale use of computerization. The authority of Gosplan seemed to be curtailed.

Mikhail Gorbachev

Test Yourself

1. In recent years, has the Soviet Union's rate of economic growth tended to decline? Has its rate of productivity growth (that is, the rate of growth of output relative to input) tended to decline as well? If so, why?

2. Describe the system of economic planning in the Soviet Union. To what extent is this system to be found in the writings of Karl Marx?

3. Discuss the differences between the United States and the Soviet Union in the way in which prices are determined. What are some of the most important economic effects of these differences?

4. Has the state "withered away" in the Soviet version of communism? Explain. What are some of the problems in Soviet planning?

The Chinese Economy

In 1949, another of the world's major powers—China—joined the Communist ranks. With Mao Tse-tung at its head, the Communist army entered Peking, the capital of a nation containing one-fourth of the world's population. China was a poor country, with little capital, little technology, and little education—a less developed country par excellence, despite its ancient civilization. Further, the Communists inherited an economy marred by many years of war with the Japanese. The country needed as much economic growth as possible, and quickly.

THE FIRST FIVE-YEAR PLAN

The Chinese Communists responded with a ruthless drive toward industrialization. China's Five-Year Plan of 1952–57 emphasized investment in heavy industry like steel and machinery and some expansion of light industry. It also called for a massive reorganization of agriculture, involving collective ownership of some farms and transfer of land from the rich to the poor. To permit the high rate of investment called for by the plan, the Chinese government pared consumption to the bone. The Chinese people were asked to work long and hard—for little return in goods and services.

Most observers agree that the plan achieved its goal of rapid economic growth. Even though China's population increased considerably, output per capita increased by about 4 or 5 percent per year during the 1950s. This was an enormous achievement for a country whose economy had been stagnant for centuries. To accomplish these objectives, China adopted measures that seem stern even when compared with the Soviet Union. (China, like the USSR, operates a command economy, but this has not prevented the development of considerable tension between them. To buttress its own position, each nation claims that the other has abandoned the true faith of Marxism.)

THE GREAT LEAP FORWARD

Having succeeded in pushing the economy ahead in the Five-Year Plan of 1952–57, in 1958 China's leaders launched a more ambitious plan, called the Great Leap Forward. Its aim was to increase per capita output by 25 percent. The large number of underemployed workers in China were to be swept into the employed labor force, and there was to be a great increase in investment. It all sounded very impressive on paper, but it turned out to be a disaster. Despite all the slogans and propaganda, the plan was unrealistic. Literally millions of people were asked to produce steel in primitive furnaces in their back yards. The result was a lot of unusable scrap metal. Also, poor planning directed millions of workers to produce other goods of little or no value. And too many people were ordered to leave agriculture and enter factories, with the result that far too little food was produced.

By 1960, the Great Leap Forward was obviously a failure of catastrophic proportions, and China's leaders had little choice but to alter their policies. In 1961, they published their new economic plan, which called for more emphasis on agriculture and less on industry. Industries that contributed to agricultural productivity—like the tractor industry—would receive more capital, while less would be devoted to industries that did not affect agriculture. Also, higher priority was given to the production of consumer goods for the peasants. Despite the new emphasis, the gains in agricultural production and efficiency seem to have been modest during the 1960s. Apparently, the Great Leap Forward had wreaked so much havoc that it was difficult to get agriculture moving ahead.

THE CULTURAL REVOLUTION

The so-called Cultural Revolution that began in 1968 saw large-scale political disorders in Communist China. Because the data on Chinese economic performance are meager and unreliable, even the experts find it difficult to estimate the effects of this social turmoil on the economy. But by 1971, it seemed likely that the economy had recovered in large part from the economic disorders arising from the Cultural Revolution. According to recent estimates by Thomas Rawski, Chinese industrial production in 1971 was perhaps double what it had been in 1963.

MOVEMENTS TOWARD DECENTRALIZATION

Workers in a farm equipment factory

During the late 1970s and early 1980s, China, under the leadership of Vice-Premier Teng Hsiao-p'ing, began to move toward a more decentralized economic system where market forces were allowed to play an important role. In December 1978, China's Central Committee approved a new system of incentives for China's 800 million peasants, under which those that produced more were rewarded. The result was a sharp increase in farm output, and China's communes began to break up as individual households became the basic agricultural unit.

In October 1984, China announced sweeping changes in its urban economy. About a million state-owned enterprises were to be given greater independence—and the necessity to compete to survive. Extensive government subsidies for consumer products like food and clothing were to be phased out. Central planning was to be limited, and the prices of many products and services were to be determined by supply and demand. Unquestionably, this was a very important shift in China's economic system, but whether these changes will be permanent or temporary remains to be seen.

In any event, during 1983 and 1984, China's real economic growth was about 8 percent per year, which was impressive. According to many reports, the new emphasis on decentralization and greater economic freedom was having beneficial results.

Economic Life in China

Despite the economic gains it has achieved, China is still a less developed country. In 1980, its per capita income was less than one-seventh that in the United States. Over 50 percent of the typical wage earner's income goes for food, and many consumer goods, like rice and cloth, have been rationed, so that a family could buy only a certain amount per month. Automobiles are uncommon in China; the bicycle is the usual means of private transportation in cities. Workers have been divided into a number of strata, and wages have been uniform within each strata. The government has played an important role in determining where and in what position a particular person works. Labor markets have not been nearly as free as in the United States. In 1979, the government, in an attempt to control population growth, adopted a policy limiting each couple to one child.

CAPITAL FORMATION

To step up its rate of economic growth, China has devoted about 25 percent of its national output to capital formation. This is a high rate of investment, relative to developed countries as well as to other less developed countries. However, it must be recognized that this does not come from voluntary saving. Instead, it is due to government action. Because the educational and skill level of the population is low, it is difficult to invest this forced saving as productively as would otherwise be the case. The Russians, when they were on better terms with the Chinese, provided some technical assistance, but those days are long gone. At present, China finds it difficult to absorb the technology it so badly needs.

INDUSTRY AND AGRICULTURE

About four-fifths of China's population is engaged in agriculture, which contributes about 40 percent of GNP. Industrial production has been growing more rapidly than agricultural output. In 1983, industrial output increased by about 10 percent; in 1984, it increased by over 13 percent, according to Chinese officials.

INCOME DISTRIBUTION

The distribution of income in China is much less unequal than it was 30 years ago. Some economists, like John Gurley of Stanford University, believe that China has been able to eradicate abject poverty despite her economic adversities. According to Gurley,

> The basic, overriding economic fact about China is that for twenty years she has fed, clothed, and housed everyone. . . . Millions have not starved; sidewalks and

streets have not been covered with multitudes of sleeping, begging, hungry, and illiterate human beings; millions are not disease-ridden.[2]

It is difficult, however, to obtain reliable information about living conditions in so huge and diverse a country, particularly when very few Americans were allowed in China before President Nixon's visit in 1972. Many economists are less enthusiastic than Gurley about China's economic performance.[3] Also, some call attentioh to the price the Chinese have paid in what we would regard as regimentation and lack of political and social freedom.

U.S.-CHINA RELATIONS

In 1979, Chinese Vice-Premier Teng Hsiao-p'ing visited the United States —this being the first official visit by a high government official of China in about 30 years. The American government agreed to sell China a communications satellite system, among other things; and Teng expressed the hope that further American credit and technology would be made available to his country.

According to some estimates, U.S. exports to China in 1980 were about $3 billion, and China's exports to the U.S. were about $1 billion. During the early 1980s, the United States and China engaged in a variety of scientific and technological exchange programs. The Reagan administration and American firms tried in many ways to promote trade with China. Although Sino-American relations may not have improved as rapidly as some optimists forecasted in the late 1970s, they are certainly much warmer than they were several decades ago.

Democratic Socialism

We have described two brands of Communism—Russian and Chinese. And in previous chapters, we have described capitalism. Now we must stress that there are other types of economic systems besides capitalism and Communism. One of the most important of these is *democratic socialism,* which has included France's and Sweden's socialist governments and Britain's Labor government, among others. In many ways, the democratic socialist economies occupy a middle ground between our more capitalist system and the Communist systems. They generally favor government ownership of heavy industry like coal and steel (although the fervor for nationalization of such industries has died down in recent years); heavy taxation of the rich; and extensive welfare programs (social security, medical care, and so on); as well as a certain amount of economic planning, rather than the unfettered play of market forces.

But in contrast to the Communists, the democratic socialists generally do not favor violent revolution. Instead, they believe that democratic

---

[2] John Gurley, "Maoist Economic Development," in E. Mansfield, *Principles of Microeconomics: Readings, Issues, and Cases,* 4th ed., New York: Norton, 1983.

[3] For example, see James Tobin, "The Economy of China: A Tourist's View," in Mansfield, *Principles of Microeconomics: Readings, Issues, and Cases,* 4th ed.

means should be used to obtain power. A good example is the British Labor government, which came into office after World War II. During the 1920s and 1930s, the Labor party had worked within the existing political system and gained strength. Finally, after the war it got its hands on the reins. Since then the Labor party has remained a major influence in British politics (although it has been in and out of office). As it has gathered further experience, its goals have changed somewhat. Thus, because government ownership of industry seems to have been inefficient, the socialists are much more tolerant of private property, and less interested in nationalizing industry, than they were 25 years ago.

CHANGES IN THE U.S.

To a considerable extent, the more capitalist countries—like the United States—have taken over many of the socialist programs. The United States has moved a long way toward heavy taxation of the rich and toward extensive welfare programs. If Calvin Coolidge could be retrieved from the Great Beyond—and if Silent Cal could be induced to comment—he surely would be impressed (and perhaps dismayed) by how far the United States has traveled toward socialism since his presidency in the 1920s. Even though *planning* is viewed with suspicion in the United States, the government has become more and more involved in various aspects of our economic life, as we have seen in earlier chapters. The adoption by essentially capitalistic countries of many of their programs has taken some of the appeal—and some of the vitality and direction—from the socialists.

Radical Economics

RADICAL ECONOMICS AND THE NEW LEFT

In the United States in recent years, a new force in economics has appeared: *radical economics.* The radical economists, mainly young and still in the process of shaping their own contributions to the field, draw heavily on the views of Karl Marx. Looking at the urban, racial, environmental, and poverty problems of today, they argue that the conventional tools of economics are too biased toward maintaining the *status quo* to analyze many of these problems properly. They challenge the methods and assumptions of conventional economics, criticize conventional economists for neglecting many important social problems, and question the reasonableness of many of our society's economic goals.

The analytical framework underlying radical economics consists largely of the following hypotheses. First, following Marx, the radical economists argue that the structure of any society is determined principally by the society's dominant mode of production, and that the most distinctive features of the mode of production under capitalism is the use of the wage-contract, the dominance of impersonal markets, and the private ownership of capital. Second, according to the radical economists, the pressure under capitalism for capital accumulation and riches tends to create a momentum in and of itself, which creates important contradictions and social problems. Third, according to the radical economists, the United States

THE MAMMOTH DEBT PROBLEMS OF ARGENTINA, BRAZIL, AND MEXICO

During the early 1980s, the financial pages of the newspapers (and the front pages and editorials as well) were full of stories concerning the very severe debt problems of third-world countries, particularly Argentina, Brazil, and Mexico (which together owed over $200 billion). In 1982, Mexico announced that it was unable to meet its obligations to foreign creditors. The U.S. government responded by mounting a rescue operation involving banks (to whom much of the debt was owed) and the International Monetary Fund. Subsequently, Brazil and Argentina also found it necessary to look for debt relief from their creditors, and ways were found to keep them afloat, at least temporarily.

The major American banks have lent an enormous amount of money to these countries. For example, Manufacturers Hanover, a major New York bank, has lent over $1 billion—40 percent of its capital—to Argentina alone. During the 1970s, the banks increased their loans to these countries at a rapid rate. Because their exports were growing fast, the banks felt that these countries would be able to earn the dollars to pay off the loans. (As shown in Table 1, the ratio of debt to exports was lower in 1980 than in 1974.) However, during 1980–82, the real rate of interest increased, thus increasing the interest payments on these loans. Moreover, the 1980–82 world recession reduced the export earnings of the debtor countries. Because of these and other factors, including major mistakes made by the debtor nations themselves, each of these nations was unable to meet its financial obligations.

Should these countries be granted new loans? According to some observers, this is throwing good money after bad, since the loans will never be repaid. In their opinion, the debt should be written off, at least in part. But others, including President Reagan's Council of Economic Advisers, argue that the problem is only temporary, and that continued lending is justified. Among other things, they stress the importance of avoiding unnecessary damage to the economies of the debtor nations. The banks to whom the debts are owed are anxious, of course, to collect as much as they can, while the debtor countries want to have the interest rates and fees on the loans reduced.

Table 1

DEBT, RATIO OF DEBT TO EXPORTS, AND INTEREST PAYMENTS OF ARGENTINA, BRAZIL, AND MEXICO COMBINED, 1974–83

	1974	1977	1980	1981	1982	1983
Debt (billions of dollars)	43.4	75.7	143.2	185.1	205.3	213.9
Debt divided by exports	2.1	2.7	2.4	2.7	3.2	3.2
Interest payments (billions of dollars)	2.7	4.9	15.1	22.6	28.4	26.2

By 1983, interest payments were over $26 billion, and banks were reluctant to extend enough new loans to these countries to cover these payments. There was a widespread feeling that the banks had made unwise loans, and that they should reap the consequences. After all, an important aspect of the price system is that firms should accept the losses imposed by the market place, not go hat in hand to the government. But the government, faced with what it regarded as an extremely hazardous situation, helped to put together a set of actions and policies aimed at improving the situation. As part of this cooperative effort, the banks granted about $9 billion in new loans to Argentina, Brazil, and Mexico in 1983.

The debtor countries themselves improved their aggregate trade balance in goods and services (excluding interest) by $28 billion between 1981 and 1983. Imports were cut by about 52 percent in Argentina, 30 percent in Brazil, and 66 percent in Mexico. Each of these countries experienced severe recessions that resulted in a cut in expenditures on traded goods. According to the debtors, they have accepted bitter medicine to help pay their debts. In some quarters, there is a fear that, if pushed too hard, some of these countries might repudiate their debts. Although such a drastic step would result in the ostracism of the country from the world banking community, it cannot be ruled out completely.

The International Monetary Fund has played a major role in trying to manage the debt problem. As pointed out in Chapter 33, the IMF lends money to any of its member governments that is having difficulties with its balance of payments. In 1983, Congress approved the U.S. share of an increase in resources for the IMF. In that same year, the IMF lent about $4 billion to Argentina, Brazil, and Mexico. But the size of the loans made by the IMF is often less significant than its role as a catalyst. If a debtor country agrees to follow particular policies, the IMF can give the country a "seal of approval," which enables it to borrow from banks and elsewhere. In recent years, in order for such a seal of approval to be given, the banks to which the country owes money must also agree to extend new loans.

The governments of the creditor countries have also extended credit directly to the debtor countries. Because of the lack of private credit, some U.S. firms that normally export to these countries are unable to do so. The U.S. Export-Import Bank can raise its levels of credit in such circumstances. Other countries have similar agencies. In 1983, government financing for Argentina, Brazil, and Mexico was about $3 billion.

This combination of actions by the banks, the IMF, and the governments of the creditor and debtor countries has thus far kept the situation from deteriorating further, but the mammoth debt problems of these countries will continue to haunt them and their creditors for many years to come.[1]

[1] For further discussion, see 1984 Annual Report of the Council of Economic Advisers, and *Business Week*, February 6, 1984.

has reached a state of economic development where class struggles are not necessary or rational, since there is enough productive capacity so that all citizens can share adequately in wealth and leisure. To solve existing social problems, the radicals argue that the basic institutions of our society must change. In their eyes, nothing less will suffice.

The flavor of the radical position is well conveyed by this quotation from David Gordon:

> Radicals criticize capitalist society essentially because it evolves irrationally. Its basic mode of production and the structures of its institutions create conflicts which do not need to exist. In the language of economics, it forces "trade-offs" that are not necessary. Fundamentally, radicals argue, capitalism forces a conflict between the aggregate wealth of society (and obviously the enormous wealth of some individuals) and the freedom of most individuals. In another, truly democratic, humanist and socialist society, radicals argue, conditions could be forged in which increases in aggregate social wealth complemented the personal freedom of all individuals. Edwards and Mac-Ewan mention some of the other unnecessary conflicts created (or sustained) by capitalist societies: "income growth versus a meaningful work environment, employment versus stable prices, private versus social costs, public versus private consumption, and income versus leisure." Other conflicts can be specified, but the criticisms gain force in the context of the radical vision of a "better" society. It should be emphasized in discussing the radical vision that many modern socialist radicals, though socialist, do not view most modern socialist countries with great approval. To many Western radicals, the purposes and the realities of the socialist revolution in Cuba provide the closest manifest approximation to their ideals. Che Guevara, in many ways a more important ideologue of that revolution than Fidel Castro, has often expressed those ideals most eloquently.[4]

RESPONSE TO RADICAL ECONOMICS

As you would expect, the economics profession has responded in a variety of ways to the emergence of radical economics, with its relatively small number of followers. Some economists have chosen to ignore them, while others, like Robert Solow of M.I.T., have responded sharply. In Solow's view,

> Radical economics may conceivably be the wave of the future, but I do not think that it is the wave of the present. In fact, to face the issue head on, I think that radical economics as it is practiced contains more cant, not less cant; more role-playing, not less role-playing; less facing of the facts, not more facing of the facts, than conventional economics. In short, we neglected radical economics because it is negligible. There is little evidence that radical political economics is capable of generating a line of normal science, or even that it wants to.[5]

Since radical economists are still engaged in the work that will tell whether theirs is really a contribution to science, it is premature to attempt to evaluate the accuracy or importance of their efforts. Admittedly, they

[4] D. Gordon, *Problems in Political Economy: An Urban Perspective,* Boston: Heath, 1971, p. 7.

[5] R. Solow, "The State of Economics," *American Economic Review,* May 1971.

have attracted considerable attention, despite the smallness of their numbers, but attention and agreement are two different things. The vast majority of the economics profession unquestionably would disagree with their conclusions. Most economists do not believe that capitalism should be replaced. Nor do they agree with the radicals' view of how our society works, or with their indictment of conventional economics.

Does Capitalism Have a Future?

Basic Idea #70: The major capitalist economies in Asia, Europe, and North America have shown great vitality in recent decades. The Marxist prediction that the lot of the workers would get worse and worse seems completely out of tune with the facts. Although we do not lack challenges, our kind of economic system seems to be performing effectively.

Most economists today do not seem to believe that our modern version of capitalism is about to wither on the vine. This is particularly noteworthy, since at the end of World War II, many distinguished non-Marxist economists and social seers, as well as the Marxists, were predicting the demise of capitalism and the rise of socialism. One of the most significant developments of the past 40 years has been the extent to which these prophecies have fallen flat on their faces.

The essentially capitalistic economies of the West have shown a tremendous vitality, have grown at a relatively rapid rate, and have avoided any deep depressions (although stagflation has proved to be a persistent difficulty). This is a tremendous achievement, and one that should be recognized and appreciated. It does not mean that we do not have many problems. On the contrary, much of this book has been devoted to the discussion of our important social problems. But it does mean that our modern version of capitalism seems to be more than holding its own in today's world.

Test Yourself

1. "In a field where controlled experimentation is impossible, the relative performance of India and China gives some idea of whether a Communist or a democratic system results in faster economic development." Comment and evaluate.

2. There have been complaints in Chinese newspapers that the centralized system of job allocation has been unable to find work for all the entrants into the labor force. According to some estimates, about 20 million people were waiting for job assignments. Does this amount to what would be called unemployment in the West? Explain.

3. According to some critics, like Assar Lindbeck, whereas either markets or centralized power can be used to organize a modern economy, the radical economists are against both. How then can an economy like ours be organized?

4. Compare the economic systems of the Soviet Union and China. To what extent have they departed from Marx's teachings? To what extent are their economic institutions much the same? What are the major differences in the way economic decisions are made? Which of them seems to be performing best economically? Which of them seems to be performing worst?

Summary

1. Karl Marx viewed history as a series of class struggles, the present class struggle being between the capitalists, who own the means of production, and the workers. In Marx's view, capitalists and workers struggle because the workers are exploited. Marx, who subscribed to a labor theory of value, believed that the workers create a surplus value, the difference between the value of what they produce and the subsistence wage they receive. Capital formation, in Marx's view, comes about as a consequence of this surplus value.

2. According to Marx, the lot of the workers would inevitably get worse. Consequently, capitalism would eventually be overthrown and succeeded by socialism, then by communism. Socialism would be a "dictatorship of the proletariat." After an unspecified period of time, Marx felt that socialism would give way to communism, which would be characterized by a classless society, the withering away of the state, and the distribution of income according to the principle: "From each according to his ability, to each according to his needs."

3. The Soviet Union, the first country to embrace Marxian socialism, has a command economy where power is concentrated in the hands of a relatively few Communist officials who make the big decisions on what is to be produced, how it is to be produced, and who is to receive how much. The government owns the factories, mines, equipment, and other means of production—and gives no evidence of withering away.

4. The top officials of the Communist party establish the overall goals for the economy. The detailed production plans to realize these broad goals are drawn up by Gosplan, the State Planning Commission. These plans are reviewed by individual industries and plants, and after negotiations and revision, Gosplan issues the final plan.

5. In the Soviet Union, the government, not the market, sets prices. Prices facing producers are set in such a way that a firm of average efficiency will make neither a profit nor a loss. Prices facing consumers are set to ration the consumer goods produced and to raise the planned revenue needed for investment. The difference between the price to the consumer and the price to the producer is the turnover tax.

6. Another type of Communist system is found in China, which is a very poor country despite its ancient civilization. China's first Five-Year Plan was an ambitious drive toward industrialization that seemed to achieve its objectives, but Mao's Great Leap Forward was a disaster that set back the country's economic development. More recently, China's industrial output seems to have grown relatively rapidly.

7. In the United States, a new force in recent years has been radical economics, which is based largely on Marxism. The radical economists challenge the methods and assumptions of conventional economics, and advocate basic institutional change. Many economists question whether radical economics is a contribution to science at all. At present, it is difficult to say, since radical economics is so new.

8. The essentially capitalist economies of the West have shown great vitality in the postwar period. They have grown at a relatively rapid rate, and have managed to avoid any deep depressions. Contrary to many predictions of over 40 years ago by some distinguished social seers, our modern version of capitalism seems to be more than holding its own in the world of today, although it obviously is beset by many serious problems.

Concepts for Review

Communism	Marxism	Quota
Capitalist	Five-year plan	Turnover tax
Proletariat	Gosplan	Piece rates
Socialism	Gosbank	Democratic socialism
Value	Command economy	Radical economics
Surplus value		

APPENDICES:

Digging Deeper into the Economist's Tool Box

In this final section of the book, we present five appendices, each of which contains important material that is sometimes considered too advanced for the elementary course. Appendix A takes up *IS* and *LM* curves, with particular reference to the Keynesian-monetarist controversy. Appendix B deals with isoquants, isocost curves, and the optimal input combination. Appendix C is concerned with linear programming. Appendix D deals with general equilibrium analysis and input-output models. Appendix E is concerned with welfare economics, optimal resource allocation and perfect competition.

Appendix A: *IS* and *LM* Curves and the Keynesian-Monetarist Controversy[1]

To understand more completely the argument between the Keynesians and the monetarists, it is worthwhile to enlarge the model of national output determination in Chapters 10 to 12 to include monetary factors. The simplest extension of this sort involves the use of *IS* and *LM* curves, both of which will be discussed in detail below. These curves, originated by Oxford's Nobel laureate, Sir John Hicks, help to put the debate between the monetarists and the Keynesians into somewhat deeper perspective.

[1] To understand this appendix, the reader should be familiar with Chapters 10 to 17.

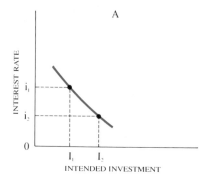

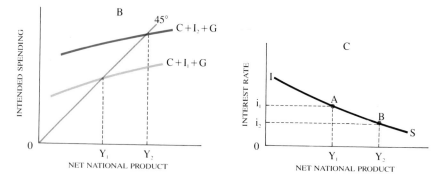

Figure A.1

Derivation of the* IS *Curve *If the interest rate is* i_1*, intended investment is* I_1*. If the interest rate is* i_2*, intended investment is* I_2*.*

If intended investment is I_1*, equilibrium NNP is* Y_1*. If intended investment is* I_2*, equilibrium NNP is* Y_2*.*

The IS *curve shows, for each level of the interest rate, the level of NNP that will satisfy the equilibrium condition that intended spending on output must equal NNP. Points A and B are derived in the panels above, which show that equilibrium NNP equals* Y_1 *if the interest rate is* i_1 *and* Y_2 *if the interest rate is* i_2*.*

Before describing how *IS* and *LM* curves are constructed, it is important to be clear concerning the basic assumptions that are being made. First, it is assumed that the price level is fixed, and that the public has a fixed demand curve for real money balances, a fixed consumption function, and a fixed investment function, Second, foreign trade is ignored. Third, the money supply is fixed by the monetary authorities, and does not vary with NNP or the interest rate. Fourth, tax rates are fixed, and fiscal policy takes the form of varying government expenditure.

THE *IS* CURVE: DEFINITION AND DERIVATION

The IS *curve shows, for each possible level of the interest rate, the level of NNP that will satisfy the equilibrium condition that intended spending on output must equal NNP.* (If this equilibrium condition is a bit hazy, review Chapter 10.) This equilibrium condition is equivalent to saying that the public must be spending the intended amount relative to its income. (We put a great deal of stress on this equilibrium condition in Chapter 10.) To construct the *IS* curve, it is essential to recognize two things. First, the level of intended investment is inversely related to the interest rate. (In other words, for reasons described in Chapter 10, the higher the rate of interest, the lower the amount of intended investment, as shown in panel A of Figure A.1.) Second, the level of intended investment (as well as consumption and government expenditure) will determine the equilibrium level of NNP. (See panel B of Figure A.1.) Thus, since the interest rate determines the level of intended investment, and the level of intended investment determines the equilibrium level of NNP, there will be a relationship between the level of the interest rate and the equilibrium level of NNP. This relationship is the *IS* curve, shown in panel C of Figure A.1.

To see more precisely what the *IS* curve is, it is useful to derive some points on such a curve. Let's derive two points—*A* and *B*—on the *IS* curve in panel C of Figure A.1. To derive point *A*, note that, if the interest rate is i_1, intended investment will be I_1, according to panel A of Figure A.1. And if intended investment is I_1, total intended spending at each level of NNP will be as shown by the $C + I_1 + G$ line in panel B of Figure A.1, with the result that the equilibrium level of NNP will be Y_1. Thus, if the interest rate is i_1, the equilibrium level of NNP is Y_1—which explains the coordinates of point *A*.

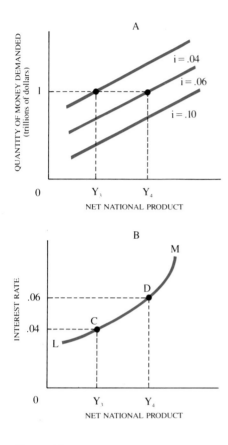

To explain point *B*, note that if the interest rate is i_2, intended investment will be I_2, according to panel A of Figure A.1. And if intended investment is I_2, total intended spending at each level of NNP will be as shown by the $C + I_2 + G$ line in panel B of Figure A.1, with the result that the equilibrium level of NNP will be Y_2. Thus, if the interest rate is i_2, the equilibrium level of NNP is Y_2—which explains the coordinates of point *B*.

Note that the *IS* curve slopes downward to the right. That is, the lower the interest rate, the higher the level of NNP on the *IS* curve. For example, when the interest rate fell from i_1 to i_2 in Figure A.1, panel A, intended investment increased from I_1 to I_2. And when intended investment rose from I_1 to I_2, the equilibrium level of NNP increased from Y_1 to Y_2, as shown in panel B of Figure A.1. More generally, since the level of intended investment is inversely related to the interest rate, but directly related to the equilibrium level of NNP, it follows that the interest rate must be inversely related to the level of NNP on the *IS* curve.

THE *LM* CURVE: DEFINITION AND DERIVATION

The LM *curve shows, for each possible level of the interest rate, the level of NNP that will satisfy the equilibrium condition that the public be satisfied to hold the existing quantity of money.* Chapter 14 stressed the importance of this equilibrium condition. Clearly, the quantity of money demanded for transactions purposes is dependent upon the value of NNP. Further, the quantity of money demanded is dependent on the rate of interest. Thus, as stressed in Chapter 14, the total quantity of money demanded by the public is dependent both on the value of NNP and on the interest rate.

More specifically, the total quantity of money demanded by the public is *directly* related to the value of NNP and *inversely* related to the interest rate. (Recall the discussion in Chapter 14.) As NNP increases (and incomes rise), people want to keep more money on hand to carry out the larger volume of transactions. Thus the quantity of money demanded by the public is directly related to the value of NNP (as shown in panel A of Figure A.2). On the other hand, the higher the interest rate, the more costly it is to hold money (because the more interest is forgone by holding money rather than buying bonds or other securities). Thus the higher the interest rate, the smaller the amount of money that is demanded. In other words, the quantity of money demanded by the public is inversely related to the interest rate. (This is shown in panel A of Figure A.2 by the fact that, if NNP is held constant, the quantity of money demanded increases as i decreases.)

Let's derive two points, *C* and *D*, on the *LM* curve, shown in panel B of Figure A.2. Recall that any *LM* curve is based on the supposition that the money supply is *fixed,* and that the money supply must be just equal to the quantity of money demanded (for an equilibrium to occur). The *LM* curve in panel B of Figure A.2 shows, for each interest rate, the value of NNP that will result in the public's demanding this fixed amount of money, say \$1 trillion. If the relationships in panel A of Figure A.2 hold, the quantity of money demanded will equal \$1 trillion if the interest rate is 4 percent and NNP is Y_3. Thus, if the interest rate is 4 percent, NNP (on

Figure A.2

Derivation of the LM Curve *Holding constant the interest rate,* i, *the quantity of money demanded increases as NNP increases. Holding constant NNP, the quantity of money demanded increases as the interest rate decreases. If* i = .04 *and NNP* = Y_3, *the quantity of money demanded equals \$1 trillion. If* i = .06 *and NNP* = Y_4, *the quantity of money demanded equals \$1 trillion. These correspond to points* C *and* D *in panel* B.

The LM *curve shows, for each possible level of the interest rate, the level of NNP that will satisfy the equilibrium condition that the quantity of money demanded equal the supply of money. Points* C *and* D *are derived in panel* A.

this *LM* curve) must be Y_3—which explains the coordinates of point *C*. Panel A of Figure A.2 shows that the quantity of money demanded will also equal \$1 trillion if the interest rate is 6 percent and the NNP is Y_4. Thus, if the interest rate is 6 percent, NNP (on this *LM* curve) must be Y_4—which explains the coordinates of point *D*.

Note that to maintain the quantity of money demanded equal to the fixed money supply (\$1 trillion in this case), an increase in the interest rate must be accompanied by an increase in NNP. Why? Because, holding NNP constant, an increase in the interest rate will reduce the quantity of money demanded, as shown in panel A of Figure A.2. Thus, unless NNP is increased, the quantity of money demanded will be less than the fixed money supply. To bring it back into equality with the fixed money supply, and thus to maintain the equilibrium on which the *LM* curve is based, NNP must be increased. Similarly, a decrease in the interest rate must be accompanied by a decrease in NNP, if the quantity of money demanded is to equal the fixed money supply. For these reasons, *the* LM *curve slopes upward to the right.* That is, the higher the interest rate, the higher the level of NNP that satisfies the equilibrium condition underlying the *LM* curve.

THE EQUILIBRIUM LEVEL OF NNP

As pointed out in an earlier section, a full-scale equilibrium requires *both* that households and firms be spending the intended amounts relative to their incomes *and* that they be satisfied to hold the existing amount of money. In other words, both the equilibrium condition underlying the *IS* curve and the equilibrium condition underlying the *LM* curve must be satisfied. For this to be so, the equilibrium combination of NNP and interest rate must be at a point lying both on the *IS* curve (which means that it satisfies the equilibrium condition underlying this curve) and on the *LM* curve (which means that it satisfies the equilibrium condition underlying this curve).

If we plot the IS *and* LM *curves on the same diagram, as in Figure A.3, the equilibrium combination of NNP and interest rate must therefore be the one that is given by the intersection of the two curves.* Only this combination lies on both curves, and thus satisfies both equilibrium conditions. For example, in Figure A.3, the equilibrium level of NNP must be Y_5, and the equilibrium level of the interest rate must be i_5. This is the only combination of NNP and interest rate that will satisfy both equilibrium conditions, given that the money supply, the public's demand curve for money, its consumption function, its investment function, and government expenditures (and taxes) remain fixed.

EFFECTS OF FISCAL POLICY ON THE *IS* CURVE

The IS *curve will shift to the right if government expenditures increase or taxes decrease.* The reason why these factors shift the *IS* curve to the right is that, holding the interest rate constant, each of these factors increases the level of NNP that satisfies the equilibrium condition underlying the *IS* curve.

To see why this is so, take as an example the effect of a \$10 billion increase in government expenditures in Figure A.1. Before the increase

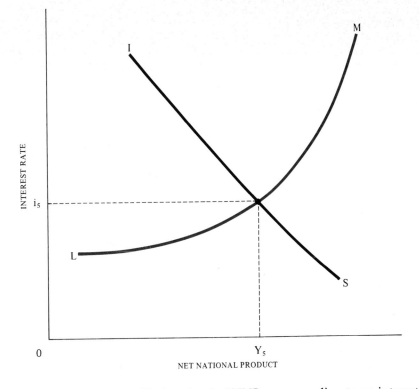

Figure A.3
Determination of Equilibrium NNP and
Interest Rate *The equilibrium level of*
NNP (and of the interest rate) must be at
the intersection of the IS *and* LM *curves.*
The equilibrium NNP equals Y_5, *and the*
equilibrium interest rate equals i_5.

occurs, what is the equilibrium level of NNP corresponding to an interest rate of i_1? As we saw in Figure A.1, it is Y_1. But after the increase occurs, it is no longer Y_1. Due to the increased government expenditure, the $C + I + G$ line in panel B of Figure A.1 is raised from $C + I_1 + G$ to $C + I_1 + (G + 10)$, as shown in Figure A.4. Thus the equilibrium level of

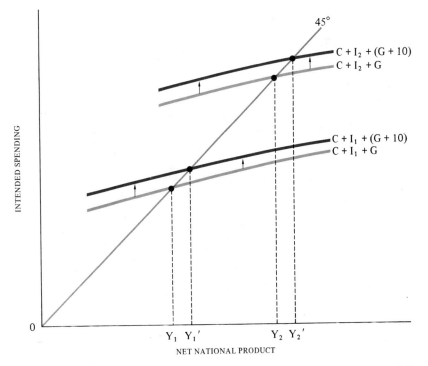

Figure A.4
Effect of a $10 Billion Increase in
Government Expenditures on IS **Curve**
If government expenditures are increased
by $10 billion, and the interest rate is i_1,
equilibrium NNP increases from Y_1 *to*
Y_1'. *If the interest rate is* i_2, *it increases*
from Y_2 *to* Y_2'. *Since the level of NNP*
on the IS *curve corresponding to any*
level of the interest rate is increased, the
effect of the increase in government
expenditures must be to shift the IS *curve*
to the right.

NNP is increased to Y_1', as shown in Figure A.4. Similarly, if the interest rate is i_2, the equilibrium level of NNP is increased from Y_2 to Y_2'. Since the level of NNP on the *IS* curve corresponding to each level of the interest rate is increased, the effect of the increase in government expenditure is to shift the *IS* curve to the right.

EFFECTS OF MONETARY POLICY ON THE *LM* CURVE

The LM *curve will shift to the right if the monetary authorities increase the money supply, and it will shift to the left if they decrease the money supply.* To see why, consider first an increase in the money supply. Under such circumstances, if the interest rate stays the same, NNP must increase in order to bring the quantity of money demanded into equality with the new money supply. Why? Because the quantity of money demanded, if it is to equal the new money supply, must increase, and an increase in NNP will be required to produce such an increase in the quantity of money demanded. Thus, since the level of NNP where this equality holds (the interest rate being unchanged) is greater than before, the effect of the increase in the money supply must be to shift the *LM* curve to the right.

Next, consider a decrease in the money supply. If the interest rate stays the same, NNP must decrease in order to bring the quantity of money demanded into equality with the new money supply. Why? Because decreases in NNP will decrease the quantity of money demanded, which is required if the quantity of money demanded is to equal the diminished money supply. Thus, since the level of NNP where this equality holds (the interest rate being unchanged) is smaller than before, the effect of the decrease in the money supply must be to shift the *LM* curve to the left.

EFFECTS OF FISCAL POLICY ON NNP

To understand the difference between Keynesian and monetarist views concerning the effects of fiscal policy on NNP, it is useful to consider three alternative assumptions:

1. Let's assume that the economy is operating at a point where *the* LM *curve is neither close to being vertical nor close to being horizontal.* Under these circumstances, what are the effects of an expansionary fiscal policy (that is, an increase in government expenditures or a cut in taxes)? Since it shifts the *IS* curve to the right, an expansionary fiscal policy will increase both NNP and the interest rate, if the *LM* curve has such a shape. Panel A of Figure A.5 shows that this is the case. A shift to the right of the *IS* curve (such as from I_1S_1 to $I_1'S_1'$) increases both NNP (from Y_6 to Y_7) and the interest rate (from i_6 to i_7).

2. Let's assume that the economy is operating at a point where *the* LM *curve is close to being vertical.* Indeed, to make things simple, let's assume that it is vertical. If so, an expansionary fiscal policy results in an increase in the interest rate, but no increase in NNP. For example, in panel B of Figure A.5, a shift to the right of the *IS* curve (such as from I_2S_2 to $I_2'S_2'$) increases the interest rate (from i_8 to i_9), but not NNP. This is the so-called *classical range* of the *LM* curve, where fiscal policy cannot increase NNP.

3. Let's assume that the economy is operating at a point where *the* LM

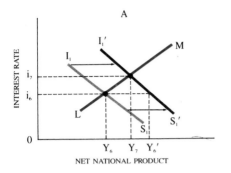

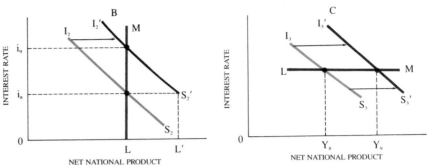

curve is horizontal (or nearly so). If so, an expansionary fiscal policy results in an increase in NNP, but no increase in the interest rate. For example, in panel C of Figure A.5, a shift to the right of the *IS* curve (such as from $I_3 S_3$ to $I_3' S_3'$) increases NNP (from Y_8 to Y_9), but not the interest rate. This is sometimes called the *liquidity-trap range.*

Although both a perfectly vertical and a perfectly horizontal *LM* curve are polar extremes, they are useful in indicating the differences that have existed between the monetarists and the Keynesians. *The monetarists have tended to believe that the* LM *curve is close to vertical, whereas the Keynesians have tended to believe that it is much closer to horizontal.* (Why? Because of the differences in their assumptions, indicated in Figures 17.1 to 17.3.) Given their different views concerning the shape of the *LM* curve, it is easy to see why they have come to quite different conclusions concerning the effects of fiscal policy on NNP. Clearly, the monetarists, based on their assumptions, have tended to conclude that fiscal policy has less impact on NNP than the Keynesians have been willing to accept.[2]

EFFECTS OF MONETARY POLICY ON NNP

To understand the difference between Keynesian and monetarist views concerning the effects of monetary policy on NNP, it is useful to consider three alternative assumptions:

1. Let's assume that the economy is operating at a point where the IS *curve is neither close to being horizontal nor close to being vertical.* Under these circumstances, what are the effects of an expansionary monetary policy (that is, an increase in the money supply)? Since it shifts the *LM* curve to the right, an expansionary monetary policy will increase NNP and reduce the interest rate, if the *IS* curve has this shape. Panel A of Figure A.6 shows that this is the case. A shift to the right of the *LM* curve (from $L_1 M_1$ to $L_1' M_1'$) increases NNP (from Y_{10} to Y_{11}) and reduces the interest rate (from i_{10} to i_{11}).

2. Let's assume that the economy is operating at a point where *the* IS

[2] The crowding-out effect, cited earlier in Chapter 17, is measured by the difference between (1) the equilibrium value of NNP if the interest rate remained at its original level, and (2) the equilibrium level of NNP at the new interest rate. In panel A of Figure A.5, the crowding-out effect equals $Y_6' - Y_7$; in panel B, it equals $L' - L$; and in panel C, it equals zero. If the crowding-out effect is zero, the effect on NNP of government expenditure conforms to the simple multiplier given in Chapter 12.

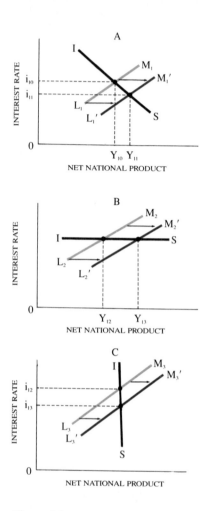

Figure A.6

Effects of Monetary Policy *An increase
in the money supply shifts the LM curve
to the right. If the IS curve is downward
sloped (as in panel A), an increase in the
money supply will increase NNP and
reduce the interest rate. If the IS curve is
horizontal (as in panel B), it will increase
NNP, but have no effect on the interest
rate. If the IS curve is vertical (as in
panel C), it will reduce the interest rate,
but have no effect on NNP. The monetarists have tended to believe that the IS
curve is close to horizontal, whereas
some Keynesians have tended to believe
that it is closer to vertical.*

curve is horizontal (or very nearly so). If so, expansionary monetary policy
results in an increase in NNP, but little or no decrease in the interest rate.
For example, in panel B of Figure A.6, a shift to the right of the *LM* curve
(from L_2M_2 to $L_2'M_2'$) increases NNP (from Y_{12} to Y_{13}) but does not
reduce the interest rate.

3. Let's assume that the economy is operating at a point where *the IS
curve is close to being vertical.* If so, an expansionary monetary policy
results in a decrease in the interest rate, but little or no increase in NNP.
For example, in panel C of Figure A.6, a shift to the right of the *LM* curve
(from L_3M_3 to $L_3'M_3'$) decreases the interest rate (from i_{12} to i_{13}) but does
not affect NNP.

Although both a perfectly horizontal and a perfectly vertical *IS* curve
are polar extremes, they are useful in indicating the differences between
the monetarists and the Keynesians. *Some Keynesians have believed that
the IS curve is close to vertical, whereas the monetarists have believed that it
is closer to horizontal.* (Why? Because of the differences in their assumptions, indicated in Figures 17.1 to 17.3.) Given their different views concerning the shape of the *IS* curve, it is easy to see why they have come to
different conclusions concerning the effects of monetary policy on NNP.
Clearly, the monetarists, based on their assumptions, have tended to conclude that monetary policy has a greater impact on NNP than the Keynesians have been willing to accept.

Appendix B: Isoquants, Isocost Curves, and the Optimal Input Combination[3]

In this Appendix, we present a somewhat different way of finding a firm's
optimal input combination. This approach is based on the use of isoquants
and isocost curves. There are advantages in being acquainted with this
approach, as well as the one presented in Chapter 23.

ISOQUANTS

In the case of a crude-oil pipeline, a given amount of oil can be carried per
day either by using a large diameter of pipe and relatively small horsepower or by using a smaller diameter of pipe and greater horsepower.
Similar opportunities to vary inputs to achieve a given output rate exist in
practically all industries. To describe these opportunities, economists use
the concept of an isoquant. *An **isoquant** is a curve showing all possible
efficient combinations of inputs capable of producing a certain quantity of
output.* An *inefficient* combination of inputs is one that includes more of at
least one input, and as much of other inputs, as some other combination of
inputs that can produce the same quantity of output. Inefficient combinations cannot minimize costs or maximize profits. On a wheat farm, it may
be possible to produce 1 unit of output with 2 units of land and 3 units of
labor. It may also be possible to produce 1 unit of output with 3 units of
land and 3 units of labor. The second input combination—which is inefficient—cannot be the least-cost input combination, so long as land has a

[3] To understand this Appendix, the reader should have covered Chapter 23.

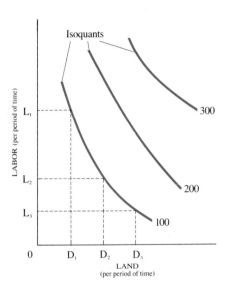

Isoquants

LABOR (per period of time)

L_1

L_2

L_3

300

200

100

0   D_1 D_2 D_3

LAND
(per period of time)

Figure B.1

Isoquants, Wheat Farm *An isoquant shows all possible efficient combinations of inputs capable of producing a certain quantity of output. These isoquants show the various combinations of inputs that can produce 100, 200, and 300 bushels of wheat per period of time. For example, 100 bushels of wheat can be produced with OL_1 units of labor and OD_1 units of land, with OL_2 units of labor and OD_2 units of land, or with OL_3 units of labor and OD_3 units of land.*

positive price. Only *efficient* input combinations are worth bothering with in the present circumstances, and they alone are included in an isoquant.

There is an isoquant pertaining to each level of production. Figure B.1 shows some isoquants for a wheat farm. These isoquants show the various combinations of inputs that can produce 100, 200, and 300 bushels of wheat per period of time. Consider the isoquant for 100 bushels of wheat per period of time. According to this isoquant, the farm can attain this output rate if OL_1 units of labor and OD_1 units of land are used per period of time. Alternatively, this output rate can be attained with OL_2 units of labor and OD_2 units of land—or OL_3 units of labor and OD_3 units of land—per period of time.

The shape and position of a firm's isoquants are derived from the firm's production function. Indeed, one way to represent the firm's production function is by showing its isoquants. Thus the firm's isoquants, like its production function, show the firm's technological possibilities—the various efficient input-output combinations that can be achieved with existing technology. The shape of an isoquant is typically like that shown in Figure B.1; that is, it slopes downward to the right, but *its slope becomes less and less steep.*

To illustrate what isoquants in an actual firm look like, consider once again our crude-oil pipeline. Figure B.2 shows the isoquants corresponding to 100,000, 200,000, and 300,000 barrels of crude oil carried per day. For example, the isoquant corresponding to 100,000 barrels per day shows all the combinations of line diameter and horsepower that permit a pipeline to carry 100,000 barrels per day (for 1,000 miles). Note that each of these isoquants slopes downward to the right. Moreover, comparing these isoquants with Table 23.2, you can readily see that, if Table 23.2 contained more detailed data on the production function, it would be simple to derive the isoquants from the data regarding the production function in Table 23.2. How? By determining from this more detailed version of Table 23.2 the various input combinations that can produce each output rate. For example, to derive the isoquant corresponding to 100,000 barrels of crude oil carried per day, one could determine from such a table the various input combinations that can produce this output rate.

Figure B.2

Isoquants for 100,000, 200,000, and 300,000 Barrels of Crude Oil Carried per Day, Crude-Oil Pipeline *This graph shows the isoquants in an actual case. Note that they are shaped as economic theory would predict.*

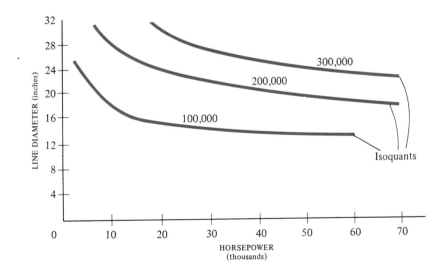

ISOCOST CURVES AND THE OPTIMAL INPUT DECISION

To determine the combination of inputs that will minimize the firm's costs, one can use the isoquant concept. All input combinations that can efficiently produce the specified level of output can be represented by the isoquant corresponding to this level of output. For example, the isoquant in Figure B.3 shows all the input combinations a wheat farm can use to produce a certain amount of wheat. The optimal input combination must lie on this isoquant, but where? A simple way to determine the optimal input combination is to draw a number of *isocost curves,* as shown in Figure B.3. *Each isocost curve shows the input combinations the firm can obtain for a given expenditure.* Consider the isocost curves corresponding to expenditures of $12,000, $16,200, and $20,000, shown in Figure B.3.

In Figure B.3 the price of labor is $8,000 per man-year, and the annual price of using land is $2,000. Given the price of each input, it is a simple matter to draw each isocost curve. Take the case of the isocost curve corresponding to annual expenditures of $12,000. If this expenditure were devoted entirely to labor, 1½ man-years could be hired. Thus this isocost curve must cut the horizontal axis in Figure B.3 at 1½ man-years of labor. Similarly, if this expenditure were devoted entirely to land, 6 acres of land could be hired. Thus this isocost curve must cut the vertical axis at 6 acres of land. Finally, if we connect the point where the isocost curve cuts the vertical axis to the point where it cuts the horizontal axis, we obtain the entire isocost curve.

Given both the isoquant and the isocost curves, one can readily determine the input combination that will minimize the firm's costs. This input combination corresponds to *that point on the isoquant that lies on the lowest isocost curve*—in other words, point *A* in Figure B.3. Input combinations on lower isocost curves (like that corresponding to $12,000) that lie below *A* are cheaper than *A,* but cannot produce the desired output. Input combinations on isocost curves (like that corresponding to $20,000) that lie above *A* will produce the desired output but at a higher cost than *A.*

What is the relationship between the input combination determined in this way and the input combination determined by means of the rule described in Chapter 23? Reassuringly enough, these input combinations will always be the same, since the rule described in Chapter 23 will always give the same answer as this geometric technique. In general, *if you find the combination of inputs where the marginal product of a dollar's worth of any one input equals the marginal product of a dollar's worth of any other input used, this will give you the same answer as if you find the point on the isoquant that lies on the lowest isocost curve.*

FINDING THE OPTIMAL INPUT COMBINATION: A CASE STUDY

To illustrate the use of isoquants and isocost curves to identify optimal input combinations, let's go back to Earl Heady's study of the production of corn, discussed in Chapter 23. Figure B.4 shows an isoquant that Heady and his coworkers estimated from the production of corn on Kansas Verdigras soil. This isoquant shows the amounts of land and fertilizer that will produce 82.6 bushels of corn. It indicates that this amount of corn can be produced if 1.19 acres of land and no fertilizer are used, or if 1.11 acres of land and 20 pounds of fertilizer are used, or if .99 acres of land and 60

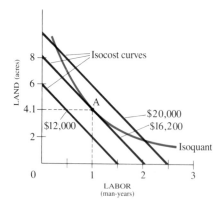
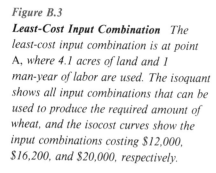

Figure B.3

Least-Cost Input Combination The *least-cost input combination is at point* A, *where 4.1 acres of land and 1 man-year of labor are used. The isoquant shows all input combinations that can be used to produce the required amount of wheat, and the isocost curves show the input combinations costing $12,000, $16,200, and $20,000, respectively.*

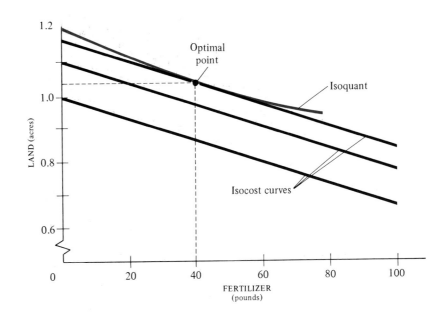

Figure B.4
Isoquant for the Production of 82.6 Bushels of Corn in Kansas *This graph shows how economic analysis has been used to help farmers make better production decisions. Given the assumed conditions, the optimal input combination would be 40 pounds of fertilizer and 1.04 acres of land.*

pounds of fertilizer are used, and so forth. (The same data are shown in Table 23.5.)

After estimating isoquants of this sort, Heady and his coworkers derived the optimal input combination farmers should use to minimize their costs. Suppose that a pound of fertilizer costs .003 times as much as an acre of land. Then the isocost curves would be as shown in Figure B.4. Under these circumstances, the minimum-cost combination would be 40 pounds of fertilizer and 1.04 acres of land. (This finding agrees with the results obtained in Chapter 23, where we took up this same case.) No matter what the ratio of the price of fertilizer to the price of land may be, the least-cost input combination can be derived this way.

Appendix C: Linear Programming[4]

In this Appendix, we look at the firm's production problems from a somewhat different angle—that of **linear programming.** Linear programming is the most famous of the mathematical programming methods that have come into existence since World War II. It is a technique that permits decision makers to solve maximization and minimization problems where there are certain constraints on what can be done. First used shortly after World War II to help schedule the procurement activities of the United States Air Force, linear programming has become an extremely important part of economic analysis and a very powerful tool for solving managerial problems. Its remarkable growth has been helped along by the development of computers, which can handle the many computations required to solve large linear programming problems.

There are at least two reasons why it is important to re-examine the theory of the firm in terms of linear programming:

---

[4] To understand this Appendix, the reader should have covered Chapter 23 and Appendix B.

1. The programming analysis is more fundamental in one respect than the conventional analysis presented up to this point. The conventional theory is based on the production function, which assumes that the efficient production processes have been determined and given to economists before they attack the problem. But in the real world, economists are usually confronted with a number of *feasible* production processes, and it is very difficult to tell which ones—or which combinations—are *efficient.* The choice of the optimal combination of production processes is an extremely important decision, and it can be analyzed more fully by linear programming.

2. The programming analysis seems to conform more closely to the way managers view production. The language and concepts of linear programming, though abstract and by no means the same as those of management, seem to be closer to those of managers and engineers than the ones used by conventional theory. This means that often it is easier to apply linear programming to many types of production problems in industry and government.

THE LINEAR-PROGRAMMING VIEW OF THE FIRM

To economists who use linear programming, *the technology available to a firm consists of a finite number of* **processes,** *each of which uses inputs and produces one or more outputs.* IBM can choose among a number of different processes to manufacture a computer, and U.S. Steel can use a number of processes to manufacture steel. Typically, a firm can use various alternative processes to do a particular job. An important assumption in linear programming is that *each process uses inputs in fixed proportions.* Consider the case of an automobile manufacturer that, among other things, assembles truck engines. Suppose that one process it can employ is Process X, which uses 10 hours of labor and 1 hour of machine time to assemble 1 truck engine. If this process uses inputs in fixed proportions—as assumed in linear programming—this 10:1 ratio of labor time to machine time must be maintained. It cannot be altered.

Any process can be operated at various activity levels; *the **activity level** of a process is the number of units of output produced with the process.* If Process X is used to assemble 3 truck engines, its activity level is 3; if it is used to assemble 100 truck engines, its activity level is 100. If the output of any process is varied, it is assumed that the inputs used by the process vary proportionately with the output of the process. Consequently, the amount of any input used by a process equals the activity level of the process—i.e., the number of units of output produced with the process—times the number of units of input the process requires to produce a unit of output. In our example, the amount of labor used by Process X to assemble 5 truck engines is 50 man-hours, since the process is operated at an activity level of 5, and Process X requires 10 man-hours of labor to assemble each truck engine.[5]

Linear programming views the firm's production problem as follows. *The firm has certain fixed amounts of a number of inputs at its disposal.*

---

[5] It is also assumed that, when two or more processes are used simultaneously, they do not interfere with one another or make each other more productive.

*Thus a manufacturing firm has available a limited amount of land, managerial labor, raw materials, and equipment of various kinds. (These limitations on the amounts of various inputs that the firm can use are called **constraints**.) Each unit of output resulting from a particular process yields the firm a certain amount of profit. This amount of profit varies in general from process to process. Knowing the profit to be made from a unit of output from each process and bearing in mind the limited amounts of inputs at its disposal, the firm must determine the activity level at which each process should be operated to maximize profit.* This is the firm's problem in a nutshell—a linear-programming nutshell, that is.

REMOVING DEFECTS FROM SHEET METAL: AN EXAMPLE

No general description of linear programming can give more than a very incomplete idea of the nature of linear programming and its power to solve real-life problems. We can get a somewhat better idea from a simple case study which concerns a metalworking firm that removes defects from sheet metal. Suppose that there are three processes the firm can use—Processes A, B, and C. Process A requires 2 man-hours of labor and 1 hour of machine time to remove the defects from 1 square foot of sheet metal, Process B does the same job with 1.5 man-hours of labor and 1.5 hours of machine time, and Process C requires 1.1 man-hours of labor and 2.2 hours of machine time. The same kind of machine is used for each process.

Assume that the firm has contracted to remove the defects from 100 square feet of sheet metal per week, and that it will receive a price of $10 a square foot for this service. Also assume that the firm must pay $3 per man-hour for labor and that the cost of an hour of machine time is $2. Given these circumstances, the firm must decide which process or processes it should use to satisfy this contract. Should it use any single process to remove the defects from all 100 square feet of sheet metal per week? If so, which process should it use? Should it use some combination of processes, such as Process A for 50 square feet and Process B for the rest? Which of the myriad of possibilities will maximize the firm's profits?

Since the firm receives $1,000 a week for the work (100 square feet × $10 per square foot) regardless of which processes it uses, the firm will maximize its profit by minimizing its costs. Thus, in this simple case,[6] the problem boils down to determining which process or processes can do the job at least cost. We begin by assuming that the firm can hire all the labor that it wants and that it has plenty of the necessary machines. (This assumption is contrary to our earlier statement that linear programming views the firm as having limited amounts of certain inputs, but we relax this assumption in a later section.) Letting Q_1 be the number of square feet of sheet metal subjected to Process A, Q_2 be the number of square feet subjected to Process B, and Q_3 be the number of square feet subjected to Process C, *the firm's problem can be regarded as the following simple linear programming problem. Choose the lowest possible value for*

$$\text{total cost} = 8.0\,Q_1 + 7.5\,Q_2 + 7.7\,Q_3 \tag{C.1}$$

---

[6] In general the problem of maximizing profit does not boil down to the minimization of cost because the firm's total revenue is not fixed as it is in this simple case.

subject to the constraints—

$$Q_1 + Q_2 + Q_3 = 100 \qquad \text{(C.2)}$$

$$Q_1 \geq 0;\ Q_2 \geq 0;\ Q_3 \geq 0. \qquad \text{(C.3)}$$

Why should the firm seek the lowest possible value for the expression in Equation (C.1)? Because this expression equals the firm's total weekly costs of doing the job. The cost of each square foot of sheet metal subjected to Process A is $8.00, since Process A requires 2 man-hours of labor (at $3 per man-hour) and 1 hour of machine time (at $2 per hour). Thus the total cost of the sheet metal subjected to Process A is 8.0 Q_1. Similarly, the total cost of sheet metal subjected to Process B is 7.5 Q_2, since the cost of each square foot of sheet metal subjected to Process B is $7.50. And the total cost of the sheet metal subjected to Process C is 7.7 Q_3, since the cost of each square foot subjected to Process C is $7.70. Clearly, the total cost of the job is the sum of whatever costs are incurred using each of the processes, which is the expression in Equation (C.1).

Why must the firm conform to the constraints in Equation (C.2) and Inequality (C.3)? Equation (C.2) must hold if the firm is to meet its contract, since it states that the sum of the amounts of sheet metal subjected to each process must equal 100 square feet. That is, $Q_1 + Q_2 + Q_3$ must equal 100. Also, the inequalities in (C.3) must hold. All they say is that the number of square feet of sheet metal subjected to each process must be either zero or more than zero, which certainly must be true. (If you wonder why such an obvious constraint must be specified, remember that electronic computers won't recognize it as being true unless they are told.)

SOLVING THE PROBLEM: NO CONSTRAINTS ON INPUTS

It is convenient to begin solving the problem by providing a graphic representation of each of the three processes. Since a process is defined to have fixed input proportions and since all points where input proportions are unchanged lie along a straight line through the origin, we can represent each process by such a line, or **ray.** In Figure C.1, the ray *OA* represents Process A. Process A uses 2 man-hours of labor and 1 hour of machine time per square foot of sheet metal—in other words, 2 man-hours of labor for every hour of machine time. Consequently, the ray *OA* includes all points where labor time is combined with machine time in the ratio of 2:1.

Two things should be noted about ray *OA*. First, *each point on this ray implies a certain output level.* For example, point U_A, where 200 man-hours of labor and 100 hours of machine time are used, implies an output of 100 square feet of sheet metal per week. Second, *every possible output rate corresponds to some point on this ray.* This is true because all possible points at which labor time is combined with machine time in the ratio of 2:1 are included in the ray *OA*.

In Figure C.2, we show the rays corresponding to all three processes: *OA* corresponds to Process A, *OB* to Process B, and *OC* to Process C. Each ray is constructed in the same way. Using these rays, we can draw the isoquant corresponding to the output of 100 square feet of sheet metal

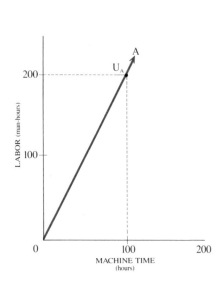

Figure C.1
Graphical Representation of Process A
The ray OA *includes all points where labor time is combined with machine time in the ratio of 2:1, since this is the ratio used by Process A. The point* U_A *corresponds to an output of 100 square feet of sheet metal per week. (Why? Because Process A uses 2 man-hours of labor and 1 hour of machine time per square foot of sheet metal. Thus 200 man-hours of labor and 100 hours of machine time are required to produce an output of 100 square feet.)*

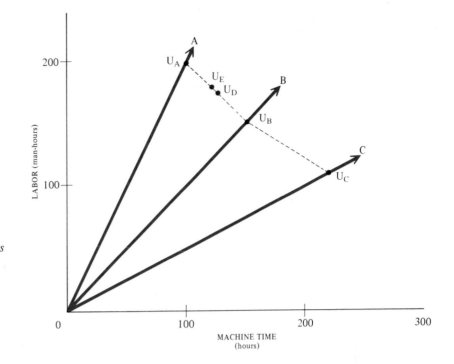

Figure C.2

Graphical Representation of Processes A, B, and C *Ray* OA *pertains to Process A, ray* OB *to Process B, and ray* OC *to Process C. Based on these rays, we derive the isoquant corresponding to an output of 100 square feet per week,* $U_A U_B U_C$. *(Since Process B uses 1.5 man-hours of labor and 1.5 hours of machine time per square foot of sheet metal, point* U_B *is at 150 man-hours of labor and 150 hours of machine time. Since Process C uses 1.1 man-hours of labor and 2.2 hours of machine time per square foot of sheet metal, point* U_C *is at 110 man-hours of labor and 220 hours of machine time.)*

processed—the curve that includes all input combinations that can produce this amount of output. Focusing first on Processes A and B, point U_A is the point corresponding to an output of 100 square feet of sheet metal with Process A, and point U_B corresponds to an output of 100 square feet with Process B. Thus U_A *and* U_B *are points on the isoquant corresponding to an output of 100 square feet of sheet metal.*

Moreover, *any point on the line segment joining* U_A *and* U_B *is also on this isoquant,* because the firm can simultaneously use both Process A and Process B to remove defects from a total of 100 square feet of sheet metal. For example, point U_D corresponds to the case in which Processes A and B are each used to remove defects from 50 square feet of the metal; and point U_E corresponds to the case in which Process A is used for 60 square feet and Process B for 40 square feet. By varying the proportion of the total output subjected to each of these two processes, one can obtain all points on the line segment that joins U_A to U_B.

To complete the isoquant, we must recognize the existence of Process C, too. In Figure C.2, U_C is the point corresponding to the use of Process C to remove defects from 100 square feet of sheet metal. Thus U_C *is also a point on this isoquant.* Moreover, *any point on the line segment joining* U_B *and* U_C *is also on this isoquant,* because the firm can simultaneously use both Process B and Process C to remove defects from a total of 100 square feet of sheet metal.[7] Consequently, *the entire isoquant is* $U_A U_B U_C$. Note that

---

[7] At first glance, one might wonder why the line segment joining U_A to U_C is not part of the isoquant. After all, it too represents various combinations of labor time and machine time that can remove the defects from 100 square feet of sheet metal. This line segment is excluded because the points on it are inefficient. They use as much of one input and more of the other input than some point on $U_A U_B U_C$. Recall from Appendix B that an isoquant contains only efficient combinations of inputs.

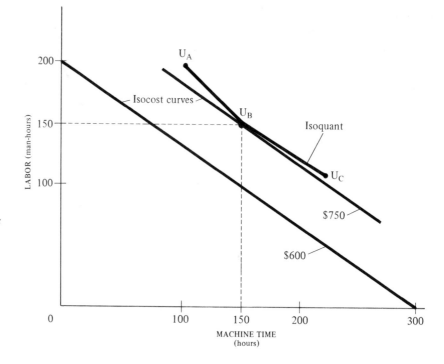

Figure C.3

Isoquant and Isocost Curves *The point on the isoquant* $U_A U_B U_C$ *that is on the lowest isocost curve is point* U_B. *(The $600 isocost curve shows all combinations of labor and machine time that can be obtained for $600. The $750 isocost curve shows all combinations of labor and machine time that can be obtained for $750.)*

this isoquant, like all in linear programming, consists of connected line segments, and, while not smooth, has the same basic shape as the isoquants of conventional theory.

Given the isoquant $U_A U_B U_C$, it is simple to solve the firm's problem. All we have to do is construct Figure C.3, which contains this isoquant as well as some isocost curves, each of which shows all input combinations that cost the firm the same amount. The isocost curves corresponding to $600 and $750 are shown in Figure C.3. To find the input combination that minimizes the cost of removing defects from 100 square feet of sheet metal, we need only follow the procedure recommended in Appendix B: *find the point on the isoquant that is on the lowest isocost curve.* This is U_B—the point corresponding to the use of Process B alone. Thus the firm should use only Process B, its total costs will be $750, and it will make a profit of $250 per week on the contract, which is the best it can do.

SOLVING THE PROBLEM: CONSTRAINT ON MACHINE TIME

The foregoing problem is simple—so simple that it can easily be solved outside the framework of linear programming.[8] Let's complicate the problem a bit and make it somewhat more realistic. In the previous section, we assumed that the firm could use all the machine time it wanted— at $2 per hour. But in the short run, the firm is likely to have only a certain

---

[8] All this problem really entails is a choice among three methods of production, the cost of producing a unit of output being constant for each process and no constraint being placed on the amount that can be produced with a certain process. In such a case, the answer is obvious. Produce the required volume of output with the process with the lowest cost per unit of output. The simplicity of this case does not detract from its usefulness as a first step in the discussion of the nature of linear programming.

number of machines available. It therefore is constrained to use no more than a certain number of machine hours per week. Specifically, suppose that the firm can use no more than 120 hours of machine time per week; this is the maximum capacity of the machines it owns or to which it has access. Now which process or processes should be used to satisfy the contract?

This problem recognizes that the firm has limited amounts of certain inputs in the short run; thus it contains constraints of the sort visualized in the linear-programming view of the firm. The objective is still to minimize the expression in Equation (C.1), and the constraints in Equation (C.2) and Inequality (C.3) must still be met, but there is now a new constraint—

$$Q_1 + 1.5\ Q_2 + 2.2\ Q_3 \le 120. \tag{C.4}$$

Why? Because the number of hours of machine time per week must be less than (or equal to) 120, and the total number of hours of machine time used per week equals $Q_1 + 1.5Q_2 + 2.2Q_3$.

To see that this is so, recall that the removal of defects from each square foot of sheet metal by Process A requires 1 hour of machine time; thus, since Q_1 is the number of square feet of sheet metal treated per week by Process A, the number of hours of machine time per week used on Process A must also equal Q_1. Similarly, the number of hours of machine time per week used on Process B must equal 1.5 Q_2 since the removal of defects from each square foot of sheet metal by Process B requires 1.5 hours of machine time. Moreover, the number of hours of machine time per week used on Process C must equal 2.2 Q_3 since Process C requires 2.2 hours of machine time per square foot of metal. Thus the *total* amount of machine time used per week on *all* processes must be $Q_1 + 1.5Q_2 + 2.2Q_3$.

How can this problem be solved? The constraint in Inequality (C.4) means that many of the points in Figure C.3 are no longer feasible, because they require more than 120 hours per week of machine time. These nonfeasible points are shown in the shaded area of Figure C.4. To solve the problem, we must find that *feasible* point on the isoquant $U_AU_BU_C$ that is on the lowest isocost curve. The feasible points on this isoquant are all on line U_AU_E in Figure C.4. Isocost curves representing costs of $600 and $780 are also shown in Figure C.4. It is evident that the point on U_AU_E that is on the lowest isocost curve is U_E. Thus the firm should use 180 man-hours of labor and 120 machine hours per week—which means that Process A should be used on 60 square feet of sheet metal per week and Process B on 40 square feet.[9] The firm's total cost is $780, and it makes $220 per week—which is the best it can do under these circumstances.

LINEAR PROGRAMMING AND MANAGEMENT SCIENCE

Linear programming is only one of a number of analytical tools that have been developed in the past 30 years to aid decision making in the private and public sectors of the economy. These techniques form the core of **management science** or **operations research**, a very rapidly growing and

---

[9] Since the total amount of man-hours used equals 180 hours, $2Q_1 + 1.5Q_2 = 180$. And since the total amount of machine time used equals 120 hours, $Q_1 + 1.5Q_2 = 120$. Solving these two equations simultaneously, $Q_1 = 60$ and $Q_2 = 40$. Thus Process A should be used on 60 square feet and Process B on 40 square feet.

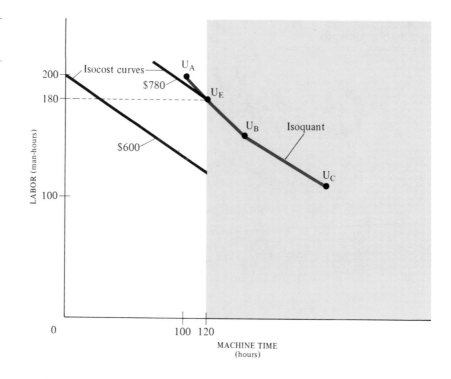

Figure C.4
Isoquant (with Constraint on Machine Time) and Isocost Curves *If the firm cannot use more than 120 hours of machine time per week, the shaded area is no longer feasible, so the feasible point on the isoquant that is on the lowest isocost curve is U_E. (The $780 isocost curve, which is the lowest isocost curve touching the line $U_A U_E$, shows all combinations of labor and machine time that can be obtained for $780.)*

exciting field that draws on economics and other disciplines. Although management is still very much an art, the development and application of techniques like linear programming are making it more and more a science. Many problems that were "solved" only 10 or 20 years ago by guesswork and seat-of-the-pants judgment are now being handled by linear programming and other such techniques, with the result that decisions are better, firms are more efficient, and society gets more out of its available resources.

Appendix D: General Equilibrium Analysis and Input-Output Models[10]

PARTIAL EQUILIBRIUM VERSUS GENERAL EQUILIBRIUM ANALYSIS

In this book, we looked in detail at the behavior of individual decision-making units and the workings of individual markets. We looked at consumers, at firms, and at various types of product markets and input markets. We almost always viewed each single market in isolation. According to the models we have used, the price and quantity in each such market are determined by supply and demand curves, with these curves drawn on the assumption that other prices are given. Each market is regarded as independent and self-contained for all practical purposes. In particular, it is assumed that *changes in price in the market under consider-*

---

[10] To understand this Appendix, the reader should have covered Chapter 25.

ation do not have serious repercussions on the prices in other markets. This is *partial equilibrium analysis.*

General equilibrium analysis recognizes that *changes in price may affect other prices, and that the changes in other prices may have an impact on the market under consideration.* No market can adjust to a change in conditions without causing *some* change in other markets, and in some cases this change may be substantial. Suppose that an upward shift occurs in the demand for barley. In previous chapters, it was generally assumed that when the price and output of barley changed in response to this change in conditions, the prices of other products would remain fixed. However, the market for barley is not sealed off from the markets for rye, corn, wheat, and other foodstuffs. (For that matter, it is not completely sealed off from the markets for nonfood products like sewing machines and autos.) Thus the market for barley cannot adjust without disturbing the equilibrium of other markets *and having these disturbances feed back on itself.*

Both partial and general equilibrium analyses are very useful, each in its own way. Partial equilibrium analysis is perfectly adequate when a change in conditions in one market has little repercussion on prices in other markets. Thus, in studying the effects of a proposed excise tax on the production of a certain commodity, we often can assume that prices of other commodities are fixed and remain close to the truth. However, if a change in conditions in one market has important repercussions on other prices, a general equilibrium analysis may be required.

INPUT-OUTPUT ANALYSIS

Input-output analysis, due largely to Nobel laureate Wassily Leontief, puts general equilibrium analysis in a form that is operationally useful to governments and firms faced with a variety of important practical problems. An important feature of input-output analysis is its emphasis on the *interdependence* of the economy. Each industry uses the outputs of other industries as its inputs, and its own output may be used as an input by the same industries whose output it uses. Recognizing this interdependence, input-output analysis attempts to determine the amount each industry must produce so that a specified amount of various final goods will be turned out by the economy. This type of analysis has been used to help predict production requirements to meet estimated demands. Economic planners have applied it to military mobilization, to problems of economic development in less developed countries, and to many other areas.

To put general equilibrium analysis in a usable form, input-output analysis makes a number of simplifying assumptions. Thus it generally uses as variables the *total* quantity of a particular good demanded or supplied, rather than the quantity demanded by a particular consumer or supplied by a particular firm. This reduces enormously the number of variables and equations in the analysis. Also, in the simpler versions of input-output analysis, it is assumed that consumer demand for all commodities is known. Input-output analysis attempts to find out what can be produced, and the amount of each input and intermediate good that must be employed to produce a given output. It views these questions as largely a matter of technology.

Finally, input-output analysis assumes that inputs are used in *fixed* proportions to produce any product and that there are *constant returns to scale.* This is a key assumption of Leontief's input-output system. In the production of steel, Leontief would assume that, for every ton of steel produced, a certain amount of iron ore, a certain amount of coke, a certain amount of fuel, and so on would be required. The amount of each input required per unit of output is assumed to be the same, whatever the level of output. If a certain amount of iron ore is required to produce 1 million tons of steel, it is assumed that 10 times that amount is required to produce 10 million tons of steel.[11]

Table D.1

AMOUNT OF EACH INPUT USED PER
DOLLAR OF OUTPUT (DOLLARS)

| Type of input | Type of output | | |
	Electric power	Coal	Chemicals
Electric power	.10	.30	.00
Coal	.50	.10	.00
Chemicals	.20	.00	.90
Labor	.20	.60	.10
Total	1.00	1.00	1.00

A NUMERICAL EXAMPLE

With some basic algebra, the essentials of input-output analysis are quickly grasped. Suppose that the economy consists of only three industries—coal, chemicals, and electric power. Each industry uses the products of the other industries in the proportions shown in Table D.1. Thus the second column of Table D.1 states that every dollar's worth of coal requires $.30 worth of electric power, $.10 worth of coal, and $.60 worth of labor. (One could just as well carry out the analysis with inputs and outputs measured in physical units—labor-hours or tons per year—as in money.)

This economy has set consumption targets of $100 million of electric power, $50 million of coal, and $50 million of chemicals. Input-output analysis takes up the question: *How much will have to be produced by each industry in order to meet these targets?* Let's begin with coal. If electric power output is E, chemical output is C, and coal output is X (E, C, and X are measured in millions of dollars), it follows from Table D.1 that

$$X = .5E + .1X + 50 \qquad (D.1)$$

if the target is met. Why? Because the electric power industry needs an amount of coal equal in value to $.5E$, the coal industry needs an amount equal in value to $.1X$, and an amount equal in value to 50 must be produced for consumption. Thus the total output of coal must be equal to the sum of these three terms, as shown in Equation (D.1).

If we construct similar equations for electric power output and chemical output, we find that

$$E = .1E + .3X + 100 \qquad (D.2)$$

$$C = .2E + .9C + 50 \qquad (D.3)$$

if the targets are to be met. For example, Equation (D.3) must hold because chemical output must equal the amount needed by the electric power industry ($.2E$) plus the amount needed by the chemical industry itself ($.9C$) plus 50 for consumption.

---

[11] In previous chapters, we said that the proportion in which inputs are combined can generally be altered. This is a direct contradiction of the assumption of fixed proportions in input-output analysis. But it often takes a fair amount of time for changes to be made and they are often gradual, with the result that Leontief's assumption of fixed proportions may work reasonably well in the short run.

WHAT'S THE ANSWER?

Since Equations (D.1) to (D.3) are three equations in three unknowns, X, E, and C, we can solve for the unknowns, which turn out to be $X = 144$, $E = 159$, and $C = 818$. We have answered our question—*$144 million of coal, $159 million of electric power, and $818 million of chemicals must be produced to meet the consumption targets.* We can also find out how much labor will be required to meet these targets, since (according to Table D.1) the total value of labor required equals

$$.2E + .6X + .1C. \tag{D.4}$$

Substituting the 144, 159, and 818 for X, E, and C, respectively, in Equation (D.4), we find that $206 million of labor is required. If this does not exceed the available labor supply, the solution is feasible; otherwise the targets must be scaled downward.

This simple example illustrates the fundamentals of input-output analysis. It also suggests why the assumption that inputs are used in fixed proportions is so convenient. Without this assumption, the input-output table in Table D.1 would not hold for each output level of the industries. Instead, the numbers in the table would vary depending on how much of each commodity was produced. The added complexity that would arise (without this assumption) is obvious. Even with this assumption, the computational and estimation problems involved in solving large input-output models can be substantial. Government agencies, such as the Departments of Commerce and Labor, have constructed a model of the U.S. economy involving several hundred industries. Usually, however, far fewer industries are included in such models.

APPLICABILITY OF INPUT-OUTPUT ANALYSIS

Whether input-output analysis can be applied fruitfully in a particular situation depends in part on whether the **production coefficients**—the numbers in Table D.1—remain constant. (See footnote 11.) There are at least two important factors that might cause changes over time in such coefficients. First, changes in technology may change the relative quantities of input used. For this reason, among others, the amount of coal required to produce many goods decreased considerably in the years since World War II. Second, changes in the relative prices of inputs may result in changes in production coefficients as cheaper inputs are substituted for more expensive ones.

Since World War II, much has been done to implement and extend input-output analysis. Basic research has been conducted by academic economists interested in the quantitative significance of various types of economic interdependence. Applied research has been devoted to formulating techniques that would be useful in decision making in government and business. In 1973–74, Anne Carter of Brandeis University and Clopper Almon of the University of Maryland used input-output analysis to estimate the effect of the Arab oil embargo on the level of unemployment in various industries. Other countries have used input-output analysis to determine the relationship of imports and exports to domestic production, as well as to analyze various problems of economic development. Also, business firms have used input-output analysis to forecast their sales.[12]

Appendix E: Optimal Resource Allocation and Perfect Competition[13]

THE NATURE OF WELFARE ECONOMICS

One of the great goals of economics is to determine how best to allocate society's scarce resources. Questions concerning the optimal allocation of inputs among industries and the optimal distribution of commodities among consumers are general equilibrium problems, since the optimal usage of any input cannot be determined by looking at the market for this input alone, and the optimal output of any commodity cannot be determined by looking at the market for this commodity alone. On the contrary, the optimal allocation of resources between two products depends on the relative strength of the demands for the products and their relative production costs.

The term **welfare economics** covers the branch of economics that studies policy issues concerning the allocation of resources. (Do not confuse welfare economics with the various government "welfare" programs you read about in Chapter 31.) It should be stressed from the start that welfare economics, although useful, is certainly no panacea. By itself, welfare economics can seldom provide a clear-cut solution to issues of public policy. But in combination with other disciplines, it can frequently show useful ways to structure and analyze these issues.

INTERPERSONAL COMPARISONS OF UTILITY

Perhaps the most important limitation of welfare economics stems from the fact that *there is no scientific way to compare the utility level of different individuals.* There is no way to show scientifically that a bottle of Château Haut-Brion will bring you more satisfaction than it will me, or that your backache is worse than mine. This is because there is no scale on which we can measure pleasure or pain so that interpersonal comparisons can be made scientifically. For this reason, the judgment of whether one distribution of income is better than another must be made on ethical, not scientific, grounds. If you receive twice as much income as I do, economists cannot tell us whether this is a better distribution of income than if I receive twice as much income as you do. This is an ethical judgment.

However, most problems of public policy involve changes in the distribution of income. A decision to increase the production of jet aircraft and to reduce the production of railroad locomotives may mean that certain stockholders and workers will gain, while others will lose. Because it is so difficult to tell whether the resulting change in the distribution of in-

---

[12] W. Leontief, *Input-Output Economics,* New York: Oxford University Press, 1966; and H. Chenery and P. Clark, *Interindustry Economics,* New York: Wiley, 1959.

[13] To understand this Appendix the reader should have covered Chapters 21 to 26 of this book.

come is good or bad, it is correspondingly difficult to conclude whether such a decision is good or bad.

Faced with this problem, economists have adopted a number of approaches, all of which have significant shortcomings. Some economists have simply paid no attention to the effects of proposed policies on the income distribution. Others have taken the existing income distribution as optimal, while still others have asserted that less unequal income distributions are preferable to more unequal ones. Purists have argued that we really cannot be sure a change is for the better unless it hurts no member of society, while others have suggested that we must accept the judgment of Congress (or the public as a whole) on what is an optimal distribution of income.

For now, the major thing to note is that the conditions for an optimal allocation of resources, described in the following sections, are incomplete, since they say nothing about the optimal income distribution. Whatever the income distribution you or I may consider best on ethical or some other (nonscientific) grounds, the conditions below must be met if resources are to be allocated optimally. Remember, however, that there may be many allocations of resources that meet these conditions, and the choice of which is best will depend on one's feelings about the optimal income distribution.

OPTIMAL RESOURCE ALLOCATION: CONDITION 1

Fundamentally, there are three necessary conditions for optimal resource allocation. The first pertains to the optimal allocation of commodities among consumers, and states that *the ratio of the marginal utilities of any two goods must be the same for any two consumers who consume both goods.* That is, if the marginal utility of good A is twice that of good B for one consumer, it must also be twice that of good B for any other consumer who consumes both goods. The proof that this condition is necessary to maximize consumer satisfaction is quite simple. We need only note that, if this ratio were unequal for two consumers, both consumers could benefit by trading.

Thus assume that the ratio of the marginal utility of good A to that of good B is 2 for one consumer, but 3 for another consumer. This means that the first consumer regards an additional unit of good A as having the same utility as 2 extra units of good B, whereas the second consumer regards an additional unit of good A as having the same utility as 3 extra units of good B. Then, if the first consumer trades 1 unit of good A for 2.5 units of good B from the second consumer, both are better off. (Why? Because the first consumer receives 2.5 units of good B, which he prefers to 1 unit of good A, and the second consumer receives 1 unit of good A, which she prefers to 2.5 units of good B.)

OPTIMAL RESOURCE ALLOCATION: CONDITION 2

The second condition, which pertains to the optimal allocation of inputs among producers, states that *the ratio of the marginal products of two inputs must be the same for any pair of producers that use both inputs.* That is, if the marginal product of input 1 is twice that of input 2 in one firm, it must also be twice that of input 2 in any other firm that uses both inputs. If this condition does not hold, total production can be increased merely by reallocating inputs among firms.

To illustrate this, suppose that for the first producer the marginal product of input 1 is twice that of input 2, whereas for the second producer the marginal product of input 1 is three times that of input 2. Then, if the first producer gives 1 unit of input 1 to the second producer in exchange for 2.5 units of input 2, both firms can expand their output. To see this, suppose that the marginal product of input 1 is M_1 for the first producer and M_2 for the second producer. Then the output of the first producer is reduced by M_1 units because of its loss of the unit of input 1, but it is increased by $2.5 \times M_1/2$ units because of its gain of the 2.5 units of input 2, so that on balance its output increases by $M_1/4$ units because of the trade. Similarly, the output of the second producer is increased by M_2 units because it gains the 1 unit of input 1, but it is decreased by $2.5 \times M_2/3$ units because it loses the 2.5 units of input 2, with the consequence that on balance its output increases by $M_2/6$ units because of the trade.

OPTIMAL RESOURCE ALLOCATION: CONDITION 3

The third condition pertains to the optimal output of a commodity. It states that *any commodity's output level, if it is optimal, must be such that the marginal social benefit from an extra unit of the commodity is equal to its marginal social cost.* If this condition is violated, social welfare can be increased by altering the output level of the commodity. Specifically, if the marginal social benefit from an extra unit of the commodity exceeds its marginal social cost, an increase in the output of the commodity will increase social welfare. (Why? Because the extra social benefit resulting from an extra unit of the commodity outweighs the extra social cost.) And if the marginal social benefit from an extra unit of the commodity is less than marginal social cost, a decrease in the output of the commodity will increase social welfare.

OPTIMAL RESOURCE ALLOCATION: A CASE STUDY

Let's turn now to a case study of how these conditions can be applied to one of our most important commodities—water. If the first condition is to hold, the ratio of the marginal utility of water to that of any other good must be the same for all consumers. To be specific, suppose that the other good is money. Then the ratio of the marginal utility of water to the marginal utility of money must be the same for all consumers. That is, if resources are allocated optimally, *the amount of money a consumer will give up to obtain an extra unit of water must be the same for all consumers.* This follows because the ratio of the marginal utility of good A to the marginal utility of good B equals the number of units of good B that the consumer will give up to get an extra unit of good A.

The common sense underlying this condition has been described well in a study of water resources done at the RAND Corporation:

> Suppose that my neighbor and I are both given rights (ration coupons, perhaps) to certain volumes of water, and we wish to consider whether it might

be in our mutual interest to trade those water rights between us for other resources—we might as well say for dollars, which we can think of as a generalized claim on other resources like clam chowders, babysitting services, acres of land, or yachts.... Now suppose that the last acre-foot of my periodic entitlement is worth $10 at most to me, but my neighbor would be willing to pay anything up to $50 for the right.... Evidently, if I transfer the right to him for any compensation between $10 and $50, we will both be better off in terms of our own preferences.... But this is not yet the end. Having given up one acre-foot, I will not be inclined to give up another on such easy terms (and) my neighbor is no longer quite so anxious to buy as he was before, since his most urgent need for one more acre-foot has been satisfied.... Suppose he is now willing to pay up to $45 (for another acre-foot), while I am willing to sell for anything over $15. Evidently, we should trade again. Obviously, the stopping point is where the last (or marginal) unit of water is valued equally (in terms of the greatest amount of dollars we would be willing to pay) by the two of us.... At this point no more mutually advantageous trades are available—and efficiency has been attained.[14]

If people can trade water rights freely—as in this hypothetical case—an efficient allocation of water rights will be achieved. But what if water rights cannot be traded freely, because certain kinds of water uses are given priority over other types of uses, and it is difficult, even impossible, for a low-priority user to purchase water rights from a high-priority user? The effect is to prevent water from being allocated so as to maximize consumer satisfaction. Unfortunately, this question is not merely an academic exercise. It focuses attention on a very practical problem. In fact, there is a wide variety of limitations on the free exchange of water rights in the United States. Thus some legal codes grant certain types of users priority over other types of users, and free exchange of water is limited. Experts believe that these limitations are a serious impediment to the optimal allocation of water resources.

PERFECT COMPETITION AND WELFARE MAXIMIZATION

One of the most fundamental findings of economic theory is that a perfectly competitive economy satisfies the three sets of conditions for welfare maximization set forth in previous sections. An argument for competition can be made in various ways. Some people favor it simply because it prevents the undue concentration of power and the exploitation of consumers. But to the economic theorist, the basic argument for a perfectly competitive economy is that such an economy satisfies these three conditions. In this section we prove that this is indeed a fact.

Condition 1—The Ratio of the Marginal Utilities of any Pair of Commodities Must Be the Same for All Consumers Buying Both Commodities. Recall that under perfect competition consumers choose their purchases so that the marginal utility of a commodity is proportional to its price. Since prices, and thus price ratios, are the same for all buyers under perfect competition, it follows that the ratio of the marginal utilities between any pair of commodities must be the same for all consumers. If every consumer can buy bread at $.50 a loaf and butter at $1 a pound, each one will

---

[14] J. Hirshleifer, J. Milliman, and J. DeHaven, *Water Supply,* Chicago: University of Chicago Press, 1960, p.38.

arrange his or her purchases so that the ratio of the marginal utility of butter to that of bread is 2. Thus the ratio will be the same for all consumers—2 for everyone.

To make sure you understand this point, let's consider any two goods, A and B. Based on our discussion in Chapter 22, we know that each consumer will buy amounts of these goods so that

$$\frac{MU_A}{P_A} = \frac{MU_B}{P_B},$$

where MU_A is the marginal utility of good A, MU_B is the marginal utility of good B, P_A is the price of good A, and P_B is the price of good B. Multiplying both sides of this equation by $P_A \div MU_B$, it follows that

$$\frac{MU_A}{MU_B} = \frac{P_A}{P_B}.$$

Since $P_A \div P_B$ is the same for all consumers, $MU_A \div MU_B$ must also be the same for all of them, which means this condition is satisfied.

Condition 2—The Ratio of the Marginal Products of any Pair of Inputs Must Be the Same for All Producers Using Both Inputs. We have already seen in Chapter 23 that under perfect competition producers will choose the quantity of each input so that the ratio of the marginal products of any pair of inputs equals the ratio of the prices of the pair of inputs. Since input prices, and thus price ratios, are the same for all producers under perfect competition, it follows that the ratio of the marginal products must be the same for all producers. If every producer can buy labor services at $4 an hour and machine tool services at $8 an hour, each one will arrange the quantity of its inputs so that the ratio of the marginal product of machine tool service to that of labor is 2. Thus the ratio will be the same for all producers: 2 for each.

To make sure you understand this point, let's consider any two inputs, X and Y. Based on our discussion in Chapter 23, we know that each firm will buy amounts of these inputs so that

$$\frac{MP_X}{P_X} = \frac{MP_Y}{P_Y},$$

where MP_X is the marginal product of input X, MP_Y is the marginal product of input Y, P_X is the price of input X, and P_Y is the price of input Y. Multiplying both sides of the equation by $P_X \div MP_Y$, it follows that

$$\frac{MP_X}{MP_Y} = \frac{P_X}{P_Y}.$$

Since $P_X \div P_Y$ is the same for all firms, $MP_X \div MP_Y$ must also be the same for all of them, which means this condition is satisfied.

Condition 3—The Marginal Social Benefit From an Extra Unit of any Commodity Must Be Equal to Its Marginal Social Cost. Recall from Chapter 25 that under perfect competition firms will choose their outputs so that price equals marginal cost. If a commodity's price is an accurate measure of the marginal social benefit from producing an extra unit of it, and if its marginal cost is an accurate measure of the marginal social cost of producing an extra unit of it, the fact that price is set equal to marginal cost insures that this condition will be met.

Thus, in summary, *all three conditions for optimal resource allocation are satisfied under perfect competition.* This is one principal reason why many economists are so enamored of perfect competition and so wary of monopoly and other market imperfections. If a formerly competitive economy is restructured so that some industries become monopolies, these conditions for optimal resource allocation are no longer met. As we know from Chapter 26, each monopolist produces less than the perfectly competitive industry that it replaces would have produced. Thus too few resources are devoted to the industries that are monopolized, and too many resources are devoted to the industries that remain perfectly competitive. This is one of the economist's chief charges against monopoly. It wastes resources because it results in overallocation of resources to competitive industries and underallocation of resources to monopolistic industries. The result is that society is less well off. Similarly, oligopoly and monopolistic competition are charged with wasting resources, since the conditions for optimal resource allocation are not met there either.

However, in evaluating this result and judging its relevance, one must be careful to note that it stems from a very simple model that ignores such things as technological change and other dynamic considerations, risk and uncertainty, and external economies and diseconomies. Also, there is the so-called *theory of the second-best,* which states that unless *all* of the conditions for optimal resource allocation are met, it may be a mistake to increase the number of such conditions that are fulfilled. Thus piecemeal attempts to preserve or impose competition may do more harm than good.

Brief Answers to Odd-Numbered Test-Yourself Questions*

Chapter 1 (p. 8)

1. (a) Iron ore that is still in the ground is included in land. (b) The 747 is capital. (c) These inventories are capital, as explained on p. 6. (d) Unless the University owns the telephone, it is not part of the university's capital, but it is capital to the telephone company.

3. Yes, use of the catalyst alters the relationship between inputs of crude oil and the refined oil output. By making the refining process more efficient, the catalyst allows a larger volume of refined oil to be gleaned from a barrel of crude oil. The services of engineers and scientists, as well as research laboratories, were used to obtain the invention.

Chapter 1 (p. 16)

1. Preparing the meal costs the family $25.00, assuming that Ms. Harris could see patients during that hour.

3. The $1,000 figure is correct because the remaining cost of room and board must be met whether the student goes to college or works instead.

* The answers provided here are meant only to be brief guides, not complete or exhaustive treatments. Many were contributed by Michael Claudon of Middlebury College, who is responsible for the *Instructor's Manual* accompanying this book.

Chapter 2 (p. 23)

1. 2 million bushels generates $2 million; 1 million bushels generates $2 million. No, I would produce 1 million bushels since I can sell it for as much as I can get for 2 million bushels.

3. The demand curve in Figure 2.2 shifts to the right when preferences change in favor of playing tennis.

Chapter 2 (p. 35)

1. (a) No. (b) Yes. (c) The combination of 20 million tons of food and 6 million tractors is inside the curve. Contributory factors: unemployment, inefficiency. or bad weather.

3. Yes, it is on the new curve. The horizontal intersection is 24 million tons, and the vertical one is 60 million tractors.

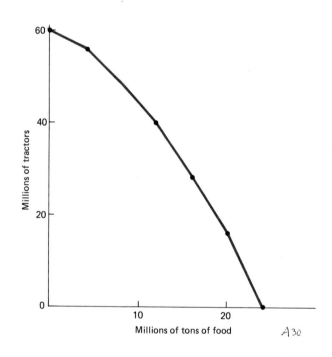

5. This statement is true. Of course, it is also important to note that not all individuals have the same number of votes, because of income inequality.

Chapter 3 (p. 47)

1. This is a direct relationship. Supply curves are generally direct relationships.

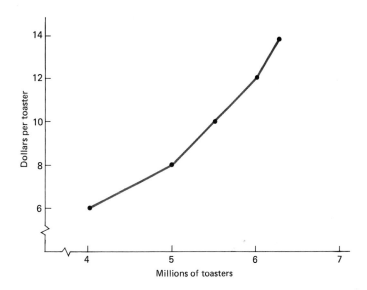

3. No, quantity demanded will exceed quantity supplied. Black markets and queues may arise. If black markets develop, the price may rise above the official price of $8. Such a ceiling might be introduced as part of an anti-inflationary program or to help the poor.

5. Equilibrium price = $3.33, and equilibrium quantity = 6.67 million pounds.

Chapter 3 (p. 61)

1. The toaster demand curve shifts: (a) right; (b) right; (c) left; (d) right; (e) no shift.

3. The impact on price is ambiguous. Equilibrium quantity rises.

5. The demand for beets and beet growers' profits rise. The opposite happens for string beans. Bean growers spy beet growers' high profits and plant beets instead of beans. Beet supply rises and string bean supply falls.

Chapter 4 (p. 75)

1. It is very difficult in many cases to know whether a certain activity can be performed better by government than private citizens can do for themselves. But the first half of this chapter indicates a number of areas where most economists believe the government has legitimate functions.

3. You can consume the services provided by national defense without depriving me of also doing so simultaneously. A rifle is not a public good; the hallmark of a public good is that it can be consumed collectively or jointly.

5. Such activities result in external economies.

Chapter 4 (p. 83)

1. The socially optimal output of paper is less than *OQ*. The supply curve reflecting true social costs lies to the left of the one shown because the latter neglects part of the social cost of paper production.

3. Government programs supported prices of dairy and grain farmers. The result has been excess supply of dairy and grain products, and huge government purchases of the excesses to support prices. Federal government programs have not solved the problem. See the section of the text on "Evaluation of Government Farm Programs."

5. The essential point here is one shared by many government programs, be they protective tariffs or farm subsidies. The benefits of the programs are concentrated on a relatively small and highly organized group of people, while the programs' costs are spread across the population at large.

Chapter 5 (p. 97)

1. The government should build the road from A to B since its benefits exceed its costs. The numbers imply that the cost of the road between B and C exceeds its benefits. The cost equals $15 million − $10 million = $5 million, while the benefit equals $22 million − $20 million = $2 million.

3. No. It is impossible to tell in which sector the inefficiency exists. The nonattainment of potential production might result from inefficiency in either sector.

Chapter 5 (p. 106)

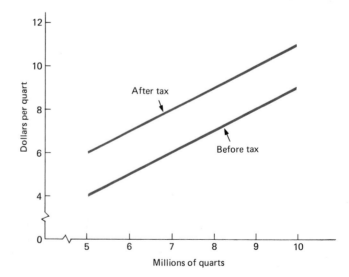

3. The equilibrium price of gin is $6 per quart both before and after the tax. None of the tax is passed on to the consumer.

Chapter 6 (p. 118)

1. The new olefins plant is not a firm; it is part of Exxon, which is a firm. A proprietorship is unlikely to build such a plant due to a lack of resources.

3. (a) and (b) are false because neither the University of Texas nor Massachusetts General Hospital are run to make profits. (c) is false because many firms are individual proprietorships with only one owner. (d) is false because many stockholders or partners do not participate in the management of the firms of which they are part owners.

5. Bondholders are not owners of the corporation, but stockholders are. Bondholders have lent money to the corporation at an agreed-upon interest rate, whereas stockholders' returns are based upon the profitability of the corporation they own.

Chapter 6 (p. 128)

1. All but (h).

3. Column 1: $700,000; Column 2: $1,100,000 and $2,000,000. The owners owe $1,600,000. The owners have contributed $400,000. The difference between current assets and fixed assets is the length of time before they will be converted into cash.

Chapter 7 (p. 140)

1. The figures are 1,000 for 1974, 1,200 for 1976, 1,820 for 1978, 2,400 for 1980, and 1,600 for 1986.

3. No. If GNP is used to gauge the net social value of economic output, pollution's costs should be subtracted from the market value of the goods produced.

Chapter 7 (p. 148)

1. GNP = $1,900 millions; NNP = $1,800 millions.

3. GNP = $93 millions, the sum of all items except for transfer payments.

5. Inventories represent goods that can be sold without drawing upon the economy's current productive capacity. Ignoring inventory increases excludes the value of these goods from the GNP calculation, even though they were produced during the year.

Chapter 8 (p. 163)

1. (i) Unemployment benefits are temporary, and averaged only about $120 per week in 1982. (ii) Unemployed workers involve an opportunity cost to the country in the form of the goods and services that these workers could produce.

3. Frictionally unemployed people have left one job (often voluntarily) and have not as yet begun a new one. Structural unemployment occurs when jobs are available for qualified workers, but the unemployed do not have the necessary qualifications. Cyclical unemployment occurs when, because of an insufficiency of aggregate demand, there are more people looking for work than there are jobs. The government should not attempt to reduce all types of unemployment to zero because severe inflation would be likely to result.

Chapter 8 (p. 173)

1. The point is that there may be tradeoffs between inflation and unemployment, and that full-employment policy should take inflation into consideration as well.

3. About 7 years.

5. Recessions tend to reduce inflation substantially. There are lots of excess capacity and unemployed resources, which put a damper on price increases.

Chapter 9 (p. 186)

1. A leftward shift in the aggregate supply curve, combined with a rightward shift in the aggregate demand curve, that kept their intersection at the same output level, would result in a constant real output but a higher price level.

3. Q falls by $2 billion from $18 billion to $16 billion.

5. The principal effect will be on the aggregate supply curve, which will shift upward and to the left. All other things equal, the result will be a higher price level and a lower real output level.

Chapter 9 (p. 192)

1. No, they tend to be caused by massive shifts to the left of the aggregate demand curve.

3. No, business cycles are movements around trend lines of this sort. Such trends are not business cycles; they are longer-term movements.

5. Policies that increase savings and investment, enhance R and D activity, and increase labor productivity will tend to shift the U.S. aggregate supply curve rightward. If we want to increase output without inflation, such a shift may be desirable.

Chapter 10 (p. 204)

1. The marginal propensity to consume = the average propensity to consume = 0.9 in this example. The consumption function has been assumed to pass through the origin. In this example, the marginal propensity to consume is unrelated to the income distribution, which is unrealistic since different socioeconomic groups have different spending and savings habits.

3. The marginal propensity to consume is not constant. The average propensity to consume falls as disposable income rises.

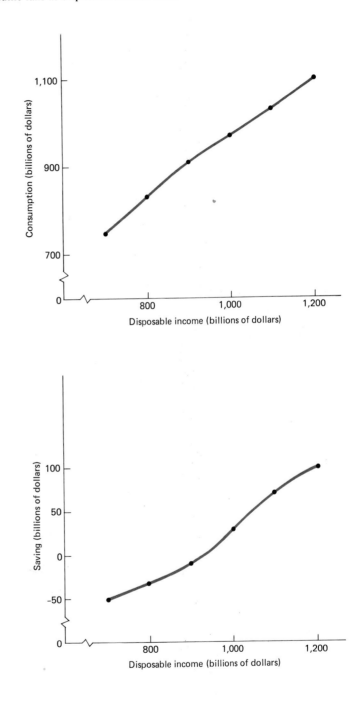

5. (a) Decrease (especially inventory investment); (b) increase; (c) increase; (d) decrease; (e) increase.

Chapter 10 (p. 215)

1. Equilibrium NNP = $500 billion. (*Note:* There is the implicit assumption that disposable income = NNP, i.e., that taxes are zero.) No, equilibrium NNP may not be full-employment NNP.

3. When NNP = $800 billions, intended saving ($330 billion) is substantially greater than intended investment ($140 billion). If NNP = $800 billions, the difference between intended investment and intended (= actual) saving becomes unintended inventory investment.

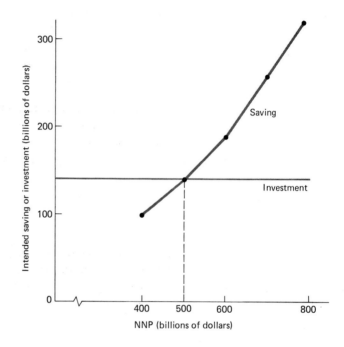

5. Intended saving equals intended investment, since this is an equilibrium. Thus saving equals $100 billion, and the average propensity to save is ⅓. Consequently, the consumption function is:

$$C = \frac{2}{3}D,$$

where C is consumption expenditure and D is disposable income.

Chapter 11 (p. 224)

1. NNP will increase by $2 billion, from $500 billion to $502 billion.

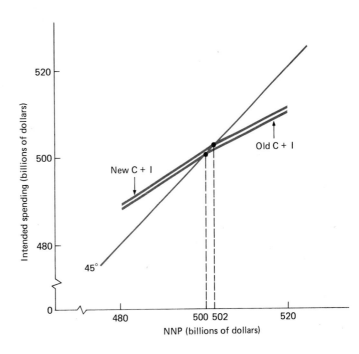

3. Multiplier = 1 ÷ .2 = 5.

5. The marginal propensity to save equals 0.25, and the multiplier is 4.

Chapter 11 (p. 232)

1. (a) Lower; (b) raise; (c) lower; (d) increase; (e) temporary increase.

3. It will shift downward, since consumers want to save $50 billion less at each level of disposable income.

5. Since the marginal propensity to save must be ⅓, the marginal propensity to consume must be ⅔.

Chapter 12 (p. 251)

1. $600 billion.

3. From top to bottom, the figures are: 500; 625; 750; 875; 1,000.

5. You cannot tell, since all you can conclude is that NNP is less than $500 billion. But if the consumption function is a straight line at all levels of disposable income, taxes will equal $75 billion and government spending will equal $50 billion, so the government will have a $25 billion surplus.

Chapter 12 (p. 264)

1. The balanced-budget multiplier indicates the influence on equilibrium NNP of an extra dollar of government spending that is financed by a one dollar increase in lump sum taxes. A simultaneous increase in both government expenditure and taxes by one dollar raises equilibrium NNP by one dollar according to the balanced-budget multiplier.

3. While it has obvious limitations, the full-employment budget has been of use to both Democratic and Republican administrations.

Chapter 13 (p. 280)

1. 1981: 0. 1982: $90,000. 1983: $90,000. 1984: $30,000. 1985: $15,000. 1986: 0.

3. If consumers acted upon their optimism and actually began to buy more autos and appliances, the consumption function might shift to the right, thus increasing NNP (and having a multiplier effect). The sales rate would increase, which, by the accelerator principle, might increase expenditures on equipment and inventory investment.

Chapter 13 (p. 292)

1. Economic cycles are not so regular that one can use them alone to forecast accurately.

3. Consumption rises by $6.52 billion in 1985–86, and by $6.53 billion in each subsequent year. Consumption levels ($ billions) for 1985 to 1989: 111.4, 117.9, 124.4, 131.0, 137.5.

5. If the estimate of $G + I = \$700$ billion $+ \$10$ billion, the $2 trillion forecast will be in error by $28.6 billion.

Chapter 14 (p. 306)

1. The paper content of a dollar has little value. Money derives value from its ability to be exchanged for goods and services, because it is a unit of account, and because it acts as a store of value.

3. Time deposits can be transformed into a medium of exchange, currency, by savings withdrawal. They represent a store of value. But the traditional argument against including them in the money supply has been that, in most instances, you could not pay directly for anything with them.

Chapter 14 (p. 317)

1. Yes, according to $MV = PQ$, V must increase by 10 percent. If people and firms conserve on the use of cash because of higher interest rates or the use of new technologies and payment methods, velocity will increase.

3. (a) Keynesian model: Changes in the money supply influence total spending through interest rates.

(b) Crude quantity theory: The quantity of money affects the price level, but not real output, thereby influencing nominal NNP.

(c) Sophisticated quantity theory: Nominal NNP is proportional to the quantity of money. In some formulations, velocity is a function of other variables like the interest rate.

Chapter 15 (p. 334)

1. Reserves, demand deposits, total assets and total liabilities rise by $50,000. Loans and investments and net worth are unchanged.

3. New balance sheet:

Assets		Liabilities	
Reserves	$20,000	Demand deposits	$50,000
Loans	$30,000	Net worth	0
Total	$50,000	Total	$50,000

Chapter 15 (p. 344)

1. The loans made by banks within the limits of reserve requirements do create money.

3. No, calling in loans and selling investments increases the bank's reserves. It does not increase demand deposits.

5. If the reserve ratio is 1/7, the system can support an additional $700 million with $100 million in excess reserves. If the reserve requirement is 1/6, $100 million in excess reserves can support a $600 million increase in the money supply.

Chapter 16 (p. 357)

1. All entries should be +$5 million.

3. No, increasing reserve requirements reduces excess reserves, but does nothing to total member bank reserves.

5. You probably should wait to invest as a dramatic increase in the discount rate is likely to mean higher interest rates and lower bond prices.

Chapter 16 (p. 369)

1. Keeping interest rates low in no way guarantees prosperity. In fact, such a policy could lead to serious inflation at times when the economy is becoming overheated.

3. The answer should focus on the material included in the section on "Should the Fed Pay More Attention to Interest Rates or the Money Supply?"

Chapter 17 (p. 380)

1. While some Keynesians may be social activists, Keynesians' preference for fiscal policy has sprung from the view that aggregate demand management is necessary for stabilizing the economy, and that fiscal policy is relatively effective at achieving this goal.

3. Although it is true that one model can be translated into the other, this does not mean that the two models are the same. As indicated in the text, they are not the same.

Chapter 17 (p. 386)

1. Whatever the size of the government, it should be possible to establish policies to move in the direction of economic stabilization.

3. No, monetarists argue that the expansionary monetary policy pursued during this period was more important than the tax cut in causing the boom that followed.

Chapter 18 (p. 399)

1. These three inflations are classic examples of demand-pull inflation.

3. The plot shows a downward-sloping Phillips curve. Friedman would reject it as a long-run Phillips curve since it is not vertical.

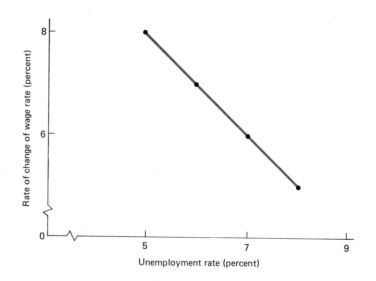

Chapter 18 (p. 411)

1. The response should include a discussion of the objections to guidelines in the section in the text on "The Kennedy-Johnson Guidelines: Criticism and Experience," as well as their possible short-term benefits.

3. To the extent that the basic causes lie with monetary or fiscal policy, this may be true.

Chapter 19 (p. 421)

1. Yes, there was an increase in output per capita. The economy was operating inside its production possibilities curve in 1985, and on its production possibilities curve in 1986.

3. 2 bushels per hour; 2 bushels per hour; zero. The law of diminishing marginal returns sets in beyond 3 million hours of labor input.

5. The equilibrium labor force occurs where the annual average product of labor is 1,400 bushels. The factors responsible are described in Figure 19.3 of the text. The technological advance would increase the equilibrium labor force.

Chapter 19 (p. 434)

1. The capital-output ratio is 2. No, this ratio can change; its value depends on technological change, among other things.

3. Ricardo did not assume that the capital-output ratio was fixed. He believed that it would increase.

Chapter 20 (p. 448)

1. No, the private costs are less than the social costs because of the required downstream water treatment.

3. The output prevailing after the industry has to reimburse others is more desirable, because it reflects the social costs of paper manufacture.

5. The total cost equals $10 - 2P + 5P = 10 + 3P$. Thus it is minimized when $P = 0$. No.

Chapter 20 (p. 456)

1. The statement is incorrect. The tax raises the price, and therefore has a greater influence on consumption the greater is the sensitivity of demand to price.

3. One disadvantage of such a fuel tax is that it might reduce our rate of economic growth.

Chapter 21 (p. 470)

1. About 0.4. About 1.4. Teenagers have lower income than adults.

3. It is price elastic.

Chapter 21 (p. 475)

1. (a) not true; (b) not true for some goods; (c) true.

3. Because of changes in tastes and incomes, and greater familiarity with cars, the demand curve may have shifted to the right between 1914 to 1916. Also, the price elasticity of demand may have been different then than in more recent years.

Chapter 22 (p. 485)

1. 2 utils. 1 util. Yes.

3. Air is cheap because its marginal utility is quite low. In general, people are willing to pay relatively higher prices for commodities having higher marginal utilities.

Chapter 22 (p. 492)

1. The quantity demanded is 26 at a price of $1, 23 at a price of $2, 19 at a price of $3, 14 at a price of $4, and 11 at a price of $5.

3. Bill's consumer's surplus = 6 cents. This number tells us how much more Bill would have been willing to spend on the two apples per day he consumes.

Chapter 23 (p. 506)

1.

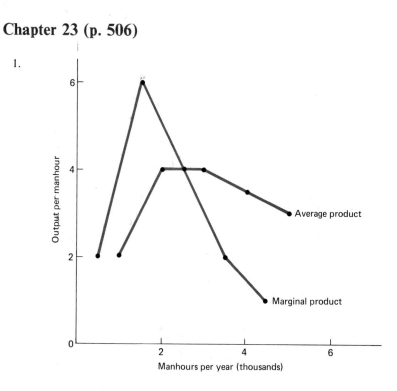

3. Labor is a variable input since the amount of labor is not fixed. Machines are a fixed input; their number cannot be changed during the period.

Chapter 23 (p. 511)

1. The price of a unit of capital is $8.00.

3. This does not seem sensible. For one thing, it denies the existence of diminishing marginal returns in the short run.

Chapter 24 (p. 523)

1. Total fixed costs = $20,000. The total variable cost of 4 units of output is $500.

3. The average costs are: $20,100, $10,100, $6,767, $5,125, and $4,160.

5. The marginal cost increases with output, since each extra unit of output increases total variable cost by more than the previous one does.

Chapter 24 (p. 531)

1. (a) False, the statement describes increasing returns to scale. (b) False, the statement confuses the short run (decreasing marginal returns) with the long run (returns to scale). (c) False, what is important in determining the optimal number of firms in an industry is the shape of the long-run average cost function.

3. No. A linear total cost curve implies constant marginal cost. If the actual marginal costs rise quickly with output, the breakeven chart is not likely to be very accurate.

Chapter 25 (p. 544)

1. Between 3 and 4 is the optimal output.

3. Marginal cost is unchanged since the total variable cost function is unchanged.

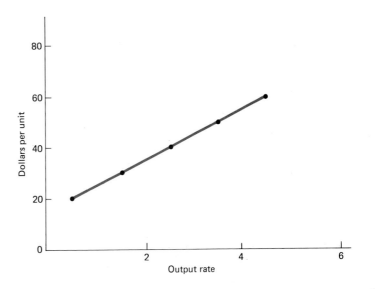

Chapter 25 (p. 554)

1. Quantity supplied increases by about 0.1 percent.

3. Price = ½. The market period supply curve is vertical.

5. For the effects on indoor tennis courts, see Example 3.2.

Chapter 26 (p. 569)

1. No, because marginal revenue is negative when demand is price inelastic. Thus a reduction in output will raise total revenue. Since it is also likely to reduce total cost, it will increase profits.

3. Marginal cost equals average variable cost over this range of output. Output will be between 2 and 3 units per year, and price will be between $6,000 and $7,000.

5. Output falls to between 1 and 2 units of output, and price increases to between $7,000 and $8,000.

Chapter 26 (p. 579)

1. See the sections in the text on "Perfect Competition and Monopoly: A Comparison" and "The Case Against Monopoly."

3. Perfectly competitive firms can earn high accounting profits if they are more efficient than are other firms. Also, in the short run, they may earn large profits.

Chapter 27 (p. 591)

1. As the slope of the demand curve becomes closer and closer to horizontal, it is tangent to the long-run average cost curve at a point that is closer and closer to the minimum point.

3. It is true that oligopolists may behave in this way.

Chapter 27 (p. 601)

1. Cartel output is 3,000 units per year.

3. If other members of the cartel hold their prices fixed (in accord with the agreement), each firm has a strong motive for lowering price, expanding sales, and increasing its profits.

Chapter 28 (p. 615)

1. The statement is incorrect. One cannot prove that perfect competition results in an optimal distribution of income. Also, the United States really hasn't opted for perfect competition, which is an abstract model.

3. The four-firm concentration ratio is 90 percent.

Chapter 28 (p. 624)

1. The issue is whether firms can escape the discipline of the market. Galbriath argues that they can: many (probably most) economists take a different view.

3. The answer should touch on the difficulties of establishing intent and, in some circumstances, its irrelevance.

Chapter 29 (p. 638)

1. The maximum is $3,600, since if the wage exceeded this amount, the firm would hire 3, not 4, man-years of labor. The minimum is $3,000, since if the wage were below this amount, the firm would hire 5, not 4, man-years of labor. These wage rates seem unrealistically low for the United States at present.

3. It would pay a lower wage. See pp. 637–38.

Chapter 29 (p. 650)

1. The focus of the answer should be upon whether the unions can be considered as monopolizers of a service.

3. This is not an easy task, as you would need data relating output responses to changes in various types of labor. No, the theory is not useless. Employers must form judgments of some sort on this score.

Chapter 30 (p. 663)

1. Borrowers might include: consumers purchasing durable goods, businesses financing inventories, and local, state, and federal governments financing expenditures.

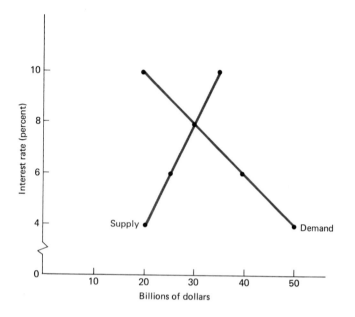

Eight percent is the equilibrium interest rate. If usury laws put a 6 percent ceiling on interest rates, there would be an excess demand for loanable funds.

3. The capitalized value of the asset is $$1,000 \div .10 = $10,000.$$

Chapter 30 (p. 670)

1. $$1,000 \div (1.08)^2 = $857.34.$$

3. As indicated in the chapter, much of the apparent increase in labor's share may have little to do with the growth of labor's power. Moreover, in recent years, it is not clear that labor's power has grown. The links to the alleged shortage of capital also are unclear.

Chapter 31 (p. 684)

1. The proportion of total income received by families with incomes of $2000 equals $40 \times 2,000 \div (40 \times 2,000 + 30 \times 4,000 + 20 \times 6,000 + 10 \times 10,000) = 19.0$ percent. The proportions received by families with incomes of $4,000, $6,000, and $10,000 are 28.6 percent, 28.6 percent, and 23.8 percent, respectively. Thus the Lorenz curve is as follows:

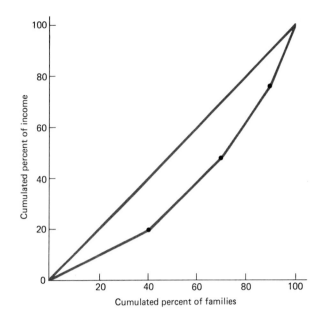

3. (a) Yes, since people can sell assets to maintain consumption. (b) No. (c) Yes.

Chapter 31 (p. 695)

1. If nonwhite and white labor are homogeneous, one would expect market forces to set the same price for them. But there are many factors that can interfere with, and postpone, such an outcome.

3. See p. 685 on "Social Insurance."

Chapter 32 (p. 708)

1. Yes, since the domestic opportunity cost of a computer is 1,000 cases of wine in the United States and 2,000 cases in France. The United States has a comparative advantage in computers, and France has one in producing wine. The United States is three times as efficient as France in computers, but only 50 percent more efficient in wine production.

3. No, forces of supply and demand will set the price of each good in world markets so that U.S. firms will find it profitable to make and export computers, while French firms will find it profitable to make and export wine.

Chapter 32 (p. 720)

1. Yes, protection is likely to reduce, not increase, a country's standard of living. On the other hand, a country's standard of living tends to be directly related to its productivity.

3. The United States may have a comparative advantage in computers, but not in TV sets.

Chapter 33 (p. 735)

1. Demanders of marks include buyers of German exports, foreign tourists in Germany, and foreign buyers of German financial assets.

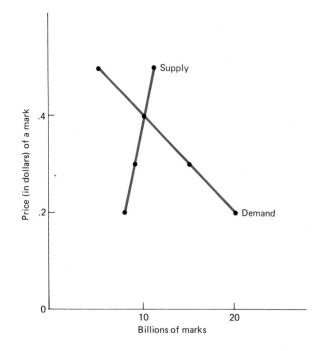

3. $.40 per mark, since at this exchange rate the quantity of marks demanded equals the quantity supplied. In recent years, there has been considerable flexibility in exchange rates, as described on p. 725.

Chapter 33 (p. 746)

1. One way to reduce a deficit is to keep inflation to a minimum. One possible problem is that policies designed to accomplish this may induce a recession.

3. The market, through changing exchange rates, tends to erase payments imbalances within a flexible exchange rate system. Reserves are required to maintain fixed exchange rates in the face of payments imbalances.

Chapter 34 (p. 760)

1. Hypotheses might include differential savings, investment, population growth, and literacy rates, a more poorly developed capital market in India, and sociological and cultural differences between the two countries.

3. No, not in the sense that population growth has been higher in India than Taiwan. In fact, the opposite was true.

Chapter 34 (p. 771)

1. No. For example, consider the case of Chile, cited on p. 762.

3. The point here is that cultural differences among nations greatly influence the countries' abilities, and even their will, to generate rapid economic development. Obviously, they also set limits on what both the developed countries and the LDCs themselves can do effectively to promote development.

Chapter 35 (p. 788)

1. Both have declined due to more emphasis on consumption rather than investment, inefficiencies inherent in the planning process, and a lack of incentive to perform, either as managers or workers.

3. The response should focus on the differences between the price mechanism and planning in solving the basic economic problems (what, how, for whom, and how much growth). See the section on "Prices in the USSR."

Chapter 35 (p. 796)

1. Some people have stated this view, but so many factors are not held equal that it is hard to see that very much can be learned from this simple comparison. Nonetheless, comparative studies of this sort, if conducted carefully, can be valuable.

3. For the views of the radical economists on this score, see the section on "Radical Economics."

Glossary of Terms

Absolute advantage the ability of one country to produce a good or service more cheaply than another country.

Aggregate demand curve a curve, slopping downward to the right, that shows the level of real national output that will be demanded at various economy-wide price levels.

Aggregate production function the relationship between the amount used of each of the inputs available in the economy and the resulting amount of potential output, i.e., the most output that existing technology permits the economy to produce from various quantities of all available inputs.

Aggregate supply curve a curve, sloping upward to the right, that shows the level of real national output that will be supplied at various economy-wide price levels.

Aid to Families with Dependent Children (AFDC) an antipoverty program that provides cash payments to families with children.

Alternative cost the value of what certain resources could have produced had they been used in the best alternative way; also called **opportunity cost.**

American Federation of Labor-Congress of Industrial Organizations (AFL-CIO) a federation of national labor unions formed in 1955 by the merger between the American Federation of Labor (originally a federation of unions organized along craft lines) and the Congress of Industrial Organizations (originally a federation of unions organized along industrial lines).

Antitrust laws legislation (such as the Sherman Act, the Clayton Act, and the Federal Trade Commission Act) intended to promote competition and control monopoly.

Appreciation of currency an increase in the value of one currency relative to another.

Automatic stabilizers structural features of the economy that tend by themselves to stabilize national output, without the help of new legislation or government policy measures.

Average fixed cost the firm's total fixed cost divided by its output.

Average product of an input total output divided by the amount of input used to produce this amount of output.

Average product of labor total output per unit of labor.

Average propensity to consume the fraction of total disposable income that is spent on consumption; equal to personal consumption expenditure divided by disposable income.

Average total cost the firm's total cost

A51

divided by its output; equal to average fixed cost plus average variable cost.

Average variable cost the firm's total variable cost divided by its output.

Backward-bending supply curve for labor a supply curve for labor inputs showing that, beyond some point, increases in price may result in smaller amounts of labor being supplied.

Balance-of-payments deficit the difference between the quantity supplied and the quantity demanded of a currency when the currency is overvalued (i.e., priced above its equilibrium price).

Balance-of-payments surplus the difference between the quantity demanded and the quantity supplied of a currency when the currency is undervalued (i.e., priced below its equilibrium price).

Balance sheet an accounting statement showing the nature of a firm's assets, the claims by creditors on those assets, and the value of the firm's ownership at a certain point in time.

Balanced budget a budget in which tax revenues cover government expenditures.

Barometric firm in an oligopolistic industry, any single firm that is the first to make changes in prices, which are then generally accepted by other firms.

Base year a year chosen as a reference point for comparison with some later or earlier year.

Bond a debt (generally long-term) of a firm or government.

Break-even chart a chart that plots a firm's total cost and total revenue, and that shows the output level that must be reached if the firm is to avoid losses.

Budget a statement of the government's anticipated expenditures and tax revenues for a fiscal year.

Budget deficit a budget in which tax revenues fall short of government expenditures.

Budget line a line showing the market baskets that the consumer can purchase, given his or her income and prevailing prices.

Budget surplus a budget in which tax revenues exceed government expenditures.

C + I + G line a curve showing total intended spending (the sum of intended consumption expenditure, investment expenditure, and government expenditure) at various levels of net national product; for simplicity, net exports are omitted.

Capital resources (such as factory buildings, equipment, raw materials, and inventories) that are created within the economic system for the purpose of producing other goods.

Capital consumption allowance the value of the capital (i.e., the plant, equipment, and structures) that is worn out in a year; also called **depreciation.**

Capital formation investment in plant and equipment.

Capital goods output consisting of plant and equipment that are used to make other goods.

Capital-output ratio the ratio of the total capital stock to annual national output.

Capitalism an economic system characterized by private ownership of the tools of production; freedom of choice and of enterprise whereby consumers and firms can pursue their own self-interest; competition for sales among producers and resource owners; and reliance on the free market.

Capitalization of assets a method of computing the value of an asset by calculating the present value of the expected future income this asset will produce.

Cartel an open, formal collusive arrangement among firms.

Central bank a government-established agency that controls the supply of money and supervises the country's commercial banks; the central bank of the United States is the Federal Reserve.

Checkoff a system whereby an employer deducts union dues from each worker's pay and hands them over to the union.

Closed shop a situation where firms can hire only workers who are already union members.

Collective bargaining process of negotiation between the union and management over wages and working conditions.

Collusion a covert arrangement whereby

firms agree on price and output levels in order to decrease competition and increase profits.

Commercial banks financial institutions that hold demand and other checkable deposits and permit checks to be written on them, and lend money to firms and individuals.

Common stock certificate of ownership of a corporation. Holders of common stock are owners of the corporation.

Comparative advantage the law that states that a nation should produce and export goods where its efficiency *relative to other nations* is highest; specialization and trade depend on comparative, not absolute advantage.

Compensation of employees the wages and salaries paid by firms and government agencies to the suppliers of labor, including supplementary payments for employee benefits (such as payments into public and private pension and welfare funds).

Complements commodities that tend to be consumed together, i.e., commodities with a negative cross elasticity of demand such that a decrease in the price of one will result in an increase in the quantity demanded of the other.

Constant dollar amounts amounts measured in base-year dollars (i.e., according to the purchasing power of the dollar in some earlier year), in order to express value in a way that corrects for changes in the price level.

Constant returns to scale a long-run situation where, if the firm increases the amount of all inputs by the same proportion, output increases by the same proportion as each of the inputs.

Consumer an individual or household that purchases the goods and services produced by the economic system.

Consumer goods output consisting of items that consumers purchase, such as clothing, food, and drink.

Consumer Price Index a measure of U.S. inflation, calculated by the Bureau of Labor Statistics, originally intended to measure changes in the prices of goods and services purchased by urban wage earners and clerical workers; in 1978, expanded to cover all urban consumers.

Consumer's surplus the difference between the maximum amount that a consumer would pay for a good or service and what he or she actually pays.

Consumption function the relationship between consumption spending and disposable income, i.e., the amount of consumption expenditure that will occur at various levels of disposable income.

Corporate profits the net income of corporations (i.e., corporate profits before income taxes), including dividends received by the stockholders, retained earnings, and the amount paid by corporations as income taxes.

Corporation a fictitious legal person separate and distinct from the stockholders who own it, governed by a board of directors elected by the stockholders.

Cost function the relationship between cost and a firm's level of output, i.e., how much cost a firm will incur at various levels of output.

Council of Economic Advisers a group established by the Employment Act of 1946, whose function is to help the president formulate and assess the economic policies of the government.

Craft union a labor union that includes all the workers in a particular craft (such as machinists or carpenters).

Creeping inflation an increase in the general price level of a few percent per year that gradually erodes the value of money.

Cross elasticity of demand the percentage change in the quantity demanded of one commodity resulting from a one percent change in the price of another commodity; may be either positive or negative.

Crowding-out effect the tendency for an increase in public sector expenditure to result in a cut in private sector expenditure.

Crude quantity theory of money and prices the theory that if the velocity of circulation of money remains constant and real net national product remains fixed at its full-employment level, it follows from the equation of exchange that the price level will be proportional to the money supply.

Cyclical unemployment joblessness that

occurs because of business cycle fluctuations.

Decreasing returns to scale a long-run situation where, if the firm increases the amount of all inputs by the same proportion, output increases by a smaller proportion than each of the inputs.

Deflating the conversion of values expressed in current dollars into values expressed in constant dollars, in order to correct for changes in the price level.

Demand curve for loanable funds a curve showing the quantity of loanable funds that will be demanded at each interest rate.

Demand curve for money a curve representing the quantity of money that will be demanded at various interest rates (holding net national product constant).

Demand deposits checking accounts; bank deposits subject to payment on demand.

Demand-pull inflation an increase in the general price level that occurs when there is too much aggregate spending, too much money chasing too few goods; also called **demand-induced inflation.**

Depreciation the value of the capital (i.e., plant, equipment, and structures) that is worn out in a year; also called a **capital consumption allowance.**

Depreciation of currency a decrease in the value of one currency relative to another.

Depression a period when national output is well below its potential (i.e., full-employment) level; a severe recession.

Derived demand demand for labor and other inputs not as ends in themselves, but as means to produce other things.

Devaluation of currency under the gold standard, a decrease in the value of a currency as a consequence of an increase in the price of gold.

Differentiated oligopoly a market structure (such as those for automobiles and machinery) where there are only a few sellers of somewhat different products.

Diffusion process the process by which the use of an innovation spreads from firm to firm and from use to use.

Direct regulation government issue of enforceable rules concerning the conduct of firms.

Discount rate the interest rate the Federal Reserve charges for loans to commercial banks.

Discretionary fiscal policy government tax and spending programs that supplement the effects of the automatic stabilizers in managing the economy.

Disposable income the total amount of income people can keep after personal taxes.

Dominant firm in an oligopolistic industry, a single large firm that sets the price for the industry but lets the small firms sell all they want at that price.

Easy monetary policy a monetary policy that increases the money supply substantially and reduces interest rates.

Economic profits the excess of a firm's profits over what it could make in other industries.

Economic resources resources that are scarce and thus command a nonzero price.

Economics the study of how resources are allocated among alternative uses to satisfy human wants.

Economies of scale efficiencies that result from carrying out a process (such as production or sales) on a large scale.

Effluent fee a fee that a polluter must pay to the government for discharging waste.

Equation of exchange a way of restating the definition of the velocity of circulation of money, such that the amount received for the final goods and services during a period equals the amount spent on those final goods and services during the same period (that is, $MV = PQ$).

Equilibrium a situation in which there is no tendency for change.

Equilibrium level of net national product the value of national output at which the flow of income generated by this level of output results in a level of spending precisely sufficient to buy this level of output.

Equilibrium price a price that shows no tendency for change, because it is the price at which the quantity demanded equals the quantity supplied; the price toward which the actual price of a good always tends to move.

Exchange rate the number of units of one currency that can purchase a unit of another currency.

Excise tax a tax imposed on each unit sold of a particular product, such as cigarettes or liquor.

Expansion the phase in the business cycle after the trough during which national output rises.

Explicit cost the cost of resources for which there is an explicit payment.

Exports the goods and services that a nation sells to other nations.

External diseconomy an uncompensated cost to one person or firm resulting from the consumption or output of another person or firm.

External economy an uncompensated benefit to one person or firm resulting from the consumption or output of another person or firm.

Featherbedding a practice whereby a union restricts output per worker in order to increase the amount of labor required to do a certain job.

Federal Open Market Committee (FOMC) a group, composed of the seven members of the Federal Reserve Board plus five presidents of Federal Reserve Banks, which makes decisions concerning the purchase and sale of government securities, in order to control bank reserves and the money supply.

Federal Reserve Board the Board of Governors of the Federal Reserve System, composed of seven members appointed by the president for 14-year terms, whose function is to promote the nation's economic welfare by supervising the operations of the U.S. money and banking system.

Federal Reserve System a system established by Congress in 1913 that includes the member banks (commercial banks), the twelve Federal Reserve Banks, and the seven-member Board of Governors of the Federal Reserve System.

Final goods and services goods and services that are destined for the ultimate user (such as flour purchased for family consumption).

Firm an organization that produces a good or service for sale in an attempt to make a profit.

Firm's demand curve for labor a curve showing the relationship between the price of labor and the amount of labor demanded by a firm, i.e., the amount of labor that will be demanded by a firm at various wage rates.

Firm's supply curve a curve, usually sloping upward to the right, showing the quantity of output a firm will produce at each price.

Fixed input a resource used in the production process (such as plant and equipment) whose quantity cannot be changed during the particular period under consideration.

Food programs federal antipoverty programs that distribute food to the poor, either directly from surpluses produced by farm programs or indirectly via stamps that can be exchanged for food.

45-degree line a line that contains all points where the amount on the horizontal axis equals the amount on the vertical axis.

Fractional-reserve banking the practice whereby banks hold less cash than the amount they owe their depositors.

Free resources resources (such as air) that are so abundant that they can be obtained without charge.

Frictional unemployment temporary joblessness, such as that occurring among people who have quit jobs, people looking for their first job, and seasonal workers.

Full employment the minimum level of joblessness that the economy could achieve without undesirably high inflation, recognizing that there will always be some frictional and structural unemployment.

Full-employment budget the difference between tax revenues and government expenditures that would result if the economy were operating at full employment.

Functional finance a budgetary policy whereby the government's budget is set to promote the socially optimal combination of unemployment and inflation, even if this means that the budget is unbalanced over considerable periods of time.

Gold exchange standard an exchange rate system developed after World War II, under which the dollar was directly convertible into gold at a fixed price, and other currencies, since they could be converted into dollars at fixed exchange rates, were thus indirectly convertible into gold at a fixed price.

Gold standard a method of exchange rate determination prevailing until the 1930s, under which currencies were convertible into a certain amount of gold.

Government purchases federal, state, and local government spending on final goods and services, excluding transfer payments.

Gross national product (GNP) the value of the total amount of final goods and services produced by the economy during a period of time; this value can be measured either by the expenditure on the final goods and services, or by the income generated by the output.

Gross private domestic investment all additions to the nation's stock of investment goods, i.e., all investment spending by firms, including purchases of tools, equipment, and machinery, all construction expenditures, and the change in total inventories.

Historical cost of assets what a firm actually paid for its assets.

Implicit cost the cost (for which there may not be an explicit payment) of the resources that are provided by the owner of a firm, measured by what these resources could bring if they were used in their best alternative employment.

Imports the goods and services that a nation buys from other nations.

Income effect the change in the quantity demanded by the consumer of a good due to the change in the consumer's level of utility resulting from a change in the price of the good.

Income elasticity of demand the percentage change in the quantity demanded of a commodity resulting from a one percent increase in total money income (all prices being held constant).

Income statement an accounting statement showing a firm's sales, costs, and profits during a particular period (often a quarter or a year).

Income tax a federal, state, or local tax imposed on personal income and corporate profits.

Incomes policy a policy to control inflation that sets some targets for wages and prices in the economy as a whole; gives particular firms and industries detailed guides for making wage and price decisions; and provides some inducements for firms and unions to follow these guidelines.

Increasing returns to scale a long-run situation where, if a firm increases the amount of all inputs by the same proportion, output increases by a larger proportion than each of the inputs.

Indifference curve a curve representing market baskets among which the consumer is indifferent.

Indirect business taxes taxes (such as general sales taxes, excise taxes, and customs duties) that are imposed not directly on the business itself but on its products or services, and hence are treated by firms as costs of production.

Individual demand curve a curve showing the relationship between individual consumer demand and prices, i.e., how much of a good an individual consumer will demand at various prices.

Industrial union a labor union that includes all the workers in a particular plant or industry (such as autos or steel).

Inflation an increase in the general level of prices economy-wide.

Innovation the first commercial application of a new technology.

Innovator a firm that is first to apply a new technology.

Input any resource used in the production process.

Interest the payment of money by borrowers to suppliers of money capital.

Interest rate the annual amount that a

borrower must pay for the use of a dollar for a year.

Intermediate good a good that is not sold to the ultimate user, but is used as an input in producing final goods and services (such as flour to be used in manufacturing bread).

IS curve a curve showing, for each level of the interest rate, the level of NNP that will satisfy the equilibrium condition that intended spending on output must equal NNP.

Isocost curve a curve showing the input combinations the firm can obtain for a given expenditure.

Isoquant a curve showing all possible efficient combinations of inputs capable of producing a certain quantity of output.

Keynesians economists who share many of the beliefs of John Maynard Keynes. His principal tenet was that a capitalist system does not automatically tend toward a full-employment equilibrium (due in part to the rigidity of wages). Keynesians tend to believe that a free-enterprise economy has weak self-regulating mechanisms that should be supplemented by activist fiscal (and other) policies.

Labor human effort, both physical and mental, used to produce goods and services.

Labor force the number of people employed plus the number of those unemployed (i.e., actively looking for work and willing to take a job if one were offered).

Labor productivity the average amount of output that can be obtained for every unit of labor.

Laffer curve a curve representing the relationship between the amount of income tax revenue collected by the government and the marginal tax rate, i.e., how much revenue will be collected at various marginal tax rates.

Land natural resources, including minerals as well as plots of ground, used to produce goods and services.

Law of diminishing marginal returns the principle that if equal increments of a given input are added (the quantities

of other inputs being held constant), the resulting increments of product obtained from the extra unit of input (i.e., the marginal product) will begin to decrease beyond some point.

Law of diminishing marginal utility the principle that if a person consumes additional units of a given commodity (the consumption of other commodities being held constant), the resulting increments of utility derived from the extra unit of the commodity (i.e., the commodity's marginal utility) will begin to decrease beyond some point.

Law of increasing cost the principle that as more and more of a good is produced, the production of each additional unit of the good is likely to entail a larger and larger opportunity cost.

Legal reserve requirements regulations, imposed by the Federal Reserve System in order to control the money supply, requiring banks (and other institutions) to hold a certain fraction of deposits as reserves.

Liabilities the debts of a firm.

LM curve a curve showing, for each level of the interest rate, the level of NNP that will satisfy the equilibrium condition that the public be satisfied to hold the existing quantity of money.

Loanable funds funds (including those supplied by households and firms that find the rate of interest high enough to get them to save) that are available for borrowing by consumers, businesses, and government.

Local unions labor unions, organized around either craft or industrial lines, that are set up in particular geographical areas or plants, and which may or may not belong to a larger national union.

Long run the period of time during which all of a firm's inputs are variable, i.e., during which the firm could completely change the resources used in the production process.

Long-run average cost function a representation of the minimum average cost of producing various output levels when any desired type or scale of plant can be built.

Lorenz curve a curve that measures income inequality by showing what percentage of the people receive what percentage of total income.

M-1 narrowly defined money supply, which includes coins, currency, demand deposits, and other checkable deposits.

M-2 broadly defined money supply, which includes savings deposits, small time deposits, money market mutual fund balances, and money market deposit accounts, as well as the components of the narrowly defined money supply, M-1 (coins, currency, demand deposits, and other checkable deposits).

Marginal cost the addition to total cost resulting from the addition of the last unit of output.

Marginal cost pricing a pricing rule whereby the price of a product is set equal to its marginal cost.

Marginal product of an input the addition to total output that results from the addition of an extra unit of input (the quantities of all other inputs being held constant).

Marginal product of labor the additional output resulting from the addition of an extra unit of labor.

Marginal propensity to consume the fraction of an extra dollar of disposable income that is spent on consumption.

Marginal propensity to save the fraction of an extra dollar of disposable income that is saved.

Marginal revenue the change in total revenue that results from the addition of one unit to the quantity sold.

Marginal tax rate the proportion of an extra dollar of income that must be paid in taxes.

Marginal utility the additional satisfaction derived from consuming an additional unit of a commodity.

Market a group of firms and individuals that are in touch with each other in order to buy or sell some good or service.

Market demand curve a curve, usually sloping downward to the right, showing the relationship between a product's price and the quantity demanded of the product.

Market demand curve for labor a curve showing the relationship between the price of labor and the total amount of labor demanded in the market.

Market period the relatively short period of time during which the supply of a particular good is fixed and output is unaffected by price.

Market structure the type or organization of a market. Markets differ with regard to the number and size of buyers and sellers in the market, the ease with which new firms can enter, the extent of product differentiation, and other factors.

Market supply curve a curve, usually sloping upward to the right, showing the relationship between a product's price and the quantity supplied of the product.

Market supply curve for labor a curve showing the relationship between the price of labor and the total amount of labor supplied in the market.

Markup in cost-plus pricing, an addition to a product's estimated average cost that is meant to include certain costs that cannot be allocated to any specific product, and to provide a return on the firm's investment.

Medicare a compulsory hospitalization program plus a voluntary insurance plan for doctors' fees for people over 65, included under the Social Security program.

Member banks the commercial banks (all of the national banks and many of the larger state banks) that belong to the Federal Reserve System.

Model a theory composed of assumptions that simplify and abstract from reality, from which conclusions or predictions about the real world are deduced.

Monetarists economists generally sharing the belief that business cycle fluctuations are due largely to changes in the money supply. Many monetarists think that a free-enterprise economy has effective self-regulating mechanisms that activist fiscal and monetary policies tend to disrupt. Some monetarists, like Milton Friedman, advocate a rule for stable growth in the money supply of 3 to 5 percent per year.

Monetary base the reserves of Federal Reserve member banks plus currency outside of the member banks.

Monetary policy the exercise of the central bank's control over the quantity of money and the level of interest rates in order to promote the objectives of national economic policy.

Money anything that serves as a medium of exchange and a standard and store of value; the unit in which the prices of goods and services are measured.

Money income income measured in current dollars (i.e., actual money amounts).

Monopolistic competition a market structure in which there are many sellers of somewhat differentiated products, where entry is easy, and where there is no collusion among sellers. Retailing seems to have many of the characteristics of monopolistic competition.

Monopoly a market structure (such as those for public utilities) in which there is only one seller of a product.

Monopsony a market structure (such as that for the single firm that employs all the labor in a company town) in which there is only a single buyer.

Moral suasion the Federal Reserve's practice of exhorting member banks to go along with its wishes, in the absence of any actual power to force the banks' compliance.

Multinational firm a firm that makes direct investments in other countries, and produces and markets its products abroad.

National banks commercial banks chartered by the federal government.

National debt the amount owed by the government. To cover the difference between its expenditures and its tax revenues, the government sells bonds, notes, and other forms of IOUs.

National income the total amount of income paid out (or owed) by employees, approximately equal to gross national product minus indirect business taxes and depreciation.

Natural monopoly an industry in which the average costs of producing the product reach a minimum at an output rate large enough to satisfy the entire market, so that competition among firms cannot be sustained and one firm becomes a monopolist.

Near-money assets (such as government bonds) that can be converted into cash, though not quite as easily as time and savings accounts.

Negative income tax a system whereby families with incomes below a certain break-even level would receive, rather than make, a government income tax payment.

Net exports the amount spent by foreigners on a nation's goods and services (exports) minus the amount a nation spends on foreign goods and services (imports).

Net national product (NNP) gross national product minus depreciation. (Depreciation equals the value of the plant, equipment, and structures that are worn out during the relevant period of time.)

Nominal expressed in current dollars (i.e., actual money amounts).

Normative economics economic propositions about what ought to be, or about what a person, organization, or nation ought to do.

Old-age insurance benefits paid under the Social Security program to retired workers, from taxes imposed on both workers and employers.

Oligopoly a market structure (such as those for autos and steel) in which there are only a few sellers of products that can be either identical or differentiated.

Open market operations the purchase and sale of U.S. government securities on the open market by the Federal Reserve in order to control the quantity of bank reserves.

Open shop a situation where a firm can hire both union and nonunion workers, with no requirement that nonunion workers ever join a union.

Opportunity cost the value of what certain resources could have produced had they been used in the best alternative way; also called **alternative cost.**

Overvaluation of currency the setting of a currency's price above the equilibrium price.

Parity the principle that a farmer should

be able to exchange a given quantity of farm output for the same quantity of nonfarm goods and services he would have been able to purchase at some point in the past; in effect, the principle that farm prices should increase at the same rate as the prices of the goods and services that farmers buy.

Partnership a form of business organization whereby two or more people agree to own and conduct a business, with each party contributing some proportion of the capital and/or labor and receiving some proportion of the profit or loss.

Peak the point in the business cycle where national output is highest relative to its potential (i.e., full-employment) level.

Perfect competition a market structure in which there are many sellers of identical products, where no one seller or buyer has control over the price, where entry is easy, and where resources can switch readily from one use to another. Many agricultural markets have many of the characteristics of perfect competition.

Personal consumption expenditures the spending by households on durable goods, nondurable goods, and services.

Phillips curve a curve representing the relationship between the rate of increase in wages and the level of unemployment.

Positive economics descriptive statements, propositions, and predictions about the economic world that are generally testable by an appeal to the facts.

Potential gross national product the total amount of goods and services that could have been produced had the economy been operating at full capacity or full employment.

Precautionary demand for money the demand for money because of uncertainty about the timing and size of future disbursements and receipts.

Price discrimination the practice whereby one buyer is charged more than another buyer for the same product.

Price elastic the demand for a good if its price elasticity of demand is greater than one.

Price elasticity of demand the percentage change in quantity demanded resulting from a one percent change in price; by convention, always expressed as a positive number.

Price elasticity of supply the percentage change in quantity supplied resulting from a one percent change in price.

Price index the ratio of the value of a set of goods and services in current dollars to the value of the same set of goods and services in constant dollars.

Price inelastic the demand for a good if its price elasticity of demand is less than one.

Price leader in an oligopolistic industry, a firm that sets a price that other firms are willing to follow.

Price supports price floors imposed by the government on a certain good.

Price system a system under which every good and service has a price, and which in a purely capitalistic economy carries out the basic functions of an economic system (determining what goods and services will be produced, how the output will be produced, how much of it each person will receive, and what the nation's growth of per capita income will be).

Primary inputs resources (such as labor and land) that are produced outside of the economic system.

Private cost the price paid by the individual user for the use of a resource.

Product differentiation the process by which producers create real or apparent differences between products that perform the same general function.

Product group a group of firms that produce similar products that are fairly close substitutes for one another.

Product market a market where products are bought and sold.

Production function the relationship between the quantities of various inputs used per period of time and the maximum quantity of output that can be produced per period of time, i.e., the most output that existing technology permits the firm to produce from various quantities of inputs.

Production possibilities curve a curve showing the combinations of amounts of various goods that a society can produce with given (fixed) amounts of resources.

Profit the difference between a firm's revenue and its costs.

Progressive tax a tax whereby the rich pay a larger proportion of their income for the tax than do the poor.

Prohibitive tariff a tariff so high that it prevents imports of a good.

Property tax a tax imposed on real estate and/or other property.

Proprietors' income the net income of unincorporated businesses (i.e., proprietorships and partnerships).

Proprietorship a firm owned by a single individual.

Prosperity a period when national output is close to its potential (i.e., full-employment) level.

Public goods goods and services that can be consumed by one person without diminishing the amount of them that others can consume. Often there is no way to prevent citizens from consuming public goods whether they pay for them or not.

Public sector the governmental sector of the economy.

Pure oligopoly a market structure (such as those for steel, cement, tin cans, and petroleum) in which there are only a few sellers of an identical product.

Pure rate of interest the interest rate on a riskless loan.

Quota a limit imposed on the amount of a commodity that can be imported annually.

Rate of return the annual profit per dollar invested that business can obtain by building new structures, adding new equipment, or increasing their inventories; the interest rate earned on the investment in a particular asset.

Rational expectations theory the theory put forth by Robert Lucas, Thomas Sargent, and others that markets clear quickly and expectations are rational. Under these circumstances, predictable macroeconomic policies may not influence real output or unemployment.

Real expressed in constant dollars.

Real income income measured in constant dollars (i.e., the amount of goods and services that can be bought with the income).

Recession the phase in the business cycle after the peak during which national output falls.

Regressive tax a tax whereby the rich pay a smaller proportion of their income for the tax than do the poor.

Rent in the context of Chapter 30, the return derived from an input that is fixed in supply.

Reproduction cost of assets what the firm would have to pay to replace its assets.

Resource market a market where resources are bought and sold.

Resources inputs used to produce goods and services.

Retained earnings the total amount of profit that the stockholders of a corporation have reinvested in the business, rather than withdrawing as dividends.

Rule of reason the idea that not all trusts, but only unreasonable combinations in restraint of trade, require conviction under the antitrust laws.

Runaway inflation a very rapid increase in the general price level that wipes out practically all of the value of money.

Sales tax a tax imposed on the goods consumers buy (with the exception, in some states, of food and medical care).

Saving the process by which people give up a claim on present consumption goods in order to receive consumption goods in the future.

Saving function the relationship between total saving and disposable income, i.e., the total amount of saving that will occur at various levels of disposable income.

Say's Law the principle that the production of a certain amount of goods and services results in the generation of an amount of income precisely sufficient to buy that output.

Short run the period of time during which at least one of a firm's inputs (generally its plant and equipment) is fixed.

Social Security a program that imposes taxes on wage earners and employers, and provides old-age, survivors, disability, medical, and unemployment benefits to workers covered under the Social Security Act.

Special drawing rights (SDRs) a reserve asset established since 1968 by the International Monetary Fund, which member countries can use to exchange for other currencies, much as they used gold in the past.

Stagflation a simultaneous combination of high unemployment and high inflation.

State banks commercial banks chartered by the states.

Structural unemployment joblessness that occurs when new goods or new technologies call for new skills, and workers with older skills cannot find jobs.

Substitutes commodities with a positive cross elasticity of demand (that is, a decrease in the price of one commodity will result in a decrease in the quantity demanded of the other commodity).

Substitution effect the change in the quantity demanded (by a consumer) of a commodity resulting from a change in the commodity's price, if the consumer's level of utility is held constant.

Supply curve for loanable funds a curve showing the relationship between the quantity of loanable funds supplied and the pure interest rate.

Supply-side economics a set of propositions concerned with influencing the aggregate supply curve through the use of financial incentives such as tax cuts.

Tariff a tax imposed by the government on imported goods (designed to cut down on imports and thus protect domestic industry and workers from foreign competition).

Tax avoidance legal steps taken by taxpayers to reduce their tax bill.

Tax evasion misreporting of income or other illegal steps taken by taxpayers to reduce their tax bill.

Technological change new methods of producing existing products, new designs that make it possible to produce new products, and new techniques of organization, marketing, and management.

Technology society's pool of knowledge concerning how goods and services can be produced from a given amount of resources.

Terms of trade the ratio of an index of export prices to an index of import prices.

Tight monetary policy a monetary policy that restrains or reduces the money supply and raises interest rates.

Total cost the sum of a firm's total fixed cost and total variable cost.

Total fixed cost a firm's total expenditure on fixed inputs per period of time.

Total revenue a firm's total dollar sales volume.

Total variable cost a firm's total expenditure on variable inputs per period of time.

Trading possibilities curve a curve showing the various combinations of products that a nation can get if it specializes in one product and trades that specialty for foreign goods.

Transactions demand for money the holding of money in cash or in checking accounts in order to pay for final goods and services; the higher the level of NNP, the greater the quantity of money demanded for transactions purposes.

Transfer payments payments made by the government or private business to individuals who do not contribute to the production of goods and services in exchange for them.

Trough the point in the business cycle where national output is lowest relative to its potential (i.e., full-employment) level.

Tying contract the practice whereby buyers must purchase other items in order to get the product they want.

Undervaluation of currency the setting of a currency's price below the equilibrium price.

Unemployment according to the definition of the Bureau of Labor Statistics, joblessness among people who are actively looking for work and would take a job if one were offered.

Unemployment rate the number of people who are unemployed divided by the number of people in the labor force.

Union shop a situation where firms can

hire nonunion workers who must then become union members within a certain length of time after being hired.

Unitary elasticity a price elasticity of demand equal to one.

Utility a number representing the level of satisfaction that a consumer derives from a particular masket basket.

Value-added the amount of value added by a firm or industry to the total worth of a product.

Value of the marginal product of labor the marginal product of labor (i.e., the additional output resulting from the addition of an extra unit of labor) multiplied by the product's price.

Variable input a resource used in the production process (such as labor or raw material) whose quantity can be changed during the particular period under consideration.

Velocity of circulation of money the rate at which the money supply is used to make transactions for final goods and services, i.e., the average number of times per year that a dollar is used to buy the final goods and services produced by the economy. It equals NNP divided by the money supply.

Wage and price controls limits imposed by the government on the amount by which wages and prices can increase, in order to reduce the inflation rate at a given unemployment rate.

Wage-price spiral a series of steps whereby higher wage demands by workers prompt firms to raise their prices to consumers, which in turn raises the general cost of living and prompts workers to make yet higher wage demands.

Wage rate the price of labor.

Photograph Credits

Bureau of Land Management (6, 68); U.S. Department of Labor (6); Sperry New Holland (7); Warder Collection (13, 30, 51, 158, 163, 253, 368, 418, 422, 619, 703, 724, 775, 778, 782); Free-Lance Photo Guild, photo by Kerwin B. Roche (33); photo by Amanda Adams (40); photos by Jeremy Townsend (58, 113, 202, 330); Food and Drug Administration (66); Official U.S. Coast Guard Photo (68); U.S. Air Force Photo (73); AP/Wide World (75, 642, 787); Caterpillar Tractor Company (76); U.S. Congressional Budget Office (87); Project Double Discovery Summer Math Class—Neville Dowe, Teacher—Courtesy Upward Bound and Talent Search of Columbia University (88); Internal Revenue Service (96); Department of Treasury (105); IBM (110, 428); Wide World (115); Edward C. Topple, NYSE Photographer (116); Copyright Gilles Peress, Magnum Photos (153); New York Public Library (160); Sheffield City Museums (161); Courtesy of the New York Historical Society (162); Courtesy of British Airways (172); Billie B. Shaddix/The White House (249); U.S. Senate (254); Jack Kightlinger/The White House (255); Courtesy of U.S. Senator Patrick Moynihan (256); U.S. Government Printing Office (257); White House Photo (258, left and right); The Norwegian Information Service (275); The Bank of America (323); Chase Manhattan Bank (328); Vermont National Bank (329); Federal Reserve (349, 365); Courtesy of Robert Lucas (383); General Motors (431); National Archives, photo by Joseph Sterling (439); E. I. Du Pont de Nemours & Co. (440); German Information Center (442, 719); Uniphoto (466); Ford Archives (468); Historical Pictures Service (480); Courtesy of Gary Becker (490); Courtesy of Ken Scala—Century 21/Scala and Clark Co., Inc. (509); Chicago Mercantile Exchange (536); Courtesy of Charles Plott (548); United Nations/Carlton Read (576); Harvard University News Office (586); Burk Uzzle, Magnum Photos (587); Courtesy of William Baumol (599); Harvard University Archives (607); Photo © by Jim Kalett (608); Department of Justice (613); © Pabst Brewing Company, Milwaukee, Wisconsin (617); Courtesy of Michael Spence (636); AFL-CIO News Photo (641); Jacques E. Levy (662); NYPL Ford Collection (665); Reprinted from the *Journal of Political Economy,* Vol. 81, No. 3, May/June 1973. Copyright © 1973 by the University of Chicago (668); UPI/Bettmann Newsphotos (678); United Nations/S. Potner (682); U. P. Laffont/Sygma (686); Burt Glinn/Magnum Photos (706); The Picture Group (712); Copyright by Christian Baur, Photograph basel Missionsstr 10 (741); International Monetary Fund (743); United Nations (752, 757, 764, 765, 776, 785, 790); World Bank photo by Ray Witlin (770); Sygma Photos (789).

Index

Definitions of terms appear on pages set in **boldface** type.

ability-to-pay principle, 93–94
accelerationists, **395**–99
acceleration principle, 269–73, **271,** 274
   multiplier and, 271–73, 275
   numerical example of, 270–71
accounting in firms, 121–26
accounts payable, **122**
activity level, **A12**
Acton, Jan, 490
Adams, Henry, 479–80
Adams, Walter, 550n, 567n, 595
Adelman, Morris, 610–11
advertising, 480n
   in monopolistic competition, 535, 586–87
   in oligopoly, 535, 588–89, 597–98
Affluent Society, The (Galbraith), 65
aggregate demand, 383
   consumption and, 176–77, 181–82
aggregate demand curves, 175, **176**–78, 309n
   business fluctuations and, 186, 189, 191
   income-expenditure analysis reconciled with, 208
   monetary policy and, 181–83, 347, 356
   reasons for shape of, 177
   shifts in, 180–84, 189, 191
aggregate models, in forecasts of GNP, 283–84
aggregate production function, **415**

aggregate supply, *see* supply-side economics
aggregate supply curves, 175, 176, **178**–80, 381, 384–86
   business fluctuations and, 186, 189, 192
   income-expenditure analysis reconciled with, 209–10
   inflation and, 384–85, 390, 391, 395
   ranges of, 179–80, 181–82
   ratchet effect on, 185
   shifts in, 183, 184
Agricultural Adjustment Act (1933), 79
agriculture, 77–83, 790
   Brannan plan in, 81, 470–71
   diminishing marginal returns in, 416–17
   in less developed countries, 751, 757, 758
   markets in, 77–78, 79–83
   perfect competition in, 534, 545, 550–51, 552
   price supports in, 59, 79–81, 82, 83
   surpluses in, 59, 78, 80–81
   see also corn; farm problem; farm programs; wheat
Agriculture and Consumer Protection Act (1973), 81
Agriculture Department, U.S., 40n, 42n, 79, 475, 506, 681
aid to families with dependent children, 687

Air Force, U.S., 73
airlines, government regulation of, 4
air pollution, 437–38, 438–39, 446
   control of, 439–40, 454–55
   as external diseconomy, 64, 69
Aliber, R., 361n
Allen, B. T., 610n
Allen, Frederick Lewis, 323n
Almon, Clopper, A22
alternative cost, *see* opportunity cost
Altman, S., 637n
Aluminum Company of America (Alcoa), 559, 565–66, 613
aluminum industry, monopoly of, 66, 559, 565–66
Amacher, Peter, 587
American Bankers Association, 105
American Cyanamid, 598
American Economic Association, 381, 399
   John Bates Clark medal of, 258, 490, 637
American Express, 322n
American Federation of Labor (AFL), 639, 640–41, 642
American Federation of Labor-Congress of Industrial Organizations (AFL-CIO), 639, 642–43
American Meat Institute, 541
American Motors, 589
American Petroleum Institute, 454

"American Plan," 641
American Statistical Association and National Bureau of Economic Research (ASA-NBER) Survey, 289
American Stock Exchange, 115
American Telephone and Telegraph Company (AT&T), 118, 534
American Tobacco Company, 612
Ando, Albert, 200–201
antipoverty programs, 686–90
antitrust laws, 4, 66, 567, **611**–15
  Berkey Photo vs. Eastman Kodak, 620–21
  collusion and, 591, 592, 593
  effectiveness of, 617
  Justice Department and, 612, 613–15
  labor unions and, 649
  post-World-War-II developments in, 614–15
  standards for, 616
  Supreme Court and, 559, 611, 612–13, 614, 618
apples, production of, 552
appreciation of currency, **726**–27, 728
arc elasticity of demand, **465**
Argentina, 81, 793
Arkwright, Richard, 30
Armco (steel corporation), 452
Armstrong, Anne, 117
army, all-volunteer, wages and, 635–37
Arnold, M., 437n
Arnold, Thurman, 613
assets:
  on balance sheets, 121–22, 325, 327, 337–38, 349–50
  capitalization of, **660**, 661
  current, **121**
  of Federal Reserve Banks, 349–50
  fixed, **121**
  of hundred largest firms, 609–10
  of manufacturing firms, 4
  near-money as, **299**
  rate of return of, **653**–54
Austria, market demand in, 42
automatic stabilizers,, **248**–50
automatic transfer service (ATS) accounts, 298
automobile industry, 108–10, 154, 529
  business organization in, 112, 113
  competition in, 3, 109, 649
  income policies and, 403–4
  labor unions and, 639, 642, 649
  oligopoly in, 535, 583, 588–89, 596–97, 610
automobiles:
  pollution from, 437–38, 439
  price elasticity of demand for, 468
average costs:
  in long run, 523–24, 527, 529, 549, 560
  marginal cost in relation to, 520–21
  measurement of, 527
  in monopolistic competition, 585
  in monopoly, 559–60
  returns to scale and, 525–26
  in short run, 516–18, 520–21, 524, 539–40
average fixed cost, **517**, 520

average product, **503**
  of labor, **417**, 503, 504–5
average propensity to consume, **198**
average total cost, **518**, 520–21
average variable cost, **517**, 520
  in perfect competition, 539–40

Babbage, Charles, 428
backward bending supply curve, **631**
Bain, Joe, 588, 600
Bakke, E. W., 158n
balance of merchandise trade, **735**
balance of payments, **731**–35
  accounts, **731**–35
  deficits, **730**–31, 737–40
  surpluses, **730**–31, 737
balance sheets, **121**
  of banks, 325–27, 331–32, 333–34, 334–37, 349–51, 353–54
  of firms, 121–22, 350–51
bank, in anti-pollution measures, **453**
Bank of America, 322–24, 325
banks, banking system, 319–45
  central, **320**, 780–81; see also Federal Reserve System
  commercial, see commercial banks; reserves, bank
  depressions and, 302
  functions of, 321, 324–25, 328–29
  international, 765, 769–70
  monopoly, 334, 339
  savings, 322
barometric-firm model, **594**
barriers to entry, 535, 583–84, 589
barter, 296, 301
base year, **133**
Baumol, W., 445n
Becker, Gary, 426–27, 490
Beckerman, W., 139n
beef, market demand curves for, 463
beer, demand for, 473
Belgium, 560, 719
Bell Telephone Laboratories, 64
benefit-cost analysis, 87–89, 92
benefit principle of taxation, 93
Benson, Ezra Taft, 470
Bergland, Bob, 82
Berkey Photo, 620–21
Berle, A. A., 609
Bernstein, E., 745n
Bethlehem Steel, 595–96
Bituminous Coal Act (1937), 624
Blank, C. J., 8
Blatz Brewing Company, 617–18
board of directors, corporate, **113**, 117
Bond, D., 779n
bonds, 95, 96
  corporate, **114**
  interest on, 306, 308, 361, 652–53
  price of, 306, 308
  U.S. government, 105, 169, 170, 324, 349, 652
bonds payable, **122**
B-1 bomber, 73
borrowers, borrowing:
  aggregate demand curves and, 176–78
  ease and cheapness of, 225
  inflation's impact on, 169

  see also credit; interest, interest rates
Boskin, Michael, 100, 385
Boston and Maine Railroad, direct market experiment of, **461**–63
Bowen, H., 8
Bower, B., 442n
Bradley, William, 96
Brannan, Charles F., 81, 470–71
Brannan plan, 81, 470–71
Brazil, 171, 751, 793–95
break-even charts, **527**–30
break-even income, **687**–88
break-even point, **530**
Bretton Woods conference (1944), 736, 743
Brezhnev, Leonid, 778
Bromley, D. Allan, 667
brown-lung disease, benefit-cost analysis of, 92
Brown Shoe case, 614
bubble, in antipollution measures, **452**
budget, federal, 14, **86**–87
  balancing of, 255–57
  full-employment budget vs., 259–61
  Keynesian emphasis on, 372
budget allocation rule, 482–85
budget line, 496–**97**
Buick Motor Company, 109
building construction, business fluctuations and, 188n
Bureau of Economic Analysis, 131, 286, 288–89
Bureau of Labor Statistics, 154, 165
Bureau of Mines, U.S., 543
Burke, Edmund, 93
Burke, Kelly, 73
Burns, Arthur F., 329, 348, 363
Burrows, James, 712n
business, see corporations; firms; *specific companies and industries*
business fluctuations (business cycles), 175, 186–92, **187**, 268–93
  avoidance of, 297
  budget balanced over, 257–58
  causes of, 268–79, 373
  forecasting of, 280–89
  as inventory cycle, 275–76
  monetarists vs. Keynesians on, 372–73
  overview of (1929–85), 188–92
  phases of, 187–88
  political, 277–78
  rational expectations and, 382–84
  turning points in, 273, 281–83, 289
  unemployment and, 153, 175, 186–91
  U.S., since 1860, 188–92
Butz, Earl, 81
Byrns, R., 15n

cable manufacturing, break-even chart and, 530
Canada, 171, 172, 451, 639n, 698
Cantor, A., 57n
capital, 161, 790
  accumulation of, 13, 34
  economic growth and, 30, 423–27
  as economic resource, 6
  existing stock of, in investment decision, 203

expected rate of return from, **201**, 202
firm's stock of, 270–71, 273
less developed countries' need for, 752–54
marginal product of, **423**–24
private ownership of, 31
roundabout production methods and, 659–60
capital budgeting, **658**
capital gains, **95**, 114
capital goods, 29–31, 219
capitalism, **31**–35
characteristics of, 31–33
future of, 161, 162, 796
in mixed economy, 34–35, 60
profits and losses as mainsprings of, 669–70
tasks of economic system and, 33–34
capitalists, **775**
capitalization of assets, **660**–61
capital-output ratio, **426**
Carpenters' Union, 639, 642
cartels, 591–92
price and output of, 592
see also Organization of Petroleum Exporting Countries
Carter, Anne, A21
Carter, Jimmy, 263, 289, 576, 791
Federal Reserve and, 349, 361, 363–64
Caves, R., 707n
Celler-Kefauver Anti-Merger Act (1950), 612, 614
Census Bureau, U.S., 688
central banks, **321**, 379n
see also Federal Reserve System
Chamberlin, Edward, 585, 588n
Chase Econometrics, 286, 289, 291
Chase Manhattan Bank, 350–51
checking accounts, *see* demand deposits
checkoff, **644**
Chenery, H., A22n
Chernenko, Konstantin, 787
China, People's Republic of, 32, 760, 788–91
Chiswick, B., 676n
choice:
freedom of, **32**, 65
public, theory of, 89–91
rational, 482–83
technology and, 7
Chorus Line, A, ticket pricing for, 57–58, 546
Chrysler, 124, 589
circular flows of money and products, 60, 140
Civil Aeronautics Board (CAB), 573
Civilisation (Clark), 413
Civil Rights Act (1964), 695
Civil War, U.S., 300–301, 389
Clark, Kenneth, 413
Clark, P., A22n
Clark medal, John Bates, 258, 490, 637
classical economics, 372
crude quantity theory in, 312–13, 313–15
rent in, 665
unemployment in, 158–60, 162–63, 215

class struggle, 774
Clausen, A. W., 770
Clayton Act (1914), 66, **611–12**
Clean Air Amendments (1970), 444
Cleveland, Grover, 613
Clorox, 614
closed shop, 644, **648**
Clothing Workers, 645
coal, coal industry, 437, 451–55, 624
perfect competition in, 546, 550, 553–54
supply curve for, 546
coincident series, **281**
coins, **297**
Coleman, Alan, 331n
collective bargaining, 400, 639, 641, **648**–49
college costs, opportunity cost and, 11
college teachers, exodus of, 667
collusion, 4, 35, 591–94, 606
barriers to, 593–94
cartels as, **591**, 592, 595
monopolistic competition and, 583–84
Comanor, W., 598n
command economy, **781**
Commerce Department, U.S., 131, 282, 283, 291, 681n, A21–A22
commercial banks, 303, 320, 321–44
balance sheets of, 325–26, 331, 333–34, 335–38
creation of money and, 331–39
functions of, 322
loans to, 350, 354–55
operations of, 324–25
reserves of, *see* reserves, bank
safety of, 328–31
Committee for Economic Development, 173
common stock, **113–14,** 115–17
risks of, 113, 115, 119
communism, 160–61, 774–92
capital and, 31–32, 790
interest rates and, 657–58
see also Soviet Union
Communist Manifesto (Marx), 775
competition, 4, 12, 32–33
of banks, 333, 339
government regulation and, 4–5, 66–67, 559, 575–76, 605, 617–24
in labor force, 160
labor productivity and, 3–4
monopolistic, *see* monopolistic competition
nonprice, 535, 597–98
perfect, *see* perfect competition
U.S. vs. foreign, 4, 110, 649, 706–7
complements, **475**–76
Comptroller of the Currency, 329
computers, 117, 428–29, 534, 615
in international trade, 699–703
conglomerate mergers, **589**, 614–15
Congress, U.S., 12, 67, 79, 153, 184–85, 278, 401, 447, 622
agricultural legislation and, 78, 79, 81–82
antitrust legislation and, 4, 66, 611
Armed Services Committee of, 73
in budgetary process, 87

Federal Reserve and, 320, 321, 348, 349, 352, 357, 365
Joint Economic Committee of, 247–48, 368
labor unions and, 641, 642, 643–44, 648
patents and, 619, 622
social insurance and, 684, 685–86
tax bills and, 91–93, 252–55, 263
see also House of Representatives, U.S.; Senate, U.S.
Congressional Budget and Impoundment Control Act (1974), 87
Congressional Budget Office, 87, 247, 695
Congress of Industrial Organizations (CIO), 639, 641–43
Connally, John, 365
Conoco, 4
conservatives, 259, 769
Federal Reserve and, 361, 367
government's role as viewed by, 63–64, 65
constant cost industries, **628**
constant dollars, 133–**34**
income in, **167**
price indexes and, 134–35
wages in, **168,** 382–83, 390, 629
constant returns to scale, **525,** 526
constraints, **A13**
consumer behavior model, 477–99
in decision making, 477
equilibrium market basket and, 482–85, **497**–98
indifference curves and, **497**–98
individual demand curves and, **486**–92
rational choice in, 482–85
tastes and preferences in, 479–81, 486–87
utility and, 480–85, 488, 496, 497–98
consumer credit, 652, 654
consumer demand curves, *see* individual demand curves
"consumer finance" companies, 322
Consumer Price Index, 165–66, 168, 289, 361, 388, 681n
consumers:
changes in market demand curves and, 41–42, 528–29
income levels of, 41–42, 53
price elasticity of demand and, 466
variety of, 53, 478
consumers' goods, **29**–31
consumer sovereignty, **33**–34, 35
consumers' surplus, **489**
consumer tastes and preferences, 479–81
individual demand curves and, 486–87
market demand curves and, 42, 51
utility and, 480–81
consumption, 141, 237–38, 377, 477–78
aggregate demand and, 177, 181, 182
changes in output and, 225–27, 229–30
economic growth and, 414
life-cycle hypothesis and, 200–201
nonincome determinants of, 225–26
permanent-income hypothesis and, 200–201, 254
stability of, 381
taxes on, 101
U.S., 269

consumption function, **196**–98
  changes in money supply and, 306*n*
  shifts in, 226–28, 228–30
contracts, 66
  tying, **612**
  yellow-dog, **641**
Cookenboo, Leslie, 501–2, 521*n*
Coolidge, Calvin, 500, 792
Cooper, Richard, 720
corn:
  demand and supply curves for, 462
  optimal input decisions and, 510–11, A10–A11
  perfect competition and, 550–53
Corn Laws, 422
corporations, **112**–18
  board of directors of, **113,** 117
  giant, 117
  income tax of, 97, 113, 248, 254, 255, 256, 386
  organization of, 109, 110, 116–17
  pros and cons of, 113
  separation of ownership from control in, 118, 119
  stock in, **113**–17
  types of securities issued by, 113–14
  unlimited life of, 113
  see also specific corporations
cosmetics, retail price maintenance and, **622**
cost functions, **514**–30
  average, *see* average costs
  break-even charts and, 527–30
  diminishing marginal returns and, **505,** 519
  long-run, 523–26, 527, 549, 560, 584–85
  marginal, *see* marginal cost
  measurement and application of, 526–30
  in monopolistic competition, 584–85
  in monopoly, 560, 562–65, 569, 580–81
  in perfect competition, 535–41, 542, 549–50, 570–71
  short-run, 514–23, 524, 527, 538–41, 584–85
  total, *see* total costs
Cost of Living Council, 400
cost-plus pricing, **596**–97
cost-push inflation, **389**–92, 405, 649
  Federal Reserve and, 390
costs, **513**–14
  alternative, *see* opportunity cost
  of goods sold, **122**–23
  historical, **572**
  implicit, **514**
  law of increasing, 26–27
  manufacturing, 122–26
  minimizing of, 507–11
  opportunity, *see* opportunity cost
  private, **438**
  reproduction, **572**
  social, *see* social costs
  of unemployment, 156–58
cotton, market demand curve for, 463
Council of Economic Advisers (CEA), 96, 105, 138, 156–57, 167, 171, 248,

249, 254, 255, 258, 290*n,* 367, 368, 391, 443, 447, 578, 691, 695, 745, 793
  forecasts by, 283, 285, 288, 289
  income policies and, 404
  tools of discretionary fiscal policy and, 251–53
  wage and price controls and, 400, 401
Council on Environmental Quality, 443–44
craft unions, **640,** 641, 642
Crandall, Robert, 92, 453
credit:
  availability of, 306–7, 309
  consumer, 652, 654
  for mortgages, 662
credit control, selective, **357**
credit items, **731**–35
credit unions, 327*n*
cross elasticity of demand, **475**
crowding-out effect, **378,** A8
Crown Packing Company, 541
crude-oil pipeline:
  cost functions and, 521–22, 524
  isoquants for, A8
  production function and, 501–2
crude quantity theory of money and prices, 312, 313–14, 372
Cultural Revolution, 789
currency, 295–**96,** 321, 341–43, 348
  appreciation of, **726**–27
  as debt, 300–301
  depreciation of, **726**–27, 738
  devaluation of, 81, **727**
  overvaluation of, **730,** 738
  undervaluation of, **730**–31
  see also dollars, U.S.; exchange rates
current assets, **121**
current dollars, **133**
  income in, *see* money income
  NNP in, 310
  price indexes and, 133–34
  wages in, **168,** 382, 390, 629
current liabilities, **122**
Customs Service, U.S., 105
cyclical unemployment, **153**

dairy farms, costs of, 522
damages assessment, opportunity cost and, 10, 15
dams, benefit-cost analysis and, 88
Danziger, S., 689*n*
Data Resources, Inc., 286, 289, 291
Dean, Joel, 527
debit items, **731**–35
debt, *see* liabilities; national debt
decision making, 33, 51, 202–4
  bank loans and, 329–31
  consumer behavior model and, 477
  in Federal Reserve, 360–61
  income elasticity of demand and, **474**–75
  market demand curves and, 459, 460, 461–63, 471–72
  price elasticity of demand and, 466–69, 470–72
  public goods and, 68
  role of economics in, 14

see also optimal input decisions
decreasing cost industries, **557**
decreasing returns to scale, **525,** 526
Defense Department, U.S., 88, 90, 511, 577, 635
defense expenditures, 64, 68, 71, 88, 190, 253, 737
  as destabilizing force, 276
  inefficiency and, 90–91
deficit financing, 247, 255–56, 264
  effects of, 261, 377
  full-employment budget vs., 259–61
  interpretation of, 262
deficits, **255**
  balance-of-payments, **730,** 731, 737–40
  elimination of, 738–39
DeHaven, J., 581*n,* A25*n*
demand, 459–99
  aggregate, 176–77, 178, 181–82, 383
  derived, **631**
  income elasticity of, 472–74, **474**
  market, *see* market demand
  for money, *see* money demand
  price elasticity of, *see* price elasticity of demand
demand curves:
  aggregate, *see* aggregate demand curves
  for energy, 450–51, 454
  firm, **472,** 561, 562, **629**–30
  foreign exchange market and, 725–26
  industry, *see* market demand curves
  kinked, 590–91
  for loanable funds, **653**
  market, *see* market demand curves
  money, *see* money demand curves
demand deposits, **297**–98, 322, 325
  as debts, 299
  insurance on, 330
  reserves in relation to, 331–32, 334–44, 352–54
demand management, supply-side economics vs., 385–86
demand-pull inflation, **388**–89, 391–92
democratic socialism, **791**–92
dentistry, price discrimination in, 574
depreciation, 123–26, 136–37, 144
  straight-line, **126**
depreciation of currency, **726**–27, 728, 738
depression, **187,** 189
  agriculture and, 76–77
  probability of, 279
  see also Great Depression
deregulation, in 1970s and 1980s, 4, 575–76
Desmond, Ralph, 329
devaluation of currency, 81, **727**
diamond-water paradox, 484
diffusion process in technological change, **427**
Dillon, Douglas, 253
diminishing marginal returns, law of, **416**–17, 419–20, 423, 427
  cost functions and, 505, 519
  optimal input combination and, 505–6
direct market experiment, **461**–63
direct regulation, **439,** 440–41, 442
discount rate, **354**–55, 360, 363

discrimination:
  balance-of-payments deficits and,
    737–38
  in employment, 156, 643
  poverty and, 690–95
  racial, 690–91
  reduction of, 695
  against women, 694–95
disinvestment, **214**–15
disposable income, **148**
  consumption function and, **196**–98,
    200–201
  life-cycle hypothesis and, 200–201
  NNP as equal to, 195, 205–6
  permanent-income hypothesis and,
    200–201
  saving function and, 198–200
  spending determined by, 205–6
dividends, **114,** 250
dollars, U.S.:
  constant, *see* constant dollars
  current, *see* current dollars
  deflation of, **134**
  devaluations of, 363
Domar, Evsey, 425n
Domencich, Thomas, 712n
dominant-firm model, **594**–96
Dornbusch, R., 304n
Doyle, Arthur Conan, 709–10
drugs, government regulation of, 66
Duchesneau, T., 554n
Duesenberry, James, 302, 361n
Dunlop, John, 401
Du Pont, 4, 202, 459, 622, 666
durable goods, 225, 375
Durant, William C., 109

Eastburn, D., 16n
Eastman Kodak, 598, 612, 620–21
Eaton, D., 437n
Eckert, J. Presper, 428
econometric models, **285**–88
  accuracy of, 288, 312
  large, 285–86
  nuts and bolts of, 286–88
economic growth, 413–57
  aggregate production function and,
    415–16
  in agriculture, 76
  capital formation and, 423–26
  diminishing marginal returns and,
    415–17, 419, 423, 427–28
  education and, 426–27, 429–30
  environmental and energy problems
    and, 436–57
  exchange rates and, 727
  human capital's role in, 426–27
  in less developed countries, 23, 413,
    760–71
  measures of, 414
  natural resources and, 415
  output gap and, 433
  population growth and, 417–21
  price system and, 54
  production possibilities curve and,
    28–31, 414–15, 429
  Ricardo's contributions to theory of,
    422–25

social environment and, 431–33
in Soviet Union, 761, 784–87
as task of economic system, 23, 34
technological change and, 415, 417,
  420, 425, 427–30
economic measurements, 20–22
economic models, *see* models, economic
economic problems, 1–17
  analysis and, 1–17
  sampler of, 1–5
economic resources, **5**–6
economics, **5**–8
  contemporary influence of, 12–14
  introduction to, 1–36
  methodology of, 19–20
  social impact of, 11–16
Economics of Welfare (Pigou), 158
Economic Stabilization Agency, 400
economic systems, 22–35
  capitalism as, 31–34
  introductory model for, 23–34
  tasks of, 7–8, 22–23, 26–31, 33–34,
    50–56
economies of scale, 559, 588–89, 706
Edison, Thomas, 589–90
education, 11, 71, 636
  economic growth and, 426–27, 430
  investment in, 426–27
  as public good, 68
  wage differentials and, 633, 636
efficiency, 4, 27–28, 33–34, 35, 54, 59, 415
  of government, 89–91
  income inequality and, 679–80
  of incomes policies, 404
  of monopolistic competition, 585,
    586–87
  of monopoly, 571, 576–77
  profits as reward for, 669
  regulation and, 576–78
  of Soviet economy, 786–87
  of U.S. agriculture, 76, 78
  of wage and price controls, 400
effluent fees, **439,** 441–42
Eisenhower, Dwight D., 259, 289, 712
elasticity of demand:
  arc, **465**
  cross, 475
  income, 473–**74**
  price, *see* price elasticity of demand
elasticity of supply, price, **545**
elderly, inflation's impact on, 167–69
electrical equipment industry, 117, 588
  collusion in, 591–93, 594
Electrical Workers, 639
electric power industry:
  as monopoly, 559–60, 572
  pollution and, 437, 438–39
electronics industry, external economies
  in, 64
Elzinga, Kenneth, 473
employment:
  agricultural, 76
  discrimination in, 156–57, 643
  full, *see* full employment
  as measure of job availability, 159
  see also unemployment
Employment Act (1946), 67, 153, 173,
  247

energy, 436, 448–56
  economic growth and, 449–50
  electrical, 437, 438–39, 559–60, 572
  environment and, 437–38
  new technologies and, 451–55
  public policy toward, 450–55
  R and D, 451
  shortages, 448–49
  see also coal, coal industry; oil;
    Organization of Petroleum Exporting
    Countries
Engels, Friedrich, 775
ENIAC, 428
entrepreneurs:
  economic growth and, 431–33
  in less-developed countries, 757
environmental policy, recent directions
  in, 447
environmental problems, 436–48
  energy and, 437–38
  see also pollution
Environmental Protection Agency (EPA),
  90, 444, 447, 448, 452
environmental quality:
  goals of, 444–47
  government regulation of, 65, 69,
    439–444
  as public good, 64
Equal Pay Act (1963), 695
equation of exchange, 311–12, 314–15,
  372
equilibrium, **44, 205**
  interest and, 359–60, 376–77, 653–56
  in long run, 549–50, 556–57, 565–66,
    584–85
  monopolistic competition and, 584–85
  monopoly and, 564
  partial vs. general, A18–A19
  perfect competition and, 546, 549–50,
    554, 556–57, 629–30, 632–33
  in short run, 546–47, 564, 584
  wages and, 629–30, 637–38
equilibrium market basket, 482–83,
  497–98
equilibrium NNP, 205–15, 227–28, 230,
  236–45, **243,** 308, 309–10, 395
  full employment and, 215, 245, 309
  government expenditures and, 236–38,
    242–44, 266–67
  graphical determination of, 208–9
  income determined by, 205
  IS-LM analysis and, A4
  spending as equal to, 205, 206–8,
    237–38
  taxation and, 236–37, 239–44
equilibrium price, **44**–50, 53
  actual price vs., 45–46
  aggregate demand and supply and, 180
  in agriculture, 44–45, 48, 77–78, 79–80
  foreign exchange and, 725–27
  labor and, 632
  market demand curves and, 44–45,
    48–49
  market supply curves and, 44–45,
    49–50
  tax incidence and, 98–100
Essay on the Principle of Population
  (Malthus), 418

European Economic Community (EEC; Common Market), 617, 706, **716,** 719

Evans, Michael, 288*n*

excess reserves, **335,** 336–44, 348, 350, 375

exchange rates, 723–48, **724**
  balance of payments and, 730–35, 737–40, 745–46, 747
  fixed, 728–29, 740–42, 743
  flexible, 725–28, 740–42, 744
  under gold standard, **724**–25, 727
  international transactions and, 723–24
  pre-World War II experience with, 736

excise taxes, 75, 98–100, 677*n*

expansions in business cycle, **187,** 188, 190–91, 268–69, 272, 278, 281–82

expectations:
  business, 203, 273–74
  business fluctuations and, 273–74
  changes in discount rate and, 355
  consumption and, 226
  inflation and, 397, 404
  in less developed countries, 750–51
  rational, 371, 382–84
  short-run Phillips curve and, 397

expected rate of return from capital, **201**–2

expenditures:
  aggregate demand curves and, 177–78, 180–83
  consumption, *see* consumption
  crowding-out effect and, **378**
  disposable income as determiner of, 205–6
  government, *see* government expenditures
  investment, *see* investment
  total, interest rate and 375
  total, unemployment determined by, 158
  see also income-expenditure analysis

expenditures approach to GNP, **140,** 141–43

Export-Import Bank, U.S., 794

exports, **697**–98
  balance between imports and, 724–25
  net, **142**

export subsidies, **711**–12

external diseconomies, **64, 438**
  social costs of, 64, 69, 438–39

external economies, **64**–65, 69

Exxon Corporation, 117, 118

Fair, Ray C., 289

Fairchild (electronics firm), 64

Fair Labor Standards Act, 692

farm problem, 76–79
  causes of, 77–79
  price elasticity of demand and, 470–72
  solution of, 83

farm programs, 59, 78–83
  as automatic stabilizer, 250
  evaluation of, 82–83

featherbedding, **647**

Fechter, A., 635*n*

Federal Advisory Council, 321

Federal Bank Commission, 329

Federal Communications Commission (FCC), 4, 572

Federal Deposit Insurance Corporation (FDIC), 73, 325, 329, 330

Federal Energy Regulatory Commission, 572, 573

Federal Labor Relations Authority, 646

Federal Mediation Service, 644

Federal Open Market Committee (FOMC), 320, 321, 348, 352, 406–7

Federal Reserve Bank of Minneapolis, 320, 383

Federal Reserve Bank of New York, 320, 352, 364

Federal Reserve Bank of Philadelphia, 288, 320

Federal Reserve Bank of St. Louis, 310, 320, 368

Federal Reserve Bank of San Francisco, 320, 327

Federal Reserve Banks, 320, 321, 327
  consolidated balance sheet of, 349–50, 354
  reserves held by, *see* reserves, bank
  Treasury deposits in, 350

Federal Reserve Board, 285, 348, 349, 358, 362, 695
  functions of, 320–21
  legal reserve requirements changed by, 352–54
  vacancies on, 349, 364

Federal Reserve System, 72–73, 251, 278, 319–21, 655, 656
  Board of Governors of, *see* Federal Reserve Board
  cost-push inflation and, 390
  decision making in, 360–61
  functions of, 321
  independence of, 365
  open market operations of, **350**–52, 354, 355
  organization of, 320–21, 348, 365
  performance of, 366–67
  rule-governed, 368–69, 379, 381
  tools of, 349–57
  see also interest rates; money supply

Federal Trade Commission (FTC), 66, 612, 622*n*

Federal Trade Commission Act (1914), 612

Feldstein, Martin, 154, 258, 685

Fellner, W., 676*n*

financial reform act (1980), 298, 322*n*

Finger, J., 771*n*

firm demand curves, **472,** 561, 562
  for labor, **629**–30

firms, 108–29
  balance sheets of, **121**–22, 350–51
  case study of, 108–9
  characteristics of, 110–12
  competition of, 4, 12, 32–33, 66
  concentration of economic power and, 609
  expectations of, 203, 273–74
  importance of, 108
  incomes policies and, 402–5
  income statements of, **122**–27
  inputs of, **120**

legal structures of, 111–13

linear programming theory of, **A11**–A18

losses of, 34, 51, 112–14, 160, 539–41, 565

market structure and, 533–625

motivation of, 118–19

multinational, **707**–8, 768

net worth of, **122**

organization of, 109, 110, 111–13, 117

profit maximization as assumption for, 118–19, 121

size of, 4, 110, 111

stock of capital of, 270–71, 273

see also corporations; cost functions; investment; production function; research and development

firm supply curves, **541,** 542, 544

First Pennsylvania Bank and Trust Company, 322

fiscal policy, 184–85, 236–67
  aggregate demand curves and, 180–83
  case studies of, 253–55
  deficit vs. surplus financing and, 247, 255–59, 259–61
  income policies vs., 405
  IS curves and, A4–A6
  Keynesian emphasis on, 372
  makers of, 246–48
  monetarists vs. Keynesians on effects of, 377–79, 380–82, A4–A8
  monetary policy vs. 346, 347, 367
  national output and, 236–67, 310, A6–A8
  nature and objectives of, 245–46
  political use of, 277–78
  recent American experience with, 262–64
  tools of, 251–52
  see also tax cuts; taxes

Fischer, S., 304*n*

Fisher, Frank, 598

Fisher, Irving, 171, 310

five-year plans, 764–65, 779, 788

fixed assets, **121**

fixed exchange rates, 728–30, 740–42
  IMF under, 743

fixed inputs, **502**

flexible exchange rates, 725–28, 740–43
  adjustment mechanism under, 728
  determinants of, 727–28
  IMF under, 744

Fogarty, Thomas, 473

Food and Agricultural Act (1977), 82

Food and Commercial Workers, 639

food-stamp program, 686–87, 688

Ford, Gerald, 244, 254, 289
  fiscal policy of, 262–63
  inflation control and, 183, 262–63

Ford, Henry, 468, 666

Ford Foundation, 757

Ford Motor Company, 459, 468, 589

forecasts, economic, 131, 220, 268, 280–93, 290
  accuracy of, 228–30, 280–81, 288–89
  with econometric models, **285**–89, 310–11, 384–85
  of GNP, 228–29, 281–82

good performance in, 281, 288
in investment decision, 203
leading indicators in, **281**–82
monetary policy and, 364–67
noneconomic forecasts vs., 281
politics and, 289
simple aggregate models in, 283–84
foreign aid, 753, 766–69
Fortune magazine, 164, 283, 624
Fox, Karl, 464
fractional-reserve banking, **326**–27
France, 75, 172, 719, 791
  international trade of, 697–98, 699–703
Franklin National Bank, 329
Fraser, Douglas, 639
freedom of choice, **32**, 65, 786
free enterprise, 12, 13, **32**
Freeman, Richard, 427
free resources, **6**
free trade, 422–23
  barriers to, 709–18, 739
frictional unemployment, **152**, 156–57
Friedland, Claire, 573
Friedman, Milton, 36n, 65, 75n, 89, 250, 315–16, 372, 381, 411
  Great Depression and, 379
  indexation and, 170
  long-run Phillips curve and, 395, 399
  permanent-income hypothesis of, 200–201
  quantity of money as viewed by, 310
  rule for Federal Reserve advocated by, 368–69, 379
Friend, Irwin, 286n
Friend-Taubman model, 286n, 288
Frisch, Ragnar, 275
full employment, 67, **156–57**, 273, 388
  as assumption of crude quantity theory, 313, 314
  creation of money and, 106, 346
  economic growth and, 433
  NNP and, 215, 245, 309, 372, 373, 426
  price and wage reductions and, 163
  production possibilities curve and, 27
  range of aggregate supply curve and, 179
full-employment budget, **259**–60
functional finance, **259**

Galbraith, John Kenneth, 65, 89, 624
  monopoly defended by, 607–8, 609
games, theory of, oligopoly and, 602–4
Gandhi, Indira, 765
Gary, Elbert, 594–95, 641
gasoline:
  rationing of, 59
  taxes on, 75, 94, 466
Gebhardt, Richard, 96
General Agreement on Tariffs and Trade (GATT), 716
General Electric, 117, 145, 567, 614, 620–21
  econometric forecasts by, 289
  as oligopoly, 589, 594, 596
general equilibrium analysis, A18–A22
General Motors Corporation, 350–51, 526
  economic power of, 609

as oligopoly, 588–89, 596–97
organization chart for, 177
securities issued by, 114, 115
in short run vs. long run, 502–3
General Theory of Employment, Interest, and Money (Keynes), 162, 384
geologists, wages of, 634
George, Henry, 665
Germany, Federal Republic of, 75, 172, 617, 719
  exchange rates and, 725–26, 727–28, 729
  foreign aid by, 769
  international trade of, 697–98
  labor productivity in, 3
  pollution control in, 442
Germany, Weimar, inflation in, 164–65, 170, 301, 313
Giannini, Amadeo Peter, 322–23
Gill, Richard, 757, 765n
GNP, *see* gross national product
gold, 296
  discovery of, 313–14
  paper, 744
  price of, 296, 313
gold-exchange standard, 736–**37**
Goldfeld, Stephen, 304n
Goldschmid, H., 600n
gold standard, **724**, 736–37, 745
  exchange rates under, 724–25, 727
Gompers, Samuel, 640–41
goods:
  capital, **29**–31, 219
  consumers', **29**–31
  durable, 225, 375
  intermediate, **132**
  public, **64**, 68
  publicly provided vs. privately provided, 89
  quality changes in, limitations of GNP and NNP and, 138
  secondhand, GNP and, 133
goods and services:
  distribution of, 22–23, 34, 53–54, 55–56
  final, **132**
  government purchases of, 142, 277
  production decisions for, 22–23, 27–29, 33, 51–53
Gorbachev, Mikhail, 787
Gordon, David, 795
Gordon, Robert J., 362, 366n, 382n, 402
Gorsuch, Anne, 447
Gosbank, 780
Gosplan, 779
government, 60, 63–85
  agricultural role of, 59, 76–83
  bonds issued by, 169, 170–71, 324, 349–50
  bureaucratic inefficiency in, 90–91
  capitalism vs., 32, 34–35
  capital owned by, 32
  changes in views of responsibilities of, 72–73
  conservatives vs. liberals on, 63, 65
  control of balance-of-payments deficits by, 738–40
  criticism of, 5, 11, 65, 89–91

demand and supply of loanable funds and, 654, 655–56
economic stability as responsibility of, 67
goods and services purchased by, 142, 276
inflation control by, 2–3, 68, 183, 190, 191, 236, 251–52, 263, 279, 346, 347, 358–68, 394, 399, 400–410
monopoly created by, 559
pollution control and, 439–44
price system vs., 58–59, 63–64, 83
"rules of the game" set by, 66
scope and efficiency of, 89
size and nature of, 69–71
summary of economic role of, 84–85
unemployment combated by, 67, 153, 162, 182–83, 191, 236, 251–55, 263, 399
  see also regulation, regulatory agencies; *specific agencies*
government expenditures, U.S., 86–106
  alternative financing of, 104–6
  balanced-budget multiplier and, 244, 266–67
  benefit-cost analysis of, 87–88
  budget for, 86–87
  changes in money supply and, 306n
  for defense, 64, 68, 71, 90–91, 190, 253–54, 276, 737
  fiscal, 72
  forecasts of, 283
  for foreign aid, 766–69
  as injection, 243–44
  national debt and, 102–4, 105
  NNP and, 236–39, 242–44, 266–67
  optimal level of, 252
  state and local expenditures vs., 71–72
  taxation and, 91–93
  theory of public choice and, 89–91
  variation in, business fluctuations and, 276
government intervention, exchange rates and, 729–30
government role, in less developed countries, 758–60
Gramlich, E., 88n
graphs, construction and interpretation of, 21–22
Great Britain, 30, 75, 172, 426, 610, 719
  banks in, 321
  economic growth in, 761
  exchange rates and, 724–25, 728, 729–30
  international trade of, 697–98, 703n, 704–5
  socialism in, 791–92
Great Depression, 67, 110, 368, 372, 410
  aggregate demand curve and, 189
  agriculture in, 76
  excess reserves in, 343, 375
  Keynes and, 162, 179
  labor unions in, 641
  monetarists vs. Keynesians on causes of, 379
  unemployment in, 1, 67, 153, 155, 182, 189
Great Leap Forward, 788–89

Greenleigh Associates, 88
green revolution, **757**
Griliches, Zvi, 598
gross national product (GNP), **131**–46, 290–91
  avoiding double counting in, 132
  exclusions from, 132–33
  expenditures approach to, **140**–43
  forecasting of, 228–30, 281–89
  gap, 433
  importance of, 131
  income approach to, **140**, 143–46
  limitations of, 137–38
  national income derived from, 147
  potential, **156**–57, **187**, 189, 415, 433
  price changes and, 133–35
  real, **134**–35, 176, 186–87, 189, 190, 366n, 414
  tax cuts and, 252
  valuation at cost in, 132
  value-added in calculation of, 135–**36**
gross private domestic investment, **141**–42, 189, 269
growth, growth rates, *see* economic growth
Gurley, John, 790

Hamermesh, Daniel, 693
Hamilton, Alexander, 713
Hansen, Alvin, 188n
Hargreaves, James, 432
Harrod, R. F., 425n
Harrod-Domar growth model, 425n
Hartford Fire Insurance Company, 614
Hartke-Burke bill, 718
Heady, Earl, 25n, 510, A10–A11
health care, as public good, 68
Heilbroner, R., 418n
Heller, Walter W., 253
Hemingway, Ernest, 171
Hendry, J. B., 550n
Heraclitus, 48
Heston, Alan, 750n
Hicks, Sir John, 271–72, 643, A1
Hildebrand, George, 719
Hirshleifer, J., 581n, A25n
historical costs, **572**
Hollomon, Herbert, 427
horizontal mergers, **589**
Hotelling, Harold, 580–81
House of Representatives, U.S.:
  Budget Committee of, 87, 247
  Ways and Means Committee of, 93, 247
housing, price ceilings and, 58–59
Houthakker, Hendrik, 465n, 720
Howe Company, investment at, 272
Howrey, Phillip, 385
Hudson, Edward, 450
human wants, **5**–6
Hume, David, 698, 725, 736
Humphrey-Hawkins Act (1978), 153n
Hunt family, 54
Husic, F., 609n
Hutcheson, William, 642
Hymans, Saul, 385

illegal aliens, economic effects of, 676
implicit costs, **514**

imports, **698**
  balance between exports and, 725
income:
  break-even, **687**
  capital gains, 95, **114**
  changes in market demand and, 42, 76
  disposable, *see* disposable income
  farm vs. nonfarm, 76–77
  future, present value of, 661–63
  individual demand curves and, 486–87
  in less developed countries, 5, 749–50, 751, 752
  money, **167**–69, 474, 482
  national, 131, 147, 148
  NNP as determiner of, 205–6
  personal, 147, **148**
  proprietors', 144
  real, **167**
income approach to GNP, **140**, 143–44
income distribution, 627–95
  in China, 790–91
  by country, 673
  as determinant of consumption, 226
  determinants of wages and, 627–51
  functional, 669–70
  government's role in, 34–35, 63–64, 67, 676–77
  inequality of, *see* income inequality
  inflation's impact on, 167–70
  interest, rent, and profits and, 652–70
  in monopoly, 571
  price system and, 53–54, 63–64
  production possibilities curve and, 28–29
  Ricardo on, 422–23
  in Soviet Union, 783–84
  taxes and, 35, 67, 676–78
  U.S., 5, 479, 673
income effect, individual demand curves and, 488–89
income elasticity of demand, 472–**74**
income-expenditure analysis, 195–216
  aggregate demand and supply curves reconciled with, 209
  aggregate flows in, 205–7
  consumption function and, **196**–98, 200–201
  investment and, 200–204, 214–15
  leakage-injection approach to, 210–15, 243–44
  saving function and, 198–200
  simplifying assumptions for, 195–96
income inequality, 672–96
  effects of tax structure on, 676–78
  efficiency and, 679–80
  in less developed countries, 750–52
  Lorenz curve and, **674**–75, 677
  pros and cons of, 678–79
  quantity of, 672–73
  reasons for, 674
  trends in, 675
  see also poverty
incomes policies, **402**–4, 410
  Kennedy-Johnson guidelines as, 403, 404–5
  tax-based, 405–9
income statemens, **122**–27
income tax, 68, 74–75, 94–96, 263, 677–78

ability-to-pay principle and, 94
  as automatic stabilizer, 248
  capital gains, **95**
  corporate, 97, 113, 248, 253–54, 255, 263, 385–86
  double, 97, **113**
  effect on income inequality of, 95
  legal tax avoidance and, 95–97
  marginal tax rate and, **95**
  negative, **687**–88
  reduction of, 100–102, 254, 262–63, 385–86
  schedule for, 95
increasing cost, law of, 26–27
increasing cost industries, **556**–57
increasing returns to scale, **525**–26
indexation, inflation and, 170–71
India, 751, 760, 761
  development planning in, 764–65
indifference curves, **494**–99
  budget line and, 496–**97**
  characteristics of, 495–96
  utility and, 496
individual demand curves, **486**–92
  downward slope of, 488–89, 492
  indifference curves in derivation of, 498–99
  influences on, 486–87
  market demand curves derived from, 491–92
industrial bank, proposed, 125
industrial concentration, 610–11
industrial policy, 124–25
industrial unions, 641, 642
industry demand curves, *see* market demand curves
inflation, 151, 164–74, 388–412
  aggregate supply curves and, 384–85, 390, 391, 395
  anticipated vs. unanticipated, 169
  as arbitrary "tax," 169–70
  automatic stabilizers of, **248**–50
  balance-of-payments deficits and, 738
  cost-push, **389**–91, 400, 405, 649
  creeping, **164**, 165, 170
  demand-pull, **388**–89, 391–92, 405
  econometric models and, 289
  fiscal policy for, 256
  government vs., 2, 67, 183, 190, 191, 236, 251–52, 263, 279, 346, 347, 359–69, 394
  impact of, 167–70
  incomes policies as control on, 402–9
  indexation and, 170–71
  measurement of, 165–66
  new money as cause of, 104
  Phillips curve and, 392–99
  rational expectations and, 398
  redistributive effects of, 167–69
  runaway, **164**, 165, 301, 308, 313
  unemployment and, 1–2, 60, 106, 171–73, 190, 262–63, 392–94, 395, 410
  wars and, 166, 190, 252, 276, 300–301, 362, 368, 389
inflationary gaps, **245**
injections, **210**
  see also leakage-injection approach
injunctions, **640**

innovation, **427**–28
  irregularity of, 219
  profits and, 54, 666–68
  timing of, 274–75
innovators, **427**–28, **666**–68
input-output analysis, A19–A22
  applicability of, A21–A22
  numerical example of, A20
inputs, **120**
  average product of, **417, 503,** 504–5
  economic growth and, 415–27
  marginal product of, **417,** 419–20,
    423–24, 506–11, 630
  monopoly of, 559
  prices of, 44, 381, 542–43
  primary, **659**–60
  production function and, 501–2
  in short run vs. long run, 502–3
  types of, 502
  see also optimal input decisions
interest, interest rates, 143, 160, **201**–2,
    358–59, **652**–63
  on bonds, 306, 307–9, 361, 652–53
  capital budgeting and, **658**
  capitalization of assets and, **660**–61
  ceilings on, 355–57
  as determinants of investment, 202,
    358–59
  determination of, 653–56
  discount rate of, **354**–55, 360, 363
  equilibrium level of, 359–60, 375–76,
    653–56
  exchange rates and, 728
  functions of, 656–57
  increases in money supply and, 306–7,
    347
  increases in price levels and, 177
  investment decision and, 204, 375
  monetarists vs. Keynesians on, 373–79
  money demand curves and, 304–5,
    307, 308–9, 360, 374–75, 376–77
  money supply vs., 359–60
  nature of, 652–53
  present value of future income and,
    661–63
  pure rate of, **653**
  real vs. nominal, **358**
  taxes on, 95–96, 97
  total expenditures and, 375, 376–77
  total output reduced by increases in,
    177–78
intermediate goods, **132**
Internal Revenue Service, 92, 105, 409
International Bank for Reconstruction and
    Development (World Bank), 765,
    769–70
International Business Machines
    Corporation (IBM), 108–10, 428
International Development Agency, 770
International Finance Corporation, 770
International Harvester, 612–13
International Ladies' Garment Workers,
    646
international lender, U.S. as, 745–46
International Monetary Fund (IMF),
    743–46, 794, 823
International Nickel Company, 559
International Telephone and Telegraph
    (ITT), 614

international trade, 422–23, 697–722
  absolute advantage and, 699–**700**
  barriers to, 709–18, 738–39
  comparative advantages and, 700–702,
    701, 703–5
  economies of scale and learning in, 706
  individual markets and, 703–5
  innovation and, 706–7
  multinational firms in, **707**–8
  specialization and, 698–99, 703
  U.S. exports vs. imports in, 697–98
international unions, 639
Interstate Commerce Commission (ICC),
    72, 572, 575–76
inventors, independent, 429
inventory cycles, **275**–76
investment, 189, 218–24, 230, 237–38,
    276
  acceleration principle and, 269–73
  actual vs. intended, 214–15
  aggregate demand and, 177, 181–82
  autonomous change in, **220**–24, 230
  business fluctuations and, 268–73
  in classical economies, 158–60
  economic growth and, 423–27
  gross private domestic, **141**–42, 189,
    269
  induced change in, **220**, 230
  interest rates and, 204, 306–8, 358–59,
    375, 378, 652–54, 658
  in less developed countries, 753–54,
    766
  magnified percentage changes in, 271
  net private domestic, 141–**42**, 201–2,
    202–4
  savings in relation to, 160, 163,
    214–15, **221**–22, 322
  U.S. balance-of-payments deficits,
    737–38, 739
  volatility of, 218–19, 269
Investment Bankers Association, 105
investment function, **213**
  effects of increases in money supply on,
    306–7, 347
  shifts in, 231, 306–7, 308
investment tax credit, 254–55, 262
"invisible hand," Smith on, 12, 13
IS curves, 371n, A1–A8
  definition and derivation of, A2–A3
  fiscal policy and, A4–A6
isocost curves, A8–A11, **A10**
  linear programming and, A14–A18
isoquants, **A8**–A11
  linear programming and, A14–A18
Israel, 171, 449
Italy, 172, 719
  economic growth in, 697–98
  international trade of, 697–98

Japan, 80, 172, 529, 610, 617, 698
  economic growth in, 762
  foreign aid by, 769
  investment rate in, 426
  unemployment in, 172
  U.S. competition with, 3, 649, 707, 737
Johnson, Lyndon B., 73, 183, 253–54,
    289, 635
  see also Kennedy-Johnson guidelines
Johnson, Samuel, 119, 686

Jones, R., 707n
Jorgensen, Dale, 450
Justice Department, U.S., 592
  Antitrust Division of, 612, 613–15

Kapital, Das (Marx), 160–61, 775–77
Kasten, Robert, 96
Kaysen, Carl, 598, 616
Kemp, Jack, 96
Kennedy, John F., 73, 182, 253, 289
Kennedy-Johnson guidelines, 403
  criticism of, 404–5
"Kennedy Round" negotiations, 716
Keynes, John Maynard, 116, 117,
    162–63, 373, 384, 743
  classical economics criticized by,
    162–63
  Great Depression and, 162–63, 179
  liquidity preference theory of, 656
  saving as viewed by, 385
Keynesian-monetarist debate, 309–10,
    347, 371–82
  business fluctuations and, 373
  current state of, 380–82
  fiscal policy effects and, 377–79
  historical background of, 372
  interest rates and, 374–75
  IS-LM model of, 371n, A1–A8
  monetary policy effects and, 376–77
  monetary rule and, 379–80
  stability of economy and, 373
Khrushchev, Nikita, 778
Kindleberger, Charles, 707n
kinked demand curve, 590–91
Kinney, R. G., 614
Kirkland, Lane, 643
Kneese, Allen, 440n, 442n, 445
Knight, Frank, 668
Korean War, 400
  inflation and, 166, 190, 276
Krause, Lawrence, 707
Kravis, Irving, 750n
Kreps, Juanita, 399, 695
Kuznets, Simon, 131, 188n, 760
Kuznets cycles, 188n

labor, labor force, 13, **154,** 404, 627–51,
    636
  average product of, **417,** 503, 504–5
  economic growth and, 414–17
  as economic resource, 6
  equilibrium price and, 632
  firm demand curve for, **629**–30
  government's role in, 73–74, 641–42,
    643, 646
  marginal product of, 403–5, **417,**
    419–20, 630
  market demand curves for, **630**–31,
    645, 647
  market supply curves for, **631**–32, 645,
    647–48
  mobility of, **637**
  monopsony and, **637**–38, 646
  perfect competition and, 629–37
  price of, 628–29, 632–33, 647–48
  as primary input, **659**–60
  profit-maximizing quantity of, 629–30
  U.S. occupational composition of, 628
  see also income; unemployment; wages

laboratory experimentation in economics, 548
Labor Department, U.S., 291, A21
labor productivity, 2–3, **393**, 389–90, 403–4
  slowdowns in, 2–3
  technological change and, 430
labor unions, 639–49
  big, pros and cons of, 649
  cost-push inflation and, 389–90, 391, 649
  early history of, 640–41
  incomes policies and, 403–9
  internal problems of, 643–44
  national vs. local, **639**
  in New Deal and World War II, 641–42
  post-World War II developments in, 642–43
  recent membership trends in, 644–46
  technological change and, 430
  wages increased by, 647–48
  see also specific unions
Laffer, Arthur, 100–102
Laffer curve, **102**
lagging series, **281**
Lamb, Charles, 631, 652
Lampman, Robert, 683
land, **664**
  as economic resource, 6
  opportunity cost and, 10–11
  as primary input, **659**
Landrum-Griffin Act (1959), 644
Lave, Lester, 438n, 447
leading indicators, **281**–82, 283
leading series, **281**
leakage-injection approach, 210–15, 243–44
  actual saving equals actual investment and, 214–15
  graphical view of, 213
  numerical example of, 212–13
  usefulness of, 215
leakages, **210**
Leftwich, R., 454n
Lehrman, L., 745n
leisure, GNP and, 137–38, 414
Lenin, V. I., 778
Leontief, Wassily, A19–A20
Leo, XIII, Pope, 151
Lerner, Abba, 259n, 580
L'Esperance, W., 545n
less developed countries (LDCs), 81, **749**–73
  balanced growth in, 760–62
  barriers to development in, 752–54
  characteristics of, 749–52
  development planning in, 762–65
  economic growth in, 23, 413, 760–71
  entrepreneurship and social institutions in, 757
  foreign aid to, **753**, 766–69
  government's role in, 758–60
  industrialization in, 761–62, 763
  investment selection in, 766
  labor in, 753, 759
  lack of capital in, 752–54
  natural resources in, 758

population growth in, 420, 754–56
poverty in, 749–57
technology in, 756–57, 768
Lever Brothers, 603–4
Levine, H., 779n
Lewis, John L., 641–42
Lewis, W. Arthur, 759
liabilities:
  on balance sheets, 121–22, 325–26, 335–37, 349–50
  current, **122**
  of Federal Reserve Banks, 349, 350
  long-term, **122**
  type of business organization and, 111–13
liberals, 769
  Federal Reserve criticized by, 364, 367
  government's role as viewed by, 63–64, 65–66
  rational expectations theory challenged by, 383
life-cycle hypothesis, 200–201
lighthouses, as public goods, 68
Limits to Growth, The, 449
linear programming, 763, **A11**–A18
  case study of, A13–A18
  management science and, A18
Ling-Temco-Vought, 614
liquidity preference theory, **656**
Little, S., 57n
Litton Industries, 614
LM curves, 371n, A1–A8
  definition and derivation of, A3–A4
  monetary policy and, A6
loanable funds theory, **653**–54
local governments:
  bonds issued by, 95, 324
  expenditures of, 72
  tax revenues of, 75
local unions, **639**, 643
Lone Star National Bank, 329
long run, **502**–3
  cost functions in, 523–24, 527, 549, 560, 584–85
  equilibrium in, 549–50, 554, 556–57, 565, 584–85
  government expenditures in, 252
  monopolistic competition in, 584–85
  monopoly in, 564–65
  NNP in, 310
  perfect competition in, 547–50, 551–53, 556–57
  Phillips curve in, 395–99
  as planning horizon, 502–3
  price and output in, 547, 565–56
long-term liabilities, **122**
Lorenz curves, **674**–75, 677
Lucas, Robert, 482–83
Luxembourg, 719

M-1, *see* money supply, narrow definition of
M-2, *see* money supply, broad definition of
McDonald's, 693
Machinists' Union, 639
McKean, R., 97n
McKinsey and Company, 513

McNamara, Robert, 770
McNees, Stephen, 289n
Madison, A., 754n
Malkiel, Burton, 116
Malthus, Thomas, 417–20, 422, 755
management, 500, 645, 648
  economic growth and, 429–30, 431
  in Soviet Union, 781
management science, linear programming and, A18–A19
Mancke, R., 450n
Mandatory Oil Import Quota (1959), 712
Mann, H. M., 600n
Mansfield, E., 55n, 65n, 93n, 97n, 418n, 428n, 440n, 608n, 617n, 680n, 791n
marginal cost, **518**–21, **562**
  average costs in relation to, 519–21
  diminishing returns and, 519
  measurement of, 527
  in monopolistic competition, 584–85
  in monopoly, 564–65, 567, 569, 580–81
  in perfect competition, 538–40, 541, 549–50, 570
marginal-cost pricing, 572n, **580**–81
marginal product, **504**
  of capital, 423–24
  optimal input decisions and, 507–11
marginal product of labor, **417**, 419–20, 503–4
  value of, **630**
marginal propensity to consume, 196–**97**, 200, 220
marginal propensity to save, **199**–200, 220
marginal returns, law of diminishing, 415–17, **416**, 419, 423, 427, 505–6
marginal revenue, **561**–62
  in monopolistic competition, 584–85
  in monopoly, 560–62, 564–65
  in oligopoly, 591
marginal tax rate, **95**
marginal utility, **481**–85, 498
  law of diminishing, **481**–82, 488
  marginal product and, **504**
margin requirements, **357**
market concentration ratio, **610**–11
market demand, 40–43, 44, 55–58
  cross elasticity of demand and, 475
  income elasticity of demand and, 473–74
  increase vs. decrease in, 42
market demand curves, **40**–43, 175, 459–76
  aggregate demand curves compared to, 176–77, 180–81
  changes in, 41–43, 48–49, 180–81, 460
  effects of externalities on, 69
  equilibrium price and, 44–45, 48–49
  for farm products, 77–78, 81, 462, 463, 464, 470–72
  individual demand curves compared to, 486
  individual demand curves in derivation of, 491–92
  for labor, **630**–31, 645, 647–48
  market supply curves compared to, 545
  measurement of, 460–61

in monopoly, 559–60, 561–62
in perfect competition, 546–47, 552, 556–57, 566–67, 630–31
price elasticity of demand and, **463**–72, 630–31
production decisions and, 51, 459, 460
speculation and, 462
tax incidence and, 98–100
market performance, **616**
market period, **546,** 547
markets:
in agriculture, 77–78, 79–81, 82–83
capitalism's reliance on, 33
foreign exchange, 725–28
international trade and, 703–5
product, **60**
resource, **60**
stock, 95, 115–17, 189, 357
technological change and, 430
market structure, 533–625
economic performance and, 533–35
measures of, 610–11
standards for antitrust policy and, 616
types of, 534
market supply, 40, 43–44, 55–58
market supply curves, **43**–44, 176, 500–531, **542**
aggregate supply curves compared to, 178–79
backward bending, **631**
changes in, 44, 49–50
derivation of, 542–43
determinants of location and shape of, 544
effects of externalities on, 69
equilibrium price and, **44**–45, 50, 51
for farm products, 77–78, 462, 470
firm's supply curves and, **541,** 542–43
for labor, **632,** 645, 647–48
in perfect competition, 535–36, 541–47, 553–54, 556–57, 566–67, 631, 632
price elasticity of supply and, 544–45
in short run, 542–44, 546–47
tax incidence and, 98–100
Marks, Leonard, 331n
markups, **596**
Marshall, Alfred, 8, 158, 171, 310
Marston, Stephen, 154
Martin, William McChesney, 253, 348, 369
Marx, Karl, 160–61, 668, 775–77, 792
Marxist economics, 775–77
unemployment and, 160–61
see also communism; radical economics; socialism
Mason, Edward, 617
Massachusetts, 124
Mass Transportation Commission of, 461
NOW accounts in, 298
Mauchly, John, 428
Mayer, T., 361n, 367n
Meadows, D., 449n
measurements, economic, 20
meat, consumer's surplus and, **489**
meat-processing plants, closing down of, 541

Medicare, 685–86, 688
member banks in Federal Reserve, **320,** 321, 349, 350
mercury, supply of, 543
mergers, 4
conglomerate, **589**–90, 614–15
horizontal, **589**
oligopoly and, 589
vertical, **589**
Merrill Lynch, 258, 322n, 350n, 351
metalworking firm, linear programming used by, A13–A18
Michigan, University of, 284, 286, 288
Research Seminar in Quantitative Economics of, 288
Survey Research Center at, 284
milk, production theory and, 506
Mill, John Stuart, 158, 160, 698
Miller, G. William, 348, 363, 365
Miller-Tydings Act (1937), 622
Milliman, J., 581n, A25
Minarik, Joseph, 167–69
minimum wage, teenage unemployment and, 692–94
minorities:
discrimination against, 690–91
unemployment and, 156, 157, 158
Mitchell, Wesley, C., 281
Mobil, 117
models, economic, **19**–20, 23–31
econometric, *see* econometric models
predictive function of, 19–20
quantification of, 20–21
as simplification, 19
Modigliani, Franco, 200–201, 380, 381, 384, 399
monetarists, 312
Keynesians vs., *see* Keynesian-monetarist debate
money supply as viewed by, 309–11, 314–16, 347, 359, 372, 374–75
monetary base, **359,** 361, 366
monetary factors, in business fluctuations, 278–79, 301–2
monetary policy, 184, **346**–70
aggregate demand curves and, 183–84, 347, 356
aims of, 346–47, 364–66
business fluctuations and, 189, 190
central role of bank reserves in, 347–48
fiscal policy vs., 346, 347, 367
income policies vs., 405–9
lags in impact of, 361, 365, 366
LM curves and, A6–A7
makers of, 348–49
monetarist emphasis on, 372, 375, 377
monetarists vs. Keynesians on effects of, 376–77, 380–81, A6, A7–A8
political use of, 277–78
problems in formulation of, 364–66
tight vs. easy, 347, 358–59, 364, 366, 367, 656
tools of, 349–56
U.S., since 1960, 362–64
monetary rule, 368–69, 370
monetarists vs. Keynesians on, 379–80
money, 295–318
circular flows of, 60, 140–41

creation of, 104–6, 331–39
federal borrowing of, 102–4
"fiat," 297
importance of, 316
as medium of exchange, 296
quantity theory of, 309–16, 347, 372
as standard of value, 296
as store of value, 296
value of, 300–301
velocity of, **310**–16
money demand, 177, 302–5
empirical evidence on, 304
monetarists vs. Keynesians on, 374–75
precautionary, 303
speculative motive and, 304n
transactions, 303, 309n, 377
money demand curves, **305,** 308n, 310
interest rates and, 304–5, 306, 308, 359–60, 374–75, 377
money income, **167, 482**
demand and, *see* income elasticity of demand
fixed, 167–69
money market mutual funds, 298
money supply, 346–70
broad definition of (M-2), 299–300, 315n
changes in, NNP and, 306–7
decreases in, 189, 308–9, 346–47, 348
determinants of, 302–3
FOMC and, 352
increases in, 190–91, 253, 278, 298, 301–2, 307, 346, 347, 348, 359–63, 366
inflation and, 301–2, 347, 358–69
interest rates vs., 359–60
Keynesian model of, 307–9, 309–10, 317–18, 347, 358, 375
monetarists' views on, 309–11, 314–16, 347, 359, 372, 375
narrow definition of (M-1), 297–99, 315n, 363, 407–8
in World War II, 190
money supply curve, **376**
money wages, **168**
monopolistic competition, **582**–88
barriers to entry in, 535, 583
case against, 606
characteristics of, 582–84
control over price in, 534
equilibrium and, 584–85
excess capacity in, 585, 586
in long run, 584–85
monopoly compared to, 583, 586
nonprice competition in, 535
number of firms in, 534, 583, 584, 585
oligopoly compared to, 583
perfect competition compared to, 583, 586–87
price and output in, 584–85
in short run, 584
type of product in, 534–35
monopoly, 19, 35, 66, 534, **558**–81
antitrust policy vs., 605, 611–18
barriers to entry in, 535
case against, 569–71
causes of, 559–60, 618–22
control over price in, 534

cost functions in, 559–60, 562–65,
    569–70, 580–81
defense of, 607–9
equilibrium and, 564
firm demand curve in, 560–61
Golden Rule of Output Determination
    for, 563–64
labor unions as, 649
in long run, 565–66
marginal-cost pricing and, 572n,
    580–81
market demand curves in, 560, 561–62
monopolistic competition compared to,
    583, 586
natural, **559**–60
nonprice competition in, 535
oligopoly compared to, 590–91
OPEC as, 449
optimal power of, 608–9
perfect competition compared to, 558,
    560–61, 564, 566–68, 570, 607
price and output in, 562–67, 606
profits and, 562–66, 668–69
regulation of, 559, 571–78, 580–81,
    605
resource allocation in, 567–68, 569,
    570, 605
in short run, 562–65
technological change and, 571, 607,
    608
type of product in, 534–35
monopoly banks, 333, 339
monopsony, **637**–38, 649
Montgomery, D., 437n
Montgomery, M., 437n
moral suasion, 355
Moran, William, 140
Morgenstern, O., 602n
mortgages, 662
Motor Age, 468
Mueller, Willard, 610
multinational firms, **707**–8, 768
multiplier, **223**–24, 227
    acceleration principle and, **271**–73, 275
    algebraic derivation of, 233–35
    balanced-budget, 244, 266–67
    in forecasts, 228–30
    for government expenditures, 238–39
    graphical derivation of size of, 223–24
Musgrave, Peggy, 87n
Musgrave, Richard, 87n, 677

Nader, Ralph, 485, 573
National Advisory Commission on Rural
    Poverty, 76
national banks, **320,** 322
National Bureau of Economic Research,
    131, 281
national debt, 102–4, 656
    as burden on future generations, 102–4
    externally held, 104
    internally held, 104
    size and growth of, 102–4, 258
    Treasury Department and, 105
national defense:
    expenditures for, 64, 68, 71, 89, 90–91,
        190, 191, 253, 276, 277, 737
    measured economic welfare and, 139

as public good, 64, 68
tariffs and quotas and, 711–12
National Education Association, 639
National Foreign Trade Council, 742
national income, 131, **147**–48
national income accounts, **131**
National Labor Relations Board, 641,
    642n
national product, *see* gross national
    product; net national product
National Steel, 593
national unions, **639**, 642–43
natural monopoly, **559**
natural resources:
    economic growth and, 415
    in less developed countries, 758
near-money, **299**
negotiable order of withdrawal (NOW)
    accounts, 298, 330
Nelson, J., 581n
neo-Keynesians, 309, 371, 381
Nerlove, Marc, 554
net exports, **142**
Netherlands, the, 719
net national product (NNP), **136**–39, 193,
    195–245, 432
    changes in, 218–35
    changes in money demand and, 303–5
    changes in money supply and, 307–18,
        346–47
    determination of, 195–245, A1–A8
    equilibrium level, of *see* equilibrium
        NNP
    fiscal policy and, A6–A7
    forecasting of, 280, 281, 312, 316
    foreign trade and, 721–22
    Keynesian-monetarist debate and, 372,
        373, 377
    limitations of, 137–38
    monetary policy and, A7–A8
    nominal, **310**–18
    real, 176, 311–12, 314, 346–47, 383–84
net private domestic investment, **142**
    decision making and, 202–4
    determinants of, 201–2
net worth, **122**
New Deal, labor unions and, 641–42
New Economic Policy, 363
New England Electric System, 452
new international economic order,
    770–71
New York City:
    Municipal Assistance Corp., 124
    pollution control in, 441
    poverty in, 682
    rent control in, 59
    sales tax in, 75
New York Stock Exchange, 115
New York Times, 102, 116, 264, 289, 682
Nixon, Richard M., 251, 260, 289, 712,
    791
    fiscal policy of, 363
    wage and price controls and, 363,
        400–401, 402
NNP, *see* net national product
nominal interest rates, **358**
nominal NNP, **310**–16
    velocity of money and, 310–12

noncompeting groups, **633**
Nordhaus, William, 138, 139
normative economics, **14**
    positive economics vs., **14**–16, 79
    values and, 15, 16
Norris-La Guardia Act (1932), 641
notes payable, **122**
Nove, Alec, 783n
nuclear power, 437

Oates, W., 445n
occupational expenses, wage differentials
    and, 633–34
Occupational Safety and Health
    Administration (OSHA), 92
Office of Economic Opportunity, U.S., 88
Office of Management and Budget, U.S.,
    86, 248, 255
offset, in anti-pollution measures, **452**
oil, oil industry, 59, 117, 364, 437
    cost functions and, 521–22, 524–25
    decontrol of price of, 454
    oligopoly in, 583, 586, 588, 589, 595
    pre-1973 import quotas on, 712–13
    price elasticity of demand for, 466
    price increases for, 262, 289, 391, 395,
        436, 448–49
    production function and, 501–2
    synthetic, 451–55
    U.S. payments for imports of, 448–49
oil embargo, 289, 448–49, 711
Okner, B., 677–78n
Okun, Arthur, 169–70, 253n, 409, 680,
    689
old-age insurance, **684**–86
oligopoly, **583**, 588–91
    barriers to entry in, 535, 588–89
    case against, 605–6
    collusion and, 591–94, 606
    control over price in, 534
    cost-plus pricing in, **596**–97
    differentiated, **583**
    economies of scale in, 588–89
    game theory and, 602–4
    kinked demand curve in, 590
    mergers and, 589–90
    monopolistic competition compared to,
        583
    monopoly compared to, 590
    nonprice competition in, 535, 597–98
    number of firms in, 534
    perfect competition compared to, 583,
        590, 598–600
    price leadership and, **594**–96
    price stability and, 591
    pure, **583**
    type of product in, 534–35
Omenn, Gilbert, 447
open market operations, **350**–52, 355
open shop, **648**
opportunity cost (alternative cost), 9–11,
    10, 26, 514
    examples of, 10, 11, 15
    of government programs, 104–6
    parks and, 10–11
optimal input decisions, 500–512
    case studies of, 510–11
    determination of, 507–11

isoquants and isocost curves in,
A8–A11
numerical example of, 507–8
Organization for Economic Cooperation
and Development, 431, 529
Organization of Petroleum Exporting
Countries (OPEC), 59, 262, 448–49
other oil sources and, 595
output, **1**
acceleration principle and, 269–73
actual vs. potential, 433
aggregate demand curves and, 175,
176–78, 180–83, 189
aggregate supply curves and, 175,
178–80, 184–85
agricultural, restrictions on, 80–81
determination of, 195–217
fiscal policy and, 236–67, 310, A6–A7
government expenditures in relation to,
71
growth of, *see* economic growth
inflation's effects on, 170
level and composition of, 22, 23–26,
33, 50–51
measures of, *see* gross national product;
net national product
national debt as percent of, 103
price levels and, 180
see also price and output

Pabst Brewing Company, 617–18
parity, concept of, **79–80**
Parker, Dave, 674
Parker Pen Company, 461
parks, national, opportunity cost and,
10–11
partial equilibrium analysis, **A19**
partnerships, **112**, 113, 144
patents, 589, 706
monopoly caused by, 559, 618–22
Pay Board, 400–401
payoff in game theory, **602**
payoff matrix, **602**
Peabody Coal Company, 513
peaks in business cycle, **187**, 190–91, 268,
273
variables and, 281–82
Pechman, Joseph, 93*n*, 264, 677
Peck, Merton J., 91*n*
Penner, R., 745*n*
pensions, 143, 147–48*n*, 170
perfect competition, 32, **533–57**, **535**
in agriculture, 535, 544–45, 550–53
barriers to entry in, 535
constant cost industries in, **556**
control over price in, 534, 536
cost functions in, 536–41, 542, 549–50,
570
decreasing cost industries, **557**
equilibrium and, 546–47, 549–50,
553–54, 629–30, 632–33
firm demand curve in, 560–61, 562,
629–30
Golden Rule of Output Determination
in, 538–39, 540, 565
identical products in, 535, 536
increasing cost industries in, **556–57**
in labor market, 629–37

in long run, 547–50, 551–53, 556–57
market demand curves in, 546–47,
553–54, 556–57, 566–67, 630–32
in market period, **546**, 547
market supply curves in, 541–47,
553–54, 556–57, 566–67, 631
monopolistic competition compared to,
583, 586–87
monopoly compared to, 558, 560–61,
565, 566–68, 576, 607
number of firms in, 534, 535–36
oligopoly compared to, 583, 590,
598–600
optimal output in, 570
price and input in, 535–41, 546–50,
566–67
resource allocation in, 550–54, 567–68,
A25–A27
in short run, 535–44, 546–47
wage differentials and, 633–35
welfare maximization and, A25–A27
permanent-income hypothesis, 200–201,
381
personal income, 147, **148**–49
Phelps, Edmund, 395
Philadelphia, Pa., pollution control in, 441
Philadelphia Inquirer, 52*n,* 73
Phillips, A., 560*n*
Phillips, A. W., 392
Phillips curve, **392–99**
instability of, 394–95
in long run, 395–99
in short run, 397–99
Phillips Petroleum, 453
piece rates, **784**
Pigou, A. C., 158, 678
plant and equipment:
forecasts on expenditures for, 283–84
investment in, 423–24, 426
plastics industry, innovation in, 706
players in game theory, **602**
Plotnick, R., 689*n*
Plott, Charles, 548
politics:
business fluctuations and, 277–78
economic forecasts and, 289
in Keynesian-monetarist debate,
381–82
pollution, 436, 437–47
air, 65, 69, 436–37, 439–40, 446,
452–53
direct regulation of, **439**, 440–41
effluent fees and, **439**–40, 441–42
as external diseconomy, 65, 69, **438**–39
public policy toward, 439–42
reducing costs of control of, 445
U.S. control programs for, 443–44
in U.S. vs. foreign countries, 439
water, 65, 69, 437, 439–41, 442
zero, 446–47
population control, 420
"birth rights" and, 419
population growth, 417–21, 754–56
economic growth and, 417–21
in industrialized nations, 1913–59, 421
positive economics, **14**
normative economics vs., 14–16
poverty, 12, 680–83, 749–57

in agricultural sector, 76, 82–83
case studies of, 681–82
characteristics of, 682–83
declining incidence of, 682
discrimination and, 690–95
"dollar votes" and, 64*n*
elimination of, 4–5, 35, 684–90
in history, 413
reasons for, 683
see also welfare
precautionary demand for money, 304
preferred stock, **114**
present value of future income, 661–63
president, U.S.:
in budgetary process, 86–87
Economic Report of, 248
Federal Reserve and, 321, 349, 365
tax changes and, 91–93, 105
price and output:
market period and, **546**
in monopolistic competition, 584–85
in monopoly, 562–66, 606
in perfect competition, 535–41,
546–50, 566–67
Price Commission, 400
price controls (price ceilings), 58–59,
400–401, 403–4
disadvantages of, 400–401
in 1970s, 191, 262–63, 363–64, 401–2
in World War II, 190, 400
price discrimination, **574, 612**
in dentistry, 574
price elastic, **466–69**, 473–74, 544–45,
546–47
price elasticity of demand, **463–72**, 476,
630–31
for automobiles, 468
calculation of, 464–65
determinants of, 465–66
farm problem and, 470–72
in retailing, 587
total money expenditure and, 466–69
U.S., for selected commodities, 465
price elasticity of supply, 544–**45**
price-escalator clauses, 170–71
price indexes, 134–35, **134**
see also Consumer Price Index
price inelastic, **446**–69, 470, 544–45
price leadership, **594–96**
price levels:
aggregate demand curves and, 175,
176–78, 180–83, 189, 190
aggregate supply curves and, 175,
178–80, 183–84, 192
changes in market demand curves and,
42–43
changes in market supply curves and,
44
exchange rates and, 727–28, 739
GNP adjusted for changes in, 133–35
money supply and, 346–47
money's value dependent on, 300–301
stability of, as responsibility of
government, 67
U.S. changes in, 2, 3, 166
see also depression; inflation
prices:
agricultural, 44–47, 48–49, 59, 76–80,

82, 83, 191, 401, 460, 461, 463, 464–65, 470–72
crude quantity theory of, 312–13, 314–15, 372
equilibrium, *see* equilibrium price
flexibility of, 160, 163, 381
regulation and, 571–76
in Soviet Union, 781–82
price supports (price floors), 59, 79–81, 82, 83
price system, **33**–34, 39–60, 77–78, 438–39
in Broadway theater, 56–58
government regulation vs., 58–59, 63–65, 83
limits of, 34–35, 63–65, 66, 83
population control and, 419
in prisoner-of-war camp, 55–56
tasks of economic system and, 33–34, 50–57
printing industry, industrial concentration in, 610
prisoner-of-war camp, price system in, 55–56, 546
private costs, **438**
processes in linear programming, **A12**
Procter & Gamble, 603–4, 614
Producer Price Index, 166
product differentiation, 582-**83**, 587
product group, **583**–84
production:
agricultural, 76, 79–81
capital and roundabout methods of, 659–60
production coefficients, **A21**–A22
production function, **120, 501**–2
aggregate, **415**–16
average product and, 503, 504–5
isoquants and, A8–A9
linear programming vs., A11–A13
marginal product and, 504–5
production possibilities curve, 23–31, **24, 702**
"bowed out" vs. "bowed in" shape of, 26
determination of how goods are produced and, 27–28
determination of what is produced and, 23–26
economic growth and, 429
income distribution and, 28–31
law of increasing cost and, 26–27
publicly provided vs. privately provided goods and, 89
productive capacity, 415, 425
GNP forecasts compared to, 285
variations in, 219
productivity, labor, *see* labor productivity
product markets, **60**
products:
circular flows of money and, 60, 140–41
development of, 598
market structure and, 534–35
Professional Air Traffic Controllers Organization (PATCO), 646
profits, 34, 51, 109, **118**–19, 121–27, 144, 389, 395, 396, 666–69

of banks, 324
economic vs. accounting, 127
functions of, 54, 668–69
innovation, uncertainty, and monopoly power and, 666–68
maximization of, 119
in monopolistic competition, 584–85
in monopoly, 562–66, 668
in perfect competition, 536–38, 549–50, 607, 629–30
statistics on, 666
Progress and Poverty (George), 665
proletariat, **775,** 776
property:
assessed vs. market values of, 98
personal, **98**
property taxes, 68, 74, 75, 94, **98,** 165, 677
Proposition 13, 74
proprietorships, **111**–12, 113, 144
prosperity, **187**
Protestant ethic, 431
public choice, theory of, 89–91
public debt, *see* national debt
public employment, labor unions and, 646
public goods, **64,** 68
Public Law 480, 81
public policy:
importance of economics in, 12–14
see also government, U.S.; government expenditures, U.S.
public works, government expenditures for, 251
Pure Food and Drug Act, 66

quantity theory of money, 309–18, 347
crude, 312, 313–14, 372
equation of exchange and, 312, 313, 314–15, 372
sophisticated version of, 314–16
Quink, market demand curve for, 461
quotas, 705*n,* **710**–13, 739
argument for, 711–12
social costs of, 710
in Soviet Union, **781,** 786

racial problems, poverty and, 5, 690–91
Radford, R. A., 55*n*
radical economics, **792**–96
Rae, John B., 468*n*
railroads:
government regulation of, 4, 575, 576
market demand curves for, 461–63
RAND Corporation, 490, 581, A24–A25
random shocks, business fluctuations and, 275
Rapoport, J., 609*n*
rate of return, **653**–54, 766
rational choice, 482–85
rational expectations theory, 372, 382–84, 398
Rawski, Thomas, 789
Reagan, Ronald, 14, 73, 74, 204, 289, 576, 646, 687, 743, 745
antitrust law and, 615
fiscal policy of, 255, 263–64

price and wage controls and, 410*n,* 411
price supports and, 82
supply-side economics and, 100, 184, 398
real estate investment, 509
real GNP, **134**–35, 176, 190
in Great Depression, 189
as measure of economic growth, 414
U.S., since 1918, 186–87
real income, **167**
real interest rates, **358**
real NNP, 176, 310–11, 314, 346–48
real wages, **168**
recessionary gaps, **245**
recessions, **187,** 188, 190, 191, 255–56, 279, 381
causes of, 302
fiscal policy for, 255–56
leading indicators in, 281–82
monetary policy and, 346, 347–48, 360–61, 363, 364
of 1953–54, 276
of 1957–58, 276, 389–91
of 1974–75, 274, 276, 363
rational expectations and, 382, 383
variations in, 268–69
Regan, Donald, 258, 745
regulation, regulatory agencies, 4, 67
competition reduced by, 559, 575–76, 605, 618–24
monopoly and, 559–60, 571–78, 580–81, 605
price setting by, 572–73
prices increased by, 575–76
see also specific agencies
Regulation Q, **355**–57
regulatory lag, **577**–78
Remington Rand, 428
rent, 143, **664**–65
nature and significance of, 664–65
rent control, 59
reproduction costs, **572**
resale price maintenance, **622**
research and development (R and D), 73, 429
for energy, 451–55
interindustry differences in, 431
reserves, bank, 334–44, 347–48, 349–54
on consolidated balance sheets, 349–50
deficiency of, 340–41, 344, 348
deposits equal to, 331–32
effects of decrease in, 340–41, 348
excess, **335,** 334–44, 348, 375
fractional, **326**–28, 331–32
legal requirements for, **327**–28, 332–34, 335–41, 352–54, 360
secondary, 328
resource allocation, 5–7, 438
choice in, 7
effects of wage and price controls on, 400
in monopoly, 567–68, 569–70, 571, 605
opportunity cost and, 9–11
in perfect competition, 550–54, 567–68, A25–A27
profits and, 669
Smith's views on, 12, 13

as task of economic system, 22–23, 23–28
welfare economics and, A23–A25
resource markets, **60**
resources, **6**
diminishing marginal returns and, 415–**16**, 419–20, 422, 427, 505–6, 519
economic, **6–7**
economic growth and, 414–27
efficiency of use of, 33, 34, 54
free, **6**
international trade and, 699, 700
natural, 415, 758
Retail Clerks, 646
retailing, monopolistic competition in, 587–88
retained earnings, **122,** 307n
Revolutionary War, 301, 389
Ricardo, David, 422–24, 434, 698, 701
risks:
of common stock, 114, 115, 119
of innovation, 427
of lending, 324–25, 343, 653
profit maximization and, 118, 654
Risser, Hubert, 546
River, Charles, Associates, 712
Rivlin, Alice, 87, 695
Robinson-Patman Act (1936), 622
robots, unemployment and, 432, 528
Rockefeller, John D., 586, 589
Rockefeller Foundation, 757
Rohatyn, Felix, 124
Rohrer, D., 437n
Romeo, A., 609n
Roosevelt, Theodore, 613
Rose, Pete, 674
Rosinski, E., 8
Ruhr valley, effluent fees in, 442
rule of reason, **612**
rules of the game, **602**
Ruttan, V., 464n

Sackrin, S. M., 475
sales, investment in relation to, 270–71, 272, 273, 276
sales taxes, 67, 68, 75, **98**–100, 676
Samuelson, Paul, 36n, 65n, 271–72
Sargent, Thomas, 382
saving function, **198**–200
shifts in, 226–27, 230–31
savings, 12, 30, 322, 659–**60**
actual vs. intended, 214–15
as automatic stabilizer, 250
checking vs., 297, 298
inflation's impact on, 169
investment in relation to, 160, 162, 214–15, 221, 322
paradox of thrift and, 230–31
supply-side view of, 384–85
savings and loan associations, 322, 327n, 357
savings banks, 322, 327n
Say, J. B., 158
Say's Law, **158–60**
scale, returns to, 525–26
Scherer, F. M., 91, 589n, 592–93
Schultz, Henry, 465n

Schultz, Theodore, 426
Schultze, Charles, 445
Schumpeter, Joseph, 427, 607, 667
Schwartz, Anna, 379
Science, 456
scrubbers, in pollution control, 440, 451
Sears Roebuck, 322n
second best, theory of, A27
Securities and Exchange Commission, 73, 118, 283
Security National Bank, 329
Seidman, Lawrence, 409
selective credit control, **357**
self-interest, 32, 51
Smith's views on, 12, 13
Senate, U.S.:
Budget Committee of, 87, 247
Finance Committee of, 93, 247
McClellan Committee of, 643, 644
Subcommittee on Antitrust and Monopoly of, 601
Service Employees, 639
shale, as fuel source, 451
Sharp, A., 454n
Shepherd, William, 610n
Sherman Antitrust Act (1890), 66, 72, 592, 611, 613, 615, 620–21
shoes, tariffs and, 717
short run, **502**–3
cost functions in, 514–23, 524, 527, 538–41, 584
equilibrium in, 546–47, 564, 584
government expenditures in, 251–52
market supply curves in, 542–44, 546–47
monopolistic competition in, 584
monopoly in, 562–65
NNP in, 311
perfect competition in, 535–44, 546–47
Phillips curve in, 397–99
price and output in, 535–41, 546–47, 562–65
Siegelman, L., 465n
Sierra Club, 444
silver, 296, 297
skill, wage differentials and, 633–34
slingshots:
estimated demand curve for, 461
price elasticity of demand for, 463, 464
price elasticity of supply for, 545
Sloan, Alfred, 109
Smith, Adam, 12, 13, 14, 16, 34, 184, 422, 593, 698, 760
monopoly as viewed by, 567, 571, 605
Smith, Vernon, 548
Smoot-Hawley Tariff (1930), 715
social costs:
external diseconomies and, 64, 69, 438–39
limitations of GNP and NNP and, 138
pollution and, 437–38, 439–40, 442, 446–47
private costs equal to, 438–39
of quotas, **710**
of tariffs, 709
of unemployment, 157–58
socialism, 161, **775–77**
capital and, 31

democratic, **791**–92
interest rates and, 657–58
marginal cost pricing in, 580
social security, 71, 684–85
Social Security Act (1935), 684, 686
Social Security Administration, 682
Social Security Taxes, 75, 677, 685
solar energy, 455
Solow, Robert, 119n, 795
Soviet Union, 32, 439n, 769, 770, 777–87
economic growth in, 762, 784–85
economic planning in, 778–80
evaluation of economy of, 786–87
income distribution in, 783–84
prices in, 781–82, 783
priorities and performance in, 780–81
production possibilities curve of, 28
U.S. grain sales to, 81
special drawing rights (SDRs), 744
special-interest groups, 90
specialization, 12, 422–23
incomplete, 703
returns to scale and, 526
trade and, 698–702, 703
speculation:
in inflationary periods, 170
market demand curves and, 462
Spence, Michael, 636
Spencer, M., 465n
spending, *see* expenditures
stabilization policy, 346–412
current state of, 410
see also fiscal policy; monetary policy
stabilization policy, controversies over, 371–87
monetarists vs. Keynesians and, 309–10, 347, 371–82
rational expectations theory and, 372, 382–84
supply-side economics and, 371, 384–85
stagflation, **2,** 263, 410
Stalin, Josef, 778
Standard Oil Company, 589, 612
State, County, and Municipal Employees, 639, 646n
state banks, **320,** 322
state governments:
bonds issued by, 96, 324
expenditures of, 71, 72
pollution control by, 443–44
tax revenues of, 75
statistical methods, demand curves estimated by, 461
Stealth bomber, 73
steel industry, 4, 117, 612–13
business organization, 112, 113
labor unions and, 639, 642
oligopoly in, 588, 589, 593, 594–96
optimal input decisions in, 511
price leadership in, 594–96
Stern Robert, 703n
Stigler, George, 75n, 573, 588n
stock, **113**–117
common, **113,** 115–17
dividends from, **113,** 250
preferred, **114**
stock market, 95, 115–17

comeback of, 115
  Great Crash in (1929), 155, 189, 357
  margin requirements and, **357**
Stokes, Charles, 530*n*
Stone, G., Jr., 15*n*
strategy in game theory, **602**
strikes, 641, 644, 646, 648–49
structural unemployment, **152**–53,
  156–57, 396
Studebaker-Packard, 589
subsistence economy, **751**–52
substitutes, **475**
  price elasticity of demand and, 465–66
substitution effect, individual demand
  curves and, 488
Suits, Daniel, 545*n*
Sullivan, Leon, 117
Summers, Robert, 750*n*
sunk cost, 509
Supplemental Security Income, **686**
supply:
  aggregate, *see* supply-side economics
  market, 40, 43–44, 55–58
  of money, *see* money supply
  price elasticity of, **544**–45
supply curves:
  aggregate, *see* aggregate supply curves
  energy, 450
  foreign exchange market and, 725–26
  for loanable funds, 654–55
  market, *see* market supply curves
  money, **376**–77
supply-side economics, 100–102, 184–85
  controversies over stabilization policies
  and, 371, **384**–86
Supreme Court, U.S., antitrust laws and,
  559, 611, 612–13, 614, 618
surgeons, market for, 632–33
surpluses, **256**
  agricultural, 59, 78, 79–81
  balance-of-payments, **730**–31, 737
  consumer's, **489**
surplus financing, 247, 255–59, 259–61
  effects of, 261, 377–78
  full-employment budget vs., 259–60
surplus value, 668, **776**
Survey of Current Business, 283
Sweden, 75, 380*n*, 791
Sweezy, Paul, 590
Swift, Robert, 329
Switzerland, international trade of,
  709–10
Sylvania Corp., 620–21
synthetic fuel, 451

Tacitus, 500
Taft-Hartley Act (1947), 642, **644**, 648
target rate of return, **596**
tariffs, 705*n*, **709**–10, 713–18, 739, 771
  arguments for, 711–13, 714–15
  prohibitive, **709**
  social costs of, 709
  U.S. changes in, 715–18
tar sands, as source of fuel, 451
tastes, *see* consumer tastes and
  preferences
Taubman, Paul, 286*n*
tax avoidance, 67, 95, **96**, 385

tax-based incomes policies, 405–9
tax credits, 254–55, 263
  investment, 254, 263
  for pollution-control equipment, **440**,
  442–43
tax cuts, 100–102
  on capital income, 100
  on labor income, 100
  of 1964, 190, 253, 255, 377
  of 1975, 244, 252, 254, 263
  of 1978, 263
  of 1981, 255, 385–86
  supply-side views on, 385
taxes, 14, 32, 74–75, 91–102, 104
  burden of, by income level, 677–78
  death, 74, 94, 677
  estate, 94, 677
  excise, 74, 75, 98–100, 677–78*n*
  as fiscal policy tool, 252
  flat, 96
  fuel, 450
  government's receipts from, 74–75
  incidence of, 98–100, **677**
  income, *see* income tax
  in income redistribution, 35, 67,
  676–78
  indexation and, 170–71
  indirect business, 144
  as leakage, 243–44
  legislative process and, 91–93
  net rate of, **677**
  principles of, 93–94
  progressive vs. regressive, **676**–78
  property, 68, 74, 75, 94, **98**, 165, 677
  Proposition 13 and, 74
  public goods supported by, 68
  sales, 67, 68, 75, **98**–100, 677
  simplification, 96
  single, 665
  Social Security, 75, 677, 685
  supply-side economics and, 100–102,
  384–85
  turnover, **782**
tax evasion, 95, **96**
tax surcharge (1968), 254, 372
Taylor, L., 465*n*
Taylor, Reese, 576
Teamsters Union, 639, 643
technological change:
  case study of, 428–29
  determinants of, 429–30
  diffusion process in, **427**
  diminishing marginal returns and, 417
  economic growth and, 415, 417, 420,
  424, 427–30
  first application of, *see* innovation
  labor productivity and, 430
  monopoly and, 571, 607–9
technology, **7**, 43–44, 120, **427**
  agriculture and, 76, 77
  changes in market supply curves and,
  43–44
  choice and, 7–8
  efficiency of resource use and, 54
  in investment decision, 124, 202–3
  in less-developed countries, 756–57, 768
  unemployment and, 432
technology gap, 706–7, 737

technology transfer, 430, 768
teenagers, unemployment among, 154,
  155, 156, 692–94
Teeters, Nancy, 695
Teigen, R., 303*n*
Teng Hsiao-p'ing, 791
Tennessee Valley Authority, 32
tennis, supply vs. demand for, 52
Texaco, 117
Texas Instruments, 64
Thackeray, William M., 660*n*
thrift, paradox of, 230–31
time, role in consumption of, 490
time deposits, 322, 343*n*
  in money supply, 298
  reserves in relation to, 352–54
Time magazine, 258, 291
tobacco industry, 117
Tobin, James, 138, 139, 303*n*, 791*n*
Torrio, Joseph, 157–58
total cost, **516**, 521–22
  measurement of, 526–27
  in monopoly, 562–63
  in perfect competition, 537–38, 540
total fixed cost, **514**–15, 516
  in perfect competition, 537, 540
total revenue, **536**–38, **561**
  in monopoly, 560–61, 562–63
  in perfect competition, 536–37, 540
total utility, 480–81, 482
total variable cost, **515**, 516
  in perfect competition, 536–37, 540
Townes, Charles, 117
trade:
  international, *see* international trade
  terms of, **702**–3, 713–14
Trade Agreements Act (1934), 716
Trade Reform Act (1974), 718, 771
trading possibilities curve, **702**
training, wage differentials and, 633
transactions demand for money, 303–5,
  377, 309*n*
transfer payments:
  business, 147*n*–48*n*
  GNP's exclusion of, 133
  government, **71**, **133**
  private, **133**
  see also welfare
Treasury Department, U.S., 92, 105, 170,
  248, 255, 285
  Brannan Plan and, 470–72
  Federal Reserve and, 321, 348–49, 350,
  367, 368–69
Trebing, H., 573*n*
troughs in business cycle, **187**–88,
  190–91, 268, 273
  variables and, 281–82
trucking, regulation of, 575–76
Truman administration, 81, 403, 470
Turner, Donald, 616
turnover tax, **782**
Twain, Mark, 1
Tweeten, L., 510*n*
two-person games, **602**
tying contracts, **612**

uncertainty, profits and, 119, 666–68
underemployment, 153–54

unemployment, 151–63, 188, 367
    automatic stabilizers of, **248**–50
    business fluctuations and, 153, 175,
        186–92
    costs of, 156–58
    cyclical, **153**
    economic growth and, 433
    frictional, **152**, 156
    government, vs., 67, 153, 162, 182–83,
        190, 236, 251–55, 262–63
    in Great Depression, 2, 67, 153, 155,
        182, 189
    inadequate growth of money supply
        and, 309
    inflation and, 1–3, 60, 106, 171–73,
        190–91, 263, 392–94, 395, 410
    measurement and incidence of, 153–56
    natural rate of, 396–98
    production possibilities curve and,
        27–28
    quantity of money and, 302, 309
    rational expectations and, 383
    shape of aggregate supply curves and,
        179–80
    structural, **152**–53, 156, 396
    tariffs and, 713
    theories of, 158–62
    types of, 152–53
    U.S., 2, 154–55
    voluntary, 152
    wage-increase rate in relation to, *see*
        Phillips curve
unemployment insurance, 154, 251, 686
    as automatic stabilizer, 250
unions, *see* labor unions, *specific unions*
union shops, **648**
unitary elasticity, **466**–69
United Auto Workers, 639
United Mine Workers, 639, 641, 642
United Nations Relief and Rehabilitation
    Administration (UNRRA), 767
United Shoe Machinery Company, 559
United States Steel Corporation, 501,
    526, 589, 612, 642
    price leadership and, 594–96
United Steelworkers, 639, 641
Univac I, 428
Upward Bound program, benefit-cost
    analysis of, 88
urban blight, economics of, 70
U.S. National Bank, 329
utility, 480–82, **481**
    indifference curves and, 496
    marginal, **481**–85, 488, 504
    maximizing of, 482–85, 496, 497–98
    total, 480–81, 482
    welfare economics and, A22

value:
    of currency, 296
    of marginal product of labor, **630**
    Marx's theory of, 668, 775–76
    money as standard of, 295
    money as store of, 295–96
    of output, limitations of GNP and
        NNP and, 137–38
    surplus, 668, **776**
value-added, 135–**36**
values:
    economic role of, 15, 16
    income redistribution and, 67
variable inputs, **502**
variables:
    in business fluctuations, 281
    direct vs. inverse relationship between,
        21
    graphs and, 21–22
Vernon, R., 707*n*
vertical mergers, **589**, 614
veterans' benefits, 252
Vietnam War, 190, 737
    inflation and, 166, 190, 252, 276, 389
Villani, E., 609*n*
Volcker, Paul A., 348, 361, 364
von Neumann, John, 428
Von's Grocery case, 614

wage controls, 191, 363, **400**–401, 402,
    403–4
    disadvantages of, 400
wage differentials, 628, 633–35
wage-price guidelines, *see* incomes
    policies
wage-price spiral, **389**–91
wages, 143, 161
    determinants of, 627–51
    equilibrium, 629–30, 637–38
    flexibility of, 160, 163
    as incentive, 33
    indexing of, 170
    Marx's theory of, 775–76, 777
    money vs. real, **168**, 382–83, 390,
        628–29
    monopsony and, **637**–38
    perfect competition and, 629–37
    unemployment insurance vs., 154
    unemployment related to increases in,
        see Phillips curve
    see also income; income distribution
Wagner, S., 609*n*
Wagner Act (1935), 641, 644
Wallich, Henry, 409, 745
Wallis, W. Allen, 61
Wall Street Journal, 102, 594, 634
War of 1812, 300
Warren, Earl, 614
Washington, D.C., gas tax in, 466
watermelons, price elasticity of supply
    for, 545
water pollution, 437
    control of, 439–41, 442–43
    as external diseconomy, 64, 69
Water Pollution Act, 1972 amendments
    to, 444
Water Quality Improvement Act (1970),
    443
Watt, James, 30
wealth:
    as determinant of consumption, 225
    inflation's impact on, 167–69
Wealth of Nations, The (Smith), 12, 13,
    16, 567
Webb-Pomerene Act (1918), 624
Weintraub, Sidney, 409
Weiss, Leonard, 522, 560*n*, 587, 589,
    600*n*, 623
welfare, 5, 35, 67, 71, 72, 686–**87**
    as automatic stabilizer, 250
    as fiscal policy tool, 251–52
    measured economic, **139**
welfare economics, **A22**–A27
    nature of, A22
    perfect competition and, A25–A27
    resource allocation and, A23–A25
Westinghouse, 614
Weston, J. F., 600*n*
Wharton model, 285–86, 288–89
"what if" questions, NNP and, 211
wheat:
    equilibrium price of, 44–45, 48–49
    isoquants for, A8, A10
    marginal cost and, 519
    market demand curves for, 40–43, 51,
        464–65, 472
    market supply curves for, 43–44
    optimal input decisions and, 507–8
    perfect competition and, 534, 550–53
    price elasticity of demand for, 464–65,
        466
White, L., 598*n*
Whitman, Marina, 695
Whitney, Eli, 431
Wholesale Price Index, 166
Wicksteed, Phillip, 4–5
Williams, Roy, 639
Willkie, Wendell, 642*n*
Wilson, Joseph, 669
Wilson, T., 598*n*
Witt, L., 464*n*
Wold, Herman, 474, 475
women:
    discrimination against, 691–95
    in labor unions, 645–46
World Bank, 765, 769–70
World War I, 71, 301
    labor in, 641, 642
World War II, 71, 172, 190, 642
    aggregate demand curves in, 190
    agriculture in, 76–77
    inflation and, 166, 190, 276, 298–99,
        368
    national debt and, 102, 656
    national output in, 187
    price system in, 55–56, 59
    production possibilities curve and, 28

Xerox, 622*n*, 669

yellow-dog contracts, **641**

zero-sum games, **602**

70 BASIC IDEAS IN ECONOMICS:

 # 1   Functions of any economic system · *page 7*

 # 2   Nature and usefulness of the concept of opportunity cost · *page 10*

 # 3   Effects of unemployment of resources or of inefficiency on opportunity cost · *page 27*

 # 4   Role of the price system in organizing the economy · *page 34*

 # 5   Nature of an equilibrium price, and how it can be determined · *page 47*

 # 6   Effects and disadvantages of government-imposed price ceilings and price floors · *page 59*

 # 7   Limitations of the price system · *page 64*

 # 8   Limitations of the government as an organizer of the economy · *page 83*

 # 9   Usefulness of a comparison of benefits and costs to determine whether a program is worthwhile · *page 87*

 # 10   A tax on a particular commodity frequently can be shifted by its producers to consumers · *page 98*

 # 11   Usefulness of the assumption that firms maximize profit · *page 119*

 # 12   The importance of the economist's definition of profit, in contrast to the accountant's definition · *page 127*

 # 13   How price indexes can be used to correct output measures for changes in the price level · *page 135*

 # 14   GNP can be viewed either as total expenditure on output or total income stemming from the production of output · *page 140*

 # 15   Unemployment results in both less goods and services being produced, and in obvious and acute personal hardships · *page 156*

 # 16   Inflation results in an arbitrary redistribution of income and wealth; major inflations can cripple output as well · *page 167*

 # 17   The government may shift the aggregate demand curve to the right to reduce unemployment, and to the left to combat inflation · *page 182*

 # 18   Rightward shifts of the aggregate supply curve are apt to result in more output and less inflationary pressure · *page 185*

 # 19   Personal consumption expenditure is closely, and directly, related to disposable income · *page 201*

 # 20   For NNP to be at its equilibrium value, total intended spending on final goods and services must equal NNP · *page 207*

 # 21   Under the assumptions in Chapter 11, a dollar of extra investment results in (1/MPS) dollars of extra NNP · *page 223*

 # 22   A dollar shift upward in the consumption function results in (1/MPS) dollars of extra NNP · *page 228*

 # 23   Increases in government spending and decreases in taxes result in higher values of NNP · *page 243*

 # 24   Real disadvantages and social costs of the national debt, in contrast to imagined disadvantages and costs · *page 261*

 # 25   Gross investment is likely to fall when sales begin to increase by decreasing amounts; this is one reason for a business cycle peak · *page 273*

 # 26   Nature, importance, and limitations of economic forecasting techniques · *page 288*

 # 27   Ways that the quantity of money affects the level of NNP, according to the simple Keynesian model · *page 308*

 # 28   Ways that the quantity of money affects the price level, according to the quantity theory · *page 313*

 # 29   If every bank has to maintain reserves equal to deposits, banks cannot create new money · *page 332*

 # 30   Under the assumptions in Chapter 15, the banking system can increase the money supply by $(1/r)$ dollars for every \$1 in excess reserves, where r is the required ratio of reserves to deposits · *page 339*

 # 31   Ways that the Federal Reserve influences the money supply and interest rates · *page 354*

 # 32   How to determine how tight or easy monetary policy is · *page 359*

 # 33   Differences between monetarists and Keynesians in their assessment of the role of the quantity of money · *page 380*

 # 34   Political, as well as economic, differences between monetarists and Keynesians · *page 381*

 # 35   Short-run and long-run relationships between the unemployment rate and the inflation rate, and their policy implications · *page 399*